Haynes

THE BOOK ®

Peugeot 306
Service and Repair Manual

Mark Coombs and Steve Rendle

(3073 - 448 - 7AK6)

Models covered
Peugeot 306 models with petrol & diesel engines, including special/limited editions;
3- & 5-door Hatchback, 4-door Sedan/Saloon and 5-door Estate

1124 cc, 1360 cc, 1587 cc, 1761 cc & 1998 cc petrol engines
1769 cc, 1868 cc, 1905 cc & 1997 cc diesel & turbo-diesel engines

Does NOT cover features specific to Cabriolet and Roadster
Does not cover GTi-6 model

© Haynes Publishing 2006

ABCDE
FGHIJ
K

3

A book in the **Haynes Service and Repair Manual Series**

ISBN-10: **1 84425 180 2**
ISBN-13: **978 1 84425 180 3**

British Library Cataloguing in Publication Data
A catalogue record for this book is available from the British Library.

Printed in the USA

Haynes Publishing
Sparkford, Yeovil, Somerset BA22 7JJ, England

Haynes North America, Inc
861 Lawrence Drive, Newbury Park, California 91320, USA

Editions Haynes
4, Rue de l'Abreuvoir
92415 COURBEVOIE CEDEX, France

Haynes Publishing Nordiska AB
Box 1504, 751 45 UPPSALA, Sweden

Contents

LIVING WITH YOUR PEUGEOT 306

Roadside repairs

Weekly checks

Lubricants and fluids

Tyre pressures

MAINTENANCE

Routine maintenance and servicing

Contents

Advanced driving

Many people see the words 'advanced driving' and believe that it won't interest them or that it is a style of driving beyond their own abilities. Nothing could be further from the truth. Advanced driving is straightforward safe, sensible driving - the sort of driving we should all do every time we get behind the wheel.

An average of 10 people are killed every day on UK roads and 870 more are injured, some seriously. Lives are ruined daily, usually because somebody did something stupid. Something like 95% of all accidents are due to human error, mostly driver failure. Sometimes we make genuine mistakes - everyone does. Sometimes we have lapses of concentration. Sometimes we deliberately take risks.

For many people, the process of 'learning to drive' doesn't go much further than learning how to pass the driving test because of a common belief that good drivers are made by 'experience'.

Learning to drive by 'experience' teaches three driving skills:

☐ Quick reactions. (Whoops, that was close!)
☐ Good handling skills. (Horn, swerve, brake, horn).
☐ Reliance on vehicle technology. (Great stuff this ABS, stop in no distance even in the wet...)

Drivers whose skills are 'experience based' generally have a lot of near misses and the odd accident. The results can be seen every day in our courts and our hospital casualty departments.

Advanced drivers have learnt to control the risks by controlling the position and speed of their vehicle. They avoid accidents and near misses, even if the drivers around them make mistakes.

The key skills of advanced driving are **concentration,** effective all-round **observation, anticipation** and **planning.** When **good vehicle handling** is added to

these skills, all driving situations can be approached and negotiated in a safe, methodical way, leaving nothing to chance.

Concentration means applying your mind to safe driving, completely excluding anything that's not relevant. Driving is usually the most dangerous activity that most of us undertake in our daily routines. It deserves our full attention.

Observation means not just looking, but seeing and seeking out the information found in the driving environment.

Anticipation means asking yourself what is happening, what you can reasonably expect to happen and what could happen unexpectedly. (One of the commonest words used in compiling accident reports is 'suddenly'.)

Planning is the link between seeing something and taking the appropriate action. For many drivers, planning is the missing link.

If you want to become a safer and more skilful driver and you want to enjoy your driving more, contact the Institute of Advanced Motorists at www.iam.org.uk, phone 0208 996 9600, or write to IAM House, 510 Chiswick High Road, London W4 5RG for an information pack.

Working on your car can be dangerous. This page shows just some of the potential risks and hazards, with the aim of creating a safety-conscious attitude.

General hazards

Scalding

• Don't remove the radiator or expansion tank cap while the engine is hot.
• Engine oil, automatic transmission fluid or power steering fluid may also be dangerously hot if the engine has recently been running.

Burning

• Beware of burns from the exhaust system and from any part of the engine. Brake discs and drums can also be extremely hot immediately after use.

Crushing

• When working under or near a raised vehicle, always supplement the jack with axle stands, or use drive-on ramps. *Never venture under a car which is only supported by a jack.*
• Take care if loosening or tightening high-torque nuts when the vehicle is on stands. Initial loosening and final tightening should be done with the wheels on the ground.

Fire

• Fuel is highly flammable; fuel vapour is explosive.
• Don't let fuel spill onto a hot engine.
• Do not smoke or allow naked lights (including pilot lights) anywhere near a vehicle being worked on. Also beware of creating sparks (electrically or by use of tools).
• Fuel vapour is heavier than air, so don't work on the fuel system with the vehicle over an inspection pit.
• Another cause of fire is an electrical overload or short-circuit. Take care when repairing or modifying the vehicle wiring.
• Keep a fire extinguisher handy, of a type suitable for use on fuel and electrical fires.

Electric shock

• Ignition HT voltage can be dangerous, especially to people with heart problems or a pacemaker. Don't work on or near the ignition system with the engine running or the ignition switched on.

• Mains voltage is also dangerous. Make sure that any mains-operated equipment is correctly earthed. Mains power points should be protected by a residual current device (RCD) circuit breaker.

Fume or gas intoxication

• Exhaust fumes are poisonous; they often contain carbon monoxide, which is rapidly fatal if inhaled. Never run the engine in a confined space such as a garage with the doors shut.
• Fuel vapour is also poisonous, as are the vapours from some cleaning solvents and paint thinners.

Poisonous or irritant substances

• Avoid skin contact with battery acid and with any fuel, fluid or lubricant, especially antifreeze, brake hydraulic fluid and Diesel fuel. Don't syphon them by mouth. If such a substance is swallowed or gets into the eyes, seek medical advice.
• Prolonged contact with used engine oil can cause skin cancer. Wear gloves or use a barrier cream if necessary. Change out of oil-soaked clothes and do not keep oily rags in your pocket.
• Air conditioning refrigerant forms a poisonous gas if exposed to a naked flame (including a cigarette). It can also cause skin burns on contact.

Asbestos

• Asbestos dust can cause cancer if inhaled or swallowed. Asbestos may be found in gaskets and in brake and clutch linings. When dealing with such components it is safest to assume that they contain asbestos.

Special hazards

Hydrofluoric acid

• This extremely corrosive acid is formed when certain types of synthetic rubber, found in some O-rings, oil seals, fuel hoses etc, are exposed to temperatures above 400°C. The rubber changes into a charred or sticky substance containing the acid. *Once formed, the acid remains dangerous for years. If it gets onto the skin, it may be necessary to amputate the limb concerned.*
• When dealing with a vehicle which has suffered a fire, or with components salvaged from such a vehicle, wear protective gloves and discard them after use.

The battery

• Batteries contain sulphuric acid, which attacks clothing, eyes and skin. Take care when topping-up or carrying the battery.
• The hydrogen gas given off by the battery is highly explosive. Never cause a spark or allow a naked light nearby. Be careful when connecting and disconnecting battery chargers or jump leads.

Air bags

• Air bags can cause injury if they go off accidentally. Take care when removing the steering wheel and/or facia. Special storage instructions may apply.

Diesel injection equipment

• Diesel injection pumps supply fuel at very high pressure. Take care when working on the fuel injectors and fuel pipes.

⚠️ *Warning: Never expose the hands, face or any other part of the body to injector spray; the fuel can penetrate the skin with potentially fatal results.*

Remember...

DO

• Do use eye protection when using power tools, and when working under the vehicle.

• Do wear gloves or use barrier cream to protect your hands when necessary.

• Do get someone to check periodically that all is well when working alone on the vehicle.

• Do keep loose clothing and long hair well out of the way of moving mechanical parts.

• Do remove rings, wristwatch etc, before working on the vehicle – especially the electrical system.

• Do ensure that any lifting or jacking equipment has a safe working load rating adequate for the job.

DON'T

• Don't attempt to lift a heavy component which may be beyond your capability – get assistance.

• Don't rush to finish a job, or take unverified short cuts.

• Don't use ill-fitting tools which may slip and cause injury.

• Don't leave tools or parts lying around where someone can trip over them. Mop up oil and fuel spills at once.

• Don't allow children or pets to play in or near a vehicle being worked on.

The Peugeot 306 range was introduced in the UK in the Spring of 1993. Originally, the 306 was available with a choice of 1.4 litre (1360 cc), 1.6 litre (1587 cc) and 1.8 litre (1761 cc) petrol engines. At first, models were only available in a five-door Hatchback form.

All engines are derived from the well-proven TU and XU series engines, which have appeared in many Peugeot and Citroën vehicles. The engine is of four-cylinder overhead camshaft design, mounted transversely and inclined to the rear, with the transmission mounted on the left-hand side. All models have a four- or five-speed manual transmission; the 1.8 litre model also being offered with the option of a four-speed automatic transmission.

In Summer 1993, the 1.9 litre (1905 cc) diesel engine was introduced into the range. The engine is from the well-proven XUD series, with both non-turbo and turbo versions of the engine being available.

In early 1994, a three-door version of all models was introduced, and at the same time the 2.0 litre (1998 cc) petrol engine models were also brought into the range. In the summer of 1994, the 306 Cabriolet was introduced. To complete the range, in the Autumn, the four-door Sedan (Saloon) versions of most models were introduced.

Additional new and revised models, including limited and special editions, have been regularly added to the range with a major styling facelift taking place in Spring 1997. Together with detailed styling and mechanical revisions to existing model versions, this facelift saw the launch of an Estate model and the introduction of 16-valve versions of the 1.8 and 2.0 litre petrol engines.

During 1999, further revisions were carried out to the range including revised headlights and direction indicators, upgraded driver and passenger restraint systems and other minor cosmetic changes. This year also saw the introduction of a new 1.9 litre (1868 cc) diesel engine to replace the existing 1.9 litre non-turbo unit, together with a turbocharged 2.0 litre (1997 cc) High pressure Diesel injection (HDi) engine.

Peugeot 306 Hatchback

All models have fully-independent front suspension. The rear suspension is semi-independent, with torsion bars and trailing arms.

A wide range of standard and optional equipment is available within the 306 range to suit most tastes, including central locking, electric windows, electric sunroof, and driver and passenger airbags. An anti-lock braking system and air conditioning system are available as options on certain models.

Provided that regular servicing is carried out in accordance with the manufacturer's recommendations, the Peugeot 306 should prove reliable and very economical. The engine compartment is well-designed, and most of the items requiring frequent attention are easily accessible.

Your Peugeot 306 Manual

The aim of this manual is to help you get the best value from your vehicle. It can do so in several ways. It can help you decide what work must be done (even should you choose to get it done by a garage), provide information on routine maintenance and servicing, and give a logical course of action and diagnosis when random faults occur. However, it is hoped that you will use the manual by tackling the work yourself. On simpler jobs it may even be quicker than booking the car into a garage and going there twice, to leave and collect it. Perhaps most important, a lot of money can be saved by avoiding the costs a garage must charge to cover its labour and overheads.

The manual has drawings and descriptions to show the function of the various components so that their layout can be understood. Tasks are described and photographed in a clear step-by-step sequence.

References to the 'left' and 'right' of the vehicle are in the sense of a person in the driver's seat, facing forwards.

Acknowledgements

Certain illustrations are the copyright of the Peugeot Talbot Motor Company Limited, and are used with their permission. Special thanks to Bakers of Gillingham who provided several of the project vehicles used in the origination of this manual. Thanks are also due to Draper Tools Limited, who provided some of the workshop tools.

We take great pride in the accuracy of information given in this manual, but vehicle manufacturers make alterations and design changes during the production run of a particular vehicle of which they do not inform us. No liability can be accepted by the authors or publishers for loss, damage or injury caused by errors in, or omissions from, the information given.

Illegal copying

Peugeot 306 Sedan

The following pages are intended to help in dealing with common roadside emergencies and breakdowns. You will find more detailed fault finding information at the back of the manual, and repair information in the main chapters.

If your car won't start and the starter motor doesn't turn

- [ ] If it's a model with automatic transmission, make sure the selector is in P or N.
- [ ] Open the bonnet and make sure that the battery terminals are clean and tight.
- [ ] Switch on the headlights and try to start the engine. If the headlights go very dim when you're trying to start, the battery is probably flat. Get out of trouble by jump starting (see page 0•9) using a friend's car.

If your car won't start even though the starter motor turns as normal

- [ ] Is there fuel in the tank?
- [ ] Is there moisture on electrical components under the bonnet? Switch off the ignition, then wipe off any obvious dampness with a dry cloth. Spray a water-repellent aerosol product (WD-40 or equivalent) on ignition and fuel system electrical connectors like those shown in the photos. Pay special attention to the ignition coil wiring connector and HT leads. (Note that diesel engines don't normally suffer from damp.)

A Check that the spark plug HT leads (where applicable) are securely connected by pushing them home.

B The throttle potentiometer wiring plug may cause problems if not connected securely.

C Check the ECU multi-plug for security (where applicable) with the ignition switched off.

Check that electrical connections are secure (with the ignition switched off) and spray them with a water dispersant spray like WD-40 if you suspect a problem due to damp.

D Check the security and condition of the battery connections.

E Check that the ignition coil wiring plug is secure, and spray with a water-dispersant spray if necessary.

Wheel changing

Some of the details shown here will vary according to model. For instance, the location of the spare wheel and jack is not the same on all cars. However, the basic principles apply to all vehicles.

Warning: Do not change a wheel in a situation where you risk being hit by another vehicle. On busy roads, try to stop in a lay-by or a gateway. Be wary of passing traffic while changing the wheel – it is easy to become distracted by the job in hand.

Preparation

☐ When a puncture occurs, stop as soon as it is safe to do so.
☐ Park on firm level ground, if possible, and well out of the way of other traffic.
☐ Use hazard warning lights if necessary.

☐ If you have one, use a warning triangle to alert other drivers of your presence.
☐ Apply the handbrake and engage first or reverse gear (or Park on models with automatic transmission).

☐ Chock the wheel diagonally opposite the one being removed – a couple of large stones will do for this.
☐ If the ground is soft, use a flat piece of wood to spread the load under the jack.

Changing the wheel

1 From inside the boot area, use the wheelbrace to lower the spare wheel cradle.

2 Slide the spare wheel out from the underside of the car.

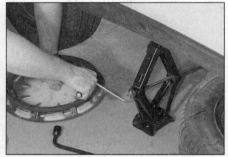

3 For safety in the event of the jack slipping, position the spare wheel under the sill, close to the jacking point.

4 Remove the wheel trim (where fitted) then slacken each wheel bolt by a half turn.

5 Locate the jack below the reinforced jacking point and on firm ground (don't jack the car at any other point on the sill).

6 Turn the jack handle clockwise until the wheel is raised clear of the ground, remove the bolts and lift the wheel clear.

7 Position the spare wheel and fit the bolts. Tighten moderately with the wheelbrace, then lower the car to the ground.

8 Tighten the wheel bolts in the sequence shown, fit the wheel trim, and secure the punctured wheel in the spare wheel cradle.

Finally...

☐ Remove the wheel chocks.

☐ Stow the jack and tools in the correct locations in the car.

☐ Check the tyre pressure on the wheel just fitted. If it is low, or if you don't have a pressure gauge with you, drive slowly to the nearest garage and inflate the tyre to the right pressure.

☐ Have the damaged tyre or wheel repaired as soon as possible.

Jump starting

Jump starting will get you out of trouble, but you must correct whatever made the battery go flat in the first place. There are three possibilities:

1 *The battery has been drained by repeated attempts to start, or by leaving the lights on.*

2 *The charging system is not working properly (alternator drivebelt slack or broken, alternator wiring fault or alternator itself faulty).*

3 *The battery itself is at fault (electrolyte low, or battery worn out).*

When jump-starting a car using a booster battery, observe the following precautions:

✔ Before connecting the booster battery, make sure that the ignition is switched off.

✔ Ensure that all electrical equipment (lights, heater, wipers, etc) is switched off.

✔ Take note of any special precautions printed on the battery case.

✔ Make sure that the booster battery is the same voltage as the discharged one in the vehicle.

✔ If the battery is being jump-started from the battery in another vehicle, the two vehicles MUST NOT TOUCH each other.

✔ Make sure that the transmission is in neutral (or PARK, in the case of automatic transmission).

1 Connect one end of the red jump lead to the positive (+) terminal of the flat battery

2 Connect the other end of the red lead to the positive (+) terminal of the booster battery.

3 Connect one end of the black jump lead to the negative (-) terminal of the booster battery

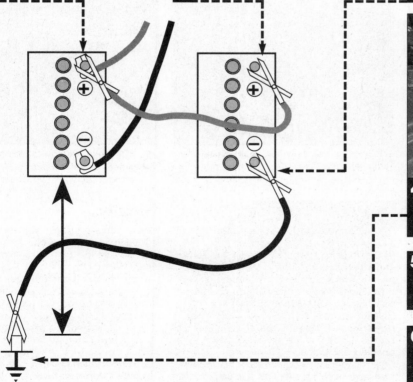

4 Connect the other end of the black jump lead to a bolt or bracket on the engine block, well away from the battery, on the vehicle to be started.

5 Make sure that the jump leads will not come into contact with the fan, drive-belts or other moving parts of the engine.

6 Start the engine using the booster battery and run it at idle speed. Switch on the lights, rear window demister and heater blower motor, then disconnect the jump leads in the reverse order of connection. Turn off the lights etc.

Identifying leaks

Puddles on the garage floor or drive, or obvious wetness under the bonnet or underneath the car, suggest a leak that needs investigating. It can sometimes be difficult to decide where the leak is coming from, especially if the engine bay is very dirty already. Leaking oil or fluid can also be blown rearwards by the passage of air under the car, giving a false impression of where the problem lies.

 Warning: Most automotive oils and fluids are poisonous. Wash them off skin, and change out of contaminated clothing, without delay.

 The smell of a fluid leaking from the car may provide a clue to what's leaking. Some fluids are distinctively coloured. It may help to clean the car carefully and to park it over some clean paper overnight as an aid to locating the source of the leak.
Remember that some leaks may only occur while the engine is running.

Sump oil

Engine oil may leak from the drain plug...

Oil from filter

...or from the base of the oil filter.

Gearbox oil

Gearbox oil can leak from the seals at the inboard ends of the driveshafts.

Antifreeze

Leaking antifreeze often leaves a crystalline deposit like this.

Brake fluid

A leak occurring at a wheel is almost certainly brake fluid.

Power steering fluid

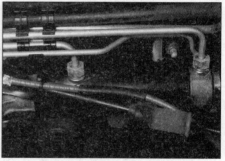

Power steering fluid may leak from the pipe connectors on the steering rack.

Towing

When all else fails, you may find yourself having to get a tow home – or of course you may be helping somebody else. Long-distance recovery should only be done by a garage or breakdown service. For shorter distances, DIY towing using another car is easy enough, but observe the following points:

☐ Use a proper tow-rope – they are not expensive. The vehicle being towed must display an ON TOW sign in its rear window.
☐ Always turn the ignition key to the 'on' position when the vehicle is being towed, so that the steering lock is released, and that the direction indicator and brake lights will work.

☐ Only attach the tow-rope to the towing eyes provided.
☐ Before being towed, release the handbrake and select neutral on the transmission. On models with automatic transmission, special precautions apply. If in doubt, do not tow, or transmission damage may result.
☐ Note that greater-than-usual pedal pressure will be required to operate the brakes, since the vacuum servo unit is only operational with the engine running.
☐ On models with power steering, greater-than-usual steering effort will also be required.
☐ The driver of the car being towed must

keep the tow-rope taut at all times to avoid snatching.
☐ Make sure that both drivers know the route before setting off.
☐ Only drive at moderate speeds and keep the distance towed to a minimum. Drive smoothly and allow plenty of time for slowing down at junctions.

⚠ *Warning: To prevent damage to the catalytic converter, a vehicle must not be push-started, or started by towing, when the engine is at operating temperature. Use jump leads (see 'Jump starting').*

Introduction

There are some very simple checks which need only take a few minutes to carry out, but which could save you a lot of inconvenience and expense.

These *Weekly checks* require no great skill or special tools, and the small amount of time they take to perform could prove to be very well spent, for example:

☐ Keeping an eye on tyre condition and pressures, will not only help to stop them wearing out prematurely, but could also save your life.
☐ Many breakdowns are caused by electrical problems. Battery-related faults are particularly common, and a quick check on a regular basis will often prevent the majority of these.

☐ If your car develops a brake fluid leak, the first time you might know about it is when your brakes don't work properly. Checking the level regularly will give advance warning of this kind of problem.
☐ If the oil or coolant levels run low, the cost of repairing any engine damage will be far greater than fixing the leak, for example.

Underbonnet check points

◄ 1.4 litre petrol

A *Engine oil level dipstick*
B *Engine oil filler cap*
C *Coolant expansion tank*
D *Brake fluid reservoir*
E *Washer fluid reservoir*
F *Battery*

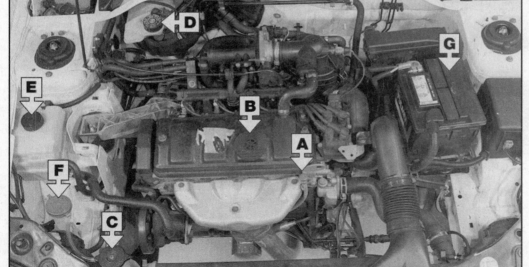

◄ 1.6 litre petrol

A *Engine oil level dipstick*
B *Engine oil filler cap*
C *Coolant expansion tank*
D *Brake fluid reservoir*
E *Power steering fluid reservoir*
F *Washer fluid reservoir*
G *Battery*

◄ **2.0 litre 8-valve petrol (1.8 litre similar)**

A *Engine oil level dipstick*

B *Engine oil filler cap*

C *Coolant expansion tank*

D *Brake fluid reservoir*

E *Power steering fluid reservoir*

F *Washer fluid reservoir*

G *Battery*

◄ **Non-turbo diesel**

A *Engine oil level dipstick and filler cap*

B *Coolant expansion tank*

C *Brake fluid reservoir*

D *Power steering fluid reservoir*

E *Washer fluid reservoir*

F *Battery*

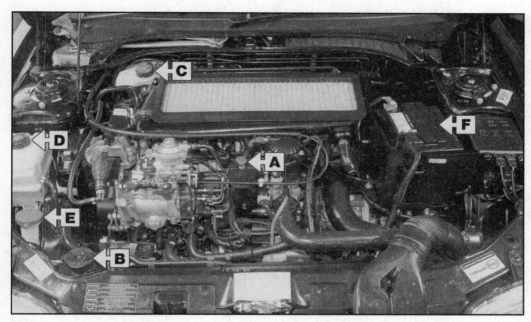

◄ 1.9 litre turbo diesel

A *Engine oil level dipstick and filler cap*

B *Coolant expansion tank*

C *Brake fluid reservoir*

D *Power steering fluid reservoir*

E *Washer fluid reservoir*

F *Battery*

◄ 2.0 litre turbo diesel

A *Engine oil level dipstick*

B *Engineoil filler cap*

C *Coolant expansion tank*

D *Brake fluid reservoir*

E *Power steering fluid reservoir*

F *Washer fluid reservoir*

G *Battery*

Engine oil level

Before you start

✔ Make sure that your car is on level ground.
✔ Check the oil level before the car is driven, or at least 5 minutes after the engine has been switched off.

 HAYNES HINT *If the oil is checked immediately after driving the vehicle, some of the oil will remain in the upper engine components, resulting in an inaccurate reading on the dipstick.*

The correct oil

Modern engines place great demands on their oil. It is very important that the correct oil for your car is used (see *Lubricants and fluids*).

Car Care

● If you have to add oil frequently, you should check whether you have any oil leaks. Place some clean paper under the car overnight, and check for stains in the morning. If there are no leaks, the engine may be burning oil.

● Always maintain the level between the upper and lower dipstick marks (see photo 3). If the level is too low severe engine damage may occur. Oil seal failure may result if the engine is overfilled by adding too much oil.

1 The dipstick is located at the rear of the engine on 1.8 litre petrol engine models, and at the front of the engine on all other models.

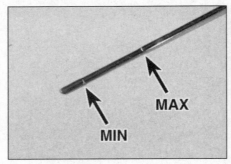

MAX

MIN

3 Note the oil level on the end of the dipstick, which should be between the upper (MAX) mark and lower (MIN) mark. Approximately 1.5 litres of oil will raise the level from the lower mark to the upper mark.

2 Withdraw the dipstick. Using a clean rag or paper towel, wipe all the oil from the dipstick. Insert the clean dipstick into the tube as far as it will go, then withdraw it again.

4 Oil is added through the filler cap. Unscrew the cap and top-up the level; a funnel may help to reduce spillage. Add the oil slowly, checking the level on the dipstick often. Don't overfill (see *Car Care*).

Power steering fluid level

Before you start

✔ Park the vehicle on level ground.
✔ Set the steering wheel straight-ahead.
✔ The engine should be turned off.

HAYNES HINT *For the check to be accurate, the steering must not be turned once the engine has been stopped.*

Safety First!

● The need for frequent topping-up indicates a leak, which should be investigated immediately.

1 The power steering fluid reservoir is located on the right-hand side of the engine compartment. The fluid level should be checked with the engine stopped. A translucent reservoir is fitted, with MAXI and MINI markings on the top of the reservoir.

2 The fluid level should be between the MAXI and MINI marks. If topping-up is necessary, and before removing the cap, wipe the surrounding area so that dirt does not enter the reservoir.

3 Unscrew the cap, allowing the fluid to drain from the bottom of the cap as it is removed. Top-up the fluid level to the MAXI mark, using the specified type of fluid (do not overfill the reservoir), then refit and tighten the filler cap.

Coolant level

 Warning: DO NOT attempt to remove the expansion tank pressure cap when the engine is hot, as there is a very great risk of scalding. Do not leave open containers of coolant about, as it is poisonous.

Car Care

● With a sealed-type cooling system, adding coolant should not be necessary on a regular basis. If frequent topping-up is required, it is likely there is a leak. Check the radiator, all hoses and joint faces for signs of staining or wetness, and rectify as necessary.

● It is important that antifreeze is used in the cooling system all year round, not just during the winter months. Don't top-up with water alone, as the antifreeze will become too diluted.

1 The coolant level varies with engine temperature. The level is checked in the expansion tank, which is built into the side of the radiator on petrol engine models and early diesel engine models. When the engine is cold, the coolant level should be between the MAXI and MINI marks.

2 On later diesel engine models, the expansion tank is located at the front of the engine compartment and the level can only be checked by removing the expansion tank cap (see next step). The coolant level is correct when it is just below the MAXI mark indicated on the side of the tank.

3 If topping-up is necessary, wait until the engine is cold then turn the pressure cap on the expansion tank slowly anti-clockwise, and pause until any pressure remaining in the system is released. Unscrew the cap and lift off.

4 Add a mixture of water and antifreeze to the expansion tank, until the coolant level is up to the MAXI level mark. Refit the cap, turning it clockwise as far as it will go until it is secure. Recheck that the cap is securely tightened once the engine is warm.

Washer fluid level

Screenwash additives not only keep the windscreen clean during foul weather, they also prevent the washer system freezing in cold weather – which is when you are likely to need it most. Don't top up using plain water as the screenwash will become too diluted, and will freeze during cold weather.

On no account use coolant antifreeze in the washer system – this could discolour or damage paintwork.

1 The windscreen/tailgate/headlight washer fluid reservoir is located at the front right-hand side of the engine compartment. If topping-up is necessary, open the cap

2 When topping-up the reservoir a screenwash additive should be added in the quantities recommended on the bottle.

Brake fluid level

Warning:
● Brake fluid can harm your eyes and damage painted surfaces, so use extreme caution when handling and pouring it.
● Do not use fluid that has been standing open for some time, as it absorbs moisture from the air, which can cause a dangerous loss of braking effectiveness.

HAYNES HiNT

• *Make sure that your car is on level ground.*

• *The fluid level in the reservoir will drop slightly as the brake pads wear down, but the fluid level must never be allowed to drop below the MIN mark.*

Safety First!

● If the reservoir requires repeated topping-up this is an indication of a fluid leak somewhere in the system, which should be investigated immediately.

● If a leak is suspected, the car should not be driven until the braking system has been checked. Never take any risks where brakes are concerned.

1 The MAX and MIN marks are indicated on the side of the reservoir, which is located on the front of the vacuum servo unit in the engine compartment. The fluid level must be kept between these two marks.

2 If topping-up is necessary, first wipe the area around the filler cap with a clean rag before removing the cap. When adding fluid, it's a good idea to inspect the reservoir. The system should be drained and refilled if dirt is seen in the fluid (see Chapter 9).

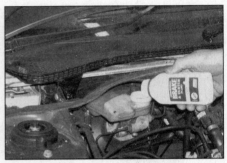

3 Carefully add fluid, avoiding spilling it on surrounding paintwork. Use only the specified hydraulic fluid; mixing different types of fluid can cause damage to the system and/or a loss of braking effectiveness. After filling to the correct level, refit the cap securely and wipe off any spilt fluid.

Tyre condition and pressure

It is very important that tyres are in good condition, and at the correct pressure - having a tyre failure at any speed is highly dangerous. Tyre wear is influenced by driving style - harsh braking and acceleration, or fast cornering, will all produce more rapid tyre wear. As a general rule, the front tyres wear out faster than the rears. Interchanging the tyres from front to rear ("rotating" the tyres) may result in more even wear. However, if this is completely effective, you may have the expense of replacing all four tyres at once! Remove any nails or stones embedded in the tread before they penetrate the tyre to cause deflation. If removal of a nail does reveal that the tyre has been punctured, refit the nail so that its point of penetration is marked. Then immediately change the wheel, and have the tyre repaired by a tyre dealer.

Regularly check the tyres for damage in the form of cuts or bulges, especially in the sidewalls. Periodically remove the wheels, and clean any dirt or mud from the inside and outside surfaces. Examine the wheel rims for signs of rusting, corrosion or other damage. Light alloy wheels are easily damaged by "kerbing" whilst parking; steel wheels may also become dented or buckled. A new wheel is very often the only way to overcome severe damage.

New tyres should be balanced when they are fitted, but it may become necessary to re-balance them as they wear, or if the balance weights fitted to the wheel rim should fall off. Unbalanced tyres will wear more quickly, as will the steering and suspension components. Wheel imbalance is normally signified by vibration, particularly at a certain speed (typically around 50 mph). If this vibration is felt only through the steering, then it is likely that just the front wheels need balancing. If, however, the vibration is felt through the whole car, the rear wheels could be out of balance. Wheel balancing should be carried out by a tyre dealer or garage.

1 *Tread Depth - visual check*
The original tyres have tread wear safety bands (B), which will appear when the tread depth reaches approximately 1.6 mm. The band positions are indicated by a triangular mark on the tyre sidewall (A).

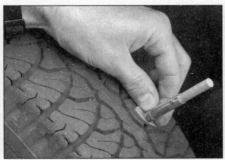

2 *Tread Depth - manual check*
Alternatively, tread wear can be monitored with a simple, inexpensive device known as a tread depth indicator gauge.

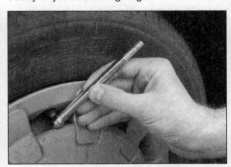

3 *Tyre Pressure Check*
Check the tyre pressures regularly with the tyres cold. Do not adjust the tyre pressures immediately after the vehicle has been used, or an inaccurate setting will result. Tyre pressures are shown on page 0•21.

Tyre tread wear patterns

Shoulder Wear

Underinflation (wear on both sides)
Under-inflation will cause overheating of the tyre, because the tyre will flex too much, and the tread will not sit correctly on the road surface. This will cause a loss of grip and excessive wear, not to mention the danger of sudden tyre failure due to heat build-up.
Check and adjust pressures
Incorrect wheel camber (wear on one side)
Repair or renew suspension parts
Hard cornering
Reduce speed!

Centre Wear

Overinflation
Over-inflation will cause rapid wear of the centre part of the tyre tread, coupled with reduced grip, harsher ride, and the danger of shock damage occurring in the tyre casing.
Check and adjust pressures

If you sometimes have to inflate your car's tyres to the higher pressures specified for maximum load or sustained high speed, don't forget to reduce the pressures to normal afterwards.

Uneven Wear

Front tyres may wear unevenly as a result of wheel misalignment. Most tyre dealers and garages can check and adjust the wheel alignment (or "tracking") for a modest charge.
Incorrect camber or castor
Repair or renew suspension parts
Malfunctioning suspension
Repair or renew suspension parts
Unbalanced wheel
Balance tyres
Incorrect toe setting
Adjust front wheel alignment
Note: *The feathered edge of the tread which typifies toe wear is best checked by feel.*

Battery

Caution: Before carrying out any work on the vehicle battery, read the precautions given in 'Safety first!' at the start of this manual.

✔ Make sure that the battery tray is in good condition, and that the clamp is tight. Corrosion on the tray, retaining clamp and the battery itself can be removed with a solution of water and baking soda. Thoroughly rinse all cleaned areas with water. Any metal parts damaged by corrosion should be covered with a zinc-based primer, then painted.

✔ Periodically (approximately every three months), check the charge condition of the battery as described in Chapter 5A.

✔ If the battery is flat, and you need to jump start your vehicle, see *Roadside Repairs*.

1 The battery is located on the left-hand side of the engine compartment. The exterior of the battery should be inspected periodically for damage such as a cracked case or cover.

2 Check the tightness of the battery cable clamps to ensure good electrical connections. You should not be able to move them. Also check each cable for cracks and frayed conductors.

Battery corrosion can be kept to a minimum by applying a layer of petroleum jelly to the clamps and terminals after they are reconnected.

3 If corrosion (white, fluffy deposits) is evident, remove the cables from the battery terminals, clean them with a small wire brush, then refit them. Automotive stores sell a useful tool for cleaning the battery post and terminals.

4 Note that the battery positive lead terminal can be disconnected by unscrewing the nut located under the plastic cover.

Electrical systems

✔ Check all external lights and the horn. Refer to the appropriate Sections of Chapter 12 for details if any of the circuits are found to be inoperative.

✔ Visually check all accessible wiring connectors, harnesses and retaining clips for security, and for signs of chafing or damage.

HAYNES HiNT *If you need to check your brake lights and indicators unaided, back up to a wall or garage door and operate the lights. The reflected light should show if they are working properly.*

1 If a single indicator light, brake light or headlight has failed, it is likely that a bulb has blown and will need to be renewed. Refer to Chapter 12 for details. If both brake lights have failed, it is possible that the brake light switch operated by the brake pedal has failed. Refer to Chapter 9 for details.

2 If more than one indicator light or tail light has failed it is likely that either a fuse has blown or that there is a fault in the circuit (see Chapter 12). The main fuses are located in the fuseboxes situated below the steering column and in the engine compartment (refer to Chapter 12).

3 To renew a blown fuse, remove it, where applicable, using the plastic tool provided. Fit a new fuse of the same rating, available from car accessory shops. It is important that you find the reason that the fuse blew (see 'Electrical fault finding' in Chapter 12).

Wiper blades

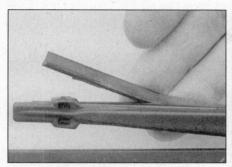

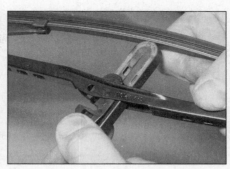

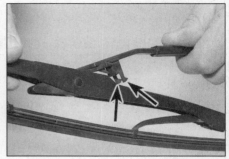

1 Check the condition of the wiper blades; if they are cracked or show any signs of deterioration, or if the glass swept area is smeared, renew them. Wiper blades should be renewed annually.

2 To remove a windscreen wiper blade, pull the arm fully away from the screen until it locks. Swivel the blade through 90°, then depress the locking clip at the base of the mounting block and slide the blade from the arm.

3 Don't forget to check the tailgate wiper blade as well (where applicable). Pull the arm away from the glass then swivel the blade through 90° to release the side locking tabs.

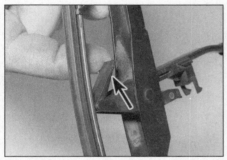

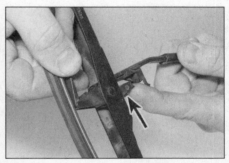

4 Hold the blade and lift up the front locking clip.

5 Depress the tab and withdraw the blade from the arm.

Lubricants and fluids

Engine

Petrol . . . . Synthetic or semi-synthetic multigrade engine oil, viscosity SAE 5W-40 or 10W-40 to specification API SH/SJ and/or ACEA A3: ESSO ULTRA/ULTRON or TOTAL QUARTZ

Diesel . . . . Synthetic or semi-synthetic multigrade engine oil, viscosity SAE 10W-40 to specification API CF/CD and/or ACEA B3: ESSO ULTRA DIESEL or TOTAL QUARTZ DIESEL 7000

Cooling system

Up to 2000 model year . . . . Mixture of ethylene glycol based antifreeze (PROCOR 3000 or REVKOGEL 107) and clean de-ionised water

Model year 2001 and onwards . . . . Mixture of monoethylene glycol based antifreeze (PROCOR TM 108, GLYSANTIN G33 or REVKOGEL 2000) and clean de-ionised water

Manual gearbox . . . . ESSO BV 75W-80W or TOTAL TRANSMISSION BV 75W-80 **only**

Automatic transmission

4 HP 14 transmission . . . . ESSO ATF D or TOTAL FLUIDE AT42

AL 4 transmission . . . . ESSO ATF 4HP20-AL4 **only**

Power steering reservoir . . . . ESSO ATF D or TOTAL FLUIDE ATX

Brake fluid reservoir . . . . Hydraulic fluid to SAE J1703, DOT 4

Choosing your engine oil

Engines need oil, not only to lubricate moving parts and minimise wear, but also to maximise power output and to improve fuel economy.

HOW ENGINE OIL WORKS

• *Beating friction*

Without oil, the moving surfaces inside your engine will rub together, heat up and melt, quickly causing the engine to seize. Engine oil creates a film which separates these moving parts, preventing wear and heat build-up.

• *Cooling hot-spots*

Temperatures inside the engine can exceed 1000° C. The engine oil circulates and acts as a coolant, transferring heat from the hot-spots to the sump.

• *Cleaning the engine internally*

Good quality engine oils clean the inside of your engine, collecting and dispersing combustion deposits and controlling them until they are trapped by the oil filter or flushed out at oil change.

OIL CARE - FOLLOW THE CODE

To handle and dispose of used engine oil safely, always:

OIL BANK LINE
0800 66 33 66
www.oilbankline.org.uk

• *Avoid skin contact with used engine oil. Repeated or prolonged contact can be harmful.*
• *Dispose of used oil and empty packs in a responsible manner in an authorised disposal site. Call 0800 663366 to find the one nearest to you. Never tip oil down drains or onto the ground.*

Tyre pressures - tyres cold

Note: *Tyre pressures should be checked when the tyres are cold (before a journey); do not forget to check the spare. Refer to the tyre pressure data plate on the rear edge of the driver's door (visible when the door is open) for the correct tyre pressures for your particular vehicle; those given below are a guide only. Pressures apply only to original-equipment tyres, and may vary if any other make or type is fitted; check with the tyre manufacturer or supplier for correct pressures if necessary.*

Note: *Where a space-saver spare wheel/tyre is supplied, the tyre must be maintained at a pressure of 4.2 bars (61 psi). Note also that such tyres must never be used at speeds in excess of 50 mph (80 km/h).*

1993 to 1997 model year vehicles	Front	Rear
165/70 R 13 T tyres - Hatchback:		
Manual steering	2.2 bars (32 psi)	2.2 bars (32 psi)
Power steering	2.0 bars (29 psi)	2.0 bars (29 psi)
165/70 R 13 T tyres - Sedan	2.2 bars (32 psi)	2.2 bars (32 psi)
165/70 R 13 T tyres - Van:		
Normal load	2.3 bars (33 psi)	2.4 bars (35 psi)
Fully-laden	2.3 bars (33 psi)	2.8 bars (41 psi)
175/70 R 13 T tyres - Hatchback:		
Petrol models, manual steering	2.2 bars (32 psi)	2.3 bars (33 psi)
Petrol models, power steering	2.0 bars (29 psi)	2.1 bars (30 psi)
Diesel models, manual steering	2.3 bars (33 psi)	2.4 bars (35 psi)
Diesel models, power steering	2.2 bars (32 psi)	2.2 bars (32 psi)
175/70 R 13 T tyres - Sedan:		
Petrol models	2.2 bars (32 psi)	2.2 bars (32 psi)
Diesel models, manual steering	2.3 bars (33 psi)	2.4 bars (35 psi)
Diesel models, power steering	2.2 bars (32 psi)	2.2 bars (32 psi)
175/70 R 13 T tyres - Van:		
Manual steering, normal load	2.3 bars (33 psi)	2.4 bars (35 psi)
Manual steering, fully-laden	2.3 bars (33 psi)	2.9 bars (42 psi)
Power steering, normal load	2.2 bars (32 psi)	2.3 bars (33 psi)
Power steering, fully-laden	2.2 bars (32 psi)	2.8 bars (41 psi)
165/70 R 14 T tyres	2.3 bars (33 psi)	2.3 bars (33 psi)
175/65 R 14 T tyres - Hatchback:		
Manual steering	2.2 bars (32 psi)	2.3 bars (33 psi)
Power steering	2.0 bars (29 psi)	2.1 bars (30 psi)
175/65 R 14 T tyres - Sedan:		
Petrol models, manual steering	2.2 bars (32 psi)	2.3 bars (33 psi)
Petrol models, power steering	2.3 bars (33 psi)	2.3 bars (33 psi)
Diesel models, manual steering	2.2 bars (32 psi)	2.3 bars (33 psi)
Diesel models, power steering	2.0 bars (29 psi)	2.1 bars (30 psi)
175/65 R 14 H tyres:		
Petrol models	2.0 bars (29 psi)	2.1 bars (30 psi)
Diesel models	2.3 bars (33 psi)	2.4 bars (35 psi)
185/60 R 14 H tyres - Hatchback:		
Early models	2.2 bars (32 psi)	2.2 bars (32 psi)
Later petrol models	2.3 bars (33 psi)	2.3 bars (33 psi)
Later Diesel models	2.3 bars (33 psi)	2.4 bars (35 psi)
185/60 R 14 H tyres - Sedan:		
Petrol models	2.4 bars (35 psi)	2.4 bars (35 psi)
Diesel models, manual steering	2.2 bars (32 psi)	2.2 bars (32 psi)
Diesel models, power steering	2.4 bars (35 psi)	2.4 bars (35 psi)
185/55 R 15 V tyres:		
Hatchback models	2.2 bars (32 psi)	2.2 bars (32 psi)
Cabriolet models	2.3 bars (33 psi)	2.3 bars (33 psi)
195/55 R 15 V tyres	2.3 bars (33 psi)	2.3 bars (33 psi)

1998-on model year vehicles	Front	Rear
165/70 R 13 T tyres - Hatchback:		
Manual steering	2.5 bars (36 psi)	2.5 bars (36 psi)
Power steering	2.4 bars (35 psi)	2.4 bars (35 psi)
165/70 R 13 T tyres - Sedan	2.4 bars (35 psi)	2.4 bars (35 psi)
175/70 R 13 T tyres - Hatchback:		
Petrol models	2.3 bars (33 psi)	2.3 bars (33 psi)
Diesel models	2.4 bars (35 psi)	2.4 bars (35 psi)
175/70 R 13 T tyres - Sedan:		
Petrol models, manual steering	2.4 bars (35 psi)	2.4 bars (35 psi)
Petrol models, power steering	2.3 bars (33 psi)	2.3 bars (33 psi)
Diesel models	2.4 bars (35 psi)	2.4 bars (35 psi)
175/70 R 13 T tyres - Estate:		
Petrol models, manual steering, normal load	2.4 bars (35 psi)	2.4 bars (35 psi)
Petrol models, manual steering, fully-laden	2.4 bars (35 psi)	3.0 bars (44 psi)
Petrol models, power steering, normal load	2.3 bars (33 psi)	2.3 bars (33 psi)
Petrol models, power steering, fully-laden	2.3 bars (33 psi)	3.0 bars (44 psi)
Diesel models, normal load	2.4 bars (35 psi)	2.4 bars (35 psi)
Diesel models, fully-laden	2.4 bars (35 psi)	3.0 bars (44 psi)
175/70 R 13 T tyres - Van	2.5 bars (36 psi)	2.5 bars (36 psi)
185/65 R 14 T tyres - Hatchback	2.4 bars (35 psi)	2.4 bars (35 psi)
185/65 R 14 T tyres - Sedan:		
Petrol models	2.4 bars (35 psi)	2.4 bars (35 psi)
Diesel models, manual steering	2.5 bars (36 psi)	2.5 bars (36 psi)
Diesel models, power steering	2.4 bars (35 psi)	2.4 bars (35 psi)
185/65 R 14 T tyres - Estate:		
Normal load	2.4 bars (35 psi)	2.4 bars (35 psi)
Fully-laden	2.4 bars (35 psi)	3.0 bars (44 psi)
185/65 R 14 H tyres - Hatchback:		
Models with LFZ engine and manual gearbox or DJY engine	2.3 bars (33 psi)	2.3 bars (33 psi)
2.0 litre models with automatic transmission	2.5 bars (36 psi)	2.5 bars (36 psi)
All other models	2.4 bars (35 psi)	2.4 bars (35 psi)
185/65 R 14 H tyres - Sedan:		
Models with DJY engine	2.3 bars (33 psi)	2.3 bars (33 psi)
1.8 and 2.0 litre models with automatic transmission, models with LFY or DHY engines	2.5 bars (36 psi)	2.5 bars (36 psi)
All other models	2.4 bars (35 psi)	2.4 bars (35 psi)
185/65 R 14 H tyres - Estate:		
2.0 litre models with automatic transmission, normal load	2.5 bars (36 psi)	2.5 bars (36 psi)
2.0 litre models with automatic transmission, fully-laden	2.5 bars (36 psi)	3.0 bars (44 psi)
All other models, manual steering, normal load	2.5 bars (36 psi)	2.5 bars (36 psi)
All other models, manual steering, fully-laden	2.5 bars (36 psi)	3.0 bars (44 psi)
All other models, power steering, normal load	2.4 bars (35 psi)	2.4 bars (35 psi)
All other models, power steering, fully-laden	2.4 bars (35 psi)	3.0 bars (44 psi)
185/65 R 14 tyres - Cabriolet:		
1.6 litre models	2.5 bars (36 psi)	2.5 bars (36 psi)
1.8 litre models	2.4 bars (35 psi)	2.4 bars (35 psi)
195/55 R 15 V tyres - Hatchback and Cabriolet	2.5 bars (36 psi)	2.5 bars (36 psi)

Chapter 1 Part A:
Routine maintenance and servicing – petrol models

Contents

Degrees of difficulty

Easy, suitable for novice with little experience	**Fairly easy,** suitable for beginner with some experience	**Fairly difficult,** suitable for competent DIY mechanic	**Difficult,** suitable for experienced DIY mechanic	**Very difficult,** suitable for expert DIY or professional

Lubricants and fluids

Refer to *Weekly checks*

Capacities (approximate)

Engine oil (including filter)

	With steel sump	With aluminium sump
1.1, 1.4 and 1.6 litre models	3.2 litres	
1.8 litre 8-valve models:		
Up to 1994 model year	4.9 litres	4.4 litres
From 1995 model year	4.7 litres	4.2 litres
1.8 litre 16-valve models	4.7 litres	4.2 litres
2.0 litre 8-valve models:		
Up to 1994 model year	4.7 litres	4.4 litres
From 1995 model year	4.5 litres	4.2 litres
2.0 litre 16-valve models	4.7 litres	4.2 litres
Difference between MAX and MIN dipstick marks	1.5 litres	

Cooling system

1.1 and 1.4 litre models	6.5 litres
1.6 litre models	7.0 litres
1.8 and 2.0 litre models	7.5 litres

Transmission

Manual	2.0 litres
Automatic:	
4 HP 14 transmission:	
From dry	6.2 litres
Drain and refill	2.4 litres
AL4 transmission:	
From dry	6.0 litres
Drain and refill	4.5 litres

Power-assisted steering .... 1.7 litres

Fuel tank .... 60.0 litres

Cooling system

Antifreeze mixture:
  50% antifreeze .... Protection down to –35°C
Note: *Refer to antifreeze manufacturer for latest recommendations.*

Fuel system

Idle speed:	
Carburettor models	850 ± 50 rpm
Fuel injected models*	850 ± 50 rpm
Idle mixture CO content:	
Carburettor models	1.0 %
Fuel injected models*	Less than 1.0 %

* *Not adjustable – controlled by ECU*
Note: *See the relevant Part of Chapter 4 for further information.*

Ignition system

Ignition timing .... Refer to Chapter 5B

Spark plugs:	Type	Electrode gap
All engines	Bosch FR7 D+	0.9 mm

Brakes

Brake pad friction material minimum thickness	2.0 mm
Brake shoe friction material minimum thickness	1.5 mm

Tyre pressures

See end of *Weekly checks*

Torque wrench settings

	Nm	lbf ft
Oil filter cover (later 1.4 and 1.6 litre engines)	25	18
Roadwheel bolts	85	63
Spark plugs	25	18
Transmission filler/level and drain plugs	25	18

Note: *This maintenance schedule is a guide recommended by Haynes for servicing your own vehicle. For the manufacturer's maintenance schedule, check with your local dealer.*

The maintenance intervals in this manual are provided with the assumption that you, not the dealer, will be carrying out the work. These are the minimum maintenance intervals recommended by us for vehicles driven daily. If you wish to keep your vehicle in peak condition at all times, you may wish to perform some of these procedures more often. We encourage frequent maintenance, because it enhances the efficiency, performance and resale value of your vehicle.

If the vehicle is driven in dusty areas, used to tow a trailer, or driven frequently at slow speeds (idling in traffic) or on short journeys, more frequent maintenance intervals are recommended.

When the vehicle is new, it should be serviced by a factory-authorised dealer service department, in order to preserve the factory warranty.

Every 250 miles (400 km) or weekly
☐ Refer to *Weekly checks*

Every 5000 miles (7500 km) or 6 months – whichever comes first
☐ Renew the engine oil and filter (Section 3).

Note: *Frequent oil and filter changes are good for the engine. The manufacturer has extended the oil change interval for later models, provided their specified lubricant is used. Consult your dealer for more information. We recommend changing the oil at the mileage specified here, or at least twice a year if the mileage covered is a less.*

Every 10 000 miles (15 000 km) or 12 months – whichever comes first
In addition to all the items listed above, carry out the following:
☐ Check all underbonnet components or fluid leaks (Section 4).
☐ Check the steering and suspension components (Section 5).
☐ Check the condition of the driveshaft rubber gaiters (Section 6).
☐ Check the automatic transmission fluid level – 4 HP 14 transmission (Section 7).

Every 20 000 miles (30 000 km)
In addition to all the items listed above, carry out the following:
☐ Check the air conditioning system refrigerant (see Section 8).
☐ Renew the spark plugs (Section 9).
☐ Renew the fuel filter – carburettor models (Section 10).
☐ Renew the automatic transmission fluid – 4 HP 14 transmission (Section 11).
☐ Check the ignition system and ignition timing (Section 12).
☐ Check the idle speed and mixture adjustment (Section 13).
☐ Check the emissions control system components (Section 14).
☐ Check the condition of the auxiliary drivebelt (Section 15).
☐ Check the clutch adjustment (Section 16).
☐ Lubricate the clutch control mechanism (Section 16).
☐ Check the condition of the front brake pads (Section 17).
☐ Check the operation of the handbrake (Section 18).
☐ Carry out a road test (Section 19).

Every 40 000 miles (60 000 km)
In addition to all the items listed above, carry out the following:
☐ Check the automatic transmission fluid level – AL4 transmission (Section 7).
☐ Lubricate all hinges and locks (Section 20).
☐ Renew the air filter (Section 21).
☐ Check the condition of the rear drum brake shoes (Section 22).
☐ Check the condition of the rear disc brake pads (Section 23).
☐ Check the manual transmission oil level (Section 24).
☐ Renew the fuel filter – fuel injected models (Section 25).
☐ Renew the timing belt (Section 26)*.

* Note: *Although the normal interval for timing belt renewal is 80 000 miles (120 000 km), it is strongly recommended that the interval is halved to 40 000 miles (60 000 km), especially on vehicles which are subjected to intensive use, ie, mainly short journeys or a lot of stop-start driving. The actual belt renewal interval is therefore very much up to the individual owner, but bear in mind that severe engine damage will result if the belt breaks.*

Every 2 years (regardless of mileage)
☐ Renew the coolant (Section 27)*.
☐ Renew the brake fluid (Section 28).

* *The manufacturer has extended the coolant renewal interval for later models, provided their specified antifreeze is used. Consult your dealer for more information.*

Underbonnet view of a 1.6 litre model

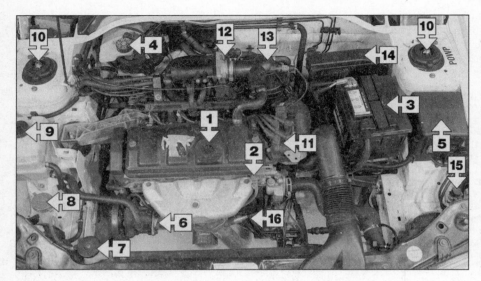

1 Engine oil filler cap
2 Engine oil dipstick
3 Battery
4 Master cylinder brake fluid reservoir
5 Relay box
6 Power steering pump
7 Radiator filler cap
8 Windscreen/tailgate washer fluid
  reservoir filler cap
9 Power steering fluid reservoir filler
  cap
10 Suspension strut upper mounting
11 DIS coil
12 Throttle housing
13 Air cleaner housing
14 Fuel injection ECU box
15 Anti-theft alarm switch
16 Lambda sensor

Underbonnet view of a 2.0 litre 8-valve model

1 Engine oil filler cap
2 Engine oil dipstick
3 Battery
4 Master cylinder brake fluid reservoir
5 Relay box
6 Alternator
7 Radiator filler cap
8 Windscreen/tailgate washer fluid
  reservoir filler cap
9 Power steering fluid reservoir filler
  cap
10 Suspension strut upper mounting
11 DIS coil
12 Throttle body
13 Air cleaner housing
14 Fuel injection ECU box
15 Anti-theft alarm switch
16 Fuel pressure regulator

Front underbody view of a 1.6 litre model

1 Engine oil filter
2 Sump drain plug
3 Power steering pump
4 Screen washer reservoir
5 Engine/transmission rear mounting
6 Exhaust front pipe
7 Front suspension subframe
8 Front brake caliper
9 Front suspension lower arm
10 Track rod balljoint
11 Front anti-roll bar
12 Steering gear assembly
13 Fuel pipes
14 Brake pipes

Rear underbody view of a 1.6 litre model

1 Spare wheel
2 Rear silencer
3 Fuel tank
4 Handbrake cable
5 Rear suspension torsion bar
6 Rear suspension tubular crossmember
7 Rear shock absorber
8 Rear suspension trailing arm

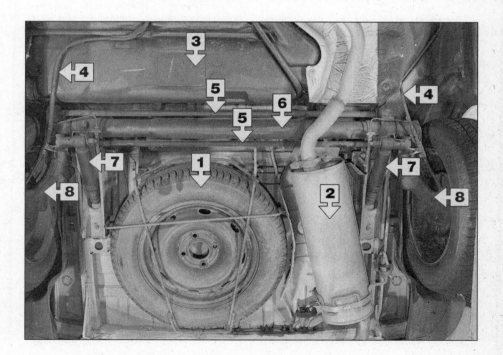

1 General information

This Chapter is designed to help the home mechanic maintain his/her vehicle for safety, economy, long life and peak performance.

The Chapter contains a master maintenance schedule, followed by Sections dealing specifically with each task in the schedule. Visual checks, adjustments, component renewal and other helpful items are included. Refer to the accompanying illustrations of the engine compartment and the underside of the vehicle for the locations of the various components.

Servicing your vehicle in accordance with the mileage/time maintenance schedule and the following Sections will provide a planned maintenance programme, which should result in a long and reliable service life. This is a comprehensive plan, so maintaining some items but not others at the specified service intervals, will not produce the same results.

As you service your vehicle, you will discover that many of the procedures can – and should – be grouped together, because of the particular procedure being performed, or because of the proximity of two otherwise-unrelated components to one another. For example, if the vehicle is raised for any reason, the exhaust can be inspected at the same time as the suspension and steering components.

The first step in this maintenance programme is to prepare yourself before the actual work begins. Read through all the Sections relevant to the work to be carried out, then make a list and gather all the parts and tools required. If a problem is encountered, seek advice from a parts specialist, or a dealer service department.

Service interval display

Later models are equipped with a service interval display indicator in the instrument panel. When the ignition is initially switched on, a spanner appears in the display window and the total number of miles remaining until the next service is due is also shown.

The display should not necessarily be used as a definitive guide to the servicing needs of your 306, but it is useful as a reminder, to ensure that servicing is not accidentally overlooked. Owners of cars covering a small annual mileage, may feel inclined to service their car more often, in which case the service interval display is perhaps less relevant.

The display should be reset whenever a service is carried out, and this is achieved using the trip meter reset button on the instrument panel as follows.

With the ignition switched off, press and hold down the trip meter reset button. Switch the ignition on and the mileage remaining until the next service will flash. Continue to hold the button down for a further ten seconds. The spanner symbol will disappear and the mileage will return to zero.

2 Regular maintenance

1 If, from the time the vehicle is new, the routine maintenance schedule is followed closely, and frequent checks are made of fluid levels and high-wear items, as suggested throughout this manual, the engine will be kept in relatively good running condition, and the need for additional work will be minimised.
2 It is possible that there will be times when the engine is running poorly due to the lack of regular maintenance. This is even more likely if a used vehicle, which has not received regular and frequent maintenance checks, is purchased. In such cases, additional work may need to be carried out, outside of the regular maintenance intervals.
3 If engine wear is suspected, a compression test or leakdown test (refer to relevant Part of Chapter 2) will provide valuable information regarding the overall performance of the main internal components. Such a test can be used as a basis to decide on the extent of the work to be carried out. If, for example, a compression or leakdown test indicates serious internal engine wear, conventional maintenance as described in this Chapter will not greatly improve the performance of the engine, and may prove a waste of time and money, unless extensive overhaul work is carried out first.
4 The following series of operations are those most often required to improve the performance of a generally poor-running engine:

Primary operations

a) Clean, inspect and test the battery (See 'Weekly checks').
b) Check all the engine-related fluids (See 'Weekly checks').
c) Check the condition and tension of the auxiliary drivebelt (Section 15).
d) Renew the spark plugs (Section 9).
e) Inspect the distributor cap, rotor arm and HT leads – as applicable (Section 12).
f) Check the condition of the air filter, and renew if necessary (Section 21).
g) Renew the fuel filter (Section 10 or 25).
h) Check the condition of all hoses, and check for fluid leaks (Section 4).
i) Check the idle speed and mixture settings – carburettor models (Section 13).

5 If the above operations do not prove fully effective, carry out the following secondary operations:

Secondary operations

All items listed under *Primary operations*, plus the following:

a) Check the charging system (Chapter 5A).
b) Check the ignition system (Chapter 5B).
c) Check the fuel system (relevant Part of Chapter 4).
d) Renew the distributor cap and rotor arm – as applicable (Section 12).
e) Renew the ignition HT leads (Section 12).

Every 5000 miles or 6 months – whichever comes first

3 Engine oil and filter renewal

Note: *A suitable square-section wrench may be required to undo the sump drain plug on some models. These wrenches can be obtained from most motor factors or your Peugeot dealer.*
1 Frequent oil and filter changes are the most important preventative maintenance procedures which can be undertaken by the DIY owner. As engine oil ages, it becomes diluted and contaminated, which leads to premature engine wear.
2 Before starting this procedure, gather together all the necessary tools and materials. Also make sure that you have plenty of clean rags and newspapers handy, to mop-up any spills. Ideally, the engine oil should be warm, as it will drain better, and more built-up sludge will be removed with it. Take care, however, not to touch the exhaust or any other hot parts of the engine when working under the vehicle. To avoid any possibility of scalding, and to protect yourself from possible skin irritants and other harmful contaminants in used engine oils, it is advisable to wear gloves when carrying out this work. Access to the underside of the vehicle will be greatly improved if it can be raised on a lift, driven onto ramps, or jacked up and supported on axle stands (see *Jacking and vehicle support*). Whichever method is chosen, make sure that the vehicle remains level, or if it is at an angle, that the drain plug is at the lowest point.

3 Slacken the drain plug about half a turn **(see illustration)**. Position the draining container under the drain plug, then remove

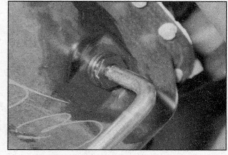

3.3 Slackening the sump drain plug with a square-section wrench

HAYNES HINT

As the drain plug releases from the threads, move it away sharply so the stream of oil issuing from the sump runs into the container, not up your sleeve.

the plug completely. If possible, try to keep the plug pressed into the sump while unscrewing it by hand the last couple of turns (**see Haynes Hint**). Recover the sealing washer from the drain plug.

4 Allow some time for the old oil to drain, noting that it may be necessary to reposition the container as the oil flow slows to a trickle.

5 After all the oil has drained, wipe off the drain plug with a clean rag, and fit a new sealing washer. Clean the area around the drain plug opening, and refit the plug. Tighten the plug securely.

6 Move the container into position under the oil filter, which is located on the front facing side of the cylinder block.

7 On most engines, the oil filter is of the disposable metal canister type screwed into the front of the cylinder block or into the oil filter housing on the front of the cylinder block. However, on later 1.4 and 1.6 litre engines, the oil filter consists of a separate disposable cartridge contained in a plastic housing. The housing is located on the front of the cylinder block adjacent to the radiator hoses (**see illustration**). Proceed as follows according to filter type.

Metal canister type filter

8 Using an oil filter removal tool if necessary,

slacken the filter initially, then unscrew it by hand the rest of the way (**see illustration**). Empty the oil in the old filter into the container. To ensure that the old filter is completely empty before disposal, puncture the filter dome in at least two places and allow any remaining oil to drain through the punctures and into the container.

9 Use a clean rag to remove all oil and dirt from the filter sealing area on the engine. Check the old filter to make sure that the rubber sealing ring hasn't stuck to the engine. If it has, carefully remove it.

10 Apply a light coating of clean engine oil to the sealing ring on the new filter, then screw it into position on the engine. Tighten the filter firmly by hand only – do not use any tools.

Disposable cartridge type filter

11 Using a 27 mm socket or spanner, slacken the oil filter cover initially, then unscrew it by hand the rest of the way. As the cover is unscrewed, the plunger tube located internally in the housing will be lifted off its seat allowing the oil remaining in the housing to drain back into the sump (**see illustration**).

12 Lift the filter cover off the housing and remove the filter cartridge. Withdraw the plunger tube from the oil filter cover. Note that a new plunger tube should always be fitted when renewing the oil filter. The tube should be supplied together with the new oil filter, but if this is not the case, obtain a new plunger tube from your Peugeot dealer.

13 Use a clean rag to remove all oil and dirt from the oil filter housing and clean the filter cover inside and out using a suitable solvent.

14 Place the new oil filter on the filter housing then insert the new plunger tube into its location in the cover. Lightly lubricate the seal in the filter cover and the O-ring on the end of the plunger tube with clean engine oil.

15 Screw the filter cover onto the housing and tighten it to the specified torque.

All filter types

16 Remove the old oil and all tools from under the car. Lower the car to the ground (if applicable).

3.7 Cartridge type oil filter housing location (arrowed) – later 1.4 and 1.6 litre engines

17 Remove the dipstick, then unscrew the oil filler cap from the cylinder head cover or oil filler/breather neck (as applicable). Fill the engine, using the correct grade and type of oil (see *Weekly checks*). An oil can spout or funnel may help to reduce spillage. Pour in half the specified quantity of oil first, then wait a few minutes for the oil to run to the sump. Continue adding oil a small quantity at a time until the level is up to the lower mark on the dipstick. Adding approximately 1.5 litres will bring the level up to the upper mark on the dipstick. Refit the filler cap.

18 Start the engine and run it for a few minutes; check for leaks around the oil filter seal and the sump drain plug. Note that there may be a delay of a few seconds before the oil pressure warning light goes out when the engine is first started, as the oil circulates through the engine oil galleries and the new oil filter before the pressure builds-up.

19 Switch off the engine, and wait a few minutes for the oil to settle in the sump once more. With the new oil circulated and the filter completely full, recheck the level on the dipstick, and add more oil as necessary.

20 Dispose of the used engine oil and filter safely, with reference to *General repair procedures* at the rear of this manual. Do not discard the old filter with domestic household waste. The facility for waste oil disposal provided by many local council refuse tips generally has a filter receptacle alongside.

3.8 Using an oil filter removal tool to slacken the canister type oil filter

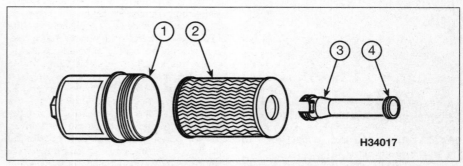

H34017

3.11 Cartridge type oil filter components – later 1.4 and 1.6 litre engines

1 Oil filter cover   2 Oil filter cartridge   3 Plunger tube   4 Plunger tube O-ring

Every 10 000 miles or 12 months – whichever comes first

4 Hose and fluid leak check

1 Visually inspect the engine joint faces, gaskets and seals for any signs of water or oil leaks. Pay particular attention to the areas around the camshaft cover, cylinder head, oil filter and sump joint faces. Bear in mind that, over a period of time, some very slight seepage from these areas is to be expected – what you are really looking for is any indication of a serious leak. Should a leak be found, renew the offending gasket or oil seal by referring to the appropriate Chapters in this manual.

2 Also check the security and condition of all the engine-related pipes and hoses. Ensure that all cable ties or securing clips are in place, and in good condition. Clips which are broken or missing can lead to chafing of the hoses, pipes or wiring, which could cause more serious problems in the future.

3 Carefully check the radiator hoses and heater hoses along their entire length. Renew any hose which is cracked, swollen or deteriorated. Cracks will show up better if the hose is squeezed. Pay close attention to the hose clips that secure the hoses to the cooling system components. Hose clips can pinch and puncture hoses, resulting in cooling system leaks. If the original Peugeot crimped-type hose clips are used, it may be a good idea to use standard worm-drive clips.

4 Inspect all the cooling system components (hoses, joint faces, etc) for leaks **(see Haynes Hint)**.

5 Where any problems are found on system components, renew the component or gasket with reference to Chapter 3.

6 Where applicable, inspect the automatic transmission fluid cooler hoses for leaks or deterioration.

7 With the vehicle raised, inspect the petrol tank and filler neck for punctures, cracks and other damage. The connection between the

HAYNES HINT

A leak in the cooling system will usually show up as white- or rust-coloured deposits on the area adjoining the leak.

filler neck and tank is especially critical. Sometimes a rubber filler neck or connecting hose will leak due to loose retaining clamps or deteriorated rubber.

8 Carefully check all rubber hoses and metal fuel lines leading away from the petrol tank. Check for loose connections, deteriorated hoses, crimped lines, and other damage. Pay particular attention to the vent pipes and hoses, which often loop up around the filler neck and can become blocked or crimped. Follow the lines to the front of the vehicle, carefully inspecting them all the way. Renew damaged sections as necessary.

9 From within the engine compartment, check the security of all fuel hose attachments and pipe unions, and inspect the fuel hoses and vacuum hoses for kinks, chafing and deterioration.

10 Where applicable, check the condition of the power steering fluid hoses and pipes.

5 Steering and suspension check

Front suspension and steering

1 Firmly apply the handbrake, then jack up the front of the car and support it securely on axle stands (see *Jacking and vehicle support*).

2 Visually inspect the balljoint dust covers and the steering rack-and-pinion gaiters for splits, chafing or deterioration. Any wear of these components will cause loss of lubricant, together with dirt and water entry, resulting in rapid deterioration of the balljoints or steering gear.

3 On vehicles with power steering, check the fluid hoses for chafing or deterioration, and the pipe and hose unions for fluid leaks. Also check for signs of fluid leakage under pressure from the steering gear rubber gaiters, which would indicate failed fluid seals within the steering gear.

4 Grasp the roadwheel at the 12 o'clock and 6 o'clock positions, and try to rock it **(see illustration)**. Very slight free play may be felt,

5.4 Check for wear in the hub bearings by grasping the wheel and trying to rock it

but if the movement is appreciable, further investigation is necessary to determine the source. Continue rocking the wheel while an assistant depresses the footbrake. If the movement is now eliminated or significantly reduced, it is likely that the hub bearings are at fault. If the free play is still evident with the footbrake depressed, then there is wear in the suspension joints or mountings.

5 Now grasp the wheel at the 9 o'clock and 3 o'clock positions, and try to rock it as before. Any movement felt now may again be caused by wear in the hub bearings or the steering track rod balljoints. If the inner or outer balljoint is worn, the visual movement will be obvious.

6 Using a large screwdriver or flat bar, check for wear in the suspension mounting bushes by levering between the relevant suspension component and its attachment point. Some movement is to be expected as the mountings are made of rubber, but excessive wear should be obvious. Also check the condition of any visible rubber bushes, looking for splits, cracks or contamination of the rubber.

7 With the car standing on its wheels, have an assistant turn the steering wheel back-and-forth about an eighth of a turn each way. There should be very little, if any, lost movement between the steering wheel and roadwheels. If this is not the case, closely observe the joints and mountings previously described, but in addition, check the steering column universal joints for wear, and the rack-and-pinion steering gear itself.

Strut/shock absorber

8 Check for any signs of fluid leakage around the suspension strut/shock absorber body, or from the rubber gaiter around the piston rod. Should any fluid be noticed, the suspension strut/shock absorber is defective internally, and should be renewed. **Note:** *Suspension struts/shock absorbers should always be renewed in pairs on the same axle.*

9 The efficiency of the suspension strut/shock absorber may be checked by bouncing the vehicle at each corner. Generally speaking, the body will return to its normal position and stop after being depressed. If it rises and returns on a rebound, the suspension strut/shock absorber is probably suspect. Examine also the suspension strut/shock absorber upper and lower mountings for any signs of wear.

6 Driveshaft gaiter check

1 With the vehicle raised and securely supported on axle stands (see *Jacking and vehicle support*), turn the steering onto full lock, then slowly rotate the roadwheel. Inspect

6.1 Check the condition of the driveshaft gaiters (arrowed)

7.1 Withdrawing the automatic transmission fluid dipstick – 4 HP 14 transmission

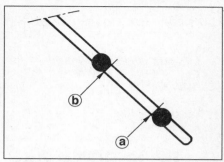

7.2 4 HP 14 automatic transmission fluid dipstick lower (a) and upper (b) fluid level markings – dipstick with two notches shown

the condition of the outer constant velocity (CV) joint rubber gaiters, squeezing the gaiters to open out the folds **(see illustration)**. Check for signs of cracking, splits or deterioration of the rubber, which may allow the grease to escape, and lead to water and grit entry into the joint. Also check the security and condition of the retaining clips. Repeat these checks on the inner CV joints. If any damage or deterioration is found, the gaiters should be renewed (see Chapter 8).

2 At the same time, check the general condition of the CV joints themselves by first holding the driveshaft and attempting to rotate the wheel. Repeat this check by holding the inner joint and attempting to rotate the driveshaft. Any appreciable movement indicates wear in the joints, wear in the driveshaft splines, or a loose driveshaft retaining nut.

7 Automatic transmission fluid level check

Note: *Refer to Chapter 7B for transmission identification according to model.*

4 HP 14 transmission

1 Take the vehicle on a moderate journey, to warm the transmission up to normal operating temperature, then park the vehicle on level ground. Leave the engine idling and move the selector lever to the P (Park) position. The fluid level is checked using the dipstick located at the front of the engine compartment, directly in front of the engine unit **(see illustration)**. The dipstick top is brightly-coloured for easy identification.

2 With the engine idling, move the selector lever to the 1 position, then back to the P position twice, stopping briefly in each position. With the selector lever returned to the P position, withdraw the dipstick from the tube, and wipe all the fluid from its end with a clean rag or paper towel. Insert the clean dipstick back into the tube as far as it will go, then withdraw it once more. Note the fluid level on the end of the dipstick. On models with two notches on the dipstick, the level should be between the upper and lower marks **(see illustration)**. On models with three

notches on the dipstick, the level should be between the two upper marks on the dipstick (the marks located on either side of the number 80).

3 If topping-up is necessary, add the required quantity of the specified fluid to the transmission via the dipstick tube. Use a funnel with a fine-mesh gauze, to avoid spillage, and to ensure that no foreign matter enters the transmission. **Note:** *Never overfill the transmission so that the fluid level is above the upper mark.*

4 After topping-up, take the vehicle on a short run to distribute the fresh fluid, then recheck the level again, topping-up if necessary.

5 Always maintain the level between the two dipstick marks. If the level is allowed to fall below the lower mark, fluid starvation may result, which could lead to severe transmission damage.

6 Frequent need for topping-up indicates that there is a leak, which should be found and corrected before it becomes serious.

AL4 transmission

Note: *The transmission unit is equipped with a fluid wear sensor to inform the driver when the fluid needs renewing (the ECU flashes the Sport and Snow mode indicator lights when fluid renewal is necessary). Every time the transmission unit is topped-up, this sensor*

should be adjusted to compensate for the new fluid being added, however this can only be done using the Peugeot diagnostic test box. Adding fluid without adjusting the sensor will not cause any problems but will mean the sensor is giving an inaccurate reading, resulting in fluid renewal being recommended earlier than is actually necessary.

7 Take the vehicle on a short journey, to warm the transmission up to normal operating temperature, then park the vehicle on level ground. Firmly apply the handbrake and place the selector lever in the P position.

8 Where necessary, remove the air cleaner and air inlet duct as described in Chapter 4C, for improved access to the filler plug on the top of the transmission. Wipe clean the area around the filler plug, then unscrew the plug and recover the sealing washer **(see illustration)**.

9 Carefully add 0.5 litre of the specified type of fluid to the transmission via the filler plug aperture. Fit a new sealing washer to the filler plug then refit the plug, tightening it to the specified torque.

10 Position a suitable container under the drain/filler plug arrangement, situated on the base of the transmission. The level plug is the smaller plug fitted to the centre of the larger drain plug **(see illustration)**.

Caution: Do not remove the drain plug by mistake.

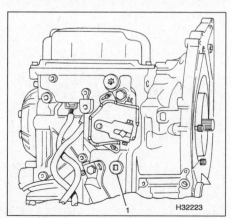

7.8 Automatic transmission fluid filler plug (1), viewed from above – AL4 transmission

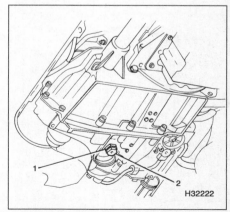

7.10 Automatic transmission fluid level plug (2) is located inside the drain plug (1) – AL4 transmission

11 Start the engine and allow it to idle. With the engine running, retain the drain plug then slacken and remove the level plug and sealing washer.

 Warning: The fluid will be hot, take precautions against scalding.

12 If there is sufficient fluid in the transmission unit, fluid should trickle out the centre of the drain plug before slowing to a drip. **Note:** *If no fluid trickles out, or just a few drips appear when the plug is removed, the fluid level is too low. Refit the level plug then switch off the engine. Add a further 0.5 litre of*

fluid to the transmission then refit the filler plug and repeat the check.
13 Once the flow of fluid stops, the level is correct. Fit a new sealing washer to the level plug then refit the plug and tighten it to the specified torque. Switch off the engine and refit any components removed for access.

Every 20 000 miles

8 Air conditioning system refrigerant check

Warning: The system should be drained and recharged only by a Peugeot dealer or air conditioning specialist. Do not attempt to carry out the work yourself, as the refrigerant is a highly-dangerous substance (refer to Chapter 3).
1 In order to check the condition of the refrigerant, a humidity indicator and a sight glass are provided on top of the drier bottle, located in the front, right-hand corner of the engine compartment **(see illustration)**.

Refrigerant humidity check

2 Check the colour of the humidity indicator. Blue indicates that the condition of the refrigerant is satisfactory. Red indicates that the refrigerant is saturated with humidity. If the indicator shows red, the system should be drained and recharged, and a new drier bottle should be fitted.
Warning: Do not attempt to open the refrigerant circuit. Refer to the precautions in Chapter 3.

Refrigerant flow check

3 Run the engine, and switch on the air conditioning.

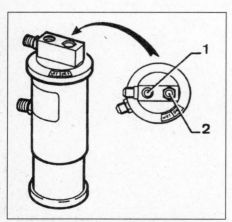

8.1 Air conditioning system drier bottle sight glass (1) and humidity indicator (2)

4 After a few minutes, inspect the sight glass, and check the fluid flow. Clear fluid should be visible – if not, the following will help to diagnose the problem:
 a) *Clear fluid flow – the system is functioning correctly.*
 b) *No fluid flow – have the system checked for leaks by a Peugeot dealer or air conditioning specialist.*
 c) *Continuous stream of clear air bubbles in fluid – refrigerant level low – have the system recharged by a Peugeot dealer or air conditioning specialist.*
 d) *Milky air bubbles visible – high humidity (see paragraph 2).*

9 Spark plug renewal

1 The correct functioning of the spark plugs is vital for the correct running and efficiency of the engine. It is essential that the plugs fitted are appropriate for the engine (a suitable type is specified at the beginning of this Chapter). If this type is used and the engine is in good condition, the spark plugs should not need attention between scheduled renewal intervals. Spark plug cleaning is rarely necessary, and should not be attempted unless specialised equipment is available, as damage can easily be caused to the firing ends.
2 On 16-valve models, to gain access to the spark plugs, the ignition coil unit fitted in the centre of the cylinder head cover must first be

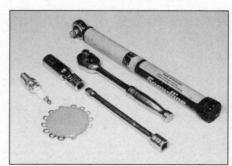

9.6 Tools required for spark plug removal, gap adjustment and refitting

removed. Disconnect the wiring connector at the left-hand end of the coil unit, then undo the six retaining bolts and lift the coil unit upwards, off the spark plugs and from its location in the cylinder head cover.
3 On certain models, to improve access to some of the plugs, it may be necessary to remove the air inlet ducting (refer to the relevant Part of Chapter 4 for further information).
4 On 8-valve models, if the marks on the original-equipment spark plug (HT) leads cannot be seen, mark the leads 1 to 4, to correspond to the cylinder the lead serves (No 1 cylinder is at the transmission end of the engine). Pull the leads from the plugs by gripping the end fitting, not the lead, otherwise the lead connection may be fractured.
5 It is advisable to remove the dirt from the spark plug recesses using a clean brush, vacuum cleaner or compressed air before removing the plugs, to prevent dirt dropping into the cylinders.
6 Unscrew the plugs using a spark plug spanner, suitable box spanner or a deep socket and extension bar **(see illustration)**. Keep the socket aligned with the spark plug – if it is forcibly moved to one side, the ceramic insulator may be broken off. As each plug is removed, examine it as follows.
7 Examination of the spark plugs will give a good indication of the condition of the engine. If the insulator nose of the spark plug is clean and white, with no deposits, this is indicative of a weak mixture or too hot a plug (a hot plug transfers heat away from the electrode slowly, a cold plug transfers heat away quickly).
8 If the tip and insulator nose are covered with hard black-looking deposits, then this is indicative that the mixture is too rich. Should the plug be black and oily, then it is likely that the engine is fairly worn, as well as the mixture being too rich.
9 If the insulator nose is covered with light tan to greyish-brown deposits, then the mixture is correct and it is likely that the engine is in good condition.
10 The spark plug electrode gap is of considerable importance as, if it is too large or too small, the size of the spark and its efficiency will be seriously impaired. Where

9.10 Measuring the spark plug gap with a wire gauge

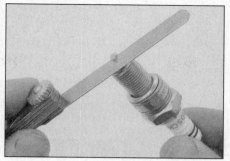

9.11 Measuring the spark plug gap with a feeler blade

It is very often difficult to insert spark plugs into their holes without cross-threading them. To avoid this possibility, fit a short length of 5/16 inch internal diameter rubber hose over the end of the spark plug. The flexible hose acts as a universal joint to help align the plug with the plug hole. Should the plug begin to cross-thread, the hose will slip on the spark plug, preventing thread damage to the cylinder head.

given, the gap should be set as specified **(see illustration)**. Note: *Spark plugs with multiple earth electrodes are becoming an increasingly common fitment, especially to vehicles equipped with catalytic converters. Unless there is clear information to the contrary, no attempt should be made to adjust the plug gap on a spark plug with more than one earth electrode.*

11 To set the gap, measure it with a feeler blade, and then bend open, or closed, the outer plug electrode until the correct gap is achieved **(see illustration)**. The centre electrode should never be bent, as this may crack the insulator and cause plug failure, if nothing worse. If using feeler blades, the gap is correct when the appropriate-size blade is a firm sliding fit.

12 Special spark plug electrode gap adjusting tools are available from most motor accessory shops, or from spark plug manufacturers.

13 Before fitting the spark plugs, check that the threaded connector sleeves are tight, and that the plug exterior and threads are clean **(see Haynes Hint)**.

14 Remove the rubber hose (if used), and tighten the plug to the specified torque using the spark plug socket and a torque wrench. Refit the remaining spark plugs in the same manner.

15 On 16-valve models, refit the ignition coil unit to the cylinder head cover and secure with the six bolts tightened securely. Reconnect the coil unit wiring connectors.

16 On 8-valve models, connect the HT leads in the correct order, and refit any components removed for access.

10 Fuel filter renewal – carburettor models

Warning: Before carrying out the following operation, refer to the precautions given in 'Safety first!' at the beginning of this manual, and follow them implicitly. Petrol is a highly-dangerous and volatile liquid, and the precautions necessary when handling it cannot be overstressed.

1 The fuel filter is situated underneath the rear of the vehicle, adjacent to the fuel tank. To gain access to the filter, chock the front wheels then jack up the rear of the vehicle and support it on axle stands (see *Jacking and vehicle support*).

2 Seal off the fuel hoses leading to and from the filter, using proprietary hose clamps, with rounded jaws – do not use G-clamps, Mole Grips or similar with flat or square jaws as these could damage the hose internally, causing leakage later.

3 Unclip the filter retaining strap from the fuel tank **(see illustration)**.

4 Noting the direction of the arrow marked on the filter body, release the retaining clips or quick-release fittings and disconnect the fuel hoses from the filter **(see illustration)**. Where

the original Peugeot crimped-type clips are still fitted, cut and discard them; use standard worm-drive hose clips on installation.

5 Remove the filter from the car. Dispose safely of the old filter; it will be highly inflammable, and may explode if thrown on a fire.

6 Slide the new filter into position, ensuring that the arrow on the filter body is pointing in the direction of the fuel flow, as noted when removing the old filter. The flow direction can otherwise be determined by tracing the fuel hoses back along their length.

7 Connect the fuel hoses to the filter, securing them in position with their retaining clips (where applicable). Where quick-release hose unions are fitted, press each hose onto its respective filter port until it 'snaps' into position.

8 Start the engine, check the filter hose connections for leaks, then lower the vehicle to the ground.

11 Automatic transmission fluid renewal – 4 HP 14 transmission

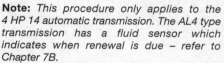

Note: *This procedure only applies to the 4 HP 14 automatic transmission. The AL4 type transmission has a fluid sensor which indicates when renewal is due – refer to Chapter 7B.*

1 Take the vehicle on a short run, to warm the transmission up to operating temperature.

2 Park the car on level ground, then switch off the ignition and apply the handbrake firmly. Chock the rear wheels then jack up the front of the car and support it on axle stands (see *Jacking and vehicle support*). Note that, when refilling and checking the fluid level, the car

10.3 Release the fuel filter strap from the tank . . .

10.4 . . . then detach the hoses and remove the filter. Note the direction of the arrow (arrowed) on the filter body

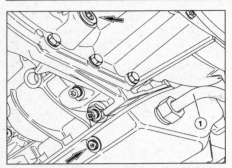

11.3 Automatic transmission fluid drain plugs (arrowed). Transmission is refilled via the dipstick tube (1) – 4 HP 14 transmission

must be lowered to the ground, and level, to ensure accuracy.

3 Remove the dipstick, then position a suitable container under the transmission. The transmission has two drain plugs: one on the sump, and another on the bottom of the differential housing **(see illustration)**.

⚠️ *Warning: If the fluid is hot, take precautions against scalding.*

4 Unscrew both drain plugs, and allow the fluid to drain completely into the container. Clean the drain plugs, being especially careful to wipe any metallic particles off the magnetic insert. Discard the original sealing washers; these should be renewed whenever they are disturbed.

5 When the fluid has finished draining, clean the drain plug threads and those of the transmission casing. Fit a new sealing washer to each drain plug, and refit the plugs to the transmission, tightening each securely. If the car was raised for the draining operation, now lower it to the ground. Make sure that the car is level (front-to-rear and side-to-side).

6 Refilling the transmission is an awkward operation, adding the specified type of fluid to the transmission a little at a time via the dipstick tube. Use a funnel with a fine-mesh gauze, to avoid spillage, and to ensure that no foreign matter enters the transmission. Allow

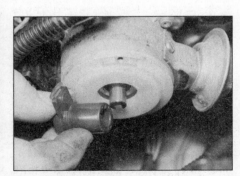

HAYNES HINT

Ensure that the leads are numbered before removing them, to avoid confusion when refitting.

plenty of time for the fluid level to settle properly. On models with two notches on the dipstick, fill the transmission until the level reaches the upper mark. On models with three notches on the dipstick, fill the transmission until the level reaches the maximum cold mark. This is the middle notch of the three, next to the number 50.

7 Once the level is up to the appropriate mark on the dipstick, refit the dipstick. Start the engine, and allow it to idle for a few minutes. Switch the engine off, then recheck the level, topping-up if necessary. Take the car on a moderate journey to fully distribute the new fluid around the transmission, then recheck the fluid level as described in Section 7.

12 Ignition system check

⚠️ *Warning: Due to the high voltages produced, extreme care must be taken when working on the system with the ignition switched on. Persons with surgically-implanted cardiac pacemaker devices should keep well clear of the ignition circuits, components and test equipment.*

1 The ignition system components should be checked carefully for damage or deterioration as described under the relevant sub-heading.

Carburettor models

General component check

2 The spark plug (HT) leads should be checked whenever new spark plugs are fitted.

3 Pull the leads from the plugs by gripping the end fitting, not the lead, otherwise the lead connection may be fractured **(see Haynes Hint)**.

4 Check inside the end fitting for signs of corrosion, which will look like a white crusty powder. Push the end fitting back onto the spark plug, ensuring that it is a tight fit on the plug. If not, remove the lead again and use pliers to carefully crimp the metal connector inside the end fitting until it fits securely on the end of the spark plug.

12.9 On carburettor models, the rotor arm is a push-fit on the distributor shaft

5 Using a clean rag, wipe the entire length of the lead to remove any built-up dirt and grease. Once the lead is clean, check for burns, cracks and other damage. Do not bend the lead excessively, nor pull the lead lengthwise – the conductor inside is quite fragile, and might break.

6 Disconnect the other end of the lead from the distributor cap. Again, pull only on the end fitting. Check for corrosion and a tight fit in the same manner as the spark plug end. Refit the lead securely on completion.

7 Check the remaining leads one at a time, in the same way.

8 If new spark plug (HT) leads are required, purchase a set for your specific car and engine.

9 Unscrew its retaining screws and remove the distributor cap. Wipe it clean, and carefully inspect it inside and out for signs of cracks, black carbon tracks (tracking) and worn, burned or loose contacts; check that the cap's carbon brush is unworn, free to move against spring pressure, and making good contact with the rotor arm. Also inspect the cap seal for signs of wear or damage, and renew if necessary. Remove the rotor arm from the distributor shaft and inspect the rotor arm **(see illustration)**. It is common practice to renew the cap and rotor arm whenever new spark plug (HT) leads are fitted.

HAYNES HINT

When fitting a new cap, remove the leads from the old cap one at a time, and fit them to the new cap in the exact same location

10 Do not simultaneously remove all the leads from the old cap, or firing order confusion may occur. When refitting, ensure that the arm is securely pressed onto the shaft, and tighten the cap retaining screws securely.

11 Even with the ignition system in first-class condition, some engines may still occasionally experience poor starting attributable to damp ignition components. To disperse moisture, a water-dispersant aerosol can be very effective.

Ignition timing – check and adjustment

12 Check the ignition timing as described in Chapter 5B.

Fuel injected models

General component check

13 Check the condition of the HT leads (where applicable) as described above in paragraphs 3 to 8.

Ignition timing – check and adjustment

14 Refer to the information contained in Chapter 5B.

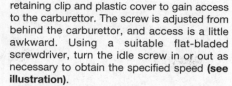

13 Idle speed and mixture check and adjustment

1 Before checking the idle speed and mixture setting, always check the following first:
 a) *Check the ignition timing (Chapter 5B).*
 b) *Check that the spark plugs are in good condition and correctly gapped (Section 9).*
 c) *Check that the accelerator cable and, on carburettor models, the choke cable is correctly adjusted (see relevant Part of Chapter 4).*
 d) *Check that the crankcase breather hoses are secure, with no leaks or kinks (Section 14).*
 e) *Check that the air cleaner filter element is clean (Section 21).*
 f) *Check that the exhaust system is in good condition (see relevant Part of Chapter 4).*
 g) *If the engine is running very roughly, check the compression pressures and valve clearances as described in Chapter 2A or 2B.*
 h) *On fuel injected models, check that the fuel injection/ignition system warning light is not illuminated (see Chapter 4B or 4C).*

2 Take the car on a journey of sufficient length to warm it up to normal operating temperature. Proceed as described under the relevant sub-heading. **Note:** *Adjustment should be completed within two minutes of return, without stopping the engine. If this cannot be achieved, or if the radiator electric cooling fan operates, first wait for the cooling fan to stop. Clear any excess fuel from the inlet manifold by racing the engine two or three times to between 2000 and 3000 rpm, then allow it to idle again.*

Carburettor models

3 Ensure that all electrical loads are switched off and the choke lever is pushed fully in; if the car does not have a tachometer (rev counter), connect one to the engine, following its manufacturer's instructions. Note the idle speed, and compare it with that specified.
4 The idle speed adjusting screw is on the throttle linkage on the right-hand side of the carburettor. It may be necessary to remove a

retaining clip and plastic cover to gain access to the carburettor. The screw is adjusted from behind the carburettor, and access is a little awkward. Using a suitable flat-bladed screwdriver, turn the idle screw in or out as necessary to obtain the specified speed **(see illustration)**.
5 The idle mixture (exhaust gas CO level) is set at the factory, and should require no further adjustment. If, due to a change in engine characteristics (carbon build-up, bore wear, etc) or after a major carburettor overhaul, the mixture setting is lost, it can be reset. Note, however, that an exhaust gas analyser (CO meter) will be required to check the mixture, in order to set it with the necessary standard of accuracy; if this is not available, the car must be taken to a Peugeot dealer for the work to be carried out.
6 If an exhaust gas analyser is available, follow its manufacturer's instructions to check the exhaust gas CO level. If adjustment is required, it is made by mixture adjustment screw. The screw is located at the right-hand rear corner of the carburettor base and is covered with a tamperproof plug to prevent adjustment. To gain access to the screw, use a sharp instrument to hook out the plug.
7 Using a suitable flat-bladed screwdriver, turn the mixture adjustment screw (in very small increments) until the CO level is correct **(see illustration)**. Turning the screw in (clockwise) weakens the mixture and reduces the CO level, turning it out will richen the mixture and increase the CO level.
8 When adjustments are complete, disconnect any test equipment, and fit a new tamperproof plug to the mixture screw. Recheck the idle speed and, if necessary, readjust.

Fuel injected models

9 Experienced home mechanics with a considerable amount of skill and equipment (including a good-quality tachometer and a good-quality, carefully-calibrated exhaust gas analyser) may be able to *check* the exhaust CO level and the idle speed. However, if these are found to be in need of *adjustment*, the car **must** be taken to a Peugeot dealer.
10 On models with a Magneti Marelli 8P engine management (fuel injection/ignition)

system, adjustment of the mixture setting (exhaust gas CO level) is possible, but adjustments can only be made by reprogramming the engine management ECU using special electronic test equipment which is connected to the diagnostic connector (see Chapter 4B or 4C).
11 On all other vehicles, adjustments are not possible. If the idle speed and/or exhaust gas CO level is incorrect, there must be a fault in the engine management system, and the vehicle should be taken to a Peugeot dealer for testing (see Chapter 4B or 4C).

14 Emissions control systems check

1 Details of the emissions control system components are given in Chapter 4F.
2 Checking consists simply of a visual check for obvious signs of damaged or leaking hoses and joints.
3 Detailed checking of the evaporative and/or exhaust emissions systems (as applicable) should be entrusted to a Peugeot dealer.

15 Auxiliary drivebelt check and renewal

Note: *Peugeot specify the use of a special electronic tool (SEEM C.TRONIC type 105 belt tensioning measuring tool) to correctly set the auxiliary drivebelt tension on manually-adjusted drivebelts. This is an involved process that varies significantly according to engine type, model year, and belt type and condition. The following procedure is an alternative method assuming that the electronic equipment is not being used. If any problems arise (such as screeching noises when driving) the tension should be checked by a Peugeot dealer using the special electronic tool at the earliest opportunity.*
1 Depending on specification, either one or two auxiliary drivebelts are fitted. Where two belts are fitted, it will obviously be necessary to remove the outer belt in order to renew the inner belt.

Check

2 Chock the rear wheels then jack up the front of the vehicle and support it on axle stands (see *Jacking and vehicle support*). Remove the right-hand front roadwheel.
3 From underneath the front of the car, prise out the retaining clips, and remove the plastic cover from the wing valance to gain access to the crankshaft sprocket/pulley bolt. Where necessary, unclip the coolant hoses from the wing to improve access further.
4 Using a suitable socket and extension bar fitted to the crankshaft sprocket/pulley bolt, rotate the crankshaft so that the entire length of the drivebelt(s) can be examined. Examine

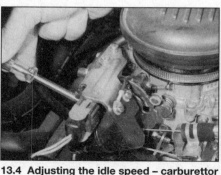

13.4 Adjusting the idle speed – carburettor models

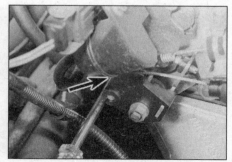

13.7 Adjusting the idle mixture (exhaust gas CO level) – carburettor models

the drivebelt(s) for cracks, splitting, fraying or damage. Check also for signs of glazing (shiny patches) and for separation of the belt plies. Renew the belt if worn or damaged.

5 If the condition of the belt is satisfactory, on models where the belt is adjusted manually, check the drivebelt tension as described below, bearing in mind the Note at the start of this Section. On models with an automatic spring-loaded tensioner, there is no need to check the drivebelt tension.

Manual adjuster on lower mounting

Removal

6 If not already done, proceed as described in paragraphs 2 and 3.

7 Disconnect the battery negative terminal (refer to *Disconnecting the battery* in the Reference Chapter).

8 Slacken both the alternator upper and lower mounting nuts/bolts (as applicable).

9 Back off the adjuster bolt(s) to relieve the tension in the drivebelt, then slip the drivebelt from the pulleys **(see illustrations). Note:** *If the belt is going to be re-used, mark the direction of rotation on the belt prior to removal. This will ensure it is refitted the correct way around.*

Refitting

10 If the belt is being renewed, ensure that the correct type is used and if the original belt is being refitted, use the mark made on removal to ensure it is fitted the correct way around. Fit the belt around the pulleys, and take up the slack in the belt by tightening the adjuster bolt.

11 Tension the drivebelt as described in the following paragraphs.

Tensioning

12 If not already done, proceed as described in paragraphs 2 and 3.

13 The belt should be tensioned so that, under firm thumb pressure, there is about 5.0 mm of free movement at the mid-point between the pulleys on the longest belt run (see the note at the start of this Section).

HAYNES HINT *Correct tensioning of the drivebelt will ensure it has a long life. A belt which is too slack will slip and squeal. Beware of overtightening, as this can cause wear in the alternator bearings.*

14 To adjust, with the upper mounting nut/bolt just holding the alternator firm, and the lower mounting nut/bolt loosened, turn the adjuster bolt until the correct tension is achieved.

15 Rotate the crankshaft a couple of times, recheck the tension, then tighten both the alternator mounting nuts/bolts. Where applicable, also tighten the bolt securing the adjuster strap to its mounting bracket.

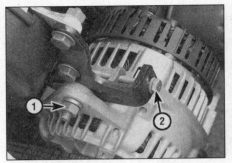
15.9a Alternator upper mounting nut (1) and adjuster bolt (2)

16 Reconnect the battery negative terminal.

17 Clip the coolant hoses into position (where necessary), then refit the plastic cover to the wing valance. Refit the roadwheel, and lower the vehicle to the ground.

Manually-adjusted pulley

Removal

18 If not already done, proceed as described in paragraphs 2 and 3.

19 Disconnect the battery negative terminal (refer to *Disconnecting the battery* in the Reference Chapter).

20 Slacken the two screws securing the tensioning pulley assembly to the engine **(see illustrations)**.

21 Rotate the adjuster bolt to move the tensioner pulley away from the drivebelt until there is sufficient slack for the drivebelt to be removed from the pulleys. **Note:** *If the belt is going to be re-used, mark the direction of rotation on the belt prior to removal. This will ensure it is refitted the correct way around.*

Refitting

22 If the belt is being renewed, ensure that

15.9b On 1.1, 1.4 and 1.6 litre engines, loosen the alternator mountings, then slacken the adjuster bolt (arrowed)

the correct type is used and if the original belt is being refitted, use the mark made on removal to ensure it is fitted the correct way around. Fit the drivebelt around the pulleys in the following order:

a) *Power steering pump and/or air conditioning compressor.*
b) *Crankshaft.*
c) *Alternator.*
d) *Tensioner roller.*

23 Ensure that the ribs on the belt are correctly engaged with the grooves in the pulleys, and that the drivebelt is correctly routed. Take all the slack out of the belt by turning the tensioner pulley adjuster bolt. Tension the belt as follows.

Tensioning

24 If not already done, proceed as described in paragraphs 2 and 3.

25 Correct tensioning of the drivebelt will ensure that it has a long life - see Haynes Hint above.

26 The belt should be tensioned so that, under firm thumb pressure, there is approximately 5.0 mm of free movement at the

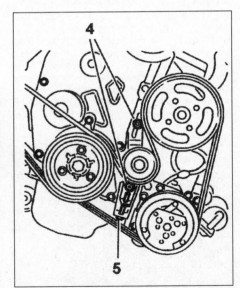
15.20a Tensioning pulley securing screws (4) and adjuster bolt (5) - models with low-mounted tensioner

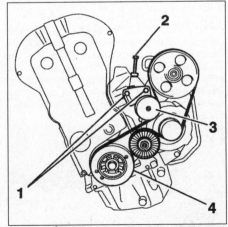
15.20b Tensioning pulley arrangement - models with high-mounted tensioner

1 *Pulley bracket securing screws*
2 *Adjuster bolt*
3 *Tensioner pulley*
4 *Crankshaft pulley*

mid-point between the pulleys on the longest belt run (see Note at the start of this Section).

27 To adjust the tension, with the two tensioner pulley assembly retaining screws slackened, rotate the adjuster bolt until the correct tension is achieved. Once the belt is correctly tensioned, rotate the crankshaft a couple of times and recheck the tension.

28 When the belt is correctly tensioned, securely tighten the tensioner pulley assembly retaining screws, then reconnect the battery negative terminal.

29 Clip the coolant hoses into position, then refit the plastic cover to the wing valance. Refit the roadwheel, and lower the vehicle to the ground.

Spring-loaded pulley

Removal

30 If not already done, proceed as described in paragraphs 2 and 3.

31 Disconnect the battery negative terminal (refer to *Disconnecting the battery* in the Reference Chapter).

32 Where necessary, remove the retaining screws from the power steering pump pulley shield, and remove the shield to gain access to the top of the drivebelt.

33 Move the tensioner pulley away from the drivebelt, using a ratchet handle or extension bar with the same size square-section end as the hole in the base of the automatic tensioner arm. Once the tensioner is released, retain it in the released position by inserting a 4.0 mm Allen key in the hole provided. Disengage the drivebelt from all the pulleys, noting its correct routing. Remove the drivebelt from the engine, noting that in some cases, it may be necessary to slacken the automatic tensioner mounting bolts to disengage the belt from behind the tensioner pulley. **Note:** *If the belt is going to be re-used, mark the direction of rotation on the belt prior to removal. This will ensure it is refitted the correct way around.*

Refitting and tensioning

34 If the belt is being renewed, ensure that the correct type is used and if the original belt is being refitted, use the mark made on

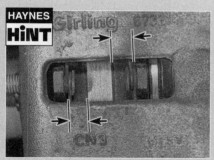

For a quick check, the thickness of friction material on each brake pad can be measured through the aperture in the caliper body.

removal to ensure it is fitted the correct way around. Fit the drivebelt around the pulleys in the following order:

a) *Automatic tensioner pulley.*
b) *Crankshaft.*
c) *Air conditioning compressor.*
d) *Power steering pump.*
e) *Idler pulley.*
f) *Alternator.*

35 Where necessary, securely tighten the automatic tensioner mounting bolts.

36 Ensure that the ribs on the belt are correctly engaged with the grooves in the pulleys. Take the load off the tensioner arm and remove the Allen key. Release the tensioner arm; the tensioner is spring-loaded, removing the need to manually adjust the belt tension.

37 Refit the power steering pump pulley shield (where removed), and securely tighten its retaining screws.

38 Reconnect the battery negative terminal.

39 Clip the coolant hoses into position, then refit the plastic cover to the wing valance. Refit the roadwheel, and lower the vehicle to the ground.

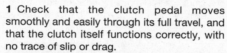

16 Clutch adjustment check and control mechanism lubrication

1 Check that the clutch pedal moves smoothly and easily through its full travel, and that the clutch itself functions correctly, with no trace of slip or drag.

2 Adjust the clutch as described in Chapter 6 (where necessary).

3 If excessive effort is required to operate the clutch, check first that the cable is correctly routed and undamaged, then remove the pedal and check that its pivot is properly greased. See Chapter 6 for more information.

17 Front brake pad check

1 Firmly apply the handbrake, then jack up the front of the car and support it securely on axle stands (see *Jacking and vehicle support*). Remove the front roadwheels.

2 If any pad's friction material is worn to the specified thickness or less, *all four pads must be renewed as a set.*

3 For a comprehensive check, the brake pads should be removed and cleaned **(see Haynes Hint)**. The operation of the caliper can then be checked, and the brake disc itself can be fully examined on both sides. Refer to Chapter 9 for details.

18 Handbrake check and adjustment

Refer to Chapter 9.

19 Road test

Instruments and electrical equipment

1 Check the operation of all instruments and electrical equipment.

2 Make sure that all instruments read correctly, and switch on all electrical equipment in turn to check it functions properly.

Steering and suspension

3 Check for any abnormalities in the steering, suspension, handling or road 'feel'.

4 Drive the vehicle, and check that there are no unusual vibrations or noises.

5 Check that the steering feels positive, with no excessive 'sloppiness', or roughness, and check for any suspension noises when cornering, or when driving over bumps.

Drivetrain

6 Check the performance of the engine, clutch, transmission and driveshafts.

7 Listen for any unusual noises from the engine, clutch and transmission.

8 Make sure the engine idles smoothly, and that there is no hesitation when accelerating.

9 Check that the clutch action is smooth and progressive, that the drive is taken up smoothly, and that the pedal travel is not excessive. Also listen for any noises when the clutch pedal is depressed.

10 Check that all gears can be engaged smoothly, without noise, and that the gear lever action is smooth and not vague or 'notchy'.

11 Listen for a metallic clicking sound from the front of the vehicle, as the vehicle is driven slowly in a circle with the steering on full lock. Carry out this check in both directions. If a clicking noise is heard, this indicates wear in a driveshaft joint, in which case, the complete driveshaft must be renewed (see Chapter 8).

Braking system

12 Make sure that the vehicle does not pull to one side when braking, and that the wheels do not lock prematurely when braking hard.

13 Check that there is no vibration through the steering when braking.

14 Check that the handbrake operates correctly, without excessive movement of the lever, and that it holds the vehicle on a slope.

15 Test the operation of the brake servo unit as follows. With the engine off, depress the footbrake four or five times to exhaust the vacuum. Start the engine, holding the brake pedal depressed. As the engine starts, there should be a noticeable 'give' in the brake pedal as vacuum builds-up. Allow the engine to run for at least two minutes, and then switch it off. If the brake pedal is depressed now, it should be possible to detect a hiss from the servo as the pedal is depressed. After about four or five applications, no further hissing should be heard, and the pedal should feel considerably firmer.

Every 40 000 miles

20 Hinge and lock lubrication

1 Work around the vehicle, and lubricate the hinges of the bonnet, doors and tailgate with a small amount of general-purpose oil.
2 Lightly lubricate the bonnet release mechanism and exposed section of inner cable with a smear of grease.
3 Check carefully the security and operation of all hinges, latches and locks, adjusting them where required. Check the operation of the central locking system (if fitted).
4 Check the condition and operation of the tailgate struts, renewing them if either is leaking or no longer able to support the tailgate securely when raised.

21 Air filter renewal

1.1 and 1.4 litre models

1 Slacken the retaining clips (where fitted), and disconnect the vacuum hose and breather hose from the front of the air cleaner housing-to-carburettor duct (**see illustration**). Where the crimped-type Peugeot hose clips are fitted, cut the clips and discard them; use standard worm-drive hose clips on refitting.
2 Slacken the retaining clip securing the duct to the carburettor/throttle body. Release the retaining clips securing the lid to the top of the air cleaner housing. Lift the duct and air cleaner lid assembly away, and place it clear of the air cleaner housing (**see illustrations**).
3 Lift the air cleaner element out of the housing (**see illustration**).
4 Wipe clean the inside of the filter housing and fit the new element.
5 Refit the sealing ring to the top of the filter (where fitted), and refit the air cleaner-to-carburettor duct. Ensure that the duct and its sealing rings are correctly seated, and securely tighten the retaining clips.
6 Reconnect the vacuum and breather hoses to the duct, and secure them in position with the retaining clips (where fitted).

1.6 litre models

7 Disconnect the intake air temperature sensor wiring, and unclip the hose union from the front of the air cleaner housing lid.
8 Release the lid retaining clips, then slacken the clips securing the lid to the intake duct and throttle housing.
9 Remove the lid, recover the sealing ring from the top of the filter housing, then lift out the element. Inspect the sealing ring for signs of damage, and renew if necessary.
10 Wipe clean the inside of the housing and fit the new element, making sure that it is correctly seated.
11 Refit the sealing ring to the top of the housing, and refit the housing lid, securing it in position with its retaining clips.
12 Securely tighten the hose clips, and reconnect the air temperature sensor wiring.

1.8 and 2.0 litre 8-valve models

13 Slacken the retaining clip, and disconnect the intake duct from the front of the cylinder head cover (**see illustration**).
14 Slacken and remove the two retaining screws situated at the front of the cylinder head cover, then release the two air filter cover retaining clips. Remove the filter cover from the cylinder head cover, and withdraw the filter element (**see illustrations**).
15 Fit the new element in position in the cylinder head cover. Refit the filter cover, securing it in position with its retaining screws and clips.

21.1 On 1.1 and 1.4 litre engines, disconnect the hoses from the front of the duct . . .

21.2a . . . then release the air cleaner lid retaining clips, and the duct clip . . .

21.2b . . . and remove the duct, positioning it clear of the air cleaner housing

21.3 Removing the air cleaner element – 1.1 and 1.4 litre models

21.13 On 1.8 and 2.0 litre 8-valve models, disconnect the intake duct from the front of the cylinder head cover . . .

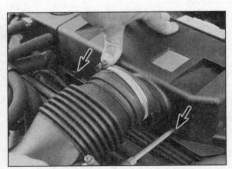

21.14a . . . then slacken the retaining screws (arrowed) . . .

21.14b . . . and release the retaining clips

21.14c Lift off the filter cover . . .

21.14d . . . and withdraw the filter element

16 Reconnect the intake duct to the cylinder head cover, and tighten its retaining clip.

1.8 and 2.0 litre 16-valve models

17 Slacken the retaining clip and disconnect the air inlet duct from the air filter housing lid.
18 Undo the screws securing the lid to the air cleaner housing body and lift off the lid.
19 Lift out the filter element and wipe clean the housing body and lid.
20 Place the new element in position in the housing body. Refit the lid and secure it in position with the retaining screws.
21 Reconnect the inlet duct to the lid and tighten its retaining clip.

22 Rear brake shoe check – models with rear drum brakes

1 Remove the rear brake drums, and check the brake shoes for signs of wear or contamination. At the same time, also inspect the wheel cylinders for signs of leakage, and the brake drum for signs of wear. Refer to the relevant Sections of Chapter 9 for further information.

23 Rear brake pad check – models with rear disc brakes

1 Chock the front wheels then jack up the rear of the vehicle and support it on axle stands (see *Jacking and vehicle support*). Remove the rear roadwheels.
2 For a quick check, the thickness of friction material remaining on each brake pad can be measured through the top of the caliper body. If any pad's friction material is worn to the specified thickness or less, all four pads must be renewed as a set.
3 For a comprehensive check, the brake pads should be removed and cleaned. This will permit the operation of the caliper to be checked, and the condition of the brake disc

itself to be fully examined on both sides. Refer to Chapter 9 for further information.

24 Manual transmission oil level check

Note: *A suitable square-section wrench may be required to undo the transmission filler/level plug on some models. These wrenches can be obtained from most motor factors or your Peugeot dealer.*

> **HAYNES HiNT** *It may be possible to use the square end fitting on a ratchet handle (as found in a typical socket set) to undo the plug.*

1 Park the car on a level surface. The oil level must be checked before the car is driven, or at least 5 minutes after the engine has been switched off. If the oil is checked immediately after driving the car, some of the oil will remain distributed around the transmission, resulting in an inaccurate level reading.
2 Prise out the clips and remove the access cover from the left-hand wheel arch liner.
3 Wipe clean the area around the filler/level plug, which is on the left-hand end of the transmission **(see illustration)**. Unscrew the plug and clean it; discard the sealing washer.

4 The oil level should reach the lower edge of the filler/level hole. A certain amount of oil will have gathered behind the filler/level plug, and will trickle out when it is removed; this does **not** necessarily indicate that the level is correct. To ensure that a true level is established, wait until the initial trickle has stopped, then add oil as necessary until a trickle of new oil can be seen emerging **(see illustration)**. The level will be correct when the flow ceases; use only good-quality oil of the specified type (refer to *Lubricants and fluids*).
5 Filling the transmission with oil is an extremely awkward operation; above all, allow plenty of time for the oil level to settle properly before checking it. If a large amount is added to the transmission, and a large amount flows out on checking the level, refit the filler/level plug and take the vehicle on a short journey so that the new oil is distributed fully around the transmission components, then recheck the level when it has settled again.
6 If the transmission has been overfilled so that oil flows out as soon as the filler/level plug is removed, check that the car is completely level (front-to-rear and side-to-side), and allow the surplus to drain off into a container.
7 When the level is correct, fit a new sealing washer to the filler/level plug. Refit the plug, tightening it to the specified torque setting. Wash off any spilt oil then refit the access cover securing it in position with the clips.

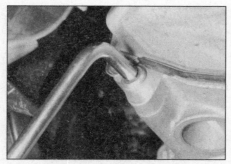

24.3 Using a square-section wrench to unscrew the transmission filler/level plug (MA transmission shown)

24.4 Topping-up the transmission oil level

25 Fuel filter renewal –
fuel injected models

 Warning: Before carrying out the following operation, refer to the precautions given in 'Safety first!' at the beginning of this manual, and follow them implicitly. Petrol is a highly-dangerous and volatile liquid, and the precautions necessary when handling it cannot be overstressed.

1 Refer to the information given for carburettor models in Section 10, noting that it will be necessary to depressurise the fuel system before the fuel hoses are disconnected from the filter (see Chapter 4B or 4C).

26 Timing belt renewal

Refer to Chapter 2A or 2B.

Every 2 years (regardless of mileage)

27 Coolant renewal

 Warning: Wait until the engine is cold before starting this procedure. Do not allow antifreeze to come in contact with your skin, or with the painted surfaces of the vehicle. Rinse off spills immediately with plenty of water. Never leave antifreeze lying around in an open container, or in a puddle in the driveway or on the garage floor. Children and pets are attracted by its sweet smell, but antifreeze can be fatal if ingested.

Cooling system draining

1 With the engine completely cold, remove the expansion tank filler cap. Turn the cap anti-clockwise until it reaches the first stop. Wait until any pressure remaining in the system is released, then push the cap down, turn it anti-clockwise to the second stop, and lift it off.
2 Position a suitable container beneath the coolant drain outlet at the lower left-hand side of the radiator.
3 Loosen the drain plug (there is no need to remove it completely) and allow the coolant to drain into the container. If desired, a length of tubing can be fitted to the drain outlet to direct the flow of coolant during draining **(see illustration)**.
4 To assist draining, open the cooling system bleed screws. These are located in the heater

matrix outlet hose union (to improve access, it may be located in an extension hose), on the engine compartment bulkhead, and on the top of the thermostat housing. On some models, there may also be a bleed screw in the top left-hand end of the radiator **(see illustrations)**.
5 When the flow of coolant stops, reposition the container below the cylinder block drain plug. On 1.1, 1.4, 1.6 and 1.8 litre models, the drain plug is located at the front of the cylinder block. On 2.0 litre models, the drain plug is located at the rear of the cylinder block.
6 Remove the drain plug, and allow the coolant to drain into the container.
7 If the coolant has been drained for a reason other than renewal, then provided it is clean and less than two years old, it can be re-used, though this is not recommended.
8 Refit the radiator and cylinder block drain plugs on completion of draining.

Cooling system flushing

9 If coolant renewal has been neglected, or if the antifreeze mixture has become diluted, then in time, the cooling system may gradually lose efficiency, as the coolant passages become restricted due to rust, scale deposits, and other sediment. The cooling system efficiency can be restored by flushing the system clean.
10 The radiator should be flushed separately from the engine, to avoid excess contamination.

Radiator flushing

11 To flush the radiator, first tighten the

radiator drain plug, and the radiator bleed screw, where applicable.
12 Disconnect the top and bottom hoses and any other relevant hoses from the radiator, with reference to Chapter 3.
13 Insert a garden hose into the radiator top inlet. Direct a flow of clean water through the radiator, and continue flushing until clean water emerges from the radiator bottom outlet.
14 If after a reasonable period, the water still does not run clear, the radiator can be flushed with a good proprietary cleaning agent. It is important that their manufacturer's instructions are followed carefully. If the contamination is particularly bad, insert the hose in the radiator bottom outlet, and reverse-flush the radiator.

Engine flushing

15 To flush the engine, first refit the cylinder block drain plug, and tighten the cooling system bleed screws.
16 Remove the thermostat (see Chapter 3), then temporarily refit the thermostat cover.
17 With the top and bottom hoses disconnected from the radiator, insert a garden hose into the radiator top hose. Direct a clean flow of water through the engine, and continue flushing until clean water emerges from the radiator bottom hose.
18 When flushing is complete, refit the thermostat and reconnect the hoses with reference to Chapter 3.

Cooling system filling

19 Before attempting to fill the cooling system, make sure that all hoses and clips are

27.3 Tubing fitted to the radiator drain plug (arrowed) – seen from above

27.4a Heater hose bleed screw (arrowed) – 1.6 litre model

27.4b Radiator bleed screw (arrowed) – 1.6 litre model

in good condition, and that the clips are tight. Note that an antifreeze mixture must be used all year round, to prevent corrosion of the engine components (see following sub-Section). Also check that the radiator and cylinder block drain plugs are in place and tight.

20 Remove the expansion tank filler cap.

21 Open all the cooling system bleed screws (see paragraph 4).

22 Some of the cooling system hoses are positioned at a higher level than the top of the radiator expansion tank. It is therefore necessary to use a 'header tank' when refilling the cooling system, to reduce the possibility of air being trapped in the system. Although Peugeot dealers use a special header tank, the same effect can be achieved by using a suitable bottle, with a seal between the bottle and the expansion tank **(see Haynes Hint)**.

23 Fit the 'header tank' to the expansion tank and slowly fill the system. Coolant will emerge from each of the bleed screws in turn, starting with the lowest screw. As soon as coolant free from air bubbles emerges from the lowest screw, tighten that screw, and watch the next bleed screw in the system. Repeat the procedure until the coolant is emerging from the highest bleed screw in the cooling system and all bleed screws are securely tightened.

24 Ensure that the 'header tank' is full (at least 0.5 litres of coolant). Start the engine, and run it at a fast idle speed (do not exceed 2000 rpm) until the cooling fan cuts in, and then cuts out. Stop the engine. **Note:** *Take great care not to scald yourself.*

25 Allow the engine to cool, then remove the 'header tank'.

26 When the engine has cooled, check the coolant level with reference to *Weekly checks*. Top-up the level if necessary, and refit the expansion tank cap.

Antifreeze mixture

27 The antifreeze should always be renewed at the specified intervals. This is necessary not only to maintain the antifreeze properties, but also to prevent corrosion which would otherwise occur as the corrosion inhibitors become progressively less effective.

28 Always use an ethylene-glycol or monoethylene-glycol based antifreeze of the specified type (see *Lubricants and fluids*). The quantity of antifreeze and level of protection are indicated in the Specifications.

29 Before adding antifreeze, the cooling system should be completely drained, preferably flushed, and all hoses checked for condition and security.

30 After filling with antifreeze, a label should be attached to the expansion tank, stating the type and concentration of antifreeze used, and the date installed. Any subsequent topping-up should be made with the same type and concentration of antifreeze.

31 Do not use engine antifreeze in the windscreen/tailgate washer system, as it will damage the vehicle paintwork. A screenwash additive should be added to the washer system in the quantities stated on the bottle.

28 Brake fluid renewal

⚠️ *Warning: Brake hydraulic fluid can harm your eyes and damage painted surfaces, so use extreme caution when handling and pouring it. Do not use fluid that has been standing open for some time, as it absorbs moisture from the air. Excess moisture can cause a dangerous loss of braking effectiveness.*

1 The procedure is similar to that for the bleeding of the hydraulic system as described in Chapter 9, except that the brake fluid reservoir should be emptied by syphoning, using a clean poultry baster or similar before starting, and allowance should be made for the old fluid to be expelled when bleeding a section of the circuit.

2 Working as described in Chapter 9, open the first bleed screw in the sequence, and

Cut the bottom off an old antifreeze container to make a 'header tank' for use when refilling the cooling system. The seal at the point arrowed must be as airtight as possible.

pump the brake pedal gently until nearly all the old fluid has been emptied from the master cylinder reservoir.

 Old hydraulic fluid is invariably much darker in colour than the new, making it easy to distinguish the two.

3 Top-up to the MAX level with new fluid, and continue pumping until only the new fluid remains in the reservoir, and new fluid can be seen emerging from the bleed screw. Tighten the screw, and top the reservoir level up to the MAX level line.

4 Work through all the remaining bleed screws in the sequence until new fluid can be seen at all of them. Be careful to keep the master cylinder reservoir topped-up to above the MIN level at all times, or air may enter the system and increase the length of the task.

5 When the operation is complete, check that all bleed screws are securely tightened, and that their dust caps are refitted. Wash off all traces of spilt fluid, and recheck the master cylinder reservoir fluid level.

6 Check the operation of the brakes before taking the car on the road.

Chapter 1 Part B:
Routine maintenance and servicing – diesel models

Contents

Degrees of difficulty

| **Easy,** suitable for novice with little experience | **Fairly easy,** suitable for beginner with some experience | **Fairly difficult,** suitable for competent DIY mechanic | **Difficult,** suitable for experienced DIY mechanic | **Very difficult,** suitable for expert DIY or professional |

Lubricants and fluids

Refer to *Weekly checks*

Capacities (approximate)

Engine oil (including filter)

1.8 and 1.9 litre XUD engines:	
With steel sump	4.5 litres
With aluminium sump	4.2 litres
1.9 litre DW engines:	
With steel sump	4.7 litres
With aluminium sump	4.5 litres
2.0 litre engines:	
With steel sump	4.5 litres
With aluminium sump	4.2 litres
Difference between MAX and MIN dipstick marks	1.5 litres

Cooling system

1.8 and 1.9 litre XUD engines	9.0 litres
1.9 litre DW engines	8.2 litres
2.0 litre engines	8.5 litres

Transmission

From dry	2.0 litres
Drain and refill	1.9 litres
Power-assisted steering	1.7 litres
Fuel tank	60.0 litres

Cooling system

Antifreeze mixture:

50% antifreeze	Protection down to –35°C

Note: *Refer to antifreeze manufacturer for latest recommendations.*

Fuel system

Note: *2.0 litre engines cannot be adjusted.*

Idle speed:	
1.8 and 1.9 litre XUD engines:	
Models without air conditioning	750 to 800 rpm
Models with air conditioning	800 to 850 rpm
1.9 litre DW engines:	
Models without air conditioning	800 to 850 rpm
Models with air conditioning	850 to 900 rpm
Fast idle speed:	
1.8 and 1.9 litre XUD engines	900 to 1000 rpm
1.9 litre DW engines	925 to 975 rpm
Anti-stall speed:	
1.8 and 1.9 litre XUD engines:	
Lucas fuel injection pump (4.0 mm shim)	1500 rpm
Bosch fuel injection pump:	
1.8 litre models (1.0 mm shim)	770 to 820 rpm
1.9 litre non-turbo models with DJZ and DJY engine*	
(1.0 mm shim)	795 to 845 rpm
1.9 litre non-turbo models with D9B engine* (3.0 mm shim) ...	1200 to 1300 rpm
1.9 litre turbo models (3.0 mm shim)	1200 to 1300 rpm
1.9 litre DW engines (3.0 mm shim)	1600 to 1800 rpm

* *Refer to Chapters 2C and 2D for information on engine identification*

Brakes

Brake pad friction material minimum thickness	2.0 mm
Brake shoe friction material minimum thickness	1.5 mm

Tyre pressures

See end of *Weekly checks*

Torque wrench settings

	Nm	lbf ft
Roadwheel bolts	85	63
Transmission filler/level and drain plugs	25	18

Note: *This maintenance schedule is a guide recommended by Haynes for servicing your own vehicle. For the manufacturer's maintenance schedule, check with your local dealer.*

The maintenance intervals in this manual are provided with the assumption that you, not the dealer, will be carrying out the work. These are the minimum maintenance intervals recommended by us for vehicles driven daily. If you wish to keep your vehicle in peak condition at all times, you may wish to perform some of these procedures more often. We encourage frequent maintenance, because it enhances the efficiency, performance and resale value of your vehicle.

If the vehicle is driven in dusty areas, used to tow a trailer, or driven frequently at slow speeds (idling in traffic) or on short journeys, more frequent maintenance intervals are recommended.

When the vehicle is new, it should be serviced by a factory-authorised dealer service department, in order to preserve the factory warranty.

Every 250 miles (400 km) or weekly
☐ Refer to *Weekly checks*

Every 6000 miles (10 000 km) or 12 months – whichever comes first
☐ Renew the engine oil and filter (Section 3)*.
☐ Drain any water from the fuel filter (Section 4).
☐ Check all underbonnet components for fluid leaks (Section 5).
☐ Check the steering and suspension components (Section 6).
☐ Check the condition of the driveshaft rubber gaiters (Section 7).
* Note: *Frequent oil and filter changes are good for the engine. The manufacturer has extended the oil change interval for later models, provided their specified lubricant is used. Consult your dealer for more information. We recommend changing the oil at the mileage specified here, or at least twice a year if the mileage covered is a less.*

Every 12 000 miles (20 000 km) or 2 years – whichever comes first
In addition to all the items listed above, carry out the following:
☐ Check the air conditioning system refrigerant (see Section 8).
☐ Check the idle speed and anti-stall speed (Section 9).
☐ Check the emissions control system hoses (Section 10).
☐ Check the auxiliary drivebelt, and renew if necessary – 1.8 and 1.9 litre XUD engines (Section 11).
☐ Check the auxiliary drivebelt, and renew if necessary – 1.9 and 2.0 litre DW engines (Section 12).
☐ Check the clutch adjustment (Section 13).
☐ Lubricate the clutch control mechanism (Section 13).
☐ Check the front brake pads, and renew if necessary (Section 14).
☐ Check the operation of the handbrake (Section 15).
☐ Carry out a road test (Section 16).

Every 36 000 miles (60 000 km)
In addition to all the items listed above, carry out the following:
☐ Renew the fuel filter (Section 17).
☐ Lubricate all hinges and locks (Section 18).
☐ Renew the air filter (Section 19).
☐ Check the condition of the rear drum brake shoes (Section 20).
☐ Check the condition of the rear disc brake pads (Section 21).
☐ Check the manual transmission oil level (Section 22).
☐ Renew the timing belt (Section 23)*.
* Note: *It is strongly recommended that the timing belt renewal interval is reduced to 36 000 miles (60 000 km) on vehicles which are subjected to intensive use, ie mainly short journeys or a lot of stop-start driving. The actual belt renewal interval is therefore very much up to the individual owner, but bear in mind that severe engine damage will result if the belt breaks.*

Every 2 years (regardless of mileage)
☐ Renew the coolant (Section 24)*.
☐ Renew the brake fluid (Section 25).
* *The manufacturer has extended the coolant renewal interval for later models, provided their specified antifreeze is used. Consult your dealer for more information.*

Underbonnet view of a 1.9 litre XUD non-turbo model

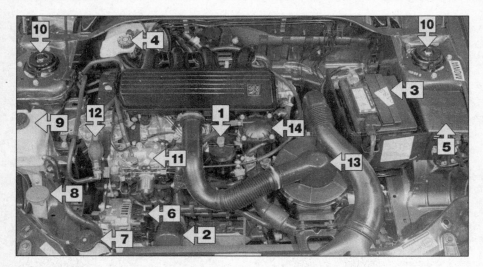

1 Engine oil filler cap/dipstick
2 Engine oil filter and oil cooler
3 Battery
4 Master cylinder brake fluid reservoir
5 Relay box
6 Alternator
7 Radiator filler cap
8 Windscreen/tailgate washer fluid reservoir filler cap
9 Power steering fluid reservoir filler cap
10 Suspension strut upper mounting
11 Injection pump
12 Fuel system priming pump
13 Air cleaner housing
14 Fuel filter

Underbonnet view of a 1.9 litre XUD turbo model

1 Engine oil filler cap/dipstick
2 Intercooler
3 Battery
4 Master cylinder brake fluid reservoir
5 Relay box
6 Alternator
7 Radiator filler cap
8 Windscreen/tailgate washer fluid reservoir filler cap
9 Power steering fluid reservoir filler cap
10 Suspension strut upper mounting
11 Injection pump
12 Fuel system priming pump
13 Air cleaner housing
14 Fuel filter

Underbonnet view of a 2.0 litre DW turbo model

1 Engine oil level dipstick
2 Engine oil filler cap
3 Battery
4 Master cylinder brake fluid reservoir
5 Relay box
6 Power steering pump
7 Expansion tank filler cap
8 Windscreen/tailgate washer fluid reservoir filler cap
9 Power steering fluid reservoir filler cap
10 Suspension strut upper mounting
11 Injection pump
12 ABS hydraulic modulator
13 Air cleaner housing
14 Fuel filter

Front underbody view (petrol model shown – diesel similar)

1 Engine oil filter
2 Sump drain plug
3 Power steering pump
4 Screen washer reservoir
5 Engine/transmission rear mounting
6 Exhaust front pipe
7 Front suspension subframe
8 Front brake caliper
9 Front suspension lower arm
10 Track rod balljoint
11 Front anti-roll bar
12 Steering gear assembly
13 Fuel pipes
14 Brake pipes

Rear underbody view (petrol model shown – diesel similar)

1 Spare wheel
2 Rear silencer
3 Fuel tank
4 Handbrake cable
5 Rear suspension torsion bar
6 Rear suspension tubular crossmember
7 Rear shock absorber
8 Rear suspension trailing arm

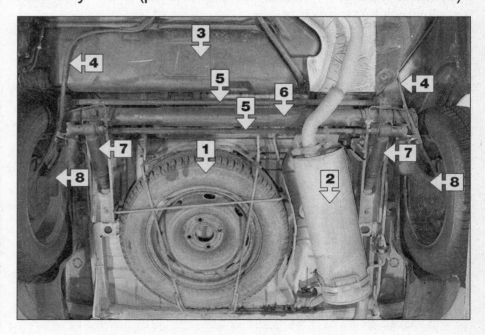

1 General information

This Chapter is designed to help the home mechanic maintain his/her vehicle for safety, economy, long life and peak performance.

The Chapter contains a master maintenance schedule, followed by Sections dealing specifically with each task in the schedule. Visual checks, adjustments, component renewal and other helpful items are included. Refer to the accompanying illustrations of the engine compartment and the underside of the vehicle for the locations of the various components.

Servicing your vehicle in accordance with the mileage/time maintenance schedule and the following Sections will provide a planned maintenance programme, which should result in a long and reliable service life. This is a comprehensive plan, so maintaining some items but not others at the specified service intervals, will not produce the same results.

As you service your vehicle, you will discover that many of the procedures can – and should – be grouped together, because of the particular procedure being performed, or because of the proximity of two otherwise-unrelated components to one another. For example, if the vehicle is raised for any reason, the exhaust can be inspected at the same time as the suspension and steering components.

The first step in this maintenance programme is to prepare yourself before the actual work begins. Read through all the Sections relevant to the work to be carried out, then make a list and gather all the parts and tools required. If a problem is encountered, seek advice from a parts specialist, or a dealer service department.

Service interval display

Later models are equipped with a service interval display indicator in the instrument panel. When the ignition is initially switched on, a spanner appears in the display window and the total number of miles remaining until the next service is due is also shown.

The display should not necessarily be used as a definitive guide to the servicing needs of your 306, but it is useful as a reminder, to ensure that servicing is not accidentally overlooked. Owners of cars covering a small annual mileage may feel inclined to service their car more often, in which case the service interval display is perhaps less relevant.

The display should be reset whenever a service is carried out, and this is achieved using the trip meter reset button on the instrument panel as follows.

With the ignition switched off, press and hold down the trip meter reset button. Switch the ignition on and the mileage remaining until the next service will flash. Continue to hold the button down for a further ten seconds. The spanner symbol will disappear and the mileage will return to zero.

2 Regular maintenance

1 If, from the time the vehicle is new, the routine maintenance schedule is followed closely, and frequent checks are made of fluid levels and high-wear items, as suggested throughout this manual, the engine will be kept in relatively good running condition, and the need for additional work will be minimised.

2 It is possible that there will be times when the engine is running poorly due to the lack of regular maintenance. This is even more likely if a used vehicle, which has not received regular and frequent maintenance checks, is purchased. In such cases, additional work may need to be carried out, outside of the regular maintenance intervals.

3 If engine wear is suspected, a compression test or leakdown test (refer to the relevant Part of Chapter 2) will provide valuable information regarding the overall performance of the main internal components. Such a test can be used as a basis to decide on the extent of the work to be carried out. If, for example, a compression or leakdown test indicates serious internal engine wear, conventional maintenance as described in this Chapter will not greatly improve the performance of the engine, and may prove a waste of time and money, unless extensive overhaul work is carried out first.

4 The following series of operations are those most often required to improve the performance of a generally poor-running engine:

Primary operations

a) Clean, inspect and test the battery (See 'Weekly checks').
b) Check all the engine-related fluids (See 'Weekly checks').
c) Check the condition and tension of the auxiliary drivebelt (Sections 11 and 12).
d) Check the condition of the air filter, and renew if necessary (Section 19).
e) Check the fuel filter (Sections 4 and 17).
f) Check the condition of all hoses, and check for fluid leaks (Section 5).
g) Check the idle speed and anti-stall speed (Section 9).

5 If the above operations do not prove fully effective, carry out the following secondary operations:

Secondary operations

All items listed under *Primary operations*, plus the following:
a) Check the charging system (Chapter 5A).
b) Check the preheating system (Chapter 5C).
c) Check the fuel system (relevant Part of Chapter 4).

Every 6000 miles or 12 months – whichever comes first

3 Engine oil and filter renewal

Note: *A suitable square-section wrench may be required on some models to undo the sump drain plug. These wrenches can be obtained from most motor factors, or from your Peugeot dealer.*

1 Frequent oil and filter changes are among the most important preventative maintenance procedures for the DIY owner. As engine oil ages, it becomes diluted and contaminated, which leads to premature engine wear.

2 Before starting this procedure, gather together all the necessary tools and materials. Also make sure that you have plenty of clean rags and newspapers handy, to mop up any spills. Ideally, the engine oil should be warm, as it will drain better, and more built-up sludge will be removed with it. Take care, however, not to touch the exhaust or any other hot parts of the engine when working under the vehicle. To avoid any possibility of scalding, and to protect yourself from possible skin irritants and other harmful contaminants in used engine oils, it is advisable to wear gloves when carrying out this work. Access to the underside of the vehicle will be greatly improved if it can be raised on a lift, driven onto ramps, or jacked up and supported on axle stands (see *Jacking and vehicle support*). Whichever method is chosen, make sure that the vehicle remains level, or if it is at an angle, that the drain plug is at the lowest point.

3 Slacken the drain plug about half a turn; on some models **(see illustration)**. Position the draining container under the drain plug, then

3.3 Slackening the sump drain plug with a square-section wrench

HAYNES HINT

As the drain plug releases from the threads, move it away sharply so the stream of oil issuing from the sump runs into the container, not up your sleeve.

remove the plug completely. If possible, try to keep the plug pressed into the sump while unscrewing it by hand the last couple of turns **(see Haynes Hint)**. Recover the sealing ring from the drain plug.

4 Allow some time for the old oil to drain, noting that it may be necessary to reposition the container as the oil flow slows to a trickle.

5 After all the oil has drained, wipe off the drain plug with a clean rag, and fit a new sealing washer. Clean the area around the drain plug opening, and refit the plug. Tighten the plug securely.

6 Move the container into position under the oil filter, which is located on the front side of the cylinder block, below the inlet manifold.

7 Using an oil filter removal tool if necessary,

3.7 Using an oil filter removal tool to slacken the oil filter

slacken the filter initially, then unscrew it by hand the rest of the way **(see illustration)**. Empty the oil in the old filter into the container.

8 Use a clean rag to remove all oil, dirt and sludge from the filter sealing area on the engine. Check the old filter to make sure that the rubber sealing ring hasn't stuck to the engine. If it has, carefully remove it.

9 Apply a light coating of clean engine oil to the sealing ring on the new filter, then screw it into position on the engine. Tighten the filter firmly by hand only – **do not** use any tools.

10 Remove the old oil and all tools from under the car, then lower the car to the ground (if applicable).

11 Remove the dipstick, then unscrew the oil filler cap from the cylinder head cover or oil filler/breather neck (as applicable). Fill the engine, using the correct grade and type of oil (see *Weekly checks*). An oil can spout or funnel may help to reduce spillage. Pour in

half the specified quantity of oil first, then wait a few minutes for the oil to fall to the sump. Continue adding oil a small quantity at a time until the level is up to the lower mark on the dipstick. Adding approximately 1.5 litres will bring the level up to the upper mark on the dipstick. Refit the filler cap.

12 Start the engine and run it for a few minutes; check for leaks around the oil filter seal and the sump drain plug. Note that there may be a brief delay before the oil pressure warning light goes out when the engine is first started, as the oil circulates through the engine oil galleries and the new oil filter (where fitted) before the pressure builds-up.

13 Switch off the engine, and wait a few minutes for the oil to settle in the sump once more. With the new oil circulated and the filter completely full, recheck the level on the dipstick, and add more oil as necessary.

14 Dispose of the used engine oil and filter safely, with reference to *General repair procedures* at the rear of this manual. Do not discard the old filter with domestic household waste. The facility for waste oil disposal provided by many local council refuse tips generally has a filter receptacle alongside.

4 Fuel filter water draining

HAYNES HINT

This is a somewhat messy operation. Wear disposable plastic gloves and spread out a good quantity of rags or newspapers to catch any spillage. Be particularly careful not to spill fuel onto cooling system hoses, wiring harnesses, engine mountings or accessory drivebelts; protect them with a plastic sheet. Catch the fuel in a clean container in order to be able to observe any water or foreign bodies drained from the filter.

1.8 and 1.9 litre XUD engines

1 A water drain plug and tube are provided at the base of the fuel filter housing.

2 Place a suitable container beneath the drain tube, and cover the clutch bellhousing.

3 Open the drain plug by turning it anti-clockwise, and allow fuel and water to drain until fuel, free from water, emerges from the end of the tube **(see illustration)**. Close the drain plug, and tighten it securely.

4 Dispose of the drained fuel safely.

5 Start the engine. If difficulty is experienced, prime the fuel system (see Chapter 4D).

1.9 litre DW engines

6 Release the fasteners from the right-hand side and top of the engine cover then lift off the cover, taking care not to lose its mounting rubbers **(see illustrations)**.

4.3 Opening the fuel filter drain plug – XUD engines

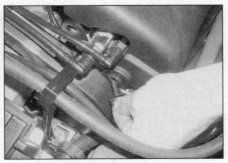

4.6a On 1.9 litre DW engines, remove the fasteners from the right-hand side . . .

4.6b . . . and top of the engine cover . . .

4.6c . . . then remove the cover from the engine

4.7 Fuel filter drain plug location – 1.9 litre DW engines

4.11a Release the fixings by turning them through 90° . . .

4.11b . . . and remove the engine cover

7 Wipe clean the exterior of the fuel filter housing then position a suitable container beneath the drain plug at the base of the housing (see illustration). If necessary attach a short length of hose to the housing drain outlet to allow the flow of fuel to be directed into the container (on some models a hose may be fitted in production).

8 Open the drain plug by turning it anti-clockwise. Operate the priming pump on the side of the filter housing to allow fuel and water to drain. Continue until fuel, free from water, emerges from the end of the hose. Close the drain plug, and tighten it securely.

9 Dispose of the drained fuel safely.

10 Refit the engine cover and start the engine. If difficulty is experienced, prime the fuel system (see Chapter 4E).

2.0 litre engines

Caution: It is vital to observe the intervals specified for draining the water from the fuel filter. The high pressure injection system is particularly susceptible to the presence of water in the fuel, which can cause seizure of the injectors and/or injection pump. The result is the destruction of the engine, either as a result of the 'blowlamp' effect of an injector stuck open, or by breakage of the timing belt consequent upon the seizure of the pump.

Note: *Always renew the drain plug and its O-ring after each draining. On completion, prime*

the fuel system (see Chapter 4E) and make sure that there are no signs of leakage at the drain plug after restarting the engine.

11 Release the fixings by turning them through 90°, and remove the engine cover (see illustrations).

12 Cover the clutch bellhousing with rags to protect it from any fuel spillage.

13 Clean the outside of the filter housing, then place a suitable container below the drain plug at the base of the housing (see illustration). If necessary attach a short length of hose to the housing drain outlet to allow the flow of fuel to be directed into the container (on some models a hose may be fitted in production).

14 Undo the drain plug and allow the contents of the filter housing to drain into the container. Note that it may be necessary to release one of the fuel hose unions on the filter housing cover to allow the draining to take place. Discard the drain plug and its O-ring.

15 Once the housing is empty, fit a new drain plug and O-ring. Tighten the drain plug and, if necessary, reconnect the hose union on the housing cover, making sure it is correctly engaged.

16 Move the container away and if necessary remove the hose. Wipe up any spillage and recover the rags.

17 Dispose of the drained fuel safely.

4.13 Fuel filter drain plug location – 2.0 litre engines

HAYNES HINT

A leak in the cooling system will usually show up as white- or rust-coloured deposits on the area adjoining the leak.

18 Prime the fuel system as described in Chapter 4E, then refit the engine cover.

5 Hose and fluid leak check

1 Visually inspect the engine joint faces, gaskets and seals for any signs of water or oil leaks. Pay particular attention to the areas around the camshaft cover, cylinder head, oil filter and sump joint faces. Bear in mind that, over a period of time, some very slight seepage from these areas is to be expected – what you are really looking for is any indication of a serious leak. Should a leak be found, renew the gasket or oil seal by referring to the appropriate Chapters in this manual.

2 Also check the security and condition of all the engine-related pipes and hoses. Ensure that all cable ties or securing clips are in place, and in good condition. Clips which are broken or missing can lead to chafing of the hoses, pipes or wiring, which could cause more serious problems in the future.

3 Carefully check the radiator hoses and heater hoses along their entire length. Renew any hose which is cracked, swollen or deteriorated. Cracks will show up better if the hose is squeezed. Pay close attention to the hose clips that secure the hoses to the cooling system components. Hose clips can pinch and puncture hoses, resulting in cooling system leaks. If the original Peugeot crimped-type hose clips are used, it may be a good idea to use standard worm-drive clips.

4 Inspect all the cooling system components (hoses, joint faces, etc) for leaks (see Haynes Hint).

5 Where any problems are found on system components, renew the component or gasket with reference to Chapter 3.

6 With the vehicle raised, inspect the fuel tank and filler neck for punctures, cracks and other damage. The connection between the filler neck and tank is especially critical. Sometimes a rubber filler neck or connecting hose will leak due to loose retaining clamps or deteriorated rubber.

7 Carefully check all rubber hoses and metal

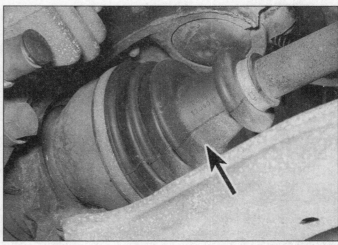

6.4 Check for wear in the hub bearings by grasping the wheel and trying to rock it

7.1 Check the condition of the driveshaft gaiters (arrowed)

fuel lines leading away from the fuel tank. Check for loose connections, deteriorated hoses, crimped lines, and other damage. Pay particular attention to the vent pipes and hoses, which often loop up around the filler neck and can become blocked or crimped. Follow the lines to the front of the vehicle, carefully inspecting them all the way. Renew damaged sections as necessary.

8 From within the engine compartment, check the security of all fuel hose attachments and pipe unions, and inspect the fuel hoses and vacuum hoses for kinks, chafing and deterioration.

9 Where applicable, check the condition of the power steering fluid hoses and pipes.

6 Steering and suspension check

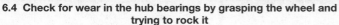

Front suspension and steering

1 Raise the front of the vehicle, and securely support it on axle stands (see *Jacking and vehicle support*).

2 Inspect the balljoint dust covers and the steering rack-and-pinion gaiters for splits, chafing or damage. Any wear of these parts will cause loss of lubricant, together with dirt and water entry, resulting in rapid deterioration of the balljoints or steering gear.

3 On models with power steering, check the fluid hoses for chafing or damage, and the pipe and hose unions for leaks. Also check for signs of leakage under pressure from the steering gear rubber gaiters, which would indicate failed fluid seals within the steering gear.

4 Grasp the roadwheel at the 12 o'clock and 6 o'clock positions, and try to rock it **(see illustration)**. Very slight free play may be felt,

but if the movement is appreciable, further investigation is necessary to determine the source. Continue rocking the wheel while an assistant depresses the footbrake. If the movement is now eliminated or significantly reduced, it is likely that the hub bearings are at fault. If the free play is still evident with the footbrake depressed, then there is wear in the suspension joints or mountings.

5 Now grasp the wheel at the 9 o'clock and 3 o'clock positions, and try to rock it as before. Any movement felt now may again be caused by wear in the hub bearings or the steering track rod balljoints. If the inner or outer balljoint is worn, the movement will be obvious.

6 Using a large screwdriver or flat bar, check for wear in the suspension mounting bushes by levering between the relevant suspension component and its attachment point. Some movement is to be expected as the mountings are made of rubber, but excessive wear should be obvious. Also check the condition of any visible rubber bushes, looking for splits, cracks or contamination of the rubber.

7 With the car standing on its wheels, have an assistant turn the steering wheel back-and-forth about an eighth of a turn each way. There should be very little, if any, lost movement between the steering wheel and roadwheels. If this is not the case, closely observe the joints and mountings previously described, but in addition, check the steering column universal joints for wear, and the steering gear itself.

Strut/shock absorber

8 Check for any signs of fluid leakage around the suspension strut/shock absorber body, or from the rubber gaiter around the piston rod. Should any fluid be noticed, the suspension strut/shock absorber is defective internally, and should be renewed. **Note:** *Suspension*

struts/shock absorbers should always be renewed in pairs on the same axle.

9 The efficiency of the suspension strut/shock absorber may be checked by bouncing the vehicle at each corner. Generally speaking, the body will return to its normal position and stop after being depressed. If it rises and returns on a rebound, the suspension strut/shock absorber is probably suspect. Examine also the suspension strut/shock absorber upper and lower mountings for any signs of wear.

7 Driveshaft gaiter check

1 With the vehicle raised and securely supported on axle stands (see *Jacking and vehicle support*), turn the steering onto full lock, then slowly rotate the roadwheel. Inspect the condition of the outer constant velocity (CV) joint rubber gaiters, squeezing the gaiters to open out the folds **(see illustration)**. Check for signs of cracking, splits or deterioration of the rubber, which may allow the grease to escape, and lead to water and grit entry into the joint. Also check the security and condition of the retaining clips. Repeat these checks on the inner CV joints. If any damage or deterioration is found, the gaiters should be renewed (see Chapter 8).

2 At the same time, check the general condition of the CV joints themselves by first holding the driveshaft and attempting to rotate the wheel. Repeat this check by holding the inner joint and attempting to rotate the driveshaft. Any appreciable movement indicates wear in the joints, wear in the driveshaft splines, or a loose driveshaft retaining nut.

Every 12 000 miles or 2 years – whichever comes first

8 Air conditioning system refrigerant check

⚠ Warning: Do not attempt to open the refrigerant circuit. Refer to the precautions given in Chapter 3.

1 In order to check the condition of the refrigerant, a humidity indicator and a sight glass are provided on top of the drier bottle, located in the front, right-hand corner of the engine compartment **(see illustration)**.

Refrigerant humidity check

2 Check the colour of the humidity indicator. Blue indicates that the condition of the refrigerant is satisfactory. Red indicates that the refrigerant is saturated with humidity. If the indicator shows red, the system should be drained and recharged, and a new drier bottle should be fitted.

⚠ Warning: The system should be drained and recharged only by a Peugeot dealer or air conditioning specialist. Do not attempt to carry out the work yourself, as the refrigerant is a highly-dangerous substance (refer to Chapter 3).

Refrigerant flow check

3 Run the engine, and switch on the air conditioning.

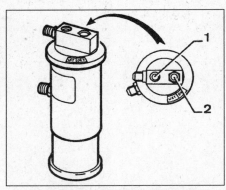

8.1 Air conditioning system drier bottle sight glass (1) and humidity indicator (2)

4 After a few minutes, inspect the sight glass, and check the fluid flow. Clear fluid should be visible – if not, the following will help to diagnose the problem:

a) *Clear fluid flow – the system is functioning correctly.*
b) *No fluid flow – have the system checked for leaks by a Peugeot dealer or air conditioning specialist.*
c) *Continuous stream of clear air bubbles in fluid – refrigerant level low – have the system recharged by a Peugeot dealer or air conditioning specialist.*
d) *Milky air bubbles visible – high humidity (see paragraph 2).*

9 Idle speed and anti-stall speed check and adjustment

Note: *2.0 litre engines cannot be adjusted.*
1 The usual type of tachometer (rev counter), which works from ignition system pulses, cannot be used on diesel engines. A diagnostic socket is provided for the use of Peugeot test equipment, but this will not normally be available to the home mechanic. If it is not felt that adjusting the idle speed 'by ear' is satisfactory, it will be necessary to purchase or hire an appropriate tachometer, or else leave the task to a Peugeot dealer or other suitably equipped specialist.
2 Before making adjustments, warm up the engine to normal operating temperature. Make sure that the accelerator cable and fast idle cables are correctly adjusted as described in the relevant Part of Chapter 4.

Lucas fuel injection pump

3 On 1.9 litre DW engine models, release the fasteners from the right-hand side and top of the engine cover then lift off the cover, taking care not to lose its mounting rubbers. On all models, with the engine idling, place a shim of the correct thickness (see Specifications), between the pump control lever and the anti-stall adjustment screw **(see illustrations)**.
4 Push the manual stop lever back against its

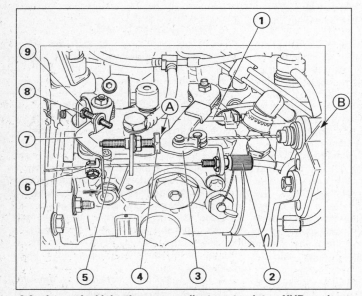

9.3a Lucas fuel injection pump adjustment points – XUD engines

1 *Maximum speed screw*	7 *Fast idle lever*
2 *Fast idle cable screw*	8 *Idle speed adjustment*
3 *Pump control lever*	*screw*
4 *Anti-stall adjustment screw*	9 *Manual stop lever*
5 *Fast idle cable*	A *Anti-stall shim location*
6 *Fast idle cable end fitting*	B *Accelerator cable screw*

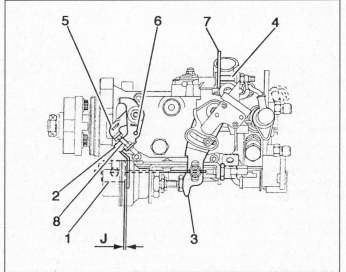

9.3b Lucas fuel injection pump adjustment points – 1.9 litre DW engines

1 *Fast idle cable end fitting*	7 *Shim for anti-stall speed*
2 *Fast idle lever*	*adjustment*
3 *Pump control lever*	8 *Idle speed adjustment*
4 *Anti-stall adjustment screw*	*screw*
5 *Manual stop lever*	J *Fast idle cable end fitting*
6 *Fast idle lever hole*	*clearance*

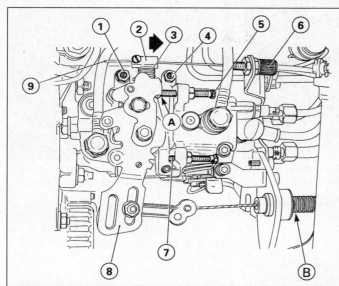

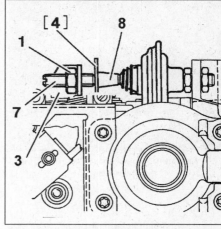

1 Fast idle lever stop screw
2 Fast idle cable end fitting
3 Fast idle lever
4 Idle speed adjustment screw
5 Anti-stall speed adjustment screw
6 Fast idle cable screw
7 Maximum speed adjustment screw
8 Pump control lever
9 Fast idle cable
A Anti-stall adjustment shim location
B Accelerator cable screw

9.14 Bosch fuel injection pump adjustment points – non-turbo engines (turbo similar)

9.24 Fuel injection pump damper adjustment details – turbo models

1 Locknut
3 Pump control lever
4 Shim
7 Adjustment screw
8 Damper rod

stop, and hold it in position by inserting a 3.0 mm diameter rod/drill through the hole in the fast idle lever.

5 The engine speed should be as specified for the anti-stall speed (see Specifications).

6 If adjustment is necessary, loosen the locknut, turn the anti-stall adjustment screw as required, then tighten the locknut.

7 Remove the rod/drill and the shim, and check that the engine is idling at the specified speed (see Specifications).

8 If adjustment is necessary, loosen the locknut on the idle speed adjustment screw. Turn the screw as required, and retighten the locknut.

9 Move the pump control lever to increase the engine speed to approximately 3000 rpm, then quickly release the lever. The deceleration period should be between 2.5 and 3.5 seconds, and the engine speed should drop to approximately 50 rpm below idle.

10 If the deceleration is too fast and the engine stalls, unscrew the anti-stall adjustment screw a quarter-turn towards the control lever. If the deceleration is too slow, resulting in poor engine braking, turn the screw a quarter-turn away from the lever.

11 Retighten the locknut after making an adjustment. Recheck the idle speed, and adjust if necessary as described previously.

12 With the engine idling, check the operation of the manual stop control by turning the stop lever clockwise. The engine must stop instantly.

13 Where applicable, disconnect the tachometer on completion, and refit the engine cover.

Bosch fuel injection pump

Non-turbo models

14 Loosen the locknut, and unscrew the anti-

stall adjustment screw until it is clear of the pump control lever (see illustration).

15 Start the engine and allow it to idle. If the idle speed is incorrect (see Specifications), loosen the locknut and turn the idle speed screw as required, then retighten the locknut.

16 Insert a shim or feeler blade of the correct thickness (see Specifications) between the pump control lever and the anti-stall adjustment screw.

17 The engine speed should be as specified for the anti-stall speed (see Specifications).

18 If adjustment is necessary, loosen the locknut and turn the anti-stall adjustment screw as required. Retighten the locknut.

19 Remove the shim or feeler blade and allow the engine to idle.

20 Move the fast idle lever fully towards the flywheel end of the engine, and check that the engine speed increases to the specified fast idle speed. If necessary, loosen the locknut and turn the fast idle adjusting screw as required, then retighten the locknut.

21 With the engine idling, check the operation of the manual stop control by turning the stop lever. The engine must stop instantly.

22 Where applicable, disconnect the tachometer on completion.

Turbo models

23 Carry out the operations described above in paragraphs 14 to 19.

24 Slacken the locknut and unscrew the control lever damper adjustment screw, located on the rear of the lever, and insert the shim or feeler blade between the damper rod and adjustment screw (see illustration). Make sure the pump control lever is in the idle position then position the adjustment screw so that the feeler blade/shim is a light, sliding fit between the screw and damper rod. Hold the screw in this position, and tighten its locknut.

25 Carry out the operations described in paragraphs 19 to 22.

10 Emissions control systems check

1 Details of the emissions control system components are given in Chapter 4F.

2 Checking consists simply of a visual check for obvious signs of damaged or leaking hoses and joints.

3 Detailed checking and testing of the evaporative and/or exhaust emissions systems (as applicable) should be entrusted to a Peugeot dealer.

11 Auxiliary drivebelt check and renewal – 1.8 and 1.9 litre XUD engines

Note: *Peugeot specify the use of a special electronic tool (SEEM C.TRONIC type 105 belt tensioning measuring tool) to correctly set the auxiliary drivebelt tension on manually-adjusted drivebelts. This is an involved process that varies significantly according to engine type, model year, and belt type and condition. The following procedure is an alternative method assuming that the electronic equipment is not being used. If any problems arise (such as screeching noises when driving) the tension should be checked by a Peugeot dealer using the special electronic tool at the earliest opportunity.*

1 Depending on specification, either one or two auxiliary drivebelts are fitted. Where two belts are fitted, it will obviously be necessary to remove the outer belt in order to renew the inner belt.

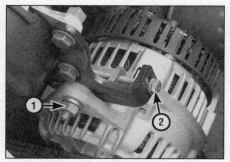

11.9 Alternator upper mounting nut (1) and adjuster bolt (2)

11.20 Slacken the two tensioner roller retaining screws (arrowed) . . .

11.21 . . . then turn the tensioner roller adjuster bolt to release the belt tension

Check

2 Chock the rear wheels then jack up the front of the vehicle and support it on axle stands (see *Jacking and vehicle support*). Remove the right-hand front roadwheel.

3 From underneath the front of the car, prise out the retaining clips, and remove the plastic cover from the wing valance to gain access to the crankshaft sprocket/pulley bolt. Where necessary, unclip the coolant hoses from the wing to improve access further.

4 Using a suitable socket and extension bar fitted to the crankshaft sprocket/pulley bolt, rotate the crankshaft so that the entire length of the drivebelt(s) can be examined. Examine the drivebelt(s) for cracks, splitting, fraying or damage. Check also for signs of glazing (shiny patches) and for separation of the belt plies. Renew the belt if worn or damaged.

5 If the condition of the belt is satisfactory, on models where the belt is adjusted manually, check the drivebelt tension as described below, bearing in mind the Note at the start of this Section. On models with an automatic spring-loaded tensioner, there is no need to check the drivebelt tension.

Manual adjuster on lower mounting

Removal

6 If not already done, proceed as described in paragraphs 2 and 3.

7 Disconnect the battery negative terminal (refer to *Disconnecting the battery* in the Reference Chapter).

8 Slacken both the alternator upper and lower mounting nuts/bolts (as applicable).

9 Back off the adjuster bolt(s) to relieve the tension in the drivebelt, then slip the drivebelt from the pulleys **(see illustration)**. **Note:** *If the belt is going to be re-used, mark the direction of rotation on the belt prior to removal. This will ensure it is refitted the correct way around.*

Refitting

10 If the belt is being renewed, ensure that the correct type is used and if the original belt is being refitted, use the mark made on removal to ensure it is fitted the correct way around. Fit the belt around the pulleys, and take up the slack in the belt by tightening the adjuster bolt.

11 Tension the drivebelt as described in the following paragraphs.

Tensioning

> **HAYNES HINT** *Correct tensioning of the drivebelt will ensure that it has a long life. A belt which is too slack will slip and squeal. Beware, however, of overtightening, as this can cause wear in the alternator bearings.*

12 If not already done, proceed as described in paragraphs 2 and 3.

13 The belt should be tensioned so that, under firm thumb pressure, there is about 5.0 mm of free movement at the mid-point between the pulleys on the longest belt run (see the note at the start of this Section).

14 To adjust, with the upper mounting nut/bolt just holding the alternator firm, and the lower mounting nut/bolt loosened, turn the adjuster bolt until the correct tension is achieved.

15 Rotate the crankshaft a couple of times, recheck the tension, then securely tighten both the alternator mounting nuts/bolts. Where applicable, also tighten the bolt securing the adjuster strap to its mounting bracket.

16 Reconnect the battery negative terminal.

17 Clip the coolant hoses into position (where necessary), then refit the plastic cover to the wing valance. Refit the roadwheel, and lower the vehicle to the ground.

Manually-adjusted pulley

Removal

18 If not already done, proceed as described in paragraphs 2 and 3.

19 Disconnect the battery negative terminal (refer to *Disconnecting the battery* in the Reference Chapter).

20 Slacken the two screws securing the tensioning pulley assembly to the engine **(see illustration)**.

21 Rotate the adjuster bolt to move the tensioner pulley away from the drivebelt until there is sufficient slack for the drivebelt to be

removed from the pulleys **(see illustration)**. **Note:** *If the belt is going to be re-used, mark the direction of rotation on the belt prior to removal. This will ensure it is refitted the correct way around.*

Refitting

22 If the belt is being renewed, ensure that the correct type is used and if the original belt is being refitted, use the mark made on removal to ensure it is fitted the correct way around. Fit the drivebelt around the pulleys ensuring that the ribs on the belt are correctly engaged with the pulley grooves, and that the drivebelt is correctly routed.

23 Take all the slack out of the belt by turning the tensioner pulley adjuster bolt, then tension the belt as follows.

Tensioning

24 If not already done, proceed as described in paragraphs 2 and 3.

25 Correct tensioning of the drivebelt will ensure that it has a long life – see Haynes Hint above.

26 The belt should be tensioned so that, under firm thumb pressure, there is approximately 5.0 mm of free movement at the mid-point between the pulleys on the longest belt run.

27 To adjust the tension, with the two tensioner pulley assembly retaining screws slackened, rotate the adjuster bolt until the correct tension is achieved. Once the belt is correctly tensioned, rotate the crankshaft a couple of times and recheck the tension.

28 When the belt is correctly tensioned, securely tighten the tensioner pulley assembly retaining screws, then reconnect the battery negative terminal.

29 Clip the coolant hoses into position, then refit the plastic cover to the wing valance. Refit the roadwheel, and lower the vehicle to the ground.

Spring-loaded pulley (early models)

Removal

30 If not already done, proceed as described in paragraphs 2 and 3.

31 Disconnect the battery negative terminal

(refer to *Disconnecting the battery* in the Reference Chapter).

32 Where necessary, remove the retaining screws from the power steering pump pulley shield, and remove the shield to gain access to the top of the drivebelt.

33 Move the tensioner pulley away from the drivebelt, using a ratchet handle or extension bar with the same size square-section end as the hole in the base of the automatic tensioner arm. Disengage the drivebelt from all the pulleys, noting its correct routing. Remove the drivebelt from the engine, noting that in some cases, it may be necessary to slacken the automatic tensioner mounting bolts to disengage the belt from behind the tensioner pulley. **Note:** *If the belt is going to be re-used, mark the direction of rotation on the belt prior to removal. This will ensure it is refitted the correct way around.*

Refitting and tensioning

34 If the belt is being renewed, ensure that the correct type is used and if the original belt is being refitted, use the mark made on removal to ensure it is fitted the correct way around. Fit the drivebelt around the pulleys ensuring that the ribs on the belt are correctly engaged with the pulley grooves, and that the drivebelt is correctly routed.

35 Where necessary, securely tighten the automatic tensioner mounting bolts.

36 Whilst holding the tensioner arm away from the belt, ensure that the ribs on the belt are correctly engaged with the grooves in the pulleys. Release the tensioner arm; the tensioner is spring-loaded, removing the need to manually adjust the belt tension.

37 Refit the power steering pump pulley shield (where removed), and securely tighten its retaining screws.

38 Reconnect the battery negative terminal.

39 Clip the coolant hoses into position, then refit the plastic cover to the wing valance. Refit the roadwheel, and lower the vehicle to the ground.

Spring-loaded pulley (later models)

Removal

40 If not already done, proceed as described in paragraphs 2 and 3.

41 Disconnect the battery negative terminal (refer to *Disconnecting the battery* in the Reference Chapter).

42 Where necessary, remove the retaining screws from the power steering pump pulley shield, and remove the shield to gain access to the top of the drivebelt.

43 Working under the wheel arch, slacken the retaining bolt located in the centre of the eccentric tensioner pulley.

44 Insert a cranked 7.0 mm square section bar (a quarter-inch square section drive socket bar for example) into the square hole on the front face of the eccentric tensioner pulley.

45 Using the bar, turn the eccentric tensioner pulley until the hole in the arm of the automatic tensioner pulley is aligned with the hole in the mounting bracket behind. When the holes are aligned, slide a suitable setting tool (a bolt or cranked length of bar of approximately 8.0 mm diameter) through the hole in the arm and into the mounting bracket.

46 With the automatic tensioner locked, turn the eccentric tensioner pulley until the drivebelt tension is released sufficiently to enable the belt to be removed. **Note:** *If the belt is going to be re-used, mark the direction of rotation on the belt prior to removal. This will ensure it is refitted the correct way around.*

Refitting and tensioning

47 If the belt is being renewed, ensure that the correct type is used and if the original belt is being refitted, use the mark made on removal to ensure it is fitted the correct way around. Fit the drivebelt around the pulleys ensuring that the ribs on the belt are correctly engaged with the pulley grooves, and that the drivebelt is correctly routed.

48 Turn the eccentric tensioner pulley to apply tension to the drivebelt, until the load is released from the setting bolt. Without altering the position of the eccentric tensioner pulley, tighten its retaining bolt securely.

49 Remove the setting bolt from the automatic tensioner arm, then rotate the crankshaft four complete revolutions in the normal direction of rotation.

50 Check that the holes in the automatic adjuster arm and the mounting bracket are still aligned by re-inserting the setting bolt. If the bolt will not slide in easily, repeat the tensioning procedure from paragraph 48 onward.

51 On completion, reconnect the battery negative terminal, and all other disturbed components.

---

12 Auxiliary drivebelt check and renewal – 1.9 and 2.0 litre DW engines

Note: *On models without power steering and air conditioning, Peugeot specify the use of a special electronic tool (SEEM C.TRONIC type 105 belt tensioning measuring tool) to correctly set the auxiliary drivebelt tension. This is an involved process that varies significantly according to engine type, model year, and belt type and condition. The following procedure is an alternative method assuming that the electronic equipment is not being used. If any problems arise (such as screeching noises when driving) the tension should be checked by a Peugeot dealer using the special electronic tool at the earliest opportunity.*

Check

1 Chock the rear wheels then jack up the front of the vehicle and support it on axle stands (see *Jacking and vehicle support*). Remove the right-hand front roadwheel.

2 From underneath the front of the car, prise out the retaining clips, and remove the plastic cover from the wing valance to gain access to the crankshaft sprocket bolt. Where necessary, unclip the coolant hoses from the wing to improve access further.

3 Using a suitable socket and extension bar fitted to the crankshaft sprocket bolt, rotate the crankshaft so that the entire length of the drivebelts can be examined. Examine the drivebelts for cracks, splitting, fraying or damage. Check also for signs of glazing (shiny patches) and for separation of the belt plies. Renew the belt if worn or damaged.

4 On all 2.0 litre models, and 1.9 litre models with power steering (without air conditioning), which are equipped with an automatic belt tensioner, check the position of the wear indicators on the tensioner pulley arm and backplate **(see illustration)**. The indicator mark on the backplate must be positioned between the two marks on the tensioner arm. If not, the belt is stretched and should be renewed.

5 Clip the coolant hoses into position (where applicable), then refit the plastic cover to the wing valance. Refit the roadwheel, and lower the vehicle to the ground.

1.9 litre without power steering

Removal

6 If not already done, proceed as described in paragraphs 1 and 2.

7 Disconnect the battery negative terminal (refer to *Disconnecting the battery* in the Reference Chapter).

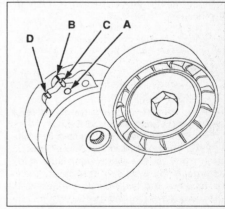

12.4 Auxiliary drivebelt automatic tensioner details

A Tensioner arm locking pin hole
B Backplate indicator mark and locking pin locating hole
C Tensioner arm right-hand (zero) wear mark
D Tensioner arm left-hand (maximum) wear mark

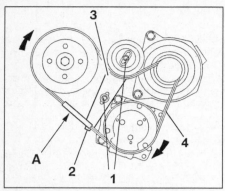

12.8 Auxiliary drivebelt and tensioner details – 1.9 litre engines without power steering

1 *Retaining bolts*
2 *Adjuster bolt*
3 *Tensioner pulley assembly*
4 *Drivebelt*
A *Tension checking point*

8 Slacken the two bolts securing the tensioner pulley assembly to the engine (see illustration).
9 Rotate the adjuster bolt to move the tensioner pulley away from the drivebelt until there is sufficient slack for the drivebelt to be removed from the pulleys. **Note:** *If the belt is going to be re-used, mark the direction of rotation on the belt prior to removal. This will ensure it is refitted the correct way around.*

Refitting

10 If the belt is being renewed, ensure that the correct type is used and if the original belt is being refitted, use the mark made on removal to ensure it is fitted the correct way around.
11 Fit the drivebelt around the pulleys ensuring that the ribs on the belt are correctly engaged with the pulley grooves, and that the drivebelt is correctly routed.
12 Take all the slack out of the belt by turning the tensioner pulley adjuster bolt, then tension the belt as follows.

Tensioning

13 If not already done, proceed as described in paragraphs 1 and 2.

HAYNES HINT *Correct tensioning of the drivebelt will ensure that it has a long life. A belt which is too slack will slip and squeal. Beware, however, of overtightening, as this can cause wear in the alternator bearings.*

14 The belt should be tensioned so that, under firm thumb pressure, there is approximately 5.0 mm of free movement at the mid-point between the pulleys on the longest belt run.
15 To adjust the tension, with the two tensioner pulley assembly retaining bolts

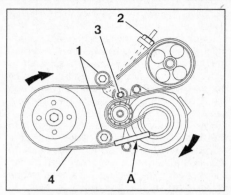

12.21 Auxiliary drivebelt and tensioner details – 1.9 litre engines with power steering and manual tensioner assembly

1 *Idler pulleys*
2 *Adjuster nut*
3 *Tensioner pulley backplate bolt*
4 *Drivebelt*
A *Tension checking point*

slackened, rotate the adjuster bolt until the correct tension is achieved. Once the belt is correctly tensioned, rotate the crankshaft a couple of times and recheck the tension.
16 When the belt is correctly tensioned, securely tighten the tensioner pulley assembly retaining bolts, then reconnect the battery negative terminal.
17 Clip the coolant hoses into position (where applicable), then refit the plastic cover to the wing valance. Refit the roadwheel, and lower the vehicle to the ground.

1.9 litre with power steering and manual tensioner (no air conditioning)

Removal

18 If not already done, proceed as described in paragraphs 1 and 2.
19 Disconnect the battery negative terminal (refer to *Disconnecting the battery* in the Reference Chapter).
20 Release the fasteners from the right-hand side and top of the engine cover then lift off the cover, taking care not to lose its mounting rubbers.

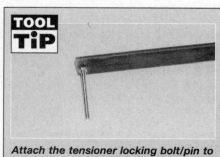

TOOL TIP

Attach the tensioner locking bolt/pin to a length of metal bar. This will enable you to manoeuvre the bolt/pin easily down between the engine and body and into position.

21 Slacken the tensioner pulley backplate bolt and back off the pulley adjuster nut, located behind the power steering pump, to move the pulley away from the drivebelt (see illustration). Once there is sufficient slack in the drivebelt, slip the belt off the pulleys and remove it from the engine. **Note:** *If the belt is going to be re-used, mark the direction of rotation on the belt prior to removal. This will ensure it is refitted the correct way around.*

Refitting

22 If the belt is being renewed, ensure that the correct type is used and if the original belt is being refitted, use the mark made on removal to ensure it is fitted the correct way around. Fit the belt around the pulleys in the following order:
  a) *Power steering pump.*
  b) *Tensioner pulley.*
  c) *Alternator.*
  d) *Lower idler pulley.*
  e) *Crankshaft.*
  f) *Upper idler pulley.*
23 Ensure that the ribs on the belt are correctly engaged with the pulley grooves, then take up the slack in the belt by tightening the adjuster bolt. Tension the drivebelt as described in the following paragraphs.

Tensioning

24 If not already done, proceed as described in paragraphs 1 and 2.
25 Correct tensioning of the drivebelt will ensure that it has a long life – see Haynes Hint above.
26 The belt should be tensioned so that, under firm thumb pressure, there is approximately 5.0 mm of free movement at the mid-point between the alternator and idler pulleys on the lower belt run.
27 To adjust the tension, with the tensioner pulley backplate bolt slackened, rotate the adjuster nut until the correct tension is achieved. Once the belt is correctly tensioned, rotate the crankshaft a couple of times and recheck the tension.
28 When the belt is correctly tensioned, securely tighten the tensioner pulley backplate bolt, then lightly tighten the adjuster nut.
29 Clip the coolant hoses into position (where applicable), then refit the plastic cover to the wing valance. Refit the roadwheel, and lower the vehicle to the ground.
30 Ensure that the mounting rubbers are all correctly fitted then install the engine cover, securing it in position with the fasteners.
31 On completion, reconnect the battery negative terminal.

1.9 litre with power steering and automatic tensioner (no air conditioning)

Note: *A 4.0 mm diameter bolt or pin will be required to lock the spring-loaded tensioner pulley in position (see Tool Tip).*

Removal

32 If not already done, proceed as described in paragraphs 1 and 2.

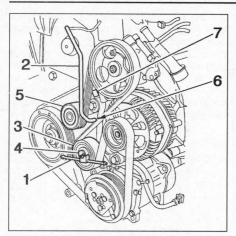

12.43 Auxiliary drivebelt and tensioner details – 1.9 litre engines with air conditioning

1 Peugeot tool for moving the manual tensioner pulley
2 Peugeot locking pin for spring-loaded tensioner
3 Drivebelt
4 Manual tensioner pulley
5 Spring-loaded tensioner pulley
6 Spring-loaded tensioner pulley arm locking hole
7 Spring-loaded tensioner pulley arm square-section hole (only accessible with drivebelt removed)

33 Disconnect the battery negative terminal (refer to *Disconnecting the battery* in the Reference Chapter).
34 Using a spanner/socket fitted to the spring-loaded tensioner pulley centre bolt, move the tensioner pulley away from the belt until it is possible to slip the drivebelt off one of the pulleys. Once the drivebelt has been displaced, align the tensioner arm right-hand (zero) wear mark **(see illustration 12.4)** with the backplate indicator mark and lock the tensioner in position by inserting the 4.0 mm diameter bolt/pin **(see illustrations 12.54a and 12.54b)**. Ensure the bolt/pin is correctly located in the backplate, then release the tensioner.
35 Disengage the drivebelt from all the pulleys, noting its correct routing, and remove it from the engine. **Note:** *If the belt is going to*

12.54a Using a spanner/socket on the tensioner pulley bolt, align the arm zero wear mark with the backplate indicator . . .

be re-used, mark the direction of rotation on the belt prior to removal. This will ensure it is refitted the correct way around.

Refitting and tensioning
36 If the belt is being renewed, ensure that the correct type is used and if the original belt is being refitted, use the mark made on removal to ensure it is fitted the correct way around. Fit the belt around the pulleys in the following order:
 a) Power steering pump.
 b) Upper idler pulley.
 c) Alternator.
 d) Lower idler pulley.
 e) Crankshaft.
37 Fit the spanner/socket to the spring-loaded tensioner pulley bolt. Move the tensioner pulley away from the belt until it is possible to withdraw the locking bolt/pin, then slip the belt over the pulley. Ensure the belt ribs are correctly seated in all the pulley grooves, then slowly release the spring-loaded tensioner to tension the drivebelt.
38 Clip the coolant hoses into position (where applicable), then refit the plastic cover to the wing valance. Refit the roadwheel, and lower the vehicle to the ground.
39 On completion, reconnect the battery negative terminal.

1.9 litre with air conditioning
Note: *A 6.0 mm diameter bolt or pin will be required to lock the spring-loaded tensioner pulley in position.*
40 If not already done, proceed as described in paragraphs 1 and 2.
41 Disconnect the battery negative terminal (refer to *Disconnecting the battery* in the Reference Chapter).
42 Slacken the manual tensioner pulley bolt.
43 Pivot the manual tensioner pulley in a clockwise direction, using a square-section key fitted to the hole in the pulley hub, to move the spring-loaded tensioner pulley. Position the tensioner pulley so that the hole in its arm aligns with the corresponding hole in the bracket, then lock the pulley in position by inserting the 6.0 mm diameter bolt/pin **(see illustration)**. Ensure that the spring-loaded tensioner pulley is locked securely in position, then release the manual tensioner pulley.
44 Disengage the drivebelt from all the pulleys, noting its correct routing, and remove

12.54b . . . and lock it in position by inserting the bolt/pin through the arm and backplate holes – 2.0 litre engines

it from the engine. **Note:** *If the belt is going to be re-used, mark the direction of rotation on the belt prior to removal. This will ensure it is refitted the correct way around.*

Refitting and tensioning
45 Ensure that the spring loaded tensioner pulley is locked in position (see paragraph 43). **Note:** *The pulley arm has a square-section cut-out to allow the pulley to be moved using a ratchet/bar, but this hole is only accessible with the drivebelt removed.*
46 If the belt is being renewed, ensure that the correct type is used and if the original belt is being refitted, use the mark made on removal to ensure it is fitted the correct way around. Fit the belt around the pulleys in the following order:
 a) Power steering pump.
 b) Manual tensioner pulley.
 c) Alternator.
 d) Air conditioning compressor.
 e) Crankshaft.
 f) Spring-loaded tensioner pulley.
47 Ensure the belt ribs are correctly seated in all the pulley grooves, then rotate the manual tensioner pulley in a clockwise direction to remove all slack from the belt.
48 To correctly set the drivebelt tension, position the manual tensioner pulley so that all spring pressure is removed from the locking bolt/pin fitted to the spring-loaded tensioner arm. Once the manual tensioner pulley is correctly positioned, securely tighten its retaining bolt.
49 Remove the locking bolt/pin then rotate the crankshaft through four complete revolutions. Check that the locking bolt/pin can still be easily inserted. If not, slacken the manual tensioner pulley bolt and repeat the adjustment procedure.
50 Once the belt is correctly tensioned, remove the locking bolt/pin, clip the coolant hoses into position (where applicable), then refit the plastic cover to the wing valance. Refit the roadwheel, and lower the vehicle to the ground.
51 On completion, reconnect the battery negative terminal.

2.0 litre

Removal
Note: *A 4.0 mm diameter bolt or pin will be required to lock the spring-loaded tensioner pulley in position (see Tool Tip above).*
52 If not already done, proceed as described in paragraphs 1 and 2.
53 Disconnect the battery negative terminal (refer to *Disconnecting the battery* in the Reference Chapter).
54 Using a spanner/socket fitted to the spring-loaded tensioner pulley centre bolt, move the tensioner pulley away from the belt until it is possible to slip the drivebelt off one of the pulleys. Once the drivebelt has been displaced, align the tensioner arm right-hand (zero) wear mark **(see illustration 12.4)** with the backplate indicator mark and lock the tensioner in position by inserting the 4.0 mm diameter bolt/pin **(see illustrations)**. Ensure

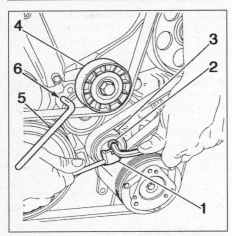

12.63 Auxiliary drivebelt adjustment details – 2.0 litre engines

1 *Peugeot tool for moving the manual tensioner pulley*
2 *Manual tensioner pulley retaining bolt*
3 *Manual tensioner pulley*
4 *Spring-loaded tensioner pulley*
5 *Peugeot locking pin for spring-loaded tensioner*
6 *Spring-loaded tensioner pulley arm locking hole*

the bolt/pin is correctly located in the backplate, then release the tensioner.
55 Disengage the drivebelt from all the pulleys, noting its correct routing, and remove it from the engine. **Note:** *If the belt is going to be re-used, mark the direction of rotation on the belt prior to removal. This will ensure it is refitted the correct way around.*

Refitting used belt

56 If the original belt is being refitted, use the mark made on removal to ensure it is fitted the correct way around. Fit the belt around the pulleys in the following order:
 a) *Power steering pump.*
 b) *Manual tensioner pulley.*
 c) *Alternator.*
 d) *Air conditioning compressor/lower idler pulley (as applicable).*
 e) *Crankshaft.*
57 Fit the spanner/socket to the spring-loaded tensioner pulley bolt. Move the tensioner pulley away from the belt until it is possible to withdraw the locking bolt/pin, then slip the belt over the pulley. Ensure the belt ribs are correctly seated in all the pulley grooves, then slowly release the spring-loaded tensioner to tension the drivebelt.
58 Clip the coolant hoses into position (where applicable), then refit the plastic cover to the wing valance. Refit the roadwheel, and lower the vehicle to the ground.
59 On completion, reconnect the battery negative terminal.

Fitting new belt

60 Ensure that the spring-loaded tensioner pulley is locked in position with its right-hand

(zero) wear mark correctly aligned with the backplate indicator (see paragraph 54).
61 Slacken the manual tensioner pulley bolt, then fit the new drivebelt around the pulleys in the following order:
 a) *Power steering pump.*
 b) *Manual tensioner pulley.*
 c) *Alternator.*
 d) *Air conditioning compressor/lower idler pulley (as applicable).*
 e) *Crankshaft.*
 f) *Spring-loaded tensioner pulley.*
62 Ensure the belt ribs are correctly seated in all the pulley grooves, then rotate the manual tensioner pulley in a clockwise direction to remove all slack from the belt. Rotate the pulley using a square-section key fitted to the hole in the pulley hub.
63 To correctly set the drivebelt tension, position the manual tensioner pulley so that all spring pressure is removed from the locking bolt/pin fitted to the spring-loaded tensioner pulley backplate **(see illustration)**. Once the manual tensioner pulley is correctly positioned, securely tighten its retaining bolt.
64 Remove the locking bolt/pin then rotate the crankshaft through four complete revolutions. Check that the holes in the tensioner pulley and backplate are still aligned, and that it is now possible to insert a setting tool of 2.0 mm diameter through both holes. If not, slacken the manual tensioner pulley bolt and repeat the adjustment procedure.
65 Once the belt is correctly tensioned, remove the setting tool, clip the coolant hoses into position (where applicable), then refit the plastic cover to the wing valance. Refit the roadwheel, and lower the vehicle to the ground.
66 On completion, reconnect the battery negative terminal.

13 Clutch adjustment check and control mechanism lubrication

1 Check that the clutch pedal moves smoothly and easily through its full travel, and that the clutch itself functions correctly, with no trace of slip or drag.
2 Adjust the clutch as described in Chapter 6 (where necessary).
3 If excessive effort is required to operate the clutch, check first that the cable is correctly routed and undamaged, then remove the pedal and check that its pivot is properly greased. Refer to Chapter 6 for further information.

14 Front brake pad check

1 Firmly apply the handbrake, then jack up the front of the car and support it securely on axle stands (see *Jacking and vehicle support*). Remove the front roadwheels.

2 If any pad's friction material is worn to the specified thickness or less, *all four pads must be renewed as a set.*
3 For a comprehensive check, the brake pads should be removed and cleaned. The operation of the caliper can then also be checked, and the condition of the brake disc itself can be fully examined on both sides. Refer to Chapter 9 for further information.

15 Handbrake check and adjustment

Refer to Chapter 9.

16 Road test

Instruments and electrical equipment

1 Check the operation of all instruments and electrical equipment.
2 Make sure that all instruments read correctly, and switch on all electrical equipment in turn to check that it works properly.

Steering and suspension

3 Check for any abnormalities in the steering, suspension, handling or road 'feel'.
4 Drive the vehicle, and check that there are no unusual vibrations or noises.
5 Check that the steering feels positive, with no excessive 'sloppiness', or roughness, and check for any suspension noises when cornering, or when driving over bumps.

Drivetrain

6 Check the performance of the engine, clutch, transmission and driveshafts.
7 Listen for any unusual noises from the engine, clutch and transmission.
8 Make sure that the engine runs smoothly when idling, and that there is no hesitation when accelerating.
9 Check that the clutch action is smooth and progressive, that the drive is taken up smoothly, and that the pedal travel is not excessive. Also listen for any noises when the clutch pedal is depressed.
10 Check that all gears can be engaged smoothly, without noise, and that the gear lever action is smooth and not abnormally vague or 'notchy'.
11 Listen for a metallic clicking sound from the front of the vehicle, as the vehicle is driven slowly in a circle with the steering on full lock. Carry out this check in both directions. If a clicking noise is heard, this indicates wear in a driveshaft joint, in which case, the complete driveshaft must be renewed (see Chapter 8).

Braking system

12 Make sure that the vehicle does not pull to one side when braking, and that the wheels do not lock prematurely when braking hard.

13 Check that there is no vibration through the steering when braking.

14 Check that the handbrake operates correctly, without excessive movement of the lever, and that it holds the vehicle stationary on a slope.

15 Test the operation of the brake servo unit as follows. With the engine off, depress the footbrake four or five times to exhaust the vacuum. Start the engine, holding the brake pedal depressed. As the engine starts, there should be a noticeable 'give' in the brake pedal as vacuum builds-up. Allow the engine to run for at least two minutes, and then switch it off. If the brake pedal is depressed now, it should be possible to detect a hiss from the servo as the pedal is depressed. After about four or five applications, no further hissing should be heard, and the pedal should feel considerably firmer.

Every 36 000 miles

Caution: Take care not to allow dirt into the fuel filter housing during this procedure or to spill fuel onto the clutch assembly.

1.8 and 1.9 litre XUD engines

1 The fuel filter is located in a plastic housing at the front of the engine.

2 Where applicable, cover the clutch bellhousing with a piece of plastic sheeting, to protect the clutch from fuel spillage.

3 Remove all traces of dirt from the exterior of the filter housing then drain the fuel filter as described in Section 4.

4 Undo the four retaining bolts and lift off the filter housing cover **(see illustration)**.

5 Lift the filter from the housing **(see illustration)**. Ensure that the rubber sealing ring comes away with the filter, and does not stick to the housing/lid.

6 Remove all traces of dirt or debris from inside the filter housing then, making sure its sealing ring is in position, fit the new fuel filter.

7 Coat the threads of the filter cover securing bolts with thread-locking compound, then refit the cover and secure with the bolts.

8 Prime the fuel system as described in Chapter 4D.

1.9 litre DW engines

9 Release the fasteners from the right-hand side and top of the engine cover then lift off the cover, taking care not to lose its mounting rubbers.

10 Remove all traces of dirt from the exterior of the filter housing then drain the fuel filter as described in Section 4.

11 Release the retaining clip and detach the fuel outlet pipe from the filter housing cover **(see illustration)**.

12 Unclip the filter housing cover retaining clip then position the cover clear of the housing **(see illustration)**. Discard the cover sealing ring – a new ring must be used on refitting.

13 Lift the fuel filter and sealing ring out of the housing **(see illustration)**.

14 Remove all traces of dirt or debris from inside the filter housing.

15 Ensure that the housing and cover are spotlessly clean then fit the new fuel filter.

16 Ensure that the new small sealing ring is correctly fitted to the top of the filter, then fit the new large sealing ring to the cover **(see illustrations)**.

17.4 Lift off the fuel filter cover . . .

17.5 . . . then lift the filter from the housing – XUD engines

17.11 Release the retaining clip and detach the fuel outlet pipe from the filter housing cover – 1.9 litre DW engines

17.12 Release the clip and lift off the filter housing cover – 1.9 litre DW engines

17.13 Lift the fuel filter and sealing ring out of the housing – 1.9 litre DW engines

17.16a Ensure that the new small sealing ring (arrowed) is correctly fitted to the fuel filter . . .

17.16b . . . and the new large sealing ring (arrowed) is correctly fitted to the housing cover – 1.9 litre DW engines

17.23 Disconnect the fuel supply and return hose quick-release fittings (arrowed) from the filter housing cover – 2.0 litre engines

17 Locate the cover correctly on the filter housing and refit the retaining clip. Ensure that the clip is correctly engaged with the housing and cover and secure it firmly in position.

18 Reconnect the fuel outlet pipe to the cover.

19 Check that the filter housing drain plug is securely closed, then prime the fuel system as described in Chapter 4E.

20 Once the engine is idling smoothly, ensure that the mounting rubbers are all correctly fitted then install the engine cover, securing it in position with the fasteners.

2.0 litre engines

Caution: The need for scrupulous cleanliness when working on the fuel system of HDi engines cannot be over-emphasised. It is particularly important to keep foreign matter – dust, water or any other contaminant – out of the fuel lines. Bear in mind also, the following specific points:

● *When renewing the fuel filter element, the filter housing must be cleaned in a solvent bath using injector test fluid, paraffin or similar. DO NOT use compressed air or ordinary rags to dry it off; special 'Resistel' cleaning cloths, available from Peugeot dealers, are the only items approved for this purpose.*

● *Before undertaking any work on the high pressure side of the system, remove any loose debris with a vacuum cleaner, then clean around the components to be removed with a paintbrush and an approved solvent ('Sodimac No 35', 'Mecanet' or equivalent).*

● *DO NOT clean the engine using a steam cleaner or a high pressure water jet; use one of the solvents mentioned above.*

● *After disconnection of any fuel union, cover the open ends immediately to keep dirt out. Special plugs for this purpose can be obtained from your dealer.*

21 Release the fixings by turning them through 90°, and remove the engine cover.

22 Remove all traces of dirt from the exterior of the filter housing then drain the fuel filter as described in Section 4.

23 At the connections on the filter housing cover, disconnect the fuel supply and return hose quick-release fittings using a small screwdriver to release the locking clip **(see illustration)**. Suitably plug or cover the open hose unions to prevent dirt entry.

24 Using a suitable socket engaged with the hexagonal moulding on the filter housing cover, turn the cover approximately a quarter turn anti-clockwise to release the locking lugs.

25 Lift off the housing cover, and collect the metal sealing ring and the O-ring seal, then lift out the filter element **(see illustrations)**.

26 Remove all traces of dirt or debris from inside the filter housing then fit the new fuel filter element.

27 Locate the new O-ring seal in position, followed by the metal sealing ring.

28 Refit the housing cover and turn it clockwise until the arrow on the housing cover is in line with the filter drain outlet.

29 Reconnect the fuel supply and return hoses, then prime the fuel system as described in Chapter 4E.

30 On completion, refit the engine cover.

18 Hinge and lock lubrication

1 Work around the vehicle, and lubricate the hinges of the bonnet, doors and tailgate with a general-purpose light oil.

2 Lightly lubricate the bonnet release mechanism and exposed section of inner cable with a smear of grease.

3 Check carefully the security and operation of all hinges, latches and locks, adjusting them where required. Check the operation of the central locking system (if fitted).

4 Check the condition and operation of the

17.25a Lift off the filter housing cover . . .

17.25b . . . remove the metal sealing ring . . .

17.25c . . . and the O-ring seal . . .

17.25d . . . then lift out the filter element – 2.0 litre engines

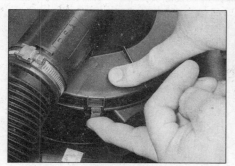

19.2a On non-turbo models, release the clips securing the air cleaner cover . . .

19.2b . . . then lift off the cover . . .

19.3 . . . and withdraw the air filter

tailgate struts, renewing them if either is leaking or no longer able to support the tailgate securely when raised.

19 Air filter renewal

1.8 and 1.9 litre engines

Non-turbo models

1 Slacken the retaining clip and disconnect the intake duct from the top of the filter housing. Slacken the retaining clips, and remove the duct linking the intake to the rear of the air cleaner housing.
2 Release the retaining clips, then lift off the filter housing lid **(see illustrations)**.
3 Remove the filter element from the housing **(see illustration)**.
4 Wipe clean the inside of the filter housing and fit the new filter element, making sure that it is correctly seated.
5 Refit the lid, and secure it in position with the retaining clips.
6 Reconnect the intake ducts, securing them in position with the retaining clips.

Turbo models

7 Access to the air filter is obtained from under the front of the vehicle. If necessary, to improve access, firmly apply the handbrake then jack up the front of the vehicle and support it on axle stands (see *Jacking and vehicle support*).
8 Release the retaining clips, and remove the cover from the base of the air cleaner housing **(see illustration)**.
9 Withdraw the filter from the housing **(see illustration)**.
10 Wipe clean the inside of the filter housing, then fit the new filter.
11 Refit the base to the housing, and secure it in position with the retaining clips. Where necessary, lower the vehicle to the ground.

2.0 litre engines

12 Disconnect the wiring connector from the airflow meter on the air filter housing lid.

13 Undo the screws securing the lid to the air filter housing **(see illustration)**.
14 Lift up the lid and withdraw the filter element from the housing **(see illustration)**.
15 Wipe clean the inside of the filter housing, then fit the new filter element.
16 Refit the lid to the filter housing and secure with the retaining screws.
17 Reconnect the airflow meter wiring connector.

20 Rear brake shoe check – models with rear drum brakes

1 Remove the rear brake drums, and check the brake shoes for wear or contamination. At

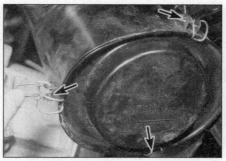

19.8 On 1.9 litre turbo models, release the air cleaner cover clips (arrowed) . . .

19.13 On 2.0 litre engines, undo the screws securing the lid to the air filter housing . . .

the same time, also inspect the wheel cylinders for signs of leakage, and the brake drum for signs of wear. Refer to the relevant Sections of Chapter 9 for further information.

21 Rear brake pad check – models with rear disc brakes

1 Chock the front wheels then jack up the rear of the vehicle and support it on axle stands (see *Jacking and vehicle support*). Remove the rear roadwheels.
2 If any pad's friction material is worn to the specified thickness or less, all four pads must be renewed as a set.
3 For a comprehensive check, the brake pads

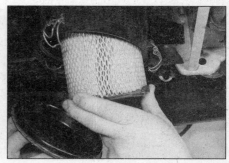

19.9 . . . and withdraw the air filter element from the housing

19.14 . . . then lift up the lid and withdraw the filter element

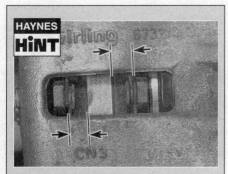

HAYNES HiNT

For a quick check, the thickness of friction material remaining on each brake pad can be measured through the aperture in the caliper body.

should be removed and cleaned **(see Haynes Hint)**. This will permit the operation of the caliper to be checked, and the condition of the brake disc itself to be fully examined on both sides. Refer to Chapter 9 for further information.

22 Manual transmission oil level check

1 Park the car on a level surface. The oil level must be checked before the car is driven, or at least 5 minutes after the engine has been switched off. If the oil is checked immediately after driving the car, some of the oil will remain distributed around the transmission, resulting in an inaccurate level reading.

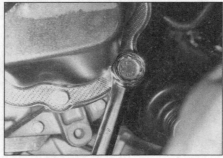

22.3 Removing the manual transmission filler/level plug

2 Prise out the clips and remove the access cover from the left-hand wheel arch liner.
3 Wipe clean the area around the filler/level plug, which is on the left-hand end of the transmission **(see illustration)**. Unscrew the plug and clean it; discard the sealing washer.
4 The oil level should reach the lower edge of the filler/level hole. A certain amount of oil will have gathered behind the filler/level plug, and will trickle out when it is removed; this does not necessarily indicate that the level is correct. To ensure that a true level is established, wait until the initial trickle has stopped, then add oil as necessary until a trickle of new oil can be seen emerging **(see illustration)**. The level will be correct when the flow ceases; use only good-quality oil of the specified type (refer to *Lubricants and fluids*).
5 Filling the transmission with oil is an extremely awkward operation; above all, allow plenty of time for the oil level to settle properly before checking it. If a large amount is added to the transmission, and a large amount flows

22.4 Oil level is correct when the oil stops flowing out of the filler/level hole

out on checking the level, refit the filler/level plug and take the vehicle on a short journey so that the new oil is distributed fully around the transmission components, then recheck the level when it has settled again.
6 If the transmission has been overfilled so that oil flows out as soon as the filler/level plug is removed, check that the car is completely level (front-to-rear and side-to-side), and allow the surplus to drain off into a suitable container.
7 When the level is correct, fit a new sealing washer to the filler/level plug. Refit the plug, tightening it to the specified torque wrench setting. Wash off any spilt oil then refit the access cover securing it in position with the retaining clips.

23 Timing belt renewal

Refer to the relevant Part of Chapter 2.

Every 2 years (regardless of mileage)

24 Coolant renewal

⚠️ *Warning: Wait until the engine is cold before starting this procedure. Do not allow antifreeze to come in contact with your skin, or with the painted surfaces of the vehicle. Rinse off spills immediately with plenty of water. Never leave antifreeze lying around in an open container, or in a puddle in the driveway or on the garage floor. Children and pets are attracted by its sweet smell, but antifreeze can be fatal if ingested.*

Cooling system draining

1 With the engine completely cold, remove the expansion tank filler cap. Turn the cap anti-clockwise until it reaches the first stop. Wait until any pressure remaining in the system is released, then push the cap down, turn it anti-clockwise to the second stop, and lift it off.

2 Position a suitable container beneath the coolant drain outlet at the lower left-hand side of the radiator.
3 Loosen the drain plug (there is no need to remove it completely) and allow the coolant to drain into the container. If desired, a length of tubing can be fitted to the drain outlet to direct the flow of coolant during draining **(see illustration)**.

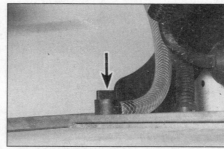

24.3 Fit a length of tubing to the radiator drain plug (arrowed) to assist draining – viewed from above

4 To assist draining, open the cooling system bleed screws. These are located in the heater matrix outlet hose union (to improve access, it may be located in an extension hose), on the engine compartment bulkhead, and on the top of the thermostat housing. On some models, there may also be a bleed screw in the top left-hand end of the radiator **(see illustrations)**.

24.4a Heater hose bleed screw (arrowed)

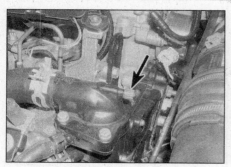

24.4b Thermostat housing bleed screw (arrowed)

24.4c Radiator bleed screw (arrowed)

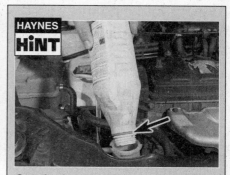

HAYNES HINT

Cut the bottom off an old antifreeze container to make a 'header tank' for use when refilling the cooling system. The seal at the point arrowed should be as airtight as possible – use an O-ring if available, or seal the joint by some other means.

5 When the flow of coolant stops, reposition the container below the cylinder block drain plug. The drain plug is located at the rear of the cylinder block.

6 Remove the drain plug, and allow the coolant to drain into the container.

7 If the coolant has been drained for a reason other than renewal, then provided it is clean and less than two years old, it can be re-used, though this is not recommended.

8 Refit the radiator and cylinder block drain plugs on completion of draining.

Cooling system flushing

9 If coolant renewal has been neglected, or if the antifreeze mixture has become diluted, then in time, the cooling system may gradually lose efficiency, as the coolant passages become restricted due to rust, scale deposits, and other sediment. The cooling system efficiency can be restored by flushing the system clean.

10 The radiator should be flushed independently of the engine, to avoid unnecessary contamination.

Radiator flushing

11 To flush the radiator, first tighten the radiator drain plug, and the radiator bleed screw, where applicable.

12 Disconnect the top and bottom hoses and any other relevant hoses from the radiator, with reference to Chapter 3.

13 Insert a garden hose into the radiator top inlet. Direct a flow of clean water through the radiator, and keep flushing until clean water emerges from the radiator bottom outlet.

14 If after a reasonable period the water still does not run clear, the radiator can be flushed with a good proprietary cleaning agent. It is important that their manufacturer's instructions are followed carefully. If the contamination is particularly bad, insert the hose in the radiator bottom outlet, and reverse-flush the radiator.

Engine flushing

15 To flush the engine, first refit the cylinder block drain plug, and tighten the cooling system bleed screws.

16 Remove the thermostat as described in Chapter 3, then temporarily refit the thermostat cover.

17 With the top and bottom hoses disconnected from the radiator, insert a garden hose into the radiator top hose. Direct a clean flow of water through the engine, and continue flushing until clean water emerges from the radiator bottom hose.

18 On completion of flushing, refit the thermostat and reconnect the hoses with reference to Chapter 3.

Cooling system filling

19 Before attempting to fill the cooling system, make sure that all hoses and clips are in good condition, and that the clips are tight. An antifreeze mixture must be used all year round, to prevent corrosion of the engine components (see following sub-Section). Also check that the radiator and cylinder block drain plugs are in place and tight.

20 Remove the expansion tank filler cap.

21 Open all the cooling system bleed screws (see paragraph 4).

22 Some of the cooling system hoses are positioned at a higher level than the top of the radiator expansion tank. It is therefore necessary to use a 'header tank' when refilling the cooling system, to reduce the possibility of air being trapped in the system. Although Peugeot dealers use a special header tank, the same effect can be achieved by using a suitable bottle, with a seal between the bottle and the expansion tank **(see Haynes Hint)**.

23 Fit the 'header tank' to the expansion tank and slowly fill the system. Coolant will emerge from each of the bleed screws in turn, starting with the lowest screw. As soon as coolant free from air bubbles emerges from the lowest screw, tighten that screw, and watch the next bleed screw in the system. Repeat the procedure until the coolant is emerging from the highest bleed screw in the cooling system and all bleed screws are securely tightened.

24 Ensure that the 'header tank' is full (at least 0.5 litres of coolant). Start the engine, and run it at a fast idle speed (do not exceed 2000 rpm) until the cooling fan cuts in, and then cuts out. Stop the engine. **Note:** *Take great care not to scald yourself with the hot coolant during this operation.*

25 Allow the engine to cool, then remove the 'header tank'.

26 When the engine has cooled, check the coolant level as described in *Weekly checks*.

Top-up the level if necessary, and refit the expansion tank cap.

Antifreeze mixture

27 The antifreeze should always be renewed at the specified intervals. This is necessary not only to maintain the antifreeze properties, but also to prevent corrosion which would otherwise occur as the corrosion inhibitors become progressively less effective.

28 Always use an ethylene-glycol or monoethylene-glycol based antifreeze of the specified type (see *Lubricants and fluids*). The quantity of antifreeze and level of protection are indicated in the Specifications.

29 Before adding antifreeze, the cooling system should be completely drained, preferably flushed, and all hoses checked for condition and security.

30 After filling with antifreeze, a label should be attached to the expansion tank, stating the type and concentration of antifreeze used, and the date installed. Any subsequent topping-up should be made with the same type and concentration of antifreeze.

31 Do not use engine antifreeze in the windscreen/tailgate washer system, as it will cause damage to the vehicle paintwork. A screenwash additive should be added to the washer system in the quantities stated on the bottle.

25 Brake fluid renewal

⚠ *Warning: Brake hydraulic fluid can harm your eyes and damage painted surfaces, so use extreme caution when handling and pouring it. Do not use fluid that has been standing open for some time, as it absorbs moisture from the air. Excess moisture can cause a dangerous loss of braking effectiveness.*

1 The procedure is similar to that for the bleeding of the hydraulic system as described in Chapter 9, except that the brake fluid reservoir should be emptied by syphoning, using a clean poultry baster or similar before starting, and allowance should be made for the old fluid to be expelled when bleeding a section of the circuit.

2 Working as described in Chapter 9, open the first bleed screw in the sequence, and pump the brake pedal gently until nearly all the old fluid has been emptied from the master cylinder reservoir.

 Old hydraulic fluid is invariably much darker in colour than the new, making it easy to distinguish the two.

3 Top-up to the MAX level with new fluid, and continue pumping until only the new fluid remains in the reservoir, and new fluid can be seen emerging from the bleed screw. Tighten the screw, and top the reservoir level up to the MAX level line.

4 Work through all the remaining bleed screws in the sequence until new fluid can be seen at all of them. Be careful to keep the master cylinder reservoir topped-up to above the MIN level at all times, or air may enter the system and greatly increase the length of the task.

5 When the operation is complete, check that all bleed screws are securely tightened, and that their dust caps are refitted. Wash off all traces of spilt fluid, and recheck the master cylinder reservoir fluid level.

6 Check the operation of the brakes before taking the car on the road.

Chapter 2 Part A:
1.1, 1.4 and 1.6 litre petrol engine in-car repair procedures

Contents

Degrees of difficulty

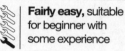

Easy, suitable for novice with little experience	**Fairly easy,** suitable for beginner with some experience	**Fairly difficult,** suitable for competent DIY mechanic	**Difficult,** suitable for experienced DIY mechanic	**Very difficult,** suitable for expert DIY or professional

Specifications

Engine (general)

Designation:
 1.1 litre (1124 cc) engine TU1
 1.4 litre (1360 cc) engine TU3
 1.6 litre (1587 cc) engine TU5
Engine codes*:
 1.1 litre engine:
  Up to mid-1997 . . . . HDZ and HDY (TU1M)
  Mid-1997 onward . . . . HDZ and HDY (TU1M+)
 1.4 litre carburettor engine:
  Up to mid-1997 . . . . K2D (TU3F 2K)
  Mid-1997 onward . . . . K5A (TU3.2 TR)
 1.4 litre fuel injected engine:
  Up to mid-1996 . . . . KDX (TU3MC)
  Mid-1996 to mid-2000 . . . . KFX (TU3JP)
  Mid-2000 onward . . . . KFW (TU3JP)
 1.6 litre fuel injected engine:
  Up to mid-2000 . . . . NFZ (TU5JP)
  Mid-2000 onward . . . . NFT (TU5JP)
Bore:
 1.1 litre engine . . . . 72.00 mm
 1.4 litre engine . . . . 75.00 mm
 1.6 litre engine . . . . 78.50 mm
Stroke:
 1.1 litre engine . . . . 69.00 mm
 1.4 litre engine . . . . 77.00 mm
 1.6 litre engine . . . . 82.00 mm
Direction of crankshaft rotation . . . . Clockwise (viewed from right-hand side of vehicle)
No 1 cylinder location . . . . At transmission end of block
The engine code is situated on the front left-hand end of the cylinder block. It is either stamped on a plate which is riveted to the block (aluminium block engines) or stamped directly on the cylinder block (cast-iron block engines).

Camshaft

Drive	Toothed belt
Number of bearings	5

Camshaft bearing journal diameter (outside diameter):

No 1	36.950 to 36.925 mm
No 2	40.650 to 40.625 mm
No 3	41.250 to 41.225 mm
No 4	41.850 to 41.825 mm
No 5	42.450 to 42.425 mm

Cylinder head bearing journal diameter (inside diameter):

No 1	37.000 to 37.039 mm
No 2	40.700 to 47.739 mm
No 3	41.300 to 41.339 mm
No 4	41.900 to 41.939 mm
No 5	42.500 to 42.539 mm

Valve clearances (engine cold)

Inlet	0.20 mm
Exhaust	0.40 mm

Lubrication system

Oil pump type	Gear-type, chain-driven off the crankshaft
Minimum oil pressure at 90°C	4 bars at 4000 rpm
Oil pressure warning switch operating pressure	0.8 bars

Torque wrench settings

	Nm	lbf ft
Big-end bearing cap nuts*	38	28
Camshaft sprocket retaining bolt	80	59
Camshaft thrust fork retaining bolt	16	12
Crankshaft pulley retaining bolts	8	6
Crankshaft sprocket retaining bolt	110	81
Cylinder head bolts (aluminium block engine):		
Stage 1	20	15
Stage 2	Angle-tighten a further 240°	
Cylinder head bolts (cast-iron block engine):		
Stage 1	20	15
Stage 2	Angle-tighten a further 120°	
Stage 3	Angle-tighten a further 120°	
Cylinder head cover nuts	16	12
Engine-to-transmission bolts	35	26
Engine/transmission left-hand mounting:		
Mounting bracket-to-transmission nuts	20	15
Mounting bracket-to-body bolts	25	18
Mounting rubber nuts	20	15
Centre nut	65	48
Engine/transmission rear mounting:		
Mounting-to-cylinder block bolts	40	30
Mounting link-to-mounting bolt	70	52
Mounting link-to-body bolt	50	37
Engine/transmission right-hand mounting bracket nuts	45	33
Flywheel/driveplate retaining bolts*	65	48
Main bearing cap bolts (cast-iron block engine):		
Stage 1	20	15
Stage 2	Angle-tighten a further 50°	
Main bearing ladder casting (aluminium block engine):		
11 mm bolts:		
Stage 1	20	15
Stage 2	Angle-tighten a further 50°	
6 mm bolts	8	6
Oil pump retaining bolts	8	6
Piston oil jet spray tube bolts (1.6 litre engine)	10	7
Sump drain plug	30	22
Sump retaining nuts and bolts	8	6
Timing belt cover bolts	8	6
Timing belt tensioner pulley nut	23	17

New nuts/bolts must be used.

1 General information

Using this Chapter

Chapter 2 is divided into five Parts; A, B, C, D and E. Repair operations that can be carried out with the engine in the vehicle are described in Parts A (1.1, 1.4 and 1.6 litre TU series petrol engines), B (1.8 and 2.0 litre XU series petrol engines), C (1.8 and 1.9 litre XUD series diesel engines) and D (1.9 and 2.0 litre DW series diesel engines). Part E covers the removal of the engine/transmission as a unit, and describes the engine dismantling and overhaul procedures.

In Parts A, B, C and D, the assumption is made that the engine is installed in the vehicle, with all ancillaries connected. If the engine has been removed for overhaul, the preliminary dismantling information which precedes each operation may be ignored.

TU series engine description

The TU series engine is a well-proven engine which has been fitted to many previous Peugeot and Citroën vehicles. The engine is of the in-line four-cylinder, overhead camshaft (OHC) type, mounted transversely at the front of the car. The clutch and transmission are attached to its left-hand end. The 306 range is fitted with 1124 cc, 1360 cc and 1587 cc versions of this engine type.

The crankshaft runs in five main bearings. Thrustwashers are fitted to No 2 main bearing (upper half) to control crankshaft endfloat.

The connecting rods rotate on horizontally-split bearing shells at their big-ends. The pistons are attached to the connecting rods by gudgeon pins, which are an interference fit in the connecting rod small-end eyes. The aluminium-alloy pistons are fitted with three piston rings – two compression rings and an oil control ring.

On 1.1 and 1.4 litre engines, the cylinder block is made of aluminium, and renewable wet liners are fitted to the cylinder bores. Sealing O-rings are fitted at the base of each liner, to prevent the escape of coolant into the sump.

On 1.6 litre engines, the cylinder block is made from cast-iron, and the cylinder bores are an integral part of the cylinder block. On this type of engine, the cylinder bores are sometimes referred to as having dry liners.

The inlet and exhaust valves are each closed by coil springs, and operate in guides pressed into the cylinder head; the valve seat inserts are also pressed into the cylinder head, and can be renewed separately if worn.

The camshaft is driven by a toothed timing belt, and operates the eight valves via rocker arms. Valve clearances are adjusted by a screw-and-locknut arrangement. The camshaft rotates directly in the cylinder head. The timing belt also drives the coolant pump.

Lubrication is by means of an oil pump, which is driven (via a chain and sprocket) off the right-hand end of the crankshaft. It draws oil through a strainer located in the sump, and then forces it through an externally-mounted filter into galleries in the cylinder block/crankcase. From there, the oil is distributed to the crankshaft (main bearings) and camshaft. The big-end bearings are supplied with oil via internal drillings in the crankshaft, while the camshaft bearings also receive a pressurised supply. The camshaft lobes and valves are lubricated by splash, as are all other engine components.

Throughout this manual, it is often necessary to identify the engines not only by their capacity, but also by their engine code which can be found on the left-hand end of the front face of the cylinder block. On models with an aluminium cylinder block, the code is stamped on a plate which is riveted to the block; on models with a cast-iron cylinder block, the number is stamped on a machined surface on the cylinder block, at the flywheel end. The first part of the engine number gives the engine code – eg KDX (see illustration).

Operations with engine in car

The following work can be carried out with the engine in the car:

a) Compression pressure – testing.
b) Cylinder head cover – removal and refitting.
c) Timing belt covers – removal and refitting.
d) Timing belt – removal, refitting and adjustment.
e) Timing belt tensioner and sprockets – removal and refitting.
f) Camshaft oil seal(s) – renewal.
g) Camshaft and rocker arms – removal, inspection and refitting*.
h) Cylinder head – removal and refitting.
i) Cylinder head and pistons – decarbonising.
j) Sump – removal and refitting.
k) Oil pump – removal, overhaul and refitting.
l) Crankshaft oil seals – renewal.
m) Engine/transmission mountings – inspection and renewal.

1.11 Engine code is stamped on a plate (arrowed) attached to the front of the cylinder block – viewed from above

n) Flywheel/driveplate – removal, inspection and refitting.
* The cylinder head must be removed for the successful completion of this work. Refer to Section 11 for details.

2 Compression test – description and interpretation

1 When engine performance is down, or if misfiring occurs which cannot be attributed to the ignition or fuel systems, a compression test can provide diagnostic clues as to the engine's condition. If the test is performed regularly, it can give warning of trouble before any other symptoms become apparent.

2 The engine must be fully warmed-up to normal operating temperature, the battery must be fully-charged, and all the spark plugs must be removed (Chapter 1A). The aid of an assistant will also be required.

3 On carburettor models, disable the ignition system by disconnecting the ignition HT coil lead from the distributor cap and earthing it on the cylinder block. Use a jumper lead or similar wire to make a good connection.

4 On fuel injected models, disable the ignition system by disconnecting the LT wiring connector from the ignition HT coil(s), referring to Chapter 5B for further information. Referring to Chapter 12, disable and depressurise the fuel system by identifying and removing the fuel pump fuse from the engine compartment fusebox. Start the engine, and run it until it cuts out.

5 Fit a compression tester to the No 1 cylinder spark plug hole – the type of tester which screws into the plug thread is to be preferred.

6 Have the assistant hold the throttle wide open, and crank the engine on the starter motor; after one or two revolutions, the compression pressure should build-up to a maximum figure, and then stabilise. Record the highest reading obtained.

7 Repeat the test on the remaining cylinders, recording the pressure in each.

8 All cylinders should produce very similar pressures; a difference of more than 2 bars between any two cylinders indicates a fault. Note that the compression should build-up quickly in a healthy engine; low compression on the first stroke, followed by gradually-increasing pressure on successive strokes, indicates worn piston rings. A low compression reading on the first stroke, which does not build-up during successive strokes, indicates leaking valves or a blown head gasket (a cracked head could also be the cause). Deposits on the undersides of the valve heads can also cause low compression.

9 Although Peugeot do not specify exact compression pressures, as a guide, any cylinder pressure of below 10 bars can be considered as less than healthy. Refer to a Peugeot dealer or other specialist if in doubt

as to whether a particular pressure reading is acceptable.

10 If the pressure in any cylinder is low, carry out the following test to isolate the cause. Introduce a teaspoonful of clean oil into that cylinder through its spark plug hole, and repeat the test.

11 If the addition of oil temporarily improves the compression pressure, this indicates that bore or piston wear is responsible for the pressure loss. No improvement suggests that leaking or burnt valves, or a blown head gasket, may be to blame.

12 A low reading from two adjacent cylinders is almost certainly due to the head gasket having blown between them; the presence of coolant in the engine oil will confirm this.

13 If one cylinder is about 20 percent lower than the others and the engine has a slightly rough idle, a worn camshaft lobe could be the cause.

14 If the compression reading is unusually high, the combustion chambers are probably coated with carbon deposits. If this is the case, the cylinder head should be removed and decarbonised.

15 On completion of the test, refit the spark plugs, reconnect the ignition system wiring and, where applicable, refit the fuel pump fuse.

3.4 Insert a 6 mm bolt (arrowed) through hole in cylinder block flange and into timing hole in the flywheel . . .

the crankshaft and camshaft are correctly positioned when assembling the engine (to prevent the possibility of the valves contacting the pistons when refitting the cylinder head), or refitting the timing belt. When the timing holes are aligned with access holes in the cylinder head and the front of the cylinder block, suitable diameter pins can be inserted to lock both the camshaft and crankshaft in position, preventing them from rotating. Proceed as follows.

2 Remove the timing belt upper cover as described in Section 5.

3 The crankshaft must now be turned until the timing hole in the camshaft sprocket is aligned with the corresponding hole in the cylinder head. The holes are aligned when the camshaft sprocket hole is in the 2 o'clock position, when viewed from the right-hand end of the engine. The crankshaft can be turned by using a spanner on the crankshaft sprocket bolt, noting that it should always be rotated in a clockwise direction (viewed from the right-hand end of the engine).

4 With the camshaft sprocket hole correctly positioned, insert a 6 mm diameter bolt or drill through the hole in the front, left-hand flange of the cylinder block, and locate it in the timing hole in the rear of the flywheel **(see illustration)**. Note that it may be necessary to rotate the crankshaft slightly, to get the holes to align.

5 With the flywheel correctly positioned, insert a 10 mm diameter bolt or a drill through the timing hole in the camshaft sprocket, and

3.5 . . . then insert a 10 mm bolt through the camshaft sprocket timing hole, and locate it in the cylinder head

locate it in the hole in the cylinder head **(see illustration)**.

6 The crankshaft and camshaft are now locked in position, preventing unnecessary rotation.

4 Cylinder head cover – removal and refitting

Removal

1 Disconnect the battery negative terminal (refer to *Disconnecting the battery* in the Reference Chapter).

2 Where necessary, undo the bolts securing the HT lead retaining clips to the rear of the cylinder head cover, and position the clips clear of the cover.

3 Slacken the retaining clip (or release the quick-release fitting), and disconnect the breather hose from the left-hand end of the cylinder head cover **(see illustration)**. Where the original crimped-type Peugeot hose clip is still fitted, cut it off and discard it. Use a standard worm-drive clip on refitting.

4 Undo the two retaining nuts, and remove the washer from each of the cylinder head cover studs **(see illustration)**.

5 Lift off the cylinder head cover, and remove it along with its rubber seal **(see illustration)**. Examine the seal for signs of damage and deterioration, and if necessary, renew it.

3 Engine assembly/valve timing holes – general information and usage

Caution: Do not attempt to rotate the engine whilst the crankshaft/camshaft are locked in position. If the engine is to be left in this state for a long period of time, it is a good idea to place warning notices inside the vehicle, and in the engine compartment. This will reduce the possibility of the engine being accidentally cranked on the starter motor, which is likely to cause damage with the locking pins in place.

1 On all models, timing holes are drilled in the camshaft sprocket and in the rear of the flywheel. The holes are used to ensure that

4.3 Disconnect the breather hose from the cylinder head cover . . .

4.4 . . . then slacken and remove the cover retaining nuts and washers (arrowed) . . .

4.5 . . . and lift off the cylinder head cover

4.6a Lift off the spacers (second one arrowed) . . .

4.6b . . . and remove the oil baffle plate

4.8 On refitting, ensure the rubber seal is correctly located on the cylinder head cover

6 Remove the spacer from each stud, and lift off the oil baffle plate **(see illustrations)**.

Refitting

7 Carefully clean the cylinder head and cover mating surfaces, and remove all traces of oil.
8 Fit the rubber seal over the edge of the cylinder head cover, ensuring that it is correctly located along its entire length **(see illustration)**.
9 Refit the oil baffle plate to the engine, and locate the spacers in their recesses in the baffle plate.
10 Carefully refit the cylinder head cover to the engine, taking great care not to displace the rubber seal.
11 Check that the seal is correctly located, then refit the washers and cover retaining nuts, and tighten them to the specified torque.
12 Where necessary, refit the HT lead clips to the rear of the head cover, and securely tighten their retaining bolts.

13 Reconnect the breather hose to the cylinder head cover, securely tightening its retaining clip (where applicable), and reconnect the battery negative terminal.

---

5 Timing belt covers – removal and refitting

Removal

Upper cover

1 Slacken and remove the two retaining bolts (one at the front and one at the rear), and remove the upper timing cover from the cylinder head **(see illustrations)**.

Centre cover

Note: *On later engines the centre cover is*

combined with the lower cover and is not a separate component.
2 Remove the upper cover as described in paragraph 1, then free the wiring from its retaining clips on the centre cover **(see illustration)**.
3 Slacken and remove the three retaining bolts (one at the rear of the cover, beneath the engine mounting plate, and two directly above the crankshaft pulley), and manoeuvre the centre cover out from the engine compartment **(see illustration)**.

Lower cover

4 Remove the auxiliary drivebelt as described in Chapter 1A.
5 Remove the upper and, where applicable, the centre covers as described in paragraphs 1 to 3.
6 Undo the three crankshaft pulley retaining bolts and remove the pulley, noting which way round it is fitted **(see illustrations)**.

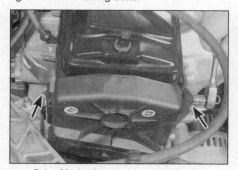

5.1a Undo the two retaining bolts (arrowed) . . .

5.1b . . . and remove the timing belt upper cover

5.2 Free the wiring loom from its clip . . .

5.3 . . . then undo the three bolts (locations arrowed) and remove the centre cover

5.6a Undo the three bolts (arrowed) . . .

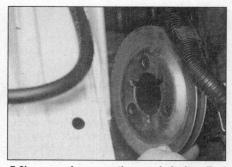

5.6b . . . and remove the crankshaft pulley

5.7 Undo the retaining bolt and remove the timing belt lower cover

7 On engines with a separate centre cover, slacken and remove the single retaining bolt, and slide the lower cover off the end of the crankshaft **(see illustration)**. On engines with a combined centre and lower cover, it will also be necessary to slacken and remove the three retaining bolts (one at the rear of the cover, beneath the engine mounting plate, and two directly above the crankshaft pulley).

Refitting

Upper cover

8 Refit the cover, ensuring it is correctly located with the centre cover, and tighten its retaining bolts.

Centre cover

9 Manoeuvre the centre cover back into position, ensuring it is correctly located with the lower cover, and tighten its retaining bolts.
10 Clip the wiring loom into its retaining clips on the front of the centre cover, then refit the upper cover as described in paragraph 8.

Lower cover

11 Locate the lower cover over the timing belt sprocket, and tighten its retaining bolt(s).
12 Fit the pulley to the end of the crankshaft, ensuring it is fitted the correct way round, and tighten its bolts to the specified torque.
13 Refit the centre (where applicable) and upper covers as described above, then refit and tension the auxiliary drivebelt as described in Chapter 1A.

---

6 Timing belt – general information, removal and refitting

Note: *On early engines, Peugeot specify the use of a special electronic tool (SEEM C.TRONIC type 105 belt tensioning measuring tool, and valve rocker contact plate (–).0132 AE) to correctly set the timing belt tension. If access to this equipment cannot be obtained, an approximate setting can be achieved using the method described below. If this method described is used, the tension must be checked using the special electronic tool at the earliest possible opportunity. Do not drive the vehicle over large distances, or use high engine speeds, until the belt tension is known*

to be correct. Refer to a Peugeot dealer for advice.

General information

1 The timing belt drives the camshaft and coolant pump from a toothed sprocket on the front of the crankshaft. If the belt breaks or slips in service, the pistons are likely to hit the valve heads, resulting in extensive (and expensive) damage.
2 The timing belt should be renewed at the specified intervals (see Chapter 1A) or earlier if it is contaminated with oil, or if it is at all noisy in operation (a 'scraping' noise due to uneven wear).
3 If the timing belt is being removed, it is a wise precaution to check the condition of the coolant pump at the same time (check for signs of coolant leakage). This may avoid the need to remove the timing belt again at a later stage, should the coolant pump fail.
4 On later engines an automatic timing belt tensioner is used to maintain the correct tension on the timing belt after the initial setting procedure has been carried out. This later type tensioner can be identified by the index arm and tension position marks on the side of the tensioner body **(see illustration 6.32)**. If this type of tensioner is fitted, follow the procedures for 'later engines' when refitting the timing belt.

Removal

5 Disconnect the battery negative terminal (refer to *Disconnecting the battery* in the Reference Chapter).
6 Align the engine assembly/valve timing holes as described in Section 3, and lock both the camshaft sprocket and the flywheel in position.
Caution: Do not attempt to rotate the engine whilst the locking tools are in position.
7 Remove the remaining timing belt cover(s) as described in Section 5.
8 Loosen the timing belt tensioner pulley retaining nut **(see illustration)**. Pivot the pulley approximately 60° in a clockwise direction, using a key fitted to the hole in the pulley hub, then retighten the retaining nut. On early engines, an 8 mm square section key will be required **(see Tool Tip)**, and on later

6.8 Slacken the nut then pivot the tensioner pulley clockwise to relieve the timing belt tension

engines with an automatic tensioner, an Allen key will be needed.
9 If the timing belt is to be re-used, use white paint or similar to mark the direction of rotation on the belt (if markings do not already exist). Slip the belt off the sprockets.
10 Check the timing belt carefully for any signs of uneven wear, splitting, or oil contamination. Pay particular attention to the roots of the teeth. Renew the belt if there is the slightest doubt about its condition. If the engine is undergoing an overhaul, and has covered more than 36 000 miles (60 000 km) with the existing belt fitted, renew the belt as a matter of course, regardless of its apparent condition. The cost of a new belt is nothing when compared to the cost of repairs, should the belt break in service. If signs of oil contamination are found, trace the source of the oil leak, and rectify it. Wash down the engine timing belt area and all related components, to remove all traces of oil.

Refitting – early engines

11 Prior to refitting, thoroughly clean the timing belt sprockets. Check that the tensioner pulley rotates freely, without any sign of roughness. If necessary, renew the tensioner pulley as described in Section 7. Make sure that the locking tools are still in place, as described in Section 3.
12 Manoeuvre the timing belt into position, ensuring that the arrows on the belt are pointing in the direction of rotation (clockwise, when viewed from the right-hand end of the engine).
13 Do not twist the timing belt sharply while refitting it. Fit the belt over the crankshaft and camshaft sprockets. Make sure that the 'front run' of the belt is taut – ie, ensure that any slack is on the tensioner pulley side of the belt. Fit the belt over the coolant pump sprocket and tensioner pulley. Ensure that the belt teeth are seated centrally in the sprockets.

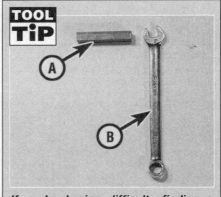

TOOL TiP

If you're having difficulty finding a square-section tool that will fit the tensioner pulley, obtain a length of standard 8 mm door handle rod from a DIY shop and cut it to length (A). Insert the rod into the pulley hub and rotate the pulley with an 8 mm spanner (B).

14 Loosen the tensioner pulley retaining nut. Pivot the pulley anti-clockwise to remove all free play from the timing belt, then retighten the nut **(see illustration)**. Tension the timing belt as described under the relevant sub-heading.

Without the electronic tool

Note: *If this method is used, ensure that the belt tension is checked by a Peugeot dealer at the earliest possible opportunity.*

15 Slacken the tensioner pulley retaining nut and pivot the pulley anti-clockwise until it is just possible to twist the timing belt through 90° by finger and thumb, midway between the crankshaft and camshaft sprockets. The deflection of the belt at the mid-point between the sprockets should be approximately 6.0 mm. Hold the tensioner pulley in this position and tighten the retaining nut.

16 Remove the locking tools from the camshaft sprocket and flywheel.

17 Using a suitable socket and extension bar on the crankshaft sprocket bolt, rotate the crankshaft through four complete rotations in a clockwise direction (viewed from the right-hand end of the engine).

Caution: Do not at any time rotate the crankshaft anti-clockwise.

18 Slacken the tensioner pulley nut, retension the belt as described in paragraph 15, then tighten the tensioner pulley nut to the specified torque.

19 Rotate the crankshaft through a further two turns clockwise, and check that both the camshaft sprocket and flywheel timing holes are still correctly aligned.

20 If all is well, refit the timing belt covers as described in Section 5, and reconnect the battery negative terminal.

Using the electronic tool

21 Fit the special belt tensioning measuring equipment to the front run of the timing belt, approximately midway between the camshaft and crankshaft sprockets. Position the tensioner pulley so that the belt is tensioned to a setting of 44 SEEM units, then retighten its retaining nut.

22 Remove the locking tools from the camshaft sprocket and flywheel, and remove the measuring tool from the belt.

6.14 Pivot the tensioner pulley anti-clockwise to remove all freeplay from the timing belt then tighten the pulley nut

23 Using a suitable socket and extension bar on the crankshaft sprocket bolt, rotate the crankshaft through four complete rotations in a clockwise direction (viewed from the right-hand end of the engine). *Do not* at any time rotate the crankshaft anti-clockwise. Refit the locking tool to the flywheel and check that the camshaft sprocket timing hole is aligned.

24 To ensure an accurate reading, it is necessary to remove the valve spring load from the camshaft by fitting the valve rocker contact plate (–) 0132 AE). Remove the cylinder head cover (see Section 4), then slacken the eight rocker arm contact bolts in the valve rocker contact plate. Fit the contact plate to the cylinder head cover studs, observing the correct fitted direction, and secure it with the cover nuts **(see illustration)**. Tighten each rocker arm contact bolt until the rockers are just free of the camshaft lobes. Do not overtighten the contact bolts otherwise the valves will contact the pistons.

25 Refit the measuring tool to the belt, slacken the tensioner pulley retaining nut, and gradually release the tensioner pulley until a setting of between 29 and 33 SEEM units is indicated on the measuring tool. Retighten the tensioner pulley retaining nut to the specified torque.

26 Remove the measuring tool from the belt then unscrew the nuts and remove the rocker arm contact plate from the cylinder head.

27 Remove the flywheel locking tool, then rotate the crankshaft through another four complete rotations in a clockwise direction. Refit the flywheel locking tool and check that the camshaft timing hole is correctly aligned with the cylinder head hole.

28 If all is well, refit the timing belt covers and cylinder head cover as described in Sections 4 and 5. **Note:** *If the rocker arm adjusting screws were moved, adjust the valve clearances before refitting the cylinder head cover.*

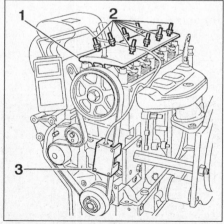

6.24 Fit the rocker arm plate (1) to the cylinder head and use the contact bolts (2) to lift the rocker arms clear of the camshaft (see text). Note the correct location for the measuring tool (3)

Refitting – later engines

29 Prior to refitting, thoroughly clean the timing belt sprockets. Check that the tensioner pulley rotates freely, without any sign of roughness. If necessary, renew the tensioner pulley as described in Section 7. Make sure that the locking tools are still in place, as described in Section 3.

30 Manoeuvre the timing belt into position, ensuring that the arrows on the belt are pointing in the direction of rotation (clockwise, when viewed from the right-hand end of the engine).

31 Do not twist the timing belt sharply while refitting. Fit the belt over the crankshaft and camshaft sprockets. Make sure that the 'front run' of the belt is taut – ie, ensure that any slack is on the tensioner pulley side of the belt. Fit the belt over the coolant pump sprocket and tensioner pulley. Ensure that the belt teeth are seated centrally in the sprockets.

32 Remove the crankshaft and camshaft locking tools, then slacken the tensioner pulley nut and, using an Allen key, rotate the pulley anti-clockwise until the index arm is in the maximum tension position **(see illustration)**. Tighten the pulley retaining nut.

33 Using a socket on the crankshaft pulley bolt, rotate the crankshaft clockwise 10 complete revolutions, and refit the crankshaft locking tool as described in Section 3.

34 Check the timing is correct by inserting the camshaft sprocket locking tool (Section 3). If the tool cannot be inserted, slacken the tensioner, remove the belt, refit the locking tools, and start again from Paragraph 30.

35 Remove the crankshaft and camshaft locking tools.

36 Hold the Allen key in the tensioner pulley to maintain the tension, then slacken the pulley nut, and rotate the tensioner to bring the index arm to the normal tension position **(see illustration 6.32)**. Tighten the pulley nut to the specified torque.

37 Rotate the crankshaft two complete revolutions, and check that the crankshaft and camshaft locking tools can still be inserted.

38 The remainder of refitting is a reversal of removal.

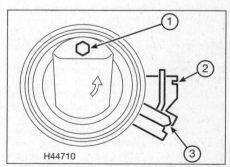

6.32 Timing belt tensioner – later engines

1 Hole for Allen key
2 Normal tension position
3 Maximum tension position

TOOL TiP

Using a home-made tool to hold the camshaft sprocket stationary whilst the retaining bolt is slackened or tightened (shown with the cylinder head removed).

7 Timing belt tensioner and sprockets – removal, inspection and refitting

Removal

Camshaft sprocket

1 Remove the timing belt as described in Section 6.

2 Withdraw the crankshaft and camshaft locking tools, and using a spanner or socket on the crankshaft pulley bolt, rotate the crankshaft backwards (anti-clockwise) 90°. This is to prevent any accidental contact between the pistons and valves.

3 Slacken the camshaft sprocket retaining bolt and remove it, along with its washer. To prevent the camshaft rotating as the bolt is slackened, a sprocket-holding tool will be required. In the absence of the special Peugeot tool, an acceptable substitute can be fabricated as follows. Use two lengths of steel strip (one long, the other short), and three nuts and bolts; one nut and bolt forms the pivot of a forked tool, with the remaining two nuts and bolts at the tips of the 'forks' to engage with the sprocket spokes **(see Tool Tip)**.
Caution: Do not attempt to use the sprocket locking pin to prevent the sprocket from rotating whilst the bolt is slackened.

4 With the retaining bolt removed, slide the

sprocket off the end of the camshaft. If the sprocket locating pin is a loose fit, remove it for safe-keeping. Examine the camshaft oil seal for signs of oil leakage and, if necessary, renew it as described in Section 8.

Crankshaft sprocket

5 Remove the timing belt as described in Section 6.

6 Slacken the crankshaft sprocket bolt. To prevent crankshaft rotation on manual transmission models, select top gear, and have an assistant apply the brakes firmly. If the engine has been removed from the vehicle or the vehicle is equipped with automatic transmission, it will be necessary to lock the flywheel/driveplate (see Section 15).
Caution: Do not be tempted to use the flywheel/driveplate locking pin to prevent the crankshaft from rotating; temporarily remove the locking pin prior to slackening the pulley bolt, then refit it once the bolt has been slackened.

7 Unscrew the retaining bolt and washer, then slide the sprocket off the end of the crankshaft **(see illustrations)**.

8 If the Woodruff key is a loose fit in the crankshaft, remove it and store it with the sprocket for safe-keeping. If necessary, also slide the flanged spacer (where fitted) off the end of the crankshaft **(see illustration)**. Examine the crankshaft oil seal for signs oil leakage and, if necessary, renew as described in Section 14.

Tensioner pulley

9 On engines with a three-piece timing belt cover arrangement, remove the centre cover as described in Section 5. On engines with a two-piece cover, remove the lower cover.

10 Lock the camshaft and crankshaft at TDC on No 1 cylinder as described in Section 3.

11 Slacken and remove the timing belt tensioner pulley retaining nut, and slide the pulley off its mounting stud. Examine the mounting stud for signs of damage and, if necessary, renew it.

Inspection

12 Clean the sprockets thoroughly, and renew any that show signs of wear, damage or cracks.

13 Clean the tensioner assembly, but do not use any strong solvent which may enter the

pulley bearing. Check that the pulley rotates freely about its hub, with no sign of stiffness or of free play. Renew the tensioner pulley if there is any doubt about its condition, or if there are any obvious signs of wear or damage.

14 Inspect the timing belt (see Section 6). Renew the belt is there is any doubt about its condition.

Refitting

Camshaft sprocket

15 Refit the locating pin (where removed) then locate the sprocket on the end of the camshaft. Ensure that the locating pin is correctly engaged with the sprocket and the cut-out in the camshaft end.

16 Refit the sprocket retaining bolt and washer. Tighten the bolt to the specified torque, whilst retaining the sprocket with the tool used on removal.

17 Realign the timing hole in the camshaft sprocket (see Section 3) with the corresponding hole in the cylinder head, and refit the locking pin.

18 Rotate the crankshaft 90° in the normal direction of rotation (clockwise), until the crankshaft locking pin can be inserted.

19 Refit the timing belt as described in Section 6.

Crankshaft sprocket

20 Locate the Woodruff key in the crankshaft end, then slide on the flanged spacer (where fitted) aligning its slot with the Woodruff key.

21 Align the crankshaft sprocket slot with the Woodruff key, and slide it onto the end of the crankshaft.

22 Temporarily remove the locking pin from the rear of the flywheel/driveplate, then refit the crankshaft sprocket retaining bolt and washer. Tighten the bolt to the specified torque, whilst preventing crankshaft rotation using the method employed on removal. Refit the locking pin to the rear of the flywheel/driveplate.

23 Refit the timing belt as described in Section 6.

Tensioner pulley

24 Refit the tensioner pulley to its mounting stud, ensuring that on later engines with an automatic tensioner, the cut-out aligns with the pin, then fit the retaining nut.

25 Ensure that the 'front run' of the belt is taut – ie, ensure that any slack is on the pulley

7.7a Remove the crankshaft sprocket bolt . . .

7.7b . . . then slide off the sprocket

7.8 Remove the flanged spacer if necessary

side of the belt. Check that the belt is centrally located on all its sprockets. Rotate the pulley anti-clockwise to remove all free play from the timing belt, then tighten the pulley retaining nut securely.

26 Tension the timing belt as described in Section 6.

27 Once the belt is correctly tensioned, refit the timing belt covers as described in Section 5.

8 Camshaft oil seal – renewal

Note: *If the camshaft oil seal has been leaking, check the timing belt for signs of oil contamination; the belt must be renewed if signs of oil contamination are found. Ensure that all traces of oil are removed from the sprockets and surrounding area before the new belt is fitted.*

1 Remove the camshaft sprocket as described in Section 7.

2 Punch or drill two small holes opposite each other in the oil seal. Screw a self-tapping screw into each, and pull on the screws with pliers to extract the seal.

3 Clean the seal housing, and polish off any burrs or raised edges, which may have caused the seal to fail in the first place.

4 Lubricate the lips of the new seal with clean engine oil, and drive it into position until it seats on its locating shoulder. Use a suitable tubular drift, such as a socket, which bears only on the hard outer edge of the seal. Take care not to damage the seal lips during fitting. Note that the seal lips should face inwards.

5 Refit the camshaft sprocket as described in Section 7.

9 Valve clearances – checking and adjustment

Note: *The valve clearances must be checked and adjusted only when the engine is cold.*

1 The importance of having the valve clearances correctly adjusted cannot be overstressed, as they vitally affect the performance of the engine. If the clearances are too big, the engine will be noisy (characteristic rattling or tapping noises) and engine efficiency will be reduced, as the valves open too late and close too early. A more serious problem arises if the clearances are too small, however. If this is the case, the valves may not close fully when the engine is hot, resulting in serious damage to the engine (eg, burnt valve seats and/or cylinder head warping/cracking). The clearances are checked and adjusted as follows.

2 Remove the cylinder head cover as described in Section 4.

3 The engine can now be turned using a suitable socket and extension bar fitted to the crankshaft sprocket/pulley bolt.

 HAYNES HiNT *Turning the engine will be easier if the spark plugs are removed first – see Chapter 1A.*

4 It is important that the clearance of each valve is checked and adjusted only when the valve is fully closed, with the rocker arm resting on the heel of the cam (directly opposite the peak). This can be ensured by carrying out the adjustments in the following sequence, noting that No 1 cylinder is at the transmission end of the engine. The correct valve clearances are given in the Specifications at the start of this Chapter. The valve locations can be determined from the position of the manifolds.

Valve fully open	Adjust valves
No 1 exhaust	No 3 inlet and No 4 exhaust
No 3 exhaust	No 4 inlet and No 2 exhaust
No 4 exhaust	No 2 inlet and No 1 exhaust
No 2 exhaust	No 1 inlet and No 3 exhaust

5 With the relevant valve fully open, check the clearances of the two valves specified. The clearances are checked by inserting a feeler blade of the correct thickness between the valve stem and the rocker arm adjusting screw. The feeler blade should be a light, sliding fit. If adjustment is necessary, slacken the adjusting screw locknut, and turn the screw as necessary. Once the correct clearance is obtained, hold the adjusting screw and securely tighten the locknut. Recheck the valve clearance, and adjust again if necessary.

6 Rotate the crankshaft until the next valve in the sequence is fully open, and check the clearances of the next two specified valves.

7 Repeat the procedure until all eight valve clearances have been checked (and if necessary, adjusted), then refit the cylinder head cover as described in Section 4.

10 Camshaft and rocker arms – removal, inspection and refitting

General information

1 The rocker arm assembly is secured to the top of the cylinder head by the cylinder head bolts. Although in theory it is possible to undo the head bolts and remove the rocker arm assembly without removing the head, in practice, this is not recommended. Once the bolts have been removed, the head gasket will be disturbed, and the gasket will almost certainly leak or blow after refitting. For this reason, removal of the rocker arm assembly cannot be done without removing the cylinder head and renewing the head gasket.

2 The camshaft is slid out of the right-hand end of the cylinder head, and it therefore cannot be removed without first removing the cylinder head, due to a lack of clearance.

Removal

Rocker arm assembly

3 Remove the cylinder head as described in Section 11.

4 To dismantle the rocker arm assembly, carefully prise off the circlip from the right-hand end of the rocker shaft; retain the rocker pedestal, to prevent it being sprung off the end of the shaft. Slide the various components off the end of the shaft, keeping all components in their correct fitted order **(see illustration)**. Make a note of each component's correct fitted position and orientation as it is removed, to ensure it is fitted correctly on reassembly.

5 To separate the left-hand pedestal and shaft, first unscrew the cylinder head cover retaining stud from the top of the pedestal; this can be achieved using a stud extractor, or two nuts locked together. With the stud removed, unscrew the grub screw from the top of the pedestal, and withdraw the rocker shaft **(see illustrations)**.

10.4 Remove the circlip, and slide the components off the end of the rocker arm

10.5a To remove the left-hand pedestal, lock two nuts together and unscrew the stud . . .

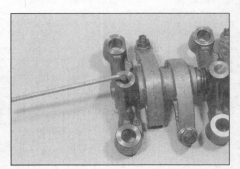

10.5b . . . then remove the grub screw

10.8 Undo the retaining bolt, and remove the camshaft thrust fork (arrowed) . . .

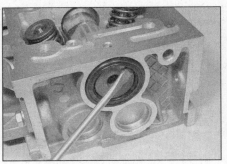

10.9a . . . prise out the oil seal . . .

10.9b . . . and slide out the camshaft

Camshaft

6 Remove the cylinder head as described in Section 11.

7 With the head on a bench, remove the locking pin, then remove the camshaft sprocket as described in paragraphs 3 and 4 of Section 7.

8 Unbolt the housing from the left-hand end of the cylinder head, then undo the retaining bolt, and remove the camshaft thrust fork from the cylinder head **(see illustration)**.

9 Using a large flat-bladed screwdriver, carefully prise the oil seal out of the right-hand end of the cylinder head, then slide out the camshaft **(see illustrations)**. Discard the seal – a new one must be used on refitting.

Inspection

Rocker arm assembly

10 Examine the rocker arm bearing surfaces which contact the camshaft lobes for wear ridges and scoring. Renew any rocker arms on which these conditions are apparent. If a rocker arm bearing surface is badly scored, also examine the corresponding lobe on the camshaft for wear, as both will likely be worn. On later engines, roller rocker arms are used incorporating a roller bearing at the camshaft lobe contact point. On this type of rocker, check for any sign of excess play of the roller bearing or any roughness as it is rotated. Renew any worn components as necessary. The rocker arm assembly can be dismantled as described in paragraphs 4 and 5.

11 Inspect the ends of the valve clearance adjusting screws for signs of wear or damage, and renew as required.

12 If the rocker arm assembly has been dismantled, examine the rocker arm and shaft bearing surfaces for wear ridges and scoring. If there are obvious signs of wear, the relevant rocker arm(s) and/or the shaft must be renewed.

Camshaft

13 Examine the camshaft bearing surfaces and cam lobes for signs of wear ridges and scoring. Renew the camshaft if any of these conditions are apparent. Examine the condition of the bearing surfaces, both on the camshaft journals and in the cylinder head. If the head bearing surfaces are worn

excessively, the cylinder head will need to be renewed. If the necessary measuring equipment is available, camshaft bearing journal wear can be checked by direct measurement, noting that No 1 journal is at the transmission end of the head.

14 Examine the thrust fork for signs of wear or scoring, and renew as necessary.

Refitting

Rocker arm assembly

15 If the rocker arm assembly was dismantled, refit the rocker shaft to the left-hand pedestal, aligning its locating hole with the pedestal threaded hole. Refit the grub screw, and tighten it securely. With the grub screw in position, refit the cylinder head cover mounting stud to the pedestal, and tighten it securely. Apply a smear of clean engine oil to the shaft, then slide on all removed components, ensuring each is correctly fitted in its original position. Once all components are in position on the shaft, compress the right-hand pedestal and refit the circlip. Ensure that the circlip is correctly located in its groove on the shaft.

16 Refit the cylinder head and rocker arm assembly as described in Section 11.

Camshaft

17 Ensure that the cylinder head and camshaft bearing surfaces are clean, then liberally oil the camshaft bearings and lobes. Slide the camshaft back into position in the cylinder head. On carburettor engines, take care that the fuel pump operating lever is not trapped by the camshaft as it is slid into position. To prevent this, remove the fuel pump before refitting the camshaft, then refit it afterwards.

18 Locate the thrust fork with the left-hand end of the camshaft. Refit the fork retaining bolt, tightening it to the specified torque setting.

19 Ensure that the housing and cylinder head mating surfaces are clean and dry, then apply a smear of sealant to the housing mating surface. Refit the housing to the left-hand end of the head, and securely tighten its retaining bolts.

20 Lubricate the lips of the new seal with clean engine oil, then drive it into position until

it seats on its locating shoulder. Use a suitable tubular drift, such as a socket, which bears only on the hard outer edge of the seal. Take care not to damage the seal lips during fitting. Note that the seal lips should face inwards.

21 Refit the camshaft sprocket as described in paragraphs 15 to 17 of Section 7.

22 Refit the cylinder head as described in Section 11.

---

11 Cylinder head – removal and refitting

Removal

1 Disconnect the battery negative terminal (refer to *Disconnecting the battery* in the Reference Chapter).

2 Drain the cooling system as described in Chapter 1A.

3 Remove the cylinder head cover as described in Section 4.

4 Align the engine assembly/valve timing holes as described in Section 3, and lock both the camshaft sprocket and flywheel in position. *Do not* attempt to rotate the engine whilst the tools are in position.

5 Note that the following text assumes that the cylinder head will be removed with both inlet and exhaust manifolds attached; this is easier, but makes it a bulky and heavy assembly to handle. If it is wished to remove the manifolds first, proceed as described in the relevant Part of Chapter 4.

6 Working as described in the relevant Part of Chapter 4, disconnect the exhaust system front pipe from the manifold. Where fitted, disconnect or release the lambda sensor wiring, so that it is not strained by the weight of the exhaust.

7 Remove the air cleaner housing and inlet duct assembly as described in the relevant Part of Chapter 4.

8 On carburettor engines, disconnect the following from the carburettor and inlet manifold as described in Chapter 4A:

a) *Fuel feed hose from the pump and the return hose from the anti-percolation chamber (plug all openings, to prevent*

loss of fuel and the entry of dirt into the
system).
b) *Accelerator cable.*
c) *Choke cable.*
d) *Carburettor heating element and idle cut-
off solenoid wiring connector(s).*
e) *Vacuum servo unit vacuum hose, coolant
hose and all other relevant
breather/vacuum hoses from the
manifold.*

9 On fuel injection engines, carry out the
following operations as described in the
relevant Part of Chapter 4:
a) *Depressurise the fuel system, and
disconnect the fuel feed and return hoses
from the throttle body/fuel rail (plug all
openings, to prevent loss of fuel and entry
of dirt into the fuel system).*
b) *Disconnect the accelerator cable.*
c) *On single-point injection models,
disconnect the relevant electrical
connectors from the throttle body.*
d) *On multi-point injection models,
disconnect the relevant electrical
connectors from the throttle housing, fuel
injectors and (where necessary) the idle
speed auxiliary air valve/stepper motor.*
e) *Disconnect the vacuum servo unit hose,
coolant hose(s) and all the other
relevant/breather hoses from the
manifold.*
f) *Where necessary unbolt the support
bracket from the inlet manifold.*
g) *On 1.4 litre models with air injection,
disconnect the hose from the injection
valve which is fitted to the exhaust
manifold.*

10 On engines with a three-piece timing belt
cover arrangement, remove the upper and
centre covers as described in Section 5. On
engines with a two-piece cover arrangement,
remove both covers.
11 Loosen the timing belt tensioner pulley
retaining nut. Pivot the pulley in a clockwise
direction, using a suitable key fitted to the
hole in the pulley hub, then retighten the
retaining nut.
12 Disengage the timing belt from the
camshaft sprocket, and position the belt clear
of the sprocket. Ensure that the belt is not
bent or twisted sharply.
13 Slacken the retaining clips, and
disconnect the coolant hoses from the
thermostat housing (on the left-hand end of
the cylinder head).
14 Depress the retaining clip(s), and
disconnect the wiring connector(s) from the
electrical switch and/or sensor(s) which are
screwed into the thermostat housing/cylinder
head (as appropriate). Also where necessary
release the TDC connector from its support
on the distributor bracket on the left-hand end
of the cylinder head.
15 On models with power steering, referring
to Chapter 10, unbolt the power steering
pump from its mounting bracket. Undo the
power steering pipe retaining clip screws then
position the pump clear of the engine.

Support the weight of the pump by tying it to
the vehicle body to prevent any excess strain
being placed on the hydraulic pipes/hoses.
Note: *There is no need to disconnect the
pipe/hose from the pump.*

Carburettor engines

16 Disconnect the LT wiring connectors from
the distributor and HT coil. Release the TDC
sensor wiring connector from the side of the
coil mounting bracket, and disconnect the
vacuum pipe from the distributor vacuum
diaphragm unit. If the cylinder head is to be
dismantled for overhaul, remove the
distributor and ignition HT coil as described in
Chapter 5B. If the cylinder numbers are not
already marked on the HT leads, number each
lead, to avoid the possibility of the leads being
incorrectly connected on refitting. Disconnect
the HT leads from the spark plugs, and
remove the distributor cap and lead
assembly.

Fuel injection engines

17 Disconnect the wiring connector from the
ignition HT coil. If the cylinder head is to be
dismantled for overhaul, remove the ignition
HT coil as described in Chapter 5B. If the
cylinder numbers are not already marked on
the HT leads, number each lead, to avoid the
possibility of the leads being incorrectly
connected on refitting. Note that the HT leads
should be disconnected from the spark plugs
instead of the coil, and the coil and leads
removed as an assembly.

All engines

18 Slacken and remove the bolt securing the
engine oil dipstick tube to the cylinder head.
19 Working in the *reverse* of the sequence
shown in illustration 11.39a, progressively
slacken the ten cylinder head bolts by half a
turn at a time, until all bolts can be unscrewed
by hand.
20 With all the cylinder head bolts removed,
lift the rocker arm assembly off the cylinder
head. Note the locating pins which are fitted
to the base of each rocker arm pedestal. If
any pin is a loose fit in the head or pedestal,
remove it for safe-keeping.
21 On engines with a cast-iron cylinder
block, lift the cylinder head away; seek
assistance if possible, as it is a heavy
assembly, especially if it is being removed
complete with the manifolds.
22 On engines with an aluminium cylinder
block, the joint between the cylinder head and
gasket and the cylinder block/crankcase must
now be broken without disturbing the wet
liners. To break the joint, obtain two L-shaped
metal bars which fit into the cylinder head bolt
holes. Gently 'rock' the cylinder head free
towards the front of the car **(see illustration)**.
Do not try to swivel the head on the cylinder
block/crankcase; it is located by dowels, as
well as by the tops of the liners. **Note:** *If care
is not taken and the liners are moved, there is
also a possibility of the bottom seals being
disturbed, causing leakage after refitting the*

head. When the joint is broken, lift the cylinder
head away; seek assistance if possible, as it is
a heavy assembly, especially if it is being
removed complete with the manifolds.
23 On all engines, remove the gasket from
the top of the block, noting the two locating
dowels. If the locating dowels are a loose fit,
remove them and store them with the head for
safe-keeping. Do not discard the gasket – on
some models it will be needed for
identification purposes (see paragraphs 29
and 30).
*Caution: On aluminium block engines, do
not attempt to rotate the crankshaft with
the cylinder head removed, otherwise the
wet liners may be displaced. Operations
that require the rotation of the crankshaft
(eg, cleaning the piston crowns), should
only be carried out once the cylinder liners
are firmly clamped in position.*
24 In the absence of the special Peugeot
liner clamps, the liners can be clamped in
position using large flat washers positioned
underneath suitable-length bolts.
Alternatively, the original head bolts could be
temporarily refitted, with suitable spacers
fitted to their shanks.
25 If the cylinder head is to be dismantled for
overhaul, remove the camshaft as described
in Section 10, then refer to Part E of this
Chapter.

Preparation for refitting

26 The mating faces of the cylinder head and
cylinder block/crankcase must be perfectly
clean before refitting the head. Use a hard
plastic or wood scraper to remove all traces of
gasket and carbon; also clean the piston
crowns. Refer to paragraph 24 before turning
the crankshaft on aluminium block engines.
Take particular care during the cleaning
operations, as aluminium alloy is easily
damaged. Also, make sure that the carbon is
not allowed to enter the oil and water
passages – this is particularly important
for the lubrication system, as carbon could
block the oil supply to the engine's
components. Using adhesive tape and paper,
seal the water, oil and bolt holes in the
cylinder block/crankcase. To prevent carbon
entering the gap between the pistons and

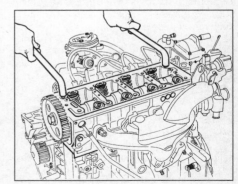

**11.22 Using two angled metal rods to free
the cylinder head from the block**

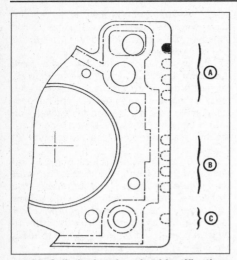

11.30 Cylinder head gasket identification markings

A *Engine type identification cut-outs*
B *Gasket manufacturer identification cut-outs*
C *Gasket thickness identification cut-out*

bores, smear a little grease in the gap. After cleaning each piston, use a small brush to remove all traces of grease and carbon from the gap, then wipe away the remainder with a clean rag. Clean all the pistons in the same way.

27 Check the mating surfaces of the cylinder block/crankcase and the cylinder head for nicks, deep scratches and other damage. If slight, they may be removed carefully with a file, but if excessive, machining may be the only alternative to renewal.

28 If warpage of the cylinder head gasket surface is suspected, use a straight-edge to check it for distortion. Refer to Part E of this Chapter if necessary.

29 When purchasing a new cylinder head gasket, it is essential that a gasket of the correct thickness is obtained. On some models only one thickness of gasket is

available, so this is not a problem. However on other models, there are two different thicknesses available – the standard gasket which is fitted at the factory, and a slightly thicker 'repair' gasket (+ 0.2 mm), for use once the head gasket face has been machined. If the cylinder head has been machined, it should have the letter R stamped adjacent to the No 3 exhaust port, and the gasket should also have the letter R stamped adjacent to No 3 cylinder on its front upper face. The gaskets can also be identified as described in the following paragraph, using the cut-outs on the left-hand end of the gasket.

30 With the gasket fitted the correct way up on the cylinder block, there will be a single cut-out, or no cut-out at all, at the rear of the left-hand side of the gasket identifying the engine type (ie, TU engine). In the centre of the gasket there will likely be another series of between 0 and 4 cut-outs, identifying the manufacturer of the gasket and whether or not it contains asbestos (these cut-outs are of little importance). The important cut-out location is at the front of the gasket; on the standard gasket there will be no cut-out in this position, whereas on the thicker 'repair' gasket there will be a single cut-out **(see illustration)**. Identify the gasket type, and ensure that the new gasket obtained is of the correct thickness. If there is any doubt as to which gasket is fitted, take the old gasket along to your Peugeot dealer, and have him confirm the gasket type. Note that on engines manufactured from approximately mid-1996 onward, there are even more variations of gasket type. This is due to various changes that have been made to the cylinder head to meet the latest exhaust emission requirements, and vary according to specific engine type. If working on a post-1995 model it is essential that the engine type, code and serial numbers are taken to a Peugeot dealer to ensure that the correct gasket is obtained.

31 Check the condition of the cylinder head

bolts, and particularly their threads, whenever they are removed. Wash the bolts in suitable solvent, and wipe them dry. Check each for any sign of visible wear or damage, renewing any bolt if necessary. Measure the length of each bolt, from the end of the thread to the underside of the bolt head, to check for stretching. If the length of any bolt exceeds 176.5 mm it must be renewed. It is strongly recommended that the bolts should be renewed as a complete set whenever they are disturbed.

32 On aluminium block engines, prior to refitting the cylinder head, check the cylinder liner protrusion as described in Part E of this Chapter.

Refitting

33 Wipe clean the mating surfaces of the cylinder head and cylinder block/crankcase. Check that the two locating dowels are in position at each end of the cylinder block/crankcase surface and, if necessary, remove the cylinder liner clamps.

34 Position a new gasket on the cylinder block/crankcase surface, ensuring that its identification cut-outs are at the left-hand end of the gasket **(see illustration)**.

35 Check that the flywheel/driveplate and camshaft sprocket are still correctly locked in position with their respective tools then, with the aid of an assistant, carefully refit the cylinder head assembly to the block, aligning it with the locating dowels **(see illustration)**.

36 Ensure that the locating pins are in position in the base of each rocker pedestal, then refit the rocker arm assembly to the cylinder head **(see illustration)**.

37 Apply a smear of grease to the threads, and to the underside of the heads, of the cylinder head bolts. Peugeot specify Molykote G Rapid Plus grease (available from your Peugeot dealer – a sachet is supplied with the top-end gasket set); in the absence of the specified grease, a good-quality high-melting-point grease may be used.

11.34 Locate the cylinder head gasket on the block . . .

11.35 . . . then lower the cylinder head into position . . .

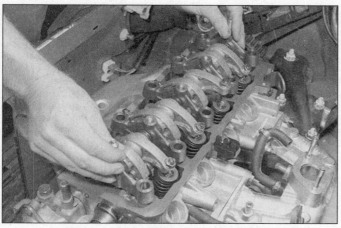

11.36 . . . and refit the rocker arm assembly

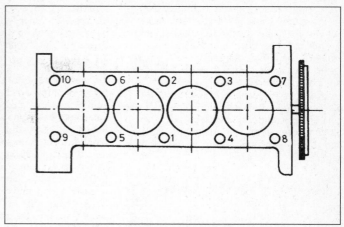

11.39a Cylinder head bolt tightening sequence

11.39b Working in the sequence, tighten the head bolts first to
the Stage 1 torque setting . . .

11.40 . . . then through the angle specified for Stage 2

38 Carefully enter each bolt into its relevant hole (*do not drop them in*) and screw in, by hand only, until finger-tight.

39 Working progressively and in sequence, tighten the cylinder head bolts to their Stage 1 torque setting, using a torque wrench and suitable socket **(see illustrations)**.

40 Once all the bolts have been tightened to their Stage 1 setting, working again in the given sequence, angle-tighten the bolts through the specified Stage 2 angle, using a socket and extension bar. It is recommended that an angle-measuring gauge is used during this stage of the tightening, to ensure accuracy **(see illustration)**. If a gauge is not available, use white paint to make alignment marks between the bolt head and cylinder head prior to tightening; the marks can then be used to check that the bolt has been rotated through the correct angle during tightening.

41 On cast-iron block engines, it will then be necessary to tighten the bolts through the specified Stage 3 angle setting.

42 With the cylinder head bolts correctly tightened, refit the dipstick tube retaining bolt and tighten it securely.

43 Refit the timing belt to the camshaft sprocket. Ensure that the 'front run' of the belt is taut – ie, ensure that any slack is on the tensioner pulley side of the belt. Do not twist the belt sharply while refitting it, and ensure that the belt teeth are seated centrally in the sprockets.

44 Loosen the tensioner pulley retaining nut. Pivot the pulley anti-clockwise to remove all free play from the timing belt, then retighten the nut.

45 Tension the belt as described under the relevant sub-heading in Section 6, then refit the timing belt covers as described in Section 5.

Carburettor engines

46 If the head was stripped for overhaul, refit the distributor and HT coil as described in Chapter 5B, ensuring that the HT leads are correctly reconnected. If the head was not stripped, reconnect the wiring connector and vacuum pipe to the distributor, and the HT lead to the coil; clip the TDC sensor wiring connector onto the coil bracket.

Fuel injection engines

47 If the head was stripped for overhaul, refit the ignition HT coil and leads as described in

Chapter 5B, ensuring that the leads are correctly reconnected. If the head was not stripped, simply reconnect the wiring connector to the HT coil.

All engines

48 Reconnect the wiring connector(s) to the coolant switch/sensor(s) on the left-hand end of the head.

49 Reconnect the coolant hoses to the thermostat housing.

50 On models with power steering, ensure the mounting spacer (where fitted) is correctly fitted to the rear mounting then locate the pump on its mounting bracket Apply locking compound (Peugeot recommend the use of Loctite Frenetanch) to the pump lower front mounting bolt then install all the bolts; tighten the pump front (drivebelt pulley end) bolts to the specified torque first then tighten the rear bolts (see Chapter 10).

51 Working as described in the relevant Part of Chapter 4, carry out the following tasks:

 a) *Refit all disturbed wiring, hoses and control cable(s) to the inlet manifold and fuel system components.*

b) On carburettor models, reconnect and adjust the choke and accelerator cables.

c) On fuel injection models, reconnect and adjust the accelerator cable.

d) Reconnect the exhaust system front pipe to the manifold. If applicable, reconnect the lambda sensor wiring connector.

e) Refit the air cleaner and inlet duct.

52 Check and, if necessary, adjust the valve clearances as described in Section 9.

53 On completion, reconnect the battery, and refill the cooling system as described in Chapter 1A.

12 Sump – removal and refitting

Removal

1 Disconnect the battery negative terminal (refer to *Disconnecting the battery* in the Reference Chapter). Firmly apply the handbrake, then jack up the front of the car and support it securely on axle stands (see *Jacking and vehicle support*).

2 Drain the engine oil, then clean and refit the engine oil drain plug, tightening it to the specified torque. If the engine is nearing its service interval when the oil and filter are due for renewal, it is recommended that the filter is also removed, and a new one fitted. After reassembly, the engine can then be refilled with fresh oil. Refer to Chapter 1A for further information.

3 Remove the exhaust system front pipe as described in the relevant Part of Chapter 4.

4 Progressively slacken and remove all the sump nuts and bolts. On cast-iron block engines, it may be necessary to unbolt the flywheel cover plate from the transmission to gain access to the left-hand sump fasteners.

5 Break the joint by striking the sump with the palm of your hand, then lower and withdraw the sump from under the car **(see illustration)**.

6 While the sump is removed, take the opportunity to check the oil pump pick-up/strainer for signs of clogging or splitting. If necessary, remove the pump as described in Section 13, and clean or renew the strainer.

Refitting

7 Clean all traces of sealant from the mating surfaces of the cylinder block/crankcase and sump, then use a clean rag to wipe out the sump and the engine's interior.

8 Ensure that the sump and cylinder block/crankcase mating surfaces are clean and dry, then apply a coating of suitable sealant to the sump mating surface.

9 Offer up the sump, locating it on its retaining studs, and refit its retaining nuts and bolts. Tighten the nuts and bolts evenly and progressively to the specified torque.

10 Refit the exhaust front pipe as described in the relevant Part of Chapter 4.

11 Replenish the engine with oil (see Chapter 1A).

13 Oil pump – removal, inspection and refitting

Removal

1 Remove the sump (see Section 12).

2 Slacken and remove the three bolts securing the oil pump in position **(see illustration)**. Disengage the pump sprocket from the chain, and remove the oil pump. If the pump locating dowel is a loose fit, remove and store it with the bolts for safe-keeping.

Inspection

3 Examine the oil pump sprocket for signs of damage and wear, such as chipped or missing teeth. If the sprocket is worn, the pump assembly must be renewed, as the sprocket is not available separately. It is also recommended that the chain and drive sprocket, fitted to the crankshaft, are renewed at the same time. On aluminium block engines, renewal of the chain and drive sprocket is an involved operation requiring the removal of the main bearing ladder, and therefore cannot be carried out with the engine still fitted to the vehicle. On cast-iron block engines, the oil pump drive sprocket and chain can be removed with the engine in situ, once the crankshaft sprocket has been removed and the crankshaft oil seal housing has been unbolted. See Part E for further information.

4 Slacken and remove the bolts securing the strainer cover to the pump body, then lift off the strainer cover. Remove the relief valve piston and spring (and guide pin – cast-iron block engines only), noting which way round they are fitted.

5 Examine the pump rotors and body for signs of wear ridges and scoring. If worn, the complete pump assembly must be renewed.

6 Examine the relief valve piston for signs of wear or damage, and renew if necessary. The condition of the relief valve spring can only be measured by comparing it with a new one; if there is any doubt about its condition, it should also be renewed. Both the piston and spring are available individually.

7 Thoroughly clean the oil pump strainer with a suitable solvent, and check it for signs of clogging or splitting. If the strainer is damaged, the strainer and cover assembly must be renewed.

8 Locate the relief valve spring, piston and (where fitted) the guide pin in the strainer cover, then refit the cover to the pump body. Align the relief valve piston with its bore in the pump. Refit the cover retaining bolts, tightening them securely.

Refitting

9 Ensure that the locating dowel is in position, then engage the pump sprocket with its drive chain. Locate the pump on its dowel, and refit the pump retaining bolts, tightening them to the specified torque setting.

10 Refit the sump as described in Section 12.

12.5 Slacken and remove the sump nuts and bolts, then remove the sump from the engine

13.2 Oil pump is retained by three bolts

14 Crankshaft oil seals – renewal

Right-hand oil seal

1 Remove the crankshaft sprocket and flanged spacer as described in Section 7. Secure the timing belt clear of the working area, so that it cannot be contaminated with oil. Make a note of the correct fitted depth of the seal in its housing.

2 Punch or drill two small holes opposite each other in the seal. Screw a self-tapping screw into each, and pull on the screws with pliers to extract the seal. Alternatively, the seal can be levered out of position using a suitable flat-bladed screwdriver, taking great care not to damage the crankshaft shoulder or seal housing **(see illustration)**.

3 Clean the seal housing, and polish off any burrs or raised edges, which may have caused the seal to fail in the first place.

4 Lubricate the lips of the new seal with clean engine oil, and carefully locate the seal on the end of crankshaft. Note that its sealing lip must face inwards. Take care not to damage the seal lips during fitting.

5 Using a suitable tubular drift (such as a socket) which bears only on the hard outer edge of the seal, tap the seal into position, to the same depth in the housing as the original was prior to removal. The inner face of the seal must be flush with the inner wall of the crankcase.

6 Wash off any traces of oil, then refit the crankshaft sprocket as described in Section 7.

Left-hand oil seal

7 Remove the flywheel/driveplate (see Section 15).

8 Make a note of the correct fitted depth of the seal in its housing. Punch or drill two small holes opposite each other in the seal. Screw a self-tapping screw into each, and pull on the screws with pliers to extract the seal.

9 Clean the seal housing, and polish off any burrs or raised edges, which may have caused the seal to fail in the first place.

10 Lubricate the lips of the new seal with clean engine oil, and carefully locate the seal on the end of the crankshaft.

11 Using a suitable tubular drift, which bears only on the hard outer edge of the seal, drive the seal into position, to the same depth in the housing as the original was prior to removal.

12 Wash off any traces of oil, then refit the flywheel/driveplate as described in Section 15.

15 Flywheel/driveplate – removal, inspection and refitting

Flywheel

Removal

1 Remove the manual transmission as described in Chapter 7A, then remove the clutch assembly as described in Chapter 6.

2 Prevent the flywheel from turning by locking the ring gear teeth with a suitable tool **(see illustration)**. Alternatively, bolt a strap between the flywheel and the cylinder block/crankcase. *Do not* attempt to lock the flywheel in position using the locking pin described in Section 3.

3 Slacken and remove the flywheel retaining bolts, and discard them; they must be renewed whenever they are disturbed.

4 Remove the flywheel. Do not drop it, as it is very heavy. If the locating dowel is a loose fit in the crankshaft end, remove and store it with the flywheel for safe-keeping.

Inspection

5 If the flywheel's clutch mating surface is deeply scored, cracked or otherwise damaged, the flywheel must be renewed.

However, it may be possible to have it surface-ground; seek the advice of a Peugeot dealer or engine reconditioning specialist.

6 If the ring gear is badly worn or has missing teeth, it must be renewed. This job is best left to a Peugeot dealer or engine reconditioning specialist. The temperature to which the new ring gear must be heated for installation is critical and, if not done accurately, the hardness of the teeth will be destroyed.

Refitting

7 Clean the mating surfaces of the flywheel and crankshaft. Remove any locking compound from the threads of the crankshaft holes, using the correct-size tap, if available.

> **HAYNES HINT** *If a suitable tap is not available, cut two slots into the threads of one of the old flywheel bolts and use the bolt to remove the locking compound from the threads.*

8 If the new flywheel retaining bolts are not supplied with their threads already precoated, apply a small amount of suitable thread-locking compound to the threads of each bolt.

9 Ensure that the locating dowel is in position. Offer up the flywheel, locating it on the dowel, and fit the new retaining bolts.

10 Lock the flywheel using the method employed on dismantling, and tighten the retaining bolts to the specified torque.

11 Refit the clutch as described in Chapter 6. Remove the locking tool, and refit the transmission as described in Chapter 7A.

Driveplate

Removal

12 Remove the automatic transmission as described in Chapter 7B.

13 Prevent the driveplate from turning by locking the ring gear teeth with a similar arrangement to that shown in illustration 15.2.

14.2 Using a screwdriver to lever out the crankshaft oil seal

15.2 Use the tool shown to lock flywheel ring gear and prevent the crankshaft rotating

Alternatively, bolt a strap between the driveplate and the cylinder block/crankcase. **Caution: Do not attempt to lock the driveplate in position using the locking pin described in Section 3.**

14 Slacken and remove the driveplate retaining bolts and remove the outer spacer plate and torque converter mounting plate. Discard the retaining bolts; they must be renewed whenever they are disturbed.

15 Remove the driveplate and inner spacer plate from the end of the crankshaft. If the locating dowel is a loose fit in the crankshaft end, remove and store it with the driveplate for safe-keeping. **Note:** *The inner and outer spacer plates are different and are not interchangeable.*

Inspection

16 Inspect the driveplate and torque converter mounting plate for signs of wear or damage. If damage is found, the worn component must be renewed (it is not possible to renew the driveplate ring gear separately).

Refitting

17 Ensure all mating surfaces are clean and dry.

18 If the new flywheel retaining bolts are not supplied with their threads already precoated, apply a small amount of suitable thread-locking compound to the threads of each bolt.

19 Ensure that the locating dowel is in position then refit the inner spacer plate, driveplate, torque converter mounting plate and outer spacer plate. Ensure all components are correctly located on the dowel then fit the retaining bolts.

20 Lock the driveplate using the method employed on dismantling, and tighten the retaining bolts evenly and progressively to the specified torque.

21 Refit the transmission as described in Chapter 7B.

16 Engine/transmission mountings – inspection and renewal

Inspection

1 If improved access is required, raise the front of the car and support it on axle stands (see *Jacking and vehicle support*).

2 Check the mounting rubber to see if it is cracked, hardened or separated from the metal at any point; renew the mounting if any such damage or deterioration is evident.

3 Check that all the mounting's fasteners are securely tightened; use a torque wrench to check if possible.

4 Using a large screwdriver or a crowbar, check for wear in the mounting by carefully levering against it to check for free play. Where this is not possible, enlist the aid of an assistant to move the engine/transmission back-and-forth, or from side-to-side, while you watch the mounting. While some free play is to be expected even from new components, excessive wear should be obvious. If excessive free play is found, check first that the fasteners are secure, then renew any worn components as described below.

Renewal

Right-hand mounting

5 Disconnect the battery negative terminal (refer to *Disconnecting the battery* in the Reference Chapter).

6 Place a jack beneath the engine, with a block of wood on the jack head. Raise the jack until it is supporting the weight of the engine.

7 Slacken and remove the three nuts securing the right-hand engine mounting upper bracket to the bracket on the cylinder block. Remove the nut securing the bracket to the mounting rubber, and lift off the bracket.

8 Lift the buffer plate off the mounting rubber stud, then unscrew the rubber from the body.

9 Check for signs of wear or damage on all components, and renew as necessary.

10 On reassembly, securely tighten the mounting rubber in the body.

11 Refit the buffer plate (where fitted) to the mounting rubber stud, then install the mounting bracket.

12 Tighten the mounting bracket retaining nuts to the specified torque wrench setting.

13 Remove the jack from under the engine, and reconnect the battery negative terminal.

Left-hand mounting

14 Remove the battery and tray as described in Chapter 5A.

15 Place a jack beneath the transmission, with a block of wood on the jack head. Raise the jack until it is supporting the weight of the transmission.

16 Slacken and remove the mounting rubber's centre nut, and two retaining nuts and remove the mounting from the engine compartment.

17 If necessary, undo the two retaining bolts and remove the mounting bracket from the body. Where applicable, disconnect the clutch cable from the transmission (see Chapter 6) then unscrew the retaining nuts and remove the bracket from the top of the transmission.

18 Check carefully for signs of wear or damage on all components, and renew them where necessary.

19 Refit the bracket to the transmission, tightening its mounting nuts to the specified torque. Where applicable, reconnect the clutch cable and adjust as described in Chapter 6. Refit the mounting bracket to the vehicle body and tighten its bolts to the specified torque.

20 Fit the mounting rubber to the bracket and tighten its retaining nuts to the specified torque. Refit the mounting centre nut, and tighten it to the specified torque.

21 Remove the jack from underneath the transmission, then refit the battery as described in Chapter 5A.

Rear mounting

22 If not already done, chock the rear wheels then jack up the front of the vehicle and support it on axle stands (see *Jacking and vehicle support*).

23 Unscrew and remove the bolt securing the rear mounting link to the mounting on the rear of the cylinder block.

24 Remove the bolt securing the rear mounting link to the bracket on the underbody. Withdraw the link.

25 To remove the mounting assembly it will first be necessary to remove the right-hand driveshaft as described in Chapter 8.

26 With the driveshaft removed, undo the retaining bolts and remove the mounting from the rear of the cylinder block.

27 Check carefully for signs of wear or damage on all components, and renew them where necessary.

28 On reassembly, fit the rear mounting assembly to the rear of the cylinder block, and tighten its retaining bolts to the specified torque. Refit the driveshaft as described in Chapter 8.

29 Refit the rear mounting link, and tighten both its bolts to their specified torque settings.

30 Lower the vehicle to the ground.

Chapter 2 Part B:
1.8 and 2.0 litre petrol engine
in-car repair procedures

Contents

Degrees of difficulty

| Easy, suitable for novice with little experience | Fairly easy, suitable for beginner with some experience | Fairly difficult, suitable for competent DIY mechanic 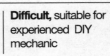 | Difficult, suitable for experienced DIY mechanic | Very difficult, suitable for expert DIY or professional |

Specifications

Engine (general)
Designation:
    1.8 litre (1761 cc) engine XU7
    2.0 litre (1998 cc) engine XU10
Engine codes*:
    1.8 litre:
        8-valve engine . . . . LFZ (XU7JP)
        16-valve engine . . . . LFY (XU7JP4)
    2.0 litre:
        8-valve engine . . . . RFX (XU10J2C)
        16-valve engine . . . . RFV (XU10J4R)
Bore:
    1.8 litre engine . . . . 83.00 mm
    2.0 litre engine . . . . 86.00 mm
Stroke:
    1.8 litre engine . . . . 81.00 mm
    2.0 litre engine . . . . 86.00 mm
Direction of crankshaft rotation . . . . Clockwise (viewed from the right-hand side of vehicle)
No 1 cylinder location . . . . At the transmission end of block

The engine code is stamped on a plate attached to the front left-hand end of the cylinder block on 1.8 litre engines and stamped directly onto the front face of the cylinder block (just to the left of the oil filter) on 2.0 litre engines.

Camshaft
Drive . . . . Toothed belt
No of bearings 5
Camshaft bearing journal diameter . . . . Not available at time of writing
Cylinder head bearing journal diameter . . . . Not available at time of writing

Valve clearances (8-valve engines only)

Inlet . . . . 0.20 mm
Exhaust . . . . 0.40 mm

Lubrication system

Oil pump type . . . . Gear-type, chain-driven off the crankshaft right-hand end
Minimum oil pressure at 80°C . . . . 5.3 bars (approximate) at 4000 rpm
Oil pressure warning switch operating pressure . . . . 0.8 bars

Torque wrench settings

	Nm	lbf ft
1.8 litre 8-valve engine		
Big-end bearing cap nuts:*		
Stage 1	20	15
Stage 2	Angle-tighten a further 70°	
Camshaft bearing cap nuts	15	11
Camshaft sprocket retaining bolt	35	26
Crankshaft pulley retaining bolt	120	89
Cylinder head bolts:		
Torx head type bolts:		
Stage 1	60	44
Fully slacken then tighten to:		
Stage 2	20	15
Stage 3	Angle-tighten a further 107°	
Stage 4	Angle-tighten a further 100°	
Stage 5	Angle-tighten a further 100°	
Hexagon head type bolts:		
Stage 1	60	44
Fully slacken then tighten to:		
Stage 2	20	15
Stage 3	Angle-tighten a further 120°	
Run engine until warm then allow to cool fully. Fully slacken then tighten to:		
Stage 4	20	15
Stage 5	Angle-tighten a further 120°	
Cylinder head cover nuts/bolts	10	7
Left-hand engine/transmission mounting:		
Mounting bracket-to-body bolts	25	18
Mounting stud	25	18
Centre nut	65	48
Engine-to-transmission fixing bolts	45	33
Engine/transmission rear mounting:		
Mounting assembly-to-block bolts	45	33
Mounting bracket-to-mounting bolt	50	37
Mounting bracket-to-subframe bolt	50	37
Engine/transmission right-hand mounting:		
Bracket-to-engine bolts	45	33
Mounting bracket retaining nuts	45	33
Flywheel/driveplate retaining bolts*	50	37
Main bearing cap nuts/bolts:		
Retaining nuts/bolts	54	40
Centre bearing cap side bolts	23	17
Oil pump retaining bolts	16	12
Oil seal carrier bolts	16	12
Sump retaining bolts	10	7
Timing belt cover bolts	8	6
Timing belt tensioner pulley bolt	20	15
New nuts/bolts must be used.		
1.8 litre 16-valve engine		
Big-end bearing cap nuts:*		
Stage 1	20	15
Stage 2	Angle-tighten a further 70°	
Camshaft bearing housings:		
Stage 1	5	4
Stage 2	10	7
Camshaft sprocket-to-hub retaining bolts	10	7
Camshaft sprocket hub-to-camshaft retaining bolts	75	55
Crankshaft pulley retaining bolt	120	89
Cylinder head cover nuts/bolts	10	7

Torque wrench settings

	Nm	lbf ft
1.8 litre 16-valve engine (continued)		
Cylinder head bolts:		
Torx head type bolts:		
Stage 1	60	44
Fully slacken then tighten to:		
Stage 2	20	15
Stage 3	Angle-tighten a further 107°	
Stage 4	Angle-tighten a further 100°	
Stage 5	Angle-tighten a further 100°	
Hexagon head type bolts:		
Stage 1	60	44
Fully slacken then tighten to:		
Stage 2	20	15
Stage 3	Angle-tighten a further 120°	
Run engine until warm then allow to cool fully. Fully slacken then tighten to:		
Stage 4	20	15
Stage 5	Angle-tighten a further 120°	
Engine-to-transmission fixing bolts	45	33
Flywheel/driveplate retaining bolts*	50	37
Left-hand engine/transmission mounting:		
Mounting bracket-to-body bolts	25	18
Mounting stud	50	36
Centre nut	65	48
Lower engine movement limiter to driveshaft bearing housing	50	37
Lower engine movement limiter to subframe	50	37
Main bearing cap bolts:		
Bearing bolts	55	41
Side securing bolts	25	18
Oil pump retaining bolts	16	12
Oil seal carrier bolts	16	12
Piston oil jet spray tube bolt	10	7
Right-hand engine/transmission mounting:		
Mounting bracket-to-engine nuts	45	33
Mounting bracket-to-engine bolts	50	37
Mounting bracket-to-rubber mounting nut	45	33
Rubber mounting-to-body nut	40	30
Upper engine movement limiter bolts	50	37
Sump retaining bolts	10	7
Timing belt cover bolts	8	6
Timing belt tensioner pulley bolt	20	15

New nuts/bolts must be used.

	Nm	lbf ft
2.0 litre 8-valve engine		
Big-end bearing cap nuts:*		
Stage 1	20	15
Stage 2	Angle-tighten a further 70°	
Camshaft bearing cap nuts/bolts	16	12
Camshaft sprocket retaining bolt	35	26
Crankshaft pulley retaining bolt	110	81
Cylinder head bolts:		
Stage 1	35	26
Stage 2	70	52
Stage 3	Angle-tighten a further 160°	
Cylinder head cover nuts/bolts	10	7
Engine/transmission left-hand mounting:		
Mounting rubber-to-body bolts	20	15
Mounting stud	50	37
Centre nut	65	48
Engine/transmission rear mounting:		
Mounting assembly-to-block bolts	45	33
Mounting link-to-mounting bolt	50	37
Mounting link-to-subframe bolt	70	52
Engine/transmission right-hand mounting:		
Mounting bracket retaining nuts	45	33
Curved retaining plate	20	15
Flywheel/driveplate retaining bolts*	50	37

Torque wrench settings

	Nm	lbf ft
2.0 litre 8-valve engine (continued)		
Main bearing cap bolts	70	52
Oil pump retaining bolts	13	10
Oil seal carrier bolts	16	12
Piston oil jet spray tube bolt	10	7
Sump retaining bolts	16	12
Timing belt cover bolts	8	6
Timing belt tensioner pulley bolt	20	15
* New nuts/bolts must be used.		
2.0 litre 16-valve engine		
Big-end bearing cap nuts:*		
Stage 1	20	15
Stage 2	Angle-tighten a further 70°	
Camshaft bearing housings:		
Stage 1	5	4
Stage 2	10	7
Camshaft sprocket-to-hub retaining bolts	10	7
Camshaft sprocket hub-to-camshaft retaining bolts	75	55
Crankshaft pulley retaining bolt	120	89
Cylinder head cover nuts/bolts	10	7
Cylinder head bolts:		
Stage 1	35	26
Stage 2	70	52
Stage 3	Angle-tighten a further 160°	
Engine-to-transmission fixing bolts	45	33
Flywheel/driveplate retaining bolts	50	37
Left-hand engine/transmission mounting:		
Mounting bracket-to-body bolts	25	18
Mounting stud	50	37
Centre nut	65	48
Lower engine movement limiter to driveshaft intermediate bearing housing	50	37
Lower engine movement limiter to subframe	85	63
Main bearing cap bolts	70	52
Oil pump retaining bolts	16	12
Oil seal carrier bolts	16	12
Piston oil jet spray tube bolt	10	7
Right-hand engine/transmission mounting:		
Mounting bracket-to-engine nuts	45	33
Mounting bracket-to-engine bolts	50	37
Mounting bracket-to-rubber mounting nut	45	33
Rubber mounting-to-body nut	40	30
Upper engine movement limiter bolts	50	37
Sump retaining bolts	10	7
Timing belt cover bolts	8	6
Timing belt tensioner pulley bolt	20	15
* New nuts/bolts must be used.		

1 General information

Using this Chapter

Chapter 2 is divided into five Parts; A, B, C, D and E. Repair operations that can be carried out with the engine in the vehicle are described in Parts A (1.1, 1.4 and 1.6 litre TU series petrol engines), B (1.8 and 2.0 litre XU series petrol engines), C (1.8 and 1.9 litre XUD series diesel engines) and D (1.9 and 2.0 litre DW series diesel engines). Part E covers the removal of the engine/transmission as a unit, and describes the engine dismantling and overhaul procedures.

In Parts A, B, C and D, the assumption is made that the engine is installed in the vehicle, with all ancillaries connected. If the engine has been removed for overhaul, the preliminary dismantling information which precedes each operation may be ignored.

XU series engine description

The XU series engine is a well-proven engine which has been fitted to many previous Peugeot and Citroën vehicles. The engine is of the in-line four-cylinder type, mounted transversely at the front of the car. The clutch and transmission are attached to its left-hand end.

The crankshaft runs in five main bearings. Thrustwashers are fitted to No 2 main bearing cap, to control crankshaft endfloat.

The connecting rods rotate on horizontally-split bearing shells at their big-ends. The pistons are attached to the connecting rods by gudgeon pins. The gudgeon pins are an interference fit in the connecting rod small-end eyes (except 2.0 litre 16-valve engines) or fully-floating and secured by circlips (2.0 litre 16-valve engines). The aluminium alloy pistons are fitted with three piston rings – two compression rings and an oil control ring.

On aluminium block engines, the cylinder block is of the 'wet-liner' type. The cylinder block is cast in aluminium alloy, and the bores have renewable cast-iron liners that are located from the top of the cylinder block. Sealing O-rings are fitted at the base of each liner, to prevent the escape of coolant into the sump.

On cast-iron block engines, the engine is of the conventional 'dry-liner' type. The cylinder block is cast in iron, and no separate bore liners are fitted.

On all models, the camshaft(s) is/are driven by a toothed timing belt, and operate the eight or sixteen valves via followers located beneath each cam lobe. On 8-valve engines, the valve clearances are adjusted by shims, positioned between the followers and the tip of the valve stem. On all other models the valve clearances are self-adjusting by means of hydraulic tappets fitted to the cam followers. The camshaft runs in bearing caps which are bolted to the top of the cylinder head. The inlet and exhaust valves are each closed by coil springs, and operate in guides pressed into the cylinder head. Both the valve seats and guides can be renewed separately if worn.

The coolant pump is driven by the timing belt.

Lubrication is by means of an oil pump which is driven (via a chain and sprocket) off the crankshaft right-hand end. It draws oil through a strainer located in the sump, and then forces it through an externally-mounted filter into galleries in the cylinder block/crankcase. From there, the oil is distributed to the crankshaft (main bearings) and camshaft. The big-end bearings are supplied with oil via internal drillings in the crankshaft; the camshaft bearings also receive a pressurised supply. The camshaft lobes and valves are lubricated by splash, as are all other engine components. On certain models, an oil cooler is mounted beneath the oil filter cartridge, to keep the oil temperature constant under severe operating conditions. The oil cooler is supplied with coolant from the engine cooling system.

Throughout the manual, it is often necessary to identify the engines not only by their cubic capacity, but also by their engine code. The engine code, consists of three letters (eg, LFZ). On 1.8 litre models the code is stamped on a plate attached to the front, left-hand end of the cylinder block, and on 2.0 litre models the engine code is stamped directly onto the front face of the cylinder block, on the machined surface located just to the left of the oil filter (next to the crankcase vent hose union).

Operations with engine in car

The following work can be carried out with the engine in the car:

a) Compression pressure – testing.
b) Cylinder head cover – removal and refitting.
c) Crankshaft pulley – removal and refitting.
d) Timing belt covers – removal and refitting.
e) Timing belt – removal, refitting and adjustment.
f) Timing belt tensioner and sprockets – removal and refitting.
g) Camshaft oil seal – renewal.
h) Camshaft and followers – removal, inspection and refitting.
i) Valve clearances – checking and adjustment.
j) Cylinder head – removal and refitting.
k) Cylinder head and pistons – decarbonising.
l) Sump – removal and refitting.
m) Oil pump – removal, overhaul and refitting.
n) Crankshaft oil seals – renewal.
o) Engine/transmission mountings – inspection and renewal.
p) Flywheel/driveplate – removal, inspection and refitting.

2 Compression test – description and interpretation

Refer to Chapter 2A, Section 2.

3 Engine assembly/valve timing holes – general information and usage

Caution: Do not attempt to rotate the engine whilst the crankshaft/camshaft are locked in position. If the engine is to be left in this state for a long period of time, it is a good idea to place suitable warning notices inside the vehicle, and in the engine compartment. This will reduce the possibility of the engine being accidentally cranked on the starter motor, which is likely to cause damage with the locking pins in place.

1 On all models, timing holes are drilled in the camshaft sprocket(s) and crankshaft pulley. The holes are used to align the crankshaft and camshaft(s), to prevent the possibility of the valves contacting the pistons when refitting the cylinder head, or when refitting the timing belt. When the holes are aligned with their corresponding holes in the cylinder head and cylinder block (as appropriate), suitable diameter pins can be inserted to lock both the camshaft(s) and crankshaft in position, preventing them rotating unnecessarily. Proceed as follows.

2 Remove the timing belt upper cover as described in Section 6.

3 Firmly apply the handbrake, then jack up the front of the car and support it securely on axle stands (see Jacking and vehicle support). Remove the right-hand front roadwheel.

4 From underneath the front of the car, prise out the two retaining clips and remove the plastic cover from the wing valance, to gain access to the crankshaft pulley bolt. Where necessary, unclip the coolant hoses from the bracket, to improve access further. The crankshaft can then be turned using a suitable socket and extension bar fitted to the pulley bolt. Note that the crankshaft must always be turned in a clockwise direction (viewed from the right-hand side of vehicle).

8-valve models

5 Rotate the crankshaft pulley until the timing hole in the camshaft sprocket is aligned with its corresponding hole in the cylinder head. Note that the holes are aligned when the sprocket hole is in the 8 o'clock position, when viewed from the right-hand end of the engine.

6 With the camshaft sprocket timing hole correctly positioned, insert an 8 mm diameter bolt or an 8 mm drill through the timing hole in the crankshaft pulley, and locate it in the corresponding hole in the end of the cylinder block (see illustration). Note that it may be necessary to rotate the crankshaft slightly, to get the holes to align.

7 Once the crankshaft pulley is locked in position, insert a suitable 9.5 mm diameter (approximate) bolt or a drill through the camshaft sprocket hole, and locate it in the cylinder head (see illustration).

8 The crankshaft and camshaft are now locked in position, preventing unnecessary rotation.

16-valve models

9 Rotate the crankshaft pulley until the timing holes in both camshafts are aligned with their corresponding holes in the cylinder head. The holes are aligned when the inlet camshaft sprocket hole is in approximately the 5 o'clock position and the exhaust camshaft sprocket hole is in approximately the

3.6 8.0 mm drill inserted through the crankshaft pulley timing hole – 8-valve models

3.7 9.5 mm diameter drill inserted through the camshaft pulley timing hole – 8-valve models

7 o'clock position, when viewed from the right-hand end of the engine.

10 With the camshaft sprocket holes correctly positioned, insert a 6 mm diameter bolt or drill through the timing hole in the crankshaft pulley, and locate it in the corresponding hole in the end of the engine. Note that the hole size may vary according to the type of pulley fitted and auxiliary drivebelt arrangement. If the bolt or drill is not a snug fit, try a larger size until a good fit is achieved in both the pulley and cylinder block.

11 With the crankshaft locked in position, insert a suitable bolt or drill through the timing hole in each camshaft sprocket and locate it in the cylinder head **(see illustration)**.

12 The crankshaft and camshafts are now locked in position, preventing rotation.

4 Cylinder head cover – removal and refitting

Note: *Depending on model and engine, there may not be enough clearance to remove the cylinder head cover past the brake master cylinder. If this should prove to be the case, it will be necessary to support the engine on a jack and unbolt the engine right-hand mounting (see Section 19) so that the engine can then be lowered sufficiently to permit the removal of the cylinder head cover.*

Removal

1 Disconnect the battery negative terminal (refer to *Disconnecting the battery* in the Reference Chapter).

8-valve models

2 Slacken the retaining clips, and disconnect the breather hoses from the front right-hand end of the cover. Where the original crimped-type Peugeot hose clips are still fitted, cut them off and discard them; use standard worm-drive hose clips on refitting.

3 Slacken the retaining clip, and disconnect the air cleaner-to-throttle housing duct from the front of the cylinder head cover. Also

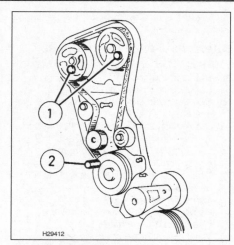

3.11 Camshaft sprocket timing hole (1) and crankshaft pulley timing hole (2) locked with suitable timing pins – 16-valve models

remove the inlet duct from the left-hand side of the head cover.

4 Release the two retaining clips, then undo the two retaining screws located at the front, and remove the air cleaner element cover from the cylinder head cover. Remove the air cleaner element, and store it with the cover.

5 Evenly and progressively unscrew the ten cylinder head cover retaining nuts, lift off the cylinder head cover, and remove it along with its rubber seal **(see illustration)**. Examine the seal for signs of damage and deterioration, and if necessary, renew it.

16-valve models

Note: *Later engines are fitted with plastic camshaft covers, rather than aluminium alloy as before. The procedure given below is not greatly affected by this change, except that the number of retaining bolts for each cover increases, and the bolts are located around the edge of each cover. No tightening sequence for the cover bolts is quoted by Peugeot, so this stage can be ignored for later engines.*

6 Disconnect the wiring connector at the left-hand end of the ignition coil unit, located in

the centre of the cylinder head covers. Undo the six retaining bolts and lift the coil unit upwards, off the spark plugs and from its location between the cylinder head covers.

7 Slacken the retaining clips, and disconnect the breather hoses from the front left-hand side of the front cover. Where the original crimped-type Peugeot hose clips are still fitted, cut them off and discard them; use standard worm-drive hose clips on refitting.

8 Undo the four bolts on the front of the inlet camshaft cover and recover the thrustwashers.

9 Working in a spiral sequence starting from the outside and working inwards, progressively slacken, then remove the retaining bolts of each cylinder head cover, noting the correct fitted position of any brackets or clips.

10 Lift off each cover in turn and remove it along with its rubber seal.

Refitting

8-valve models

11 Clean the cylinder head and cover mating surfaces, and remove all traces of oil.

12 Locate the rubber seal in the cover groove, ensuring that it is correctly located along its entire length.

13 Apply a smear of suitable sealant to each camshaft end bearing cap around the area where the cap contacts the cylinder head mating surface.

14 Carefully refit the cylinder head cover to the engine, taking great care not to displace the rubber seal.

15 Check that the seal is correctly located, then refit the cover retaining nuts and, working in sequence, tighten them evenly and progressively to the specified torque **(see illustration)**.

16 Refit the air cleaner element, and install the element cover. Securely tighten the cover retaining screws, and secure it in position with the retaining clips.

17 Reconnect the breather hoses, inlet duct and throttle housing duct to the cover, tightening their retaining clips securely. Reconnect the battery.

4.5 Cylinder head cover retaining nuts (arrowed) – 8-valve models

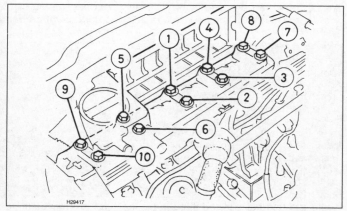

4.15 Tighten the cylinder head cover retaining nuts in sequence – 8-valve models

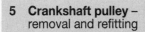

4.21 Tighten the aluminium cylinder head cover retaining nuts in sequence – 16-valve models

16-valve models

18 Clean the cylinder head and cover mating surfaces, and remove all traces of oil.
19 Locate the rubber seal in the groove of each cover, ensuring that it is correctly located along its entire length.
20 Carefully refit the cylinder head covers to the engine, taking great care not to displace the rubber seals.
21 Check that the seal is correctly located, then refit the cover retaining nuts and, working in sequence, tighten them evenly and progressively to the specified torque **(see illustration)**.
22 Reconnect the breather hoses to the front cover and securely tighten the retaining clips.
23 Refit the four bolts and thrustwashers to the front of the inlet camshaft cover and tighten them securely.
24 Refit the ignition coil unit between the cylinder head covers. Refit the retaining bolts, tightening them securely, then reconnect the coil unit wiring connectors.
25 Reconnect the battery negative terminal. On completion, start the engine and check the fuel hose unions for signs of leakage.

5 Crankshaft pulley – removal and refitting

Removal

1 Remove the auxiliary drivebelt (see Chapter 1A).
2 To prevent crankshaft turning whilst the pulley retaining bolt is being slackened on manual transmission models, select top gear and have an assistant apply the brakes firmly. On automatic transmission models, remove the starter motor (Chapter 5A) and use a suitable tool in the driveplate teeth to stop crankshaft rotation. Alternatively, the flywheel ring gear can be locked using a suitable tool made from steel angle **(see Tool Tip)**. Remove the cover plate from the base of the transmission bellhousing and bolt the tool to the bellhousing flange so it engages with the ring gear teeth. *Do not* attempt to lock the

Use a fabricated tool like this one to lock the flywheel ring gear and prevent crankshaft rotation.

pulley by inserting a bolt/drill through the timing hole. If the timing hole bolt/drill is in position, temporarily remove it prior to slackening the pulley bolt, then refit it once the bolt has been slackened.
3 Unscrew the retaining bolt and washer, then slide the pulley off the end of the crankshaft **(see illustrations)**. If the pulley locating roll pin or Woodruff key (as applicable) is a loose fit, remove it and store it with the pulley for safe-keeping. If the pulley is a tight fit, it can be drawn off the crankshaft using a suitable puller.

Refitting

4 Ensure that the Woodruff key is correctly located in its crankshaft groove, or that the roll pin is in position (as applicable). Refit the pulley to the end of the crankshaft, aligning its locating groove or hole with the Woodruff key or pin.
5 Thoroughly clean the threads of the pulley retaining bolt, then apply a coat of locking compound to the bolt threads. Peugeot recommend the use of Loctite (available from your Peugeot dealer); in the absence of this, any good-quality locking compound may be used.
6 Refit the crankshaft pulley retaining bolt and washer. Tighten the bolt to the specified torque, preventing the crankshaft from turning using the method employed on removal.
7 Refit and tension the auxiliary drivebelt as described in Chapter 1A.

6 Timing belt covers – removal and refitting

Removal – 1.8 litre 8-valve models

Upper cover

1 Release the retaining clips, and free the fuel hoses from the top of the cover.
2 Undo the two cover retaining bolts (situated at the base of the cover), and remove the cover from the engine compartment.

Centre cover

3 Slacken and remove the two cover retaining bolts (located directly beneath the mounting bracket). Move the cover upwards to free it from the two locating pins situated at the base of the cover, and remove it from the engine compartment.

Lower cover

4 Remove the crankshaft pulley as described in Section 5.
5 Remove the centre cover as described in paragraph 3.
6 Undo the two cover retaining bolts, and remove the cover from the engine. Note that on some models it may be necessary to unbolt the auxiliary drivebelt tensioner assembly and remove it from the engine in order to allow the cover to be removed.

Removal – 2.0 litre 8-valve models

Upper cover

7 Release the retaining clip, and free the fuel hoses from the top of the timing belt cover.
8 Slacken and remove the two cover retaining bolts, then lift the upper cover upwards and out of the engine compartment.

Lower cover

9 Remove the crankshaft pulley as described in Section 5.
10 Slacken and remove the three retaining bolts, then remove the lower timing belt cover from the engine. Note that on some models it may be necessary to unbolt the auxiliary drivebelt tensioner assembly and remove it

5.3a Removing the crankshaft pulley retaining bolt

5.3b Removing the crankshaft pulley from the end of the crankshaft

from the engine in order to allow the cover to be removed.

Removal – 16-valve models

Upper (outer) cover

11 Undo the upper and lower retaining bolts securing the outer cover to the inner cover. Slide the cover retaining clip upwards to release it from its fasteners.
12 Ease the outer cover upwards and away from the engine, freeing it from its lower locations.

Lower cover

13 Remove the crankshaft pulley as described in Section 5.
14 Remove the upper (outer) cover as described above.
15 Slacken and remove the three retaining bolts, then remove the lower timing belt cover from the engine. Note that on some models it may be necessary to unbolt the auxiliary drivebelt tensioner assembly and remove it from the engine in order to allow the cover to be removed.

Upper (inner) cover

16 Remove the timing belt as described in Section 8.
17 Remove both camshaft sprockets as described in Section 9.
18 Remove the six bolts securing the cover to the side of the cylinder head, and remove the cover from the engine.

Refitting

19 Refitting is a reversal of the relevant removal procedure, ensuring that each cover section is correctly located, and that the cover retaining nuts and/or bolts are securely tightened (to the specified torque, where given).

---

7 Timing belt (8-valve models) – general information, removal and refitting

Note: *Peugeot specify the use of an electronic belt tension checking tool (SEEM 4122-T) to correctly set the timing belt tension. The following procedure assumes that this equipment (or suitable alternative equipment calibrated to display belt tension in SEEM units) is available. Accurate tensioning of the timing belt is essential, and if the electronic equipment is not available, it is recommended that the work is entrusted to a Peugeot dealer or suitably-equipped garage.*

General information

1 The timing belt drives the camshaft(s) and coolant pump from a toothed sprocket on the front of the crankshaft. If the belt breaks or slips in service, the pistons are likely to hit the valve heads, resulting in extensive (and expensive) damage.
2 The timing belt should be renewed at the

specified intervals (see Chapter 1A) or earlier if it is contaminated with oil, or if it is at all noisy in operation (a 'scraping' noise due to uneven wear).
3 If the timing belt is being removed, it is a wise precaution to check the condition of the coolant pump at the same time (check for signs of coolant leakage). This may avoid the need to remove the timing belt again at a later stage, should the coolant pump fail.

Removal

4 Disconnect the battery negative terminal (refer to *Disconnecting the battery* in the Reference Chapter).
5 Align the engine assembly/valve timing holes as described in Section 3, and lock the camshaft sprocket and crankshaft pulley in position. *Do not* attempt to rotate the engine whilst the pins are in position.
6 Remove the centre and/or lower timing belt cover(s) as described in Section 6 (as applicable).
7 Loosen the timing belt tensioner pulley retaining bolt. Pivot the pulley in a clockwise direction, using a suitable square-section key fitted to the hole in the pulley hub, then securely retighten the retaining bolt **(see Tool Tip)**.
8 On 1.8 litre models, position a jack beneath the engine, with a block of wood on the jack head. Raise the jack until it is supporting the weight of the engine. Slacken and remove the three nuts securing the engine/transmission right-hand mounting bracket to the engine bracket. Remove the single nut securing the bracket to the mounting rubber, and lift off the bracket. Undo the three bolts securing the engine bracket to the end of the cylinder head/block, and remove the bracket.
9 If the timing belt is to be re-used, use white paint or chalk to mark the direction of rotation

TOOL TIP

A square section tool to fit the timing belt tensioner pulley can be made from a length of standard 8 mm door handle rod (A), obtained from a DIY shop, and then cut to size. Once the rod has been fitted to the tensioner, the timing belt can be tensioned by turning the rod with an 8 mm spanner (B).

on the belt (if markings do not already exist), then slip the belt off the sprockets. Note that the crankshaft must not be rotated whilst the belt is removed.
10 Check the timing belt carefully for any signs of uneven wear, splitting, or oil contamination. Pay particular attention to the roots of the teeth. Renew it if there is the slightest doubt about its condition. If the engine is undergoing an overhaul, and has covered more than 36 000 miles (60 000 km) with the existing belt fitted, renew the belt as a matter of course, regardless of its apparent condition. The cost of a new belt is nothing compared with the cost of repairs, should the belt break in service. If signs of oil contamination are found, trace the source of the oil leak and rectify it. Wash down the engine timing belt area and all related components, to remove all traces of oil.

Refitting

11 Before refitting, thoroughly clean the timing belt sprockets. Check that the tensioner pulley rotates freely, without any sign of roughness. If necessary, renew the tensioner pulley as described in Section 9.
12 Ensure that the camshaft sprocket locking pin is still in position. Temporarily refit the crankshaft pulley, and insert the locking pin through the pulley timing hole to ensure that the crankshaft is still correctly positioned.
13 Remove the crankshaft pulley. Manoeuvre the timing belt into position, ensuring that any arrows on the belt are pointing in the direction of rotation (clockwise when viewed from the right-hand end of the engine).
14 Do not twist the timing belt sharply while refitting it. Fit the belt over the crankshaft and camshaft sprockets. Ensure that the belt 'front run' is taut – ie, any slack should be on the tensioner pulley side of the belt. Fit the belt over the water pump sprocket and tensioner pulley. Ensure that the belt teeth are seated centrally in the sprockets.
15 Loosen the tensioner pulley retaining bolt. Using the square-section key, pivot the pulley anti-clockwise to remove all free play from the timing belt, then retighten the bolt. Tension the timing belt as follows.

Tensioning

16 Fit the sensor head of the electronic belt tension measuring equipment to the 'front run' of the timing belt, approximately midway between the camshaft and crankshaft sprockets.
17 Loosen the tensioner pulley retaining bolt. Using the square-section key, pivot the pulley anti-clockwise until an initial setting of 16 ± 2 SEEM units on 2.0 litre models, and 30 ± 2 SEEM units on 1.8 litre models is displayed on the tension measuring equipment. Hold the tensioner pulley in that position and retighten the retaining bolt.
18 Remove the locking tool from the camshaft sprocket, and remove the tension measuring equipment from the belt.

19 Refit the crankshaft pulley and tighten the bolt moderately to allow the crankshaft to be rotated.

20 Using a suitable socket and extension bar on the crankshaft pulley bolt, rotate the crankshaft through two complete rotations in a clockwise direction (viewed from the right-hand end of the engine). *Do not* at any time rotate the crankshaft anti-clockwise. Both camshaft and crankshaft timing holes should be aligned so that the locking tools can be easily inserted. This indicates that the valve timing is correct. If all is well, remove the locking tools.

21 If the timing holes are not correctly positioned, repeat the fitting procedure so far.

22 Rotate the crankshaft two more turns without turning backwards and refit the camshaft locking tool. Refit the tension measuring equipment to the timing belt.

23 The final belt tension on the 'front run' of the belt on all models should be 44 ± 2 SEEM units. Readjust the tensioner pulley position as required, then retighten the retaining bolt to the specified torque. Remove the tools and rotate the crankshaft through a further two rotations clockwise, and recheck the tension. Repeat this procedure as necessary until the correct tension reading is obtained after rotating the crankshaft.

24 With the belt tension correctly set, on 1.8 litre models, refit the mounting bracket to the side of the cylinder head, apply a drop of locking compound to the retaining bolts and tighten them to the specified torque. Refit the right-hand engine mounting bracket, and tighten its retaining nuts to the specified torque. The jack can then be removed from underneath the engine.

25 On all models, remove the camshaft locking tool, then remove the crankshaft pulley and refit the timing belt cover(s).

26 Refit the crankshaft pulley as described in Section 5, and reconnect the battery negative terminal.

8 Timing belt (16-valve models) – general information, removal and refitting

Note: *On engines with a manual tensioner pulley, Peugeot specify the use of an electronic belt tension checking tool (SEEM 4122-T) to correctly set the timing belt tension. The procedure assumes that this equipment (or suitable alternative equipment calibrated to display belt tension in SEEM units) is available. Accurate tensioning of the timing belt is essential, and if the electronic equipment is not available, it is recommended that the work is entrusted to a Peugeot dealer or suitably-equipped garage.*

General information

1 The timing belt drives the camshafts and coolant pump from a toothed sprocket on the front of the crankshaft. If the belt breaks or slips in service, the pistons are likely to hit the valve heads, resulting in extensive (and expensive) damage.

2 The timing belt should be renewed at the specified intervals (see Chapter 1A), or earlier if it is contaminated with oil, or if it is at all noisy in operation (a 'scraping' noise due to uneven wear).

3 If the timing belt is being removed, it is a wise precaution to check the condition of the coolant pump at the same time (check for signs of coolant leakage). This may avoid the need to remove the timing belt again at a later stage, should the coolant pump fail.

4 Two types of timing belt tensioner pulley may be encountered. On early engines a manual tensioner pulley is used, and the belt tension must be set using an electronic tension checking tool. On later engines (from approximately mid-1999) a dynamic tensioner pulley is used which automatically adjusts the belt tension.

Removal

5 Disconnect the battery negative terminal (refer to *Disconnecting the battery* in the Reference Chapter).

6 Remove the auxiliary drivebelt as described in Chapter 1A.

7 Where applicable, unbolt and remove the auxiliary drivebelt tensioner.

8 Move the engine wiring harness and relevant hoses clear of the working area as necessary. This will entail the disconnection of certain connectors, and the removal of the harness from various cable clips and supports. Label any disconnected wiring and components as an aid to refitting.

9 Remove the timing belt upper (outer) cover as described in Section 6.

10 Determine the type of timing belt tensioner pulley fitted, by referring to the accompanying illustrations, then proceed as described in the appropriate following sub-sections **(see illustrations)**.

Manual tensioner pulley

11 To improve access, refer to Section 19 and remove the engine right-hand mounting. This is not essential, but it does make several of the timing belt components much easier to remove with the engine in the car.

12 Align the engine assembly/valve timing holes as described in Section 3, and lock the camshaft sprocket hubs in position. *Do not attempt to rotate the engine whilst the locking tools are in place.*

13 Remove the crankshaft pulley as described in Section 5.

14 Unbolt and remove the timing belt lower cover (refer to Section 6 if necessary).

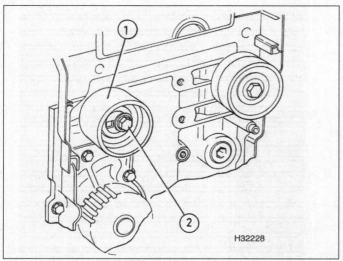

8.10a Early type manual timing belt tensioner pulley – 16-valve models

1 Manual tensioner pulley   2 Retaining bolt

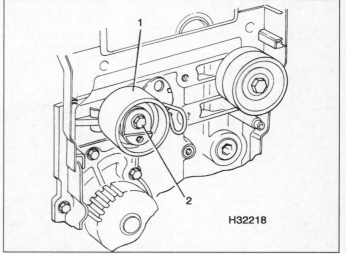

8.10b Later type dynamic timing belt tensioner pulley – 16-valve models

1 Dynamic tensioner pulley   2 Retaining bolt

8.15 Loosen the manual timing belt tensioner retaining bolt and pivot the pulley in a clockwise direction – 16-valve models

15 Loosen the timing belt tensioner pulley retaining bolt **(see illustration)**. Pivot the pulley in a clockwise direction, using a suitable square-section key fitted to the hole in the pulley hub, then securely retighten the retaining bolt **(see Tool Tip in Section 7)**.

16 If the timing belt is to be re-used, use white paint or chalk to mark the direction of rotation on the belt (if markings do not already exist), then slip the belt off the sprockets. Note that the crankshaft must not be rotated whilst the belt is removed.

17 Check the timing belt carefully for any signs of uneven wear, splitting, or oil contamination. Pay particular attention to the roots of the teeth. Renew it if there is the slightest doubt about its condition. If the engine is undergoing an overhaul, and has covered more than 36 000 miles (60 000 km) with the existing belt fitted, renew the belt as a matter of course, regardless of its apparent condition. The cost of a new belt is nothing compared with the cost of repairs, should the belt break in service. If signs of oil contamination are found, trace the source of the oil leak and rectify it. Wash down the engine timing belt area and all related components, to remove all traces of oil.

Using a home-made tool to retain the camshaft sprocket whilst the sprocket retaining bolt is tightened (TU series engine shown)

Dynamic tensioner pulley

18 To improve access, refer to Section 19 and remove the engine right-hand mounting. This is not essential, but it does make several of the timing belt components much easier to remove with the engine in the car.

19 Align the engine assembly/valve timing holes as described in Section 3, and lock the camshaft sprocket hubs in position. *Do not attempt to rotate the engine whilst the locking tools are in position.*

20 Remove the crankshaft pulley as described in Section 5.

21 Unbolt and remove the timing belt lower cover (refer to Section 6 if necessary).

22 Slacken the camshaft sprocket centre retaining bolt on each camshaft. To prevent the sprockets rotating as the bolts are slackened, a sprocket holding tool will be required. In the absence of the special Peugeot tool, an acceptable substitute can be fabricated at home **(see Tool Tip)**. *Do not attempt to use only the sprocket hub locking tools inserted in the engine assembly/valve timing holes to prevent the sprockets from rotating whilst the bolts are slackened.*

23 Slacken the timing belt tensioner pulley retaining bolt and insert a suitable Allen key into the hexagonal hole on the front face of the tensioner pulley.

24 Using the Allen key, turn the tensioner pulley anti-clockwise (as viewed from the

right-hand side of the car) until the index pointer is below the reference hole **(see illustration)**. Insert a small drill bit or short length of welding rod into the reference hole to retain the index pointer in this position.

25 Now turn the tensioner pulley clockwise until the hexagonal Allen key hole is positioned approximately adjacent to the upper edge of the coolant pump flange. Tighten the tensioner pulley retaining bolt to retain the pulley in this position.

26 If the timing belt is to be re-used, use white paint or chalk to mark the direction of rotation on the belt (if markings do not already exist), then slip the belt off the sprockets. Note that the crankshaft must not be rotated whilst the belt is removed.

27 Inspect the belt as described in paragraph 17.

Refitting and tensioning

Manual tensioner pulley

28 Before refitting, thoroughly clean the timing belt sprockets. Check that the tensioner and idler pulleys rotate freely, without any sign of roughness. If necessary, renew the pulleys as described in Section 9.

29 Ensure that the camshaft sprocket hub locking tools are still in position. Temporarily refit the crankshaft pulley, insert the locking tool through the pulley timing hole to ensure that the crankshaft is still correctly positioned, then remove the pulley.

30 Without removing the locking tools, on early engines, slacken the six camshaft sprocket retaining bolts (three on each sprocket). On later engines, only the single bolt securing each camshaft sprocket need be slackened. Check that both sprockets are free to turn within the limits of their elongated bolt holes, or that the protruding lug on single-bolt sprockets can move within its limits **(see illustrations)**. To prevent the single-bolt sprockets rotating as the bolts are slackened, a sprocket holding tool will be required. In the absence of the special Peugeot tool, an acceptable substitute can be fabricated at home **(see Tool Tip above)**. *Do not attempt to use only the sprocket hub locking tools to prevent the sprockets from rotating whilst the bolts are slackened.*

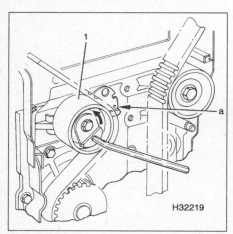

8.24 Rotate the dynamic tensioner pulley (1) anti-clockwise until the index pointer is below the reference hole (a) – 16-valve models

8.30a Slacken the camshaft sprocket retaining bolts (arrowed) – 16-valve models

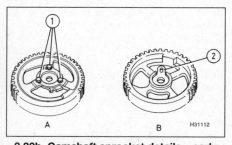

8.30b Camshaft sprocket details – early models (A) have three retaining bolts (1) in elongated slots, while later models (B) have a single bolt and a protruding lug (2) – 16-valve models

31 Tighten the camshaft sprocket retaining bolts finger-tight, then slacken them all by one sixth of a turn.

32 Again without removing the locking tools, turn each camshaft sprocket clockwise to the ends of their retaining bolt slots, or until the protruding lug reaches the end of its travel.

33 Ensuring that any arrows on the belt are pointing in the direction of rotation (clockwise when viewed from the right-hand end of the engine), manoeuvre the timing belt into position on the exhaust camshaft sprocket. Retain the belt on the sprocket using a cable tie.

34 With the sprockets still positioned fully clockwise as far as they will go, feed the belt over the inlet camshaft sprocket, keeping it tight on its top run.

35 Engage the belt around the idler pulley, crankshaft sprocket, coolant pump sprocket and finally around the tensioner pulley.

36 Fit the sensor head of the electronic belt tension measuring equipment to the 'front run' of the timing belt, approximately midway between the idler pulley and crankshaft sprocket.

37 Slacken the tensioner pulley retaining bolt and pivot the tensioner pulley anti-clockwise, using the square-section key, until an initial setting of 45 SEEM units is displayed on the tension measuring equipment. Hold the tensioner pulley in that position and retighten the retaining bolt.

38 Check that the sprockets have not been turned so far that the retaining bolts are at the end of their slots, or that the protruding lug on single-bolt sprockets is at the end of its travel. If either condition is evident, repeat the refitting operation. If all is satisfactory, tighten the sprocket retaining bolts to the specified torque.

39 Remove the belt tension measuring equipment, the crankshaft and camshaft locking tools, and the cable tie used to retain the belt on the exhaust camshaft sprocket.

40 Refit the timing belt lower cover and the crankshaft pulley as described in Sections 6 and 5 respectively.

41 Rotate the crankshaft through two complete rotations in a clockwise direction (viewed from the right-hand end of the engine). Realign the engine assembly/valve timing holes and refit the crankshaft pulley and camshaft sprocket hub locking tools.

42 Slacken the camshaft sprocket retaining bolts, retighten them finger-tight, then slacken them all by one sixth of a turn.

43 Slacken the tensioner pulley retaining bolt once again. Refit the belt tension measuring equipment to the front run of the belt, and turn the tensioner pulley to give a final setting of 26 SEEM units (engines with three bolts per camshaft sprocket) or 32 SEEM units (single-bolt sprocket engines) on the tensioning gauge. Hold the tensioner pulley in this position and tighten the retaining bolt to the specified torque. Remove the tension measuring equipment.

44 Retighten all sprocket retaining bolts to the specified torque.

45 The belt tension must now be checked as follows. Remove the locking tools, then rotate the crankshaft once again through two complete rotations in a clockwise direction. Realign the engine assembly/valve timing holes and refit the crankshaft pulley and camshaft sprocket hub locking tools.

46 Slacken the camshaft sprocket retaining bolts, then retighten them to the specified torque.

47 Remove the camshaft and crankshaft locking tools. Turn the crankshaft approximately one quarter of a turn in the normal direction of rotation, until the locking tool hole in the crankshaft pulley is aligned with the timing belt lower cover front retaining bolt. It is important that this position is achieved ONLY by turning the belt forwards – if the belt is turned back at all to achieve alignment, the belt tension check will not be valid.

48 In this position, refit the tension measuring equipment to the front run of the belt, and check that the reading is between 32 and 40 SEEM units. If not, the entire belt tensioning procedure must be repeated from the start.

49 Once the belt tension has been correctly set, refit the engine right-hand mounting components (if removed) as described in Section 19.

50 Refit the timing belt upper (outer) cover as described in Section 6.

51 Reconnect any hoses and wiring disturbed for access.

52 Refit the auxiliary drivebelt tensioner then refit and tension the drivebelt with reference to Chapter 1A.

53 Reconnect the battery negative terminal.

Dynamic tensioner pulley

54 Before refitting, thoroughly clean the timing belt sprockets. Check that the tensioner and idler pulleys rotate freely, without any sign of roughness. If necessary, renew the pulleys as described in Section 9.

55 Ensure that the camshaft sprocket hub locking tools are still in position. Temporarily refit the crankshaft pulley, insert the locking tool through the pulley timing hole to ensure that the crankshaft is still correctly positioned, then remove the pulley.

56 With the camshaft sprocket retaining bolts still slackened, turn each camshaft sprocket clockwise to the end of its travel. Tighten the sprocket retaining bolts slightly to hold the sprockets in this position.

57 Ensuring that any arrows on the belt are pointing in the direction of rotation (clockwise when viewed from the right-hand end of the engine), manoeuvre the timing belt into position on the exhaust camshaft sprocket. Retain the belt on the sprocket using a cable tie.

58 With the sprockets still positioned fully clockwise as far as they will go, feed the belt over the inlet camshaft sprocket, keeping it tight on its top run.

59 Engage the belt around the idler pulley, crankshaft sprocket, coolant pump sprocket and finally around the tensioner pulley.

60 With the timing belt in position, slacken the camshaft sprocket retaining bolts once more.

61 Remove the drill bit or welding rod from the reference hole in the tensioner pulley.

62 Slacken the tensioner pulley retaining bolt and turn the tensioner pulley, by means of the Allen key, so that the index pointer is positioned in its maximum position (ie, below the reference hole). Hold the tensioner in this position and tighten the retaining bolt.

63 Hold the camshaft sprockets with the tool used during removal, and tighten the sprocket centre retaining bolts to the specified torque.

64 Refit the timing belt lower cover and the crankshaft pulley as described in Sections 6 and 5 respectively.

65 Remove the locking tools and rotate the crankshaft through four complete rotations in a clockwise direction (viewed from the right-hand end of the engine). Realign the engine assembly/valve timing holes and refit the crankshaft pulley and camshaft sprocket hub locking tools.

66 Hold the camshaft sprockets with the tool used during removal, and once again slacken the sprocket centre retaining bolts.

67 Hold the tensioner pulley in position by means of the Allen key and slacken the tensioner pulley retaining bolt. Turn the tensioner clockwise until the index pointer is aligned with the slot in the centre of the index plate, then tighten the retaining bolt to the specified torque **(see illustration)**.

68 Hold the camshaft sprockets and tighten the sprocket centre retaining bolts to the specified torque.

69 Remove the locking tools and rotate the crankshaft through two complete rotations in a clockwise direction (viewed from the right-hand end of the engine). Realign the engine assembly/valve timing holes and refit the

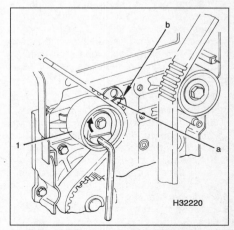

8.67 Turn the dynamic tensioner pulley (1) clockwise until the index pointer (a) is aligned with the slot (b) in the index plate – 16-valve models

crankshaft pulley and camshaft sprocket hub locking tools.

70 Check that the index pointer on the tensioner pulley is still aligned with the slot in the centre of the index plate. If not, repeat the procedure from paragraph 65 to 69.

71 Once the belt tension has been correctly set, refit the engine right-hand mounting components (if removed) as described in Section 19.

72 Refit the timing belt upper (outer) cover as described in Section 6.

73 Reconnect any hoses and wiring disturbed for access.

74 Refit the auxiliary drivebelt tensioner then refit and tension the drivebelt with reference to Chapter 1A.

75 Reconnect the battery negative terminal.

9 Timing belt tensioner and sprockets – removal, inspection and refitting

Camshaft sprocket removal

8-valve models

1 Remove the timing belt as described in Section 7.

2 Remove the locking tool from the camshaft sprocket. Disengage the timing belt from the sprocket and position it clear, taking care not to bend or twist the belt sharply.

3 Remove the locking tool from the camshaft sprocket. Slacken the sprocket retaining bolt and remove it, along with its washer. To prevent the camshaft rotating as the bolt is slackened, a sprocket holding tool will be required. In the absence of the special Peugeot tool, an acceptable substitute can be fabricated at home (see **Tool Tip** in Section 8). *Do not* attempt to use the engine assembly/valve timing hole locking tool to prevent the sprocket from rotating whilst the bolt is slackened.

4 With the retaining bolt removed, slide the sprocket off the end of the camshaft. If the locating peg is a loose fit in the rear of the sprocket, remove it for safe-keeping. Examine the camshaft oil seal for signs of oil leakage and, if necessary, renew it as described in Section 10.

Early 16-valve models

Note: *The early type camshaft sprockets have a large centre retaining bolt to secure the sprocket hub to the camshaft, and three smaller bolts that secure the sprocket to the hub. If the sprocket being worked on does not have the three smaller bolts, it is a later type – refer to the procedures contained in the following sub-Section.*

5 Remove the timing belt as described in Section 8.

6 If the sprockets are to be removed without their hubs, undo the three retaining bolts and remove the relevant sprocket. Suitably mark the sprockets inlet and/or exhaust as they are

removed (although in fact the sprockets are identical).

7 If both the sprockets and the hubs are to be removed, remove the relevant sprocket hub locking tool, then slacken the sprocket hub centre retaining bolt. To prevent the sprocket rotating as the bolt is slackened, a sprocket holding tool will be required. In the absence of the special Peugeot tool, an acceptable substitute can be fabricated at home (see **Tool Tip** in Section 8). *Do not* attempt to use the engine assembly/valve timing hole locking tool to prevent the sprocket from rotating whilst the bolt is slackened.

8 Undo the three retaining bolts and remove the relevant sprocket from its hub. Remove the previously-slackened hub retaining bolt, and withdraw the hub from the end of the camshaft. Note that the hubs are marked for identification with a single digit on their front face. On 1.8 litre models, the inlet hub is marked 1 and the exhaust hub is marked 2. On 2.0 litre models, the inlet hub is marked 3 and the exhaust hub is marked 4. Make your own markings if none are visible.

Later 16-valve models

Note: *The later type camshaft sprockets have only a centre sprocket/hub retaining bolt to secure the assembly to the camshaft. If the sprocket being worked on has three additional smaller bolts, securing the sprocket to the hub, it is an early type – refer to the procedures contained in the previous sub-Section.*

9 Remove the timing belt as described in Section 8.

10 Remove the relevant sprocket hub locking tool, then slacken the sprocket centre retaining bolt. To prevent the sprocket rotating as the bolt is slackened, a sprocket holding tool will be required. In the absence of the special Peugeot tool, an acceptable substitute can be fabricated at home (see **Tool Tip** in Section 8). *Do not* attempt to use the engine assembly/valve timing hole locking tool to prevent the sprocket from rotating whilst the bolt is slackened.

11 Remove the previously-slackened hub retaining bolt, and withdraw the relevant sprocket and hub from the end of the camshaft. Suitably mark the sprockets and hubs inlet and/or exhaust as they are removed (although in fact they are identical).

Crankshaft sprocket removal

All models

12 Remove the timing belt as described in Section 7 or 8 as applicable.

13 Slide the crankshaft sprocket off the end of the crankshaft. Remove the Woodruff key from the crankshaft, and store it with the sprocket for safe-keeping. Where necessary, also slide the spacer (where fitted) off the end of the crankshaft.

14 Examine the crankshaft oil seal for signs of oil leakage and, if necessary, renew it as described in Section 17.

Pulley removal

8-valve models

15 Remove the timing belt as described in Section 7.

16 Slacken and remove the timing belt tensioner pulley retaining bolt, and slide the pulley off its mounting stud. Examine the mounting stud for signs of damage and if necessary, renew it.

16-valve models

17 Remove the timing belt as described in Section 8.

18 Undo the tensioner and idler pulley retaining bolts and remove the relevant pulley from the engine. On engines with a dynamic tensioner pulley, recover the small drill bit or welding rod inserted in the reference hole as the assembly is removed.

Inspection

19 Clean the camshaft/crankshaft sprockets thoroughly, and renew any that show signs of wear, damage or cracks.

20 Clean the tensioner/idler pulleys, but do not use any strong solvent which may enter the pulley bearings. Check that the pulleys rotate freely, with no sign of stiffness or free play. Renew them if there is any doubt about their condition, or if there are any obvious signs of wear or damage.

Camshaft sprocket refitting

8-valve models

21 Refit the locating peg (where removed) to the rear of the sprocket. Locate the sprocket on the end of the camshaft, ensuring that the locating peg is correctly engaged with the cut-out in the camshaft end.

22 Refit the sprocket retaining bolt and washer, and tighten it to the specified torque. Retain the sprocket with the tool used on removal.

23 Realign the hole in the camshaft sprocket with the corresponding hole in the cylinder head, and refit the locking tool. Check that the crankshaft pulley locking tool is still in position.

24 Refit and tension the timing belt as described in Section 7.

Early 16-valve models

25 If both the sprockets and the hubs have been removed, engage the sprocket hub with the camshaft. Ensure that the correct hub is fitted to the relevant camshaft by observing the hub identification markings described in paragraph 8.

26 Refit the sprocket retaining bolt and washer, and tighten it to the specified torque. Temporarily refit the sprocket to allow the hub to be held stationary, with the tool used on removal, as the bolt is tightened.

27 Turn the hub so that the locking tool can be engaged.

28 If the sprockets have been removed, leaving the hubs in place, position the sprocket on its hub and refit the three bolts finger tight only at this stage. Ensure that the correct sprocket is fitted to the relevant camshaft according to the identification made on removal.

29 Refit and tension the timing belt as described in Section 8.

Later 16-valve models

30 Engage the sprocket hub with the camshaft. Ensure that the correct hub is fitted to the relevant camshaft according to the identification made on removal.

31 Position the relevant sprocket on the hub and refit the sprocket retaining bolt and washer. Tighten the retaining bolt just tight enough to hold the sprocket/hub in place at this stage.

32 Turn the hub so that the locking tool can be engaged.

33 Refit and tension the timing belt as described in Section 8.

Crankshaft sprocket refitting

All models

34 Slide the spacer (where fitted) into position, taking great care not to damage the crankshaft oil seal, and refit the Woodruff key to its slot in the crankshaft end.

35 Slide on the crankshaft sprocket, aligning its slot with the Woodruff key.

36 Temporarily refit the crankshaft pulley, and insert the locking tool through the pulley timing hole, to ensure that the crankshaft is still correctly positioned.

37 Remove the crankshaft pulley, then refit and tension the timing belt as described in Section 7 or 8 as applicable.

Pulley refitting

8-valve models

38 Refit the tensioner pulley to its mounting stud, and fit the retaining bolt.

39 Refit and tension the timing belt as described in Section 7.

16-valve models

40 Refit the tensioner and idler pulleys and secure with the retaining bolts. On engines with a dynamic tensioner pulley, ensure that the pulley body correctly engages with the projection on the cylinder block, and position the index pointer as described in Section 8, paragraphs 24 and 25.

41 Relocate and tension the timing belt as described in Section 8.

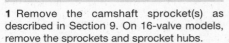

10 Camshaft oil seal(s) – renewal

1 Remove the camshaft sprocket(s) as described in Section 9. On 16-valve models, remove the sprockets and sprocket hubs.

2 Punch or drill two small holes opposite each other in the oil seal. Screw a self-tapping screw into each, and pull on the screws with pliers to extract the seal.

11.5 Removing the oil supply pipe from the camshaft bearing caps – 8-valve models

3 Clean the seal housing, and polish off any burrs or raised edges, which may have caused the seal to fail in the first place.

4 Lubricate the lips of the new seal with clean engine oil, and drive it into position until it seats on its locating shoulder. Use a suitable tubular drift, such as a socket, which bears only on the hard outer edge of the seal. Take care not to damage the seal lips during fitting. Note that the seal lips should face inwards.

5 Refit the camshaft sprocket(s) as described in Section 9.

11 Camshaft and followers – removal, inspection and refitting

Note: On 8-valve models the camshaft will have to be removed again if the valve clearances are incorrect (Paragraph 29), so measure the clearances first (Section 12) so the shim selection can be performed while the camshaft is removed.

Removal

1 Disconnect the battery negative terminal (refer to *Disconnecting the battery* in the Reference Chapter), then proceed as described under the relevant sub-heading.

8-valve models

2 Remove the cylinder head cover (Section 4) and the camshaft sprocket (Section 9).

3 Remove the ignition HT coil as described in Chapter 5B.

4 With the coil removed, slacken the upper

11.8 . . . and remove the camshaft bearing caps . . .

11.7 Working as described in the text, unscrew the retaining nuts . . .

bolt securing the thermostat housing to the left-hand end of the cylinder head. Remove the bolt, along with its sealing washer. This is necessary since the bolt screws into the left-hand (No 1) camshaft bearing cap.

5 Carefully ease the oil supply pipe out from the top of the camshaft bearing caps, and remove it **(see illustration)**. Note the O-ring seals fitted to each of the pipe unions.

6 The camshaft bearing caps should be numbered 1 to 5, number 1 being at the transmission end of the engine. If not, make identification marks on the caps, using white paint or a suitable marker pen. Also mark each cap in some way to indicate its correct fitted orientation. This will avoid the possibility of installing the caps the wrong way around on refitting.

7 Evenly and progressively slacken the camshaft bearing cap retaining nuts by one turn at a time. This will relieve the valve spring pressure on the bearing caps gradually and evenly. Once the pressure has been relieved, the nuts can be fully unscrewed and removed **(see illustration)**.

8 Note the correct fitted orientation of the bearing caps, then remove them from the cylinder head **(see illustration)**.

9 Lift the camshaft away from the cylinder head, and slide the oil seal off the camshaft end **(see illustration)**.

10 Obtain eight small, clean plastic containers, and number them 1 to 8; alternatively, divide a larger container into eight compartments. Using a rubber sucker, withdraw each follower in turn, and place it in its respective container. Do not interchange

11.9 . . . then lift the camshaft away from the cylinder head – 8-valve models

the cam followers, or the rate of wear will be much-increased. If necessary, also remove the shim from the top of the valve stem, and store it with its respective follower. Note that the shim may stick to the inside of the follower as it is withdrawn. If this happens, take care not to allow it to drop out as the follower is removed.

16-valve models

11 Remove both cylinder head covers as described in Section 4.
12 Refer to Section 9 and remove both camshaft sprockets together with their hubs, and also remove the timing belt tensioner pulley.
13 Remove the timing belt upper (inner) cover as described in Section 6.
14 Progressively slacken, by a few turns at a time, the twelve bolts securing each camshaft bearing housing to the cylinder head. Release the bearing housings from their dowels and cylinder head locations. When each housing is free, remove the bolts and washers completely, and lift off the bearing housings.
15 As both camshafts are identical, suitably mark them inlet and exhaust, or front and rear before removal.
16 Tilt the camshafts by pressing them down at their transmission end to release the centralising bearing at the timing belt end. Carefully lift the camshafts up and out of their locations and slide the oil seal off each camshaft end.
17 Obtain sixteen small, clean plastic containers, and number them inlet 1 to 8 and exhaust 1 to 8; alternatively, divide a larger container into sixteen compartments and number each compartment accordingly. Using a rubber sucker, withdraw each hydraulic tappet in turn, and place it in its respective container. Do not interchange the tappets, or the rate of wear will be much-increased.

Inspection

18 Examine the camshaft bearing surfaces and cam lobes for signs of wear ridges and scoring. Renew the camshaft if any of these conditions are apparent. Examine the condition of the bearing surfaces, both on the camshaft journals and in the cylinder head/bearing caps. If the head bearing surfaces are worn excessively, the cylinder head will need to be renewed. If suitable measuring equipment is available, camshaft bearing journal wear can be checked by direct measurement (where the necessary specifications have been quoted by Peugeot), noting that No 1 journal is at the transmission end of the head.
19 Examine the cam follower/hydraulic tappet bearing surfaces which contact the camshaft lobes for wear ridges and scoring. Renew any follower/tappet on which these conditions are apparent. If a follower/tappet bearing surface is badly scored, also examine the corresponding lobe on the camshaft for wear, as it is likely that both will be worn. Renew worn components as necessary.

Refitting

8-valve models

20 Where removed, refit each shim to the top of its original valve stem. *Do not* interchange the shims, as this will upset the valve clearances (see Section 12).
21 Liberally oil the cylinder head cam follower bores and the followers. Carefully refit the followers to the cylinder head, ensuring that each follower is refitted to its original bore. Some care will be required to enter the followers squarely into their bores.
22 Liberally oil the camshaft bearings and lobes, then refit the camshaft to the cylinder head. Temporarily refit the sprocket to the end of the shaft, and position it so that the sprocket timing hole is aligned with the corresponding cut-out in the cylinder head. Also ensure that the crankshaft is still locked in position (see Section 3).
23 Ensure that the bearing cap and head mating surfaces are completely clean, unmarked, and free from oil. Apply a smear of sealant to the thermostat housing mating surface of the left-hand (No. 1) bearing cap, then refit all the caps, using the identification marks noted on removal to ensure that each is installed correctly and in its original location.
24 Evenly and progressively tighten the camshaft bearing cap nuts by one turn at a time until the caps touch the cylinder head. Then go round again and tighten all the nuts to the specified torque setting. Work only as described, to impose the pressure of the valve springs gradually and evenly on the bearing caps.
25 Examine the oil supply pipe union O-rings for signs of damage or deterioration, and renew as necessary. Apply a smear of clean engine oil to the O-rings. Ease the pipe into position in the top of the bearing caps, taking great care not to displace the O-rings.
26 Examine the sealing washer for signs of damage or deterioration, and renew it if necessary. Refit the upper retaining bolt to the thermostat housing, tightening it securely.
27 Refit the ignition HT coil as described in Chapter 5B.
28 Fit a new camshaft oil seal, using the information given in Section 10, then refit the camshaft sprocket as described in Section 9.
29 Check the valve clearances as described in Section 12.
30 Refit the cylinder head cover as described in Section 4, and reconnect the battery negative terminal.

16-valve models

31 Before refitting, remove all traces of oil from the bearing housing retaining bolt holes in the cylinder head, using a clean rag. Also ensure that both the cylinder head and bearing housing mating faces are clean and free from oil.
32 Liberally oil the cylinder head hydraulic tappet bores and the tappets. Carefully refit the tappets to the cylinder head, ensuring that each tappet is refitted to its original bore.

Some care will be required to enter the tappets squarely into their bores. Check that each tappet rotates freely in its bore.
33 Liberally oil the camshaft bearings in the cylinder head and the camshaft lobes, then refit the camshafts to the cylinder head. Turn the camshafts so that the groove at the timing belt of each camshaft is positioned as follows:

1.8 litre models: Exhaust camshaft groove positioned at 12 o'clock, inlet camshaft groove at 11 o'clock.

2.0 litre models: Exhaust camshaft groove positioned at 3 o'clock, inlet camshaft groove at 11 o'clock.

34 Ensure that the four locating dowels are in position, one at each corner of the cylinder head.
35 Apply a bead of silicone-based jointing compound around the perimeter of the mating faces and around the retaining bolt hole locations.
36 Liberally oil the camshaft bearings and carefully locate the bearing housings over the camshafts. Refit the retaining bolts ensuring that each has a washer under its head.
37 Working sequence, progressively tighten the bearing housing retaining bolts to the Stage one torque setting then to the Stage two setting **(see illustration)**.
38 Refit the timing belt upper (inner) cover as described in Section 6.
39 Refit the timing belt tensioner pulley as described in Section 9.
40 Refit the cylinder head covers as described in Section 4.
41 Fit a new camshaft oil seal(s), using the information given in Section 10, then refit the camshaft sprocket(s) and hub(s) as described in Section 9.

12 Valve clearances (8-valve models) – checking and adjustment

Checking

1 The importance of having the valve clearances correctly adjusted cannot be

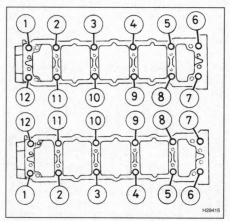

11.37 Camshaft bearing housing retaining bolt tightening sequence – 16-valve models

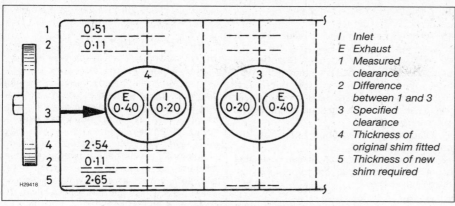
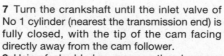

12.6 Example of valve shim thickness calculation

I Inlet
E Exhaust
1 Measured clearance
2 Difference between 1 and 3
3 Specified clearance
4 Thickness of original shim fitted
5 Thickness of new shim required

overstressed, as they vitally affect the performance of the engine. Checking should not be regarded as a routine operation, however. It should only be necessary when the valve gear has become noisy, after engine overhaul, or when trying to trace the cause of power loss. The clearances are checked as follows. The engine must be cold for the check to be accurate.

2 Firmly apply the handbrake, then jack up the front of the car and support it securely on axle stands (see *Jacking and vehicle support*). Remove the right-hand front roadwheel.

3 From underneath the front of the car, prise out the retaining clips, and remove the plastic cover from the wing valance to gain access to the crankshaft sprocket bolt. Where necessary, unclip the coolant hoses from the bracket to improve access further.

4 The engine can now be turned over using a suitable socket and extension bar fitted to the crankshaft pulley bolt.

5 Remove the cylinder head cover as described in Section 4.

6 Draw the outline of the engine on a piece of paper, numbering the cylinders 1 to 4, with No 1 cylinder at the transmission end of the engine. Show the position of each valve, together with the specified valve clearance (see paragraph 10). Above each valve, draw two lines for noting (1) the actual clearance and (2) the amount of adjustment required **(see illustration)**.

7 Turn the crankshaft until the inlet valve of No 1 cylinder (nearest the transmission end) is fully closed, with the tip of the cam facing directly away from the cam follower.

8 Using feeler blades, measure the clearance between the base of the cam and the follower **(see illustration)**. Record the clearance on line (1).

9 Repeat the measurement for the other seven valves, turning the crankshaft as necessary so that the cam lobe in question is always facing directly away from the relevant follower.

10 Calculate the difference between each measured clearance and the desired value, and record it on line (2). Since the clearance is different for inlet and exhaust valves, make sure that you are aware which valve you are dealing with. The valve sequence from either end of the engine is:

Ex – In – In – Ex – Ex – In – In – Ex

11 If all the clearances are correct, refit the cylinder head cover with reference to Section 4. Clip the coolant hoses into position (if removed) and refit the plastic cover to the wing valance. Refit the roadwheel, and lower the vehicle to the ground.

12 If any clearance measured is incorrect, adjustment must be carried out as described in the following paragraphs.

Adjustment

13 Remove the camshaft (see Section 11).

14 Withdraw the first follower from the cylinder head, and recover the shim from the top of the valve stem. Note that the shim may stick to the inside of the follower as it is withdrawn. If this happens, take care not to allow it to drop out as the follower is removed. Remove all traces of oil from the shim, and measure its thickness with a micrometer **(see illustrations)**. The shims usually carry thickness markings, but wear may have reduced the original thickness.

15 Refer to the clearance recorded for the valve concerned. If the clearance was more than that specified, the shim thickness must be *increased* by the difference recorded (2). If the clearance was less than that specified, the thickness of the shim must be *decreased* by the difference recorded (2).

16 Draw three more lines beneath each valve on the calculation paper, as shown in illustration 12.6. On line (4), note the measured thickness of the shim, then add or deduct the difference from line (2) to give the final shim thickness required on line (5).

17 Shims are available in thicknesses between 2.225 mm and 3.550 mm, in steps of 0.025 mm. Clean new shims before measuring or fitting them.

18 Repeat the procedure given in paragraphs 14 to 16 on the remaining valves, keeping each follower identified for position.

19 When reassembling, oil the shim, and fit it on the valve stem with the size marking face downwards. Oil the follower, and lower it onto the shim. Do not raise the follower after fitting, as the shim may become dislodged.

20 When all the followers are in position, complete with their shims, refit the camshaft as described in Section 11. Recheck the valve clearances before refitting the cylinder head cover, to make sure they are correct.

13 Cylinder head – removal and refitting

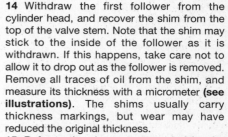

Removal

1 Disconnect the battery negative terminal (refer to *Disconnecting the battery* in the Reference Chapter).

12.8 Measuring a valve clearance using a feeler blade

12.14a Lift out the follower and remove the shim (arrowed)

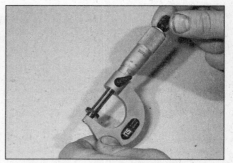

12.14b Using a micrometer to measure shim thickness

2 Drain the cooling system (see Chapter 1A).
3 Remove the timing belt as described in Section 7 or 8 as applicable.

8-valve models

4 Remove the cylinder head cover as described in Section 4.
5 Remove the air cleaner-to-throttle housing duct as described in Chapter 4C.
6 Note that the following text assumes that the cylinder head will be removed with both inlet and exhaust manifolds attached; this is easier, but makes it a bulky and heavy assembly to handle. If it is wished first to remove the manifolds, proceed as described in Chapter 4C.
7 Working as described in Chapter 4C, disconnect the exhaust system front pipe from the manifold. Where necessary, disconnect or release the lambda sensor wiring, so that it is not strained by the weight of the exhaust.
8 Carry out the following operations as described in Chapter 4C:
  a) *Depressurise the fuel system, and disconnect the fuel feed and return hoses. Plug all openings, to prevent loss of fuel and the entry of dirt into the system.*
  b) *Disconnect the accelerator cable.*
  c) *Disconnect the vacuum servo unit vacuum hose, and all the other relevant vacuum/breather hoses, from the inlet manifold and throttle housing. Release the hoses from the retaining clips on the manifold.*
  d) *Disconnect all the electrical connector plugs from the throttle housing.*
  e) *Disconnect the wiring connectors from the fuel injectors, and free the wiring loom from the manifold.*
9 Slacken the retaining clips, and disconnect the coolant hoses from the thermostat housing (on the left-hand end of the cylinder head).
10 Depress the retaining clip(s), and disconnect the wiring connector(s) from the electrical switch(es) and/or sensor(s) which are screwed into the thermostat housing, or into the left-hand end of the cylinder head (as appropriate).
11 Slacken and remove the bolt securing the engine oil dipstick tube to the left-hand end of the cylinder head, and withdraw the tube from the cylinder block.
12 Disconnect the wiring connector from the ignition HT coil. If the cylinder head is to be dismantled for overhaul, remove the ignition HT coil as described in Chapter 5B. Note that the HT leads should be disconnected from the spark plugs instead of the coil, and the coil and leads removed as an assembly. If the cylinder numbers are not already marked on the HT leads, number each lead to avoid the possibility of the leads being incorrectly connected on refitting.

16-valve models

13 Remove the air cleaner assembly and intake ducting as described in Chapter 4C.

14 Remove the cylinder head cover as described in Section 4.
15 Remove the inlet manifold as described in Chapter 4C.
16 Working as described in Chapter 4C, disconnect the exhaust system front pipe from the manifold. Where necessary, disconnect or release the lambda sensor wiring, so that it is not strained by the weight of the exhaust.
17 Disconnect the radiator hose from the coolant outlet elbow.
18 Disconnect all remaining vacuum/breather hoses, and all electrical connector plugs from the cylinder head.

All models

19 Working in the *reverse* of the sequence shown in illustration 13.37, progressively slacken the ten cylinder head bolts by half a turn at a time, until all bolts can be unscrewed by hand. Remove the bolts along with their washers (where fitted), noting the correct location of the spacer fitted to the front right-hand bolt on 1.8 litre 8-valve models.
20 With all the cylinder head bolts removed, the joint between the cylinder head and gasket and the cylinder block/crankcase must now be broken. On wet-liner engines, there is a risk of coolant and foreign matter leaking into the sump if the cylinder head is lifted carelessly. If care is not taken and the liners are moved, there is also a possibility of the bottom seals being disturbed, causing leakage after refitting the head.
21 To break the joint, obtain two L-shaped metal bars which fit into the cylinder head bolt holes, and gently 'rock' the cylinder head free towards the front of the car (see Part A, illustration 11.22). *Do not* try to swivel the head on the cylinder block/crankcase; it is located by dowels.
22 When the joint is broken, lift the cylinder head away. Seek assistance if possible, as it is a heavy assembly, especially if it is complete with the manifolds. Remove the gasket from the top of the block, noting the two locating dowels. If the locating dowels are a loose fit, remove them and store them with the head for safe-keeping. Do not discard the gasket; it will be needed for identification purposes.
23 On wet-liner engines, *do not* attempt to turn the crankshaft with the cylinder head removed, otherwise the liners may be displaced. Operations that require the crankshaft to be turned (eg, cleaning the piston crowns), should only be carried out once the cylinder liners are firmly clamped in position. In the absence of the special Peugeot liner clamps, the liners can be clamped in position as follows. Use large flat washers positioned underneath suitable-length bolts, or temporarily refit the original head bolts, with suitable spacers fitted to their shanks **(see illustration)**.
24 If the cylinder head is to be dismantled for overhaul, remove the camshaft(s) as

described in Section 11, then refer to Part E of this Chapter.

Preparation for refitting

25 The mating faces of the cylinder head and cylinder block/crankcase must be perfectly clean before refitting the head. Use a hard plastic or wooden scraper to remove all traces of gasket and carbon; also clean the piston crowns. On wet-liner engines, refer to paragraph 23 before turning the engine. Take particular care on these models, as the soft aluminium alloy is easily damaged. On all models, make sure that the carbon is not allowed to enter the oil and water passages – this is particularly important for the lubrication system, as carbon could block the oil supply to the engine's components. Using adhesive tape and paper, seal the water, oil and bolt holes in the cylinder block/crankcase. To prevent carbon entering the gap between the pistons and bores, smear a little grease in the gap. After cleaning each piston, use a small brush to remove all traces of grease and carbon from the gap, then wipe away the remainder with a clean rag. Clean all the pistons in the same way.
26 Check the mating surfaces of the cylinder block/crankcase and the cylinder head for nicks, deep scratches and other damage. If slight, they may be removed carefully with a file, but if excessive, machining may be the only alternative to renewal. If warpage of the cylinder head gasket surface is suspected, use a straight-edge to check it for distortion. Refer to Part E of this Chapter if necessary.
27 On wet-liner engines, check the cylinder liner protrusion as described in Part E of this Chapter.
28 When purchasing a new cylinder head gasket, it is essential that a gasket of the correct thickness is obtained. On some models only one thickness of gasket is available, so this is not a problem. However on other models, there are two different thicknesses available – the standard gasket which is fitted at the factory, and a slightly thicker 'repair' gasket (+ 0.2 mm), for use once the head gasket face has been machined. If the cylinder head has been machined, it should have the letter R stamped adjacent to the No 3 exhaust port, and the

13.23 Cylinder liners clamped in position using suitable bolts and large flat washers

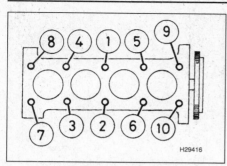

13.37 Cylinder head bolt tightening sequence

gasket should also have the letter R stamped adjacent to No 3 cylinder on its front upper face. The gaskets can also be identified as described in the following paragraph, using the cut-outs on the left-hand end of the gasket.

29 With the gasket fitted the correct way up on the cylinder block, there will be either a single hole, or a series of holes, punched in the tab on the left-hand end of the gasket. The standard (1.2 mm) gasket has only one hole punched in it (two on 2.0 litre, 16-valve models); the slightly thicker (1.4 mm) gasket has two holes punched in it (three on 2.0 litre, 16-valve models). Identify the gasket type, and ensure that the new gasket obtained is of the correct thickness. Note that modifications to the cylinder head gasket material, type, and manufacturer are constantly taking place; seek the advice of a Peugeot dealer as to the latest recommendations.

30 Check the condition of the cylinder head bolts, and particularly their threads, whenever they are removed. Wash the bolts in a suitable solvent, and wipe them dry. Check each bolt for any sign of visible wear or damage, renewing them if necessary. Measure the length of each bolt (without the washer fitted) from the underside of its head to the end of the bolt. The bolts may be re-used if their length does not exceed the following dimensions, according to bolt type.

1.8 litre 8-valve models:

Hexagon head bolt	176.5 mm
Torx head bolt	
(from engine No 2001330)	171.8 mm
1.8 litre 16-valve models	160.0 mm

2.0 litre 8-valve models:

Standard bolt without guiding	
end piece	122.0 mm
Bolt with guiding end piece at	
end of thread	124.5 mm
2.0 litre 16-valve models	112.0 mm

31 If any one bolt is longer than the specified length, *all* of the bolts should be renewed as a complete set. Note that modifications to the cylinder head bolts are constantly taking place; seek the advice of a Peugeot dealer as to the latest recommendations. Considering the stress which the cylinder head bolts are under, it is highly recommended that they are renewed, regardless of their apparent condition.

Refitting – 1.8 litre models

32 Wipe clean the mating surfaces of the cylinder head and cylinder block/crankcase. Check that the two locating dowels are in position at each end of the cylinder block/crankcase surface. Where applicable, remove the cylinder liner clamps.

33 Position a new gasket on the cylinder block/crankcase surface, ensuring that its identification holes or the projecting tongue are at the left-hand end of the gasket.

34 Check that the crankshaft pulley and camshaft sprocket(s) are still locked in position with their respective pins. With the aid of an assistant, carefully refit the cylinder head assembly to the block, aligning it with the locating dowels.

35 Apply a smear of grease to the threads, and to the underside of the heads, of the cylinder head bolts. Peugeot recommend the use of Molykote G Rapid Plus (available from your Peugeot dealer); in the absence of the specified grease, any good-quality high-melting-point grease may be used.

36 Carefully enter each bolt and washer into its relevant hole (*do not drop it in*) and screw it in finger-tight, not forgetting to fit the spacer to the rear right-hand bolt on 8-valve models.

37 The tightening procedure varies according to the type of cylinder head bolts fitted, which may be of the Torx head type, or of the conventional hexagon head type. Check which bolts are fitted, then proceed as follows according to bolt type.

Torx head bolts

a) *Working progressively and in sequence, tighten all the cylinder head bolts to their Stage 1 torque setting, using a torque wrench and a suitable socket* **(see illustration).**

b) *Starting with bolt number 1 in sequence, slacken the bolt completely then tighten it to the Stage 2 torque setting. Now angle-tighten bolt number 1 through the specified Stage 3 angle, using a socket and extension bar. It is recommended that an angle-measuring gauge is used during this stage of tightening, to ensure accuracy.*

c) *Repeat paragraph b on bolt number 2, then bolt number 3 and so on until all the bolts have been tightened to Stage 2 and Stage 3.*

d) *Angle-tighten each bolt in sequence through the specified Stage 4 angle.*

e) *Angle-tighten each bolt in sequence through the specified Stage 5 angle.*

Hexagon head bolts

a) *Working progressively and in sequence, tighten all the cylinder head bolts to their Stage 1 torque setting, using a torque wrench and a suitable socket* **(see illustration 13.37).**

b) *Once all the bolts have been tightened to their Stage 1 torque, fully slacken **all** the head bolts, working in the **reverse** of the*

tightening sequence. Once the bolts are loose, tighten all bolts to their Stage 2 torque setting, again following the specified sequence.

c) *With all the bolts tightened to their Stage 2 setting, working again in the specified sequence, angle-tighten the bolts through the specified Stage 3 angle, using a socket and extension bar. It is recommended that an angle-measuring gauge is used during this stage of tightening, to ensure accuracy.*

d) *Continue with the cylinder head refitting procedure, noting that the cylinder head bolts must be further tightened to the Stage 4 and 5 settings after the engine has been started and warmed-up, then stopped and allowed to cool completely.*

38 On 8-valve models, once the cylinder head bolts are correctly tightened, reconnect the wiring connector to the ignition HT coil. Otherwise, if the head was stripped for overhaul, refit the HT coil as described in Chapter 5B.

39 Refit and tension the timing belt as described in Section 7.

40 The remainder of the refitting procedure is a reversal of removal, noting the following points:

a) *Ensure that all wiring is correctly routed, and that all connectors are securely reconnected to the correct components.*

b) *Ensure that the coolant hoses are correctly reconnected, and that their retaining clips are securely tightened.*

c) *Ensure that all vacuum/breather hoses are correctly reconnected.*

d) *Refit the cylinder head cover as described in Section 4.*

e) *Reconnect the exhaust system to the manifold, refit the air cleaner housing and ducts, and adjust the accelerator cable, as described in Chapter 4C. If the manifolds were removed, refit these as described in Chapter 4C.*

f) *On completion, refill the cooling system as described in Chapter 1A, and reconnect the battery.*

41 On models fitted with hexagon head cylinder head bolts, carry out the following additional operations to complete the cylinder head tightening procedure.

42 Start the engine and allow it to warm-up until the cooling fan cuts in, then switch off and allow it to cool for at least two hours.

43 When the engine is completely cold, drain the cooling system as described in Chapter 1A, and remove the cylinder head cover as described in Section 4.

44 Fully slacken all the head bolts, working in the reverse of the tightening sequence. Once the bolts are loose, tighten all bolts to their Stage 4 torque setting, again following the specified sequence.

45 With all the bolts tightened to their Stage 4 setting, working again in the specified sequence, angle-tighten the bolts through the specified Stage 5 angle.

46 On completion, refit the cylinder head cover (Section 4) and refill the cooling system (Chapter 1A).

Refitting – 2.0 litre models

47 Wipe clean the mating surfaces of the cylinder head and cylinder block/crankcase. Check that the two locating dowels are in position at each end of the cylinder block/crankcase surface. Where applicable, remove the cylinder liner clamps.

48 Position a new gasket on the cylinder block/crankcase surface, ensuring that its identification holes or the projecting tongue are at the left-hand end of the gasket.

49 Refit the cylinder head as described above in paragraphs 34 to 36, ignoring the remark about the spacer fitted to the rear right-hand bolt.

50 Working progressively and in sequence **(see illustration 13.37)**, tighten the cylinder head bolts, to their Stage 1 torque setting using a torque wrench and suitable socket.

51 Once all the bolts have been tightened to their Stage 1 torque setting, tighten all bolts to their Stage 2 torque setting, again following the specified sequence.

52 With all the bolts tightened to their Stage 2 setting, working again in the specified sequence, angle-tighten the bolts through the specified Stage 3 angle, using a socket and extension bar. It is recommended that an angle-measuring gauge is used during this stage of tightening, to ensure accuracy.

53 Refit and tension the timing belt as described in Section 8.

54 The remainder of the refitting procedure is a reversal of removal, noting the points made in paragraph 40.

14 Sump – removal and refitting

Removal

1 Disconnect the battery negative terminal (refer to *Disconnecting the battery* in the Reference Chapter).

2 Drain the engine oil, then clean and refit the engine oil drain plug, tightening it securely. If the engine is nearing its service interval when the oil and filter are due for renewal, it is recommended that the filter is also removed, and a new one fitted. After reassembly, the engine can then be refilled with fresh oil. Refer to Chapter 1A for further information.

3 Firmly apply the handbrake, then jack up the front of the car and support it securely on axle stands (see *Jacking and vehicle support*).

4 On models with air conditioning, where the compressor is mounted onto the side of the sump, remove the drivebelt as described in Chapter 1A. Unbolt the compressor, and position it clear of the sump. Support the weight of the compressor by tying it to the vehicle, to prevent any excess strain being

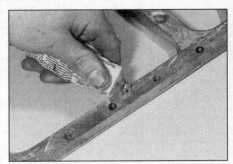

14.10a Where a sump spacer plate is fitted, apply sealant to the plate upper surface . . .

placed on the compressor lines. *Do not disconnect the refrigerant lines from the compressor* (refer to the warnings given in Chapter 3).

5 Where necessary, disconnect the wiring connector from the oil temperature sender unit, which is screwed into the sump.

6 Progressively slacken and remove all the sump retaining bolts. Since the sump bolts vary in length, remove each bolt in turn, and store it in its correct fitted order by pushing it through a clearly-marked cardboard template. This will avoid the possibility of installing the bolts in the wrong locations on refitting.

7 Break the joint by striking the sump with the palm of your hand. Lower the sump, and withdraw it from underneath the vehicle. Remove the gasket (where fitted), and discard it; a new one must be used on refitting. While the sump is removed, take the opportunity to check the oil pump pick-up/strainer for signs of clogging or splitting. If necessary, remove the pump as described in Section 15, and clean or renew the strainer.

8 On some models, a large spacer plate is fitted between the sump and the base of the cylinder block/crankcase. If this plate is fitted, undo the two retaining screws from diagonally-opposite corners of the plate. Remove the plate from the base of the engine, noting which way round it is fitted.

Refitting

9 Clean all traces of sealant/gasket from the mating surfaces of the cylinder block/crankcase and sump, then use a clean rag to wipe out the sump and the engine's interior.

10 Where a spacer plate is fitted, remove all traces of sealant/gasket from the spacer plate, then apply a thin coating of suitable sealant to the plate upper mating surface. Offer up the plate to the base of the cylinder block/crankcase, and securely tighten its retaining screws **(see illustrations)**.

11 On models where the sump was fitted without a gasket, ensure that the sump mating surfaces are clean and dry, then apply a thin coating of suitable sealant to the sump mating surface.

12 On models where the sump was fitted with a gasket, ensure that all traces of the old

14.10b . . . then refit the plate to the base of the cylinder block/crankcase

gasket have been removed, and that the sump mating surfaces are clean and dry. Position the new gasket on the top of the sump, using a dab of grease to hold it in position.

13 Offer up the sump to the cylinder block/crankcase. Refit its retaining bolts, ensuring that each is screwed into its original location. Tighten the bolts evenly and progressively to the specified torque setting.

14 Where necessary, align the air conditioning compressor with its mountings on the sump, and insert the retaining bolts. Securely tighten the compressor retaining bolts, then refit the drivebelt as described in Chapter 1A.

15 Reconnect the wiring connector to the oil temperature sensor (where fitted).

16 Lower the vehicle to the ground, then refill the engine with oil (see Chapter 1A).

15 Oil pump – removal, inspection and refitting

Removal

1 Remove the sump (see Section 14).

2 Where necessary, undo the two retaining screws, and slide the sprocket cover off the front of the oil pump.

3 Slacken and remove the three bolts securing the oil pump to the base of the cylinder block/crankcase. Disengage the pump sprocket from the chain, and remove the oil pump **(see illustration)**. Where

15.3 Removing the oil pump

15.5a Remove the oil pump cover retaining bolts . . .

15.5b . . . then lift off the cover and remove the spring . . .

15.5c . . . and relief valve piston, noting which way round it is fitted

necessary, also remove the spacer plate which is fitted behind the oil pump.

Inspection

Note: *On 1.8 litre 8-valve models from early 1994 onwards, the oil pump assembly was uprated in order to improve engine lubrication (this corresponded with the main bearing running clearance being decreased – see Chapter 2E). At overhaul, it is recommend that the uprated components are fitted in place of the originals. Refer to your Peugeot dealer for further information.*

4 Examine the oil pump sprocket for signs of damage and wear, such as chipped or missing teeth. If the sprocket is worn, the pump assembly must be renewed, since the sprocket is not available separately. It is also recommended that the chain and drive sprocket, fitted to the crankshaft, be renewed at the same time. To renew the chain and drive sprocket, first remove the crankshaft timing belt sprocket as described in Section 8. Unbolt the oil seal carrier from the cylinder block. The sprocket, spacer (where fitted) and chain can then be slid off the end of the crankshaft.

5 Slacken and remove the bolts (along with the baffle plate, where fitted) securing the strainer cover to the pump body. Lift off the strainer cover, and take off the relief valve piston and spring, noting which way round they are fitted **(see illustrations)**.

6 Examine the pump rotors and body for signs of wear ridges or scoring. If worn, the complete pump assembly must be renewed.

7 Examine the relief valve piston for signs of wear or damage, and renew if necessary. The condition of the relief valve spring can only be measured by comparing it with a new one; if there is any doubt about its condition, it should also be renewed. Both the piston and spring are available individually.

8 Thoroughly clean the oil pump strainer with a suitable solvent, and check it for signs of clogging or splitting. If the strainer is damaged, the strainer and cover assembly must be renewed.

9 Locate the relief valve spring and piston in the strainer cover. Refit the cover to the pump body, aligning the relief valve piston with its bore in the pump. Refit the baffle plate (where fitted) and the cover retaining bolts, and tighten them securely.

Refitting

10 Offer up the spacer plate (where fitted), then locate the pump sprocket with its drive chain. Seat the pump on the base of the cylinder block/crankcase. Refit the pump retaining bolts, and tighten them to the specified torque setting.

11 Where necessary, slide the sprocket cover into position on the pump. Refit its retaining bolts, tightening them securely.

12 Refit the sump as described in Section 14.

16 Oil cooler – removal and refitting

Removal

1 Firmly apply the handbrake, then jack up the front of the car and support it securely on axle stands (see *Jacking and vehicle support*).

2 Drain the cooling system as described in Chapter 1A. Alternatively, clamp the oil cooler coolant hoses directly above the cooler, and be prepared for some coolant loss as the hoses are disconnected.

16.5 Oil cooler/oil filter mounting bolt (A) and locating notch (B)

3 Position a suitable container beneath the oil filter. Unscrew the filter using an oil filter removal tool if necessary, and drain the oil into the container. If the oil filter is damaged or distorted during removal, it must be renewed. Given the low cost of a new oil filter relative to the cost of repairing the damage which could result if a re-used filter springs a leak, it is probably a good idea to renew the filter in any case.

4 Release the hose clips, and disconnect the coolant hoses from the oil cooler.

5 Unscrew the oil cooler/oil filter mounting bolt from the cylinder block, and withdraw the cooler. Note the locating notch in the cooler flange, which fits over the lug on the cylinder block **(see illustration)**. Discard the oil cooler sealing ring; a new one must be used on refitting.

Refitting

6 Fit a new sealing ring to the recess in the rear of the cooler, then offer the cooler to the cylinder block.

7 Ensure that the locating notch in the cooler flange is correctly engaged with the lug on the cylinder block, then refit the mounting bolt and tighten it securely.

8 Fit the oil filter, then lower the vehicle to the ground. Top-up the engine oil level as described in *Weekly checks*.

9 Refill or top-up the cooling system as described in Chapter 1A or *Weekly checks*. Start the engine, and check the oil cooler for signs of leakage.

17 Crankshaft oil seals – renewal

Right-hand oil seal

1 Remove the crankshaft sprocket and (where fitted) spacer as described in Section 9. Secure the timing belt clear of the working area, so that it cannot be contaminated with oil. Make a note of the correct fitted depth of the seal in its housing.

2 Punch or drill two small holes opposite each other in the seal. Screw a self-tapping

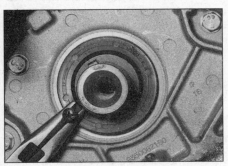

17.2 Using a self-tapping screw and pliers to remove the crankshaft oil seal

screw into each, and pull on the screws with pliers to extract the seal **(see illustration)**. Alternatively, the seal can be levered out of position. Use a flat-bladed screwdriver, and take great care not to damage the crankshaft shoulder or seal housing.

3 Clean the seal housing, and polish off any burrs or raised edges, which may have caused the seal to fail in the first place.

4 Lubricate the lips of the new seal with clean engine oil, and carefully locate the seal on the end of crankshaft. Note that its sealing lip must be facing inwards. Take care not to damage the seal lips during fitting.

5 Fit the new seal using a suitable tubular drift, such as a socket, which bears only on the hard outer edge of the seal. Tap the seal into position, to the same depth in the housing as the original was prior to removal.

6 Wash off any traces of oil, then refit the crankshaft sprocket as described in Section 8.

Left-hand oil seal

7 Remove the flywheel/driveplate as described in Section 18. Make a note of the correct fitted depth of the seal in its housing.

8 Punch or drill two small holes opposite each other in the seal. Screw a self-tapping screw into each, and pull on the screws with pliers to extract the seal.

9 Clean the seal housing, and polish off any burrs or raised edges, which may have caused the seal to fail in the first place.

10 Lubricate the lips of the new seal with

18.10 If the new flywheel bolt threads are not supplied with their threads precoated, apply a suitable thread-locking compound to them . . .

clean engine oil, and carefully locate the seal on the end of the crankshaft.

11 Fit the new seal using a suitable tubular drift, which bears only on the hard outer edge of the seal. Drive the seal into position, to the same depth in the housing as the original was prior to removal.

12 Wash off any traces of oil, then refit the flywheel/driveplate as described in Section 18.

---

18 Flywheel/driveplate – removal, inspection and refitting

Removal

Flywheel

1 Remove the transmission as described in Chapter 7A, then remove the clutch assembly as described in Chapter 6.

2 Prevent the flywheel from turning by locking the ring gear teeth with a similar arrangement to that described in Section 5. Alternatively, bolt a strap between the flywheel and the cylinder block/crankcase. *Do not* attempt to lock the flywheel in position using the crankshaft pulley locking pin described in Section 3.

3 Slacken and remove the flywheel retaining bolts, and remove the flywheel from the end of the crankshaft. Be careful not to drop it; it is heavy. If the flywheel locating dowel is a loose fit in the crankshaft end, remove it and store it with the flywheel for safe-keeping. Discard the flywheel bolts; new ones must be used on refitting.

Driveplate

4 Remove the transmission as described in Chapter 7B. Lock the driveplate as described in paragraph 2. Mark the relationship between the torque converter plate and the driveplate, and slacken all the driveplate retaining bolts.

5 Remove the retaining bolts, along with the torque converter plate and the two shims (one fitted on each side of the torque converter plate). Note that the shims are of different thickness, the thicker one being on the outside of the torque converter plate. Discard

18.12 . . . then refit the flywheel, and tighten the bolts to the specified torque

the driveplate retaining bolts; new ones must be used on refitting.

6 Remove the driveplate from the end of crankshaft. If the locating dowel is a loose fit in the crankshaft end, remove it and store it with the driveplate for safe-keeping.

Inspection

7 On models with manual transmission, examine the flywheel for scoring of the clutch face, and for wear or chipping of the ring gear teeth. If the clutch face is scored, the flywheel may be surface-ground, but renewal is preferable. Seek the advice of a Peugeot dealer or engine reconditioning specialist to see if machining is possible. If the ring gear is worn or damaged, the flywheel must be renewed, as it is not possible to renew the ring gear separately.

8 On models with automatic transmission, check the torque converter driveplate carefully for signs of distortion. Look for any hairline cracks around the bolt holes or radiating outwards from the centre, and inspect the ring gear teeth for signs of wear or chipping. If any sign of wear or damage is found, the driveplate must be renewed.

Refitting

Flywheel

9 Clean the mating surfaces of the flywheel and crankshaft. Remove any remaining locking compound from the threads of the crankshaft holes, using the correct size of tap, if available.

> **HAYNES HINT**
> *If a suitable tap is not available, cut two slots along the threads of one of the old flywheel bolts, and use the bolt to remove the locking compound from the threads.*

10 If the new flywheel retaining bolts are not supplied with their threads already precoated, apply a suitable thread-locking compound to the threads of each bolt **(see illustration)**.

11 Ensure that the locating dowel is in position. Offer up the flywheel, locating it on the dowel, and fit the new retaining bolts.

12 Lock the flywheel using the method employed on dismantling, and tighten the retaining bolts to the specified torque **(see illustration)**.

13 Refit the clutch as described in Chapter 6. Remove the flywheel locking tool, and refit the transmission as described in Chapter 7A.

Driveplate

14 Carry out the operations described above in paragraphs 9 and 10, substituting 'driveplate' for all references to the flywheel.

15 Locate the driveplate on its locating dowel.

16 Offer up the torque converter plate, with the thinner shim positioned behind the plate and the thicker shim on the outside, and align the marks made prior to removal.

17 Fit the new retaining bolts, then lock the driveplate using the method employed on dismantling. Tighten the retaining bolts to the specified torque wrench setting.

18 Remove the driveplate locking tool, and refit the transmission (see Chapter 7B).

19 Engine/transmission mountings – inspection and renewal

Inspection

1 Firmly apply the handbrake, then jack up the front of the car and support it securely on axle stands (see *Jacking and vehicle support*).

2 Check the mounting rubber to see if it is cracked, hardened or separated from the metal at any point; renew the mounting if any such damage or deterioration is evident.

3 Check that all the mounting's fasteners are securely tightened; use a torque wrench to check if possible.

4 Using a large screwdriver or a crowbar, check for wear in the mounting by carefully levering against it to check for free play. Where this is not possible, enlist the aid of an assistant to move the engine/transmission back-and-forth, or from side-to-side, while you watch the mounting. While some free play is to be expected even from new components, excessive wear should be obvious. If excessive free play is found, check first that the fasteners are correctly secured, then renew any worn components as described below.

Right-hand mounting renewal

1.8 litre 8-valve models

5 Disconnect the battery negative terminal (refer to *Disconnecting the battery* in the Reference Chapter). Release all the relevant hoses and wiring from their retaining clips, and position them clear of the mounting so that they do not hinder the removal procedure.

6 Place a jack beneath the engine, with a block of wood on the jack head. Raise the jack until it is supporting the weight of the engine.

7 Slacken and remove the three nuts securing the right-hand mounting bracket to the engine. Remove the single nut securing the bracket to the mounting rubber, and lift off the bracket.

8 Lift the rubber buffer plate off the mounting rubber stud, then unscrew the mounting rubber from the body and remove it from the vehicle. If necessary, the mounting bracket can be unbolted and removed from the side of the cylinder head.

9 Check all components carefully for signs of wear or damage, and renew them where necessary.

10 On reassembly, screw the mounting rubber into the vehicle body, and tighten it securely. Where removed, refit the mounting bracket to the side of the cylinder head, apply a drop of locking compound to the retaining bolts and tighten them to the specified torque.

11 Refit the rubber buffer plate to the mounting rubber stud, and install the mounting bracket.

12 Tighten the mounting bracket retaining nuts to the specified torque setting.

13 Remove the jack from underneath the engine, and reconnect the battery negative terminal.

2.0 litre 8-valve models

14 Disconnect the battery negative terminal (refer to *Disconnecting the battery* in the Reference Chapter). Release all the relevant hoses and wiring from their retaining clips, and position them clear of the mounting so that they do not hinder the removal procedure.

15 Place a jack beneath the engine, with a block of wood on the jack head. Raise the jack until it is supporting the weight of the engine.

16 Undo the two bolts securing the curved mounting retaining plate to the body. Lift off the plate, and withdraw the rubber damper from the top of the mounting bracket.

17 Slacken and remove the two nuts and two bolts securing the right-hand engine/transmission mounting bracket to the engine. Remove the single nut securing the bracket to the mounting rubber, and lift off the bracket.

18 Lift the rubber buffer plate off the mounting rubber stud, then unscrew the mounting rubber from the body and remove it from the vehicle. If necessary, the mounting bracket can be unbolted and removed from the front of the cylinder block.

19 Check all components carefully for signs of wear or damage, and renew as necessary.

20 On reassembly, screw the mounting rubber into the vehicle body, and tighten it securely. Where removed, refit the mounting bracket to the front of the cylinder head, and securely tighten its retaining bolts.

21 Refit the rubber buffer plate to the mounting rubber stud, and install the mounting bracket.

22 Tighten the mounting bracket retaining nuts to the specified torque setting, and remove the jack from underneath the engine.

23 Refit the rubber damper to the top of the mounting bracket, and refit the curved retaining plate. Tighten the retaining plate bolts to the specified torque, and reconnect the battery.

16-valve models

24 Disconnect the battery negative terminal (refer to *Disconnecting the battery* in the Reference Chapter). Release all the relevant hoses and wiring from their retaining clips, and position them clear of the mounting so that they do not hinder the removal procedure.

25 Place a jack beneath the engine, with a block of wood on the jack head. Raise the jack until it is supporting the weight of the engine.

26 Slacken and remove the two nuts and two bolts securing the right-hand engine/transmission mounting bracket to the engine. Remove the single nut securing the bracket to the mounting rubber.

27 Undo the bolt securing the upper engine movement limiter to the right-hand mounting bracket, and the four bolts securing the movement limiter mounting bracket to the body. Lift away the right-hand mounting bracket and the movement limiter assembly.

28 Lift the rubber buffer plate off the mounting rubber stud, then unscrew the mounting rubber from the body and remove it from the vehicle. If necessary, the mounting bracket can be unbolted and removed from the front of the cylinder block.

29 Check all components carefully for signs of wear or damage, and renew as necessary.

30 On reassembly, screw the mounting rubber into the vehicle body, and tighten it securely. Refit the mounting bracket to the front of the cylinder head, and securely tighten its retaining bolts.

31 Refit the engine movement limiter assembly to the engine mounting bracket and to the body and tighten the bolts to the specified torque.

32 Refit the rubber buffer plate to the mounting rubber stud, and install the mounting bracket.

33 Tighten the mounting bracket retaining nuts to the specified torque setting. Remove the jack from underneath the engine and reconnect the battery.

Left-hand mounting renewal

34 Remove the battery and battery tray, as described in Chapter 5A.

35 Place a jack beneath the transmission, with a block of wood on the jack head. Raise the jack until it is supporting the weight of the transmission.

36 Slacken and remove the centre nut and washer from the left-hand mounting, then undo the nuts securing the mounting in position and remove it from the engine compartment.

37 If necessary, slide the spacer (where fitted) off the mounting stud, then unscrew the stud from the top of the transmission housing, and remove it along with its washer. If the mounting stud is tight, a universal stud extractor can be used to unscrew it.

38 Check all components carefully for signs of wear or damage, and renew as necessary.

39 Clean the threads of the mounting stud, and apply a coat of thread-locking compound to its threads. Refit the stud and washer to the top of the transmission, and tighten it to the specified torque setting.

40 Slide the spacer (where fitted) onto the mounting stud, then refit the rubber mounting. Tighten both the mounting-to-body bolts and the mounting centre nut to their specified torque settings, and remove the jack from underneath the transmission.

41 Refit the battery support plate, tightening its retaining bolts securely, then refit the battery as described in Chapter 5A.

Rear mounting renewal

42 Refer to Part A of this Chapter, Section 16.

Notes

Chapter 2 Part C: 1.8 and 1.9 litre XUD diesel engine in-car repair procedures

Contents

Degrees of difficulty

Easy, suitable for novice with little experience	**Fairly easy,** suitable for beginner with some experience	**Fairly difficult,** suitable for competent DIY mechanic	**Difficult,** suitable for experienced DIY mechanic	**Very difficult,** suitable for expert DIY or professional

Specifications

General

Designation:
- 1769 cc engine XUD7
- 1905 cc engines XUD9

Engine codes*:
- 1769 cc engine . . . . A9A (XUD7 L)
- 1905 cc engine:
    - Non-turbo models . . . . D9B (XUD9A L), DJY (XUD9A) or DJZ (XUD9 Y)
    - Turbo models . . . . D8A (XUD9TE L) or DHY (XUD9TE Y)

Bore:
- 1769 cc engines . . . . 80.00 mm
- 1905 cc engines . . . . 83.00 mm

Stroke:
- 1769 cc and 1905 cc engines . . . . 88.00 mm

Direction of crankshaft rotation . . . . Clockwise (viewed from the right-hand side of vehicle)

No 1 cylinder location . . . . At the transmission end of block

Compression ratio (typical):
- 1769 cc engine . . . . 23 : 1
- 1905 cc engine:
    - Non-turbo engine . . . . 23 : 1
    - Turbo engine . . . . 21.8 : 1

*The engine code is stamped on a plate attached to the front of the cylinder block.

Compression pressures (engine hot, at cranking speed)

Normal . . . . 25 to 30 bars (363 to 435 psi)
Minimum . . . . 18 bars (261 psi)
Maximum difference between any two cylinders . . . . 5 bars (73 psi)

Camshaft

Drive . . . . Toothed belt
No of bearings 3
Endfloat . . . . 0.07 to 0.16 mm

Valve clearances (engine cold)

Inlet . . . . 0.15 ± 0.05 mm
Exhaust . . . . 0.30 ± 0.05 mm

Lubrication system

Oil pump type	Gear-type, chain-driven off the crankshaft right-hand end
Minimum oil pressure at 90°C:	
Non-turbo models	3.5 bars at 4000 rpm
Turbo models	4.9 bars at 4000 rpm
Oil pressure warning switch operating pressure	0.8 bars

Torque wrench settings

	Nm	lbf ft
Big-end bearing cap nuts:		
Stage 1	20	15
Stage 2	Tighten through a further 70°	
Camshaft bearing cap nuts	20	15
Camshaft sprocket bolt	45	33
Crankshaft front oil seal housing bolts	16	12
Crankshaft pulley bolt:		
Stage 1	40	30
Stage 2	Tighten through a further 50°	
Cylinder head bolts:		
Non-turbo models:		
Stage 1	20	15
Stage 2	60	44
Stage 3	Tighten through a further 180°	
Turbo models:		
Stage 1	20	15
Stage 2	60	44
Stage 3	Tighten through a further 220°	
Cylinder head cover bolts	20	15
Engine-to-transmission fixing bolts	45	33
Left-hand engine/transmission mounting:		
Mounting bracket-to-body bolts	25	18
Mounting stud	25	18
Centre nut	65	48
Engine/transmission rear mounting:		
Mounting assembly-to-block bolts	45	33
Mounting link-to-mounting bolt	50	37
Mounting link-to-subframe bolt	70	52
Engine/transmission right-hand mounting:		
Engine (tensioner assembly) bracket bolts	18	13
Mounting bracket retaining nuts	45	33
Curved retaining plate bolts	20	15
Flywheel/driveplate bolts	50	37
Injection pump sprocket nut	50	37
Injection pump sprocket puller retaining screws	10	7
Main bearing cap bolts	70	52
Oil pump mounting bolts	13	10
Piston oil jet spray tube bolt - Turbo models	10	7
Sump bolts	19	14
Timing belt cover bolts	8	6
Timing belt tensioner adjustment bolt	18	13
Timing belt tensioner pivot nut	18	13

1 General information

Using this Chapter

Chapter 2 is divided into five Parts; A, B, C, D and E. Repair operations that can be carried out with the engine in the vehicle are described in Parts A (1.1, 1.4 and 1.6 litre TU series petrol engines), B (1.8 and 2.0 litre XU series petrol engines), C (1.8 and 1.9 litre XUD series diesel engines) and D (1.9 and 2.0 litre DW series diesel engines). Part E covers the removal of the engine/transmission as a unit, and describes the engine dismantling and overhaul procedures.

In Parts A, B, C and D, the assumption is made that the engine is installed in the vehicle, with all ancillaries connected. If the engine has been removed for overhaul, the preliminary dismantling information which precedes each operation may be ignored.

XUD engine description

The XUD engine is a well-proven modern unit which has appeared in many Peugeot and Citroën vehicles. The engine is of four-cylinder overhead camshaft design, mounted transversely, with the transmission mounted on the left-hand side.

A toothed timing belt drives the camshaft, fuel injection pump and coolant pump. Followers are fitted between the camshaft and valves. Valve clearance adjustment is by means of shims. The camshaft is supported by three bearings machined directly in the cylinder head.

The crankshaft runs in five main bearings of the usual shell type. Endfloat is controlled by thrustwashers either side of No 2 main bearing.

The pistons are selected to be of matching weight, and incorporate fully-floating gudgeon pins retained by circlips.

The oil pump is chain-driven from the front of the crankshaft. An oil cooler is fitted to all engines.

The design of the Turbo engine is the same

as the normally-aspirated (non-turbo) version, but components such as the crankshaft, pistons and connecting rods are uprated. It also incorporates oil jets which spray oil onto the undersides of the pistons to keep them cool.

Throughout the manual, it is often necessary to identify the engines not only by their cubic capacity, but also by their engine code. The engine code, consists of three letters (eg. D9B). The code is stamped on a plate attached to the front of the cylinder block.

Repair operations possible with the engine in the vehicle

The following operations can be carried out without having to remove the engine from the vehicle:

a) Removal and refitting of the cylinder head.
b) Removal and refitting of the timing belt and sprockets.
c) Removal and refitting of the camshaft.
d) Removal and refitting of the sump.
e) Removal and refitting of the big-end bearings, connecting rods, and pistons*.
f) Removal and refitting of the oil pump.
g) Renewal of the engine/transmission mountings.
h) Removal and refitting of the flywheel/driveplate.

*Although it is possible to remove these components with the engine in place, for reasons of access and cleanliness it is recommended that the engine is removed.

2 Compression and leakdown tests - description and interpretation

Compression test

Note: *A compression tester specifically designed for Diesel engines must be used for this test.*

1 When engine performance is down, or if misfiring occurs which cannot be attributed to the fuel system, a compression test can provide diagnostic clues as to the engine's condition. If the test is performed regularly, it can give warning of trouble before any other symptoms become apparent.

2 A compression tester specifically intended for Diesel engines must be used, because of the higher pressures involved. The tester is connected to an adapter which screws into the glow plug or injector hole. On these models, an adapter suitable for use in the injector holes will be required, due to the limited access to the glow plug holes **(see illustration)**. It is unlikely to be worthwhile buying such a tester for occasional use, but it may be possible to borrow or hire one - if not, have the test performed by a garage.

3 Unless specific instructions to the contrary are supplied with the tester, observe the following points:

a) The battery must be in a good state of charge, the air filter must be clean, and the engine should be at normal operating temperature.
b) All the injectors or glow plugs should be removed before starting the test. If removing the injectors, also remove the flame shield washers, otherwise they may be blown out.
c) The stop solenoid must be disconnected, to prevent the engine from running or fuel from being discharged.

4 There is no need to hold the accelerator pedal down during the test, because the Diesel engine air inlet is not throttled.

5 The actual compression pressures measured are not so important as the balance between cylinders. Values are given in the Specifications.

6 The cause of poor compression is less easy to establish on a Diesel engine than on a petrol one. The effect of introducing oil into the cylinders ("wet" testing) is not conclusive, because there is a risk that the oil will sit in the swirl chamber or in the recess on the piston crown instead of passing to the rings. However, the following can be used as a rough guide to diagnosis.

7 All cylinders should produce very similar pressures; any difference greater than that specified indicates the existence of a fault. Note that the compression should build up quickly in a healthy engine; low compression on the first stroke, followed by gradually-increasing pressure on successive strokes, indicates worn piston rings. A low compression reading on the first stroke, which does not build up during successive strokes, indicates leaking valves or a blown head gasket (a cracked head could also be the cause). Deposits on the undersides of the valve heads can also cause low compression.

8 A low reading from two adjacent cylinders is almost certainly due to the head gasket having blown between them; the presence of coolant in the engine oil will confirm this.

9 If the compression reading is unusually high, the cylinder head surfaces, valves and pistons are probably coated with carbon deposits. If this is the case, the cylinder head should be removed and decarbonised (see Part D).

Leakdown test

10 A leakdown test measures the rate at which compressed air fed into the cylinder is lost. It is an alternative to a compression test, and in many ways it is better, since the escaping air provides easy identification of where pressure loss is occurring (piston rings, valves or head gasket).

11 The equipment needed for leakdown testing is unlikely to be available to the home mechanic. If poor compression is suspected, have the test performed by a suitably-equipped garage.

2.2 Performing a compression test

3 Engine assembly/valve timing holes - general information and usage

Caution: Do not attempt to rotate the engine whilst the crankshaft/ camshaft/injection pump are locked in position. If the engine is to be left in this state for a long period of time, it is a good idea to place suitable warning notices inside the vehicle, and in the engine compartment. This will reduce the possibility of the engine being accidentally cranked on the starter motor, which is likely to cause damage with the locking pins in place.

1 On all models, timing holes are drilled in the camshaft sprocket, injection pump sprocket and flywheel. The holes are used to align the crankshaft, camshaft and injection pump, and to prevent the possibility of the valves contacting the pistons when refitting the cylinder head, or when refitting the timing belt. When the holes are aligned with their corresponding holes in the cylinder head and cylinder block (as appropriate), suitable diameter bolts/pins can be inserted to lock both the camshaft, injection pump and crankshaft in position, preventing them from rotating unnecessarily. Proceed as follows.
Note: *With the timing holes aligned, No. 4 cylinder is at TDC on its compression stroke.*

2 Remove the upper timing belt covers as described in Section 6.

3 The crankshaft must now be turned until the three bolt holes in the camshaft and injection pump sprockets (one hole in the camshaft sprocket, two holes in the injection pump sprocket) are aligned with the corresponding holes in the engine front plate. The crankshaft can be turned by using a spanner on the pulley bolt. To gain access to the pulley bolt, from underneath the front of the car, prise out the two retaining clips and remove the plastic cover from the wing valance, to gain access to the crankshaft pulley bolt. Where necessary, unclip the coolant hoses from the bracket, to improve access further. The crankshaft can then be turned using a suitable socket and extension bar fitted to the pulley bolt. Note that the crankshaft must always be turned in a

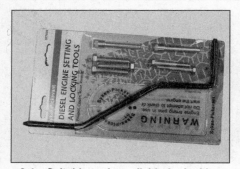

3.4a Suitable tools available for locking engine in position

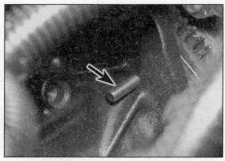

3.4b Rod (arrowed) inserted through cylinder block into timing hole in flywheel

2 Disconnect the breather hose from the front of the camshaft cover and, where necessary, remove the inlet duct from the inlet manifold.
3 Unscrew the securing bolt and remove the fuel hose bracket from the right-hand end of the cylinder head cover **(see illustration)**.
4 Note the locations of any brackets secured by the three cylinder head cover bolts, then unscrew the bolts. Recover the metal and fibre washers under each bolt **(see illustration)**.
5 Carefully move any hoses clear of the cylinder head cover.
6 Lift off the cover, and recover the rubber seal **(see illustration)**. Examine the seal for signs of damage and deterioration, and if necessary, renew it.

Refitting

7 Refitting is a reversal of removal, bearing in mind the following points:
  a) *Refit any brackets in their original positions noted before removal.*
  b) *Where applicable, refit the intercooler or the air distribution housing, as described in Chapter 4D.*

3.5a Bolt (arrowed) inserted through timing hole in camshaft sprocket

3.5b Bolts (arrowed) inserted through timing holes in injection pump sprocket

clockwise direction (viewed from the right-hand side of the vehicle).
4 Insert an 8 mm diameter rod or drill through the hole in the left-hand flange of the cylinder block by the starter motor; if necessary,

carefully turn the crankshaft either way until the rod enters the timing hole in the flywheel **(see illustrations)**.
5 Insert three 8 mm bolts through the holes in the camshaft and fuel injection pump sprockets, and screw them into the engine finger-tight **(see illustrations)**.
6 The crankshaft, camshaft and injection pump are now locked in position, preventing unnecessary rotation.

5 Crankshaft pulley - removal and refitting

1 Refer to Chapter 2B, Section 5. Although not strictly necessary, it is recommended that the retaining bolt is renewed whenever it is disturbed, due to its tightening sequence (see Specifications at the start of this Part). **Note:** *If the engine is in the car and it proves impossible to hold on the brakes, remove the starter motor and use the locking tool shown to retain the flywheel* **(see illustration)**.

4.3 Removing the fuel hose bracket from the cylinder head cover

4 Cylinder head cover - removal and refitting

Removal

1 Remove the intercooler (Turbo models) or the air distribution housing (non-turbo models with a D9B engine) - see Chapter 4D.

6 Timing belt covers - removal and refitting

Removal

Upper front cover - early models

1 If procedures are to be carried out which involve removal of the timing belt, remove the right-hand engine mounting-to-body bracket

4.4 Remove the retaining bolts and washers . . .

4.6 . . . and lift off the cylinder head cover

5.1 Notched tool (arrowed) positioned on ring gear teeth to lock flywheel

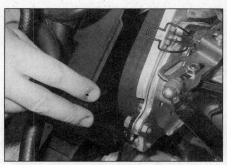

6.3 Removing the upper front timing belt cover - early models

6.5 Removing the upper rear timing belt cover - early models

6.9 Lower timing belt cover securing bolts (arrowed)

as described in Section 9. This will greatly improve access.

2 Release the upper spring clip from the cover.

3 Release the lower securing lug using a screwdriver, then lift the cover upwards from the engine **(see illustration)**.

Upper rear cover - early models

4 Remove the upper front cover as described previously.

5 Release the two securing clips, manipulate the cover over the studs on the front of the engine, then withdraw the cover upwards **(see illustration)**. Clearance is limited, and if desired, access can be improved by removing the engine mounting bracket (see Section 9).

Upper front cover - later models

6 Slacken and remove the retaining screw and

nut, and remove the cover from the engine.

Upper rear cover - later models

7 Remove the front cover as described in paragraph 6, then undo the retaining bolts and remove the rear cover from the engine.

Lower cover - early models

8 Remove the crankshaft pulley as described in Section 5.

9 Unscrew the two securing bolts and remove the cover **(see illustration)**.

Lower cover - later models

10 Remove the crankshaft pulley as described in Section 5.

11 Remove both upper covers as described previously.

12 Slacken and remove the retaining nuts and bolts, and remove the lower cover.

Refitting

13 Refitting is a reversal of the relevant removal procedure, ensuring that each cover section is correctly located, and that the cover retaining nuts and/or bolts are tightened to the specified torque.

7 Timing belt - removal, inspection, refitting and tensioning

1 The timing belt drives the camshaft, injection pump, and coolant pump from a toothed sprocket on the front of the crankshaft. The belt also drives the brake vacuum pump indirectly via the rear ("flywheel") end of the camshaft. If the belt breaks or slips in service, the pistons are likely to hit the valve heads, resulting in expensive damage.

2 The timing belt should be renewed at the specified intervals, or earlier if it is contaminated with oil, or at all noisy in operation (a "scraping" noise due to uneven wear).

3 If the timing belt is being removed, it is a wise precaution to check the condition of the coolant pump at the same time (check for signs of coolant leakage). This may avoid the need to remove the timing belt again at a later stage, should the coolant pump fail.

Removal

4 Align the engine assembly/valve timing holes as described in Section 3, and lock the camshaft sprocket, injection pump sprocket and flywheel in position. *Do not* attempt to rotate the engine whilst the pins are in position.

5 Remove the crankshaft pulley as described in Section 5.

6 Remove the right-hand engine mounting-to-body bracket as described in Section 9.

7 Loosen the timing belt tensioner pivot nut and adjustment bolt, then turn the tensioner bracket anti-clockwise to release the tension. Retighten the adjustment bolt to hold the tensioner in the released position. If available, use a 10 mm square drive extension in the hole provided, to turn the tensioner bracket against the spring tension **(see illustration)**.

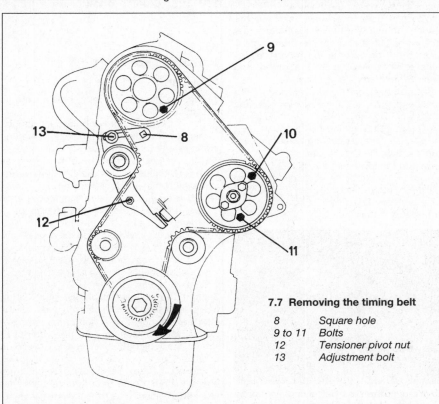

7.7 Removing the timing belt

8	Square hole
9 to 11	Bolts
12	Tensioner pivot nut
13	Adjustment bolt

7.8a Mark the timing belt with an arrow to indicate its running direction

7.8b Removing the timing belt

7.13 Locate the timing belt on the sprockets as described in text

8 Mark the timing belt with an arrow to indicate its running direction, if it is to be re-used. Remove the belt from the sprockets **(see illustrations)**.

Inspection

9 Check the timing belt carefully for any signs of uneven wear, split or oil contamination. Pay particular attention to the roots of the teeth. Renew it if there is the slightest doubt about its condition. If the engine is undergoing an overhaul, and has covered more than 36 000 miles (60 000 km) with the existing belt fitted, renew the belt as a matter of course, regardless of its apparent condition. The cost of a new belt is nothing compared with the cost of repairs, should the belt break in service. If signs of oil contamination are found, trace the source of the oil leak and rectify it. Wash down the engine timing belt area and all related components, to remove all traces of oil. Check that the tensioner and idler pulley rotates freely, without any sign of roughness. If necessary, renew as described in Sections 9 and 10 (as applicable).

Refitting and tensioning

10 Commence refitting by ensuring that the 8 mm bolts are still fitted to the camshaft and fuel injection pump sprockets, and that the rod/drill is positioned in the timing hole in the flywheel.

11 Locate the timing belt on the crankshaft sprocket, making sure that, where applicable, the direction of rotation arrow is facing the correct way.

12 Engage the timing belt with the crankshaft

sprocket, hold it in position, then feed the belt over the remaining sprockets in the following order:
  a) Idler roller.
  b) Fuel injection pump.
  c) Camshaft.
  d) Tensioner roller.
  e) Coolant pump.

13 Be careful not to kink or twist the belt. To ensure correct engagement, locate only a half-width on the injection pump sprocket before feeding the timing belt onto the camshaft sprocket, keeping the belt taut and fully engaged with the crankshaft sprocket. Locate the timing belt fully onto the sprockets **(see illustration)**.

14 Unscrew and remove the 8 mm locking bolts from the camshaft and fuel injection pump sprockets, and remove the rod/drill from the timing hole in the flywheel.

15 With the pivot nut loose, slacken the tensioner adjustment bolt while holding the bracket against the spring tension. Slowly release the bracket until the roller presses against the timing belt. Retighten the adjustment bolt and the pivot nut.

16 Rotate the crankshaft through two complete turns in the normal running direction (clockwise). **Do not** rotate the crankshaft backwards, as the timing belt must be kept tight between the crankshaft, fuel injection pump and camshaft sprockets.

17 Loosen the tensioner adjustment bolt and the pivot nut to allow the tensioner spring to push the roller against the timing belt, then tighten both the adjustment bolt and pivot nut to the specified torque.

18 Check that the timing holes are all correctly positioned by reinserting the sprocket locking bolts and the rod/drill in the flywheel timing hole, as described in Section 3. If the timing holes are not correctly positioned, the timing belt has been incorrectly fitted (possibly one tooth out on one of the sprockets) - in this case, repeat the refitting procedure from the beginning.

19 Refit the upper timing belt covers as described in Section 6, but do not lower the vehicle to the ground until the engine mounting-to-body bracket has been refitted.

20 Refit the right-hand engine mounting-to-body bracket, with reference to Section 9.

21 Refit the crankshaft pulley as described in Section 5.

8 Timing belt sprockets - removal and refitting

Camshaft sprocket

Removal

1 Remove the upper timing belt covers as described in Section 6.

2 The camshaft sprocket bolt must now be loosened. The camshaft must be prevented from turning as the sprocket bolt is unscrewed, and this can be done in one of two ways, as follows **(see illustrations)**. Do not remove the camshaft sprocket bolt at this stage.
  a) Make up a tool similar to that shown, and use it to hold the sprocket stationary by means of the holes in the sprocket.
  b) Remove the cylinder head cover as described in Section 4. Prevent the camshaft from turning by holding it with a suitable spanner on the lug between Nos 3 and 4 camshaft lobes.

3 Align the engine assembly/valve timing holes as described in Section 3, and lock the camshaft sprocket, injection pump sprocket and flywheel in position. *Do not* attempt to rotate the engine whilst the pins are in position.

4 Loosen the timing belt tensioner pivot nut and adjustment bolt, then turn the tensioner bracket anti-clockwise to release the tension, and retighten the adjustment bolt to hold the

8.2a Using a home-made tool to prevent the camshaft sprocket from turning

8.2b Holding the camshaft using a spanner on the lug between Nos 3 and 4 lobes

8.7 Withdrawing the camshaft sprocket

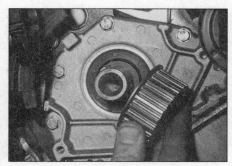

8.16 Withdrawing the crankshaft sprocket

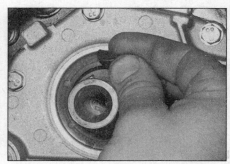

8.17 Removing the Woodruff key from the end of the crankshaft

tensioner in the released position. If available, use a 10 mm square drive extension in the hole provided, to turn the tensioner bracket against the spring tension. Slip the timing belt off the sprocket.

5 Slacken and remove the camshaft sprocket retaining bolt and washer.

6 Unscrew and remove the locking bolt from the camshaft sprocket.

7 With the retaining bolt removed, slide the sprocket off the end of the camshaft **(see illustration)**. If the locating peg is a loose fit in the rear of the sprocket, remove it for safe-keeping. Examine the camshaft oil seal for signs of oil leakage and, if necessary, renew it as described in Section 16.

Refitting

8 Where applicable, refit the Woodruff key to the end of the camshaft, then refit the camshaft sprocket. Note that the sprocket will only fit one way round (with the protruding centre boss against the camshaft), as the end of the camshaft is tapered.

9 Refit the sprocket retaining bolt and washer. Tighten the bolt to the specified torque, preventing the camshaft from turning as during removal.

10 Where applicable, refit the cylinder head cover as described in Section 4.

11 Align the holes in the camshaft sprocket and the engine front plate, and refit the 8 mm bolt to lock the camshaft in position.

12 Fit the timing belt around the fuel injection pump sprocket (where applicable) and the camshaft sprocket, and tension the timing belt as described in Section 7.

13 Refit the upper timing belt covers as described in Section 6.

Crankshaft sprocket

Removal

14 Remove the crankshaft pulley as described in Section 5.

15 Proceed as described in paragraphs 1, 3 and 4.

16 Disengage the timing belt from the crankshaft sprocket, and slide the sprocket off the end of the crankshaft **(see illustration)**.

17 Remove the Woodruff key from the crankshaft, and store it with the sprocket for safe-keeping **(see illustration)**.

18 Examine the crankshaft oil seal for signs of oil leakage and, if necessary, renew it as described in Section 16.

Refitting

19 Refit the Woodruff key to the end of the crankshaft, then refit the crankshaft sprocket (with the flange nearest the cylinder block).

20 Fit the timing belt around the crankshaft sprocket, and tension the timing belt as described in Section 7.

21 Refit the crankshaft pulley as described in Section 5.

Fuel injection pump sprocket
Removal

22 Proceed as described in paragraphs 1, 3 and 4.

23 Make alignment marks on the fuel injection pump sprocket and the timing belt, to ensure that the sprocket and timing belt are correctly aligned on refitting.

24 Remove the 8 mm bolts securing the fuel injection pump sprocket in the TDC position.

25 On certain models, the sprocket may be fitted with a built-in puller, which consists of a plate bolted to the sprocket. The plate contains a captive nut (the sprocket securing nut), which is screwed onto the fuel injection pump shaft. On models not fitted with the built-in puller, a suitable puller can be made up using a short length of bar, and two M7 bolts screwed into the holes provided in the sprocket.

26 The fuel injection pump shaft must be prevented from turning as the sprocket nut is unscrewed, and this can be achieved using a tool similar to that shown **(see illustration)**.

Use the tool to hold the sprocket stationary by means of the holes in the sprocket.

27 On models with a built-in puller, unscrew the sprocket securing nut until the sprocket is freed from the taper on the pump shaft, then withdraw the sprocket. Recover the Woodruff key from the end of the pump shaft if it is loose. If desired, the puller assembly can be removed from the sprocket by removing the two securing screws and washers.

28 On models not fitted with a built-in puller, partially unscrew the sprocket securing nut, then fit the improvised puller, and tighten the two bolts (forcing the bar against the sprocket nut), until the sprocket is freed from the taper on the pump shaft **(see illustration)**. Withdraw the sprocket, and recover the Woodruff key from the end of the pump shaft if it is loose. Remove the puller from the sprocket.

Refitting

29 Where applicable, refit the Woodruff key to the pump shaft, ensuring that it is correctly located in its groove.

30 Where applicable, if the built-in puller assembly has been removed from the sprocket, refit it, and tighten the two securing screws to the specified torque, ensuring that the washers are in place.

31 Refit the sprocket, then tighten the securing nut to the specified torque, preventing the pump shaft from turning as during removal.

32 Make sure that the 8 mm bolts are fitted to the camshaft and fuel injection pump sprockets, and that the rod/drill is positioned in the flywheel timing hole.

8.26 Using a home-made tool to prevent the injection pump sprocket from turning

8.28 Home-made puller fitted to fuel injection pump sprocket

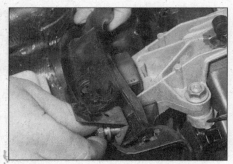

9.4 Remove the curved retaining plate . . .

9.5 . . . and lift the rubber buffer out from the engine mounting

9.6 Removing the engine mounting-to-body bracket

33 Fit the timing belt around the fuel injection pump sprocket, ensuring that the marks made on the belt and sprocket before removal are aligned.

34 Tension the timing belt (see Section 7).

35 Refit the upper timing belt covers as described in Section 6.

Coolant pump sprocket

36 The coolant pump sprocket is integral with the pump, and cannot be removed.

9 Right-hand engine mounting bracket and timing belt tensioner - removal and refitting

General

1 The timing belt tensioner is operated by a spring and plunger housed in the right-hand engine mounting bracket, which is bolted to the end face of the engine. The engine mounting is attached to the mounting on the body via the engine mounting-to-body bracket.

Right-hand engine mounting-to-body bracket

Removal

2 Before removing the bracket, the engine must be supported, preferably using a suitable hoist and lifting tackle attached to the lifting bracket at the right-hand end of the engine. Alternatively, the engine can be supported using a trolley jack and interposed

block of wood beneath the sump, in which case, be prepared for the engine to tilt backwards when the bracket is removed.

3 Release the retaining clips, and position all the relevant hoses and cables clear of the engine mounting assembly and suspension top mounting.

4 Unscrew the two retaining bolts, and remove the curved retaining plate from the top of the mounting **(see illustration)**.

5 Lift out the rubber buffer to expose the engine mounting bracket-to-body securing nut **(see illustration)**.

6 Unscrew the three nuts securing the bracket to the engine mounting, and the single nut securing the bracket to the body, then lift off the bracket **(see illustration)**.

Refitting

7 Refitting is a reversal of removal. Tighten the nuts and bolts to the specified torque.

Timing belt tensioner and right-hand engine mounting bracket

Note: *A suitable tool will be required to retain the timing belt tensioner plunger during this operation.*

Removal

8 Remove the engine mounting-to-body bracket as described previously in this Section, and remove the auxiliary drivebelt as described in Chapter 1B.

9 If not already done, support the engine with a trolley jack and interposed block of wood beneath the sump.

10 Where applicable, disconnect the hoist and lifting tackle supporting the engine from the right-hand lifting bracket (this is necessary because the lifting bracket is attached to the engine mounting bracket, and must be removed).

11 Unscrew the two retaining bolts and remove the engine lifting bracket.

12 Align the engine assembly/valve timing holes as described in Section 3, and lock the camshaft sprocket, injection pump sprocket and flywheel in position. *Do not* rotate the engine whilst the pins are in position.

13 Loosen the timing belt tensioner pivot nut and adjustment bolt, then turn the tensioner bracket anti-clockwise until the adjustment bolt is in the middle of the slot, and retighten the adjustment bolt. Use a 10 mm square drive extension in the hole provided, to turn the tensioner bracket against the spring tension.

14 Mark the timing belt with an arrow to indicate its running direction, if it is to be re-used. Remove the belt from the sprockets.

15 A tool must now be obtained in order to hold the tensioner plunger in the engine mounting bracket.

16 The Peugeot tool is designed to slide in the two lower bolt holes of the mounting bracket. It should be easy to fabricate a similar tool out of sheet metal, using 10 mm bolts and nuts instead of metal rods **(see Tool Tip)**.

17 Unscrew the two lower engine mounting bracket bolts, then fit the special tool **(see illustrations)**. Grease the inner surface of the tool, to prevent any damage to the end of the

TOOL TiP

Fabricated tool for holding tensioner plunger in engine mounting bracket

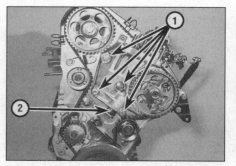

9.17a View of timing belt end of engine

1 Engine mounting bracket retaining bolts
2 Timing belt tensioner plunger

9.17b Tool in place to hold tensioner plunger in engine mounting bracket - timing belt removed for clarity

tensioner plunger. Unscrew the pivot nut and adjustment bolt, and withdraw the tensioner assembly.

18 Remove the two remaining engine mounting bracket bolts, and withdraw the bracket.

19 Compress the tensioner plunger into the engine mounting bracket, remove the special tool, then withdraw the plunger and spring.

Refitting

20 Refitting is a reversal of removal, bearing in mind the following points:
  a) *Tighten all fixings to the specified torque.*
  b) *Refit and tension the timing belt as described in Section 7.*
  c) *Refit and tighten the auxiliary drivebelt as described in Chapter 1B.*

---

10 Timing belt idler roller - removal and refitting

Removal

1 Remove the auxiliary drivebelt as described in Chapter 1B.

2 Align the engine assembly/valve timing holes as described in Section 3, and lock the camshaft sprocket, injection pump sprocket and flywheel in position. *Do not* rotate the engine whilst the pins are in position.

3 Loosen the timing belt tensioner pivot nut and adjustment bolt, then turn the tensioner bracket anti-clockwise to release the tension, and retighten the adjustment bolt to hold the tensioner in the released position. If available, use a 10 mm square drive extension in the hole provided, to turn the tensioner bracket against the spring tension.

4 Unscrew the two bolts and the stud securing the idler roller assembly to the cylinder block, noting that the upper bolt also secures the engine mounting bracket.

5 Slightly loosen the remaining four engine mounting bolts, noting that the uppermost bolt is on the inside face of the engine front plate, and also secures the engine lifting bracket. Slide out the idler roller assembly.

Refitting

6 Refitting is a reversal of removal, bearing in mind the following points:
  a) *Tighten all fixings to the specified torque.*
  b) *Tension the timing belt as described in Section 7.*
  c) *Refit and tension the auxiliary drivebelt as described in Chapter 1B.*

---

11 Camshaft and followers - removal, inspection and refitting

Removal

1 Remove the cylinder head cover as described in Section 4.

2 Remove the camshaft sprocket as described in Section 8.

3 Remove the braking system vacuum pump as described in Chapter 9.

4 The camshaft bearing caps should be numbered from the flywheel end of the engine **(see illustration)**. If the caps are not already numbered, identify them, numbering them from the flywheel end of the engine, and making the marks on the manifold side.

5 Progressively unscrew the nuts, then remove the bearing caps.

6 Lift the camshaft from the cylinder head. Remove the oil seal from the timing belt end of the camshaft. Discard the seal, a new one should be used on refitting.

7 Obtain eight small, clean plastic containers, and number them 1 to 8; alternatively, divide a larger container into eight compartments. Using a rubber sucker, withdraw each follower in turn, and place it in its respective container. Do not interchange the cam followers, or the rate of wear will be much-increased. If necessary, also remove the shim from the top of the valve stem, and store it with its respective follower. Note that the shim may stick to the inside of the follower as it is withdrawn. If this happens, take care not to allow it to drop out as the follower is removed.

Inspection

8 Examine the camshaft bearing surfaces and cam lobes for signs of wear ridges and scoring. Renew the camshaft if any of these conditions are apparent. Examine the condition of the bearing surfaces, both on the camshaft journals and in the cylinder head/bearing caps. If the head bearing surfaces are worn excessively, the cylinder head will need to be renewed. If suitable measuring equipment is available, camshaft bearing journal wear can be checked by direct measurement (where the necessary specifications have been quoted by Peugeot), noting that No 1 journal is at the transmission end of the head.

9 Examine the cam follower bearing surfaces which contact the camshaft lobes for wear ridges and scoring. Renew any follower on which these conditions are apparent. If a follower bearing surface is badly scored, also examine the corresponding lobe on the camshaft for wear, as it is likely that both will be worn. Renew worn components as necessary.

Refitting

10 To prevent any possibility of the valves contacting the pistons as the camshaft is refitted, remove the locking rod/drill from the flywheel and turn the crankshaft a quarter turn in the *opposite* direction to normal rotation, to position all the pistons at mid-stroke. Release the timing belt from the injection pump sprocket while turning the crankshaft.

11 Where removed, refit each shim to the top of its original valve stem. *Do not* interchange the shims, as this will upset the valve

11.4 Camshaft bearing cap identification mark (arrowed)

clearances (see Section 12).

12 Liberally oil the cylinder head cam follower bores and the followers. Carefully refit the followers to the cylinder head, ensuring that each follower is refitted to its original bore. Some care will be required to enter the followers squarely into their bores.

13 Lubricate the cam lobes and bearing journals with clean engine oil of the specified grade.

14 Position the camshaft in the cylinder head, passing it through the engine front plate.

15 Temporarily locate the sprocket on the end of the camshaft, and turn the shaft so that the sprocket timing hole is aligned with the corresponding cut-out in the cylinder head. Remove the sprocket.

16 Fit the centre bearing cap the correct way round as previously noted, then screw on the nuts and tighten them two or three turns.

17 Apply sealing compound to the end bearing caps on the areas shown **(see illustration)**. Fit them in the correct positions, and tighten the nuts two or three turns.

18 Tighten all the nuts progressively to the specified torque, making sure that the camshaft remains correctly positioned.

19 Check that the camshaft endfloat is as given in the Specifications, using a feeler blade. If not, the camshaft and/or the cylinder head must be renewed. To check the endfloat, push the camshaft fully towards one end of the cylinder head, and insert a feeler blade between the thrust faces of one of the camshaft lobes and a bearing cap **(see illustration)**.

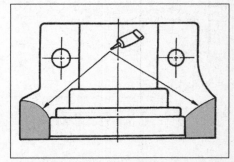

11.17 Apply sealing compound to the end camshaft bearing caps on the areas shown

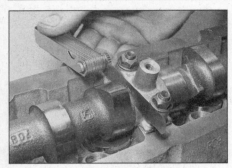

11.19 Checking the camshaft endfloat using a feeler blade

20 If the original camshaft is being refitted, and it is known that the valve clearances are correct, proceed to the next paragraph. Otherwise, check and adjust the valve clearances as described in Section 12.

21 Smear the lips of the new oil seal with clean engine oil and fit it onto the camshaft end, making sure its sealing lip is facing inwards. Press the oil seal in until it is flush with the end face of the camshaft bearing cap.

22 Refit the braking system vacuum pump as described in Chapter 9.

23 Again, temporarily locate the sprocket on the end of the camshaft, and make sure that the sprocket timing hole is aligned with the corresponding cut-out in the cylinder head.

24 Turn the crankshaft a quarter turn in the normal direction of rotation so that pistons 1 and 4 are again at TDC.

25 Refit the rod/drill to the flywheel timing hole.

26 Refit the camshaft sprocket as described in Section 8.

27 Refit the cylinder head cover as described in Section 4.

---

12 Valve clearances - checking and adjustment

Checking

1 The importance of having the valve clearances correctly adjusted cannot be overstressed, as they vitally affect the performance of the engine. Checking should not be regarded as a routine operation, however. It should only be necessary when the valve gear has become noisy, after engine overhaul, or when trying to trace the cause of power loss. The clearances are checked as follows. The engine must be cold for the check to be accurate.

2 Chock the rear wheels then jack up the front of the car and support it on axle stands (see *"Jacking and Vehicle Support"*). Remove the right-hand front roadwheel.

3 From underneath the front of the car, prise out the two retaining clips, and remove the plastic cover from the wing valance to gain access to the crankshaft sprocket bolt. Where necessary, unclip the coolant hoses from the bracket to improve access further.

4 The engine can now be turned over using a suitable socket and extension bar fitted to the crankshaft pulley bolt.

HAYNES HiNT *The engine will be easier to turn if the fuel injectors or glow plugs are removed.*

5 Remove the cylinder head cover as described in Section 4.

6 On a piece of paper, draw the outline of the engine with the cylinders numbered from the flywheel end. Show the position of each valve, together with the specified valve clearance. Above each valve, draw lines for noting (1) the actual clearance and (2) the amount of adjustment required **(see illustration)**.

7 Turn the crankshaft until the inlet valve of No 1 cylinder (nearest the transmission) is fully closed, with the tip of the cam facing directly away from the bucket tappet.

8 Using feeler blades, measure the clearance between the base of the cam and the bucket tappet **(see illustration)**. Record the clearance on line (1).

9 Repeat the measurement for the other seven valves, turning the crankshaft as necessary so that the cam lobe in question is always facing directly away from the relevant tappet.

10 Calculate the difference between each measured clearance and the desired value, and record it on line (2). Since the clearance is different for inlet and exhaust valves - make sure that you are aware which valve you are dealing with. The valve sequence from either end of the engine is:

In - Ex - Ex - In - In - Ex - Ex - In

11 If all the clearances are within tolerance, refit the cylinder head cover with reference to Section 4, and where applicable, lower the vehicle to the ground. If any clearance measured is outside the specified tolerance, adjustment must be carried out as described in the following paragraphs.

Adjustment

12 Remove the camshaft as described in Section 11.

13 Withdraw the first follower and its shim. Be careful that the shim does not fall out of the tappet. Clean the shim, and measure its thickness with a micrometer. The shims carry

---

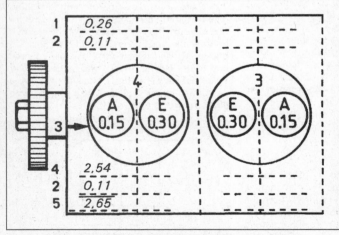

12.6 Example of valve shim thickness calculation

A	Inlet
E	Exhaust
1	Measured clearance
2	Difference between 1 and 3
3	Specified clearance
4	Thickness of shim fitted
5	Thickness of shim required

12.8 Measuring a valve clearance using a feeler blade

13.4 Disconnecting the vacuum hose from the braking system vacuum pump

13.5 Disconnecting a fuel injector leak-off hose

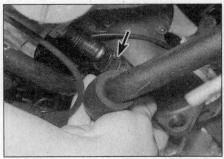

13.8 Disconnecting the coolant hose (arrowed) from the rear of the cylinder head

thickness markings, but wear may have reduced the original thickness, so be sure to check.

14 Refer to the clearance recorded for the valve concerned. If the clearance was more than that specified, the shim thickness must be increased by the difference recorded (2). If the clearance was less than that specified, the thickness of the shim must be decreased by the difference recorded (2).

15 Draw three more lines beneath each valve on the calculation paper, as shown in illustration 12.6. On line (4) note the measured thickness of the shim, then add or deduct the difference from line (2) to give the final shim thickness required on line (5).

16 Repeat the procedure given in paragraphs 13 to 15 on the remaining valves, keeping each tappet identified for position.

17 When reassembling, oil the shim and fit it into the valve retainer, with the size marking face downwards. Oil the follower, and lower it onto the shim. Do not raise the follower after fitting, as the shim may become dislodged.

18 When all the followers are in position, complete with their shims, refit the camshaft as described in Section 11. Recheck the valve clearances before refitting the camshaft cover, to make sure they are correct.

13 Cylinder head - removal and refitting

Note: *This is an involved procedure, and it is suggested that the Section is read thoroughly*

before starting work. To aid refitting, make notes on the locations of all relevant brackets and the routing of hoses and cables before removal.

Removal

1 Disconnect the battery negative terminal (refer to *"Disconnecting the battery"* in the Reference Section of this manual).

2 Drain the cooling system as described in Chapter 1B.

3 Remove the inlet and exhaust manifolds as described in Chapter 4D. Alternatively (particularly on Turbo models), remove the inlet manifold, then unscrew the exhaust manifold securing nuts, remove the spacers, and remove the manifold studs from the cylinder head (using a stud extractor or two nuts locked together). The exhaust manifold can then be left in place complete with the turbocharger. Ensure that the manifold and turbocharger are adequately supported, taking particular care not to strain the turbocharger oil feed pipe.

4 Slacken the retaining clip and disconnect the vacuum hose from the braking system vacuum pump **(see illustration)**.

5 Disconnect and remove the fuel injector leak-off hoses **(see illustration)**.

6 Disconnect the fuel pipes from the fuel injectors and the fuel injection pump, and remove the pipes as described in Chapter 4D.

7 Unscrew the securing nut and disconnect the feed wire from the relevant glow plug. Recover the washers.

8 Disconnect the coolant hose from the rear, left-hand end of the cylinder head **(see illustration)**.

9 Disconnect the small coolant hose from the front timing belt end of the cylinder head **(see illustration)**.

10 Unclip the fuel return hose from the brackets on the cylinder head, and move it to one side **(see illustration)**.

11 Disconnect the accelerator cable from the fuel injection pump (refer to Chapter 4D if necessary), and move the cable clear of the cylinder head.

12 Remove the fuel filter/thermostat housing as described in Chapter 3.

13 Unscrew the nut or stud securing the coolant hose bracket and the engine lifting bracket to the transmission end of the cylinder head.

14 Remove the camshaft sprocket as described in Section 8.

15 Remove the timing belt tensioner and the right-hand engine mounting bracket as described in Section 9.

16 Remove the timing belt idler roller as described in Section 10.

17 Remove the bolt securing the engine front plate to the fuel injection pump mounting bracket.

18 Remove the nut and bolt securing the engine front plate and the alternator mounting bracket to the fuel injection pump mounting bracket, then remove the engine front plate.

19 Progressively unscrew the cylinder head bolts, in the reverse order to that shown in illustration 13.34 **(see illustration)**.

20 Lift out the bolts and recover the spacers **(see illustration)**.

21 Release the cylinder head from the cylinder block and location dowel by rocking it.

13.9 Disconnecting the coolant hose (arrowed) from the front of the head

13.10 Unclip the fuel return hose from its brackets

13.19 Unscrewing a cylinder head bolt

13.20 Removing a cylinder head bolt and spacer

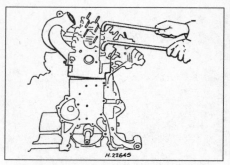

13.21 Freeing the cylinder head using angled rods

13.22 Removing the cylinder head

The Peugeot tool for doing this consists simply of two metal rods with 90-degree angled ends **(see illustration)**. Do not prise between the mating faces of the cylinder head and block, as this may damage the gasket faces.

22 Lift the cylinder head from the block, and recover the gasket **(see illustration)**.

Gasket selection

23 Check that the timing belt is clear of the fuel injection pump sprocket, then turn the crankshaft until pistons 1 and 4 are at TDC. Position a dial test indicator (dial gauge) on the cylinder block, and zero it on the block face. Transfer the probe to the centre of No 1 piston, then slowly turn the crankshaft back and forth past TDC, noting the highest reading on the indicator. Record this reading.

24 Repeat this measurement procedure on No 4 piston, then turn the crankshaft half a turn (180°) and repeat the procedure on Nos 2 and 3 pistons **(see illustration)**.

25 If a dial test indicator is not available, piston protrusion may be measured using a straight-edge and feeler blades or vernier calipers. However, this is much less accurate, and cannot therefore be recommended.

26 Note down the greatest piston protrusion measurement, and use this to determine the correct cylinder head gasket from the following table. The notches or holes at the corner of the gasket are used for thickness identification. The notches or holes near the centre-line of the gasket identify the engine capacity and type, and have no significance for the gasket thickness **(see illustration)**.

Piston protrusion	Gasket identification
0.56 to 0.67 mm	*1 notch*
0.68 to 0.71 mm	*2 notches*
0.72 to 0.75 mm	*3 notches*
0.76 to 0.79 mm	*4 notches*
0.80 to 0.83 mm	*5 notches*

Cylinder head bolt examination

27 A number of different cylinder head bolt types have been used on the XUD engines during the course of production, of both hexagon head and Torx head arrangement. If working on an engine fitted with the earlier hexagon head type bolts, these **must** be renewed once disturbed, and replaced with the latest Torx head type. The Torx head type bolts are supplied in two versions, one version with a guiding end-piece at the base of the thread, and one version without an end-piece. It is permissible to re-use the Torx type bolts providing that their length does not exceed the figures shown below. Note that, if a bolt is modified to locate the gasket (see paragraph 30), a new bolt will be required when finally refitting the cylinder head.

28 Measure the length of each bolt from the base of the head to the end of the shank (or guiding end-piece) **(see illustration)**. Compare the results with the values given in the following table, to determine whether the bolts and spacers should be renewed. **Note:** *Considering the stress which the cylinder head bolts are under, it is highly recommended that they are renewed, regardless of their apparent condition.*

Non-turbo models

Bolt length	Action required
Bolts without guiding end-piece:	
Below 121.5 mm	*Re-use bolts/spacers*
Above 121.5 mm	*Renew bolts/spacers*
Bolts with guiding end-piece:	
Below 125.5 mm	*Re-use bolts/spacers*
Above 125.5 mm	*Renew bolts/spacers*

Turbo models

Bolt length	Action required
Bolts without guiding end-piece:	
Below 146.5 mm	*Re-use bolts/spacers*
Above 146.5 mm	*Renew bolts/spacers*
Bolts with guiding end-piece:	
Below 150.5 mm	*Re-use bolts/spacers*
Above 150.5 mm	*Renew bolts/spacers*

Refitting

29 Turn the crankshaft clockwise (viewed from the timing belt end) until Nos 1 and 4 pistons pass bottom dead centre (BDC) and begin to rise, then position them halfway up their bores. Nos 2 and 3 pistons will also be at their mid-way positions, but descending their bores.

30 Fit the correct gasket the right way round on the cylinder block, with the identification notches or holes at the flywheel/driveplate end of the engine. Make sure that the locating dowel is in place at the timing belt end of the

13.24 Measuring piston protrusion

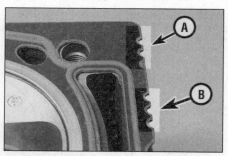

13.26 Cylinder head gasket thickness identification notches (A). Also note engine capacity and type identification notches (B)

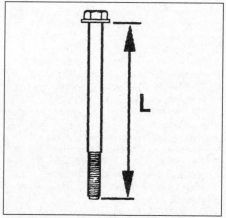

13.28 Measure the length (L) of the cylinder head bolts, to determine whether renewal is required

block. Note that, as there is only one locating dowel, it is possible for the gasket to move as the cylinder head is fitted, particularly when the cylinder head is fitted with the engine in the car (due to the inclination of the engine). In the worst instance, this can allow the pistons and/or the valves to hit the gasket, causing engine damage. To avoid this problem, saw the head off a cylinder head bolt, and file (or cut) a slot in the end of the bolt, to enable it to be turned with a screwdriver. Screw the bolt into one of the bolt holes at the flywheel/driveplate end of the cylinder block, then fit the gasket over the bolt and location dowel. This will ensure that the gasket is held in position as the cylinder head is fitted.

31 Lower the cylinder head onto the block.

32 Apply a smear of grease to the threads, and to the underside of the heads, of the cylinder head bolts. Peugeot recommend the use of Molykote G Rapid Plus (available from your Peugeot dealer); in the absence of the specified grease, any good-quality high-melting-point grease may be used.

33 Carefully enter each bolt and spacer (convex sides uppermost, where applicable) into its relevant hole (*do not drop it in*) and screw it in finger-tight. Where applicable, after fitting three or four bolts to locate the cylinder head, unscrew the modified bolt fitted in paragraph 30, and fit a new bolt in its place.

34 Working progressively and in the sequence shown, tighten the cylinder head bolts to their Stage 1 torque setting, using a torque wrench and suitable socket **(see illustration)**.

35 Once all the bolts have been tightened to their Stage 1 torque setting, working again in the specified sequence, tighten each bolt to the specified Stage 2 setting. Finally, angle-tighten the bolts through the specified Stage 3 angle. It is recommended that an angle-measuring gauge is used during this stage of tightening, to ensure accuracy.

36 The remainder of the refitting procedure is a reversal of removal, noting the following points:

a) *Ensure that all wiring is correctly routed, and that all connectors are securely reconnected to the correct components.*

b) *Ensure that the coolant hoses are correctly reconnected, and that their retaining clips are securely tightened.*

c) *Ensure that all vacuum/breather hoses are correctly reconnected.*

d) *Refit the cylinder head cover as described in Section 4.*

e) *Reconnect the exhaust system to the manifold, refit the air cleaner housing and ducts, and adjust the accelerator cable, as described in Chapter 4D. If the manifolds were removed, refit these as described in Chapter 4D.*

f) *Refill the cooling system as described in Chapter 1B.*

g) *Reconnect the battery and bleed the fuel system as described in Chapter 4D.*

14 Sump -
removal and refitting

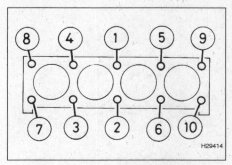

Refer to Chapter 2B, Section 13.

15 Oil pump and drive chain -
removal, inspection and refitting

Refer to Chapter 2B, Section 14.

16 Oil seals -
renewal

Crankshaft right-hand oil seal

1 Remove the timing belt crankshaft sprocket as described in Section 8.

2 Note the fitted depth of the oil seal.

3 Pull the oil seal from the housing using a hooked instrument. Alternatively, drill a small hole in the oil seal, and use a self-tapping screw and a pair of pliers to remove it **(see illustration)**.

4 Clean the oil seal housing and the crankshaft sealing surface.

5 Dip the new oil seal in clean engine oil, and press it into the housing (open end first) to the previously-noted depth, using a suitable tube or socket. A piece of thin plastic or tape wound around the front of the crankshaft is useful to prevent damage to the oil seal as it is fitted.

6 Where applicable, remove the plastic or tape from the end of the crankshaft.

7 Refit the timing belt crankshaft sprocket as described in Section 8.

Crankshaft left-hand oil seal

8 Remove the flywheel/driveplate, as described in Section 18.

9 Proceed as described in paragraphs 2 to 6, noting that when fitted, the outer lip of the oil seal must point outwards; if it is pointing inwards, use a piece of bent wire to pull it out. Take care not to damage the oil seal.

10 Refit the flywheel/driveplate, as described in Section 18.

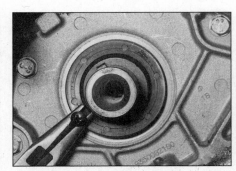

16.3 Self-tapping screw and pliers used to remove the crankshaft right-hand oil seal

16.12 Removing the camshaft right-hand oil seal

13.34 Cylinder head bolt tightening sequence

Camshaft right-hand oil seal

11 Remove the camshaft sprocket as described in Section 8. In principle there is no need to remove the timing belt completely, but remember that if the belt has been contaminated with oil, it must be renewed.

12 Pull the oil seal from the housing using a hooked instrument **(see illustration)**. Alternatively, drill a small hole in the oil seal and use a self-tapping screw and a pair of pliers to remove it.

13 Clean the oil seal housing and the camshaft sealing surface.

14 Smear the new oil seal with clean engine oil, then fit it over the end of the camshaft, open end first. A piece of thin plastic or tape wound round the front of the camshaft should prevent damage to the oil seal as it is fitted.

15 Press the seal into the housing until it is flush with the end face of the cylinder head. Use an M10 bolt (screwed into the end of the camshaft), washers and a suitable tube or socket to press the seal into position.

16 Refit the camshaft sprocket as described in Section 8.

17 Where applicable, fit a new timing belt as described in Section 7.

Camshaft left-hand oil seal

18 No oil seal is fitted to the left-hand end of the camshaft. The sealing is provided by an O-ring fitted to the vacuum pump flange. The O-ring can be renewed after unbolting the pump from the cylinder head (see Chapter 9).

16.18 Camshaft left-hand oil seal (1) and oil feed gallery O-ring (2) on rear of the brake vacuum pump

Note the smaller O-ring which seals the oil feed gallery to the pump - this may also cause leakage from the pump/cylinder head mating faces if it deteriorates or fails **(see illustration)**.

17 Oil level, temperature and pressure sensors - general

Refer to Chapter 5A for details.

18 Flywheel/driveplate - removal, inspection and refitting

Refer to Chapter 2B, Section 17.

19 Engine oil cooler - removal and refitting

Refer to Chapter 2B, Section 15.

20 Engine/transmission mountings - inspection and renewal

Inspection

1 Refer to Chapter 2B, Section 18.

Renewal

Right-hand mounting

2 Refer to Section 9.

Left-hand engine mounting

3 Refer to Chapter 2B, Section 18.

Rear mounting

4 Refer to Chapter 2A, Section 16.

Chapter 2 Part D: 1.9 and 2.0 litre
DW diesel engine in-car repair procedures

Contents

Degrees of difficulty

Easy, suitable for novice with little experience		Fairly easy, suitable for beginner with some experience		Fairly difficult, suitable for competent DIY mechanic		Difficult, suitable for experienced DIY mechanic		Very difficult, suitable for expert DIY or professional	

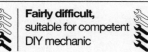
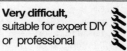

Specifications

Engine (general)
Designation:
  1.9 litre (1868 cc) engine DW8
  2.0 litre (1997 cc) engine DW10
Engine codes*:
  1.9 litre engine:
    Engines with mechanical injection pump . . . . WJZ (DW8)
    Engines with electronically-controlled injection pump . . . . WJY (DW8B)
  2.0 litre engine . . . . RHY (DW10TD)
Bore:
  1.9 litre engine . . . . 82.2 mm
  2.0 litre engine . . . . 85.0 mm
Stroke . . . . 88.00 mm
Direction of crankshaft rotation . . . . Clockwise (viewed from right-hand side of vehicle)
No 1 cylinder location . . . . At transmission end of block
*The engine code is stamped on front of the cylinder block, just to the left of the oil filter/cooler.
The code given in brackets is the factory identification number.

Compression pressures (engine hot, at cranking speed)
Normal . . . . 25 to 30 bars (363 to 435 psi)
Maximum difference between any two cylinders . . . . 5 bars (73 psi)

Camshaft
Drive . . . . Toothed belt
No of bearings:
  1.9 litre engine 3
  2.0 litre engine 5
Endfloat:
  1.9 litre engine . . . . 0.02 to 0.07 mm
  2.0 litre engine . . . . 0.07 to 0.38 mm

Valve clearances (engine cold)

1.9 litre engine:
Inlet	0.15 ± 0.07 mm
Exhaust	0.30 ± 0.07 mm
2.0 litre engine	Automatically adjusted by hydraulic tappets

Lubrication system

Oil pump type	Gear-type, chain-driven off the crankshaft right-hand end

Minimum oil pressure at 80°C:
1.9 litre engine	4.5 bars at 4000 rpm
2.0 litre engine	4 bars at 4000 rpm

Torque wrench settings

	Nm	lbf ft
Big-end bearing cap nuts:*		
Stage 1	20	15
Stage 2	Tighten through a further 70°	
Camshaft:		
Bearing cap nuts (1.9 litre engine)	20	15
Bearing cap casting bolts (2.0 litre engine)	10	7
Camshaft sprocket:		
Hub-to-camshaft bolt	43	32
Sprocket-to-hub bolts:		
1.9 litre engine	23	17
2.0 litre engine	20	15
Crankshaft right-hand oil seal housing bolts	14	10
Crankshaft pulley bolt:		
1.9 litre engine	10	7
2.0 litre engine:		
Stage 1	40	30
Stage 2	Tighten through a further 50°	
Crankshaft sprocket bolt (1.9 litre engine):		
Stage 1	40	30
Stage 2	Tighten through a further 55°	
Cylinder head bolts:		
1.9 litre engine:		
Stage 1	20	15
Stage 2	60	44
Stage 3	Tighten through a further 180°	
2.0 litre engine:		
Stage 1	20	15
Stage 2	60	44
Stage 3	Tighten through a further 220°	
Cylinder head cover bolts:		
1.9 litre engine:		
Upper cover bolts	10	7
Lower cover bolts	5	4
2.0 litre engine	10	7
Engine-to-transmission fixing bolts	55	41
Engine/transmission left-hand mounting:		
Mounting bracket-to-body bolts	19	14
Mounting stud to bracket	50	37
Mounting-to-bracket bolts	30	22
Mounting centre nut	65	48
Mounting bracket to transmission	60	44
Engine/transmission rear mounting:		
Mounting assembly-to-block bolts	45	33
Mounting link-to-mounting bolt	50	37
Mounting link-to-subframe bolt	35	26
Engine/transmission right-hand mounting:		
Vibration damper bracket-to-body bolts	22	16
Vibration damper	32	24
Mounting-to engine bracket:		
Bracket-to-cylinder block bracket bolts	61	45
Bracket-to-mounting nut	45	33
Movement restrictors	20	15
Mounting to body	40	30
Cylinder block bracket bolts:		
M8 bolts	20	15
M10 bolts	45	33

Torque wrench settings (continued)

	Nm	lbf ft
Flywheel bolts*	48	35
Fuel filter/thermostat housing bolts (1.9 litre engine)	15	11
Fuel filter plastic housing bolt (1.9 litre engine)	18	13
Injection pump sprocket:		
Sprocket-to-hub bolts (1.9 litre engine)	23	17
Sprocket nut (2.0 litre engine)	50	37
Main bearing cap bolts:		
1.9 litre engine	70	52
2.0 litre engine:		
Stage 1	25	18
Stage 2	Tighten through a further 60°	
Oil cooler centre bolt	50	37
Oil pump mounting bolts	16	12
Piston oil jet spray tube bolt	10	7
Roadwheel bolts	85	63
Sump bolts	16	12
Sump drain plug	34	25
Thermostat housing fixings (2.0 litre engine):		
Housing studs	25	18
Retaining nuts and bolts	20	15
Timing belt cover bolts	8	6
Timing belt tensioner pulley bolt	23	17
Timing belt idler pulley bolt	43	32

New nuts/bolts must be used.

1 General information

Using this Chapter

Chapter 2 is divided into five Parts; A, B, C, D and E. Repair operations that can be carried out with the engine in the vehicle are described in Parts A (1.1, 1.4 and 1.6 litre TU series petrol engines), B (1.8 and 2.0 litre XU series petrol engines), C (1.8 and 1.9 litre XUD series diesel engines) and D (1.9 and 2.0 litre DW series diesel engines). Part E covers the removal of the engine/transmission as a unit, and describes the engine dismantling and overhaul procedures.

In Parts A, B, C and D, the assumption is made that the engine is installed in the vehicle, with all ancillaries connected. If the engine has been removed for overhaul, the preliminary dismantling information which precedes each operation may be ignored.

DW series engine description

The DW series engine is a relatively new power unit based on the well-proven XUD series engine which has appeared in many Peugeot and Citroën vehicles. The engine is of four-cylinder single overhead camshaft design, mounted transversely, with the transmission mounted on the left-hand side.

The crankshaft runs in five main bearings of the usual shell type. Endfloat is controlled by thrustwashers either side of No 2 main bearing.

The connecting rods rotate on horizontally-split bearing shells at their big-ends. The pistons are attached to the connecting rods by gudgeon pins, which are secured in position with circlips. The aluminium-alloy pistons are fitted with three piston rings – two compression rings and an oil control ring.

The cylinder block is made from cast-iron, and the cylinder bores are an integral part of the cylinder block. On this type of engine, the cylinder bores are sometimes referred to as having dry liners.

The camshaft is driven by a toothed timing belt which also operates the coolant pump. On 1.9 litre engines, the camshaft operates the eight valves via bucket-type followers; valve clearances are adjusted by shims fitted between the valve stem and follower. On 2.0 litre engines, the camshaft operates the valves via followers and hydraulic tappets which automatically adjust the valve clearances. On all engines the camshaft runs in bearing caps which are bolted to the top of the cylinder head. The inlet and exhaust valves are each closed by coil springs, and operate in guides pressed into the cylinder head.

Lubrication is by means of an oil pump, which is driven (via a chain and sprocket) off the right-hand end of the crankshaft. It draws oil through a strainer located in the sump, and then forces it through an externally-mounted filter into galleries in the cylinder block/crankcase. From there, the oil is distributed to the crankshaft (main bearings) and camshaft. The big-end bearings are supplied with oil via internal drillings in the crankshaft, while the camshaft bearings also receive a pressurised supply. The camshaft lobes and valves are lubricated by splash, as are all other engine components. An oil cooler is mounted between the oil filter and cylinder block to keep the oil temperature stable under arduous operating temperatures.

Repair operations – precaution

The 2.0 litre engine is a complex unit with numerous accessories and ancillary components. The design of the engine compartment is such that every conceivable space has been utilised, and access to virtually all of the engine components is extremely limited. In many cases, ancillary components will have to be removed, or moved to one side, and wiring, pipes and hoses will have to be disconnected or removed from various cable clips and support brackets.

When working on this engine, read through the entire procedure first, look at the vehicle and engine at the same time, and establish whether you have the necessary tools, equipment, skill and patience to proceed. Allow considerable time for any operation, and be prepared for the unexpected. Any major work on this engine is not for the faint-hearted!

Because of the limited access, many of the engine photographs appearing in this Chapter were, by necessity, taken with the engine removed from the vehicle.

 Warning: It is essential to observe strict precautions when working on the fuel system components of the 2.0 litre engine, particularly the high pressure side of the system. Before carrying out any engine operations that entail working on, or near, any part of the fuel system, refer to the precautionary information given in Chapter 4E, Section 1.

Operations with engine in car

10 The following work can be carried out with the engine in the car:
a) Compression and leakdown tests.
b) Cylinder head cover – removal and refitting.

c) *Timing belt covers – removal and refitting.*
d) *Timing belt – removal, refitting and adjustment.*
e) *Timing belt sprockets and tensioner/idler pulleys – removal and refitting.*
f) *Camshaft oil seal – renewal.*
g) *Camshaft and followers – removal, inspection and refitting.*
h) *Cylinder head – removal and refitting.*
i) *Cylinder head and pistons – decarbonising.*
j) *Sump – removal and refitting.*
k) *Oil pump – removal, overhaul and refitting.*
l) *Crankshaft oil seals – renewal.*
m) *Engine/transmission mountings – inspection and renewal.*
n) *Flywheel – removal, inspection and refitting.*

2 Compression and leakdown tests – description and interpretation

Compression test

Note: *A compression tester specifically designed for diesel engines must be used for this test, because of the high pressures involved.*

1 When engine performance is down, or if misfiring occurs which cannot be attributed to the fuel system, a compression test can provide diagnostic clues as to the engine's condition. If the test is performed regularly, it can give warning of trouble before any other symptoms become apparent.

2 The tester is connected to an adapter which screws into the glow plug or injector hole. On these engines, an adapter suitable for use in the glow plug holes will be required, so as not to disturb the fuel system components. It is unlikely to be worthwhile buying such a tester for occasional use, but it may be possible to borrow or hire one – if not, have the test performed by a garage.

3 Unless specific instructions to the contrary are supplied with the tester, observe the following points:
a) *The battery must be in a good state of charge, the air filter must be clean, and the engine should be at normal operating temperature.*
b) *All the glow plugs should be removed as described in Chapter 5C before starting the test.*
c) *On 1.9 litre WJZ engines, the anti-theft system electronic engine immobiliser unit wiring connector at the rear of the injection pump must be disconnected.*
d) *On 1.9 litre WJY engines and all 2.0 litre engines, the wiring connector on the engine management system ECU must be disconnected. Refer to Chapter 4E for further information.*

4 Crank the engine on the starter motor; after one or two revolutions, the compression pressure should build-up to a maximum figure, and then stabilise. Record the highest reading obtained.

5 Repeat the test on the remaining cylinders, recording the pressure in each.

6 All cylinders should produce very similar pressures; a difference of more than 5 bars between any two cylinders indicates a fault. Note that the compression should build-up quickly in a healthy engine; low compression on the first stroke, followed by gradually-increasing pressure on successive strokes, indicates worn piston rings. A low compression reading on the first stroke, which does not build-up during successive strokes, indicates leaking valves or a blown head gasket (a cracked head could also be the cause). Deposits on the undersides of the valve heads can also cause low compression.

7 As a guide, any cylinder pressure of below 20 bars can be considered as less than healthy. Refer to a Peugeot dealer or other specialist if in doubt as to whether a particular pressure reading is acceptable.

8 The cause of poor compression is less easy to establish on a diesel engine than on a petrol one. The effect of introducing oil into the cylinders ('wet' testing) is not conclusive, because there is a risk that the oil will sit in the swirl chamber or in the recess on the piston crown instead of passing to the rings. A low reading from two adjacent cylinders is almost certainly due to the head gasket having blown between them; the presence of coolant in the engine oil will confirm this.

Leakdown test

9 A leakdown test measures the rate at which compressed air fed into the cylinder is lost. It is an alternative to a compression test, and in many ways it is better, since the escaping air provides easy identification of where pressure loss is occurring (piston rings, valves or head gasket).

10 The equipment needed for leakdown testing is unlikely to be available to the home mechanic. If poor compression is suspected,

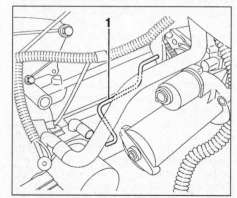

3.4 Insert the bolt/drill (Peugeot special tool shown – 1) in through the hole in the cylinder block flange (shown with the starter motor moved forwards for clarity) and locate it in the rear of the flywheel

have the test performed by a suitably-equipped garage.

3 Engine assembly/valve timing holes – general information and usage

Note: *Do not attempt to rotate the engine whilst the crankshaft/camshaft/injection pump are locked in position. If the engine is to be left in this state for a long period of time, it is a good idea to place suitable warning notices inside the vehicle, and in the engine compartment. This will reduce the possibility of the engine being accidentally cranked on the starter motor, which is likely to cause damage with the locking pins in place.*

1.9 litre engine

1 Timing holes are drilled in the camshaft sprocket hub, injection pump sprocket hub and flywheel. The holes are used to align the crankshaft, camshaft and injection pump, and to prevent the possibility of the valves contacting the pistons when refitting the cylinder head, and to ensure the valve timing/injection pump timing is correct when refitting the timing belt. When the holes are aligned with their corresponding holes in the cylinder head and cylinder block (as appropriate), suitable diameter bolts/pins can be inserted to lock the camshaft, injection pump and crankshaft in position, preventing them from rotating unnecessarily. Proceed as follows.

2 Remove the injection pump sprocket and camshaft sprocket timing belt covers as described in Section 6 to gain access to the sprockets.

3 The crankshaft must now be rotated using a spanner on the crankshaft sprocket bolt. Note that the crankshaft must always be turned in a clockwise direction (viewed from the right-hand side of the vehicle). To improve access to the pulley, undo the screws securing the front section of the right-hand wheel arch liner to the base of the bumper. Remove the fasteners (pull out the centre pin then remove the complete fastener) securing the liner section to the body then manoeuvre the front section of the liner out from underneath the wing.

4 Rotate the crankshaft until the holes in the camshaft and injection pump sprocket hubs are aligned with the corresponding holes in the cylinder head/pump. With the camshaft sprocket hole correctly positioned, insert an 8 mm diameter bolt or drill through the hole in the front, left-hand flange of the cylinder block, located behind the starter motor, and locate it in the timing hole in the rear of the flywheel **(see illustration)**. Note that it may be necessary to rotate the crankshaft slightly, to get the holes to align.

5 With the flywheel correctly positioned, lock the camshaft sprocket in position by inserting an 8 mm diameter bolt or a drill through the

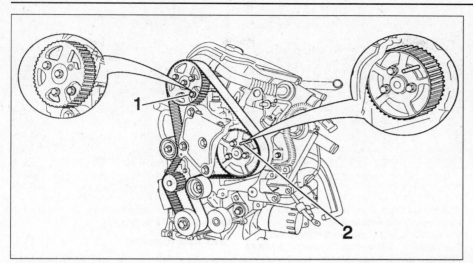

3.12 On 2.0 litre engines, peg the flywheel in position then insert a bolt/drill in through the hole in the camshaft sprocket hub and locate it in the cylinder head

3.5 On 1.9 litre engines, peg the camshaft and injection pump sprockets in position by inserting bolts/drills (1 and 2)

timing hole in the sprocket hub, and locating it in the hole in the cylinder head **(see illustration)**.

6 Lock the injection pump sprocket in position by inserting a 6 mm diameter bolt or a drill through the timing hole in the sprocket hub and locating it in the pump.

7 The crankshaft, camshaft and injection pump are now locked in position, preventing unnecessary rotation.

2.0 litre engine

8 Timing holes are drilled in the camshaft sprocket hub and flywheel. The holes are used to align the crankshaft and camshaft to prevent the possibility of the valves contacting the pistons when refitting the cylinder head, and to ensure the valve timing is correct when refitting the timing belt. When the holes are aligned with their corresponding holes in the cylinder head and cylinder block (as appropriate), suitable diameter bolts/pins can be inserted to lock both the camshaft and crankshaft in position, preventing them from rotating unnecessarily. Proceed as follows.

9 Remove the camshaft sprocket timing belt cover as described in Section 6 to gain access to the sprocket.

10 The crankshaft must now be rotated using a spanner on the crankshaft sprocket bolt. Note that the crankshaft must always be turned in a clockwise direction (viewed from the right-hand side of the vehicle). To improve access to the pulley, undo the bolts securing the right-hand inner cover to the wing valance and undercover and remove the cover from underneath the wing.

11 Rotate the crankshaft until the hole in the camshaft sprocket hub is aligned with the corresponding hole in the cylinder head. With the camshaft sprocket hole correctly positioned, insert an 8 mm diameter bolt or drill through the hole in the front, left-hand flange of the cylinder block, located behind the starter motor, and locate it in the timing hole in the rear of the flywheel **(see illustration 3.4)**. Note that it may be necessary to rotate the crankshaft slightly, to get the holes to align.

12 With the flywheel correctly positioned, lock the camshaft sprocket in position by inserting a 6 mm diameter bolt or a drill through the timing hole in the sprocket hub, and locating it in the hole in the cylinder head **(see illustration)**.

13 The crankshaft and camshaft are now locked in position, preventing unnecessary rotation.

4 Cylinder head cover – removal and refitting

1.9 litre engine

Removal

1 Release the fasteners from the right-hand side and top of the engine cover then lift off the cover, taking care not to lose its mounting rubbers **(see illustrations)**. Disconnect the battery negative terminal (refer to *Disconnecting the battery* in the Reference Chapter).

2 Remove the upper section of the inlet manifold as described in Chapter 4E.

3 Unscrew the bolts securing the EGR pipe to the top of the exhaust manifold and the cylinder head cover. Free the pipe from the manifold and position it clear of the cylinder head cover. Recover the gasket and discard it; a new one should be used on refitting.

4 Slacken the retaining clips and disconnect the breather hoses from the upper section of the cylinder head cover.

5 Unscrew the eight retaining bolts then lift off the upper section of the cylinder head cover, complete with its rubber seal.

6 Unscrew the three retaining bolts and washers then remove the lower section of the cylinder head cover, complete with its rubber seal.

4.1a On 1.9 litre engines, remove the fasteners from the right-hand side . . .

4.1b . . . and top of the engine cover . . .

4.1c . . . then remove the cover from the engine

4.14a On 2.0 litre engines rotate each fastener 90° to release it . . .

4.14b . . . then lift off the engine cover

4.18 Removing the cylinder head cover – 2.0 litre engine

7 Inspect the cover seals for signs of damage or deterioration and, if necessary, renew.

Refitting

8 Carefully clean the cylinder head and cover mating surfaces, and remove all traces of oil.

9 Fit the rubber seals to both the cylinder head cover sections, ensuring they are correctly located along their entire length.

10 Fit the lower section of the cover the cylinder head. Ensure the rubber seal is still correctly located then refit the cover retaining bolts and washers, tightening them to the specified torque.

11 Refit the upper section of the cover to the lower section, ensuring its seal remains correctly seated, and tighten its retaining bolts to the specified torque.

12 Reconnect the breather hoses to the upper section of the cover.

13 Refit the EGR pipe and inlet manifold as described in Chapter 4E.

2.0 litre engine

Removal

14 Release the fasteners (rotate them 90° to release them) and remove the engine cover **(see illustrations)**.

15 Disconnect the battery negative terminal (refer to *Disconnecting the battery* in the Reference Chapter), then disconnect the wiring connector from the camshaft sensor.

16 Unscrew the bolts and free the engine cover right-hand mounting bracket from the cylinder head cover.

17 Release the retaining clips and disconnect the breather hoses from the cylinder head cover.

18 Working in a spiral pattern from the outside bolts inwards, slacken and remove the cylinder head cover retaining bolts and washers. Lift off the cylinder head cover, complete with its rubber seal **(see illustration)**. Inspect the cover seal for signs of damage or deterioration and, if necessary, renew.

Refitting

19 Carefully clean the cylinder head and cover mating surfaces, and remove all traces of oil.

20 Fit the rubber seal to the cylinder head

cover, ensuring it is correctly located along its entire length **(see illustration)**.

21 Fit the cover the cylinder head, ensuring the rubber seal remains correctly located. Refit the cover retaining bolts and washers and tighten them to the specified torque, working in a spiral pattern from the centre bolts outwards.

22 Reconnect the breather hoses securely to the cover.

23 Reconnect the camshaft sensor wiring connector. It is recommended that the sensor air gap is checked (see Chapter 4E).

24 Refit the engine cover mounting bracket, tightening its retaining bolts securely then refit the engine cover.

25 On completion reconnect the battery.

---

5 Crankshaft pulley – removal and refitting

1.9 litre engine

Removal

1 Remove the auxiliary drivebelt as described in Chapter 1B.

2 Undo the four crankshaft pulley retaining bolts and remove the pulley, noting which way round it is fitted.

Refitting

3 Fit the pulley to the end of the crankshaft, ensuring it is fitted the correct way round, and tighten its bolts to the specified torque.

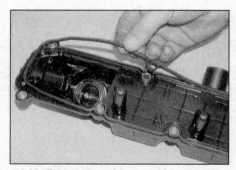

4.20 Ensure the rubber seal is correctly located in the cover groove

4 Refit and tension the auxiliary drivebelt as described in Chapter 1B.

2.0 litre engine

Removal

5 Remove the auxiliary drivebelt as described in Chapter 1B.

6 Slacken the crankshaft pulley bolt. To prevent crankshaft rotation, select top gear, and have an assistant apply the brakes firmly. If the engine has been removed from the vehicle, it will be necessary to lock the flywheel (see Section 17).

Caution: Do not be tempted to use the flywheel locking pin to prevent the crankshaft from rotating; temporarily remove the locking pin (where fitted) prior to slackening the pulley bolt, then refit it once the bolt has been slackened.

7 Unscrew the retaining bolt and washer from the crankshaft and remove the pulley **(see illustration)**. If the pulley is a tight fit, it can be drawn off the crankshaft with a suitable puller.

8 If the Woodruff key is a loose fit in the crankshaft, remove it and store it with the pulley for safe-keeping. Examine the crankshaft oil seal for signs oil leakage and, if necessary, renew as described in Section 16.

Refitting

9 Where removed, locate the Woodruff key in the crankshaft end.

10 Align the crankshaft pulley slot with the Woodruff key, and slide it onto the end of the crankshaft.

11 Remove all traces of locking compound

5.7 On 2.0 litre engines, unscrew the bolt and washer and remove the crankshaft pulley

from the threads of the pulley bolt and crankshaft. Apply a drop of locking compound (Peugeot recommend the use of Loctite Frenetanch) to the threads of the bolt then refit the bolt and washer to the crankshaft.

12 Temporarily remove the locking pin (where fitted) from the rear of the flywheel, then tighten the bolt to the specified torque Stage 1 torque setting, whilst preventing crankshaft rotation using the method employed on removal.

13 Angle-tighten the pulley bolt through the specified Stage 2 angle, using a socket and extension bar. It is recommended that an angle-measuring gauge is used during this stage of the tightening, to ensure accuracy. Check the crankshaft pulley bolt is correctly tightened by applying a torque of 195 Nm (144 lbf ft) to it; the bolt should not move.

14 Refit the auxiliary drivebelt as described in Chapter 1B.

6 Timing belt covers – removal and refitting

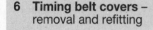

Injection pump sprocket cover

1.9 litre engine

1 Release the fasteners from the right-hand side and top of the engine cover then lift off the cover, taking care not to lose its mounting rubbers (see illustrations 4.1a to 4.1c). Disconnect the battery negative terminal (refer to *Disconnecting the battery* in the Reference Chapter).

2 Unclip the fuel pipes and position them clear of the timing belt covers (see illustration).

3 Slacken and remove the cover upper and lower retaining bolts then manoeuvre the cover out of position.

4 Refitting is the reverse of removal. Ensure that the cover is correctly located, and that the cover retaining bolts are tightened to the specified torque.

Camshaft sprocket cover

Note: *A small amount of coolant may weep from the coolant pump whilst the cover is removed. Do not worry about this, the leak will stop when the cover is refitted; ensure the coolant level is topped-up once the cover is refitted.*

1.9 litre engine

5 Remove the injection pump sprocket cover (see paragraphs 1 to 3).

6 Slacken and remove the two lower retaining bolts then manoeuvre the camshaft sprocket cover out of position.

7 Refitting is the reverse of removal. Ensure that the cover is correctly located, and that the cover retaining bolts are tightened to the specified torque.

2.0 litre engine

8 Release the fasteners (rotate the fasteners 90° to release them) and remove the engine

6.2 Unclip the fuel pipes from the top of the timing belt covers

cover (see illustrations 4.14a and 4.14b). Disconnect the battery negative terminal (refer to *Disconnecting the battery* in the Reference Chapter).

9 Unclip the fuel pipes and position them clear of the timing belt covers

10 Unscrew the cover upper and lower retaining bolts (the cover lower bolt hole is slotted) then manoeuvre the cover out of position (see illustration).

11 Refitting is the reverse of removal. Ensure that the cover is correctly located, and that the cover retaining bolts are tightened to the specified torque.

Injection pump sprocket cover

2.0 litre engine

12 Remove the camshaft sprocket cover (see paragraphs 8 to 10).

13 Slacken and remove the two lower retaining bolts (the lower bolt hole is slotted) then manoeuvre the cover out of position (see illustration).

14 Refitting is the reverse of removal. Ensure that the cover is correctly located, and that the cover retaining bolts are tightened to the specified torque.

Lower cover

15 Remove the crankshaft pulley as described in Section 5.

16 Remove the injection pump and camshaft sprocket covers as described earlier.

17 Unscrew the lower retaining bolts then manoeuvre the lower cover out of position (see illustration).

6.13 Removing the injection pump sprocket cover – 2.0 litre engine

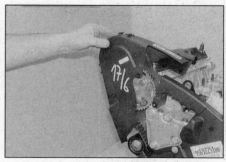

6.10 Removing the camshaft sprocket cover – 2.0 litre engine

18 Refitting is the reverse of removal. Ensure that the cover is correctly located, and that the cover retaining bolts are tightened to the specified torque.

7 Timing belt – general information, removal and refitting

Note: *Peugeot specify the use of a special electronic tool (SEEM C.TRONIC type 105.5 belt tensioning measuring tool) to correctly set the timing belt tension. If access to this equipment cannot be obtained, an approximate setting can be achieved using the method described below. If this method is used, the tension must be checked using the special electronic tool at the earliest possible opportunity. Do not drive the vehicle over large distances, or use high engine speeds, until the belt tension is known to be correct. Refer to a Peugeot dealer for advice.*

General information

1 The timing belt drives the camshaft, injection pump and coolant pump from a toothed sprocket on the front of the crankshaft. If the belt breaks or slips in service, the pistons are likely to hit the valve heads, resulting in extensive (and expensive) damage.

2 The timing belt should be renewed at the specified intervals (see Chapter 1B), or earlier if it is contaminated with oil or if it is at all noisy in operation (a 'scraping' noise due to uneven wear).

6.17 Undo the retaining bolts (arrowed) and remove the timing belt lower cover – 2.0 litre engine

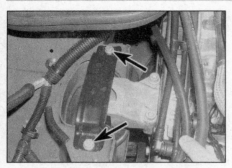

7.11 Undo the bolts and remove the bracket from the top of the right-hand engine/transmission mounting

3 If the timing belt is being removed, it is a wise precaution to check the condition of the coolant pump at the same time (check for signs of coolant leakage). This may avoid the need to remove the timing belt again at a later stage, should the coolant pump fail.

Removal

4 Disconnect the battery negative terminal (refer to *Disconnecting the battery* in the Reference Chapter).
5 Remove the camshaft sprocket and injection pump sprocket timing belt covers as described in Section 6.
6 Align the engine assembly/valve timing holes as described in Section 3, and lock both the camshaft sprocket hub and the flywheel in position. On 1.9 litre engines also lock the injection pump sprocket hub.
Caution: Do not attempt to rotate the engine whilst the locking tools are in position.
7 Remove the crankshaft pulley as described in Section 5 then remove the timing belt lower cover (see Section 6).
8 Where necessary, remove the retaining bolts, screws and clips and remove the undercover (where fitted) from beneath the engine/transmission unit.
9 On all models, unscrew the nuts and bolts and remove the mounting link securing the rear engine/transmission mounting to the subframe.
10 Place a jack with a block of wood beneath the engine, to take the weight of the engine. Alternatively, attach a couple of lifting eyes to the engine, and fit a hoist or support bar to take the engine weight.
11 Unscrew the two bolts and remove the bracket from the right-hand engine/transmission mounting **(see illustration)**.
12 Unscrew the vibration damper (where fitted) from the mounting then unscrew the nut and bolts and lift off the right-hand mounting bracket. Take care not to lose the bracket locating dowels.
13 Loosen the timing belt tensioner pulley retaining bolt. Pivot the pulley in a clockwise direction, using a square-section key fitted to the hole in the pulley hub, then retighten the retaining bolt **(see Tool Tip)**.

14 If the timing belt is to be re-used, use white paint or similar to mark the direction of rotation on the belt (if markings do not already exist). Slip the belt off the sprockets. If necessary, lower the engine slightly to enable the belt to be removed.
Caution: Take great care not to place any excess strain on the exhaust system or damage the radiator if the engine is moved. On models equipped with air conditioning, care must also be taken to ensure the auxiliary drivebelt pulleys do not damage the air conditioning pipes on the right-hand side of the engine compartment.
15 Check the timing belt carefully for any signs of uneven wear, splitting, or oil contamination. Pay particular attention to the roots of the teeth. Renew the belt if there is the slightest doubt about its condition. If the engine is undergoing an overhaul, and has covered more than 36 000 miles (60 000 km) with the existing belt fitted, renew the belt as a matter of course, regardless of its apparent condition. The cost of a new belt is nothing when compared to the cost of repairs, should the belt break in service. If signs of oil contamination are found, trace the source of the oil leak, and rectify it. Wash down the engine timing belt area and all related components, to remove all traces of oil.

Refitting

1.9 litre engine

16 Prior to refitting, thoroughly clean the timing belt sprockets. Check that the tensioner and idler pulleys rotate freely, without any sign of roughness. If necessary, renew the pulleys as described in Section 8.
17 Ensure that the locking tools are still in place, as described in Section 3.
18 Slacken the bolts securing the camshaft and injection pump sprockets to their hubs.

TOOL TiP

If you're having difficulty finding a square-section tool that will fit the tensioner pulley, obtain a length of standard 8 mm door handle rod from a DIY shop and cut it to length (A). Insert the rod into the pulley hub and rotate the pulley with an 8 mm spanner (B).

Rotate both sprockets fully clockwise on their hubs then lightly tighten the sprocket bolts.
19 Manoeuvre the timing belt into position, ensuring that the arrows on the belt are pointing in the direction of rotation (clockwise, when viewed from the right-hand end of the engine).
20 Locate the belt on the crankshaft sprocket, taking care not to twist it sharply while refitting it, and route the belt round the idler pulley.
21 Ensure the 'front run' of the belt is taut then align the belt with the injection pump sprocket. Rotate the sprocket anti-clockwise on its hub until the belt and sprocket teeth are correctly aligned then engage the belt on the sprocket. **Note:** *Do not rotate the sprocket anti-clockwise any more than is necessary and never rotate it through more than one sprocket tooth of movement.*
22 Once the belt is correctly seated on the injection pump sprocket, ensure the belt 'front' and 'top' runs are taut then align the belt with the camshaft sprocket. Rotate the camshaft sprocket anti-clockwise on its hub until the belt and sprocket teeth are correctly aligned then engage the belt on the sprocket. **Note:** *Do not rotate the sprocket anti-clockwise any more than is necessary and never rotate it through more than one sprocket tooth of movement.*
23 Ensure that any slack is on the tensioner pulley side of the belt then locate the belt behind the tensioner pulley and over the coolant pump sprocket.
24 Ensure that the belt teeth are seated centrally in the sprockets then loosen the tensioner pulley retaining bolt. Pivot the pulley anti-clockwise to remove all freeplay from the timing belt, then retighten the bolt.
25 Remove one of the sprocket bolts from both the injection pump and camshaft sprockets and check that the sprockets are not at the end of their retaining bolt slots **(see illustration)**. If they are, the sprocket was rotated through more than one tooth of movement whilst installing the belt; remove

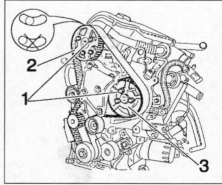

7.25 On 1.9 litre engines remove one of the bolts (1) from both the camshaft (2) and injection pump (3) sprockets and check that each sprocket is not at the end of its bolt slots (see inset)

the timing belt and repeat the refitting procedure. If the sprockets are correctly positioned, tension the timing belt as described under the relevant sub-heading.

2.0 litre engine

26 Prior to refitting, thoroughly clean the timing belt sprockets. Check that the tensioner and idler pulleys rotate freely, without any sign of roughness. If necessary, renew the pulleys as described in Section 8.

27 Ensure that the locking tools are still in place, as described in Section 3.

28 Slacken the bolts securing the camshaft sprocket to its hub. Rotate the sprocket fully clockwise on its hub then lightly tighten the sprocket bolts **(see illustration)**.

29 Manoeuvre the timing belt into position, ensuring that the arrows on the belt are pointing in the direction of rotation (clockwise, when viewed from the right-hand end of the engine).

30 Locate the belt with the crankshaft sprocket, taking care not to twist the timing belt sharply while refitting it and route the belt round the idler pulley and engage it with the injection pump sprocket. **Note:** *It is not necessary to set the injection pump timing when refitting the belt due to the nature of the fuel system.*

31 Ensure the belt 'front' and 'top' runs are taut then align the belt with the camshaft sprocket. Rotate the sprocket anti-clockwise on its hub until the belt and sprocket teeth are correctly aligned then engage the belt on the sprocket. **Note:** *Do not rotate the sprocket anti-clockwise any more than is necessary and never rotate it through more than one sprocket tooth of movement.*

32 Ensure that any slack is on the tensioner pulley side of the belt then locate the belt behind the tensioner pulley and over the coolant pump sprocket.

33 Ensure that the belt teeth are seated centrally in the sprockets then loosen the tensioner pulley retaining bolt. Pivot the pulley anti-clockwise to remove all freeplay from the timing belt, then retighten the bolt.

34 Remove one of the bolts from the camshaft sprocket and check that the sprocket is not at the end of its retaining bolt slots. If it is, the sprocket was rotated through more than one tooth of movement whilst installing the belt; remove the timing belt and repeat the refitting procedure. If the sprocket is correctly positioned, tension the timing belt as described under the relevant sub-heading.

Tensioning without electronic tool

Note: *If this method is used, ensure that the belt tension is checked by a Peugeot dealer at the earliest possible opportunity.*

35 Ensure the bolts securing the sprocket(s) to the hub(s) are loose, then slacken the tensioner pulley retaining bolt. Rotate the pulley anti-clockwise to adjust the timing belt tension until it is just possible to twist the timing belt slightly, midway between the camshaft and injection pump sprockets. Hold the tensioner pulley stationary then securely tighten its retaining bolt.

36 Tighten all the sprocket bolts to the specified torque setting then remove the locking tools from the sprocket hub(s) and flywheel.

37 Using a suitable socket and extension bar on the crankshaft sprocket bolt, rotate the crankshaft through eight complete rotations in a clockwise direction (viewed from the right-hand end of the engine). Refit the flywheel locking tool and sprocket hub locking tool(s).

Caution: Do not at any time rotate the crankshaft anti-clockwise.

38 Slacken the sprocket bolts and the tensioner pulley bolt. Retension the belt as described in paragraph 35, then tighten the tensioner pulley bolt to the specified torque.

39 Tighten the sprocket bolts to the specified torque then remove the locking tools again.

40 Rotate the crankshaft through a further two turns clockwise. Recheck the timing belt tension and ensure that the flywheel timing hole and the sprocket hub hole(s) are still correctly aligned.

41 If all is well, ensure the locating dowels (where fitted) are in position then refit the right-hand mounting bracket, tightening its nut and bolts to the specified torque. Tighten the vibration damper to the specified torque then refit the bracket to the body, tightening its bolts to the specified torque.

42 Refit the mounting link to the rear mounting, tightening its bolts to the specified torque. Where necessary, refit the undercover.

43 Refit the timing belt covers and crankshaft pulley as described in Sections 6 and 5.

44 On all models, reconnect the battery negative terminal.

Tensioning with electronic tool

45 Fit the special belt tensioning measuring equipment to the 'top run' of the timing belt, approximately midway between the camshaft and injection pump sprockets **(see illustration)**.

46 Ensure the bolts securing the sprocket(s) to the hub(s) are loose. Position the tensioner pulley so that the belt is tensioned to a setting of 106 SEEM units, then tighten the pulley retaining bolt to the specified torque.

47 Tighten all the sprocket bolts to the specified torque setting then remove the locking tools from the sprocket hub(s) and flywheel.

48 Remove the measuring tool from the belt then, using a suitable socket and extension bar on the crankshaft sprocket bolt, rotate the crankshaft through eight complete rotations in a clockwise direction (viewed from the right-hand end of the engine). Refit the flywheel locking tool and sprocket hub locking tool(s).

Caution: Do not at any time rotate the crankshaft anti-clockwise.

49 Slacken the sprocket bolts and refit the tensioning measuring equipment to the top run of the belt.

50 Slacken the tensioner pulley retaining bolt whilst holding the pulley stationary. Gradually release the tensioner pulley until a tension setting of 41 ± 2 SEEM units is indicated on 1.9 litre engines, and a setting of 54 ± 2 SEEM units is indicated on 2.0 litre engines. With the belt correctly tensioned, hold the pulley stationary and tighten its retaining bolt to the specified torque.

51 Tighten all the sprocket bolts to the specified torque

52 Release the measuring equipment then refit it again to check the belt tension. The belt tension should be between 38 and 42 SEEM units on 1.9 litre engines and between 51 and 57 SEEM units on 2.0 litre engines. If the tension is incorrect, repeat the tensioning procedure described in paragraphs 45 to 51.

53 Once the belt is correctly tensioned, remove the measuring tool and the locking tools.

54 Rotate the crankshaft through another two complete rotations in a clockwise direction. Refit the flywheel locking tool and check that the sprocket hub timing hole(s) are still correctly aligned.

55 If all is well, refit all disturbed components as described in paragraphs 41 to 44.

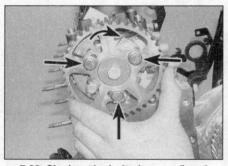

7.28 Slacken the bolts (arrowed) and rotate the camshaft sprocket fully clockwise on its hub

7.45 The timing belt measuring tool should be fitted to the centre of the belt upper run

8 Timing belt sprockets and idler/tensioner pulleys – removal, inspection and refitting

Removal

1 Disconnect the battery negative terminal (refer to *Disconnecting the battery* in the Reference Chapter).

2 Position the engine assembly/valve timing holes as described in Section 3, and lock the sprocket hub(s) and flywheel in position.

Caution: Do not attempt to rotate the engine whilst the pins are in position.

3 Remove the timing belt as described in Section 7 then proceed as described under the relevant sub-heading. **Note:** *If the timing belt is not going to be renewed, there is no need to disturb the engine mounting.*

Camshaft sprocket

4 As a precaution, remove the flywheel locking pin then rotate the crankshaft **backwards** (anti-clockwise) through 90°; this will position the pistons mid-way up the bores and remove the risk of the valves contacting the pistons during the following operation.

5 If the sprocket hub is being removed, slacken the hub bolt. To prevent the camshaft rotating as the bolt is slackened, a sprocket-

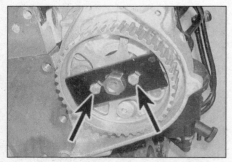

8.11a Fit the bar over the sprocket nut and screw in the two bolts (arrowed)

8.7 Unscrew the bolt and remove the sprocket hub from the camshaft

holding tool will be required. In the absence of the special Peugeot tool, an acceptable substitute can be fabricated as follows. Use two lengths of steel strip (one long, the other short); attach the short strip to the longer one with a nut a bolt to form a forked tool. Either fit a nut and bolt to the each of each of the strips to engage with the sprocket spokes or bend the ends of the strips at right-angles to engage with the sprocket spokes as shown in illustration 8.28.

6 Unscrew the three retaining bolts and remove the sprocket from its hub.

7 Unscrew the hub bolt and slide the hub off the end of the camshaft **(see illustration)**. If the Woodruff key is a loose fit, remove it for safe-keeping. Examine the camshaft oil seal for signs of oil leakage and, if necessary, renew it as described in Section 9.

Injection pump sprocket – 1.9 litre engine

8 Unscrew the three retaining bolts and remove the sprocket from its hub; The hub is an integral part of the injection pump.

Injection pump sprocket – 2.0 litre engine

9 Slacken the sprocket retaining nut whilst preventing rotation by retaining the sprocket with a holding tool (see paragraph 5).

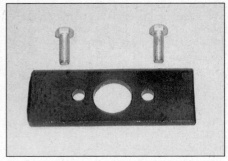

8.10 Home-made puller arrangement for removing the injection pump sprocket – 2.0 litre engine

10 The sprocket must then be freed from the injection pump shaft using a puller. In the absence of correct puller (Peugeot puller assembly 0188-R or a pattern substitute), a suitable alternative can be made out of a short length of steel bar. Drill two holes in the bar to align with the threaded holes in the pump sprocket and larger hole in the centre of the bar which pass over the hexagonal section of the sprocket nut but not the nut flange **(see illustration)**.

11 Loosen the sprocket nut then bolt the steel bar to the sprocket by screwing two M7 bolts in the threaded holes provided. Evenly tighten the bolts, so the bar is forced into contact with nut, then unscrew the sprocket nut to draw the sprocket off the pump shaft. Once the sprocket has been released, unscrew the bolts and remove the bar then unscrew the nut and remove the sprocket **(see illustrations)**.

Crankshaft sprocket – 1.9 litre engine

12 As a precaution, remove the flywheel locking pin then rotate the crankshaft **backwards** (anti-clockwise) through 90°; this will position the pistons mid-way up the bores and remove the risk of the valves contacting the pistons during the following operation.

13 Slacken the crankshaft sprocket bolt. To

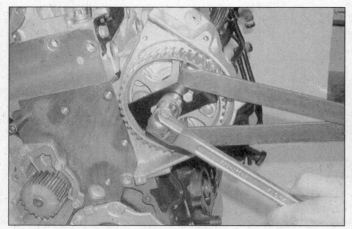

8.11b With the puller in position, retain the sprocket then unscrew the sprocket nut to release the sprocket from the pump shaft

8.11c Once the sprocket is free, remove the puller then unscrew the nut and lift off the sprocket

8.15a On 2.0 litre engines, slide the sprocket off the crankshaft . . .

8.15b . . . then remove the Woodruff key

prevent crankshaft rotation, select top gear, and have an assistant apply the brakes firmly. If the engine has been removed from the vehicle, it will be necessary to lock the flywheel (see Section 17).

14 Unscrew the retaining bolt and washer, then slide the sprocket off the end of the crankshaft. If the Woodruff key is a loose fit in the crankshaft, remove it and store it with the sprocket for safe-keeping. Examine the crankshaft oil seal for signs oil leakage and, if necessary, renew as described in Section 16.

Crankshaft sprocket – 2.0 litre engine

15 Slide the sprocket and off the end of the crankshaft. If the Woodruff key is a loose fit in the crankshaft, remove it and store it with the sprocket for safe-keeping (see illustrations). Examine the crankshaft oil seal for signs oil leakage and, if necessary, renew as described in Section 16.

Tensioner pulley

16 Unscrew the bolt and remove the pulley from its mounting pin. Examine the mounting stud for signs of damage and, if necessary, renew it.

Idler pulley

17 Unscrew the mounting bolt and remove the idler pulley from the cylinder block (see illustration).

Inspection

18 Clean the sprockets thoroughly, and renew any that show signs of wear, damage or cracks.

19 Clean the tensioner and idler pulleys, but

do not use any strong solvent which may enter the pulley bearing. Check that each pulley rotates freely about its hub, with no sign of stiffness or of free play. Renew the pulley if there is any doubt about its condition, or if there are any obvious signs of wear or damage.

20 Inspect the timing belt (see Section 7). Renew the belt is there is any doubt about its condition.

Refitting

Camshaft sprocket

21 Where necessary, refit the Woodruff key to the camshaft then refit the sprocket hub, aligning its slot with the key.

22 Seat the camshaft sprocket on the hub and lightly tighten its bolts.

23 Refit the hub bolt and tighten it to the specified torque, using the holding tool to prevent rotation (see illustration 8.28).

24 Align the hub timing hole with the cylinder head and insert the locking tool. Rotate the crankshaft 90° clockwise and lock the flywheel in position with the locking tool.

25 Refit the timing belt (see Section 7).

Injection pump sprocket – 1.9 litre engine

26 Seat the sprocket on the hub and lightly tighten its bolts.

27 Refit the timing belt (see Section 7).

Injection pump sprocket – 2.0 litre engine

28 Ensure the pump shaft and sprocket taper surfaces are clean and dry then fit the sprocket to the pump. Refit the sprocket nut

and tighten it to the specified torque, using the holding tool to prevent rotation (see illustration).

29 Refit the timing belt (see Section 7).

Crankshaft sprocket – 1.9 litre engine

30 Where removed, locate the Woodruff key in the crankshaft end.

31 Align the crankshaft sprocket slot with the Woodruff key, and slide it onto the end of the crankshaft.

32 Remove all traces of locking compound from the threads of the sprocket bolt and crankshaft. Apply a drop of locking compound (Peugeot recommend the use of Loctite Frenetanch) to the threads of the bolt then refit the bolt and washer to the crankshaft.

33 Tighten the bolt to the specified torque Stage 1 torque setting, whilst preventing crankshaft rotation using the method employed on removal.

34 Angle-tighten the sprocket bolt through the specified Stage 2 angle, using a socket and extension bar. It is recommended that an angle-measuring gauge is used during this stage of the tightening, to ensure accuracy.

35 Rotate the crankshaft 90° clockwise and lock the flywheel in position with the locking tool.

36 Refit the timing belt (see Section 7).

Crankshaft sprocket – 2.0 litre engine

37 Where removed, locate the Woodruff key in the crankshaft end.

38 Align the crankshaft sprocket slot with the Woodruff key, and slide it onto the end of the crankshaft.

39 Refit the timing belt (see Section 7).

Tensioner pulley

40 Refit the tensioner pulley to its mounting pin, and fit the retaining bolt.

41 Refit the timing belt (see Section 7).

Idler pulley

42 Refit the idler pulley to the cylinder block and tighten its retaining bolt to the specified torque.

43 Refit the timing belt (see Section 7).

| 9 | Camshaft oil seal – renewal | |

Note: If the camshaft oil seal has been leaking, check the timing belt for signs of oil contamination; the belt must be renewed if signs of oil contamination are found. Ensure that all traces of oil are removed from the sprockets and surrounding area before the new belt is fitted.

1 Remove the camshaft sprocket and hub as described in Section 8.

2 Punch or drill two small holes opposite each other in the oil seal. Screw a self-tapping screw into each, and pull on the screws with pliers to extract the seal.

8.17 Unscrew the mounting bolt and remove the idler pulley from the block

8.28 Retain the sprocket and tighten its retaining nut to the specified torque

9.4 Using a socket, a length of stud and a nut to press the camshaft oil seal into position

10.4 On 1.9 litre engines the camshaft bearing caps should be numbered (arrowed) for identification

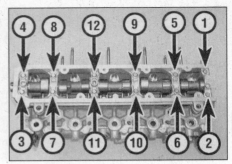

10.9 Camshaft bearing cap casting bolt slackening sequence – 2.0 litre engine

3 Clean the seal housing, and polish off any burrs or raised edges, which may have caused the seal to fail in the first place.

4 Lubricate the lips of the new seal with clean engine oil, and drive/press it into position until it seats on its locating shoulder. Use a suitable tubular drift, such as a socket, which bears only on the hard outer edge of the seal **(see illustration)**. Take care not to damage the seal lips during fitting. Note that the seal lips should face inwards.

5 Refit the camshaft sprocket and hub as described in Section 8.

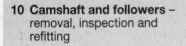

10 Camshaft and followers – removal, inspection and refitting

Note: *On 1.9 litre engines, valve clearance adjustment requires the removal of the camshaft. If the original camshaft is being refitted, it is worthwhile recording the valve clearances before it is removed, so any adjustments can be made before refitting it (see Section 11).*

Removal

1 Remove the cylinder head cover as described in Section 4.

2 Remove the braking system vacuum pump as described in Chapter 9.

3 Remove the camshaft sprocket and hub as

described in Section 8. Proceed as described under the relevant sub-heading.

1.9 litre engine

4 The camshaft bearing caps should be numbered 1 to 3, number 1 being at the transmission end of the engine **(see illustration)**. If not, make identification marks on the caps, using white paint or a suitable marker pen. Also mark each cap in some way to indicate its correct fitted orientation. This will avoid the possibility of installing the caps the wrong way around on refitting.

5 Evenly and progressively slacken the camshaft bearing cap retaining nuts by one turn at a time. This will relieve the valve spring pressure on the bearing caps gradually and evenly. Once the pressure has been relieved, the nuts can be fully unscrewed and removed. *Caution: If the bearing cap nuts are carelessly slackened, the bearing caps may break. If any bearing cap breaks then the complete cylinder head assembly must be renewed; the bearing caps are matched to the head and are not available separately.*

6 Note the correct fitted orientation of the bearing caps, then remove them from the cylinder head.

7 Lift the camshaft away from the cylinder head, and slide the oil seal off the camshaft end.

8 Obtain eight small, clean plastic containers, and number them 1 to 8; alternatively, divide a larger container into eight compartments.

Using a rubber sucker, withdraw each follower in turn, and place it in its respective container. Do not interchange the cam followers, or the rate of wear will be much-increased. If necessary, also remove the shim from the top of the valve stem, and store it with its respective follower. **Note:** *The shim may stick to the inside of the follower as it is withdrawn. If this happens, take care not to allow it to drop out as the follower is removed.*

2.0 litre engine

9 Working in sequence, evenly and progressively slacken the camshaft bearing cap casting retaining bolts by one turn at a time **(see illustration)**. This will relieve the valve spring pressure on the bearing caps gradually and evenly. Once the pressure has been relieved, the bolts can be fully unscrewed and removed. *Caution: If the bearing cap casting bolts are carelessly slackened, the casting may break. If the casting breaks then the complete cylinder head assembly must be renewed; the casting is matched to the head and is not available separately.*

10 Remove the camshaft bearing cap casting from the cylinder head **(see illustration)**. If the casting locating dowels are a loose fit in the head, remove them and store them with the casting for safe-keeping.

11 Lift the camshaft away from the cylinder head, and slide the oil seal off the camshaft end **(see illustration)**.

10.10 Remove the bearing cap casting . . .

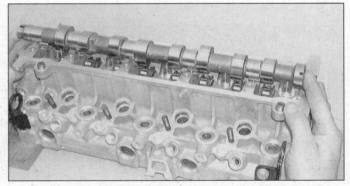

10.11 . . . then lift the camshaft out of position (shown with cylinder head removed)

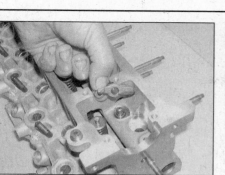

10.12a Lift the camshaft followers . . .

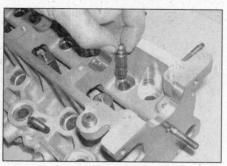

10.12b . . . and hydraulic tappets out from the cylinder head

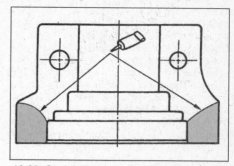

10.22 On 1.9 litre engines apply sealant to the areas shown on the camshaft end bearing caps

12 Obtain eight small, clean plastic containers, and number them 1 to 8; alternatively, divide a larger container into eight compartments. Lift each follower and hydraulic tappet out of position and place it in its respective container **(see illustrations)**. Do not interchange the cam followers or tappets, or the rate of wear will be much-increased.

Inspection

13 Examine the camshaft bearing surfaces and cam lobes for signs of wear ridges and scoring. Renew the camshaft if any of these conditions are apparent. Examine the condition of the bearing surfaces, both on the camshaft journals and in the cylinder head/bearing caps. If the head bearing surfaces are worn excessively, the cylinder head will need to be renewed.

14 Examine the cam follower bearing surfaces which contact the camshaft lobes for wear ridges and scoring. Renew any follower on which these conditions are apparent. If a follower bearing surface is badly scored, also examine the corresponding lobe on the camshaft for wear, as it is likely that both will be worn. Renew worn components as necessary.

15 On 2.0 litre engines, if the hydraulic tappets are thought to be faulty they should be renewed.

Refitting

1.9 litre engine

16 If the original camshaft is being refitted, and it is known that the valve clearances are

correct, proceed to the next paragraph, otherwise, adjust the valves as described in Section 11 using the clearances noted before camshaft removal. If a new camshaft is used, fit it as described in paragraphs 17 to 23, and the adjust the valve clearances (Section 11).

Caution: Ensure the crankshaft is correctly positioned with the pistons mid-way up the bores before rotating the camshaft.

17 Fit each shim to the top of its valve stem.

Caution: Do not interchange the shims, as this will upset the valve clearances (see Section 11).

18 Liberally oil the cylinder head cam follower bores and the followers. Carefully refit the followers to the cylinder head, ensuring that each follower is refitted to its original bore. Some care will be required to enter the followers squarely into their bores.

19 Lubricate the cam lobes and bearing journals with clean engine oil of the specified grade. Then refit the camshaft back into position on the cylinder head.

20 Temporarily refit the sprocket hub to the end of the camshaft and position it so that the hub timing hole is aligned with the corresponding cut-out in the cylinder head. Ensure the crankshaft is still positioned 90° BTDC so the pistons are mid-way up the bores.

21 Fit the centre bearing cap the correct way round as previously noted, then screw on the nuts and tighten them two or three turns.

22 Apply sealing compound to the end bearing caps on the areas shown **(see illustration)**. Fit them in the correct positions,

and tighten the nuts two or three turns.

23 Tighten all the nuts evenly and progressively to the specified torque, making sure that the camshaft remains correctly positioned.

Caution: If the bearing cap nuts are carelessly tightened, the bearing caps may break. If any bearing cap breaks then the complete cylinder head assembly must be renewed; the bearing caps are matched to the head and are not available separately.

24 Smear the lips of the new oil seal with clean engine oil and fit it onto the camshaft end, making sure its sealing lip is facing inwards. Press the oil seal in until it is flush with the end face of the camshaft bearing cap.

25 Refit the camshaft sprocket and hub as described in Section 8.

26 Refit the braking system vacuum pump as described in Chapter 9.

27 Refit the cylinder head cover as described in Section 4.

2.0 litre engine

28 Liberally oil the cylinder head tappet bores and the followers. Ensure the followers and hydraulic tappets are correctly clipped together then carefully refit them to the cylinder head, ensuring that each assembly is refitted in its original location.

29 Lubricate the cam bearing journals and followers with clean engine oil of the specified grade.

30 Ensure the crankshaft is still positioned 90° BTDC so the pistons are mid-way up the bores.

31 Ensure the mating surfaces of the camshaft bearing cap casting and cylinder head are clean and dry. Apply a thin bead of sealant (Peugeot recommend the use of Autojoint OR) to the mating surface of the casting as shown **(see illustration)**.

32 Locate the camshaft correctly in the bearing cap casting then, ensuring the locating dowels are in position, refit the camshaft and bearing cap casting assembly to the head.

33 Install the bearing cap casting bolts, tightening all bolts by hand. Working in the sequence shown, evenly and progressively tighten the bolts to draw the casting squarely down onto the cylinder head **(see illustration)**.

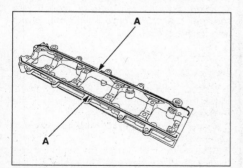

10.31 On 2.0 litre engines apply a thin bead of sealant (A) to the mating surface of the camshaft bearing cap casting as shown

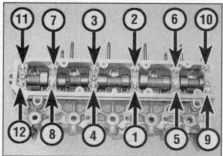

10.33 Camshaft bearing cap bolt tightening sequence – 2.0 litre engine

Once the casting is in contact with the head, go around in the specified sequence and tighten the bolts to the specified torque.

Caution: If the bearing cap casting bolts are carelessly tightened, the casting may break. If the casting breaks then the complete cylinder head assembly must be renewed; the casting is matched to the head and is not available separately.

34 Smear the lips of the new oil seal with clean engine oil and fit it onto the camshaft end, making sure its sealing lip is facing inwards. Press the oil seal in until it is flush with the end face of the camshaft bearing cap.

35 Refit the camshaft sprocket and hub as described in Section 8.

36 Refit the braking system vacuum pump as described in Chapter 9.

37 Refit the cylinder head cover as described in Section 4.

11 Valve clearances – checking and adjustment

1.9 litre engine

Checking

1 The importance of having the valve clearances correctly adjusted cannot be overstressed, as they vitally affect the performance of the engine. Checking should not be regarded as a routine operation, however. It should only be necessary when the valve gear has become noisy, after engine overhaul, or when trying to trace the cause of power loss. The clearances are checked as follows. The engine must be cold for the check to be accurate.

2 Firmly apply the handbrake, then jack up the front of the car and support it securely on axle stands (see *Jacking and vehicle support*). From underneath the front of the car, prise out the retaining clips, and remove the plastic cover from the wing valance to gain access to the crankshaft sprocket/pulley bolt. Where necessary, unclip the coolant hoses from the wing to improve access further.

3 The engine can now be turned over using a suitable socket and extension bar fitted to the crankshaft pulley bolt. Note that the crankshaft must always be turned in a clockwise direction (viewed from the right-hand side of the vehicle).

4 Remove the cylinder head cover as described in Section 4.

5 On a piece of paper, draw the outline of the engine with the cylinders numbered from the flywheel end. Show the position of each valve, together with the specified valve clearance. Above each valve, draw lines for noting (1) the actual clearance and (2) the amount of adjustment required **(see illustration)**.

6 Turn the crankshaft until the inlet valve of No 1 cylinder (nearest the transmission) is fully

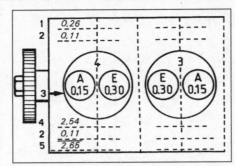

11.5 Example of valve shim thickness calculation – 1.9 litre engine

A   Inlet valve
B   Exhaust valve
1   Measured clearance
2   Difference from specified clearance (3)
3   Specified clearance
4   Thickness of shim fitted
5   Correct thickness of shim required

closed, with the tip of the cam facing directly away from the bucket tappet.

7 Using feeler blades, measure the clearance between the base of the cam and the bucket tappet. Record the clearance on line (1) **(see illustration)**.

8 Repeat the measurement for the other seven valves, turning the crankshaft as necessary so that the cam lobe in question is always facing directly away from the relevant tappet.

9 Calculate the difference between each measured clearance and the desired value, and record it on line (2). Since the clearance is different for inlet and exhaust valves – make sure that you are aware which valve you are dealing with. The valve sequence from either end of the engine is:

In – Ex – Ex – In – In – Ex – Ex – In

10 If all the clearances are within tolerance, refit the cylinder head cover with reference to Section 4, and where applicable, lower the vehicle to the ground. If any clearance measured is outside the specified tolerance, adjustment must be carried out as described in the following paragraphs.

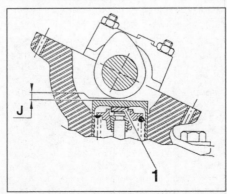

11.7 Valve clearance measurement (J). Clearance is altered by changing the shim (1)

Adjustment

11 Remove the camshaft as described in Section 10.

12 Withdraw the first follower and its shim. Be careful that the shim does not fall out of the tappet. Clean the shim, and measure its thickness with a micrometer. The shims carry thickness markings, but wear may have reduced the original thickness, so be sure to check.

13 Refer to the clearance recorded for the valve concerned. If the clearance was more than that specified, the shim thickness must be increased by the difference recorded (2). If the clearance was less than that specified, the thickness of the shim must be decreased by the difference recorded (2).

14 Draw three more lines beneath each valve on the calculation paper as shown in illustration 11.5. On line (4) note the measured thickness of the shim, then add or deduct the difference from line (2) to give the final shim thickness required on line (5).

15 Repeat the procedure given in paragraphs 13 to 15 on the remaining valves, keeping each tappet identified for position.

16 When reassembling, oil the shim and fit it into the valve retainer, with the size marking face downwards. Oil the follower, and lower it onto the shim. Do not raise the follower after fitting, as the shim may become dislodged.

17 When all the followers are in position, complete with their shims, refit the camshaft as described in Section 10. Recheck the valve clearances before refitting the cylinder head cover, to make sure they are correct.

2.0 litre engine

18 The 2.0 litre engine is equipped with hydraulic tappets which automatically adjust the valve clearances. Therefore there is no need to check or adjust the valve clearances at any time.

12 Cylinder head – removal and refitting

Note: *Ensure the engine is cold before removing the cylinder head.*

Caution: Be careful not to allow dirt into the fuel injection pump or injector pipes during this procedure.

1.9 litre engine

Removal

1 Disconnect the battery negative terminal (refer to *Disconnecting the battery* in the Reference Chapter).

2 Drain the cooling system as described in Chapter 1B.

3 Remove the braking system vacuum pump as described in Chapter 9.

4 Remove the timing belt as described in Section 7.

5 Once the timing belt has been removed,

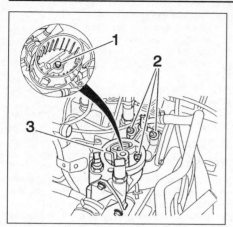

12.10 On 1.9 litre engines, unscrew the bolt (1) and remove fuel filter housing then undo the three bolts (2) and free the filter/thermostat housing (3) from the cylinder head

unscrew the single bolt securing the right-hand engine/transmission mounting bracket to the cylinder head. Leave all the bolts securing the bracket to the cylinder block then refit the upper bracket, securing the engine bracket to the mounting, and securely tighten its nuts and bolts. This will ensure the engine/transmission unit is securely supported through out the following procedure.

6 If the cylinder head is to be overhauled, remove the camshaft sprocket and camshaft (see Sections 8 and 10).

7 Referring to Chapter 4D, carry out the following operations.

a) *Remove the air cleaner housing.*
b) *Remove the inlet and exhaust manifolds.*
c) *Disconnect and remove the fuel return hose from the end injector.*
d) *Unscrew the union nuts and disconnect the fuel pipes from the fuel injectors and the fuel injection pump. Remove the pipes.*
e) *If the cylinder head is being overhauled, remove the injectors.*

8 Remove the cylinder head cover as described in Section 4.

9 Remove the fuel filter as described in Chapter 1B.

10 Unscrew the retaining bolt and remove the filter plastic housing, complete with its sealing ring **(see illustration)**. Discard the sealing ring; a new one must be used on refitting.

11 Slacken and remove the three bolts, noting the correct fitted location of the sealing washer, securing the fuel filter/thermostat housing to the front of the cylinder head. Disconnect the coolant hose connecting the housing to the coolant pipe then free the housing from the cylinder head. Recover the housing gasket and discard it; a new one must be used on refitting.

12 Unscrew the securing nut and disconnect

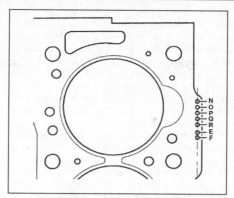

12.22 Cylinder head gasket thickness identification holes – 1.9 litre engine

the feed wire from the relevant glow plug. Recover the washers.

13 Unscrew the bolt securing the coolant pipe to the left-hand end of the cylinder head.

14 Check that the wiring and hoses is released from all the relevant clips or guides on the cylinder head and positioned clear.

15 Working in the *reverse* of the sequence shown in illustration 12.33, progressively slacken the ten cylinder head bolts by half a turn at a time, until all bolts can be unscrewed by hand.

16 With all the cylinder head bolts removed, release the cylinder head from the cylinder block and locating dowel by rocking it. The Peugeot tool for doing this consists simply of two metal rods with 90-degree angled ends. Do not prise between the mating faces of the cylinder head and block, as this may damage the gasket faces. Lift the cylinder head away; seek assistance if possible.

17 Remove the gasket from the top of the block, noting the locating dowel. If the locating dowel is a loose fit, remove it and store it with the head for safe-keeping. Do not discard the gasket – it will be needed for identification purposes (see paragraphs 22 to 25).

18 If the cylinder head is to be dismantled for overhaul, remove the camshaft and followers as described in Section 10, then refer to Part E of this Chapter.

Preparation for refitting

19 The mating faces of the cylinder head and cylinder block must be perfectly clean before refitting the head. Use a hard plastic or wood scraper to remove all traces of gasket and carbon; also clean the piston crowns. Take particular care during the cleaning operations, as aluminium alloy is easily damaged. Also, make sure that the carbon is not allowed to enter the oil and water passages – this is particularly important for the lubrication system, as carbon could block the oil supply to the engine's components. Using adhesive tape and paper, seal the water, oil and bolt holes in the cylinder block/crankcase. To prevent carbon entering the gap between the pistons and bores, smear a little grease in the

gap. After cleaning each piston, use a small brush to remove all traces of grease and carbon from the gap, then wipe away the remainder with a clean rag. Clean all the pistons in the same way.

20 Check the mating surfaces of the cylinder block and the cylinder head for nicks, deep scratches and other damage. If slight, they may be removed carefully with a file, but if excessive, machining may be the only alternative to renewal.

21 If warpage of the cylinder head gasket surface is suspected, use a straight-edge to check it for distortion. Refer to Part E of this Chapter if necessary.

22 When purchasing a new cylinder head gasket, it is essential that a gasket of the correct thickness is obtained. There are six different thicknesses of gasket available to enable the cylinder head-to-piston clearance to be accurately set. The gasket thickness can be determined by looking at the tab situated in front of No 1 cylinder **(see illustration)**. There will be between 3 and 7 holes in the tab; the first two holes (in locations E and F) identify the engine type (D8W), these are present on all gaskets and are of no real significance. It is the last group of between 1 and 5 holes (in locations N to R) which identify the gasket thickness as follows.

Number of holes (hole locations)	Gasket thickness (when compressed)
1 (N)	1.26 mm
2 (N and O)	1.30 mm
3 (N, O and P)	1.34 mm
4 (N, O, P and Q)	1.38 mm
5 (N, O, P, Q and R)	1.42 mm
2 (N and R)	1.46 mm

The correct thickness of gasket required is selected by measuring the piston protrusions as follows.

23 Ensure the flywheel is correctly locked in position so pistons 1 and 4 are exactly at TDC. Mount a dial test indicator securely on the block so that its pointer can be easily pivoted between the piston crown and block mating surfaces. Zero the dial test indicator on the gasket surface of the cylinder block then carefully move the indicator over No 1 piston and measure its protrusion **(see illustration)**. Take measurements at the front and rear of the piston, and take the average of the two measurements to be the piston

12.23 Measuring piston protrusion

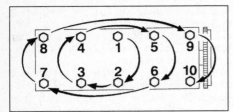

12.33 Cylinder head bolt tightening sequence

protrusion. Repeat this procedure on No 4 piston.

24 Remove the locking tool then rotate the crankshaft half-a-turn (180°) clockwise to bring pistons 2 and 3 to TDC. Ensure the crankshaft is accurately positioned then measure the protrusions of pistons No 2 and 3. Once all four pistons have been measured, rotate the crankshaft through a further half-a-turn (180°) clockwise to bring pistons 1 and 4 back to TDC then lock the flywheel in position again.

25 Using the largest protrusion measurement of the four pistons, select the correct thickness of gasket required using the following:

Piston protrusion measurement	Gasket thickness required
0.510 to 0.549 mm	1.26 mm
0.550 to 0.589 mm	1.30 mm
0.590 to 0.629 mm	1.34 mm
0.630 to 0.669 mm	1.38 mm
0.670 to 0.709 mm	1.42 mm
0.710 to 0.750 mm	1.46 mm

26 Check the condition of the cylinder head bolts, and particularly their threads, whenever they are removed. Wash the bolts in suitable solvent, and wipe them dry. Check each for any sign of visible wear or damage, renewing any bolt if necessary. Measure the length of each bolt, from the underside of its head to the bolt end, to check for stretching. There are two possible types of cylinder head bolt, those with a centring point at their end and those without. Bolts with a centring point are 124 mm long when new and must be renewed if any bolt has stretched to more than 125.5 mm. Bolts without a centring point are 120 mm long when new and must be renewed if they have stretched to more than 121.5 mm. Renew all the cylinder head bolts as a set if any bolt exceeds the maximum length. Although Peugeot do not actually specify that the bolts must be renewed, it is strongly recommended that the bolts should be renewed as a complete set, regardless of their apparent condition, whenever they are disturbed.

Refitting

27 Wipe clean the mating surfaces of the cylinder head and cylinder block. Check that the locating dowel is in position in the cylinder block.

28 Position the correct thickness new gasket on the cylinder block surface, ensuring that its identification holes are at the front, left-hand end of the gasket.

29 Check that the flywheel and camshaft sprocket are still correctly locked in position with their respective tools. **Note:** *If the camshaft/camshaft sprocket are not installed, as a precaution, remove the flywheel locking pin then rotate the crankshaft* **backwards** *(anti-clockwise) through 90°; this will position the pistons mid-way up the bores and remove the risk of the valves contacting the pistons during the following operation.*

30 With the aid of an assistant, carefully refit the cylinder head assembly to the block, aligning it with the locating dowel.

31 Lubricate the threads and underside of the heads of the cylinder head bolts with a smear of grease (Peugeot recommend the use of Molykote G Rapid Plus grease).

32 Carefully enter each bolt into its relevant hole (*do not drop them in*) and screw in, by hand only, until finger-tight.

33 Working progressively and in sequence, tighten the cylinder head bolts to their Stage 1 torque setting, using a torque wrench and suitable socket **(see illustration)**.

34 Once all the bolts have been tightened to their Stage 1 setting, working again in the given sequence, tighten the cylinder head bolts to the specified Stage 2 torque setting.

35 Finally angle-tighten the bolts through the specified Stage 3 angle, using a socket and extension bar. It is recommended that an angle-measuring gauge is used during this stage of the tightening, to ensure accuracy. If a gauge is not available, use white paint to make alignment marks between the bolt head and cylinder head prior to tightening; the marks can then be used to check that the bolt has been rotated through the correct angle during tightening.

36 Where necessary, refit the camshaft and/or camshaft sprocket (see Sections 8 and 10). If the cylinder head has been overhauled, check the valve clearances before proceeding.

37 Ensure the engine/transmission unit is securely supported then remove the mounting bracket from the right-hand engine/transmission mounting. Refit the bolt securing the bracket to the cylinder head and tighten it to the specified torque.

38 Refit the timing belt as described in Section 7.

39 Refit the coolant pipe bolt and securely reconnect the glow plug wiring.

40 Ensure the mating surfaces are clean and dry then refit the fuel filter/thermostat housing to the cylinder head, using a new gasket. Fit the housing retaining bolts, ensuring the sealing washer is fitted to the bolt located inside the filter housing, and tighten them to the specified torque. Reconnect the coolant hose securely to the housing.

41 Fit a new sealing ring to the base of the fuel filter plastic housing and refit the housing, tightening its bolt to the specified torque.

42 Refit the cylinder cover (see Section 4).

43 Referring to Chapter 4D, carry out the following.

a) *Refit the injectors (where removed).*

b) *Refit the fuel pipes connecting the injection pump to the injectors and reconnect the leak off hoses to the injectors.*

c) *Refit the manifolds and air cleaner housing.*

44 Refit the braking system vacuum pump as described in Chapter 9.

45 Fit a new fuel filter and refill the cooling system as described in Chapter 1B.

2.0 litre engine

Removal

46 Disconnect the battery negative terminal (refer to *Disconnecting the battery* in the Reference Chapter).

47 Drain the cooling system as described in Chapter 1B.

48 Remove the braking system vacuum pump as described in Chapter 9.

49 Unbolt the engine cover brackets and remove them from the cylinder head.

50 Remove the timing belt as described in Section 7. Once the timing belt has been removed, unscrew the two upper bolts securing the right-hand engine/transmission mounting bracket to the cylinder head. Leave the lower bolts securing the bracket to the cylinder block then refit the upper bracket, securing the engine bracket to the mounting, and securely tighten its nuts and bolts. This will ensure the engine/transmission unit is securely supported through out the following procedure.

51 Referring to Chapter 4E, carry out the following operations.

a) *Remove the air cleaner housing.*

b) *Remove the turbocharger.*

c) *Remove the high-pressure fuel pipe connecting the injection pump to the fuel rail and the fuel return pipe.*

d) *If the cylinder head is being overhauled, remove the fuel rail and injectors. If not disconnect the wiring connectors from the injectors and fuel rail sensor(s) then unbolt the wiring harness guide and position it clear of the head.*

52 Remove the camshaft as described in Section 10.

53 Disconnect the wiring connector from the coolant temperature sensor fitted to the thermostat housing **(see illustration)**.

12.53 Disconnect the coolant temperature sensor wiring connector – 2.0 litre engine

54 Release the retaining clips and disconnect the coolant hoses from the coolant outlet housing on the left-hand end of the cylinder head **(see illustration)**.

55 Slacken and remove the engine oil dipstick tube retaining bolt.

56 Unscrew the nuts and bolts securing the coolant outlet housing to the end of the cylinder head and remove the wiring bracket. Unscrew the two housing studs from the cylinder head; to do this, screw two nuts onto the end of the stud then lock the nuts securely together and use the inner nut to unscrew the stud from the head **(see illustration)**.

57 Free the coolant outlet housing from the end of the cylinder head and recover its gasket. Discard the gasket, a new one must be used on refitting.

58 Working in the *reverse* of the sequence shown in illustration 12.33, progressively slacken the ten cylinder head bolts by half a turn at a time, until all bolts can be unscrewed by hand.

59 With all the cylinder head bolts removed, release the cylinder head from the cylinder block and locating dowels by rocking it. The Peugeot tool for doing this consists simply of two metal rods with 90-degree angled ends. Do not prise between the mating faces of the cylinder head and block, as this may damage the gasket faces. Lift the cylinder head away; seek assistance if possible.

60 Remove the gasket from the top of the block, noting the two locating dowels. If the locating dowels are a loose fit, remove them and store them with the head for safe-keeping. Do not discard the gasket – it will be needed for identification purposes (see paragraphs 63 to 66) **(see illustration)**.

61 If the cylinder head is to be dismantled overhaul, refer to Part E of this Chapter.

Preparation for refitting

62 Clean and check the cylinder head and block mating surfaces as described in paragraphs 19 to 21.

63 When purchasing a new cylinder head gasket, it is essential that a gasket of the correct thickness is obtained. There are five different thicknesses of gasket available to enable the cylinder head-to-piston clearance to be accurately set. The gasket thickness can be determined by looking at the tab situated

12.54 On 2.0 litre engines disconnect the coolant hoses from the housing on the left-hand end of the cylinder head

in front of No 2 and 3 cylinders. There will be between 1 and 5 notches on the tab **(see illustration)**. These notches identify the gasket thickness as follows.

Number of notches (notch locations)	Gasket thickness (when compressed)
1 (R)	1.30 mm
2 (Q and R)	1.35 mm
3 (P, Q and R)	1.40 mm
4 (O, P, Q and R)	1.45 mm
5 (N, O, P, Q and R)	1.50 mm

The correct thickness of gasket required is selected by measuring the piston protrusions as follows.

64 Rotate the crankshaft 90° clockwise to bring pistons No 1 and 4 to TDC then lock the flywheel in position with the locking tool. Mount a dial test indicator securely on the block so that its pointer cam be easily pivoted between the piston crown and block mating surfaces **(see illustration 12.23)**. Zero the dial test indicator on the gasket surface of the cylinder block then carefully move the indicator over No 1 piston and measure its protrusion. Take measurements at the front and rear of the piston, and take the average of the two measurements to be the piston protrusion. Repeat this procedure on No 4 piston.

65 Remove the locking tool then rotate the crankshaft half-a-turn (180°) clockwise to bring pistons 2 and 3 to TDC. Ensure the crankshaft is accurately positioned then measure the protrusions of pistons No 2 and 3. Once all four pistons have been measured, rotate the crankshaft through

12.56 Lock two nuts together then unscrew the coolant outlet housing studs from the cylinder head

another 90° clockwise to position the pistons halfway up their bores.

66 Using the largest protrusion measurement of the four pistons, select the correct thickness of head required using the following table.

Piston protrusion measurement	Gasket thickness required
0.470 to 0.604 mm	1.30 mm
0.605 to 0.654 mm	1.35 mm
0.655 to 0.704 mm	1.40 mm
0.705 to 0.754 mm	1.45 mm
0.755 to 0.830 mm	1.50 mm

67 Check the condition of the cylinder head bolts, and particularly their threads, whenever they are removed. Wash the bolts in suitable solvent, and wipe them dry. Check each for any sign of visible wear or damage, renewing any bolt if necessary. Measure the length of each bolt, from the underside of its head to the bolt end, to check for stretching. The bolts are 131.5 mm long when new and must be renewed if any bolt has stretched to more than 133.4 mm. Renew all the cylinder head bolts as a set if any bolt exceeds the maximum length. Although Peugeot do not actually specify that the bolts must be renewed, it is strongly recommended that the bolts should be renewed as a complete set, regardless of their apparent condition, whenever they are disturbed.

Refitting

68 Bring pistons No 1 and 4 to TDC then rotate the crankshaft **backwards** (anti-clockwise) through 90°; this will position the pistons mid-way up the bores and remove the risk of the valves contacting the pistons during the following operation.

69 Wipe clean the mating surfaces of the cylinder head and cylinder block. Check that the locating dowels are in position in the cylinder block.

70 Position the correct thickness new gasket on the cylinder block surface, ensuring that its identification notches are at the front of the gasket and the gasket is the correct way up.

71 With the aid of an assistant, carefully refit the cylinder head assembly to the block, aligning it with the locating dowels.

72 Lubricate the threads and underside of the heads of the cylinder head bolts with a

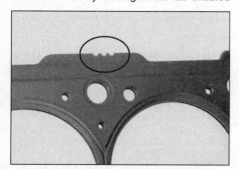

12.60 Cylinder head thickness can be identified by the cut-outs (circled)

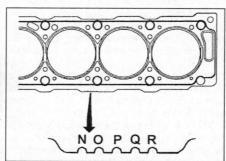

12.63 Cylinder head gasket identification notch location – 2.0 litre engine

N O P Q R

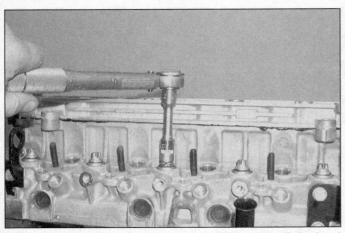

12.74 Working in the specified sequence, tighten the cylinder head bolts to the specified Stage 1 and Stage 2 torque settings . . .

12.76 . . . then angle-tighten them through the specified Stage 3 angle

smear of grease (Peugeot recommend the use of Molykote G Rapid Plus grease).

73 Carefully enter each bolt into its relevant hole (*do not drop them in*) and screw in, by hand only, until finger-tight.

74 Working progressively and in the sequence shown in illustration 12.33, tighten the cylinder head bolts to their Stage 1 torque setting, using a torque wrench and suitable socket **(see illustration)**.

75 Once all the bolts have been tightened to their Stage 1 setting, working again in the given sequence, tighten the cylinder head bolts to the specified Stage 2 torque setting.

76 Finally angle-tighten the bolts through the specified Stage 3 angle, using a socket and extension bar. It is recommended that an angle-measuring gauge is used during this stage of the tightening, to ensure accuracy **(see illustration)**. If a gauge is not available, use white paint to make alignment marks between the bolt head and cylinder head prior to tightening; the marks can then be used to check that the bolt has been rotated through the correct angle during tightening.

77 Refit the camshaft and camshaft sprocket (see Sections 8 and 10).

78 Ensure the engine/transmission unit is securely supported then remove the mounting bracket from the right-hand engine/transmission mounting. Apply thread locking compound (Peugeot recommend the use of Loctite Frenetanch) to the M10 bolt then refit both bolts securing the bracket to the cylinder head, tightening them to the specified torque.

79 Refit the timing belt as described in Section 7.

80 Ensure the mating surfaces are clean and dry then refit the thermostat housing to the cylinder head, using a new gasket. Apply locking compound to the threads of the housing studs then screw the studs into the cylinder head, ensuring they pass through the gasket holes, and tighten them to the specified torque. Refit the wiring bracket and install the housing nuts and bolts, tightening them to the specified torque.

81 Reconnect the wiring connector to the coolant temperature sensor then securely reconnect the coolant hoses to the housing.

82 Refit the engine oil dipstick tube bolt and tighten securely.

83 Refit the cylinder cover (see Section 4) then refit the engine cover brackets to the cylinder head.

84 Referring to Chapter 4E, carry out the following.

a) Refit the injectors and fuel rail (where removed) or reconnect the wiring connectors and secure the wiring harness guide in position (as applicable).

b) Refit the high-pressure fuel pipe connecting the injection pump to the fuel rail and reconnect the fuel return pipe.

c) Refit the turbocharger.

d) Refit the air cleaner housing.

85 Refit the braking system vacuum pump as described in Chapter 9.

86 Refill the cooling system as described in Chapter 1B.

13 Sump – removal and refitting

Removal

1 Firmly apply the handbrake, then jack up the front of the car and support it securely on axle stands (see *Jacking and vehicle support*). Disconnect the battery negative terminal (refer to *Disconnecting the battery* in the Reference Chapter).

2 Where necessary, remove the retaining bolts, screws and clips and remove the undercover from beneath the engine/transmission unit.

3 Drain the engine oil, then clean and refit the engine oil drain plug, tightening it to the specified torque. If the engine is nearing its service interval when the oil and filter are due for renewal, it is recommended that the filter is also removed, and a new one fitted. After

reassembly, the engine can then be refilled with fresh oil. Refer to Chapter 1B for further information.

4 On models with air conditioning, remove the auxiliary drivebelt as described in Chapter 1B. Unscrew the compressor mounting bolts and nuts. Free the compressor from the sump and support its weight by tying it to the vehicle, to prevent any excess strain being placed on the compressor lines. Take care not to lose the spacers from the compressor rear mountings (where fitted).

Caution: Do not disconnect the refrigerant lines from the compressor (refer to the warnings given in Chapter 3). Ensure the compressor is securely supported to prevent the refrigerant lines being damaged.

5 Progressively slacken and remove all the sump retaining bolts. On some models, it may be necessary to unbolt the flywheel cover plate from the transmission to gain access to the left-hand sump fasteners.

6 Break the joint by striking the sump with the palm of your hand. Lower the sump, and withdraw it from underneath the vehicle. On models with air conditioning, recover the sump locating dowel(s).

7 While the sump is removed, take the opportunity to check the oil pump pick-up/strainer for signs of clogging or splitting. If necessary, remove the pump as described in Section 14, and clean or renew the strainer.

Refitting

8 Clean all traces of sealant from the mating surfaces of the cylinder block/crankcase and sump, then use a clean rag to wipe out the sump and the engine's interior.

9 Apply a thin coating of suitable sealant to the sump mating surface.

10 On models with air conditioning ensure the sump locating dowel(s) is/are correctly fitted (as applicable).

11 Offer up the sump to the cylinder block/crankcase and refit its retaining bolts. Tighten all bolts by hand then evenly and

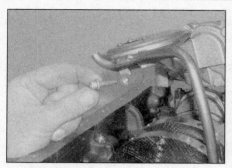

14.2a Unscrew the bolt securing the dipstick guide tube to the oil pump . . .

14.2b . . . then remove the guide tube from the block (shown with engine removed)

14.4 Note the correct fitted location of each oil pump retaining bolt (arrowed) as it is removed

progressively tighten them to the specified torque setting.

12 Where necessary, ensure the spacers (where fitted) are correctly to the rear mountings then align the air conditioning compressor with the sump. Refit the mounting bolts and nuts; tighten compressor front (drivebelt pulley end) mounting bolts to the specified torque first, then tighten the rear mounting bolts to the specified torque (see Chapter 3). Refit the auxiliary drivebelt as described in Chapter 1B.

13 Refit the undercover (where fitted) then lower the vehicle to the ground and refill the engine with oil (see Chapter 1B).

14 Oil pump – removal, inspection and refitting

Removal

1 Remove the sump (see Section 13).

2 Unscrew the bolt securing the dipstick guide tube to the oil pump and remove the guide tube from the cylinder block **(see illustrations)**.

3 On 1.9 litre engines slacken and remove the three bolts securing the oil pump in position, noting the correct fitted location of the longer bolt. Disengage the pump sprocket from the chain, and remove the oil pump and spacer plate from the engine.

4 On 2.0 litre engines slacken and remove the three bolts securing the oil pump in position, noting the correct fitted location of the each bolt (they are all different sizes) and the

sealing washer **(see illustration)**. Disengage the pump sprocket from the chain, and remove the oil pump from the engine.

Inspection

5 Examine the oil pump sprocket for signs of damage and wear, such as chipped or missing teeth. If the sprocket is worn, the pump assembly must be renewed, as the sprocket is not available separately. It is also recommended that the chain and drive sprocket, fitted to the crankshaft, is renewed at the same time. The oil pump drive sprocket and chain can be removed with the engine *in situ*, once the crankshaft sprocket has been removed and the crankshaft oil seal housing has been unbolted. See Part E for further information.

6 Slacken and remove the bolts securing the strainer cover to the pump body, then lift off the strainer cover. Remove the relief valve piston and spring (and guide pin – 2.0 litre engine only), noting which way round they are fitted **(see illustrations)**.

7 Examine the pump rotors and body for signs of wear ridges and scoring. If worn, the complete pump assembly must be renewed.

8 Examine the relief valve piston for signs of wear or damage, and renew if necessary. The condition of the relief valve spring can only be measured by comparing it with a new one; if there is any doubt about its condition, it should also be renewed. Both the piston and spring are available individually.

9 Thoroughly clean the oil pump strainer with a suitable solvent, and check it for signs of clogging or splitting. If the strainer is

damaged, the strainer and cover assembly must be renewed.

10 Locate the relief valve spring, piston and (where fitted) the guide pin in the strainer cover, then refit the cover to the pump body. Align the relief valve piston with its bore in the pump. Refit the cover retaining bolts, tightening them securely.

Refitting

11 On 1.9 litre engines, fit the spacer plate then offer up the pump, engaging the pump sprocket with its drive chain. Refit the pump retaining bolts, ensuring the longer bolt is fitted to the rear hole, and tighten them to the specified torque setting.

12 On 2.0 litre engines, engage the pump sprocket with the drive chain then install the retaining bolts. Fit the sealing washer to the rear bolt then install the pump retaining bolts, ensuring they are fitted in their original locations. Tighten the bolts to the specified torque.

13 On all models, refit the dipstick guide tube to the cylinder block and securely tighten its retaining bolt.

14 Refit the sump as described in Section 13.

15 Oil cooler – removal and refitting

Removal

1 The oil cooler is mounted on the front of the cylinder block. To gain access to the cooler,

14.6a Unscrew the retaining bolts . . .

14.6b . . . then lift off the cover and remove the spring . . .

14.6c . . . and relief valve piston, noting which way around it is fitted

15.6 Oil cooler centre bolt (A) and locating notch (B)

16.2 Using a self-tapping screw and pliers to remove the crankshaft right-hand oil seal

17.2 Lock the flywheel ring gear

firmly apply the handbrake, then jack up the front of the vehicle and support it on axle stands (see *Jacking and vehicle support*). Disconnect the battery negative terminal (refer to *Disconnecting the battery* in the Reference Chapter).

2 Where necessary, remove the retaining bolts, screws and clips and remove the undercover from beneath the engine/ transmission unit.

3 Position a suitable container beneath the oil filter. Unscrew the filter using an oil filter removal tool if necessary, and drain the oil into the container (see Chapter 1B). If the oil filter is damaged or distorted during removal, it must be renewed. Given the low cost of a new oil filter relative to the cost of repairing the damage which could result if a re-used filter springs a leak, it is probably a good idea to renew the filter in any case.

4 Using a hose clamp or similar, clamp both the oil cooler coolant hoses to minimise coolant loss during subsequent operations.

5 Slacken the retaining clips, and disconnect both coolant hoses from the oil cooler – be prepared for some coolant spillage. Wash off any spilt coolant immediately with cold water, and dry the surrounding area before proceeding further.

6 Slacken and remove the oil cooler centre bolt, and remove the cooler from the cylinder block **(see illustration)**. Remove the sealing ring (where fitted) from the rear of the cooler, and discard it; a new one must be used on refitting.

Caution: Ensure no dirt is allowed to enter the engine whilst the oil cooler is removed.

Refitting

7 Where a sealing ring was fitted to the oil cooler, fit a new sealing ring to the oil cooler. Where no sealing ring was fitted, ensure the oil cooler mating surface is clean and dry then apply a bead of suitable sealant to the cooler.

8 Clean the oil cooler centre bolt and apply a smear of fresh sealant to its threads.

9 Locate the fluid cooler on the front of the cylinder block, ensuring its locating notch its correctly located with the lug on the block. Refit the cooler centre bolt and tighten it to the specified torque.

10 Reconnect the coolant hoses to the oil

cooler, and securely tighten their retaining clips. Remove the hose clamp(s).

11 Fit the oil filter (see Chapter 1B), then refit the undercover (where fitted) and lower the vehicle to the ground.

12 Top-up the engine oil level and the cooling system as described in *Weekly checks*. Start the engine, and check the oil cooler for signs of leakage.

16 Crankshaft oil seals – renewal

Right-hand oil seal

1 Remove the crankshaft sprocket as described in Section 8.

2 Make a note of the correct fitted depth of the seal in its housing then carefully punch or drill two small holes opposite each other in the seal. Screw a self-tapping screw into each, and pull on the screws with pliers to extract the seal **(see illustration)**. Alternatively, the seal can be levered out of position using a suitable flat-bladed screwdriver, taking great care not to damage the oil pump drive gear shoulder or seal housing.

3 Clean the seal housing, and polish off any burrs or raised edges, which may have caused the seal to fail in the first place.

4 Lubricate the lips of the new seal with clean engine oil, and carefully locate the seal on the end of crankshaft. Note that its sealing lip must face inwards. Take care not to damage the seal lips during fitting.

5 Using a suitable tubular drift (such as a socket) which bears only on the hard outer edge of the seal, tap the seal into position to the same depth in the housing as the original was prior to removal. The inner face of the seal must be flush with the inner wall of the crankcase.

6 Wash off any traces of oil, then refit the crankshaft sprocket as described in Section 8.

Left-hand oil seal

7 Remove the flywheel (see Section 17).

8 Make a note of the correct fitted depth of the seal in its housing. Punch or drill two small

holes opposite each other in the seal. Screw a self-tapping screw into each, and pull on the screws with pliers to extract the seal.

9 Clean the seal housing, and polish off any burrs or raised edges, which may have caused the seal to fail in the first place.

10 Lubricate the lips of the new seal with clean engine oil, and carefully locate the seal on the end of the crankshaft.

11 Using a suitable tubular drift, which bears only on the hard outer edge of the seal, drive the seal into position, to the same depth in the housing as the original was prior to removal.

12 Wash off any traces of oil, then refit the flywheel as described in Section 17.

17 Flywheel – removal, inspection and refitting

Note: *New flywheel retaining bolts must be used on refitting.*

Removal

1 Remove the transmission as described in Chapter 7A, then remove the clutch assembly as described in Chapter 6.

2 Prevent the flywheel from turning by locking the ring gear teeth with a similar arrangement to that shown **(see illustration)**. Alternatively, bolt a strap between the flywheel and the cylinder block/crankcase.

Caution: Do not attempt to lock the flywheel in position using the locking pin described in Section 3.

3 Slacken and remove the flywheel retaining bolts. Discard the bolts; new ones must be used on refitting.

4 Remove the flywheel. Do not drop it, as it is very heavy. If the locating dowel is a loose fit in the crankshaft end, remove and store it with the flywheel for safe-keeping.

Inspection

5 If the flywheel's clutch mating surface is deeply scored, cracked or otherwise damaged, the flywheel must be renewed. However, it may be possible to have it surface-ground; seek the advice of a Peugeot dealer or engine reconditioning specialist.

6 If the ring gear is badly worn or has missing

teeth, it must be renewed. This job is best left to a Peugeot dealer or engine reconditioning specialist. The temperature to which the new ring gear must be heated for installation is critical and, if not done accurately, the hardness of the teeth will be destroyed.

Refitting

7 Clean the mating surfaces of the flywheel and crankshaft. Remove any remaining locking compound from the threads of the crankshaft holes, using the correct size of tap, if available.

HAYNES HINT *If a suitable tap is not available, cut two slots along the threads of one of the original flywheel bolts and use the bolt to remove the locking compound from the threads.*

8 Ensure that the locating dowel is in position. Offer up the flywheel, locating it on the dowel, and fit the new retaining bolts **(see illustration)**.

9 Lock the flywheel using the method employed on dismantling, and tighten the retaining bolts evenly and progressively to the specified torque **(see illustration)**.

10 Refit the clutch as described in Chapter 6. Remove the locking tool, and refit the transmission as described in Chapter 7A.

---

18 Engine/transmission mountings – inspection and renewal

Inspection

1 If improved access is required, raise the front of the car and support it on axle stands (see *Jacking and vehicle support*).

2 Check the mounting rubber to see if it is cracked, hardened or separated from the metal at any point; renew the mounting if any such damage or deterioration is evident.

3 Check that all the mounting's fasteners are securely tightened; use a torque wrench to check if possible.

4 Using a large screwdriver or a crowbar, check for wear in the mounting by carefully levering against it to check for free play. Where this is not possible, enlist the aid of an assistant to move the engine/transmission back-and-forth, or from side-to-side, while you watch the mounting. While some free play is to be expected even from new components, excessive wear should be obvious. If excessive free play is found, check first that the fasteners are secure, then renew any worn components as described below.

Renewal

Right-hand mounting

5 Disconnect the battery negative terminal

17.8 Locate the flywheel on the crankshaft then fit the new retaining bolts

(refer to *Disconnecting the battery* in the Reference Chapter).

6 On 1.9 litre engines, remove the fasteners from the right-hand side and top of the engine cover then lift off the cover, taking care not to lose its mounting rubbers **(see illustrations 4.1a to 4.1c)**, on 2.0 litre engines remove the fasteners (rotate them 90° to release them) then lift off the engine cover **(see illustrations 4.14a and 4.14b)**.

7 Remove the undercover (where fitted) then place a jack beneath the engine, with a block of wood on the jack head. Raise the jack until it is supporting the weight of the engine.

8 Slacken and remove the mounting bolts and remove the bracket from the top of the mounting **(see illustration)**.

9 Unscrew the vibration damper (where fitted) from the top of the mounting rubber then slacken and remove the nut securing the mounting bracket to the mounting rubber **(see illustration)**.

10 Slacken and remove the three bolts securing the right-hand engine mounting bracket to the bracket on the side of the cylinder block then lift off the mounting bracket, taking care not to lose the locating dowels (where fitted).

11 Make identification marks on the movement restrictors (the front and rear restrictors are different and are not interchangeable) then unscrew the nuts and remove both restrictors.

12 Using a strap wrench, unscrew the mounting rubber from the body

18.8 Unscrew the bolts and remove the bracket from the top of the right-hand mounting

17.9 Lock the flywheel (tool arrowed) then tighten the retaining bolts evenly and progressively to the specified torque

13 Check for signs of wear or damage on all components, and renew as necessary.

14 On reassembly, screw the mounting rubber into the body, tightening it to the specified torque.

15 Refit the front and rear movement restrictors in their original locations. Ensure the restrictor pegs are correctly located in their holes then securely tighten their retaining nuts.

16 Ensure the dowels (where fitted) are in position then install the mounting bracket, tightening its retaining bolts and nut to their specified torque settings.

17 Refit the vibration damper (where fitted) to the mounting, tightening it to the specified torque.

18 Fit the bracket over the vibration damper, tightening its bolts to the specified torque.

19 Remove the jack from under the engine then refit the undercover (where fitted). Reconnect the battery negative lead then refit the engine cover.

Left-hand mounting

20 Remove the battery, battery tray and mounting plate as described in Chapter 5A.

21 Remove the undercover (where fitted) and place a jack beneath the transmission, with a block of wood on the jack head. Raise the jack until it is supporting the weight of the transmission.

22 Slacken and remove the mounting rubber's centre nut and two retaining bolts and remove the mounting from the engine compartment.

18.9 Unscrew the vibration damper (where fitted) from the top of the mounting to gain access to the mounting nut

23 If necessary, undo the retaining bolts and remove the mounting bracket from the body.

24 The mounting stud is a screw-fit into its mounting bracket and the bracket is secured to the transmission by two bolts. If the mounting stud is tight, a universal stud extractor can be used to unscrew it.

25 Check carefully for signs of wear or damage on all components, and renew them where necessary.

26 Where necessary, refit the mounting bracket to the top of the transmission unit and tighten its bolts to the specified torque. Apply locking compound (Peugeot recommend the use of Loctite Frenetanch) to the stud threads then refit the stud to the bracket, tightening it to the specified torque. Slide the spacer onto the stud.

27 Refit the mounting bracket to the vehicle body and tighten its bolts to the specified torque.

28 Fit the mounting rubber to the bracket and tighten its retaining bolts to the specified torque. Refit the mounting centre nut, and tighten it to the specified torque.

29 Remove the jack from underneath the transmission and refit the undercover (where fitted).

30 Refit the battery as described in Chapter 5A.

Rear mounting

31 If not already done, firmly apply the handbrake, then jack up the front of the vehicle and support it securely on axle stands (see *Jacking and vehicle support*).

32 Where necessary, remove the retaining bolts, screws and clips and remove the undercover from beneath the engine/transmission unit.

33 Unscrew and remove the bolt securing the rear mounting link to the mounting on the rear of the cylinder block.

34 Remove the bolt securing the rear mounting link to the subframe.

35 To remove the mounting assembly it will first be necessary to remove the right-hand driveshaft as described in Chapter 8.

36 With the driveshaft removed, undo the retaining bolts and remove the mounting from the rear of the cylinder block.

37 Check carefully for signs of wear or damage on all components, and renew them where necessary.

38 On reassembly, fit the rear mounting assembly to the rear of the cylinder block, and tighten its retaining bolts to the specified torque. Refit the driveshaft as described in Chapter 8.

39 Refit the rear mounting link, and tighten both its bolts to their specified torque settings.

40 Refit the undercover (where fitted) then lower the vehicle to the ground.

Chapter 2 Part E:
Engine removal and overhaul procedures

Contents

Degrees of difficulty

Easy, suitable for novice with little experience	**Fairly easy,** suitable for beginner with some experience	**Fairly difficult,** suitable for competent DIY mechanic	**Difficult,** suitable for experienced DIY mechanic	**Very difficult,** suitable for expert DIY or professional 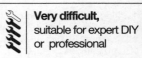

Specifications

Cylinder head

Maximum gasket face distortion:		
Petrol engines	0.05 mm	
Diesel engines	0.03 mm	
Cylinder head height:		
TU series petrol engines	111.2 ± 0.08 mm	
XU series petrol engines	157.4 to 157.7 mm	
XUD series diesel engines	157.4 to 157.7 mm	
DW series diesel engines:		
1.9 litre engines (from centre of camshaft to head mating surface) . .	139.95 to 140.25 mm	
2.0 litre engines	133.0 mm	
Swirl chamber protrusion – 1.8 and 1.9 litre diesel engines only	0 to 0.03 mm	

Valves

	Inlet	Exhaust
Valve head diameter:		
Petrol engines:		
1.1 and 1.4 litre engines	36.8 mm	29.4 mm
1.6 litre engines	39.35 mm	31.4 mm
1.8 litre:		
8-valve engines	41.6 mm	34.5 mm
16-valve engines	34.7 mm	29.7 mm
2.0 litre:		
8-valve engines	42.6 mm	34.5 mm
16-valve engines	34.7 mm	29.7 mm
Diesel engines:		
1.8 and 1.9 litre engines	38.6 mm	33.0 mm
2.0 litre engines	35.6 mm	33.8 mm

Valves (continued)

Valve stem diameter:	Inlet	Exhaust
Petrol engines:		
1.1 and 1.4 litre engines	6.96 to 6.98 mm	6.94 to 6.96 mm
1.6 litre engines	6.95 to 6.97 mm	6.95 to 6.97 mm
1.8 litre:		
8-valve engines	7.96 to 7.98 mm	7.95 to 7.97 mm
16-valve engines	6.96 to 6.98 mm	6.94 to 6.96 mm
2.0 litre:		
8-valve engines	7.97 to 7.99 mm	7.95 to 7.97 mm
16-valve engines	6.96 to 6.98 mm	6.94 to 6.96 mm
Diesel engines:		
1.8 and 1.9 litre engines	7.96 to 7.99 mm	7.95 to 7.98 mm
2.0 litre engines	5.978 ± 0.007 mm	5.968 ± 0.007 mm
Overall length:	Inlet	Exhaust
Petrol engines:		
1.1 and 1.4 litre engines	112.51 to 113.01 mm	112.31 to 112.81 mm
1.6 litre engines	111.5 mm	111.5 mm
1.8 litre:		
8-valve engines	108.59 to 108.99 mm	108.20 to 108.54 mm
16-valve engines	104.38 to 104.78 mm	102.90 to 103.30 mm
2.0 litre:		
8-valve engines	108.59 to 108.99 mm	106.12 to 106.52 mm
16-valve engines	104.38 to 104.78 mm	102.90 to 103.30 mm
Diesel engines:		
1.8 and 1.9 litre engines	112.10 to 112.70 mm	111.55 to 112.15 mm
2.0 litre engines:		
Standard	107.18 mm	107.18 mm
Minimum	106.78 mm	106.78 mm

Crankshaft

Endfloat:		
Petrol engines	0.07 to 0.27 mm	
Diesel engines	0.07 to 0.32 mm	
Main bearing journal diameter:	Standard	Undersize
Petrol engines:		
1.1, 1.4 and 1.6 litre engines	49.965 to 49.981 mm	49.665 to 49.681 mm
1.8 litre engines	59.981 to 60.000 mm	59.681 to 59.700 mm
2.0 litre engines	59.975 to 60.000 mm	59.675 to 59.700 mm
Diesel engines	59.977 to 60.000 mm	59.677 to 59.700 mm
Main bearing running clearance:		
Petrol engines:		
1.1 and 1.4 litre engines	0.010 to 0.036 mm	
1.6 litre engines	0.023 to 0.048 mm	
1.8 litre engines*:		
Models up to mid-1994	0.034 to 0.075 mm	
Mid-1994 onwards models	0.025 to 0.062 mm	
2.0 litre engines	0.038 to 0.069 mm	
Diesel engines**	0.025 to 0.050 mm	
Big-end bearing journal diameter:	Standard	Undersize
Petrol engines:		
1.1, 1.4 and 1.6 litre engines	44.992 to 45.008 mm	44.962 to 44.708 mm
1.8 litre engines	44.975 to 44.991 mm	44.675 to 44.691 mm
2.0 litre engines	49.984 to 50.000 mm	49.684 to 49.700 mm
Diesel engines	49.984 to 50.000 mm	49.681 to 49.700 mm
Big-end bearing running clearance – all models**	0.025 to 0.050 mm	
Maximum bearing journal out-of-round (all models)	0.007 mm	

On 1.8 litre engines the bearing clearance was modified during early 1994 – see text for further information:
** These are suggested figures, typical for this type of engine – no exact values are stated by Peugeot.

Piston rings

End gaps*:		
Petrol engines:		
Top compression ring	0.2 to 0.4 mm	
Second compression ring	0.3 to 0.5 mm	
Oil control ring	0.3 to 0.5 mm	
Diesel engines:		
Top and second compression rings	0.20 to 0.40 mm	
Oil control ring	0.25 to 0.50 mm	

* These are suggested figures, typical for this type of engine – no exact values are stated by Peugeot.

Cylinder block

Cylinder bore diameter:
 Petrol engines:
  1.1 litre engines:
   Size group A .... 72.000 to 72.010 mm
   Size group B .... 72.010 to 72.020 mm
   Size group C .... 72.020 to 72.030 mm
  1.4 litre engines:
   Size group A .... 75.000 to 75.010 mm
   Size group B .... 75.010 to 75.020 mm
   Size group C .... 75.020 to 75.030 mm
  1.6 litre engines .... 78.5 mm (nominal)
  1.8 litre engines:
   Size group A .... 83.000 to 83.010 mm
   Size group B .... 83.010 to 83.020 mm
   Size group C .... 83.020 to 83.030 mm
  2.0 litre engines:
   Standard .... 86.0 mm
   1st oversize .... 86.25 mm
   2nd oversize .... 86.6 mm
   3rd oversize .... 86.8 mm
 Diesel engines:
  1.8 litre engines:
   Standard size 1 .... 80.000 to 80.018 mm
   Standard size 2 .... 80.030 to 80.048 mm
   1st oversize .... 80.200 to 80.218 mm
   2nd oversize .... 80.500 to 80.518 mm
   3rd oversize .... 80.800 to 80.818 mm
  1.9 litre XUD series engines:
   Standard size 1 .... 83.000 to 83.018 mm
   Standard size 2 .... 83.030 to 83.048 mm
   1st oversize .... 83.200 to 83.218 mm
   2nd oversize .... 83.500 to 83.518 mm
   3rd oversize .... 83.800 to 83.818 mm
  1.9 litre DW series engines:
   Standard .... 82.200 to 82.218 mm
   Oversize .... 82.800 to 82.818 mm
  2.0 litre engines:
   Standard .... 85.000 to 85.018 mm
   Oversize .... 85.600 to 85.618 mm
Liner protrusion – aluminium block petrol engine only:
 Standard .... 0.03 to 0.10 mm
 Maximum difference between any two liners .... 0.05 mm

Pistons

Piston diameter:
 Petrol engines:
  1.1 litre engines:
   Size group A .... 71.940 ± 0.010 mm
   Size group B .... 71.950 ± 0.010 mm
   Size group C .... 71.960 ± 0.010 mm
  1.4 litre engines:
   Size group A .... 74.950 ± 0.010 mm
   Size group B .... 74.960 ± 0.010 mm
   Size group C .... 74.970 ± 0.010 mm
  1.6 litre engines:
   Standard .... 78.455 to 78.470 mm
   Oversize .... 78.840 to 78.855 mm
  1.8 litre engines:
   Size group A .... 82.960 ± 0.007 mm
   Size group B .... 82.970 ± 0.007 mm
   Size group C .... 82.980 ± 0.007 mm
  2.0 litre engines:
   Standard .... 85.965 ± 0.009 mm
   1st oversize .... 86.215 ± 0.009 mm
   2nd oversize .... 86.656 ± 0.009 mm
   3rd oversize .... 86.765 ± 0.009 mm

Pistons (continued)
Piston diameter: (continued)
  Diesel engines:
    1.8 litre engines:

Standard size 1	79.921 to 79.939 mm
Standard size 2	79.951 to 79.969 mm
1st oversize	80.121 to 80.139 mm
2nd oversize	80.421 to 80.439 mm
3rd oversize	80.721 to 80.739 mm

    1.9 litre XUD series engines:

Standard size 1	82.921 to 82.939 mm
Standard size 2	82.951 to 82.969 mm
1st oversize	83.121 to 83.139 mm
2nd oversize	83.421 to 83.439 mm
3rd oversize	83.721 to 83.739 mm

    1.9 litre DW series engines:

Standard	82.121 to 82.139 mm
Oversize	82.721 to 82.739 mm

    2.0 litre engines:

Standard	84.210 to 84.228 mm
Oversize	Not available

Torque wrench settings

1.1, 1.4 and 1.6 litre petrol engines
Refer to Chapter 2A Specifications.

1.8 and 2.0 litre petrol engines
Refer to Chapter 2B Specifications.

1.8 and 1.9 litre XUD series diesel engines
Refer to Chapter 2C Specifications.

1.9 and 2.0 litre DW series diesel engines
Refer to Chapter 2D Specifications.

1 General information

Included in this Part of Chapter 2 are details of removing the engine/transmission from the car and general overhaul procedures for the cylinder head, cylinder block/crankcase and all other engine internal components.

The information given ranges from advice concerning preparation for an overhaul and the purchase of new parts, to detailed step-by-step procedures covering removal, inspection, renovation and refitting of engine internal components.

After Section 6, all instructions are based on the assumption that the engine has been removed from the car. For information concerning in-car engine repair, as well as the removal and refitting of those external components necessary for full overhaul, refer to Part A, B, C or D of this Chapter (as applicable) and to Section 6. Ignore any preliminary dismantling operations described in Part A, B, C or D that are no longer relevant once the engine has been removed from the car.

Apart from torque wrench settings, which are given at the beginning of Part A, B, C or D (as applicable), all specifications relating to engine overhaul are at the beginning of this Part of Chapter 2.

2 Engine overhaul – general information

1 It is not always easy to determine when, or if, an engine should be completely overhauled, as a number of factors must be considered.

2 High mileage is not necessarily an indication that an overhaul is needed, while low mileage does not preclude the need for an overhaul. Frequency of servicing is probably the most important consideration. An engine which has had regular and frequent oil and filter changes, as well as other required maintenance, should give many thousands of miles of reliable service. Conversely, a neglected engine may require an overhaul very early in its life.

3 Excessive oil consumption is an indication that piston rings, valve seals and/or valve guides are in need of attention. Make sure that oil leaks are not responsible before deciding that the rings and/or guides are worn. Perform a compression test, as described in Part A and B (petrol engines) or C and D (diesel engines) of this Chapter, to determine the likely cause of the problem.

4 Check the oil pressure with a gauge fitted in place of the oil pressure switch, and compare it with that specified. If it is extremely low, the main and big-end bearings, and/or the oil pump, are probably worn out.

5 Loss of power, rough running, knocking or metallic engine noises, excessive valve gear noise, and high fuel consumption may also point to the need for an overhaul, especially if they are all present at the same time. If a complete service does not remedy the situation, major mechanical work is the only solution.

6 An engine overhaul involves restoring all internal parts to the specification of a new engine. During an overhaul, the cylinder liners (where applicable), the pistons and the piston rings are renewed. New main and big-end bearings are generally fitted; if necessary, the crankshaft may be reground, to restore the journals. The valves are also serviced as well, since they are usually in less-than-perfect condition at this point. While the engine is being overhauled, other components, such as the distributor, starter and alternator, can be overhauled as well. The end result should be an as-new engine that will give many trouble-free miles.

Note: *Critical cooling system components such as the hoses, thermostat and water pump should be renewed when an engine is overhauled. The radiator should be checked carefully, to ensure that it is not clogged or leaking. Also, it is a good idea to renew the oil pump whenever the engine is overhauled.*

7 Before beginning the engine overhaul, read through the entire procedure, to familiarise yourself with the scope and requirements of the

job. Overhauling an engine is not difficult if you follow carefully all of the instructions, have the necessary tools and equipment, and pay close attention to all specifications. It can, however, be time-consuming. Plan on the car being off the road for a minimum of two weeks, especially if parts must be taken to an engineering works for repair or reconditioning. Check on the availability of parts and make sure that any necessary special tools and equipment are obtained in advance. Most work can be done with typical hand tools, although a number of precision measuring tools are required for inspecting parts to determine if they must be renewed. Often the engineering works will handle the inspection of parts and offer advice concerning reconditioning and renewal. **Note:** *Always wait until the engine has been completely dismantled, and until all components (especially the cylinder block/crankcase and the crankshaft) have been inspected, before deciding what service and repair operations must be performed by an engineering works. The condition of these components will be the major factor to consider when determining whether to overhaul the original engine, or to buy a reconditioned unit. Do not, therefore, purchase parts or have overhaul work done on other components until they have been thoroughly inspected. As a general rule, time is the primary cost of an overhaul, so it does not pay to fit worn or sub-standard parts.*

8 As a final note, to ensure maximum life and minimum trouble from a reconditioned engine, everything must be assembled with care, in a spotlessly-clean environment.

3 Engine/transmission removal – methods and precautions

1 If you have decided that the engine must be removed for overhaul or major repair work, several preliminary steps should be taken.

2 Locating a suitable place to work is extremely important. Adequate work space, along with storage space for the car, will be needed. If a workshop or garage is not available, at the very least, a flat, level, clean work surface is required.

3 Cleaning the engine compartment and engine/transmission before beginning the removal procedure will help keep tools clean and organised.

4 An engine hoist or A-frame will also be necessary. Make sure the equipment is rated in excess of the combined weight of the engine and transmission. Safety is of primary importance, considering the potential hazards involved in lifting the engine/transmission out of the car.

5 If this is the first time you have removed an engine, an assistant should ideally be available. Advice and aid from someone more experienced would also be helpful. There are many instances when one person cannot simultaneously perform all of the operations required when lifting the engine out of the vehicle.

6 Plan the operation ahead of time. Before starting work, arrange for the hire of or obtain all of the tools and equipment you will need. Some of the equipment necessary to perform engine/transmission removal and installation safely and with relative ease (in addition to an engine hoist) is as follows: a heavy duty trolley jack, complete sets of spanners and sockets as described in the front of this manual, wooden blocks, and plenty of rags and cleaning solvent for mopping-up spilled oil, coolant and fuel. If the hoist must be hired, make sure that you arrange for it in advance, and perform all of the operations possible without it beforehand. This will save you money and time.

7 Plan for the car to be out of use for quite a while. An engineering works will be required to perform some of the work which the do-it-yourselfer cannot accomplish without special equipment. These places often have a busy schedule, so it would be a good idea to consult them before removing the engine, in order to accurately estimate the amount of time required to rebuild or repair components that may need work.

8 Always be extremely careful when removing and refitting the engine/transmission. Serious injury can result from careless actions. Plan ahead and take your time, and a job of this nature, although major, can be accomplished successfully.

Note: *Such is the complexity of the power unit arrangement on these vehicles, and the variations that may be encountered according to model and optional equipment fitted, that the following should be regarded as a guide to the work involved, rather than a step-by-step procedure. Where differences are encountered, or additional component disconnection or removal is necessary, make notes of the work involved as an aid to refitting.*

4 Engine and manual transmission – removal, separation and refitting

Note: *The engine can be removed from the car only as a complete unit with the transmission; the two are then separated for overhaul. This is an involved operation. Read through the procedure thoroughly before starting work, and ensure that adequate lifting tackle and jacking/support equipment is available. Make notes during dismantling to ensure that all wiring/hoses and brackets are correctly repositioned and routed on refitting.*

 Warning: It is essential to observe strict precautions when working on the fuel system components of the 2.0 litre diesel engine. Before carrying out any of the following operations, refer to the special information given in Chapter 4E, Section 2.

Removal

1 Chock the rear wheels then jack up the front of the vehicle and support it on axle stands (see *Jacking and vehicle support*). Remove the front roadwheels.

2 Set the bonnet in the upright position, and remove the battery and tray as described in Chapter 5A. Where fitted, remove the engine cover and engine undertray.

3 Remove the complete air cleaner housing and duct assembly, as described in the relevant Part of Chapter 4.

4 If the engine is to be dismantled, working as described in the relevant Part of Chapter 1, first drain the oil and remove the oil filter. Clean and refit the drain plug, tightening it securely.

5 Drain the transmission oil as described in Chapter 7A. Refit the drain and filler plugs, and tighten them to their specified torque settings.

6 Remove the alternator as described in Chapter 5A.

7 Where applicable, remove the power steering pump as described in Chapter 10.

8 On models with air conditioning, unbolt the compressor, and position it clear of the engine. Support the weight of the compressor by tying it to the vehicle body, to prevent any excess strain being placed on the compressor lines whilst the engine is removed. Do not disconnect the refrigerant lines from the compressor (refer to the warnings given in Chapter 3).

9 Remove the radiator as described in Chapter 3. Note that this is not strictly necessary on 1.4 litre models, but greatly improves clearance, and removes the risk of damaging the radiator as the engine is removed.

10 On carburettor models, carry out the following operations, using the information given in Chapter 4A:
   a) *Disconnect the fuel feed hose from the anti-percolation chamber.*
   b) *Disconnect the accelerator and choke cables from the carburettor.*
   c) *Disconnect the braking system servo vacuum hose from the inlet manifold.*
   d) *Disconnect/remove the exhaust system front pipe.*

11 On fuel injection models, carry out the following operations, using the information given in Chapter 4B or 4C (as applicable):
   a) *Depressurise the fuel system, and disconnect the fuel feed and return hoses.*
   b) *Disconnect the accelerator cable.*
   c) *Disconnect the fuel system wiring connectors.*
   d) *Disconnect the purge valve and/or braking system servo vacuum hoses from the inlet manifold (as applicable).*
   e) *Disconnect/remove the exhaust system front pipe.*

12 On diesel models, remove the preheating control unit as described in Chapter 5C, and

4.14 Disconnecting the clutch cable

carry out the following operations as described in Chapter 4D or 4E:

a) On 1.8 and 1.9 litre engines, disconnect the fuel supply hose from the fuel filter/thermostat housing and the return hose.

b) On 2.0 litre engines, disconnect the fuel supply and return hose quick-release fittings at the connections above the fuel pump.

c) On 1.9 litre turbo engines, remove the intercooler.

d) On 1.9 litre D9B engines, remove the air distribution housing.

e) Disconnect the accelerator cable from the injection pump or pedal position sensor, as applicable.

f) Disconnect the vacuum hose from the braking system pump.

g) Disconnect/remove the exhaust system front pipe/catalytic converter.

h) On 2.0 litre engines, remove the engine management ECU.

13 Referring to Chapter 3, release the retaining clip and disconnect the heater matrix hoses from their connection on the engine compartment bulkhead.

14 Working as described in Chapter 6, disconnect the clutch cable from the transmission, and position it clear of the working area **(see illustration)**.

15 Carry out the following operations, using the information given in Chapter 7A:

a) Disconnect the gearchange selector rod/link rods (as applicable) from the transmission.

b) Disconnect the speedometer cable from the speedometer drive.

c) Release the power steering pipe from the underside of the transmission.

d) Disconnect the wiring connector(s) from the reversing light switch and speedometer drive (as applicable).

16 Remove both driveshafts as described in Chapter 8.

17 Trace the wiring harness back from the engine to the wiring connector(s) in the front, left-hand corner of the engine compartment. Release the locking ring(s) by twisting them anti-clockwise and disconnect the connectors. Also trace the harness lead(s) back to the relay box, situated beside the battery. Unclip the wiring connector plate from the front of the relay box cover, then undo the retaining nut and remove the cover. Lift up the engine harness lead cover; then undo the nut(s) and release the lead(s) from

the relay box **(see illustrations)**. Check that all the relevant connectors have been disconnected, and that the wiring is released from any relevant clips or ties, so that it is free to be removed with the engine/transmission.

18 Manoeuvre the engine hoist into position, and attach it to the lifting brackets bolted onto the cylinder head. Raise the hoist until it is supporting the weight of the engine.

19 Slacken and remove the centre nut and washer from the engine/transmission left-hand mounting. Undo the two nuts and washers securing the mounting to its bracket, and remove the mounting from the engine compartment and recover the spacer (where fitted). To improve clearance (where possible) undo the two retaining bolts and remove the bracket from the body.

20 From underneath the vehicle, slacken and remove the nuts and bolts securing the rear mounting link to the mounting assembly and subframe, and remove the link.

21 Working on the right-hand engine/transmission mounting, undo the two bolts and remove the curved retaining plate and rubber damper (where fitted) from the top of the mounting. Slacken and remove the mounting bracket retaining nuts/bolts (as applicable) and lift off the bracket. Remove the rubber damper plate from the mounting, and store it with the bracket for safe-keeping.

22 Make a final check that any components which would prevent the removal of the engine/transmission from the car have been removed or disconnected. Ensure that components such as the gearchange selector rod are secured so that they cannot be damaged on removal.

23 Lift the engine/transmission out of the car, ensuring that nothing is trapped or damaged. Enlist the help of an assistant during this procedure, as it will be necessary to tilt the assembly slightly to clear the body panels. On models equipped with anti-lock brakes, great care must be taken to ensure that the anti-lock braking system unit is not damaged during the removal procedure.

24 Once the engine is high enough, lift it out over the front of the body, and lower the unit to the ground.

Separation

25 With the engine/transmission assembly removed, support the assembly on suitable blocks of wood, on a workbench (or failing that, on a clean area of the workshop floor).

26 Disconnect all the individual wiring connectors from the various components on the engine and transmission to enable the main engine wiring harness to be removed. Make notes or attach labels to each connector to aid reconnection.

27 With all wiring disconnected, detach the wiring harness support brackets and plastic ducting mountings, release the relevant cable ties and remove the complete harness assembly from the engine/transmission.

28 Undo the retaining bolts, and remove the

4.17b Undo the retaining nut . . .

4.17a Disconnecting the engine wiring harness connector

4.17c . . . and lift off the relay box cover

4.17d Lift the cover, undo the nuts and disconnect the leads from the relay box

flywheel lower cover plate (where fitted) from the transmission.

29 On models with a 'pull-type' clutch release mechanism (see Chapter 6 for further information), tap out the retaining pin or unscrew the retaining bolt (as applicable), and remove the clutch release lever from the top of the release fork shaft. This is necessary to allow the fork shaft to rotate freely, so that it disengages from the release bearing as the transmission is pulled away from the engine. Make an alignment mark across the centre of the clutch release fork shaft, using a scriber, paint or similar, and mark its relative position on the transmission housing (see Chapter 7A for further information).

30 Slacken and remove the retaining bolts, and remove the starter motor from the transmission.

31 Ensure that both engine and transmission are adequately supported, then slacken and remove the remaining bolts securing the transmission housing to the engine. Note the correct fitted positions of each bolt (and the relevant brackets) as they are removed, to use as a reference on refitting.

32 Carefully withdraw the transmission from the engine, ensuring that the weight of the transmission is not allowed to hang on the input shaft while it is engaged with the clutch friction plate.

33 If they are loose, remove the locating dowels from the engine or transmission, and keep them in a safe place.

34 On models with a 'pull-type' clutch, make a second alignment mark on the transmission housing, marking the relative position of the release fork mark after removal. This should indicate the angle at which the release fork is positioned. The mark can then be used to position the release fork prior to installation, to ensure that the fork correctly engages with the clutch release bearing as the transmission is installed.

Refitting

35 If the engine and transmission have been separated, perform the operations described below in paragraphs 36 to 45. If not, proceed as described from paragraph 46 onwards.

36 Apply a smear of high-melting-point grease (Peugeot recommend the use of Molykote BR2 plus – available from your Peugeot dealer) to the splines of the transmission input shaft. Do not apply too much, otherwise there is a possibility of the grease contaminating the clutch friction plate.

37 Ensure that the locating dowels are correctly positioned in the engine or transmission.

38 On models with a 'pull-type' clutch, before refitting, position the clutch release bearing so that its arrow mark is pointing upwards (bearing fork slots facing towards the front of the engine), and align the release fork shaft mark with the second mark made on the transmission housing (release fork positioned at approximately 60° to clutch housing face).

This will ensure that the release fork and bearing will engage correctly as the transmission is refitted to the engine.

39 Carefully offer the transmission to the engine, until the locating dowels are engaged. Ensure that the weight of the transmission is not allowed to hang on the input shaft as it is engaged with the clutch friction plate.

40 On models with a 'pull-type' clutch, with the transmission fully engaged with the engine, check that the release fork and bearing are correctly engaged. If the release fork and bearing are correctly engaged, the mark on the release fork should be aligned with the original mark made on the transmission housing (see Chapter 7A for further information).

41 Refit the transmission housing-to-engine bolts, ensuring that all the necessary brackets are correctly positioned, and tighten them securely.

42 Refit the starter motor, and securely tighten its retaining bolts.

43 Locate the main engine wiring harness on the engine and transmission and reconnect the relevant wiring connectors.

44 On models with a 'pull-type' clutch release mechanism, refit the clutch release lever to the top of the release fork shaft, securing it in position with its retaining pin or bolt (as applicable).

45 Where necessary, refit the lower flywheel cover plate to the transmission, and securely tighten its retaining bolts.

46 Reconnect the hoist and lifting tackle to the engine lifting brackets. With the aid of an assistant, lift the assembly over the engine compartment.

47 The assembly should be tilted as necessary to clear the surrounding components, as during removal; lower the assembly into position in the engine compartment, manipulating the hoist and lifting tackle as necessary.

48 With the engine/transmission in position, refit the right-hand engine/transmission mounting bracket, tightening the nuts and bolts (as applicable) by hand only at this stage.

49 Working on the left-hand mounting, refit the mounting bracket (where removed) to the body and tighten its retaining bolts to the specified torque. Refit the mounting rubber and refit the mounting retaining nuts and washers and the centre nut and washer, tightening them lightly only.

50 From underneath the vehicle, refit the rear mounting link and install both its bolts.

51 Rock the engine to settle it on its mountings, then go around and tighten all the mounting nuts and bolts to their specified torque settings. Where necessary, once the right-hand mounting bracket nuts have been tightened, refit the rubber damper and curved retaining plate, tightening its retaining bolts to the specified torque. The hoist can then be detached from the engine and removed.

52 The remainder of the refitting procedure is

a direct reversal of the removal sequence, noting the following points:

a) *Ensure that the wiring loom is correctly routed and retained by all the relevant retaining clips; all connectors should be correctly and securely reconnected.*

b) *Prior to refitting the driveshafts to the transmission, renew the driveshaft oil seals as described in Chapter 7A.*

c) *Ensure that all coolant hoses are correctly reconnected, and securely retained by their retaining clips.*

d) *Adjust the clutch cable as described in Chapter 6.*

e) *Adjust the choke cable and/or accelerator cable (as applicable) as described in the relevant Part of Chapter 4.*

f) *Refill the engine and transmission with the correct quantity and type of lubricant.*

g) *Refill the cooling system as described in the relevant Part of Chapter 1.*

h) *On diesel models, on completion bleed the fuel system (see Chapter 4D or 4E).*

5 Engine and automatic transmission – removal, separation and refitting

Note: *The engine can be removed from the car only as a complete unit with the transmission; the two are then separated for overhaul. This is an involved operation. Read through the procedure thoroughly before starting work, and ensure that adequate lifting tackle and jacking/support equipment is available. Make notes during dismantling to ensure that all wiring/hoses and brackets are correctly repositioned and routed on refitting.*

Removal

1 Carry out the operations described in paragraphs 1 to 9 of Section 4, noting that it is only necessary to drain the transmission oil on the 4 HP 14 transmission, and the draining procedure is given in Chapter 1A.

2 Carry out the following operations, using the information given in Chapter 4C:

a) *Depressurise the fuel system, and disconnect the fuel feed and return hoses.*

b) *Disconnect the accelerator cable.*

c) *Disconnect the fuel system wiring connectors.*

d) *Disconnect the purge valve and/or braking system servo vacuum hoses from the inlet manifold (as applicable).*

e) *Disconnect/remove the exhaust system front pipe.*

3 Referring to Chapter 3, release the retaining clip and disconnect the heater matrix hoses from their connection on the engine compartment bulkhead.

4 On models equipped with the 4 HP 14 transmission, carry out the following operations, using the information given in Chapter 7B:

a) *Remove the transmission dipstick tube.*

b) *Disconnect the wiring from the starter*

inhibitor/reversing light switch and the speedometer drive housing. Release the earth strap(s) from the top of the transmission housing.

c) Disconnect the selector cable.

d) Release the power steering pipe from the transmission.

e) Disconnect the speedometer cable.

5 On models equipped with the AL4 transmission, carry out the following operations, using the information given in Chapter 7B:

a) Disconnect the transmission ECU wiring connector, undo the ECU mounting bracket screws and remove the mounting bracket and ECU as an assembly.

b) Disconnect the wiring harness from the modular connector located at the rear of the transmission.

c) Disconnect the output speed sensor wiring plug located behind the modular connector.

d) Disconnect the vehicle speed sensor wiring plug.

e) Disconnect the selector cable.

6 On models equipped with the AL4 transmission, slacken the retaining clips and disconnect the coolant hoses from the transmission fluid cooler.

7 Remove the engine/transmission as described in paragraphs 16 to 24 of Section 4.

Separation

8 With the engine/transmission assembly removed, support the assembly on suitable blocks of wood, on a workbench (or failing that, on a clean area of the workshop floor).

9 On the 4 HP 14 transmission, detach the kickdown cable from the throttle cam. Work back along the cable, freeing it from any retaining clips, and noting its correct routing.

10 Undo the retaining bolts and remove the driveplate lower cover plate from the transmission, to gain access to the torque converter retaining bolts/nuts. Slacken and remove the visible bolt/nut. Rotate the crankshaft using a socket and extension bar on the pulley bolt, and undo the remaining bolts/nuts securing the torque converter to the driveplate as they become accessible. There are three bolts or three nuts in total.

11 Slacken and remove the retaining bolts, and remove the starter motor from the transmission.

12 To ensure that the torque converter does not fall out as the transmission is removed, secure it in position using a length of metal strip bolted to one of the starter motor bolt holes.

13 Ensure that both the engine and transmission are adequately supported, then slacken and remove the remaining bolts securing the transmission housing to the engine. Note the correct fitted positions of each bolt (and any relevant brackets) as they are removed, to use as a reference on refitting.

14 Carefully withdraw the transmission from

the engine. If the locating dowels are a loose fit in the engine/transmission, remove them and keep them in a safe place.

Refitting

15 If the engine and transmission have been separated, perform the operations described below in paragraphs 16 to 23. If not, proceed as described from paragraph 24 onwards.

16 Ensure that the bush fitted to the centre of the crankshaft is in good condition. Apply a little Molykote G1 grease (available from your Peugeot dealer) to the torque converter centring pin. Do not apply too much, otherwise there is a possibility of the grease contaminating the torque converter.

17 Ensure that the locating dowels are correctly positioned in the engine or transmission.

18 Carefully offer the transmission to the engine, aligning the torque converter studs with the driveplate holes on the AL4 transmission. Engage the transmission with the engine.

19 Refit the transmission housing-to-engine bolts, ensuring that all the necessary brackets are correctly positioned, and tighten them to the specified torque setting.

20 Remove the torque converter retaining strap installed prior to removal.

21 On the 4 HP 14 transmission, align the torque converter threaded holes with the retaining plate, and refit the three retaining bolts. On the AL4 transmission, refit the three retaining nuts.

22 Tighten the torque converter retaining bolts/nuts to the specified torque setting (see Chapter 7B), then refit the driveplate lower cover.

23 Refit the starter motor, and securely tighten its retaining bolts.

24 Refit the engine to the vehicle as described in paragraphs 46 to 51 of Section 4.

25 The remainder of the refitting procedure is a reversal of the removal sequence, noting the following points:

a) Ensure that the wiring loom is correctly routed, and retained by all the relevant retaining clips; all connectors should be correctly and securely reconnected.

b) On the 4 HP 14 transmission, prior to refitting the driveshafts to the transmission, renew the driveshaft oil seals (see Chapter 7B).

c) Ensure that all coolant hoses are correctly reconnected, and securely retained by their retaining clips.

d) Adjust the selector cable and, on 4 HP 14 transmissions, the kickdown cable (see Chapter 7B).

e) Adjust the accelerator cable (see relevant Part of Chapter 4).

f) Refill the engine and transmission with the correct quantity and type of lubricant (see Chapter 1A).

g) Refill the cooling system (see Chapter 1A).

6 Engine overhaul – dismantling sequence

1 It is much easier to dismantle and work on the engine if it is mounted on a portable engine stand. These stands can often be hired from a tool hire shop. Before the engine is mounted on a stand, the flywheel/driveplate should be removed, so that the stand bolts can be tightened into the end of the cylinder block/crankcase.

2 If a stand is not available, it is possible to dismantle the engine with it blocked up on a sturdy workbench, or on the floor. Be extra careful not to tip or drop the engine when working without a stand.

3 If you are going to obtain a reconditioned engine, all the external components must be removed first, to be transferred to the new engine (just as they will if you are doing a complete engine overhaul yourself). These components include the following:

a) Alternator mounting brackets.

b) Power steering pump and air conditioning compressor brackets (where fitted).

c) Thermostat and housing, and coolant outlet chamber/elbow – petrol models (Chapter 3).

d) Fuel filter/thermostat housing – diesel models

e) Dipstick tube.

f) Carburettor/fuel system components (relevant Part of Chapter 4).

g) All electrical switches and sensors.

h) Inlet and exhaust manifolds (relevant Part of Chapter 4).

i) Oil filter (relevant Part of Chapter 1).

j) Fuel pump – carburettor engines only (Chapter 4A).

k) Flywheel/driveplate (relevant Part of Chapter 2).

Note: When removing the external components from the engine, pay close attention to details that may be helpful or important during refitting. Note the fitted position of gaskets, seals, spacers, pins, washers, bolts, and other small items.

4 If you are obtaining a 'short' engine (cylinder block/crankcase, crankshaft, pistons and connecting rods all assembled), then the cylinder head, sump, oil pump, and timing belt will have to be removed also.

5 If you are planning a complete overhaul, the engine can be dismantled, and the internal components removed, in the order given below, referring to Part A, B, C or D of this Chapter unless otherwise stated.

a) Inlet and exhaust manifolds.

b) Timing belt, sprockets and tensioner(s).

c) Cylinder head.

d) Flywheel/driveplate.

e) Sump.

f) Oil pump.

g) Pistons/connecting rods (Section 10).

h) Crankshaft (Section 11).

6 Before beginning the dismantling and

7.5a Compress the valve spring using a spring compressor . . .

7.5b . . . then extract the collets and release the spring compressor

7.5c Remove the spring retainer . . .

7.5d . . . followed by the valve spring

7.5e Remove the valve stem oil seal using a pair of pliers . . .

7.5f . . . then lift out the spring seat

overhaul procedures, make sure that you have all of the tools necessary. Refer to *Tools and working facilities* for further information.

7 Cylinder head – dismantling

Note: *New and reconditioned cylinder heads are available from the manufacturer, and from engine overhaul specialists. Some specialist tools are required for dismantling and inspection, and new components may not be readily available. It may therefore be more practical and economical for the home mechanic to purchase a reconditioned head, rather than dismantle, inspect and recondition the original head.*

1 Remove the cylinder head as described in Part A, B, C or D of this Chapter (as applicable).

2 If not already done, remove the inlet and exhaust manifolds with reference to the relevant Part of Chapter 4.

3 Remove the camshaft(s), followers and shims, or rocker arms and hydraulic tappets (as applicable) as described in Part A, B, C or D of this Chapter.

4 On diesel models, remove the glow plugs as described in Chapter 5C and the injectors as described in Chapter 4D or 4E.

5 On all models, using a valve spring compressor, compress each valve spring in turn until the split collets can be removed. Release the compressor, and lift off the spring

retainer and spring. Using a pair of pliers, carefully extract the valve stem oil seal from the top of the guide, then lift out the spring seat **(see illustrations)**.

6 If, when the valve spring compressor is screwed down, the spring retainer refuses to free and expose the split collets, gently tap the top of the tool, directly over the retainer, with a light hammer. This will free the retainer.

7 Withdraw the valve through the combustion chamber.

8 It is essential that each valve is stored together with its collets, retainer, spring, and spring seat. The valves should also be kept in their correct sequence, unless they are so badly worn that they are to be renewed. If they are going to be kept and used again, place each valve assembly in a labelled polythene bag or similar small container **(see illustration)**. Note that No 1 valve is nearest to the transmission (flywheel/driveplate) end of the engine.

7.8 Place each valve and its associated components in a labelled polythene bag

8 Cylinder head and valves – cleaning and inspection

1 Thorough cleaning of the cylinder head and valve components, followed by a detailed inspection, will enable you to decide how much valve service work must be carried out during the engine overhaul.

Note: *If the engine has been severely overheated, it is best to assume that the cylinder head is warped – check carefully for signs of this.*

Cleaning

2 Scrape away all traces of old gasket material from the cylinder head.

3 Scrape away the carbon from the combustion chambers and ports, then wash the cylinder head thoroughly with paraffin or a suitable solvent.

4 Scrape off any heavy carbon deposits that may have formed on the valves, then use a power-operated wire brush to remove deposits from the valve heads and stems.

Inspection

Note: *Be sure to perform all the following inspection procedures before concluding that the services of a machine shop or engine overhaul specialist are required. Make a list of all items that require attention.*

Cylinder head

5 Inspect the head very carefully for cracks, evidence of coolant leakage, and other

8.6 Checking the cylinder head gasket surface for distortion

8.10 Checking a swirl chamber protrusion – 1.8 and 1.9 litre diesel engines

damage. If cracks are found, a new cylinder head should be obtained.

6 Use a straight-edge and feeler blade to check that the cylinder head gasket surface is not distorted **(see illustration)**. If it is, it may be possible to have it machined, provided that the cylinder head is not reduced to less than the specified height.

Note: *On diesel engines, it may be necessary to recut the valve seats if the cylinder head is machined. This is necessary in order to maintain the correct dimensions between the valve heads, valve guides and cylinder head gasket face.*

7 Examine the valve seats in each of the combustion chambers. If they are severely pitted, cracked, or burned, they will need to be renewed or recut by an engine overhaul specialist. If they are only slightly pitted, this can be removed by grinding-in the valve heads and seats with fine valve-grinding compound, as described below.

8 Check the valve guides for wear by inserting the relevant valve, and checking for side-to-side motion of the valve. A very small amount of movement is acceptable. If the movement seems excessive, remove the valve. Measure the valve stem diameter (see below), and renew the valve if it is worn. If the valve stem is not worn, the wear must be in the valve guide, and the guide must be renewed. The renewal of valve guides is best carried out by a Peugeot dealer or engine overhaul specialist, who will have the necessary tools available. Where no valve stem diameter is specified, seek the advice of a Peugeot dealer on the best course of action.

9 If renewing the valve guides, the valve seats should be recut or reground only *after* the guides have been fitted.

10 On 1.8 and 1.9 litre diesel models, inspect the swirl chambers for burning or damage such as cracking. Small cracks in the chambers are acceptable; renewal of the chambers will only be required if chamber tracts are badly burned and disfigured, or if they are no longer a tight fit in the cylinder head. If there is any doubt as to the swirl chamber condition, seek the advice of a Peugeot dealer or a suitable repairer who specialises in diesel engines. Swirl chamber renewal should be entrusted to a specialist. Using a dial test indicator, check that the swirl chamber protrusion is within the limits given in the Specifications **(see illustration)**. Zero the dial test indicator on the gasket surface of the cylinder head, then measure the protrusion of the swirl chamber. If the protrusion is not within the specified limits, the advice of a Peugeot dealer or suitable repairer who specialises in diesel engines should be sought.

Valves

11 Examine the head of each valve for pitting, burning, cracks, and general wear. Check the valve stem for scoring and wear ridges. Rotate the valve, and check for any obvious indication that it is bent. Look for pits or excessive wear on the tip of each valve stem. Renew any valve that shows any such signs of wear or damage.

12 If the valve appears satisfactory at this stage, measure the valve stem diameter at several points using a micrometer **(see illustration)**. Any significant difference in the readings obtained indicates wear of the valve stem. Should any of these conditions be apparent, the valve(s) must be renewed.

13 If the valves are in satisfactory condition, they should be ground (lapped) into their respective seats, to ensure a smooth, gas-tight seal. If the seat is only lightly pitted, or if it has been recut, fine grinding compound *only* should be used to produce the required finish. Coarse valve-grinding compound should *not* be used, unless a seat is badly burned or deeply pitted. If this is the case, the cylinder head and valves should be inspected by an expert, to decide whether seat recutting, or even the renewal of the valve or seat insert (where possible) is required.

14 Valve grinding is carried out as follows. Place the head upside-down on a bench.

15 Smear a trace of (the appropriate grade of) valve-grinding compound on the seat face, and press a suction grinding tool onto the valve head **(see illustration)**. With a semi-rotary action, grind the valve head to its seat, lifting the valve occasionally to redistribute the grinding compound. A light spring placed under the valve head will greatly ease this operation.

16 If coarse grinding compound is being used, work only until a dull, matt even surface is produced on both the valve seat and the valve, then wipe off the used compound, and repeat the process with fine compound. When a smooth unbroken ring of light grey matt finish is produced on both the valve and seat, the grinding operation is complete. *Do not* grind-in the valves any further than absolutely necessary, or the seat will be prematurely sunk into the cylinder head.

17 When all the valves have been ground-in, carefully wash off *all* traces of grinding compound using paraffin or a suitable solvent, before reassembling the cylinder head.

Valve components

18 Examine the valve springs for signs of damage and discoloration. No minimum free length is specified by Peugeot, so the only way of judging valve spring wear is by comparison with a new component.

19 Stand each spring on a flat surface, and check it for squareness. If any of the springs are damaged, distorted or have lost their tension, obtain a complete new set of springs. It is normal to fit new springs as a matter of course if a major overhaul is being carried out.

20 Renew the valve stem oil seals regardless of their apparent condition.

8.12 Measuring a valve stem diameter

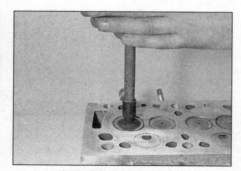

8.15 Grinding-in a valve

9 Cylinder head – reassembly

1 Lubricate the stems of the valves, and insert the valves into their original locations

9.1 Lubricate the valve stems prior to refitting

9.2 Fitting a valve stem oil seal using a socket

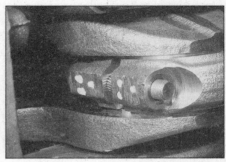

10.3 Connecting rod and big-end bearing cap identification marks (No 3 shown)

(see illustration). If new valves are being fitted, insert them into the locations to which they have been ground.

2 Refit the spring seat then, working on the first valve, dip the new valve stem seal in fresh engine oil. Carefully locate it over the valve and onto the guide. Take care not to damage the seal as it is passed over the valve stem. Use a suitable socket or tube to press the seal firmly onto the guide **(see illustration)**.

3 Locate the valve spring on top of its seat, then refit the spring retainer.

4 Compress the valve spring, and locate the split collets in the recess in the valve stem. Release the compressor, then repeat the procedure on the remaining valves.

> **HAYNES HINT** *Use a little dab of grease to hold the collets in position on the valve stem while the spring compressor is released.*

5 With all the valves installed, place the cylinder head flat on the bench and, using a hammer and interposed block of wood, tap the end of each valve stem to settle the components.

6 Refit the camshaft(s), followers and shims, or rocker arms and hydraulic tappets (as applicable) as described in Part A, B, C or D of this Chapter.

7 The cylinder head can then be refitted as described in Part A, B, C or D of this Chapter.

10 Piston/connecting rod assembly – removal

1 Remove the cylinder head, sump and oil pump as described in Part A, B, C or D of this Chapter (as applicable).

2 If there is a pronounced wear ridge at the top of any bore, it may be necessary to remove it with a scraper or ridge reamer, to avoid piston damage during removal. Such a ridge indicates excess bore wear.

3 Using a hammer and centre-punch, paint or similar, mark each connecting rod and big-end bearing cap with its respective cylinder number on the flat machined surface provided; if the engine has been dismantled

before, note carefully any identifying marks made previously **(see illustration)**. Note that No 1 cylinder is at the transmission (flywheel) end of the engine.

4 Turn the crankshaft to bring pistons 1 and 4 to BDC (bottom dead centre).

5 Unscrew the nuts from No 1 piston big-end bearing cap. Take off the cap, and recover the bottom half bearing shell **(see illustration)**. If the bearing shells are to be re-used, tape the cap and the shell together.

6 To prevent the possibility of damage to the crankshaft bearing journals, tape over the connecting rod stud threads **(see illustration)**.

7 Using a hammer handle, push the piston up through the bore, and remove it from the top of the cylinder block. Recover the bearing shell, and tape it to the connecting rod for safe-keeping.

8 Loosely refit the big-end cap to the connecting rod, and secure with the nuts – this will help to keep the components in their correct order.

9 Remove No 4 assembly in the same way.

10 Turn the crankshaft through 180° to bring pistons 2 and 3 to BDC (bottom dead centre), and remove them in the same way.

11 Crankshaft – removal

1 Remove the crankshaft sprocket and the oil pump as described in Part A, B, C or D of this Chapter (as applicable).

10.5 Removing a big-end bearing cap and shell

2 Remove the pistons and connecting rods, as described in Section 10. If no work is to be done on the pistons and connecting rods, there is no need to remove the cylinder head, or to push the pistons out of the cylinder bores. The pistons should just be pushed far enough up the bores so that they are positioned clear of the crankshaft journals.

3 Check the crankshaft endfloat as described in Section 14, then proceed as follows.

TU series petrol engines

Aluminium block engines

4 Work around the outside of the cylinder block, and unscrew all the small (6 mm) bolts securing the main bearing ladder to the base of the cylinder block. Note the correct fitted depth of both the left- and right-hand crankshaft oil seals in the cylinder block/main bearing ladder.

5 Working in a diagonal sequence, evenly and progressively slacken the ten large (11 mm) main bearing ladder retaining bolts by a turn at a time. Once all the bolts are loose, remove them from the ladder.

6 With all the retaining bolts removed, carefully lift the main bearing ladder casting away from the base of the cylinder block. Recover the lower main bearing shells, and tape them to their respective locations in the casting. If the two locating dowels are a loose fit, remove them and store them with the casting for safe-keeping.

7 Lift out the crankshaft, and discard both the oil seals. Remove the oil pump drive chain from the end of the crankshaft. Where

10.6 To protect the crankshaft journals, tape over the connecting rod stud threads

11.15 Removing the oil seal carrier from the front of the block

11.16a Remove the oil pump drive chain . . .

11.16b . . . then slide off the drive sprocket . . .

11.16c . . . and remove the Woodruff key from the crankshaft

11.17 Main bearing cap identification markings (arrowed)

necessary, slide off the drive sprocket, and recover the Woodruff key.

8 Recover the upper main bearing shells, and store them along with the relevant lower bearing shell. Also recover the two thrustwashers (one fitted either side of No 2 main bearing) from the cylinder block.

Cast-iron block engines

9 Unbolt and remove the crankshaft left- and right-hand oil seal housings from each end of the cylinder block, noting the correct fitted locations of the locating dowels. If the locating dowels are a loose fit, remove them and store them with the housings for safe-keeping.

10 Remove the oil pump drive chain, and slide the drive sprocket off the end of the crankshaft. Remove the Woodruff key, and store it with the sprocket for safe-keeping.

11 The main bearing caps should be numbered 1 to 5 from the transmission (flywheel) end of the engine. If not, mark them accordingly using a centre-punch or paint.

12 Unscrew and remove the main bearing cap retaining bolts, and withdraw the caps. Recover the lower main bearing shells, and tape them to their respective caps for safe-keeping.

13 Carefully lift out the crankshaft, taking care not to displace the upper main bearing shell.

14 Recover the upper bearing shells from the cylinder block, and tape them to their respective caps for safe-keeping. Remove the

thrust-washer halves from the side of No 2 main bearing, and store them with the bearing cap.

XU series petrol and diesel engines

15 Slacken and remove the retaining bolts, and remove the oil seal carrier from the timing belt end of the cylinder block, along with its gasket (where fitted) **(see illustration)**.

16 Remove the oil pump drive chain, and slide the drive sprocket and spacer (where fitted) off the end of the crankshaft. Remove the Woodruff key, and store it with the sprocket for safe-keeping **(see illustrations)**.

17 The main bearing caps should be numbered 1 to 5, starting from the transmission (flywheel/driveplate) end of the engine **(see illustration)**. If not, mark them accordingly using a centre-punch. Also note

the correct fitted depth of the crankshaft oil seal in the bearing cap.

18 On 1.8 litre petrol engines, undo the two bolts (one at the front of the block, and one at the rear) securing the centre main bearing cap to the block. Remove the bolts, along with their sealing washers.

19 On all engines, slacken and remove the main bearing cap retaining bolts/nuts, and lift off each bearing cap. Recover the lower bearing shells, and tape them to their respective caps for safe-keeping. Also recover the lower thrustwasher halves from the side of No 2 main bearing cap **(see illustration)**. Remove the sealing strips from the sides of No 1 main bearing cap, and discard them.

20 Lift out the crankshaft **(see illustration)**, and discard the oil seal.

21 Recover the upper bearing shells from the cylinder block **(see illustration)**, and tape

11.19 Removing No 2 main bearing cap. Note the thrustwasher (arrowed)

11.20 Lifting out the crankshaft

11.21 Remove the upper main bearing shells from the cylinder block/crankcase, and store them with their lower shells

them to their respective caps for safe-keeping. Remove the upper thrustwasher halves from the side of No 2 main bearing, and store them with the lower halves.

12 Cylinder block/crankcase – cleaning and inspection

Cleaning

1 Remove all external components and electrical switches/sensors from the block. For complete cleaning, the core plugs should ideally be removed **(see illustration)**. Drill a small hole in the plugs, then insert a self-tapping screw into the hole. Pull out the plugs by pulling on the screw with a pair of grips, or by using a slide hammer.

2 On aluminium block engines with wet liners, remove the liners – see paragraph 18.

3 Where fitted, undo the retaining bolts and remove the piston oil jet spray tubes from inside the cylinder block.

4 Scrape all traces of gasket from the cylinder block/crankcase, and from the main bearing ladder (where fitted), taking care not to damage the gasket/sealing surfaces.

5 Remove all oil gallery plugs (where fitted). The plugs are usually very tight – they may have to be drilled out, and the holes retapped. Use new plugs when the engine is reassembled.

6 If any of the castings are extremely dirty, all should be steam-cleaned.

7 After the castings are returned, clean all oil holes and oil galleries one more time. Flush all internal passages with warm water until the water runs clear. Dry thoroughly, and apply a light film of oil to all mating surfaces, to prevent rusting. On cast-iron block engines, also oil the cylinder bores. If you have access to compressed air, use it to speed up the drying process, and to blow out all the oil holes and galleries.

 Warning: Wear eye protection when using compressed air.

8 If the castings are not very dirty, you can do an adequate cleaning job with hot, soapy water and a stiff brush. Take plenty of time, and do a thorough job. Regardless of the cleaning method used, be sure to clean all oil holes and galleries very thoroughly, and to dry all components well. On cast-iron block engines, protect the cylinder bores as described above, to prevent rusting.

9 All threaded holes must be clean, to ensure accurate torque readings during reassembly. To clean the threads, run the correct-size tap into each of the holes to remove rust, corrosion, thread sealant or sludge, and to restore damaged threads **(see illustration)**. If possible, use compressed air to clear the holes of debris produced by this operation.

10 Apply suitable sealant to the new oil gallery plugs, and insert them into the holes in the block. Tighten them securely. Similarly

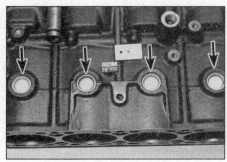

12.1 Cylinder block core plugs (arrowed)

apply sealant to new core plugs and tap them into place with a suitable-diameter tube.

11 On engines with piston oil jet spray tubes, clean the threads of each oil jet retaining bolt, and apply a drop of thread-locking compound to the bolt threads. Refit the piston oil jet spray tubes to the cylinder block, and tighten the retaining bolts to the specified torque setting.

12 If the engine is not going to be reassembled right away, cover it with a large plastic bag to keep it clean; protect all mating surfaces and the cylinder bores as described above, to prevent rusting.

Inspection

Cast-iron cylinder block

13 Visually check the castings for cracks and corrosion. Look for stripped threads in the threaded holes. If there has been any history of internal water leakage, it may be worthwhile having an engine overhaul specialist check the cylinder block/crankcase with special equipment. If defects are found, have them repaired if possible, or renew the assembly.

14 Check each cylinder bore for scuffing and scoring. Check for signs of a wear ridge at the top of the cylinder, indicating that the bore is excessively worn.

15 If the necessary measuring equipment is available, measure the bore diameter of each cylinder liner at the top (just under the wear ridge), centre, and bottom of the cylinder bore, parallel to the crankshaft axis.

16 Next, measure the bore diameter at the same three locations, at right-angles to the

12.18a On aluminium block engines, remove each liner . . .

12.9 Cleaning a cylinder block threaded hole using a suitable tap

crankshaft axis. Compare the results with the figures given in the Specifications. Where no figures are stated by Peugeot, if there is any doubt about the condition of the cylinder bores, seek the advice of a Peugeot dealer or suitable engine reconditioning specialist.

17 At the time of writing, it was not clear whether oversize pistons were available for all models. Consult your Peugeot dealer for the latest information on piston availability. If oversize pistons are available, then it may be possible to have the cylinder bores rebored and fit the oversize pistons. If oversize pistons are not available, and the bores are worn, renewal of the block seems to be the only option.

Aluminium cylinder block

18 Remove the liner clamps (where used), then use a hard wood drift to tap out each liner from the inside of the cylinder block. When all the liners are released, tip the cylinder block/crankcase on its side and remove each liner from the top of the block. As each liner is removed, stick masking tape on its left-hand (transmission side) face, and write the liner number on the tape. No 1 cylinder is at the transmission (flywheel) end of the engine. Remove the O-ring from the base of each liner, and discard **(see illustrations)**.

19 Check each cylinder liner for scuffing and scoring. Check for signs of a wear ridge at the top of the liner, indicating that the bore is excessively worn.

20 If the necessary measuring equipment is available, measure the bore diameter of each

12.18b . . . and recover the bottom O-ring seal (arrowed)

cylinder liner at the top (just under the wear ridge), centre, and bottom of the cylinder bore, parallel to the crankshaft axis.

21 Next, measure the bore diameter at the same three locations, at right-angles to the crankshaft axis. Compare the results with the figures given in the Specifications.

22 Repeat the procedure for the remaining cylinder liners.

23 If the liner wear exceeds the permitted tolerances at any point, or if the cylinder liner walls are badly scored or scuffed, then renewal of the relevant liner assembly will be necessary. If there is any doubt about the condition of the cylinder bores, seek the advice of a Peugeot dealer or engine reconditioning specialist.

24 If renewal is necessary, new liners, complete with pistons and piston rings, can be purchased from a Peugeot dealer. Note that it is not possible to buy liners individually – they are supplied only as a matched assembly complete with piston and rings.

25 To allow for manufacturing tolerances, pistons and liners are separated into three size groups. The size group of each piston is indicated by a letter (A, B or C) stamped onto its crown, and the size group of each liner is indicated by a series of 1 to 3 notches on the upper lip of the liner; a single notch for group A, two notches for group B, and three notches for group C. Ensure that each piston and its respective liner are both of the same size group. It is permissible to have different size group piston and liner assemblies fitted to the same engine, but never fit a piston of one size group to a liner in a different group.

26 Prior to installing the liners, thoroughly clean the liner mating surfaces in the cylinder block, and use fine abrasive paper to polish away any burrs or sharp edges which might damage the liner O-rings. Clean the liners and wipe dry, then fit a new O-ring to the base of each liner. To aid installation, apply a smear of oil to each O-ring and to the base of the liner.

27 If the original liners are being refitted, use the marks made on removal to ensure that each is refitted the correct way round, and is inserted into its original bore. Insert each liner into the cylinder block, taking care not to damage the O-ring, and press it home as far as possible by hand. Using a hammer and a block of wood, tap each liner lightly but fully onto its locating shoulder. Wipe clean, then lightly oil, all exposed liner surfaces, to prevent rusting.

28 With all four liners correctly installed, use a dial gauge (or a straight-edge and feeler blade) to check that the protrusion of each liner above the upper surface of the cylinder block is within the limits given in the Specifications. The maximum difference between any two liners must not be exceeded.

29 If new liners are being fitted, it is permissible to interchange them to bring the difference in protrusion within limits. Remember to keep each piston with its respective liner.

30 If liner protrusion cannot be brought within limits, seek the advice of a Peugeot dealer or engine reconditioning specialist before proceeding with the engine rebuild.

13 Piston/connecting rod assembly – inspection

1 Before the inspection process can begin, the piston/connecting rod assemblies must be cleaned, and the original piston rings removed from the pistons.

2 Carefully expand the old rings over the top of the pistons. The use of two or three old feeler blades will be helpful in preventing the rings dropping into empty grooves **(see illustration)**. Be careful not to scratch the piston with the ends of the ring. The rings are brittle, and will snap if they are spread too far. They are also very sharp – protect your hands and fingers. Note that the third ring incorporates an expander. Always remove the rings from the top of the piston. Keep each set of rings with its piston if the old rings are to be re-used.

3 Scrape away all traces of carbon from the top of the piston. A hand-held wire brush (or a piece of fine emery cloth) can be used, once the majority of the deposits have been scraped away.

4 Remove the carbon from the ring grooves in the piston, using an old ring. Break the ring in half to do this (be careful not to cut your fingers – piston rings are sharp).

Caution: Be careful to remove only the carbon deposits – do not remove any metal, and do not nick or scratch the sides of the ring grooves.

5 Once the deposits have been removed, clean the piston/connecting rod assembly with paraffin or a suitable solvent, and dry thoroughly. Make sure that the oil return holes in the ring grooves are clear.

6 If the pistons and cylinder bores are not damaged or worn excessively, and if the cylinder block does not need to be rebored, the original pistons can be refitted. Normal piston wear shows up as even vertical wear on the piston thrust surfaces, and slight looseness of the top ring in its groove. New

13.2 Removing a piston ring with the aid of a feeler blade

piston rings should always be used when the engine is reassembled.

7 Carefully inspect each piston for cracks around the skirt, around the gudgeon pin holes, and at the piston ring 'lands' (between the ring grooves).

8 Look for scoring and scuffing on the piston skirt, holes in the piston crown, and burned areas at the edge of the crown. If the skirt is scored or scuffed, the engine may have been suffering from overheating, and/or abnormal combustion which caused excessively high operating temperatures. The cooling and lubrication systems should be checked thoroughly. Scorch marks on the sides of the pistons show that blow-by has occurred. A hole in the piston crown, or burned areas at the edge of the piston crown, indicates that abnormal combustion (pre-ignition, knocking, or detonation) has been occurring. If any of the above problems exist, the causes must be investigated and corrected, or the damage will occur again. The causes may include incorrect ignition/injection pump timing, or a faulty injector (as applicable).

9 Corrosion of the piston, in the form of pitting, indicates that coolant has been leaking into the combustion chamber and/or the crankcase. Again, the cause must be corrected, or the problem may persist in the rebuilt engine.

10 On aluminium-block engines with wet liners, it is not possible to renew the pistons separately; pistons are only supplied with piston rings and a liner, as a part of a matched assembly (see Section 12). On iron-block engines, pistons can be purchased from a Peugeot dealer.

11 Examine each connecting rod carefully for signs of damage, such as cracks around the big-end and small-end bearings. Check that the rod is not bent or distorted. Damage is highly unlikely, unless the engine has been seized or badly overheated. Detailed checking of the connecting rod assembly can only be carried out by a Peugeot dealer or engine specialist with the necessary equipment.

12 The connecting rod big-end cap nuts must be renewed whenever they are disturbed. Although Peugeot do not specify that the bolts must also be renewed, it is recommended that the nuts and bolts are renewed as a complete set.

13 On all petrol engines except 2.0 litre 16-valve models, the gudgeon pins are an interference fit in the connecting rod small-end bearing. Therefore, piston and/or connecting rod renewal should be entrusted to a Peugeot dealer or engine repair specialist, who will have the necessary tooling to remove and install the gudgeon pins.

14 On 2.0 litre 16-valve petrol engines and all diesel engines, the gudgeon pins are of the floating type, secured in position by two circlips. On these engines, the pistons and connecting rods can be separated as follows.

15 Using a small flat-bladed screwdriver, prise out the circlips, and push out the

13.15a Prise out the circlip . . .

13.15b . . . withdraw the gudgeon pin . . .

13.15c . . . and separate the piston from the connecting rod – diesel engines

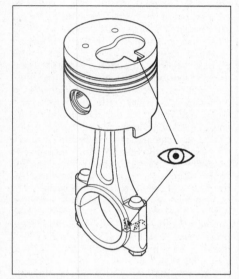

13.19a On 1.8 and 1.9 litre diesel engines, ensure that the piston cut-out is positioned as shown, in relation to the connecting rod bearing shell cut-out

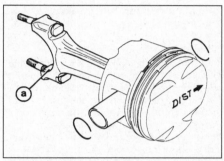

13.19b On 2.0 litre 16-valve petrol engines, the arrow on the piston crown must be positioned as shown in relation to the connecting rod bearing shell cut-out (a)

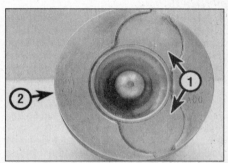

13.19c On 2.0 litre diesel engines, the valve recesses (1) on the piston crown must be on the opposite side to the connecting rod bearing shell cut-out (2 – not visible)

gudgeon pin (see illustrations). Hand pressure should be sufficient to remove the pin. Identify the piston and rod to ensure correct reassembly. Discard the circlips – new ones must be used on refitting.

16 Examine the gudgeon pin and connecting rod small-end bearing for signs of wear or damage. Wear can be cured by renewing both the pin and bush. Bush renewal, however, is a specialist job – press facilities are required, and the new bush must be reamed accurately.

17 The connecting rods themselves should not be in need of renewal, unless seizure or some other major mechanical failure has occurred. Check the alignment of the connecting rods visually, and if the rods are not straight, take them to an engine overhaul specialist for a more detailed check.

18 Examine all components, and obtain any new parts from your Peugeot dealer. If new pistons are purchased, they will be supplied complete with gudgeon pins and circlips. Circlips can also be purchased individually.

19 Position the piston so that the cut-out or arrow on the piston crown is positioned as shown in relation to the connecting rod big-end bearing shell cut-outs (see illustrations).

Apply a smear of clean engine oil to the gudgeon pin. Slide it into the piston and through the connecting rod small-end. Check that the piston pivots freely on the rod, then secure the gudgeon pin in position with two new circlips. Ensure that each circlip is correctly located in its groove in the piston.

14 Crankshaft – inspection

Checking endfloat

1 If the crankshaft endfloat is to be checked, this must be done when the crankshaft is still installed in the cylinder block/crankcase, but is free to move (see Section 11).

2 Check the endfloat using a dial gauge in contact with the end of the crankshaft. Push the crankshaft fully one way, and then zero the gauge. Push the crankshaft fully the other way, and check the endfloat. The result can be compared with the specified amount, and will give an indication as to whether new thrustwashers are required (see illustration).

3 If a dial gauge is not available, feeler blades can be used. First push the crankshaft fully towards the flywheel end of the engine, then use feeler blades to measure the gap between the web of No 2 crankpin and the thrustwasher (see illustration).

14.2 Checking crankshaft endfloat using a dial gauge

14.3 Checking crankshaft endfloat using feeler blades

14.10 Measuring a crankshaft big-end journal diameter

Inspection

4 Clean the crankshaft using paraffin or a suitable solvent, and dry it, preferably with compressed air if available. Be sure to clean the oil holes with a pipe cleaner or similar probe, to ensure that they are not obstructed. *Warning: Wear eye protection when using compressed air.*

5 Check the main and big-end bearing journals for uneven wear, scoring, pitting and cracking.

6 Big-end bearing wear is accompanied by distinct metallic knocking when the engine is running (particularly noticeable when the engine is pulling from low speed) and some loss of oil pressure.

7 Main bearing wear is accompanied by severe engine vibration and rumble – getting progressively worse as engine speed increases – and again by loss of oil pressure.

8 Check the bearing journal for roughness by running a finger lightly over the bearing surface. Any roughness (which will be accompanied by obvious bearing wear) indicates that the crankshaft requires regrinding (where possible) or renewal.

9 If the crankshaft has been reground, check for burrs around the crankshaft oil holes (the holes are usually chamfered, so burrs should not be a problem unless regrinding has been carried out carelessly). Remove any burrs with a fine file or scraper, and thoroughly clean the oil holes as described previously.

10 Using a micrometer, measure the diameter of the main and big-end bearing journals, and compare the results with the Specifications **(see illustration)**. By measuring the diameter at a number of points around each journal's circumference, you will be able to determine whether or not the journal is out-of-round. Take the measurement at each end of the journal, near the webs, to determine if the journal is tapered. Compare the results obtained with those given in the Specifications. Where no specified journal diameters are quoted, seek the advice of a Peugeot dealer.

11 Check the oil seal contact surfaces at each end of the crankshaft for wear and damage. If the seal has worn a deep groove in the surface of the crankshaft, consult an engine overhaul specialist; repair may be

possible, but otherwise a new crankshaft will be required.

12 At the time of writing, it was not clear whether Peugeot produce oversize bearing shells for all of these engines. On some engines, if the crankshaft journals have not already been reground, it may be possible to have the crankshaft reconditioned, and to fit oversize shells (see Section 18). If no oversize shells are available and the crankshaft has worn beyond the specified limits, it will have to be renewed. Consult your Peugeot dealer or engine specialist for further information on parts availability.

15 Main and big-end bearings – inspection

1 Even though the main and big-end bearings should be renewed during the engine overhaul, the old bearings should be retained for close examination, as they may reveal valuable information about the condition of the engine. The bearing shells are graded by thickness, the grade of each shell being indicated by the colour code marked on it.

2 Bearing failure can occur due to lack of lubrication, the presence of dirt or other foreign particles, overloading the engine, or corrosion **(see illustration)**. Regardless of the cause of bearing failure, the cause must be corrected (where applicable) before the engine is reassembled, to prevent it from happening again.

3 When examining the bearing shells, remove them from the cylinder block/crankcase, the main bearing ladder/caps (as appropriate), the connecting rods and the connecting rod big-end bearing caps. Lay them out on a clean

surface in the same general position as their location in the engine. This will enable you to match any bearing problems with the corresponding crankshaft journal. *Caution: Do not touch any shell's bearing surface with your fingers while checking it, or the delicate surface may be scratched.*

4 Dirt and other foreign matter gets into the engine in a variety of ways. It may be left in the engine during assembly, or it may pass through filters or the crankcase ventilation system. It may get into the oil, and from there into the bearings. Metal chips from machining operations and normal engine wear are often present. Abrasives are sometimes left in engine components after reconditioning, especially when parts are not thoroughly cleaned using the proper cleaning methods. Whatever the source, these foreign objects often end up embedded in the soft bearing material, and are easily recognised. Large particles will not embed in the bearing, and will score or gouge the bearing and journal. The best prevention for this cause of bearing failure is to clean all parts thoroughly, and keep everything spotlessly-clean during engine assembly. Frequent and regular engine oil and filter changes are also recommended.

5 Lack of lubrication (or lubrication breakdown) has a number of interrelated causes. Excessive heat (which thins the oil), overloading (which squeezes the oil from the bearing face) and oil leakage (from excessive bearing clearances, worn oil pump or high engine speeds) all contribute to lubrication breakdown. Blocked oil passages, which usually are the result of misaligned oil holes in a bearing shell, will also oil-starve a bearing, and destroy it. When lack of lubrication is the cause of bearing failure, the bearing material is wiped or extruded from the steel backing of the bearing. Temperatures may increase to the point where the steel backing turns blue from overheating.

6 Driving habits can have a definite effect on bearing life. Full-throttle, low-speed operation (labouring the engine) puts very high loads on bearings, tending to squeeze out the oil film. These loads cause the bearings to flex, which produces fine cracks in the bearing face (fatigue failure). Eventually, the bearing material will loosen in pieces, and tear away from the steel backing.

7 Short-distance driving leads to corrosion of bearings, because insufficient engine heat is produced to drive off the condensed water and corrosive gases. These products collect in the engine oil, forming acid and sludge. As the oil is carried to the engine bearings, the acid attacks and corrodes the bearing material.

8 Incorrect bearing installation during engine assembly will lead to bearing failure as well. Tight-fitting bearings leave insufficient bearing running clearance, and will result in oil starvation. Dirt or foreign particles trapped behind a bearing shell result in high spots on the bearing, which lead to failure.

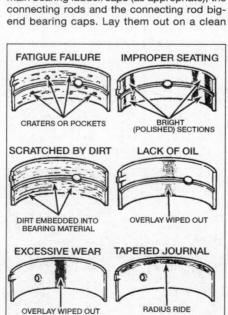

15.2 Typical bearing failures

Caution: Do not touch any shell's bearing surface with your fingers during reassembly; there is a risk of scratching the delicate surface, or of depositing particles of dirt on it.

9 As mentioned at the beginning of this Section, the bearing shells should be renewed as a matter of course during engine overhaul; to do otherwise is false economy. Refer to Section 18 and 19 for details of bearing shell selection.

16 Engine overhaul – reassembly sequence

1 Before reassembly begins, ensure that all new parts have been obtained, and that all necessary tools are available. Read through the entire procedure to familiarise yourself with the work involved, and to ensure that all items necessary for reassembly of the engine are at hand. In addition to all normal tools and materials, thread-locking compound will be needed. A suitable tube of liquid sealant will also be required for the joint faces that are fitted without gaskets. It is recommended that Peugeot's own product(s) are used, which are specially formulated for this purpose; the relevant product names are quoted in the text of each Section where they are required.

2 In order to save time and avoid problems, engine reassembly can be carried out in the following order:
a) Crankshaft (See Section 18).
b) Piston/connecting rod assemblies (See Section 19).
c) Oil pump.
d) Sump (See Part A, B, C or D – as applicable).
e) Flywheel/driveplate (See Part A, B, C or D – as applicable).
f) Cylinder head (See Part A, B, C or D – as applicable).
g) Timing belt tensioner and sprockets, and timing belt (See Part A, B, C or D – as applicable).
h) Engine external components.

3 At this stage, all engine components should be absolutely clean and dry, with all faults repaired. The components should be laid out (or in individual containers) on a completely clean work surface.

17 Piston rings – refitting

1 Before fitting new piston rings, the ring end gaps must be checked as follows.

2 Lay out the piston/connecting rod assemblies and the new piston ring sets, so that the ring sets will be matched with the same piston and cylinder during the end gap measurement and subsequent engine reassembly.

3 Insert the top ring into the first cylinder, and push it down the bore using the top of the piston. This will ensure that the ring remains square with the cylinder walls. Position the ring near the bottom of the cylinder bore, at the lower limit of ring travel. Note that the top and second compression rings are different. The second ring is easily identified by the step on its lower surface, and by the fact that its outer face is tapered.

4 Measure the end gap using feeler blades.

5 Repeat the procedure with the ring at the top of the cylinder bore, at the upper limit of its travel (see illustration), and compare the measurements with the figures given in the Specifications. Where no figures are given, seek the advice of a Peugeot dealer or engine reconditioning specialist.

6 If the gap is too small (unlikely if genuine Peugeot parts are used), it must be enlarged, or the ring ends may contact each other during engine operation, causing serious damage. Ideally, new piston rings providing the correct end gap should be fitted. As a last resort, the end gap can be increased by filing the ring ends very carefully with a fine file. Mount the file in a vice equipped with soft jaws, slip the ring over the file with the ends contacting the file face, and slowly move the ring to remove material from the ends. Take care, as piston rings are sharp, and are easily broken.

7 With new piston rings, it is unlikely that the end gap will be too large. If the gaps are too large, check that you have the correct rings for your engine and for the cylinder bore size.

8 Repeat the checking procedure for each ring in the first cylinder, and then for the rings in the remaining cylinders. Remember to keep rings, pistons and cylinders matched up.

9 Once the ring end gaps have been checked and if necessary corrected, the rings can be fitted to the pistons.

10 Fit the piston rings using the same technique as for removal. Fit the bottom (oil control) ring first, and work up. When fitting the oil control ring, first insert the expander (where fitted), then fit the ring with its gap positioned 180° from the expander gap. Ensure that the second compression ring is fitted the correct way up, with its identification mark (either a dot of paint or the word TOP stamped on the ring surface) at the top, and the stepped surface at the bottom (see illustration). Arrange the gaps of the top and second compression rings 120° either side of the oil control ring gap.

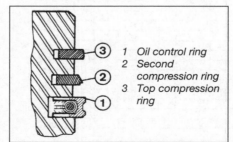

1 Oil control ring
2 Second compression ring
3 Top compression ring

17.10 Piston ring fitting diagram (typical)

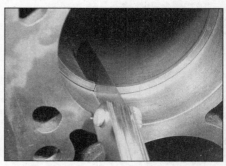

17.5 Measuring a piston ring end gap

Note: Always follow any instructions supplied with the new piston ring sets – different manufacturers may specify different procedures. Do not mix up the top and second compression rings, as they have different cross-sections.

18 Crankshaft – refitting and main bearing clearance check

Selection of new bearing shells

TU series petrol engines

1 To ensure that the main bearing running clearance can be accurately set, the bearing shells are supplied in different thicknesses (grades). On cast-iron block engines there are three different grades of bearing shell, on aluminium block engines there are three different grades on early engines and six different grades on later engines. The grades are indicated by a colour-coding marked on the edge of each shell, which denotes the shell's thickness, as listed in the following table. The upper shell on all bearings is of the same size (class B, colour code black), and the running clearance is controlled by fitting a lower bearing shell of the required thickness.

Aluminium block engine – early models

Bearing colour code	Thickness (mm)	
	Standard	Undersize
Blue (class A)	1.823	1.973
Black (class B)	1.835	1.985
Green (class C)	1.848	1.998

Aluminium block engine – later models

Bearing colour code	Thickness (mm)	
	Standard	Undersize
Blue (class A)	1.823	1.973
Orange (class B)	1.829	1.979
Black (class C)	1.835	1.985
Yellow (class D)	1.841	1.991
Green (class E)	1.847	1.998
White (class F)	1.853	2.003

Cast-iron block engine

Bearing colour code	Thickness (mm)	
	Standard	Undersize
Blue (class A)	1.844	1.994
Black (class B)	1.858	2.008
Green (class C)	1.869	2.019

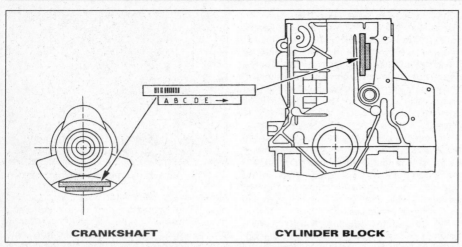

18.3 Cylinder block and crankshaft main bearing reference markings – TU series petrol engines

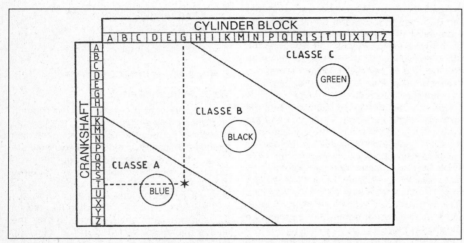

18.5a Three class main bearing shell selection chart for TU series petrol engines – see text

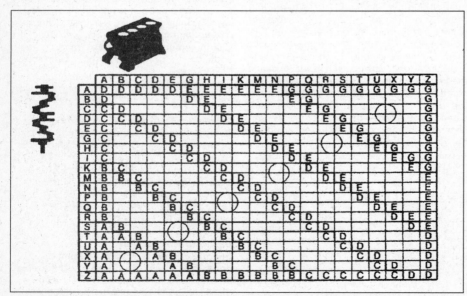

18.5b Six class main bearing shell selection chart for TU series petrol engines – see text

2 New bearing shells can be selected using the reference marks on the cylinder block/crankcase. The cylinder block marks identify the diameter of the bearing bores and the crankshaft marks, the diameter of the crankshaft journals.

3 The cylinder block reference marks are on the right-hand (timing belt) end of the block, and the crankshaft reference marks are on the right-hand (timing belt) end of the crankshaft, on the right-hand web of No 4 crankpin **(see illustration)**. These marks can be used to select bearing shells of the required thickness as follows.

4 On both the crankshaft and block there are two lines of identification: a bar code, which is used by Peugeot during production, and a row of five letters. The first letter in the sequence refers to the size of No 1 bearing (at the flywheel/driveplate end). The last letter in the sequence (which is followed by an arrow) refers to the size of No 5 main bearing. These marks can be used to select the required bearing shell grade as follows.

5 Obtain the identification letter of both the relevant crankshaft journal and the cylinder block bearing bore. Noting that the cylinder block letters are listed across the top of the chart, and the crankshaft letters down the side, trace a vertical line down from the relevant cylinder block letter, and a horizontal line across from the relevant crankshaft letter, and find the point at which both lines cross. This crossover point will indicate the grade of lower bearing shell required to give the correct main bearing running clearance. For example, illustration 18.5a shows cylinder block reference G, and crankshaft reference T, crossing at a point within the area of Class A, indicating that a blue-coded (Class A) lower bearing shell is required to give the correct main bearing running clearance **(see illustrations)**.

6 Repeat this procedure so that the required bearing shell grade is obtained for each of the five main bearing journals.

7 Seek the advice of your Peugeot dealer for the latest information on parts availability when ordering new bearing shells.

XU series petrol engines

8 On some early engines, both the upper and lower bearing shells were of the same thickness.

9 However, on later engines the main bearing running clearance was significantly reduced. To enable this to be done, four different grades of bearing shell were introduced. The grades are indicated by a colour-coding marked on the edge of each shell, which denotes the shell's thickness, as listed in the following table. The upper shell on all bearings is of the same size, and the running clearance is controlled by fitting a lower bearing shell of the required thickness. **Note:** *On all XU engines, upper shells are easily distinguished from lower shells, by their grooved bearing surface; the lower shells have a plain surface.*

1.8 litre engines

Bearing colour code	Thickness (mm)	
	Standard	Undersize
Upper bearing:		
Yellow	1.856	2.006
Lower bearing:		
Blue (class A)	1.836	1.986
Black (class B)	1.848	1.998
Green (class C)	1.859	2.009
Red (Class D)	1.870	2.020

2.0 litre engines

Bearing colour code	Thickness (mm)	
	Standard	Undersize
Upper bearing:		
Black	1.847	1.997
Lower bearing:		
Blue (class A)	1.844	1.994
Black (class B)	1.857	2.007
Green (class C)	1.866	2.016
Red (Class D)	1.877	2.027

10 On most later engines, new bearing shells can be selected using the reference marks on the cylinder block/crankcase. The cylinder block marks identify the diameter of the bearing bores and the crankshaft marks, the diameter of the crankshaft journals. Where no marks are present, the bearing shells can only be selected by checking the running clearance (see below).

11 The cylinder block reference marks are on the left-hand (flywheel/driveplate) end of the block, and the crankshaft reference marks are on the end web of the crankshaft (see illustration). These marks can be used to select bearing shells of the required thickness as follows.

12 On both the crankshaft and block there are two lines of identification: a bar code, which is used by Peugeot during production, and a row of five letters. The first letter in the sequence refers to the size of No 1 bearing (at the flywheel/driveplate end). The last letter in the sequence (which is followed by an arrow) refers to the size of No 5 main bearing. These marks can be used to select the required bearing shell grade as follows.

13 Obtain the identification number/letter of both the relevant crankshaft journal and the cylinder block bearing bore. Noting that the crankshaft references are listed across the top of the chart, and the cylinder block references down the side, trace a vertical line down from the relevant crankshaft reference, and a horizontal line across from the relevant cylinder block reference, and find the point at which both lines cross. This crossover point will indicate the grade of lower bearing shell required to give the correct main bearing running clearance. For example, the illustration shows crankshaft reference 6, and cylinder block reference H, crossing at a point within the RED area, indicating that a Red-coded (Class D) lower bearing shell is required to give the correct main bearing running clearance (see illustration).

14 Repeat this procedure so that the required bearing shell grade is obtained for each of the five main bearing journals.

15 Seek the advice of your Peugeot dealer on parts availability, and on the best course of action when ordering new bearing shells. **Note:** *On early models, at overhaul it is recommended that the later bearing shell arrangement is fitted. This, however, should only be done if the lubrication system components are upgraded (necessitating replacement of the oil pump relief valve piston and spring, as well as the pump sprocket and drive chain) at the same time. If the new bearing arrangement is to be used without uprating the lubrication system, Peugeot state that Blue (Class A) lower bearing shells should be fitted. Refer to your Peugeot dealer for further information.*

Diesel engines

16 On all diesel engines both the upper and lower bearing shells are of the same thickness. Peugeot produce both a standard set of shells and an undersize set of shells.

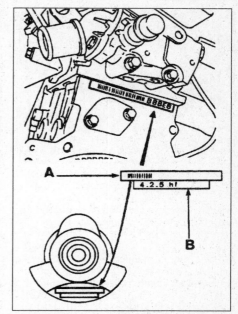

18.11 Cylinder block and crankshaft main bearing reference markings – XU series petrol engines

A Bar code (for production use only)
B Reference marks

Main bearing clearance check

TU series aluminium block engines

17 The running clearance check can be carried out using the original bearing shells. However, it is preferable to use a new set, since the results obtained will be more conclusive.

18 Clean the backs of the bearing shells, and the bearing locations in both the cylinder block/crankcase and the main bearing ladder.

19 Press the bearing shells into their locations, ensuring that the tab on each shell engages in the notch in the cylinder block/crankcase or main bearing ladder location. Take care not to touch any shell's bearing surface with your fingers. Note that the grooved bearing shells, both upper and lower, are fitted to Nos 2 and 4 main bearings (see illustration). If the original bearing shells

18.19 On TU series petrol engines, note that the grooved bearing shells are fitted to Nos 2 and 4 main bearing journals

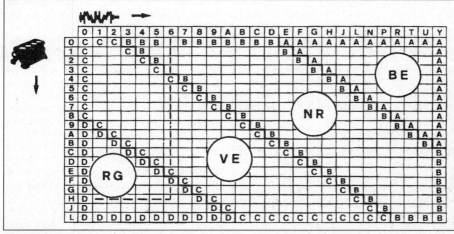

18.13 Main bearing shell selection chart, for use with XU series petrol engines – see text

RG Red   VE Green   NR Black   BE Blue

18.23 Plastigauge in place on a crankshaft main bearing journal

18.26 Measure the width of the deformed Plastigauge using the scale on the card

18.40 Refitting a crankshaft thrustwasher

are being used for the check, ensure that they are refitted in their original locations. The clearance can be checked in either of two ways.

20 One method (which will be difficult to achieve without a range of internal micrometers or internal/external expanding calipers) is to refit the main bearing ladder casting to the cylinder block/crankcase, with the bearing shells in place. With the casting retaining bolts correctly tightened, measure the internal diameter of each assembled pair of bearing shells. If the diameter of each corresponding crankshaft journal is measured and then subtracted from the bearing internal diameter, the result will be the main bearing running clearance.

21 The second (and more accurate) method is to use an American product known as Plastigauge. This consists of a fine thread of perfectly-round plastic, which is compressed between the bearing shell and the journal. When the shell is removed, the plastic is deformed, and can be measured with a special card gauge supplied with the kit. The running clearance is determined from this gauge. Plastigauge should be available from your Peugeot dealer; otherwise, enquiries at one of the larger specialist motor factors should produce the name of a stockist in your area. The procedure for using Plastigauge is as follows.

22 With the main bearing upper shells in place, carefully lay the crankshaft in position. Do not use any lubricant; the crankshaft journals and bearing shells must be perfectly clean and dry.

23 Cut several lengths of the appropriate-size Plastigauge (they should be slightly shorter than the width of the main bearings), and place one length on each crankshaft journal axis (see illustration).

24 With the main bearing lower shells in position, refit the main bearing ladder casting, tightening its retaining bolts as described in paragraph 45. Take care not to disturb the Plastigauge, and *do not* rotate the crankshaft at any time during this operation.

25 Remove the main bearing ladder casting, again taking great care not to disturb the Plastigauge or rotate the crankshaft.

26 Compare the width of the crushed Plastigauge on each journal to the scale

printed on the Plastigauge envelope, to obtain the main bearing running clearance (see illustration). Compare the clearance measured with that in the Specifications at the start of this Chapter.

27 If the clearance is significantly different from that expected, the bearing shells may be the wrong size (or excessively worn, if the original shells are being re-used). Before deciding that different-size shells are required, make sure that no dirt or oil was trapped between the bearing shells and the caps or block when the clearance was measured. If the Plastigauge was wider at one end than at the other, the crankshaft journal may be tapered.

28 If the clearance is not as specified, use the reading obtained, along with the shell thicknesses quoted above, to calculate the necessary grade of bearing shells required. When calculating the bearing clearance required, bear in mind that it is always better to have the running clearance towards the lower end of the specified range, to allow for wear in use.

29 Where necessary, obtain the required grades of bearing shell, and repeat the running clearance checking process described above.

30 On completion, carefully scrape away all traces of the Plastigauge material from the crankshaft and bearing shells. Use your fingernail, or a wooden or plastic scraper which is unlikely to score the bearing surfaces.

TU series cast-iron block engines

31 The procedure is similar to that described in paragraphs 17 to 30, except that each main bearing has a separate cap, which must be fitted and the bolts tightened to the specified torque.

XU series petrol engines

32 On early engines, if the later bearing shells are to be fitted, obtain a set of new upper bearing shells, and new blue (as applicable) lower bearing shells (see paragraph 9). On later engines where the modified bearing shells are already fitted, the running clearance check can be carried out using the original bearing shells. However, it is preferable to use a new set, since the results obtained will be more conclusive.

33 Clean the backs of the bearing shells, and the bearing locations in both the cylinder block/crankcase and the main bearing caps.

34 Press the bearing shells into their locations, ensuring that the tab on each shell engages in the notch in the cylinder block/crankcase or bearing cap. Take care not to touch any shell's bearing surface with your fingers. Note that the upper bearing shells all have a grooved bearing surface, whereas the lower shells have a plain bearing surface. If the original bearing shells are being used for the check, ensure that they are refitted in their original locations.

35 The clearance can be checked in either of two ways.

36 One method (which will be difficult to achieve without a range of internal micrometers or internal/external expanding calipers) is to refit the main bearing caps to the cylinder block/crankcase, with bearing shells in place. With the cap retaining bolts tightened to the specified torque, measure the internal diameter of each assembled pair of bearing shells. If the diameter of each corresponding crankshaft journal is measured and then subtracted from the bearing internal diameter, the result will be the main bearing running clearance.

37 The second, and more accurate, method is to use Plastigauge. The method is as described above in paragraphs 21 to 30, substituting 'main bearing caps' for all references to the main bearing ladder casting.

Diesel engines

38 The running clearance check can be carried out using the original bearing shells. However, it is preferable to use a new set, since the results obtained will be more conclusive. Perform the check using the information given in paragraphs 33 to 37.

Final crankshaft refitting

TU series aluminium block engines

39 Carefully lift the crankshaft out of the cylinder block once more.

40 Using a little grease, stick the upper thrustwashers to each side of the No 2 main bearing upper location; ensure that the oilway grooves on each thrustwasher face outwards (away from the block) (see illustration).

18.41 Ensure each bearing shell tab is located (arrowed), and apply clean oil

18.42 Refitting the oil pump drive chain and sprocket

18.43 Apply a thin film of sealant to the cylinder block/crankcase mating surface . . .

41 Place the bearing shells in their locations as described earlier. If new shells are being fitted, ensure that all traces of protective grease are cleaned off using paraffin. Wipe dry the shells and connecting rods with a lint-free cloth. Liberally lubricate each bearing shell in the cylinder block/crankcase with clean engine oil (see illustration).
42 Refit the Woodruff key, then slide on the oil pump drive sprocket, and locate the drive chain on the sprocket (see illustration). Lower the crankshaft into position so that Nos 2 and 3 cylinder crankpins are at TDC; Nos 1 and 4 cylinder crankpins will be at BDC, ready for fitting No 1 piston. Check the crankshaft endfloat as described in Section 14.
43 Thoroughly degrease the mating surfaces of the cylinder block/crankcase and the main bearing ladder. Apply a thin bead of suitable sealant to the cylinder block/crankcase mating surface of the main bearing ladder casting, then spread to an even film (see illustration).
44 Lubricate the lower bearing shells with clean engine oil, then refit the main bearing ladder, ensuring that the shells are not displaced, and that the locating dowels engage correctly (see illustration).
45 Install the ten 11 mm main bearing ladder retaining bolts, and tighten them all by hand only. Working progressively outwards from the centre bolts, tighten the ten bolts, by a turn at a time, to the specified Stage 1 torque wrench setting. Once all the bolts have been tightened to the Stage 1 setting, angle-tighten the bolts through the specified Stage 2 angle

using a socket and extension bar. It is recommended that an angle-measuring gauge is used during this stage of the tightening, to ensure accuracy (see illustrations). If a gauge is not available, use a dab of white paint to make alignment marks between the bolt head and casting prior to tightening; the marks can then be used to check that the bolt has been rotated sufficiently during tightening.
46 Refit all the 6 mm bolts securing the main bearing ladder to the base of the cylinder block, and tighten them to the specified torque. Check that the crankshaft rotates freely.
47 Refit the piston/connecting rod assemblies to the crankshaft as described in Section 19.
48 Ensuring that the drive chain is correctly located on the sprocket, refit the oil pump and

sump as described in Part A of this Chapter.
49 Fit two new crankshaft oil seals as described in Part A.
50 Refit the flywheel as described in Part A of this Chapter.
51 Where removed, refit the cylinder head as described in Part A. Also refit the crankshaft sprocket and timing belt (see Part A).

TU series cast-iron block engines

52 Carefully lift the crankshaft out of the cylinder block once more.
53 Using a little grease, stick the upper thrustwashers to each side of the No 2 main bearing upper location. Ensure that the oilway grooves on each thrustwasher face outwards (away from the cylinder block) (see illustration).
54 Place the bearing shells in their locations as described earlier (see illustration). If new

18.44 . . . then lower the main bearing ladder into position

18.45a Tighten the ten 11 mm main bearing bolts to the Stage 1 torque setting . . .

18.45b . . . then angle-tighten them through the specified Stage 2 angle

18.53 Fitting a thrustwasher to No 2 main bearing upper location

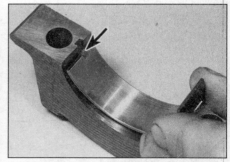

18.54 Ensure that the tab (arrowed) is correctly located in the cap when fitting the bearing shells

18.71 Applying sealant to the cylinder block No 1 main bearing cap mating face

18.72a Fitting a sealing strip to No 1 main bearing cap

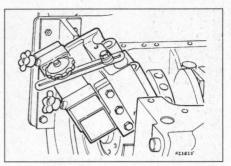

18.72b Using the Peugeot special tool to fit No 1 main bearing cap

shells are being fitted, ensure that all traces of protective grease are cleaned off using paraffin. Wipe dry the shells and connecting rods with a lint-free cloth. Liberally lubricate each bearing shell in the cylinder block/crankcase and cap with clean engine oil.

55 Lower the crankshaft into position so that Nos 2 and 3 cylinder crankpins are at TDC; Nos 1 and 4 cylinder crankpins will be at BDC, ready for fitting No 1 piston. Check the crankshaft endfloat as described in Section 14.

56 Lubricate the lower bearing shells in the main bearing caps with clean engine oil. Make sure that the locating lugs on the shells engage with the corresponding recesses in the caps.

57 Fit the main bearing caps to their correct locations, ensuring that they are fitted the correct way round (the bearing shell lug recesses in the block and caps must be on the same side). Insert the bolts loosely.

58 Tighten the main bearing cap bolts to the specified Stage 1 torque wrench setting. Once all the bolts have been tightened to the Stage 1 setting, angle-tighten the bolts through the specified Stage 2 angle, using a socket and extension bar. It is recommended that an angle-measuring gauge is used during this stage of the tightening, to ensure accuracy. If a gauge is not available, use a dab of white paint to make alignment marks between the bolt head and casting prior to tightening; the marks can then be used to check that the bolt has been rotated sufficiently during tightening.

59 Check that the crankshaft rotates freely.
60 Refit the piston/connecting rod assemblies to the crankshaft as described in Section 19.
61 Refit the Woodruff key to the crankshaft groove, and slide on the oil pump drive sprocket. Locate the drive chain on the sprocket.
62 Ensure that the mating surfaces of right-hand oil seal housing and cylinder block are clean and dry. Note the correct fitted depth of the oil seal then, using a large flat-bladed screwdriver, lever the seal out of the housing.
63 Apply a smear of suitable sealant to the oil seal housing mating surface, and make sure that the locating dowels are in position. Slide the housing over the end of the crankshaft, and into position on the cylinder block. Tighten the housing retaining bolts securely.
64 Repeat the operations in paragraphs 62 and 63, and fit the left-hand oil seal housing.
65 Fit new crankshaft oil seals as described in Part A of this Chapter.
66 Ensuring that the chain is correctly located on the drive sprocket, refit the oil pump and sump as described in Part A of this Chapter.
67 Refit the flywheel/driveplate as described in Part A of this Chapter.
68 Where removed, refit the cylinder head and install the crankshaft sprocket and timing belt as described in the relevant Sections of Part A.

XU series petrol and diesel engines

69 Carry out the operations described above in paragraphs 52 to 56.

70 Fit main bearing caps Nos 2 to 5 to their correct locations, ensuring that they are fitted the correct way round (the bearing shell tab recesses in the block and caps must be on the same side). Insert the bolts/nuts, tightening them only loosely at this stage.
71 Apply a small amount of sealant to the No 1 main bearing cap mating face on the cylinder block, around the sealing strip holes **(see illustration)**.
72 Locate the tab of each sealing strip over the pins on the base of No 1 bearing cap, and press the strips into the bearing cap grooves. It is now necessary to obtain two thin metal strips, of 0.25 mm thickness or less, in order to prevent the strips moving when the cap is being fitted. Peugeot garages use the tool shown, which acts as a clamp. Metal strips (such as old feeler blades) can be used, provided all burrs which may damage the sealing strips are first removed **(see illustrations)**.
73 Where applicable, oil both sides of the metal strips, and hold them on the sealing strips. Fit the No 1 main bearing cap, insert the bolts loosely, then carefully pull out the metal strips in a horizontal direction, using a pair of pliers **(see illustrations)**.
74 Tighten all the main bearing cap bolts/nuts evenly to the specified torque and, on 2.0 litre diesel engines, additionally through the specified angle.
75 On 1.8 litre petrol engines, refit the centre main bearing side retaining bolts and sealing washers (one at the front of the block, and one at the rear) and tighten them both to the specified torque.
76 On all engines, check that the sealing strips protrude slightly from above the cylinder block/crankcase mating surface by approximately 1 mm. If not, remove the bearing cap again and refit; the seals are supplied the correct length and should not be cut. Also check that the crankshaft rotates freely.
77 Fit a new crankshaft left-hand oil seal as described in Chapter 2B, 2C or 2D (as applicable).
78 Refit the piston/connecting rod assemblies to the crankshaft as described in Section 19.
79 Refit the Woodruff key, then slide on the

18.73a Fitting No 1 main bearing cap, using metal strips to retain the side seals

18.73b Removing a metal strip from No 1 main bearing cap using a pair of pliers

oil pump drive sprocket and spacer (where fitted), and locate the drive chain on the sprocket.

80 Ensure that the mating surfaces of the right-hand oil seal carrier and cylinder block are clean and dry. Note the correct fitted depth of the oil seal then, using a large flat-bladed screwdriver, lever the old seal out of the housing.

81 Apply a smear of suitable sealant to the oil seal carrier mating surface. Ensure that the locating dowels are in position, then slide the carrier over the end of the crankshaft and into position on the cylinder block. Tighten the carrier retaining bolts to the specified torque.

82 Fit a new crankshaft right-hand oil seal as described in Chapter 2B, 2C or 2D (as applicable).

83 Ensuring that the drive chain is correctly located on the sprocket, refit the oil pump and sump as described in Chapter 2B, 2C or 2D (as applicable).

84 Where removed, refit the cylinder head as described in Chapter 2B, 2C or 2D (as applicable).

---

19 Piston/connecting rod assembly – refitting and big-end bearing clearance check

Selection of bearing shells

1 On most engines, there are two sizes of big-end bearing shell produced by Peugeot; a standard size for use with the standard crankshaft, and an oversize for use once the crankshaft journals have been reground.

2 Consult your Peugeot dealer for the latest information on parts availability. Always quote the diameter of the crankshaft big-end crankpins when ordering bearing shells.

3 Before refitting the piston/connecting rod assemblies, we recommend that the big-end bearing running clearance is checked as follows.

Big-end bearing clearance check

4 Clean the backs of the bearing shells, and the bearing locations in both the connecting rod and bearing cap.

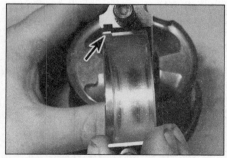

19.5 Fitting a bearing shell to a connecting rod – ensure the tab (arrowed) engages with the recess in the connecting rod

5 Press the bearing shells into their locations, ensuring that the tab on each shell engages in the notch in the connecting rod and cap. Take care not to touch any shell's bearing surface with your fingers **(see illustration)**. If the original bearing shells are being used for the check, ensure that they are refitted in their original locations. The clearance can be checked in either of two ways.

6 One method is to refit the big-end bearing cap to the connecting rod, ensuring that they are fitted the correct way around (see paragraph 20), with the bearing shells in place. With the cap retaining nuts correctly tightened, use an internal micrometer or vernier caliper to measure the internal diameter of each assembled pair of bearing shells. If the diameter of each corresponding crankshaft journal is measured and then subtracted from the bearing internal diameter, the result will be the big-end bearing running clearance.

7 The second, and more accurate method is to use Plastigauge (see Section 18).

8 Ensure that the bearing shells are correctly fitted. Place a strand of Plastigauge on each (cleaned) crankpin journal.

9 Refit the (clean) piston/connecting rod assemblies to the crankshaft, and refit the big-end bearing caps, using the marks made or noted on removal to ensure that they are fitted the correct way around.

10 Tighten the bearing cap nuts as described below in paragraph 21 or 22 (as applicable). Take care not to disturb the Plastigauge, nor rotate the connecting rod during the tightening sequence.

11 Dismantle the assemblies without rotating the connecting rods. Use the scale printed on the Plastigauge envelope to obtain the big-end bearing running clearance.

12 If the clearance is significantly different from that expected, the bearing shells may be the wrong size (or excessively worn, if the original shells are being re-used). Make sure that no dirt or oil was trapped between the bearing shells and the caps or block when the clearance was measured. If the Plastigauge was wider at one end than at the other, the crankshaft journal may be tapered.

13 Note that Peugeot do not specify a recommended big-end bearing running

clearance. The figure given in the Specifications is a guide figure, which is typical for this type of engine. Before condemning the components concerned, refer to your Peugeot dealer or engine reconditioning specialist for further information on the specified running clearance. Their advice on the best course of action to be taken can then also be obtained.

14 On completion, carefully scrape away all traces of the Plastigauge material from the crankshaft and bearing shells. Use your fingernail, or some other object which is unlikely to score the bearing surfaces.

Final refitting

15 Note that the following procedure assumes that the cylinder liners (where fitted) are in position in the cylinder block/crankcase as described in Section 12, and that the crankshaft and main bearing ladder/caps are in place (see Section 18).

16 Ensure that the bearing shells are correctly fitted as described earlier. If new shells are being fitted, ensure that all traces of the protective grease are cleaned off using paraffin. Wipe dry the shells and connecting rods with a lint-free cloth.

17 Lubricate the cylinder bores, the pistons, and piston rings, then lay out each piston/connecting rod assembly in its respective position.

18 Start with assembly No 1. Make sure that the piston rings are still spaced as described in Section 17, then clamp them in position with a piston ring compressor. Insert the piston/connecting rod assembly into the top of cylinder/liner No 1, ensuring the piston is correctly positioned as follows.

a) On petrol engines, ensure that the arrow on the piston crown is pointing towards the timing belt end of the engine.

b) On 1.8 and 1.9 litre diesel engines, ensure that the cloverleaf-shaped cut-out on the piston crown is towards the front (oil filter side) of the cylinder block.

c) On 2.0 litre diesel engines, ensure that the valve recesses on the piston crown are towards the rear of the cylinder block.

19 Using a block of wood or hammer handle against the piston crown, tap the assembly into the cylinder/liner until the piston crown is flush with the top of the cylinder/liner **(see illustration)**.

20 Ensure that the bearing shell is still correctly installed. Liberally lubricate the crankpin and both bearing shells. Taking care not to mark the cylinder/liner bores, pull the piston/connecting rod assembly down the bore and onto the crankpin. Refit the big-end bearing cap, tightening the nuts finger-tight at first. Note that the faces with the identification marks must match (which means that the bearing shell locating tabs abut each other).

21 On TU series petrol engines, tighten the bearing cap retaining nuts evenly and progressively to the specified torque setting.

22 On XU series petrol engines and all diesel

19.19 Tap the piston into the bore using a hammer handle

engines, tighten the bearing cap retaining nuts evenly and progressively to the Stage 1 torque setting **(see illustration)**. Once both nuts have been tightened to the Stage 1 setting, angle-tighten them through the specified Stage 2 angle, using a socket and extension bar. It is recommended that an angle-measuring gauge is used during this stage of the tightening, to ensure accuracy **(see illustration)**.

23 On all engines, once the bearing cap retaining nuts have been correctly tightened, rotate the crankshaft. Check that it turns freely; some stiffness is to be expected if new components have been fitted, but there should be no signs of binding or tight spots.

24 Refit the other three piston/connecting rod assemblies in the same way.

25 Refit the cylinder head and oil pump as described in Part A, B, C or D of this Chapter (as applicable).

20 Engine – initial start-up after overhaul

1 With the engine refitted in the vehicle, double-check the engine oil and coolant levels (see *Weekly checks*). Make a final check that everything has been reconnected, and that there are no tools or rags left in the engine compartment.

19.22a Tighten the big-end bearing cap nuts to the specified torque (see text)

19.22b . . . then through the angle specified for the final tightening torque

2 Switch on the ignition and immediately turn the engine on the starter (do not allow the glow plugs to heat up on diesel engines) until the oil pressure warning light goes out.

3 Pressurise/prime the fuel system as described in the relevant Part of Chapter 4, then start the engine, noting that this may take a little longer than usual, due to the fuel system components having been disturbed.

4 While the engine is idling, check for fuel, water and oil leaks. Don't be alarmed if there are some odd smells and smoke from parts getting hot and burning off oil deposits.

5 Assuming all is well, keep the engine idling until hot water is felt circulating through the top hose, then switch off the engine.

6 Allow the engine to cool then recheck the oil and coolant levels as described in *Weekly checks*, and top-up as necessary.

7 If they were tightened as described, on all engines except XU series petrol (see Chapter 2B), there is no need to retighten the cylinder head bolts once the engine has first run after reassembly.

8 If new pistons, rings or crankshaft bearings have been fitted, the engine must be treated as new, and run-in for the first 500 miles (800 km). *Do not* operate the engine at full-throttle, or allow it to labour at low engine speeds in any gear. It is recommended that the oil and filter be changed at the end of this period.

Chapter 3
Cooling, heating and ventilation systems

Contents

Degrees of difficulty

Easy, suitable for novice with little experience		Fairly easy, suitable for beginner with some experience		Fairly difficult, suitable for competent DIY mechanic		Difficult, suitable for experienced DIY mechanic		Very difficult, suitable for expert DIY or professional	

Specifications

General
Maximum system pressure .... 1.4 bars

Thermostat
Opening temperatures:
   Starts to open:
      TU series petrol engine models .... 89°C
      All other models .... 83°C
   Fully-open .... 99°C

Torque wrench settings

	Nm	lbf ft
Coolant pump housing bolts (aluminium block petrol engines):		
Smaller bolts	30	22
Larger bolts	65	48
Coolant pump securing bolts (cast-iron iron block engines)	15	11

1 General information and precautions

General information

The cooling system is of pressurised type, comprising a coolant pump driven by the timing belt, an aluminium crossflow radiator with integral expansion tank, electric cooling fan(s), a thermostat, heater matrix, and all associated hoses and switches.

The system functions as follows. Cold coolant in the bottom of the radiator passes through the bottom hose to the coolant pump, where it is pumped around the cylinder block and head passages, and through the oil cooler(s) (where fitted). After cooling the cylinder bores, combustion surfaces and valve seats, the coolant reaches the underside of the thermostat, which is initially closed. The coolant passes through the heater, and is returned via the cylinder block to the coolant pump.

When the engine is cold, the coolant circulates only through the cylinder block, cylinder head, and heater. When the coolant reaches a predetermined temperature, the thermostat opens, and the coolant passes through the top hose to the radiator. As the coolant circulates through the radiator, it is cooled by the inrush of air when the car is in forward motion. The airflow is supplemented by the action of the electric cooling fan(s) when necessary. Upon reaching the bottom of the radiator, the coolant has now cooled, and the cycle is repeated.

When the engine is at normal operating temperature, the coolant expands, and some of it is displaced into the expansion tank. Coolant collects in the tank, and is returned to the radiator when the system cools.

On models with automatic transmission, a proportion of the coolant is recirculated from the bottom of the radiator through the transmission fluid cooler mounted on the transmission. On models fitted with an engine oil cooler, the coolant is also passed through the oil cooler.

The electric cooling fan(s) mounted in front of the radiator are controlled by a thermostatic switch/sensor. At a predetermined coolant temperature, the switch/sensor actuates the fan.

Precautions

 Warning: Do not attempt to remove the expansion tank filler cap, or to disturb any part of the cooling system, while the engine is hot, as there is a high risk of scalding. If the expansion tank filler cap must be removed before the engine and radiator have fully cooled (even though this is not recommended), the pressure in the cooling system must first be relieved. Cover the cap with a thick layer of cloth to avoid scalding, and slowly unscrew the filler cap until a hissing sound is heard. When the hissing has stopped, indicating that the pressure has reduced, slowly unscrew the filler cap until it can be removed; if more hissing sounds are heard, wait until they have stopped before unscrewing the cap. At all times, keep well away from the filler cap opening, and protect your hands.

Warning: Do not allow antifreeze to come into contact with your skin, or with the painted surfaces of the vehicle. Rinse off spills immediately, with plenty of water. Never leave antifreeze lying around in an open container, or in a puddle in the driveway or on the garage floor. Children and pets are attracted by its sweet smell, but antifreeze can be fatal if ingested.

Warning: If the engine is hot, the electric cooling fan may start rotating even if the engine is not running. Be careful to keep your hands, hair and any loose clothing well clear when working in the engine compartment.

Warning: Refer to Section 11 for precautions to be observed when working on models equipped with air conditioning.

2 Cooling system hoses – disconnection and renewal

Note: *Refer to the warnings given in Section 1 of this Chapter before proceeding. Hoses should only be disconnected once the engine has cooled sufficiently to avoid scalding.*

1 If the checks described in Chapter 1A or 1B reveal a faulty hose, it must be renewed as follows.

2 First drain the cooling system (Chapter 1A or 1B). If the coolant is not due for renewal, it may be re-used, providing it is collected in a clean container.

3 To disconnect a hose, proceed as follows, according to the type of hose connection.

Conventional hose connections

4 On conventional connections, the clips

2.5 Disconnecting the radiator top hose

used to secure the hoses in position may be either standard worm-drive clips or disposable crimped types. The crimped type of clip is not designed to be re-used and a worm-drive type should be used on reassembly.

Removal

5 To disconnect a hose, use a screwdriver to slacken or release the clips, then move them along the hose, clear of the relevant inlet/outlet. Carefully work the hose free **(see illustration)**. The hoses can be removed with relative ease when new – on an older car, they may have stuck.

6 If a hose proves to be difficult to remove, try to release it by rotating its ends before attempting to free it. Gently prise the end of the hose with a blunt instrument (such as a flat-bladed screwdriver), but do not apply too much force, and take care not to damage the pipe stubs or hoses. Note in particular that the radiator inlet stub is fragile; do not use excessive force when attempting to remove the hose. If all else fails, cut the hose with a sharp knife, then slit it so that it can be peeled off in two pieces. Although this may prove expensive if the hose is otherwise undamaged, it is preferable to buying a new radiator. Check first, however, that a new hose is readily available.

Refitting

7 When fitting a hose, first slide the clips onto the hose, then work the hose into position. If crimped-type clips were originally fitted, use standard worm-drive clips when refitting the hose.

8 Work the hose into position, checking that it is correctly routed, then slide each clip back along the hose until it passes over the flared end of the relevant inlet/outlet, before tightening the clip securely.

> **HAYNES HINT** *If the hose is stiff, use a little soapy water as a lubricant, or soften the hose by soaking it in hot water. Do not use oil or grease, which may attack the rubber.*

9 Refill the cooling system (see Chapter 1A or 1B).

10 Check thoroughly for leaks as soon as possible after disturbing any part of the cooling system.

Bayonet-type hose connections

Note: *A new O-ring should be used when reconnecting the hose.*

Removal

11 On certain models, the radiator bottom and/or top hose(s) may be connected to the radiator using a plastic bayonet-type connection. To disconnect this type of connector, proceed as follows.

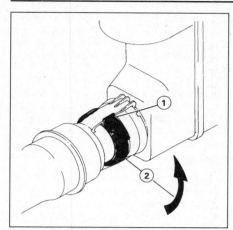

2.12 To release the bayonet-type radiator hose connection, turn the locking ring (2) until it contacts the stop (1)

12 Turn the locking ring (2) anti-clockwise until it contacts the stop (1) **(see illustration)**.
13 Press the connector away from the hose, to ensure that the two retaining lugs (3) are free **(see illustration)**.
14 Pull the hose, complete with the connector, from the radiator.
15 Recover the O-ring from the connector, and discard it; a new one must be used on refitting.

Refitting

16 Wipe the connector and the stub on the radiator thoroughly with a clean, lint-free cloth.
17 Fit a new O-ring to the male half of the connector, ensuring that it is correctly seated **(see illustration)**.
18 Turn the locking ring clockwise until it clicks.
19 Offer the hose to the stub on the radiator, with the locating cut-out in the male part of the connector located at the bottom **(see illustration)**.
20 Push the connector into the stub until both the retaining lugs click into position. Make sure that the O-ring is not trapped.
21 Pull the connector rearwards (away from the stub) to adjust the position of the retaining lugs if necessary.
22 Refill the cooling system (see Chapter 1A or 1B).
23 Check thoroughly for leaks as soon as possible after disturbing any part of the cooling system.

Spring clip type hose connections

Note: *A new sealing ring should be used when reconnecting the hose.*

Removal

24 On later models, some cooling system hoses may be secured in position using a wire spring clip. To disconnect this type of connector, proceed as follows.
25 Using a small screwdriver, extract the

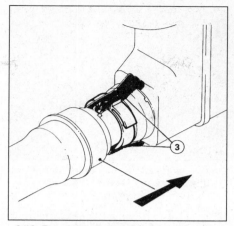

2.13 Press the connector away from the hose, to ensure that the two retaining lugs (3) are free

retaining spring clip and disconnect the hose connection **(see illustration)**. Once the hose has been disconnected, refit the spring clip to the hose union.
26 Inspect the hose unit sealing ring for signs of damage or deterioration and renew if necessary.

Refitting

27 Ensure that the sealing ring is in position and the spring clip is correctly located in the groove in the union **(see illustration)**.
28 Lubricate the sealing ring with a smear of soapy water, to ease installation, then push

2.19 Offer the hose to the stub on the radiator, cut-out (arrowed) at the bottom

2.27 Ensure that the sealing ring and spring clip (arrowed) are correctly fitted to the hose union before reconnecting

2.17 On refitting, fit a new O-ring (arrowed) to the hose union

the hose into position until it is heard to click into position.
29 Ensure that the hose is securely retained by the spring clip then refill the cooling system (see Chapter 1A or 1B).
30 Check thoroughly for leaks as soon as possible after disturbing any part of the cooling system.

Heater matrix hose connections

Note: *New O-rings should be used when reconnecting the hoses.*

Removal

31 The two hoses are connected to the matrix by means of a single connector.
32 Prise the metal retaining clip from the top of the connector **(see illustration)**.
33 Release the plastic retaining clip by

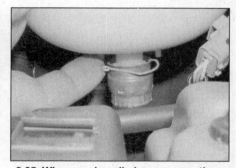

2.25 Where spring clip hose connections are used, remove the spring clip then disconnect the hose

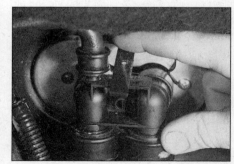

2.32 Remove the metal clip from the top of the heater matrix connector on the engine compartment bulkhead . . .

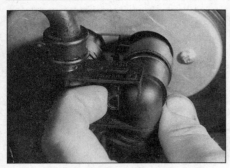

2.33 . . . then release the plastic retaining clip . . .

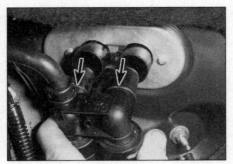

2.34 . . . and pull the connector away from the bulkhead – recover the O-rings (arrowed)

pushing it towards the left-hand hose connection **(see illustration)**.

34 Pull the connector assembly from the heater matrix. Recover the O-ring seals from the connector, and discard them; new ones should be used on refitting **(see illustration)**.

Refitting

35 Refitting is a reversal of the removal procedure, using new O-rings.

36 Refill the cooling system (see Chapter 1A or 1B).

37 Check thoroughly for leaks as soon as possible after disturbing any part of the cooling system.

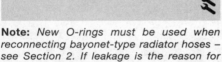

3 Radiator – removal, inspection and refitting

Note: *New O-rings must be used when reconnecting bayonet-type radiator hoses – see Section 2. If leakage is the reason for removing the radiator, bear in mind that minor leaks can often be cured using a radiator sealant with the radiator in situ.*

Removal

1 Disconnect the battery negative terminal (refer to *Disconnecting the battery* in the Reference Chapter).

2 Drain the cooling system (see Chapter 1A or 1B).

3 Where applicable, release the securing clip(s), and unscrew the bolt securing the air

inlet ducting to the front body panel and the engine, then remove the ducting.

4 On April 1997 onward diesel models, remove the windscreen washer reservoir as described in Chapter 12. Move the cooling system expansion tank (at the front of the radiator) to one side, then unbolt and remove the expansion tank support bracket.

5 Working at the bottom left-hand corner of the cooling fan shroud, disconnect the wiring connector **(see illustration)**.

6 Disconnect the coolant hoses from the radiator with reference to Section 2.

7 Working at the top of the radiator, release the four securing clips (two on each side), then lift the complete radiator/cooling fan assembly from the engine compartment, taking care not to damage the radiator fins on surrounding components **(see illustrations)**.

8 The cooling fan shroud may be secured to the radiator using a cable-tie, which must be removed before the radiator and cooling fan assembly can be separated.

Inspection

9 If the radiator has been removed due to suspected blockage, reverse-flush it as described in Chapter 1A or 1B. Clean dirt and debris from the radiator fins, using an air line (in which case, wear eye protection) or a soft brush.

Caution: Be careful, as the fins are sharp, and easily damaged.

10 If necessary, a radiator specialist can perform a 'flow test' on the radiator, to establish whether an internal blockage exists.

11 A leaking radiator must be referred to a specialist for permanent repair. Do not attempt to weld or solder a leaking radiator, as damage to the plastic components may result.

12 If the radiator is to be sent for repair or renewed, remove all hoses and the cooling fan switch (where fitted).

13 Inspect the condition of the radiator mounting rubbers, and renew them if necessary.

Refitting

14 Refitting is a reversal of removal, bearing in mind the following points:
  a) *Where applicable, use a new cable-tie to secure the cooling fan shroud to the radiator.*
  b) *Ensure that the lower lugs on the radiator are correctly engaged with the mounting rubbers in the body panel.*
  c) *Reconnect the hoses with reference to Section 2, using new O-rings where applicable.*
  d) *On completion, refill the cooling system as described in Chapter 1A or 1B.*

4 Thermostat – removal, testing and refitting

Removal

1 Disconnect the battery negative terminal (refer to *Disconnecting the battery* in the Reference Chapter).

2 On later diesel engine models, release the fasteners and remove the engine cover.

3 Drain the cooling system (see Chapter 1A or 1B).

4 Where necessary, release any relevant wiring and hoses from the retaining clips, and position clear of the thermostat housing to improve access. On some models, access is also improved if the air cleaner duct is removed (see relevant Part of Chapter 4).

5 Unscrew the retaining bolts, and carefully withdraw the thermostat housing cover to expose the thermostat. Take care not to strain the coolant hose(s) connected to the cover

3.5 Disconnecting the cooling fan/switch wiring connector

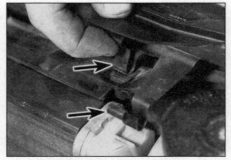

3.7a Release the securing clips (arrowed) . . .

3.7b . . . and lift the radiator assembly from the engine compartment

4.5a Thermostat housing cover retaining bolts (arrowed) – 1.4 litre petrol engine

4.5b Thermostat housing cover (arrowed) – 2.0 litre petrol engine

4.6 Removing the sealing ring from the thermostat flange

(see illustrations). Note that the design of the thermostat housing varies between engine types, but the thermostat removal procedure for each type is similar.

6 On early models with a separate thermostat, lift the thermostat from the housing, noting which way round the thermostat is fitted, and recover the sealing ring(s) **(see illustration)**.

7 On later models where the thermostat is an integral part of the housing cover, recover the sealing ring, release the retaining clip and remove the cover from the coolant hose.

Testing

8 A rough test of the thermostat may be made by suspending it with a piece of string in a container full of water. Heat the water to bring it to the boil – the thermostat must open by the time the water boils. If not, renew it.

9 If a thermometer is available, the precise opening temperature of the thermostat may be determined; compare with the figures given in the Specifications. The opening temperature is also marked on the thermostat.

10 A thermostat which fails to close as the water cools must also be renewed.

Refitting

11 Refitting is a reversal of removal, bearing in mind the following points:

a) Examine the sealing ring(s) for damage or deterioration, and if necessary, renew.

b) Ensure that the thermostat is fitted the correct way round as noted during removal.

c) On completion, refill the cooling system as described in Chapter 1A or 1B.

---

5 Electric cooling fan(s) – removal and refitting

General information

1 On models without air conditioning, the current supply to the cooling fan(s) is via the battery and a fuse (see Chapter 12). The circuit is completed by the cooling fan thermostatic switch, which (on most models) is mounted in the left-hand side of the radiator. On models with air conditioning, the cooling fans are controlled by the air conditioning system (or engine management system) electronic control unit, in conjunction with a temperature sensor located in the thermostat housing – see Section 6.

Removal

2 Remove the radiator/cooling fan assembly as described in Section 3.

3 Where applicable, release the cable-tie securing the cooling fan shroud to the radiator **(see illustration)**.

4 Disconnect the wiring plug from the rear of the motor.

5 Unscrew the three motor retaining nuts, rotating the fan blades as necessary so that the bolts can be counterheld from the front as the nuts are unscrewed **(see illustration)**. Withdraw the motor assembly, complete with the fan, from the shroud.

6 If desired, the fan blades can be removed from the motor shaft, after its retaining screw or clip (as applicable) has been removed.

7 If the motor is faulty, the complete unit must be renewed, as no spares are available.

Refitting

8 Refitting is a reversal of removal. Refit the radiator as described in Section 3.

---

6 Cooling system electrical switches and sensors – location, removal and refitting

Petrol engine models

Cooling fan switch

1 On models without air conditioning, the cooling fan switch has a blue wiring connector and is located in the left-hand side of the radiator.

2 On models with air conditioning, the cooling fans are controlled by the air conditioning system control unit in conjunction with a temperature sensor located in the top of the thermostat housing. The sensor can be identified by its brown wiring connector.

Temperature warning light switch/gauge sensor

3 The coolant temperature warning light switch/temperature gauge sensor has a blue wiring connector and is located in the thermostat housing or at the left-hand end of the cylinder head **(see illustration)**.

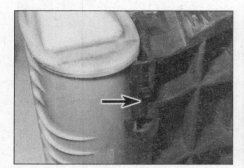

5.3 Cooling fan shroud securing cable-tie

5.5 Fan motor securing nuts (arrowed)

6.3 Coolant temperature warning light switch/temperature gauge sensor (A) and coolant temperature sensor (B) – 1.6 litre petrol engine

Engine management system coolant temperature sensor

4 The engine management system coolant temperature sensor has a green wiring connector and is located in the thermostat housing.

5 On later engines (approximately 2001 onward) the coolant temperature sensor has a blue or green wiring connector and is located above the thermostat in the coolant outlet housing at the left-hand end of the cylinder head. The temperature signal from this sensor is used by the engine management ECU for fuel injection/ignition regulation and to control the operation of the cooling fan, air conditioning system and temperature warning light/gauge.

1.8 and 1.9 litre diesel engine models

Cooling fan switch

6 On models without air conditioning, the cooling fan switch has a blue wiring connector and is located in the left-hand side of the radiator.

7 On models with air conditioning, the cooling fans are controlled by the air conditioning system control unit in conjunction with a temperature sensor located in the thermostat housing. The sensor can be identified by its brown wiring connector.

Temperature warning light switch/gauge sensor

8 The coolant temperature warning light switch/temperature gauge sensor has a blue wiring connector and is located in the thermostat housing.

Preheating/EGR system coolant temperature switch/sensor

9 The coolant temperature switch or sensor used for control of the preheating and EGR systems has a green wiring connector and is located in the thermostat housing.

2.0 litre diesel engine models

Engine management system coolant temperature sensor

10 The coolant temperature sensor has a green wiring connector and is mounted in the thermostat/coolant outlet housing at the left-hand end of the cylinder head. The temperature signal from this sensor is used by the engine management ECU for diesel injection regulation and to control the operation of the exhaust gas recirculation, cooling fans, pre/post-heating control unit, air conditioning system and temperature warning light/gauge.

Removal

 Warning: The engine should be cold before removing a cooling system switch or sensor.

11 Disconnect the battery negative terminal (refer to *Disconnecting the battery* in the Reference Chapter).

12 Partially drain the cooling system to just below the level of the switch/sensor (as described in Chapter 1A or 1B). Alternatively, have ready a suitable bung to plug the switch aperture in the housing when the switch is removed. If this method is used, take care not to use anything which will allow foreign matter to enter the cooling system.

13 Where necessary, refer to the relevant Part of Chapter 4 and remove the air cleaner and air inlet ducts for access to the switches/sensors located in the thermostat housing or cylinder head.

14 Unplug the wiring connector from the relevant switch/sensor.

15 On 2.0 litre diesel engines fitted with a plastic thermostat/coolant outlet housing, prise out the sensor retaining circlip then remove the sensor and sealing ring from the housing. If the system has not been drained, plug the sensor aperture to prevent further coolant loss.

16 On all other engines, carefully unscrew the switch/sensor from its mounting and recover the sealing ring (where applicable). If the system has not been drained, plug the switch/sensor aperture to prevent further coolant loss.

Refitting

17 On 2.0 litre diesel engines fitted with a plastic thermostat/coolant outlet housing, fit a new sealing ring to the sensor. Push the sensor firmly into the housing and secure it in position with the circlip, ensuring it is correctly located in the housing groove. Reconnect the sensor wiring connector.

18 On all other engines, if the switch/sensor was originally fitted using sealing compound, clean the switch/sensor threads thoroughly, and coat them with fresh sealing compound. If the switch was originally fitted using a sealing ring, use a new sealing ring on refitting.

19 Fit the switch/sensor to its location, tighten it securely and reconnect the wiring connector.

20 On all engines, refill and bleed the cooling system as described in Chapter 1A or 1B. Follow the bleeding instructions carefully, to ensure that all air is expelled from the cooling system.

21 On completion, refit any components removed for access, then start the engine and run it until it reaches normal operating temperature. Continue to run the engine, and check that the component(s) controlled by the switch/sensor operate correctly.

7 Coolant pump – removal and refitting

Aluminium block engines

Note: *A new impeller assembly O-ring, and where applicable, a new impeller housing O-ring, will be required on refitting.*

Removal

1 The coolant pump is driven by the timing belt, and is located in a housing at the timing belt end of the engine.

2 Drain the cooling system as described in the relevant Part of Chapter 1.

3 Remove the timing belt as described in the relevant Part of Chapter 2.

4 Remove the securing bolts, and withdraw the pump impeller assembly from the pump housing (access is most easily obtained from under the wheel arch). Recover the O-ring **(see illustrations)**.

5 If desired, the pump impeller housing can be removed from the rear of the coolant pump housing. Access is most easily obtained from underneath the vehicle (it may be necessary to remove the exhaust heat shield). Disconnect the coolant hoses from the impeller housing (be prepared for coolant spillage), then remove the securing bolts and withdraw the impeller housing. Again, recover the O-ring.

Refitting

6 Ensure that all mating faces are clean.

7 Where applicable, refit the impeller housing to the rear of the coolant pump housing, using a new O-ring. Reconnect the coolant hoses securely.

8 Refit the impeller assembly to the pump housing, using a new O-ring.

9 Refit the timing belt as described in the relevant Part of Chapter 2.

10 Refill the cooling system as described in the relevant Part of Chapter 1.

7.4a Withdraw the coolant pump . . .

7.4b . . . and recover the O-ring – 1.4 litre petrol engine

8.8a Unscrew the securing bolt (arrowed) . . .

8.8b . . . withdraw the plastic housing . . .

8.8c . . . and recover the O-ring

Cast-iron block engines

Note: *A new pump O-ring must be used on refitting.*

11 The pump is driven by the timing belt, and is located directly in the cylinder block.

12 Proceed as described previously for engines with an aluminium cylinder block, but note that there is no separate impeller housing.

8 Thermostat/fuel filter housing (1.8 and 1.9 litre diesel engine models)

Note: *A new gasket must be used when refitting the main housing.*

Removal

1 Disconnect the battery negative terminal (refer to *Disconnecting the battery* in the Reference Chapter).

2 Drain the cooling system as described in Chapter 1B.

3 Place a plastic sheet over the transmission bellhousing and the starter motor, to prevent any fuel spilled during the following procedure from causing damage.

4 Remove the fuel filter as described in Chapter 1B.

5 Disconnect the wiring plugs from the coolant sensors mounted in the top of the housing.

6 Disconnect the coolant hoses from the plastic thermostat housing.

7 Disconnect the coolant hose from the stub at the rear of the housing.

8 Unscrew the bolt securing the plastic fuel filter housing to the main housing, then withdraw the plastic housing and move it clear of the main housing. Recover the O-ring from the base of the plastic housing **(see illustrations)**.

9 Unscrew the three securing bolts, and withdraw the main housing from the cylinder head **(see illustrations)**. Recover the gasket.

10 Disconnect the coolant hose from the base of the housing, and remove the housing.

Refitting

11 Refitting is a reversal of removal, bearing in mind the following points:

a) *Examine the condition of the O-ring on the base of the plastic housing, and renew if necessary.*

b) *Use a new gasket when refitting the main housing.*

c) *Ensure that all hoses, pipes and wires are correctly reconnected.*

d) *Refill the cooling system as described in Chapter 1B.*

e) *On completion, prime and bleed the fuel system as described in Chapter 4D or 4E, as applicable.*

9 Heating and ventilation system – general information

The heating/ventilation system consists of a four-speed blower motor (housed behind the facia), face level vents in the centre and at each end of the facia, and air ducts to the front footwells.

The control unit is located in the facia, and the controls operate flap valves to deflect and mix the air flowing through the various parts of the heating/ventilation system. The flap valves are contained in the air distribution housing, which acts as a central distribution unit, passing air to the various ducts and vents.

Cold air enters the system through the grille at the rear of the engine compartment. If required, the airflow is boosted by the blower, and then flows through the various ducts, according to the settings of the controls. Stale air is expelled through ducts at the rear of the vehicle. If warm air is required, the cold air is passed over the heater matrix, which is heated by the engine coolant.

On models fitted with air conditioning, a recirculation switch enables the outside air supply to be closed off, while the air inside the vehicle is recirculated. This can be useful to prevent unpleasant odours entering from

8.9a Unscrew the three securing bolts (arrowed) . . .

8.9b . . . and withdraw the main thermostat housing

10.3 Removing the heater/ventilation control unit securing screws (arrowed)

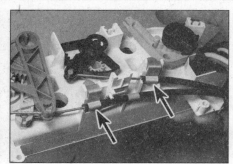

10.4a Two of the control cables are secured by metal clips (arrowed) . . .

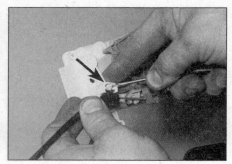

10.4b . . . the third cable is held by a plastic clip, released here using a screwdriver

outside the vehicle, but should only be used briefly, as the recirculated air inside the vehicle will soon become stale.

10 Heater/ventilation components – removal and refitting

Heater/ventilation control unit

Removal

1 Disconnect the battery negative terminal (refer to *Disconnecting the battery* in the Reference Chapter).

10.12 Disconnect the heater hoses from the matrix pipes

2 Remove the facia centre panel as described in Chapter 11.
3 Remove the four control unit securing screws, then withdraw the control unit from the facia **(see illustration)**.
4 Working at the rear of the control unit, release the securing clips, and disconnect the control cables from the unit. Note the locations of the cables to ensure correct refitting **(see illustrations)**.
5 Disconnect the wiring plug from the rear of the control unit, then withdraw the unit.

Refitting

6 Refitting is a reversal of removal, but ensure that the control cables are securely reconnected to their original locations.

Heater/ventilation control cables

Removal

7 Disconnect the cables from the heater/ventilation control unit, as described previously in this Section during the control unit removal procedure.
8 Working through the facia aperture or under the facia (it may be necessary to remove certain facia panels for access – see Chapter 11 – depending on which cable is to be removed), release the clips and disconnect the cable from the heater assembly. Note

the routing of the cable to ensure correct refitting.

Refitting

9 Refitting is a reversal of removal, ensuring that the cables are correctly routed, and securely reconnected.

Heater matrix (no air conditioning)

Note: *New heater hose connector O-rings must be used on refitting.*

Removal

10 Drain the cooling system (see Chapter 1A or 1B).
11 Remove the complete facia assembly as described in Chapter 11.
12 Working in the engine compartment, where applicable, unclip the brake servo vacuum pipe from the bulkhead to improve access to the heater hose-to-matrix connections. Disconnect the heater hoses from the matrix pipes – refer to Section 2 **(see illustration)**.
13 Again working in the engine compartment, unscrew the two nuts securing the heater assembly to the bulkhead **(see illustrations)**.
14 Working inside the vehicle, unscrew the bolt securing the bottom of the heater to the

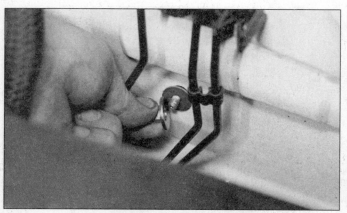

10.13a Unscrew the left-hand . . .

10.13b . . . and right-hand heater securing nuts (arrowed) – right-hand-drive model

10.14 Unscrewing the bolt securing the heater to the floor

10.15 Removing the heater assembly

10.16a Release the four securing clips . . .

bracket on the floor **(see illustration)**. Note that on certain models it may be necessary to unbolt the anti-theft alarm system immobiliser keypad and move it aside for access to the bolt.

15 With the aid of an assistant working in the engine compartment, prise the matrix pipe grommet from the bulkhead, and carefully pull the heater assembly from the bulkhead into the vehicle interior, feeding the pipes through the bulkhead **(see illustration)**.

16 With the heater assembly removed, release the four securing clips, then withdraw the matrix from the heater casing **(see illustrations)**.

Refitting

17 Refitting is a reversal of removal bearing in mind the following points.

a) Before refitting the heater assembly, lubricate the heater pipe grommet, then refit it to the matrix pipes.

b) Offer the heater assembly into position, pushing the heater pipe grommet through the bulkhead as the assembly is refitted (again, an assistant working in the engine compartment will ease the task).

c) When reconnecting the heater hoses to the pipes, fit new O-rings to the matrix pipes, then reconnect the hose connector to the pipes.

Heater matrix (with air conditioning)

Removal

18 Proceed as described in paragraphs 10 to 14 inclusive.

19 Detach the temperature sensor from the side of the heater casing.

20 If not already done, disconnect the wiring plug from the heater/ventilation control unit, and unclip the wiring harness(es) from the heater casing.

21 Remove the three screws securing the main heater casing to the evaporator/heater blower motor casing.

22 Unplug the wiring from the rear of the unit.

23 Proceed as described in paragraphs 15 and 16, but separate the main heater casing from the evaporator/heater blower motor casing as the assembly is removed (this avoids the need to disconnect the refrigerant circuit).

Refitting

24 Refitting is a reversal of removal, bearing in mind the points made in paragraph 17.

Heater blower motor

Removal

25 The blower motor assembly is located on the passenger side of the vehicle.

26 Disconnect the battery negative terminal (refer to *Disconnecting the battery* in the Reference Chapter).

27 Working inside the vehicle, unclip the lower facia trim panel from the bottom of the facia, and withdraw the panel.

28 To improve access, remove the glovebox as described in Chapter 11.

29 Unscrew the three motor securing screws. On models without air conditioning, note that two of the screws secure a wiring plug bracket, and the third screw secures the

10.16b . . . and withdraw the heater matrix

lower facia trim panel support bracket. Unclip the wiring plugs from the bracket and remove the bracket **(see illustration)**.

30 Lower the motor assembly, then pull the rubber wiring grommet away from the motor casing, and disconnect the wiring plugs **(see illustrations)**.

Refitting

31 Refitting is a reversal of removal.

Heater blower motor resistor

Removal

32 Switch on the windscreen wipers, and switch off the ignition, leaving the wiper arms in the raised position.

33 Disconnect the battery negative terminal (refer to *Disconnecting the battery* in the Reference Chapter).

34 Move the heater blower motor control to the bottom (closed) position.

10.29 Remove the wiring plug bracket from under the heater motor . . .

10.30a . . . then lower the motor . . .

10.30b . . . and pull the grommet out for access to the wiring plugs

35 Open the bonnet.

36 Working at the passenger's side of the vehicle, open the front door, and pull the weatherstrip from the edge of the scuttle cover panel to expose the scuttle panel side securing nut.

37 Remove the securing screws, then pull the passenger's side scuttle cover panel from the scuttle.

38 Unscrew the three securing bolts, and remove the scuttle cover panel bracket from the scuttle.

39 Unclip the water deflector from the scuttle.

40 Pull out the cover from the heater air inlet duct **(see illustration)**.

41 Twist the resistor anti-clockwise to release it, then disconnect the wiring plug and withdraw the unit **(see illustration)**.

 HAYNES HINT *Tie a piece of string to the wiring connector, to retrieve it if it falls back out of the duct.*

Refitting

42 Refitting is a reversal of removal.

11 Air conditioning system – general information and precautions

General information

An air conditioning system is available on certain models. It enables the temperature of incoming air to be lowered, and also dehumidifies the air, which makes for rapid demisting and increased comfort.

The cooling side of the system works in the same way as a domestic refrigerator. Refrigerant gas is drawn into a belt-driven compressor, and passes into a condenser mounted on the front of the radiator, where it loses heat and becomes liquid. The liquid passes through an expansion valve to an evaporator, where it changes from liquid

10.40 Pull the cover from the heater air intake duct . . .

under high pressure to gas under low pressure. This change is accompanied by a drop in temperature, which cools the evaporator. The refrigerant returns to the compressor, and the cycle begins again.

Air blown through the evaporator passes to the air distribution unit, where it is mixed with hot air blown through the heater matrix to achieve the desired temperature in the passenger compartment.

The heating side of the system works in the same way as on models without air conditioning (see Section 9).

The operation of the system is controlled by an electronic control unit, which controls the electric cooling fan(s), the compressor and the facia-mounted warning light. Any problems with the system should be referred to a Peugeot dealer.

Precautions

When an air conditioning system is fitted, it is necessary to observe special precautions whenever dealing with any part of the system, or its associated components. If for any reason the system must be disconnected, entrust this task to your Peugeot dealer or a refrigeration engineer.

⚠ *Warning: The refrigeration circuit may contain a liquid refrigerant, and it is therefore dangerous to disconnect any part of the system without specialised knowledge and equipment.*

The refrigerant is potentially dangerous,

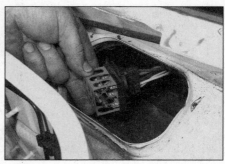

10.41 . . . then twist the resistor to release it

and should only be handled by qualified persons. If it is splashed onto the skin, it can cause frostbite. It is not itself poisonous, but in the presence of a naked flame (including a cigarette) it forms a poisonous gas. Uncontrolled discharging of the refrigerant is dangerous, and potentially damaging to the environment.

12 Air conditioning system components – removal and refitting

Note: *Do not operate the air conditioning system if it is known to be short of refrigerant, as this may damage the compressor.*

1 The only operation which can be carried out easily without discharging the refrigerant is the renewal of the auxiliary (compressor) drivebelt. This is described in Chapter 1A or 1B. (The air conditioning system control unit temperature sensor may be renewed using the information in Section 6.) All other operations must be referred to a Peugeot dealer or an air conditioning specialist.

2 If necessary, the compressor can be unbolted and moved aside, without disconnecting its flexible hoses, after removing the drivebelt.

⚠ *Warning: Do not attempt to open the refrigerant circuit. Refer to the precautions given in Section 11.*

Chapter 4 Part A:
Fuel/exhaust systems - carburettor petrol models

Contents

Degrees of difficulty

Easy, suitable for novice with little experience		Fairly easy, suitable for beginner with some experience		Fairly difficult, suitable for competent DIY mechanic		Difficult, suitable for experienced DIY mechanic		Very difficult, suitable for expert DIY or professional	

Specifications

Fuel pump
Type . . . . Mechanical, driven by eccentric on camshaft

Carburettor
Type:
    Early models . . . . Solex 32-34 Z2
    Later models . . . . Solex 32-34 CISAC
Designation:
    Early models . . . . 32-34 Z2 - 528
    Later models . . . . 32-34 CISAC 528/12
Choke type . . . . Manual, cable-operated

Carburettor data

Solex 32-34 Z2	Primary	Secondary
Venturi diameter	24 mm	25 mm
Main jet	120	122
Idle jet	40	100
Idle air jet	150	150
Air correction jet	175	180
Emulsion tube	6Z	ZC
Accelerator pump	35	
Pneumatic enrichment device	45	
Needle valve	1.8	
Float height setting	33.5 mm	
Throttle valve fast idle setting	0.5 mm	
Choke pull-down setting	3.0 mm	
Idle speed	850 ± 50 rpm	
Idle mixture CO content	1.0 %	

Solex 32-34 CISAC	Primary	Secondary
Venturi diameter	24 mm	25 mm
Main jet	120	120
Idle jet	46	70
Idle air jet	155	160
Air correction jet	160	170
Emulsion tube	8Z	ZC
Accelerator pump	40	35
Pneumatic enrichment device	45	
Needle valve	1.8	
Float height setting	33.5 mm	
Throttle valve fast idle setting	0.5 mm	
Choke pull-down setting	4.0 mm	
Idle speed	850 ± 50 rpm	
Idle mixture CO content	1.0 %	

Recommended fuel
Minimum octane rating	95 RON unleaded	

Torque wrench settings	Nm	lbf ft
Fuel pump retaining bolts	16	12
Inlet manifold retaining nuts	8	6
Exhaust manifold retaining nuts	16	12
Front pipe-to-manifold nuts	30	22
Front pipe mounting bolt	35	26

---

1 General information and precautions

The fuel system consists of a fuel tank mounted under the rear of the car, a mechanical fuel pump, and a carburettor. The fuel pump is operated by an eccentric on the camshaft, and is mounted on the rear of the cylinder head. The air cleaner contains a disposable paper filter element, and incorporates a flap valve air temperature control system; this allows cold air from the outside of the car, and warm air from the exhaust manifold, to enter the air cleaner in the correct proportions.

The fuel pump lifts fuel from the fuel tank via a filter, which is mounted on the engine compartment bulkhead, and supplies it to the carburettor via an anti-percolation chamber. The anti-percolation chamber ensures that the supply of fuel to the carburettor is kept at a constant pressure, and is free of air bubbles. Excess fuel is returned from the anti-percolation chamber to the fuel tank.

The carburettor is a Solex 32-34 twin-choke carburettor (see Section 11), mixture enrichment for cold starting is by a cable-operated choke control.

The exhaust system consists of four sections; the front pipe, the intermediate pipe, the centre silencer box, and the tailpipe and main silencer box. The system is suspended throughout its entire length by rubber mountings.

> **Warning: Many of the procedures in this Chapter require the removal of fuel lines and connections, which may result in some fuel spillage. Before carrying out any operation on the fuel system, refer to the precautions given in "Safety first!" at the beginning of this manual, and follow them implicitly. Petrol is a highly dangerous and volatile liquid, and the precautions necessary when handling it cannot be overstressed.**

2 Air cleaner assembly - removal and refitting

Removal

1 Slacken the retaining clips (where fitted), and disconnect the vacuum hose and breather hose from the front of the air cleaner housing-to-carburettor duct (see illustration). Where the crimped-type Peugeot hose clips are fitted, cut the clips and discard them; use standard worm-drive hose clips on refitting.

2 Slacken the retaining clips, then lift the duct off the top of the carburettor and air cleaner housing. Disconnect the air temperature control valve hose from the end of the duct, and remove the duct from the engine compartment (see illustrations). Recover the rubber sealing ring(s) from the top of the carburettor and/or air cleaner housing (as applicable).

2.1 Disconnect the vacuum and breather hoses (arrowed) from the front of the duct . . .

2.2a . . . slacken the retaining clips . . .

2.2b . . . and remove the duct, disconnecting the air temperature control valve hose (arrowed)

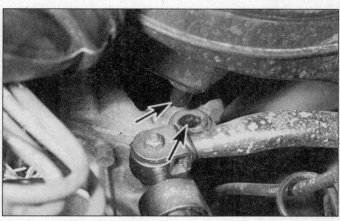

2.4 Undo the intake duct front retaining bolt then release the rear fastener, and remove the duct and hose assembly

2.5 On refitting, ensure the air cleaner housing peg is correctly located in its mounting rubber (arrowed)

3 Disconnect the intake duct from the front of the air cleaner housing, and remove the air cleaner housing from the engine compartment.

4 To remove the intake duct assembly, undo the retaining bolts securing the duct to the left-hand wing valance, then release the fastener securing the rear of the duct to the cylinder head (see illustration). Disconnect the hot-air intake hose from the exhaust manifold shroud, and remove the duct and hose assembly from the engine compartment.

Refitting

5 Refitting is a reversal of the removal procedure, noting the following points:
 a) Examine the rubber sealing ring(s) for signs of damage or deterioration, and if necessary renew. Note that, on some models, the carburettor seal is fitted with an O-ring; this should also be renewed if it is damaged.
 b) Ensure the air cleaner housing locating peg is correctly engaged with its mounting on the top of the transmission (see illustration).
 c) Prior to tightening the air cleaner-to-carburettor duct retaining clips, ensure the duct is correctly seated on both the air cleaner housing and carburettor flanges.

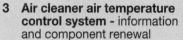

3 Air cleaner air temperature control system - information and component renewal

Information

1 The system is controlled by a heat-sensitive vacuum switch, mounted in the end of the air cleaner housing-to-carburettor duct. When the engine is started from cold, the switch is open, allowing inlet manifold depression to act on the air temperature control valve diaphragm in the intake duct. This vacuum causes the diaphragm to rise, drawing a flap valve across the cold-air intake, thus allowing only (warmed) air from the exhaust manifold to enter the air cleaner.

2 As the temperature of the exhaust-warmed air in the air cleaner-to-carburettor duct rises, the wax capsule in the vacuum switch deforms and closes the switch, cutting off the vacuum supply to the air temperature control valve assembly. As the vacuum supply is cut, the flap is gradually lowered across the hot-air intake until, when the engine is fully warmed-up to normal operating temperature, only cold air from the front of the car is entering the air cleaner.

3 To check the system, allow the engine to cool down completely, then slacken the retaining clip and disconnect the intake duct from the front of the control valve assembly; the flap valve in the duct should be securely seated

across the hot-air intake. Start the engine; the flap should immediately rise to close off the cold-air intake, and should then lower steadily as the engine warms up, until it is eventually seated across the hot-air intake again.

4 To check the vacuum switch, disconnect the vacuum pipe from the control valve when the engine is running, and place a finger over the pipe end. When the engine is cold, full inlet manifold vacuum should be present in the pipe, and when the engine is at normal operating temperature, there should be no vacuum in the pipe.

5 To check the air temperature control valve assembly, slacken the retaining clip and disconnect the intake duct from the front of the valve assembly; the flap valve should be securely seated across the hot-air intake. Disconnect the vacuum pipe, and suck hard at the control valve stub; the flap should rise to shut off the cold-air intake.

6 If either component is faulty, it must be renewed.

Vacuum switch - renewal

7 Remove the air cleaner housing-to-carburettor duct, as described in paragraphs 1 and 2 of Section 2.

8 Bend up the tangs on the switch retaining clip, then remove the clip, along with its seal, and withdraw the switch from inside the duct (see illustrations). Examine the seal for signs

3.8a Remove the retaining clip . . .

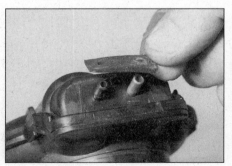

3.8b . . . and seal . . .

3.8c . . . then withdraw the vacuum switch from inside the duct

3.11 Air temperature control valve assembly

of damage or deterioration, and renew if necessary.

9 On refitting, ensure the switch and duct mating surfaces are clean and dry, and position the switch inside the duct.

10 Fit the seal over the switch unions, and refit the retaining clip. Ensure the switch is pressed firmly against the duct, and secure it in position by bending down the retaining clip tangs. Refit the duct as described in Section 2.

Air temperature control valve - renewal

11 Disconnect the vacuum pipe from the air temperature control valve, then slacken the retaining clips securing the intake ducts to the valve (see illustration).

12 Disconnect both intake ducts and the hot-air intake hose from the control valve assembly, and remove it from the vehicle.

13 Refitting is the reverse of the removal

4.3 Arrows on raised fuel pump unions indicate the direction of fuel flow

procedure, noting that the air temperature control valve assembly can only be renewed as a complete unit.

4 Fuel pump - testing, removal and refitting

Note: *Refer to the warning note in Section 1 before proceeding.*

Testing

1 To test the fuel pump on the engine, disconnect the outlet pipe which leads to the carburettor. Hold a wad of rag by the pump outlet while an assistant spins the engine on the starter. *Keep your hands away from the electric cooling fan.* Regular spurts of fuel should be ejected as the engine turns. Be careful not to spill fuel onto hot engine components.

2 The pump can also be tested by removing it. With the pump outlet pipe disconnected but the inlet pipe still connected, hold the wad of rag by the outlet. Operate the pump lever by hand, moving it in and out; if the pump is in a satisfactory condition, the lever should move and return smoothly, and a strong jet of fuel should be ejected.

Removal

3 Identify the pump inlet and outlet hoses, and slacken both retaining clips (see illustration). Where the crimped-type Peugeot hose clips are fitted, cut the clips and discard them; use standard worm-drive hose clips on refitting. Place wads of rag beneath the hose unions to catch any spilled fuel, then disconnect both hoses from the pump; plug the hose ends to minimise fuel loss.

4 Remove the insulating cover from the fuel pump, then slacken and remove the bolts securing the pump to the rear of the cylinder head. Remove the pump along with its insulating block. Discard the insulating block: a new one must be used on refitting.

Refitting

5 Ensure the pump and cylinder head mating surfaces are clean and dry, then offer up the new insulating block and refit the pump to the

cylinder head. Tighten the pump retaining bolts to the specified torque, then refit the pump insulating cover.

6 Reconnect the inlet and outlet hoses to the relevant pump unions, and securely tighten their retaining clips.

5 Fuel gauge sender unit - removal and refitting

Note: *Refer to the warning note in Section 1 before proceeding.*

Removal

1 Disconnect the battery negative terminal (refer to "*Disconnecting the battery*" in the Reference Section of this manual).

2 For access to the sender unit, fold the rear seat cushion forwards or remove the rear seats as described in Chapter 11.

3 Using a screwdriver, carefully prise the plastic access cover from the floor to expose the sender unit. It is located under the left-hand cover (see illustration).

4 Disconnect the wiring connector from the sender unit, and tape the connector to the vehicle body to prevent it from disappearing behind the tank (see illustration).

5 Mark the hoses for identification purposes, then slacken the feed and return hose retaining clips. Where the crimped-type Peugeot hose clips are fitted, cut the clips and discard them; use worm-drive hose clips on refitting. Disconnect both hoses from the top of the sender unit, and plug the hose ends.

6 Noting the alignment marks on the tank, sender unit and the locking ring, unscrew the ring and remove it from the tank. This is best accomplished by using a screwdriver on the raised ribs of the locking ring, as follows. Carefully tap the screwdriver to turn the ring anti-clockwise until it can be unscrewed by hand (see illustrations).

7 Carefully lift the sender unit from the top of the fuel tank, taking great care not to bend the sender unit float arm, or to spill fuel onto the interior of the vehicle. Recover the rubber sealing ring and discard it - a new one must be used on refitting (see illustrations).

5.3 Remove the plastic access cover . . .

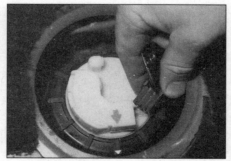

5.4 . . . and unplug the wiring from the fuel gauge sender (fuel-injected model shown)

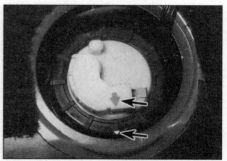

5.6a Note the alignment marks (arrowed) on the sender unit and locking ring . . .

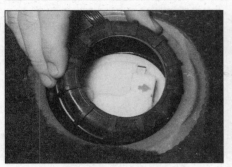

5.6b . . . then unscrew the locking ring

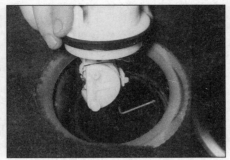

5.7a Withdraw the sender unit from the tank . . .

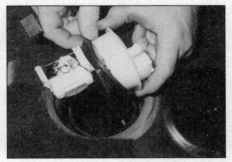

5.7b . . . and remove the rubber sealing ring

Refitting

8 Refitting is a reversal of the removal procedure, noting the following points:

a) *Prior to refitting, fit a new rubber sealing ring to the sender unit.*

b) *Refit the sender unit to the tank, aligning its arrow with the centre of the three alignment marks on the fuel tank. Secure the sender in position with the locking ring, and check that the locking ring, sender unit and fuel tank marks are all correctly aligned.*

c) *Ensure the feed and return hoses are correctly reconnected and securely retained by their clips.*

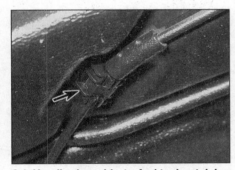

6.4 Handbrake cable-to-fuel tank retaining clip (arrowed)

6.6a Disconnect the main breather hose (arrowed) from the filler neck . . .

6 Fuel tank - removal and refitting

Note: *Refer to the warning note in Section 1 before proceeding.*

Removal

1 Before removing the fuel tank, all fuel must be drained from the tank. Since a fuel tank drain plug is not provided, it is therefore preferable to carry out the removal operation when the tank is nearly empty. Before proceeding, disconnect the battery negative terminal (refer to *"Disconnecting the battery"* in the Reference Section of this manual) and syphon or hand-pump the remaining fuel from the tank.

2 Remove the exhaust system and relevant heat shield(s) as described in Section 16.

3 Disconnect the two handbrake cables from the handbrake lever - see Chapter 9.

4 From underneath the vehicle, remove the retaining clips, and release each handbrake cable from its guides on the underside of the fuel tank **(see illustration)**. Position both cables clear of the tank, so that they will not hinder the removal procedure.

5 Disconnect the wiring connector from the fuel gauge sender unit (see Section 5).

6 Working at the right-hand side of the fuel tank, release the retaining clips then disconnect the filler neck vent pipe and main filler neck hose from the fuel tank/filler neck. Where necessary, also disconnect the

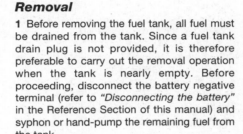

6.6b . . . and the main filler hose (arrowed) from the tank

breather hose(s). Some breather hoses are joined to the tank with quick-release fittings; to disconnect these fittings, slide the cover along the hose then depress the centre ring and pull the hose out of its fitting **(see illustrations)**.

7 Trace the fuel feed and return hoses back from the right-hand side of the tank to their union with the fuel pipes. Slacken the retaining clips and disconnect both hoses from the fuel pipes. Where the crimped-type Peugeot hose clips are fitted, cut the clips and discard them; use standard worm-drive hose clips on refitting. Plug the hose and pipe ends, to prevent the entry of dirt into the system.

8 Place a trolley jack with an interposed block of wood beneath the tank, then raise the jack until it is supporting the weight of the tank.

9 Slacken and remove the retaining nut and bolts, then remove the two support rods from the underside of the tank.

10 Slowly lower the fuel tank out of position, disconnecting any other relevant vent pipes as they become accessible (where necessary), and remove the tank from underneath the vehicle.

11 If the tank is contaminated with sediment or water, remove the sender unit (Section 5), and swill the tank out with clean fuel. The tank is injection-moulded from a synthetic material - if seriously damaged, it should be renewed. However, in certain cases, it may be possible to have small leaks or minor damage repaired. Seek the advice of a specialist before attempting to repair the fuel tank.

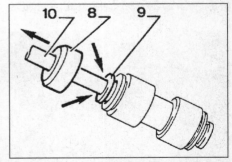

6.6c Fuel tank breather hose quick release connector

8 Cover   10 Hose
9 Centre ring

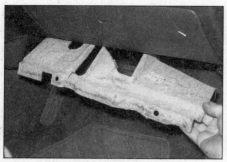

7.3 Remove the felt undercover from underneath the driver's side of the facia . . .

7.4a . . . then release the fastener . . .

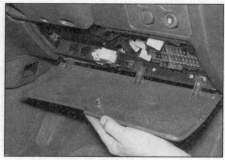

7.4b . . . and remove the fusebox cover

Refitting

12 Refitting is the reverse of the removal procedure, noting the following points:

   a) *When lifting the tank back into position, take care to ensure that none of the hoses become trapped between the tank and vehicle body.*
   b) *Ensure all pipes and hoses are correctly routed, and securely held in position with their retaining clips.*
   c) *Reconnect the handbrake cables and adjust the handbrake as described in Chapter 9.*
   d) *On completion, refill the tank with a small amount of fuel, and check for signs of leakage prior to taking the vehicle out on the road.*

7 Accelerator cable - removal, refitting and adjustment

Removal

1 Working in the engine compartment, free the accelerator inner cable from the carburettor throttle cam, then pull the outer cable out from its mounting bracket rubber grommet. Slide the flat washer off the end of the cable, and remove the spring clip.
2 Working back along the length of the cable, free it from any retaining clips or ties, noting its correct routing.
3 Release the retaining clips, and remove the felt undercover from underneath the driver's

7.14 Adjusting the accelerator cable

side of the facia panel **(see illustration)**.
4 Working from inside the vehicle, release the fastener by rotating it through a quarter of a turn anti-clockwise, and remove the fusebox cover from the facia **(see illustrations)**.
5 Release the retaining clip and detach the inner cable from the top of the accelerator pedal.
6 Release the outer cable from its retainer on the pedal mounting bracket, then tie a length of string to the end of the cable.
7 Return to the engine compartment, release the cable grommet from the bulkhead and withdraw the cable. When the end of the cable appears, untie the string and leave it in position - it can then be used to draw the cable back into position on refitting.

Refitting

8 Tie the string to the end of the cable, then use the string to draw the cable into position through the bulkhead. Once the cable end is visible, untie the string, then clip the outer cable into its pedal bracket retainer, and clip the inner cable into position in the pedal end.
9 Check that the cable is securely retained, then refit the felt undercover and fusebox cover to the facia.
10 From within the engine compartment, ensure the outer cable is correctly seated in the bulkhead grommet, then work along the cable, securing it in position with the retaining clips and ties, and ensuring that the cable is correctly routed.
11 Slide the flat washer onto the cable end and refit the spring clip.
12 Pass the outer cable through its carburettor mounting bracket grommet, and reconnect the inner cable to the throttle cam. Adjust the cable as described below.

Adjustment

13 Remove the spring clip from the accelerator outer cable. Ensuring that the throttle cam is fully against its stop, gently pull the cable out of its grommet until all free play is removed from the inner cable.
14 With the cable held in this position, refit the spring clip to the last exposed outer cable groove in front of the rubber grommet and washer. When the clip is refitted and the outer cable is released, there should be only a small

amount of free play in the inner cable **(see illustration)**.
15 Have an assistant depress the accelerator pedal, and check that the throttle cam opens fully and returns smoothly to its stop.

8 Accelerator pedal - removal and refitting

Removal

1 Disconnect the accelerator cable from the pedal as described in paragraphs 3 to 5 of Section 7.

Right-hand drive models

2 Unscrew the nut from the end of the pedal pivot shaft, whilst retaining the pivot shaft with an open-ended spanner on the flats provided.
3 Pull the pedal and pivot shaft assembly from the support bracket.
4 Examine the pivot shaft for signs of wear or damage and, if necessary, renew it. The pivot shaft is a screw fit in the pedal.

Left-hand drive models

5 Slide off the spring clip from one end of the pedal pivot shaft.
6 Withdraw the pivot shaft and remove the pedal and pivot bush assembly from the support bracket.
7 Examine the pivot bushes and shaft for signs of wear, and renew as necessary.

Refitting

8 Refitting is a reversal of the removal procedure, applying a little multi-purpose grease to the pedal pivot point. On completion, adjust the accelerator cable as described in Section 7.

9 Choke cable - removal, refitting and adjustment

Removal

1 Where necessary, prise out the retaining clip and remove plastic cover to gain access to the carburettor.

2 Free the choke inner cable from the carburettor linkage, then slacken and remove the retaining bolt and remove the outer cable retaining clamp **(see illustration)**.

3 Slacken the retaining clip securing the rubber collar to the outer cable, and slide the collar off the cable. Where the original crimped-type Peugeot hose clip is still fitted, cut the clip and discard it; use a standard worm-drive hose clip on refitting.

4 Working back along the length of the cable, free it from any retaining clips or ties, noting its correct routing. Tie a length of string to the end of the choke inner cable.

5 Working from inside the vehicle, pull the choke lever fully out, to gain access to the retaining screw. Unclip the choke lever from the facia and withdraw the lever and cable assembly from the facia, disconnecting the wiring from the lever switch (where fitted) as it becomes accessible. Once the end of the cable appears through the lever aperture, untie the string and leave it in position in the vehicle - it can then be used to draw the cable back into position on refitting.

Refitting

6 Tie the string to the end of the choke cable, then use the string to draw the cable into position through the bulkhead into the engine compartment. Once the cable end is fully in position, untie the string.

7 Reconnect the wiring connector (where fitted), and clip the choke lever in its facia panel aperture.

8 From within the engine compartment, ensure the outer cable is correctly seated in the bulkhead grommet. Work along the cable, securing it in position with all the relevant retaining clips and ties, and ensuring that the cable is correctly routed.

9 Slide the rubber collar and retaining clip onto the end of the cable, then engage the inner end of the cable with carburettor linkage. Align the rubber collar with the carburettor bracket, then refit the retaining clip and securely tighten its retaining bolt. Adjust the cable as described below.

Adjustment

10 If not already done, prise out the retaining clip and remove the plastic cover (where fitted) from the carburettor.

11 Slacken the retaining clip securing the rubber collar to the outer cable. Where the crimped-type Peugeot hose clip is still fitted, cut the clip and discard it; use a standard worm-drive hose clip on refitting **(see illustration)**.

12 Ensuring that the choke lever is flush with the facia panel and the carburettor linkage is fully against its stop, move the outer cable in the rubber collar until the position is found where there is only a small amount of free play present in the inner cable. Hold the outer cable in this position, and securely tighten the clip securing the rubber collar to the outer cable.

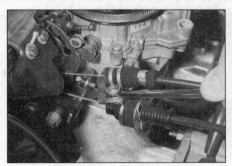

9.2 Undo the retaining bolt and remove the choke cable retaining clip

13 Have an assistant operate the choke lever, and check that the choke linkage closes fully and returns smoothly to its stop. If necessary, repeat the adjustment procedure.

14 Where necessary, clip the plastic cover back into position and refit its retaining clip.

10 Unleaded petrol -
general information and usage

Note: *The information given in this Chapter is correct at the time of writing. If updated information is thought to be required, check with a Peugeot dealer. If travelling abroad, consult one of the motoring organisations (or a similar authority) for advice on the fuel available.*

The fuel recommended by Peugeot is given in the Specifications Section of this Chapter.

All Peugeot 306 carburettor models are designed to run on 95 octane petrol. Both leaded and unleaded petrol can be used without modification. Leaded and Super unleaded (98 octane) petrol can also be used if wished, though there is no advantage in doing so.

9.11 Choke cable-to-rubber collar retaining clip (arrowed)

11 Carburettor -
general information

1 The Solex 32-34 carburettor is a downdraught progressive twin-venturi instrument **(see illustration)**. The throttle linkages are arranged so that the secondary throttle valve will not start to open until the primary valve is about two-thirds open, but at full throttle both valves are fully open. The choke control is manual.

2 An electrical heating element is fitted to the base of the throttle body. The heater warms the carburettor body quickly on cold starts, improving atomisation of the fuel/air mixture and preventing carburettor icing

3 During slow running and at idle, fuel from the float chamber passes into the idle channel through a metered idle jet. Here it is mixed with a small amount of air from a calibrated air bleed. The resulting mixture is drawn through a channel, to be discharged from the idle orifice under the primary throttle plate. A tapered mixture screw is used to vary the outlet, allowing fine control of the idle mixture.

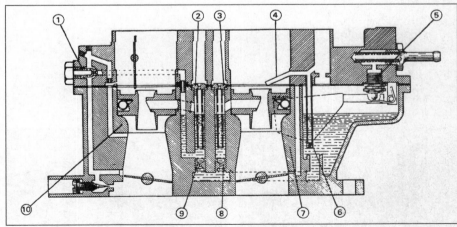

11.1 Sectional view of the Solex 32-34 Z2 carburettor

1 Idle jet
2 Primary air correction jet/emulsion tube
3 Secondary air correction jet/emulsion tube
4 Secondary fuel jet
5 Needle valve
6 Bypass jet
7 Secondary venturi
8 Secondary main jet
9 Primary main jet
10 Primary venturi

12.5 Disconnecting the carburettor wiring connector

4 An idle cut-off valve is used to prevent run-on when the engine is switched off. The valve uses a solenoid plunger to block the idle jet when the ignition is switched off.

5 A progression slot provides extra enrichment as it is uncovered by the opening of the throttle valve during initial acceleration.

6 Under normal operating conditions, the amount of fuel discharged into the airstream is controlled by a calibrated main jet. Fuel is drawn through the main jet. The fuel is then mixed with air, drawn in through the air correction jet and through the holes in the emulsion tube. The resulting mixture is discharged from the main orifice through an auxiliary vent.

7 The carburettor also has an accelerator pump to provide an initial spurt of extra fuel during sudden acceleration. During acceleration, fuel is pumped through a ball valve located in the pump injector, and is discharged into both the primary and secondary venturis.

8 The idle speed is set by an adjustable screw. The adjustable mixture screw is sealed during production with a tamperproof plug, to prevent unnecessary or inexpert adjustment.

12 Carburettor - removal and refitting

Note: *Refer to the warning note in Section 1 before proceeding. Where original crimped-type Peugeot hose clips are still fitted, the clips should be cut and discarded; obtain*

12.6 Carburettor fuel hose union

some standard worm-drive hose clips for refitting.

Removal

1 Disconnect the battery negative terminal (refer to *"Disconnecting the battery"* in the Reference Section of this manual). Where necessary, prise out the retaining clip and remove the plastic cover from the carburettor.

2 Remove the air cleaner-to-carburettor duct, with reference to paragraphs 1 and 2 of Section 2.

3 Free the accelerator inner cable from the throttle cam, then pull the outer cable out from its mounting bracket rubber grommet, along with its flat washer and spring clip.

4 Disconnect the choke inner cable from the carburettor linkage, then undo the retaining bolt and remove the retaining clamp. Position the cable clear of the carburettor.

5 Disconnect the wiring connector from the carburettor heating element and the idle cut-off solenoid **(see illustration)**.

6 Slacken the retaining clip, and disconnect the fuel feed hose from the carburettor. Place wads of rag around the union to catch any spilled fuel, and plug the hose as soon as it is disconnected, to minimise fuel loss **(see illustration)**.

7 Make a note of the correct fitted positions of all the relevant vacuum pipes and breather hoses, to ensure they are correctly positioned on refitting, then release the retaining clips (where fitted) and disconnect them from the carburettor.

8 Unscrew the four nuts and washers securing the carburettor to the inlet manifold. Remove the carburettor assembly from the car **(see illustration)**. Remove the insulating spacer and/or gasket(s). Discard the gasket(s); new ones must be used on refitting. Plug the inlet manifold port with a wad of clean cloth, to prevent the possible entry of foreign matter.

Refitting

9 Refitting is the reverse of the removal procedure, noting the following points:
   a) *Ensure the carburettor and inlet manifold sealing faces are clean and flat. Fit a new gasket, and securely tighten the carburettor retaining nuts.*

12.8 Carburettor retaining nuts (two of four arrowed)

   b) *Use the notes made on dismantling to ensure all hoses are refitted to their original positions and, where necessary, are securely held by their retaining clips.*
   c) *Where the original crimped-type Peugeot hose clips were fitted, discard them; use standard worm-drive hose clips when refitting.*
   d) *Refit and adjust the choke and accelerator cables as described in Sections 7 and 9.*
   e) *Refit the air cleaner duct (Section 2).*
   f) *On completion, check and, if necessary, adjust the idle speed and mixture settings as described in Chapter 1A.*

13 Carburettor - fault diagnosis, overhaul and adjustments

Fault diagnosis

1 If a carburettor fault is suspected, always check first that the ignition timing is correctly set, that the spark plugs are in good condition and correctly gapped, that the accelerator and choke cables are correctly adjusted, and that the air cleaner filter element is clean; refer to the relevant Sections of Chapter 1A, Chapter 5B or this Chapter. If the engine is running very roughly, first check the valve clearances as described in Chapter 1A, then check the compression pressures as described in the relevant Part of Chapter 2.

2 If careful checking of all the above produces no improvement, the carburettor must be removed for cleaning and overhaul.

3 Prior to overhaul, check the availability of component parts before starting work; note that most sealing washers, screws and gaskets are available in kits, as are some of the major sub-assemblies. In most cases, it will be sufficient to dismantle the carburettor and to clean the jets and passages.

Overhaul

Note: *Refer to the warning note in Section 1 before proceeding.*

4 Remove the carburettor from the vehicle as described in Section 12.

5 Unscrew the idle cut-off solenoid from the carburettor body, and remove it along with its plunger and spring. To test the solenoid, connect a 12-volt battery to it (positive terminal to the solenoid terminal, negative terminal to the solenoid body), and check that the plunger is retracted fully into the body. Disconnect the battery (refer to *"Disconnecting the battery"* in the Reference Section of this manual) and check that the plunger is pushed out by spring pressure. If the valve does not perform as expected, and cleaning does not improve the situation, the solenoid valve must be renewed.

6 Remove the five screws and lift off the carburettor upper body.

7 Tap out the float pivot pin and remove the float assembly, needle valve, and float chamber gasket. Check that the needle valve anti-vibration ball is free in the valve end, then examine the needle valve tip and seat for wear or damage. Examine the float assembly and pivot pin for signs of wear and damage. The float assembly must be renewed if it appears to be leaking - shake the float to detect the presence of fuel inside.

8 Unscrew the fuel inlet union and inspect the fuel filter. Clean the filter housing of debris and dirt, and renew the filter if it is blocked.

9 Undo the four screws, detach the accelerator pump cover, and remove the pump diaphragm and spring, noting which way around they are fitted. Examine the diaphragm for signs of damage and deterioration, and renew if necessary. Remove the choke pull-down diaphragm and part-load enrichment diaphragms, and examine them in the same way.

10 Unscrew the idle jet from the upper body.

11 Unscrew both the primary and secondary combined air correction jets and emulsion tubes.

12 Using a long thin screwdriver, unscrew the main jets from the bottom of the emulsion tube drillings. Invert the carburettor and catch the jets as they fall out of the drillings.

13 Remove the idle mixture adjustment screw tamperproof cap. Screw the screw in until it seats lightly, counting the exact number of turns required to do this, then unscrew it. On refitting, screw the screw in until it seats lightly, then back the screw off by the number of turns noted on removal, to return the screw to its original position.

14 Clean the jets, carburettor body assemblies, float chamber and internal drillings. An air line may be used to clear the internal passages once the carburettor is fully dismantled.

Caution: If high pressure air is directed into drillings and passages where a diaphragm is fitted, the diaphragm is likely to be damaged.

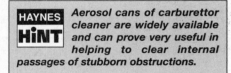
HAYNES HINT *Aerosol cans of carburettor cleaner are widely available and can prove very useful in helping to clear internal passages of stubborn obstructions.*

15 Use a straight edge to check all carburettor body assembly mating surfaces for distortion.

16 To test the carburettor heating element, connect a multimeter, set to the resistance function, between the heater wiring terminal and the carburettor body. A resistance reading of approximately 0.25 to 0.5 ohms should be obtained. If an open-circuit is present, or an extremely high resistance reading is obtained, it is likely that the heating element is faulty. A heating element repair kit is available from your Peugeot dealer. To renew the element undo the screw and

remove the retaining plate, then slide the element holder, pin, element and insulating plate, noting each component correct fitted location. Fit the new components, ensuring each one is correctly positioned, and securely tighten the retaining screws. **Note:** *Ensure the insulating plate is correctly positioned between the heating element and body so that there is no danger of the element shorting out on the carburettor body.*

17 On reassembly renew any worn components and fit a complete set of new gaskets and seals. A jet kit and a gasket and seal kit are available from your Peugeot dealer.

18 Reassembly is a reversal of the dismantling procedure. Ensure that all jets are securely locked in position, but take great care not to overtighten them. Ensure all mating surfaces are clean and dry, and that all body sections are correctly assembled with their fuel and air passages correctly aligned. Prior to refitting the carburettor to the vehicle, set the float height, throttle valve fast idle and choke pull-down settings as described below.

Adjustments

Idle speed and mixture

19 Refer to Chapter 1A.

Float height setting

20 Invert the carburettor body, so that the float is at the top and the needle valve is depressed. Measure the distance between

the upper edge of the float and the sealing face of the upper body (with its gasket fitted). This measurement should be as given in the Specifications at the start of this Chapter.

21 If necessary, the float height can be adjusted by *carefully* bending the small tang on the float arm which touches the needle valve.

Throttle valve fast idle setting

22 Invert the carburettor and pull the carburettor choke linkage to fully close the choke valve. The fast idle screw will butt against the fast idle cam and force the throttle valve open slightly.

23 Using the shank of a twist drill, measure the clearance between the edge of the throttle valve and bore, and compare this to the clearance given in the Specifications at the start of this Chapter. If necessary, adjust by turning the fast idle adjustment screw in the appropriate direction until the specified clearance is obtained **(see illustration)**.

Choke pull-down setting

24 Pull the carburettor choke linkage to fully close the choke valve, and hold the linkage in this position.

25 Attach a hand-held vacuum pump to the choke pull-down diaphragm, and apply a vacuum to the diaphragm so that the diaphragm rod is pulled fully into the diaphragm body. In the absence of a vacuum pump, the rod can be pushed into the diaphragm with a small screwdriver.

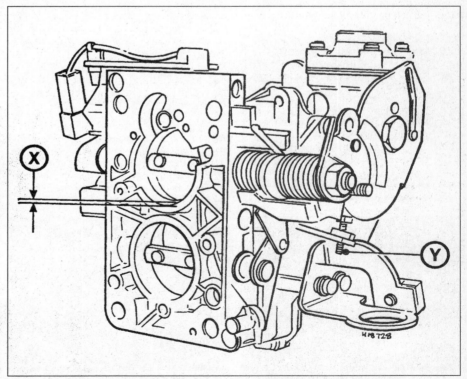

13.23 Throttle valve fast idle setting - Solex 32-34 Z2 carburettor

Adjust screw Y until clearance X is as given in the Specifications

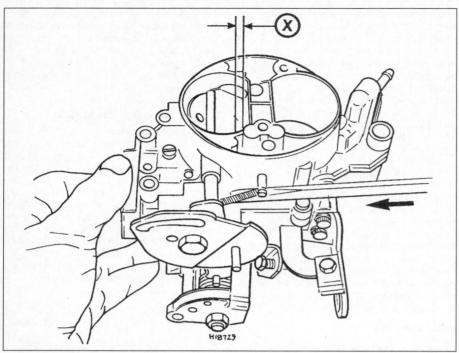

13.26 Choke pull-down setting (using a screwdriver to retract the diaphragm rod) - Solex 32-34 Z2 carburettor

Adjust until clearance X is as specified

26 With the rod fully retracted, use the shank of a twist drill to measure the clearance between the edge of the choke valve and bore, and compare this to the clearance given in the Specifications **(see illustration)**. If necessary, remove the plug from the diaphragm cover and adjust by turning the adjustment screw. Once the pull-down setting is correctly adjusted, refit the plug to the diaphragm cover and remove the vacuum pump (where used).

14 Inlet manifold - removed and refitting

Note: *Refer to the warning note in Section 1 before proceeding.*

Removal

1 Remove the carburettor as described in Section 12.

15.1 Remove the hot-air intake hose . . .

15.2 . . . then undo the three retaining screws (arrowed) and remove the exhaust manifold shroud

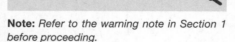

15.5 Exhaust manifold is retained by eight nuts (upper four arrowed)

2 Drain the cooling system as described in Chapter 1A.
3 Undo the bolt(s) securing the anti-percolation chamber mounting bracket to the manifold, and position the chamber clear of the manifold so that it does not hinder removal.
4 Slacken the retaining clips, then disconnect the vacuum servo unit hose from the left-hand side of the manifold, and the coolant hose from the base of the manifold.
5 Make a final check that all the necessary vacuum/breather hoses have been disconnected from the manifold.
6 Unscrew the six retaining nuts, then manoeuvre the manifold away from the head and out of the engine compartment. Note that there is no manifold gasket.

Refitting

7 Refitting is the reverse of the removal procedure, noting the following points:
  a) *Ensure that the manifold and cylinder head mating surfaces are clean and dry, and apply a thin coating of suitable sealing compound to the manifold mating surface. Install the manifold and tighten its retaining nuts to the specified torque setting.*
  b) *Ensure all relevant hoses are reconnected to their original positions and are securely held (where necessary) by their retaining clips.*
  c) *Refit the carburettor as described in Section 12.*
  d) *On completion, refill the cooling system as described in Chapter 1A.*

15 Exhaust manifold - removal and refitting

Removal

1 Disconnect the hot-air intake hose from the manifold shroud and remove it from the vehicle **(see illustration)**.
2 Slacken and remove the three retaining screws, and remove the shroud from the top of the exhaust manifold **(see illustration)**.
3 Chock the rear wheels then jack up the front of the vehicle and support it on axle stands (see *"Jacking and Vehicle Support"*).
4 Undo the nuts securing the exhaust front pipe to the manifold, then remove the bolt securing the front pipe to its mounting bracket. Disconnect the front pipe from the manifold, and recover the gasket.
5 Undo the eight retaining nuts securing the manifold to the head **(see illustration)**. Manoeuvre the manifold out of the engine compartment, and discard the manifold gaskets.

Refitting

6 Refitting is the reverse of the removal procedure, noting the following points:

a) Examine all the exhaust manifold studs for signs of damage and corrosion; remove all traces of corrosion, and repair or renew any damaged studs.

b) Ensure that the manifold and cylinder head sealing faces are clean and flat, and fit the new manifold gaskets. Tighten the manifold retaining nuts to the specified torque.

c) Reconnect the front pipe to the manifold using the information given in Section 16.

16 Exhaust system -
general information, removal and refitting

General information

1 The exhaust system consists of four sections; the front pipe, the intermediate pipe, the centre silencer box, and the tailpipe and main silencer box. All exhaust sections are joined by flanged joints. The front pipe joints are secured by nuts and bolts, the intermediate pipe joint being of the spring-loaded ball type, to allow for movement in the exhaust system, and the other joints are secured by clamping rings.

2 The system is suspended throughout its entire length by rubber mountings.

Removal

3 Each exhaust section can be removed individually, or alternatively, the complete system can be removed as a unit. Even if only one part of the system needs attention, it is often easier to remove the whole system and separate the sections on the bench.

4 To remove the system or part of the system, first jack up the front or rear of the car and support it on axle stands (see "Jacking and Vehicle Support"). Alternatively, position the car over an inspection pit or on car ramps.

Front pipe

5 Undo the nuts securing the front pipe flange joint to the manifold, and the single bolt securing the front pipe to its mounting bracket. Separate the flange joint and collect the gasket.

6 Slacken and remove the two nuts securing the front pipe flange joint to the intermediate pipe, and recover the spring cups and springs. Remove the bolts, then withdraw the front pipe from underneath the vehicle, and recover the wire-mesh gasket.

Intermediate pipe

7 Undo the two nuts securing the front pipe flange joint to the intermediate pipe. Recover the springs and spring cups, and withdraw the bolts.

8 Slacken the intermediate pipe clamping ring bolts and disengage the clamp from the flange joint.

9 Free the intermediate pipe, then withdraw it from underneath the vehicle, and recover the wire-mesh gasket from the front pipe joint.

Centre silencer

10 Slacken the clamping ring bolts and disengage the clamps from the front and rear flange joints.

11 Unhook the centre silencer from its mounting rubber and remove it from underneath the vehicle.

Tailpipe

12 Slacken the tailpipe clamping ring bolts and disengage the clamp from the flange joint.

13 Unhook the tailpipe from its mounting rubbers and remove it from the vehicle.

Complete system

14 Undo the nuts securing the front pipe flange joint to the manifold, and the single bolt securing the front pipe to its mounting bracket. Separate the flange joint and collect the gasket. Free the system from all its mounting rubbers and lower it from under the vehicle.

Heat shield(s)

15 The heat shields are secured to the underside of the body by various nuts and bolts. Each shield can be removed once the relevant exhaust section has been removed. If a shield is being removed to gain access to a component located behind it, it may prove sufficient in some cases to remove the retaining nuts and/or bolts, and simply lower the shield, without disturbing the exhaust system.

Refitting

16 Each section is refitted by reversing the removal sequence, noting the following points:

a) Ensure that all traces of corrosion have been removed from the flanges and renew all necessary gaskets.

b) Inspect the rubber mountings for signs of damage or deterioration, and renew as necessary.

c) Prior to assembling the spring-loaded joint, a smear of high-temperature grease should be applied to the joint mating surfaces.

d) Where joints are secured together by a clamping ring, apply a smear of exhaust system jointing paste to the flange joint, to ensure a gas-tight seal. Tighten the clamping ring nuts evenly and progressively, so that the clearance between the clamp halves remains equal on either side.

e) Prior to tightening the exhaust system fasteners, ensure that all rubber mountings are correctly located, and that there is adequate clearance between the exhaust system and vehicle underbody.

Notes

Chapter 4 Part B:
Fuel/exhaust systems - single-point petrol injection models

Contents

Degrees of difficulty

Easy, suitable for novice with little experience	**Fairly easy,** suitable for beginner with some experience	**Fairly difficult,** suitable for competent DIY mechanic 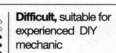	**Difficult,** suitable for experienced DIY mechanic	**Very difficult,** suitable for expert DIY or professional

Specifications

System type
1.1 litre models:
  1993 to 1997 . . . . Magneti Marelli G6
  1997 onward . . . . Bosch Monopoint MA3.1
1.4 litre models:
  1993 to 1994 . . . . Bosch Monopoint MA3.0
  1994 to 1996 . . . . Magneti Marelli G6

Fuel system data
Fuel pump type . . . . Electric, immersed in tank
Fuel pump regulated constant pressure . . . . 1.0 ± 0.1 bars
Specified idle speed (not adjustable) . . . . 850 ± 50 rpm (controlled by ECU)
Idle mixture CO content:
  Bosch system (not adjustable) . . . . Less than 1.0 % (controlled by ECU)
  Magneti Marelli system* . . . . Less than 1.0 % (controlled by ECU)
*On the Magneti Marelli system, idle mixture adjustment is possible, but only using special electronic equipment - see text

Recommended fuel
Minimum octane rating . . . . 95 RON unleaded

Torque wrench settings

	Nm	lbf ft
Inlet manifold nuts	8	6
Exhaust manifold nuts	16	12
Front pipe-to-manifold nuts	30	22
Front pipe mounting bolt	35	26
Front pipe-to-catalytic converter nuts	10	7
Exhaust clamping ring nuts	20	15

4.3 Adjust the accelerator cable as described in text

1 General information and precautions

The fuel system consists of a fuel tank (which is mounted under the rear of the car, with an electric fuel pump immersed in it), a fuel filter, fuel feed and return lines, and the throttle body assembly (which incorporates the single fuel injector and the fuel pressure regulator). In addition, there is an Electronic Control Unit (ECU) and various sensors, electrical components and related wiring. The air cleaner contains a disposable paper filter element, and incorporates a flap valve air temperature control system. This allows cold air from the outside of the car and warm air from around the exhaust manifold to enter the air cleaner in the correct proportions. Refer to Section 7 for further information on the operation of each fuel injection system, and to Section 18 for information on the exhaust system.

Throughout this Chapter, it is occasionally necessary to identify vehicles by their engine codes rather than by engine capacity. Refer to the relevant Part of Chapter 2 for further information on engine code identification.

⚠ *Warning: Many of the procedures in this Chapter require the removal of fuel lines and connections, which may result in some fuel spillage. Before carrying out any operation on the fuel system, refer to the precautions given in "Safety first!" at the beginning of this manual, and follow them implicitly. Petrol is a highly dangerous and volatile liquid, and the precautions necessary when handling it cannot be overstressed.*
Note: *Residual pressure will remain in the fuel lines long after the vehicle was last used. When disconnecting any fuel line, first depressurise the fuel system as described in Section 8.*

2 Air cleaner assembly and intake ducts - removal and refitting

Refer to Chapter 4A, Section 2, substituting "throttle body" for all references to the carburettor.

3 Air cleaner air temperature control system - information and component renewal

Refer to Chapter 4A, Section 3, substituting "throttle body" for all references to the carburettor.

4 Accelerator cable - removal, refitting and adjustment

Removal and refitting

1 Refer to Chapter 4A, Section 7 substituting "throttle body" for all references to the carburettor. Adjust the cable as described below.

Adjustment

2 Remove the spring clip from the accelerator outer cable then, ensuring that the throttle cam is fully against its stop, gently pull the cable out of its grommet until all free play is removed from the inner cable.
3 With the cable held in this position, ensure that the flat washer is pressed securely against the grommet, then fit the spring clip to the third outer cable groove visible in front of the rubber grommet and washer **(see illustration)**. This will leave a fair amount of freeplay in the inner cable which is necessary to ensure correct operation of the idle control stepper motor (see Section 14).
4 Have an assistant depress the accelerator pedal and check that the throttle cam opens fully and returns smoothly to its stop.

5 Accelerator pedal - removal and refitting

Refer to Chapter 4A, Section 8.

6 Unleaded petrol - general information and usage

Note: *The information given in this Chapter is correct at the time of writing. If updated information is thought to be required, check with a Peugeot dealer. If travelling abroad, consult one of the motoring organisations (or a similar authority) for advice on the fuel available.*

The fuel recommended by Peugeot is given in the Specifications Section of this Chapter.

All Peugeot 306 single-point injection models are designed to run on fuel with a minimum octane rating of 95 (RON). All models are equipped with catalytic converters, and therefore must be run on unleaded fuel only. Under no circumstances should leaded fuel be used, as this may damage the catalytic converter.

Super unleaded petrol (98 octane) can also be used in all models if wished, though there is no advantage in doing so.

7 Fuel injection systems - general information

Note: *The fuel injection ECU is of the "self-learning" type, meaning that as it operates, it also monitors and stores the settings which give optimum engine performance under all operating conditions. When the battery is disconnected, these settings are lost and the ECU reverts to the base settings programmed into its memory at the factory. On restarting, this may lead to the engine running/idling roughly for a short while, until the ECU has re-learned the optimum settings. This process is best accomplished by taking the vehicle on a road test (for approximately 15 minutes), covering all engine speeds and loads, concentrating mainly in the 2,500 to 3,500 rpm region.*

Bosch Monopoint MA3.0 and MA3.1 systems

1 The Bosch Monopoint MA3.0 engine management (fuel injection/ignition) system is fitted to early 1.4 litre models, and the MA3.1 system is fitted to later 1.1 litre models. Both systems are very similar in operation and incorporate a closed-loop catalytic converter and an evaporative emission control system, to comply with the latest emission control standards. The systems operate as follows.
2 The fuel pump, immersed in the fuel tank, pumps fuel from the fuel tank to the fuel injector, via a filter mounted underneath the rear of the vehicle. Fuel supply pressure is controlled by the pressure regulator in the throttle body assembly. The regulator operates by allowing excess fuel to return to the tank.
3 The electrical control system consists of the ECU, along with the following sensors.
   a) *Throttle potentiometer - informs the ECU of the throttle position, and the rate of throttle opening or closing.*
   b) *Coolant temperature sensor - informs the ECU of engine temperature.*
   c) *Inlet air temperature sensor - informs the ECU of the temperature of the air passing through the throttle body.*
   d) *Lambda sensor - informs the ECU of the oxygen content of the exhaust gases (explained in greater detail in Part E of this Chapter).*
   e) *Throttle position switch (built into the idle speed stepper motor) - informs the ECU when the throttle valve is closed (ie when the accelerator pedal is released).*
   f) *Crankshaft sensor - informs the ECU of engine speed and crankshaft position*
   g) *Vehicle speed sensor (fitted to the gearbox) - informs the ECU of the road speed.*
   h) *Idle control stepper motor - controls the position of the throttle during idling to maintain a constant engine idle speed.*
   i) *Inlet manifold heater (MA3.1 system only)*

- raises the temperature of the inlet manifold to minimise fuel condensation.

4 All the above information is analysed by the ECU and, based on this, the ECU determines the appropriate ignition and fuelling requirements for the engine. The ECU controls the fuel injector by varying its pulse width - the length of time the injector is held open - to provide a richer or weaker mixture, as appropriate. The mixture is constantly varied by the ECU, to provide the best setting for cranking, starting (with either a hot or cold engine), warm-up, idle, cruising, and acceleration. Refer to Chapter 5B for further information on the ignition system.

5 The ECU also has full control over the engine idle speed, via a stepper motor which is fitted to the throttle body. The motor pushrod rests against a cam on the throttle valve spindle. When the throttle valve is closed, the ECU uses the motor to vary the opening of the throttle valve and so controls the idle speed.

6 The ECU also controls the exhaust and evaporative emission control systems, which are described in detail in Part E of this Chapter.

7 If there is an abnormality in any of the readings obtained from either the coolant temperature sensor, the inlet air temperature sensor or the lambda sensor, the ECU enters its back-up mode. In this event, the ECU ignores the abnormal sensor signal, and assumes a pre-programmed value which will allow the engine to continue running (albeit at reduced efficiency). If the ECU enters this back-up mode, the warning light on the instrument panel will come on, and the relevant fault code will be stored in the ECU memory.

8 If the warning light comes on, the vehicle should be taken to a Peugeot dealer at the earliest opportunity. A complete test of the engine management system can then be carried out, using a special electronic diagnostic test unit which is simply plugged into the system's diagnostic connector.

Magneti Marelli G6 system

9 On 1.1 litre and later 1.4 litre models, a Magneti Marelli engine management (fuel injection/ignition) system is fitted.

10 The fuel injection side of the system operates as described in the following paragraphs. Refer to Chapter 5B for information on the ignition side of the system.

11 The fuel pump, immersed in the fuel tank, pumps fuel from the fuel tank to the fuel injector, via a filter. Fuel supply pressure is controlled by the pressure regulator in the throttle body assembly. The regulator operates by allowing excess fuel to return to the tank. To reduce emissions and to improve driveability when the engine is cold, engine coolant is passed through the manifold and around the throttle body assembly.

12 The electrical control system consists of the ECU, along with the following sensors.

a) *Manifold absolute pressure (MAP) sensor - informs the ECU of the load on the engine (expressed in terms of inlet manifold vacuum).*

b) *Crankshaft sensor - informs the ECU of the crankshaft position and engine speed.*

c) *Throttle potentiometer - informs the ECU of the throttle position, and the rate of throttle opening/closing.*

d) *Coolant temperature sensor - informs the ECU of the engine temperature.*

e) *Fuel/air mixture temperature sensor - informs the ECU of the temperature of the fuel/air mixture charge entering the cylinders.*

f) *Lambda (oxygen) sensor - informs the ECU of the oxygen content of the exhaust gases (explained in greater detail in Part E of this Chapter).*

13 In addition, the ECU senses battery voltage (adjusting the injector pulse width to suit, and using the stepper motor to increase the idle speed and, therefore, the alternator output if the voltage is too low). Short-circuit protection and diagnostic capabilities are incorporated into the ECU, and it can both receive and transmit information via the engine management circuit diagnostic connector, thus permitting engine diagnosis and tuning by special diagnostic equipment.

14 All the above signals are compared by the ECU, using digital techniques, with set values pre-programmed (mapped) into its memory. Based on this information, the ECU selects the response appropriate to those values and controls the ignition HT coil (see Chapter 5B), and the fuel injector (varying its pulse width - the length of time the injector is held open - to provide a richer or weaker mixture, as appropriate). The mixture, idle speed and ignition timing are constantly varied by the ECU, to provide the best settings for cranking, starting (with either a hot or cold engine), warm-up, idle, cruising and acceleration.

15 The ECU regulates the engine idle speed via a stepper motor which is fitted to the throttle body. The motor has a pushrod controlling the opening of an air passage which bypasses the throttle valve. When the throttle valve is closed, the ECU controls the movement of the motor pushrod, which regulates the amount of air which flows through the throttle body passage, and so controls the idle speed. The bypass passage is also used as an additional air supply during cold starting.

16 The ECU also controls the exhaust and evaporative emission control systems, which are described in detail in Part E of this Chapter.

17 If there is an abnormality in any of the readings obtained from any of the engine management circuit sensors, the ECU enters its back-up mode. In this event, the ECU ignores the abnormal sensor signal, and assumes a pre-programmed value which will allow the engine to continue running (albeit at reduced efficiency). On entering this back-up mode, the engine management warning light in the instrument panel will come on, informing the driver of the fault, and the relevant fault code will be stored in the ECU memory.

18 If the warning light comes on, the vehicle should be taken to a Peugeot dealer at the earliest opportunity. A complete test of the engine management system can then be carried out, using a special electronic diagnostic test unit which is simply plugged into the system's diagnostic connector.

8 Fuel injection system - depressurisation

Note: Refer to the warning note in Section 1 before proceeding.

Warning: The following procedure will merely relieve the pressure in the fuel system - remember that fuel will still be present in the system components, so take precautions accordingly before disconnecting any of them.

1 The fuel system referred to in this Section is defined as the tank-mounted fuel pump, the fuel filter, the fuel injector and the pressure regulator in the injector housing, and the metal pipes and flexible hoses of the fuel lines between these components. All these contain fuel which will be under pressure while the engine is running, and/or while the ignition is switched on. The pressure will remain for some time after the ignition has been switched off, and it must be relieved in a controlled fashion when any of these components are disturbed for servicing work.

2 Disconnect the battery negative terminal (refer to *"Disconnecting the battery"* in the Reference Section of this manual).

3 Place a suitable container beneath the connection or union to be disconnected, and have a large rag ready to soak up any escaping fuel not being caught by the container.

4 Slowly loosen the connection or union nut to avoid a sudden release of pressure, and position the rag around the connection, to catch any fuel spray which may be expelled. Once the pressure is released, disconnect the fuel line. Plug the pipe ends, to minimise fuel loss and prevent the entry of dirt into the fuel system.

9 Fuel pump - removal and refitting

Note: Refer to the warning note in Section 1 before proceeding.

Removal

1 Disconnect the battery negative terminal (refer to *"Disconnecting the battery"* in the Reference Section of this manual).

2 For access to the fuel pump, tilt or remove the rear seat as described in Chapter 11.

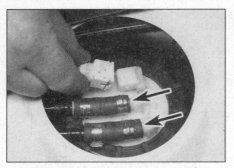

9.4 Unplug the wiring connector, then release the fuel feed and return hoses (arrowed) from the fuel pump

9.6 Unscrew the locking ring . . .

9.7a . . . then lift out the fuel pump . . .

3 Using a screwdriver, carefully prise the plastic access cover from the floor to expose the fuel pump. Where two access covers are fitted, the pump is located under the right-hand cover.

4 Disconnect the wiring connector from the fuel pump, and tape the connector to the vehicle body, to prevent it from disappearing behind the tank **(see illustration)**.

5 Mark the hoses for identification purposes, then slacken the feed and return hose retaining clips, or release the quick-release connectors. Where the crimped-type Peugeot hose clips are fitted, cut the clips and discard them; use standard worm-drive hose clips on refitting. Disconnect both hoses from the top of the pump, and plug the hose ends.

6 Noting the alignment marks on the tank, pump cover and the locking ring, unscrew the ring and remove it from the tank **(see illustration)**. This is best accomplished by using a screwdriver on the raised ribs of the locking ring. Carefully tap the screwdriver to turn the ring anti-clockwise until it can be unscrewed by hand.

7 Displace the pump cover, then reach into the tank and unclip the pump from the tank base. Lift the fuel pump assembly out of the fuel tank, taking great care not to damage the filter, or to spill fuel onto the interior of the vehicle. Recover the rubber sealing ring and discard it - a new one must be used on refitting **(see illustrations)**.

8 Note that the fuel pump is only available as a complete assembly - no components are available separately.

Refitting

9 Ensure that the fuel pump pick-up filter is clean and free of debris. Fit the new sealing ring to the top of the fuel tank.

10 Carefully manoeuvre the pump assembly into the fuel tank, and clip it into position in the base of the tank.

11 Align the mark on the fuel pump cover with the centre of the three alignment marks on the fuel tank, then refit the locking ring. Securely tighten the locking ring, then check that the locking ring, pump cover and tank marks are all correctly aligned **(see illustration)**.

12 Reconnect the feed and return hoses to the top of the fuel pump, using the marks made on removal to ensure that they are correctly reconnected, and securely tighten their retaining clips.

13 Reconnect the pump wiring connector.

14 Reconnect the battery negative terminal and start the engine. Check the fuel pump feed and return hoses unions for signs of leakage.

15 If all is well, refit the plastic access cover. Tilt or refit the rear seat as described in Chapter 11 (as applicable).

10 Fuel gauge sender unit - removal and refitting

1 On pre-April 1997 models, refer to Chapter 4A, Section 5, noting that there are no fuel pipe connections to the sender unit **(see illustration)**.

2 On April 1997 models onward, the sender unit is integral with the fuel pump - refer to Section 9 of this Chapter.

11 Fuel tank - removal and refitting

Refer to Chapter 4A, Section 6, noting that it will be necessary to depressurise the fuel system as the feed and return hoses are disconnected (see Section 8). It will also be necessary to disconnect the wiring connector from the fuel pump before lowering the tank out of position.

12 Throttle body - removal and refitting

Note: *Refer to the warning note in Section 1 before proceeding.*

Removal

1 Disconnect the battery negative terminal (refer to *"Disconnecting the battery"* in the Reference Section of this manual).

2 Remove the air cleaner housing-to-throttle body duct, with reference to Section 2.

3 Depress the retaining clips and disconnect the wiring connectors from the throttle potentiometer, the idle control stepper motor

9.7b . . . and recover the sealing ring

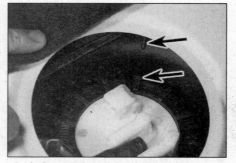

9.11 On refitting, tighten the locking ring until it is aligned with the fuel tank mark

10.1 Removing the fuel gauge sender unit

(where fitted), and the injector wiring loom connector which is situated on the side of the throttle body **(see illustrations)**.

4 Referring to Section 8 (depressurising the fuel system), release the retaining clips and disconnect the fuel feed and return hoses from the throttle body assembly. If the original crimped-type Peugeot clips are still fitted, cut the clips and discard them; use worm-drive hose clips on refitting **(see illustration)**.

5 Disconnect the accelerator inner cable from the throttle cam, then withdraw the outer cable from the mounting bracket, along with its flat washer and spring clip.

6 Where necessary, disconnect the air temperature control vacuum hose and purge valve vacuum hose from the throttle body (as applicable).

7 Slacken and remove the bolts securing the throttle body assembly to the inlet manifold, then remove the assembly along with its gasket **(see illustration)**.

8 If necessary, with the throttle body removed, undo the retaining screws and separate the upper and lower sections, noting the gasket which is fitted between the two.

Refitting

9 Refitting is a reverse of the removal procedure, bearing in mind the following points:

a) *Where applicable, ensure the mating surfaces of the upper and lower throttle body sections are clean and dry. Fit a new gasket and reassemble the two sections, tightening the retaining screws securely.*

b) *Ensure the mating surfaces of the manifold and throttle body are clean and dry, then fit a new gasket. Securely tighten the throttle body retaining bolts.*

c) *Ensure all hoses are correctly reconnected and, where necessary, that their retaining clips are securely tightened.*

12.3a Disconnect the wiring connectors from the throttle potentiometer . . .

d) *On completion, adjust the accelerator cable using the information given in Section 4.*

13 Fuel injection system - testing and adjustment

Testing

1 If a fault appears in the fuel injection system, first ensure that all the system wiring connectors are securely connected and free of corrosion. Ensure that the fault is not due to poor maintenance; ie, check that the air cleaner filter element is clean, the spark plugs are in good condition and correctly gapped, the valve clearances are correctly adjusted, the cylinder compression pressures are correct, the ignition timing is correct, and that the engine breather hoses are clear and undamaged, referring to Chapter 1A, 2A and 5B for further information.

2 If these checks fail to reveal the cause of the problem, the vehicle should be taken to a suitably-equipped Peugeot dealer for testing. A wiring block connector is incorporated in the engine management circuit, into which a special electronic diagnostic tester can be

12.3b . . . the injector wiring loom connector and the stepper motor

plugged. The connector is clipped to the rear of the ECU mounting box. The tester will locate the fault quickly and simply, alleviating the need to test all the system components individually, which is a time-consuming operation that also carries a risk of damaging the ECU.

Adjustment

3 Experienced home mechanics with a considerable amount of skill and equipment (including a tachometer and an accurately calibrated exhaust gas analyser) may be able to check the exhaust CO level and the idle speed. However, if these are found to be in need of adjustment, the car *must* be taken to a suitably-equipped Peugeot dealer for further testing.

4 On the Bosch system, no adjustment is possible. Should the idle speed or exhaust gas CO level be incorrect, then a fault must be present in the fuel injection system.

5 On the Magneti Marelli system, it is possible to adjust the mixture setting (exhaust gas CO level) and ignition timing. However, adjustments can be made only by re-programming the ECU, using special diagnostic equipment connected to the system via the diagnostic connector.

12.4 Fuel feed and return hose connections (arrowed) - later model shown

12.7 Throttle body retaining screws (arrowed)

14.3a Undo the injector cap retaining screw, noting the use of rag to catch fuel spray . . .

14.3b . . . then lift off the cap and withdraw the injector

14.3c On refitting, ensure the cap terminals are correctly aligned with the injector pins (arrowed)

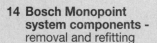

14 Bosch Monopoint system components - removal and refitting

Note: *Check the availability of individual components with your Peugeot dealer before dismantling.*

Fuel injector

Note: *Refer to the warning note in Section 1 before proceeding. If a faulty injector is suspected, before condemning the injector, it is worth trying the effect of one of the proprietary injector-cleaning treatments.*

1 Disconnect the battery negative terminal (refer to *"Disconnecting the battery"* in the Reference Section of this manual), then remove the inlet air temperature sensor as described later in this Section.

2 Lift out the injector and recover its lower sealing ring.

3 Refitting is a reversal of the removal procedure ensuring that the injector sealing ring(s) and injector cap O-ring are in good condition. When refitting the injector cap ensure that the injector pins are correctly aligned with the cap terminals, the terminals are marked '+' and '-' for identification **(see illustrations)**.

Fuel pressure regulator

Note: *Refer to the warning note in Section 1 before proceeding. At the time of writing, the fuel pressure regulator assembly was not available separately from the throttle body*

assembly. Refer to a Peugeot dealer for the latest information. Although the unit can be dismantled for cleaning, if required, it should not be disturbed unless absolutely necessary.

4 Disconnect the battery negative terminal (refer to *"Disconnecting the battery"* in the Reference Section of this manual).

5 Remove the air cleaner-to-throttle body duct, using the information given in Section 2.

6 Using a marker pen, make alignment marks between the regulator cover and throttle body, then slacken and remove the cover retaining screws **(see illustration)**. As the screws are slackened, place a clean rag over the cover to catch any fuel spray which may be released.

7 Lift off the cover, then remove the spring and withdraw the diaphragm, noting its correct fitted orientation. Remove all traces of dirt and examine the diaphragm for signs of splitting. If damage is found, it will probably be necessary to renew the throttle body assembly.

8 Refitting is a reverse of the removal procedure, ensuring that the diaphragm and cover are fitted the correct way round, and that the retaining screws are securely tightened.

Idle control stepper motor

9 Disconnect the battery negative terminal (refer to *"Disconnecting the battery"* in the Reference Section of this manual).

10 Depress the retaining clip and disconnect the wiring connector from the idle control stepper motor.

11 Undo the retaining screws and remove the motor from the front of the throttle body **(see illustration)**.

12 Refitting is a reverse of the removal procedure, ensuring that the motor retaining screws are securely tightened.

Throttle potentiometer

13 The throttle potentiometer is a sealed unit, and *under no circumstances* should it be disturbed. For this reason, on some models, it is secured to the throttle body assembly by tamperproof screws. If the throttle potentiometer is faulty, the complete throttle body assembly must be renewed - refer to your Peugeot dealer for the latest information.

Inlet air temperature sensor

Note: *Refer to the warning note in Section 1 before proceeding.*

14 The sensor is an integral part of the throttle body injector cap. To remove the cap, first disconnect the battery negative terminal (refer to *"Disconnecting the battery"* in the Reference Section of this manual), then remove the air cleaner-to-throttle body duct using the information given in Section 2.

15 Undo the three retaining screws and remove the circular plastic ring from the top of the throttle body and recover its sealing ring **(see illustrations)**.

16 Depress the retaining clip and disconnect the wiring connector from the injector **(see illustration)**.

17 Undo the injector cap retaining screw, then lift off the cap and recover the gasket

14.6 Fuel pressure regulator retaining screws (arrowed)

14.11 Idle control stepper motor retaining screws (arrowed)

14.15a Undo the three retaining screws (arrowed) . . .

14.15b ... then lift off the plastic ring and recover the sealing ring

14.16 Disconnecting the injector wiring connector. Injector retaining screw is arrowed

and/or sealing ring (as applicable). Note that as the cap screw is slackened, place a rag over the injector to catch any fuel spray which may be released **(see illustration 14.16).**

18 Refitting is a reversal of the removal procedure ensuring that the injector cap gasket and/or O-ring is in good condition. Take care to ensure that the cap terminals are correctly aligned with the injector pins and securely tighten the cap retaining screw.

Coolant temperature sensor

19 Refer to Chapter 3.

Electronic control unit (ECU)

20 The ECU is located in the plastic box which is mounted onto the rear of the battery mounting tray.
21 Disconnect the battery negative terminal (refer to *"Disconnecting the battery"* in the Reference Section of this manual).
22 Unclip the cover from the box, then lift the retaining clip and disconnect the wiring connector from the ECU.
23 Undo the retaining nut and release the relay unit from the rear of the ECU box.
24 Undo the retaining screws and remove the ECU and box assembly from the battery tray. If necessary, undo the retaining screws and separate the ECU and box.
25 Refitting is a reverse of the removal procedure ensuring that the wiring connector is securely reconnected.

Fuel injection system relay unit

26 The relay unit is mounted onto the rear of the ECU plastic box which is situated directly behind the battery.
27 Disconnect the battery negative terminal (refer to *"Disconnecting the battery"* in the Reference Section of this manual).
28 Undo the retaining nut, then disconnect the wiring connector and remove the relay unit from the vehicle.
29 Refitting is the reverse of removal, ensuring that the relay unit is securely clipped in position.

Crankshaft sensor

30 The crankshaft sensor is situated on the front face of the transmission (clutch) housing.
31 Disconnect the battery negative terminal

(refer to *"Disconnecting the battery"* in the Reference Section of this manual).
32 Trace the wiring back from the sensor to the wiring connector, and disconnect it from the main harness.
33 Prise out the rubber grommet, then undo the retaining bolt and withdraw the sensor from the transmission.
34 Refitting is a reverse of the removal procedure. Ensure that the sensor retaining bolt is securely tightened, and that the grommet is correctly seated in the transmission housing.

Vehicle speed sensor

35 The vehicle speed sensor is an integral part of the speedometer drive housing. Refer to Chapter 7A, Section 7 for removal and refitting details.

Inlet manifold heater - MA3.1 system

36 Remove the inlet manifold as described in Section 16.
37 Release the circlip and withdraw the heater from the underside of the manifold casting.
38 Refitting is a reversal of removal.

---

15 Magneti Marelli system components - removal and refitting

Note: *Check the availability of individual components with your Peugeot dealer before dismantling.*

Fuel injector

Note: *Refer to the warning note in Section 1 before proceeding.*
Note: *If a faulty injector is suspected, before condemning the injector, it is worth trying the effect of one of the proprietary injector-cleaning treatments available from car accessory shops. If this fails, the vehicle should be taken to a Peugeot dealer for testing using the appropriate specialist equipment. At the time of writing, it appears that neither the fuel injector nor its seals are available separately and, if faulty, the complete upper throttle body assembly must be renewed. Refer to your Peugeot dealer for further information on parts availability.*

1 Disconnect the battery negative terminal (refer to *"Disconnecting the battery"* in the Reference Section of this manual).
2 Remove the air cleaner-to-throttle body duct using the information given in Section 2.
3 Release the retaining tangs and disconnect the injector wiring connector.
4 Undo the retaining screw, then remove the retaining clip and lift the injector out of the housing, noting its sealing ring. Note that as the screw is slackened, place a rag over the injector to catch any fuel spray which may be released.
5 Refitting is a reverse of the removal procedure ensuring that the injector sealing ring is in good condition.

Fuel pressure regulator

Note: *Refer to the warning note at the start of this Section before proceeding.*
Note: *At the time of writing, it appears that the fuel pressure regulator is not available separately. If the fuel pressure regulator assembly is faulty, the complete upper throttle body assembly must be renewed. Refer to a Peugeot dealer for further information on parts availability. Although the unit can be dismantled for cleaning, if required, it should not be disturbed unless absolutely necessary.*
6 Disconnect the battery negative terminal (refer to *"Disconnecting the battery"* in the Reference Section of this manual).
7 Remove the air cleaner-to-throttle body duct using the information given in Section 2.
8 Using a suitable marker pen, make alignment marks between the regulator cover and throttle body, then undo the four retaining screws. Note that as the screws are slackened, place a rag over the cover to catch any fuel spray which may be released.
9 Lift off the cover, then remove the spring and withdraw the diaphragm whilst noting its correct fitted orientation. Remove all traces of dirt and examine the diaphragm for signs of splitting. If damage is found, it will be necessary to renew the complete upper throttle body assembly as described earlier in this Section.
10 Refitting is a reverse of the removal procedure ensuring that the diaphragm and cover are fitted the correct way around and the retaining screws are securely tightened.

Idle control stepper motor

11 Disconnect the battery negative terminal (refer to *"Disconnecting the battery"* in the Reference Section of this manual).
12 To remove the stepper motor, depress the retaining tabs and disconnect the wiring connector. Undo the two retaining screws and withdraw the motor from the side of the throttle body assembly.
13 Refitting is a reverse of removal.

Throttle potentiometer

14 Disconnect the battery negative terminal (refer to *"Disconnecting the battery"* in the Reference Section of this manual). Depress

the retaining tabs and disconnect the wiring connector from the throttle potentiometer.

15 Undo the two retaining screws and remove the throttle potentiometer from the side of the throttle body assembly.

16 Refitting is a reversal of the removal procedure ensuring that the throttle potentiometer tang is correctly engaged with the throttle spindle.

Inlet air temperature sensor

17 The sensor is screwed into the underside of the upper throttle body where it is situated on the left-hand side of the fuel injector.

18 Disconnect the battery negative terminal (refer to *"Disconnecting the battery"* in the Reference Section of this manual).

19 Disconnect the wiring connector, then undo the retaining screw and remove the sensor from the throttle body.

Note: *The sensor retaining screw is very difficult to reach. If it proves impossible to unscrew, the throttle body will have to be removed to permit sensor removal.*

20 Refitting is a reverse of the removal procedure.

Manifold absolute pressure (MAP) sensor

21 The MAP sensor is mounted onto a bracket which is situated on the engine compartment bulkhead, behind the throttle body.

22 Disconnect the battery negative terminal (refer to *"Disconnecting the battery"* in the Reference Section of this manual).

23 Slacken and remove the three retaining bolts, then free the MAP sensor from the bracket. Disconnect the wiring connector and vacuum hose and remove the sensor from the engine compartment.

24 Refitting is a reverse of the removal procedure.

Coolant temperature sensor

25 Refer to Chapter 3.

Crankshaft sensor

26 Refer to Section 14.

Electronic control unit (ECU)

27 Refer to Section 14.

Fuel injection system relay unit

28 Refer to Section 14.

Throttle body heating element

29 The throttle body heating element is situated in front of the throttle body.

30 Disconnect the battery negative terminal (refer to *"Disconnecting the battery"* in the Reference Section of this manual).

31 Remove the air cleaner housing-to-throttle body duct using the information given in Section 2.

32 Disconnect the wiring connectors from the inlet air temperature sensor and the injector. Also disconnect the main wiring connector from the throttle body and free the connector from its mounting bracket.

33 Undo the retaining screws and free the accelerator mounting bracket from the throttle body. As the bracket is released, recover the spring from the front of the heating element.

34 Ease the heating element out from the throttle housing and remove it along with the wiring connector and wiring harness. Examine the O-ring for signs of damage or deterioration and renew if necessary.

35 Refitting is a reversal of the removal procedure, where necessary, using a new O-ring.

16 Inlet manifold -
removal and refitting

Removal

1 Remove the throttle body as described in Section 12.

2 Drain the cooling system as described in Chapter 1A.

3 Slacken the retaining clip and disconnect the coolant hose(s) from the manifold.

4 Slacken the retaining clip and disconnect the vacuum servo unit hose from the left-hand side of the manifold.

5 Make a final check that all the necessary vacuum/breather hoses have been disconnected from the manifold.

6 Unscrew the six retaining nuts, then manoeuvre the manifold away from the head and out of the engine compartment. Note that there is no manifold gasket.

Refitting

7 Refitting is the reverse of the removal procedure, noting the following points:

a) Ensure that the manifold and cylinder head mating surfaces are clean and dry, and apply a thin coating of suitable sealing compound to the manifold mating surface. Refit the manifold and tighten its retaining nuts to the specified torque.

b) Ensure that all relevant hoses are reconnected to their original positions and securely held (where necessary) by their retaining clips.

c) Refit the throttle body as described in Section 12.

d) On completion, refill the cooling system as described in Chapter 1A.

17 Exhaust manifold -
removal and refitting

Removal

1 Refer to Chapter 4A, Section 15, noting that the lambda (oxygen) sensor wiring connectors should be disconnected. Alternatively, care must be taken to support the front pipe, to avoid any strain being placed on the sensor wiring.

Refitting

2 Refitting is the reverse of the removal procedure, noting the following points:

a) Examine all the exhaust manifold studs for signs of damage and corrosion; remove all traces of corrosion, and repair or renew any damaged studs.

b) Ensure that the manifold and cylinder head sealing faces are clean and flat, and fit the new manifold gaskets. Tighten the manifold retaining nuts to the specified torque.

c) Reconnect the front pipe to the manifold using the information given in Section 18.

18 Exhaust system -
general information, removal and refitting

General information

1 The exhaust system consists of four sections; the front pipe, the catalytic converter, the centre silencer, and the tailpipe and main silencer box. All exhaust sections are joined by a flanged joint. The front pipe joints are secured by nuts and bolts, the catalytic converter joint being of the spring-loaded ball type, to allow for movement in the exhaust system. The catalytic converter-to-intermediate pipe joint and the intermediate pipe-to-silencer joint are secured by a clamping ring.

2 The system is suspended throughout its entire length by rubber mountings.

Removal and refitting

3 Refer to Chapter 4A, Section 16 substituting "catalytic converter" for all references to the intermediate pipe. Note also that it will be necessary to disconnect the lambda (oxygen) sensor wiring connectors in order to remove the front pipe/complete system. On refitting, ensure that the sensor wiring is retained by all the relevant retaining clips so that it is in no danger of contacting the hot exhaust/engine.

Chapter 4 Part C:
Fuel/exhaust systems – multi-point petrol injection models

Contents

Degrees of difficulty

Easy, suitable for novice with little experience	**Fairly easy,** suitable for beginner with some experience 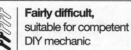	**Fairly difficult,** suitable for competent DIY mechanic	**Difficult,** suitable for experienced DIY mechanic	**Very difficult,** suitable for expert DIY or professional

Specifications

System type

1.4 litre models:
Up to mid-2000 models . . . . Magneti Marelli 1 AP
Mid-2000 models onward . . . . Sagem S2000
1.6 litre models:
Up to 1997 models . . . . Bosch Motronic MP5.1
1997 to 1999 models . . . . Bosch Motronic MP5.2
1999 to mid-2000 models . . . . Bosch Motronic MP7.2
Mid-2000 models onward . . . . Bosch Motronic ME7.4.4
1.8 litre:
8-valve models . . . . Magneti Marelli 8P
16-valve models:
Up to mid-2000 . . . . Sagem Lucas SL96
Mid-2000 models onward . . . . Bosch Motronic MP7.3
2.0 litre:
8-valve models . . . . Magneti Marelli 8P
16-valve models . . . . Bosch Motronic MP5.2

Fuel system data

Fuel pump type . . . . Electric, immersed in tank
Specified idle speed . . . . 850 ± 50 rpm (not adjustable – controlled by ECU)
Idle mixture CO content . . . . Less than 1.0 % (not adjustable– controlled by ECU)

Recommended fuel

Minimum octane rating . . . . 95 RON unleaded

Torque wrench settings

	Nm	lbf ft
Inlet manifold nuts:		
1.4 and 1.6 litre models	8	6
1.8 and 2.0 litre models	20	15
Exhaust manifold nuts:		
1.4 and 1.6 litre models	16	12
1.8 and 2.0 litre models	35	26

1 General information and precautions

The fuel supply system consists of a fuel tank (which is mounted under the rear of the car, with an electric fuel pump immersed in it), a fuel filter, fuel feed and return lines. The fuel pump supplies fuel to the fuel rail, which acts as a reservoir for the four fuel injectors which inject fuel into the inlet tracts. The fuel filter incorporated in the feed line from the pump to the fuel rail ensures that the fuel supplied to the injectors is clean.

Warning: Many of the procedures in this Chapter require the removal of fuel lines and connections, which may result in some fuel spillage. Before carrying out any operation on the fuel system, refer to the precautions given in 'Safety first!' at the beginning of this manual, and follow them implicitly. Petrol is a highly dangerous and volatile liquid, and the precautions necessary when handling it cannot be overstressed.

Refer to Section 6 for further information on the operation of each fuel injection system, and to Section 17 for information on the exhaust system. Throughout this Chapter, it is also occasionally necessary to identify vehicles by their engine codes rather than by engine capacity alone. Refer to the relevant Part of Chapter 2 for further information on engine code identification.

Note: *Residual pressure will remain in the fuel lines long after the vehicle was last used. When disconnecting any fuel line, first depressurise the fuel system as described in Section 7.*

2 Air cleaner assembly and intake ducts – removal and refitting

Removal

1.4 and 1.6 litre models

1 Slacken the retaining clips (where fitted) and disconnect the vacuum hose and breather hose from the top of the air cleaner housing. Where crimped-type hose clips or ties are fitted, cut and discard them; use standard worm-drive hose clips or new cable ties on refitting. Alternatively, the front hose union can be unclipped from the housing leaving the hoses connected **(see illustration)**.
2 Slacken the retaining clips and free the air cleaner housing from the throttle housing and disconnect the intake duct from the side of the housing **(see illustration)**.
3 Disconnect the wiring connector from the inlet air temperature sensor (where applicable) and lift the air cleaner housing assembly out of the engine compartment **(see illustration)**.
4 To remove the intake duct assembly, undo the bolt (or drill out the rivets) securing the duct to the bonnet crossmember, then release the fastener securing the rear of the duct to the cylinder head and remove the duct from the engine compartment **(see illustrations)**.

1.8 and 2.0 litre 8-valve models

5 Slacken the retaining clip(s) and disconnect the breather hose(s) from the side of the air cleaner-to-throttle housing duct. Slacken the duct retaining clips, then disconnect it from the air cleaner and throttle housing, and remove it from the vehicle. Where necessary, recover the rubber sealing ring from the throttle housing.
6 Release the two retaining clips, then slacken and remove the two retaining screws from the front of the cylinder head cover, and remove the air cleaner element cover from the head. Withdraw the air cleaner element.
7 To remove the intake duct, undo the bolt securing the rear section of the duct to the end of the cylinder head, then slacken the retaining clip and disconnect the duct from the cylinder head cover. Undo the bolt securing the front of the duct to the crossmember and manoeuvre the duct out of the engine compartment.

1.8 and 2.0 litre 16-valve models

8 Slacken the retaining clips and disconnect the intake duct from the throttle housing and air cleaner housing lid.
9 Undo the screws securing the lid to the air cleaner housing body. Lift off the lid and take out the filter element.
10 Lift the housing body upward to disengage it from the lower locating lugs. On some models, as the housing is lifted up, it will be necessary to disengage a small plastic retaining tag at the front securing the housing to the cold air intake duct underneath.

2.1 On 1.6 litre models, unclip the front hose union from the air cleaner housing . . .

2.2 . . . then slacken the clip securing the air cleaner to the throttle housing

2.3 Disconnecting the wiring connector from the inlet air temperature sensor

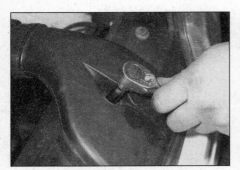

2.4a Unscrew the bolt securing the intake duct to the bonnet crossmember . . .

2.4b . . . then release the fastener securing it to the cylinder head . . .

2.4c . . . and remove the duct assembly from the engine compartment

11 To remove the cold air intake duct, undo the air cleaner housing mounting bracket bolts and withdraw the bracket. Release the cold air intake from the bracket as it is removed.

12 Release the other end of the cold air intake from its body attachments and manipulate the duct from the car.

Refitting

13 Refitting is a reversal of the removal procedure, ensuring that all hoses are properly reconnected, and that all ducts are correctly seated and securely held by their retaining clips.

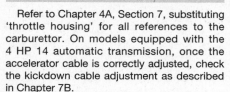

3 Accelerator cable – removal, refitting and adjustment

Refer to Chapter 4A, Section 7, substituting 'throttle housing' for all references to the carburettor. On models equipped with the 4 HP 14 automatic transmission, once the accelerator cable is correctly adjusted, check the kickdown cable adjustment as described in Chapter 7B.

Note: *On models equipped with the AL4 automatic transmission, Peugeot specify that the automatic transmission electronic control unit (ECU) should be reprogrammed every time the accelerator cable is adjusted. If the transmission performance has been adversely affected by accelerator cable adjustment, take the vehicle to a Peugeot dealer to have the transmission ECU reprogrammed with the necessary diagnostic equipment.*

4 Accelerator pedal – removal and refitting

Removal

Models with accelerator cable

1 Detach the accelerator cable from the pedal as described in the previous Section.

2 On right-hand drive models, unscrew the nut from the end of the pedal pivot shaft, whilst retaining the pivot shaft with an open-ended spanner on the flats provided. Pull the pedal and pivot shaft assembly from the support bracket.

3 On left-hand drive models, slide off the spring clip from one end of the pedal pivot shaft. Withdraw the pivot shaft and remove the pedal and pivot bush assembly from the support bracket.

Models without accelerator cable

4 Release the fasteners and remove trim panel above the pedals (see Chapter 11).

5 Disconnect the accelerator pedal position sensor wiring plug from the top of the pedal.

6 Undo the three nuts and remove the pedal assembly.

Refitting

7 Refitting is a reversal of the removal procedure. On models fitted with a cable, apply a little multi-purpose grease to the pedal pivot point, and adjust the accelerator cable as described in Section 3.

5 Unleaded petrol – general information and usage

Note: *The information given in this Chapter is correct at the time of writing. If updated information is thought to be required, check with a Peugeot dealer. If travelling abroad, consult one of the motoring organisations (or a similar authority) for advice on the fuel available.*

1 All Peugeot 306 multi-point injection models are designed to run on unleaded fuel with a minimum octane rating of 95 (RON). All engines have a catalytic converter, and so must be run on unleaded fuel **only**. Under no circumstances should leaded fuel, or lead replacement petrol (LRP) be used, as this will damage the converter.

2 Super unleaded petrol (98 octane) can also be used in all models if wished, though there is no advantage in doing so.

6 Fuel injection systems – general information

Note: *The fuel injection ECU is of the 'self-learning' type, meaning that as it operates, it also monitors and stores the settings which give optimum engine performance under all operating conditions. When the battery is disconnected, these settings are lost and the ECU reverts to the base settings programmed into its memory at the factory. On restarting, this may lead to the engine running/idling roughly for a short while, until the ECU has relearned the optimum settings. This process is best accomplished by taking the vehicle on a road test (for approximately 15 minutes), covering all engine speeds and loads, concentrating mainly in the 2500 to 3500 rpm region.*

On all models, the fuel injection and ignition functions are combined into a single engine management system. The systems fitted are manufactured by Bosch, Magneti Marelli and Sagem, and are very similar to each other in most respects, the only significant differences being in the software contained in the system ECU, and specific component location according to engine type. Each system incorporates a closed-loop catalytic converter and an evaporative emission control system,

and complies with the latest emission control standards. Refer to Chapter 5B for information on the ignition side of each system; the fuel side of the system operates as follows.

The fuel pump supplies fuel from the tank to the fuel rail, via a renewable cartridge filter mounted on the side of the fuel tank. The pump itself is mounted inside the tank, with the pump motor permanently immersed in fuel, to keep it cool. The fuel rail is mounted directly above the fuel injectors and acts as a fuel reservoir.

Fuel rail supply pressure is controlled by the pressure regulator, mounted at the end of the fuel rail or, on later models, integrated into the fuel pump assembly. The regulator contains a spring-loaded valve, which lifts to allow excess fuel to return to the tank when the optimum operating pressure of the fuel system is exceeded (eg, during low speed, light load cruising).

The fuel injectors are electromagnetic pintle valves, which spray atomised fuel into the combustion chambers under the control of the engine management system ECU. There are four injectors, one per cylinder, mounted in the inlet manifold close to the cylinder head. Each injector is mounted at an angle that allows it to spray fuel directly onto the back of the inlet valve(s). The ECU controls the volume of fuel injected by varying the length of time for which each injector is held open.

The electrical control system consists of the ECU, along with the following sensors. Note that this list is typical, and variations may be encountered according to model year, system type, emission level and optional equipment fitted:

a) Throttle potentiometer – informs the ECU of the throttle valve position, and the rate of throttle opening/closing.

b) Coolant temperature sensor – informs the ECU of engine temperature.

c) Inlet air temperature sensor – informs the ECU of the temperature of the air passing through the throttle housing.

d) Lambda (oxygen) sensors – inform the ECU of the oxygen content of the exhaust gases (explained in greater detail in Part F of this Chapter).

e) Manifold pressure sensor – informs the ECU of the load on the engine (expressed in terms of inlet manifold vacuum).

f) Crankshaft position sensor – informs the ECU of engine speed and crankshaft angular position.

g) Vehicle speed sensor – informs the ECU of the vehicle speed.

h) Knock sensor – informs the ECU of pre-ignition (detonation) within the cylinders.

i) Camshaft sensor – informs the ECU of which cylinder is on the firing stroke on systems with sequential injection.

j) Accelerator pedal position sensor – informs the ECU of the pedal position and rate of change (ME7.4.4).

k) *Accelerometer sensor – informs the ECU of the quality of the road surface on which the vehicle is being driven. This ensures the ECU does not diagnose variations in engine speed due to an uneven road surface as an ignition misfire (MP7.3).*

Signals from each of the sensors are compared by the ECU and, based on this information, the ECU selects the response appropriate to those values, and controls the fuel injectors (varying the pulse width – the length of time the injectors are held open – to provide a richer or weaker air/fuel mixture, as appropriate). The air/fuel mixture is constantly varied by the ECU, to provide the best settings for cranking, starting (with either a hot or cold engine) and engine warm-up, idle, cruising and acceleration.

The ECU also has full control over the engine idle speed, via a stepper motor fitted to the throttle housing. The stepper motor either controls the amount of air passing through a bypass drilling at the side of the throttle or controls the position of the throttle valve itself, depending on model. On some models, a sensor informs the ECU of the position, and rate of change, of the accelerator pedal. The ECU then controls the throttle valve by means of a throttle positioning motor integral with the throttle body – no accelerator cable is fitted. The ECU also carries out 'fine tuning' of the idle speed by varying the ignition timing to increase or reduce the torque of the engine as it is idling. This helps to stabilise the idle speed when electrical or mechanical loads (such as headlights, air conditioning, etc) are switched on and off.

The throttle housing may also fitted with an electric heating element. The heater is supplied with current by the ECU, warming the throttle housing on cold starts to help prevent icing of the throttle valve.

The exhaust and evaporative loss emission control systems are described in more detail in Chapter 4F.

If there is any abnormality in any of the readings obtained from the coolant temperature sensor, the inlet air temperature sensor or the lambda sensor, the ECU enters its 'back-up' mode. If this happens, the erroneous sensor signal is overridden, and the ECU assumes a preprogrammed 'back-up' value, which will allow the engine to continue running, albeit at reduced efficiency. If the ECU enters this mode, the warning lamp on the instrument panel will be illuminated, and the relevant fault code will be stored in the ECU memory.

If the warning light illuminates, the vehicle should be taken to a Peugeot dealer or specialist at the earliest opportunity. Once there, a complete test of the engine management system can be carried out, using a special electronic diagnostic test unit, which is plugged into the system's diagnostic connector.

7 Fuel system – depressurisation and pressurising

Note: *Refer to the warning note in Section 1 before proceeding.*

Depressurisation

⚠️ *Warning: The following procedure will merely relieve the pressure in the fuel system – remember that fuel will still be present in the system components and take precautions accordingly before disconnecting any of them.*

1 The fuel system referred to in this Section is defined as the tank-mounted fuel pump, the fuel filter, the fuel injectors, the fuel rail and the pipes of the fuel lines between these components. All these contain fuel which will be under pressure while the engine is running, and/or while the ignition is switched on. The pressure will remain for some time after the ignition has been switched off, and must be relieved in a controlled fashion when any of these components are disturbed for servicing work.

2 Disconnect the battery negative terminal (refer to *Disconnecting the battery* in the Reference Chapter).

3 Some models are equipped with a pressure relief valve on the fuel rail. On these models, unscrew the cap from the valve and position a container beneath the valve. Hold a wad of rag over the valve and relieve the pressure in the system by depressing the valve core with a suitable screwdriver. Be prepared for the squirt of fuel as the valve core is depressed and catch it with the rag. Hold the valve core down until no more fuel is expelled from the valve. Once the pressure is relieved, securely refit the valve cap.

4 Where no valve is fitted to the fuel rail, it will be necessary to release the pressure as the fuel pipe is disconnected. Place a container beneath the union and position a large rag around the union to catch any fuel spray which may be expelled. Slowly release and disconnect the fuel pipe and catch any spilt fuel in the container. Plug the pipe/union to minimise fuel loss and prevent the entry of dirt into the fuel system.

11.2 On early models the fuel injection diagnostic wiring plug is clipped to the ECU mounting box

Pressurising

5 After any work is carried out on the fuel system, the system should be pressurised as follows.

6 Depress the accelerator pedal fully then switch on the ignition. Hold the pedal depressed for approximately 1 second then release it. The ECU should then operate the fuel pump for between 20 and 30 seconds to refill the fuel system. Once the fuel pump stops the ignition can be switched off.

8 Fuel pump – removal and refitting

Refer to Chapter 4B, Section 9.

9 Fuel gauge sender unit – removal and refitting

1 On pre-April 1997 models, refer to Chapter 4A, Section 5, noting that there are no fuel pipe connections to the sender unit.

2 On April 1997 models onward, the sender unit is integral with the fuel pump – refer to Chapter 4B, Section 9.

10 Fuel tank – removal and refitting

Refer to Chapter 4A, Section 6, noting that it will be necessary to depressurise the fuel system as the feed and return hoses are disconnected (see Section 7). It will also be necessary to disconnect the wiring connector from the fuel pump before lowering the tank out of position.

11 Fuel injection system – testing and adjustment

Testing

1 If a fault appears in the fuel injection system, first ensure that all the system wiring connectors are securely connected and free of corrosion. Ensure that the fault is not due to poor maintenance; ie, check that the air cleaner filter element is clean, the spark plugs are in good condition and correctly gapped, the cylinder compression pressures are correct, and that the engine breather hoses are clear and undamaged, referring to the relevant Parts of Chapters 1, 2 and 4 for further information.

2 If these checks fail to reveal the cause of the problem, the vehicle should be taken to a suitably-equipped Peugeot dealer for testing. A wiring block connector is incorporated in the engine management circuit, into which a special electronic diagnostic tester can be plugged. On pre-April 1997 models, the connector is clipped to the rear of the ECU mounting box **(see illustration)**. On later

models the connector is mounted below the steering column. The tester will locate the fault quickly and simply, alleviating the need to test all the system components individually, which is a time-consuming operation that carries a risk of damaging the ECU.

Adjustment

3 Whilst experienced home mechanics with a considerable amount of skill and equipment (including a tachometer and an accurately calibrated exhaust gas analyser) may be able to check the exhaust CO level and the idle speed. However, if these are found to be in need of adjustment, the car must be taken to a suitably-equipped Peugeot dealer for further testing. Neither the mixture adjustment (exhaust gas CO level) nor the idle speed are adjustable, and should either be incorrect, a fault must be present in the fuel injection system.

12 Throttle housing – removal and refitting

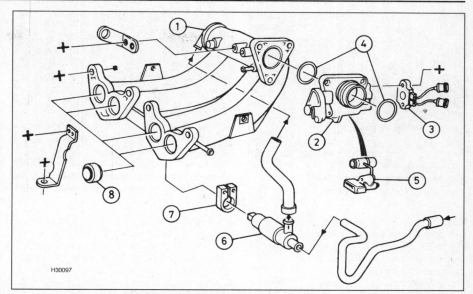

12.4 Throttle housing and inlet manifold components – early 1.6 litre models

1 Inlet manifold	4 O-ring seals	7 Mounting bracket
2 Throttle housing	5 Electric heating element	8 Sealing rings
3 Throttle potentiometer	6 Idle speed auxiliary air valve	

Removal

1 Disconnect the battery negative terminal (refer to *Disconnecting the battery* in the Reference Chapter).

1.4 and 1.6 litre models

2 Remove the air cleaner assembly as described in Section 2.
3 Where fitted, disconnect the accelerator inner cable from the throttle cam, then withdraw the outer cable from the mounting bracket, along with its rubber washer and spring clip.
4 Depress the retaining clip and disconnect the wiring connector(s) from the throttle housing assembly, inlet air temperature sensor and, where necessary, from the electric heating element, and/or the stepper motor (as applicable) **(see illustration)**.
5 Slacken and remove the retaining screws, and remove the throttle housing from the inlet manifold **(see illustrations)**. Recover the O-ring from manifold (where fitted) and discard it; a new one must be used when refitting.

1.8 and 2.0 litre models

6 Remove the air cleaner-to-throttle housing duct as described in Section 2.
7 On 1.8 litre 8-valve models, carefully lever the accelerator linkage rod off its throttle housing balljoint.
8 On all other models, where fitted, disconnect the accelerator inner cable from the throttle cam, then withdraw the outer cable from the mounting bracket along with its flat washer and spring clip. Where necessary, also disconnect the kickdown cable as described in Chapter 7B.
9 Depress the retaining clips, and disconnect the wiring connectors from the throttle housing assembly, the electric heating element, the inlet air temperature sensor and idle control stepper motor (as applicable).
10 Release the retaining clips (where fitted), and disconnect all the relevant vacuum and breather hoses from the throttle housing. Make identification marks on the hoses, to

ensure they are connected correctly on refitting.
11 Where necessary, undo the bolts or screws and release the accelerator cable bracket and housing support bracket.
12 Slacken and remove the three retaining screws, and remove the throttle housing from the inlet manifold. Remove the O-ring from the manifold, and discard it – a new one must be used on refitting.

Refitting

13 Refitting is a reversal of the removal procedure, noting the following points:
a) Fit a new O-ring to the manifold, then refit the throttle housing and securely tighten its retaining nuts or screws (as applicable).
b) Ensure all hoses are correctly reconnected and, where necessary, are securely held in position by the retaining clips.
c) Ensure all wiring is correctly routed, and that the connectors are securely reconnected.
d) On completion, adjust the accelerator cable as described in Section 3 and, where necessary, the kickdown cable as described in Chapter 7B.

13 Bosch and Sagem system components – removal and refitting

1.4 and 1.6 litre models

Fuel rail and injectors

Note: *Refer to the warning note in Section 1 before proceeding.*

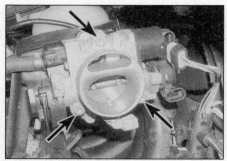

12.5a Undo the three retaining screws (arrowed) . . .

12.5b . . . then remove the throttle housing from the manifold and recover the sealing ring (arrowed) – 1.4 litre models

13.4a On early 1.6 litre models, unscrew the retaining nut . . .

13.4b . . . and remove the bolt securing the wiring/hose retaining clip to the fuel rail

13.5 Release the clips (arrowed) and detach the fuel feed and return hoses from the fuel rail – early 1.6 litre models

Note: *If a faulty injector is suspected, before condemning the injector, it is worth trying the effect of one of the proprietary injector-cleaning treatments which are available from car accessory shops.*

1 Disconnect the battery negative terminal (refer to *Disconnecting the battery* in the Reference Chapter).

2 Remove the air cleaner assembly as described in Section 2.

3 On later models with the ignition HT coil module mounted above the fuel rail, remove the coil module as described in Chapter 5B.

4 On early models, disconnect the vacuum pipe from the fuel pressure regulator. On early 1.6 litre models, undo the retaining nut and bolt and release the wiring/hose support clip from the end of the fuel rail **(see illustrations)**.

5 Bearing in mind the information given in Section 7, disconnect the fuel feed and, on early models, the return hoses by slackening the retaining clips or disconnecting the quick-release fittings **(see illustration)**.

6 Where applicable, disconnect the accelerator cable from the throttle cam and release the outer cable from the mounting bracket. Undo the bolts and remove the accelerator cable mounting bracket from the manifold/cylinder head.

7 Depress the retaining tangs and disconnect the wiring connectors from the four injectors. Slacken and remove the fuel rail retaining bolts and nuts, then carefully ease the fuel rail and injector assembly out from the inlet manifold and remove it from the engine. Remove the O-rings from the end of each

injector and discard them; they must be renewed whenever they are disturbed.

8 Slide out the retaining clip(s) and remove the relevant injector(s) from the fuel rail **(see illustration)**. Remove the upper O-ring from each disturbed injector and discard; all disturbed O-rings must be renewed.

9 Refitting is a reversal of the removal procedure, noting the following points.
  a) Fit new O-rings to all disturbed injector unions.
  b) Apply a smear of engine oil to the O-rings to aid installation, then ease the injectors and fuel rail into position ensuring that none of the O-rings are displaced.
  c) On later models, refit the ignition coil module as described in Chapter 5B.
  d) On completion, start the engine and check for fuel leaks.

Fuel pressure regulator

Note: *Refer to the warning note in Section 1 before proceeding.*

Note: *The following procedure applies to models with the fuel pressure regulator mounted on the fuel rail. On later models, the regulator is an integral part of the fuel pump assembly and is not available separately.*

10 Disconnect the battery negative terminal (refer to *Disconnecting the battery* in the Reference Chapter).

11 Disconnect the vacuum pipe from the regulator. Note that on early models, access to the regulator is poor with the fuel rail in position, if necessary, remove the fuel rail as described earlier, then remove the regulator.

12 Bearing in mind the information given in Section 7, place a wad of rag over the regulator, to catch any fuel spray which may be released, then remove the retaining clip and ease the regulator out from the fuel rail.

13 Refitting is a reversal of the removal procedure. Examine the regulator seal for signs of damage or deterioration and renew if necessary.

Throttle potentiometer

14 Disconnect the battery negative terminal (refer to *Disconnecting the battery* in the Reference Chapter).

15 Depress the retaining clip and disconnect

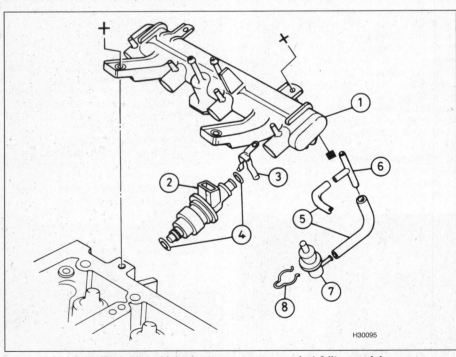

13.8 Fuel rail and injector components – early 1.6 litre models

1 *Fuel rail*	4 *O-ring seals*	7 *Fuel pressure regulator*
2 *Injector*	5 *Fuel hoses*	8 *Retaining clip*
3 *Retaining clip*	6 *T-piece*	

13.15 Disconnecting the throttle potentiometer wiring connector – 1.6 litre models

13.20a Lift the retaining clip . . .

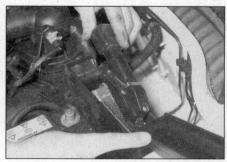

13.20b . . . and disconnect the wiring connector from the ECU

the wiring connector from the throttle potentiometer (**see illustration**).

16 Slacken and remove the two retaining screws, then disengage the potentiometer from the throttle valve spindle and remove it from the engine.

17 Refit in the reverse order of removal. Ensure that the potentiometer is correctly engaged with the throttle valve spindle.

Electronic control unit (ECU)

18 The ECU is located in the plastic box which is mounted onto the rear of the battery mounting tray.

19 Disconnect the battery negative terminal (refer to *Disconnecting the battery* in the Reference Chapter).

20 Unclip the cover from the box, then lift the retaining clip and disconnect the wiring connector from the ECU (**see illustrations**).

21 Undo the retaining nut and release the relay unit from the rear of the ECU box.

22 Undo the retaining screws and remove the ECU and box assembly from the battery tray. If necessary, undo the retaining screws and separate the ECU and box (**see illustration**).

23 Refitting is a reverse of the removal procedure ensuring the wiring connector is securely reconnected.

Idle speed auxiliary air valve

24 The auxiliary air valve is only fitted to 1.6 litre models with Bosch Motronic MP5.1 and MP5.2 systems. The valve is mounted on the underside of the inlet manifold (early models) or on the right-hand end of the inlet manifold casting (later models). On 1.4 litre models, and all other 1.6 litre models, idle speed regulation is via a stepper motor as described in the next sub-Section.

25 Disconnect the battery negative terminal (refer to *Disconnecting the battery* in the Reference Chapter).

26 Depress the retaining clip and disconnect the wiring connector.

27 Slacken the retaining clips and disconnect the air hose(s) from the end of the auxiliary air valve.

28 On early models, slide the valve out from its mounting bracket, and remove it from the engine compartment. On later models, undo

the securing screw and withdraw the valve from the manifold (**see illustration**).

29 Refitting is a reversal of the removal procedure. Examine the mounting rubber for signs of deterioration and renew it if necessary.

Idle speed stepper motor

30 The idle speed stepper motor is fitted to 1.4 litre models, and 1.6 litre models with Bosch Motronic MP7.2 and ME7.4.4 systems. The unit is located on the side of the throttle housing assembly.

31 Disconnect the battery negative terminal (refer to *Disconnecting the battery* in the Reference Chapter).

32 Release the retaining clip and disconnect the wiring connector from the motor (**see illustration**).

13.22 Undo the screws and remove the ECU and mounting box from the battery tray

13.32 Disconnect the wiring connector from the idle speed stepper motor (arrowed) . . .

33 Slacken and remove the two retaining screws, and withdraw the motor from the throttle housing (**see illustration**).

34 Refitting is a reversal of the removal procedure.

Manifold pressure sensor

35 On 1.4 litre models, the pressure sensor is mounted on the right-hand side of the inlet manifold. On early 1.6 litre models, the pressure sensor is situated remotely on the right-hand side of the engine compartment where it is mounted onto the wing valance. On later 1.6 litre models, the sensor is mounted directly on the front of the inlet manifold.

36 Disconnect the battery negative terminal (refer to *Disconnecting the battery* in the Reference Chapter).

37 On early 1.6 litre models, undo the

13.28 Idle speed auxiliary air valve securing screw (arrowed) – later 1.6 litre models

13.33 . . . then undo the retaining screws (arrowed) and remove the motor from the throttle housing – 1.4 litre models

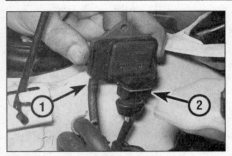

13.37 Disconnect the vacuum hose (1) and wiring connector (2) and remove the manifold pressure sensor from the engine compartment – early 1.6 litre models

13.38 Manifold pressure sensor securing screw (arrowed) – later 1.6 litre models

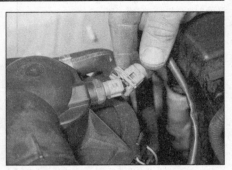

13.43 Disconnect the inlet air temperature sensor wiring connector – early 1.6 litre models

retaining nut, and free the sensor from its mounting bracket. Disconnect the wiring connector and vacuum hose and remove the sensor from the engine compartment **(see illustration)**.

38 On later models, remove the securing screw and with withdraw the sensor from the manifold **(see illustration)**. Disconnect the wiring connector, and remove the sensor from the engine.

39 Refitting is the reverse of the removal procedure.

Coolant temperature sensor

40 Refer to Chapter 3.

Inlet air temperature sensor

41 On early models, the inlet air temperature sensor is screwed into the air cleaner housing lid. On later models it is located on the underside of the throttle housing.

42 Disconnect the battery negative terminal (refer to *Disconnecting the battery* in the Reference Chapter).

43 Disconnect the wiring connector, then unscrew the sensor, or release the retaining clips and remove it from the vehicle **(see illustration)**.

44 Refitting is the reverse of removal.

Crankshaft sensor

45 The crankshaft sensor is situated on the front face of the transmission clutch housing.

46 Disconnect the battery negative terminal (refer to *Disconnecting the battery* in the Reference Chapter).

47 Trace the wiring back from the sensor to

the wiring connector and disconnect it from the main harness.

48 Prise out the rubber grommet, then undo the retaining bolt and withdraw the sensor from the transmission unit.

49 Refitting is reverse of the removal procedure ensuring the sensor retaining bolt is securely tightened and the grommet is correctly seated in the transmission housing.

Knock sensor

50 The knock sensor is screwed onto the front face of the cylinder block on 1.4 litre models, and onto the cylinder block rear face on 1.6 litre models.

51 Disconnect the battery negative terminal (refer to *Disconnecting the battery* in the Reference Chapter).

52 To gain access to the sensor, chock the rear wheels then jack up the front of the vehicle and support it on axle stands (see *Jacking and vehicle support*).

53 Trace the wiring back from the sensor to its wiring connector, and disconnect it from the main loom.

54 Slacken and remove the bolt securing the sensor to the cylinder block, and remove it from underneath the vehicle.

55 Refitting is a reversal of the removal procedure, ensuring that the sensor wiring is correctly routed and its retaining bolt is tightened securely.

Fuel injection system relay unit

56 The relay unit is mounted onto the rear of the ECU plastic box which is situated directly behind the battery.

57 Disconnect the battery negative terminal (refer to *Disconnecting the battery* in the Reference Chapter).

58 Undo the retaining nut, then disconnect the wiring connector and remove the relay unit from the vehicle **(see illustrations)**.

59 Refitting is the reverse of removal, ensuring that the relay unit is securely clipped in position.

Vehicle speed sensor

60 The vehicle speed sensor is an integral part of the speedometer drive housing. Refer to Chapter 7A or 7B, as applicable, for removal and refitting details.

1.8 and 2.0 litre 16-valve models

Fuel rail and injectors

Note: *Refer to the warning note in Section 1 before proceeding.*

Note: *If a faulty injector is suspected, before condemning the injector, it is worth trying the effect of one of the proprietary injector-cleaning treatments which are available from car accessory shops.*

61 Disconnect the battery negative terminal (refer to *Disconnecting the battery* in the Reference Chapter).

62 On early models, disconnect the vacuum pipe from the fuel pressure regulator.

63 Bearing in mind the information given in Section 7, slacken the retaining clips and disconnect the fuel feed and return hoses (as applicable) from the fuel rail and fuel pressure regulator **(see illustration)**. Where the original

13.58a Undo the retaining nut . . .

13.58b . . . and remove the relay unit from the vehicle

13.63 Disconnect the fuel feed and return hoses from the fuel rail and fuel pressure regulator – 1.8 litre 16-valve models

13.64 Disconnect the wiring connectors from the fuel injectors – 1.8 litre 16-valve models

13.65a Slacken and remove the fuel rail retaining bolts . . .

13.65b . . . then carefully ease the fuel rail and injector assembly from the inlet manifold – 1.8 litre 16-valve models

crimped-type hose clips are still fitted, cut them and discard; use standard worm-type hose clips on refitting.

64 Disconnect the wiring harness connector along the front of the fuel rail then depress the retaining tangs and disconnect the wiring connectors from the four injectors **(see illustration)**.

65 Slacken and remove the fuel rail retaining bolts, then carefully ease the fuel rail and injector assembly out from the inlet manifold and remove it from the engine **(see illustrations)**. Remove the O-rings from the end of each injector and discard them; they must be renewed whenever they are disturbed.

66 Slide out the retaining clip(s) and remove the relevant injector(s) from the fuel rail. Remove the upper O-ring from each disturbed injector and discard; all disturbed O-rings must be renewed.

67 Refitting is a reversal of the removal procedure, noting the following points.

a) *Fit new O-rings to all disturbed injector unions **(see illustration)**.*
b) *Apply a smear of engine oil to the O-rings to aid installation, then ease the injectors and fuel rail into position ensuring that none of the O-rings are displaced.*
c) *On completion, start the engine and check for fuel leaks.*

Fuel pressure regulator

Note: *Refer to the warning note in Section 1 before proceeding.*

Note: *The following procedure applies to models with the fuel pressure regulator mounted on the fuel rail. On later models, the regulator is an integral part of the fuel pump assembly and is not available separately.*

68 Disconnect the battery negative terminal (refer to *Disconnecting the battery* in the Reference Chapter).

69 Bearing in mind the information given in Section 7, slacken the retaining clips and disconnect the fuel feed and return hoses from the fuel rail and pressure regulator.

70 Disconnect the vacuum pipe from the regulator **(see illustration)**.

71 Place some rags under the regulator, to catch any spilt fuel. Remove the retaining clip and ease the regulator out from the fuel rail **(see illustrations)**.

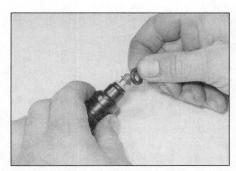

13.67 Fit new O-rings to the injectors before refitting – 1.8 litre 16-valve models

72 Refitting is a reversal of the removal procedure. Examine the regulator seal for signs of damage or deterioration and renew if necessary.

Throttle potentiometer

73 Disconnect the battery negative terminal (refer to *Disconnecting the battery* in the Reference Chapter).

74 Depress the retaining clip and disconnect the wiring connector from the throttle potentiometer located beneath the throttle housing.

75 Slacken and remove the two retaining screws, then disengage the potentiometer from the throttle valve spindle and remove it from the vehicle.

76 Refit in the reverse order of removal. Ensure that the potentiometer is correctly engaged with the throttle valve spindle.

13.71a Remove the retaining clip . . .

13.70 Disconnect the vacuum pipe from the regulator – 1.8 litre 16-valve models

Electronic control unit (ECU)

77 Refer to paragraphs 18 to 23.

Idle speed stepper motor

78 The idle speed control stepper motor is located on the side of the throttle housing assembly.

79 Disconnect the battery negative terminal (refer to *Disconnecting the battery* in the Reference Chapter).

80 Release the retaining clip, and disconnect the wiring connector from the motor.

81 Slacken and remove the two retaining screws, and withdraw the motor from the throttle housing.

82 Refitting is a reversal of the removal procedure.

13.71b . . . and ease the regulator from the fuel rail. Check the sealing ring condition (arrowed) before refitting – 1.8 litre 16-valve models

Manifold pressure sensor

83 The pressure sensor is situated on the underside of the inlet manifold.

84 Disconnect the battery negative terminal (refer to *Disconnecting the battery* in the Reference Chapter).

85 Disconnect the wiring connector from the sensor.

86 Undo the securing screw, then pull the sensor out of the manifold.

87 Refitting is the reverse of the removal procedure.

Coolant temperature sensor

88 Refer to Chapter 3.

Inlet air temperature sensor

89 The inlet air temperature sensor is located in the throttle housing.

90 Disconnect the battery negative terminal (refer to *Disconnecting the battery* in the Reference Chapter).

91 Loosen the retaining clip, and release the air inlet duct from the throttle housing. The inlet air temperature sensor is visible in the top of the housing.

92 Trace the wiring back from the sensor to its wiring connector on the throttle housing, and unplug the connector.

93 The sensor itself can be pressed out of the throttle housing. Note that it is sealed in place with sealant, to prevent air leaks; a suitable sealant will be required for refitting.

94 Refitting is the reverse of removal.

Crankshaft sensor

95 Refer to paragraphs 45 to 49.

Knock sensor

96 The knock sensor is screwed onto the rear face of the cylinder block.

97 Disconnect the battery negative terminal (refer to *Disconnecting the battery* in the Reference Chapter).

98 To gain access to the sensor, chock the rear wheels then jack up the front of the vehicle and support it on axle stands (see *Jacking and vehicle support*).

99 Trace the wiring back from the sensor to its wiring connector, and disconnect it from the main loom.

100 Slacken and remove the bolt securing the sensor to the cylinder block, and remove it from underneath the vehicle.

101 Refitting is a reversal of the removal procedure, ensuring that the sensor wiring is correctly routed and its retaining bolt is tightened securely.

Vehicle speed sensor

102 The vehicle speed sensor is an integral part of the speedometer drive housing. Refer to Chapter 7 Part A or B, as applicable, for removal and refitting details.

---

14 Magneti Marelli system components – removal and refitting

1.4 litre models

Fuel rail and injectors

1 Refer to the information given in Section 13, paragraphs 1 to 9.

Fuel pressure regulator

2 Refer to the information given in Section 13, paragraphs 10 to 13.

Throttle potentiometer

3 Refer to the information given in Section 13, paragraphs 14 to 17.

Electronic control unit (ECU)

4 Refer to the information given in Section 13, paragraphs 18 to 23.

Idle speed control stepper motor

5 The idle speed control stepper motor is located on the side of the throttle housing assembly.

6 Disconnect the battery negative terminal (refer to *Disconnecting the battery* in the Reference Chapter).

7 Release the retaining clip, and disconnect the wiring connector from the motor **(see illustration)**.

8 Slacken and remove the two retaining screws, and withdraw the motor from the throttle housing **(see illustration)**.

9 Refitting is a reversal of the removal procedure.

Manifold pressure sensor

10 On early models, the sensor is mounted on a bracket on the bulkhead at the rear of the engine compartment bulkhead. On later models, the sensor is mounted directly on the inlet manifold casting.

11 Disconnect the battery negative terminal (refer to *Disconnecting the battery* in the Reference Chapter).

12 Release the locking tab and unplug the wiring from the sensor connector.

13 On early models, disconnect the vacuum hose, then remove the screws and withdraw the sensor from the mounting bracket. On later models, remove the securing screws and withdraw the sensor from the manifold, recovering the sealing ring.

14 Refitting is a reversal of removal.

Coolant temperature sensor

15 Refer to Chapter 3.

Inlet air temperature sensor

16 The sensor is threaded into the underside of the throttle housing.

17 Disconnect the battery negative terminal (refer to *Disconnecting the battery* in the Reference Chapter).

18 Unplug the wiring from the sensor connector, then unscrew the sensor and remove it from the vehicle. Recover the sealing ring, where applicable.

19 Refitting is the reverse of removal.

Crankshaft sensor

20 Refer to the information given in Section 13, paragraphs 45 to 49.

Knock sensor

21 Refer to the information given in Section 13, paragraphs 50 to 55.

Fuel injection system relay unit

22 Refer to the information given in Section 13, paragraphs 56 to 59.

Throttle housing heating element

23 The throttle housing heating element is fitted to the side of the throttle housing.

24 Disconnect the battery negative terminal (refer to *Disconnecting the battery* in the Reference Chapter).

25 To improve access, disconnect the accelerator inner cable from the throttle cam, then withdraw the outer cable from the mounting bracket, along with its flat washer and spring clip.

26 Disconnect the element wiring connector, then undo the retaining screw, and free the wiring connector from the throttle housing.

27 Undo the screws securing the accelerator cable bracket to the side of the throttle housing. Carefully remove the bracket, and recover the spring from the top of the heating element.

28 Ease the heating element out from the throttle housing. Examine the O-ring for signs of damage or deterioration, and renew if necessary.

29 Refitting is a reversal of the removal procedure; where necessary, use a new O-ring.

14.7 Disconnect the wiring connector from the idle speed stepper motor . . .

14.8 . . . then remove the two screws and withdraw the motor from the throttle housing – 1.4 litre models

Vehicle speed sensor

30 The vehicle speed sensor is an integral part of the speedometer drive housing. Refer to Chapter 7A or 7B, as applicable, for removal and refitting details.

1.8 litre 8-valve models

Fuel injectors

Note: *Refer to the warning note in Section 1 before proceeding.*

Note: *If a faulty injector is suspected, before condemning the injector, it is worth trying the effect of one of the proprietary injector-cleaning treatments which are available from car accessory shops.*

31 Disconnect the battery negative terminal (refer to *Disconnecting the battery* in the Reference Chapter).

32 Remove the air cleaner-to-throttle housing duct as described in Section 2.

33 Undo the two bolts securing the wiring tray to the top of the manifold, and position the tray clear of the injectors.

34 Depress the retaining clip(s) and disconnect the wiring connector(s) from the injector(s).

35 Slacken the retaining screw and remove the injector retaining plate; Nos 1 and 2 injectors are retained by one plate, Nos 3 and 4 by another.

36 Place a wad of clean rag over the injector, to catch any fuel spray which may be released, then carefully ease the relevant injector(s) out of the manifold. Remove the O-rings from the end of each disturbed injector, and discard them – these must be renewed whenever they are disturbed.

37 On refitting the injectors, fit new O-rings to the end of each injector. Apply a smear of engine oil to the O-ring, to aid installation, then ease the injector(s) back into position in the manifold.

38 Ensure each injector connector is correctly positioned, then refit the retaining plate and securely tighten its retaining screw. Reconnect the wiring connector(s) to the injector(s).

39 Refit the wiring tray to the top of the manifold and securely tighten its retaining bolts.

40 Refit the air cleaner-to-throttle body duct and reconnect the battery. Start the engine and check the injectors for signs of leakage.

Fuel pressure regulator

41 Refer to the information given in Section 13, paragraphs 10 to 13.

Throttle potentiometer

42 The throttle potentiometer is fitted to the right-hand side of the throttle housing.

43 Disconnect the battery negative terminal (refer to *Disconnecting the battery* in the Reference Chapter).

44 Depress the retaining clip and disconnect the potentiometer wiring connector. Slacken and remove the two retaining screws, and remove the potentiometer from the throttle housing.

45 Refitting is the reverse of removal, ensuring that the potentiometer is correctly engaged with the throttle valve spindle.

Electronic control unit (ECU)

46 Refer to the information given in Section 13, paragraphs 18 to 23.

Idle speed control stepper motor

47 The idle speed control stepper motor is located on the front of the throttle housing assembly.

48 Disconnect the battery negative terminal (refer to *Disconnecting the battery* in the Reference Chapter).

49 Release the retaining clip and disconnect the wiring connector from the motor. Slacken and remove the two retaining screws, and withdraw the motor from the throttle housing.

50 Refitting is a reversal of the removal procedure.

Manifold pressure sensor

51 Refer to the information given in paragraphs 10 to 14 of this Section.

Coolant temperature sensor

52 Refer to Chapter 3.

Inlet air temperature sensor

53 The inlet air temperature sensor is located in the throttle housing.

54 To remove the sensor, first remove the throttle potentiometer as described in paragraphs 42 to 45.

55 Depress the retaining clip and disconnect the wiring connector from the air temperature sensor.

56 Remove the screw securing the sensor connector to the top of the throttle housing, then carefully ease the sensor out of position and remove it from the throttle housing. Examine the sensor O-ring for signs of damage or deterioration, and renew if necessary.

57 Refitting is a reversal of the removal procedure, using a new O-ring where necessary, and ensuring that the throttle potentiometer is correctly engaged with the throttle valve spindle.

Crankshaft sensor

58 Refer to the information given in Section 13, paragraphs 45 to 49.

Fuel injection system relay unit

59 Refer to the information given in Section 13, paragraphs 56 to 59.

Throttle housing heating element

60 The throttle housing heating element is fitted to the top of the throttle housing.

61 Disconnect the battery negative terminal (refer to *Disconnecting the battery* in the Reference Chapter). Depress the retaining tangs and disconnect the wiring connector from the heating element.

62 Undo the screw(s) securing the wiring connector to the throttle housing, then displace the connector and carefully withdraw the heating element from the throttle housing. Examine the element O-ring (where fitted) for signs of damage or deterioration, and renew if necessary.

63 Refitting is a reversal of the removal procedure, taking great care to ensure that the element wiring does not become trapped as the wiring connector bolt(s) are tightened.

Vehicle speed sensor

64 The vehicle speed sensor is an integral part of the transmission speedometer drive assembly. Refer to Chapter 7A or 7B for removal and refitting details.

2.0 litre 8-valve models

Fuel rail and injectors

Note: *Refer to the warning note in Section 1 before proceeding.*

Note: *If a faulty injector is suspected, before condemning the injector, it is worth trying the effect of one of the proprietary injector-cleaning treatments which are available from car accessory shops.*

65 Disconnect the battery negative terminal (refer to *Disconnecting the battery* in the Reference Chapter).

66 Remove the air cleaner-to-throttle housing duct, using the information given in Section 2.

67 Disconnect the vacuum pipe from the fuel pressure regulator.

68 Release the retaining clip and free the various hoses from the top of the fuel rail.

69 Bearing in mind the information given in Section 7, slacken the retaining clip, and disconnect the fuel feed and return hoses from the ends of the fuel rail. Where the original crimped-type Peugeot hose clips are still fitted, cut them off and discard them; use standard worm-drive hose clips on refitting.

70 Depress the retaining clips and disconnect the wiring connectors from the four injectors.

71 Slacken and remove the three fuel rail retaining bolts, then carefully ease the fuel rail and injector assembly out from the inlet manifold, and remove it from the vehicle. Remove the O-rings from the end of each injector and discard them; these must be renewed whenever they are disturbed.

72 Slide out the retaining clip(s) and remove the relevant injector(s) from the fuel rail. Remove the upper O-ring from each injector as it is removed, and discard it; all O-rings must be renewed once they have been disturbed.

73 Refitting is a reversal of the removal procedure, noting the following points:

a) Fit new O-rings to all disturbed injectors.

b) Apply a smear of engine oil to the O-rings to aid installation, then ease the injectors and fuel rail into position, ensuring that none of the O-rings are displaced.

c) On completion, start the engine and check for fuel leaks.

14.74 Fuel pressure regulator – 2.0 litre 8-valve models

14.80 Disconnecting the wiring connector from the idle speed control stepper motor – 2.0 litre 8-valve models

14.93 Disconnect the throttle housing heating element wiring connector – 2.0 litre 8-valve models

Fuel pressure regulator

74 Refer to the information given in Section 13, paragraphs 10 to 13 **(see illustration)**.

Throttle potentiometer

75 Remove the throttle housing as described in Section 12.

76 Undo the two retaining screws and remove the potentiometer from the base of the throttle housing.

77 On refitting, ensure that the potentiometer is correctly engaged with the throttle valve spindle, and securely tighten its retaining screws.

78 Refit the throttle housing as described in Section 12.

Electronic control unit (ECU)

79 Refer to the information given in Section 13, paragraphs 18 to 23.

Idle speed control stepper motor

80 Refer to the information given in paragraphs 47 to 50 of this Section **(see illustration)**.

Manifold pressure sensor

81 The manifold pressure sensor is situated on the right-hand side of the engine compartment, mounted on the front suspension mounting turret.

82 Disconnect the battery negative terminal (refer to *Disconnecting the battery* in the Reference Chapter).

83 Undo the three retaining nuts and free the sensor from the underside of the mounting bracket. Depress the retaining clip, disconnect the wiring connector and vacuum hose from the sensor, and remove the sensor from the engine compartment.

84 Refitting is a reversal of the removal procedure.

Coolant temperature sensor

85 Refer to Chapter 3.

Inlet air temperature sensor

86 The inlet air temperature sensor is located in the base of the throttle housing.

87 To remove the sensor, first remove the throttle housing as described in Section 12, then undo the two retaining screws and remove the throttle potentiometer from the base of the housing.

88 Trace the wiring back from the sensor to its wiring connector, and remove the screw securing the connector to the throttle housing.

89 Carefully ease the sensor out of position, and remove it from the throttle housing. Examine the sensor O-ring for signs of damage or deterioration, and renew if necessary.

90 Refitting is a reversal of the removal procedure, using a new O-ring where necessary.

Crankshaft sensor

91 Refer to the information given in Section 13, paragraphs 45 to 49.

Fuel injection system relay unit

92 Refer to the information given in Section 13, paragraphs 56 to 59.

Throttle housing heating element

93 Refer to the information given in paragraphs 60 to 63 of this Section **(see illustration)**.

Vehicle speed sensor

94 The vehicle speed sensor is an integral part of the transmission speedometer drive assembly. Refer to Chapter 7A or 7B for removal and refitting details.

Knock sensor

95 The knock sensor is screwed onto the rear face of the cylinder block.

96 Firmly apply the handbrake, then jack up the front of the car and support it securely on axle stands (see *Jacking and vehicle support*). Access to the sensor can then be gained from underneath the vehicle.

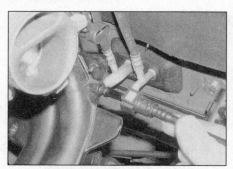

15.5a Disconnect the braking system servo vacuum pipe . . .

97 Trace the wiring back from the sensor to its wiring connector, and disconnect it from the main loom.

98 Slacken and remove the bolt securing the sensor to the cylinder block, and remove it from underneath the vehicle.

99 Refitting is a reversal of the removal procedure, ensuring that the sensor wiring is correctly routed and its retaining bolt securely tightened.

15 Inlet manifold – removal and refitting

Removal

1 Disconnect the battery negative terminal (refer to *Disconnecting the battery* in the Reference Chapter) then proceed as described under the relevant sub-heading.

1.4 and 1.6 litre models

2 Remove the air cleaner assembly as described in Section 2.

3 Remove the fuel rail and injectors as described in Section 13.

4 If not already having done so, disconnect the wiring connectors from the throttle housing components then unclip the harness and position it clear of the manifold.

5 Release the retaining clips and disconnect the vacuum servo unit pipe and purge valve pipe from the inlet manifold **(see illustrations)**.

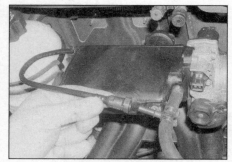

15.5b . . . and the purge valve pipe from the inlet manifold – 1.4 litre models

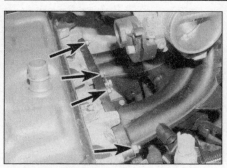

15.9a Unscrew the retaining nuts (upper nuts arrowed) . . .

15.9b . . . then manoeuvre the inlet manifold assembly out of position – 1.4 litre models

15.25 Disconnecting the inlet manifold breather hoses from the cylinder head cover – 1.8 litre 16-valve models

6 Disconnect the wiring connector from the manifold pressure sensor and unclip the wiring from the manifold.

7 Unclip the fuel pipe and position it clear of the manifold.

8 Where necessary, undo the retaining bolts and remove the support bracket from the underside of the manifold.

9 Undo the manifold retaining nuts and withdraw the manifold from the engine compartment. Recover the four manifold seals and discard them; new ones must be used on refitting **(see illustrations)**.

1.8 litre 8-valve models

10 Remove the air cleaner-to-throttle housing duct as described in Section 2.

11 Disconnect the accelerator inner cable from the throttle cam, then withdraw the outer cable from the mounting bracket along with its flat washer and spring clip. Where necessary, also disconnect the kickdown cable as described in Chapter 7B.

12 Undo the two bolts securing the wiring tray to the top of the manifold, and position the tray, and its associated wiring and hoses, clear of the manifold so that it does not hinder removal.

13 Depress the retaining clips and disconnect the wiring connectors from the four fuel injectors. Also disconnect the wiring connectors from the throttle potentiometer, stepper motor and inlet air temperature sensor.

14 Bearing in mind the information given in

Section 7, slacken the retaining clips and disconnect the fuel feed and return hoses from either side of the manifold. Where the original crimped-type Peugeot hose clips are still fitted, cut them off and discard them; use standard worm-drive hose clips on refitting.

15 Slacken the retaining clip(s) and disconnect the braking system vacuum servo unit hose, and all the relevant vacuum/breather hoses, from the top of the manifold. Where necessary, make identification marks on the hoses, to ensure they are correctly reconnected on refitting.

16 Undo the manifold retaining nuts and withdraw the manifold from the engine compartment. Recover the two manifold seals and discard them – new ones must be used on refitting.

2.0 litre 8-valve models

17 Carry out the operations described above in paragraphs 10 and 11.

18 Depress the retaining clips and disconnect the wiring connectors from the four fuel injectors.

19 Bearing in mind the information given in Section 7, slacken the retaining clips and disconnect the fuel feed and return hoses from either end of the fuel rail. Where the original crimped-type Peugeot hose clips are still fitted, cut them off and discard them; use standard worm-drive hose clips on refitting.

20 Slacken the retaining clip(s) and disconnect the braking system vacuum servo unit hose, and all the relevant

vacuum/breather hoses, from the manifold. Where necessary, make identification marks on the hoses, to ensure they are correctly reconnected on refitting.

21 Release the retaining clip and free all the disconnected hoses from the clip on the top of the fuel rail.

22 Slacken and remove the bolt securing the dipstick tube to the side of the manifold.

23 Undo the six nuts and bolts securing the manifold to the cylinder head, and remove the manifold from the engine compartment. Recover the manifold seals and discard them – new ones must be used on refitting.

1.8 and 2.0 litre 16-valve models

24 Remove the throttle housing as described in Section 12 and the fuel rail and injectors as described in Section 13.

25 Slacken the retaining clip(s), and disconnect the braking system vacuum servo unit hose, and all the relevant vacuum/breather hoses, from the manifold **(see illustration)**. Where necessary, make identification marks on the hoses, to ensure that they are correctly reconnected on refitting.

26 Where applicable, slacken and remove the bolt securing the dipstick tube to the side of the manifold **(see illustration)**.

27 Release the wiring loom from the retaining clips and brackets at the rear and at the timing belt end of the engine **(see illustrations)**.

28 Undo the nuts and bolts securing the

15.26 Slacken and remove the bolt securing the dipstick tube to the rear of the manifold – 1.8 litre 16-valve models

15.27a Unclip the wiring harness from the bracket at the rear of the manifold . . .

15.27b . . . and from the timing belt end of the manifold – 1.8 litre 16-valve models

15.28a Withdraw the inlet manifold . . .

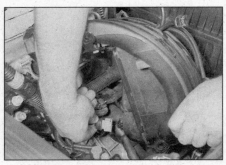

15.28b . . . and disconnect the manifold pressure sensor wiring connector – 1.8 litre 16-valve models

manifold to the cylinder head, and move the manifold away from the engine. As it is withdrawn, disconnect the wiring connector from the pressure sensor on the base of the manifold **(see illustrations)**. Remove the manifold from the engine compartment.

29 Recover the manifold gasket/seals, and discard them – new ones must be used on refitting.

Refitting

30 Refitting is a reverse of the relevant removal procedure, noting the following points:

a) *Ensure that the manifold and cylinder head mating surfaces are clean and dry, then locate the new seals in their recesses in the manifold. Refit the manifold and tighten its retaining nuts and bolts to the specified torque.*

b) *Ensure that all relevant hoses are reconnected to their original positions and are securely held (where necessary) by the retaining clips.*

c) *Adjust the accelerator cable as described in Section 3 then, where necessary, adjust the kickdown cable as described in Chapter 7B.*

---

16 Exhaust manifold – removal and refitting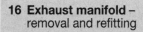

Removal

1.4 and 1.6 litre models

1 Disconnect the battery negative terminal (refer to *Disconnecting the battery* in the Reference Chapter).

2 Firmly apply the handbrake, then jack up the front of the vehicle and support it on axle stands (see *Jacking and vehicle support*). Release the screws and remove the engine undershield (where fitted).

3 Trace the lambda (oxygen) sensor(s) wiring back to the connectors and disconnect them.

4 Slacken and remove the retaining screws and remove the shroud from the top of the exhaust manifold. It may be necessary to remove the engine lifting eye bracket from the left-hand end of the cylinder head, and undo

the bolt and remove the oil dipstick tube. Feed the lambda sensor wiring through the hole in the top of the shroud as it is removed.

5 On some models, a second heat shield is fitted on the underside of the manifold, above the oil filter. Undo the bolts and remove the heat shield.

6 Undo the nuts securing the exhaust front pipe to the manifold, then remove the bolt securing the front pipe to its mounting bracket. Disconnect the front pipe from the manifold, and recover the gasket.

Caution: Do not place any strain on the flexible section of the exhaust front pipe (where fitted), it is easily damaged.

7 Undo the retaining nuts securing the manifold to the head. Manoeuvre the manifold out of the engine compartment, and discard the manifold gasket(s).

1.8 and 2.0 litre 8-valve models

8 Firmly apply the handbrake, then jack up the front of the vehicle and support it on axle stands (see *Jacking and vehicle support*).

9 Undo the two nuts securing the front pipe to the manifold. Recover the springs and spring cups, and withdraw the bolts, then disconnect the front pipe from the manifold, and recover the gasket.

10 Undo the eight retaining nuts securing the manifold to the head. Manoeuvre the manifold out of the engine compartment, complete with the gasket.

11 Undo the two retaining bolts and separate the manifold and gasket, noting the spacers which are fitted between the gasket and manifold.

1.8 and 2.0 litre 16-valve models

12 Disconnect the hot-air inlet hose from the manifold shroud and remove it from the vehicle.

13 Slacken and remove the three retaining screws, and remove the shroud from the top of the exhaust manifold.

14 Firmly apply the handbrake, then jack up the front of the vehicle and support it on axle stands (see *Jacking and vehicle support*).

15 Where necessary, disconnect the wiring from the lambda (oxygen) sensor. Alternatively, support the exhaust front pipe, to avoid any strain being placed on the sensor wiring.

16 Undo the nuts securing the exhaust front pipe to the manifold and recover the springs. Where applicable, remove the bolt securing the front pipe to its mounting bracket. Disconnect the front pipe from the manifold, and recover the gasket.

17 Undo the retaining nuts securing the manifold to the cylinder head. Manoeuvre the manifold out of the engine compartment, and discard the manifold gaskets.

Refitting

18 Refitting is the reverse of the removal procedure, noting the following points:

a) *Examine all the exhaust manifold studs for signs of damage and corrosion; remove all traces of corrosion, and repair or renew any damaged studs.*

b) *Ensure that the manifold and cylinder head sealing faces are clean and flat, and fit the new manifold gasket(s). Tighten the manifold retaining nuts to the specified torque.*

c) *Reconnect the front pipe to the manifold, using the information given in Section 17.*

---

17 Exhaust system – general information, removal and refitting

General information

1 On early 1.4 and 1.6 litre models, the exhaust system consists of four sections; the front pipe, the catalytic converter, the centre silencer, and the tailpipe and main silencer box. All exhaust sections are joined by a flanged joint. The front pipe joints are secured by nuts and bolts, the catalytic converter joint being of the spring-loaded ball type, to allow for movement in the exhaust system. The catalytic converter-to-intermediate pipe joint and the intermediate pipe-to-silencer joint are secured by a clamping ring.

2 On later 1.4 and 1.6 litre models, the exhaust system consists three sections; the front pipe with integral catalytic converter, the intermediate pipe, and rear silencer with tailpipe. The front pipe and intermediate pipe sections are joined by flanged joints. All other joints are secured by clamping rings.

3 On 1.8 and 2.0 litre models, the exhaust system consists of three sections; the front pipe/catalytic converter, the intermediate pipe and centre silencer and the tailpipe and main silencer. The front pipe-to-manifold joint is of the spring-loaded ball type, to allow for movement in the exhaust system and all other joints are secured by a clamping ring.

4 The system is suspended throughout its entire length by rubber mountings.

Removal – 1.4 and 1.6 litre models

5 Each exhaust section can be removed individually, or alternatively, the complete system can be removed as a unit. Even if only one part of the system needs attention, it is often easier to remove the whole system and separate the sections on the bench.

6 To remove the system or part of the system, first jack up the front or rear of the car and support it on axle stands (see *Jacking and vehicle support*). Alternatively, position the car over an inspection pit or on car ramps.

Front pipe

Note: *On later models, the catalytic converter is integral with the front pipe.*

7 Trace the wiring back from the lambda sensor to its wiring connectors, which are clipped to the transmission housing, and disconnect them from the main harness.

8 Undo the nuts securing the front pipe flange joint to the manifold, and the single bolt securing the front pipe to its mounting bracket. Separate the flange joint and collect the gasket.

9 Slacken and remove the two nuts securing the front pipe flange joint to the catalytic converter, and recover the spring cups and springs. Remove the bolts, then withdraw the front pipe from underneath the vehicle, and recover the wire-mesh gasket.

Catalytic converter

Note: *On later models, the catalytic converter is integral with the front pipe.*

10 Later 1.4 litre models have a second lambda sensor located 'downstream' of the catalytic converter. On models so equipped, trace the wiring back from the lambda sensor to its wiring connectors, and disconnect them from the main harness.

11 Undo the two nuts securing the front pipe flange joint to the catalytic converter. Recover the springs and spring cups, and withdraw the bolts.

12 Slacken the catalytic converter clamping ring bolts and disengage the clamp from the flange joint.

13 Free the converter, then withdraw it from underneath the vehicle, and recover the wire-mesh gasket from the front pipe joint.

Intermediate pipe

14 Slacken the clamping ring bolts and disengage the clamps from the front and rear flange joints.

15 Unhook the intermediate pipe from its mounting rubber and remove it from underneath the vehicle.

Tailpipe

16 Slacken the tailpipe clamping ring bolts

and disengage the clamp from the flange joint.

17 Unhook the tailpipe from its mounting rubbers and remove it from the vehicle.

Complete system

18 Disconnect the lambda sensor wiring connectors from the main wiring harness.

19 Undo the nuts securing the front pipe flange joint to the manifold, and the single bolt securing the front pipe to its mounting bracket. Separate the flange joint and collect the gasket. Free the system from all its mounting rubbers and lower it from under the vehicle.

Heat shield(s)

20 The heat shields are secured to the underside of the body by various nuts and bolts. Each shield can be removed once the relevant exhaust section has been removed. If a shield is being removed to gain access to a component located behind it, it may prove sufficient in some cases to remove the retaining nuts and/or bolts, and simply lower the shield, without disturbing the exhaust system.

Removal – 1.8 and 2.0 litre models

21 Each exhaust section can be removed individually, or alternatively, the complete system can be removed as a unit. Even if only one part of the system needs attention, it is often easier to remove the whole system and separate the sections on the bench.

22 To remove the system or part of the system, first jack up the front or rear of the car and support it on axle stands (see *Jacking and vehicle support*). Alternatively, position the car over an inspection pit or on car ramps.

Front pipe/catalytic converter

23 Trace the wiring back from the lambda sensor to its wiring connectors, which are clipped to the transmission housing, and disconnect them from the main harness.

24 Slacken and remove the two nuts securing the front pipe flange joint to the manifold, and recover the spring cups and springs. Remove the bolts, separate the joint and recover the sealing ring.

25 Slacken the catalytic converter clamping ring bolts and disengage the clamp from the flange joint. Withdraw the front pipe/catalytic converter from underneath the vehicle.

Intermediate pipe

26 Slacken the clamping ring bolts and

disengage the clamps from the front and rear flange joints.

27 Unhook the intermediate pipe from its mounting rubber and remove it from underneath the vehicle.

Tailpipe

28 Slacken the tailpipe clamping ring bolts and disengage the clamp from the flange joint.

29 Unhook the tailpipe from its mounting rubbers and remove it from the vehicle.

Complete system

30 Disconnect the lambda sensor wiring connectors from the main wiring harness.

31 Slacken and remove the two nuts securing the front pipe flange joint to the manifold, and recover the spring cups and springs. Remove the bolts, separate the joint and recover the sealing ring.

32 Free the system from all its mounting rubbers and lower it from under the vehicle.

Heat shield(s)

33 Refer to paragraph 20.

Refitting – all models

34 Each section is refitted by reversing the removal sequence, noting the following points:

a) *Ensure that all traces of corrosion have been removed from the flanges and renew all necessary gaskets.*

b) *Inspect the rubber mountings for signs of damage or deterioration, and renew as necessary.*

c) *Prior to assembling the spring-loaded joint, a smear of high-temperature grease should be applied to the joint mating surfaces.*

d) *Where joints are secured together by a clamping ring, apply a smear of exhaust system jointing paste to the flange joint, to ensure a gas-tight seal. Tighten the clamping ring nuts evenly and progressively, so that the clearance between the clamp halves remains equal on either side.*

e) *Prior to tightening the exhaust system fasteners, ensure that all rubber mountings are correctly located, and that there is adequate clearance between the exhaust system and vehicle underbody.*

f) *Ensure that the lambda sensor wiring is reconnected correctly and secured to the underbody by the relevant retaining clips.*

Chapter 4 Part D:
Fuel/exhaust systems - 1.8 and 1.9 litre XUD diesel models

Contents

Degrees of difficulty

Easy, suitable for novice with little experience	**Fairly easy,** suitable for beginner with some experience	**Fairly difficult,** suitable for competent DIY mechanic	**Difficult,** suitable for experienced DIY mechanic	**Very difficult,** suitable for expert DIY or professional

Specifications

General
System type . . . . Rear-mounted fuel tank, distributor fuel injection pump with integral transfer pump, indirect injection. Turbocharger and intercooler on some engines

Firing order . . . . 1-3-4-2 (No 1 at flywheel end)

Fast idle speed
Fast idle speed . . . . 950 ± 50 rpm

Maximum speed
1.8 litre and 1.9 litre non-turbo engines . . . . 5150 ± 125 rpm
1.9 litre Turbo engines . . . . 5100 ± 80 rpm

Injection pump (Lucas)
Direction of rotation . . . . Clockwise, viewed from sprocket end
Static timing:
    Engine position . . . . No 4 piston at TDC
    Pump position . . . . Value shown on pump - see text
Dynamic timing (at idle speed) . . . . 12° ± 1°

Injection pump (Bosch)

Direction of rotation .... Clockwise, viewed from sprocket end
Static timing:
  Engine position .... No 4 piston at TDC
  Pump timing measurement:*
    1.8 litre engine .... 0.90 ± 0.02 mm
    1.9 litre non-turbo engines:
      D9B engine .... 1.07 ± 0.02 mm
      DJZ engine .... 0.77 ± 0.02 mm
      DJY engine .... 0.90 ± 0.02 mm
    1.9 litre Turbo engines:
      D8A engine .... 0.66 ± 0.02 mm
      DHY engine .... 0.63 ± 0.02 mm
Dynamic timing (at idle speed):*
  1.8 litre engine .... 15° ± 1°
  1.9 litre non-turbo engines:
    D9B engine .... 18° ± 1°
    DJZ engine .... 12° ± 1°
    DJY engine .... No values available
  1.9 litre Turbo engines:
    D8A engine .... 11° ± 1°
    DHY engine .... 10.5° ± 1°

Injectors

Type .... Pintle
Opening pressure:*
  Models with Lucas CAV/Roto-Diesel fuel injection pump:
    Pre-April 1997 models .... 130 ± 5 bars
    April 1997 models onward:
      1.8 litre (A9A) engine .... 130 ± 10 bars
      1.9 litre Turbo (DHY) engine .... 150 ± 5 bars
  Models with Bosch fuel injection pump:
    Non-turbo models:
      Pre-April 1997 models .... 130 to 135 bars
      April 1997 models onward - 1.9 litre (DJY) engine .... 130 ± 10 bars
    Turbo models .... 175 to 180 bars
Refer to Chapter 2C for further information on engine code identification

Turbocharger

Type .... KKK K14, or Garrett T2
Boost pressure (approximate) .... 1 bar at 3000 rpm

Torque wrench settings

	Nm	lbf ft
Exhaust system:		
Manifold joint bolt nuts	10	7
Clamping ring nuts	20	15
Fuel pipe union nuts	20	15
Injection pump mounting nuts/bolts	20	15
Injection pump sprocket nut	50	37
Injection pump sprocket puller bolts	10	7
Injection pump timing hole blanking plug:		
Lucas pump	6	4
Bosch pump	15	11
Injectors to cylinder head	90	66
No 4 cylinder TDC blanking plug	30	22
Stop solenoid:		
Lucas pump	15	11
Bosch pump	20	15
Turbocharger mounting bolts	55	41
Turbocharger oil pipe unions	20	15

1.9a Hand-operated stop lever (arrowed) - Lucas pump

1.9b Hand-operated stop lever (arrowed) - Bosch pump

1 General information and precautions

General information

1 The fuel system consists of a rear-mounted fuel tank, a fuel filter with integral water separator, a fuel injection pump, injectors and associated components. Before passing through the filter, the fuel is heated by coolant flowing through the base of the fuel filter/thermostat housing. A turbocharger and intercooler are fitted to some models.

2 Fuel is drawn from the fuel tank to the fuel injection pump by a vane-type transfer pump incorporated in the fuel injection pump. Before reaching the pump, the fuel passes through a fuel filter, where foreign matter and water are removed. Excess fuel lubricates the moving components of the pump, and is then returned to the tank.

3 The fuel injection pump is driven at half-crankshaft speed by the timing belt. The high pressure required to inject the fuel into the compressed air in the swirl chambers is achieved by a cam plate acting on a single piston on the Bosch pump, or by two opposed pistons forced together by rollers running in a cam ring on the Lucas (CAV) pump. The fuel passes through a central rotor with a single outlet drilling which aligns with ports leading to the injector pipes.

4 Fuel metering is controlled by a centrifugal governor, which reacts to accelerator pedal position and engine speed. The governor is linked to a metering valve, which increases or decreases the amount of fuel delivered at each pumping stroke. On turbocharged models, a separate device also increases fuel delivery with increasing boost pressure.

5 Basic injection timing is determined when the pump is fitted. When the engine is running, it is varied automatically to suit the prevailing engine speed by a mechanism which turns the cam plate or ring.

6 The four fuel injectors produce a homogeneous spray of fuel into the swirl chambers located in the cylinder head. The injectors are calibrated to open and close at critical pressures to provide efficient and even combustion. Each injector needle is lubricated by fuel, which accumulates in the spring chamber and is channelled to the injection pump return hose by leak-off pipes.

7 Bosch or Lucas fuel system components may be fitted, depending on the model. Components from the latter manufacturer are marked either "CAV", "Roto-Diesel" or "Con-Diesel", depending on their date and place of manufacture. With the exception of the fuel filter assembly, replacement components must be of the same make as those originally fitted.

8 Cold starting is assisted by preheater or "glow" plugs fitted to each swirl chamber. A thermostatic sensor in the cooling system operates a fast idle lever on the injection pump to increase the idling speed when the engine is cold. On turbocharged models, the injection timing is advanced when the engine is cold by a coolant-fed capsule.

9 A stop solenoid cuts the fuel supply to the injection pump rotor when the ignition is switched off, and there is also a hand-operated stop lever for use in an emergency (see illustrations).

10 Provided that the specified maintenance is carried out, the fuel injection equipment will give long and trouble-free service. The injection pump itself may well outlast the engine. The main potential cause of damage to the injection pump and injectors is dirt or water in the fuel.

11 Servicing of the injection pump and injectors is very limited for the home mechanic, and any dismantling or adjustment other than that described in this Chapter must be entrusted to a Peugeot dealer or fuel injection specialist.

Precautions

 Warning: It is necessary to take certain precautions when working on the fuel system components, particularly the fuel injectors. Before carrying out any operations on the fuel system, refer to the precautions given in "Safety first!" at the beginning of this manual, and to any additional warning notes at the start of the relevant Sections.

2 Fuel system - priming and bleeding

1 After disconnecting part of the fuel supply system or running out of fuel, it is necessary to prime the system and bleed off any air which may have entered the system components.

2 All models are fitted with a hand-operated priming pump, consisting of a rubber bulb, which is located on the right-hand side of the engine compartment (see illustration).

3 An automatic bleed valve is fitted to certain engines, which bleeds the air from the low pressure circuit when it is primed. On engines without an automatic bleed valve, a bleed screw is fitted to the injection pump fuel inlet

2.2 Hand-operated fuel system priming pump

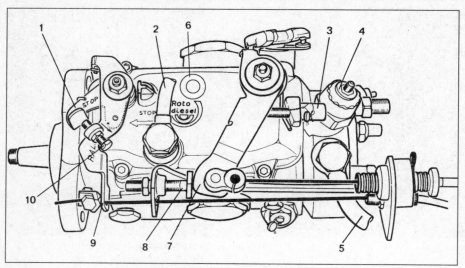

3.3a Lucas fuel injection pump adjustment points

1 Manual stop lever	4 Stop solenoid	8 Anti-stall adjustment screw
2 Fuel return pipe	5 Fuel inlet	9 Fast idle lever
3 Maximum speed adjustment screw	6 Timing access plug	10 Idle speed adjustment screw
	7 Control (accelerator) lever	

pipe union bolt. Where a bleed screw is fitted, slacken the screw half a turn.

4 Pump the priming pump until fuel free from air bubbles emerges from the bleed screw (where fitted), or until resistance is felt. Retighten the bleed screw.

5 Switch on the ignition (to activate the stop solenoid) and continue pumping the priming plunger until firm resistance is felt, then pump a few more times.

6 If a large amount of air has entered the pump, place a wad of rag around the fuel return union on the pump (to absorb spilt fuel), then slacken the union. Operate the priming plunger (with the ignition switched on to activate the stop solenoid), or crank the engine on the starter motor in 10 second bursts, until fuel free from air bubbles emerges from the fuel union. Tighten the union and mop up split fuel.

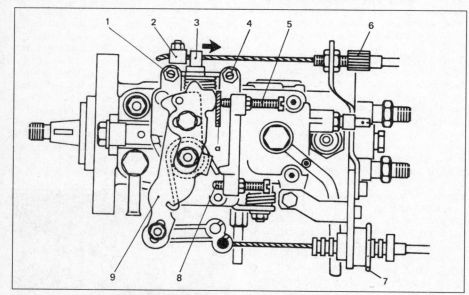

3.3b Bosch fuel injection pump adjustment points

1 Fast idle adjustment screw	5 Anti-stall adjustment screw	8 Maximum speed adjustment screw
2 Cable end fitting	6 Fast idle cable adjustment screw	9 Control (accelerator) lever
3 Fast idle lever	7 Accelerator cable adjustment grommet	a Shim for anti-stall adjustment
4 Idle speed adjustment screw		

 Warning: Be prepared to stop the engine if it should fire, to avoid excessive fuel spray and spillage.

7 If air has entered the injector pipes, place wads of rag around the injector pipe unions at the injectors (to absorb spilt fuel), then slacken the unions. Crank the engine on the starter motor until fuel emerges from the unions, then stop cranking the engine and retighten the unions. Mop up spilt fuel. *Refer to the warning given in the previous paragraph.*

8 Start the engine with the accelerator pedal fully depressed. Additional cranking may be necessary to finally bleed the system before the engine starts.

3 Maximum speed - checking and adjustment

Caution: The maximum speed adjustment screw is sealed by the manufacturers at the factory, using paint or a locking wire and a lead seal. There is no reason why it should require adjustment. Do not disturb the screw if the vehicle is still within the warranty period, otherwise the warranty will be invalidated. This adjustment requires the use of a tachometer suitable for use on diesel engines.

1 Run the engine to normal operating temperature.

2 Have an assistant fully depress the accelerator pedal, and check that the maximum engine speed is as given in the Specifications. Do not keep the engine at maximum speed for more than two or three seconds.

3 If adjustment is necessary, stop the engine, then loosen the locknut, turn the maximum speed adjustment screw as necessary, and retighten the locknut **(see illustrations)**.

4 Repeat the procedure in paragraph 2 to check the adjustment.

5 Stop the engine and disconnect the tachometer.

4 Fast idle thermostatic sensor - removal, refitting and adjustment

Removal

Note: *A new sealing washer must be used when refitting the sensor.*

1 The thermostatic sensor is located in the side of the thermostat/fuel filter housing.

2 For improved access, on Turbo models remove the intercooler, and on non-turbo models with D9B engine remove the air distribution housing. If necessary, also remove the intake duct, and disconnect the breather hose from the engine oil filler tube. Refer to the relevant Sections of this Chapter for further information.

4.4a Fast idle cable end fitting clamp nut (arrowed) - Lucas pump

4.4b Loosening the fast idle cable end fitting clamp screw (arrowed) - Bosch pump

4.5 Sliding the fast idle cable from the adjustment screw - Bosch pump

3 Drain the cooling system as described in Chapter 1B.

4 Loosen the clamp screw or nut (as applicable), and disconnect the fast idle cable end fitting from the inner cable at the fuel injection pump fast idle lever **(see illustrations)**.

5 Slide the cable from the adjustment screw located in the bracket on the fuel injection pump **(see illustration)**.

6 Using a suitable open-ended spanner, unscrew the thermostatic sensor from the fuel filter/thermostat housing, and withdraw the sensor complete with the cable **(see illustration)**. Recover the sealing washer, where applicable.

Refitting

7 If sealing compound was originally used to fit the sensor in place of a washer, thoroughly clean all traces of old sealing compound from the sensor and housing. Ensure that no traces of sealant are left in the internal coolant passages of the housing.

8 Fit the sensor, using suitable sealing compound or a new washer as applicable, and tighten it.

9 Insert the adjustment screw into the bracket on the fuel injection pump, and screw on the locknut finger-tight.

10 Insert the inner cable through the fast idle lever, and position the end fitting on the cable, but do not tighten the clamp screw or nut (as applicable).

11 Adjust the cable as described in the following paragraphs.

Adjustment

12 With the engine cold, push the fast idle lever fully towards the flywheel end of the engine. Tighten the clamp screw or nut with the cable end fitting touching the lever.

13 Adjust the screw to ensure that the fast idle lever is touching its stop, then tighten the locknut.

14 Measure the exposed length of the inner cable.

15 Where necessary, refit the intercooler or the air distribution housing, and reconnect the breather hose to the engine oil filler tube.

16 Refill the cooling system as described in Chapter 1B, and run the engine to its normal operating temperature.

17 Check that the fast idle cable is slack. If not, it is likely that the sensor is faulty.

18 With the engine hot, check that there is approximately 0.5 to 1 mm of free play in the cable on Lucas injection pumps and 5 to 6 mm of free play in the cable on Bosch injection pumps. This indicates that the thermostatic sensor is functioning correctly.

19 Check that the engine speed increases when the fast idle lever is pushed towards the flywheel end of the engine. With the lever against its stop, the fast idle speed should be as specified (refer to Chapter 1B for details of how to check engine speed accurately).

20 Stop the engine.

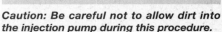

5 Stop solenoid - description, removal and refitting

Caution: Be careful not to allow dirt into the injection pump during this procedure.

Description

1 The stop solenoid is located on the end of the fuel injection pump **(see illustrations)**. Its purpose is to cut the fuel supply when the ignition is switched off. If an open-circuit occurs in the solenoid or supply wiring, it will be impossible to start the engine, as the fuel will not reach the injectors. The same applies if the solenoid plunger jams in the "stop" position. If the solenoid jams in the "run" position, the engine will not stop when the ignition is switched off.

2 If the solenoid has failed and the engine will not run, a temporary repair may be made by removing the solenoid as described in the following paragraphs. Refit the solenoid body without the plunger and spring. Tape up the wire so that it cannot touch earth. The engine can now be started as usual, but it will be necessary to use the manual stop lever (see Section 1, paragraph 9) on the fuel injection pump (or to stall the engine in gear) to stop it.

Removal

3 Disconnect the battery negative terminal (refer to *"Disconnecting the battery"* in the Reference Section of this manual).

4.6 Fast idle thermostatic sensor (arrowed)

5.1a Removing the stop solenoid wiring cover (arrowed) - Bosch pump

5.1b Removing the stop solenoid wiring cover - Lucas pump

6.9a Disconnecting the fuel pump fuel supply banjo union. Note sealing washers (arrowed) - Bosch pump

6.9b Refitting the fuel supply banjo bolt with a small section of fuel hose (arrowed) to prevent dirt ingress - Bosch pump

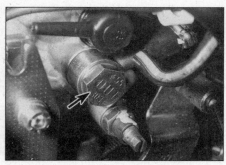

6.10 Injection pump fuel return pipe banjo union (arrowed) - Bosch pump

4 On models fitted with a Bosch fuel injection pump, it may be necessary to unbolt the fast idle cable support bracket from the side of the fuel injection pump, to improve access. Refer to Section 4 if it proves necessary to disconnect the cable from the bracket.

5 Withdraw the rubber boot (where applicable), then unscrew the terminal nut and disconnect the wire from the top of the solenoid.

6 Carefully clean around the solenoid, then unscrew and withdraw the solenoid, and recover the sealing washer or O-ring (as applicable). Recover the solenoid plunger and spring if they remain in the pump. Operate the hand-priming pump as the solenoid is removed, to flush away any dirt.

Refitting

7 Refitting is a reversal of removal, using a new sealing washer or O-ring and tightening the solenoid to the specified torque setting.

8 If the fast idle cable was disconnected, reconnect and adjust it as described in Section 4.

---

6 Fuel injection pump - removal and refitting

Caution: Be careful not to allow dirt into the injection pump or injector pipes during this procedure. New sealing rings should be used on the fuel pipe banjo unions when refitting.

Removal

1 Disconnect the battery negative terminal (refer to *"Disconnecting the battery"* in the Reference Section of this manual).

2 Cover the alternator with a plastic bag, as a precaution against spillage of Diesel fuel.

3 For improved access, on Turbo models remove the intercooler, and on non-turbo models with D9B engine remove the air distribution housing. If necessary, also remove the intake duct, and disconnect the breather hose from the engine oil filler tube. Refer to the relevant Sections of this Chapter for further information.

4 On manual transmission models, chock the rear wheels and release the handbrake. Jack up the front right-hand corner of the vehicle until the wheel is just clear of the ground. Support the vehicle on an axle stand (*see "Jacking and Vehicle Support"*) and engage 4th or 5th gear. This will enable the engine to be turned easily by turning the right-hand wheel. On automatic transmission models, turn the engine using a spanner on the crankshaft pulley bolt. It will be easier to turn the engine if the glow plugs are removed (see Chapter 5C).

5 Remove the upper timing belt covers with reference to Chapter 2C.

6 Where necessary, disconnect the hoses from the vacuum converter on the end of the fuel injection pump. Where applicable, on some Bosch pump equipped Turbo models, disconnect and plug the coolant hoses to and from the cold start advance capsule. Be prepared for some coolant spillage.

7 Disconnect the accelerator cable from the fuel injection pump, with reference to Section 11. On models with automatic transmission, also disconnect the kickdown cable.

8 Disconnect the fast idle cable from the fuel injection pump, with reference to Section 4.

9 Loosen the clip, or undo the banjo union, and disconnect the fuel supply hose. Recover the sealing washers from the banjo union, where applicable. Cover the open end of the hose, and refit and cover the banjo bolt to keep dirt out (**see illustrations**).

10 Disconnect the main fuel return pipe and the injector leak-off return pipe banjo union (**see illustration**). Recover the sealing washers from the banjo union. Again, cover the open end of the hose and the banjo bolt to keep dirt out. Take care not to get the inlet and outlet banjo unions mixed up.

11 Disconnect all relevant wiring from the pump. Note that on certain Bosch pumps, this can be achieved by simply disconnecting the wiring connectors at the brackets on the pump (**see illustration**). On some pumps, it will be necessary to disconnect the wiring from the individual components (some connections may be protected by rubber covers).

12 Unscrew the union nuts securing the injector pipes to the fuel injection pump and injectors. Counterhold the unions on the pump, while unscrewing the pipe-to-pump union nuts. Remove the pipes as a set. Cover open unions to keep dirt out, using small plastic bags, or fingers cut from discarded (but clean!) rubber gloves (**see illustrations**).

13 Turn the crankshaft until the two bolt

6.11 Disconnecting a fuel injection pump wiring plug - Bosch pump

6.12a Unscrewing a fuel pipe-to-injector union

6.12b Cover the open end of the injector to prevent dirt ingress

6.12c Unscrewing a fuel pipe-to-pump union - Bosch pump

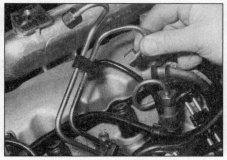

6.12d Removing a fuel pipe assembly

6.14 Bolts inserted through timing holes in injection pump sprocket

6.15 Mark the injection pump in relation to the mounting bracket (arrowed)

6.16a Unscrewing an injection pump front mounting nut - Bosch pump

6.16b Unscrewing an injection pump rear mounting nut (arrowed) - Bosch pump

holes in the fuel injection pump sprocket are aligned with the corresponding holes in the engine front plate.

14 Insert two M8 bolts through the holes, and hand-tighten them. Note that the bolts must retain the sprocket while the fuel injection pump is removed, thereby making it unnecessary to remove the timing belt **(see illustration)**.

15 Mark the fuel injection pump in relation to the mounting bracket, using a scriber or felt tip pen **(see illustration)**. This will ensure the correct pump timing is retained when refitting.

16 Unscrew the three front mounting nuts, and recover the washers. Unscrew and remove the rear mounting nut and bolt, noting the locations of the washers, and support the injection pump on a block of wood **(see illustrations)**.

17 Release the injection pump sprocket from the pump shaft, as described in Chapter 2C, Section 8. Note that the sprocket can be left engaged with the timing belt as the pump is withdrawn from its mounting bracket. Refit the M8 bolts to retain the sprocket in position while the pump is removed.

18 Carefully withdraw the pump. Recover the Woodruff key from the end of the pump shaft if it is loose, and similarly recover the bush from the rear of the mounting bracket **(see illustrations)**.

Refitting

19 Commence refitting the injection pump by fitting the Woodruff key to the shaft groove (if removed).

20 Offer the pump to the mounting bracket, and support on a block of wood, as during removal.

21 Engage the pump shaft with the sprocket, and refit the sprocket as described in Chapter 2C, Section 8. Ensure that the Woodruff key does not fall out of the shaft as the sprocket is engaged.

22 Align the marks made on the pump and mounting bracket before removal. If a new pump is being fitted, transfer the mark from the old pump to give an approximate setting.

23 Refit and lightly tighten the pump mounting nuts and bolt.

24 Set up the injection timing, as described in Sections 7, 8 and 9 (as applicable).

25 Refit and reconnect the injector fuel pipes.

26 Reconnect all relevant wiring to the pump.

27 Reconnect the fuel supply and return hoses, and tighten the unions, as applicable. Use new sealing washers on the banjo unions.

28 Reconnect the fast idle cable, and adjust it as described in Section 4.

29 Reconnect and adjust the accelerator

cable with reference to Section 11. Also reconnect the kickdown cable where applicable.

30 Where necessary, reconnect the hoses to the vacuum converter. Where applicable, unplug and reconnect the coolant hoses to and from the cold start advance capsule. Check, and if necessary top-up, the coolant level as described in *"Weekly checks"*.

31 Refit the upper timing belt covers.

32 Lower the vehicle to the ground.

33 Where applicable, refit the intercooler or the air distribution housing.

34 Remove the plastic bag used to cover the alternator.

35 Reconnect the battery negative terminal.

36 Bleed the fuel system as described in Section 2.

37 Start the engine, and check the fuel injection pump adjustments as described in Chapter 1B.

6.18a Removing an injection pump - Bosch pump

6.18b Recover the bush from the rear of the pump mounting bracket

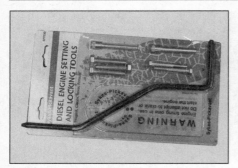

7.3 TDC setting and locking tools for setting injection timing on Peugeot diesels

7 Injection timing - checking methods and adjustment

1 Checking the injection timing is not a routine operation. It is only necessary after the injection pump has been disturbed.

2 Dynamic timing equipment does exist, but it is unlikely to be available to the home mechanic. The equipment works by converting pressure pulses in an injector pipe into electrical signals. If such equipment is available, use it in accordance with its maker's instructions.

3 Static timing as described in this Chapter gives good results if carried out carefully. A dial test indicator will be needed, with probes and adaptors appropriate to the type of injection pump **(see illustration)**. Read through the procedures before starting work, to find out what is involved.

8 Injection timing (Lucas fuel injection pump) - checking and adjustment

Caution: The maximum engine speed and transfer pressure settings, together with

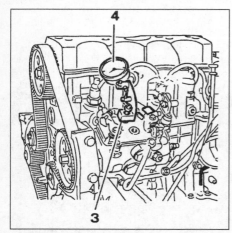

8.4 Peugeot injection pump timing gauge (4) and mounting bracket (3) in position on the injection pump

8.3 Removing the injection pump timing inspection plug - Lucas pump

timing access plugs, are sealed by the manufacturers at the factory using locking wire and lead seals. Do not disturb the wire if the vehicle is still within the warranty period otherwise the warranty will be invalidated. Also do not attempt the timing procedure unless accurate instrumentation is available. Suitable special tools for carrying out pump timing should be available from larger motor factors or your Peugeot dealer. Refer to the precautions given in Section 1 of this Chapter before proceeding.

Note: *To check the injection pump timing a special timing probe and mounting bracket (Peugeot tool No. 0117AM) is required* **(see illustration 8.4)**. *Without access to this piece of equipment, injection pump timing should be entrusted to a Peugeot dealer or other suitably equipped specialist.*

1 If the injection timing is being checked with the pump in position on the engine unit, rather than as part of the pump refitting procedure, disconnect the battery negative terminal (refer to *"Disconnecting the battery"* in the Reference Section of this manual), and cover the alternator with a clean cloth or plastic bag to prevent the possibility of fuel being spilt onto it. Remove the injector pipes as described in paragraph 12 of Section 6.

2 Referring to Chapter 2C, align the engine assembly/valve timing holes to lock the crankshaft in position. Remove the crankshaft locking tool, then turn the crankshaft **backwards** (anti-clockwise) approximately a quarter of a turn.

3 Unscrew the access plug from the guide on the top of the pump body and recover the sealing washer **(see illustration)**. Insert the special timing probe into the guide, making sure it is correctly seated against the guide sealing washer surface.

Note: *The timing probe must be seated against the guide sealing washer surface and not the upper lip of the guide for the measurement to be accurate.*

4 Mount the bracket on the pump guide (Peugeot tool No. 0117AM) and securely mount the dial gauge (dial test indicator) in the bracket so that its tip is in contact with the bracket linkage **(see illustration)**. Position the dial gauge so that its plunger is at the mid-point of its travel and zero the gauge.

5 Rotate the crankshaft slowly in the correct direction of rotation (clockwise) until the crankshaft locking tool can be re-inserted.

6 With the crankshaft locked in position read the dial gauge; the reading should correspond to the value marked on the pump (there is a tolerance of ± 0.04 mm). The timing value may be marked on a plastic disc attached to the front of the pump, or alternatively on a tag attached to the pump control lever **(see illustrations)**.

7 If adjustment is necessary, slacken the front pump mounting nuts and the rear mounting bolt, then slowly rotate the pump body until the point is found where the specified reading is obtained on the dial gauge. When the pump is correctly positioned, tighten both its front mounting nuts and the rear bolt to their specified torque settings. To improve access to the pump nuts, undo the two screws and remove the cover panel from the side of the radiator.

8 Withdraw the timing probe slightly, so that it is positioned clear of the pump rotor dowel, and remove the crankshaft locking pin. Rotate the crankshaft through one and three quarter rotations in the normal direction of rotation.

9 Slide the timing probe back into position ensuring that it is correctly seated against the guide sealing washer surface, not the upper lip, then zero the dial gauge.

10 Rotate the crankshaft slowly in the correct direction of rotation until the crankshaft locking tool can be re-inserted. Recheck the timing measurement.

8.6a Pump timing value (x) marked on plastic disc - Lucas pump

8.6b Pump timing values marked on label (1) and tag (2) - Lucas pump

11 If adjustment is necessary, slacken the pump mounting nuts and bolt and repeat the operations in paragraphs 7 to 10.

12 When the pump timing is correctly set, remove the dial gauge and mounting bracket and withdraw the timing probe.

13 Refit the screw and sealing washer to the guide and tighten it securely.

14 If the procedure is being carried out as part of the pump refitting sequence, proceed as described in Section 6.

15 If the procedure is being carried out with the pump fitted to the engine, refit the injector pipes tightening their union nuts to the specified torque setting. Reconnect the battery, then bleed the fuel system - see Section 2. Start the engine and adjust the idle speed and anti-stall speeds - see Chapter 1B.

9 Injection timing (Bosch fuel injection pump) - checking and adjustment

Caution: Some of the injection pump settings and access plugs may be sealed by the manufacturers at the factory, using paint or locking wire and lead seals. Do not disturb the seals if the vehicle is still within the warranty period, otherwise the warranty will be invalidated. Also do not attempt the timing procedure unless accurate instrumentation is available.

1 If the injection timing is being checked with the pump in position on the engine unit, rather than as part of the pump refitting procedure, disconnect the battery negative terminal (refer to *"Disconnecting the battery"* in the Reference Section of this manual), and cover the alternator with a clean cloth or plastic bag to prevent the possibility of fuel being spilt onto it. Remove the injector pipes as described in paragraph 12 of Section 6.

2 If not already having done so, slacken the clamp screw and/or nut (as applicable) and slide the fast idle cable end fitting arrangement along the cable so that it is no longer in contact with the pump fast idle lever (ie. so the fast idle lever returns to its stop) (see Section 4). On certain Turbo models, disconnect the cold start advance capsule as follows **(see illustration)**. Undo the grub screw (4), push the lever (6) back toward the delivery pipes, rotate the collar (5) through 90° and release the lever (6). This ensures that the cold start capsule is in the non-advanced state.

3 Referring to Chapter 2C, align the engine assembly/valve timing holes to lock the crankshaft in position. Remove the crankshaft locking tool, then turn the crankshaft **backwards** (anti-clockwise) approximately a quarter of a turn.

4 Unscrew the access screw, situated in the centre of the four injector pipe unions, from the rear of the injection pump. As the screw is removed, position a suitable container beneath the pump to catch any escaping fuel. Mop up any spilt fuel with a clean cloth.

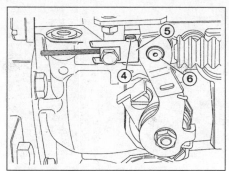

9.2 Cold start advance capsule details - Turbo models

    4 Grub screw   *6 Lever*
    5 Collar

5 Screw the adaptor into the rear of the pump and mount the dial gauge in the adaptor **(see illustration)**. If access to the special adaptor cannot be gained (Peugeot tool No. 0117F), they can be purchased from most good motor factors. Position the dial gauge so that its plunger is at the mid-point of its travel and securely tighten the adaptor locknut.

6 Slowly rotate the crankshaft back and forth whilst observing the dial gauge, to determine when the injection pump piston is at the bottom of its travel (BDC). When the piston is correctly positioned, zero the dial gauge.

7 Rotate the crankshaft slowly in the correct direction until the crankshaft locking tool can be re-inserted.

8 The reading obtained on the dial gauge should be equal to the specified pump timing measurement given in the Specifications at the start of this Chapter. If adjustment is necessary, slacken the front and rear pump mounting nuts and bolts and slowly rotate the pump body until the point is found where the specified reading is obtained. When the pump is correctly positioned, tighten both its front and rear mounting nuts and bolts securely.

9 Rotate the crankshaft through one and three quarter rotations in the normal direction

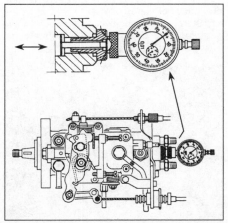

9.5 Dial test indicator and timing probe for use with Bosch pump

of rotation. Find the injection pump piston BDC as described in paragraph 6 and zero the dial gauge.

10 Rotate the crankshaft slowly in the correct direction of rotation until the crankshaft locking tool can be re-inserted (bringing the engine back to TDC). Recheck the timing measurement.

11 If adjustment is necessary, slacken the pump mounting nuts and bolts and repeat the operations in paragraphs 8 to 10.

12 When the pump timing is correctly set, unscrew the adaptor and remove the dial gauge.

13 Refit the screw and sealing washer to the pump and tighten it securely.

14 If the procedure is being carried out as part of the pump refitting sequence, proceed as described in Section 6.

15 If the procedure is being carried out with the pump fitted to the engine, refit the injector pipes tightening their union nuts to the specified torque setting. Where applicable, reset the cold start advance capsule by reversing the instructions given in paragraph 2. Reconnect the battery then bleed the fuel system as described in Section 2. Start the engine and adjust the idle speed and anti-stall speeds as described in Chapter 1B. Also adjust the fast idle cable as described in Section 4.

10 Fuel injectors - testing, removal and refitting

⚠️ *Warning: Exercise extreme caution when working on the fuel injectors. Never expose the hands or any part of the body to injector spray, as the high working pressure can cause the fuel to penetrate the skin, with possibly fatal results. You are strongly advised to have any work which involves testing the injectors under pressure carried out by a dealer or fuel injection specialist.*

Testing

1 Injectors do deteriorate with prolonged use, and it is reasonable to expect them to need reconditioning or renewal after 60 000 miles (100 000 km) or so. Accurate testing, overhaul and calibration of the injectors must be left to a specialist. A defective injector which is causing knocking or smoking can be located without dismantling as follows.

2 Run the engine at fast idle. Slacken each injector union in turn, placing rag around the union to catch spilt fuel, and being careful not to expose the skin to any spray. When the union on the defective injector is slackened, the knocking or smoking will stop.

Removal

3 For improved access, on Turbo models remove the intercooler, and on non-turbo models with D9B engine remove the air

10.5 Pulling a leak-off pipe from a fuel injector

10.7 Unscrewing an injector pipe union nut

10.8 Unscrew the injectors and remove them from the cylinder head

10.9a Removing a fuel injector copper washer . . .

10.9b . . . fire seal washer . . .

10.9c . . . and sleeve

distribution housing. If necessary, also remove the intake duct, and disconnect the breather hose from the engine oil filler tube. Refer to the relevant Sections of this Chapter for further information.

4 Carefully clean around the injectors and injector pipe union nuts.

5 Pull the leak-off pipes from the injectors (see illustration).

6 Unscrew the union nuts securing the injector pipes to the fuel injection pump. Counterhold the unions on the pump when unscrewing the nuts. Cover open unions to keep dirt out, using small plastic bags, or fingers cut from discarded (but clean!) rubber gloves.

7 Unscrew the union nuts and disconnect the pipes from the injectors (see illustration). If necessary, the injector pipes may be completely removed. Note carefully the locations of the pipe clamps, for use when refitting. Cover the ends of the injectors, to prevent dirt ingress.

8 Unscrew the injectors using a deep socket or box spanner (27 mm across-flats), and remove them from the cylinder head (see illustration).

9 Recover the copper washers and fire seal washers from the cylinder head. Also recover the sleeves if they are loose (see illustrations).

Refitting

10 Obtain new copper washers and fire seal washers. Also renew the sleeves, if they are damaged.

11 Take care not to drop the injectors, or allow the needles at their tips to become

damaged. The injectors are precision-made to fine limits, and must not be handled roughly. In particular, never mount them in a bench vice.

12 Commence refitting by inserting the sleeves (if removed) into the cylinder head, followed by the fire seal washers (convex face uppermost), and copper washers.

13 Insert the injectors and tighten them to the specified torque.

14 Refit the injector pipes and tighten the union nuts. Make sure the pipe clamps are in their previously-noted positions. If the clamps are wrongly positioned or missing, problems may be experienced with pipes breaking or splitting.

15 Reconnect the leak-off pipes.

16 Refit the intercooler or air distribution housing where applicable.

17 Start the engine. If difficulty is experienced, bleed the fuel system as described in Section 2.

11.1 Releasing the accelerator cable inner from the lever on the injection pump

11 Accelerator cable - removal, refitting and adjustment

Removal

1 Working in the engine compartment, operate the pump control lever on the fuel injection pump, and release the cable inner from the lever (see illustration).

2 Pull the cable outer from the grommet in the fuel injection pump bracket (see illustration).

3 Release the cable from the remaining clips and brackets in the engine compartment, noting its routing.

4 Working in the passenger compartment, release the securing clips, and remove the felt trim panel from under the facia in the driver's footwell.

11.2 Pulling the accelerator cable outer from the bracket

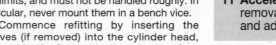

5 Working from inside the vehicle, release the fastener by rotating it through a quarter of a turn anti-clockwise, and remove the fusebox cover from the facia. Release the retaining clips, and remove the felt undercover from underneath the driver's side of the facia panel.
6 Release the securing clip, and disconnect the cable inner from the pedal.
7 Slide the cable outer grommet from the bracket on the pedal.
8 Carefully feed the cable through the bulkhead grommet from the engine compartment into the vehicle interior, and remove it from the vehicle.

Refitting

9 Refitting is a reversal of removal, but ensure that the cable is routed as noted before removal, and on completion, adjust the cable as follows.

Adjustment

10 Remove the spring clip from the accelerator outer cable. Ensuring that the control lever is against its stop, gently pull the cable out of its grommet until all free play is removed from the inner cable.
11 With the cable held in this position, refit the spring clip to the last exposed outer cable groove in front of the rubber grommet and washer. When the clip is refitted and the outer cable is released, there should be only a small amount of free play in the inner cable.
12 Have an assistant depress the accelerator pedal, and check that the control lever opens fully and returns smoothly to its stop.

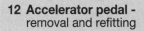

12 Accelerator pedal -
removal and refitting

Refer to Chapter 4A, Section 8.

13 Fuel level sender -
removal and refitting

Refer to Chapter 4A, Section 5, noting that there are no fuel pipe connections to the sender unit.

14.4 Note the flow direction arrows (arrowed) on the fuel pick-up unit

14 Fuel pick-up unit -
removal and refitting

Removal

1 Disconnect the battery negative terminal (refer to *"Disconnecting the battery"* in the Reference Section of this manual).
2 For access to the pick-up unit, tilt or remove the rear seats, according to model, as described in Chapter 11.
3 Using a screwdriver, carefully prise the plastic access cover from the floor to expose the fuel pump. Where two access covers are fitted, the pump is located under the right-hand cover (viewed facing towards the front of the vehicle).
4 Mark the hoses for identification purposes, then slacken the feed and return hose retaining clips. Where the crimped-type hose clips are fitted, cut the clips and discard them, replace them with standard worm-drive hose clips on refitting. On later models quick-release fittings may be fitted to the fuel hoses; these are released by depressing their metal collars with a small, flat-bladed screwdriver **(see illustration)**.
5 Note the alignment arrows on the pick-up unit and the locking ring **(see illustration)**.
6 The locking ring which secures the unit in the fuel tank must now be unscrewed. This is best accomplished by using a screwdriver on the raised ribs of the locking ring. Carefully tap the screwdriver to turn the ring anti-

14.5 Alignment arrows (arrowed) on fuel pick-up unit and locking ring

clockwise until it can be unscrewed by hand **(see illustration)**.
7 Unscrew the locking ring, and carefully lift the unit from the top of the fuel tank. Recover the rubber sealing ring if it is loose **(see illustrations)**.

Refitting

8 Before refitting, examine the condition of the sealing ring, and renew if necessary. Similarly, examine the condition of the filter at the end of the pick-up pipe, and clean or renew as necessary.
9 Refitting is a reversal of removal, ensuring that the hoses are correctly reconnected, as noted before removal. Also ensure that the arrows on the pick-up unit and the locking ring are aligned as previously noted (tighten the locking ring using a screwdriver as during removal).

15 Fuel tank -
removal and refitting

Refer to Chapter 4A, Section 6.

16 Manifolds -
removal and refitting

Note: *On Turbo models, the inlet and exhaust manifolds share the same gasket. Therefore, it is recommended that both manifolds are*

14.6 Releasing the fuel pick-up unit locking ring using a screwdriver

14.7a Lifting the fuel pick-up unit from the tank

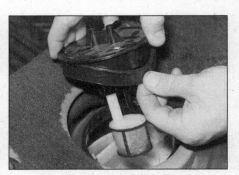

14.7b Recovering the sealing ring

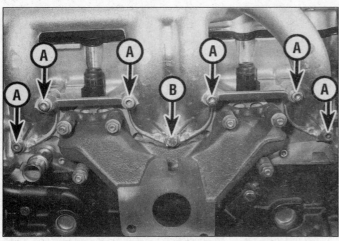

16.7 Inlet manifold securing bolts (A) and hex bolt (B - loosen, do not remove) on Turbo models - viewed with engine removed for clarity

16.8 Withdrawing the inlet manifold from the cylinder head

removed, whenever one is removed, in order that the gasket can be renewed. It is possible to remove the manifolds individually, in which case the original gasket would be re-used, but this is not recommended.

Inlet manifold

Note: *Renew the manifold gasket(s) when refitting.*

Removal

1 Disconnect the battery negative terminal (refer to *"Disconnecting the battery"* in the Reference Section of this manual).

2 For improved access, on Turbo models remove the intercooler, and on non-turbo models with D9B engine remove the air distribution housing. If necessary, also remove the intake duct, and disconnect the breather hose from the engine oil filler tube. Refer to the relevant Sections of this Chapter for further information.

3 Disconnect the end of the accelerator cable from the fuel injection pump, with reference to Section 11. Release the cable from its clips, noting their locations, and position the cable to one side, clear of the manifolds.

4 Similarly, disconnect the brake servo vacuum hose from the vacuum pump, and move the hose to one side.

5 On models equipped with an exhaust gas recirculation (EGR) system, disconnect the vacuum hoses from the flow valve and recirculation valve. Slacken and remove the nuts and bolts securing each valve to the manifolds and remove both valves as an assembly. Recover the gasket fitted between each valve and its relevant manifold.

6 On Turbo models, release the hose clips and disconnect the air hoses from the air tube which connects the turbocharger to the air cleaner tubing. Manipulate the air tube from the inlet manifold, and remove it from the engine compartment. Push a wad of (clean!) rag into the open end of the turbocharger air hose (or the turbocharger itself, if the hose has been removed completely), to prevent the possibility of dirt ingress. Also release the securing clip, and remove the intercooler air hose from the turbocharger.

7 Using a suitable hexagon bit or Allen key, remove the six bolts securing the inlet manifold. Loosen, but do not remove, the central hexagon manifold securing bolt - the manifold is slotted **(see illustration)**.

8 Withdraw the manifold from the cylinder head **(see illustration)**.

Refitting

9 Refitting is a reversal of removal, bearing in mind the following points.

a) *Renew the gasket(s) when refitting the manifold.*

b) *Tighten all fixings to the specified torques, where applicable.*

c) *Reconnect the accelerator cable to the fuel injection pump. Adjust the cable if necessary, with reference to Section 11.*

d) *Ensure that all relevant hoses and pipes are correctly reconnected and routed.*

Exhaust manifold

Note: *Renew the manifold gasket(s) when refitting.*

Removal

10 For improved access, remove the inlet manifold as described previously in this Section. This is essential on Turbo models.

11 If the inlet manifold is to be left in place, proceed as described in paragraphs 1 to 4, then proceed as follows. On models with an exhaust gas recirculation (EGR) system also carry out the operation described in paragraph 5.

12 On non-turbo models, disconnect the exhaust front pipe from the manifold, with reference to Section 22.

13 On Turbo models, remove the turbocharger as described in Section 18.

14 On certain models, it may be necessary to unbolt the resonator chamber from the manifold, to allow sufficient clearance for the manifold to be removed.

15 Unscrew the six exhaust manifold securing nuts, and recover the spacers from the studs **(see illustration)**.

16 Lift the exhaust manifold from the cylinder head, and recover the gasket(s) (where fitted) **(see illustration)**.

17 It is possible that some of the manifold studs may be unscrewed from the cylinder head when the manifold securing nuts are unscrewed. In this event, the studs should be screwed back into the cylinder head once the manifolds have been removed, using two manifold nuts locked together.

16.15 Exhaust manifold securing nuts (arrowed) on Turbo models - viewed with engine removed for clarity

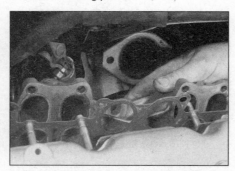

16.16 Lifting the exhaust manifold and gasket from the cylinder head

18.2 Disconnecting the oil feed pipe from the turbocharger

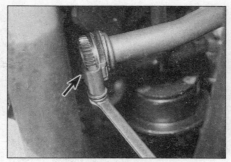

18.5 Remove the hose (arrowed) connecting the turbocharger oil return pipe to the pipe on the cylinder block

18.6 Remove the screw (arrowed) securing the oil feed pipe

Refitting

18 Refitting is a reversal of removal, bearing in mind the following points.

a) *Renew the manifold gasket(s) on refitting (where fitted). Where no gaskets are fitted, apply a smear of suitable sealant to the manifold mating surface.*

b) *Where applicable, refit the turbocharger as described in Section 18.*

c) *Where applicable, reconnect the exhaust front pipe to the exhaust manifold as described in Section 22.*

d) *Tighten all fixings to the specified torque, where applicable.*

e) *Reconnect the accelerator cable to the fuel injection pump. Adjust the cable if necessary, with reference to Section 11.*

f) *Ensure that all relevant hoses and pipes are correctly reconnected and routed.*

17 Turbocharger -
description and precautions

Description

1 A turbocharger is fitted to some engines. It increases engine efficiency by raising the pressure in the inlet manifold above atmospheric pressure. Instead of the air simply being sucked into the cylinders, it is forced in. Additional fuel is supplied by the injection pump in proportion to the increased air intake.

2 Energy for the operation of the turbocharger comes from the exhaust gas. The gas flows through a specially-shaped housing (the turbine housing) and in so doing, spins the turbine wheel. The turbine wheel is attached to a shaft, at the end of which is another vaned wheel known as the compressor wheel. The compressor wheel spins in its own housing, and compresses the inlet air on the way to the inlet manifold.

3 Between the turbocharger and the inlet manifold, the compressed air passes through an intercooler. This is an air-to-air heat exchanger, mounted over the engine, and supplied with cooling air ducted through bonnet insulation. The purpose of the intercooler is to remove from the inlet air

some of the heat gained in being compressed. Because cooler air is denser, removal of this heat further increases engine efficiency.

4 Boost pressure (the pressure in the inlet manifold) is limited by a wastegate, which diverts the exhaust gas away from the turbine wheel in response to a pressure-sensitive actuator. A pressure-operated switch operates a warning light on the instrument panel in the event of excessive boost pressure developing.

5 The turbo shaft is pressure-lubricated by an oil feed pipe from the main oil gallery. The shaft "floats" on a cushion of oil. A drain pipe returns the oil to the sump.

Precautions

6 The turbocharger operates at extremely high speeds and temperatures. Certain precautions must be observed, to avoid premature failure of the turbo, or injury to the operator.

7 Do not operate the turbo with any of its parts exposed, or with any of its hoses removed. Foreign objects falling onto the rotating vanes could cause excessive damage, and (if ejected) personal injury.

8 Do not race the engine immediately after start-up, especially if it is cold. Give the oil a few seconds to circulate.

9 Always allow the engine to return to idle speed before switching it off - do not blip the throttle and switch off, as this will leave the turbo spinning without lubrication.

10 Allow the engine to idle for several minutes before switching off after a high-speed run.

11 Observe the recommended intervals for oil and filter changing, and use a reputable oil of the specified quality. Neglect of oil changing, or use of inferior oil, can cause carbon formation on the turbo shaft, leading to subsequent failure.

18 Turbocharger -
removal and refitting

Removal

1 Remove the inlet manifold as described in Section 16.

2 Unscrew the union nut, and disconnect the oil feed pipe from the top of the turbocharger **(see illustration)**.

3 Apply the handbrake, then jack up the front of the vehicle and support securely on axle stands (see *"Jacking and Vehicle Support"*).

4 Disconnect the exhaust front pipe from the turbocharger, with reference to Section 22.

5 Working under the vehicle, loosen the securing clips, and remove the hose connecting the turbocharger oil return pipe to the pipe on the cylinder block **(see illustration)**.

6 Remove the screw securing the oil feed pipe to the support bracket at the rear of the cylinder block **(see illustration)**.

7 Unscrew the union nut securing the oil feed pipe to the cylinder block, then withdraw the oil feed pipe from above the engine **(see illustrations)**.

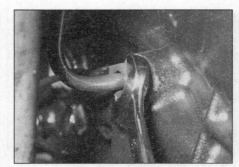

18.7a Unscrew the union nut . . .

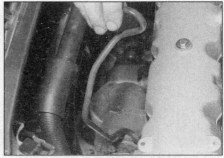

18.7b . . . and withdraw the oil feed pipe

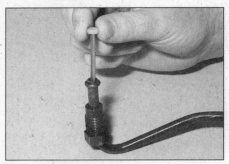

18.8 Removing the filter from the oil feed pipe

18.9 Turbocharger lower securing bolts (arrowed) - viewed from underneath

18.10 Unscrewing the turbocharger upper securing bolt

8 Remove the filter from the cylinder block end of the oil feed pipe (where fitted), and examine it for contamination **(see illustration)**. Clean or renew if necessary.
9 Working under the vehicle, unscrew and remove the two lower turbocharger securing bolts **(see illustration)**.
10 Support the turbocharger, then remove the upper turbocharger securing bolt, and recover the spacer **(see illustration)**.
11 Carefully manipulate the turbocharger out through the top of the engine compartment **(see illustration)**. If it is to be refitted, store the turbocharger carefully, and plug its openings to prevent dirt ingress.

Refitting

12 Refitting is a reversal of removal, bearing in mind the following points:
a) If a new turbocharger is being fitted, change the engine oil and filter. Also

renew the filter in the oil feed pipe.
b) Do not fully tighten the oil feed pipe unions until both ends of the pipe are in place. When tightening the oil return pipe union, position it so that the return hose is not strained.
c) Before starting the engine, prime the turbo lubrication circuit by disconnecting the stop solenoid lead at the fuel pump, and cranking the engine on the starter for three ten-second bursts.

19 Turbocharger -
examination and renovation

1 With the turbocharger removed, inspect the housing for cracks or other visible damage.
2 Spin the turbine or the compressor wheel, to verify that the shaft is intact and to feel for

excessive shake or roughness. Some play is normal, since in use, the shaft is "floating" on a film of oil. Check that the wheel vanes are undamaged.
3 On the KKK turbo, the wastegate and actuator are integral, and cannot be checked or renewed separately. On the Garrett turbo, the wastegate actuator is a separate unit. Consult a Peugeot dealer or other specialist if it is thought that testing or renewal is necessary.
4 If the exhaust or induction passages are oil-contaminated, the turbo shaft oil seals have probably failed. (On the induction side, this will also have contaminated the intercooler, which should if necessary be flushed with solvent.)
5 No DIY repair of the turbo is possible. A new unit may be available on an exchange basis.

20 Intercooler -
removal and refitting

Removal

1 To remove the intercooler, follow the procedure shown in the accompanying sequence of photographs **(see illustrations)**.

Refitting

2 Refitting is a reversal of removal.

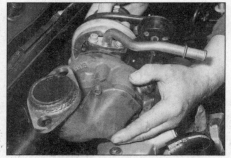

18.11 Withdrawing the turbocharger

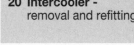

20.1a Disconnect the hose (arrowed) from the front edge of the intercooler

20.1b Detach the hoses (arrowed) from the valve on the left-hand side of the intercooler

20.1c Disconnect the hose from the right-hand end of the intercooler

20.1d Lift the surround from the top of the intercooler

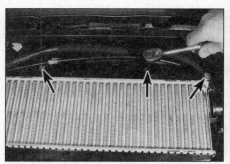

20.1e Unscrew the three upper securing bolts (arrowed) . . .

20.1f . . . and the two front securing bolts . . .

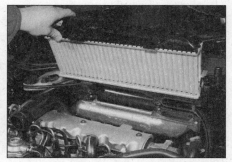

20.1g . . . and remove the intercooler

21 Air cleaner and associated components - removal and refitting

Removal

Air cleaner - non-turbo models

1 Slacken the retaining clips securing the air cleaner to manifold duct in position and, where necessary, remove the duct mounting bolt. Disconnect the duct and remove it from the engine unit. On D9B engines recover the seal from the air distribution housing.
2 Slacken and remove the bolt securing the intake duct to the crossmember then unclip the duct from the side of the air cleaner and remove it from the vehicle.
3 Slacken and remove the bolts securing the air cleaner and mounting bracket in position and remove both items as an assembly.

Air cleaner - turbo models

4 Slacken the retaining clips securing the air cleaner to manifold duct in position and undo the duct mounting bolt. Manoeuvre the duct assembly out from the engine compartment. Recover the seal fitted to each end of the duct.

5 Slacken and remove the bolt securing the intake duct to the crossmember then unclip the duct from the side of the air cleaner and remove it from the vehicle.
6 Slacken and remove the retaining bolts and remove the air cleaner from the engine compartment.

Air distribution housing - non-turbo models fitted with D9B engine

7 Disconnect the air hose and the crankcase breather hose from the front of the air distribution housing.
8 Unscrew the two bolts securing the housing to the front mounting brackets **(see illustration)**. Recover the spacer plates.
9 Unscrew the four bolts securing the housing to the inlet manifold. Recover the washers **(see illustration)**.
10 Lift the housing from the inlet manifold, and recover the seal(s).

Refitting

11 Refitting is the reverse of the relevant removal procedure. Examine the condition of the seal(s) (where fitted) and renew if necessary.

22 Exhaust system - general information and component renewal

General information

1 On models not fitted with a catalytic converter the exhaust system consists of two sections: the front pipe and the tailpipe. The front pipe to manifold joint is of the spring-loaded ball type, to allow for movement in the exhaust system, and the tailpipe joint is secured by a clamping ring.
2 On models with a catalytic converter the exhaust system consists of three sections: the catalytic converter, the intermediate pipe and the tailpipe. The catalytic converter to manifold joint is of the spring-loaded ball type, to allow for movement in the exhaust system, and both the other joints are secured by clamping rings.
3 The system is suspended throughout its entire length by rubber mountings.

Removal

4 Each exhaust section can be removed individually, or alternatively, the complete

21.8 Front air distribution housing securing bolt (arrowed)

21.9 Air distribution housing-to-inlet manifold bolts (arrowed)

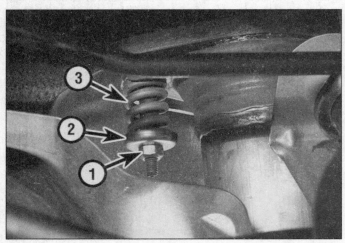

22.7a Exhaust front pipe-to-turbocharger securing nut (1), spring seat (2) and spring (3) - viewed from underneath vehicle

22.7b Exhaust front pipe-to-turbocharger securing bolts (arrowed) - viewed from engine compartment

system can be removed as a unit. Even if only one part of the system needs attention, it is often easier to remove the whole system and separate the sections on the bench.

5 To remove the system or part of the system, first jack up the front or rear of the car, and support it on axle stands (see *"Jacking and Vehicle Support"*). Alternatively, position the car over an inspection pit, or on car ramps.

Front pipe - non-catalyst models

6 Slacken the front pipe clamping ring bolts, and disengage the clamp from the flange joint.

7 Slacken and remove the two nuts securing the front pipe flange joint to the manifold, and recover the spring cups and springs. Remove the bolts, then free the front pipe from its mounting rubber(s) and remove it from underneath the vehicle **(see illustrations)**. Recover the wire-mesh gasket from the manifold joint.

Catalytic converter

8 Slacken the catalytic converter clamping ring bolts, and disengage the clamp from the flange joint.

9 Slacken and remove the two nuts securing the catalytic converter to the manifold, and recover the spring cups and springs. Withdraw the bolts and remove the catalytic converter

from underneath the vehicle. Recover the wire-mesh gasket from the manifold joint.

Intermediate pipe - models with catalytic converter

10 Slacken the clamping ring bolts, and disengage both clamps from the flange joints.

11 Release the pipe from its mounting rubber and remove it from underneath the vehicle.

Tailpipe

12 Slacken the tailpipe clamping ring bolts, and disengage the clamp from the flange joint.

13 Unhook the tailpipe from its mounting rubbers, and remove it from the vehicle.

Complete system

14 Slacken and remove the two nuts securing the front pipe flange joint to the manifold, and recover the spring cups and springs. Remove the bolts, then free the system from its mounting rubbers and remove it from underneath the vehicle. Recover the wire-mesh gasket from the manifold joint.

Heat shield(s)

15 The heat shields are secured to the underside of the body by various nuts and bolts. Each shield can be removed once the relevant exhaust section has been removed. If a shield is being removed to gain access to a component located behind it, it may prove

sufficient in some cases to remove the retaining nuts and/or bolts, and simply lower the shield, without disturbing the exhaust system.

Refitting

16 Each section is refitted by reversing the removal sequence, noting the following points:

a) Ensure that all traces of corrosion have been removed from the flanges, and renew all necessary gaskets.

b) Inspect the rubber mountings for signs of damage or deterioration, and renew as necessary.

c) Prior to assembling the spring-loaded joint, a smear of high-temperature grease should be applied to the joint mating surfaces.

d) Where joints are secured together by a clamping ring, apply a smear of exhaust system jointing paste to the flange joint, to ensure a gas-tight seal. Tighten the clamping ring nuts evenly and progressively to the specified torque setting, so that the clearance between the clamp halves remains equal on either side.

e) Prior to tightening the exhaust system fasteners, ensure that all rubber mountings are correctly located, and that there is adequate clearance between the exhaust system and vehicle underbody.

Chapter 4 Part E:
Fuel/exhaust systems –
1.9 and 2.0 litre DW diesel models

Contents

Degrees of difficulty

Easy, suitable for novice with little experience	**Fairly easy,** suitable for beginner with some experience	**Fairly difficult,** suitable for competent DIY mechanic	**Difficult,** suitable for experienced DIY mechanic	**Very difficult,** suitable for expert DIY or professional

Specifications

General
System type:
1.9 litre engine:	
Engine code WJZ	Indirect injection system incorporating a distributor fuel injection pump
Engine code WJY	Indirect injection system incorporating a semi-electronically controlled distributor fuel injection pump
2.0 litre engine	High-pressure Diesel injection (HDi) direct injection 'common-rail' system incorporating an electronically controlled fuel injection pump and injectors

Injection pump type:
1.9 litre engine:	
Engine code WJZ	Lucas DWLP11
Engine code WJY	Lucas DWLP12
2.0 litre engine	Bosch EDC 15C2

Adjustment data
Idle speed:
1.9 litre engines:	
Models without air conditioning	800 to 850 rpm
Models with air conditioning	850 to 900 rpm
2.0 litre engine	800 ± 20 rpm – controlled by ECU

Maximum speed:
1.9 litre engine	Not available
2.0 litre engine	5000 rpm – controlled by ECU

Injectors
Opening pressure:
1.9 litre engine	135 ± 5 bars
2.0 litre engine	Controlled by ECU

Turbocharger

Type	KKK K03
Boost pressure (approximate)	1 bar at 3000 rpm

Torque wrench settings

	Nm	lbf ft
1.9 litre engine		
Exhaust manifold nuts	30	22
Fuel pipe union nuts	25	18
Inlet manifold:		
Lower section nuts/bolts	20	15
Upper section:		
M6 bolts	8	6
M8 bolts	18	13
Injection pump:		
Front mounting bolts	20	15
Rear mounting bolt	23	17
Mounting bracket-to-cylinder head bolts	20	15
Injection pump sprocket-to-hub bolts	23	17
Injectors to cylinder head	90	66
2.0 litre engine		
EGR valve bolts	10	7
Exhaust manifold nuts	20	15
Fuel filter bracket bolts	18	13
Fuel pipe union nuts	20	15
Fuel pressure sensor	35	26
Fuel rail mounting bolts	23	17
Inlet manifold nuts and bolts	23	17
Injection pump:		
Front mounting bolts/nut	23	17
Rear bracket bolts	20	15
Mounting bracket-to-cylinder head bolts	20	15
Injection pump sprocket nut	50	37
Injector retaining clamp nut	30	22
Turbocharger:		
Mounting nuts	25	18
Exhaust flange bolts	23	17
Support bracket:		
Bracket-to-cylinder block bolts	23	17
Bracket-to-turbo bolt	30	22
Oil feed pipe:		
Pipe-to-turbo union bolt	22	16
Pipe-to-cylinder block union nut	48	35
Oil return hose union bolts	12	9

1 General information and precautions

1.9 litre WJZ engine

1 The fuel system consists of a fuel tank (which is mounted under the rear of the car), a fuel filter with integral water separator, a fuel injection pump, injectors and associated components.

2 The injection pump draws fuel from the tank through the fuel filter, which is mounted on the thermostat housing on the left-hand end of the cylinder head. The fuel filter removes all foreign matter and water, and ensures that the fuel supplied to the injection pump is clean. Excess fuel is returned from the bleed outlet on the filter housing lid to the tank. The filter housing incorporates a thermostat. When the temperature of the fuel in the filter housing is below 15°C, the filter housing thermostat opens and allows the fuel to circulate between the filter housing and thermostat housing which effectively warms the fuel. When the fuel in the filter housing reaches 35°C, the thermostat closes.

3 The fuel injection pump is driven at half-crankshaft speed by the timing belt. The high pressure required to inject the fuel into the compressed air in the swirl chambers is achieved by two opposed pistons forced together by rollers running in a cam ring. The fuel passes through a central rotor with a single outlet drilling which aligns with ports leading to the injector pipes.

4 Fuel metering is controlled by a centrifugal governor, which reacts to accelerator pedal position and engine speed. The governor is linked to a metering valve, which increases or decreases the amount of fuel delivered at each pumping stroke.

5 Basic injection timing is determined when the timing belt is fitted. When the engine is running, it is varied automatically to suit the prevailing engine speed by a mechanism which turns the cam plate or ring.

6 The four fuel injectors produce a homogeneous spray of fuel into the swirl chambers located in the cylinder head. The injectors are calibrated to open and close at critical pressures to provide efficient and even combustion. Each injector needle is lubricated by fuel, which accumulates in the spring chamber and is channelled to the injection pump return hose by leak-off pipes.

7 Cold starting is assisted by preheater or 'glow' plugs fitted to each swirl chamber. A thermostatic sensor in the cooling system operates a fast idle lever on the injection pump to increase the idling speed when the engine is cold.

8 A stop solenoid cuts the fuel supply to the injection pump rotor when the ignition is switched off, and there is also a hand-operated stop lever for use in an emergency **(see illustration)**.

9 Provided that the specified maintenance is carried out, the fuel injection equipment will give long and trouble-free service. The injection pump itself may well outlast the engine. The main potential cause of damage to the injection pump and injectors is dirt or water in the fuel.

10 A catalytic converter and exhaust gas recirculation (EGR) system are fitted to the engine to reduce exhaust emissions. Refer to Part F of this Chapter for further information.

11 Servicing of the injection pump and injectors is very limited for the home mechanic, and any dismantling or adjustment other than that described in this Chapter must be entrusted to a Peugeot dealer or fuel injection specialist.

 Warning: It is necessary to take certain precautions when working on the fuel system components, particularly the fuel injectors. Before carrying out any operations on the fuel system, refer to the precautions given in 'Safety first!' at the beginning of this manual, and to any additional warning notes at the start of the relevant Sections.

1.9 litre WJY engine

12 Later 1.9 litre WJY engines are fitted with an electronically controlled fuel injection pump to improve emissions in order to meet the next level of emission standards being introduced. The fuel system is very similar to that described in paragraphs 1 to 11, with the following changes to the injection pump.

13 The fuel injection pump electrical control system consists of the ECU, along with the following sensors:

a) *Throttle potentiometer – informs the injection pump accelerator lever position, and the rate of throttle opening/closing.*

b) *Coolant temperature sensor – informs the ECU of engine temperature.*

c) *Crankshaft sensor – informs the ECU of the crankshaft position and speed of rotation.*

d) *Vehicle speed sensor – informs the ECU of the vehicle speed.*

e) *Injector needle lift sensor – informs the ECU when the start of injection occurs at No 1 injector.*

f) *Atmospheric pressure sensor (incorporated in the ECU) – measures the atmospheric pressure to prevent problems when driving at high altitude.*

14 All the above signals are analysed by the ECU which controls the injection timing via the advance solenoid valve which is fitted to the injection pump. By opening and closing the solenoid valve, the ECU can advance and retard the injection timing as necessary. When the advance solenoid is open, the hydraulic pressure on the pump piston is reduced which results in the injection timing being retarded. To advance the injection timing, the

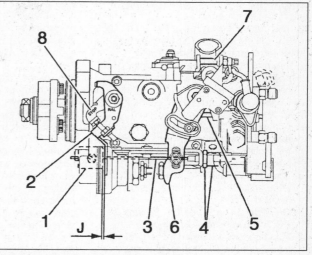

1 Fast idle cable end fitting
2 Fast idle lever
3 Fast idle cable
4 Fast idle cable adjustment screw and locknut
5 Maximum speed adjustment screw
6 Accelerator lever
7 Anti-stall speed adjustment screw
8 Manual stop lever
J Fast idle cable end fitting clearance

1.8 Injection pump details – 1.9 litre engine

ECU closes the solenoid valve which increases the pressure on the piston.

15 The ECU also controls the exhaust gas recirculation (EGR) system, described in detail in Part F of this Chapter, and the engine cooling fan.

16 If there is an abnormality in any of the readings obtained from the various sensors, the ECU enters its back-up mode. In this event, it ignores the abnormal sensor signal and assumes a preprogrammed value which will allow the engine to continue running (albeit at reduced efficiency). If the ECU enters this back-up mode, the warning light on the instrument panel will come on, and the relevant fault code will be stored in the ECU memory.

17 If the warning light comes on, the vehicle should be taken to a Peugeot dealer at the earliest opportunity. A complete test of the engine management system can then be carried out, using a special electronic diagnostic test unit which is simply plugged into the system's diagnostic connector (located next to the fusebox).

 Warning: It is necessary to take certain precautions when working on the fuel system components, particularly the fuel injectors. Before carrying out any operations on the fuel system, refer to the precautions given in 'Safety first!' at the beginning of this manual, and to any additional warning notes at the start of the relevant Sections.

2.0 litre engine

18 All 2.0 litre engines are fitted with a high-pressure diesel injection (HDi) system which incorporates the very latest in diesel injection technology. On the HDi system, the injection pump is used purely to provide the pressure required for the injection system and has no control over the injection timing (unlike conventional diesel injection systems). The

injection timing is controlled by the electronic control unit (ECU) via the electrically operated injectors. The system operates as follows.

19 The fuel system consists of a fuel tank (which is mounted under the rear of the car, with an electric fuel pump immersed in it), a fuel filter with integral water separator, a fuel injection pump, injectors and associated components.

20 The fuel pump supplies fuel to the fuel filter housing which is located at the front of the engine. The fuel filter removes all foreign matter and water and ensures that the fuel supplied to the injection pump is clean. Excess fuel is returned from the outlet on the filter housing lid to the tank via the fuel cooler. The fuel cooler is fitted to the underside of the vehicle and is cooled by the passing airflow to ensure the fuel is cool before it enters the fuel tank.

21 The fuel is heated to ensure no problems occur when the ambient temperature is very low. On early models the filter housing is connected to the coolant outlet housing on the left-hand end of the cylinder head and is fitted with a thermostat. When the temperature of the fuel in the filter housing is below 15ºC, the filter housing thermostat opens and allows the fuel to circulate around the coolant outlet housing which effectively warms the fuel. When the fuel in the filter housing reaches 25ºC, the thermostat closes. On later models an electrically operated fuel heater is fitted to the fuel feed pipe to the filter housing, the heater is controlled by the ECU.

22 The fuel injection pump is driven at half-crankshaft speed by the timing belt. The high pressure required in the system (up to 1350 bar) is produced by the three pistons in the pump. The injection pump supplies high pressure fuel to the fuel rail, which acts as a reservoir for the four injectors. Since the injection pump has no control over the injection timing (unlike conventional diesel injection systems), this means that there is no need to time the injection pump when installing the timing belt.

23 The electrical control system consists of the ECU, along with the following sensors:

a) *Accelerator pedal position sensor – informs the ECU of the accelerator pedal position, and the rate of throttle opening/closing.*

b) *Coolant temperature sensor – informs the ECU of engine temperature.*

c) *Airflow meter (incorporating the intake air temperature sensor – informs the ECU of the amount and temperature of air passing through the intake duct.*

d) *Crankshaft sensor – informs the ECU of the crankshaft position and speed of rotation.*

e) *Camshaft position sensor – informs the ECU of the positions of the pistons.*

f) *Fuel temperature sensor (where fitted) – informs the ECU of the temperature of the fuel in the fuel rail.*

g) *Fuel pressure sensor – informs the ECU of the fuel pressure present in the fuel rail.*

h) *Atmospheric pressure sensor (incorporated in the ECU) – measures the atmospheric pressure to prevent problems when driving at high altitude.*

i) *Vehicle speed sensor – informs the ECU of the vehicle speed.*

j) *Power steering pressure switch – informs the ECU when the power steering pump is under load.*

k) *Air conditioning system relay – informs ECU when the air conditioning compressor is under load.*

24 All the above signals are analysed by the ECU which selects the fuelling response appropriate to those values. The ECU controls the fuel injectors (varying the pulse width – the length of time the injectors are held open – to provide a richer or weaker mixture, as appropriate. The mixture is constantly varied by the ECU, to provide the best setting for cranking, starting (with either a hot or cold engine), warm-up, idle, cruising and acceleration. The injectors are operated 'semi-sequentially', injectors No 1 and 4 being operated as one pair and injectors No 2 and 3 as the other.

25 The ECU also has full control over the fuel pressure present in the fuel rail via the high-pressure fuel regulator and third piston deactivator solenoid valve which are fitted to the injection pump. To reduce the pressure, the ECU opens the high-pressure fuel regulator which allows the excess fuel to return direct to the tank from the pump. The third piston deactivator is used mainly to reduce the load on the engine, but can also be used to lower the fuel pressure. The deactivator solenoid valve relieves the fuel pressure from the third piston of the pump which results in only two of the pistons pressurising the fuel system.

26 The ECU also controls the exhaust gas recirculation (EGR) system, described in detail in Part F of this Chapter, and the engine cooling fan.

27 A turbocharger is fitted to increases engine efficiency. It does this by raising the pressure in the inlet manifold above atmospheric pressure. Instead of the air simply being sucked into the cylinders, it is forced in.

28 Energy for the operation of the turbocharger comes from the exhaust gas. The gas flows through a specially-shaped housing (the turbine housing) and in so doing, spins the turbine wheel. The turbine wheel is attached to a shaft, at the end of which is another vaned wheel known as the compressor wheel. The compressor wheel spins in its own housing, and compresses the inlet air on the way to the inlet manifold. The turbo shaft is pressure-lubricated by an oil feed pipe from the main oil gallery. The shaft 'floats' on a cushion of oil. A drain pipe returns the oil to the sump. Boost pressure (the pressure in the inlet manifold) is limited by a wastegate, which diverts the exhaust gas away from the turbine wheel in response to a pressure-sensitive actuator.

29 If there is an abnormality in any of the readings obtained from the various sensors, the ECU enters its back-up mode. In this event, it ignores the abnormal sensor signal and assumes a preprogrammed value which will allow the engine to continue running (albeit at reduced efficiency). If the ECU enters this back-up mode, the warning light on the instrument panel will come on, and the relevant fault code will be stored in the ECU memory.

30 If the warning light comes on, the vehicle should be taken to a Peugeot dealer at the earliest opportunity. A complete test of the engine management system can then be carried out, using a special electronic diagnostic test unit which is simply plugged into the system's diagnostic connector (located next to the fusebox).

Warnings and precautions

31 It is essential to observe strict precautions when working on the fuel system components, particularly the high pressure side of the system. Before carrying out any operations on the fuel system, refer to the precautions given in *Safety first!* at the beginning of this manual, and to the following additional information.

• *Do not carry out any repair work on the high pressure fuel system unless you are competent to do so, have all the necessary tools and equipment required, and are aware of the safety implications involved.*

• *Before starting any repair work on the fuel system, wait at least 30 seconds after switching off the engine to allow the fuel circuit to return to atmospheric pressure.*

• *Never work on the high pressure fuel system with the engine running.*

• *Keep well clear of any possible source of fuel leakage, particularly when starting the engine after carrying out repair work. A leak in the system could cause an*

extremely high pressure jet of fuel to escape, which could result in severe personal injury.

• *Never place your hands or any part of your body near to a leak in the high pressure fuel system.*

• *Do not use steam cleaning equipment or compressed air to clean the engine or any of the fuel system components.*

Repairs and general information

32 Strict cleanliness must be observed at all times when working on any part of the fuel system. This applies to the working area in general, the person doing the work, and the components being worked on.

33 Before working on the fuel system components, they must be thoroughly cleaned with a suitable degreasing fluid. Peugeot recommend the use of a specific product (SODIMAC degreasing fluid – available from Peugeot dealers). Alternatively, a suitable brake cleaning fluid may be used. Cleanliness is particularly important when working on the fuel system connections at the following components:

a) *Fuel filter.*

b) *Injection pump.*

c) *Fuel rail.*

d) *Fuel injectors.*

e) *High pressure fuel pipes.*

34 After disconnecting any fuel pipes or components, the open union or orifice must be immediately sealed to prevent the entry of dirt or foreign material. Plastic plugs and caps in various sizes are available in packs from motor factors and accessory outlets, and are particularly suitable for this application **(see illustration)**. Fingers cut from disposable rubber gloves should be used to protect components such as fuel pipes, fuel injectors and wiring connectors, and can be secured in place using elastic bands. Suitable gloves of this type are available at no cost from most petrol station forecourts.

35 Whenever any of the high pressure fuel pipes are disconnected or removed, a new pipe(s) must be obtained for refitting.

36 On the completion of any repair on the

1.34 Typical plastic plug and cap set for sealing disconnected fuel pipes and components

1.37 Two crow-foot adaptors will be necessary for tightening the fuel pipe unions

2.6 Disconnect the flexible air inlet duct from the airflow meter and turbocharger rigid inlet duct – 2.0 litre engine

2.8a Disconnect the wiring connector from the airflow meter . . .

high pressure fuel system, Peugeot recommend the use of ARDROX 9D1 BRENT leak-detecting compound. This is a powder which is applied to the fuel pipe unions and connections and turns white when dry. Any leak in the system will cause the product to darken indicating the source of the leak.

37 The torque wrench settings given in the Specifications must be strictly observed when tightening component mountings and connections. This is particularly important when tightening the high pressure fuel pipe unions. To enable a torque wrench to be used on the fuel pipe unions, two crow-foot adaptors are required (Peugeot special tools (-). 1603-G and (-). 1603-F). Suitable alternatives are available from motor factors and accessory outlets **(see illustration)**.

<table><tr><td>**2**</td><td>**Air cleaner assembly and intake ducts** – removal and refitting</td><td></td></tr></table>

Removal

1.9 litre engine

1 Release the fasteners from the right-hand side and top of the engine cover then lift off the cover, taking care not to lose its mounting rubbers.
2 Slacken the retaining clips securing the inlet duct to the air cleaner lid and EGR valve

housing. Undo the mounting bolt at the base of the resonator, then disconnect the duct and remove it from the engine.
3 Slacken and remove the bolt securing the intake duct to the crossmember then unclip the duct from the side of the air cleaner and remove it from the vehicle.
4 Slacken and remove the bolts securing the air cleaner and mounting bracket in position and remove both items as an assembly.

2.0 litre engine

5 Remove the fasteners (rotate them 90º to release them) and remove the engine cover.
6 Slacken the retaining clips and free the flexible duct from the airflow meter and turbocharger rigid inlet duct **(see illustration)**.
7 Unscrew the two bolts and free the accelerator pedal position sensor bracket from the side of the air cleaner housing.
8 Disconnect the wiring connector from the airflow meter on the side of the air cleaner lid. Lift the air cleaner housing assembly off of its mounting bracket and remove it from the engine compartment **(see illustrations)**.
9 To remove the air cleaner air inlet duct, undo the bolt securing the front of the duct to the crossmember. Undo the bolts securing the flexible tube to the air cleaner support bracket and remove the duct from the engine compartment.
10 To remove the turbocharger rigid inlet duct, release the retaining clips and free the flexible duct and breather hose from the top

of the rigid duct and unscrew the duct upper mounting bolt. Firmly apply the handbrake then jack up the front of the car and support it on axle stands (see *Jacking and vehicle support*). Unscrew the bolt securing the rigid duct to the side of the turbocharger then manoeuvre the duct out of position **(see illustrations)**. Recover the sealing ring fitted between the duct and turbocharger.

Refitting

11 Refitting is a reversal of the removal procedure, ensuring that all hoses and ducts are properly reconnected and correctly seated and are securely held by their retaining clips/bolts.

<table><tr><td>**3**</td><td>**Accelerator cable** – removal, refitting and adjustment</td><td></td></tr></table>

Removal

1 On 1.9 litre engines, release the fasteners from the right-hand side and top of the engine cover then lift off the cover, taking care not to lose its mounting rubbers. Free the accelerator inner cable from the injection pump accelerator lever, then pull the outer cable out from the mounting bracket, complete with its spring clip. Whilst the cable is disconnected, remove the cable locating

2.8b . . . then lift the air cleaner housing upward at the rear and disengage the front locating lugs – 2.0 litre engine

2.10a Undo the upper mounting bolt (arrowed) securing the rigid inlet duct to the inlet manifold

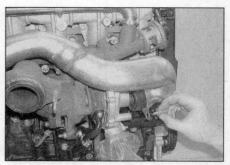

2.10b Undo the bolt securing the rigid inlet duct to the turbocharger and remove the duct – 2.0 litre engine

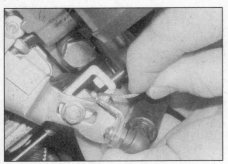

3.1a On 1.9 litre engines, free the accelerator inner cable from the lever . . .

3.1b . . . then withdraw the outer cable from the pump bracket, complete with spring clip

3.1c Remove the cable locating collar from the pump whilst the cable is removed

collar from the mounting bracket for safe-keeping (see illustrations).

2 On 2.0 litre engines, working in the engine compartment, unscrew the two bolts and free the accelerator pedal position sensor bracket from the side of the air cleaner housing. Detach the accelerator inner cable from the sensor, then pull the outer cable out from sensor bracket, complete with the spring clip (see illustrations).

3 On all engines, working back along the length of the cable, free it from any retaining clips or ties, noting its correct routing.

4 Working in the passenger compartment, release the securing clips, and remove the felt trim panel from under the facia in the driver's footwell.

5 Working from inside the vehicle, release the fastener by rotating it through a quarter of a turn anti-clockwise, and remove the fusebox cover from the facia. Release the retaining clips, and remove the felt undercover from underneath the driver's side of the facia panel.

6 Reach up behind the facia then release the retaining clip and detach the inner cable from the top of the accelerator pedal.

7 Remove the retaining clip (where fitted) which secures the outer cable end fitting to the bulkhead then tie a length of string to the end of the cable.

8 Return to the engine compartment, release the cable grommet from the bulkhead and withdraw the cable. When the end of the cable appears, untie the string and leave it in position – it can then be used to draw the cable back into position on refitting.

Refitting

9 Tie the string to the end of the cable, then use the string to draw the cable into position through the bulkhead. Once the cable end is visible, untie the string, then secure the outer cable in position and fit the inner cable into the pedal end.

10 From within the engine compartment, ensure the outer cable is correctly seated in the bulkhead grommet, then work along the cable, securing it in position with the retaining clips and ties, and ensuring that the cable is correctly routed.

11 On 1.9 litre engines, fit the locating collar to the mounting bracket then pass the cable through the collar and reconnect the inner cable to the accelerator lever. Adjust the cable as described below, then refit the facia trim panels.

12 On 2.0 litre engines, pass the outer cable through the sensor bracket grommet and reconnect the inner cable to the accelerator pedal position sensor. Refit the sensor bracket to the side of the air cleaner housing, tightening its retaining bolts securely. Adjust the cable as described below, then refit the facia trim panels.

Adjustment

13 On 1.9 litre engines, release the fasteners from the right-hand side and top of the engine cover then lift off the cover, taking care not to lose its mounting rubbers.

14 On all engines, remove the spring clip from the accelerator outer cable (see illustration). Ensuring that the injection pump lever/accelerator pedal position sensor is fully against its stop, gently pull the cable out of its grommet until all free play is removed from the inner cable.

15 With the cable held in this position, refit the spring clip to the last exposed outer cable groove in front of the rubber grommet and washer (see illustration). When the clip is refitted and the outer cable is released, there should be only a small amount of free play in the inner cable.

16 Have an assistant depress the accelerator pedal, and check that the accelerator lever/pedal position sensor opens fully and returns smoothly to its stop.

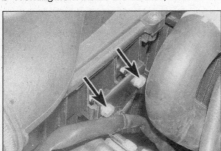

3.2a On 2.0 litre engines, undo the two bolts (arrowed) and free the accelerator pedal sensor from the air cleaner housing . . .

3.2b . . . then detach the cable from the sensor

3.14 Slide off the spring clip and adjust the accelerator cable as described in text – 1.9 litre engine

3.15 Remove all freeplay from the cable then fit the spring clip to the last exposed groove on the outer cable – 2.0 litre engine

17 On 1.9 litre engines, ensure the mounting rubbers are all correctly fitted then install the engine cover, securing it in position with the fasteners.

4 Accelerator pedal – removal and refitting

Removal

1 Disconnect the accelerator cable from the pedal as described in Section 3.

Right-hand drive models

2 Unscrew the nut from the end of the pedal pivot shaft, whilst retaining the pivot shaft with an open-ended spanner on the flats provided.
3 Pull the pedal and pivot shaft assembly from the support bracket.
4 Examine the pivot shaft for signs of wear or damage and, if necessary, renew it. The pivot shaft is a screw fit in the pedal.

Left-hand drive models

5 Slide off the spring clip from one end of the pedal pivot shaft.
6 Withdraw the pivot shaft and remove the pedal and pivot bush assembly from the support bracket.
7 Examine the pivot bushes and shaft for signs of wear, and renew as necessary.

Refitting

8 Refitting is a reversal of the removal procedure, applying a little multi-purpose grease to the pedal pivot point. On completion, adjust the accelerator cable as described in Section 3.

5 Fuel system – priming and bleeding

1 After disconnecting part of the fuel supply system or running out of fuel, it is necessary to prime the fuel system and bleed off any air which may have entered the system components, as follows.

1.9 litre engine

2 All models are fitted with a hand-operated priming pump which is built into the fuel filter housing. To gain access to the pump, release the fasteners from the right-hand side and top of the engine cover then lift off the cover, taking care not to lose its mounting rubbers.
3 Pump the priming pump until resistance is felt then pump a few more times **(see illustration)**. This will prime the fuel system components and remove all air from the system.
4 Start the engine as normal. If difficulty is encountered, pump the priming pump a few times with the ignition switched on.
5 Once the engine has started, ensure the mounting rubbers are all correctly fitted then

5.3 Priming the fuel system – 1.9 litre engine

install the engine cover, securing it in position with the fasteners.

2.0 litre engine

Note: *A new fuel filter drain plug and O-ring will be required for this operation.*
6 On completion of work on the fuel system slacken, or leave loose (as appropriate), the **new** fuel filter drain plug. Operate the low pressure pump 4 or 5 times by switching on the ignition each time for a period of 5 seconds. Switch off the ignition and wait for a period of 5 to 10 seconds to allow the pressure to fall in the fuel supply circuit. Tighten the drain plug and wipe away all spilt fuel. Start the engine and check that there is no sign whatever of fuel seepage from the filter drain plug once the engine is running.

6 Fuel supply pump (2.0 litre engine) – removal and refitting

The diesel fuel supply pump is located in the same position as the conventional fuel pump on petrol engine models, and the removal and refitting procedures are virtually identical. Refer to Chapter 4B, Section 9.

7 Fuel gauge sender unit – removal and refitting

The fuel gauge sender unit can be removed as described in Chapter 4B, Section 9. **Note:** *On 1.9 litre engines the fuel gauge sender unit does not have the fuel pump as part of the assembly. On 2.0 litre engines the fuel gauge sender unit is an integral part of the fuel pump and is not available separately.*

8 Fuel tank – removal and refitting

Refer to Chapter 4A, Section 6, noting that it will be necessary to disconnect the fuel lines and wiring connectors at the fuel supply pump/fuel gauge sender unit before lowering the tank out of position.

9 Maximum speed – checking and adjustment

Caution: The maximum speed adjustment screw is sealed by the manufacturers at the factory, using paint or an anti-tamper cap. There is no reason why it should require adjustment. Do not disturb the screw if the vehicle is still within the warranty period, otherwise the warranty will be invalidated.
Note: *This adjustment requires the use of a tachometer suitable for use on diesel engines.*

1.9 litre engine

Note: *At the time of writing, Peugeot did not specify a maximum speed for the 1.9 litre engine. Refer to your Peugeot dealer for the latest available information.*
1 Run the engine to normal operating temperature.
2 Have an assistant fully depress the accelerator pedal, and check that the maximum engine speed is as specified by the dealer. Do not keep the engine at maximum speed for more than two or three seconds.
3 If adjustment is necessary, stop the engine, release the fasteners from the right-hand side and top of the engine cover then lift off the cover, taking care not to lose its mounting rubbers.
4 Loosen the locknut, turn the maximum speed adjustment screw as necessary, and retighten the locknut **(see illustration)**.
5 Repeat the procedure in paragraph 2 to check the adjustment.
6 Stop the engine and disconnect the tachometer.
7 Where necessary, ensure the mounting rubbers are all correctly fitted then install the engine cover, securing it in position with the fasteners.

2.0 litre engine

8 The maximum speed is controlled by the ECU and cannot be adjusted by the home mechanic. The speed can be checked as described above (see paragraphs 1 and 2) but if adjustment is needed, the vehicle will have to be taken to a Peugeot dealer for testing (see Section 1).

9.4 Maximum speed adjustment screw fitted with tamperproof cap (arrowed) – 1.9 litre engine

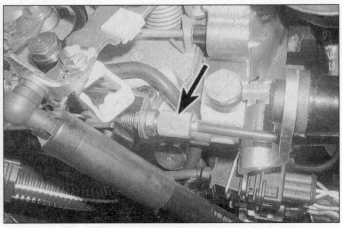

10.4 Slacken the retaining screw (arrowed) then slide the end fitting off the fast idle cable

10.13 Fast idle cable adjustment screw and locknut

10 Fast idle thermostatic sensor (1.9 litre engine) – removal, refitting and adjustment

Removal

Note: *A new sealing washer must be used when refitting the sensor.*

1 The thermostatic sensor is located in the side of the thermostat/fuel filter housing.

2 To gain access to the sensor, remove the intake duct connecting the air cleaner housing to the inlet manifold as described in Section 2.

3 Drain the cooling system as described in Chapter 1B.

4 Loosen the clamp screw or nut (as applicable), and disconnect the fast idle cable end fitting from the inner cable at the fuel injection pump fast idle lever **(see illustration)**.

5 Slide the cable from the adjustment screw located in the bracket on the fuel injection pump.

6 Using a suitable open-ended spanner, unscrew the thermostatic sensor from the fuel filter/thermostat housing, and withdraw the sensor complete with the cable. Recover the sealing washer and discard it; a new one should be used on refitting.

Refitting

7 Fit the sensor, complete with a new sealing washer, and tighten it securely.

8 Ensure the cable is correctly routed then pass it through the adjustment screw on the bracket.

9 Insert the inner cable through the fast idle lever, and position the end fitting on the cable, but do not tighten the clamp screw or nut (as applicable).

10 Adjust the cable as described in the following paragraphs.

Adjustment

11 Release the fasteners from the right-hand side and top of the engine cover then lift off the cover, taking care not to lose its mounting rubbers.

12 With the engine cold, slacken the fast idle cable end fitting clamp screw/nut. Push the fast idle lever fully towards the flywheel end of the engine then remove all slack from the cable. With the fast idle lever against its stop and the end fitting firmly against the lever, securely tighten the clamp screw or nut.

13 Check the fast idle lever is firmly against its stop. If necessary, adjust the cable using the screw and locknut arrangement fitted to the injection pump bracket **(see illustration)**.

14 Ensure the end fitting clamp screw/nut and adjuster locknut are securely tightened then measure the exposed length of the fast idle inner cable.

15 Refit the intake duct assembly (where removed – see Section 2).

16 Refill the cooling system as described in Chapter 1B, and run the engine to its normal operating temperature.

17 With the engine at its normal operating temperature, the thermostatic sensor cable should be slack with approximately 0.5 to 1.0 mm of freeplay present. If no freeplay is present in the cable, it is likely that the sensor is faulty. If the thermostatic sensor is functioning correctly, the cable travel should be at least 6 mm from cold to hot.

18 Check that the engine speed increases when the fast idle lever is pushed towards the flywheel end of the engine.

19 If all is well, stop the engine.

20 Ensure the mounting rubbers are all correctly fitted then install the engine cover, securing it in position with the fasteners.

11 Injection system electrical components – removal and refitting

1.9 litre WJZ engine

Stop solenoid

1 The stop solenoid is part of the immobiliser unit which is located on the top of the fuel

injection pump, its purpose being to cut the fuel supply when the ignition is switched off. Renewal of the immobiliser/solenoid unit is a complex operation which should be entrusted to a Peugeot dealer or Lucas injection specialist. The immobiliser unit is secured in position with shear bolts which have to drilled out (a high-risk operation which could lead to damage if carried out carelessly) and the new unit will have to be initialised on refitting.

Fuel cut-off inertia switch

Note: *A fuel cut-off inertia switch is not fitted to all models.*

2 The fuel cut-off inertia switch is located in the left-hand rear corner of the engine compartment. To remove it, first disconnect the battery negative terminal (refer to *Disconnecting the battery* in the Reference Chapter).

3 Unscrew the retaining bolts then disconnect the wiring connector and remove the switch from the vehicle.

4 Refitting is the reverse of removal. On completion, reset the switch by firmly depressing its button.

1.9 litre WJY engine

Stop solenoid

5 See paragraph 1.

Electronic control unit

6 The ECU is located in the plastic box which is mounted onto the rear of the battery mounting tray.

7 Disconnect the battery negative terminal (refer to *Disconnecting the battery* in the Reference Chapter).

8 Unclip the cover from the box, then lift the retaining clip and disconnect the wiring connector from the ECU.

9 Undo the retaining nut and release the relay unit from the rear of the ECU box.

10 Undo the retaining screws and remove the ECU and box assembly from the battery tray. If necessary, undo the retaining screws and separate the ECU and box.

11.14a Slacken the mounting bolt . . .

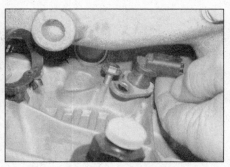

11.14b . . . then free the crankshaft sensor from the bolt and manoeuvre it out of position

11 Refitting is a reverse of the removal procedure ensuring the wiring connector is securely reconnected.

Crankshaft sensor

12 The crankshaft sensor is situated on the top of the transmission unit.
13 To remove the sensor, first disconnect the battery negative terminal (refer to *Disconnecting the battery* in the Reference Chapter).
14 Disconnect the wiring connector from the sensor then slacken the mounting bolt and remove the sensor from the transmission unit (the sensor is slotted to ease removal) **(see illustrations)**.
15 Refitting is reverse of the removal procedure.

Vehicle speed sensor

16 The vehicle speed sensor is an integral part of the speedometer drive. Refer to Chapter 7A for removal and refitting details.

Injector needle lift sensor

17 The needle lift sensor is an integral part of No 1 cylinder injector. See Section 14 for removal and refitting details.

Injection system relay unit

18 The relay unit is mounted onto the rear of the ECU plastic box which is situated directly behind the battery.
19 Disconnect the battery negative terminal (refer to *Disconnecting the battery* in the Reference Chapter).
20 Undo the retaining nut, then disconnect the wiring connector and remove the relay unit from the vehicle.
21 Refitting is the reverse of removal, ensuring that the relay unit is securely clipped in position.

Coolant temperature sensor

22 The coolant temperature sensor is screwed into the fuel filter/thermostat housing. Refer to Chapter 3 for removal and refitting information.

Throttle potentiometer and advance solenoid

23 These components are both fitted to the injection pump. If either of the above are faulty, renewal should be entrusted to a Peugeot dealer who will have the necessary special equipment to adjust and calibrate the new components.

Fuel cut-off inertia switch

Note: *A fuel cut-off inertia switch is not fitted to all models.*
24 Proceed as described in paragraphs 2 to 4.

2.0 litre engine

Electronic control unit

25 Proceed as described in paragraphs 6 to 11.

Crankshaft sensor

26 Proceed as described in paragraphs 12 to 15. Access to the sensor is poor; remove the battery and battery tray to improve access (see Chapter 5A)

Vehicle speed sensor

27 The vehicle speed sensor is an integral part of the speedometer drive. Refer to Chapter 7A for removal and refitting details.

Injection system relay unit

28 Proceed as described in paragraphs 18 to 21.

Coolant temperature sensor

29 The coolant temperature sensor is fitted to the side of the coolant outlet/thermostat housing on the left-hand end of the cylinder head **(see illustration)**. Refer to Chapter 3 for removal and refitting information.

11.29 Coolant temperature sensor (arrowed) is fitted to the coolant outlet housing on the left-hand end of the cylinder head

Airflow meter

30 The airflow meter is attached to the lid of the air cleaner housing. Prior to removal, disconnect the battery negative terminal (refer to *Disconnecting the battery* in the Reference Chapter), then remove the fasteners (rotate them 90° to release them) and remove the engine cover.
31 Slacken the retaining clips and free the flexible duct from the airflow meter and turbocharger rigid inlet duct.
32 Disconnect the wiring connector from the side of the airflow meter. Undo the screws securing the air cleaner lid to the housing and lift off the lid, complete with airflow meter.
33 Undo the two screws and withdraw the airflow meter from the air cleaner lid.
34 Refitting is the reverse of removal.

Camshaft position sensor

35 The camshaft position sensor is fitted to the top of the cylinder head cover right-hand end. Prior to removal, disconnect the battery negative terminal (refer to *Disconnecting the battery* in the Reference Chapter). Remove the fasteners (rotate them 90° to release them) and remove the engine cover.
36 Remove the camshaft sprocket timing belt cover (see Chapter 2D).
37 Disconnect the camshaft sensor wiring connector.
38 Unscrew the retaining bolt and remove the sensor from the engine.
39 On refitting, align the camshaft hub timing hole with the cylinder head hole (see Chapter 2D, Section 3). Insert the flywheel locking tool to ensure the camshaft is correctly positioned.
40 Fit the sensor to its mounting bracket and lightly tighten its bolt.
41 If a new sensor is being fitted, position the sensor so its fitting lug is in contact with the rear of the camshaft hub then securely tighten the sensor bolt. The lug automatically sets the sensor air gap to the correct distance and will be knocked off the first time the engine is started.
42 If the original sensor is being refitted, using feeler gauges, set the gap between the sensor tip and camshaft hub to 1.2 mm. Ensure the sensor is correctly positioned then securely tighten its retaining bolt **(see illustration)**. Check the air gap and, if necessary, readjust.

11.42 On 2.0 litre engines, adjust the camshaft sensor air gap as described in text

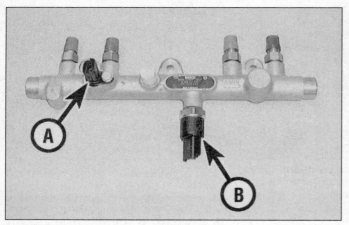

11.45 Fuel temperature sensor (A) and fuel pressure sensor (B) locations on the fuel rail (shown removed for clarity)

11.72 Fuel heater assembly – later models

43 Once the sensor is correctly positioned, refit the timing belt cover and remove the flywheel locking tool (where fitted).

44 Reconnect the sensor wiring connector and battery negative terminal, then securely refit the engine cover.

Fuel temperature sensor

 Warning: Refer to the precautionary information contained in Section 1 before proceeding.

Note: *Do not remove the sensor from the fuel rail unless there is a valid reason to do so. At the time of writing there was no information as to the availability of the sensor seal as a separate item. Consult a Peugeot parts stockist for the latest information before proceeding.*

45 The fuel temperature sensor is located towards the right-hand end of the fuel rail **(see illustration)**. Prior to removal, disconnect the battery negative terminal (refer to *Disconnecting the battery* in the Reference Chapter).

46 Remove the fasteners (rotate them 90° to release them) and remove the engine cover.

47 Disconnect the fuel temperature sensor wiring connector.

48 Thoroughly clean the area around the sensor and its location on the fuel rail.

49 Suitably protect the components below the sensor and have plenty of clean rags handy. Be prepared for considerable fuel spillage.

50 Undo the retaining bolt and withdraw the sensor from the fuel rail. Plug the opening in the fuel rail as soon as the sensor is withdrawn.

51 Prior to refitting, if the original sensor is to be refitted, renew the sensor seal, where applicable (see the note at the start of this sub-Section).

52 Locate the sensor in the fuel rail and refit the retaining bolt, tightened securely.

53 Refit the sensor wiring connector and reconnect the battery.

54 Observing the precautions listed in Section 1, prime the fuel system as described in Section 5, then start the engine and allow it to idle. Check for leaks at the fuel temperature sensor with the engine idling. If satisfactory, increase the engine speed to 4000 rpm and check again for leaks. Take the car for a short road test and check for leaks once again on return. If any leaks are detected, obtain and fit a new sensor.

55 Refit the engine cover on completion.

Fuel pressure sensor

 Warning: Refer to the precautionary information contained in Section 1 before proceeding.

Note: *A 27 mm forked adaptor and a new sensor sealing ring will be required for this operation.*

56 The fuel pressure sensor is located centrally on the underside of the fuel rail.

57 Disconnect the battery negative terminal (refer to *Disconnecting the battery* in the Reference Chapter), then release the fasteners (rotate them 90° to release them) and remove the engine cover.

58 Release the retaining clip and disconnect the crankcase ventilation hose from the cylinder head cover.

59 Disconnect the fuel supply and return hose quick-release fittings at the fuel filter, using a small screwdriver to release the locking clip. Suitably plug or cover the open unions to prevent dirt entry. Release the fuel hoses from the relevant retaining clips.

60 Disconnect the fuel pressure sensor wiring connector.

61 Thoroughly clean the area around the sensor and its location on the fuel rail.

62 Suitably protect the components below the sensor and have plenty of clean rags handy. Be prepared for considerable fuel spillage.

63 Using the 27 mm forked adaptor and a socket bar, unscrew the fuel pressure sensor from the base of the fuel rail.

64 Obtain and fit a new sealing ring to the sensor prior to refitting.

65 Locate the sensor in the fuel rail and tighten it to the specified torque.

66 Reconnect the sensor wiring connector, fuel hoses, crankcase ventilation hose and battery.

67 Observing the precautions listed in Section 1, prime the fuel system as described in Section 5, then start the engine and allow it to idle. Check for leaks at the fuel pressure sensor with the engine idling. If satisfactory, increase the engine speed to 4000 rpm and check again for leaks. Take the car for a short road test and check for leaks once again on return. If any leaks are detected, obtain and fit another new sensor sealing ring.

68 Refit the engine cover on completion.

Third piston deactivator solenoid valve

69 The solenoid valve is mounted on the top of the injection pump; it is an integral part of the pump and cannot be renewed. If the valve is faulty the injection pump will have to be renewed or repaired. Never attempt to remove the solenoid from the pump.

High-pressure fuel regulator

70 The high-pressure fuel regulator is mounted on the rear of the injection pump; it is an integral part of the pump and cannot be renewed. If the regulator is faulty the injection pump will have to be renewed or repaired. Never attempt to remove the regulator from the pump.

Fuel cut-off inertia switch

71 Refer to paragraphs 2 to 4.

Electrically-operated fuel heater

 Warning: Refer to the precautionary information contained in Section 1 before proceeding.

72 The fuel heater is fitted to the fuel feed pipe to the filter housing **(see illustration)**.

73 Disconnect the battery negative terminal

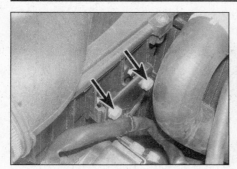

11.79a Undo the two bolts (arrowed) . . .

11.79b . . . and free the accelerator pedal sensor from the side of the air cleaner housing

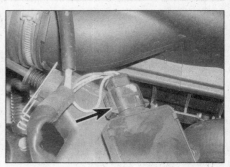

11.80 Disconnect the wiring connector (arrowed) . . .

(refer to *Disconnecting the battery* in the Reference Chapter), then release the fasteners (rotate them 90° to release them) and remove the engine cover.

74 Disconnect the wiring connector from the heater.

75 Remove all traces of dirt from around the heater; the heater and its surrounding area must be clean and dry before proceeding. Position a wad of rag beneath the heater to catch any spilt fuel.

76 Release the clips and disconnect the fuel pipes from the heater. Plug the fuel pipes to prevent the entry of dirt into the fuel system.

77 Unscrew the retaining bolt and remove the fuel heater from the engine.

78 Refitting is the reverse of removal. On completion, prime the fuel system as described in Section 5.

Accelerator pedal position sensor

79 Working in the engine compartment, unscrew the two bolts and free the accelerator pedal position sensor bracket from the side of the air cleaner housing **(see illustrations)**.

80 Disconnect the sensor wiring connector **(see illustration)**.

81 Free the accelerator inner cable from the sensor then free the outer cable from sensor bracket, complete with the spring clip, and remove the sensor from the vehicle **(see illustration)**.

82 Refitting is the reverse of removal, adjusting the accelerator cable as described in Section 3.

11.81 . . . then detach the cable and remove the accelerator pedal position sensor from the vehicle

<table>
<tr><td>

12 Fuel injection pump –
removal and refitting

</td></tr>
</table>

Caution: Be careful not to allow dirt into the injection pump or injector pipes during this procedure.

1.9 litre engine

Removal

Note: *If the injection pump is being taken to a injection specialist for repair, unlock the immobiliser module as follows before disconnecting the battery. Switch on the ignition and lower the driver's door window. Get out of the vehicle and close all the doors then switch off the ignition. Reach in through the window and switch on the ignition again, wait at least ten seconds then switch the ignition off. Immediately disconnect the battery negative terminal (refer to 'Disconnecting the battery' in the Reference Chapter) then disconnect the wiring connectors from the injection pump (the pump must be disconnected within ten minutes of the ignition being switched off). If the immobiliser module is not unlocked it will not be possible for the pump repairers to test the pump.*

1 Disconnect the battery negative terminal (refer to *Disconnecting the battery* in the Reference Chapter).

2 Release the fasteners from the right-hand side and top of the engine cover then lift off the cover, taking care not to lose its mounting rubbers.

12.11 On 1.9 litre engines, disconnect the wiring connectors (arrowed) from the rear of the injection pump

3 Remove the intake duct connecting the air cleaner housing to the manifold (see Section 2).

4 Cover the components beneath the injection pump with a plastic bag, as a precaution against fuel spillage.

5 Remove the injection pump sprocket as described in Chapter 2D, Section 8.

6 Remove the upper section of the inlet manifold (see Section 18).

7 Disconnect the accelerator cable from the fuel injection pump (see Section 3).

8 Disconnect the fast idle cable from the fuel injection pump (see Section 10).

9 Trace the injection pump fuel feed pipe back to the filter. Wipe clean the pipe end fitting then release and disconnect the pipe from the filter. Plug the pipe end and filter housing union to minimise fuel loss and prevent the entry of dirt into the system.

10 Wipe clean the area around the injection pump fuel return metal pipe unions. Disconnect the return pipe and hose from the metal pipe and plug the pipe and union ends to minimise fuel loss and prevent the entry of dirt into the system.

11 Disconnect the wiring connectors from the injection pump **(see illustration)**.

12 Remove all traces of dirt from all the injector pipe unions. Unscrew the union nuts securing the injector pipes to the fuel injection pump and injectors. Counterhold the adaptors on the pump, while unscrewing the pipe-to-pump union nuts. Remove the pipes as a set. Plug the injection pump/injector unions to prevent the entry of dirt.

13 Slacken the pump rear mounting bolt.

14 Unscrew the three front mounting bolts securing the pump to the mounting bracket then manoeuvre the pump out of position.

15 If necessary, unbolt the pump mounting bracket and remove it from the cylinder head, taking care not to lose its locating dowels.

Refitting

16 If necessary, ensure the locating dowels are in position, then refit the mounting bracket to the cylinder head. Tighten the bracket bolts to the specified torque

17 Ensure the pump rear mounting bolt, spacer, washer and nut are correctly fitted to the mounting bracket.

18 Manoeuvre the pump into position and seat it correctly in the mounting bracket.

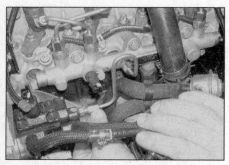

12.35 On 2.0 litre engines, counterhold the adapters while slackening the union nuts to remove the high-pressure pipe linking the pump and the fuel rail

1 High-pressure pipe
2 High-pressure fuel regulator wiring connector
3 Rear bracket-to-pump bolts
4 Rear bracket-to-mounting bracket bolt
5 Rear bracket
6 Fuel return hose
7 Pump front mounting nut/bolts
8 Fuel feed hose
9 Third piston deactivator solenoid valve wiring connector
10 Fuel pipe adaptor

12.36 Injection pump details – 2.0 litre engine

19 Refit the pump front mounting bolts, tightening them to the specified torque. Once the front mounting bolts have been tightened, tighten the rear mounting bolt to the specified torque.

20 Refit and reconnect the injector fuel pipes. Loosely tighten all the union nuts to ensure all pipes are correctly seated then go around and tighten them to the specified torque. Counterhold the injection pump adaptors whilst tightening the injection pump end nuts.

21 Reconnect all relevant wiring to the pump.

22 Securely reconnect the feed and return pipes to the injection pump and fuel filter housing.

23 Reconnect and adjust the accelerator cable as described in Section 3.

24 Reconnect and adjust the fast idle cable as described in Section 10.

25 Refit the injection pump sprocket and timing belt as described in Chapter 2D, Section 8.

26 Refit the inlet manifold as described in Section 18.

27 Prime the fuel system as described in Section 5. Start the engine and check for signs of fuel leaks before refitting the engine cover.

2.0 litre engine

 Warning: Refer to the precautionary information contained in Section 1 before proceeding.

Removal

Note: A new high-pressure fuel pipe will be required on refitting. The pipe should be renewed whenever a union nut is slackened.

28 Disconnect the battery negative terminal (refer to Disconnecting the battery in the Reference Chapter).

29 Remove the injection pump sprocket as described in Chapter 2D, Section 8.

30 Cover the components beneath the injection pump with a plastic bag, as a precaution against fuel spillage.

31 Drain the fuel filter housing (see Chapter 1B).

32 Wipe clean the area around the fuel outlet unions on the top of the fuel filter housing. Disconnect the pipes from the housing and plug the pipe and union ends to minimise fuel loss and prevent the entry of dirt into the system.

33 Free the fuel filter housing from its mounting bracket and position it clear of the injection pump. Slacken and remove the bolts and remove the filter housing mounting bracket.

34 Remove all traces of dirt from the injection pump feed and return hose unions, and the high-pressure fuel pipe unions; the pump and its surrounding area must be clean and dry before proceeding. Position a wad of rag beneath the pipe to catch any spilt fuel.

35 Counterhold the adaptors then slacken the union nuts securing the high-pressure fuel pipe to the injection pump/fuel rail. Remove the fuel pipe and plug the pump/fuel rail unions to prevent the entry of dirt into the fuel system **(see illustration)**. Discard the pipe; a new one should be used on refitting.

Caution: Never unscrew the adaptors from the fuel rail or injection pump.

36 Release the retaining clips and disconnect the fuel feed and return hoses from the pump **(see illustration)**. Plug the hoses ends and pump unions to prevent the entry of dirt.

37 Disconnect the wiring connectors from the injection pump third piston deactivator solenoid and the high-pressure fuel regulator.

38 Unscrew the two bolts securing the rear bracket to the injection pump. Slacken the bolt securing the bracket to the mounting bracket and pivot the bracket away from the pump.

39 Slacken and remove the three front mounting nut/bolts securing the pump to the mounting bracket. Remove the injection pump and recover the spacers fitted between the pump and bracket.

40 If necessary, unbolt the pump mounting bracket and remove it from the cylinder head, taking care not to lose its locating dowels.

Refitting

41 If necessary, ensure the locating dowels are in position, then refit the mounting bracket to the cylinder head. Tighten the bracket bolts to the specified torque.

42 Ensure the rear bracket, spacer, captive nut and bolt are correctly fitted to the pump mounting bracket.

43 Manoeuvre the pump into position and engage it with the mounting stud. Align the rear mounting bracket with the pump and fit the bolts, tightening them lightly only at this stage.

44 Ensure the spacers are correctly positioned between the pump and bracket then refit the front mounting bolts. Fit the nut to the mounting stud then tighten the pump front mounting nut and bolts to the specified torque.

45 Tighten the bolts securing the rear bracket to the pump to the specified torque then tighten the bolt securing the bracket to the pump mounting bracket to the specified torque.

46 Reconnect the wiring connectors to the injection pump.

47 Fit the new high-pressure fuel pipe to the injection pump/fuel rail, and tighten both its union nuts by hand to ensure the pipe is correctly positioned. Using a torque wrench and crow-foot adaptor, tighten the union nuts to the specified torque whilst counterholding the pump/fuel rail adaptor **(see illustration)**.

12.47 On 2.0 litre engines, when refitting the new high-pressure pipe to the pump and fuel rail, counterhold their adapters to tighten the union nuts to the specified torque wrench setting

48 Reconnect the feed and return hoses to the pump, tightening the retaining clips securely.

49 Refit the fuel filter mounting bracket and tighten its retaining bolts to the specified torque. Securely refit the filter housing to the bracket then reconnect the fuel pipes.

50 Refit the injection pump sprocket and timing belt as described in Chapter 2D, Section 8.

51 Prime the fuel system as described in Section 5. Start the engine and check for signs of fuel leaks before refitting the engine cover.

13 Injection timing – checking and adjustment

1.9 litre engine

1 The injection timing is set when the timing belt is installed. If at any time a fault is suspected, referring to Chapter 2D, Section 3, remove the timing belt covers and check that the flywheel, camshaft and injection pump timing holes are all correctly aligned so the locking tools can be inserted. If the timing holes are correctly aligned, the injection pump timing is correct (Peugeot do not specify any static or dynamic timing figures for this engine – on the WJY engine the timing is being constantly altered by the ECU anyway). If not, remove and refit the timing belt as described in Chapter 2D.

2.0 litre engine

2 On the 2.0 litre engine the injection timing is determined by the ECU using the information from its various sensors. Checking and adjustment can only be carried out using specialist diagnostic equipment (see Section 1).

14 Fuel injectors – removal and refitting

⚠️ **Warning: Exercise extreme caution when working on the fuel injectors. Never expose the hands or any part of the body to injector spray, as the high working pressure can cause the fuel to penetrate the skin, with possibly fatal results. You are strongly advised to have any work which involves testing the injectors under pressure carried out by a dealer or fuel injection specialist.**

1.9 litre engine

Caution: Be careful not to allow dirt into the injection pump or injectors during this procedure.

Removal

1 Remove the upper section of the inlet manifold as described in Section 18.

2 Disconnect the leak-off pipe(s) from the injector to be removed **(see illustration)**.

3 Remove all traces of dirt from all the injector pipe unions. Unscrew the union nuts securing the injector pipes to the fuel injection pump and injectors **(see illustration)**. Counterhold the adaptors on the pump, while unscrewing the pipe-to-pump union nuts. Remove the pipes as a set. Plug the injection pump/injector unions to prevent the entry of dirt.

4 On WJY engines, if No 1 injector is being removed, trace the needle lift sensor wiring back from the injector and disconnect its wiring connector from the main harness.

5 Remove all traces of dirt from around the injector then unscrew the injector from the cylinder head. Recover the injector fire seal washer from the cylinder head and discard it; a new one must be used on refitting.

Caution: Take care not to drop the injectors, or allow the needles at their tips to become damaged. The injectors are precision-made to fine limits, and must not be handled roughly. In particular, never mount them in a bench vice.

Refitting

6 Fit the new fire seal washer ensuring its convex surface is facing upwards (towards the injector).

7 Carefully refit the injector to the cylinder head, tightening it to the specified torque.

8 Reconnect the leak-off pipe(s) to the injector. Where necessary, reconnect the needle lift sensor wiring connector.

9 With all the injectors correctly installed, refit and reconnect the injector pipes. Loosely tighten all the union nuts to ensure all pipes are correctly seated then go around and tighten them to the specified torque. Counterhold the injection pump adaptors whilst tightening the injection pump end nuts.

10 Refit the inlet manifold as described in Section 18.

11 Prime the fuel system as described in Section 5. Start the engine and check for signs of fuel leaks before refitting the engine cover.

2.0 litre engine

⚠️ **Warning: Refer to the precautionary information contained in Section 1 before proceeding.**
Caution: Be careful not to allow dirt into the fuel rail or injectors during this procedure.
Note: A new high-pressure fuel pipe will be required for each injector on refitting. They should be renewed whenever a union nut is slackened.

Removal

12 Disconnect the battery negative terminal (refer to *Disconnecting the battery* in the Reference Chapter).

13 Remove the fasteners (rotate them 90° to release them) and remove the engine cover.

14 Each injector can then be removed as follows; if necessary unbolt the engine cover bracket/wiring harness guide and/or disconnect the breather hose to improve access.

15 Disconnect the wiring connector from the injector.

16 Remove all traces of dirt from the injector and high-pressure fuel pipe unions, the injector and its surrounding area must be clean and dry before proceeding. Position a wad of rag beneath the pipe to catch any spilt fuel.

17 Counterhold the adaptor then slacken the union nuts securing the high-pressure fuel pipe to the injector/fuel rail **(see illustration)**. Remove the fuel pipe and plug the injector/fuel rail unions to prevent the entry of dirt into the fuel system. Discard the pipe; a new one should be used on refitting.

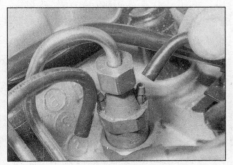

14.2 Disconnecting the leak-off pipe from the injector – 1.9 litre engine

14.3 Unscrewing an injector pipe nut – 1.9 litre engine

14.17 On 2.0 litre engines, retain the adaptors whilst slackening the union nuts then remove and discard the high-pressure pipe linking the injector to the fuel rail

14.18 Remove the retaining clip and disconnect the leak-off pipe connector from the injector

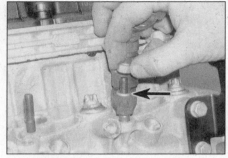

14.19 Slacken and remove the injector retaining nut and lift off the domed washer (arrowed)

14.20a Remove the injector and retaining clamp from the cylinder head . . .

Caution: Never unscrew the adaptors from the fuel rail or injector.

18 Remove the retaining clip and disconnect the leak-off pipe connector from the injector **(see illustration)**.

19 Slacken and remove the injector retaining nut and domed washer **(see illustration)**.

20 Carefully remove the injector and retaining clamp from the cylinder head, noting which way up the clamp is fitted. If the retaining clamp pin is a loose fit, remove it and store it with the clamp for safe-keeping **(see illustrations)**.

> **HAYNES HINT**
> *If the injector is a tight fit, remove the retaining clamp stud (using two nuts locked together) and free the injector by rotating it with an open-ended spanner located on the retaining clamp flats. Never rotate the injector using a spanner on the large nut on the upper end of the injector as this will seriously damage the injector.*

Caution: Take care not to knock or drop the injector. The injectors are precision-made to fine limits, and must not be handled roughly. In particular, never mount them in a bench vice.

21 Recover the injector sealing washer and collar and discard them; new ones must be used on refitting.

Refitting

22 Where necessary, refit the injector retaining clamp stud to the cylinder head. Ensure the stud is fitted the correctly way around (shorter length of thread screwed into the cylinder head) then tighten it securely.

23 Fit a new sealing collar and washer to the injector **(see illustrations)**.

24 Engage the retaining clamp with the injector flats, ensuring the flat surface of the clamp is facing downwards.

25 Ensure the clamp pin is correctly fitted to the cylinder head then manoeuvre the injector and retaining clamp into position.

26 Ensure the injector and clamp are correctly located then fit the domed washer with its convex surface facing downwards. Refit the retaining clamp nut, tighten it lightly only at this stage.

27 Fit the new high-pressure fuel pipe and lightly tighten its union nuts.

28 Ensure the high-pressure pipe is correctly seated then tighten the injector retaining clamp nut to the specified torque.

29 Using a torque wrench and crow-foot adaptor, tighten the high-pressure fuel pipe union nuts to the specified torque whilst counterholding the injector/fuel rail adaptor.

30 Reconnect the wiring connector and leak-off pipe connector securely to the injector.

31 Reconnect the battery then prime the fuel system as described in Section 5.

32 Start the engine and check for fuel leaks before refitting the engine cover.

15 Fuel rail (2.0 litre engine) – removal and refitting

> ⚠ *Warning: Refer to the precautionary information contained in Section 1 before proceeding.*

Caution: Be careful not to allow dirt into the injection pump or injectors during this procedure.

Note: *New high-pressure fuel pipes will be required on refitting. They should be renewed whenever a union nut is slackened.*

Removal

1 Disconnect the battery negative terminal (refer to *Disconnecting the battery* in the Reference Chapter). Release the fasteners (rotate them 90° to release them) and remove the engine cover.

2 Disconnect the breather hose from the cylinder head cover and position it clear of the fuel rail.

3 Unscrew the bolts and remove the engine cover mounting bracket from the right-hand side of the cylinder head. Undo the nuts and free the injector wiring harness guide from the cylinder head.

4 Remove all traces of dirt from the injector and high-pressure fuel pipe unions, the fuel rail and its surrounding area must be clean and dry before proceeding. Position a wad of rag beneath the fuel rail to catch any spilt fuel.

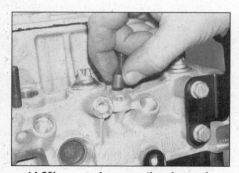

14.20b . . . and remove the clamp pin

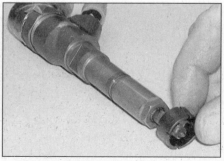

14.23a Slide the new sealing collar onto the injector . . .

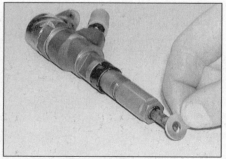

14.23b . . . then fit the new sealing washer

15.6a Retain the adaptors whilst slackening the union nuts then remove and discard the high-pressure pipes linking the pump and injectors to the fuel rail

15.6b Plug/cap all unions to prevent the entry of dirt into the fuel system

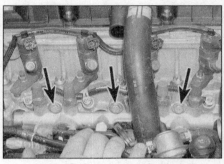

15.8a Undo the mounting bolts (arrowed) . . .

5 Wipe clean the area around the fuel outlet unions on the top of the fuel filter housing. Disconnect the pipes from the housing and plug the pipe and union ends to minimise fuel loss and prevent the entry of dirt into the system. Free the fuel filter housing from its mounting bracket and position it clear of the injection pump.

6 Counterhold the adaptors then slacken the union nuts securing the high-pressure fuel pipes to the fuel rail/injection pump/injectors. Remove the fuel pipes and plug all the fuel unions to prevent the entry of dirt into the fuel system **(see illustrations)**. Discard the pipes; new ones should be used on refitting.
Caution: Never unscrew the adaptors from the fuel rail, injection pump or injectors.

7 Disconnect the wiring connectors from the fuel temperature sensor (where fitted) and pressure sensor which are fitted to the fuel rail.

8 Unscrew the three mounting bolts then remove the fuel rail from the cylinder head **(see illustrations)**.

Refitting

9 Manoeuvre the fuel rail into position and lightly tighten its mounting bolts. Reconnect the wiring connectors to the fuel temperature and pressure sensors.

10 Fit the new high-pressure fuel pipes and tighten all the union nuts by hand to ensure each pipe is correctly positioned. Using a torque wrench and crow-foot adaptor, tighten

the union nuts to the specified torque counterholding each adaptor as the nut is tightened **(see illustration)**. **Note:** *If it is not possible to connect the pipes to the injectors. Remove the injectors and refit them, connecting the pipe to the injectors before tightening the retaining clamp nuts (see Section 14).*

11 Once all pipe union nuts are correctly tightened, tighten the fuel rail mounting bolts to the specified torque.

12 Refit the fuel filter housing to its bracket then reconnect the fuel hoses.

13 Refit the engine cover bracket to the cylinder head and reconnect the breather hose.

14 Reconnect the battery then prime the fuel system as described in Section 5.

15 Start the engine and check for fuel leaks before refitting the engine cover.

16 Fuel cooler (2.0 litre engine) – removal and refitting

⚠ **Warning: Refer to the precautionary information contained in Section 1 before proceeding.**
Caution: Be careful not to allow dirt into the fuel system during this procedure.

Removal

1 Chock the rear wheels, firmly apply the handbrake then jack up the front of the vehicle and support it on axle stands (*see Jacking and vehicle support*).

2 Remove all traces of dirt from fuel cooler and its surrounding area on the vehicle underbody. Position a container underneath the cooler to catch any spilt fuel.

3 Release the retaining clips and disconnect the fuel pipes from the cooler **(see illustration)**. Plug the pipe ends to minimise fuel loss and prevent the entry of dirt into the fuel system.

4 Unscrew the mounting nuts and remove the fuel cooler from the vehicle. Inspect the cooler mounting rubber for signs of damage or deterioration and renew if necessary.

Refitting

5 Ensure the mounting rubber is correctly fitted to the body then engage the fuel cooler peg in the rubber. Locate the cooler on its mounting studs and refit the mounting nuts, tightening them securely.

6 Reconnect the fuel pipes securely to the cooler then lower the vehicle to the ground.

7 Prime the fuel system (see Section 5) then start the engine and check for signs of fuel leaks.

17 Turbocharger – removal and refitting

Removal

1 Firmly apply the handbrake then jack up the front of the vehicle and support it on axle sands (see *Jacking and vehicle support*).

2 Remove the right-hand driveshaft as described in Chapter 8.

15.8b . . . and manoeuvre the fuel rail out of position

15.10 Using a torque wrench and crow-foot adaptor, tighten the fuel pipe union nuts

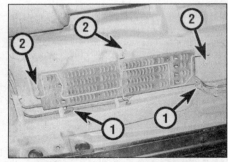

16.3 Fuel cooler fuel pipe unions (1) and mounting nuts (2) – 2.0 litre engine

17.8 Removing the connecting sleeve from the turbocharger

17.11 Turbocharger oil feed pipe union and return hose union

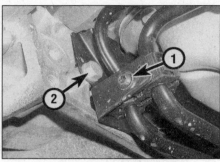

17.13 Undo the power steering pipe clip screw (1) then undo the bolts (2) and remove the flywheel lower cover plate from the transmission unit

3 Unscrew the nuts and bolts and remove the mounting link securing the rear engine/transmission mounting to the subframe. Undo the retaining bolts and remove the rear mounting assembly from the rear of the cylinder block.

4 Remove the exhaust system catalytic converter as described in Section 20.

5 Unscrew the bolts and remove the exhaust outlet flange from the turbocharger.

6 Slacken the retaining clip and free the flexible duct from the top of the turbocharger intake pipe. Also unscrew the pipe upper mounting bolt. Unscrew the bolt securing the intake pipe to the side of the turbocharger then manoeuvre the pipe out of position. Recover the sealing ring fitted between the pipe and turbocharger.

7 Slacken the retaining clips securing the outlet pipe to its connecting sleeves on the turbocharger and inlet manifold then unclip and remove the pipe.

8 Slacken the retaining clip and remove the connecting sleeve from the turbocharger **(see illustration)**.

9 Remove the EGR valve as described in Part F of this Chapter.

10 Unscrew the retaining bolts and remove the support bracket from the base of the turbocharger.

11 Wipe clean the area around the oil feed and return unions on the cylinder block **(see illustration)**. Where the feed pipe is secured by a union nut, unscrew the nut then free the pipe from the block and recover the filter (where fitted) from inside the pipe. Where the feed pipe is secured in position with a union bolt, unscrew the bolt and recover the sealing washers; discard the sealing washers, new ones should be used on refitting.

12 Release the retaining clip and detach the oil return hose from the block.

13 Undo the power steering pipe clip screws and free the pipes from the underside of the engine/transmission unit **(see illustration)**. Unscrew the retaining bolts and remove the flywheel lower cover plate from the transmission unit.

14 Unscrew the nuts securing the turbocharger to the exhaust manifold then manoeuvre the turbocharger downwards and out of position. If necessary, tilt the engine

slightly forwards to gain the necessary clearance required to remove the turbocharger. Discard the nuts; new ones should be used on refitting.

15 Do not attempt to dismantle the turbocharger any further. If the unit is thought to be faulty take it to a turbo specialist for testing and examination. They will be able to inform you if the unit can be overhauled or will need renewing.

Refitting

16 Refitting is the reverse of removal, noting the following.
   a) *Ensure all mating surfaces are clean and dry.*
   b) *Secure the turbocharger to the exhaust manifold with new nuts.*
   c) *Prime the turbocharger by injecting clean engine oil through the oil feed pipe union before reconnecting the union.*
   d) *Tighten all fixings to the specified torque (where given).*
   e) *Refit the EGR valve as described in Part F of this Chapter.*
   f) *Refit the driveshaft as described in Chapter 8 and check the transmission oil level as described in 'Weekly checks').*
   g) *Ensure all turbocharger ducts are correctly and securely reconnected.*
   h) *If a new turbocharger is being fitted, change the engine oil and filter as described in Chapter 1B. Also renew the filter (where fitted) in the oil feed pipe.*

---

18 Inlet manifold – removal and refitting

1.9 litre engine
Removal

1 Disconnect the battery negative terminal (refer to *Disconnecting the battery* in the Reference Chapter).

2 Release the fasteners from the right-hand side and top of the engine cover then lift off the cover, taking care not to lose its mounting rubbers.

3 Slacken the retaining clip and detach the intake duct from the EGR valve. Release the retaining clip and detach the EGR pipe from

the side of the EGR valve. **Note:** *If the pipe is secured in position with a crimped-type clip, discard the clip and obtain a new one for use on refitting.*

4 Disconnect the breather hose from the left-hand end of the manifold upper section.

5 Unscrew the bolts securing the manifold upper section to the cylinder head and lower section.

6 Remove the manifold upper section, complete with EGR valve, disconnecting the wiring connector and vacuum hose from the EGR valve solenoid. Recover the four seals fitted between the upper and lower sections.

7 To remove the lower section of the manifold, unscrew the bolts securing the EGR pipe to the top of the exhaust manifold and the cylinder head cover. Free the pipe from the manifold and recover its gasket. Discard the gasket; a new one should be used on refitting.

8 Slacken and remove the nuts and bolt securing the inlet manifold to the cylinder head. Remove the manifold and EGR pipe as an assembly. Recover the manifold gaskets and discard them; new ones must be used on refitting.

Refitting

9 Examine all the manifold studs for signs of damage and corrosion; remove all traces of corrosion, and repair or renew any damaged studs.

10 Ensure that the mating surfaces are clean and flat, and fit the new manifold gaskets.

11 Route the EGR pipe through the lower section of the manifold then install both as an assembly. Tighten the manifold retaining nuts and bolt to the specified torque.

12 Fit a new gasket to the exhaust manifold then reconnect the EGR pipe, tightening its retaining bolts securely.

13 Fit a new seal to each of the upper manifold section joints then refit the upper section of the manifold, reconnecting the wiring connector and vacuum hose to the EGR solenoid valve. Refit the retaining bolts, tightening them to the specified torque, and reconnect the breather hose.

14 Reconnect the intake duct and EGR pipe to the manifold upper section, secure them in position with their retaining clips.

15 Ensure the mounting rubbers are all correctly fitted then install the engine cover, securing it in position with the fasteners. Reconnect the battery negative terminal.

2.0 litre engine

Removal

16 Remove the exhaust manifold as described in Section 19.

17 Slacken and remove the nuts and bolt securing the inlet manifold to the cylinder head. Remove the manifold and recover the manifold gasket. Discard the gasket; a new one must be used on refitting.

Refitting

18 Examine all the manifold studs for signs of damage and corrosion; remove all traces of corrosion, and repair or renew any damaged studs.

19 Ensure that the mating surfaces are clean and flat, and fit the new manifold gasket.

20 Refit the manifold and tighten its retaining nuts and bolt to the specified torque.

21 Refit the exhaust manifold as described in Section 19.

19 Exhaust manifold –
removal and refitting

1.9 litre engine

Removal

1 Disconnect the battery negative terminal (refer to *Disconnecting the battery* in the Reference Chapter).

2 Release the fasteners from the right-hand side and top of the engine cover then lift off the cover, taking care not to lose its mounting rubbers.

3 Release the retaining clip and detach the EGR pipe from the side of the EGR valve. **Note:** *If the pipe is secured in position with a crimped-type clip, discard the clip and obtain a new one for use on refitting*

4 Unscrew the bolts securing the EGR pipe to the top of the exhaust manifold and the cylinder head cover. Free the pipe from the manifold and recover its gasket. Discard the gasket; a new one should be used on refitting.

5 Disconnect the exhaust pipe from the manifold as described in Section 20.

6 Unscrew the exhaust manifold retaining nuts and remove the spacers from the manifold studs.

7 Remove the exhaust manifold and recover the manifold gaskets. Discard the gaskets; new ones must be used on refitting.

Refitting

8 Examine all the manifold studs for signs of damage and corrosion; remove all traces of corrosion, and repair or renew any damaged studs.

9 Ensure that the mating surfaces are clean and flat, and fit the new manifold gaskets.

10 Refit the manifold then fit the spacers to the mounting studs and screw on the retaining nuts. Tighten the nuts evenly and progressively to the specified torque.

11 Fit a new gasket then reconnect the EGR pipe to the manifold, tightening its retaining bolts securely. Reconnect the pipe to the EGR valve, securing it in position with the retaining clip, and refit the bolt securing the pipe to the cylinder head cover.

12 Reconnect the exhaust front pipe as described in Section 20.

13 Refit the engine cover then reconnect the battery.

2.0 litre engine

Removal

14 Remove the turbocharger as described in Section 17.

15 Unscrew the exhaust manifold retaining nuts and remove the spacers from the manifold studs.

16 Remove the exhaust manifold and recover the manifold gasket. Discard the gasket; a new one must be used on refitting.

Refitting

17 Examine all the manifold studs for signs of damage and corrosion; remove all traces of corrosion, and repair or renew any damaged studs.

18 Ensure that the mating surfaces are clean and flat, and fit the new manifold gaskets.

19 Refit the manifold then fit the spacers to the mounting studs and screw on the retaining nuts. Tighten the nuts evenly and progressively to the specified torque.

20 Refit the turbocharger as described in Section 17.

20 Exhaust system – general
information, removal and
refitting

General information

1 According to model, the exhaust system consists of either two or three sections. Three section systems consist of a catalytic converter, an intermediate pipe and a tailpipe. On two section systems, the catalytic converter and intermediate pipe are combined to form a single section.

2 The exhaust system joints are either of the spring-loaded ball type, to allow for movement in the exhaust system, or clamp-ring type.

3 The system is suspended throughout its entire length by rubber mountings.

4 Each exhaust section can be removed individually or, alternatively, the complete system can be removed as a unit. Even if only one part of the system needs attention, it is often easier to remove the whole system and separate the sections on the bench.

5 To remove the system or part of the system, first jack up the front or rear of the car and support it on axle stands (see *Jacking and*

vehicle support). Alternatively, position the car over an inspection pit or on car ramps.

Removal

Catalytic converter

6 Undo the nuts securing the flange joint to the manifold, and recover the spring cups and springs. Remove the bolts and recover the wire-mesh gasket.

7 Have an assistant support the front end of the pipe, then slacken and remove the nut, washer and bolt from the clamping ring and disengage the clamp from the flange joint.

8 Free the catalytic converter from its mounting rubber(s) and remove it from underneath the vehicle.

Intermediate pipe

9 Slacken the clamping ring bolts, and disengage both clamps from the flange joints.

10 Release the pipe from its mounting rubber and remove it from underneath the vehicle.

Tailpipe

11 Slacken and remove the nut, washer and bolt from the tailpipe clamping ring and disengage the clamp from the flange joint.

12 Unhook the tailpipe from its mounting rubbers and remove it from the vehicle.

Complete system

13 Undo the nuts securing the flange joint to the manifold, and recover the spring cups, springs and bolts.

14 With the aid of an assistant, free the system from all its mounting rubbers and lower it from under the vehicle. Recover the wire-mesh gasket from the manifold joint.

Heatshield(s)

15 The heat shields are secured to the underside of the body by various nuts and fasteners. If a shield is being removed to gain access to a component located behind it, remove the retaining nuts and/or fastener (unscrew the centre screw then pull out the complete fastener), and manoeuvre the shield out of position. On some models it may be necessary to free the exhaust system from its mountings to gain the clearance necessary to remove the larger heat shield.

Refitting

16 Each section is refitted by reversing the removal sequence, noting the following points:

a) Ensure that all traces of corrosion have been removed from the flanges and renew all necessary gaskets.

b) Inspect the rubber mountings for signs of damage or deterioration, and renew as necessary.

c) Where joints are secured together by a clamping ring, apply a smear of exhaust system jointing paste to the flange joint to ensure a gas-tight seal.

d) Prior to tightening the exhaust system fasteners, ensure that all rubber mountings are correctly located, and that there is adequate clearance between the exhaust system and vehicle underbody.

Notes

Chapter 4 Part F:
Emission control systems

Contents

Degrees of difficulty

Easy, suitable for novice with little experience

Fairly easy, suitable for beginner with some experience

Fairly difficult, suitable for competent DIY mechanic

Difficult, suitable for experienced DIY mechanic

Very difficult, suitable for expert DIY or professional

---

1 General information

All petrol engines have the ability to use unleaded petrol and also have various other features built into the fuel system to help minimise harmful emissions. In addition, all engines are equipped with the crankcase emission control system described below. Fuel injected engines are also equipped with a catalytic converter and an evaporative emission control system. Certain later engines to emission standard L4 also utilise a secondary air injection system to quickly bring the catalytic converter up to normal working temperature.

All diesel engines are also designed to meet the strict emission requirements and are also equipped with a crankcase emission control system. To further reduce exhaust emissions, a catalytic converter and an exhaust gas recirculation (EGR) system are fitted to the majority of engines.

The emission control systems function as follows.

Petrol engines
Crankcase emission control

To reduce the emission of unburned hydrocarbons from the crankcase into the atmosphere, the engine is sealed and the blow-by gases and oil vapour are drawn from inside the crankcase, through a wire mesh oil separator, into the inlet tract to be burned by the engine during normal combustion.

Under conditions of high manifold depression (idling, deceleration) the gases will be sucked positively out of the crankcase. Under conditions of low manifold depression (acceleration, full-throttle running) the gases are forced out of the crankcase by the (relatively) higher crankcase pressure; if the engine is worn, the raised crankcase pressure (due to increased blow-by) will cause some of the flow to return under all manifold conditions.

Exhaust emission control

To minimise the amount of pollutants which escape into the atmosphere, fuel injected engines are fitted with a catalytic converter in the exhaust system. The system is of the closed-loop type, in which one or two lambda sensors in the exhaust system provides the engine management ECU with constant feedback, enabling the ECU to adjust the air/fuel mixture ratio to provide the best possible conditions for the converter to operate.

The lambda sensor has a heating element built-in that is controlled by the ECU through the lambda sensor relay to quickly bring the sensor's tip to an efficient operating temperature. The sensor's tip is sensitive to oxygen and sends the ECU a varying voltage depending on the amount of oxygen in the exhaust gases; if the intake air/fuel mixture is too rich, the exhaust gases are low in oxygen so the sensor sends a low-voltage signal, the voltage rising as the mixture weakens and the amount of oxygen rises in the exhaust gases. Peak conversion efficiency of all major pollutants occurs if the intake air/fuel mixture is maintained at the chemically-correct ratio for the complete combustion of petrol of 14.7 parts (by weight) of air to 1 part of fuel (the 'stoichiometric' ratio). The sensor output voltage alters in a large step at this point, the ECU using the signal change as a reference point and correcting the intake air/fuel mixture accordingly by altering the fuel injector pulse width.

Evaporative emission control

To minimise the escape into the atmosphere of unburned hydrocarbons, an evaporative emission control system is fitted to fuel injected engines. The fuel tank filler cap is sealed and a charcoal canister is mounted underneath the right-hand front wing to collect the petrol vapours generated in the tank when the car is parked. It stores them until they can be cleared from the canister (under the control of the engine management ECU) via the purge valve into the inlet tract to be burned by the engine during normal combustion.

To ensure that the engine runs correctly when it is cold and/or idling and to protect the catalytic converter from the effects of an over-rich mixture, the purge control valve(s) is/are not opened by the ECU until the engine has warmed up, and the engine is under load; the valve solenoid is then modulated on and off to allow the stored vapour to pass into the inlet tract.

Secondary air injection

Certain later engines to emission standard L4 are also equipped with a secondary air injection system. This system is designed to reduce exhaust emissions in the period after starting the engine until the catalytic converter reaches operating (functioning) temperature. Introduction of air into the exhaust system during the initial start-up period, creates an 'afterburner' effect which quickly increases the temperature in the exhaust system front pipe, thus bringing the catalytic converter up to normal operating temperatures very quickly.

The system consists of an air pump, an air injection valve, and interconnecting air hoses.

The system operates for between 10 and 45 seconds after engine start-up, dependant on coolant temperature.

Diesel engines

Crankcase emission control

Refer to paragraphs 4 and 5.

Exhaust emission control

To minimise the level of exhaust pollutants released into the atmosphere, a catalytic converter is fitted in the exhaust system of later models.

The catalytic converter consists of a canister containing a fine mesh impregnated with a catalyst material, over which the hot exhaust gases pass. The catalyst speeds up the oxidation of harmful carbon monoxide, unburnt hydrocarbons and soot, effectively reducing the quantity of harmful products released into the atmosphere via the exhaust gases.

Exhaust gas recirculation system

This system is designed to recirculate small quantities of exhaust gas into the inlet tract, and therefore into the combustion process. This process reduces the level of oxides of nitrogen present in the final exhaust gas which is released into the atmosphere.

The volume of exhaust gas recirculated is controlled by vacuum supplied from the brake servo vacuum pump, via a solenoid valve controlled by the glow plug preheating system, or by an electronic control unit.

A vacuum-operated valve is fitted to the exhaust manifold, to regulate the quantity of exhaust gas recirculated. The valve is operated by the vacuum supplied via the solenoid valve.

Additionally, on certain models, a butterfly valve mounted on the inlet manifold allows the ratio of air-to-recirculated exhaust gas to be controlled. The butterfly valve also enables the exhaust gases to be drawn into the inlet manifold at idle or under light load, when the valve on the exhaust manifold is fully open.

The system is controlled by an electronic control unit, which receives information on coolant temperature, engine load, and engine speed, via the coolant temperature switch/sensor, throttle position switch/sensor and crankshaft sensor respectively.

2.4a Undo the retaining bolt . . .

2.4b . . . and lower the charcoal canister out from underneath the right-hand wing

2.5 To release the quick-release hose connectors, depress their center collars with a small flat-bladed screwdriver

2.7 The purge valve is located in the right-hand rear corner of the engine compartment

2 Emission control systems (petrol engines) – testing and component renewal

Crankcase emission control

1 The components of this system require no attention other than to check that the hose(s) are clear and undamaged at regular intervals.

Evaporative emission control

Testing

2 If the system is thought to be faulty, disconnect the hoses from the charcoal canister and purge control valve and check that they are clear by blowing through them. If the purge control valve(s) or charcoal canister are thought to be faulty, they must be renewed.

Charcoal canister renewal

3 The charcoal canister is located behind the right-hand front wing. To gain access to the canister, firmly apply the handbrake, then jack up the front of the car and support it securely on axle stands (see *Jacking and vehicle support*). Undo the retaining screw from the base of the wheel arch liner then prise out the retaining clips and remove the liner from underneath the wing.

4 Slacken and remove the retaining bolt then free the canister from its mounting clamp and lower it out from underneath the wing. Mark the hoses for identification purposes **(see illustrations)**.

5 Slacken the retaining clips then disconnect both hoses and remove the canister from the vehicle. Where the crimped-type hose clips are fitted, cut the clips and discard them; use standard worm-drive hose clips on refitting. Where the hoses are equipped with quick-release fittings, depress the centre collar of the fitting with a small flat-bladed screwdriver then detach the hose from the canister **(see illustration)**.

6 Refitting is a reverse of the removal procedure ensuring the hoses are correctly reconnected.

Purge valve(s) renewal

7 The purge valve is located in the right-hand rear corner of the engine compartment **(see illustration)**.

8 Disconnect the battery negative terminal (refer to *Disconnecting the battery* in the Reference Chapter).

9 Depress the retaining clip and disconnect the wiring connector from the valve. Disconnect the hoses from either end of the valve then release the valve from its retaining clip or strap and remove it from the engine compartment, noting which way around it is fitted.

10 Refitting is a reversal of the removal procedure, ensuring the valve is fitted the correct way around and the hoses are securely connected.

Exhaust emission control

Testing

11 The performance of the catalytic converter can only be checked by measuring the exhaust gases using a good-quality, carefully-calibrated exhaust gas analyser. If access to such equipment can be gained, it should be connected and used according with the maker's instructions.

12 If the CO level at the tailpipe is too high, the vehicle should be taken to a Peugeot dealer so that the complete engine management system, can be thoroughly checked using the special diagnostic equipment. Once these have been checked and are known to be free from faults, the fault must be in the catalytic converter, which must be renewed as described in Chapter 4B or 4C (as applicable).

Catalytic converter renewal

13 Refer to Chapter 4B or 4C (as applicable).

Lambda sensor(s) renewal

Note 1: *The lambda sensor is delicate and will not work if it is dropped or knocked, if its power supply is disrupted, or if any cleaning materials are used on it.*

Note 2: *Later engines to emission standard L4 are fitted with a 'downstream' lambda sensor located after the catalytic converter. Removal and refitting procedures are the same for both sensors.*

14 Trace the wiring back from the lambda sensor (which is screwed into the top of the exhaust front pipe or into the exhaust manifold), to the top of the transmission unit. Disconnect both wiring connectors and free the wiring from any relevant retaining clips or ties **(see illustration)**.

15 Unscrew the sensor from the exhaust system front pipe or manifold and remove it along with its sealing washer **(see illustration)**.

16 Refitting is a reverse of the removal procedure using a new sealing washer. Prior to installing the sensor, apply a smear of high temperature grease to the sensor threads. Ensure the sensor is securely tightened and that the wiring is correctly routed and in no danger of contacting either the exhaust system or engine.

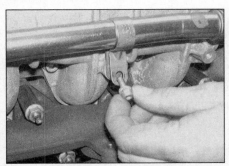

3.14 On 2.0 litre diesel engines, undo the bolts securing the EGR pipe support clips to the inlet manifold . . .

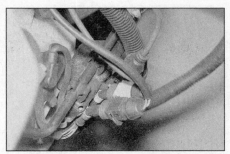

2.14 On early 1.1, 1.4 and 1.6 litre petrol engines the lambda sensor wiring connectors are clipped onto the front of the transmission . . .

Secondary air injection

Testing

17 The components of this system require no attention other than to check that the hose(s) are clear and undamaged at regular intervals.

18 Accurate testing of the system operation entails the use of diagnostic test equipment and should be entrusted to a Peugeot dealer.

Component renewal

19 At the time of writing, no specific information was available regarding removal and refitting of the system components.

---

3 Emission control systems (diesel engines) – testing and component renewal

Crankcase emission control

1 The components of this system require no attention other than to check that the hose(s) are clear and undamaged at regular intervals.

Exhaust emission control

Testing

2 The performance of the catalytic converter can only be checked by measuring the exhaust gases using a good-quality, carefully-calibrated exhaust gas analyser. If access to such equipment can be gained, it should be connected and used according with the maker's instructions.

3.15 . . . and the two nuts securing the EGR valve to the exhaust manifold

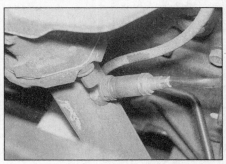

2.15 . . . and the sensor is screwed into the top of the exhaust front pipe

3 If the exhaust emissions are excessive, before assuming the catalytic converter is faulty, it is worth checking the problem is not due to a faulty injector(s), or other diesel fuel system fault. Refer to your Peugeot dealer for further information.

Catalytic converter renewal

4 Refer to Chapter 4D or 4E as applicable.

Exhaust gas recirculation system

Testing

5 Testing of the system should be entrusted to a Peugeot dealer.

EGR component renewal

1.8 and 1.9 litre XUD series engines

6 At the time of writing, no specific information was available regarding removal and refitting of the system components.

1.9 litre DW series engines

7 Disconnect the battery negative terminal (refer to *Disconnecting the battery* in the Reference Chapter).

8 Remove the upper section of the inlet manifold as described in Chapter 4E.

9 Unscrew the EGR valve housing from the manifold and recover the O-ring seal.

10 To remove the EGR pipe, undo the two bolts securing the pipe to the exhaust manifold and release the pipe side support strap.

11 Remove the inlet manifold as described in Chapter 4E, and lift out the EGR pipe.

12 Refitting is a reverse of the removal procedure, bearing in mind the following points:
a) Ensure that the EGR valve and exhaust manifold mating faces are clean.
b) Refit the inlet manifold as described in Chapter 4E.

2.0 litre DW series engines

13 Firmly apply the handbrake, then jack up the front of the car and support it securely on axle stands (see *Jacking and vehicle support*).

14 Undo the bolts securing the EGR pipe support clips to the inlet manifold **(see illustration)**.

15 Disconnect the vacuum hose, then undo the two nuts securing the EGR valve to the exhaust manifold **(see illustration)**.

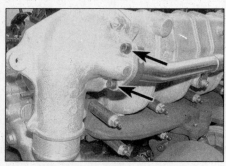

3.16a Undo the two bolts (arrowed) securing the EGR pipe to the inlet manifold elbow . . .

16 Undo the two bolts securing the EGR pipe to the inlet manifold elbow. Withdraw the EGR valve and pipe assembly from the manifold and recover the gasket at the EGR pipe-to-inlet manifold flange **(see illustrations)**.

17 To separate the EGR pipe from the valve, remove the clip securing the upper flexible portion of the pipe to the valve. If the original crimped clip is still in place, cut it off; new clips are supplied by Peugeot parts stockists with a screw clamp fixing. If a screw clamp type clip is fitted, undo the screw and manipulate the clip off the pipe.

18 To remove the EGR solenoid valve, disconnect the two vacuum hoses and the wiring connector. Undo the mounting bracket bolts and remove the valve from the engine compartment.

19 Refitting is a reverse of the removal procedure, bearing in mind the following points:

a) *Ensure that the EGR valve and exhaust manifold mating faces are clean.*

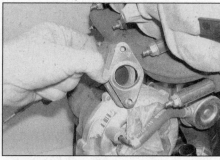

3.16b . . . then withdraw the valve and pipe assembly and recover the gasket at the EGR pipe flange

b) *Secure the EGR pipe with new screw clamp type clips, if crimped type clips were initially fitted.*

---

4 Catalytic converter – general information and precautions

1 The catalytic converter is a reliable and simple device which needs no maintenance in itself, but there are some facts of which an owner should be aware if the converter is to function properly for its full service life.

Petrol engines

a) *DO NOT use leaded petrol in a car equipped with a catalytic converter – the lead will coat the precious metals, reducing their converting efficiency and will eventually destroy the converter.*

b) *Always keep the ignition and fuel systems well-maintained in accordance with the manufacturer's schedule.*

c) *If the engine develops a misfire, do not drive the car at all (or at least as little as possible) until the fault is cured.*

d) *DO NOT push- or tow-start the car – this will soak the catalytic converter in unburned fuel, causing it to overheat when the engine does start.*

e) *DO NOT switch off the ignition at high engine speeds.*

f) *DO NOT use fuel or engine oil additives – these may contain substances harmful to the catalytic converter.*

g) *DO NOT continue to use the car if the engine burns oil to the extent of leaving a visible trail of blue smoke.*

h) *Remember that the catalytic converter operates at very high temperatures. DO NOT, therefore, park the car in dry undergrowth, over long grass or piles of dead leaves after a long run.*

i) *Remember that the catalytic converter is FRAGILE – do not strike it with tools during servicing work.*

j) *In some cases a sulphurous smell (like that of rotten eggs) may be noticed from the exhaust. This is common to many catalytic converter-equipped cars and once the car has covered a few thousand miles the problem should disappear.*

k) *The catalytic converter, used on a well-maintained and well-driven car, should last for between 50 000 and 100 000 miles – if the converter is no longer effective it must be renewed.*

Diesel engines

2 Refer to parts f, g, h and i of the petrol engine information given above.

Chapter 5 Part A:
Starting and charging systems

Contents

Degrees of difficulty

Easy, suitable for novice with little experience	Fairly easy, suitable for beginner with some experience	Fairly difficult, suitable for competent DIY mechanic	Difficult, suitable for experienced DIY mechanic	Very difficult, suitable for expert DIY or professional

Specifications

System type . . . .   12-volt, negative earth

Battery
Type . . . .   Fulmen, Delco or Steco
Charge condition:
  Poor . . . .   12.5 volts
  Normal . . . .   12.6 volts
  Good . . . .   12.7 volts

Alternator
Type . . . .   Valeo or Bosch (depending on model)

Starter motor
Type . . . .   Valeo or Bosch (depending on model)

---

1 General information and precautions

General information

The engine electrical system consists mainly of the charging and starting systems. Because of their engine-related functions, these components are covered separately from the body electrical devices such as the lights, instruments, etc (which are covered in Chapter 12). On petrol engine models refer to Part B for information on the ignition system, and on Diesel models refer to Part C for information on the preheating system.

The electrical system is of the 12-volt negative earth type.

The battery is of the low maintenance or "maintenance-free" (sealed for life) type and is charged by the alternator, which is belt-driven from the crankshaft pulley.

The starter motor is of the pre-engaged type incorporating an integral solenoid. On starting, the solenoid moves the drive pinion into engagement with the flywheel ring gear before the starter motor is energised. Once the engine has started, a one-way clutch prevents the motor armature being driven by the engine until the pinion disengages from the flywheel.

Further details of the various systems are given in the relevant Sections of this Chapter. While some repair procedures are given, the usual course of action is to renew the component concerned. The owner whose interest extends beyond mere component renewal should obtain a copy of the *"Automotive Electrical & Electronic Systems Manual"*, available from the publishers of this manual.

Precautions

It is necessary to take extra care when working on the electrical system to avoid damage to semi-conductor devices (diodes and transistors), and to avoid the risk of personal injury. In addition to the precautions given in *"Safety first!"* at the beginning of this manual, observe the following when working on the system:

Always remove rings, watches, etc before working on the electrical system. Even with the battery disconnected, capacitive discharge could occur if a component's live terminal is earthed through a metal object. This could cause a shock or nasty burn.

Do not reverse the battery connections. Components such as the alternator, electronic control units, or any other components having semi-conductor circuitry could be irreparably damaged.

If the engine is being started using jump leads and a slave battery, connect the batteries positive-to-positive and negative-to-negative (see "Booster battery (jump) starting"). This also applies when connecting a battery charger.

Never disconnect the battery terminals, the alternator, any electrical wiring or any test instruments when the engine is running.

Do not allow the engine to turn the alternator when the alternator is not connected.

Never "test" for alternator output by "flashing" the output lead to earth.

Never use an ohmmeter of the type incorporating a hand-cranked generator for circuit or continuity testing.

Always ensure that the battery negative terminal is disconnected when working on the electrical system.

Before using electric-arc welding equipment on the car, disconnect the battery, alternator and components such as the fuel injection/ignition electronic control unit to protect them from the risk of damage.

Several systems fitted to the vehicle require battery power to be available at all times, either to ensure their continued operation (such as the clock) or to maintain control unit memories or security codes which would be wiped if the battery were to be disconnected. To ensure that there are no unforeseen consequences of this action, Refer to "Disconnecting the battery" in the Reference Section of this manual for further information.

2 Electrical fault finding - general information

Refer to Chapter 12.

3 Battery - testing and charging

Standard and low maintenance battery - testing

1 If the vehicle covers a small annual mileage, it is worthwhile checking the specific gravity of the electrolyte every three months to determine the state of charge of the battery. Use a hydrometer to make the check and compare the results with the following table. Note that the specific gravity readings assume an electrolyte temperature of 15°C (60°F); for every 10°C (18°F) below 15°C (60°F) subtract 0.007. For every 10°C (18°F) above 15°C (60°F) add 0.007.

	Above 25°C (77°F)	Below 25°C (77°F)
Fully-charged	1.210 to 1.230	1.270 to 1.290
70% charged	1.170 to 1.190	1.230 to 1.250
Discharged	1.050 to 1.070	1.110 to 1.130

2 If the battery condition is suspect, first check the specific gravity of electrolyte in each cell. A variation of 0.040 or more between any cells indicates loss of electrolyte or deterioration of the internal plates.

3 If the specific gravity variation is 0.040 or more, the battery should be renewed. If the cell variation is satisfactory but the battery is discharged, it should be charged as described later in this Section.

Maintenance-free battery - testing

4 In cases where a "sealed for life" maintenance-free battery is fitted, topping-up and testing of the electrolyte in each cell is not possible. The condition of the battery can therefore only be tested using a battery condition indicator or a voltmeter.

5 Certain models may be fitted with a "Delco" type maintenance-free battery, with a built-in charge condition indicator. The indicator is located in the top of the battery casing, and indicates the condition of the battery from its colour. If the indicator shows green, then the battery is in a good state of charge. If the indicator turns darker, eventually to black, then the battery requires charging, as described later in this Section. If the indicator shows clear/yellow, then the electrolyte level in the battery is too low to allow further use, and the battery should be renewed. **Do not** attempt to charge, load or jump start a battery when the indicator shows clear/yellow.

6 If testing the battery using a voltmeter, connect the voltmeter across the battery and compare the result with those given in the Specifications under "charge condition". The test is only accurate if the battery has not been subjected to any kind of charge for the previous six hours. If this is not the case, switch on the headlights for 30 seconds, then wait four to five minutes before testing the battery after switching off the headlights. All other electrical circuits must be switched off, so check that the doors and tailgate are fully shut when making the test.

7 If the voltage reading is less than 12.2 volts, then the battery is discharged, whilst a reading of 12.2 to 12.4 volts indicates a partially discharged condition.

8 If the battery is to be charged, remove it from the vehicle (Section 4) and charge it as described later in this Section.

Standard and low maintenance battery - charging

Note: *The following is intended as a guide only. Always refer to the manufacturer's recommendations (often printed on a label attached to the battery) before charging a battery.*

9 Charge the battery at a rate of 3.5 to 4 amps and continue to charge the battery at this rate until no further rise in specific gravity is noted over a four hour period.

10 Alternatively, a trickle charger charging at the rate of 1.5 amps can safely be used overnight.

11 Specially rapid "boost" charges which are claimed to restore the power of the battery in 1 to 2 hours are not recommended, as they can cause serious damage to the battery plates through overheating.

12 While charging the battery, note that the temperature of the electrolyte should never exceed 37.8°C (100°F).

Maintenance-free battery - charging

Note: *The following is intended as a guide only. Always refer to the manufacturer's recommendations (often printed on a label attached to the battery) before charging a battery.*

13 This battery type takes considerably longer to fully recharge than the standard type, the time taken being dependent on the extent of discharge, but it can take anything up to three days.

14 A constant voltage type charger is required, to be set, when connected, to 13.9 to 14.9 volts with a charger current below 25 amps. Using this method, the battery should be usable within three hours, giving a voltage reading of 12.5 volts, but this is for a partially discharged battery and, as mentioned, full charging can take considerably longer.

15 If the battery is to be charged from a fully discharged state (condition reading less than 12.2 volts), have it recharged by your Peugeot dealer or local automotive electrician, as the charge rate is higher and constant supervision during charging is necessary.

4 Battery - removal and refitting

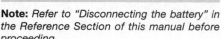

Note: *Refer to "Disconnecting the battery" in the Reference Section of this manual before proceeding.*

Removal

1 The battery is located on the left-hand side of the engine compartment.

2 Slacken the clamp bolts and disconnect the clamp from the battery negative (earth) terminal.

3 Remove the insulation cover (where fitted) and disconnect the positive terminal lead(s) in the same way.

4 Unscrew the nut/bolts (as applicable) and remove the battery retaining clamp.

5 Lift the battery out of the engine compartment. If necessary, undo the retaining bolts then release all the relevant clips securing the wiring to the tray and remove the battery tray from the engine compartment. On petrol engine models, where the electronic control unit (ECU) is housed in the end of the battery tray, it will be necessary to disconnect the wiring connector from the ECU and fuel injection relay unit (where fitted) to allow the tray to be removed **(see illustrations)**.

6 If necessary, with the tray removed, undo the retaining bolts and remove the mounting plate from the top of the left-hand engine/transmission mounting **(see illustration)**.

4.5a Release all the relevant wiring clips from the battery tray . . .

4.5b . . . then undo the retaining bolts . . .

4.5c . . . and remove the tray assembly from the engine compartment

Refitting

7 Refitting is a reversal of removal, but smear petroleum jelly on the terminals when reconnecting the leads, and always reconnect the positive lead first, negative lead last.

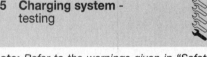

5 Charging system - testing

Note: *Refer to the warnings given in "Safety first!" and in Section 1 of this Chapter before starting work.*

1 If the ignition warning light fails to illuminate when the ignition is switched on, first check the alternator wiring connections for security. If satisfactory, check that the warning light bulb has not blown, and that the bulbholder is

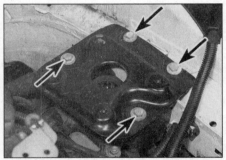

4.6 Battery mounting plate is secured to the engine mounting by four bolts

secure in its location in the instrument panel. If the light still fails to illuminate, check the continuity of the warning light feed wire from the alternator to the bulbholder. If all is satisfactory, the alternator is at fault and should be renewed or taken to an auto-electrician for testing and repair.

2 If the ignition warning light illuminates when the engine is running, stop the engine and check that the drivebelt is correctly tensioned (see Chapter 1A or 1B) and that the alternator connections are secure. If all is so far satisfactory, have the alternator checked by an auto-electrician for testing and repair.

3 If the alternator output is suspect even though the warning light works correctly, the regulated voltage may be checked as follows.

4 Connect a voltmeter across the battery terminals and start the engine.

5 Increase the engine speed until the voltmeter reading remains steady; the reading should be approximately 12 to 13 volts, and no more than 14 volts.

6 Switch on as many electrical accessories (eg, the headlights, heated rear window and heater blower) as possible, and check that the alternator maintains the regulated voltage at around 13 to 14 volts.

7 If the regulated voltage is not as stated, the fault may be due to worn brushes, weak brush springs, a faulty voltage regulator, a faulty diode, a severed phase winding or worn or damaged slip rings. The alternator should be renewed or taken to an auto-electrician for testing and repair.

6 Alternator drivebelt - removal, refitting and tensioning

Refer to the procedure given for the auxiliary drivebelt(s) in Chapter 1A or 1B.

7 Alternator - removal and refitting

Removal

1 Disconnect the battery negative terminal (refer to *"Disconnecting the battery"* in the Reference Section of this manual).

2 Slacken and remove the auxiliary drivebelt from the alternator pulley (refer to Chapter 1A or 1B).

3 Remove the rubber covers (where fitted) from the alternator terminals, then unscrew the retaining nuts and disconnect the wiring from the rear of the alternator **(see illustration)**.

4 Unscrew the nut and/or bolt securing the alternator to the upper mounting bracket. Unscrew the lower nut and/or mounting bolt, or undo the nut securing the adjuster bolt bracket to the alternator (as applicable). Note that, where a long through-bolt is used to secure the alternator in position, the bolt does not need to be fully removed; the alternator can be disengaged from the bolt once it has been slackened sufficiently **(see illustrations)**.

7.3 Undo the nuts and disconnect the wiring from the alternator - Diesel shown

7.4a Slacken and remove the alternator upper mounting bolt . . .

7.4b . . . and lower bolt (arrowed) and remove the alternator - 2.0 litre model

On some models, it may be necessary to remove the drivebelt idler/tensioner pulley to gain access to the alternator mounting nuts and bolts (depending on specification). On Diesel models, prise out the cover shield fastener to allow the cover to be lifted slightly to improve access to the upper bolt.

5 Manoeuvre the alternator away from its mounting brackets and out of the engine bay.

Refitting

6 Refitting is a reversal of removal, tensioning the auxiliary drivebelt with reference to Chapter 1A or 1B, and ensuring that the alternator mountings are securely tightened.

8 Alternator - testing and overhaul

If the alternator is thought to be suspect, it should be removed from the vehicle and taken to an auto-electrician for testing. Most auto-electricians will be able to supply and fit brushes at a reasonable cost. However, check on the cost of repairs before proceeding as it may prove more economical to obtain a new or exchange alternator.

9 Starting system - testing

Note: *Refer to the precautions given in "Safety first!" and in Section 1 of this Chapter before starting work.*

1 If the starter motor fails to operate when the ignition key is turned to the appropriate position, the following possible causes may be to blame.

a) *The battery is faulty.*
b) *The electrical connections between the switch, solenoid, battery and starter motor are somewhere failing to pass the*

necessary current from the battery through the starter to earth.
c) *The solenoid is faulty.*
d) *The starter motor is mechanically or electrically defective.*

2 To check the battery, switch on the headlights. If they dim after a few seconds, this indicates that the battery is discharged - recharge (see Section 3) or renew the battery. If the headlights glow brightly, operate the ignition switch and observe the lights. If they dim, then this indicates that current is reaching the starter motor, therefore the fault must lie in the starter motor. If the lights continue to glow brightly (and no clicking sound can be heard from the starter motor solenoid), this indicates that there is a fault in the circuit or solenoid - see following paragraphs. If the starter motor turns slowly when operated, but the battery is in good condition, then this shows that either the starter motor is faulty, or there is considerable resistance in the circuit.

3 If a fault in the circuit is suspected, disconnect the battery leads (including the earth connection to the body), the starter/solenoid wiring and the engine/transmission earth strap. Thoroughly clean the connections, and reconnect the leads and wiring, then use a voltmeter or test lamp to check that full battery voltage is available at the battery positive lead connection to the solenoid, and that the earth is sound. Smear petroleum jelly around the battery terminals to prevent corrosion - corroded connections are amongst the most frequent causes of electrical system faults.

4 If the battery and all connections are in good condition, check the circuit by disconnecting the wire from the solenoid blade terminal. Connect a voltmeter or test lamp between the wire end and a good earth (such as the battery negative terminal), and check that the wire is live when the ignition switch is turned to the 'start' position. If it is, then the circuit is sound - if not the circuit

wiring can be checked as described in Chapter 12.

5 The solenoid contacts can be checked by connecting a voltmeter or test lamp between the battery positive feed connection on the starter side of the solenoid, and earth. When the ignition switch is turned to the "start" position, there should be a reading or lighted bulb, as applicable. If there is no reading or lighted bulb, the solenoid is faulty and should be renewed.

6 If the circuit and solenoid are proved sound, the fault must lie in the starter motor. In this event, it may be possible to have the starter motor overhauled by a specialist, but check on the cost of spares before proceeding, as it may prove more economical to obtain a new or exchange motor.

10 Starter motor - removal and refitting

Removal

1 Disconnect the battery negative terminal (refer to *"Disconnecting the battery"* in the Reference Section of this manual).

2 So that access to the motor can be gained both from above and below, firmly apply the handbrake then jack up the front of the vehicle and support it on axle stands (see *"Jacking and Vehicle Support"*). On 1.1, 1.4 and 1.6 litre models, to improve access to the motor remove the air cleaner housing as described in the relevant Part of Chapter 4.

3 Slacken and remove the two retaining nuts and disconnect the wiring from the starter motor solenoid. Recover the washers under the nuts **(see illustration)**.

4 Undo the three mounting bolts, supporting the motor as the bolts are withdrawn **(see illustration)**. Recover the washers from under the bolt heads and note the locations of any wiring or hose brackets secured by the bolts.

10.3 Unscrew the two nuts (arrowed) and disconnect the wiring from the rear of the starter motor - 1.8 litre model shown

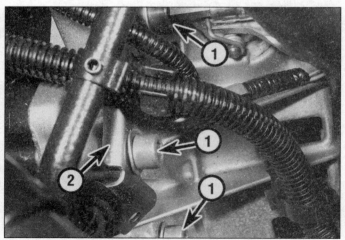

10.4 Unscrew the starter motor securing bolts (1). Note the location of the bracket (2) - 1.8 litre model shown

14.2 Removing the oil level sensor from the cylinder block

5 Manoeuvre the starter motor out from underneath the engine and recover the locating dowel(s) from the motor/transmission (as applicable).

Refitting

6 Refitting is a reversal of removal, ensuring that the locating dowel(s) are correctly positioned. Also make sure that any wiring or hose brackets are in place under the bolt heads as noted prior to removal.

11 Starter motor - testing and overhaul

If the starter motor is thought to be suspect, it should be removed from the vehicle and taken to an auto-electrician for testing. Most auto-electricians will be able to supply and fit brushes at a reasonable cost. However, check on the cost of repairs before proceeding as it may prove more economical to obtain a new or exchange motor.

12 Ignition switch - removal and refitting

The ignition switch is integral with the steering column lock, and can be removed as described in Chapter 10.

13 Oil pressure warning light switch - removal and refitting

Removal

1 The switch is located at the front of the cylinder block, above the oil filter mounting. Note that on some models access to the switch may be improved if the vehicle is jacked up and supported on axle stands so that the switch can be reached from underneath (see *"Jacking and Vehicle Support"*).
2 Disconnect the battery negative terminal (refer to *"Disconnecting the battery"* in the Reference Section of this manual).
3 Remove the protective sleeve from the wiring plug (where applicable), then disconnect the wiring from the switch.
4 Unscrew the switch from the cylinder block, and recover the sealing washer. Be prepared for oil spillage, and if the switch is to be left removed from the engine for any length of time, plug the hole in the cylinder block.

Refitting

5 Examine the sealing washer for signs of damage or deterioration and if necessary renew.
6 Refit the switch, complete with washer, and tighten it securely. Reconnect the wiring connector.
7 Lower the vehicle to the ground then check and, if necessary, top up the engine oil as described in *"Weekly checks"*.

14 Oil level sensor - removal and refitting

1 The sensor is located on the front side of the cylinder block, just to the right of the oil filter.
2 The removal and refitting procedure is as described for the oil pressure switch in

15.1 Oil temperature sensor is screwed into the rear of the sump

Section 13. Access is most easily obtained from underneath the vehicle **(see illustration)**.

15 Oil temperature sensor - removal and refitting

Removal

1 The oil temperature sensor is screwed into the sump **(see illustration)**.
2 To gain access to the sensor, firmly apply the handbrake then jack up the front of the vehicle and support it on axle stands (see *"Jacking and Vehicle Support"*).
3 Drain the engine oil into a clean container then refit the drain plug and tighten it to the specified torque setting (see Chapter 1A or 1B).
4 Disconnect the wiring connector then unscrew the sensor from the sump, and remove it from underneath the vehicle along with its sealing washer.

Refitting

5 Examine the sealing washer for signs of damage or deterioration and if necessary renew.
6 Refit the sensor, tightening it securely, and reconnect the wiring connector.
7 Lower the vehicle to the ground and refill the engine with oil as described in Chapter 1A or 1B.

Chapter 5 Part B:
Ignition system (petrol models)

Contents

Degrees of difficulty

Easy, suitable for novice with little experience	**Fairly easy,** suitable for beginner with some experience	**Fairly difficult,** suitable for competent DIY mechanic	**Difficult,** suitable for experienced DIY mechanic	**Very difficult,** suitable for expert DIY or professional

Specifications

System type
Carburettor models .... Breakerless electronic ignition system
Fuel injected models .... Static (distributorless) ignition system controlled by engine
management ECU

Firing order .... 1-3-4-2 (No 1 cylinder at transmission end)
Spark plugs .... See Chapter 1A Specifications

Ignition timing
Carburettor models .... 8° BTDC @ 750 rpm
Fuel injected models .... Controlled by the ECU – see text

Ignition HT coil
Resistances*:
  Carburettor models:
    Primary windings .... 0.8 ohms
    Secondary windings .... 6.5 K ohms
  Fuel injected models:
    Early TU series and all XU series 8-valve engines:
      Primary windings .... 0.5 to 0.8 ohms
      Secondary windings – Bosch coil .... 14.6 K ohms
      Secondary windings – Valeo coil .... 8.6 K ohms
* The above results are approximate values and are accurate only when the coil is at 20°C. See text for further information

Torque wrench setting

	Nm	lbf ft
Distributor mounting nuts	8	6

1 Ignition system – general information

Carburettor models

On all carburettor models a breakerless electronic ignition system is used. The system comprises solely of the HT ignition coil and the distributor, both of which are mounted on the left-hand end of the cylinder head, the distributor being driven off the end of the camshaft.

The distributor contains a reluctor mounted onto its shaft and a magnet and stator fixed to its body. The ignition amplifier unit is also mounted onto the side of the distributor body. The system operates as follows.

When the ignition is switched on but the engine is stationary the transistors in the amplifier unit prevent current flowing through the ignition system primary (LT) circuit.

As the crankshaft rotates, the reluctor moves through the magnetic field created by the stator. When the reluctor teeth are in alignment with the stator projections a small AC voltage is created. The amplifier unit uses this voltage to switch the transistors in the unit and complete the ignition system primary (LT) circuit.

As the reluctor teeth move out of alignment with the stator projections the AC voltage changes and the transistors in the amplifier unit are switched again to interrupt the primary (LT) circuit. This causes a high voltage to be induced in the coil secondary (HT) windings which then travels down the HT lead to the distributor and onto the relevant spark plug.

A TDC sensor is fitted to the rear of the flywheel but the sensor is not part of the ignition system. It is there to be used for diagnostic purposes only.

Fuel injected models

Early TU and all XU 8-valve engines

The ignition system is integrated with the fuel injection system to form a combined engine management system under the control of one ECU (see the relevant Part of Chapter 4 for further information). The ignition side of the system is of the static (distributorless) type, consisting only of a four output ignition coil. The ignition coil actually consists of two separate HT coils which supply two cylinders each (one coil supplies cylinders 1 and 4, and the other cylinders 2 and 3). Under the control of the ECU, the ignition coil operates on the 'wasted spark' principle, ie, each spark plug sparks twice for every cycle of the engine, once on the compression stroke and once on the exhaust stroke. The ECU uses its inputs from the various sensors to calculate the required ignition advance setting and coil charging time.

On 2.0 litre models a knock sensor is incorporated into the ignition system. The sensor is mounted onto the cylinder head and

prevents the engine 'pinking' under load. The sensor is sensitive to vibration and detects the knocking which occurs when the engine starts to 'pink' (pre-ignite). The knock sensor sends an electrical signal to the ECU which in turn retards the ignition advance setting until the 'pinking' ceases.

Later TU and all XU 16-valve engines

On these engines, the ignition side of the system is also of the static (distributorless) type and operates as described previously. The primary difference is that the ignition coils are housed in a single unit mounted directly above the spark plugs. The coils are integral with the spark plug caps and are pushed directly onto the spark plugs, one for each plug. This removes the need for any HT leads connecting the coils to the plugs.

2 Ignition system – testing

![Warning triangle] **Warning: Voltages produced by an electronic ignition system are considerably higher than those produced by conventional ignition systems. Extreme care must be taken when working on the system with the ignition switched on. Persons with surgically-implanted cardiac pacemaker devices should keep well clear of the ignition circuits, components and test equipment.**

Carburettor models

Note: *Refer to the warning given in Section 1 of Part A of this Chapter before starting work. Always switch off the ignition before disconnecting or connecting any component and when using a multimeter to check resistances.*

General

1 The components of electronic ignition systems are normally very reliable; most faults are far more likely to be due to loose or dirty connections or to 'tracking' of HT voltage due to dirt, dampness or damaged insulation than to the failure of any of the system's components. **Always** check all wiring thoroughly before condemning an electrical component and work methodically to eliminate all other possibilities before deciding that a particular component is faulty.

2 The old practice of checking for a spark by holding the live end of an HT lead a short distance away from the engine is not recommended; not only is there a high risk of a powerful electric shock, but the HT coil or amplifier unit will be damaged. Similarly, **never** try to 'diagnose' misfires by pulling off one HT lead at a time.

Engine will not start

3 If the engine either will not turn over at all, or only turns very slowly, check the battery and starter motor. Connect a voltmeter across

the battery terminals (meter positive probe to battery positive terminal), disconnect the ignition coil HT lead from the distributor cap and earth it, then note the voltage reading obtained while turning over the engine on the starter for (no more than) ten seconds. If the reading obtained is less than approximately 9.5 volts, first check the battery, starter motor and charging system as described in the relevant Sections of this Chapter.

4 If the engine turns over at normal speed but will not start, check the HT circuit by connecting a timing light (following the manufacturer's instructions) and turning the engine over on the starter motor; if the light flashes, voltage is reaching the spark plugs, so these should be checked first. If the light does not flash, check the HT leads themselves followed by the distributor cap, carbon brush and rotor arm using the information given in Chapter 1A.

5 If there is a spark, check the fuel system for faults referring to the relevant Part of Chapter 4 for further information.

6 If there is still no spark, check the voltage at the ignition HT coil '+' terminal; it should be the same as the battery voltage (ie, at least 11.7 volts). If the voltage at the coil is more than 1 volt less than that at the battery, check the feed back through the fusebox and ignition switch to the battery and its earth until the fault is found.

7 If the feed to the HT coil is sound, check the coil's primary and secondary winding resistance as described later in this Section; renew the coil if faulty, but be careful to check carefully the condition of the LT connections themselves before doing so, to ensure that the fault is not due to dirty or poorly-fastened connectors.

8 If the HT coil is in good condition, the fault is probably within the amplifier unit or distributor stator assembly. Testing of these components should be entrusted to a Peugeot dealer.

Engine misfires

9 An irregular misfire suggests either a loose connection or intermittent fault on the primary circuit, or an HT fault on the coil side of the rotor arm.

10 With the ignition switched off, check carefully through the system ensuring that all connections are clean and securely fastened. If the equipment is available, check the LT circuit as described above.

11 Check that the HT coil, the distributor cap and the HT leads are clean and dry. Check the leads themselves and the spark plugs (by substitution, if necessary), then check the distributor cap, carbon brush and rotor arm as described in Chapter 1A.

12 Regular misfiring is almost certainly due to a fault in the distributor cap, HT leads or spark plugs. Use a timing light (paragraph 4 above) to check whether HT voltage is present at all leads.

13 If HT voltage is not present on any

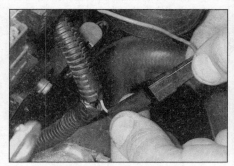

3.3 On carburettor models, disconnect the capacitor wiring connector, and release the TDC sensor connector . . .

3.4a . . . then disconnect the HT lead . . .

3.4b . . . and wiring connector (arrowed) from the ignition HT coil

particular lead, the fault will be in that lead or in the distributor cap. If HT is present on all leads, the fault will be in the spark plugs; check and renew them if there is any doubt about their condition.

14 If no HT is present, check the HT coil; its secondary windings may be breaking down under load.

Fuel injected models

15 If a fault appears in the engine management (fuel injection/ignition) system first ensure that the fault is not due to a poor electrical connection or poor maintenance; ie; check that the air cleaner filter element is clean, the spark plugs are in good condition and correctly gapped, that the engine breather hoses are clear and undamaged, referring to Chapter 1A for further information.

Also check that the accelerator cable is correctly adjusted as described in the relevant Part of Chapter 4. If the engine is running very roughly, check the compression pressures and the valve clearances as described in the relevant Part of Chapter 2.

16 If these checks fail to reveal the cause of the problem the vehicle should be taken to a suitably equipped Peugeot dealer for testing. A wiring block connector is incorporated in the engine management circuit into which a special electronic diagnostic tester can be plugged. The tester will locate the fault quickly and simply alleviating the need to test all the system components individually which is a time consuming operation that carries a high risk of damaging the ECU.

17 The only ignition system checks which can be carried out by the home mechanic are

those described in Chapter 1A, relating to the spark plugs, and on certain models, the ignition coil test described in this Chapter. If necessary, the system wiring and wiring connectors can be checked as described in Chapter 12 ensuring that the ECU wiring connector(s) have first been disconnected.

3 Ignition HT coil – removal, testing and refitting

Removal

Carburettor models

1 Disconnect the battery negative terminal (refer to *Disconnecting the battery* in the Reference Chapter).

2 Disconnect the hot air intake hose from the exhaust manifold shroud and air temperature control valve and remove it from the engine. Release the intake duct fastener and position the duct clear of the coil.

3 Disconnect the wiring connector from the capacitor mounted on the coil mounting bracket and release the TDC sensor wiring connector from the front of the bracket **(see illustration)**.

4 Disconnect the HT lead from the coil then depress the retaining clip and disconnect the coil wiring connector **(see illustrations)**.

5 Slacken and remove the two retaining bolts and remove the coil and mounting bracket from the cylinder head. Where necessary, slacken and remove the four screws and nuts, and separate the HT coil and mounting bracket **(see illustrations)**.

Early TU and all XU 8-valve fuel injected models

6 The ignition HT coil is mounted on the left-hand end of the cylinder head.

7 Disconnect the battery negative terminal (refer to *Disconnecting the battery* in the Reference Chapter), then depress the retaining clip and disconnect the wiring connector from the HT coil **(see illustration)**.

8 Make a note of the correct fitted positions of the HT leads then disconnect them from the coil terminals **(see illustration)**.

3.5a Undo the two retaining bolts (arrowed) . . .

3.5b . . . and remove the coil and mounting bracket from the cylinder head

3.7 Disconnect the wiring connector from the HT coil

3.8 Disconnect the HT leads from the coil terminals

3.9 Undo the four retaining screws and remove the ignition HT coil from the mounting bracket

3.12 Unplug the wiring connector from the top of the ignition coil unit

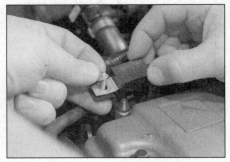

3.13a Remove radio suppresser from the right-hand end of the coil unit . . .

9 Undo the four retaining screws securing the coil to its mounting bracket and remove it from the engine compartment **(see illustration)**.

Later TU fuel injected models

10 Disconnect the battery negative terminal (refer to *Disconnecting the battery* in the Reference Chapter).
11 Disconnect the engine breather hose at the quick-release connections on the air cleaner air inlet duct, cylinder head cover and inlet manifold. Move the hose to one side.
12 Unplug the wiring connector from the top of the ignition coil unit **(see illustration)**.
13 Where applicable, unscrew the securing nut and remove radio suppresser from the right-hand end of the coil unit, together with its mounting bracket **(see illustrations)**.
14 Undo the nut securing each end of the ignition coil unit to the mounting studs **(see illustration)**. Note that it is quite likely that the stud will be released with the nut.
15 Lift the ignition coil unit upwards off the mounting studs and at the same time carefully ease the HT extension pillars away from the tops of the spark plugs. Lift the unit off the plugs and withdraw it from the engine **(see illustration)**.

XU 16-valve fuel injected models

16 Disconnect the battery negative terminal (refer to *Disconnecting the battery* in the Reference Chapter).
17 There are four separate ignition HT coils,

one on the top of each spark plug. To gain access to the coils, disconnect the wiring connectors at the left-hand end of the coil unit, then undo the six retaining bolts and lift the coil unit upwards, off the spark plugs and from its location in the cylinder head cover. The individual coils can now be removed as required.

Testing

Early TU and all XU 8-valve models

18 Testing of the coil consists of using a multimeter set to its resistance function, to check the primary (LT '+' to '–' terminals) and secondary (LT '+' to HT lead terminal) windings for continuity, bearing in mind that on the four output, static type HT coil there are two sets of each windings. Compare the results obtained to those given in the Specifications at the start of this Chapter. Note the resistance of the coil windings will vary slightly according to the coil temperature, the results in the Specifications are approximate values for when the coil is at 20°C.
19 Check that there is no continuity between the HT lead terminal and the coil body/mounting bracket.
20 If the coil is thought to be faulty, have your findings confirmed by a Peugeot dealer before renewing the coil.

Later TU and all XU 16-valve models

21 The circuitry arrangement of the ignition

coils and the coil unit on these engines is such that testing of an individual coil in isolation from the remainder of the engine management system is unlikely to prove effective in diagnosing a particular fault. Should there be any reason to suspect a faulty individual coil, the engine management system should be tested by a Peugeot dealer using diagnostic test equipment (see Section 2).

Refitting

22 Refitting is a reversal of the relevant removal procedure ensuring the wiring connectors are securely reconnected and, where necessary, the HT leads are correctly connected.

---

4 Distributor (carburettor models) – removal and refitting

Removal

1 Disconnect the battery negative terminal (refer to *Disconnecting the battery* in the Reference Chapter). If necessary, to improve access to the distributor, remove the ignition HT coil as described in Section 3 and the intake duct as described in Chapter 4A.
2 Peel back the waterproof cover then slacken and remove the distributor cap retaining screws then remove the cap and

3.13b . . . together with its mounting bracket

3.14 Remove the securing nuts . . .

3.15 . . . and lift the ignition coil unit from the mounting studs

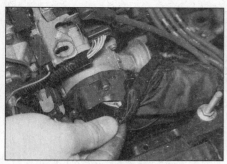

4.2a Peel back the waterproof cover . . .

4.2b . . . then undo the retaining screws . . .

4.2c . . . and remove the cap from the end of the distributor

4.3a Disconnect the distributor wiring connector . . .

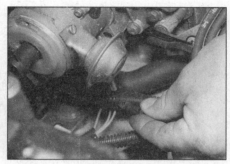

4.3b . . . and the vacuum diaphragm hose . . .

4.4 . . . then undo the retaining nuts and remove the distributor

position it clear of the distributor body **(see illustrations)**. Recover the seal from the cap.

3 Depress the retaining clip and disconnect the wiring connector from the distributor. Disconnect the hose from the vacuum diaphragm unit **(see illustrations)**.

4 Check the cylinder head and distributor flange for signs of alignment marks. If no marks are visible, using a scriber or suitable marker pen, mark the relationship of the distributor body to the cylinder head. Slacken and remove the two mounting nuts and withdraw the distributor from the cylinder head **(see illustration)**. Remove the O-ring from the end of the distributor body and discard it; a new one must be used on refitting.

Refitting

5 Lubricate the new O-ring with a smear of engine oil and fit it to the groove in the distributor body. Examine the distributor cap seal for wear or damage and renew if necessary.

6 Align the distributor rotor shaft drive coupling key with the slots in the camshaft end noting that the slots are offset to ensure that the distributor can only be fitted in one position. Carefully insert the distributor into the cylinder head whilst rotating the rotor arm slightly to ensure the coupling is correctly engaged.

7 Align the marks noted or made (as applicable) on removal and install the distributor retaining nuts, tightening them lightly only.

8 Ensure that the seal is correctly located in its groove then refit the cap assembly to the distributor and tighten its retaining screws securely. Fold the waterproof cover back over the distributor cap ensuring it is correctly located.

9 Reconnect the vacuum hose to the diaphragm unit and the distributor wiring connector. Where necessary, refit the ignition HT coil as described in Section 3, and the intake duct as described in Chapter 4A.

10 Check and, if necessary, adjust the ignition timing as described in Section 6 then tighten the distributor mounting nuts to the specified torque.

5 Ignition system amplifier unit (carburettor models) – removal and refitting

Removal

1 Disconnect the battery negative terminal (refer to *Disconnecting the battery* in the Reference Chapter).

2 The amplifier unit is mounted onto the side of the distributor body **(see illustration)**. To improve access to the unit, disengage the hot air intake hose from the control valve and manifold shroud and remove it from the vehicle.

3 Disconnect the wiring connector then undo the two retaining screws and remove the amplifier unit.

Refitting

4 Refitting is a reverse of the removal procedure.

6 Ignition timing – checking and adjustment

Carburettor models

1 To check the ignition timing, a stroboscopic timing light will be required. It is also recommended that the flywheel timing mark is highlighted as follows.

2 Remove the plug from the aperture on the front of the transmission clutch housing. Using a socket and suitable extension bar on the crankshaft pulley bolt, slowly turn the

5.2 On carburettor models, the ignition amplifier unit is secured to the side of the distributor by two screws

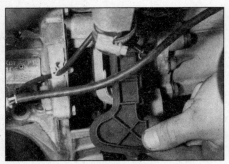

6.2a On carburettor models, remove the plug from the transmission housing . . .

6.2b . . . to reveal the timing plate and flywheel timing mark (arrowed)

engine over until the timing mark (a straight line) scribed on the edge of the flywheel appears in the aperture. Highlight the line with quick-drying white paint – typist's correction fluid is ideal **(see illustrations)**.

3 Start the engine, allow it to warm-up to normal operating temperature, and then stop it.

4 Disconnect the vacuum hose from the distributor diaphragm, and plug the hose end.

5 Connect the timing light to No 1 cylinder spark plug lead (No 1 cylinder is at the transmission end of the engine) as described in the timing light manufacturer's instructions.

6 Start the engine, allowing it to idle at the specified speed, and point the timing light at the transmission housing aperture. The flywheel timing mark should be aligned with the appropriate notch on the timing plate (refer to the Specifications for the correct

timing setting). The numbers on the plate indicate degrees Before Top Dead Centre (BTDC).

7 If adjustment is necessary, slacken the two distributor mounting nuts, then slowly rotate the distributor body as required until the flywheel mark and the timing plate notch are brought into alignment. Once the marks are correctly aligned, hold the distributor stationary and tighten its mounting nuts. Recheck that the timing marks are still correctly aligned and, if necessary, repeat the adjustment procedure.

8 When the timing is correctly set, increase the engine speed, and check that the flywheel mark advances to beyond the beginning of the timing plate reference marks, returning to the specified mark when the engine is allowed to idle. This shows that the centrifugal advance mechanism is functioning; if a

detailed check is thought necessary, this must be left to a Peugeot dealer having the necessary equipment. Reconnect the vacuum hose to the distributor, and repeat the check. The rate of advance should significantly increase if the vacuum diaphragm is functioning correctly, but again a detailed check must be left to a Peugeot dealer.

9 When the ignition timing is correct, stop the engine and disconnect the timing light.

Fuel injected models

10 On all fuel injected models, there are no timing marks on the flywheel or crankshaft pulley. The timing is constantly being monitored and adjusted by the engine management ECU, and nominal values cannot be given. Therefore, it is not possible for the home mechanic to check the ignition timing.

11 The only way in which the ignition timing can be checked is using special electronic test equipment, connected to the engine management system diagnostic connector (refer to the relevant Part of Chapter 4 for further information).

12 On models, with Magneti Marelli engine management systems, adjustment of the ignition timing is possible. However, adjustments can be made only by reprogramming the ECU using the special test equipment (see relevant Part of Chapter 4).

13 On all other models, no adjustment of the ignition timing is possible. Should the ignition timing be incorrect, then a fault is likely to be present in the engine management system.

Chapter 5 Part C:
Preheating system (diesel models)

Contents

Degrees of difficulty

Easy, suitable for novice with little experience	**Fairly easy,** suitable for beginner with some experience	**Fairly difficult,** suitable for competent DIY mechanic	**Difficult,** suitable for experienced DIY mechanic	**Very difficult,** suitable for expert DIY or professional

Specifications

Glow plugs

Resistance (typical)	Less than 1 ohm
Type:	
XUD engine	Bosch 0 250 201 039
DW engine:	
1.9 litre	Bosch 0 250 202 020
2.0 litre	Bosch 0 250 202 032

Torque wrench setting

	Nm	lbf ft
Glow plugs	22	16

1 Preheating system – description and testing

Description

1 Each swirl chamber has a heater plug (commonly called a glow plug) screwed into it. The plugs are electrically-operated before and during start-up when the engine is cold.

2 The electrical feed to the glow plugs is controlled by the preheating system control unit. With the exception of later 1.9 litre WJY engines and all 2.0 litre engines, the control unit operates using signals received from the coolant temperature sensor and accelerator switch on the injection pump. On later 1.9 litre WJY engines and all 2.0 litre engines, the control unit is operated by the injection system ECU (see Chapter 4E).

3 On certain models, the glow plugs provide a 'post-heating' function, whereby the glow plugs remain switched on for a period after the engine has started. Once the starter has been switched off, the glow plugs begin a timed 'post-heating' cycle. Post-heating only takes place if the engine is cold (coolant temperature below 60° on 1.8 and 1.9 litre engines, and below 20° on 2.0 litre engines) and the supply to the glow plugs will be interrupted if the engine is placed under load.

4 A warning light in the instrument panel tells the driver that preheating is taking place. When the light goes out, the engine is ready to be started. The voltage supply to the glow plugs continues for several seconds after the light goes out. If no attempt is made to start, the timer then cuts off the supply, in order to avoid draining the battery and overheating the glow plugs.

Testing

1.8 and 1.9 litre engines

5 If the system malfunctions, testing is ultimately by substitution of known good units, but some preliminary checks may be made as follows.

6 Where applicable, release the fasteners from the right-hand side and top of the engine cover, then lift off the cover, taking care not to lose its mounting rubbers.

7 Connect a voltmeter or 12 volt test lamp between the glow plug supply cable and earth (engine or vehicle metal). Make sure that the live connection is kept clear of the engine and bodywork.

8 Have an assistant switch on the ignition, and check that voltage is applied to the glow plugs. Note the time for which the warning light is lit, and the total time for which voltage is applied before the system cuts out. Switch off the ignition.

9 At a coolant temperature of 20°C, typical times noted should be 5 or 6 seconds for warning light operation, followed by a further 10 seconds supply after the light goes out. Warning light time will increase with lower temperatures and decrease with higher temperatures.

10 If there is no supply at all, the control unit or associated wiring is at fault.

11 To locate a defective glow plug, on turbo models remove the intercooler, and on non-turbo models with D9B engine remove the air distribution housing. If necessary, also remove the inlet duct, and disconnect the breather hose from the engine oil filler tube. Refer to Chapter 4D for further information. Disconnect the main supply cable and the interconnecting wire or strap from the top of the glow plugs. Be careful not to drop the nuts and washers.

12 Use a continuity tester, or a 12 volt test lamp connected to the battery positive terminal, to check for continuity between each glow plug terminal and earth. The resistance of a glow plug in good condition is very low (less than 1 ohm), so if the test lamp does not light or the continuity tester shows a high resistance, the glow plug is certainly defective.

13 If an ammeter is available, the current draw of each glow plug can be checked. After an initial surge of 15 to 20 amps, each plug should draw 12 amps. Any plug which draws much more or less than this is probably defective.

14 As a final check, the glow plugs can be removed and inspected as described in the following Section.

2.0 litre engines

15 The system can be checked as described in paragraphs 7 to 14. However testing will be difficult due to the temperatures at which the preheating system functions; at coolant temperatures above 0°C, preheating is virtually unnecessary. Approximate times for preheating duration are as follows:

Coolant temperature	Preheating time
–30°C	20 seconds
–10°C	5 seconds
0°C	0.5 seconds
18°C	No preheating necessary

2 Glow plugs – removal, inspection and refitting

Caution: If the preheating system has just been energised, or if the engine has been running, the glow plugs will be very hot.

Removal

1 Disconnect the battery negative terminal (refer to *Disconnecting the battery* in the Reference Chapter).

2 On 1.9 litre turbo models remove the intercooler, and on non-turbo models with D9B engine remove the air distribution housing. If necessary, also remove the inlet duct, and disconnect the breather hose from the engine oil filler tube. Refer to Chapter 4D for further information.

3 On 1.9 litre models with an engine cover, release the fasteners from the right-hand side and top of the engine cover, then lift off the cover, taking care not to lose its mounting rubbers. On 2.0 litre models, release the fasteners (rotate them through 90° to release them) and remove the engine cover.

4 Unscrew the nut from the relevant glow plug terminal(s), and recover the washer(s) **(see illustration)**. Note that the main supply cable is connected to No 1 cylinder glow plug and an interconnecting wire is fitted between the four plugs.

5 Where applicable, carefully move any obstructing pipes or wires to one side to enable access to the relevant glow plug(s).

6 Unscrew the glow plug(s) and remove from the cylinder head **(see illustration)**.

Inspection

7 Inspect each glow plug for physical damage. Burnt or eroded glow plug tips can be caused by a bad injector spray pattern. Have the injectors checked if this sort of damage is found.

8 If the glow plugs are in good physical condition, check them electrically using a 12 volt test lamp or continuity tester as described in the previous Section.

9 The glow plugs can be energised by applying 12 volts to them to verify that they heat up evenly and in the required time. Observe the following precautions.

2.4 Unscrew the nut (arrowed) and disconnect the wiring from the glow plug terminal (later 1.9 litre engine)

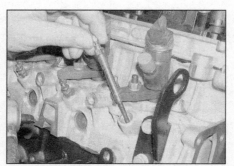

2.6 Unscrew the glow plug(s) and remove them from the cylinder head (2.0 litre engine with fuel rail removed)

a) *Support the glow plug by clamping it carefully in a vice or self-locking pliers. Remember it will become red-hot.*

b) *Make sure that the power supply or test lead incorporates a fuse or overload trip to protect against damage from a short-circuit.*

c) *After testing, allow the glow plug to cool for several minutes before attempting to handle it.*

10 A glow plug in good condition will start to glow red at the tip after drawing current for 5 seconds or so. Any plug which takes much longer to start glowing, or which starts glowing in the middle instead of at the tip, is defective.

Refitting

11 Refit by reversing the removal operations. Apply a smear of copper-based anti-seize compound to the plug threads and tighten the glow plugs to the specified torque. Do not overtighten, as this can damage the glow plug element.

3 Preheating system control unit – removal and refitting

Removal

1 The unit is located on the left-hand side of the engine compartment where it is mounted onto the rear of the battery box.

2 Disconnect the battery negative terminal (refer to *Disconnecting the battery* in the Reference Chapter).

3 Unscrew the retaining nut securing the unit to the battery box.

4 Disconnect the wiring connector from the base of the unit then unscrew the two retaining nuts and free the main feed and supply wires from the unit **(see illustration)**. Remove the unit from the engine compartment.

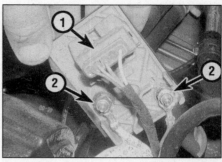

3.4 Disconnect the wiring connector (1) then unscrew the nuts (2) and disconnect the feed and supply wires from the control unit

Refitting

5 Refitting is a reversal of removal, ensuring that the wiring connectors are correctly connected.

Notes

Chapter 6
Clutch

Contents

Degrees of difficulty

| Easy, suitable for novice with little experience | | Fairly easy, suitable for beginner with some experience | | Fairly difficult, suitable for competent DIY mechanic | 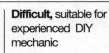 | Difficult, suitable for experienced DIY mechanic | | Very difficult, suitable for expert DIY or professional | |

Specifications

Type .... Single dry plate with diaphragm spring, cable-operated

Clutch pedal travel* .... 131 to 141 mm
*On most models the clutch cable is automatically adjusted and therefore the pedal travel is not adjustable - see text

Friction plate diameter
Petrol models:
    1.1 and 1.4 litre models .... 180 mm
    1.6 and 1.8 litre models .... 200 mm
    2.0 litre models .... 215 mm
Diesel models:
    Turbo models .... 215 mm
    Non-turbo models .... 200 mm

Torque wrench settings	**Nm**	**lbf ft**
Pressure plate retaining bolts:		
1.1, 1.4 and 1.6 litre models	15	11
1.8 litre and larger models	25	18

1 General information

The clutch consists of a friction plate, a pressure plate assembly, a release bearing and the release mechanism; all of these components are contained in the large cast-aluminium alloy bellhousing, sandwiched between the engine and the transmission. The release mechanism is mechanical, being operated by a cable.

The friction plate is fitted between the engine flywheel and the clutch pressure plate, and is allowed to slide on the transmission input shaft splines.

The pressure plate assembly is bolted to the engine flywheel. When the engine is running, drive is transmitted from the crankshaft, via the flywheel, to the friction plate (these components being clamped securely together by the pressure plate assembly) and from the friction plate to the transmission input shaft.

To interrupt the drive, the spring pressure must be relaxed. On the models covered in this manual, two different types of clutch release mechanism are used. The first is a conventional "push-type" mechanism, where an independent clutch release bearing, fitted concentrically around the transmission input shaft, is pushed onto the pressure plate assembly. The second is a "pull-type" mechanism, where the clutch release bearing is an integral part of the pressure plate assembly, and is lifted away from the friction plate.

On models with the conventional "push-type" mechanism, at the transmission end of the clutch cable, the outer cable is retained by a fixed mounting bracket, and the inner cable is attached to the release fork lever. Depressing the clutch pedal pulls the control cable inner wire, and this rotates the release fork by acting on the lever at the fork's upper end. The release fork then presses the release bearing against the pressure plate spring fingers. This causes the springs to deform and releases the clamping force on the pressure plate.

On models with the "pull-type" mechanism, at the transmission end of the clutch cable, the inner cable is attached to a fixed mounting bracket, and the outer cable acts against the release fork lever. Depressing the clutch pedal rotates the release fork. The release fork then lifts the release bearing, which is attached to the pressure plate springs, away from the friction plate, and releases the clamping force exerted at the pressure plate periphery.

On some early 1.1, 1.4 and 1.6 litre (TU engine) models, to ensure correct operation, the clutch must be regularly adjusted. On all 1.8 litre and larger (XU and XUD engine) and later 1.1, 1.4 and 1.6 litre models the clutch cable has an automatic adjuster built into the cable.

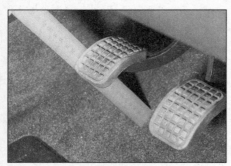

2.2 To check clutch adjustment, measure the clutch pedal travel as described in text

2 Clutch - adjustment

1.1, 1.4 and 1.6 litre models

Early models (with manually adjusted cable)

1 The clutch adjustment is checked by measuring the clutch pedal travel. If a new cable has been fitted, settle it in position by depressing the clutch pedal at least 20 times.

2 Ensure that there are no obstructions beneath the clutch pedal then measure the distance from the centre of the clutch pedal pad to the base of the steering wheel with the pedal in the at-rest position. Depress the clutch pedal fully to the floor, and measure the distance from the centre of the clutch pedal pad to the base of the steering wheel **(see illustration)**.

3 Subtract the first measurement from the second to obtain the clutch pedal travel. If this is not with the range given in the Specifications at the start of this Chapter, adjust the clutch as follows.

4 The clutch cable is adjusted by means of the adjuster nut on the transmission end of the cable. On some models, access to the locknut is limited and, if required, the air cleaner duct or housing component can be removed or disconnected to improve access. Refer to the relevant Part of Chapter 4 for further information.

5 Working in the engine compartment, slacken the locknut from the end of the clutch cable. Adjust the position of the adjuster nut, then re-measure the clutch pedal travel. Repeat this procedure until the clutch pedal travel is as specified **(see illustration)**.

6 Once the adjuster nut is correctly positioned, and the pedal travel is correctly set, securely tighten the cable locknut. Where necessary, refit any disturbed air cleaner duct/housing components (see the relevant Part of Chapter 4).

Later models (with automatic adjuster built into cable)

7 On these models no adjustment of the clutch is necessary. The cable automatically adjusts during use. The pedal assist spring can be adjusted as described below.

1.8 litre and larger models

8 On these models the cable has an automatic adjuster built into it and requires no manual adjustment. The only adjustment possible is to the clutch pedal assist spring as follows.

9 Working inside the vehicle, release the fastener by turning it through a quarter of a turn, and remove the fusebox cover from the facia. Remove the heater duct which is situated behind the cover. Prise out the retaining clips and remove the undercover from beneath the facia. Loosen the screw securing the pedal assist spring bracket in position then lift the clutch pedal up to its stop. Hold the pedal in this position and securely tighten the spring bracket screw. Refit the components removed for access.

3 Clutch cable - removal and refitting

Removal

1 If necessary, to improve access remove the air cleaner duct or housing components as described in the relevant Part of Chapter 4. Where necessary, also remove the battery, battery tray and mounting plate (see Chapter 5A).

2 Working in the engine compartment, release the inner cable and outer cable fittings from the clutch release lever and mounting bracket, and free the cable from the transmission housing **(see illustrations)**. On early 1.1, 1.4 and 1.6 litre models, where necessary, fully slacken the locknut and adjuster nut from the end of the clutch cable to aid removal.

3 Working inside the vehicle, release the fastener by turning it through a quarter of a turn, and remove the fusebox cover from the facia. Remove the heater duct which is situated behind the cover.

4 Prise out the retaining clips and remove the undercover from beneath the facia.

5 Reach up and unhook the cable from the upper end of the clutch pedal.

6 Return to the engine compartment, then release the cable guide from the bulkhead and withdraw the cable forwards, releasing it from any relevant retaining clips and guides. Note its correct routing, and remove it from the car.

7 Examine the cable, looking for worn end fittings or a damaged outer casing, and for signs of fraying of the inner wire. Check the cable's operation; the inner wire should move smoothly and easily through the outer casing. Remember that a cable that appears serviceable when tested off the car may well be much heavier in operation when in its working position. Renew the cable if it shows signs of excessive wear or any damage.

Refitting

8 Apply a thin smear of multi-purpose grease to the cable end fittings, then pass the cable through the engine compartment bulkhead.

9 From inside the vehicle, hook the inner cable onto the clutch pedal, and check that it is correctly located. Clip the felt undercover back into position, then refit the heater duct, ensuring it is correctly located at both ends, and install the fusebox cover.

10 Ensuring that the cable is correctly routed and retained by all the relevant retaining clips and guides, clip the guide back into position and pass the lower end through the release lever/mounting bracket (as applicable) and engage the inner cable. Ensure that the cable spacers and washers are correctly positioned against the lever/mounting bracket.

11 Adjust the clutch as described in Section 2 (where necessary) then refit any components removed for access.

2.5 Adjusting the clutch cable

3.2a Slacken the clutch cable locknut and adjuster nut (where necessary), then free the inner cable end fittings . . .

3.2b . . . and outer cable end fittings from the release lever and mounting bracket

4 Clutch pedal - removal and refitting

Removal

1 Detach the clutch cable from the upper end of the pedal as described in paragraphs 1 to 5 of Section 3. Proceed as described under the relevant sub-heading.

Right-hand drive models

2 Slacken the bolt securing the clutch pedal spring bracket in position. As the bolt is withdrawn, support the spring bracket then release it slowly to gently relieve the spring pressure.

3 Slacken and remove the pivot nut and bolt then remove the pedal assembly from the vehicle, and recover the spacer (where fitted) which is positioned between the brake and clutch pedal mounting brackets. Do not attempt to dismantle the pedal assembly as no spare parts are available. If it is damaged, the complete assembly must be renewed.

1.1, 1.4 and 1.6 litre left-hand drive models

4 Noting their correct fitted positions, carefully unhook the springs from the pedal to relieve spring tension.

5 Slacken and remove the pivot bolt nut and withdraw the bolt. Remove the pedal assembly from the bracket. Recover the spacer and springs.

6 Inspect the spacer and springs for signs of wear or damage and renew as necessary.

1.8 litre and larger left-hand drive models

7 Noting its correct fitted position, unhook the return spring and remove it from the pedal.

8 Remove the pedal as described above in paragraphs 2 and 3.

Refitting

9 Refitting is the reverse of the removal procedure, noting the following points.

  a) Prior to refitting, apply a smear of grease to the pedal pivot bolt shank.
  b) Ensure that the pedal springs are

5.14 Ensure the friction plate is fitted the correct way around, then install the pressure plate

correctly fitted then reconnect the cable and adjust the clutch as described in Section 2 (where necessary).

5 Clutch assembly - removal, inspection and refitting

Note: Although some friction materials may no longer contain asbestos, it is safest to assume they do, and to take precautions accordingly.

Removal

⚠️ **Warning: Dust created by clutch wear and deposited on the clutch components may contain asbestos, which is a health hazard. DON'T blow it out with compressed air, nor inhale any of it. DO NOT use petrol or petroleum-based solvents to clean off the dust. Brake system cleaner or methylated spirit should be used to flush the dust into a suitable receptacle. After the clutch components are wiped clean with rags, dispose of the contaminated rags and cleaner in a sealed, marked container.**

1 Unless the complete engine/transmission is to be removed from the car and separated for major overhaul (see the relevant Part of Chapter 2), the clutch can be reached by removing the transmission as described in Chapter 7A.

2 Before disturbing the clutch, use chalk or a marker pen to mark the relationship of the pressure plate assembly to the flywheel.

3 Working in a diagonal sequence, slacken the pressure plate bolts by half a turn at a time, until spring pressure is released and the bolts can be unscrewed by hand.

4 Prise the pressure plate assembly off its locating dowels, and collect the friction plate, noting which way round the plate is fitted.

Inspection

Note: Due to the amount of work necessary to remove and refit clutch components, it is considered good practice to renew the clutch friction plate, pressure plate assembly and release bearing as a matched set, even if only one of these is worn enough to require renewal. It is worth considering the renewal of the clutch components on a preventive basis if the engine and/or transmission have been removed for some other reason.

5 Remove the clutch assembly.

6 When cleaning clutch components, read first the warning at the beginning of this Section; remove dust using a clean, dry cloth, and working in a well-ventilated atmosphere.

7 Check the friction plate facings for signs of wear, damage or oil contamination. If the friction material is cracked, burnt, scored or damaged, or if it is contaminated with oil or grease (shown by shiny black patches), the friction plate must be renewed.

8 If the friction material is still serviceable,

check that the centre boss splines are unworn, that the torsion springs are in good condition and securely fastened, and that all the rivets are tight. If any wear or damage is found, the friction plate must be renewed.

9 If the friction material is fouled with oil, this must be due to an oil leak from the crankshaft left-hand oil seal, from the sump-to-cylinder block joint, or from the transmission input shaft. Renew the seal or repair the joint, as appropriate, as described in the relevant Part of Chapter 2 or 7, before installing the new friction plate.

10 Check the pressure plate assembly for obvious signs of wear or damage; shake it to check for loose rivets or worn or damaged fulcrum rings, and check that the drive straps securing the pressure plate to the cover do not show signs (such as a deep yellow or blue discoloration) of overheating. If the diaphragm spring is worn or damaged, or if its pressure is in any way suspect, the pressure plate assembly should be renewed.

11 Examine the machined bearing surfaces of the pressure plate and of the flywheel; they should be clean, completely flat, and free from scratches or scoring. If either is discoloured from excessive heat, or shows signs of cracks, it should be renewed - although minor damage of this nature can sometimes be polished away using emery paper.

12 Check that the release bearing contact surface rotates smoothly and easily, with no sign of noise or roughness. Also check that the surface itself is smooth and unworn, with no signs of cracks, pitting or scoring. If there is any doubt about its condition, the bearing must be renewed. On clutches with a "pull-type" release mechanism, this means that the complete pressure plate assembly must also be renewed.

Refitting

13 On reassembly, ensure that the bearing surfaces of the flywheel and pressure plate are completely clean, smooth, and free from oil or grease. Use solvent to remove any protective grease from new components.

14 Fit the friction plate so that its spring hub assembly faces away from the flywheel; there may be a marking showing which way round the plate is to be refitted **(see illustration)**.

15 Refit the pressure plate assembly, aligning the marks made on dismantling (if the original pressure plate is re-used), and locating the pressure plate on its three locating dowels. Fit the pressure plate bolts, but tighten them only finger-tight, so that the friction plate can still be moved.

16 The friction plate must now be centralised, so that when the transmission is refitted, its input shaft will pass through the splines at the centre of the friction plate.

17 Centralisation can be achieved by passing a screwdriver or other long bar through the friction plate and into the hole in the crankshaft; the friction plate can then be moved around until it is centred on the

5.17 Using a clutch-aligning-tool to centralise the friction plate

crankshaft hole. Alternatively, a clutch-aligning-tool can be used to eliminate the guesswork; these can be obtained from most accessory shops **(see illustration)**.

 A home-made aligning tool can be fabricated from a length of metal rod or wooden dowel which fits closely inside the crankshaft hole, and has insulating tape wound around it to match the diameter of the friction plate splined hole.

18 When the friction plate is centralised, tighten the pressure plate bolts evenly and in a diagonal sequence to the specified torque setting **(see illustration)**.

19 Apply a thin smear of molybdenum disulphide grease (Peugeot recommend the use of Molykote BR2 Plus - available from your Peugeot dealer) to the splines of the friction plate and the transmission input shaft, and also to the release bearing bore and release fork shaft.

20 Refit the transmission as described in Chapter 7A.

6 Clutch release mechanism - removal, inspection and refitting

Note: *Refer to the warning concerning the dangers of asbestos dust at the beginning of Section 5.*

Removal

1 Unless the complete engine/transmission is to be removed from the car and separated for major overhaul (see the relevant Part of Chapter 2), the clutch release mechanism can be reached by removing the transmission only, as described in Chapter 7A.

2 On models with a conventional "push-type" release mechanism, unhook the release bearing from the fork, and slide it off the input shaft. Drive out the roll pin, and remove the release lever from the top of the release fork shaft. Discard the roll pin - a new one must be used on refitting.

3 On both types of clutch, depress the retaining tabs, then slide the upper bush off the end of the release fork shaft. Disengage the shaft from its lower bush, and manoeuvre it out from the transmission. Depress the retaining tabs, and remove the lower pivot bush from the transmission housing.

Inspection

4 Check the release mechanism, renewing any component which is worn or damaged. Carefully check all bearing surfaces and points of contact.

5 When checking the release bearing itself, note that it is often considered worthwhile to renew it as a matter of course. Check that the contact surface rotates smoothly and easily, with no sign of noise or roughness, and that the surface itself is smooth and unworn, with

5.18 Once the friction plate is centralised, tighten the pressure plate retaining bolts to the specified torque

no signs of cracks, pitting or scoring. If there is any doubt about its condition, the bearing must be renewed. On models with a "pull-type" release mechanism, this means that the complete pressure plate assembly must be renewed, as described in Section 5.

Refitting

6 Apply a smear of molybdenum disulphide grease to the shaft pivot bushes and the contact surfaces of the release fork.

7 Locate the lower pivot bush in the transmission, ensuring it is securely retained by its locating tangs, and refit the release fork. Slide the upper bush down the release fork shaft, and clip it into position in the transmission housing **(see illustrations)**.

8 On models with a conventional "push-type" release mechanism, refit the release lever to the shaft. Align the lever with the shaft hole, and secure it in position by tapping a new roll pin fully into position. Slide the release bearing onto the input shaft, and engage it with the release fork.

9 Refit the transmission as described in Chapter 7A.

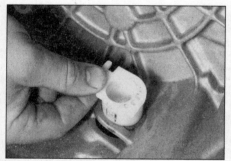

6.7a Clip the lower pivot bush into position in the transmission housing . . .

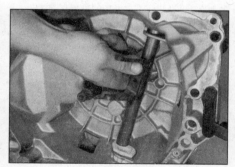

6.7b . . . locate the release fork shaft in the lower bush . . .

6.7c . . . and slide the upper pivot down the shaft, and into position in the transmission housing - BE3 transmission shown

Chapter 7 Part A:
Manual transmission

Contents

Degrees of difficulty

Easy, suitable for novice with little experience	Fairly easy, suitable for beginner with some experience	Fairly difficult, suitable for competent DIY mechanic	Difficult, suitable for experienced DIY mechanic	Very difficult, suitable for expert DIY or professional

Specifications

General
Type .... Manual, five forward speeds and reverse. Synchromesh on all forward speeds

Designation:
  1.1, 1.4 and 1.6 litre models .... MA
  1.8 litre and larger-engine models BE3
Transmission code:
  Petrol models:
    1.1 litre models 2CB 62
    1.4 litre models .... 2CB 60, 2CB 61 or 2CB 97
    1.6 litre models 2CB 88
    1.8 litre models .... CL 36, CL 75 or CL 78
    2.0 litre models .... CJ 76
  Diesel models .... CM29 or CL 77

Note: *Transmission code is stamped on the front of the clutch housing on 1.1, 1.4 and 1.6 litre models, and onto the front face of the transmission housing on 1.8 litre and larger-engine models.*

Lubrication
Recommended oil type .... See *"Lubricants and fluids"*
Recommended gearchange linkage grease .... Esso Norva 275

Torque wrench settings

	Nm	lbf ft
MA transmission - 1.1, 1.4 and 1.6 litre models		
Clutch release bearing guide sleeve bolts	12	9
Engine-to-transmission fixing bolts	35	26
Gearchange selector rod pivot bolts:		
Gearchange lever bolt	15	11
Transmission lever bolt	20	15
Left-hand engine/transmission mounting:		
Mounting bracket-to-transmission nuts	20	15
Mounting bracket-to-body bolts	25	18
Centre nut	65	48
Oil drain plug	25	18
Oil filler/level plug	25	18
Reversing light switch	25	18
Roadwheel bolts	85	62
Selector lever mounting bracket nuts	17	13

Torque wrench settings (continued)

	Nm	lbf ft
BE3 transmission - 1.8 litre and larger-engine models		
Clutch cable bracket retaining bolts ("pull-type" clutch only)	18	13
Clutch release bearing guide sleeve bolts	12	9
Engine-to-transmission fixing bolts	45	33
Gearchange linkage bellcrank pivot bolt	28	21
Gearchange selector rod to lever pivot bolt	15	11
Left-hand engine/transmission mounting:		
Mounting bracket-to-body bolts	25	18
Mounting stud	25	18
Centre nut	65	48
Oil drain plug	35	26
Oil filler/level plug	22	16
Reversing light switch	25	18
Roadwheel bolts	85	62

1 General information

The transmission is contained in a cast-aluminium alloy casing bolted to the engine's left-hand end, and consists of the gearbox and final drive differential - often called a transaxle.

Drive is transmitted from the crankshaft via the clutch to the input shaft, which has a splined extension to accept the clutch friction plate, and rotates in sealed ball-bearings. From the input shaft, drive is transmitted to the output shaft, which rotates in a roller bearing at its right-hand end, and a sealed ball-bearing at its left-hand end. From the output shaft, the drive is transmitted to the differential crownwheel, which rotates with the differential case and planetary gears, thus driving the sun gears and driveshafts. The rotation of the planetary gears on their shaft allows the inner roadwheel to rotate at a slower speed than the outer roadwheel when the car is cornering.

The input and output shafts are arranged side by side, parallel to the crankshaft and driveshafts, so that their gear pinion teeth are in constant mesh. In the neutral position, the output shaft gear pinions rotate freely, so that drive cannot be transmitted to the crownwheel.

Gear selection is via a floor-mounted lever and selector rod mechanism. The selector rod causes the appropriate selector fork to move its respective synchro-sleeve along the shaft, to lock the gear pinion to the synchro-hub. Since the synchro-hubs are splined to the output shaft, this locks the pinion to the shaft, so that drive can be transmitted. To ensure that gear-changing can be made quickly and quietly, a synchro-mesh system is fitted to all forward gears, consisting of baulk rings and spring-loaded fingers, as well as the gear pinions and synchro-hubs. The synchro-mesh cones are formed on the mating faces of the baulk rings and gear pinions.

Two different manual transmissions are used on the models covered in this manual; 1.1, 1.4 and 1.6 litre models have the "MA" transmission, whereas 1.8 litre and larger-engined models are fitted with the "BE3" unit.

2 Manual transmission - draining and refilling

Note: *A suitable square section wrench may be required to undo the transmission filler/level and drain plugs on some models. These wrenches can be obtained from most motor factors or your Peugeot dealer.*

1 This operation is much quicker and more efficient if the car is first taken on a journey of sufficient length to warm the engine/transmission up to normal operating temperature.

2 Park the car on level ground, switch off the ignition and apply the handbrake firmly. For improved access, jack up the front of the car and support it securely on axle stands (see *"Jacking and Vehicle Support"*). Note that the car must be lowered to the ground and level, to ensure accuracy, when refilling and checking the oil level.

3 Prise out the retaining clips and remove the access cover from underneath the left-hand wheelarch liner.

4 Wipe clean the area around the filler/level plug, which is situated on the left-hand end of the transmission, next to the end cover. Unscrew the filler/level plug from the transmission and recover the sealing washer **(see illustration)**.

5 Position a suitable container under the drain plug (situated at the rear of the transmission) and unscrew the plug. On 1.1, 1.4 and 1.6 litre models, the plug is on the left-hand side of the differential housing; on 1.8 litre and larger-engine models, it is on the base of the differential housing **(see illustration)**.

6 Allow the oil to drain completely into the container. If the oil is hot, take precautions against scalding. Clean both the filler/level and the drain plugs, being especially careful to wipe any metallic particles off the magnetic inserts. Discard the original sealing washers; they should be renewed whenever they are disturbed.

7 When the oil has finished draining, clean the drain plug threads and those of the transmission casing, fit a new sealing washer and refit the drain plug, tightening it to the specified torque wrench setting. If the car was raised for the draining operation, now lower it to the ground.

8 Refilling the transmission is an extremely awkward operation. Above all, allow plenty of time for the oil level to settle properly before checking it. Note that the car must be parked on flat level ground when checking the oil level.

9 Refill the transmission with the exact amount of the specified type of oil then check the oil level as described in Chapter 1A or 1B; if the correct amount was poured into the transmission and a large amount flows out on

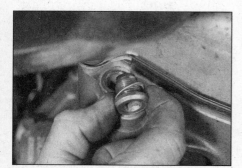

2.4 Removing the filler/level plug and sealing washer from the transmission (1.4 litre model shown)

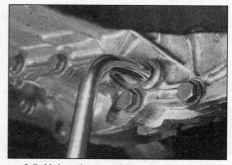

2.5 Using the special square-section wrench to unscrew the transmission drain plug (1.4 litre model shown)

checking the level, refit the filler/level plug and take the car on a short journey so that the new oil is distributed fully around the transmission components, then check the level again on your return. Refit the access cover and secure it in position with the retaining clips.

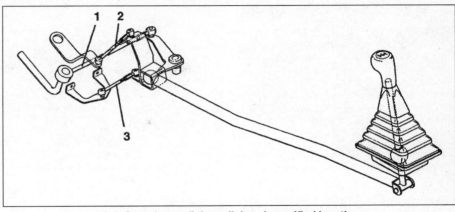

3.5 Gearchange linkage link rod specified lengths

1 260.5 ± 1 mm   2 106 ± 1 mm   3 106.5 ± 1 mm

3 Gearchange linkage - general information and adjustment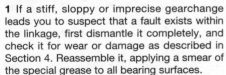

1 If a stiff, sloppy or imprecise gearchange leads you to suspect that a fault exists within the linkage, first dismantle it completely, and check it for wear or damage as described in Section 4. Reassemble it, applying a smear of the special grease to all bearing surfaces.

2 If this does not cure the fault, the car should be examined by an expert, as the fault must lie within the transmission itself. There is no adjustment as such in the linkage.

3 On 1.8 litre and larger-engined models, note that, while the length of the link rods can be altered as described below, this is for initial setting-up only, and is not intended to provide a form of compensation for wear. If the link rods have been renewed, or if the length of the originals is incorrect, adjust them as follows.

Link rod adjustment - 1.8 litre and larger-engined models

4 Firmly apply the handbrake, then jack up the front of the vehicle and support it on axle stands (see *"Jacking and Vehicle Support"*). Access to the link rods is poor, but can be gained both from above and below the vehicle.

5 Working in (or under) the engine compartment, measure the length of each link rod, and compare this to the length specified **(see illustration)**. Note that the measurements given are the distances between the centre points of the link rod balljoints, and not the total length of the rod.

6 If adjustment is necessary, slacken the locknut, then carefully lever the relevant link rod off its balljoint on the transmission. Turn the end of the rod until the specified distance between the link rod balljoint centres is obtained, then press the disconnected end of the rod firmly back onto its balljoint and securely tighten the link rod locknut.

7 Once all link rod lengths are correctly set, check that all gears can be selected, and that the gearchange lever returns properly to its correct at-rest (neutral) position.

4 Gearchange linkage - removal and refitting

Removal

1 Firmly apply the handbrake, then jack up the front of the vehicle and support it on axle stands (see *"Jacking and Vehicle Support"*).

1.1, 1.4 and 1.6 litre models

2 To improve access to the transmission end of the linkage, remove the air cleaner housing as described in the relevant Part of Chapter 4.

3 Slacken and remove the nut and washer, then withdraw the pivot bolt from each end of the selector rod. Disengage the rod from the gearchange lever and selector lever, and remove it from underneath the vehicle **(see illustration)**. If it is loose, remove the spacer from the transmission selector lever.

4 Undo the two nuts securing the selector lever mounting bracket to the transmission housing, then remove the bracket and lever assembly from the transmission.

5 Inspect all the linkage components for signs of wear or damage, paying particular attention to the pivot bushes, and renew worn components as necessary. If necessary, remove the gearchange lever as follows.

6 Unclip the gearchange lever gaiter from the centre console then unscrew the knob from the gearchange lever and remove the gaiter.

7 Slacken and remove the selector lever retaining nuts and lift off the retaining plate then lower the lever out from underneath the vehicle **(see illustration)**.

4.3 Transmission selector lever arrangement - 1.1, 1.4 and 1.6 litre models. Selector rod pivot bolt (arrowed)

4.7 Remove the four retaining nuts then remove the gearchange lever from underneath the vehicle

4.8a Peel back the lower gaiter . . .

4.8b . . . then disengage the mounting plate . . .

4.8c . . . and peel the upper gaiter away from the lever baseplate

8 Peel back the lower gaiter from the base of the gearchange lever, then disengage the lever mounting plate, and slide the upper gaiter up the lever to gain access to the gearchange lever pivot ball. Examine the lever components for signs of wear or damage, paying particular attention to the rubber gaiters, and renew components as necessary. The lever can be separated from its baseplate after the retaining ring has been unclipped **(see illustrations)**.

1.8 litre and larger-engined models

9 Slacken and remove the nut, and withdraw the pivot bolt securing the selector rod to the base of the gearchange lever.
10 Using a flat-bladed screwdriver, carefully lever the three link rods off their balljoints on the transmission **(see illustration)**. Disengage the selector rod from the bellcrank pivot, and remove it from underneath the vehicle.
11 Carefully prise the plastic cap off the bolt securing the gearchange linkage bellcrank to the subframe.
12 Slacken and remove the bellcrank pivot bolt and washer, then manoeuvre the bellcrank and link rod out from under the vehicle, and recover the spacer and pivot bushes from the centre of the bellcrank.
13 Inspect all the linkage components for signs of wear or damage, paying particular attention to the pivot bushes and link rod balljoints, and renew worn components as necessary. If necessary, the gearchange lever can be removed and inspected as described above in paragraphs 6 to 8.

Refitting

1.1, 1.4 and 1.6 litre models

14 Refitting is a reversal of the removal procedure, noting the following points:
  a) *Before refitting, apply a smear of the special grease (see Specifications) to the selector lever and rod pivots.*

  b) *Ensure that the gearchange lever rubber gaiters are correctly seated before refitting the lever assembly to the vehicle.*

  c) *Tighten the selector rod pivot bolts to the specified torque setting.*

1.8 litre and larger-engined models

15 Refitting is a reversal of the removal procedure, noting the following points:
  a) *Before refitting, check and if necessary adjust the link rod lengths as described in Section 3.*

  b) *Apply a smear of the special grease (see Specifications) to the gearchange lever pivot ball, the link rod balljoints and the bellcrank ball and pivot bushes.*

  c) *Ensure that the gearchange lever rubber gaiters are correctly seated before refitting the lever assembly to the vehicle.*

  d) *Tighten the bellcrank and selector rod pivot bolts to their specified torques, and ensure that the link rods are securely pressed onto their balljoints.*

5 Oil seals - renewal

Driveshaft oil seals

1 Chock the rear wheels, apply the handbrake, then jack up the front of the car and support it on axle stands (see *"Jacking and Vehicle Support"*). Remove the appropriate front roadwheel.
2 Drain the transmission oil (Section 2).
3 Slacken and remove the lower balljoint nut and clamp bolt and free the balljoint shank from the swivel hub (see Chapter 10, Section 2). Proceed as described under the relevant sub-heading.

Right-hand seal

4 Loosen the two intermediate bearing retaining bolt nuts, then rotate the bolts through 90° so that their offset heads are clear of the bearing outer race.
5 Carefully pull the swivel hub assembly outwards, and pull on the inner end of the driveshaft to free the intermediate bearing from its mounting bracket.
6 Once the driveshaft end is free from the transmission, slide the dust seal off the inner end of the shaft, noting which way around it is fitted, and support the inner end of the driveshaft to avoid damaging the constant velocity joints or gaiters.
7 Carefully prise the oil seal out of the transmission, using a large flat-bladed screwdriver **(see illustration)**.

4.8d The lever and baseplate can be separated once the retaining ring has been unclipped

4.10 On 1.8 litre and larger-engined models, detach the three gearchange linkage link rods from their balljoints

5.7 Use a large flat-bladed screwdriver to prise the driveshaft oil seals out of position

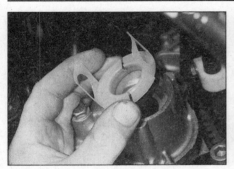

5.8a **Fit the new seal to the transmission, noting the plastic seal protector . . .**

5.8b **. . . and tap it into position using a tubular drift**

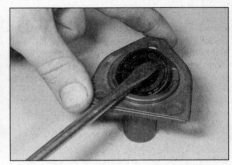

5.22 **Removing the input shaft seal from the guide sleeve**

8 Remove all traces of dirt from the area around the oil seal aperture, then apply a smear of grease to the outer lip of the new oil seal. Fit the new seal into its aperture, and drive it squarely into position using a suitable tubular drift (such as a socket) which bears only on the hard outer edge of the seal, until it abuts its locating shoulder. If the seal was supplied with a plastic protector sleeve, leave this in position until the driveshaft has been refitted **(see illustrations)**.

9 Thoroughly clean the driveshaft splines, then apply a thin film of grease to the oil seal lips and to the driveshaft inner end splines.

10 Slide the dust seal into position on the end of the shaft, ensuring that its flat surface is facing the transmission.

11 Carefully locate the inner driveshaft splines with those of the differential sun gear, taking care not to damage the oil seal, then align the intermediate bearing with its mounting bracket, and push the driveshaft fully into position. If necessary, use a soft-faced mallet to tap the outer race of the bearing into position in the mounting bracket.

12 Ensure that the intermediate bearing is correctly seated, then rotate its retaining bolts back through 90° so that their offset heads are resting against the bearing outer race, and tighten the retaining nuts to the specified torque. Remove the plastic seal protector (where supplied), and slide the dust seal tight up against the oil seal.

13 Engage the balljoint shank with the lower arm, making sure that the balljoint protector is correctly seated in the hub. Refit the clamp

bolt and nut and tighten it to the specified torque setting (see Chapter 10).

14 Refit the roadwheel, then lower the vehicle to the ground and tighten the roadwheel bolts to the specified torque.

15 Refill the transmission with the specified type and amount of fluid/oil, and check the level using the information given in Chapter 1A or 1B.

Left-hand seal

16 Pull the swivel hub assembly outwards and withdraw the driveshaft inner constant velocity joint from the transmission, taking care not to damage the driveshaft oil seal. Support the driveshaft, to avoid damaging the constant velocity joints or gaiters.

17 Renew the oil seal as described above in paragraphs 7 to 9.

18 Carefully locate the inner constant velocity joint splines with those of the differential sun gear, taking care not to damage the oil seal, and push the driveshaft fully into position. Where fitted, remove the plastic protector from the oil seal.

19 Carry out the operations described above in paragraphs 13 to 15.

Input shaft oil seal

20 Remove the transmission as described in Section 8.

21 Undo the three bolts securing the clutch release bearing guide sleeve in position, and slide the guide off the input shaft, along with its O-ring or gasket (as applicable). Recover any shims or thrustwashers which have stuck

to the rear of the guide sleeve, and refit them to the input shaft.

22 Carefully lever the oil seal out of the guide using a suitable flat-bladed screwdriver **(see illustration)**.

23 Before fitting a new seal, check the input shaft's seal rubbing surface for signs of burrs, scratches or other damage, which may have caused the seal to fail in the first place. It may be possible to polish away minor faults of this sort using fine abrasive paper; however, more serious defects will require the renewal of the input shaft. Ensure that the input shaft is clean and greased, to protect the seal lips on refitting.

24 Dip the new seal in clean oil, and fit it to the guide sleeve.

25 Fit a new O-ring or gasket (as applicable) to the rear of the guide sleeve, then carefully slide the sleeve into position over the input shaft. Refit the retaining bolts and tighten them to the specified torque setting **(see illustrations)**.

26 Take the opportunity to inspect the clutch components if not already done (Chapter 6). Finally, refit the transmission as described in Section 8.

Selector shaft oil seal

1.1, 1.4 and 1.6 litre models

27 On these models, to renew the selector shaft seal, the transmission must be dismantled. This task should therefore be entrusted to a Peugeot dealer or transmission specialist.

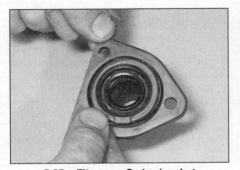

5.25a **Fit a new O-ring/gasket (as applicable) . . .**

5.25b **. . . refit the guide sleeve over the input shaft . . .**

5.25c **. . . and secure it in position with its three retaining bolts**

1.8 litre and larger-engined models

28 Apply the handbrake, then jack up the front of the vehicle and support it on axle stands (see *"Jacking and Vehicle Support"*). Remove the left-hand front roadwheel, and unclip the access cover from the centre of the wheel arch liner.

29 Using a large flat-bladed screwdriver, lever the link rod balljoint off the transmission selector shaft, and disconnect the link rod.

30 Using a large flat-bladed screwdriver, carefully prise the selector shaft seal out of the housing, and slide it off the end of the shaft **(see illustrations)**.

31 Before fitting a new seal, check the selector shaft's seal rubbing surface for signs of burrs, scratches or other damage, which may have caused the seal to fail in the first place. It may be possible to polish away minor faults of this sort using fine abrasive paper; however, more serious defects will require the renewal of the selector shaft.

32 Apply a smear of grease to the new seal's outer edge and sealing lip, then carefully slide the seal along the selector rod. Press the seal fully into position in the transmission housing.

33 Refit the link rod to the selector shaft, ensuring that its balljoint is pressed firmly onto the shaft. Refit the roadwheel and lower the car to the ground.

5.30a On 1.8 litre and larger-engined models, use a screwdriver to prise the selector shaft seal out of position . . .

Removal

3 Where necessary, to improve access to the switch, it may be necessary to remove the air inlet duct(s) as described in the relevant Part of Chapter 4. If necessary, also remove the battery mounting tray (see Chapter 5A).

4 Disconnect the wiring connector, then unscrew it from the transmission casing along with its sealing washer **(see illustration)**.

Refitting

5 Fit a new sealing washer to the switch, then screw it back into position in the top of the transmission housing and tighten it to the specified torque setting. Refit the wiring plug, and test the operation of the circuit. Refit any components removed for access.

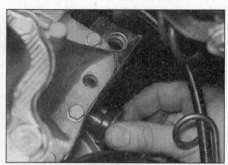

5.30b . . . then slide the seal off the shaft

pin, and disconnect the cable from the speedometer drive. Where necessary, disconnect the wiring connector from the speedometer drive.

3 Slacken and remove the retaining bolt, along with the heat shield (where fitted), and withdraw the speedometer drive and driven pinion assembly from the transmission housing, along with its O-ring **(see illustrations)**.

4 If necessary, the pinion can be slid out of the housing, and the oil seal can be removed from the top of the housing. Examine the pinion for signs of damage, and renew if necessary. Renew the housing O-ring as a matter of course.

5 If the driven pinion is worn or damaged, also examine the drive pinion in the transmission housing for similar signs.

6 On 1.1, 1.4 and 1.6 litre models, to renew the drive pinion, the transmission must be dismantled and the differential gear removed. This task should therefore be entrusted to a Peugeot dealer or a transmission specialist.

7 On 1.8 litre and larger-engined models, to remove the drive pinion, first disengage the right-hand driveshaft from the transmission, as described in paragraphs 1 to 7 of Section 5. Undo the three retaining bolts, and remove the speedometer drive housing from the transmission, along with its O-ring. Remove the drive pinion from the differential gear, and recover any adjustment shims from the gear **(see illustrations)**.

---

6 Reversing light switch - testing, removal and refitting

Testing

1 The reversing light circuit is controlled by a plunger-type switch screwed into the top of the transmission casing. If a fault develops, first ensure that the circuit fuse has not blown.

2 To test the switch, disconnect the wiring connector, and use a multimeter (set to the resistance function) or a battery-and-bulb test circuit to check that there is continuity between the switch terminals only when reverse gear is selected. If this is not the case, and there are no obvious breaks or other damage to the wires, the switch is faulty, and must be renewed.

7 Speedometer drive - removal and refitting

Removal

1 Chock the rear wheels, firmly apply the handbrake, then jack up the front of the car and support it on axle stands (see *"Jacking and Vehicle Support"*). The speedometer drive is on the rear of the transmission housing, next to the inner end of the right-hand driveshaft.

2 Pull out the speedometer cable retaining

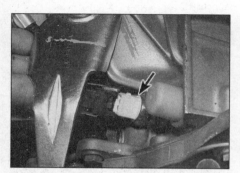

6.4 Disconnecting the wiring connector from the reversing light switch (arrowed)

7.3a Slacken and remove the retaining bolt . . .

7.3b . . . then withdraw the speedometer drive from the transmission (transmission removed for clarity - type BE3 shown)

7.7a On 1.8 litre and larger-engined models (BE3 transmission), undo the three bolts . . .

7.7b . . . and remove the housing, O-ring and drive pinion from the transmission (transmission removed for clarity)

7.8 On refitting, ensure the drive pinion dogs are correctly engaged with the gear slots (arrowed)

Refitting

8 On 1.8 litre and larger-engined models, where the drive pinion has been removed, refit the adjustment shims to the differential gear, then locate the speedometer drive on the gear, ensuring it is correctly engaged in the gear slots **(see illustration)**. Fit a new O-ring to the rear of the speedometer drive housing, then refit the housing to the transmission and securely tighten its retaining bolts. Inspect the driveshaft oil seal for signs of wear, and renew if necessary. Refit the driveshaft to the transmission, with reference to Section 5.

9 On all models, apply a smear of grease to the lips of the seal and to the driven pinion shaft, and slide the pinion into position in the speedometer drive.

10 Fit a new O-ring to the speedometer drive and refit it to the transmission, ensuring that the drive and driven pinions are correctly engaged.

11 Refit the retaining bolt and the heat shield (where fitted), and tighten the bolt. Where necessary, reconnect the wiring connector to the speedometer drive.

12 Apply a smear of oil to the speedometer cable O-rings, then reconnect the cable to the drive, and secure it in position with the rubber retaining pin. Lower the vehicle to the ground.

---

8 Manual transmission - removal and refitting 🔧

Removal

1 Chock the rear wheels, then firmly apply the handbrake. Jack up the front of the vehicle, and securely support it on axle stands (see *"Jacking and Vehicle Support"*). Remove both front roadwheels. Prise out the retaining clips and remove the plastic cover from inside the left-hand wheel arch.

2 Drain the transmission oil as described in Section 2, then refit the drain and filler plugs, and tighten to their specified torque settings.

3 Remove the battery, battery tray and mounting plate as described in Chapter 5A.

4 Where necessary, to improve access to the top of the transmission remove the air cleaner housing and/or inlet duct (as applicable) as described in the relevant Part of Chapter 4. On Turbo diesel models also remove the intercooler.

5 Remove the starter motor (Chapter 5A).

6 Working in the engine compartment, release the inner cable and outer cable fittings from the clutch release lever and mounting bracket, and free the cable from the transmission housing. On 1.1, 1.4 and 1.6 litre models, where necessary, fully slacken the locknut and adjuster nut from the end of the clutch cable to aid removal.

7 Disconnect the wiring connector from the reversing light switch and, where necessary, the speedometer drive housing. Undo the retaining nut(s), and disconnect the earth straps from the top of the transmission housing. Free the wiring from any relevant retaining clips, and position it clear of the transmission.

8 On 1.1, 1.4 and 1.6 litre models, slacken and remove the nut and washer, then withdraw the pivot bolt and disconnect the selector rod from the transmission lever. Where necessary, undo the bolt securing the exhaust front pipe to its transmission mounting bracket.

9 On 1.8 litre and larger-engined models, using a flat-bladed screwdriver, carefully lever the three gearchange mechanism link rods off their respective balljoints on the transmission **(see illustration)**. Position the rods clear of the transmission.

10 On models with power steering, undo the retaining nuts (where fitted) and release the retaining clips securing the power steering pipe to the transmission. Position the pipe clear of the unit so that it will not be damaged during the removal procedure.

11 Undo the retaining bolt(s), and remove the flywheel lower cover plate (where fitted) from the transmission **(see illustration)**.

12 Withdraw the rubber retaining pin, disconnect the speedometer cable from the drive housing, and free it from any relevant retaining clips **(see illustrations)**.

13 Remove both driveshafts as described in Chapter 8.

8.9 On 1.8 litre and larger-engined models (BE3 transmission), lever the gearchange link rods off their balljoints using a large flat-bladed screwdriver

8.11 On larger-engined models, remove the flywheel lower cover plate

8.12a Withdraw the rubber retaining pin (arrowed) . . .

8.12b . . . and disconnect the speedometer cable from the transmission - BE3 transmission shown

8.18a Remove the centre nut and washer from the left-hand mounting . . .

8.18b . . . then undo the two retaining bolts and remove the mounting bracket assembly

14 On 1.8 litre and larger-engined models, remove the speedometer drive gear housing and gear assembly from the transmission as described in Section 7.

15 Place a jack with a block of wood beneath the engine, to take the weight of the engine. Alternatively, attach a couple of lifting eyes to the engine, and fit a hoist or support bar to take the engine weight.

16 Place a jack and block of wood beneath the transmission, and raise the jack to take the weight of the transmission.

17 Where necessary, to improve access to the left-hand engine transmission mounting on models fitted with ABS, undo the modulator retaining nuts then, taking great care not to place any undue strain on the brake pipes, carefully position the modulator clear of the mounting assembly (see Chapter 9).

18 Slacken and remove the centre nut and washer from the left-hand engine/transmission mounting. Undo the two bolts securing the mounting bracket assembly to the vehicle body, and remove the mounting bracket assembly (where possible). Where the bracket is welded in position undo the nuts

and washers and remove the rubber mounting **(see illustrations)**.

19 On 1.1, 1.4 and 1.6 litre models, undo the three retaining nuts and remove the mounting plate from the top of the transmission.

20 On 1.8 litre and larger-engined models, slide the spacer (where fitted) off the mounting stud, then unscrew the stud from the top of the transmission housing and remove it along with its washer. If the mounting stud is tight, a universal stud extractor can be used to unscrew it **(see illustrations)**.

21 On models with a "pull-type" clutch release mechanism (see Chapter 6), tap out the retaining pin or unscrew the retaining bolt (as applicable) and remove the clutch release lever from the top of the release fork shaft. This is necessary to allow the fork shaft to rotate freely, to disengage from the release bearing as the transmission is pulled away from the engine. Make an alignment mark across the centre of the clutch release fork shaft using a scriber, paint or similar, and mark its position relative to the transmission housing **(see illustrations)**. Undo the retaining bolts, and remove the clutch cable

bracket from the top of the transmission housing.

22 With the jack positioned beneath the transmission taking the weight, slacken and remove the remaining bolts securing the transmission housing to the engine. Note the correct fitted positions of each bolt, and the necessary brackets, as they are removed, to use as a reference on refitting. Make a final check that all components have been disconnected, and are positioned clear of the transmission so that they will not hinder the removal procedure.

23 With the bolts removed, move the trolley jack and transmission to the left, to free it from its locating dowels then pivot the differential end of the transmission upwards (to disengage it from the subframe).

24 Once the transmission is free, lower the jack and manoeuvre the unit out from under the car. Remove the locating dowels from the transmission or engine if they are loose, and keep them in a safe place.

25 On models with a "pull-type" clutch, make a second alignment mark on the transmission housing, marking the relative position of the release fork mark after removal, noting the

8.20a On 1.8 litre and larger-engined models, slide the spacer off the mounting stud . . .

8.20b . . . and unscrew the mounting stud. If the stud is tight, use a stud extractor

8.21a On models with a "pull-type" clutch, withdraw the retaining pin . . .

8.21b . . . then remove the clutch release lever . . .

8.21c . . . and make an alignment mark between the release fork shaft and transmission housing (arrowed)

angle at which the release fork is positioned **(see illustration 8.26a)**. This mark can then be used to position the release fork before refitting, to ensure that the fork correctly engages with the clutch release bearing as the transmission is installed.

Refitting

26 The transmission is refitted by a reversal of the removal procedure, bearing in mind the following points:

a) *Apply a little high-melting-point grease (Peugeot recommend the use of Molykote BR2 plus - available from your Peugeot dealer) to the splines of the transmission input shaft. Do not apply too much, otherwise there is a possibility of the grease contaminating the clutch friction plate.*

b) *Ensure that the locating dowels are correctly positioned prior to installation.*

c) *On models with a "pull-type" clutch, before refitting, position the clutch release bearing so that its arrow mark is pointing upwards (bearing fork slots facing towards the front of the engine), and align the release fork shaft mark with the*

second mark made on the transmission housing (release fork positioned at approximately 60° to clutch housing face) **(see illustration)**. This will ensure that the release fork and bearing will engage correctly as the transmission is refitted to the engine. If the bearing and fork are correctly engaged, the mark on the shaft should be aligned with the original mark made on the transmission housing. Ensure that the release fork and bearing are correctly engaged before bolting the transmission to the engine.

d) *On 1.8 litre and larger-engined models, apply thread-locking fluid to the left-hand engine/transmission mounting stud threads, prior to refitting it to the transmission **(see illustration)**. Tighten the stud to the specified torque.*

e) *Tighten all nuts and bolts to the specified torque (where given).*

f) *Renew the driveshaft oil seals, then refit the driveshafts (see Chapter 8).*

g) *Adjust the clutch (see Chapter 6).*

h) *On completion, refill the transmission with the specified type and quantity of lubricant, as described in Chapter 1A or 1B.*

9 Manual transmission overhaul - general information

Overhauling a manual transmission is a difficult and involved job for the DIY home mechanic. In addition to dismantling and reassembling many small parts, clearances must be precisely measured and, if necessary, changed by selecting shims and spacers. Internal transmission components are also often difficult to obtain, and in many instances, extremely expensive. Because of this, if the transmission develops a fault or becomes noisy, the best course of action is to have the unit overhauled by a specialist repairer, or to obtain an exchange reconditioned unit.

Nevertheless, it is not impossible for the more experienced mechanic to overhaul the transmission, provided the special tools are available, and the job is done in a deliberate step-by-step manner, so that nothing is overlooked.

The tools necessary for an overhaul include

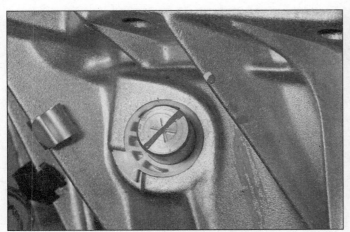

8.26a On models with a "pull-type" clutch, prior to refitting the transmission, align the release fork mark with the second mark made on removal

8.26b On 1.8 litre and larger-engined models, apply thread-locking fluid to the mounting stud threads

internal and external circlip pliers, bearing pullers, a slide hammer, a set of pin punches, a dial test indicator, and possibly a hydraulic press. In addition, a large, sturdy workbench and a vice will be required.

During dismantling of the transmission, make careful notes of how each component is fitted, to make reassembly easier and more accurate.

Before dismantling the transmission, it will help if you have some idea what area is malfunctioning. Certain problems can be closely related to specific areas in the transmission, which can make component examination and replacement easier. Refer to the Fault finding Section for more information.

Chapter 7 Part B:
Automatic transmission

Contents

Degrees of difficulty

Easy, suitable for novice with little experience	Fairly easy, suitable for beginner with some experience	Fairly difficult, suitable for competent DIY mechanic	Difficult, suitable for experienced DIY mechanic	Very difficult, suitable for expert DIY or professional 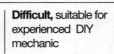

Specifications

General

Type	Automatic, four forward speeds and reverse
Designation:	
Up to mid-1999	4 HP 14
Mid-1999 onward	AL4

Lubrication

Recommended fluid	See *Lubricants and fluids*

Torque wrench settings

	Nm	lbf ft
4 HP 14 transmission		
Dipstick tube-to-sump union nut	45	33
Engine-to-transmission securing bolts	40	30
Fluid cooler centre bolt	50	37
Left-hand engine/transmission mounting	See Chapter 2B	
Selector cable fixings:		
Outer cable locknuts	10	7
Mounting bracket-to-transmission bolts	20	15
Cable-to-mounting bracket screws	10	7
Selector lever retaining nuts	7	5
Torque converter-to-driveplate bolts	35	26
Transmission selector lever retaining nut	30	22
AL4 transmission		
Engine-to-transmission securing bolts	35	26
Engine/transmission left-hand mounting	See Chapter 2A or 2B	
Fluid cooler retaining bolt	50	37
Fluid drain plug	33	24
Fluid filler and level plugs	25	18
Input speed sensor	10	7
Output speed sensor	10	7
Selector lever position switch bolts	15	11
Torque converter-to-driveplate bolts:		
Stage 1	10	7
Stage 2	30	22
Transmission selector shaft lever clamp bolt and nut	15	11

1 General information

4 HP 14 transmission

Certain petrol engine models are optionally available with a four-speed fully-automatic transmission, consisting of a torque converter, an epicyclic geartrain, and hydraulically-operated clutches and brakes **(see illustration)**.

The torque converter provides a fluid coupling between engine and transmission, which acts as an automatic clutch, and also provides a degree of torque multiplication when accelerating.

The epicyclic geartrain provides either of the four forward or one reverse gear ratios, according to which of its component parts are held stationary or allowed to turn. The components of the geartrain are held or released by brakes and clutches which are activated by a hydraulic control unit. A fluid pump within the transmission provides the necessary hydraulic pressure to operate the brakes and clutches.

Driver control of the transmission is by a seven-position selector lever. The transmission has a 'drive' position, and a 'hold' facility on the first three gear ratios. The drive position D provides automatic changing throughout the range of all four gear ratios, and is the one to select for normal driving. An automatic kickdown facility shifts the transmission down a gear if the accelerator pedal is fully depressed. The hold facility is very similar, but limits the number of gear ratios available – ie, when the selector lever is in the 3 position, only the first three ratios can be selected; in the 2 position, only the first two can be selected, and so on. The lower ratio hold is useful for providing engine braking when travelling down steep gradients, or for preventing unwanted selection of top gear on twisty roads. Note, however, that the transmission should never be shifted down a position if the engine speed exceeds 4000 rpm.

AL4 transmission

The AL4 transmission, optionally available on later petrol engine models, is a development of the earlier 4 HP 14 unit, and incorporates electronic control; the automatic gearchanges are electronically controlled, rather than hydraulically as with the 4 HP 14 type. The advantage of electronic management is to provide a faster gearchange response. A kickdown facility is also provided, to enable a faster acceleration response when required.

The torque converter incorporates an automatic lock-up feature which eliminates any possibility of converter slip in the top two gears; this aids performance and economy. In addition to the normal alternative of manual change, the three-position mode switch on the centre console (adjacent to the selector lever) provides 'normal', 'sport' or 'snow' settings, as required. In sport mode, upshifts are delayed longer, to make full use of engine power. In snow mode, either 2nd or 3rd gear is used to pull away from rest, maximising traction in slippery conditions.

Another feature of this transmission is the Park lock, which is partly a safety, and partly a security, feature. Moving the lever out of the P position requires the ignition to be on, and the brake pedal must also be depressed.

The gear selector cable has an automatic adjuster mechanism, meaning that routine cable adjustment should not normally be required.

Routine transmission fluid changes are not featuring in the manufacturer's maintenance schedule; the transmission unit is equipped with a fluid wear sensor to inform the driver when the fluid needs renewing (the ECU flashes the Sport and Snow mode indicator lights when fluid renewal is necessary).

In the event of a problem developing with the transmission, the transmission ECU may select one of two emergency back-up modes, to enable the car to continue being driven. When operating in this back-up mode, shifting out of N or R will become more jerky, or the

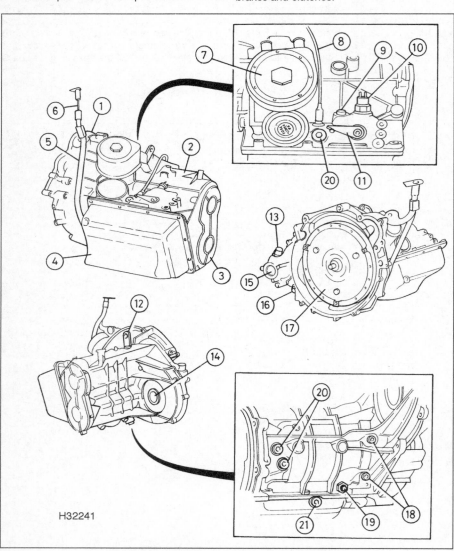

H32241

1.1 External components of the 4 HP 14 transmission

1 Torque converter housing	9 Breather	15 Final drive right-hand output
2 Main casing	10 Starter inhibitor/reversing light switch	16 Final drive drain plug
3 End cover	11 Selector lever	17 Torque converter
4 Sump	12 Lifting eye	18 Output shaft bearing bolts
5 Dipstick tube	13 Speedometer drive	19 Brake band adjuster
6 Dipstick	14 Final drive left-hand output	20 Pressure test points
7 Fluid cooler		21 Sump drain plug
8 Kickdown cable		

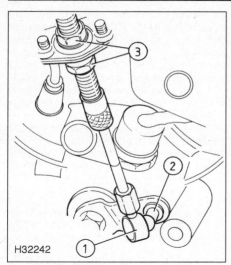

2.5 Selector cable transmission end fixings – 4 HP 14 transmission

1 *Cable end fitting*
2 *Selector lever balljoint*
3 *Outer cable locknuts*

transmission will only select 3rd gear (no gearchanges). If a fault is suspected, your Peugeot dealer will be able to download fault codes from the transmission ECU memory, to speed up diagnosis.

All transmission types

Due to the complexity of the automatic transmission, any repair or overhaul work must be left to a Peugeot dealer with the necessary special equipment for fault diagnosis and repair. The contents of the following Sections are therefore confined to supplying general information, and any service information and instructions that can be used by the owner.

2 Selector cable – adjustment

4 HP 14 transmission

1 Position the selector lever firmly against its detent in the N (neutral) position.
2 To improve access to the transmission end of the selector cable, remove the battery, battery tray and mounting plate as described in Chapter 5A. To further improve access, it may also be necessary to remove the air inlet duct(s) (see the relevant Part of Chapter 4).
3 Using a large flat-bladed screwdriver, carefully lever the selector cable end fitting off the transmission selector lever balljoint, whilst ensuring that the lever does not move.
4 Ensure that the cable end fitting is screwed onto at least 5 mm of the inner cable thread.
5 With both the selector levers in the N position, the selector cable end fitting should be correctly aligned with the transmission

lever balljoint, so that the cable can be connected to the lever without the balljoint moving. If necessary, adjust the position of the end fitting by screwing or unscrewing it (as applicable) on the cable thread, bearing in mind the point made above in paragraph 4. If this proves impossible, further adjustments can be made by slackening the locknuts securing the outer cable to its mounting bracket **(see illustration)**. Reposition the nuts as required until the end fitting and balljoint are correctly aligned, then tighten the nuts.
6 Once the end fitting is correctly positioned, press it firmly onto the balljoint, and check that it is securely retained.
7 Refit any components removed to improve access.

AL4 transmission

8 Position the selector lever firmly against its detent in the P (park) position.
9 To improve access to the transmission end of the selector cable, remove the battery, battery tray and mounting plate as described in Chapter 5A. To further improve access, it may also be necessary to remove the air inlet duct(s) (see the relevant Part of Chapter 4).
10 Working on the cable end fitting at the transmission end of the cable, release the locking plunger retaining clip and allow the orange coloured locking plunger to extend fully from the end fitting.
11 Ensure that the selector lever on the transmission is pushed fully towards the rear then lock the adjustment mechanism by depressing the locking plunger back into the end fitting.
12 Check the operation of the selector lever, then refit the components removed to improve access.

3 Selector lever and cable – removal and refitting

Note: *At the time of writing, the selector lever and cable were only available as a complete assembly. Refer to a Peugeot dealer for parts availability.*

Removal

4 HP 14 transmission

1 Firmly apply the handbrake, then jack up the front of the car and support it securely on axle stands (see *Jacking and vehicle support*). Position the selector lever in the N position.
2 Remove the battery, battery tray and mounting plate as described in Chapter 5A.
3 Remove the exhaust system heat shield(s) to gain access to the base of the selector lever assembly (see the relevant Part of Chapter 4). On some models, it may also be necessary to remove the air inlet duct(s) as described in the relevant Part of Chapter 4.
4 Working on the transmission end of the cable, undo the two screws securing the outer

cable to its retaining bracket, and carefully lever the inner cable end fitting off its balljoint on the transmission selector lever. Note that the transmission selector lever must not be disturbed until the cable is refitted. As a precaution, mark the position of the lever in relation to the transmission housing.
5 Work back along the selector cable, releasing it from any relevant retaining clips, and noting its correct routing.
6 Working from inside the vehicle, carefully prise the selector lever trim panel out from the centre console.
7 Slacken and remove the screws securing the handle to the shaft of the selector lever. Depress the selector lever handle detent knob, then rotate the handle through 90° anti-clockwise, lift the assembly up, and rotate it back 90° clockwise to release the detent button from the selector lever pushrod. With the handle removed, withdraw the detent button and spring from the handle.
8 Undo the four nuts securing the selector lever to the floor.
9 Working underneath the vehicle, disengage the selector lever assembly from the body, and remove the lever and cable assembly, noting the correct routing of the cable.

AL4 transmission

10 Release the Park lock by switching on the ignition and pressing the brake pedal. Position the selector lever in the 2nd gear position, then switch off the ignition.
11 Remove the air cleaner assembly and air inlet ducting as described in the relevant Part of Chapter 4.
12 Remove the battery, battery tray and mounting plate as described in Chapter 5A.
13 Using a suitable forked tool (a fork-type balljoint splitter could be used, or failing that, a large flat-bladed screwdriver), carefully prise the selector cable balljoint off the selector lever **(see illustration)**.

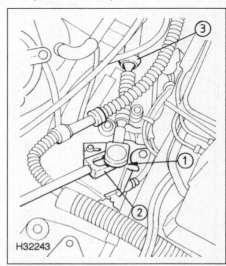

3.13 Prise off the selector cable balljoint (1) using a forked tool (2), then remove the cable from the bracket (3) – AL4 transmission

14 Extract the retaining C-clip and release the outer cable and cable grommet from the transmission bracket.

15 Firmly apply the handbrake, then jack up the front of the car and support it securely on axle stands (see *Jacking and vehicle support*).

16 Detach and lower the exhaust system in the area below the passenger compartment selector lever, and remove the heat shield in order to release the selector cable retaining clamp (see the relevant Part of Chapter 4).

17 Remove the centre console as described in Chapter 12.

18 Undo the two screws and withdraw the Park lock solenoid valve from the front of the selector lever upper housing.

19 Pull the selector lever knob upwards off the lever, without twisting it.

20 Undo the two nuts securing the selector lever upper housing to the lower housing and lift off the upper housing. On later models, there may be two additional upper housing retaining screws which are accessible through the selector lever gate.

21 Undo the remaining nuts and bolts securing the selector lever lower housing to the floor, then withdraw the lower housing and cable from the car.

Refitting

4 HP 14 transmission

22 Ensuring that the cable is correctly routed, manoeuvre the lever and cable assembly back into position from underneath the vehicle.

23 From inside the vehicle, pull the lever up into position, and tighten all four selector lever retaining nuts.

24 Refit the spring and detent button to the selector lever handle, and press the button fully into the handle. Keeping the button depressed, slide the handle assembly onto the lever then, exerting light downward pressure on the handle, rotate the handle through 90° clockwise, then back 90° anti-clockwise to engage the detent button with the lever pushrod. Release the detent button, then refit the four handle retaining screws and tighten them securely. Check the operation of the selector lever detent button before proceeding.

25 From underneath the vehicle, work along the length of the selector cable, ensuring that it is retained by all the relevant clips. Align the outer cable bracket with its mounting bracket on the transmission, then refit and tighten its retaining bolts.

26 Ensure that the selector lever is in the N position and the transmission selector lever is still in the neutral position, then adjust the cable and connect it to the transmission lever as described in paragraphs 4 to 6 of Section 2.

27 Refit the heat shield(s) as described in the relevant Part of Chapter 4, then lower the vehicle to the ground.

28 Refit all components removed for access.

AL4 transmission

29 Refit the selector lever upper and lower housing, the Park lock solenoid and centre console, using the reverse of the removal procedure.

30 Move the gear selection lever in the passenger compartment to the P position.

31 Under the car, fit the selector cable retaining clamp, exhaust heatshield and other disturbed exhaust system components as necessary.

32 In the engine compartment, move the transmission selector lever to the P position (fully towards the engine compartment bulkhead).

33 Fit the cable and grommet to the transmission bracket and secure with the C-clip. Reconnect the selector cable balljoint to the transmission selector lever, pressing it firmly into place.

34 Adjust the selector cable as described in paragraphs 8 to 12 of Section 2.

35 Final refitting is now a reversal of removal. Check for satisfactory operation of the selector cable on completion.

4 Kickdown cable (4 HP 14 transmission) – adjustment

Note: *This Section does not apply to the AL4 transmission, as the kickdown function is controlled electronically.*

1 Warm the engine up to its normal operating temperature, then check that the engine idle speed is correctly set. If necessary, adjust the idle speed as described in the relevant Part of Chapter 4.

2 Detach the kickdown inner cable from the throttle body cam then, referring to the relevant Part of Chapter 4, check that the accelerator cable is correctly adjusted.

3 Pull the kickdown inner cable fully out of its outer cable, and measure the distance between the end of the lug on the inner cable and the threaded end of the outer cable **(see illustration)**. This should be approximately 39 mm. If necessary, slacken the two outer cable locknuts, and position the nuts as required so that the distance is as specified.

4 Reconnect the kickdown cable to the throttle body cam, then check the clearance once more between the inner cable lug and the threaded end of the outer cable. Ensuring that the throttle body cam is fully against its stop, there should be a gap of 0.5 to 1.0 mm **(see illustration)**. If not, adjust the gap by repositioning the outer cable locknuts as required. Once the outer cable is correctly positioned and the gap is as specified, securely tighten the cable locknuts.

5 Kickdown cable (4 HP 14 transmission) – renewal

Renewal of the kickdown cable is a complex task, which should be entrusted to a Peugeot dealer. To detach the cable at the transmission end requires removal of the hydraulic valve block, which is a task that should not be undertaken by the home mechanic.

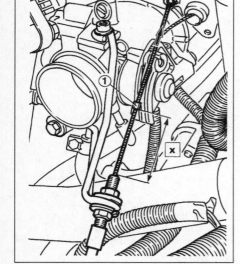

4.3 Fully extend the kickdown cable, and measure distance (X) between the cable lug (1) and the outer cable end – 4 HP 14 transmission

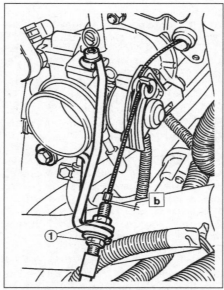

4.4 Reconnect the kickdown cable and check that clearance (b) is as given in the text. If necessary, adjust by repositioning the locknuts (1) – 4 HP 14 transmission

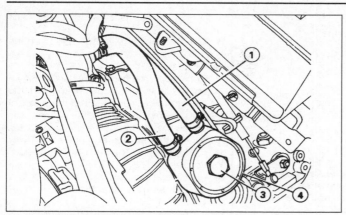

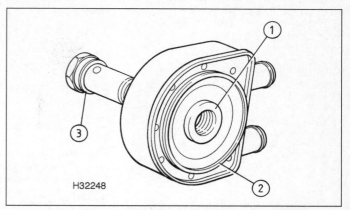

8.2 Transmission fluid cooler details – 4 HP 14 transmission

1 Coolant hose   2 Coolant hose   3 Centre bolt   4 Fluid cooler

8.5a Transmission fluid cooler seals – 4 HP 14 transmission

1 Cooler inner seal   2 Cooler outer seal   3 Centre bolt seal

6 Speedometer drive – removal and refitting

Refer to Chapter 7A.

7 Oil seals – renewal

Driveshaft oil seals

1 Refer to Chapter 7A.

Selector shaft oil seal

4 HP 14 transmission

2 Position the selector lever firmly against its detent mechanism in the N position.

3 To improve access to the transmission end of the selector cable, remove the battery, battery tray and mounting plate as described in Chapter 5A. To further improve access, it may also be necessary to remove the inlet duct(s) as described in the relevant Part of Chapter 4.

4 Undo the two screws securing the outer cable to its retaining bracket, and carefully lever the inner cable end fitting off its balljoint on the transmission selector lever. Note the transmission selector shaft must not be

disturbed until the cable is refitted. As a precaution, mark the position of the lever in relation to the transmission housing.

5 Undo the retaining nut, and remove the lever from the transmission selector shaft.

6 Punch or drill two small holes opposite each other in the seal. Screw a self-tapping screw into each, and pull on the screws with pliers to extract the seal.

7 Clean the seal housing, and polish off any burrs or raised edges, which may have caused the seal to fail in the first place. Small imperfections can be removed using emery paper, but larger defects will require the renewal of the selector shaft.

8 Lubricate the lips of the new seal with clean engine oil, and carefully ease the seal into position over the end of the shaft, taking great care not to damage its sealing lip. Tap the seal into position until it is flush with the transmission casing, using a suitable tubular drift (such as a socket) which bears only on the hard outer edge of the seal. Note that the seal lips should face inwards.

9 Refit the selector lever to the shaft and tighten its retaining nut.

10 Align the outer cable bracket with its mounting bracket on the transmission, then refit and tighten its retaining bolts.

11 Ensure that the selector lever is in the N position and the transmission selector lever is still in the neutral position, then adjust the

cable and connect it to the transmission lever as described in paragraphs 4 to 6 of Section 2.

AL4 transmission

12 Remove the selector lever position switch as described in Section 10 for access to the oil seal.

13 Renew the seal as described above in paragraphs 6 to 8.

14 Refit the selector lever position switch as described in Section 10.

8 Fluid cooler – removal and refitting

Removal

1 The fluid cooler is mounted on the front (4 HP 14) or rear (AL4) of the transmission housing. To gain access to the fluid cooler, remove the air inlet duct(s) as described in the relevant Part of Chapter 4. Slacken and remove the bolts securing the hose retaining bracket in position, and position the bracket clear of the fluid cooler.

2 Using a hose clamp or similar, clamp both the fluid cooler coolant hoses to minimise coolant loss during subsequent operations **(see illustration)**.

3 Slacken the retaining clips, and disconnect both coolant hoses from the fluid cooler – be prepared for some coolant spillage. Wash off any spilt coolant immediately with cold water, and dry the surrounding area before proceeding further.

4 Slacken and remove the fluid cooler centre bolt, and remove the cooler from the transmission. Remove the seal from the centre bolt, and the two seals fitted to the base of the cooler, and discard them; new ones must be used on refitting.

Refitting

5 Lubricate the new seals with clean automatic transmission fluid, then fit the two new seals to the base of the fluid cooler, and a new seal to the centre bolt **(see illustrations)**.

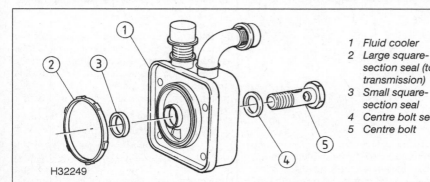

8.5b Transmission fluid cooler details – AL4 transmission

1 Fluid cooler
2 Large square-section seal (to transmission)
3 Small square-section seal
4 Centre bolt seal
5 Centre bolt

6 Locate the fluid cooler on the transmission housing, ensuring its flat edge is parallel to the mating surface of the housing. Refit the centre bolt, and tighten it to the specified torque setting.

7 Reconnect the coolant hoses to the fluid cooler, and securely tighten their retaining clips. Remove the hose clamp.

8 Refit the disturbed inlet duct/air cleaner housing components (as applicable) as described in the relevant Part of Chapter 4.

9 On completion, top-up and bleed the cooling system, and check the automatic transmission fluid level as described in Chapter 1A.

9 Starter inhibitor/reversing light switch (4 HP 14 transmission)

General information

1 The starter inhibitor/reversing light switch is a dual-function switch which is screwed into the top of the transmission housing. The inhibitor function of the switch ensures that the engine can only be started with the selector lever in either the N or P positions, therefore preventing the engine being started with the transmission in gear. This is achieved by the switch cutting the supply to the starter motor solenoid. If at any time it is noted that the engine can be started with the selector lever in any position other than P or N, then it is likely that the inhibitor function of the switch is suspect. The switch also performs the function of the reversing light switch, illuminating the reversing lights whenever the selector lever is in the R position.

Removal

2 To improve access to the switch, remove the battery, battery tray and mounting plate as described in Chapter 5A, then remove the air inlet duct(s) as described in the relevant Part of Chapter 4.

3 Trace the wiring back from the switch, and disconnect it at the wiring connector.

4 Unscrew the switch, and remove it from the top of the transmission housing, along with its washer.

Testing

⚠ **Warning: Ensure that the transmission selector lever is in the N or P position during the following tests.**

5 Temporarily refit and reconnect the battery and reconnect the switch wiring.

6 With the ignition switched on and the starter inhibitor/reversing light switch plunger pressed fully in, check that the reversing lights are illuminated.

7 With the switch plunger released, check that it is possible to start the engine.

8 With the switch plunger in the mid-position check that it is not possible to start the engine and that the reversing lights are not illuminated.

9 If the switch does not operate as described, check the security and continuity of the switch wiring connections. If the wiring is satisfactory, the switch should be renewed.

Refitting

10 Fit a new washer to the switch, screw it back into the transmission, and tighten it securely. Note that washers of various thicknesses are available in the form of a shim kit from Peugeot dealers. If the original switch is being refitted, a washer 0.2 mm thicker than the original should be used. If a new switch is being fitted, a washer at least 1.6 mm thick should be used.

11 Temporarily reconnect the battery, reconnect the switch wiring and carry out the following tests.

12 Firmly apply the handbrake and footbrake and check that it is possible to start the engine with the selector lever in the P and N positions, but not in any other positions.

13 Check that it is not possible to start the engine with the selector lever moved half-way between the N and R positions and N and D positions.

14 Check that the reversing lights are only illuminated with the selector lever in the R position.

15 If the switch does not operate as described, fit a slightly thicker washer and repeat the procedure until the correct operation is achieved.

16 On completion, refit the mounting plate, battery tray and battery as described in Chapter 5A, then refit the air inlet duct(s).

10 AL4 transmission electronic system components – removal and refitting

Electronic control unit

Note: *If a new electronic control unit is being fitted, it will be necessary for the transmission ECU to be initialised and matched electronically to the engine management ECU on completion – this work must be referred to a Peugeot dealer.*

1 The transmission ECU is located behind the battery. To gain access, first remove the battery and battery tray as described in Chapter 5A, then remove the air inlet ducts as described in the relevant Part of Chapter 4.

2 Disconnect the ECU wiring connector, then undo the three ECU mounting bracket screws.

3 Lift out the ECU and its mounting bracket, then undo the bolts and separate the ECU from the bracket.

4 Refitting is a reversal of removal, ensuring that the ECU wiring connector is securely connected.

Input speed sensor

5 The input speed sensor is located on the left-hand end of the transmission, in front of the driveshaft.

6 Remove the battery, battery tray and mounting plate as described in Chapter 5A, then remove the air cleaner and air inlet ducts as described in the relevant Part of Chapter 4.

7 Remove the two securing screws from the modular connector located at the rear of the transmission, and disconnect the wiring as it is removed.

8 Extract the yellow three-way wiring connector from the modular connector.

9 Detach the wiring harness from the transmission as necessary for access to the sensor. Unscrew and remove the sensor retaining bolt, then withdraw the sensor from the transmission (**see illustration**).

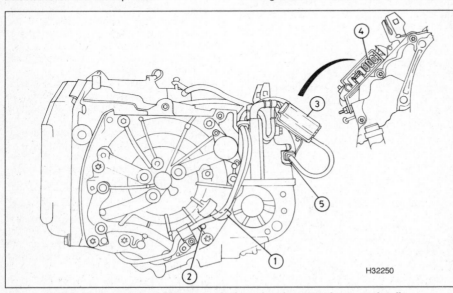

10.9 End-on view of AL4 transmission, showing speed sensor details

1 Input speed sensor
2 Input speed sensor retaining bolt
3 Modular connector
4 Input speed sensor wiring connector (yellow)
5 Output speed sensor

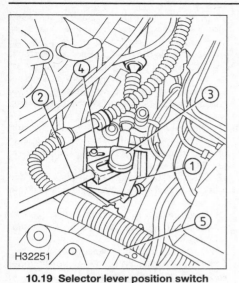

10.19 Selector lever position switch details – AL4 transmission

1 *Selector lever position switch*
2 *Forked tool*
3 *Selector cable balljoint*
4 *Transmission selector lever clamp bolt and nut*
5 *Wiring support bracket*

Recover the sensor O-ring seal, and discard it.

10 Refitting is a reversal of removal. Use a new O-ring seal when refitting the sensor, and tighten its retaining bolt to the specified torque. Ensure that all wiring connections are securely remade.

Output speed sensor

11 The output speed sensor is fitted to the rear of the transmission, just below the selector cable bracket **(refer to illustration 10.9)**.
12 Disconnect the battery negative terminal (refer to *Disconnecting the battery* in the Reference Chapter).
13 Disconnect the speed sensor wiring plug located behind the modular connector.
14 Unscrew and remove the sensor retaining bolt, then withdraw the sensor from the transmission. Recover the sensor O-ring seal, and discard it.
15 Refitting is a reversal of removal. Use a new O-ring seal when refitting the sensor, and tighten its retaining bolt to the specified torque. Ensure that the wiring connection is securely remade.

Selector lever position switch

16 The selector lever position switch is situated on top of the transmission, attached to the selector cable.
17 Remove the battery, battery tray and mounting plate as described in Chapter 5A, then remove the air inlet duct as described in the relevant Part of Chapter 4.
18 From inside the car, move the selector lever to the N position.

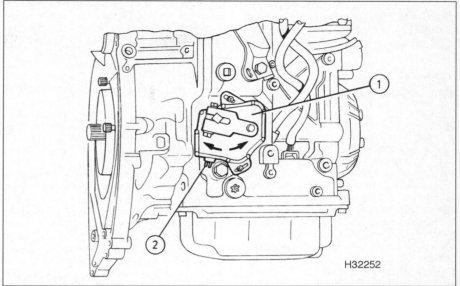

10.30 Turn switch (1) until resistance measured at terminals (2) falls to zero – AL4 transmission

19 Using a suitable forked tool (a fork-type balljoint splitter could be used, or failing that, a large flat-bladed screwdriver), carefully prise the selector cable balljoint off the transmission selector lever **(see illustration)**. Take care not to bend the transmission selector lever during this operation.
20 Mark the position of the transmission selector lever in relation to the splined shaft of the switch, for use when refitting. Unscrew and remove the clamp bolt and nut from the selector lever, and remove the lever from the shaft splines.
21 Detach the wiring harness and its support bracket from in front of the switch.
22 If the original switch is to be refitted, mark the position of the two switch retaining bolts in the slotted holes of the switch. If the switch is refitted in exactly the same position, there should be no need to check the switch resistance on refitting.
23 Unscrew the switch retaining bolts, disconnect the switch wiring, and remove the switch from the engine compartment.
24 With the switch removed, check the condition of the selector shaft oil seal. If signs of leakage are evident, renew the seal as described in Section 7.
25 Refitting is a reversal of removal, but the switch position must be set to ensure correct operation.
26 If the original switch is being refitted, the switch bolts can be aligned in the switch slots as marked on removal.
27 If a new switch is being fitted, or the marks have been lost, connect an ohmmeter between the two pins provided on the front of the switch (do not use a test light, or any multimeter which supplies more than 100 mA, or the switch will be damaged). Fit the switch retaining bolts loosely at this stage.

28 Refit the transmission selector lever to the splined shaft of the switch and tighten the clamp bolt and nut to the specified torque.
29 Ensure that the transmission selector lever is in the neutral N position.
30 Turn the switch body until the resistance measured on the ohmmeter falls to zero **(see illustration)**.
31 When the switch position is correct, tighten the retaining bolts to the specified torque.
32 Refit all remaining components removed for access, and check for satisfactory operation on completion.

Park lock solenoid

33 The Park lock solenoid is located on the front of the gear selector lever housing in the passenger compartment.
34 To gain access to the solenoid, remove the centre console as described in Chapter 12.
35 Unscrew the two retaining bolts, disconnect the wiring plug, and remove the solenoid.
36 Refitting is a reversal of removal.
37 In the event of a fault in the system, such that the selector lever cannot be moved out of P with the ignition on and the brake pedal depressed, the system can be disabled manually, as follows.
38 Carefully prise out the trim panel around the selector lever, and remove it.
39 Using a suitable flat-bladed screwdriver, carefully ease the central plunger away from the switch body to release the locking mechanism. Move the selector lever to the N position and it should now be possible to start the engine and drive the car.

11 Automatic transmission – removal and refitting

Removal

4 HP 14 transmission

1 Chock the rear wheels, apply the handbrake, and place the selector lever in the N (neutral) position. Jack up the front of the vehicle, and securely support it on axle stands (see *Jacking and vehicle support*). Remove both front roadwheels.

2 Drain the transmission fluid as described in Chapter 1A, then refit the drain plugs, tightening them securely.

3 Remove the battery, battery tray and mounting plate as described in Chapter 5A.

4 Remove the starter motor as described in Chapter 5A.

5 Remove the air inlet duct(s) as described in the relevant Part of Chapter 4.

6 Undo the union nut securing the dipstick tube to the transmission sump, then undo the bolt securing the tube to the transmission housing, and remove the dipstick from the transmission.

7 Disconnect the wiring connector from the starter inhibitor/reversing light switch and, where necessary, the speedometer drive housing. Undo the retaining nut/bolt(s) and disconnect the earth strap(s) from the top of the transmission housing.

8 Using a hose clamp or similar, clamp both the fluid cooler coolant hoses to minimise coolant loss. Slacken the retaining clips and disconnect both coolant hoses from the fluid cooler – be prepared for some coolant spillage. Wash off any spilt coolant immediately with cold water.

9 Undo the two screws securing the outer selector cable to its retaining bracket, and carefully lever the inner cable end fitting off its balljoint on the transmission selector lever. Note that the transmission selector lever must not be disturbed until the cable is refitted. As a precaution, mark the position of the lever in relation to the transmission housing. Work back along the selector cable, releasing it from any relevant retaining clips, and position it clear of the transmission.

10 Detach the kickdown inner cable from the throttle body cam, then slacken the outer cable locknuts and free the cable from its mounting bracket. Release the kickdown cable from any relevant retaining clips, so that it is free to be removed with the transmission.

11 On models with power steering, undo the nut/release the retaining clips (as necessary) and free the power steering pipe from the transmission.

12 Undo the retaining bolts and remove the lower driveplate cover plate from the transmission, to gain access to the torque converter retaining bolts. Slacken and remove the visible bolt then, using a socket and extension bar to rotate the crankshaft pulley, undo the remaining bolts securing the torque converter to the driveplate as they become accessible. There are three bolts in total.

13 To ensure that the torque converter does not fall out as the transmission is removed, secure it in position using a length of metal strip bolted to one of the starter motor bolt holes.

14 Withdraw the rubber retaining pin, disconnect the speedometer cable from the drive, and free it from any retaining clips.

15 Remove the driveshafts as described in Chapter 8.

16 Place a jack with a block of wood beneath the engine, to take the weight of the engine. Alternatively, attach a couple of lifting eyes to the engine, and fit a hoist or support bar to take the weight of the engine.

17 Place a jack and block of wood beneath the transmission, and raise the jack to take the weight of the transmission.

18 Slacken and remove the centre nut and washer from the left-hand engine/transmission mounting. Undo the two nuts and washers securing the mounting rubber in position and remove it from the engine compartment.

19 Slide the spacer (where fitted) off the mounting stud, then unscrew the stud from the top of the transmission housing and remove it along with its washer. If the mounting stud is tight, a universal stud extractor can be used to unscrew it.

20 With the jack positioned beneath the transmission taking the weight, slacken and remove the remaining bolts securing the transmission housing to the engine. Note the correct fitted positions of each bolt as it is removed, to use as a reference on refitting. Make a final check that all necessary components have been disconnected, and positioned clear of the transmission so that they will not hinder the removal procedure.

21 With the bolts removed, move the trolley jack and transmission to the left, to free it from its locating dowels.

22 Once the transmission is free, lower the jack and manoeuvre the unit out from under the car. If they are loose, remove the locating dowels from the transmission or engine, and keep them in a safe place.

AL4 transmission

Note: *If a new transmission unit is being fitted, it will be necessary for the transmission ECU to be initialised and matched electronically to the engine management ECU on completion – this work must be referred to a Peugeot dealer.*

23 Chock the rear wheels, apply the handbrake, and place the selector lever in the N (neutral) position. Jack up the front of the vehicle, and securely support it on axle stands (see *Jacking and vehicle support*). Remove both front roadwheels.

24 Drain the transmission fluid (see Section 12) then refit the drain and level plugs; tighten them to the specified torque.

25 Remove the battery, battery tray and mounting plate as described in Chapter 5A, then remove the air cleaner and air inlet duct as described in the relevant Part of Chapter 4.

26 Slacken the locking rings and disconnect the two circular main wiring loom connectors – one located behind the transmission ECU, and one located forward of the battery tray location.

27 Disconnect the transmission ECU wiring connector, then undo the three ECU mounting bracket screws. Lift out the mounting bracket and ECU as an assembly.

28 Disconnect the wiring harness from the modular connector located at the rear of the transmission.

29 Disconnect the output speed sensor wiring plug located behind the modular connector.

30 Disconnect the vehicle speed sensor wiring plug located directly above the inner end of the right-hand driveshaft.

31 Using a hose clamp or similar, clamp both the fluid cooler coolant hoses to minimise coolant loss during subsequent operations.

32 Slacken the retaining clips, and disconnect both coolant hoses from the fluid cooler – be prepared for some coolant spillage. Wash off any spilt coolant immediately with cold water, and dry the surrounding area before proceeding further.

33 Undo the retaining bolt(s and disconnect the earth straps from the top of the transmission housing.

34 Using a suitable forked tool (a fork-type balljoint splitter could be used, or failing that, a large flat-bladed screwdriver), carefully prise the selector cable balljoint off the selector lever.

35 Extract the retaining C-clip and release the selector outer cable and cable grommet from the transmission bracket.

36 Disconnect and release the wiring connectors and relevant support brackets running along the top of the transmission.

37 Disconnect the wiring connectors at the engine speed sensor and lambda sensor located below the thermostat housing and radiator top hose.

38 Remove the exhaust system catalytic converter/front pipe as described in the relevant Part of Chapter 4.

39 Remove the starter motor as described in Chapter 5A.

40 Undo the retaining bolts and remove the lower driveplate cover plate from the transmission, to gain access to the torque converter retaining nuts. Slacken and remove the visible nut then, using a socket and extension bar to rotate the crankshaft pulley, undo the remaining nuts securing the torque converter to the driveplate as they become accessible. There are three nuts in total.

41 To ensure that the torque converter does not fall out as the transmission is removed, secure it in position using a length of metal strip bolted to one of the starter motor bolt holes.

42 Remove the driveshafts as described in Chapter 8.

43 Place a jack with a block of wood beneath the engine, to take the weight of the engine. Alternatively, attach a couple of lifting eyes to the engine, and fit a hoist or support bar to take the weight of the engine.

44 Place a jack and block of wood beneath the transmission, and raise the jack to take the weight of the transmission.

45 Slacken and remove the centre nut and washer from the left-hand engine/transmission mounting. Undo the two nuts and washers securing the mounting rubber in position and remove it from the engine compartment.

46 Slide the spacer (where fitted) off the mounting stud, then unscrew the stud from the top of the transmission housing and remove it along with its washer. If the mounting stud is tight, a universal stud extractor can be used to unscrew it.

47 With the jack positioned beneath the transmission taking the weight, slacken and remove the remaining bolts securing the transmission housing to the engine. Note the correct fitted positions of each bolt as it is removed, to use as a reference on refitting. Make a final check that all necessary components have been disconnected, and positioned clear of the transmission so that they will not hinder the removal procedure.

48 With the bolts removed, move the trolley jack and transmission to the left, to free it from its locating dowels.

49 Once the transmission is free, lower the jack and manoeuvre the unit out from under the car. If they are loose, remove the locating dowels from the transmission or engine, and keep them in a safe place.

Refitting

50 Both transmission types are refitted using a reversal of the removal procedure, bearing in mind the following points:

a) *Ensure that the bush fitted to the centre of the crankshaft is in good condition, and apply a little Molykote G1 grease to the torque converter centring pin. Do not apply too much, otherwise there is a possibility of the grease contaminating the torque converter.*

b) *On the AL4 transmission, turn the torque converter so that one of the mounting studs is positioned opposite the right-hand driveshaft output shaft (approximately the 9 o'clock position). Turn the engine crankshaft so that the corresponding mounting hole in the driveplate is in the same position. The torque converter mounting studs and the corresponding holes in the driveplate should then be in alignment when the transmission is fitted.*

c) *Ensure that the engine/transmission locating dowels are correctly positioned prior to installation.*

d) *Once the transmission and engine are correctly joined, refit the securing bolts, tightening them to the specified torque setting, then remove the metal strip used to retain the torque converter.*

e) *Apply thread-locking fluid to the left-hand engine/transmission mounting stud threads prior to refitting it to the transmission. Tighten the stud to the specified torque.*

f) *Tighten all nuts and bolts to the specified torque (where given).*

g) *On the 4 HP 14 transmission, renew the driveshaft oil seals as described in Chapter 7A.*

h) *Refit the driveshafts to the transmission as described in Chapter 8.*

i) *Adjust the selector cable and, on the 4 HP 14 transmission, the kickdown cable as described in Sections 2 and 5.*

j) *On completion, top-up the cooling system then refill the transmission with the specified type and quantity of fluid as described in Chapter 1A (4 HP 14 transmission) or Section 12 (AL4 transmission).*

12 Automatic transmission fluid
– draining and refilling

4 HP 14 transmission

1 Refer to Chapter 1A.

AL4 transmission

Note: *The transmission unit is equipped with a fluid wear sensor to inform the driver when the fluid needs renewing (the ECU flashes the Sport and Snow mode indicator lights when fluid renewal is necessary). If the transmission is drained and refilled with new fluid, this sensor should be reset. This can only be done using the Peugeot diagnostic test box.*

2 The fluid must be drained when it is hot, so take the car on a moderate journey (at least 30 minutes), to warm the transmission up to normal operating temperature.

3 To improve access to the fluid drain and level plugs on the base of the housing, it may be preferable to jack up the front and rear of the car, and support it on axle stands (see *Jacking and vehicle support*). Note that it will be essential that the car is level when checking the oil level after refilling.

4 Place a container of sufficient capacity under the transmission. Unscrew and remove the level plug, then the drain plug, from the base of the transmission **(see illustration)**.

⚠️ *Warning: Take precautions against scalding as the oil will be very hot.*

5 Allow the fluid to drain, then refit the drain plug and tighten to the specified torque. Do not refit the level plug in the centre of the drain plug at this stage.

6 Where necessary, remove the air cleaner and air inlet duct as described in the relevant Part of Chapter 4, for improved access to the filler plug on the top of the transmission. Wipe clean the area around the filler plug, then unscrew the plug and recover the sealing washer **(see illustration)**.

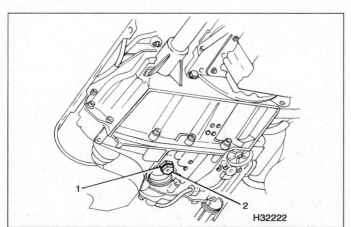

12.4 Transmission oil drain plug (1) and oil level plug (2), inside drain plug – AL4 transmission

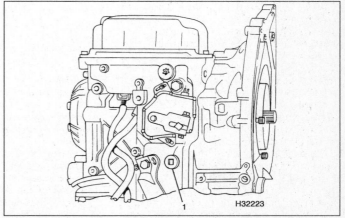

12.6 Transmission oil filler plug (1) as viewed from above – AL4 transmission

7 Make sure that the car is level (front-to-rear and side-to-side), then add the specified fluid until it runs out of the level plug in the base of the transmission.

8 Fit and tighten the level plug and filler plug to the specified torque, then lower the car to the ground.

9 Final level checking must be done with the transmission oil at normal operating temperature, so once again take the car on a moderate journey (at least 30 minutes), to warm-up the transmission.

10 With the transmission fluid hot, carry out the level checking procedure described in Chapter 1A, Section 7.

13 Automatic transmission overhaul – general information

In the event of a fault occurring with the transmission, it is first necessary to determine whether it is of an electrical, mechanical or hydraulic nature, and to do this, special test equipment is required. It is therefore essential to have the work carried out by a Peugeot dealer if a transmission fault is suspected.

Do not remove the transmission from the car for possible repair before professional fault diagnosis has been carried out, since most tests require the transmission to be in the vehicle.

Chapter 8
Driveshafts

Contents

Degrees of difficulty

Easy, suitable for novice with little experience	Fairly easy, suitable for beginner with some experience	Fairly difficult, suitable for competent DIY mechanic	Difficult, suitable for experienced DIY mechanic	Very difficult, suitable for expert DIY or professional

Specifications

Lubrication (overhaul only - see text)

Lubricant type/specification . . . . Use only special grease supplied in sachets with gaiter kits - joints are otherwise pre-packed with grease and sealed

Torque wrench settings

	Nm	lbf ft
Driveshaft retaining nut:		
M20x150 nut	265	194
M24x150 nut	320	235
Lower suspension arm balljoint retaining nuts	50	37
Right-hand driveshaft intermediate bearing retaining bolt nuts	17	13
Roadwheel bolts	85	63

1 General information

Drive is transmitted from the differential to the front wheels by means of two solid-steel driveshafts of unequal length.

Both driveshafts are splined at their outer ends, to accept the wheel hubs, and are threaded so that each hub can be fastened by a large nut. The inner end of each driveshaft is splined, to accept the differential sun gear.

Constant velocity (CV) joints are fitted to each end of the driveshafts, to ensure that the smooth and efficient transmission of power at all suspension and steering angles. On 1.4 and 1.6 litre engine models, the outer constant velocity joints are of the spider-and-yoke type; on all other models, they are of the ball-and-cage type. The inner constant velocity joints are of the tripod type on all models.

On the right-hand side, due to the length of the driveshaft, the inner constant velocity joint is situated approximately halfway along the shaft's length, and an intermediate support bearing is mounted in the engine/transmission rear mounting bracket. The inner end of the driveshaft passes through the bearing (which prevents any lateral movement of the driveshaft inner end) and the inner constant velocity joint outer member.

2.4 On 1.4 and 1.6 litre engine models, relieve the retaining nut staking with a suitable chisel-nosed tool

2.10a On the right-hand driveshaft, slacken the two intermediate bearing retaining bolt nuts . . .

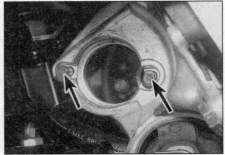

2.10b . . . then turn the bolts through 90° to disengage their offset heads (arrowed) from the bearing (driveshaft removed for clarity)

2 Driveshafts - removal and refitting

Removal

Note: *Do not allow the vehicle to rest on its wheels with one or both driveshafts removed, as damage to the wheel bearing(s) may result. If moving the vehicle is unavoidable, temporarily insert the outer end of the driveshaft(s) in the hub(s) and tighten the hub nut(s): in this case, the inner end(s) of the driveshaft(s) must be supported, for example by suspending with string from the vehicle underbody. Do not allow the driveshaft to hang down under its own weight. On models with a staked driveshaft nut, a new nut must be used on refitting. New lower arm balljoint nuts must be used on refitting.*

1 Chock the rear wheels of the car, firmly apply the handbrake, then jack up the front of the car and support it on axle stands (see *"Jacking and Vehicle Support"*). Remove the appropriate front roadwheel.
2 Drain the transmission oil or fluid as described in the relevant Part of Chapter 1 or 7 as applicable.
3 On models equipped with ABS, trace the wiring connector back from the wheel sensor,

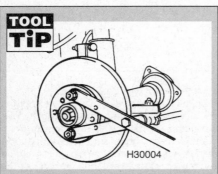

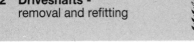

Using a fabricated tool to hold the front hub stationary whilst the driveshaft retaining nut is slackened

freeing it from its retaining clips, and disconnect it at its wiring connector.
4 On models where the driveshaft nut is staked, using a hammer and a chisel or similar tool, tap up the staking securing the driveshaft retaining nut in position **(see illustration)**. Note that a new retaining nut must be used on refitting.
5 On models where the driveshaft nut is secured by an R-clip, withdraw the R-clip and remove the locking cap from the driveshaft retaining nut.
6 Refit at least two roadwheel bolts to the front hub, and tighten them securely. Have an assistant firmly depress the brake pedal to prevent the front hub from rotating, then using a socket and a long extension bar, slacken and remove the driveshaft retaining nut. Alternatively, a tool can be fabricated from two lengths of steel strip (one long, one short) and a nut and bolt; the nut and bolt forming the pivot of a forked tool. Bolt the tool to the hub using two wheel bolts, and hold the tool to prevent the hub from rotating as the driveshaft retaining nut is undone **(see Tool Tip)**. This nut is very tight; make sure that there is no risk of pulling the car off the axle stands (see *"Jacking and Vehicle Support"*). (If the roadwheel trim allows access to the driveshaft nut, the initial slackening can be done with the wheels chocked and on the ground.)
7 Slacken and remove the three nuts securing the balljoint to the lower suspension arm, then withdraw the bolts and free the balljoint from the arm. Discard the nuts - new ones must be used on refitting.

Left-hand driveshaft

8 Carefully pull the swivel hub assembly outwards, and withdraw the driveshaft outer constant velocity joint from the hub assembly. If necessary, the shaft can be tapped out of the hub using a soft-faced mallet.
9 Support the driveshaft, then withdraw the inner constant velocity joint from the transmission, taking care not to damage the driveshaft oil seal. Remove the driveshaft from the vehicle.

Right-hand driveshaft

10 Loosen the two intermediate bearing retaining bolt nuts, then rotate the bolts through 90°, so that their offset heads are clear of the bearing outer race **(see illustrations)**.
11 Carefully pull the swivel hub assembly outwards, and withdraw the driveshaft outer constant velocity joint from the hub assembly. If necessary, the shaft can be tapped out of the hub using a soft-faced mallet.
12 Support the outer end of the driveshaft, then pull on the inner end of the shaft to free the intermediate bearing from its mounting bracket.
13 Once the driveshaft end is free from the transmission, slide the dust seal off the inner end of the shaft, noting which way around it is fitted, and remove the driveshaft.

Refitting

14 Before installing the driveshaft, examine the driveshaft oil seal in the transmission for signs of damage or deterioration and, if necessary, renew it, referring to Chapter 7A for further information. (Having got this far it is worth renewing the seal as a matter of course.)
15 Thoroughly clean the driveshaft splines, and the apertures in the transmission and hub assembly. Apply a thin film of grease to the oil seal lips, and to the driveshaft splines and shoulders. Check that all gaiter clips are securely fastened.

Left-hand driveshaft

16 Offer up the driveshaft, and locate the joint splines with those of the differential sun gear, taking great care not to damage the oil seal. Push the joint fully into position.
17 Locate the outer constant velocity joint splines with those of the swivel hub, and slide the joint back into position in the hub.
18 Align the balljoint with the lower arm, and fit the three retaining bolts. Fit new retaining nuts to the bolts, and tighten them to the specified torque setting.
19 Lubricate the inner face and threads of the driveshaft retaining nut with clean engine oil, and refit it to the end of the driveshaft. Use the

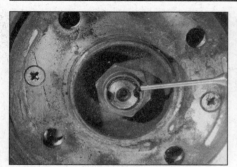

2.20 On 1.4 and 1.6 litre engine models, tighten the nut and stake it firmly into the driveshaft groove

2.21a On all except 1.4 and 1.6 litre engine models, refit the locking cap . . .

2.21b . . . and secure it in position with the R-clip

method employed on removal to prevent the hub from rotating, and tighten the driveshaft retaining nut to the specified torque. Check that the hub rotates freely.

20 On models where the driveshaft nut is staked, stake the new nut into the driveshaft grooves using a hammer and punch **(see illustration).**

21 On models where the driveshaft nut is secured by an R-clip, engage the locking cap with the driveshaft nut so that one of its cut-outs is aligned with the driveshaft hole. Secure the cap in position with the R-clip **(see illustrations).**

22 Where necessary, reconnect the ABS wheel sensor wiring connector, ensuring that the wiring is correctly routed and retained by all the necessary clips and ties.

23 Refit the roadwheel, then lower the vehicle to the ground and tighten the roadwheel bolts to the specified torque.

24 Refill the transmission with the specified type and amount of fluid/oil, and check the level using the information given in Chapter 1A or 1B.

Right-hand driveshaft

25 Check that the intermediate bearing rotates smoothly, without any sign of roughness or undue free play between its inner and outer races. If necessary, renew the bearing as described in Section 5. Examine

the dust seal for signs of damage or deterioration, and renew if necessary.

26 Apply a smear of grease to the outer race of the intermediate bearing, and to the inner lip of the dust seal.

27 Pass the inner end of the shaft through the bearing mounting bracket, then carefully slide the dust seal into position on the driveshaft, ensuring that its flat surface is facing the transmission **(see illustration).**

28 Carefully locate the inner driveshaft splines with those of the differential sun gear, taking care not to damage the oil seal. Align the intermediate bearing with its mounting bracket, and push the driveshaft fully into position. If necessary, use a soft-faced mallet to tap the outer race of the bearing into position in the mounting bracket.

29 Locate the outer constant velocity joint splines with those of the swivel hub, and slide the joint back into position in the hub **(see illustration).**

30 Ensure that the intermediate bearing is correctly seated, then rotate its retaining bolts back through 90°, so that their offset heads are resting against the bearing outer race. Tighten the retaining nuts to the specified torque. Ensure that the dust seal is tight against the driveshaft oil seal **(see illustration).**

31 Carry out the operations described above in paragraphs 19 to 24.

3 Driveshaft rubber gaiters - renewal

Outer joint

1 Remove the driveshaft from the car as described in Section 2.

1.4 and 1.6 litre engine models

2 Remove the inner constant velocity joint and gaiter as described below in paragraphs 24 to 29. It is recommended that the inner gaiter is also renewed, regardless of its apparent condition.

3 Release the two outer gaiter retaining clips, then slide the gaiter off the inner end of the driveshaft.

4 Thoroughly clean the outer constant velocity joint using paraffin, or a suitable solvent, and dry it thoroughly. Carry out a visual inspection of the joint.

5 Check the driveshaft spider and outer member yoke for signs of wear, pitting or scuffing on their bearing surfaces. Also check that the outer member pivots smoothly and easily, with no traces of roughness.

6 If on inspection, the spider or outer member reveals signs of wear or damage, it will be necessary to renew the complete driveshaft as an assembly, since no components are

2.27 Locate the dust seal on the inner end of the right-hand driveshaft, ensuring it is fitted the correct way round

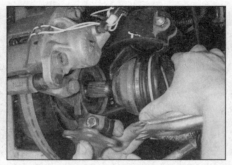

2.29 Pull out the swivel hub assembly, and locate the outer constant velocity joint splines with those of the swivel hub

2.30 Secure the intermediate bearing in position, then slide the dust seal up tight against the driveshaft oil seal

3.21a Fit the hard plastic rings to the outer CV joint gaiter . . .

3.21b . . . then slide on the new plastic bush (arrowed) and seat it in its recess in the shaft. Slide the gaiter onto the shaft . . .

3.21c . . . and seat the gaiter inner end on top of the plastic bush

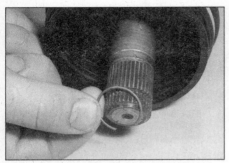

3.21d Fit the new circlip to its groove in the driveshaft splines . . .

3.21e . . . then locate the joint outer member on the splines and slide into position over the circlip. Ensure that the joint is firmly retained by the circlip before proceeding

3.21f Pack the joint with the grease supplied, working it well into the ball tracks while twisting the joint, then locate the gaiter outer lip in its groove on the outer member

3.21g Fit the outer gaiter retaining clip and, using a hook fabricated out of welding rod and a pair of pliers, pull the clip tightly to remove all slack

3.21h Bend the clip end back over the buckle, then cut off the excess clip

3.21i Fold the clip end underneath the buckle . . .

3.21j . . . then fold the buckle firmly down onto the clip to secure the clip in position

3.21k Carefully lift the gaiter inner end to equalise air pressure in the gaiter, then secure the inner gaiter retaining clip in position using the same method

available separately. If the joint components are in satisfactory condition, obtain a repair kit from your Peugeot dealer, consisting of a new gaiter, retaining clips, and the correct type and quantity of grease.

7 Tape over the splines on the inner end of the driveshaft, then carefully slide the outer gaiter onto the shaft.

8 Pack the joint with the grease supplied in the repair kit. Work the grease well into the bearing tracks whilst twisting the joint, and fill the rubber gaiter with any excess.

9 Ease the gaiter over the joint, and ensure that the gaiter lips are correctly located in the grooves on both the driveshaft and constant velocity joint. Lift the outer sealing lip of the gaiter, to equalise the air pressure in the gaiter.

10 Fit the large metal retaining clip to the gaiter. Remove any slack in the gaiter retaining clip by carefully compressing the raised section of the clip. In the absence of the special tool, a pair of side cutters may be used. Secure the small retaining clip using the same procedure. Check that the constant velocity joint moves freely in all directions before proceeding further.

11 Refit the inner constant velocity joint as described in paragraphs 32 to 39.

All except 1.4 and 1.6 litre engine models

12 Secure the driveshaft in a vice equipped with soft jaws, and release the two rubber gaiter retaining clips. If necessary, the gaiter retaining clips can be cut to release them.

13 Slide the rubber gaiter down the shaft, to expose the outer constant velocity joint. Scoop out the excess grease.

14 Using a hammer and suitable soft metal drift, sharply strike the inner member of the outer joint to drive it off the end of the shaft. The joint is retained on the driveshaft by a circlip, and striking the joint in this manner forces the circlip into its groove, so allowing the joint to slide off.

15 Once the joint assembly has been removed, remove the circlip from the groove in the driveshaft splines, and discard it. A new circlip must be fitted on reassembly.

16 Withdraw the rubber gaiter from the driveshaft, and slide off the gaiter inner end plastic bush.

17 With the constant velocity joint removed from the driveshaft, thoroughly clean the joint using paraffin, or a suitable solvent, and dry it thoroughly. Carry out a visual inspection of the joint.

18 Move the inner splined driving member from side to side, to expose each ball in turn at the top of its track. Examine the balls for cracks, flat spots, or signs of surface pitting.

19 Inspect the ball tracks on the inner and outer members. If the tracks have widened, the balls will no longer be a tight fit. At the same time, check the ball cage windows for wear or cracking between the windows.

20 If on inspection, any of the constant velocity joint components are found to be worn or damaged, it will be necessary to renew the complete joint assembly (where available), or even the complete driveshaft (where no joint components are available separately). Refer to your Peugeot dealer for further information on parts availability. If the joint is in satisfactory condition, obtain a repair kit consisting of a new gaiter, circlip, retaining clips, and the correct type and quantity of grease.

21 To install the new gaiter, refer to the accompanying illustrations, and perform the operations shown **(see illustrations 3.21a to 3.21k)**. Be sure to stay in order, and follow the captions carefully. Note that the hard plastic rings are not fitted to all gaiters, and the gaiter retaining clips supplied with the repair kit may be different to those shown in the sequence. To secure this other type of clip in position, lock the ends of the clip together, then remove any slack in the clip by carefully compressing the raised section of the clip using a pair of side cutters.

22 Check that the constant velocity joint moves freely in all directions, then refit the driveshaft to the car as described in Section 2.

Inner joint

23 Remove the driveshaft from the vehicle as described in Section 2.

1.4 and 1.6 litre engine models

24 Secure the driveshaft in a vice equipped with soft jaws then, using a suitable pair of pliers, carefully peel back the lip of the constant velocity joint outer member cover.

25 Once the lip of the cover is fully released, pull the joint outer member out from the cover, and recover the spring and thrust cap from the end of the shaft. Remove the O-ring from the outside of the outer member, and discard it.

26 Fold the gaiter back, and wipe away the excess grease from the tripod joint. If the rollers are not secured to the joint with circlips, wrap adhesive tape around the joint to hold them in position.

27 Using a dab of paint, or a hammer and punch, mark the relative position of the tripod joint in relation to the driveshaft. Using circlip pliers, extract the circlip securing the joint to the driveshaft.

28 The tripod joint can now be removed. If it is tight, draw the joint off the driveshaft end, using a two or three-legged bearing puller. Ensure that the legs of the puller are located behind the joint inner member, and do not contact the joint rollers. Alternatively, support the inner member of the tripod joint, and press the shaft out of the joint using a hydraulic press, ensuring that no load is applied to the joint rollers.

29 With the tripod joint removed, slide the gaiter and inner retaining collar off the end of the driveshaft.

30 Thoroughly clean all the constant velocity joint components using paraffin, or a suitable solvent, and dry them thoroughly - take great care not to remove the alignment marks made on dismantling, especially if paint was used. Carry out a visual inspection of the joint.

31 Examine the tripod joint, rollers and outer member for any signs of scoring or wear, and for smoothness of movement of the rollers on the tripod stems. If any component is worn, the complete driveshaft assembly must be renewed; no joint components are available separately. If the joint components are in good condition, obtain a repair kit from your Peugeot dealer, consisting of a new rubber gaiter and outer cover, circlip, thrust cap, spring, O-ring, and the correct quantity of special grease.

32 Slide the gaiter into position inside the metal outer cover, then tape over the splines on the end of the driveshaft, and carefully slide the inner retaining collar and gaiter/cover assembly onto the shaft.

33 Remove the tape then, aligning the marks made on dismantling, engage the tripod joint with the driveshaft splines. Use a hammer and soft metal drift to tap the joint onto the shaft, taking great care not to damage the driveshaft splines or joint rollers.

34 Secure the tripod joint in position with the new circlip, ensuring that it is correctly located in the driveshaft groove.

35 Remove the tape (where fitted), and evenly distribute the special grease contained in the repair kit around the tripod joint and outer member. Pack the gaiter/cover with the remainder, then draw the cover over the tripod joint.

36 Fit the new O-ring, spring and thrust cap to the joint outer member.

37 Position the outer member assembly over the tripod joint, and locate the thrust cap against the end of the driveshaft. Push the outer member onto the shaft, compressing the spring, and locate it inside the outer cover. Secure the outer member in position by peening the end of the cover evenly over the joint outer edge.

38 Briefly lift the inner gaiter lip, using a blunt instrument such as a knitting needle, to equalise the air pressure within the gaiter. Secure the inner clip in position.

39 Check that the constant velocity joint moves freely in all directions, then refit the driveshaft to the car as described in Section 2.

All except 1.4 and 1.6 litre engine models

40 Remove the outer constant velocity joint as described above in paragraphs 1 to 5.

41 Tape over the splines on the driveshaft, and carefully remove the outer constant velocity joint rubber gaiter, and the gaiter inner end plastic bush. It is recommended that the outer joint gaiter is also renewed, regardless of its apparent condition.

3.42a Release the inner gaiter retaining clips, and remove the joint outer member

3.42b Slide the gaiter off the end of the driveshaft . . .

3.42c . . . and remove the plastic bush

42 Release the retaining clips, then slide the gaiter off the shaft, and remove its plastic bush. As the gaiter is released, the joint outer member will also be freed from the end of the shaft **(see illustrations)**.

43 Thoroughly clean the joint using paraffin, or a suitable solvent, and dry it thoroughly. Check the tripod joint bearings and joint outer member for signs of wear, pitting or scuffing on their bearing surfaces. Check that the bearing rollers rotate smoothly and easily around the tripod joint, with no traces of roughness.

44 If on inspection, the tripod joint or outer member reveal signs of wear or damage, it will be necessary to renew the complete driveshaft assembly, since the joint is not available separately. If the joint is in satisfactory condition, obtain a repair kit consisting of a new gaiter, retaining clips, and the correct type and quantity of grease. Although not strictly necessary, it is also recommended that the outer constant velocity joint gaiter is renewed, regardless of its apparent condition.

45 On reassembly, pack the inner joint with the grease supplied in the gaiter kit. Work the grease well into the bearing tracks and rollers, while twisting the joint.

46 Clean the shaft, using emery cloth to remove any rust or sharp edges which may damage the gaiter, then slide the plastic bush

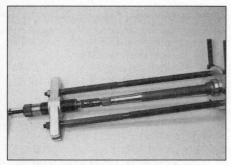

5.3 Using a long-reach bearing puller to remove the intermediate bearing from the right-hand driveshaft

and inner joint gaiter along the driveshaft. Locate the plastic bush in its recess on the shaft, and seat the inner end of the gaiter on top of the bush.

47 Fit the outer member over the end of the shaft, and locate the gaiter in the groove on the joint outer member. Push the outer member onto the joint, so that its spring-loaded plunger is compressed, then lift the outer edge of the gaiter to equalise air pressure in the gaiter. Fit both the inner and outer retaining clips, securing them in position using the information given in paragraph 21. Ensure that the gaiter retaining clips are securely tightened, then check that the joint moves freely in all directions.

48 Refit the outer constant velocity joint components using the information given in paragraph 21.

4 Driveshaft overhaul - general information

1 If any of the checks described in Chapter 1A or 1B reveal wear in any driveshaft joint, first remove the roadwheel trim or centre cap (as appropriate).

2 On models with a staked driveshaft nut, if the staking is still effective, the driveshaft nut should be correctly tightened; if in doubt, relieve the staking, then tighten the nut to the specified torque and restake it into the driveshaft grooves. Refit the roadwheel trim or centre cap (as applicable), and repeat the check on the remaining driveshaft nut.

3 On models where the driveshaft nut is secured by an R-clip, if the R-clip is fitted, the driveshaft nut should be correctly tightened; if in doubt, remove the R-clip and locking cap, and use a torque wrench to check that the nut is securely fastened. Once tightened, refit the locking cap and R-clip, then refit the centre cap or trim. Repeat this check on the remaining driveshaft nut.

4 Road test the vehicle, and listen for a metallic clicking from the front as the vehicle is driven slowly in a circle on full-lock. If a

clicking noise is heard, this indicates wear in the outer constant velocity joint. This means that the joint must be renewed; reconditioning is not possible.

5 If vibration, consistent with road speed, is felt through the car when accelerating, there is a possibility of wear in the inner constant velocity joints.

6 To check the joints for wear, remove the driveshafts, then dismantle them as described in Section 3; if any wear or free play is found, the affected joint must be renewed. In the case of the inner joints (and on some models, the outer joints), this means that the complete driveshaft assembly must be renewed, as the joints are not available separately. Refer to your Peugeot dealer for information on the availability of driveshaft components.

5 Right-hand driveshaft intermediate bearing - renewal

Note: *A suitable bearing puller will be required, to draw the bearing and collar off the driveshaft end.*

1 Remove the right-hand driveshaft as described in Section 2 of this Chapter.

2 Check that the bearing outer race rotates smoothly and easily, without any signs of roughness or undue free play between the inner and outer races. If necessary, renew the bearing as follows.

3 Using a long-reach universal bearing puller, carefully draw the collar and intermediate bearing off the driveshaft inner end **(see illustration)**. Apply a smear of grease to the inner race of the new bearing, then fit the bearing over the end of the driveshaft. Using a hammer and suitable piece of tubing which bears only on the bearing inner race, tap the new bearing into position on the driveshaft, until it abuts the constant velocity joint outer member. Once the bearing is correctly positioned, tap the bearing collar onto the shaft until it contacts the bearing inner race.

4 Check that the bearing rotates freely, then refit the driveshaft as described in Section 2.

Chapter 9
Braking system

Contents

Degrees of difficulty

| Easy, suitable for novice with little experience | | Fairly easy, suitable for beginner with some experience | | Fairly difficult, suitable for competent DIY mechanic | | Difficult, suitable for experienced DIY mechanic | | Very difficult, suitable for expert DIY or professional | |

Specifications

Front brakes

Disc thickness:
  New:
    Solid disc . . . . 10.0 mm
    Ventilated disc . . . . 20.4 mm
  Minimum thickness:
    Solid disc . . . . 8.0 mm
    Ventilated disc . . . . 18.4 mm
Maximum disc run-out . . . . 0.07 mm
Brake pad minimum thickness . . . . See Chapter 1A or 1B

Rear drum brakes

Drum internal diameter:
  All except models with Bendix rear brakes and ABS, and Van models:
    New . . . . 180.0 mm
    Maximum diameter after machining . . . . 181.0 mm
  Models with Bendix rear brakes and ABS, and Van models:
    New . . . . 228.6 mm
    Maximum diameter after machining . . . . 230.0 mm
Brake shoe thickness:
  New . . . . 4.85 mm
  Minimum . . . . See Chapter 1A or 1B

Rear disc brakes

Disc thickness:
  New . . . . 8.0 mm
  Minimum thickness . . . . 6.0 mm
Maximum disc run-out . . . . 0.07 mm
Brake pad minimum thickness . . . . See Chapter 1A or 1B

Torque wrench settings

	Nm	lbf ft
Front brake caliper:		
Guide pin bolts (Lucas/Girling caliper)*	35	26
Guide bolts (ATE Teves caliper)*	30	22
Caliper mounting bolts (Bendix caliper)*	110	81
Mounting bracket-to-swivel hub bolts	120	89
Rear brake caliper mounting bolts	110	81
Rear hub nut:		
Models with rear drum brakes:		
All except models with Bendix rear brakes and ABS, and		
Van models	200	148
Models with Bendix rear brakes and ABS, and Van models	185	136
Models with rear disc brakes	185	136
Master cylinder-to-servo unit nuts	10	7
Brake pedal pivot shaft nut	20	15
Vacuum servo unit mounting nuts	20	15
ABS wheel sensor retaining bolts*	10	7
ABS hydraulic modulator bolts	20	15
Roadwheel bolts	85	63

*Use thread-locking compound.

1 General information

The braking system is of the servo-assisted, dual-circuit hydraulic type. The arrangement of the hydraulic system is such that each circuit operates one front and one rear brake from a tandem master cylinder. Under normal circumstances, both circuits operate in unison. However, in the event of hydraulic failure in one circuit, full braking force will still be available at two wheels.

Some large-capacity engine models have disc brakes all round as standard; all other models not equipped with the Anti-lock Braking System (ABS) are fitted with front disc brakes and rear drum brakes. ABS is fitted as standard to certain models, and is offered as an option on most other models (refer to Section 22 for further information on ABS operation).

The front disc brakes are actuated by single-piston sliding type calipers, which ensure that equal pressure is applied to each disc pad.

On models with rear drum brakes, the rear brakes incorporate leading and trailing shoes, which are actuated by twin-piston wheel cylinders. The wheel cylinders incorporate integral pressure-regulating valves, which control the hydraulic pressure applied to the rear brakes. The regulating valves help to prevent rear wheel lock-up during emergency braking. A self-adjust mechanism is incorporated, to automatically compensate for brake shoe wear. As the brake shoe linings wear, the footbrake operation automatically operates the adjuster mechanism, which effectively lengthens the shoe strut and repositions the brake shoes, to remove the lining-to-drum clearance.

On models with rear disc brakes, the brakes are actuated by single-piston sliding calipers which incorporate mechanical handbrake mechanisms. On early models, a pressure-regulating valve is situated in the brake line to each rear caliper. The regulating valve is similar to that fitted to the rear wheel cylinders on drum brake models, and helps to prevent rear wheel lock-up during emergency braking. On later models, a load-sensitive pressure regulating valve assembly is fitted into the hydraulic circuit to each rear brake. The valve is mounted on the underside of the vehicle at the rear and is attached to the rear suspension by means of an operating rod and spring. The valve measures the load on the rear of the vehicle via the movement of the rear suspension and regulates the hydraulic pressure applied to the rear brakes accordingly.

On all models, the handbrake provides an independent mechanical means of rear brake application.

On Diesel engines, there is insufficient vacuum in the inlet manifold to operate the braking system servo effectively at all times. To overcome this problem, a vacuum pump is fitted to the engine, to provide sufficient vacuum to operate the servo unit. The vacuum pump is mounted on the end of the cylinder head, and driven directly off the end of the camshaft.

Note: *When servicing any part of the system, work carefully and methodically; also observe scrupulous cleanliness when overhauling any part of the hydraulic system. Always renew components (in axle sets, where applicable) if in doubt about their condition, and use only genuine Peugeot replacement parts, or at least those of known good quality. Note the warnings given in "Safety first" and at relevant points in this Chapter concerning the dangers of asbestos dust and hydraulic fluid.*

2 Hydraulic system - bleeding

Warning: Hydraulic fluid is poisonous; wash off immediately and thoroughly in the case of skin contact, and seek immediate medical advice if any fluid is swallowed or gets into the eyes. Certain types of hydraulic fluid are inflammable, and may ignite when allowed into contact with hot components; when servicing any hydraulic system, it is safest to assume that the fluid is inflammable, and to take precautions against the risk of fire as though it is petrol that is being handled. Hydraulic fluid is also an effective paint stripper, and will attack plastics; if any is spilt, it should be washed off immediately, using copious quantities of fresh water. Finally, it is hygroscopic (it absorbs moisture from the air) - old fluid may be contaminated and unfit for further use. When topping-up or renewing the fluid, always use the recommended type, and ensure that it comes from a freshly-opened sealed container.

General

1 The correct operation of any hydraulic system is only possible after removing all air from the components and circuit; this is achieved by bleeding the system.

2 During the bleeding procedure, add only clean, unused hydraulic fluid of the recommended type; never re-use fluid that has already been bled from the system. Ensure that sufficient fluid is available before starting work.

3 If there is any possibility of incorrect fluid being already in the system, the brake components and circuit must be flushed

completely with uncontaminated, correct fluid, and new seals should be fitted to the various components.

4 If hydraulic fluid has been lost from the system, or air has entered because of a leak, ensure that the fault is cured before proceeding further.

5 Park the vehicle on level ground, switch off the engine and select first or reverse gear, then chock the wheels and release the handbrake.

6 Check that all pipes and hoses are secure, unions tight and bleed screws closed. Clean any dirt from around the bleed screws.

7 Unscrew the master cylinder reservoir cap, and top the master cylinder reservoir up to the "MAX" level line; refit the cap loosely, and remember to maintain the fluid level at least above the "MIN" level line throughout the procedure, or there is a risk of further air entering the system.

8 There are a number of one-man, do-it-yourself brake bleeding kits currently available from motor accessory shops. It is recommended that one of these kits is used whenever possible, as they greatly simplify the bleeding operation, and also reduce the risk of expelled air and fluid being drawn back into the system. If such a kit is not available, the basic (two-man) method must be used, which is described in detail below.

9 If a kit is to be used, prepare the vehicle as described previously, and follow the kit manufacturer's instructions, as the procedure may vary slightly according to the type being used; generally, they are as outlined below in the relevant sub-section.

10 Whichever method is used, the same sequence must be followed (paragraphs 11 and 12) to ensure the removal of all air from the system.

Bleeding sequence

11 If the system has been only partially disconnected, and suitable precautions were taken to minimise fluid loss, it should be necessary only to bleed that part of the system (ie the primary or secondary circuit).

12 If the complete system is to be bled, then it should be done working in the following sequence:

Non-ABS models

  a) Left-hand rear brake.
  b) Right-hand front brake.
  c) Right-hand rear brake.
  d) Left-hand front brake.

Models with Bendix (2-wheel) ABS

Note: *Before carrying out any bleeding, switch off the ignition, and disconnect the wiring connector (8-pin, black) from the hydraulic modulator assembly (see illustration).*
  a) Rear brake furthest from master cylinder.
  b) Rear brake nearest master cylinder.
  c) Front brake furthest from master cylinder.
  d) Front brake nearest master cylinder.
  e) Hydraulic modulator assembly (see illustration).

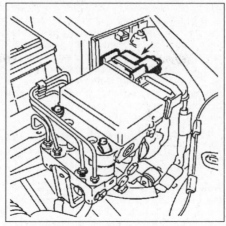

2.12a Disconnect the wiring connector (arrowed) from the hydraulic modulator assembly - Bendix ABS

Models with Bosch (4-wheel) ABS

  a) Left-hand front brake.
  b) Right-hand front brake.
  c) Left-hand rear brake.
  d) Right-hand rear brake.

Note: *If difficulty is experienced in bleeding the braking circuit on models with Bosch (4-wheel) ABS, using the above sequence, try bleeding the complete system working in the following order:*
  a) Right-hand rear brake.
  b) Left-hand rear brake.
  c) Left-hand front brake.
  d) Right-hand front brake.

Bleeding - basic (two-man) method

13 Collect a clean glass jar, a suitable length of plastic or rubber tubing which is a tight fit over the bleed screw, and a ring spanner to fit the screw. The help of an assistant will also be required.

14 Remove the dust cap from the first screw in the sequence **(see illustration)**. Fit the spanner and tube to the screw, place the other end of the tube in the jar, and pour in sufficient fluid to cover the end of the tube.

15 Ensure that the master cylinder reservoir fluid level is maintained at least above the "MIN" level line throughout the procedure.

16 Have the assistant fully depress the brake pedal several times to build up pressure, then maintain it on the final downstroke.

17 While pedal pressure is maintained, unscrew the bleed screw (approximately one turn) and allow the compressed fluid and air to flow into the jar. The assistant should maintain pedal pressure, following it down to the floor if necessary, and should not release it until instructed to do so. When the flow stops, tighten the bleed screw again, have the assistant release the pedal slowly, and recheck the reservoir fluid level.

18 Repeat the steps given in paragraphs 16 and 17 until the fluid emerging from the bleed

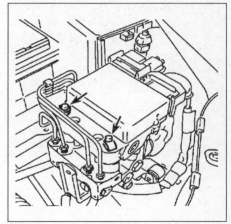

2.12b Hydraulic modulator assembly bleed screws (arrowed) - Bendix ABS

screw is free from air bubbles. If the master cylinder has been drained and refilled, and air is being bled from the first screw in the sequence, allow approximately five seconds between cycles for the master cylinder passages to refill.

19 When no more air bubbles appear, tighten the bleed screw securely, remove the tube and spanner, and refit the dust cap. Do not overtighten the bleed screw.

20 Repeat the procedure on the remaining screws in the sequence, until all air is removed from the system and the brake pedal feels firm again.

Bleeding - using a one-way valve kit

21 As their name implies, these kits consist of a length of tubing with a one-way valve fitted, to prevent expelled air and fluid being drawn back into the system; some kits include a translucent container, which can be positioned so that the air bubbles can be more easily seen flowing from the end of the tube.

22 The kit is connected to the bleed screw, which is then opened. The user returns to the driver's seat, depresses the brake pedal with a smooth, steady stroke, and slowly releases it; this is repeated until the expelled fluid is clear of air bubbles **(see illustration)**.

2.14 Rear brake wheel cylinder dust cap (arrowed) - model with rear drum brakes

2.22 Bleeding a rear brake caliper using a one-way valve kit

23 Note that these kits simplify work so much that it is easy to forget the master cylinder reservoir fluid level; ensure that this is maintained at least above the "MIN" level line at all times.

Bleeding - using a pressure-bleeding kit

24 These kits are usually operated by the reservoir of pressurised air contained in the spare tyre. However, note that it will probably be necessary to reduce the pressure to a lower level than normal; refer to the instructions supplied with the kit.
25 By connecting a pressurised, fluid-filled container to the master cylinder reservoir, bleeding can be carried out simply by opening each screw in turn (in the specified sequence), and allowing the fluid to flow out until no more air bubbles can be seen in the expelled fluid.
26 This method has the advantage that the large reservoir of fluid provides an additional safeguard against air being drawn into the system during bleeding.
27 Pressure-bleeding is particularly effective when bleeding "difficult" systems, or when bleeding the complete system at the time of routine fluid renewal.

All methods

28 When bleeding is complete, and firm pedal feel is restored, wash off any spilt fluid, tighten the bleed screws, and refit their dust caps.
29 Check the hydraulic fluid level in the master cylinder reservoir, and top-up if necessary (see "Weekly checks").
30 Discard any fluid that has been bled from the system; it will not be fit for re-use.

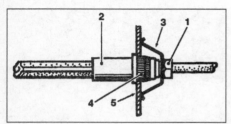

3.2 Hydraulic pipe-to-flexible hose connection

1 Union nut	4 Splined end
2 Flexible hose	fitting
3 Spring clip support	5 Mounting bracket

31 Check the feel of the brake pedal. If it feels at all spongy, air must still be present in the system, and further bleeding is required. Failure to bleed properly after a reasonable repetition of the bleeding procedure may be due to worn master cylinder seals.
32 On models with Bendix 2-wheel ABS, reconnect the wiring connector to the hydraulic modulator assembly.

3 Hydraulic pipes and hoses - renewal

Note: *Before starting work, refer to the note at the beginning of Section 2 concerning the dangers of hydraulic fluid.*
1 If any pipe or hose is to be renewed, minimise fluid loss by first removing the master cylinder reservoir cap, then tightening it down onto a piece of polythene to obtain an airtight seal. Alternatively, flexible hoses can be sealed, if required, using a proprietary brake hose clamp; metal brake pipe unions can be plugged (if care is taken not to allow dirt into the system) or capped immediately they are disconnected. Place a wad of rag under any union that is to be disconnected, to catch any spilt fluid.
2 If a flexible hose is to be disconnected, unscrew the brake pipe union nut before removing the spring clip which secures the hose to its mounting bracket **(see illustration)**.
3 To unscrew the union nuts, it is preferable to obtain a brake pipe spanner of the correct size; these are available from most large motor accessory shops. Failing this, a close-fitting open-ended spanner will be required, though if the nuts are tight or corroded, their flats may be rounded-off if the spanner slips. In such a case, a self-locking wrench is often the only way to unscrew a stubborn union, but it follows that the pipe and the damaged nuts must be renewed on reassembly. Always clean a union and surrounding area before disconnecting it. If disconnecting a component with more than one union, make a careful note of the connections before disturbing any of them.
4 If a brake pipe is to be renewed, it can be obtained, cut to length and with the union nuts and end flares in place, from Peugeot dealers. All that is then necessary is to bend it to shape, following the line of the original, before fitting it

4.2 Disconnect the brake pad wear sensor wiring from the connector (arrowed)

to the car. Alternatively, most motor accessory shops can make up brake pipes from kits, but this requires very careful measurement of the original, to ensure that the replacement is of the correct length. The safest answer is usually to take the original to the shop as a pattern.
5 On refitting, do not overtighten the union nuts. It is not necessary to exercise brute force to obtain a sound joint.
6 Ensure that the pipes and hoses are correctly routed, with no kinks, and that they are secured in the clips or brackets provided. After fitting, remove the polythene from the reservoir, and bleed the hydraulic system as described in Section 2. Wash off any spilt fluid, and check carefully for fluid leaks.

4 Front brake pads - renewal

⚠️ *Warning: Renew both sets of front brake pads at the same time - never renew the pads on only one wheel, as uneven braking may result. Note that the dust created by wear of the pads may contain asbestos, which is a health hazard. Never blow it out with compressed air, and don't inhale any of it. An approved filtering mask should be worn when working on the brakes. DO NOT use petrol or petroleum-based solvents to clean brake parts; use brake cleaner or methylated spirit only.*

1 Apply the handbrake, then jack up the front of the vehicle and support it on axle stands (see "Jacking and Vehicle Support"). Remove the front roadwheels.
2 Trace the brake pad wear sensor wiring back from the pads, and disconnect it from the wiring connector **(see illustration)**. Note the routing of the wiring, and free it from any relevant retaining clips.
3 Push the piston into its bore by pulling the caliper outwards.
4 Several different types of front brake caliper are fitted. The situation is generally as follows, but exceptions may be found:
a) Bendix Series IV+ - early models with solid discs and no ABS.
b) ATE Teves FN 48 - models (except 2.0 litre) with ventilated discs but without ABS.
c) Lucas/Girling C54 - 2.0 litre engine models, Estate models with ventilated discs, other models with ventilated discs and ABS.
d) Bendix SV ZO, or Bosch Series 4G or 5 - later models with solid and ventilated discs.
In some cases, especially with the later Bendix/Bosch caliper, the manufacturer's material refers to the same unit by more than one make and type. To be sure of getting the correct replacement parts, clean the caliper carefully and note all maker's names and identifying marks before ordering. All calipers are of the single-piston sliding type, with very similar pad renewal and overhaul procedures. In particular the Lucas/Girling and the later Bendix/Bosch units are virtually identical.

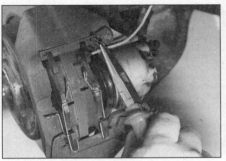

4.5a On the Bendix caliper, remove the spring clip . . .

4.5b . . . then slide out the retaining plate . . .

4.6 . . . and remove the pads. Note the correct fitted positions of pad springs (arrowed)

Bendix caliper

5 Using pliers, extract the small spring clip from the pad retaining plate, and then slide the plate out of the caliper (see illustrations).

6 Withdraw the pads from the caliper, then make a note of the correct fitted position of each anti-rattle spring, and remove the spring from each pad (see illustration).

7 First measure the thickness of each brake pad's friction material. If either pad is worn at any point to the specified minimum thickness or less, all four pads must be renewed (see illustration). Also, the pads should be renewed if any are fouled with oil or grease; there is no proper way of degreasing friction material, once contaminated. If any of the brake pads are worn unevenly, or are fouled with oil or grease, trace and rectify the cause before reassembly. New brake pads and spring kits are available from Peugeot dealers.

8 If the brake pads are still serviceable, carefully clean them using a clean, fine wire brush or similar, paying particular attention to the sides and back of the metal backing. Clean out the grooves in the friction material, and pick out any large embedded particles of dirt or debris. Carefully clean the pad locations in the caliper body/mounting bracket.

9 Prior to fitting the pads, check that the guide pins are free to slide easily in the caliper body/mounting bracket, and check that the rubber guide pin gaiters are undamaged (see illustration). Brush the dust and dirt from the caliper and piston, but do not inhale it, as it is injurious to health. Inspect the dust seal around the piston for damage, and the piston

for evidence of fluid leaks, corrosion or damage. If attention to any of these components is necessary, refer to Section 10.

10 If new brake pads are to be fitted, the caliper piston must be pushed back into the cylinder to make room for them. Either use a G-clamp or similar tool, or use suitable pieces of wood as levers. Provided that the master cylinder reservoir has not been overfilled with hydraulic fluid, there should be no spillage, but keep a careful watch on the fluid level while retracting the piston. If the fluid level rises above the "MAX" level line at any time, the surplus should be siphoned off or ejected via a plastic tube connected to the bleed screw (see Section 2).

⚠️ Warning: Do not syphon the fluid by mouth, as it is poisonous; use a syringe or an old poultry baster.

11 Fit the anti-rattle springs to the pads; when the pads are installed in the caliper, the spring end must be located at the opposite end of the pad in relation to the pad retaining plate.

12 Locate the pads in the caliper, ensuring that the friction material of each pad is against the brake disc, and check that the anti-rattle spring ends are at the opposite end of the pad to which the retaining plate is to be inserted. Note that if the pads are installed correctly, looking at the pads from the front of the vehicle, the innermost pad groove must be higher than the outer pad groove. Ensure that the pads are fitted correctly before proceeding (see illustration).

13 Slide the retaining plate into place, and install the new small spring clip at its inner end. It may be necessary to file an entry chamfer on the edge of the retaining plate, to enable it to be fitted without difficulty.

14 Reconnect the brake pad wear sensor wiring connectors, ensuring that the outer wire is correctly routed through the anti-rattle spring loops, and that both wires pass through the loop of the bleed screw cap.

15 Depress the brake pedal repeatedly, until the pads are pressed into firm contact with the brake disc, and normal (non-assisted) pedal pressure is restored.

16 Repeat the above procedure on the remaining front brake caliper.

17 Refit the roadwheels, then lower the vehicle to the ground and tighten the roadwheel bolts to the specified torque.

18 Check the hydraulic fluid level as described in "Weekly checks".

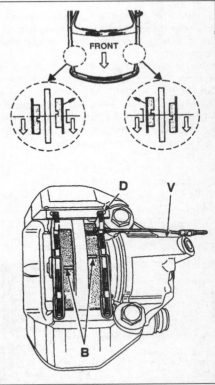

4.12 Correct fitting of brake pads - Bendix caliper

B Grooves
V Bleed screw
D Pad retaining plate spring clip

4.7 Measuring brake pad friction material thickness

4.9 Check the condition of the guide pins and gaiters - Lucas/Girling caliper shown

4.19 Using a screwdriver, carefully prise out the pad retaining spring from the caliper - ATE caliper

4.20 Remove the guide bolt dust caps . . .

4.21a . . . then unscrew the guide bolts . . .

4.21b . . . and slide off the caliper and inner pad assembly - ATE caliper

4.24 Clip the inner pad securely into the caliper piston . . .

4.25 . . . and fit the outer pad to the caliper mounting bracket - ATE caliper

ATE Teves caliper

19 Using a screwdriver, prise the pad retaining spring from the outer edge of the caliper, noting its correct fitted position (see illustration).

20 Prise out the two guide bolt dust caps from the inner edge of the caliper (see illustration).

21 Unscrew the guide bolts from the caliper, and lift the caliper and inner pad away from the mounting bracket. Tie the caliper to the suspension strut using a suitable piece of wire (see illustrations).

Caution: Do not allow the caliper to hang unsupported on the flexible brake hose.

22 Remove the inner pad from the caliper piston, noting that it is retained by a clip attached to the pad backing plate, and recover the outer pad from the mounting bracket.

23 Proceed as described in paragraphs 7 to 10.

24 Fit the inner pad to the caliper, ensuring that its clip is correctly located in the caliper piston (see illustration).

25 Fit the outer pad to the caliper mounting bracket, ensuring that its friction material is facing the brake disc (see illustration).

26 Slide the caliper and inner pad into position over the outer pad, and locate it in the mounting bracket.

27 Install the caliper guide bolts, and tighten them to the specified torque (see illustration).

28 Refit the guide bolt dust caps to the caliper.

29 Refit the pad retaining spring to the caliper, ensuring that its ends are correctly located in the caliper holes (see illustration).

30 Depress the brake pedal repeatedly, until normal (non-assisted) pedal pressure is restored, and the pads are pressed into firm contact with the brake disc.

31 Repeat the above procedure on the remaining front brake caliper.

32 Reconnect the brake pad wear sensor wiring connectors, ensuring that the wiring is correctly routed, as noted before removal.

33 Refit the roadwheels, then lower the vehicle to the ground and tighten the road-wheel bolts to the specified torque setting.

34 Check the hydraulic fluid level as described in *"Weekly checks"*.

Lucas/Girling caliper

Note: *New guide pin bolts must be used on refitting.*

35 Where applicable, prise off the dust covers, then slacken and remove the upper and lower caliper guide pin bolts, using a slim open-ended spanner to prevent the guide pin itself from rotating (see illustration). Discard the guide pin bolts - new bolts must be used on refitting.

4.27 Slide the caliper into position and install the guide bolts, tightening them to the specified torque - ATE caliper

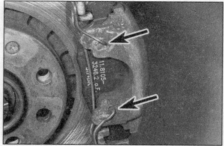

4.29 When refitting, ensure that the pad retaining spring ends are correctly located in the caliper holes (arrowed)

4.35 On the Lucas/Girling caliper, retain the guide pin with an open-ended spanner while slackening the guide pin bolt

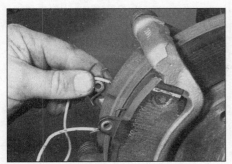

4.38 Ensure that the brake pads are fitted the correct way around, with friction material facing the disc . . .

36 With the guide pin bolts removed, lift the caliper away from the brake pads and mounting bracket, and tie it to the suspension strut using a suitable piece of wire.
Caution: Do not allow the caliper to hang unsupported on the flexible brake hose.
37 Withdraw the two brake pads from the caliper mounting bracket, and examine them as described above in paragraphs 7 to 10.
38 Install the pads in the caliper mounting bracket, ensuring that the friction material of each pad is against the brake disc **(see illustration)**.
39 Position the caliper over the pads, and pass the pad warning sensor wiring through the caliper aperture and underneath the retaining clip **(see illustration)**. If the threads of the new guide pin bolts are not already pre-coated with locking compound, apply a suitable thread-locking compound to them. Press the caliper into position, then install the guide pin bolts, tightening them to the specified torque, retaining the guide pins with an open-ended spanner. Where applicable, refit the dust covers to the guide pins.
40 Reconnect the brake pad wear sensor wiring connectors, ensuring that the wiring is correctly routed through the loop of the caliper bleed screw cap.
41 Depress the brake pedal repeatedly, until the pads are pressed into firm contact with the brake disc, and normal (non-assisted) pedal pressure is restored.
42 Repeat the above procedure on the remaining front brake caliper.

43 Refit the roadwheels, then lower the vehicle to the ground and tighten the roadwheel bolts to the specified torque.
44 Finally, check the fluid level (see *"Weekly checks"*).

All calipers
45 New pads will not give full braking efficiency until they have bedded in. Be prepared for this, and avoid hard braking as far as possible for the first hundred miles or so after pad renewal.

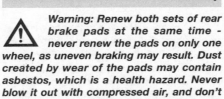

5 Rear brake pads - renewal

⚠️ *Warning: Renew both sets of rear brake pads at the same time - never renew the pads on only one wheel, as uneven braking may result. Dust created by wear of the pads may contain asbestos, which is a health hazard. Never blow it out with compressed air, and don't inhale any of it. An approved filtering mask should be worn when working on the brakes. DO NOT use petrol or petroleum-based solvents to clean brake parts; use brake cleaner or methylated spirit only.*

1 Chock the front wheels, then jack up the rear of the vehicle and support it on axle stands (see *"Jacking and Vehicle Support"*). Remove the rear wheels.
2 Extract the small spring clip from the pad retaining plate, and then slide the plate out of the caliper **(see illustrations)**. Discard the spring clip - a new one must be used on refitting.
3 Using pliers if necessary, withdraw both the inner and outer pads from the caliper **(see illustration)**. Make a note of the correct fitted position of the anti-rattle springs, and remove the springs from each pad.
4 First measure the thickness of the friction material of each brake pad. If either pad is worn at any point to the specified minimum thickness or less, all four pads must be renewed. Also, the pads should be renewed if any are fouled with oil or grease; there is no satisfactory way of degreasing friction

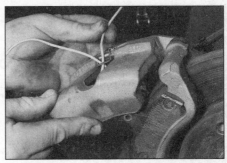

4.39 . . . then refit the caliper, feeding the pad wiring through the caliper aperture

material, once contaminated. If any of the brake pads are worn unevenly, or fouled with oil or grease, trace and rectify the cause before reassembly. New brake pads and spring kits are available from Peugeot dealers.
5 If the brake pads are still serviceable, carefully clean them using a clean, fine wire brush or similar, paying particular attention to the sides and back of the metal backing. Clean out the grooves in the friction material, and pick out any large embedded particles of dirt or debris. Carefully clean the pad locations in the caliper body/mounting bracket.
6 Prior to fitting the pads, check that the guide sleeves are free to slide easily in the caliper body, and check that the rubber guide sleeve gaiters are undamaged. Brush the dust and dirt from the caliper and piston, but **do not** inhale it, as it is injurious to health. Inspect the dust seal around the piston for damage, and the piston for evidence of fluid leaks, corrosion or damage. If attention to any of these components is necessary, refer to Section 11.
7 If new brake pads are to be fitted, it will be necessary to retract the piston fully into the caliper bore, by rotating it in a clockwise direction. This can be achieved using a suitable square-section bar, such as the shaft of a screwdriver, which locates snugly in the caliper piston slots **(see illustration)**. Provided that the master cylinder reservoir has not been overfilled with hydraulic fluid, there should be no spillage, but keep a careful watch on the fluid level while retracting the piston. If the fluid level rises above the "MAX

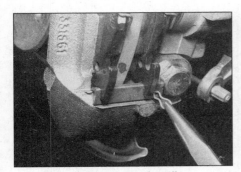

5.2a Extract the spring clip . . .

5.2b . . . then slide out the pad retaining plate . . .

5.3 . . . and withdraw the brake pads from the caliper

5.7 Retract the piston using a square-section bar . . .

level line at any time, the surplus should be siphoned off, or ejected via a plastic tube connected to the bleed screw (see Section 2).

⚠️ *Warning: Do not syphon the fluid by mouth, as it is poisonous; use a syringe or an old poultry baster.*

8 Position the caliper piston so that its piston reference slot (A) is positioned horizontally, above or below the piston groove (B); this is necessary to ensure that the lug on the inner pad will locate with the caliper piston slot on installation **(see illustration)**.

9 The brake pad with the lug on its backing plate is the inner pad. Refit the anti-rattle springs to the pads, so that when the pads are fitted in the caliper, the spring end will be located at the opposite end of the pad, in relation to the pad retaining plate **(see illustration)**.

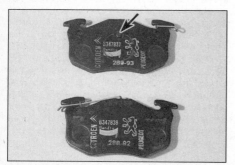

5.9 Inner brake pad can be identified by its locating lug (arrowed). Note the correct fitted positions of the anti-rattle springs

5.10 Install the inner pad, ensuring its locating lug is correctly engaged in the piston slot

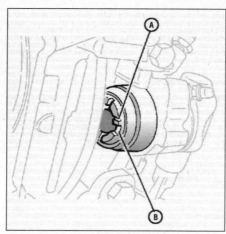

5.8 . . . and position the piston so that the reference slot (A) is positioned horizontally above or below the piston groove (B)

10 Locate the outer brake pad in the caliper body, ensuring that its friction material is against the brake disc. Slide the inner pad into position in the caliper, ensuring that the lug on its backing plate is aligned with the slot in the caliper piston **(see illustration)**.

11 Ensure that the anti-rattle spring ends on both pads are correctly positioned, then slide the retaining plate into place, and secure it in position with a new spring clip. It may be necessary to file an entry chamfer on the edge of the retaining plate, to enable it to be fitted without difficulty.

12 Depress the brake pedal repeatedly until the pads are pressed into firm contact with

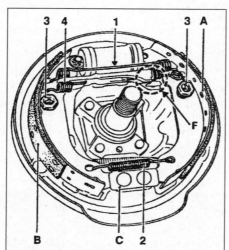

6.6a Correct fitted positions of the Bendix rear brake components

A Leading shoe
B Trailing shoe
C Lower pivot point
F Adjuster strut mechanism
1 Upper return spring

2 Lower return spring
3 Retaining pin, spring and spring cup
4 Adjuster strut-to-trailing shoe spring

the brake disc, and normal (non-assisted) pedal pressure is restored. Check that the inner pad lug is correctly engaged with one of the caliper piston slots.

13 Repeat the above procedure on the remaining rear brake caliper.

14 Check the handbrake cable adjustment as described in Section 17, then refit the roadwheels and lower the vehicle to the ground. Tighten the roadwheel bolts to the specified torque setting.

15 Check the hydraulic fluid level as described in *"Weekly checks"*.

16 New pads will not give full braking efficiency until they have bedded in. Be prepared for this, and avoid hard braking as far as possible for the first hundred miles or so after pad renewal.

6 Rear brake shoes - renewal

⚠️ *Warning: Brake shoes must be renewed on both rear wheels at the same time - never renew the shoes on only one wheel, as uneven braking may result. Also, the dust created by wear of the shoes may contain asbestos, which is a health hazard. Never blow it out with compressed air, and don't inhale any of it. An approved filtering mask should be worn when working on the brakes. DO NOT use petrol or petroleum-based solvents to clean brake parts; use brake cleaner or methylated spirit only.*

1 Remove the brake drum (see Section 9).

2 Working carefully, and taking the necessary precautions, remove all traces of brake dust from the brake drum, backplate and shoes.

3 Measure the thickness of the friction material of each brake shoe at several points; if either shoe is worn at any point to the specified minimum thickness or less, all four shoes must be renewed as a set. The shoes should also be renewed if any are fouled with oil or grease; there is no proper way of degreasing friction material, once contaminated.

4 If any of the brake shoes are worn unevenly, or fouled with oil or grease, trace and rectify the cause before reassembly.

5 To renew the brake shoes, proceed as described under the relevant sub-heading.

Bendix brake shoes

Note: *The components encountered may vary in detail, but the principles described in the following paragraphs are equally applicable to all models. Make a careful note of the fitted positions of all components before dismantling.*

6 Using a pair of pliers, remove the shoe retainer spring cups by depressing and turning them through 90° **(see illustrations)**. With the cups removed, lift off the springs and withdraw the retainer pins.

7 Ease the shoes out one at a time from the lower pivot point, to release the tension of the

6.6b Removing a shoe retainer spring cup

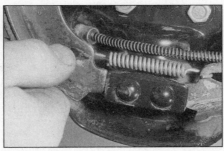

6.7 On Bendix rear brake shoes, ease the shoes out of the lower pivot point, and disconnect the lower return spring

6.12 Correct fitted position of Bendix adjuster strut components

return spring, then disconnect the lower return spring from both shoes **(see illustration)**.

8 Ease the upper end of both shoes out from their wheel cylinder locations, taking care not to damage the wheel cylinder seals, and disconnect the handbrake cable from the trailing shoe. The brake shoe and adjuster strut assembly can then be manoeuvred out of position and away from the backplate. Do not depress the brake pedal until the brakes are reassembled; wrap an elastic band around the wheel cylinder pistons to retain them.

9 With the shoe and adjuster strut assembly on a bench, make a note of the correct fitted positions of the springs and adjuster strut, to use as a guide on reassembly. Release the handbrake lever stop-peg (if not already done), then carefully detach the adjuster strut bolt retaining spring from the leading shoe. Disconnect the upper return spring, then detach the leading shoe and return spring from the trailing shoe and strut assembly. Unhook the spring securing the adjuster strut to the trailing shoe, and separate the two.

10 If genuine Peugeot brake shoes are being installed, it will be necessary to remove the handbrake lever from the original trailing shoe, and install it on the new shoe. Secure the lever in position with a new retaining clip. All return springs should be renewed, regardless of their apparent condition; spring kits are also available from Peugeot dealers.

11 Withdraw the adjuster bolt from the strut, and carefully examine the assembly for signs of wear or damage. Pay particular attention to the threads of the adjuster bolt and the knurled

6.16 Apply a little high-melting-point grease to the shoe contact points on the backplate

adjuster wheel, and renew if necessary. Note that left-hand and right-hand struts are not interchangeable - they are marked "G" (left) and "D" (right) respectively. Also note that the strut adjuster bolts are not interchangeable; the left-hand strut bolt has a left-handed thread, and the right-hand bolt a right-handed thread.

12 Ensure that the components on the end of the strut are correctly positioned, then apply a little high-melting-point grease to the threads of the adjuster bolt **(see illustration)**. Screw the adjuster wheel onto the bolt until only a small gap exists between the wheel and the head of the bolt, then fit the bolt in the strut.

13 Fit the adjuster strut retaining spring to the trailing shoe, ensuring that the shorter hook of the spring is engaged with the shoe. Attach the adjuster strut to the spring end, then ease the strut into its slot in the trailing shoe.

14 Engage the upper return spring with the trailing shoe, then hook the leading shoe onto the other end of the spring, and lever the leading shoe down until the adjuster bolt head is correctly located in its groove. Once the bolt is correctly located, hook its retaining spring into the slot on the leading shoe.

15 Peel back the rubber protective caps, and check the wheel cylinder for fluid leaks or other damage; check that both cylinder pistons are free to move easily. Refer to Section 12, if necessary, for information on wheel cylinder renewal.

16 Prior to installation, clean the backplate, and apply a thin smear of high-temperature brake grease or anti-seize compound to all those surfaces of the backplate which bear on the shoes, particularly the wheel cylinder pistons and lower pivot point **(see illustration)**. Do not allow the lubricant to foul the friction material.

17 Ensure that the handbrake lever stop-peg is correctly located against the edge of the trailing shoe, and remove the elastic band fitted to the wheel cylinder.

18 Manoeuvre the shoe and strut assembly into position on the vehicle, and locate the upper end of both shoes with the wheel cylinder pistons. Attach the handbrake cable to the trailing shoe lever. Fit the lower return spring to both shoes, and ease the shoes into position on the lower pivot point.

19 Tap the shoes to centralise them with the

backplate, then refit the shoe retainer pins and springs, and secure them in position with the spring cups.

20 Using a screwdriver, turn the strut adjuster wheel to expand the shoes until the brake drum just slides over the shoes.

21 Refit the brake drum (see Section 9).

22 Repeat the above procedure on the remaining rear brake.

23 Once both sets of rear shoes have been renewed, adjust the lining-to-drum clearance by repeatedly depressing the brake pedal. Whilst depressing the pedal, have an assistant listen to the rear drums, to check that the adjuster strut is functioning correctly; if so, a clicking sound will be emitted by the strut as the pedal is depressed.

24 Check and, if necessary, adjust the handbrake as described in Section 17.

25 On completion, check the hydraulic fluid level as described in *"Weekly checks"*.

Girling brake shoes

Note: *The components encountered may vary in detail, but the principles described in the following paragraphs are equally applicable to all models. Make a careful note of the fitted positions of all components before dismantling.*

26 Make a note of the correct fitted positions of the springs and adjuster strut, to use as a guide on reassembly **(see illustration)**.

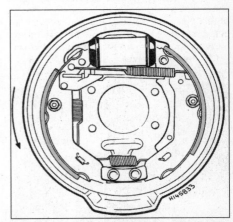

6.26 Correct fitted positions of Girling rear brake components

Arrow indicates direction of wheel rotation

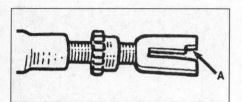

6.37 On Girling rear brake shoes, adjuster strut fork cut-out (A) must engage with leading shoe adjusting lever on refitting

27 Carefully unhook both the upper and lower return springs, and remove them from the brake shoes.

28 Using a pair of pliers, remove the leading shoe retainer spring cup by depressing it and turning through 90°. With the cup removed, lift off the spring, then withdraw the retainer pin and remove the shoe from the backplate. Unhook the adjusting lever spring, and remove it from the leading shoe.

29 Detach the adjuster strut, and remove it from the trailing shoe.

30 Remove the trailing shoe retainer spring cup, spring and pin as described above, then detach the handbrake cable and remove the shoe from the vehicle. Do not depress the brake pedal until the brakes are reassembled; wrap a strong elastic band around the wheel cylinder pistons to retain them.

31 If genuine Peugeot brake shoes are being installed, it will be necessary to remove the adjusting lever from the original leading shoe, and install it on the new shoe. All return springs should be renewed, regardless of their apparent condition; spring kits are also available from Peugeot dealers.

32 Withdraw the forked end from the strut, and carefully examine the assembly for signs of wear or damage. Pay particular attention to the threads and the knurled adjuster wheel, and renew if necessary. Note that left-hand and right-hand struts are not interchangeable; the left-hand fork has a right-handed thread, and the right-hand fork a left-handed thread.

33 Peel back the rubber protective caps, and check the wheel cylinder for fluid leaks or other damage; check that both cylinder pistons are free to move easily. Refer to Section 12, if necessary, for information on wheel cylinder renewal.

34 Prior to installation, clean the backplate,

7.3 Using a micrometer to measure disc thickness

and apply a thin smear of high-temperature brake grease or anti-seize compound to all those surfaces of the backplate which bear on the shoes, particularly the wheel cylinder pistons and lower pivot point. Do not allow the lubricant to foul the friction material.

35 Ensure that the handbrake lever stop-peg is correctly located against the edge of the trailing shoe, and remove the elastic band fitted to the wheel cylinder.

36 Locate the upper end of the trailing shoe in the wheel cylinder piston, then refit the retainer pin and spring, and secure it in position with the spring cup. Connect the handbrake cable to the lever.

37 Screw in the adjuster wheel until the minimum strut length is obtained, then hook the strut into position on the trailing shoe. Rotate the adjuster strut forked end, so that the cut-out of the fork will engage with the leading shoe adjusting lever once the shoe is installed **(see illustration)**.

38 Fit the spring to the leading shoe adjusting lever, so that the shorter hook of the spring engages with the lever.

39 Slide the leading shoe assembly into position, ensuring that it is correctly engaged with the adjuster strut fork, and that the fork cut-out is engaged with the adjusting lever. Ensure that the upper end of the shoe is located in the wheel cylinder piston, then secure the shoe in position with the retainer pin, spring and spring cup.

40 Install the upper and lower return springs, then tap the shoes to centralise them with the backplate.

41 Using a screwdriver, turn the strut adjuster wheel to expand the shoes until the brake drum just slides over the shoes.

42 Refit the brake drum as described in Section 9.

43 Repeat the above procedure on the remaining rear brake.

44 Once both sets of rear shoes have been renewed, adjust the lining-to-drum clearance by repeatedly depressing the brake pedal. Whilst depressing the pedal, have an assistant listen to the rear drums, to check that the adjuster strut is functioning correctly; if so, a clicking sound will be emitted by the strut as the pedal is depressed.

45 Check and, if necessary, adjust the handbrake as described in Section 17.

7.4 Checking disc run-out using a dial gauge

46 On completion, check the hydraulic fluid level as described in *"Weekly checks"*.

All shoes

47 New shoes will not give full braking efficiency until they have bedded in. Be prepared for this, and avoid hard braking as far as possible for the first hundred miles or so after shoe renewal.

7 Front brake disc - inspection, removal and refitting

Note: *Before starting work, refer to the note at the beginning of Section 4 concerning the dangers of asbestos dust.*

Inspection

Note: *If either disc requires renewal, BOTH should be renewed at the same time, to ensure even and consistent braking. New brake pads should also be fitted.*

1 Apply the handbrake, then jack up the front of the car and support it on axle stands (see *"Jacking and Vehicle Support"*). Remove the appropriate front roadwheel.

2 Slowly rotate the brake disc so that the full area of both sides can be checked; remove the brake pads if better access is required to the inboard surface. Light scoring is normal in the area swept by the brake pads, but if heavy scoring or cracks are found, the disc must be renewed.

3 It is normal to find a lip of rust and brake dust around the disc's perimeter; this can be scraped off if required. If, however, a lip has formed due to excessive wear of the brake pad swept area, then the disc's thickness must be measured using a micrometer **(see illustration)**. Take measurements at several places around the disc, at the inside and outside of the pad swept area; if the disc has worn at any point to the specified minimum thickness or less, the disc must be renewed.

4 If the disc is thought to be warped, it can be checked for run-out. Either use a dial gauge mounted on any convenient fixed point, while the disc is slowly rotated, or use feeler blades to measure (at several points all around the disc) the clearance between the disc and a fixed point, such as the caliper mounting bracket **(see illustration)**. If the measurements obtained are at the specified maximum or beyond, the disc is excessively warped, and must be renewed; however, it is worth checking first that the hub bearing is in good condition (Chapters 1 and/or 10). Also try the effect of removing the disc and turning it through 180°, to reposition it on the hub; if the run-out is still excessive, the disc must be renewed.

5 Check the disc for cracks, especially around the wheel bolt holes, and any other wear or damage, and renew if necessary.

Removal

6 On models with Bendix calipers, remove the brake pads as described in Section 4.

7 On models with ATE Teves and Lucas/Girling calipers, remove the caliper as described in Section 10, but note that there is no need to disconnect the fluid hose from the caliper **(see illustrations)**. Using a piece of wire or string, tie the caliper to the front suspension coil spring, to avoid placing any strain on the fluid hose.

8 Use chalk or paint to mark the relationship of the disc to the hub, then remove the screws securing the brake disc to the hub, and remove the disc **(see illustration)**. If it is tight, lightly tap its rear face with a hide or plastic mallet.

Refitting

9 Refitting is the reverse of the removal procedure, noting the following points:
  a) Ensure that the mating surfaces of the disc and hub are clean and flat.
  b) Align (if applicable) the marks made on removal, and securely tighten the disc retaining screws.
  c) If a new disc has been fitted, use a suitable solvent to wipe any preservative coating from the disc, before refitting the caliper.
  d) On models with ATE Teves and Lucas/Girling calipers, refit the calipers as described in Section 10.
  e) On models with Bendix calipers, refit the pads as described in Section 4.
  f) Refit the roadwheel, then lower the vehicle to the ground and tighten the roadwheel bolts to the specified torque. On completion, repeatedly depress the brake pedal until normal (non-assisted) pedal pressure returns.

8 Rear brake disc - inspection, removal and refitting

Note: Before starting work, refer to the note at the beginning of Section 5 concerning the dangers of asbestos dust.

Inspection

Note: If either disc requires renewal, BOTH should be renewed at the same time, to ensure even and consistent braking. New brake pads should also be fitted.

1 Firmly chock the front wheels, then jack up the rear of the car and support it on axle stands (see "Jacking and Vehicle Support"). Remove the appropriate rear roadwheel.

2 Inspect the disc as described in Section 7.

Removal

3 Remove the brake pads as described in Section 5.

4 Use chalk or paint to mark the relationship of the disc to the hub, then remove the screw securing the brake disc to the hub, and remove

7.7a Undo the two mounting bolts . . .

the disc **(see illustration)**. If it is tight, lightly tap its rear face with a hide or plastic mallet.

Refitting

5 Refitting is the reverse of the removal procedure, noting the following points:
  a) Ensure that the mating surfaces of the disc and hub are clean and flat.
  b) Align (if applicable) the marks made on removal, and securely tighten the disc retaining screws.
  c) If a new disc has been fitted, use a suitable solvent to wipe any preservative coating from the disc, before refitting the caliper.
  d) Refit the brake pads as described in Section 5.
  e) Refit the roadwheel, then lower the vehicle to the ground and tighten the roadwheel bolts to the specified torque.

9 Rear brake drum - removal, inspection and refitting

Note: Before starting work, refer to the note at the beginning of Section 6 concerning the dangers of asbestos dust.

All except models with Bendix rear brakes and ABS, and Van models

Removal

Note: A new rear hub nut and hub cap must be used on refitting.

7.8 Undo the two retaining screws and remove the disc

7.7b . . . then slide the caliper assembly off the disc

1 Chock the front wheels, then jack up the rear of the vehicle and support it on axle stands (see "Jacking and Vehicle Support"). Remove the appropriate rear wheel.

2 Using a hammer and a large flat-bladed screwdriver, carefully tap and prise the cap out of the centre of the brake drum. Discard the cap - a new one must be used on refitting. Using a hammer and chisel, tap up the staking securing the hub retaining nut to the groove in the stub axle.

3 Using a socket and long bar, slacken and remove the rear hub nut, and withdraw the thrustwasher. Discard the hub nut - a new nut must used on refitting.

4 It should now be possible to withdraw the brake drum and hub bearing assembly from the stub axle by hand. It may be difficult to remove the drum due to the tightness of the hub bearing on the stub axle, or due to the brake shoes binding on the inner circumference of the drum. If the bearing is tight, tap the periphery of the drum using a hide or plastic mallet, or use a universal puller, secured to the drum with the wheel bolts, to pull it off. If the brake shoes are binding, first check that the handbrake is fully released, then proceed as follows.

5 Referring to Section 17 for further information, fully slacken the handbrake cable adjuster nut, to obtain maximum free play in the cable.

6 Insert a screwdriver through one of the wheel bolt holes in the brake drum, so that it contacts the handbrake operating lever on the trailing brake shoe. Push the lever until the

8.4 Removing a rear brake disc

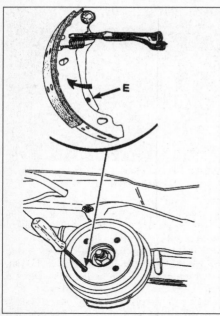

9.6a Using a screwdriver inserted through the brake drum to release the handbrake operating lever

E Handbrake operating lever stop-peg location

stop-peg slips behind the brake shoe web, allowing the brake shoes to retract fully **(see illustrations)**. The brake drum can now be withdrawn, and the seal slid off the stub axle.

Inspection

Note: *If either drum requires renewal, BOTH should be renewed at the same time, to ensure even and consistent braking. New brake shoes should also be fitted.*

7 Working carefully, remove all traces of brake dust from the drum, but *avoid inhaling the dust, as it is injurious to health.*

8 Clean the outside of the drum, and check it for obvious signs of wear or damage, such as cracks around the roadwheel bolt holes; renew the drum if necessary.

9 Examine carefully the inside of the drum. Light scoring of the friction surface is normal, but if heavy scoring is found, the drum must be renewed. It is usual to find a lip on the drum's inboard edge which consists of a mixture of

rust and brake dust; this should be scraped away, to leave a smooth surface which can be polished with fine (120- to 150-grade) emery paper. If, however, the lip is due to the friction surface being recessed by excessive wear, then the drum must be renewed.

10 If the drum is thought to be excessively worn, or oval, its internal diameter must be measured at several points using an internal micrometer. Take measurements in pairs, the second at right-angles to the first, and compare the two, to check for signs of ovality. Provided that it does not enlarge the drum to beyond the specified maximum diameter, it may be possible to have the drum refinished by skimming or grinding; if this is not possible, the drums on both sides must be renewed. Note that if the drum is to be skimmed, BOTH drums must be refinished, to maintain a consistent internal diameter on both sides.

Refitting

11 If a new brake drum is to be installed, use a suitable solvent to remove any preservative coating that may have been applied to its interior. Note that it may also be necessary to shorten the adjuster strut length, by rotating the strut wheel, to allow the drum to pass over the brake shoes.

12 Ensure that the handbrake lever stop-peg is correctly repositioned against the edge of the brake shoe web **(see illustration)**, then apply a smear of clean engine oil to the stub axle, and slide on the seal and brake drum.

13 Fit the thrustwasher and new hub nut, and tighten the hub nut to the specified torque. Stake the nut firmly into the groove on the stub axle, to secure it in position, then tap the new hub cap into place in the centre of the brake drum.

14 Depress the footbrake several times to operate the self-adjusting mechanism.

15 Repeat the above procedure on the remaining rear brake assembly (where necessary), then check and, if necessary, adjust the handbrake cable as described in Section 17.

16 On completion, refit the roadwheel(s), then lower the vehicle to the ground and tighten the wheel bolts to the specified torque.

Models with Bendix rear brakes and ABS, and Van models
Removal

17 Chock the front wheels, then jack up the rear of the vehicle and support it on axle

stands (see *"Jacking and Vehicle Support"*). Remove the appropriate rear roadwheel.

18 Remove the drum retaining screw.

19 It should now be possible to withdraw the brake drum by hand. It may be difficult to remove the drum due to the brake shoes binding on the inner circumference of the drum. If the brake shoes are binding, first check that the handbrake is fully released, then proceed as described in paragraphs 5 and 6.

Inspection

20 Refer to paragraphs 7 to 10 inclusive.

Refitting

21 Proceed as described in paragraphs 11 and 12.

22 Refit and tighten the drum retaining screw.

23 Proceed as described in paragraphs 14 to 16 inclusive.

10 Front brake caliper - removal, overhaul and refitting

Note: *Before starting work, refer to the note at the beginning of Section 2 concerning the dangers of hydraulic fluid, and to the warning at the beginning of Section 4 concerning the dangers of asbestos dust.*

Note: *Several different types of front brake caliper are fitted. In some cases, especially with the later Bendix/Bosch caliper, the manufacturer's material refers to the same unit by more than one make and type. To be sure of getting the correct replacement parts, clean the caliper carefully and note all maker's names and identifying marks before ordering. All calipers are of the single-piston sliding type, with very similar pad renewal and overhaul procedures. In particular the Lucas/Girling and the later Bendix/Bosch units are virtually identical.*

Removal

1 Apply the handbrake, then jack up the front of the vehicle and support it on axle stands (see *"Jacking and Vehicle Support"*). Remove the appropriate roadwheel.

2 Minimise fluid loss by first removing the master cylinder reservoir cap, and then tightening it down onto a piece of polythene, to obtain an airtight seal. Alternatively, use a brake hose clamp, a G-clamp or a similar tool to clamp the flexible hose.

Bendix caliper

3 Remove the brake pads as described in Section 4.

4 Clean the area around the union, then loosen the fluid hose union nut.

5 Slacken the two bolts securing the caliper assembly to the swivel hub and remove them along with the mounting plate, noting which way around the plate is fitted. Lift the caliper assembly away from the brake disc, and unscrew it from the end of the fluid hose.

9.6b Releasing the handbrake operating lever

9.12 Check that the handbrake lever stop-peg is positioned against the shoe edge

ATE Teves caliper

6 Disconnect the brake pad wear sensor wiring, and free it from any retaining clips.

7 Clean the area around the union, then loosen the fluid hose union nut.

8 Using a screwdriver, prise the pad retaining spring from the outer edge of the caliper, noting its correct fitted position.

9 Prise out the two guide bolt dust caps from the inner edge of the caliper.

10 Unscrew the guide bolts from the caliper, and lift the caliper and inner pad away from the mounting bracket. Unscrew the caliper from the end of the fluid hose. The outer pad can be left in the caliper mounting bracket.

11 Remove the inner pad from the caliper piston, noting that it is retained by a clip attached to the pad backing plate.

Lucas/Girling caliper

Note: *New guide pin bolts must be used on refitting.*

12 Clean the area around the hose union, then loosen the union. Disconnect the pad wear warning sensor wiring connector, and free it from any relevant retaining clips.

13 Slacken and remove the upper and lower caliper guide pin bolts, using a slim open-ended spanner to prevent the guide pin itself from rotating. Discard the guide pin bolts - new bolts must be used on refitting. With the guide pin bolts removed, lift the caliper away from the brake disc, then unscrew the caliper from the end of the brake hose. Note that the brake pads need not be disturbed, and can be left in position in the caliper mounting bracket.

Overhaul

14 The caliper can be overhauled after obtaining the relevant repair kit from a Peugeot dealer. Ensure that the correct repair kit is obtained for the caliper being worked on. Note the locations of all components to ensure correct refitting, and lubricate the new seals using clean brake fluid. Follow the assembly instructions supplied with the repair kit.

Refitting

Bendix caliper

15 Screw the caliper fully onto the flexible hose union, then position the caliper over the brake disc.

16 If the threads of the new caliper mounting bolts are not already pre-coated with locking compound, apply a suitable locking compound to them. Refit the bolts along with the mounting plate, ensuring that the plate is fitted so that its bend curves away from the caliper body. With the plate correctly positioned, tighten the caliper bolts to the specified torque.

17 Securely tighten the brake hose union nut, then refit the brake pads (see Section 4).

18 Remove the brake hose clamp or polythene, as applicable, and bleed the hydraulic system (see Section 2). Providing

the precautions described were taken to minimise brake fluid loss, it should only be necessary to bleed the relevant front brake.

19 Refit the roadwheel, then lower the vehicle to the ground and tighten the roadwheel bolts to the specified torque.

ATE Teves caliper

20 Refit the inner brake pad to the caliper, ensuring that the clip engages correctly with the piston.

21 Screw the caliper fully onto the flexible hose union, then position the caliper over the brake disc. Ensure that the outer pad is in position in the caliper mounting bracket.

22 Slide the caliper and inner pad into position over the outer pad, and locate the caliper in the mounting bracket.

23 Fit the caliper guide bolts, and tighten them to the specified torque setting.

24 Refit the guide bolt dust caps.

25 Refit the pad retaining spring to the caliper, ensuring that its ends are correctly located in the caliper holes.

26 Reconnect the pad wear sensor wiring, ensuring that it is correctly routed as noted before removal.

27 Tighten the brake hose union securely, then remove the brake hose clamp or polythene, where fitted, and bleed the hydraulic system (see Section 2). Providing the precautions described were taken to minimise brake fluid loss, it should only be necessary to bleed the relevant front brake.

28 Depress the brake pedal repeatedly, until normal (non-assisted) pedal pressure is restored, and the pads are pressed into firm contact with the brake disc.

29 Refit the roadwheel, then lower the vehicle to the ground and tighten the roadwheel bolts to the specified torque.

Lucas/Girling caliper

30 Screw the caliper body fully onto the flexible hose union, then check that the brake pads are still correctly fitted in the caliper mounting bracket.

31 Position the caliper over the pads, and pass the pad warning sensor wiring through the caliper aperture. If the threads of the new guide pin bolts are not already pre-coated with locking compound, apply a suitable locking compound to them. Fit the new lower guide pin bolt, then press the caliper into position and fit the new upper guide pin bolt. Securely tighten both the guide pin bolts, while retaining the guide pin with an open-ended spanner.

32 Reconnect the brake pad wear sensor wiring connectors, ensuring that the wiring is correctly routed through the loop of the caliper bleed screw cap.

33 Tighten the brake hose union nut securely, then remove the brake hose clamp or polythene, where fitted, and bleed the hydraulic system (see Section 2). Providing the precautions described were taken to minimise brake fluid loss, it should only be necessary to bleed the relevant front brake.

11.3a Disconnect the handbrake inner cable from the caliper lever . . .

34 Depress the brake pedal repeatedly, until the pads are pressed into firm contact with the brake disc, and normal (non-assisted) pedal pressure is restored.

35 Refit the roadwheel, then lower the vehicle to the ground and tighten the roadwheel bolts to the specified torque.

11 Rear brake caliper - removal, overhaul and refitting

Note: *Before starting work, refer to the note at the beginning of Section 2 concerning the dangers of hydraulic fluid, and to the warning at the beginning of Section 5 concerning the dangers of asbestos dust.*

Removal

Note: *New caliper mounting bolts must be used on refitting.*

1 Chock the front wheels, then jack up the rear of the vehicle and support on axle stands (see *"Jacking and Vehicle Support"*). Remove the relevant rear wheel.

2 Remove the brake pads (see Section 5).

3 Ensure that the handbrake is fully released, then free the handbrake inner cable from the caliper handbrake operating lever. Tap the outer cable out of its bracket on the caliper body **(see illustrations)**.

4 Minimise fluid loss by first removing the master cylinder reservoir cap, and then tightening it down onto a piece of polythene, to obtain an airtight seal. Alternatively, use a brake hose clamp, a G-clamp or a similar tool

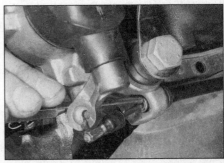

11.3b . . . then tap the outer cable out from the caliper body

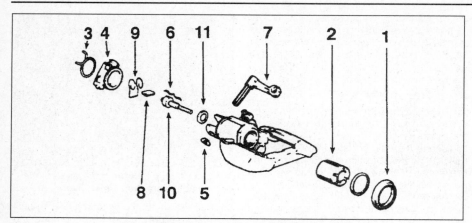

11.7 Exploded view of the rear brake caliper

1 *Dust seal*	5 *Circlip*	8 *Plunger cam*
2 *Piston*	6 *Spring washers*	9 *Return spring*
3 *Retaining clip*	7 *Handbrake operating*	10 *Adjusting screw*
4 *Handbrake mechanism*	*lever*	11 *Thrustwasher*
dust cover		

to clamp the flexible hose at the nearest convenient point to the brake caliper.

5 Wipe away all traces of dirt around the brake pipe union on the caliper, and slacken the union nut.

6 Slacken the two bolts securing the caliper assembly to the trailing arm, and remove them along with the mounting plate, noting which way around the plate is fitted. Lift the caliper assembly away from the brake disc, and unscrew it from the end of the brake hose. Discard the caliper mounting bolts - they should be renewed whenever they are disturbed.

Overhaul

7 The caliper can be overhauled after obtaining the relevant repair kit from a Peugeot dealer. Ensure that the correct repair kit is obtained for the caliper being worked on. Note the locations of all components (this applies particularly if the handbrake mechanism is dismantled) to ensure correct refitting, and lubricate the new seals using brake fluid **(see illustration)**. Follow the assembly instructions supplied with the repair kit.

Refitting

8 Screw the caliper fully onto the brake hose, then position the caliper over the brake disc. If the threads of the new caliper mounting bolts are not already pre-coated with locking compound, apply a suitable locking compound to them. Install the new caliper mounting bolts and the mounting plate, noting that the mounting plate must be fitted so that its bend curves away from the caliper body. With the plate correctly positioned, tighten the caliper bolts to the specified torque, tightening the lower bolt first.

9 Tighten the brake hose union securely, then remove the clamp from the flexible brake hose, or the polythene from the master cylinder reservoir (as applicable).

10 Insert the handbrake cable through its bracket on the caliper, and tap the outer cable into position using a hammer and suitable pin punch. Reconnect the inner cable to the caliper operating lever.

11 Refit the brake pads (see Section 5).

12 Bleed the hydraulic system as described in Section 2. Note that, providing the precautions described were taken to minimise brake fluid loss, it should only be necessary to bleed the relevant rear brake.

13 Repeatedly apply the brake pedal until normal (non-assisted) pedal pressure returns. Check and if necessary adjust the handbrake cable as described in Section 17.

14 Refit the roadwheel, then lower the vehicle to the ground and tighten the wheel bolts to the specified torque. Finally, check the fluid level as described in *"Weekly checks"*.

---

12 Rear wheel cylinder - removal and refitting

Note: *Before starting work, refer to the note at the beginning of Section 2 concerning the dangers of hydraulic fluid, and to the warning at the beginning of Section 6 concerning the dangers of asbestos dust.*

Removal

1 Remove the brake drum (see Section 9).

2 Using pliers, carefully unhook the upper brake shoe return spring, and remove it from both brake shoes. Pull the upper ends of the shoes away from the wheel cylinder to disengage them from the pistons.

3 Minimise fluid loss by first removing the master cylinder reservoir cap, and then tightening it down onto a piece of polythene, to obtain an airtight seal. Alternatively, use a brake hose clamp, a G-clamp or a similar tool to clamp the flexible hose at the nearest convenient point to the wheel cylinder **(see illustration)**.

4 Wipe away all traces of dirt around the brake pipe union at the rear of the wheel cylinder, and unscrew the union nut **(see illustration)**. Carefully ease the pipe out of the wheel cylinder, and plug or tape over its end to prevent dirt entry. Wipe off any spilt fluid immediately.

5 Unscrew the two wheel cylinder retaining bolts from the rear of the backplate, and remove the cylinder, taking great care not to allow surplus hydraulic fluid to contaminate the brake shoe linings.

6 Note that it is not possible to overhaul the cylinder, since no components are available separately. If faulty, the complete wheel cylinder assembly must be renewed.

Refitting

7 Ensure that the backplate and wheel cylinder mating surfaces are clean, then spread the brake shoes and manoeuvre the wheel cylinder into position.

8 Engage the brake pipe, and screw in the union nut two or three turns to ensure that the thread has started.

9 Insert the two wheel cylinder retaining bolts, and tighten them securely. Now fully tighten the brake pipe union nut.

10 Remove the clamp from the flexible brake hose, or the polythene from the master cylinder reservoir (as applicable).

12.3 To minimise fluid loss, fit a brake hose clamp to the flexible hose

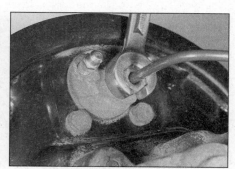

12.4 Using a brake pipe spanner to unscrew the wheel cylinder union nut

13.2 Disconnecting the wiring connector from the master cylinder fluid level sender

13.3 Using a brake pipe spanner to unscrew the master cylinder union nut

13.4 Master cylinder retaining nuts (arrowed)

11 Ensure that the brake shoes are correctly located in the cylinder pistons, then carefully refit the brake shoe upper return spring. Use a screwdriver to stretch the spring into position.

12 Refit the brake drum (see Section 9).

13 Bleed the brake hydraulic system as described in Section 2. Providing suitable precautions were taken to minimise loss of fluid, it should only be necessary to bleed the relevant rear brake.

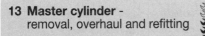

13 Master cylinder -
removal, overhaul and refitting

Note: *Before starting, refer to the warning in Section 2 on the dangers of hydraulic fluid.*

Removal

Note: *A new O-ring must be used when refitting the master cylinder.*

1 On left-hand-drive models, to provide improved access, remove the battery and battery tray as described in Chapter 5A.

2 On all models, remove the master cylinder reservoir cap, and syphon the hydraulic fluid from the reservoir. **Note:** *Do not syphon the fluid by mouth, as it is poisonous; use a syringe or an old poultry baster.* Alternatively, open any convenient bleed screw in the system, and gently pump the brake pedal to expel the fluid through a plastic tube connected to the screw (see Section 2). Disconnect the wiring connector from the brake fluid level sender unit **(see illustration)**.

3 Wipe clean the area around the brake pipe unions on the side of the master cylinder, and place absorbent rags beneath the pipe unions to catch any surplus fluid. Make a note of the correct fitted positions of the unions, then unscrew the union nuts and carefully withdraw the pipes **(see illustration)**. Plug or tape over the pipe ends and master cylinder orifices, to minimise the loss of brake fluid, and to prevent the entry of dirt into the system. Wash off any spilt fluid immediately with cold water.

4 Slacken and remove the two nuts securing the master cylinder to the vacuum servo unit, then withdraw the unit from the engine compartment **(see illustration)**. Remove the

O-ring from the rear of the master cylinder, and discard it.

Overhaul

5 The master cylinder can be overhauled after obtaining the relevant repair kit from a Peugeot dealer. Ensure that the correct repair kit is obtained for the master cylinder being worked on. Note the locations of all components to ensure correct refitting, and lubricate the new seals using clean brake fluid. Follow the assembly instructions supplied with the repair kit.

Refitting

6 Remove all traces of dirt from the master cylinder and servo unit mating surfaces, and fit a new O-ring to the groove on the master cylinder body.

7 Fit the master cylinder to the servo unit, ensuring that the servo unit pushrod enters the master cylinder bore centrally. Refit the master cylinder mounting nuts, and tighten them to the specified torque.

8 Wipe clean the brake pipe unions, then refit them to the master cylinder ports and tighten them securely.

9 On left-hand-drive models, refit the battery

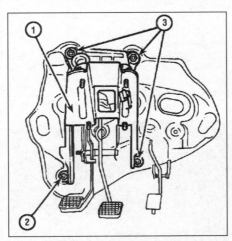

14.5 Steering column bracket mounting details

1 Bracket
2 Nut with conventional thread
3 Nuts with left-hand thread

tray and battery (see Chapter 5A).

10 On all models, refill the master cylinder reservoir with new fluid, and bleed the complete hydraulic system (see Section 2).

14 Brake pedal -
removal and refitting

Removal

Note: *A new pedal securing nut should be used on refitting.*

1 Remove the steering column (Chapter 10).

2 Remove the complete facia assembly as described in Chapter 11.

3 Disconnect the accelerator cable from the pedal and the steering column mounting bracket, with reference to the relevant Part of Chapter 4 if necessary.

4 Unclip any wiring harnesses and/or cables from the steering column mounting bracket.

5 Unscrew the four steering column bracket securing nuts, and withdraw the bracket from the bulkhead **(see illustration)**. **Note:** *The two top and the bottom right-hand securing nuts have a left-hand thread.*

6 Prise off the securing clip, and withdraw the clevis pin securing the servo pushrod to the pedal **(see illustration)**.

7 Unscrew the nut from the end of the pedal through-bolt (counterhold the through-bolt if necessary).

8 Withdraw the through-bolt from the pedal, and recover the spacer bush if it is loose. Withdraw the pedal.

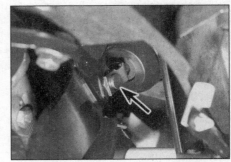

14.6 Prise off the securing clip, and withdraw the clevis pin (arrowed)

Refitting

9 Refitting is a reversal of removal, bearing in mind the following points.

   a) Fit a new nut to the pedal through-bolt.
   b) Refit the facia assembly (Chapter 11).
   c) Refit the steering column (Chapter 10).
   d) On completion, check the accelerator cable adjustment as described in the relevant Part of Chapter 4.

15 Vacuum servo unit - testing, removal and refitting

Testing

1 To test the operation of the servo unit, depress the footbrake several times to exhaust the vacuum, then start the engine whilst keeping the pedal firmly depressed. As the engine starts, there should be a noticeable "give" in the brake pedal as the vacuum builds up. Allow the engine to run for at least two minutes, then switch it off. If the brake pedal is now depressed it should feel normal, but further applications should result in the pedal feeling firmer, with the pedal stroke decreasing with each application.

2 If the servo does not operate as described, first inspect the servo unit check valve as described in Section 16. On Diesel engine models, also check the operation of the vacuum pump as described in Section 25.

3 If the servo unit still fails to operate satisfactorily, the fault lies within the unit itself. Repairs to the unit are not possible - if faulty, the servo unit must be renewed.

Removal

Note: *On certain right-hand-drive models, to gain the clearance required to remove the servo unit, it may prove necessary to split the right-hand engine/transmission mounting and move the engine forwards slightly; this is due to the lack of clearance between the servo unit and the rear of the engine. If this proves necessary, refer to the relevant Part of Chapter 2 for further information on supporting the engine and dismantling the mounting. Additionally, on some models, it may be necessary to remove the inlet manifold (relevant Part of Chapter 4) and/or the camshaft cover and surrounding components - refer to the relevant Chapter for details. A new servo mounting gasket will be required on refitting.*

4 Remove the steering column (Chapter 10).

5 Remove the complete facia assembly as described in Chapter 11.

6 Disconnect the accelerator cable from the pedal and the steering column mounting bracket, with reference to the relevant Part of Chapter 4 if necessary.

7 Unclip any wiring harnesses and/or cables from the steering column mounting bracket.

8 Unscrew the four steering column bracket securing nuts, and withdraw the bracket from the bulkhead. **Note:** *The two top and the*

15.14 Recover the gasket from the rear of the servo unit

bottom right-hand securing nuts have a left-hand thread.

9 Remove the master cylinder (Section 13).

10 Slacken the retaining clip (where fitted) and disconnect the vacuum hose from the servo unit check valve.

11 Where applicable, on right-hand-drive models, release the servo vacuum pipe from the clips on the bulkhead, and move the pipe clear of the servo.

12 Prise off the spring clip, then withdraw the clevis pin securing the servo unit pushrod to the brake pedal.

13 Prise back the sound insulation from the pedal mounting bracket for access to the servo mounting nuts (for improved access, remove the brake pedal (Section 14), and the clutch pedal (Chapter 6).

14 Undo the four retaining nuts securing the servo unit to the pedal mounting bracket, then return to the engine compartment and manoeuvre the servo unit out of position, noting the gasket which is fitted to the rear of the unit **(see illustration)**.

Refitting

15 Check the servo unit check valve sealing grommet for signs of damage or deterioration, and renew if necessary.

16 Fit a new gasket to the rear of the servo unit, and reposition the unit in the engine compartment.

17 From inside the vehicle, refit and tighten the servo unit mounting nuts. If the brake pedal is in place, ensure that the servo unit pushrod is engaged with the brake pedal.

18 Where applicable, refit the brake pedal

16.3 Servo unit check valve is a push-fit in the sealing grommet (master cylinder removed for clarity)

and the clutch pedal - see Section 14, and Chapter 6 respectively.

19 Refit the servo unit pushrod-to-brake pedal clevis pin, and secure it in position with the spring clip.

20 Reconnect the vacuum hose to the servo unit check valve and, where necessary, securely tighten its retaining clip. Where applicable, refit the vacuum pipe to the clips on the bulkhead.

21 Refit the master cylinder (Section 13).

22 Refit the facia assembly (Chapter 11).

23 Refit the steering column (Chapter 10).

24 Where applicable, reconnect the engine/transmission mounting, and/or refit any components removed to provide access.

25 On completion, start the engine and check for air leaks at the vacuum hose-to-servo unit connection; check the operation of the braking system. Also check the accelerator cable adjustment - see the relevant Part of Chapter 4.

16 Vacuum servo unit check valve - removal, testing and refitting

Removal

Note: *If it is necessary to remove the fluid reservoir for access to the valve, it may be necessary to use new seals on refitting.*

1 On certain models, the check valve is obscured by the master cylinder fluid reservoir. Where this is the case, the reservoir must be removed for access to the valve as follows:

   a) Disconnect the battery negative terminal (refer to "Disconnecting the battery" in the Reference Section of this manual), then disconnect the wiring plug from the brake fluid level sensor.
   b) Remove the master cylinder reservoir cap, and syphon the hydraulic fluid from the reservoir. Note: Do not syphon the fluid by mouth, as it is poisonous; use a syringe or an old poultry baster. Alternatively, open any convenient bleed screw in the system, and gently pump the brake pedal to expel the fluid through a plastic tube connected to the screw (see Section 2).
   c) Remove the spring clip, then withdraw the reservoir securing pin, and lift the reservoir from the master cylinder. Plug the openings in the master cylinder to prevent dirt ingress.

2 Slacken the retaining clip (where fitted), and disconnect the vacuum hose from the servo unit check valve.

3 Withdraw the valve from its rubber sealing grommet, using a pulling and twisting motion. Remove the grommet from the servo **(see illustration)**.

Testing

4 Examine the check valve for signs of damage, and renew if necessary. The valve may be tested by blowing through it in both directions. Air should flow through the valve in

17.4 Handbrake adjuster nut (arrowed)

18.3 Handbrake lever nuts (arrowed)

3 Slacken and remove the three handbrake lever retaining nuts, and remove the lever from the vehicle **(see illustration)**.

Refitting

4 Refitting is a reversal of removal. Prior to refitting the handbrake lever cover panel, adjust the handbrake (see Section 17).

19 Handbrake cables - removal and refitting

Removal

1 Remove the centre console (Chapter 11). The handbrake cable consists of two sections, a right and a left-hand section, which are linked to the lever by an equaliser plate. Each section can be removed individually.

2 Slacken the handbrake lever adjusting nut to obtain maximum free play in the cable(s), and disengage the inner cables from the handbrake lever plate.

3 Firmly chock the front wheels, then jack up the rear of the vehicle and support it on axle stands (see *"Jacking and Vehicle Support"*).

4 Slacken and remove the retaining nuts, then release the exhaust system heat shield(s) from the vehicle underbody, to gain access to the front of the relevant handbrake cable. Free the front end of the outer cable from the body, and withdraw the cable from its support guide.

5 Working back along the length of the cable, where applicable prise off the retaining clip and free it from its guide, then depress the retaining tangs and free the cable from its trailing arm bracket **(see illustration)**.

6 On models with rear drum brakes, remove the rear brake shoes from the relevant side as described in Section 6. Using a hammer and pin punch, carefully tap the outer cable out from the brake backplate, and remove it from underneath the vehicle **(see illustration)**.

7 On models with rear disc brakes, disengage the inner cable from the caliper handbrake lever then, using a hammer and pin punch, tap the outer cable out of its mounting bracket on the caliper, and remove the cable from underneath the vehicle **(see illustration)**.

---

one direction only - when blown through from the servo unit end of the valve. Renew the valve if this is not the case.

5 Examine the rubber sealing grommet and flexible vacuum hose for signs of damage or deterioration, and renew as necessary.

Refitting

6 Fit the sealing grommet into the servo unit.

7 Ease the check valve into position, taking care not to displace or damage the grommet. Reconnect the vacuum hose to the valve, and tighten its retaining clip (as applicable).

8 If the master cylinder fluid reservoir has been removed, proceed as follows.
  a) *Refit the reservoir, using new seals if necessary, then refit the securing pin and the spring clip.*
  b) *Reconnect the fluid level sensor wiring, then reconnect the battery negative terminal.*
  c) *Fill the reservoir with fluid, then bleed the complete hydraulic system (Section 2).*

9 On completion, start the engine and check the check valve-to-servo unit connection for signs of air leaks.

17 Handbrake - adjustment

1 To check the handbrake adjustment, first apply the footbrake firmly several times to establish correct shoe-to-drum/pad-to-disc clearance, then apply and release the handbrake several times to ensure that the self-adjust mechanism is fully adjusted.

Applying normal moderate pressure, pull the handbrake lever to the fully-applied position, counting the number of clicks emitted from the handbrake ratchet mechanism. If adjustment is correct, there should be 4 to 7 clicks before the handbrake is fully applied. If this is not the case, adjust as follows.

2 For access to the handbrake adjuster nut, remove the centre console (Chapter 11).

3 Chock the front wheels, then jack up the rear of the vehicle and support it on axle stands (see *"Jacking and Vehicle Support"*).

4 With the handbrake set on the first notch of the ratchet mechanism, rotate the adjusting nut until only a slight drag can be felt when the rear wheels/hubs are turned **(see illustration)**. Once this is so, fully release the handbrake lever, and check that the wheels/hubs rotate freely. Check the adjustment by applying the handbrake fully, counting the clicks from the handbrake ratchet and, if necessary, re-adjust.

5 Refit the centre console, then lower the vehicle to the ground.

18 Handbrake lever - removal and refitting

Removal

1 Remove the centre console (Chapter 11).

2 Slacken the handbrake lever adjusting nut to obtain maximum free play in the cables, and disengage the inner cables from the handbrake lever plate.

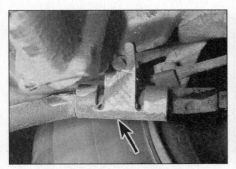

19.5 Free the handbrake cable from the trailing arm bracket (arrowed)

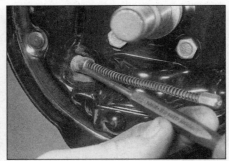

19.6 On drum brake models, drive the outer cable from the brake backplate

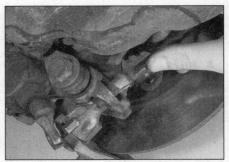

19.7 On disc brake models, disconnect the cable from the brake caliper

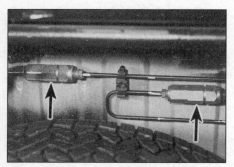

20.1 Rear disc brake pressure-regulating valves (arrowed) - 1.6 litre engine model

Refitting

8 Refitting is a reversal of the removal procedure, adjusting the handbrake as described in Section 17.

20 Rear brake pressure-regulating valves (rear disc brakes models) - removal and refitting

Note: *Certain later models are fitted with a load-sensitive pressure regulating valve assembly fitted to the underside of the vehicle at the rear and connected to the rear suspension by means of an operating rod and spring. Any work on this type of valve should be entrusted to a Peugeot dealer as specialist equipment is required to check and adjust the hydraulic pressure settings according to vehicle loading.*

1.4, 1.6 and 1.8 litre petrol engine and non-Turbo Diesel engine models

Note: *Before starting work, refer to the warning at the beginning of Section 2 concerning the dangers of hydraulic fluid.*

Removal

1 The pressure-regulating valves are located just in front of the rear axle assembly; there are two valves, one for each rear brake caliper **(see illustration)**.

2 Firmly chock the front wheels, then jack up the rear of the vehicle and support it on axle stands (see *"Jacking and Vehicle Support"*).
3 Minimise fluid loss by first removing the master cylinder reservoir cap, and then tightening it down onto a piece of polythene, to obtain an airtight seal.
4 Wipe clean the area around the brake pipe unions on the relevant valve, and place absorbent rags beneath the pipe unions to catch any surplus fluid. Retain the relevant pressure-regulating valve with a suitable open-ended spanner, then slacken the union nuts, disconnect both brake pipes, and remove the valve from underneath the vehicle. Plug or tape over the pipe ends and valve orifices, to minimise the loss of brake fluid, and to prevent the entry of dirt into the system. Wash off any spilt fluid immediately with cold water.

Refitting

5 Refitting is a reverse of the removal procedure, ensuring that the pipe union nuts are securely tightened. On completion, bleed the complete braking system (see Section 2).

1.8 and 2.0 litre petrol engine and Turbo Diesel engine models

Note: *Before starting work, refer to the warning at the beginning of Section 2 concerning the dangers of hydraulic fluid.*

Removal

6 Two valves are incorporated in a single assembly, mounted just behind the rear axle.
7 Proceed as described in paragraphs 2 and 3.
8 Wipe clean the area around the brake pipe unions on the valve, and place absorbent rags beneath the pipe unions to catch any surplus fluid.
9 Remove the screws securing the valve bracket to the underside of the vehicle, and withdraw the valve.

Refitting

10 Refitting is a reversal of removal. Note that it is possible to adjust the valves, but this operation requires the use of special equipment, and should be entrusted to a Peugeot dealer.

21 Stop-light switch - removal, refitting and adjustment

Removal

1 The stop-light switch is located on the pedal bracket behind the facia.
2 Remove the complete facia, as described in Chapter 11.
3 Remove the securing clip, and unscrew the switch from the bracket.

Refitting and adjustment

4 Screw the switch back into position in the mounting bracket, until the gap between the end of the main body of the switch and the lug on the brake pedal is approximately 2 to 3 mm.
5 Once the stop-light switch is correctly positioned, reconnect the wiring connector, and check the operation of the stop-lights. The stop-lights should illuminate after the brake pedal has travelled approximately 5 mm.
6 Refit the facia as described in Chapter 11.

22 Anti-lock braking system (ABS) - general information

1 ABS is available as an option on certain models covered by this manual, and is fitted as standard equipment on some models. The purpose of the system is to prevent the wheel(s) locking during heavy braking. This is achieved by automatic release of the brake on the relevant wheel, followed by re-application of the brake. The system comprises an electronic control module, a hydraulic modulator block, the hydraulic solenoid valves and accumulators, the electrically-driven return pump, and the roadwheel sensors.
2 One of two different systems may be fitted, depending on model.
3 The Bendix 2-wheel ABS system operates on the front wheels only **(see illustration)**. This system will prevent front-wheel lock-up by regulating the hydraulic pressure to the front calipers. The ABS has no control over the rear brakes, but conventional pressure regulating valves are fitted to prevent the rear wheels locking before the front wheels under heavy braking - see Section 20. Models with this system are fitted with front disc brakes, and rear drum brakes.
4 The Bosch 4-wheel ABS system operates on all four wheels. Models with this system may be fitted with rear drum or rear disc brakes.
5 The solenoids (which control the fluid pressure to the calipers) are controlled by the electronic control unit, which itself receives signals from the wheel sensors (fitted to the front wheels on the 2-wheel system or all four wheels on the 4-wheel system), which monitor the speed of rotation of each wheel.

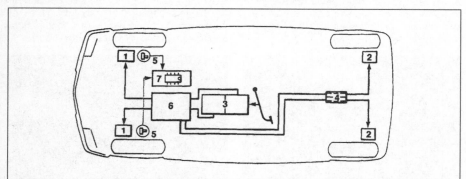

22.3 Schematic layout of Bendix ABS system

1 Front brake calipers
2 Rear brake wheel cylinders (drum brakes)
3 Master cylinder
4 Rear brake pressure-regulating valve
5 Wheel sensors
6 Modulator assembly
7 Electronic control unit

By comparing these speed signals from the wheels, the control unit can determine the speed at which the vehicle is travelling. It can then use this speed to determine when a wheel is decelerating at an abnormal rate, compared to the speed of the vehicle, and therefore predicts when a wheel is about to lock. During normal operation, the system functions in the same way as a non-ABS braking system.

23 Anti-lock braking system (ABS) components - removal and refitting

Bendix 2-wheel ABS

Modulator assembly

Note: *Before starting, refer to the warning in Section 2 on the dangers of hydraulic fluid.*
Removal
1 Disconnect the battery negative terminal (refer to *"Disconnecting the battery"* in the Reference Section of this manual).
2 Disconnect the wiring connectors from the modulator assembly.
3 Mark the locations of the hydraulic fluid pipes to ensure correct refitting, then unscrew the union nuts, and disconnect the pipes from the modulator assembly. Be prepared for fluid spillage, and plug the open ends of the pipes and the modulator, to prevent dirt ingress and further fluid loss. Note the position of the clip on the brake pipes to ensure correct refitting.

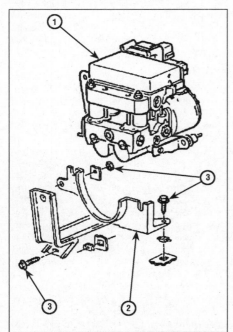

23.5 Bendix ABS hydraulic modulator mounting details

1 Modulator assembly
2 Mounting bracket
3 Bracket fixings

4 Remove the upper securing nut from the modulator mounting bracket.
5 Working under the modulator mounting bracket, unscrew the two lower mounting screws, then withdraw the assembly, complete with the mounting bracket **(see illustration)**.
6 If desired, the modulator assembly can be removed from the bracket after unscrewing the securing nuts.
Refitting
Caution: Do not reconnect the wiring connectors to the modulator until the hydraulic circuits have been bled as described in Section 2.
7 Check the condition of the modulator mounting rubbers, and renew if necessary.
8 Where applicable, refit the modulator to the mounting bracket, ensuring that the mounting rubbers are correctly positioned.
9 Position the assembly in the engine compartment, then refit the lower securing screws, and the upper securing nut.
10 Reconnect the fluid pipes to the assembly, as noted before removal, ensuring that no dirt enters the system. Ensure that the brake pipe clip is fitted as noted before removal.
11 Bleed the complete hydraulic system as described in Section 2.
12 Reconnect the modulator wiring plugs.
13 Reconnect the battery negative terminal.

Electronic control unit

Removal
14 The control unit is mounted on the side of the hydraulic modulator unit.
15 Disconnect the battery negative terminal (refer to *"Disconnecting the battery"* in the Reference Section of this manual).
16 Disconnect the two wiring connectors from the control unit.
17 Remove the four securing screws, and

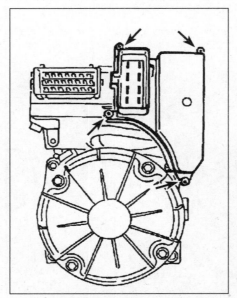

23.17 Bendix ABS electronic control module securing screws (arrowed)

withdraw the control unit from the hydraulic modulator unit **(see illustration)**.
Refitting
18 Refitting is a reversal of removal.

Wheel sensor

Note: *Thread-locking compound must be applied to the sensor stud on refitting.*
Removal
19 Disconnect the battery negative terminal (refer to *"Disconnecting the battery"* in the Reference Section of this manual).
20 Apply the handbrake, then jack up the front of the vehicle and support securely on axle stands (see *"Jacking and Vehicle Support"*). If desired, remove the appropriate front roadwheel to improve access.
21 Follow the wiring back from the sensor, and separate the two halves of the wiring connector. Release the wiring from the securing clips, noting its routing.
22 Unscrew the securing nut, and withdraw the shield from the sensor.
23 Unscrew the stud, and withdraw the sensor from the swivel hub **(see illustration)**.
Refitting
24 Refitting is a reversal of removal, bearing in mind the following points:
a) Ensure that the mating faces of the sensor and the swivel hub are clean, and apply a little grease to the swivel hub bore before refitting.
b) Ensure that the end face of the sensor is clean.
c) Apply thread-locking compound to the threads of the sensor securing stud, and tighten to the specified torque.
d) Ensure that the sensor wiring is routed as noted before removal.

Bosch 4-wheel ABS

Note: *Later models are fitted with Bosch 5.3 ABS. At the time of writing, no information was available regarding component removal and refitting on this system.*

Modulator assembly

Note: *Before starting, refer to the note in Section 2 on the dangers of hydraulic fluid.*
Removal
25 Proceed as described previously in this Section for the Bendix ABS modulator assembly, but note that it will be necessary to

23.23 Slacken and remove the stud and remove the sensor from the swivel hub

23.25 Disconnecting a Bosch ABS modulator assembly wiring plug

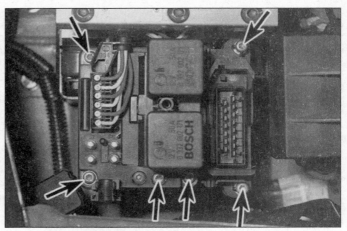

23.27 Bosch ABS electronic control unit securing screws (arrowed)

unclip the control unit cover for access to the wiring plugs **(see illustration)**.

Electronic control unit

Removal

26 Disconnect the battery negative terminal (refer to *"Disconnecting the battery"* in the Reference Section of this manual), then unclip the control unit cover from the top of the modulator assembly.

27 Unplug the three wiring connectors from the control unit, then slacken and remove the six Torx screws, and lift the control unit away from the modulator assembly **(see illustration)**.

Refitting

28 Refitting is a reversal of the removal procedure. Ensure that the wiring connectors are securely reconnected, and do not overtighten the retaining screws.

Front wheel sensor

29 Proceed as described previously in this Section for the Bendix system wheel sensor.

Rear wheel sensor

Note: *Thread-locking compound must be applied to the sensor stud on refitting.*

Removal

30 Chock the front wheels, then jack up the rear of the vehicle and support it on axle stands (see *"Jacking and Vehicle Support"*). Remove the appropriate roadwheel.

31 Trace the wiring back from the sensor to its wiring connector, then free the connector from its retaining clip, and disconnect the wiring from the main wiring loom.

32 Work back along the sensor wiring, and free it from any relevant retaining clips.

33 Slacken and remove the bolt securing the sensor unit to the trailing arm, and remove the sensor and lead assembly **(see illustration)**.

Refitting

34 Refitting is a reversal of removal, bearing in mind the following points:

a) *The mating faces of the sensor and the trailing arm must be clean. Apply grease to the trailing arm bore before refitting.*

b) *Ensure the end face of the sensor is clean.*

c) *Apply thread-locking compound to the threads of the sensor securing bolt, and tighten to the specified torque.*

d) *Ensure that the sensor wiring is routed as noted before removal.*

Relays

35 Both the solenoid relay and return pump relay are located on the top of the electronic control unit, which is mounted on the modulator block assembly. To gain access to the relays, unclip the control unit cover from the top of the modulator assembly. Either relay can then be simply pulled out of position **(see illustration)**. Refer to Chapter 12 for further information on relays.

24 Vacuum pump (Diesel engine models) - removal and refitting

Removal

Note: *New O-rings must be used on refitting.*

1 To improve access, remove the intercooler (where fitted) and the air cleaner and air inlet ducts as described in the relevant Part of Chapter 4.

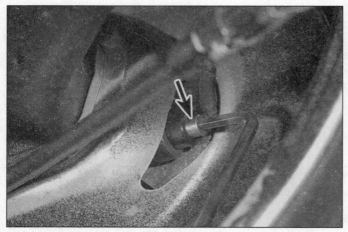

23.33 Remove the securing bolt and remove the rear wheel sensor - Bosch ABS

23.35 Removing a Bosch ABS relay

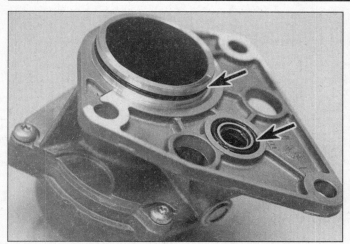

24.4a Fit new O-rings (arrowed) to the pump recesses . . .

24.4b . . . then refit the pump to the cylinder head, ensuring the drive dog is correctly aligned with the camshaft slot (arrowed)

2 Release the retaining clip and disconnect the vacuum hose from the pump.
3 Slacken and remove the three bolts and washers securing the pump to the left-hand end of the cylinder head, then remove the pump, along with its two O-rings. Discard the O-rings - new ones must be used on refitting.

Refitting

4 Fit new O-rings to the pump recesses, then align the drive dog with the slot in the end of the camshaft, and refit the pump to the cylinder head, ensuring that the O-rings remain correctly seated **(see illustrations)**.
5 Refit the pump mounting bolts and washers, and tighten them securely.

6 Reconnect the vacuum hose to the pump, and tighten its securing clip.
7 Refit the air cleaner, air inlet ducts and intercooler (as applicable) as described in the relevant Part of Chapter 4.

25 Vacuum pump (Diesel engine models) - testing and overhaul

Testing

1 The operation of the braking system vacuum pump can be checked using a vacuum gauge.
2 Disconnect the vacuum pipe from the pump, and connect the gauge to the pump union using a suitable length of hose.
3 Start the engine and allow it to idle, then measure the vacuum created by the pump. As a guide, after one minute, a minimum of approximately 500 mm Hg should be recorded. If the vacuum registered is significantly less than this, it is likely that the pump is faulty. However, seek the advice of a Peugeot dealer before condemning the pump.

Overhaul

4 Overhaul of the vacuum pump is not possible, since no components are available separately for it. If faulty, the complete pump assembly must be renewed.

Notes

Chapter 10
Suspension and steering

Contents

Degrees of difficulty

Easy, suitable for novice with little experience		Fairly easy, suitable for beginner with some experience		Fairly difficult, suitable for competent DIY mechanic		Difficult, suitable for experienced DIY mechanic		Very difficult, suitable for expert DIY or professional	

Specifications

Steering
Power steering fluid type .... See "Weekly checks"

Wheel alignment and steering angles
Front wheel toe setting:
   Manual steering .... 1.0 ± 0.5 mm (0°10') toe-out
   Power-assisted steering .... 1.0 ± 0.5 mm (0°10') toe-in

Roadwheels
Type .... Pressed-steel or aluminium alloy (depending on model)
Size .... 5B x 13, 5.5B x 13, 5.5B x 14, 5.5J x 14 or 6J x 15 (depending on model)
Maximum run-out at rim .... 1.2 mm
Maximum eccentricity on tyre bead locating surface .... 0.8 mm

Torque wrench settings

	Nm	lbf ft
Front suspension		
Anti-roll bar:		
Mounting clamp bolts	55	41
Connecting link securing nuts	40	30
Lower arm balljoint clamp bolt	40	30
Lower arm balljoint retaining nuts	50	37
Lower arm front pivot bolt	75	55
Lower arm rear pivot bush mounting bolts:		
8 mm bolt	27	20
10 mm bolt	55	41
Strut upper mounting bolts	20	15
Strut upper mounting retaining nut	45	33
Strut-to-swivel hub bolt (see text in Section 2):		
Standard swivel hub	55	41
Modified swivel hub	45	33
Subframe mounting bolts	85	63
Rear suspension		
Rear axle mountings:		
Front mounting-to-body nuts	55	41
Rear mounting nuts	45	33
Rear hub nut::		
Models with rear drum brakes:		
All except models with Bendix rear brakes and ABS, and Van models	200	148
Models with Bendix rear brakes and ABS, and Van models	185	136
Models with rear disc brakes	185	136
Shock absorber lower mounting bolt	100	74
Shock absorber upper mounting bolt	75	55
Steering		
Steering column mounting nuts	17	13
Steering column shaft-to-intermediate shaft universal joint clamp bolt	20	15
Steering gear mounting bolts	50	37
Steering intermediate shaft-to-steering gear pinion universal joint clamp nut	25	18
Steering wheel nut	35	26
Track rod balljoint-to-swivel hub nut	35	26
Track rod-to-steering rack	50	37
Roadwheels		
Wheel bolts	85	63

1 General information

The independent front suspension is of the MacPherson strut type, incorporating coil springs and integral telescopic shock absorbers. The MacPherson struts are located by transverse lower suspension arms, which utilise rubber inner mounting bushes, and incorporate a balljoint at the outer ends. The front swivel hubs, which carry the wheel bearings, brake calipers and the hub/disc assemblies, are bolted to the MacPherson struts, and connected to the lower arms via the balljoints. A front anti-roll bar is fitted to all models. The anti-roll bar is rubber-mounted onto the subframe, and is connected directly to the front suspension struts.

The rear suspension is of the independent trailing arm type, which consists of two trailing arms, linked by a tubular crossmember. Torsion bars linking the trailing arms are situated in front of and behind the crossmember, and a stabilizer bar linking the arms passes through the centre of the crossmember.

The complete rear axle assembly is mounted onto the vehicle underbody by four "self-steering" rubber mountings. These mountings are designed to move slightly under extreme cornering forces. This movement of the rear axle assembly has the effect of actually turning the rear wheels slightly, to help steer the vehicle in the required direction. This improves the handling of the vehicle when cornering at high speeds.

The steering column has a universal joint fitted in the centre of its length, which is connected to an intermediate shaft having a second universal joint at its lower end. The lower universal joint is clamped to the steering gear pinion by means of a clamp bolt .

The steering gear is mounted onto the front subframe, and is connected by two track rods, with balljoints at their outer ends, to the steering arms projecting rearwards from the swivel hubs. The track rod ends are threaded, to facilitate adjustment.

Power-assisted steering is fitted as standard on some models, and is available as an option on all others. The hydraulic steering system is powered by a belt-driven pump, which is driven off the crankshaft pulley.

2 Front swivel hub assembly - removal and refitting

Removal

Note: *All Nyloc nuts disturbed on removal must be renewed as a matter of course. These nuts have threads which are pre-coated with locking compound (this is only effective once), and include the track rod balljoint nut, lower suspension arm balljoint nuts, and the swivel hub clamp bolt nut. New brake caliper mounting bolts must be used on refitting, and suitable thread-locking compound may be required for the bolts.*

2.6 Remove the bolt securing the wiring retaining bracket to the swivel hub

2.9 Remove the three lower suspension arm balljoint retaining nuts

2.11 Removing the swivel hub assembly. Note the use of the screwdriver to open up the hub clamp

Caution: Do not allow the vehicle to rest on its wheels with one or both driveshafts disconnected from the swivel hubs, as damage to the wheel bearing(s) may result. If moving the vehicle is unavoidable, temporarily insert the outer end of the driveshaft(s) in the hub(s) and tighten the hub nut(s).

1 Chock the rear wheels, then firmly apply the handbrake. Jack up the front of the vehicle, and support it on axle stands (see *"Jacking and Vehicle Support"*). Remove the appropriate front roadwheel.

2 On models with a staked driveshaft nut, using a hammer and a chisel-nosed tool, tap up the staking securing the driveshaft retaining nut in position. Note that a new retaining must be used on refitting.

3 On models where the driveshaft nut is secured by an R-clip, withdraw the R-clip, and remove the locking cap from the driveshaft retaining nut.

4 Refit at least two roadwheel bolts to the front hub, and tighten them securely. Have an assistant firmly depress the brake pedal, to prevent the front hub from rotating, then using a socket and extension bar, slacken and remove the driveshaft retaining nut. Alternatively, a tool can be fabricated from two lengths of steel strip (one long, one short) and a nut and bolt; the nut and bolt forming the pivot of a forked tool. Bolt the tool to the hub using two wheel bolts, and hold the tool to prevent the hub from rotating as the driveshaft nut is undone (see Chapter 8, Section 2).

5 If the hub bearings are to be disturbed, remove the brake disc as described in Chapter 9. If not, unscrew the two bolts securing the brake caliper/mounting bracket assembly to the swivel hub, and slide the caliper assembly off the disc. Using a piece of wire or string, tie the caliper to the front suspension coil spring, to avoid placing any strain on the hydraulic brake hose. Discard the caliper mounting bolts - they must be renewed whenever they are disturbed.

6 Where applicable, slacken and remove the bolt securing the wiring retaining bracket to the top of the swivel hub **(see illustration)**.

7 On models with ABS, remove the wheel sensor as described in Chapter 9.

8 On all models, slacken and remove the nut securing the steering gear track rod balljoint to the swivel hub, and release the balljoint tapered shank using a balljoint separator.

9 Slacken and remove the three nuts securing the balljoint to the lower suspension arm, then withdraw the bolts and free the balljoint from the arm **(see illustration)**.

10 Undo the nut and withdraw the swivel hub-to-suspension strut clamp bolt, noting that the bolt fits from the rear of the vehicle.

11 Free the swivel hub assembly from the end of the strut, then release it from the outer constant velocity joint splines, and remove it from the vehicle. If the swivel hub is a tight fit on the strut, use a large flat-bladed

screwdriver to carefully open up the clamp a little **(see illustration)**.

Refitting

12 Note that all Nyloc nuts disturbed on removal must be renewed as a matter of course. These nuts have threads which are pre-coated with locking compound (this is only effective once), and include the track rod balljoint nut, lower suspension arm balljoint nuts, and the swivel hub clamp bolt nut.

13 Ensure that the driveshaft outer constant velocity joint and hub splines are clean, then slide the hub fully onto the driveshaft splines.

14 Slide the hub assembly fully onto the suspension strut, aligning the split in the hub clamp with the lug on the base of the strut. Also ensure that the stop bosses on the strut are in contact with the top surface of the swivel hub. Insert the swivel hub-to-suspension strut clamp bolt from the rear side of the strut, then fit a new nut to the clamp bolt, and tighten it to the specified torque **(see illustration)**. Note that certain later models are fitted with a modified swivel hub assembly which can be identified by the presence of a hole directly above the hub bearing location **(see illustrations)**. If working on the modified assembly, note that the torque setting for the swivel hub-to-suspension strut clamp bolt has altered. Ensure that the correct torque setting is used according to swivel hub type.

2.14a Ensure the swivel hub clamp is aligned with the lug (arrowed) on the strut prior to inserting the clamp bolt

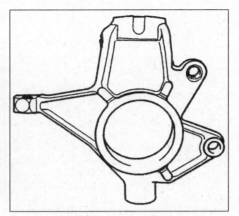

2.14b Standard type front swivel hub assembly

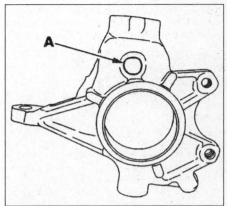

2.14c Modified type front swivel assembly identified by the hole (A)

3.3 Front hub bearing retaining circlip (arrowed)

15 Align the balljoint with the lower arm, and fit the three retaining bolts. Fit new retaining nuts to the bolts, and tighten them to the specified torque.

16 Engage the track rod balljoint in the swivel hub, then fit a new retaining nut and tighten it to the specified torque.

17 Where necessary, refit the brake disc to the hub, referring to Chapter 9 for further information. If the threads of the new caliper mounting bolts are not already pre-coated with locking compound, apply a suitable locking compound to them. Slide the caliper assembly into position over the disc, then fit the mounting bolts and tighten them to the specified torque (see Chapter 9).

18 Where necessary, refit the ABS wheel sensor as described in Chapter 9.

19 Where applicable, refit the wiring retaining bracket to the top of the swivel hub, and tighten its retaining bolt securely.

20 Lubricate the inner face and threads of the driveshaft retaining nut with clean engine oil (a new nut must be used on models with a staked nut), and refit it to the end of the driveshaft. Use the method employed on removal to prevent the hub from rotating, and tighten the driveshaft retaining nut to the specified torque (see Chapter 8). Check that the hub rotates freely.

21 On models with a staked driveshaft nut, stake the nut firmly into the driveshaft grooves using a hammer and punch.

22 On models where the driveshaft nut is secured with an R-clip, engage the locking cap with the driveshaft nut so that one of its cut-outs is aligned with the driveshaft hole.

4.4 Unscrewing the swivel hub-to-suspension strut clamp bolt

Secure the cap with the R-clip.

23 Refit the roadwheel, then lower the vehicle to the ground and tighten the roadwheel bolts to the specified torque.

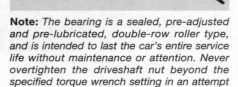

3 Front hub bearings - renewal

Note: *The bearing is a sealed, pre-adjusted and pre-lubricated, double-row roller type, and is intended to last the car's entire service life without maintenance or attention. Never overtighten the driveshaft nut beyond the specified torque wrench setting in an attempt to "adjust" the bearing.*

Note: *A press will be required to dismantle and rebuild the assembly; if such a tool is not available, a large bench vice and spacers (such as large sockets) will serve as an adequate substitute. The bearing's inner races are an interference fit on the hub; if the inner race remains on the hub when it is pressed out of the hub carrier, a knife-edged bearing puller will be required to remove it. A new bearing retaining circlip must be used on refitting.*

1 Remove the swivel hub assembly as described in Section 2.

2 Support the swivel hub securely on blocks or in a vice. Using a tubular spacer which bears only on the inner end of the hub flange, press the hub flange out of the bearing. If the bearing's outboard inner race remains on the hub, remove it using a bearing puller (see note above).

3 Extract the bearing retaining circlip from the inner end of the swivel hub assembly **(see illustration)**.

4 Where necessary, refit the inner race back in position over the ball cage, and securely support the inner face of the swivel hub. Using a tubular spacer which bears only on the inner race, press the complete bearing assembly out of the swivel hub.

5 Thoroughly clean the hub and swivel hub, removing all traces of dirt and grease, and polish away any burrs or raised edges which might hinder reassembly. Check both for cracks or any other signs of wear or damage, and renew them if necessary. Renew the circlip, regardless of its apparent condition.

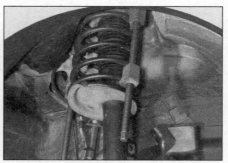

4.5 Coil spring compressors fitted to strut spring

6 On reassembly, apply a light film of oil to the bearing outer race and hub flange shaft, to aid installation of the bearing.

7 Securely support the swivel hub, and locate the bearing in the hub. Press the bearing fully into position, ensuring that it enters the hub squarely, using a tubular spacer which bears only on the bearing outer race.

8 Once the bearing is correctly seated, secure the bearing in position with the new circlip, ensuring that it is correctly located in the groove in the swivel hub.

9 Securely support the outer face of the hub flange, and locate the swivel hub bearing inner race over the end of the hub flange. Press the bearing onto the hub, using a tubular spacer which bears only on the inner race of the hub bearing, until it seats against the hub shoulder. Check that the hub flange rotates freely, and wipe off any excess oil or grease.

10 Refit the swivel hub assembly as described in Section 2.

4 Front suspension strut - removal and refitting

Removal

Note: *All Nyloc nuts disturbed on removal must be renewed as a matter of course. These nuts have threads which are pre-coated with locking compound (this is only effective once), and include the swivel hub clamp bolt nut, and the anti-roll bar connecting link nut. Suitable thread-locking compound may be required for the brake caliper securing bolts. Suitable spring compressor tools will be required for this operation.*

1 Chock the rear wheels, apply the handbrake, then jack up the front of the vehicle and support it on axle stands (see *"Jacking and Vehicle Support"*). Remove the appropriate roadwheel.

2 Where applicable, unclip any wiring and/or hoses from the strut.

3 Unscrew the nut (and recover the washer) securing the anti-roll bar connecting link to the strut, and position the link clear of the strut. Discard the nut - a new one must be used on refitting.

4 Undo the nut and withdraw the swivel hub-to-suspension strut clamp bolt, noting that the bolt fits from the rear of the strut. Discard the nut - a new one must be used on refitting **(see illustration)**.

5 The coil spring must now be compressed to enable the strut to be removed. Working under the wheel arch, fit suitable spring compressors to the spring and compress the spring sufficiently to enable the lower end of the strut to be disconnected from the swivel hub **(see illustration)**.

6 Release the strut from the swivel hub. If the swivel hub is a tight fit on the strut, carefully open up the clamp a little using a large flat-bladed screwdriver or similar tool. Take care not to strain the brake hose and the wiring attached to the brake caliper and swivel hub.

7 Working in the engine compartment, slacken and remove the suspension strut upper mounting bolts (A), then withdraw the strut from under the wheel arch **(see illustration)**.

Refitting

8 With the coil spring compressors in place, as during removal, manoeuvre the strut assembly into position, ensuring that the top mounting plate locating pin is correctly located in the corresponding hole in the body. Engage the lower end of the strut with the swivel hub, aligning the split in the hub clamp with the lug on the base of the strut (if necessary, slacken the spring compressors to aid positioning of the lower end of the strut). Also ensure that the stop bosses on the strut are in contact with the top surface of the swivel hub.

9 Insert the strut upper mounting bolts, and tighten them to the specified torque.

10 Insert the swivel hub-to-suspension strut clamp bolt from the rear side of the strut. Fit a new nut to the clamp bolt, and tighten it to the specified torque. Note that two types of swivel hub are used and the clamp bolt torque setting is different for each - refer to Section 2, paragraph 14.

11 Carefully slacken and then remove the spring compressors.

12 Reconnect the anti-roll bar connecting link to the strut. Fit a new nut to the connecting link, and tighten it to the specified torque.

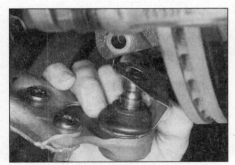

6.3 Release the balljoint from the swivel hub, and remove the protector plate from the balljoint shank

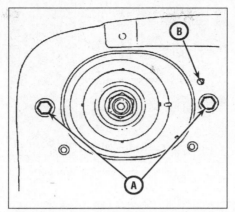

4.7 Suspension strut upper mounting bolts (A) and top mounting plate locating pin (B)

13 Where applicable, clip any wiring/hoses into position on the strut.

14 Refit the roadwheel, then lower the vehicle to the ground and tighten the roadwheel bolts to the specified torque.

5 Front suspension strut - overhaul

⚠️ *Warning: Before attempting to dismantle the front suspension strut, a suitable tool to hold the coil spring in compression must be obtained. Adjustable coil spring compressors are readily-available, and are recommended for this operation. Any attempt to dismantle the strut without such a tool is likely to result in damage or personal injury.*

1 With the strut removed from the vehicle as described in Section 4, dismantling and overhaul is self-explanatory, but note the following points:

a) *Ensure that suitable spring compressors are securely fitted in accordance with their manufacturer's instructions.*

b) *To unscrew the upper mounting retaining nut, counterhold the strut piston with an Allen key.*

c) *Note the location and orientation of all components to ensure correct refitting.*

6 Front suspension lower arm - removal, overhaul and refitting

Removal

Note: *All Nyloc nuts disturbed on removal must be renewed as a matter of course. These nuts have threads which are pre-coated with locking compound (this is only effective once), and include the lower arm balljoint clamp nut.*

1 Chock the rear wheels then jack up the front of the vehicle and support it on axle stands (see *"Jacking and Vehicle Support"*). Remove the appropriate front roadwheel.

2 Slacken and remove the nut, then withdraw the lower arm balljoint clamp bolt from the swivel hub. Discard the nut - a new one must be used on refitting.

3 Lever the arm downwards to release the balljoint from the swivel hub, and remove the protector plate which is fitted to the balljoint shank **(see illustration)**.

4 Slacken and remove the lower arm front pivot bolt and nut. Recover the nut from its housing if it is loose **(see illustration)**.

5 Unscrew the two bolts securing the lower arm rear mounting bush to the subframe, noting that the larger bolt also secures the anti-roll bar mounting clamp (counterhold the nut if necessary) **(see illustration)**. Recover the nut from the top of the anti-roll bar mounting clamp.

6 Manoeuvre the lower arm assembly out from underneath the vehicle **(see illustration)**.

Overhaul

Note: *If the lower arm balljoint is renewed, new retaining nuts must be used on refitting.*

7 Thoroughly clean the lower arm and the area around the arm mountings, removing all traces of dirt and underseal if necessary, then check carefully for cracks, distortion or any other signs of wear or damage, paying particular attention to the pivot bushes, and renew components as necessary.

8 Check that the lower arm balljoint moves freely, without any sign of roughness; check also that the balljoint gaiter shows no sign of deterioration, and is free from cracks and splits. If renewal is necessary, slacken and

6.4 Remove the lower arm front pivot bolt . . .

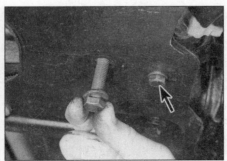

6.5 . . . and the two rear mounting bush bolts (second bolt arrowed) . . .

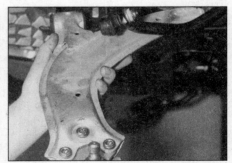

6.6 . . . then remove the lower arm from the vehicle

remove its retaining bolts, and remove the balljoint from the arm. Fit the new balljoint, and insert its retaining bolts. Fit new nuts to the bolts, and tighten them to the specified torque.

9 Examine the shank of the pivot bolt for signs of wear or scoring, and renew if necessary.

Refitting

10 Manoeuvre the lower arm assembly into position, and refit the front pivot bolt, tightening it finger-tight only. Ensure that the nut is located in its housing.

11 Refit the rear pivot bush retaining bolts and nut, ensuring that the bush bracket is located between the subframe and the anti-roll bar clamp. Tighten the fixings to the specified torque.

12 Refit the protector plate to the lower arm balljoint, then locate the balljoint shank in the swivel hub, ensuring that the lug on the protector plate is correctly located in the clamp split. Insert the balljoint clamp bolt (from the rear of the swivel hub), then fit the new retaining nut and tighten it to the specified torque.

13 Refit the roadwheel, then lower the vehicle and tighten the roadwheel bolts to the specified torque. Rock the vehicle to settle the disturbed components, then tighten the lower arm front pivot bolt to the specified torque.

7 Front suspension lower arm balljoint - removal and refitting

Removal

Note: *A new balljoint clamp nut, and new balljoint securing nuts must be used on refitting.*

1 Release the balljoint from the swivel hub as described in Section 6, paragraphs 1 to 3.

2 Slacken and remove the three nuts, then withdraw the balljoint retaining bolts and remove the balljoint from the lower arm **(see illustrations)**. Discard the nuts - new ones must be used on refitting.

3 Check that the lower arm balljoint moves freely, without any sign of roughness. Check

8.12 Slacken and remove the bolt and nut (arrowed) and remove the anti-roll bar mounting clamp

7.2a Remove the three retaining bolts . . .

also that the balljoint gaiter shows no sign of deterioration, and is free from cracks and splits. Renew worn or damaged components as necessary.

Refitting

4 Locate the balljoint in the end of the suspension arm, and insert the three retaining bolts. Fit new nuts to the bolts, and tighten them to the specified torque.

5 Carry out the operations described in paragraphs 12 and 13 of Section 6.

8 Front suspension anti-roll bar - removal and refitting

Removal

Note: *All Nyloc nuts disturbed on removal must be renewed as a matter of course. These nuts have threads which are pre-coated with locking compound (this is only effective once), and include the track rod balljoint nuts, connecting link nuts, engine mounting bolt nut, and the intermediate shaft clamp bolt nut (and pinch-bolt).*

1 Chock the rear wheels, firmly apply the handbrake, then jack up the front of the vehicle and support it on axle stands (see *"Jacking and Vehicle Support"*). Remove both front roadwheels.

2 Undo the nut and washer securing the left-hand connecting link to the anti-roll bar, and position the link clear of the bar. Repeat the procedure on the right-hand side.

3 Where applicable, unclip the clutch cable from the brackets on the subframe.

4 On models with power steering, using brake hose clamps, clamp both the supply and return hoses near the power steering fluid reservoir. This will minimise fluid loss during subsequent operations. Trace the fluid feed and return pipes back from the steering gear, and disconnect the flexible hoses from the ends of the pipes. Be prepared for fluid spillage, and position a suitable container beneath the pipes to catch escaping fluid. If the original Peugeot hose clips are still fitted, discard the clips and fit new ones when reconnecting the hoses.

7.2b . . . and remove the lower arm balljoint

5 Working in the engine compartment, unscrew the securing nut from the intermediate shaft-to-steering gear pinion pinch-bolt, then carefully tap the pinch-bolt from the universal joint - discard the pinch-bolt and nut, new ones must be used on refitting. Pull off the metal clip securing the intermediate shaft to the pinion.

6 Make alignment marks on the universal joint and the steering gear pinion, then push the universal joint upwards to separate it from the pinion.

7 Slacken and remove the nut securing the left-hand steering gear track rod balljoint to the swivel hub, and release the balljoint tapered shank using a universal balljoint separator. Repeat the procedure on the right-hand side.

8 On all models with manual transmission, except 1.4 and 1.6 litre engine models, using a large screwdriver, carefully lever the three gearchange linkage link rods off their balljoints on the transmission.

9 Slacken and remove the engine/transmission rear mounting through-bolt and nut.

10 Make a final check to ensure that all pipes, hoses and wiring harnesses have been moved clear of the subframe to allow the rear of the subframe to be lowered.

11 Slacken and remove the four rear subframe mounting bolts. Loosen the two front subframe mounting bolts by a few turns, until it is possible to lower the rear edge of the subframe approximately 65 mm. Wedge a block of wood between the rear of the subframe and the vehicle underbody, to hold the subframe in this position.

12 Slacken the two anti-roll bar mounting clamp retaining bolts, and recover the nuts from the top of the clamps **(see illustration)**. Remove both clamps from the subframe.

13 Manoeuvre the anti-roll bar out from underneath the vehicle, and remove the mounting bushes from the bar.

14 Carefully examine the anti-roll bar components for signs of wear, damage or deterioration, paying particular attention to the mounting bushes. Renew worn components as necessary.

Refitting

15 Fit the rubber mounting bushes to the anti-roll bar, ensuring that the lugs on the inside of each bush engage with the corresponding cut-outs in the anti-roll bar. The bushes are correctly positioned when the alignment marks on the edges of the bushes are aligned with the paint marks on the anti-roll bar.

16 Offer up the anti-roll bar, and manoeuvre it into position on the subframe. Refit the mounting clamps, ensuring that their ends are correctly located in the hooks on the subframe, and refit the retaining bolts and nuts. Ensure that the bush markings are still aligned with the paint marks on the bars, then tighten the mounting clamp retaining bolts to the specified torque.

17 The remainder of the refitting is a reversal of the removal procedure, noting the following points:

a) All Nyloc nuts disturbed on removal must be renewed as a matter of course. These nuts have threads which are pre-coated with locking compound (this is only effective once), and include the track rod balljoint nuts, connecting link nuts, and the engine mounting bolt nut.

b) Tighten all nuts and bolts to the specified torque settings (where given).

c) Ensure that the metal clip is correctly refitted to the steering intermediate shaft universal joint.

d) Fit a new intermediate shaft pinch-bolt and nut, ensuring that the lugs on the bolt engage with the cut-outs in the universal joint.

e) On models with power steering, where applicable use new hose clips when connecting the fluid hoses, and on completion, bleed the hydraulic system as described in Section 22.

f) On completion check and, if necessary, adjust the front wheel alignment as described in Section 26.

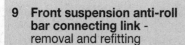

9 Front suspension anti-roll bar connecting link - removal and refitting

Removal

Note: *New connecting link securing nuts must be used on refitting.*

1 Firmly apply the handbrake, then jack up the front of the car and support it on axle stands (see *"Jacking and Vehicle Support"*).

2 Slacken and remove the upper and lower connecting link retaining nuts and washers, and remove the link from the vehicle.

3 Examine the connecting link for signs of damage, paying particular attention to the mounting bushes or balljoints (as applicable), and renew if necessary. It is not possible to renew the bushes or balljoints separately. Note that the connecting link retaining nuts must be renewed as a matter of course.

Refitting

4 Refitting is a reversal of the removal procedure, using new retaining nuts and tightening them to the specified torque setting.

10.10a Front subframe left-hand rear mounting bolts (arrowed) . . .

10 Front suspension subframe - removal and refitting

Removal

Note: *All Nyloc nuts disturbed on removal must be renewed as a matter of course. These nuts have threads which are pre-coated with locking compound (this is only effective once), and include the connecting link nuts, lower arm balljoint nuts, engine mounting bolt nuts and steering gear bolt nuts.*

1 Chock the rear wheels, firmly apply the handbrake, then jack up the front of the vehicle and support it on axle stands (see *"Jacking and Vehicle Support"*). Remove both front roadwheels.

2 Remove the anti-roll bar connecting links as described in Section 9.

3 Slacken and remove the rear engine/transmission through-bolt and nut, then undo the nut and bolt securing the mounting bracket to the subframe and remove the bracket.

4 Slacken and remove the three nuts, then withdraw the balljoint bolts and disengage the left-hand balljoint from the lower arm. Repeat the procedure on the right-hand side.

5 Slacken the steering gear mounting bolts, and recover the nuts. Withdraw the mounting bolts, and recover the spacers from the subframe apertures.

6 On all models with manual transmission, except 1.4 and 1.6 litre engine models, using a large screwdriver, carefully lever the three gearchange linkage link rods off their balljoints on the transmission. Slacken and remove the pivot bolt securing the selector rod to the gearchange lever.

7 On models with power steering, undo the bolt(s) securing the steering gear pipe(s) to the mounting bracket(s) on the subframe, and free the pipe(s) from any subframe retaining clips.

8 Where applicable, release the clutch cable from the clips on the subframe.

9 Place a jack and a suitable block of wood under the subframe to support the subframe as it is lowered.

10 Slacken and remove the four rear subframe mounting bolts, and the two front bolts, then carefully lower the subframe assembly out of position and remove it from

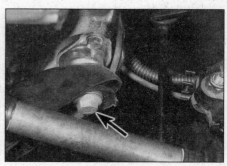

10.10b . . . and front mounting bolt (arrowed)

underneath the vehicle **(see illustrations)**. Where applicable, recover the washers fitted between the subframe and the body. On models with power steering, ensure that the subframe assembly does not catch the power steering pipes as it is lowered out of position.

Refitting

11 Refitting is a reversal of the removal procedure, noting the following points:

a) Where applicable, ensure that the washers are in position between the subframe and the body.

b) All Nyloc nuts disturbed on removal must be renewed as a matter of course. These nuts have threads which are pre-coated with locking compound (this is only effective once), and include the connecting link nuts, lower arm balljoint nuts, engine mounting bolt nuts and steering gear bolt nuts.

c) Tighten all nuts and bolts to the specified torque settings (where given).

d) On completion check and, if necessary, adjust the front wheel alignment as described in Section 26.

11 Rear hub assembly - removal and refitting

Rear drum brakes

All except models with Bendix rear brakes and ABS, and Van models

1 On these models, the rear hub is an integral part of the brake drum. Refer to Chapter 9 for drum removal and refitting details.

Models with Bendix rear brakes and ABS, and Van models

Note: *Do not remove the hub assembly unless it is absolutely necessary. A puller will be required to draw the hub assembly off the stub axle, and the hub bearing will almost certainly be damaged by the removal procedure. A new hub nut, and a new hub cap must be used on refitting.*

2 Remove the rear brake drum as described in Chapter 9.

3 Proceed as described for disc brake models in paragraphs 6 to 14.

11.6a Tap off the hub centre cap . . .

11.6b . . . then tap up the rear hub staking using a hammer and suitable punch

11.8 Use a suitable legged puller to draw the hub assembly off the stub axle

4 On completion, refit the brake drum as described in Chapter 9.

Rear disc brakes

Note: *Do not remove the hub assembly unless it is absolutely necessary. A puller will be required to draw the hub assembly off the stub axle, and the hub bearing will almost certainly be damaged by the removal procedure. A new hub nut, and a new hub cap must be used on refitting.*

Removal

5 Remove the rear brake disc as described in Chapter 9.

6 Using a hammer and a large flat-bladed screwdriver, carefully tap and prise the cap out of the centre of the hub. Discard the cap - a new one must be used on refitting. Using a hammer and a chisel-nosed tool, tap up the staking securing the hub retaining nut to the groove in the stub axle **(see illustrations)**.

11.14a Fit the thrustwasher and new hub nut, and tighten to the specified torque

7 Using a socket and long bar, slacken and remove the rear hub nut, and withdraw the thrustwasher. Discard the hub nut - a new nut must used on refitting.

8 Using a puller, draw the hub assembly off the stub axle, along with the outer bearing race **(see illustration)**. With the hub removed, use the puller to draw the inner bearing race off the stub axle, then remove the hub spacer, noting which way around it is fitted.

9 Refit the races to the hub bearing, and check the hub bearing for signs of roughness. It is recommended that the bearing should be renewed as a matter of course, as it is likely to have been damaged during removal. This means that the complete hub assembly must be renewed, since it is not possible to obtain the bearing separately.

10 With the hub removed, examine the stub axle shaft for signs of wear or damage, and if necessary renew it. The stub axle is an interference fit in the trailing arm, and can either be tapped out of position, using a hammer and a soft-metal drift, or pushed out using a heavy-duty bearing puller. When installing the new stub axle, align its splines with those of the trailing arm, and drift or press it fully into position in the arm.

Refitting

11 Lubricate the stub axle shaft with clean engine oil, then slide on the spacer, ensuring it is fitted the correct way round.

12 Fit the new bearing inner race, and tap it fully onto the stub axle using a hammer and a tubular drift which bears only on the flat inside edge of the race.

13 Ensure that the bearing is packed with grease, then slide the hub assembly onto the stub axle. Fit the new outer bearing race, and tap it into position using the tubular drift.

14 Fit the thrustwasher and new hub nut, and tighten the hub nut to the specified torque. Stake the nut firmly into the groove on the stub axle to secure it in position, then tap the new hub cap into place in the centre of the hub **(see illustrations)**.

15 Refit the rear brake disc (see Chapter 9).

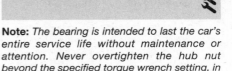

12 Rear hub bearings - renewal

Note: *The bearing is intended to last the car's entire service life without maintenance or attention. Never overtighten the hub nut beyond the specified torque wrench setting, in an attempt to "adjust" the bearings.*

Rear drum brakes

All except models with Bendix rear brakes and ABS, and Van models

1 Remove the rear brake drum (Chapter 9).
2 Using circlip pliers, extract the bearing retaining circlip from the centre of the brake drum **(see illustration)**.
3 Prise the oil seal seating ring from the rear of the hub **(see illustration)**.
4 Securely support the drum hub, then press or drive the bearing out of position, using a tubular drift which bears on the bearing inner race. Alternatively, the bearing can be

11.14b Using a hammer and suitable punch . . .

11.14c . . . stake the hub nut firmly into the stub axle groove . . .

11.14d . . . then fit the new hub cap

12.2 Extracting the rear hub bearing circlip

12.3 Prising the oil seal seating ring from the rear hub

12.4 Drawing the hub bearing from the hub using improvised tools

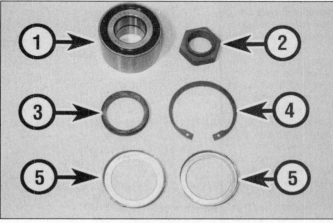

12.5 Rear hub bearing kit

1	Bearing	3	Oil seal	5	Seal seating rings (alternative sizes)
2	Hub nut	4	Circlip		

12.6 Fitting a new oil seal to the stub axle. Note spacer (arrowed)

removed using an improvised tool made up from a suitable socket or tube, washers, nut and a suitable long bolt or threaded rod **(see illustration)**.

5 Thoroughly clean the hub, removing all traces of dirt and grease, and polish away any burrs or raised edges which might hinder reassembly. Check the hub for cracks or any other signs of wear or damage, and renew them if necessary. The bearing and its circlip must be renewed whenever they are disturbed. Note that a replacement bearing kit, which consists of the bearing, circlip and spacer, is available from Peugeot dealers **(see illustration)**.

6 Carefully prise the oil seal from the stub axle, and fit the new seal supplied in the bearing kit. Note the spacer fitted behind the oil seal **(see illustration)**.

7 Examine the stub axle shaft for signs of wear or damage, and if necessary renew it. The stub axle is an interference fit in the trailing arm, and can either be tapped out of position, using a hammer and a soft-metal drift, or pushed out using a heavy-duty bearing puller. When installing the new stub axle, align its splines with those of the trailing arm, and drive or press it fully into position in the arm. **Note:** *Check for availability of parts; it might be necessary to renew the trailing arm and stub axle as an assembly.*

8 On reassembly, apply a light film of clean engine oil to the bearing outer race, to aid installation of the bearing.

9 Securely support the drum, and locate the bearing in the hub. Press the bearing fully into position, ensuring it enters the hub squarely, using a tubular spacer which bears only on the bearing outer race. Alternatively, the bearing can be drawn into position with the improvised tool used previously, but note that a different socket or tube will be required, to bear on the bearing outer race **(see illustrations)**.

10 Ensure that the bearing is correctly seated against the hub shoulder, and secure it in position with the new circlip. Ensure that the circlip is correctly seated in its hub groove.

11 Tap the new oil seal seating ring into position in the rear of the hub, taking care not to damage the oil seal seating surface **(see illustrations)**. Note that two different-size oil seal seating rings may be supplied in the bearing kit - ensure the correct ring is used.

12 Refit the brake drum (see Chapter 9).

12.9a Locate the bearing in the hub . . .

12.9b . . . then draw the bearing into position

12.11a Fit the new oil seal seating ring . . .

12.11b . . . and tap it into position

Models with Bendix rear brakes and ABS, and Van models

13 On these models, the rear hub bearing is integral with the rear hub, and it is not possible to renew the hub bearing separately. If the bearing is worn, the complete rear hub assembly must be renewed. See Section 11 for hub removal and refitting procedures.

Rear disc brakes

14 On models with rear disc brakes, it is not possible to renew the rear hub bearing separately. If the bearing is worn, the complete rear hub assembly must be renewed. Refer to Section 11 for hub removal and refitting procedures.

13 Rear suspension components - general

Although it is possible to remove the rear suspension torsion bars, trailing arms and stabilizer bar independently of the complete rear axle assembly, it is essential to have certain special tools available to complete the work successfully.

Due to the complexity of the tasks, and the requirement for special tools to accurately set the suspension geometry on refitting, the removal and refitting of individual rear suspension components is considered to be beyond the scope of DIY work, and should be entrusted to a Peugeot dealer.

Procedures for removal and refitting of the rear shock absorbers, and the complete rear suspension assembly are given in Sections 14 and 15 respectively.

14 Rear shock absorber - removal, testing and refitting

Removal

Note: *New shock absorber mounting nuts must be used on refitting.*

1 Chock the front wheels, then jack up the rear of the vehicle and support it on axle stands (see *"Jacking and Vehicle Support"*). Remove the relevant rear roadwheel.

2 On some models, note that if the left-hand shock absorber is to be removed, it will first be necessary to remove the exhaust tailpipe and tailpipe heatshield, in order to allow the shock absorber upper mounting bolt to be withdrawn. If this is the case, refer to the relevant Part of Chapter 4 for information on exhaust system removal. Similarly, if removing the right-hand shock absorber, it may be necessary to remove the spare wheel from its cradle.

3 Using a trolley jack, raise the trailing arm until the shock absorber is slightly compressed.

4 Unscrew the securing bolt, and detach the handbrake cable/brake pipe bracket from the trailing arm. Where applicable, take care not to strain the brake pipe.

5 Slacken and remove the nuts and washers from both the upper and lower shock absorber mounting bolts. Counterhold the bolts.

6 Withdraw the mounting bolts, noting which way round they are fitted, and manoeuvre the shock absorber out from underneath the vehicle. Recover the washer from the top mounting bolt. Note that a brake pipe bracket may be secured by the lower mounting bolt on certain models.

Testing

7 Examine the shock absorber for signs of fluid leakage or damage. Test the operation of the shock absorber, while holding it in an upright position, by moving the piston through a full stroke and then through short strokes of 50 to 100 mm. In both cases, the resistance felt should be smooth and continuous. If the resistance is jerky, or uneven, or if there is any visible sign of wear or damage, renewal is necessary. Also check the rubber mounting bushes for damage and deterioration. Renew the complete unit if any damage or excessive wear is evident; the mounting bushes are not available separately. Inspect the shanks of the mounting bolts for signs of wear or damage, and renew as necessary.

Refitting

8 Prior to refitting the shock absorber, mount it upright in the vice, and operate it fully through several strokes in order to prime it. Apply a smear of multi-purpose grease to both the shock absorber mounting bolts.

9 Manoeuvre the shock absorber into position, and insert its mounting bolts; ensure that the upper bolt is inserted from the inside of the trailing arm (with the washer in position), and the lower bolt from the outside.

10 Fit the washers and new nuts to the mounting bolts, but do not tighten the fixings at this stage. Where applicable, ensure that the brake pipe bracket is in place on the lower mounting bolt.

11 Measure the distance between the shock absorber bolt head centres, and adjust the position of the jack under the trailing arm until a distance of 288.0 mm is obtained between the bolt centres. Tighten the shock absorber mounting nuts and bolts to the specified torque.

12 Refit the handbrake cable/brake pipe bracket and tighten the securing bolt.

13 Refit the roadwheel, then lower the car to ground and tighten the roadwheel bolts to the specified torque.

14 Where necessary, refit the heat shield and tailpipe as described in the relevant Part of Chapter 4. Similarly, where applicable, refit the spare wheel.

15 Rear axle assembly - removal and refitting

Removal

1 Firmly chock the front wheels, then jack up the rear of the vehicle and support it on axle stands (see *"Jacking and Vehicle Support"*). Remove both rear roadwheels, then lower the spare wheel out from underneath the rear of the vehicle, and unhook the wheel carrier.

2 Remove the relevant exhaust system components and heat shield(s) (see relevant Part of Chapter 4).

3 Remove the centre console, and fully slacken the handbrake cable adjuster nut. Refer to Chapter 9 for further information.

4 On models with rear drum brakes, disconnect both cables from the handbrake lever. From underneath the vehicle, work along the length of each cable, and free them from any retaining clips which secure them to the vehicle underbody. Note the routing of the cables to ensure correct refitting.

5 On models with rear disc brakes, free the end of the handbrake inner cable from the caliper handbrake lever, then tap the outer cable out of the caliper using a hammer and punch.

6 Where necessary, disconnect the ABS wheel sensors at the wiring connectors, and free them from any retaining clips.

7 Trace the brake pipes back from the caliper/backplate to their unions, which are situated on the brackets attached to the top of the axle mounting brackets. Slacken the union nuts, and disconnect the pipes. Plug the pipe ends, to minimise fluid loss and prevent the entry of dirt into the hydraulic system.

15.10a Rear axle assembly front mounting nuts (arrowed)

8 Make a final check that all necessary components have been disconnected and positioned so that they will not hinder the removal procedure, then position a trolley jack beneath the centre of the rear axle assembly. Raise the jack until it is supporting the weight of the axle.

9 Working in the luggage compartment, lift up the luggage compartment carpet to gain access to the rear axle nuts. Prise the covers from the floor to reveal the retaining nuts.

10 Slacken and remove the two retaining nuts and washers from each front mounting assembly, and the single nut and washer securing each rear mounting assembly to the vehicle **(see illustrations)**.

11 Lower the jack and axle assembly out of position, and remove it from underneath the car.

12 Examine the rear axle mountings for signs of damage or deterioration of the mounting rubber, and renew if necessary. Note that all four mountings should be renewed as a set; do not renew the mountings individually.

Refitting

13 Refitting is a reversal of the removal procedure, bearing in mind the following points:

a) *Take care not to crush the brake pipes when positioning the axle assembly under the body.*

b) *Raise the rear axle assembly into position, and tighten the mounting retaining nuts to their specified torque settings.*

c) *Ensure that the brake pipes, handbrake cables and wiring (as applicable) are correctly routed, and retained by all the necessary retaining clips.*

---

d) *Tighten the brake pipe union nuts.*

e) *Adjust the handbrake cable (Chapter 9).*

f) *On completion, lower the vehicle to the ground, and bleed the braking system hydraulic circuit (see Chapter 9).*

g) *On completion, have the vehicle ride height checked at the earliest opportunity (see Section 16).*

16 Vehicle ride height - checking

Checking of the vehicle ride height requires the use of Peugeot special tools to accurately compress the suspension in a suspension checking bay.

The operation should be entrusted to a Peugeot dealer, as it not possible to carry out checking accurately without the use of the appropriate tools.

17 Steering wheel - removal and refitting

Note: *Models equipped with an air bag can be identified from the red air bag warning light located in the bottom spoke of the steering wheel.*

Models without air bag

Removal

1 Set the front wheels in the straight-ahead position, and release the steering lock by inserting the ignition key.

2 Carefully ease off the steering wheel centre pad/trim plate, then slacken and remove the steering wheel retaining nut. Recover the washer **(see illustrations)**.

3 Mark the steering wheel and steering column shaft in relation to each other, then lift the steering wheel off the column splines.

HAYNES HINT *If the wheel is tight, tap it up near the centre, using the palm of your hand, or twist it from side to side, whilst pulling to release it from the shaft splines.*

15.10b Rear axle assembly rear mounting nut (arrowed)

Refitting

4 Refitting is a reversal of removal, noting the following points:

a) *Prior to refitting, ensure that the indicator switch stem is in its central position. Failure to do this could lead to the steering wheel lug breaking the switch tab as the steering wheel is refitted.*

b) *On refitting, align the marks made on removal, and tighten the retaining nut to the specified torque.*

Models with an air bag

⚠ **Warning: Refer to the precautions given in Chapter 12, Section 25 before proceeding. Note that the air bag control module is integral with the steering wheel.**

Additionally, note the following points:

a) *Do not drop the steering wheel, or subject it to impacts.*

b) *Do not try to dismantle the steering wheel.*

c) *Do not attempt to fit a steering wheel from another model of vehicle (even a different model of Peugeot 306), as the air bag control module is calibrated for each particular model.*

Removal

5 Remove the air bag unit (see Chapter 12).

6 Set the front wheels in the straight-ahead position, and engage the steering lock.

7 Unscrew the steering wheel retaining nut by several threads.

8 Release the steering wheel from the column splines (see paragraph 3).

9 Separate the two halves of the air bag control unit wiring connector **(see illustration)**.

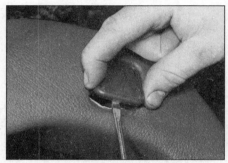

17.2a Prise out the steering wheel trim plate . . .

17.2b . . . and unscrew the steering wheel retaining nut

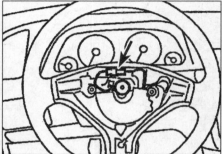

17.9 Separate the two halves of the air bag control unit wiring connector (arrowed)

18.6 Disconnect the wiring connectors . . .

18.7a . . . then unscrew the three securing screws . . .

18.7b . . . and withdraw the stalk switch/mounting assembly

10 Remove the steering wheel retaining nut, and recover the washer.

11 Carefully withdraw the steering wheel, feeding the wiring harness (connecting the rotary connector to the air bag control unit) through the wheel as it is withdrawn. Do not disturb the air bag control unit wiring connector (located in the steering wheel).

Refitting

12 Refitting is a reversal of removal, noting the points listed in paragraph 4. On completion, refit the air bag unit (Chapter 12).

18 Steering column - removal, inspection and refitting

Removal

Note: *Where applicable, a new intermediate shaft-to-steering gear pinion nut and bolt must be used on refitting.*

1 Disconnect the battery negative terminal (refer to *"Disconnecting the battery"* in the Reference Section of this manual).

2 Remove the steering wheel (see Section 17).

3 Release the securing clip, and remove the fusebox cover panel from the lower facia.

4 Remove the three securing screws, and withdraw the lower steering column shroud. Where applicable, remove the securing screws, and separate the radio/cassette player remote control switch and (where applicable) the cruise control switch from the shroud. Similarly, where applicable, remove

the securing clip, and withdraw the alarm switch from the shroud.

5 If necessary, lower the column, then unclip the upper column shroud.

6 Disconnect the steering column stalk switch and the ignition switch wiring connectors **(see illustration)**.

7 Unscrew the three securing screws, and withdraw the stalk switch/mounting assembly from the steering column **(see illustrations)**.

8 Unplug the lower relay(s) from the relay board.

9 Unscrew the two securing screws, and lower the relay carrier from the facia, taking care not to strain the wiring.

10 Make alignment marks on the universal joint and the intermediate shaft, then unscrew the column-to-intermediate shaft pinch-bolt **(see illustration)**.

11 Unscrew the two lower steering column securing nuts **(see illustration)**.

12 Unscrew the two upper steering column securing nuts, and carefully withdraw the column from the vehicle **(see illustration)**.

13 To remove the intermediate shaft, proceed as follows. Note that on certain models, it will be necessary to jack up the front of the vehicle and support on axle stands (see *"Jacking and Vehicle Support"*) for access to the intermediate shaft-to-steering gear joint. On some models, the joint can be reached through the engine compartment.

a) *Unscrew the securing nut from the intermediate shaft-to-steering gear pinion pinch-bolt, then carefully tap the pinch-bolt from the universal joint - discard the*

pinch-bolt and nut, new ones must be used on refitting.

b) *Pull off the metal clip securing the intermediate shaft to the pinion.*

c) *Make alignment marks on the universal joint and the steering gear pinion, then push the universal joint upwards to separate it from the pinion.*

d) *Release the shaft from the pinion splines, and remove it from the vehicle.*

Inspection

14 The steering column incorporates a telescopic safety feature. In the event of a front-end crash, the shaft collapses and prevents the steering wheel injuring the driver. Before refitting the steering column, examine the column and mountings for signs of damage and deformation, and renew as necessary.

15 Check the steering shaft for signs of free play in the column bushes, and check the universal joints for signs of damage or roughness in the joint bearings. If any damage or wear is found on the steering column universal joints or shaft bushes, the column must be renewed as an assembly.

16 The steering column nuts (and, where disturbed, the intermediate shaft-to-steering gear pinch-bolt and nut) must be renewed as a matter of course.

Refitting

17 Where removed, refit the intermediate shaft, engaging the universal joint with the steering gear drive pinion splines (align the marks made on removal). Ensure that the

18.10 Unscrew the column-to-intermediate shaft pinch-bolt (arrowed)

18.11 Unscrew the two lower steering column securing nuts (arrowed) . . .

18.12 . . . and the two upper nuts

metal clip is correctly refitted to the intermediate shaft-to-steering gear universal joint, then fit a new pinch-bolt and nut, ensuring that the lugs on the bolt engage with the cut-outs in the universal joint. Tighten the nut to the specified torque.

18 Where applicable, ensure that the column adjuster handle is positioned in the "locked" position.

19 Manoeuvre the steering column assembly into position then, aligning the marks made prior to removal, engage the universal joint with the intermediate shaft splines.

20 Fit the column over its mounting studs, and refit the steering column mounting nuts, and tighten them to the specified torque.

21 Refit the universal joint clamp bolt, but do not tighten it at this stage.

22 Temporarily refit the steering wheel (with reference to Section 17), and tighten the securing nut to the specified torque.

23 Measure the clearance between the lower edge of the steering wheel, and the top edge of the steering column tube. The clearance should be approximately 2.0 mm. If the clearance is not as specified, adjust the position of the inner column shaft as required (by pushing or pulling on the steering wheel), then tighten the universal joint clamp bolt to secure the column shaft in position.

24 Remove the steering wheel.

25 Further refitting is a reversal of removal, bearing in mind the following points:
a) Ensure that all wiring is routed correctly and is not trapped.
b) Refit the steering wheel with reference to Section 17.

---

19 Ignition switch/steering column lock -
removal and refitting

Removal

1 Disconnect the battery negative terminal (refer to "Disconnecting the battery" in the Reference Section of this manual).

2 Release the securing clip, and remove the fusebox cover panel from the lower facia.

3 Remove the three securing screws, and withdraw the lower steering column shroud. Where applicable, take care not to strain the radio/cassette player remote control and (where applicable) the cruise control switch wiring. If desired, the switches can be removed from the shroud. Similarly, where applicable, the alarm switch can be removed after withdrawing the securing clip.

4 If necessary, lower the column, then unclip the upper column shroud.

5 Tilt the steering column fully downwards, then trace the wiring back from the ignition switch, and disconnect its wiring connectors from the main wiring loom.

6 Slacken and remove the lock retaining screw and washer from the side of the lock (see illustration).

19.6 Removing the lock retaining screw

7 Insert the key, and rotate it so that is aligned with the mark positioned between the "A" and "S" marks on the barrel. Using a small flat-bladed screwdriver, depress the lock retaining lug, then withdraw the lock assembly from the steering column (see illustration).

Refitting

8 Refitting is a reversal of the removal procedure, ensuring that the lock assembly is securely held in position by its retaining lug. Prior to refitting the column shrouds, remove the ignition key and check that the steering lock functions correctly.

---

20 Steering gear assembly -
removal, overhaul and refitting

Removal

Note: All Nyloc nuts disturbed on removal must be renewed as a matter of course. These nuts have threads which are pre-coated with locking compound (this is only effective once), and include the track rod balljoint nuts, steering gear mounting bolt nuts, and the intermediate shaft pinch-bolt nut. A balljoint separator tool will be required for this operation.

1 Chock the rear wheels, firmly apply the handbrake, then jack up the front of the vehicle and support on axle stands (see "Jacking and Vehicle Support"). Remove both front roadwheels.

20.2 Releasing a track rod balljoint using a balljoint separator

19.7 Depress the lock retaining lug (arrowed), then withdraw the lock assembly

2 Slacken and remove the nuts securing the steering gear track rod balljoints to the swivel hubs, and release the balljoint tapered shanks using a universal balljoint separator (see illustration).

3 Unscrew the nut from the intermediate shaft-to-steering gear pinion pinch-bolt, then carefully tap the pinch-bolt from the universal joint - discard the pinch-bolt and nut, new ones must be used on refitting. Pull off the metal clip securing the intermediate shaft to the pinion.

4 Make alignment marks on the universal joint and the steering gear pinion, then push the universal joint upwards to separate it from the pinion.

5 Where necessary, undo the two retaining screws, then unclip the heat shield and remove it from the top of the steering gear assembly.

Manual steering gear

6 Slacken the steering gear mounting bolts, and recover the nuts. Withdraw the mounting bolts, and recover the spacers from the subframe apertures (see illustration).

7 The steering gear assembly can then be manoeuvred out from underneath the right-hand wheel arch. Note that on certain left-hand-drive models with manual transmission, it may be necessary to disconnect one or more of the gearchange linkage link rods from their balljoints on the transmission, to gain the necessary clearance required to withdraw the steering gear.

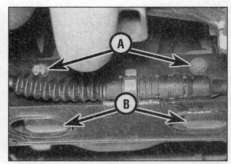

20.6 Withdraw the steering gear mounting bolts (A) and recover the spacers from the subframe apertures (B)

Power-assisted steering gear

8 Using brake hose clamps, clamp both the supply and return hoses near the power steering fluid reservoir. This will minimise fluid loss during subsequent operations.

9 Mark the unions to ensure that they are correctly positioned on reassembly, then unscrew the feed and return pipe union nuts from the steering gear assembly; be prepared for fluid spillage, and position a suitable container beneath the pipes whilst unscrewing the union nuts. Disconnect both pipes, and plug the pipe ends and steering gear orifices, to prevent fluid leakage and to keep dirt out of the hydraulic system.

10 Free the power steering pipes from any retaining clips, and position them clear of the steering gear so that they will not hinder the removal procedure.

11 Remove the steering gear as described above in paragraphs 6 and 7.

Overhaul

12 Examine the steering gear assembly for signs of wear or damage, and check that the rack moves freely throughout the full length of its travel, with no signs of roughness or excessive free play between the steering gear pinion and rack. It is possible to overhaul the steering gear assembly housing components, but this task should be entrusted to a Peugeot dealer. The only components which can be renewed easily by the home mechanic are the steering gear gaiters, the track rod balljoints and the track rods. Track rod, track rod balljoint and steering gear gaiter renewal procedures are covered in Sections 25, 24 and 21 respectively.

13 On models with power steering, inspect all the steering gear fluid unions for signs of leakage, and check that all union nuts are securely tightened. Also examine the steering gear hydraulic ram for signs of fluid leakage or damage, and if necessary renew it.

Refitting

14 Note that all Nyloc nuts disturbed on removal must be renewed as a matter of course. These nuts have threads which are pre-coated with locking compound (this is only effective once), and include the track rod balljoint nuts, and the steering gear mounting bolt nuts.

15 Manoeuvre the steering gear assembly into position from the right-hand side of the vehicle.

16 Position the spacers in the subframe apertures, then insert the mounting bolts. Fit the new nuts onto the steering gear, then tighten the mounting bolts to the specified torque. Where necessary, clip the gearchange linkage link rods onto their balljoints.

17 Where applicable, clip the heat shield onto the top of the steering gear, and securely tighten its two retaining screws.

18 Engage the intermediate shaft universal joint with the steering gear pinion splines (align the marks made before removal).

Ensure that the metal clip is correctly refitted to the intermediate shaft-to-steering gear universal joint, then fit a new pinch-bolt and nut, ensuring that the lugs on the bolt engage with the cut-outs in the universal joint. Tighten the nut to the specified torque.

19 Engage the track rod balljoints in the swivel hubs, then fit a new retaining nut to each one. Tighten the nuts to the specified torque.

20 On models with power steering, wipe clean the feed and return pipe unions, then refit them to their respective positions on the steering gear, and tighten the union nuts securely. Ensure that the pipes are correctly routed, and are securely held by all the necessary retaining clips.

21 On all models, refit the roadwheels, then lower the vehicle to the ground and tighten the roadwheel bolts to the specified torque.

22 Where necessary, remove the hose clamps from the power steering hoses, then top-up the fluid reservoir and bleed the hydraulic system as described in Section 22.

23 On completion check and, if necessary, adjust the front wheel alignment as described in Section 26.

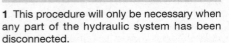

21 Steering gear rubber gaiters - renewal

Manual steering gear

1 Remove the track rod balljoint as described in Section 24.

2 Mark the correct fitted position of the gaiter on the track rod, then release the retaining clips and slide the gaiter off the steering gear housing and track rod end.

3 Thoroughly clean the track rod and the steering gear housing, using fine abrasive paper to polish off any corrosion, burrs or sharp edges, which might damage the new gaiter's sealing lips on installation. Scrape off all the grease from the old gaiter, and apply it to the track rod inner balljoint. (This assumes that grease has not been lost or contaminated as a result of damage to the old gaiter. Use fresh grease if in doubt.)

4 Carefully slide the new gaiter onto the track rod end, and locate it on the steering gear housing. Align the outer edge of the gaiter with the mark made on the track rod prior to removal, then secure it in position with new retaining clips.

5 Refit the track rod balljoint as described in Section 24.

Power-assisted steering gear

6 On power-assisted steering gear assemblies, it is only possible to renew the gaiter nearest the drive pinion, ie the right-hand gaiter on right-hand-drive models, and the left-hand gaiter on left-hand-drive models. This can be renewed as described above in paragraphs 1 to 5.

7 The task of renewing the opposite gaiter should be entrusted to a Peugeot dealer. This is necessary since it is not possible to pass the gaiter over the steering rack stud to which the hydraulic ram is fixed. Therefore, the steering gear must be dismantled and the rack removed from the housing to allow the gaiter to be renewed.

8 The only task on this end of the assembly which can be carried out by the home mechanic is the renewal of the track rod inner balljoint dust cover. The dust cover can be renewed once the track rod balljoint has been removed as described in Section 24. On refitting, ensure that the dust cover is correctly located on the track rod and steering rack, then refit the balljoint.

22 Power steering system - bleeding

1 This procedure will only be necessary when any part of the hydraulic system has been disconnected.

2 Referring to "Weekly checks", remove the fluid reservoir filler cap, and top-up with the specified fluid to the maximum level mark.

3 With the engine stopped, slowly move the steering from lock-to-lock several times to purge out the trapped air, then top-up the level in the fluid reservoir. Repeat this procedure until the fluid level in the reservoir does not drop any further.

4 Start the engine, then slowly move the steering from lock-to-lock several times to purge out any remaining air in the system. Repeat this procedure until bubbles cease to appear in the fluid reservoir.

5 If, when turning the steering, an abnormal noise is heard from the fluid lines, it indicates that there is still air in the system. Check this by turning the wheels to the straight-ahead position and switching off the engine. If the fluid level in the reservoir rises, then air is present in the system, and further bleeding is necessary.

6 Once all traces of air have been removed from the power steering hydraulic system, turn the engine off and allow the system to cool. Once cool, check that the fluid level is up to the maximum mark on the power steering fluid reservoir, topping-up if necessary.

23 Power steering pump - removal and refitting

Removal

Note: A new fluid feed pipe union O-ring must be used on refitting.

1 Release the drivebelt tension as described in Chapter 1A or 1B, and unhook the drivebelt from the pump pulley. The power steering pump is mounted directly above, or directly below the alternator, depending on the engine type and the specification level of the vehicle (if the pump is mounted below the alternator, access is most easily obtained from underneath the vehicle).

2 Using brake hose clamps, clamp both the supply and return hoses near the power steering fluid reservoir. This will minimise fluid loss during subsequent operations.

3 Undo the retaining nut, and free the fluid hose retaining clip from the rear of the pump, where necessary.

4 Slacken the retaining clip, and disconnect the fluid supply hose from the pump. If the original Peugeot clip is still fitted, cut the clip and discard it; replace it with a standard worm-drive hose clip on refitting **(see illustration)**. Slacken the union nut, and disconnect the feed pipe from the pump, along with its O-ring. Be prepared for some fluid spillage as the pipe and hose are disconnected, and plug the hose/pipe end and pump unions, to minimise fluid loss and prevent the entry of dirt into the system.

5 To improve access to the front pump securing bolts, remove the pulley from the pump. The pump spindle can be counterheld using a suitable bit whilst unscrewing the four pulley bolts **(see illustration)**.

6 Unscrew the four pump securing bolts, and withdraw the pump from its bracket.

Refitting

7 Manoeuvre the pump into position, then refit its mounting bolts and tighten them securely.

8 Where applicable, refit the pump pulley and tighten the securing bolts.

9 Fit a new O-ring to the feed pipe union, then reconnect the pipe to the pump and securely tighten the union nut. Refit the supply pipe to the pump, and securely tighten its retaining clip. Remove the brake hose clamps used to minimise fluid loss.

10 Where applicable, refit the fluid hose retaining clip to the rear of the pump, and securely tighten its retaining nut.

11 Refit the drivebelt to the pump pulley, and tension it as described in Chapter 1A or 1B.

12 On completion, bleed the hydraulic system as described in Section 22.

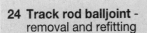

24 Track rod balljoint - removal and refitting

Removal

Note: *A new track rod end-to-swivel hub nut must be used on refitting.*

1 Apply the handbrake, then jack up the front of the vehicle and support it on axle stands (see *"Jacking and Vehicle Support"*). Remove the appropriate front roadwheel.

2 If the balljoint is to be re-used, use a

23.4 **Cut the clip (arrowed) and disconnect the power steering pump supply hose**

straight-edge and a scriber, or similar, to mark its relationship to the track rod.

3 Hold the track rod, and unscrew the balljoint locknut by a quarter of a turn. Do not move the locknut from this position, as it will serve as a handy reference mark on refitting.

4 Slacken and remove the nut securing the track rod balljoint to the swivel hub, and release the balljoint tapered shank using a universal balljoint separator. Discard the nut - a new one must be used when refitting.

5 Counting the **exact** number of turns necessary to do so, unscrew the balljoint from the track rod end.

6 Count the number of exposed threads between the end of the balljoint and the locknut, and record this figure. If a new balljoint is to be fitted, unscrew the locknut from the old balljoint.

7 Carefully clean the balljoint and the threads. Renew the balljoint if its movement is sloppy or too stiff, if excessively worn, or if damaged in any way; carefully check the stud taper and threads. If the balljoint gaiter is damaged, the complete balljoint assembly must be renewed; it is not possible to obtain the gaiter separately.

Refitting

8 If a new balljoint is to be fitted, screw the locknut onto its threads, and position it so that the same number of exposed threads are visible, as was noted prior to removal.

9 Screw the balljoint into the track rod by the number of turns noted on removal. This should bring the balljoint locknut to within a

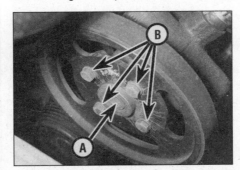

23.5 **Counterhold the pump spindle (A) and unscrew the pulley bolts (B)**

quarter of a turn from the locknut, with the alignment marks that were made on removal (if applicable) lined up.

10 Refit the balljoint shank to the swivel hub, then fit a new retaining nut and tighten it to the specified torque.

11 Refit the roadwheel, then lower the vehicle to the ground and tighten the roadwheel bolts to the specified torque.

12 Check and, if necessary, adjust the front wheel toe setting as described in Section 26, then securely tighten the balljoint locknut.

25 Track rod - removal and refitting

Removal

Note: *A new inner balljoint lockwasher must be used on refitting.*

1 Remove the track rod balljoint as described in Section 24.

2 Either release the retaining clips and slide the steering gear gaiter off the end of the track rod, or release the track rod balljoint dust cover from the rack, and slide it off the track rod (as applicable). Refer to Section 21 for further information.

3 Unscrew the track rod inner balljoint from the steering rack end, preventing the steering rack from turning by holding the balljoint lockwasher with a pair of grips. Take great care not to mark the surfaces of the rack and balljoint.

4 Remove the track rod assembly, and discard the lockwasher - a new one must be used on refitting.

5 Examine the track rod inner balljoint for signs of slackness or tight spots, and check that the track rod itself is straight and free from damage. If necessary, renew the track rod; it is also recommended that the steering gear gaiter/dust cover is renewed.

Refitting

6 Locate the new lockwasher assembly on the end of the steering rack, and apply a few drops of locking fluid to the track rod inner balljoint threads.

7 Screw the balljoint into the steering rack, and tighten it to the specified torque whilst retaining the lockwasher with a pair of grips. Again, take great care not to damage or mark the track rod balljoint or steering rack.

8 Where a gaiter was removed, carefully slide on the new gaiter, and locate it on the steering gear housing. Turn the steering fully from lock-to-lock, to check that the gaiter is correctly positioned on the track rod, then secure it in position with new retaining clips.

9 Where a dust cover was removed, carefully slide on the new cover, and locate it in its grooves on the steering rack collar and track rod.

10 Refit the track rod balljoint (Section 24).

26.11 Adjusting the front wheel alignment

26 Wheel alignment and steering angles - general information

General

1 A car's steering and suspension geometry is defined in four basic settings - all angles are expressed in degrees (toe settings are also expressed as a measurement); the relevant settings are camber, castor, steering axis inclination, and toe-setting. With the exception of front wheel toe-setting, none of these settings are adjustable.

Front wheel toe setting - checking and adjustment

2 Due to the special measuring equipment necessary to accurately check the wheel alignment, and the skill required to use it properly, checking and adjustment is best left to a Peugeot dealer or similar expert. Note that most tyre-fitting shops now possess sophisticated checking equipment. The following is provided as a guide, should the owner decide to carry out a DIY check.

3 The front wheel toe setting is checked by measuring the distance between the front and rear inside edges of the roadwheel rims. Proprietary toe measurement gauges are available from motor accessory shops. Adjustment is made by screwing the balljoints in or out of their track rods, to alter the effective length of the track rod assemblies.

4 For **accurate** checking, the vehicle **must** be at the kerb weight, ie unladen and with a full tank of fuel, and the ride height must be correct (see Section 16).

5 Before starting work, check first that the tyre sizes and types are as specified, then check the tyre pressures and tread wear, the roadwheel run-out, the condition of the hub bearings, the steering wheel free play, and the condition of the front suspension components (Chapter 1A or 1B). Correct any faults found.

6 Park the vehicle on level ground, check that the front roadwheels are in the straight-ahead position, then rock the rear and front ends to settle the suspension. Release the handbrake, and roll the vehicle backwards 1 metre, then forwards again, to relieve any stresses in the steering and suspension components.

7 Measure the distance between the front edges of the wheel rims and the rear edges of the rims. Subtract the rear measurement from the front measurement, and check that the result is within the specified range.

8 If adjustment is necessary, apply the handbrake, then jack up the front of the vehicle and support it securely on axle stands (see *"Jacking and Vehicle Support"*). Turn the steering wheel onto full-left lock, and record the number of exposed threads on the right-hand track rod end. Now turn the steering onto full-right lock, and record the number of threads on the left-hand side. If there are the same number of threads visible on both sides, then subsequent adjustment should be made equally on both sides. If there are more threads visible on one side than the other, it will be necessary to compensate for this during adjustment. **Note:** *It is most important that after adjustment, the same number of threads are visible on each track rod end.*

9 First clean the track rod threads; if they are corroded, apply penetrating fluid before starting adjustment. Release the rubber gaiter outboard clips (where necessary), and peel back the gaiters; apply a smear of grease to the inside of the gaiters, so that both are free, and will not be twisted or strained as their respective track rods are rotated.

10 Use a straight-edge and a scriber or similar to mark the relationship of each track rod to its balljoint then, holding each track rod in turn, unscrew its locknut fully.

11 Alter the length of the track rods, bearing in mind the note made in paragraph 8. Screw them into or out of the balljoints, rotating the track rod using an open-ended spanner fitted to the flats provided on the track rod. Shortening the track rods (screwing them into their balljoints) will reduce toe-in/increase toe-out **(see illustration)**.

12 When the setting is correct, hold the track rods and securely tighten the balljoint locknuts. Check that the balljoints are seated correctly in their sockets, and count the exposed threads to check the length of both track rods. If they are not the same, then the adjustment has not been made equally, and problems will be encountered with tyre scrubbing in turns; also, the steering wheel spokes will no longer be horizontal when the wheels are in the straight-ahead position.

13 If the track rod lengths are the same, lower the vehicle to the ground and re-check the toe setting; re-adjust if necessary. When the setting is correct, securely tighten the track rod balljoint locknuts. Ensure that the rubber gaiters are seated correctly, and are not twisted or strained, and secure them in position with new retaining clips (where necessary).

Chapter 11
Bodywork and fittings

Contents

Degrees of difficulty

| **Easy,** suitable for novice with little experience | **Fairly easy,** suitable for beginner with some experience | **Fairly difficult,** suitable for competent DIY mechanic | **Difficult,** suitable for experienced DIY mechanic | **Very difficult,** suitable for expert DIY or professional |

Specifications

Torque wrench settings	Nm	lbf ft
Seat mounting bolts	20	15
Seat belt mounting bolts	20	15
Longitudinal roof bar mounting bolts - Estate models	10	7

1 General information

The bodyshell is made of pressed steel sections, and is available in three and five-door Hatchback, four-door Sedan and five-door Estate versions. Most components are welded together, but some use is made of structural adhesives. The front wings are bolted on.

The bonnet, doors and some other vulnerable panels are made of zinc-coated metal, and are further protected by being coated with an anti-chip primer prior to being sprayed.

Extensive use is made of plastic materials, mainly in the interior, but also in exterior components. The front and rear bumpers and the front grille are injection-moulded from a synthetic material which is very strong, and yet light. Plastic components such as wheelarch liners are fitted to the underside of the vehicle, to improve the body's resistance to corrosion.

2 Maintenance -
bodywork and underframe

The general condition of a vehicle's bodywork is the one thing that significantly affects its value. Maintenance is easy, but needs to be regular. Neglect, particularly after minor damage, can lead quickly to further deterioration and costly repair bills. It is important also to keep watch on those parts of the vehicle not immediately visible, for instance the underside, inside all the wheelarches, and the lower part of the engine compartment.

The basic maintenance routine for the bodywork is washing - preferably with a lot of water, from a hose. This will remove all the loose solids which may have stuck to the vehicle. It is important to flush these off in such a way as to prevent grit from scratching the finish. The wheelarches and underframe need washing in the same way, to remove any accumulated mud which will retain moisture and tend to encourage rust. Paradoxically enough, the best time to clean the underframe and wheelarches is in wet weather, when the mud is thoroughly wet and soft. In very wet weather, the underframe is usually cleaned of large accumulations automatically, and this is a good time for inspection.

Periodically, except on vehicles with a wax-based underbody protective coating, it is a good idea to have the whole of the underframe of the vehicle steam-cleaned, engine compartment included, so that a thorough inspection can be carried out to see what minor repairs and renovations are necessary. Steam-cleaning is available at many garages, and is necessary for the removal of the accumulation of oily grime, which sometimes is allowed to become thick in certain areas. If steam-cleaning facilities are not available, there are one or two excellent grease solvents available, which can be brush-applied; the dirt can then be simply hosed off. Note that these methods should not be used on vehicles with wax-based underbody protective coating, or the coating will be removed. Such vehicles should be inspected annually, preferably just prior to winter, when the underbody should be washed down, and any damage to the wax coating repaired using underseal. Ideally, a completely fresh coat should be applied. It would also be worth considering the use of wax-based protection for injection into door panels, sills, box sections, etc, as an additional safeguard against rust damage, where such protection is not provided by the vehicle manufacturer.

After washing paintwork, wipe off with a chamois leather to give an unspotted clear finish. A coat of clear protective wax polish will give added protection against chemical pollutants in the air. If the paintwork sheen has dulled or oxidised, use a cleaner/polisher combination to restore the brilliance of the shine. This requires a little effort, but such dulling is usually caused because regular washing has been neglected. Care needs to be taken with metallic paintwork, as a special non-abrasive cleaner/polisher is required to avoid damage to the finish. Always check that the door and ventilator opening drain holes and pipes are completely clear, so that water can be drained out. Brightwork should be treated in the same way as paintwork. Windscreens and windows can be kept clear of the smeary film which often appears, by the use of proprietary glass cleaner. Never use any form of wax or other body or chromium polish on glass.

3 Maintenance - upholstery and carpets

Mats and carpets should be brushed or vacuum-cleaned regularly, to keep them free of grit. If they are badly stained, remove them from the vehicle for scrubbing or sponging, and make quite sure they are dry before refitting. Seats and interior trim panels can be kept clean by wiping with a damp cloth and a proprietary upholstery cleaner. If they do become stained (which can be more apparent on light-coloured upholstery), use a little liquid detergent and a soft nail brush to scour the grime out of the grain of the material. Do not forget to keep the headlining clean in the same way as the upholstery. When using liquid cleaners inside the vehicle, do not over-wet the surfaces being cleaned. Excessive damp could get into the seams and padded interior, causing stains, offensive odours or even rot. If the inside of the vehicle gets wet accidentally, it is worthwhile taking some trouble to dry it out properly, particularly where carpets are involved.

Caution: Do not leave oil or electric heaters inside the vehicle for this purpose.

4 Minor body damage - repair

Note: *For more detailed information about bodywork repair, Haynes Publishing produce a book called "The Car Bodywork Repair Manual". This incorporates information on such aspects as rust treatment, painting and glass-fibre repairs, as well as details on more ambitious repairs involving welding and panel beating.*

Repairs of minor scratches in bodywork

If the scratch is very superficial, and does not penetrate to the metal of the bodywork, repair is very simple. Lightly rub the area of the scratch with a paintwork renovator, or a very fine cutting paste, to remove loose paint from the scratch, and to clear the surrounding bodywork of wax polish. Rinse the area with clean water.

Apply touch-up paint to the scratch using a fine paint brush; continue to apply fine layers of paint until the surface of the paint in the scratch is level with the surrounding paintwork. Allow the new paint at least two weeks to harden, then blend it into the surrounding paintwork by rubbing the scratch area with a paintwork renovator or a very fine cutting paste. Finally apply wax polish.

Where the scratch has penetrated right through to the metal of the bodywork, causing the metal to rust, a different repair technique is required. Remove any loose rust from the bottom of the scratch with a penknife, then apply rust-inhibiting paint, to prevent the formation of rust in the future. Using a rubber or nylon applicator, fill the scratch with bodystopper paste. If required, this paste can be mixed with cellulose thinners, to provide a very thin paste which is ideal for filling narrow scratches. Before the stopper-paste in the scratch hardens, wrap a piece of smooth cotton rag around the top of a finger. Dip the finger in cellulose thinners, and quickly sweep it across the surface of the stopper-paste in the scratch; this will ensure that the surface of the stopper-paste is slightly hollowed. The scratch can now be painted over as described earlier in this Section.

Repairs of dents in bodywork

When deep denting of the vehicle's bodywork has taken place, the first task is to pull the dent out, until the affected bodywork almost attains its original shape. There is little point in trying to restore the original shape completely, as the metal in the damaged area will have stretched on impact, and cannot be reshaped fully to its original contour. It is better to bring the level of the dent up to a point which is about 3 mm below the level of the surrounding bodywork. In cases where the dent is very shallow anyway, it is not worth trying to pull it out at all. If the underside of the

dent is accessible, it can be hammered out gently from behind, using a mallet with a wooden or plastic head. Whilst doing this, hold a suitable block of wood firmly against the outside of the panel, to absorb the impact from the hammer blows and thus prevent a large area of the bodywork from being "belled-out".

Should the dent be in a section of the bodywork which has a double skin, or some other factor making it inaccessible from behind, a different technique is called for. Drill several small holes through the metal inside the area - particularly in the deeper section. Then screw long self-tapping screws into the holes, just sufficiently for them to gain a good purchase in the metal. Now the dent can be pulled out by pulling on the protruding heads of the screws with a pair of pliers.

The next stage of the repair is the removal of the paint from the damaged area, and from an inch or so of the surrounding "sound" bodywork. This is accomplished most easily by using a wire brush or abrasive pad on a power drill, although it can be done just as effectively by hand, using sheets of abrasive paper. To complete the preparation for filling, score the surface of the bare metal with a screwdriver or the tang of a file, or alternatively, drill small holes in the affected area. This will provide a really good "key" for the filler paste.

To complete the repair, see the Section on filling and respraying.

Repairs of rust holes or gashes in bodywork

Remove all paint from the affected area, and from an inch or so of the surrounding "sound" bodywork, using an abrasive pad or a wire brush on a power drill. If these are not available, a few sheets of abrasive paper will do the job most effectively. With the paint removed, you will be able to judge the severity of the corrosion, and therefore decide whether to renew the whole panel (if this is possible) or to repair the affected area. New body panels are not as expensive as most people think, and it is often quicker and more satisfactory to fit a new panel than to attempt to repair large areas of corrosion.

Remove all fittings from the affected area, except those which will act as a guide to the original shape of the damaged bodywork (eg headlight shells etc). Then, using tin snips or a hacksaw blade, remove all loose metal and any other metal badly affected by corrosion. Hammer the edges of the hole inwards, in order to create a slight depression for the filler paste.

Wire-brush the affected area to remove the powdery rust from the surface of the remaining metal. Paint the affected area with rust-inhibiting paint; if the back of the rusted area is accessible, treat this also.

Before filling can take place, it will be necessary to block the hole in some way. This can be achieved by the use of aluminium or plastic mesh, or aluminium tape.

Aluminium or plastic mesh, or glass-fibre matting, is probably the best material to use for a large hole. Cut a piece to the approximate size and shape of the hole to be filled, then position it in the hole so that its edges are below the level of the surrounding bodywork. It can be retained in position by several blobs of filler paste around its periphery.

Aluminium tape should be used for small or very narrow holes. Pull a piece off the roll, trim it to the approximate size and shape required, then pull off the backing paper (if used) and stick the tape over the hole; it can be overlapped if the thickness of one piece is insufficient. Burnish down the edges of the tape with the handle of a screwdriver or similar, to ensure that the tape is securely attached to the metal underneath.

Bodywork repairs - filling and respraying

Before using this Section, see the Sections on dent, minor scratch, rust holes and gash repairs.

Many types of bodyfiller are available, but generally speaking, those proprietary kits which contain a tin of filler paste and a tube of resin hardener are best for this type of repair; some can be used directly from the tube. A wide, flexible plastic or nylon applicator will be found invaluable for imparting a smooth and well-contoured finish to the surface of the filler.

Mix up a little filler on a clean piece of card or board - measure the hardener carefully (follow the maker's instructions on the pack), otherwise the filler will set too rapidly or too slowly. Using the applicator, apply the filler paste to the prepared area; draw the applicator across the surface of the filler to achieve the correct contour and to level the surface. As soon as a contour that approximates to the correct one is achieved, stop working the paste - if you carry on too long, the paste will become sticky and begin to "pick-up" on the applicator. Continue to add thin layers of filler paste at 20-minute intervals, until the level of the filler is just proud of the surrounding bodywork.

Once the filler has hardened, the excess can be removed using a metal plane or file. From then on, progressively-finer grades of abrasive paper should be used, starting with a 40-grade production paper, and finishing with a 400-grade wet-and-dry paper. Always wrap the abrasive paper around a flat rubber, cork, or wooden block - otherwise the surface of the filler will not be completely flat. During the smoothing of the filler surface, the wet-and-dry paper should be periodically rinsed in water. This will ensure that a very smooth finish is imparted to the filler at the final stage.

At this stage, the "dent" should be surrounded by a ring of bare metal, which in turn should be encircled by the finely "feathered" edge of the good paintwork. Rinse the repair area with clean water, until all of the dust produced by the rubbing-down operation has gone.

Spray the whole area with a light coat of primer - this will show up any imperfections in the surface of the filler. Repair these imperfections with fresh filler paste or bodystopper, and once more smooth the surface with abrasive paper. If bodystopper is used, it can be mixed with cellulose thinners, to form a really thin paste which is ideal for filling small holes. Repeat this spray-and-repair procedure until you are satisfied that the surface of the filler, and the feathered edge of the paintwork, are perfect. Clean the repair area with clean water, and allow to dry fully.

The repair area is now ready for final spraying. Paint spraying must be carried out in a warm, dry, windless and dust-free atmosphere. This condition can be created artificially if you have access to a large indoor working area, but if you are forced to work in the open, you will have to pick your day very carefully. If you are working indoors, dousing the floor in the work area with water will help to settle the dust which would otherwise be in the atmosphere. If the repair area is confined to one body panel, mask off the surrounding panels; this will help to minimise the effects of a slight mismatch in paint colours. Bodywork fittings (eg chrome strips, door handles etc) will also need to be masked off. Use genuine masking tape, and several thicknesses of newspaper, for the masking operations.

Before commencing to spray, agitate the aerosol can thoroughly, then spray a test area (an old tin, or similar) until the technique is mastered. Cover the repair area with a thick coat of primer; the thickness should be built up using several thin layers of paint, rather than one thick one. Using 400 grade wet-and-dry paper, rub down the surface of the primer until it is really smooth. While doing this, the work area should be thoroughly doused with water, and the wet-and-dry paper periodically rinsed in water. Allow to dry before spraying on more paint.

Spray on the top coat, again building up the thickness by using several thin layers of paint. Start spraying in the centre of the repair area, and then, using a circular motion, work outwards until the whole repair area and about 2 inches of the surrounding original paintwork is covered. Remove all masking material 10 to 15 minutes after spraying on the final coat of paint.

Allow the new paint at least two weeks to harden, then, using a paintwork renovator or a very fine cutting paste, blend the edges of the paint into the existing paintwork. Finally, apply wax polish.

Plastic components

With the use of more and more plastic body components by the vehicle manufacturers (eg bumpers, spoilers, and in some cases major body panels), rectification of more serious damage to such items has become a matter of either entrusting repair work to a specialist in this field, or renewing complete components. Repair of such damage by the DIY owner is not really feasible, owing to the cost of the equipment and materials required for effecting such repairs. The basic technique involves making a groove along the line of the crack in the plastic, using a rotary burr in a power drill. The damaged part is then welded back together, using a hot air gun to heat up and fuse a plastic filler rod into the groove. Any excess plastic is then removed, and the area rubbed down to a smooth finish. It is important that a filler rod of the correct plastic is used, as body components can be made of a variety of different types (eg polycarbonate, ABS, polypropylene).

Damage of a less serious nature (abrasions, minor cracks etc) can be repaired by the DIY owner using a two-part epoxy filler repair material. Once mixed in equal proportions, this is used in similar fashion to the bodywork filler used on metal panels. The filler is usually cured in twenty to thirty minutes, ready for sanding and painting.

If the owner is renewing a complete component himself, or if he has repaired it with epoxy filler, he will be left with the problem of finding a suitable paint for finishing which is compatible with the type of plastic used. At one time, the use of a universal paint was not possible, owing to the complex range of plastics encountered in body component applications. Standard paints, generally speaking, will not bond to plastic or rubber satisfactorily. However, it is now possible to obtain a plastic body parts finishing kit which consists of a pre-primer treatment, a primer and coloured top coat. Full instructions are normally supplied with a kit, but basically, the method of use is to first apply the pre-primer to the component concerned, and allow it to dry for up to 30 minutes. Then the primer is applied, and left to dry for about an hour before finally applying the special-coloured top coat. The result is a correctly-coloured component, where the paint will flex with the plastic or rubber, a property that standard paint does not normally posses.

5 Major body damage - repair

Where serious damage has occurred, or large areas need renewal due to neglect, it means that complete new panels will need welding-in, and this is best left to professionals. If the damage is due to impact, it will also be necessary to check completely the alignment of the bodyshell, and this can only be carried out accurately by a Peugeot dealer using special jigs. If the body is left misaligned, it is primarily dangerous, as the car will not handle properly, and secondly, uneven stresses will be imposed on the steering, suspension and possibly transmission, causing abnormal wear, or complete failure, particularly to such items as the tyres.

6.2 Removing a splash shield from the lower wheelarch

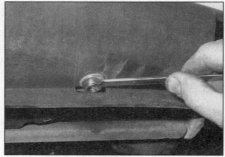

6.5 Removing a front bumper lower securing screw

6.6 Front bumper side securing nuts (arrowed) - spanner shown on hidden nut (viewed from underneath vehicle)

6.9 Front bumper to crossmember lower mountings (arrowed)

6.15a Front bumper rubber mounting buffer (arrowed)

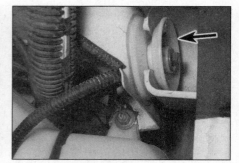

6.15b Ensure the bumper engages correctly with the buffer (arrowed) on refitting

6 Front bumper - removal and refitting

Removal

Pre-April 1997 models

1 For improved access, apply the handbrake, then jack up the front of the vehicle and support securely on axle stands (see *"Jacking and Vehicle Support"*).

2 Working at each side of the bumper, remove the screws, and where applicable drill out the rivets securing the splash shields and/or the wheelarch liners to the sides of the bumper **(see illustration)**.

3 On certain models, it may be necessary to remove the washer fluid reservoir for access to the right-hand bumper securing nuts.

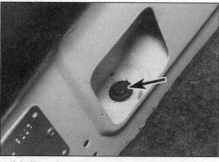

7.3 Rear bumper upper securing screw (arrowed)

4 On models with foglights, disconnect the battery negative terminal (refer to *"Disconnecting the battery"* in the Reference Section of this manual), then disconnect the foglight wiring connectors.

5 Working under the bumper, remove the remaining two self-tapping securing screws securing the bumper to the front body panel **(see illustration)**.

6 Again working under the bumper, unscrew the four nuts (two on each side) securing the bumper to the front body panel. Reach up behind the bumper for access to the bolts **(see illustration)**.

7 Carefully withdraw the bumper from the front of the vehicle.

April 1997 models onward

8 For improved access, apply the handbrake, then jack up the front of the vehicle and support securely on axle stands (see *"Jacking and Vehicle Support"*).

9 Undo the three bolts securing the bumper lower mountings to the crossmember **(see illustration)**.

10 Working at each side of the bumper, remove the screws, clips and where applicable drill out the rivets securing the splash shields and/or the wheelarch liners to the sides of the bumper.

11 Remove the washer fluid reservoir for access to the bumper right-hand attachments.

12 On models with foglights, disconnect the battery negative terminal (refer to *"Disconnecting the battery"* in the Reference Section of this manual), then disconnect the foglight wiring connectors.

13 Again working under the bumper, unscrew the four nuts (two on each side) securing the bumper to the front body panel. Reach up behind the bumper for access to the bolts.

14 Carefully withdraw the bumper from the front of the vehicle.

Refitting

All models

15 Refitting is a reversal of removal, but note that the fit of the bumper can be adjusted by altering the position of the eccentric rubber mounting buffers at the sides of the bumper. Ensure that the bumper engages with the buffers on refitting **(see illustrations)**.

7 Rear bumper - removal and refitting

Removal

Pre-April 1997 models

1 For improved access, chock the front wheels, then jack up the rear of the vehicle and support securely on axle stands (see *"Jacking and Vehicle Support"*).

2 Disconnect the battery negative terminal (refer to *"Disconnecting the battery"* in the Reference Section of this manual).

3 Open the tailgate, and remove the four upper bumper securing screws **(see illustration)**.

7.4 Disconnecting the rear number plate light wiring connector

7.5 Remove the screws securing the wheelarch liners to the rear bumper

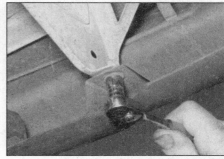

7.6a Unscrew the lower bumper securing screws . . .

4 Working at the rear left-hand side of the luggage compartment, remove the two securing nuts and withdraw the rear cover from the light unit, then disconnect the rear number plate light wiring connector (**see illustration**).

5 Working under the bumper, remove the two screws securing the wheelarch liners to the bumper (**see illustration**).

6 Working under the bumper, unscrew the two lower bumper securing screws, then unscrew the bolts (one on each side) securing the corners of the bumper to the body - prise back the insulation for access to the two side bolts (**see illustrations**).

7 Carefully withdraw the bumper from the vehicle, withdrawing the number plate wiring from the rear body panel as the bumper is withdrawn. Note the routing of the wiring.

April 1997 models onward

8 Chock the front wheels, then jack up the rear of the vehicle and support securely on axle stands (see *"Jacking and Vehicle Support"*). Remove the rear roadwheels.

9 Disconnect the battery negative terminal (refer to *"Disconnecting the battery"* in the Reference Section of this manual).

10 Working at each side of the bumper, remove the screws, clips and where applicable drill out the rivets securing the splash shields and/or the wheelarch liners to the sides and rear of the bumper (**see illustrations**).

11 Open the boot lid or tailgate and withdraw the weatherstrip along the base of the luggage compartment aperture (**see illustration**).

12 Unscrew the six screws securing the upper edge of the bumper to the body (**see illustration**).

13 Working under the bumper, disconnect the wiring harness connectors then undo the bolt securing the bumper to the bumper bracket each side (**see illustration**).

14 Unscrew the bolts (one on each side, just to the rear of the wheelarch) securing the sides of the bumper to the body.

15 Carefully withdraw the bumper from the rear of the vehicle.

Refitting

16 Refitting is a reversal of removal but, where applicable, make sure that the rear number plate wiring is correctly routed as noted before removal.

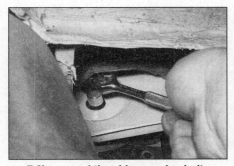

7.6b . . . and the side securing bolts

7.10a Splash shield to rear bumper retaining screw at the side of the bumper (arrowed) . . .

7.10b . . . and at the rear (arrowed)

7.11 Withdraw the weatherstrip along the base of the luggage compartment aperture

7.12 Undo the six screws securing the upper edge of the bumper

7.13 Undo the bolt (arrowed) securing the bumper to the bracket each side

9.3 Removing the bonnet release lever securing bolt

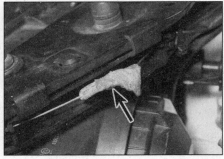

9.5 Bonnet release cable connecting plate (arrowed)

8 Bonnet and support struts - removal, refitting and adjustment

Bonnet

Removal

1 Open the bonnet and have an assistant support it, then, using a pencil or felt tip pen, mark the outline of each bonnet hinge relative to the bonnet, to use as a guide on refitting.
2 On later models, release the spring clips using a screwdriver and pull the bonnet support struts from the balljoints on the bonnet.
3 Disconnect the windscreen washer fluid pipe from its non-return valve on the left-hand side of the bonnet.
4 Unscrew the bonnet retaining bolts and, with the help of the assistant, carefully lift the bonnet from the vehicle. Store the bonnet out of the way in a safe place.
5 Inspect the bonnet hinges for signs of wear and free play at the pivots, and if necessary renew. Each hinge is secured to the body by two bolts. On refitting, apply a smear of multi-purpose grease to the hinges.

Refitting and adjustment

6 With the aid of an assistant, offer up the bonnet and loosely fit the retaining bolts. Align the hinges with the marks made on removal, then tighten the retaining bolts securely, and reconnect the windscreen washer fluid pipe.
7 On later models, reconnect the support struts and secure with the spring clips.

9.18 Disconnect the bonnet release cable from the lock lever (arrowed)

8 Close the bonnet, and check for alignment with the adjacent panels. If necessary, slacken the hinge bolts and re-align the bonnet to suit. Once the bonnet is correctly aligned, tighten the hinge bolts securely.
9 Once the bonnet is correctly aligned, check that the bonnet fastens and releases in a satisfactory manner. If adjustment is necessary, slacken the bonnet lock retaining bolts, and adjust the position of the lock to suit. Once the lock is operating correctly, securely tighten its retaining bolts.

Support struts

10 On later models fitted with bonnet support struts, proceed as described for the tailgate support struts on Hatchback models in Section 15.

9 Bonnet release cable - removal and refitting

General

1 The cable consists of two halves, joined at a connecting plate in the engine compartment.

Release lever-to-connecting plate cable

Removal

2 Working in the footwell, carefully prise the weather seal from the edge of the door aperture.
3 Unscrew the release lever assembly securing bolt, then withdraw the lever from the footwell (see illustration).
4 Unscrew the lower facia securing bolt, then pull the facia forward slightly from the bulkhead, and insert a wedge (ideally a rubber block) between the facia and the door pillar to hold the facia clear of the bulkhead.
5 Working in the engine compartment, locate the cable connecting plate, which is positioned in a housing at the front of the engine compartment (see illustration).
6 Remove the anti-squeal foam from the cable connector, then disconnect the release lever cable from the connector.
7 Remove the end fitting from the cable.
8 Tie a length of string to the end of the cable

in the engine compartment, then release the cable from any securing clips in the engine compartment, and carefully pull the cable through into the vehicle interior, noting its routing.
9 Untie the string from the end of the cable, and leave it in position to aid refitting.

Refitting

10 Commence refitting by tying the end of the new cable to the string in the vehicle interior.
11 Use the string to pull the cable through into the engine compartment, routing it as noted before removal.
12 Pull the bulkhead grommet into position, and make sure that it is securely seated in the bulkhead aperture. Note that it may be necessary to push the grommet into position using a suitable long screwdriver or similar tool inserted between the facia and the body.
13 Further refitting is a reversal of removal.

Connecting plate-to-lock cable

Removal

14 Working in the engine compartment, locate the cable connecting plate, which is positioned in a housing at the front of the engine compartment.
15 Remove the anti-squeal foam from the cable connector, then disconnect the release lever cable from the connector.
16 Remove the end fitting from the cable.
17 To improve access to the lock, remove the front grille panel as described in Section 27.
18 Disconnect the end of the cable from the lock, then unclip the cable outer from the bracket on the lock, release the cable from any clips on the body, and withdraw the cable, noting its routing (see illustration).

Refitting

19 Refitting is a reversal of removal.

10 Bonnet lock - removal and refitting

Removal

1 Open the bonnet. If desired for improved access, remove the front grille panel as described in Section 27.
2 Unscrew the two bolts securing the lock assembly to the body front panel, then lift out the lock and disconnect the bonnet release cable from the lock lever. Where applicable, disconnect the wiring plug from the alarm switch mounted on the lock.

Refitting

3 Refitting is a reversal of removal, but when reconnecting the release cable to the lock lever, make sure that the anti-squeal grommet is in place in the lever hole.
4 On completion, check the operation of the lock. If necessary, adjust the position of the lock within the elongated bolt holes to achieve satisfactory operation.

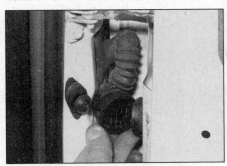

11.2 Disconnecting a front door wiring connector

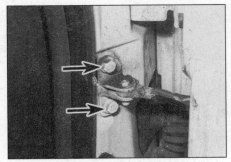

11.3 Unscrew the two bolts (arrowed) securing the check strap to the door pillar

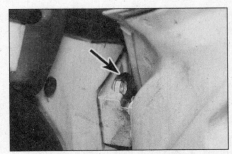

11.6 Working through the wheelarch, loosen the hinge bolts (arrowed) to adjust the position of the door

11 Door -
removal, refitting and adjustment

Front door

Removal

1 Disconnect the battery negative terminal (refer to *"Disconnecting the battery"* in the Reference Section of this manual).
2 Open the door, then release the locking ring and disconnect the door wiring connector from the socket in the front door pillar **(see illustration)**.
3 Unscrew the two securing bolts, and disconnect the door check strap from the door pillar **(see illustration)**.
4 Ensure that the door is adequately supported, then unscrew the bolts securing

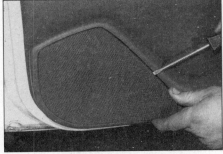

12.2 Prising out the front door loudspeaker cover panel

the hinges to the door, and lift the door from the vehicle.
5 If desired, the hinges can be unbolted from the body.

Refitting and adjustment

6 Refitting is a reversal of removal, but on completion, check the fit of the door in relation to the surrounding body panels, and if necessary adjust as follows:
a) *Jack up the front of the vehicle, and support securely on axle stands (see "Jacking and Vehicle Support").*
b) *Remove the roadwheel and wheelarch liner.*
c) *Close the door.*
d) *Using a suitable spanner through the wheelarch, loosen the bolts securing the door hinges to the body, and adjust the position of the door to provide a satisfactory fit (see illustration). Tighten the bolts on completion.*
e) *If necessary, the bolts securing the hinges to the door can also be loosened to provide additional adjustment.*

Rear door

7 The procedure is as described for the front doors, bearing in mind the following points:
a) *In order to disconnect the door electrical wiring, it will be necessary to remove the door inner trim panel (see Section 12) and disconnect the wiring inside the door.*
b) *The hinge-to-body bolts can be accessed with the front door open.*

12 Door inner trim panel -
removal and refitting

Front door -
pre-April 1997 models

Removal

1 Disconnect the battery negative terminal (refer to *"Disconnecting the battery"* in the Reference Section of this manual).
2 Where applicable (on models with basic trim), remove the screws securing the loudspeaker cover panel. Alternatively, prise the cover panel from the door **(see illustration)**.
3 Remove the securing screws, then withdraw the loudspeaker from its housing and disconnect the wiring plug.
4 Remove the trim panel securing screws from the edge of the door pocket, and remove the remaining lower trim panel securing screw, which is accessible through the loudspeaker housing **(see illustrations)**.
5 Where applicable, prise out the armrest trim plate then, where applicable, push out the electric mirror switch, and reach through the aperture to push out the electric window switches. Disconnect the wiring plugs from the switches **(see illustration)**.
6 Prise out the cover plate and unscrew the front armrest securing nut. Remove the securing screws, and withdraw the armrest **(see illustrations)**.

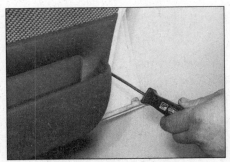

12.4a Remove the trim panel screws from the edge of the door pocket . . .

12.4b . . . and from the loudspeaker housing

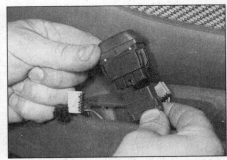

12.5 Prise the switches from the door pocket, and disconnect the wiring plugs

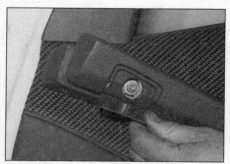

12.6a Prise out the cover plate to expose the armrest securing nut . . .

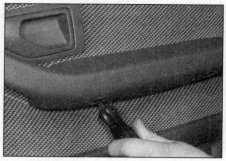

12.6b . . . then remove the securing screws . . .

12.6c . . . and withdraw the armrest

7 Unclip the interior handle surround **(see illustration)**.
8 Unclip the mirror trim panel **(see illustration)**.
9 On models with manual windows, pull the

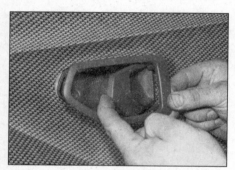

12.7 Unclip the interior handle surround

winder handle off the spindle, and then remove the spindle trim plate.
10 Lift up the inner door lock operating button, then, using a small screwdriver, depress the retaining tab, and slide off the button **(see illustration)**.
11 Using a suitable forked tool, work around the edge of the door trim panel, and release the panel securing clips.
12 Pull the panel from the door, and feed the wiring looms through the panel.

Refitting

13 Refitting is a reversal of removal, bearing in mind the following points:
a) *Before refitting, check whether any of the trim panel retaining studs were broken on removal, and renew them as necessary.*
b) *To refit the inner door lock operating button, first lock the door, to ensure that*

the link rod is in its lowest position. *Position the button locating tab in the lower of its two holes, then firmly push the button onto the rod, until it clips into position and the retaining tab appears in the upper hole (see illustrations).*

Front door - April 1997 models onward

Removal

14 Disconnect the battery negative terminal (refer to *"Disconnecting the battery"* in the Reference Section of this manual).
15 Using a small screwdriver, carefully prise out the trim cap covering the panel front upper securing screw then undo the screw now exposed **(see illustration)**.
16 Undo the door panel centre securing screw located below the front of the armrest **(see illustration)**.

12.8 Unclip the mirror trim panel

12.10 Remove the lock operating button

12.13a Position the lock button locating tab in the lower position

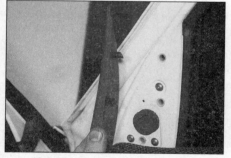

12.13b Push the button onto the rod until the retaining tab appears in the upper hole

12.15 Prise out the trim cap and undo the screw now exposed

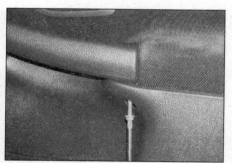

12.16 Undo the centre securing screw below the armrest

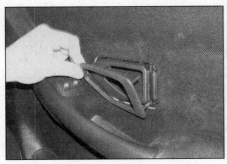

12.17 Withdraw the interior handle surround

12.19a Prise out the switch control panel . . .

12.19b . . . and disconnect the wiring plugs

17 Release the interior handle surround at the rear, then withdraw the surround from the door panel **(see illustration)**.
18 On models with manual windows, pull the

winder handle off the spindle, and then remove the spindle trim plate.
19 Where applicable, prise out the electric window and mirror switch control panel using a wide spatula. Disconnect the wiring plugs from the switches and remove the control panel **(see illustrations)**.
20 Undo the panel securing bolt located in the switch control panel aperture **(see illustration)**.
21 Carefully prise off the exterior mirror inner trim panel **(see illustration)**.
22 Prise off the loudspeaker cover panel then undo the screws securing the loudspeaker to the door panel. Withdraw the loudspeaker and disconnect the wiring connectors **(see illustrations)**.
23 Using a suitable forked tool, work around the edge of the door trim panel, and release the panel securing clips **(see illustration)**.

24 Pull the panel from the door, and feed the wiring looms through the panel.

Refitting

25 Before refitting, check whether any of the trim panel retaining studs were broken on removal. Renew the panel retaining studs as necessary, then refit the panel using a reversal of removal.

Rear door- pre-April 1997 models

Removal

26 On models with electric windows and/or central locking, disconnect the battery negative terminal (refer to *"Disconnecting the battery"* in the Reference Section of this manual).
27 Remove the securing screws and withdraw the armrest **(see illustration)**.

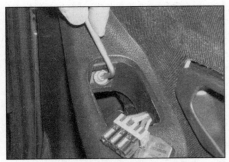

12.20 Undo the bolt located in the switch panel aperture

12.21 Prise off the mirror trim panel

12.22a Remove the loudspeaker cover panel . . .

12.22b . . . Undo the loudspeaker securing screws . . .

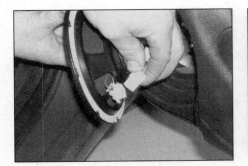

12.22c . . . remove the loudspeaker and disconnect the wiring

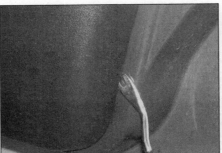

12.23 Release the trim panel clips using a forked tool

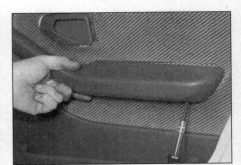

12.27 Removing a rear door armrest securing screw

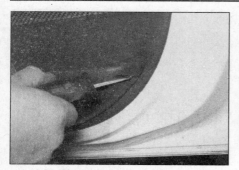

12.28 Removing a rear door pocket securing screw

12.32 Remove the trim panel securing screw from the lock button surround

13.2 Remove the interior door handle, and disconnect the link rod (arrowed)

28 Remove the securing screws and withdraw the door pocket **(see illustration)**.

29 Unclip the interior handle surround.

30 On models with manual windows, pull the winder handle off the spindle, and then remove the spindle trim plate.

31 Lift up the inner door lock operating button. Using a small screwdriver, depress the retaining tab, and slide off the button.

32 Remove the screw from the bottom of the door lock button surround **(see illustration)**.

33 Using a suitable forked tool, work around the edge of the door trim panel, and release the panel securing clips.

34 Pull the panel from the door, and disconnect all relevant wiring connectors.

Refitting

35 Refitting is a reversal of removal, bearing in mind the points made in paragraph 13.

Rear door-
April 1997 models onward

Removal

36 Using a small screwdriver, carefully prise out the trim cap covering the panel upper securing screw then undo the screw now exposed.

37 Undo the door panel centre securing screw located below the front of the armrest.

38 Release the interior handle surround at the rear, then withdraw the surround from the door panel.

39 On models with manual windows, pull the winder handle off the spindle, and then remove the spindle trim plate.

40 Using a suitable forked tool, work around the edge of the door trim panel, and release the panel securing clips.

41 Pull the panel from the door and lift up to remove.

Refitting

42 Refitting is a reversal of removal.

13 Door handle and lock components - removal and refitting

Interior door handle

Removal

1 Remove the door inner trim panel, as described in Section 12.

2 Slide the handle assembly towards the front of the door, then pull the assembly from the door aperture, and disconnect the link rod (if necessary, release the link rod from the clips on the door) **(see illustration)**.

Refitting

3 Refitting is a reversal of removal, but ensure that the link rod is correctly reconnected, and refit the inner trim panel (see Section 12).

Exterior door handle

Removal

Note: *A new door sealing sheet will be required on refitting.*

4 Remove the door inner trim panel (Section 12).

5 Remove the appropriate plastic sealing sheet for access to the handle through the aperture in the inside of the door.

6 Working inside the door, unscrew the front handle securing nut **(see illustration)**.

7 Working outside the door, unscrew the rear handle securing screw **(see illustration)**.

8 Withdraw the handle from the outside of the door, and disconnect the lock operating rod from the handle as it is removed **(see illustration)**.

Refitting

9 Refitting is a reversal of removal, but fit a new sealing sheet to the door, and refit the inner trim panel as described in Section 12.

Front door lock cylinder

10 The lock cylinder can be removed as follows, without the need to remove the door inner trim panel:

a) *Make up a suitable tool using a medium-size self-tapping screw brazed to a length of rod, bent at a right-angle.*

b) *Open the door, and prise the cover plate from the rear edge of the door.*

c) *Insert the tool through the aperture in the edge of the door **(see illustration)**, and screw the self-tapping screw into the lock securing clip to the end of the thread on the screw.*

d) *Pull the tool to release the securing clip, and withdraw the lock cylinder from outside the door **(see illustration)**. Leave the tool engaged with the clip.*

e) *Refit the lock, and use the tool to push the securing clip into position.*

13.6 Unscrew the front handle securing nut . . .

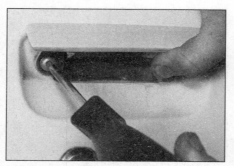

13.7 . . . and the rear securing screw . . .

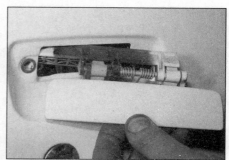

13.8 . . . then withdraw the door exterior handle

f) Ensure that the clip is securely engaged with the lock cylinder, then unscrew the tool from the clip, and refit the cover plate.

Removal

Note: *A new door sealing sheet will be required on refitting.*

11 Remove the door inner trim panel (Section 12).

12 Remove the relevant plastic sealing sheet for access to the lock through the aperture in the door.

13 Working inside the door, pull the clip from the rear of the lock cylinder, then remove the lock cylinder from the outside of the door.

Refitting

14 Refitting is a reversal of removal, but ensure that the lock cylinder securing clip is securely refitted, and use a new plastic sealing sheet. Refit the door inner trim panel (Section 12).

Front door lock

Removal

Note: *A new door sealing sheet will be required on refitting.*

15 Remove the door inner trim panel (Section 12).

16 Remove the relevant plastic sealing sheet for access to the door lock through the aperture in the door.

17 Remove the door lock cylinder, and the interior and exterior door handles, as described previously in this Section.

13.10a Insert the tool through the aperture in the rear of the door

18 Remove the lock rod clip, and the plastic trim clip from the door. It will be necessary to slide the retaining plate from the trim clip before it can be removed **(see illustrations)**.

19 Push the lock button operating rod forwards before removing assembly.

20 Unscrew the three lock securing screws from the rear edge of the door.

21 Pull back the insulation from the lock button operating rod, then twist the assembly, and manipulate the assembly out through the top door aperture **(see illustrations)**.

Refitting

22 Refitting is a reversal of removal, bearing in mind the following points:

a) Feed the assembly into position, top end first, and ensure the lock rods are between the inner door skin and the window regulator channel (see illustration).

13.10b Withdrawing the lock cylinder

b) As the lock is refitted, feed the lock button rod up through the hole in the door.

c) Fit a new plastic sealing sheet to the door. Refit the inner trim panel (see Section 12).

Rear door lock

Removal

Note: *A new door sealing sheet will be required on refitting.*

23 Remove the door inner trim panel as described in Section 12.

24 Remove the plastic sealing sheets from the inside of the door.

25 Slide the door interior handle assembly towards the rear of the door, then pull the assembly from the door aperture, and disconnect the link rod. Release the link rod from the clips on the door **(see illustration)**.

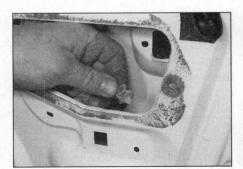

13.18a Remove the lock rod clip . . .

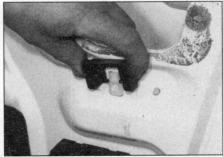

13.18b . . . then slide off the retaining plate . . .

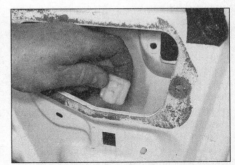

13.18c . . . and remove the trim clip

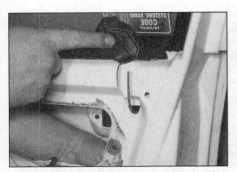

13.21a Pull the insulation from the lock button operating rod

13.21b Manipulate the lock assembly out through the top door aperture

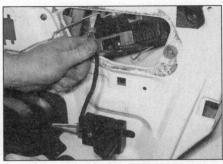

13.22 Feed the lock into position, top end first

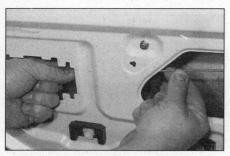

13.25 Release the rear door interior handle link rod from the clips

13.26 Release the securing clip, and push the bellcrank from the door panel

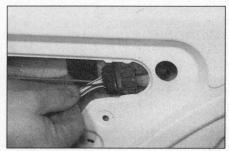

13.27 Disconnect the wiring plug from the lock

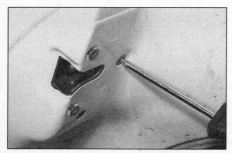

13.28 Unscrew the three lock securing screws

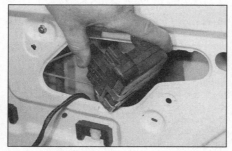

13.30 Withdraw the lock assembly through the top door aperture

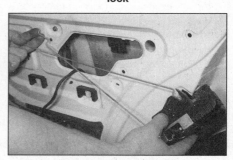

13.31 Make sure that the link rods are crossed over before refitting

26 Working at the front of the door, release the securing clip, and push the lock button rod bellcrank from the inside of the door panel (see illustration).
27 Disconnect the wiring plug from the lock (see illustration).
28 Working at the rear edge of the door, remove the three lock securing screws (see illustration).
29 Push the longer link rod down towards the bottom of the door.
30 Withdraw the lock assembly through the top door aperture, bending the longer link rod as necessary (see illustration).

Refitting

31 Refitting is a reversal of removal, bearing in mind the following points:
  a) Make sure that the link rods are crossed over before refitting (see illustration).
  b) Make sure that the child-proof lock lever is in the "down" position.

  c) Fit the lower part of the lock first.
  d) Ensure that the link rods pass between the regulator and the inner door skin.
  e) Push the longer link rod down, and bend it to allow the lock to be fitted.

14 Door window glass and regulator - removal and refitting

Front door window glass

Removal

Note: *A new door sealing sheet will be required on refitting.*

1 Remove the door inner trim panel (Section 12).
2 Lower the window two-thirds of the way.
3 Pull the weatherstrip from the lower edge of the window aperture (see illustration).

4 Partially pull the weatherstrip from the rear and upper edge of the window aperture (see illustration).
5 If applicable, disconnect the wiring plug from the electric windows control unit, and move the wiring to one side (see illustration).
6 Remove the moulded sealing sheet from the door (see illustration).
7 Working inside the door, remove the plastic clip securing the glass to the regulator mechanism (see illustrations).
8 Lift the glass from the outside of the door.

Refitting

9 Refitting is a reversal of removal, bearing in mind the following points:
  a) To ease refitting, coat the weatherstrips with soapy water (washing-up liquid is ideal).
  b) Fit a new moulded sealing sheet.
  c) Refit the door inner trim panel with reference to Section 12.

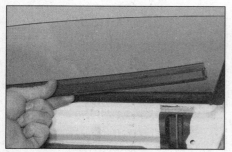

14.3 Pull the weatherstrip from the lower edge of the window aperture . . .

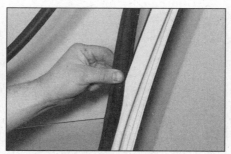

14.4 . . . and release the weatherstrip from the rear and upper edge

14.5 Disconnect the wiring plug from the electric windows control unit

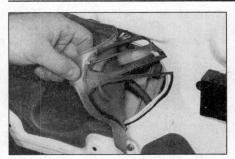

14.6 Remove the moulded sealing sheet

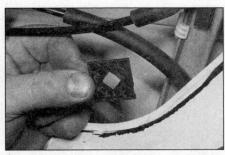

14.7a Remove the plastic clip securing the glass to the regulator

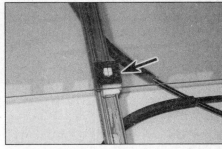

14.7b Plastic glass retaining clip (arrowed) viewed with assembly removed from door

14.11 Disconnect the wiring plug from the window lift motor

14.12 Drill out the rivets securing the regulator mechanism to the door

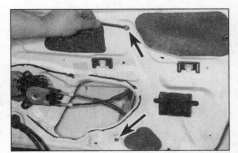

14.13 Remove the two nuts securing the window lift rail

Front door regulator

Note: *Three 6.0 mm nuts and bolts will be needed for the regulator assembly on refitting.*

Removal

10 Remove the window glass as described previously.
11 If applicable, disconnect the wiring plug(s) from the window lift motor **(see illustration)**.

14.14 Lift the assembly out through the door aperture

12 Using a 6.0 mm drill, drill out the rivets securing the regulator mechanism to the door **(see illustration)**.
13 Remove the two nuts securing the window lift rail **(see illustration)**.
14 Tilt the assembly, and lift it out through the aperture in the door **(see illustration)**.
15 Remove the rivet swarf from inside the bottom of the door.

Refitting

16 Refitting is a reversal of removal, but refit the regulator mechanism using 6.0 mm nuts and bolts instead of rivets, and refit the window glass as described previously in this Section. Note that the cables must be "crossed" when refitting.

Rear door sliding window glass

Note: *A new door sealing sheet will be required on refitting.*
17 Proceed as described previously for the front door glass, noting the following points:
 a) Fully lower the window glass.

b) Unclip the weatherstrip from the window aperture as necessary to allow sufficient clearance to remove the glass.

Rear door fixed window glass

Removal

18 Fully lower the sliding window glass.
19 Unclip the weatherstrip from the rear glass channel, and from the top of the sliding window aperture **(see illustration)**.
20 Remove the upper and lower screws securing the rear glass channel to the door, and withdraw the channel **(see illustrations)**.
21 Carefully pull the fixed glass panel towards the front of the door, and withdraw it.

Refitting

22 Refer to paragraph 9.

Rear door regulator

23 The procedure is as described previously for the front door regulator. Note that there is no need to remove the fixed window glass.

14.19 Unclip the weatherstrip from the window aperture . . .

14.20a . . . for access to the upper (arrowed) . . .

14.20b . . . and lower (arrowed) window channel securing screws

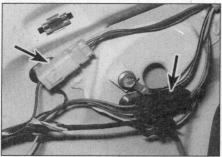

15.4 Disconnect the tailgate wiring connectors (arrowed)

15 Tailgate and support struts (Hatchback models) - removal and refitting

Tailgate

Removal

1 Disconnect the battery negative terminal (refer to *"Disconnecting the battery"* in the Reference Section of this manual).

2 The tailgate wiring can be disconnected at the connectors behind the rear quarter light trim panels, or the wiring can be disconnected from the individual components inside the tailgate, as desired. Proceed as follows according to which option is to be followed.

Disconnecting wiring behind rear quarter light trim panel

3 Remove the rear side trim or rear quarter light and wheelarch trim panels, according to model, as described in Section 30.

4 Separate the two halves of each tailgate wiring connector, then tie lengths of string to each wiring harness **(see illustration)**.

5 Pull the wiring through the body panel to emerge from the top of the rear body panel in front of the tailgate. Untie the string from the harnesses, and leave the string in position to aid refitting.

6 Similarly, disconnect the washer fluid hose.

7 Proceed to paragraph 16.

Disconnecting wiring from components inside tailgate

8 Remove the screws securing the tailgate trim panel, then withdraw the panel from the tailgate.

9 Disconnect the heated rear window wiring connectors from the contacts on the tailgate.

10 Disconnect the wiring plug from the luggage compartment light switch, and from the alarm sensor switch, where applicable.

11 Where applicable, working through the aperture in the tailgate, disconnect the tailgate wiper motor and the central locking motor wiring plugs.

12 Disconnect the washer fluid hose from the wiper motor assembly.

13 Release the wiring and the washer fluid hose from any clips inside the tailgate.

14 Pull the wiring grommets from the top corners of the tailgate **(see illustration)**.

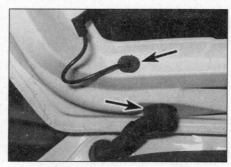

15.14 Pull the wiring grommets (arrowed) from the tailgate

15 If the original tailgate is to be refitted, tie a string to the ends of all the relevant wiring, then feed the wiring through the top of the tailgate. Untie the string, leaving it in position in the tailgate to assist refitting.

All procedures

16 Support the tailgate, then prise out the support strut spring clips, and pull the struts from the balljoints on the tailgate.

17 Unscrew the bolts securing the hinges to the top of the tailgate, and carefully lift the tailgate from the vehicle.

Refitting

18 If a new tailgate is to be fitted, transfer all serviceable components (rubber buffers, lock mechanism, etc) to it.

19 Refitting is a reversal of removal, bearing in mind the following points:

a) If the original tailgate is being refitted, draw the wiring and washer fluid hose (where applicable) through the tailgate, or through the body panel (as applicable) using the string.

b) If necessary, adjust the rubber buffers to obtain a good fit when the tailgate is shut.

c) If necessary, adjust the position of the tailgate lock within its elongated holes to achieve satisfactory lock operation.

Adjustment

20 If necessary, the position of the tailgate in relation to the body can be adjusted by loosening the bolts securing the tailgate hinges to the body, and moving the hinges (the bolt holes are elongated).

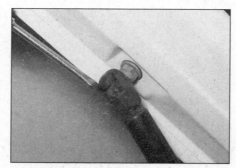

15.24 Use a screwdriver to release the tailgate support strut spring clips

21 For access to the hinge-to-body bolts, prise the weatherstrips from the edges of the tailgate aperture, then prise off the rear roof trim panel. If necessary, prise out the rear courtesy light, and lower the rear of the headlining for improved access.

22 If necessary, the rubber buffers at the lower corners of the tailgate can be adjusted to obtain a good fit when the tailgate is shut. The tailgate lock can be adjusted by altering the position of the lock in its elongated holes.

Support struts

Removal

23 Support the tailgate in the open position, with the help of an assistant, or using a stout piece of wood.

24 Using a suitable flat-bladed screwdriver, release the spring clip, and pull the support strut from its balljoint on the tailgate **(see illustration)**.

25 Similarly, release the strut from the balljoint on the body, and withdraw the strut from the vehicle.

Refitting

26 Refitting is a reversal of removal, but ensure the spring clips are correctly engaged.

16 Tailgate and support struts (Estate models) - removal and refitting

Tailgate

Removal

Note: *The following procedure describes removal and refitting of the tailgate and the adjustments that can be carried out at the rubber buffers and tailgate lock. If the fit of the tailgate in relation to the body aperture is excessively out of adjustment after refitting, it will be necessary to reposition the tailgate hinges by slackening the hinge to body retaining bolts. Access to these bolts, however, entails partial removal of the headlining which is a difficult and involved procedure (see Section 30). Be prepared for the additional work that may be needed to achieve accurate adjustment after refitting, or have the adjustment carried out by a Peugeot dealer.*

1 Disconnect the battery negative terminal (refer to *"Disconnecting the battery"* in the Reference Section of this manual).

2 The tailgate wiring can be disconnected at the connectors behind the rear quarter window trim panels, or the wiring can be disconnected from the individual components inside the tailgate, as desired. Proceed as follows according to which option is to be followed.

Disconnecting wiring behind rear quarter window trim panels

3 Remove the rear quarter window trim panels from the rear passenger compartment, as described in Section 30.

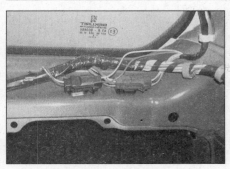

16.4 Tailgate wiring connectors located behind the trim panel on Estate models

16.17 Tailgate left-hand hinge retaining bolts (arrowed) on Estate models

4 Separate the two halves of each tailgate wiring connector on both sides of the vehicle, then tie lengths of string to each wiring harness **(see illustration)**. Release the cable clips securing the wiring to the body.
5 Release the wiring grommets located between the body and tailgate, then pull the wiring through the body panel to emerge from the top of the rear body panel in front of the tailgate. Untie the string from the harnesses, and leave the string in position to aid refitting.
6 Similarly, disconnect the washer fluid hose.
7 Proceed to paragraph 16.

Disconnecting wiring from components inside tailgate

8 Remove the tailgate trim panel as described in Section 30.
9 Disconnect the heated rear window wiring connectors from the contacts on the tailgate.
10 Disconnect the wiring plug from the luggage compartment light switch, and from the alarm sensor switch, where applicable.
11 Where applicable, working through the aperture in the tailgate, disconnect the tailgate wiper motor and the central locking motor wiring plugs.
12 Disconnect the washer fluid hose from the wiper motor assembly.
13 Release the wiring and the washer fluid hose from any clips inside the tailgate.
14 Pull the wiring grommets from the top corners of the tailgate.
15 If the original tailgate is to be refitted, tie a string to the ends of all the relevant wiring, then feed the wiring through the top of the tailgate. Untie the string, leaving it in position in the tailgate to assist refitting.

All procedures

16 Support the tailgate, then prise out the support strut spring clips, and pull the struts from the balljoints on the tailgate.
17 Unscrew the bolts securing the hinges to the top of the tailgate, and carefully lift the tailgate from the vehicle **(see illustration)**.

Refitting

18 If a new tailgate is to be fitted, transfer all serviceable components (rubber buffers, lock mechanism, etc) to it.
19 Refitting is a reversal of removal, bearing in mind the following points:

a) If the original tailgate is being refitted, draw the wiring and washer fluid hose (where applicable) through the tailgate, or through the body panel (as applicable) using the string.
b) If necessary, adjust the rubber buffers to obtain a good fit when the tailgate is shut.
c) If necessary, adjust the position of the tailgate lock within its elongated holes to achieve satisfactory lock operation.

Adjustment

20 If necessary, the rubber buffers at the lower corners of the tailgate can be adjusted to obtain a good fit when the tailgate is shut. The tailgate lock can be adjusted by altering the position of the lock in its elongated holes.
21 The position of the tailgate in relation to the body can be adjusted by loosening the bolts securing the tailgate hinges to the body, and moving the hinges (the bolt holes are elongated).

22 For access to the hinge-to-body bolts, it will be necessary to locally detach the rear portion of the headlining as described in Section 30.

Support struts

23 Proceed as described for the tailgate support struts on Hatchback models in Section 15.

---

17 Tailgate lock components (Hatchback and Estate models) - removal and refitting

Tailgate lock

Removal

1 Remove the tailgate trim panel as described in Section 30.
2 Working through the aperture in the lower edge of the tailgate, disconnect the lock operating rod.
3 Unscrew the two lock securing screws, and withdraw the lock **(see illustration)**.

Refitting

4 Refitting is a reversal of removal, but ensure that the lock lever engages correctly as the lock is positioned in the tailgate.

Tailgate lock cylinder

Removal

5 Open the tailgate.
6 Remove the tailgate trim panel as described in Section 30.
7 Where fitted, remove the tailgate wiper motor as described in Chapter 12.
8 Working at the lower edge of the tailgate, unscrew the right-hand central locking motor securing screws, and loosen the left-hand screw sufficiently to allow the motor to be slid from its location. Slide the motor from the tailgate, then unhook the lock operating rod and disconnect the wiring plug from the motor **(see illustrations)**.
9 Unhook the lock cylinder rod from the lock.
10 Remove the two securing screws and withdraw the lock cylinder from outside the tailgate **(see illustrations)**.

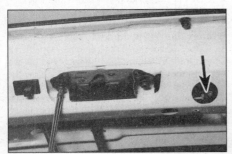

17.3 Disconnect the lock operating rod (arrowed), then unscrew the lock securing screws

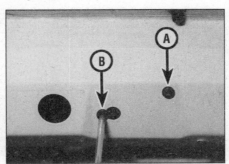

17.8a Remove the right-hand screw (A) and loosen the left-hand screw (B) ...

17.8b ... then withdraw the central locking motor

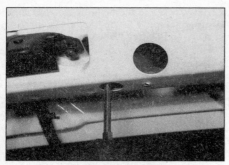

17.10a Removing a lock securing screw

17.10b Withdraw the lock cylinder . . .

17.11 . . . and recover the inner lock

11 Recover the inner lock section from inside the tailgate **(see illustration)**.

Refitting

12 Refitting is a reversal of removal, bearing in mind the following points:
  a) *Ensure that the operating rod is in position on the lock cylinder when refitting.*
  b) *Feed the operating rod through the inner section of the lock as it is refitted.*
  c) *Check that the lock mechanism operates correctly before refitting the tailgate trim panel.*

Tailgate lock striker

Removal

13 On Estate models, undo the screws and remove the cover panels for access to the striker plate bolts.
14 Mark the position of the striker on the body, for use when refitting. Unscrew the two securing bolts, and remove the striker from the body.

Refitting

15 Refitting is a reversal of removal. Before tightening the securing bolts, the position of the striker should be altered (the securing bolt holes are elongated) until satisfactory lock operation is obtained. Use the marks made prior to removal, if appropriate.

---

18 Boot lid and support struts (Sedan models) - removal and refitting

Boot lid

Removal

1 Disconnect the battery negative terminal (refer to *"Disconnecting the battery"* in the Reference Section of this manual).
2 Remove the clips securing the trim panel, then withdraw the panel from the boot lid.
3 Disconnect the wiring plug from all relevant components in the boot lid.
4 Release the wiring harnesses and the washer fluid hose from any clips inside the boot lid.
5 Pull the wiring grommet(s) from the top corner(s) of the boot lid.

6 If the original boot lid is to be refitted, tie string to the ends of all the relevant wiring, then feed the wiring through the top of the tailgate. Untie the string, leaving it in position in the boot lid to assist refitting.
7 Support the boot lid, then prise out the support strut spring clips, and pull the struts from the balljoints on the boot lid.
8 Unscrew the bolts securing the hinges to the top of the boot lid, and carefully lift the boot lid from the vehicle.

Refitting

9 If a new boot lid is to be fitted, transfer all serviceable components (rubber buffers, lock mechanism, etc) to it.
10 Refitting is a reversal of removal, bearing in mind the following points:
  a) *If the original boot lid is being refitted, draw the wiring through the boot lid, using the string.*
  b) *If necessary, adjust the rubber buffers to obtain a good fit when the boot lid is shut.*
  c) *If necessary, adjust the position of the lock within its elongated holes to achieve satisfactory lock operation.*

Adjustment

11 If necessary, the position of the boot lid in relation to the body can be adjusted by loosening the hinge bolts moving the boot lid (the bolt holes are elongated) as necessary.
12 If necessary, the rubber buffer stops at the lower corners of the boot lid can be adjusted to obtain a good fit when the boot is shut. The lock operation can be adjusted by altering the position of the lock within its elongated holes.

19.9 Boot lid central locking motor securing screws (arrowed)

Support struts

13 Proceed as described for the tailgate support struts on Hatchback models in Section 15.

---

19 Boot lid lock components (Sedan models) - removal and refitting

Boot lid lock

Removal

1 Prise out the securing clips, and remove the boot lid trim panel.
2 Working through the aperture in the lower edge of the boot lid, disconnect the lock operating rod.
3 Unscrew the two lock securing screws, and withdraw the lock.

Refitting

4 Refitting is a reversal of removal, but ensure that the lock lever engages correctly as the lock is positioned in the boot lid.
5 Adjust the position of the lock within its elongated holes as necessary to achieve satisfactory lock operation.

Boot lid lock cylinder

Removal

6 Disconnect the battery negative terminal (refer to *"Disconnecting the battery"* in the Reference Section of this manual).
7 Open the boot lid.
8 Prise out the securing clips, and remove the boot lid trim panel.
9 Working at the lower edge of the boot lid, unscrew the left-hand central locking motor securing screw, and loosen the right-hand screw sufficiently to allow the motor to be slid from its location **(see illustration)**. Slide the motor from the boot lid, then unhook the lock operating rod and disconnect the wiring plug from the motor. If necessary, unclip the wiring harness from the boot lid.
10 Unhook the lock cylinder rod from the lock.
11 Remove the two securing screws, and withdraw the lock cylinder from outside the boot lid **(see illustration)**.

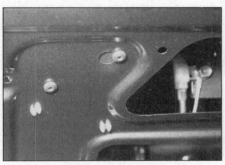

19.11 Boot lid lock cylinder securing screws

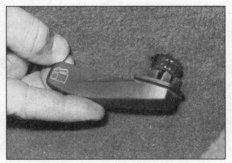

20.8 Prise the release lever from the operating mechanism

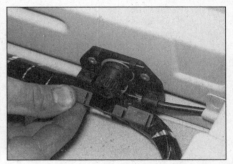

20.10 Unclip the metal cover from the release mechanism

12 Recover the inner lock section from inside the boot lid.

Refitting

13 Refitting is a reversal of removal, bearing in mind the following points:
a) *Ensure that the operating rod is in position on the lock cylinder when refitting.*
b) *Feed the operating rod through the inner section of the lock as it is refitted.*
c) *Check that the lock operates correctly before refitting the boot lid trim panel.*

Boot lid lock striker

Removal

14 Remove the rear bumper (see Section 7).
15 Prise out the plastic covers, then unscrew the two bolts, and withdraw the lock striker.

Refitting

16 Refitting is a reversal of removal.

20 Fuel filler flap release cable - removal and refitting

Removal

1 Chock the front wheels, then jack up the rear of the vehicle and support securely on axle stands (see *"Jacking and Vehicle Support"*).
2 Remove the right-hand rear wheel, then remove the appropriate securing screws and clips, and withdraw the wheelarch liner.

3 Open the fuel filler flap, and unscrew the two lock securing screws.
4 Working under the wheelarch, release the lock from the body panel.
5 Remove the rear seat backrest and seat cushion (see Section 28). On models with split rear seats, it is only necessary to remove the right-hand seat assembly.
6 Remove the driver's seat as described in Section 28.
7 Remove the rear passenger compartment side trim panel (3-door models), or the rear wheelarch trim panel (5-door models), as applicable for access to the cable.
8 Using a suitable screwdriver, prise the operating lever from the end of the release mechanism **(see illustration)**.
9 Pull the weatherstrip from the edge of the door aperture, then fold back the carpet for access to the release cable.
10 Unclip the metal cover from the release mechanism **(see illustration)**.
11 Release the lever return spring from the lug on the bracket, then slide the release lever from the pivot, and unhook the end of the release cable from the lever **(see illustrations)**.
12 Unclip the cable from the bracket, then tie a length of string to the end of the cable to aid refitting.
13 Working under the rear wheelarch, pull the cable to draw it through from the vehicle interior, and withdraw the lock/cable assembly from the vehicle.
14 It may be necessary to lift the carpet to release the cable from the securing clips.

15 Untie the string from the end of the cable, and leave it in position to aid refitting.
16 If desired, the release mechanism can be removed after drilling out the securing rivets.

Refitting

17 Refitting is a reversal of removal, bearing in mind the following points:
a) *Lightly grease the cable before refitting.*
b) *Use the string to pull the cable into position.*
c) *Ensure that the cable is routed as noted before removal.*
d) *Ensure that the release lever return spring is correctly located on its retaining lug.*

21 Central locking components - removal and refitting

Note: *Before working on any of the central locking system components, disconnect the battery negative terminal (refer to "Disconnecting the battery" in the Reference Section of this manual). Reconnect the terminalon completion of work.*

Electronic control unit

1 The central locking system's electronic control unit has changed locations several times during the course of production. Refer to the relevant procedure in this and other Chapters to gain access to it.
2 On early Hatchback and Sedan models, the

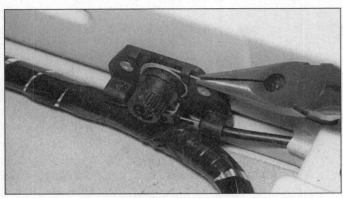

20.11a Release the return spring . . .

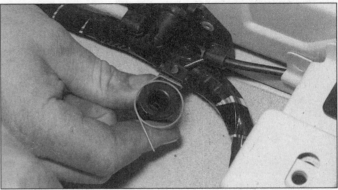

20.11b . . . then slide the release lever from the pivot

unit is under the rear seat cushion, on the left-hand side. On later models, it is on the right-hand side, behind the rear seat backrest. With the seat component(s) removed, lift the floor covering as necessary to find the unit.

3 On Hatchback, Sedan and Estate models (between 1997 and 2000, approximately), the unit is under the floor carpet at the base of the right-hand A-pillar. Remove the driver's seat and dismantle the trim panels and seat belt mountings as required to reach the unit.

4 On Hatchback, Sedan and Estate models from 2001-on, the unit is behind the facia centre panel (Section 32), approximately on the level of the row of push-button switches.

5 On early Cabriolet models, the unit is in the left-hand rear corner of the luggage compartment, behind the trim panel. On later models it is in the rear passenger compartment, behind the right-hand trim panel.

Door lock motor

6 The motor is integral with the door lock assembly. Removal and refitting of the lock assembly is described in Section 13.

Tailgate lock motor

7 Removal of the tailgate lock motor is described as part of the tailgate lock cylinder removal procedure in Section 17.

Boot lid lock motor

8 Removal of the boot lid lock motor is described as part of the boot lid lock cylinder removal procedure in Section 19.

Remote control receiver unit

Removal

9 Carefully prise the trim panel from the roof console to expose the two console securing screws.

10 Remove the securing screws, and lower the panel.

11 Disconnect the wiring plug and slide the receiver unit from the console **(see illustration)**.

Refitting

12 Refitting is a reversal of removal.

Remote control transmitter batteries - renewal

13 Using a small screwdriver, carefully prise

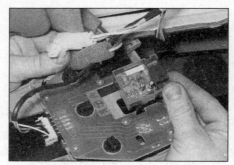

21.11 Removing the central locking remote control receiver unit

the two halves of the transmitter apart, and remove the two batteries, noting which way round they are fitted.

14 Fit the two new batteries, ensuring that they are fitted the correct way round; the battery and transmitter terminals are marked "+" and "-" to avoid confusion. Clip the transmitter back together.

---

22 Electric window components renewal - general information

Electronic control unit

Removal

1 The electronic control unit is located in the driver's door, behind the trim panel.

2 Remove the door inner trim panel as described in Section 12.

3 Disconnect the wiring from the control unit.

4 Remove the two securing screws, and withdraw the unit from the door.

Refitting

5 Refitting is a reversal of removal.

Window switches

6 Refer to Chapter 12.

Window regulator motors

7 The regulator motors are integral with the regulator assemblies, and cannot be obtained separately.

8 Removal and refitting details for the regulator assemblies are given in Section 14.

23.2 Prise the mirror trim plate from the edge of the door

---

23 Exterior mirrors and associated components - removal and refitting

Mirror assembly

Removal

1 On models with electric mirrors, disconnect the battery negative terminal (refer to "Disconnecting the battery" in the Reference Section of this manual).

2 Prise the mirror trim plate from the inner edge of the door. Where applicable, remove the screw securing the adjuster knob to the trim plate, and withdraw the trim plate. Where applicable, pull the adjuster grommet from the door **(see illustration)**.

3 Remove the three mirror securing screws, then withdraw the mirror from the door (complete with adjuster mechanism, where applicable). Where applicable, unclip the wiring from the door, and separate the two halves of the connector **(see illustrations)**.

Refitting

4 Refitting is a reversal of removal. Where applicable, ensure that the adjuster knob is securely fastened to the trim plate by the securing screw.

Mirror glass

Removal

5 Working at the bottom edge of the mirror glass, locate the ends of the spring clip which secures the glass.

23.3a Remove the mirror securing screws . . .

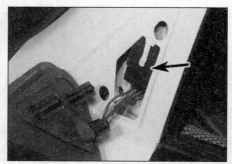

23.3b . . . then withdraw the mirror and unclip the wiring connector (arrowed)

23.3c Separate the two halves of the wiring connector

23.6 Prise the ends of the clip apart (seen with mirror removed and inverted) . . .

23.7a . . . then withdraw the glass and disconnect the wiring

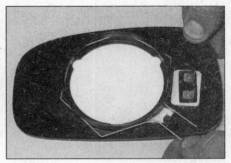

23.7b Recover the spring clip if it is loose

6 Using a suitable screwdriver, prise the ends of the clip apart to release the glass **(see illustration)**.

7 Withdraw the glass, and disconnect the wiring, where applicable. Recover the spring clip if it is loose **(see illustrations)**.

Refitting

8 Fit the spring clip to the rear of the mirror glass, ensuring the clip is correctly located in the slots in the rear of the mirror glass.

9 Push the mirror glass into the mirror until the spring clip locks into position in the mirror adjuster groove **(see Haynes Hint)**.

HAYNES HINT *Lightly grease the plastic ring on the mirror adjuster to aid refitting of the spring clip.*

Electric mirrors - general

10 No spare parts are available for the electric adjustment mechanism, and if faulty, the complete mirror assembly must be renewed. The mirror glass can be renewed as described previously in this Section. Switch removal and refitting is described in Chapter 12.

24 Windscreen, tailgate and fixed rear quarter window glass - general information

These areas of glass are secured by the tight fit of the weatherstrip in the body aperture, and are bonded in position with a special adhesive. Renewal of such fixed glass is a difficult, messy and time-consuming task, which is considered beyond the scope of the home mechanic. It is difficult, unless one has plenty of practice, to obtain a secure, waterproof fit. Furthermore, the task carries a high risk of breakage; this applies especially to the laminated glass windscreen. In view of this, owners are strongly advised to have this sort of work carried out by one of the many specialist windscreen fitters.

25 Rear quarter window (three-door models) - removal and refitting

Removal

1 Open the window.

2 Support the glass, then working inside the vehicle, remove the screws securing the glass panel to the hinges and the handle. Withdraw the panel, taking care not to damage the surrounding paintwork. Where applicable, recover the plastic nuts and the trim from the panel.

3 To remove the handle, drill out the rivets securing the assembly to the body.

Refitting

4 Refitting is a reversal of removal. Where applicable, use new rivets to secure the handle to the body. Take care not to overtighten the glass panel securing screws (it is easy to strip the threads of the plastic nuts).

26 Sunroof - general information

The factory-fitted sunroof is of the electric tilt/slide type.

Due to the complexity of the sunroof mechanism, considerable expertise is required to repair, replace or adjust the sunroof components successfully. Removal of the roof first requires the headlining to be removed, which is a tedious operation, and not a task to be undertaken lightly. Any problems with the sunroof should be referred to a Peugeot dealer.

For sunroof switch removal, see Chapter 12.

27 Body exterior fittings - removal and refitting

Front grille panel - pre-April 1997 models

Removal

1 Open the bonnet.

2 Remove the four upper securing clips, or prise off the covers and remove the screws, as applicable **(see illustration)**.

3 Working through the front of the panel, unscrew the two front securing screws **(see illustration)**.

4 Release the clips securing the grille panel to the headlight lower trim strips, then withdraw the grille panel.

Refitting

5 Refitting is a reversal of removal, but ensure that the panel engages correctly with the headlight lower trim strips.

Front grille panel - April 1997 models onward

Removal

6 Open the bonnet then undo the bolt in the front centre of the grille panel **(see illustration)**.

27.2 Remove the grille upper screws . . .

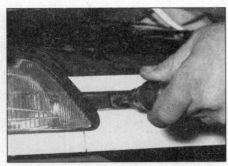

27.3 . . . and the front securing screws

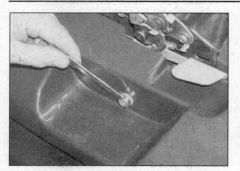

27.6 Undo the grille panel centre bolt

27.7a Lift out the centre portion of the four stud fasteners . . .

27.7b . . . then remove the fastener base

7 Using a screwdriver or forked tool, lift out the centre portion of the four stud fasteners along the top edge of the grille panel. Once the centre portion is withdrawn, remove the fastener base **(see illustrations)**.

8 Carefully release each end of the grille panel where it attaches to the trim strips below the headlights, then withdraw the grille **(see illustrations)**. Note that the end attachment is by means of a moulded plastic clip on each side which is easily broken if care is not taken.

Refitting

9 Refitting is a reversal of removal, but ensure that the panel engages correctly with the headlight lower trim strips.

Wheelarch liners and mud shields

10 The wheelarch liners are secured by a combination of self-tapping screws, and push-fit clips. Removal is self-evident, and normally

the clips can be released by pulling the liner away from the wheelarch **(see illustration)**.

11 The mud shields are secured in a similar manner, although certain panels may be secured using pop-rivets **(see illustration)**. Where applicable, drill out the pop-rivets, and use new rivets on refitting.

Body trim strips and badges

12 The various body trim strips and badges are held in position with a special adhesive tape. Removal requires the trim/badge to be heated, to soften the adhesive, and then cut away from the surface. Due to the high risk of damage to the vehicle paintwork during this operation, it is recommended that this task should be entrusted to a Peugeot dealer.

Longitudinal roof bars - Estate models

Removal

13 Using a small screwdriver, carefully prise off the trim covers at each end of the roof bar.
14 Similarly, prise off the trim cover from the side of the centre brace.
15 Undo the front, centre and rear mounting bolts now exposed and lift off the roof bar. Recover the roof bar to body seals located at each mounting. Examine the seals for deterioration and renew as necessary.

Refitting

16 Refitting is a reversal of removal ensuring that the seals are correctly located. Tighten the mounting bolts to the specified torque.

28 Seats - removal and refitting

Front seat

⚠ **Warning: On models with seat belt pre-tensioners, observe the following precautions before attempting to remove the seat:**
a) *Remove the ignition key.*
b) *Disconnect the battery negative terminal (refer to "Disconnecting the battery" in the Reference Section of this manual), and wait for two minutes before carrying out any further work.*
c) *Disconnect the pre-tensioner wiring plug from the tensioner unit.*

⚠ **Warning: On models with side air bags incorporated in the seat assembly, entrust the work of seat removal to a Peugeot dealer. DO NOT attempt to remove the seat on vehicles so equipped.**

Removal

1 Move the seat fully forwards.
2 Tilt the seat backrest forwards.
3 Remove the bolts (one bolt on each side) securing the rear of the seat rails to the floor **(see illustration)**.
4 Move the seat fully rearwards.
5 Remove the bolts (one bolt on each side) securing the front of the seat rails to the floor **(see illustration)**.

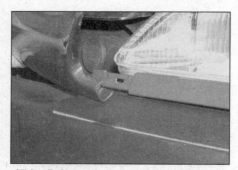

27.8a Release the ends of the grille panel from the headlight trim strips . . .

27.8b . . . and withdraw the grille

27.10 Removing a front wheelarch liner

27.11 Removing a front wheelarch mud shield

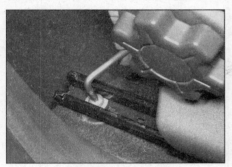

28.3 Remove the rear . . .

28.5 . . . and the front seat securing bolts

28.7 Recover the plates from the floor

6 Recover the washers, where applicable, then lift the seat from the vehicle.
7 Recover the plastic plates from the floor (see illustration).

⚠️ **Warning: Do not tamper with the pre-tensioner unit in any way, and do not attempt to test the unit. Note that the unit is triggered if the mechanism is supplied with an electrical current (including via an ohmmeter), or if the assembly is subjected to a temperature of greater than 100°C.**

Refitting

8 Refitting is a reversal of removal, but ensure that the plastic plates are in position on the floor, and tighten the mounting bolts to the specified torque.

Rear seat back

Removal

9 Tilt the rear seat cushion forwards.
10 Release the securing catches, and tilt the seat back forwards against the front seats.
11 Working at the rear of the seat back, unscrew the bolts securing the hinges to the vehicle floor, then withdraw the seat back (see illustration).

Refitting

12 Refitting is a reversal of removal, but ensure that the seat belts are not trapped.

Rear seat cushion - Hatchback and Estate models

Removal

13 Tilt the seat cushion forwards, through 90°, then lift the cushion to release it from the hinges, and withdraw the cushion from the vehicle.

Refitting

14 Refitting is a reversal of removal, but ensure that the seat belts are not trapped.

Rear seat cushion - Sedan models

Removal

15 Working at the front of the seat cushion, where applicable, unclip the trim plates from the hinges, then remove the screws securing the hinges to the floor.

16 Lift the seat cushion from the vehicle. It may be necessary to pull the rear of the seat cushion up and forwards to release it from the locking catch.

Refitting

17 Refitting is a reversal of removal.

29 Seat belt components - removal and refitting

Front seat belt - 3-door Hatchback models

Removal

1 Remove the rear passenger compartment side trim panel, as described in Section 30.
2 Feed the seat belt and the upper mounting plate through the aperture in the trim panel.
3 Prise off the trim cap from the lower belt anchorage bolt. Remove the bolt and washers, then pull out the anchorage bar, and free the seat belt from the bar.
4 Remove the inertia reel securing bolt, and withdraw the seat belt from the vehicle.

Refitting

5 Refitting is a reversal of removal. Ensure that all washers and/or spacers are positioned as noted before removal, and tighten all mounting bolts to the specified torque.

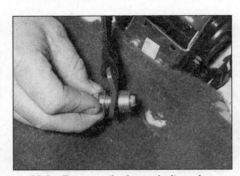

29.8a Remove the lower belt anchor bolt . . .

28.11 Rear seat back hinge securing bolts (arrowed) - Hatchback model

Front seat belt - 5-door Hatchback, Sedan and Estate models

Removal

6 If desired, to improve access, remove the relevant front seat as described in Section 28.
7 Remove the centre pillar trim panels as described in Section 30.
8 Where applicable prise off the trim cap, then remove the lower belt anchor bolt, and recover the washer. Prise the carpet trim panel back from the body to expose the inertia reel securing bolt (see illustrations).
9 Unscrew the inertia reel securing bolt, then withdraw the seat belt assembly from the vehicle.

Refitting

10 Refitting is a reversal of removal. Tighten the mounting bolts to the specified torque.

29.8b . . . and prise back the carpet for access to the inertia reel bolt (arrowed)

Front seat belt stalk

⚠️ *Warning: On models with seat belt pre-tensioners, do not attempt to remove the seat belt stalk assembly, which incorporates the pre-tensioner assembly. Refer the operation to a Peugeot dealer.*

Removal

11 Each stalk is secured to the front seat frame by a bolt and washer.

Refitting

12 Tighten the securing bolt to the specified torque.

Rear side seat belts Hatchback and Estate models

Removal

13 Remove the rear quarter light trim panel (Hatchback models) or the rear quarter window trim panel (Estate models) as described in Section 30.
14 Unbolt the upper seat belt anchor, then remove the bolt securing the inertia reel **(see illustration)**. Note the locations of any washers and spacers on the bolts.
15 Fold the rear seat cushion forwards for access to the lower seat belt anchor bolt, then unscrew the bolt and withdraw the seat belt assembly from the vehicle.

Refitting

16 Refitting is a reversal of removal, but ensure that any washers and spacers are positioned as noted before removal, and tighten the mounting bolts to the specified torque.

Rear centre belt and buckles - Hatchback and Estate models

Removal

17 The assemblies can simply be unbolted from the floor panel, after folding the rear seat cushion forwards. Note the locations of any washers and spacers, to ensure correct refitting.

Refitting

18 Refitting is a reversal of removal. Ensure that all washers and/or spacers are positioned as noted before removal, and tighten all mounting bolts to the specified torque.

29.14 Remove the rear quarter trim panel to expose the rear belt inertia reel

Rear seat belts - Sedan models

Removal

19 Disconnect the battery negative terminal (refer to *"Disconnecting the battery"* in the Reference Section of this manual).
20 Fold the rear seat cushion forwards, and unbolt the relevant lower seat belt anchor from the floor.
21 Fold down the rear seat backs.
22 Working in the luggage compartment, disconnect the wiring plugs from the loudspeakers.
23 Prise out the three securing clips, then release the rear parcel shelf trim panel from the side trim panels.
24 Lift the parcel shelf up, and pull it forwards to release it from the body.
25 Prise the relevant seat belt surround plate from the parcel shelf.
26 Unbolt the inertia reel from the rear body panel, then feed the belt and the lower anchor plate through the hole in the parcel shelf, and withdraw the seat belt.

Refitting

27 Refitting is a reversal of removal, but tighten the bolts to the specified torque.

---

30 Interior trim - removal and refitting 🔧

Door trim panels

1 Refer to Section 12.

Rear passenger compartment side trim panel - 3-door models

Removal

2 Remove the upper centre pillar trim panel as described later in this Section.
3 Remove the rear seat cushion, with reference to Section 28, and fold the seat back fully forwards.
4 Open the rear quarterlight, and prise the weatherstrip from the edge of the window aperture.
5 Unbolt the rear seat belt lower anchor bolt, then carefully pull the panel from the body to release the securing clips.
6 Feed the seat belts and anchor brackets through the aperture in the trim panel. Withdraw the trim panel from the vehicle.

Refitting

7 Refitting is a reversal of removal, but tighten the seat belt mountings to the specified torque.

Rear quarter light and wheelarch trim panels - 5-door Hatchback models

Removal

8 Open the tailgate, and prise the weatherstrip from the edge of the panel, and from the rear roof trim panel **(see illustration)**.
9 Prise the rear roof trim panel from its retaining clips **(see illustration)**.
10 Fold the rear seat back forwards.
11 Where applicable, disconnect the battery negative terminal (refer to *"Disconnecting the battery"* in the Reference Section of this manual, and prise the luggage compartment light and the switch from the trim panel.
12 Remove the top screw securing the quarter light trim panel **(see illustration)**.
13 Unscrew the two lower quarter light trim panel securing screws **(see illustration)**.
14 Remove the two screws securing the rear wheelarch trim panel **(see illustration)**.
15 Pull the quarter light trim panel from the body to release the securing clips, and unclip the panel from the wheelarch trim panel **(see illustration)**.
16 Feed the seat belt through the panel, and withdraw the panel from the vehicle.
17 Release any remaining clips and remove the wheelarch trim panel.

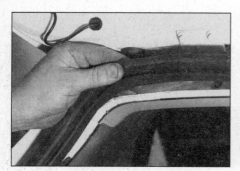

30.8 Prise the weatherstrip from the trim panels

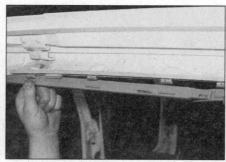

30.9 Prise the rear roof trim panel from its retaining clips

30.12 Remove the top panel securing screw

30.13 Remove the two lower panel securing screws

30.14 Remove the two wheelarch panel securing screws

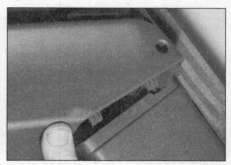

30.15 Unclip the panel from the wheelarch trim panel

Refitting

18 Refitting is a reversal of removal, but ensure that the retaining clips are correctly engaged, and that the seat belt is correctly routed through the panel.

Centre pillar trim panels - 3-door Hatchback models

Removal

19 Where applicable, unclip the trim plate, then unbolt the upper seat belt anchor bolt **(see illustration)**.
20 Using a flat-bladed screwdriver, prise out the centre of the seat belt height adjuster button, then pull off the adjuster button **(see illustration)**.
21 Open the doors, and prise the weatherstrips from the edge of the trim panel **(see illustration)**.
22 Pull the upper panel from the pillar to release the securing clips.

Refitting

23 Refitting is a reversal of removal. Tighten the seat belt anchor bolt to the specified torque.

Centre pillar trim panels - 5-door Hatchback, Sedan and Estate models

Removal

24 Remove the upper trim panel as described previously for 3-door Hatchback models.
25 If desired, the lower trim panel can now be removed from the pillar as follows.
26 Remove the two upper securing clips, exposed by removal of the upper panel.
27 Remove the two lower securing screws, then withdraw the lower panel.

Refitting

28 Refitting is a reversal of removal. Tighten the seat belt anchor bolt to the specified torque.

Rear quarter window trim panel - Estate models

Removal

29 Disconnect the battery negative terminal (refer to *"Disconnecting the battery"* in the Reference Section of this manual).
30 Remove the luggage cover from the load compartment.
31 Pull away the rear door weatherstrip in the area adjacent to the quarter window trim panel.
32 Undo the quarter window trim front securing screw located below the courtesy light **(see illustration)**.
33 Open the rear storage compartment door and undo the two screws at the top of the storage compartment aperture **(see illustration)**.
34 Undo the screws securing the rear of the trim panel to the body pillar **(see illustration)**.

30.19 Unbolt the upper seat belt anchor bolt

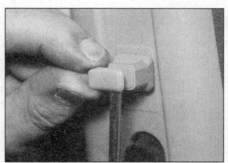

30.20 Prise out the centre of the seat belt height adjuster button

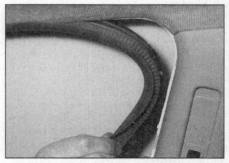

30.21 Prise the weatherstrips from the edge of the trim panel

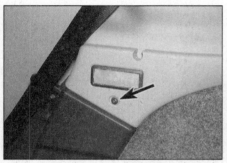

30.32 Undo the quarter window trim front securing screw (arrowed) . . .

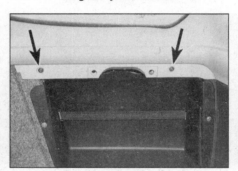

30.33 . . . the two screws at the top of the storage compartment (arrowed) . . .

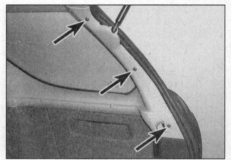

30.34 . . . and the screws securing the rear of the panel to the body pillar (arrowed)

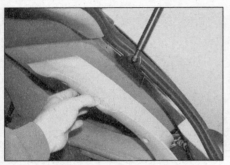

30.35 Release the retaining clips and withdraw the panel

30.37a Undo the screws securing the tailgate trim panel at the side . . .

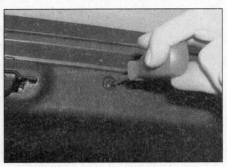

30.37b . . . and along the lower edge

35 Carefully ease the panel away from the body to release the plastic retaining clips **(see illustration)**. When sufficient clearance exists, reach behind the panel and disconnect the courtesy light wiring connectors.

Refitting

36 Refitting is a reversal of removal, but ensure that the retaining clips are correctly engaged.

Tailgate trim panel - Hatchback and Estate models

Removal

37 Open the tailgate and undo the screws at the sides and along the lower edge of the trim panel **(see illustrations)**.
38 Withdraw the panel from the tailgate, releasing any clips as necessary.

Refitting

39 Refitting is a reversal of removal, but ensure that the retaining clips (where applicable) are correctly engaged.

Carpets

40 The passenger compartment floor carpet is in one piece, and is secured at its edges by screws or various types of clips.
41 Carpet removal and refitting is reasonably straightforward, but time-consuming, due to the fact that all adjoining trim panels must be removed first, as must components such as the seats and centre console.

Headlining

Note: *Headlining removal requires considerable skill and experience if it is to be carried out without damage, and is therefore best entrusted to a Peugeot dealer or bodywork specialist. A general overview of the procedure is given below for those with the expertise to attempt the operation on a DIY basis.*
42 The headlining is clipped and glued to the roof, and can be withdrawn only once all fittings such as the grab handles, courtesy lights, sun visors, sunroof (if fitted), overhead console (if fitted), front, centre and rear pillar trim panels, and associated additional panels have been removed. The door, tailgate and sunroof aperture weatherstrips will also have to be prised clear and any additional screws

and clips removed. Once the headlining attachments are released, the adhesive bonding in the centre panels must be broken using a hot air gun and spatula, starting at the front and working rearwards.
43 When refitting, a coat of neoprene adhesive (available from Peugeot dealers) must be applied to the centre panels in the locations noted during removal. Position the headlining carefully and refit all components disturbed during removal. Clean the headlining with soap and water or white spirit on completion.

---

31 Centre console - removal and refitting

Handbrake console

Removal

1 Fully apply the handbrake.
2 Remove the handbrake lever grip. If the grip proves difficult to remove, use a hair dryer to heat it gently until it can be pulled from the end of the lever.
3 Unclip the ashtray from the rear of the console.
4 Unscrew the four console securing screws - two accessible through the ashtray aperture, and two in the oddments tray.
5 Withdraw the console, and pull it forwards over the handbrake lever.

Refitting

6 Refitting is a reversal of removal.

31.14 Unclip the gear lever gaiter to expose the two centre console nuts (arrowed)

Gear lever console

Removal

7 Unclip the gear lever gaiter from the console, and slide it up the gear lever.
8 Lift the rubber mat from the console oddments tray.
9 Unscrew the two console securing nuts, accessible through the gear lever aperture.
10 Unscrew the console securing screws, accessible in the oddments tray.
11 Withdraw the console over the gear lever, passing the lever gaiter through the hole in the console.

Refitting

12 Refitting is a reversal of removal.

Full-length console

Removal

13 Disconnect the battery negative terminal (refer to *"Disconnecting the battery"* in the Reference Section of this manual).
14 On models with a manual gearbox, unclip the gear lever gaiter from the console, and slide it up the gear lever **(see illustration)**.
15 On models with automatic transmission, unclip the selector lever position indicator trim plate from the console.
16 Lift the rubber mat from the console oddments tray **(see illustration)**.
17 Carefully prise the trim panel from the middle of the console **(see illustration)**.
18 Fully apply the handbrake.
19 Remove the handbrake lever grip. If the grip proves difficult to remove, use a hair

31.16 Lift out the rubber mat to expose the front centre console screw (arrowed)

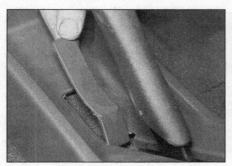

31.17 Prise the trim panel from the middle of the centre console

31.19 Remove the handbrake lever grip

31.20 Unclip the ashtray to expose the two rear centre console screws (arrowed)

dryer to heat it gently until it can be pulled from the end of the lever **(see illustration)**.

20 Unclip the ashtray from the rear of the console **(see illustration)**.

21 Unscrew the two central console nuts.

22 Unscrew the two rear console securing screws, accessible through the ashtray aperture, and the front securing screw, accessible in the oddments tray.

23 Lift the console upwards, and disconnect all relevant wiring connectors, noting their locations to ensure correct refitting.

24 Withdraw the console over the handbrake and gear levers (and the selector lever trim plate, where applicable).

Refitting

25 Refitting is a reversal of removal, but ensure that all relevant wiring connectors are correctly reconnected as noted before removal.

32 Facia panel assembly - removal and refitting

Facia centre panel

Removal

1 Prise the switch/clock trim panel from the facia centre panel **(see illustration)**.

2 Remove the radio/cassette player as described in Chapter 12, or prise out the blanking panel, as applicable.

3 Working through the radio/cassette player aperture, unscrew the two centre panel securing nuts.

4 Working at the sides of the clock, unscrew the two centre panel securing screws, then unclip the panel from the facia and disconnect the wiring connectors from the switches and

the clock **(see illustrations)**. Note the locations of the wiring connectors to ensure correct refitting.

Refitting

5 Refitting is a reversal of removal, but ensure that the wiring connectors are reconnected to their correct locations as noted before removal.

Steering column shrouds

Removal

6 Disconnect the battery negative terminal (refer to *"Disconnecting the battery"* in the Reference Section of this manual).

7 Working under the steering column, unscrew the securing screws, then withdraw the lower column shroud **(see illustrations)**.

8 Where applicable, unclip the wiring harness(es) from the shroud, then remove the securing screws and withdraw the stalk switch(es) from the inside of the shroud.

9 Where applicable, remove the clip securing the alarm switch to the shroud, then tilt the switch and withdraw it through the inside of the shroud **(see illustration)**.

10 Unclip the upper column shroud, and withdraw it from the column **(see illustration)**.

Refitting

11 Refitting is a reversal of removal.

32.1 Prise the trim panel from the facia centre panel

32.4a Remove the two centre panel securing screws . . .

32.4b . . . then unclip the panel from the facia

32.7a Unscrew the securing screws . . .

32.7b . . . and withdraw the lower column shroud

32.9 Removing the alarm switch securing clip

32.10 Unclip the upper column shroud

32.13 Withdrawing the upper glovebox assembly

Upper glovebox

Removal

12 Open the glovebox lid.

13 Unscrew the six securing screws, and withdraw the glovebox assembly (complete with lid) from the facia **(see illustration)**.

Refitting

14 Refitting is a reversal of removal.

Complete facia assembly

Removal

⚠️ *Warning: On models fitted with a passenger's air bag, seek the advice of a Peugeot dealer before proceeding. At the time of writing, no information was available concerning the passenger's air bag attachments or connections in the facia.*

15 Disconnect the battery negative terminal (refer to *"Disconnecting the battery"* in the Reference Section of this manual).

16 Remove the facia centre panel, the steering column shrouds and the upper glovebox as described previously in this Section.

17 Remove the steering wheel (Chapter 10).

18 Remove the windscreen wiper motor assembly, as described in Chapter 12.

19 Working under the facia, loosen the two lower steering column mounting nuts. Remove the two upper column mounting nuts (see Chapter 10).

20 Remove the instrument panel as described in Chapter 12.

21 Release the securing clip and remove the fusebox lid.

22 Unscrew the three screws securing the stalk switch housing to the steering column, then disconnect the wiring plugs from the

switches and withdraw the complete switch assembly.

23 Trace the wiring back from the ignition switch, then separate the two halves of the wiring connector.

24 Working in the engine compartment, locate the main facia wiring harness connector. The connector is located on the right-hand side of the scuttle on right-hand-drive models, or on the left-hand side of the scuttle on left-hand-drive models. Disconnect the plug from the connector as follows:

a) *Pull the plastic cover from the connector.*

b) *Using a suitable Allen key, unscrew the wiring plug retaining screw cover (see illustration).*

c) *Unscrew the Torx screw securing the wiring plug to the connector.*

d) *Pull out the wiring plug (see illustration).*

25 Again working in the scuttle, pull off the rubber covers, then unscrew the two nuts securing the main wiring connector to the bulkhead **(see illustration)**.

26 Working at the opposite side of the scuttle from the wiper motor, unscrew the three securing bolts, and remove the remaining scuttle cover panel bracket **(see illustration)**.

27 Unclip the rubber cover from the scuttle to expose the facia upper securing nut **(see illustrations)**.

28 Unscrew the three upper facia nuts (one at each side, and one in the centre, all accessible from the scuttle) **(see illustration)**.

29 Working in the engine compartment, pull the speedometer cable ball from the grommet in the bulkhead **(see illustration)**.

32.24a Unscrewing the facia wiring harness plug retaining screw cover

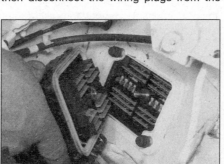

32.24b Disconnecting the main facia wiring harness plug

32.25 Unscrew the main wiring connector securing nuts

32.26 Remove the scuttle cover panel bracket . . .

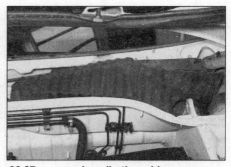

32.27a . . . and unclip the rubber cover . . .

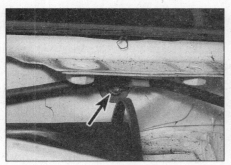

32.27b . . . to expose the facia securing nut (arrowed)

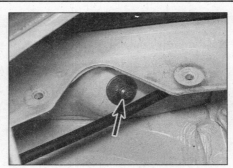

32.28 Right-hand upper facia securing nut (arrowed)

32.29 Pull the speedometer cable ball (arrowed) from the bulkhead grommet

30 Working inside the vehicle, locate the radio aerial wiring connector. The connector is located at the lower right-hand side of the facia on right-hand-drive models, or at the

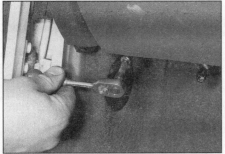

32.31 Removing the left-hand lower facia securing screw

lower left-hand side of the facia on left-hand-drive models. Separate the two halves of the connector.

31 Working at each lower corner of the facia, remove the lower facia securing screws (one screw on each side) **(see illustration)**.

32 Remove the four screws securing the heater control unit to the facia.

33 Working through the instrument panel aperture, unscrew the centre facia securing screw **(see illustration)**.

34 Unclip the heater air distribution control cable from the heater control unit **(see illustration)**.

35 Working through the radio aperture, unclip the upper heater wiring plug from the facia.

36 Working at the left-hand side of the facia,

unclip the two lower heater wiring connectors, and separate the two halves of the connectors **(see illustration)**.

37 Working at the left-hand side of the facia on right-hand-drive models, or the right-hand side of the facia on left-hand-drive models, unbolt the earth lead from the body panel, and unclip the wiring connectors under the fusebox. Separate the two halves of each wiring connector **(see illustrations)**.

38 Working through the radio aperture, unclip the alarm LED wiring connector from the back of the facia, and separate the connector halves.

39 Working at each side of the lower centre facia panel, unscrew the two securing screws (one screw on each side) and withdraw the panel **(see illustrations)**.

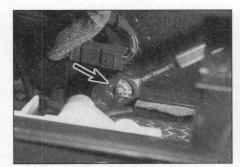

32.33 Using a wrench (arrowed) to unscrew the centre facia securing screw

32.34 Unclip the air distribution control cable from the control unit

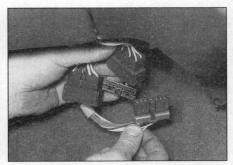

32.36 Disconnect the heater lower wiring connectors

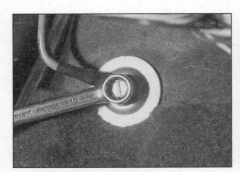

32.37a Unbolt the earth lead from the body panel

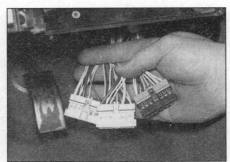

32.37b Disconnect the wiring connectors beneath the fusebox

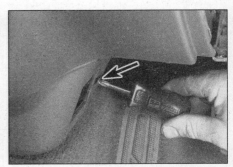

32.39a Unscrew the securing screws . . .

32.39b . . . and withdraw the lower centre facia panel

32.40a Remove the left-hand . . .

32.40b . . . and centre screws securing the facia to the heater unit

32.41 Remove the air duct through the glovebox aperture

32.42 Remove the lower right-hand heater duct

32.46 Withdraw the facia assembly with the aid of an assistant

40 Working at the bottom of the heater assembly, remove the two screws securing the facia to the heater unit **(see illustrations)**.

41 Unclip the upper air duct from the heater and the facia vent. Working through the upper glovebox aperture, remove the duct **(see illustration)**.

42 Unclip the lower right-hand heater duct and remove it **(see illustration)**.

43 Pull the facia assembly rearwards from the bulkhead.

44 Reach behind the facia, and disconnect the wiring plug from the stop light switch.

45 Disconnect the remaining wiring connectors.

46 With the aid of an assistant, withdraw the facia assembly through one of the door apertures **(see illustration)**.

Refitting

47 Offer the facia into position, and reconnect the stop light switch wiring.

48 As the facia is refitted, feed the main facia wiring connector into position on the bulkhead, and fit the securing screws **(see Haynes Hint)**.

49 Ensure that the heater air ducts are reconnected securely as the facia is refitted. Also ensure that the speedometer cable housing is correctly positioned in the appropriate facia aperture.

50 Engage the facia assembly with the locating pins on the bulkhead, then refit and tighten the upper facia securing nuts, and the lower screws.

51 Further refitting is a reversal of removal, bearing in mind the following points:

a) *Ensure that all wiring connectors are correctly reconnected and clipped into position.*

b) *Refit the wiper motor assembly as described in Chapter 12.*

c) *Refit the steering wheel with reference to Chapter 10.*

HAYNES HiNT

Screw an M6 bolt into the facia wiring connector to allow it to be pulled into position in the bulkhead

Chapter 12
Body electrical systems

Contents

Degrees of difficulty

Easy, suitable for novice with little experience	**Fairly easy,** suitable for beginner with some experience	**Fairly difficult,** suitable for competent DIY mechanic	**Difficult,** suitable for experienced DIY mechanic	**Very difficult,** suitable for expert DIY or professional

Specifications

General
System type . . . . 12-volt negative earth

Fuses - pre-April 1997 models

Facia fusebox with 13 fuses

Fuse No	Rating (amps)	Circuit(s) protected
F1	10	Instrument panel warning lights, "lights-on" warning buzzer
F2	25	Heater blower motor, coolant thermostat ECU
F3	25	Air conditioning system, heated rear window, cooling fan relay
F4	25	Direction indicators, rear window wipe, rear roof light
F5	30	Heated rear window
F6	10	Hazard warning lights
F7	10	Fuel gauge, dim-dip relay (UK models), water-in-fuel sensor (Diesel models), reversing lights, instrument panel warning lights
F8	20	Horns, radio memory, clock, courtesy lights, boot light
F9	30	Windscreen wiper motor and timer, rear window wiper control, screen wash, "lights on" warning buzzer, instrument panel warning lights, radio, courtesy light, stop-lights, load warning light, front roof light
F10	20	Cooling system control, cooling fan relay, cigar lighter
F11	5	Rear foglights
F12	5	Front sidelights and LH tail light, switch illumination, instrument panel lights
F13	10	RH tail light

Fuses - pre-April 1997 models (continued)

Facia fusebox with 30 fuses

Fuse No	Rating (amps)	Circuit(s) protected
F1A	10	Radio memory
F2	5	Instrument panel warning lights, fuel gauge, dim-dip relay (UK models), tachometer
F3	15	Not used
F4	10	Front sidelights, RH tail light
F5	10	Heater blower, cooling fan relay, coolant temperature unit (carburettor models), heating control unit, air conditioning switch, pressostat and cut-out control relay
F6	10	Front foglights
F7	20	Horns, cooling fan relay and thermal switch, coolant thermostat ECU, dip beam supply relay for anti-theft alarm
F8	-	Shunt (fuse 15, fuse 25)
F9	5	Left-hand tail light, instrument panel illumination lights
F10	30	Rear electric windows
F11	30	Electrically-operated hood (Cabriolet)
F12	10	Reversing lights, instrument panel warning lights, alarm system, starter inhibitor switch/relay (automatic transmission), water-in-fuel sensor (Diesel models), cruise control, catalytic converter temperature control unit
F13	15	Hazard warning light switch
F14	15	Dip beam supply relay for anti-theft alarm
F15	20	Central locking control unit and remote control unit, courtesy lights, boot light, electric aerial
F16	20	Cigarette lighter
F16A	20	Cigarette lighter
F17	-	Not used
F18	10	Rear foglights
F19	10	"Lights on" warning circuit, instrument panel lighting and dimmer, clock
F20	30	Heated seats
F21	30	Heating and ventilation
F22	20	Rear window wiper motor, rear roof light, central locking unit
F23	15	Heated rear window, exterior mirror heating, air conditioning
F24	30	Windscreen and rear window wiper motors, front wiper switch and timer, headlight and screen washers
F25	5	Radio memory, clock, alarm LED
F26	15	Alarm control unit
F27	30	Heated rear window, heated mirrors
F28	15	Load warning light, additional regulation unit, stop-lights, clock, sunroof, electric windows, electrically-operated hood (Cabriolet), instrument warning lights
F29	30	Front electric windows, sunroof
F30	15	Map reading lights, vanity mirror light, glovebox light, "lights on" warning buzzer, direction indicators, electric mirrors, pulse window winders, courtesy lights, remote central locking unit

Engine compartment fuses

Fuse No	Rating (amps)	Circuit(s) protected
F31	30	ABS
F32	-	Shunt
F33	30	Cooling system
F34	30	Cooling system
F35	10	Fuel pump
F36	30	Oxygen sensor

Fuses – April 1997 to August 2000

Facia fusebox with 13 fuses

Fuse No	Rating (amps)	Circuit(s) protected
F1	10	Instrument panel, warning light switch, audio equipment, air conditioning, ashtray and lighter illumination, heated rear window switch, hazard warning lights
F2	25	Ventilation
F3	10	Heated rear window switch and timer relay, heated seats switch
F4	25	Hazard warning switch, rear window wiper motor
F5	30	Heated rear window timer relay
F6	10	Hazard warning switch, engine ECU
F7	10	Instrument panel, reversing lights, catalytic converter temperature unit, engine immobiliser
F8	20	Caravan connector, courtesy light, instrument panel, cigarette lighter, audio equipment, luggage compartment light switch, engine immobiliser
F9	30	Windscreen wiper timer and motor switch, instrument panel, audio equipment, brake switch, courtesy light
F10	25	Fan, thermostat, lighting switch
F11	5	Rear foglights, lighting switch
F12	10	RH tail light
F13	5	LH tail light, front side lights

Facia fusebox with 23 fuses

Fuse No	Rating (amps)	Circuit(s) protected
F1	10	Audio equipment
F2	5	Engine immobiliser, thermostat, automatic transmission selector lever illumination, shift lock relay, instrument panel
F3	-	Not used
F4	10	RH tail light
F5	10	Heated rear window switch, heated rear window timer relay, courtesy light, ventilation supply relay
F6	-	Not used
F7	20	Lighting switch, dip beam and anti-theft alarm supply relay
F8	-	Shunt
F9	5	LH tail light, front side lights
F10	-	Not used
F11	-	Not used
F12	20	Reversing lights, catalytic converter temperature control unit, ABS, pressure switch, air conditioning compressor relay, fan, day running lights and dip beam headlight relay
F13	-	Not used
F14	15	Central locking control unit, audio equipment
F15	30	Hazard warning lights, fan, thermostat, courtesy light, engine ECU
F16	20	Cigarette lighter
F17	-	Not used
F18	10	Rear foglights
F19	10	Air conditioning, lighting rheostat, switch illumination, rear window locking switch, audio equipment, hazard warning switch, heated rear window switch, clock and temperature display
F20	20	Heated seats
F21	30	Air conditioning and ventilation
F22	-	Not used
F23	-	Shunt
F24	30	Windscreen wiper motor, relay, switch and timer,
F25	5	Luggage compartment lighting, electric aerial, clock and temperature display, engine immobiliser, instrument panel, anti-theft alarm
F26	20	Caravan connector
F27	30	Heated rear window timer relay
F28	15	Central locking control unit, electric front windows and sun roof relay, brake switch, instrument panel, clock and temperature display, rear window wiper motor
F29	30	Engine running supply, electric front windows and sun roof relay
F30	15	Rain sensor, hazard warning switch, glovebox illumination, electric windows and mirrors switch, courtesy light

Fuses – April 1997 to August 2000 (continued)

Facia fusebox with 30 fuses

Fuse No	Rating (amps)	Circuit(s) protected
F1	10	Audio equipment
F1A	-	Not used
F2	5	Engine immobiliser, thermostat, automatic transmission selector lever illumination, shift lock relay, instrument panel
F3	15	Over-speeding buzzer, anti-theft alarm control unit, automatic transmission
F4	10	RH tail light
F5	10	Heated rear window switch, heated rear window timer relay, courtesy light, ventilation supply relay
F6	10	Front fog lights
F7	20	Lighting switch, dip beam and anti-theft alarm supply relay
F8	-	Shunt
F9	5	LH tail light, front side lights
F10	30	Rear window relay
F11	-	Not used
F12	20	Reversing lights, catalytic converter temperature control unit, ABS, pressure switch, air conditioning compressor relay, fan, day running lights and dip beam headlight relay
F13	-	Not used
F14	15	Central locking control unit, audio equipment, anti-theft alarm control unit
F15	30	Hazard warning lights, fan, thermostat, courtesy light, engine ECU
F16	20	Cigarette lighter
F16A	-	Not used
F17	-	Anti-theft alarm headlight relay
F18	10	Rear foglights
F19	10	Air conditioning, lighting rheostat, switch illumination, rear window locking switch, audio equipment, hazard warning switch, heated rear window switch, clock and temperature display
F20	20	Heated seats switch
F21	30	Air conditioning and ventilation
F22	20	Rear windows relay
F23	-	Shunt
F24	30	Windscreen wiper motor, relay, switch and timer,
F25	5	Luggage compartment lighting, electric aerial, clock and temperature display, engine immobiliser, instrument panel, anti-theft alarm
F26	20	Caravan connector
F27	30	Heated rear window timer relay
F28	15	Central locking control unit, electric front windows and sun roof relay, brake switch, instrument panel, clock and temperature display, rear window wiper motor
F29	30	Engine running supply, electric front windows and sun roof relay
F30	15	Rain sensor, hazard warning switch, glovebox illumination, electric windows and mirrors switch, courtesy light

Engine compartment fuses

Fuse No	Rating (amps)	Circuit(s) protected
F1	-	Not used
F2	40	Fan
F3	40	Fan, instrument panel
F4	-	Not used
F5	-	Not used
F6	20	Headlight wash timer relay
F7	-	Not used
F8	-	Not used
F9	15	Fuel pump
F10	-	Not used
F11	10	Fuel pump control, oxygen sensor
F12	10	LH headlight main beam
F13	10	RH headlight main beam
F14	10	LH headlight dip beam
F15	10	RH headlight dip beam

Fuses – August 2000 onwards

Facia fusebox with 28 fuses

Fuse No	Rating (amps)	Circuit(s) protected
F1		Not used
F2	7.5	Automatic transmission ECU
F3		Not used
F4	5	Passenger airbag neutralisation, instrument panel, passenger compartment protection unit, coolant temperature unit, automatic transmission selector illumination, lever locking (automatic transmission)
F5	25	Stop-lights, pressostat. Anti-lock brake control unit, air conditioning compressor, left-hand fan
F6	5	Clock and outside temperature display, passenger compartment protection unit, instrument panel, luggage compartment lighting
F7	30	Heated rear window
F8	20	Passenger compartment protection unit, radio
F9	20	Engine ECU (XU10J4R, TU5JP/L3) (automatic transmission), air conditioning compressor, fan
F10	20	Hazard warning signal switch, front and rear courtesy lights
F11	10	Hazard warning signal switch – lighting switch, clock and outside temperature display, radio, ashtray illumination, headlamp height corrector, lighting rheostat, front cigar lighter, heated rear window, heated driver's seat, air conditioning control unit, automatic transmission programme selector
F12	10	Rear foglamps
F13	30	Electric hood relay power
F14	30	Rear electric window and heated seats
F15	20	Tow bar
F16	30	Front electric window and sunroof
F17	20	Lighting switch
F18	10	Front foglamps
F19	10	Right-hand tail lamp
F20	30	Air conditioning blower unit, air conditioning ECU, mixer motor, air inlet flap
F21	10	Headlamps, left-hand tail lamp, running lights or lighting switch
F22	10	Heated rear window, air conditioning blower unit
F23	20	Front cigar lighter
F24	10	Radio
F25	10	Electric hood, central unit supply and switch
F26	30	Front screen wash/wipe
F27	15	Hazard warning signal switch, rain sensor, front and rear courtesy lights, map reading lamp, vanity mirror (passenger), passenger compartment air thermistor
F28	15	Battery light, clock and outside temperature display, rear electric window and heated seat, electric front windows and sunroof, rear wiper

Engine compartment fuses

Fuse No	Rating (amps)	Circuit(s) protected
F29	10	Left-hand dipped beam headlight
F30	10	Right-hand dipped beam headlight
F31	10	Left-hand main beam headlight
F32	10	Right-hand main beam headlight
F33	15 (DW10 engine)	Control unit
F34	10 (not DW10 engine)	Oxygen sensor
F35	15	Petrol pump
F36	20	Headlight wash timer
F37	40	Fan unit
F38		Not used
F39	40	Spare fuses (fan unit)
F40	40	Fan unit

Bulbs	Type	Wattage
Headlights:		
Dip/main beam (single headlights system)	H4	60/55
Individual main beam (twin headlight system):		
Pre-April 1997 models	H1	55
April 1997 models onward	H7	55
Individual dip beam (twin headlight system):		
Pre-April 1997 models	H1	55
April 1997 models onward	H7	55
Front foglight	H3	55
Front sidelights	Push-fit	5
Direction indicator light	Bayonet	21
Direction indicator side repeater	Push-fit	5
Stop/tail light	Bayonet	21/5
Rear foglight	Bayonet	21
Reversing light	Bayonet	21
Number plate light	Push-fit	5
High-level stoplight	Push-fit	5

Torque wrench setting	Nm	lbf ft
Air bag unit securing screws	8	6

1 General information and precautions

⚠ *Warning: Before carrying out any work on the electrical system, read through the precautions given in "Safety first!" at the beginning of this manual, and in the relevant Parts of Chapter 5.*

The electrical system is of 12-volt negative earth type. Power for the lights and all electrical accessories is supplied by a lead/acid type battery, which is charged by the alternator.

This Chapter covers repair and service procedures for the various electrical components not associated with the engine. Information on the battery, alternator and starter motor can be found in Chapter 5A.

It should be noted that, prior to working on any component in the electrical system, the battery negative terminal should first be disconnected, to prevent the possibility of electrical short-circuits and/or fires.

Caution: Before proceeding, refer to "Disconnecting the battery" in the Reference Section of this manual for further information.

2 Electrical fault-finding - general information

Note: *Refer to the precautions given in "Safety first!" and in Section 1 of this Chapter before starting work. The following tests relate to testing of the main electrical circuits, and should not be used to test delicate electronic circuits (such as anti-lock braking systems), particularly where an electronic control module is used.*

General

1 A typical electrical circuit consists of an electrical component, any switches, relays, motors, fuses, fusible links or circuit breakers related to that component, and the wiring and connectors which link the component to both the battery and the chassis. To help to pinpoint a problem in an electrical circuit, wiring diagrams are included at the end of this manual.

2 Before attempting to diagnose an electrical fault, first study the appropriate wiring diagram, to obtain a more complete understanding of the components included in the particular circuit concerned. The possible sources of a fault can be narrowed down by noting whether other components related to the circuit are operating properly. If several components or circuits fail at one time, the problem is likely to be related to a shared fuse or earth connection.

3 Electrical problems usually stem from simple causes, such as loose or corroded connections, a faulty earth connection, a blown fuse, a melted fusible link, or a faulty relay (refer to Section 3 for details of testing relays). Visually inspect the condition of all fuses, wires and connections in a problem circuit before testing the components. Use the wiring diagrams to determine which terminal connections will need to be checked, in order to pinpoint the trouble-spot.

4 The basic tools required for electrical fault-finding include a circuit tester or voltmeter (a 12-volt bulb with a set of test leads can also be used for certain tests); a self-powered test light (sometimes known as a continuity tester); an ohmmeter (to measure resistance); a battery and set of test leads; and a jumper wire, preferably with a circuit breaker or fuse incorporated, which can be used to bypass suspect wires or electrical components. Before attempting to locate a problem with test instruments, use the wiring diagram to determine where to make the connections.

5 To find the source of an intermittent wiring fault (usually due to a poor or dirty connection, or damaged wiring insulation), a "wiggle" test can be performed on the wiring. This involves wiggling the wiring by hand, to see if the fault occurs as the wiring is moved. It should be possible to narrow down the source of the fault to a particular section of wiring. This method of testing can be used in conjunction with any of the tests described in the following sub-Sections.

6 Apart from problems due to poor connections, two basic types of fault can occur in an electrical circuit - open-circuit, or short-circuit.

7 Open-circuit faults are caused by a break somewhere in the circuit, which prevents current from flowing. An open-circuit fault will prevent a component from working, but will not cause the relevant circuit fuse to blow.

8 Short-circuit faults are caused by a "short" somewhere in the circuit, which allows the current flowing in the circuit to "escape" along an alternative route, usually to earth. Short-circuit faults are normally caused by a breakdown in wiring insulation, which allows a feed wire to touch either another wire, or an earthed component such as the bodyshell. A short-circuit fault will normally cause the relevant circuit fuse to blow.

Finding an open-circuit

9 To check for an open-circuit, connect one lead of a circuit tester or voltmeter to either the negative battery terminal or a known good earth.

10 Connect the other lead to a connector in the circuit being tested, preferably nearest to the battery or fuse.

11 Switch on the circuit, bearing in mind that some circuits are live only when the ignition switch is moved to a particular position.

12 If voltage is present (indicated either by the tester bulb lighting or a voltmeter reading, as applicable), this means that the section of the circuit between the relevant connector and the battery is problem-free.

13 Continue to check the remainder of the circuit in the same fashion.

14 When a point is reached at which no voltage is present, the problem must lie between that point and the previous test point with voltage. Most problems can be traced to a broken, corroded or loose connection.

Finding a short-circuit

15 To check for a short-circuit, first disconnect the load(s) from the circuit (loads are the components which draw current from a circuit, such as bulbs, motors, heating elements, etc).

16 Remove the relevant fuse from the circuit, and connect a circuit tester or voltmeter to the fuse connections.

17 Switch on the circuit, bearing in mind that some circuits are live only when the ignition switch is moved to a particular position.

18 If voltage is present (indicated either by the tester bulb lighting or a voltmeter reading, as applicable), this means that there is a short-circuit.

19 If no voltage is present, but the fuse still blows with the load(s) connected, this indicates an internal fault in the load(s).

Finding an earth fault

20 The battery negative terminal is connected to "earth" - the metal of the engine/transmission and the car body - and most systems are wired so that they only receive a positive feed, the current returning via the metal of the car body. This means that the component mounting and the body form part of that circuit. Loose or corroded mountings can therefore cause a range of electrical faults, ranging from total failure of a circuit, to a puzzling partial fault. In particular, lights may shine dimly (especially when another circuit sharing the same earth point is in operation), motors (eg wiper motors or the radiator cooling fan motor) may run slowly, and the operation of one circuit may have an apparently-unrelated effect on another. Note that on many vehicles, earth straps are used between certain components, such as the engine/transmission and the body, usually where there is no metal-to-metal contact between components, due to flexible rubber mountings, etc.

21 To check whether a component is properly earthed, disconnect the battery, and connect one lead of an ohmmeter to a known good earth point. Connect the other lead to the wire or earth connection being tested. The resistance reading should be zero; if not, check the connection as follows.

22 If an earth connection is thought to be faulty, dismantle the connection, and clean back to bare metal both the bodyshell and the wire terminal or the component earth connection mating surface. Be careful to remove all traces of dirt and corrosion, then use a knife to trim away any paint, so that a clean metal-to-metal joint is made. On

reassembly, tighten the joint fasteners securely; if a wire terminal is being refitted, use serrated washers between the terminal and the bodyshell, to ensure a clean and secure connection. When the connection is remade, prevent the onset of corrosion in the future by applying a coat of petroleum jelly or silicone-based grease, or by spraying on (at regular intervals) a proprietary ignition sealer or water-dispersant lubricant.

3 Fuses and relays - general information

Fuses

1 Fuses are designed to break a circuit when a predetermined current is reached, in order to protect the components and wiring which could be damaged by excessive current flow. Any excessive current flow will be due to a fault in the circuit, usually a short-circuit (see Section 2).

2 The main fuses are located in the fusebox, below the steering column on the driver's side of the facia. According to model, year of manufacture, and equipment fitted, the fusebox will contain either 13, 23 or 30 fuses.

3 For access to the fuses, turn the securing clip through a quarter-turn, then pull the fusebox cover from the facia (**see illustration**).

4 On certain models, additional fuses may be located in the fuse/relay box in the engine compartment, attached to the left-hand suspension turret.

5 A blown fuse can be recognised from its melted or broken wire.

6 To remove a fuse, first ensure that the relevant circuit is switched off.

7 Using the plastic tool provided in the fusebox, pull the fuse from its location.

8 Spare fuses are provided in the blank terminal positions in the fusebox.

9 Before renewing a blown fuse, trace and rectify the cause, and always use a fuse of the correct rating. Never substitute a fuse of a higher rating, or make temporary repairs using wire or metal foil; more serious damage, or even fire, could result.

10 Note that the fuses are colour-coded as

3.3 Removing the fusebox cover

follows. Refer to the wiring diagrams for details of the fuse ratings and the circuits protected:

Colour	Rating
Orange	5A
Red	10A
Blue	15A
Yellow	20A
Clear or white	25A
Green	30A

11 Additional fuses and circuit breakers may be located in the fuse/relay box in the engine compartment.

Relays

12 A relay is an electrically-operated switch, which is used for the following reasons:

a) *A relay can switch a heavy current remotely from the circuit in which the current is flowing, allowing the use of lighter-gauge wiring and switch contacts.*

b) *A relay can receive more than one control input, unlike a mechanical switch.*

c) *A relay can have a timer function - for example, the intermittent wiper relay.*

13 Most of the relays are located at the rear of the main fusebox (remove the securing screws and pull the fusebox forwards to improve access). Additional relays are located in the fuse/relay box mounted on the left-hand side of the engine compartment (**see illustrations**). Depending on model and equipment fitted, further relays may be located on or adjacent to the components they control.

14 If a circuit or system controlled by a relay develops a fault, and the relay is suspect, operate the system. If the relay is functioning, it should be possible to hear it "click" as it is

3.13a Early type engine compartment fuse/relay box (arrowed) - viewed with cover removed

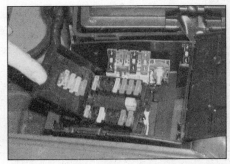

3.13b Later type fuse/relay box shown with cover removed

4.4 Unscrew the stalk switch securing screws . . .

4.5 . . . then withdraw the switch and disconnect the wiring plug

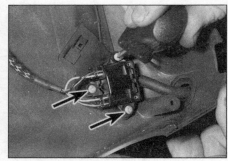

4.8 Removing the radio/cassette player switch securing screws (arrowed)

energised. If this is the case, the fault lies with the components or wiring of the system. If the relay is not being energised, then either the relay is not receiving a main supply or a switching voltage, or the relay itself is faulty. Testing is by the substitution of a known good unit, but be careful - while some relays are identical in appearance and in operation, others look similar but perform different functions.

15 To remove a relay, first ensure that the relevant circuit is switched off. The relay can then simply be pulled out from the socket, and pushed back into position.

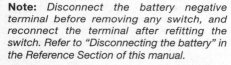

4 Switches - removal and refitting

Note: *Disconnect the battery negative terminal before removing any switch, and reconnect the terminal after refitting the switch. Refer to "Disconnecting the battery" in the Reference Section of this manual.*

Ignition switch/steering column lock

1 Refer to Chapter 10.

Steering column combination switches

2 Remove the three securing screws, and withdraw the lower steering column shroud. Where applicable, remove the securing screws and separate the radio/cassette player remote control switch and (where applicable) the cruise control switch from the shroud.

3 If necessary, lower the column, then unclip the upper column shroud.
4 Remove the two securing screws **(see illustration)**, and withdraw the relevant switch from the housing on the steering column. Where applicable, note the location of the insulating foam around the switch body.
5 Disconnect the wiring plug(s) from the rear of the switch **(see illustration)**.
6 Refitting is a reversal of removal, ensuring that, where applicable, the insulating foam is positioned around the switch as noted before removal.

Radio/cassette player remote control and cruise control stalk switches

7 Remove the three securing screws, and withdraw the lower steering column shroud.
8 Unscrew the three securing screws, and withdraw the switch from the column shroud **(see illustration)**.
9 If the cruise control switch is being removed, trace the wiring back from the switch, and disconnect the wiring connector, then withdraw the switch. Note the routing of the wiring.
10 If the radio/cassette player switch is being removed, remove the radio/cassette player as described in Section 20, then disconnect the switch wiring connector from the rear of the unit, and feed the wiring through behind the facia to enable removal of the switch. Note the routing of the wiring.
11 Refitting is a reversal of removal, ensuring that the switch wiring is routed as noted before removal.

4.12a Prise out the switch trim panel . . .

Facia-mounted push-button switches

Centre facia-mounted switches

12 Carefully prise the trim panel from the switches and clock **(see illustrations)**.
13 Using two small flat-bladed screwdrivers or similar tools, carefully lever the switch forwards to release the retaining clips **(see illustration)**.
14 Pull the switch forwards to release it from the facia, then disconnect the wiring plug and remove the switch.
15 Refitting is a reversal of removal.

Driver's side facia-mounted switches

16 To remove the instrument panel light dimmer switch or the headlight beam adjuster switch, carefully prise the switch from the facia panel using a screwdriver (take care not to damage the trim), then disconnect the wiring plug and remove the switch **(see illustration)**. Refitting is a reversal of removal.

4.12b . . . to release the securing clips (arrowed)

4.13 Lever the switch forwards to release the retaining clips

4.16 Removing the instrument panel light dimmer switch

4.17a Prise the switch surround panel from the facia . . .

17 For the push-button switches, proceed as follows:
 a) *Prise the switch surround panel from the facia, then disconnect the wiring plug(s) from the instrument panel light dimmer and/or headlight beam adjustment switch(es) and withdraw the panel (see illustration).*
 b) *Reach in through the aperture in the facia, then pull the relevant push-button switch from the facia, and disconnect the wiring plug (see illustration).*
 c) *Refitting is a reversal of removal.*

Heater blower motor switch

18 The heater blower motor switch is an integral part of the heater/ventilation control panel, and cannot be renewed separately. If the switch is faulty, the complete control panel must be renewed - refer to Chapter 3 for details.

4.17b . . . then reach in through the aperture in the facia and pull out the switch

Centre console-mounted switches

19 Using a suitable flat-bladed screwdriver, carefully prise the switch panel from the centre console **(see illustration)**.
20 Disconnect the switch wiring connectors.
21 Unscrew the securing screws, and remove the trim panel from the top of the switch panel **(see illustrations)**.
22 Release the securing clips, and withdraw the switch from the panel **(see illustration)**.
23 Refitting is a reversal of removal.

Door-mounted switches - pre-April 1997 models

Electric door mirror adjustment switch

24 Carefully prise the switch trim panel from the door pocket **(see illustration)**.
25 Using a flat-bladed screwdriver, prise the

4.19 Prise the switch panel from the centre console

switch from the door pocket, and disconnect the wiring plug **(see illustration)**.
26 Refitting is a reversal of removal.

Electric window switches

27 Prise the switch trim panel from the door pocket, then remove the blanking plate, or the electric door mirror adjustment switch (see previous paragraphs), as applicable.
28 Reach in through the aperture in the door pocket, and push out the relevant window switch **(see illustration)**.
29 Disconnect the wiring plugs and withdraw the switch **(see illustration)**.
30 Refitting is a reversal of removal.

Door-mounted switches - April 1997 models onward

31 On later models, the electric door mirror adjustment switch and electric window switches are combined in a single switch unit

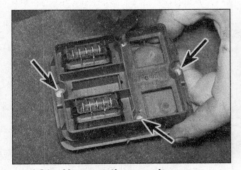

4.21a Unscrew the securing screws (arrowed) . . .

4.21b . . . and remove the trim panel . . .

4.22 . . . then withdraw the switch

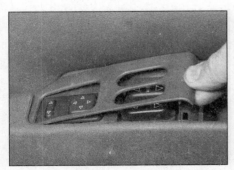

4.24 Prise the trim panel from the door pocket . . .

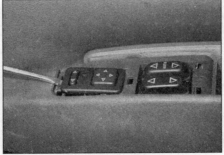

4.25 . . . then prise out the electric door mirror adjustment switch

4.28 Push the electric window switches from the door pocket

4.29 Where applicable, use a screwdriver to release the smaller wiring plug clip

4.32 Release the combined electric mirror and window switch unit . . .

4.33 . . . and disconnect the wiring plugs

mounted in the door pocket. The switch unit is removed as a complete assembly, the switches cannot be individually separated.

32 Using a flat-bladed screwdriver, prise the switch unit from the door pocket (see illustration).

33 Release the wiring plug clip and disconnect the wiring plugs (see illustration).

34 Refitting is a reversal of removal.

Courtesy light switches

Door-pillar-mounted switches

35 Open the door, then prise the rubber gaiter from the switch (see illustration).

36 Remove the securing screw, then withdraw the switch from the door pillar. Disconnect the wiring connector as it becomes accessible.

> **HAYNES HINT**
> Tape the wiring to the door pillar, to prevent it falling back into the door pillar. Alternatively, tie a piece of string to the wiring, to retrieve it.

37 Refitting is a reversal of removal, but ensure that the rubber gaiter is correctly seated on the switch.

Roof panel-mounted switches

38 The switches are integral with the relevant panel, and are not available separately.

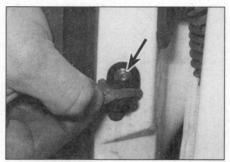

4.35 Prising the gaiter from a courtesy light switch to expose the securing screw

Glovebox light switch

39 The switch is located in the rear of the facia, above the glovebox.

40 Remove the glovebox with reference to Chapter 11.

41 Carefully prise the switch from its location in the facia, and disconnect the wiring plug.

42 Refitting is a reversal of removal.

Luggage compartment light switch

43 The light is operated by a tilt-sensitive switch fitted inside the tailgate/boot lid.

44 Open the tailgate/boot lid, then remove the securing clips, and withdraw the trim panel.

45 Remove the screw securing the switch to the tailgate/boot lid panel. Recover the

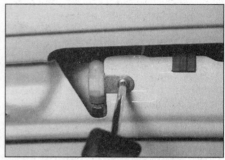

4.45 Removing the luggage compartment light switch securing screw - Hatchback models

lockwasher (see illustration).

46 Disconnect the wiring plug and withdraw the switch.

47 Refitting is a reversal of removal.

Map reading light switches

48 The switches are integral with the roof console, and are not available separately.

Electric sunroof switch

49 Prise the cover panel from the roof console, to expose the two console securing screws.

50 Remove the two securing screws, then lower the console from the roof, and disconnect the wiring plugs (see illustrations).

51 Remove the screws securing the printed circuit board and the light/switch housing to the console, then lift off the circuit board and the light/switch housing (see illustration).

4.50a Remove the securing screws . . .

4.50b . . . and withdraw the roof console

4.51 Lift off the circuit board and the light/switch housing . . .

4.52 . . . then prise the sunroof switch from the housing

52 Carefully prise the sunroof switch from the light/switch housing (see illustration).
53 Refitting is a reversal of removal.

5 Bulbs (exterior lights) - renewal

General

1 Whenever a bulb is renewed, note the following points:

a) *Disconnect the battery negative terminal before starting work. Refer to "Disconnecting the battery" in the Reference Section of this manual.*
b) *Remember that, if the light has just been in use, the bulb may be extremely hot.*
c) *Always check the bulb contacts and holder, ensuring that there is clean metal to metal contact between the bulb and its live(s) and earth. Clean off any corrosion or dirt before fitting a new bulb.*
d) *Wherever bayonet-type bulbs are fitted (see Specifications), ensure that the live contact(s) bear firmly against the bulb contact.*
e) *Always ensure that the new bulb is of the correct rating, and that it is completely clean before fitting it; this applies particularly to headlight/foglight bulbs (see below).*

Headlight

Models with single headlights

2 Working in the engine compartment, twist the headlight rear cover anti-clockwise, and remove it from the headlight (see illustration).
3 Disconnect the wiring plug from the rear of the headlight bulb (see illustration).
4 Release the spring clip by pushing it towards the right-hand side of the vehicle, then withdraw the bulb (see illustrations).
5 When handling the new bulb, use a tissue or clean cloth, to avoid touching the glass with the fingers; moisture and grease from the skin can cause blackening and rapid failure of this type of bulb. If the glass is accidentally touched, wipe it clean using methylated spirit.
6 Install the new bulb, ensuring that its locating tabs are correctly seated in the light cut-outs. Secure the bulb in position with the spring clip, and reconnect the wiring plug.
7 Refit the plastic cover, ensuring that it is correctly seated on the headlight.

Models with twin headlights

8 Working in the engine compartment, unclip the headlight rear cover.
9 Disconnect the wiring from the relevant bulb.
10 Where applicable, release the spring clip, then withdraw the bulb.
11 When handling the new bulb, use a tissue or clean cloth, to avoid touching the glass with the fingers; moisture and grease from the skin can cause blackening and rapid failure of this type of bulb. If the glass is accidentally touched, wipe it clean using methylated spirit.
12 Install the new bulb, ensuring that, where applicable, its locating tabs are correctly seated in the light cut-outs. Secure the bulb in position with the spring clip (where applicable), and reconnect the wiring plug.
13 Refit the plastic cover, ensuring that it is correctly seated on the headlight.

Front sidelight

14 Working in the engine compartment, unclip the rear cover from the headlight. On models with a round headlight cover, twist the cover anti-clockwise to release it.
15 Twist the bulbholder anti-clockwise, then withdraw it from the headlight unit (see illustration).
16 The bulb is a push-fit in the bulbholder (see illustration).
17 Refitting is the reverse of the removal procedure, ensuring that the bulbholder seal is in good condition.

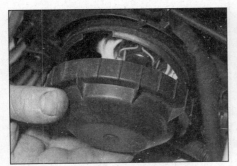

5.2 Remove the headlight cover . . .

5.3 . . . then disconnect the wiring plug from the headlight bulb

5.4a Release the spring clip . . .

5.4b . . . then withdraw the bulb

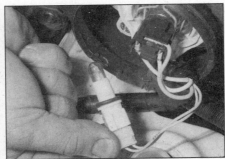

5.15 Withdrawing a sidelight bulbholder

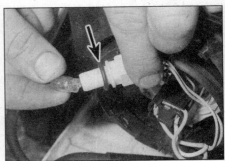

5.16 The bulb is a push-fit in the bulbholder. Note the seal (arrowed)

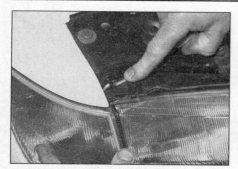

5.18 Depress the retaining lever to release the indicator light unit

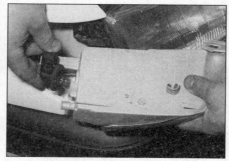

5.19 Withdraw the bulbholder

5.20 The bulb is a bayonet fit in the bulbholder

Front direction indicator - pre-April 1997 models

18 Working in the engine compartment, depress the indicator light retaining lever, then pull the light unit forwards from the wing panel **(see illustration)**.

19 Twist the bulbholder anti-clockwise to release it from the light unit **(see illustration)**.

20 The bulb is a bayonet fit in the bulbholder **(see illustration)**.

21 Refitting is a reversal of removal, but ensure that the light unit retaining lever is securely engaged.

Front direction indicator - April 1997 models onward

22 Working in the engine compartment, twist the bulbholder anti-clockwise to release it from the rear of the headlight unit **(see illustration)**.

23 The bulb is a bayonet fit in the bulbholder.

5.22 Front direction indicator bulbholder (arrowed) on later models

24 Refitting is a reversal of the removal procedure.

Front direction indicator side repeater - pre-April 1997 models

25 Push the light unit towards the rear of the vehicle, to free its retaining clips, then withdraw it from the wing panel.

26 Pull the bulbholder out of the light unit, then pull the bulb out of its holder (the bulb is a push-fit) **(see illustration)**.

27 Refitting is a reversal of the removal procedure.

Front direction indicator side repeater - April 1997 models onward

28 Pull the rear part of the transparent cover to release the assembly.

29 Support the connector, turn the transparent cover anti-clockwise then pull the bulb out of its holder (the bulb is a push-fit).

5.26 Pull the bulbholder from the side repeater light unit, then pull out the bulb

30 Refitting is a reversal of the removal procedure.

Front foglight

Note: *Some models are fitted with front foglights which have no securing screws visible from the front of the lens. At the time of writing, no information was available for this type of foglight.*

31 Working at the front of the light unit, remove the two securing screws, and withdraw the glass, surround and reflector assembly **(see illustration)**.

32 Disconnect the bulb wiring connector.

33 Release the spring clip, and remove the bulb from the rear of the light unit **(see illustration)**.

34 When handling the new bulb, use a tissue or clean cloth, to avoid touching the glass with the fingers; moisture and grease from the skin can cause blackening and rapid failure of this type of bulb. If the glass is accidentally touched, wipe it clean using methylated spirit.

35 Install the new bulb, ensuring that its locating tabs are correctly located in the light unit cut-outs. Secure the bulb in position with the clip, and reconnect the wiring connector.

36 Refit the glass, surround and reflector assembly, and tighten the securing screws.

Rear light cluster - Hatchback and Sedan models

37 Working in the luggage compartment, unscrew the two retaining nuts from the rear of the light unit.

38 Pull the cover from the rear of the light unit, then disconnect the wiring plugs **(see illustrations)**.

5.31 Remove the two securing screws and withdraw the glass, surround and reflector assembly from the foglight . . .

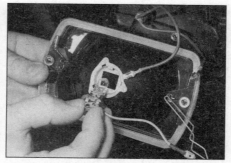

5.33 . . . then release the spring clip and withdraw the bulb

5.38a Remove the cover from the rear of the light unit . . .

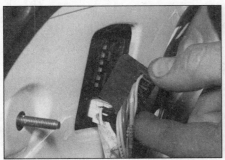

5.38b . . . then disconnect the wiring plugs

5.39 Withdraw the light unit . . .

5.40a . . . then squeeze the retaining tab . . .

39 Withdraw the light unit rearwards from the body panel **(see illustration)**.

40 Release the bulbholder from the light unit by squeezing the retaining tab **(see illustrations)**.

41 The bulbs are a bayonet fit in the bulbholder.

42 Refitting is a reversal of the removal procedure.

Rear light cluster - Estate models

43 Working in the luggage compartment, open the lid of the side storage compartment **(see illustration)**.

44 From inside the storage compartment, open the access flap **(see illustration)**.

45 Reach in through the aperture and unscrew the light unit plastic wing nut **(see illustration)**.

46 Open the tailgate and unscrew the second

plastic wing nut from the outside **(see illustration)**.

47 Withdraw the light unit rearwards from the body panel and disconnect the wiring plug **(see illustration)**.

5.40b . . . and withdraw the bulbholder

48 Release the bulbholder from the light unit by squeezing the retaining tabs **(see illustration)**.

49 The bulbs are a bayonet fit in the bulbholder **(see illustration)**.

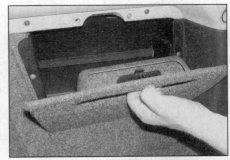

5.43 Open the lid of the storage compartment on Estate models

5.44 From inside the storage compartment, open the access flap

5.45 Reach through the aperture and unscrew the wing nut (arrowed)

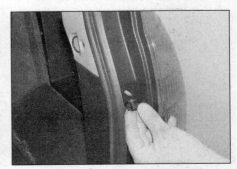

5.46 Unscrew the second wing nut from the outside

5.47 Withdraw the light unit and disconnect the wiring plug

5.48 Squeeze the retaining tabs to release the bulbholder

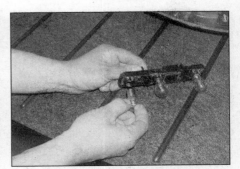

5.49 The bulbs are a bayonet fit in the bulbholder

5.51 Release the rear foglight on Estate models using a small screwdriver

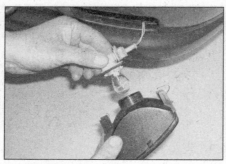

5.52 Withdraw the light unit and remove the bulbholder . . .

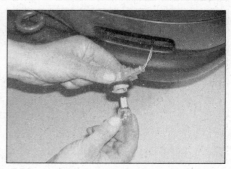

5.53 . . . then remove the bayonet fit bulb

50 Refitting is a reversal of the removal procedure.

Rear foglight - Estate models

51 Using a small screwdriver, release the retaining clip on the side of the light unit **(see illustration)**.

5.55a Depress the retaining tags . . .

52 Withdraw the light unit from the rear bumper and twist the bulbholder anti-clockwise to release it from the light unit **(see illustration)**.

53 The bulb is a bayonet fit in the bulbholder **(see illustration)**.

54 Refitting is a reversal of the removal procedure.

High-level stoplight

55 Using a small screwdriver, depress the retaining tags on the side of the light unit cover and remove the cover **(see illustrations)**.

56 Release the bulbholder from the light unit by squeezing the retaining tabs **(see illustration)**.

57 The bulbs are a push-fit in the bulbholder **(see illustration)**.

58 Refitting is a reversal of the removal procedure.

Number plate light

59 Using a suitable screwdriver, carefully prise the lens from the light unit **(see illustration)**.

60 Pull the bulb from its holder (the bulb is a push-fit) **(see illustration)**.

61 Refitting is a reversal of removal.

6 Bulbs (interior lights) - renewal

General

1 Refer to Section 5, paragraph 1.

Courtesy light

2 Carefully prise the lens from the courtesy light for access to the bulb **(see illustration)**.

3 The bulb is a push-fit in the holder.

4 Refitting is a reversal of removal.

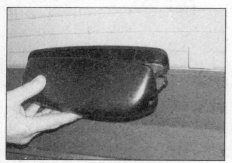

5.55b . . . and remove the high-level stoplight cover

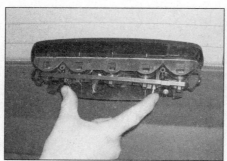

5.56 Squeeze the retaining tabs to remove the bulbholder . . .

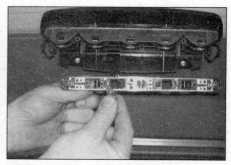

5.57 . . . then remove the push-fit bulbs from the holder

5.59 Prise the lens from the number plate light . . .

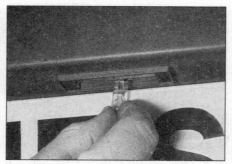

5.60 . . . then pull the bulb from the bulbholder

6.2 Prise the lens from the courtesy light for access to the bulb

6.5 Removing a map reading light bulb

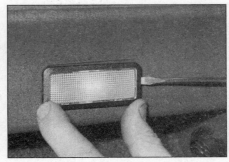

6.10 Prising out the luggage compartment light

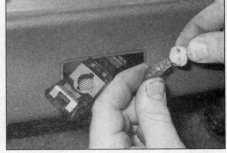

6.11a Twist the bulbholder anti-clockwise to remove, then pull out the push-fit bulb

6.11b Alternatively, depress the side tags to remove the bulbholder

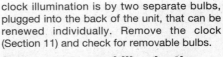

6.15 Carefully prise the front panel from the heater/ventilation control unit for access to the bulbs

clock illumination is by two separate bulbs, plugged into the back of the unit, that can be renewed individually. Remove the clock (Section 11) and check for removable bulbs.

Instrument panel illumination and warning light bulbs

19 Remove the instrument panel as described in Section 9.
20 Twist the relevant bulbholder anti-clockwise to remove it from the rear of the panel **(see illustration)**.
21 The bulbs are integral with the bulbholders.
22 On completion, refit the instrument panel with reference to Section 9.

Map reading light

5 Proceed as described previously for the courtesy light **(see illustration)**.

Glovebox light

6 Open the glovebox, then carefully prise out the light unit, and disconnect the wiring plug.
7 Twist the bulbholder anti-clockwise to release it from the rear of the light unit.
8 The bulb is a push-fit in the bulbholder.
9 Refitting is a reversal of removal.

Luggage compartment light

10 Carefully prise the light unit from its location in the luggage compartment **(see illustration)**.
11 Either twist the bulbholder anti-clockwise or depress the side retaining tags, according to type, to remove it from the rear of the light unit. The bulb is a push-fit in the bulbholder **(see illustrations)**.
12 Refitting is a reversal of removal.

Heater/ventilation control unit illumination bulbs

13 Remove the facia centre panel as described in Chapter 11.
14 Turn all the control knobs fully clockwise.
15 Using a suitable flat-bladed screwdriver, carefully prise the front panel from the control unit **(see illustration)**.
16 Carefully pull the relevant bulb from the circuit board.
17 Refitting is a reversal of removal, but ensure that all the heater control switches and knobs are turned fully clockwise before refitting the control unit front panel.

Clock and facia switch illumination bulbs

18 For the switches, the illumination is integral with each switch and cannot be renewed independently; according to the manufacturer, the same applies to the clock. However, it would seem that in some cases,

7 Exterior light units - removal and refitting

Note: *Disconnect the battery negative terminal before removing any light unit, and reconnect the terminal after refitting the unit. Refer to "Disconnecting the battery" in the Reference Section of this manual.*

Headlight - pre-April 1997 models

Removal

1 Note: *The headlight glass can be renewed after proceeding as described in paragraphs 2 to 7, and then unclipping the trim strip from the bottom of the headlight. Use a suitable screwdriver to release the glass securing clips, then pull the glass from the front of the*

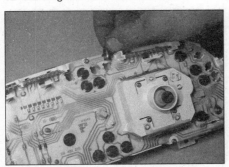

6.20 Removing an instrument panel bulb

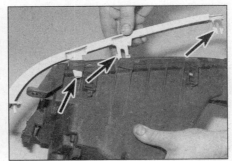

7.1a Unclip the headlight trim strip (clips arrowed) . . .

7.1b . . . then release the glass securing clips . . .

7.1c ... and withdraw the headlight glass

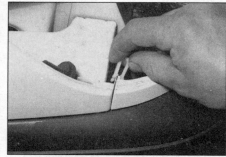

7.3 Remove the clip securing the headlight trim strip

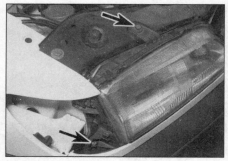

7.7a Remove the upper headlight securing screw, and the outer nut (arrowed) ...

7.7b ... and inner nut (arrowed) ...

7.7c ... then withdraw the headlight assembly

7.10 On later models, release the clip legs and withdraw the headlight trim strip

headlight, and recover the seal **(see illustrations)**. *Fit the new glass using a new seal and new clips.*

2 Remove the front grille panel (refer to Chapter 11), then remove the direction indicator unit as described later in this Section.

3 Remove the clip securing the trim strip below the headlight to the body **(see illustration)**.

4 Working in the engine compartment, remove the plastic cover from the rear of the headlight, then disconnect the wiring plugs from the rear of the bulbs.

5 Where applicable, disconnect the wiring plug from the headlight adjuster motor.

6 Unclip the wiring harness from the rear of the headlight.

7 Remove the upper headlight securing screw, then unscrew the lower headlight

securing nuts, and withdraw the headlight from the vehicle, complete with the trim strip **(see illustrations)**. Note that if desired, the balljoint and adjuster units (and the electric adjuster motor, where applicable) can be removed from the light unit after twisting the adjuster itself (or the locking collar, as applicable) to release the adjuster from the aperture in the light unit.

Refitting

8 Refitting is a reversal of removal, but on completion have the headlight beam alignment checked at the earliest opportunity.

Headlight - April 1997 models onward

Removal

9 Remove the front grille panel as described in Chapter 11.

10 Carefully release the plastic clip legs and withdraw the trim strip below the headlight **(see illustration)**.

11 Working in the engine compartment, twist the direction indicator bulbholder anti-clockwise to release it from the rear of the headlight unit.

12 Disconnect the headlight wiring plug and, where applicable, the wiring plug for the headlight adjuster motor **(see illustrations)**.

13 Undo the headlight unit upper, left-hand and right-hand mounting bolts and withdraw the unit from the front body panel **(see illustrations)**. Note that if desired, the balljoint and adjuster units (and the electric adjuster motor, where applicable) can be removed from the light unit after twisting the adjuster itself (or the locking collar, as applicable) to release the adjuster from the aperture in the light unit.

7.12a Disconnect the headlight wiring plug ...

7.12b ... and, where applicable, the headlight adjuster motor wiring plug

7.13a Undo the headlight unit upper mounting bolt (arrowed) ...

7.13b . . . left-hand mounting bolt
(arrowed) . . .

7.13c . . . and right-hand mounting bolt
(arrowed) . . .

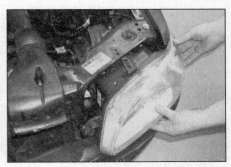

7.13d . . . then withdraw the light unit from
the front body panel

Refitting

14 Refitting is a reversal of removal, but on completion have the headlight beam alignment checked at the earliest opportunity.

Front direction indicator light - pre-April 1997 models

Removal

15 Open the bonnet.
16 Depress the indicator light unit retaining clip, located at the top outer corner of the headlight **(see illustration 5.18)**.
17 Pull the light unit out from the wing panel, and disconnect the wiring plug.

Refitting

18 Refitting is a reversal of removal, but make sure that the retaining clip engages correctly with the light unit.

Front direction indicator light - April 1997 models onward

19 On later models the direction indicator and headlight unit are all one assembly. Refer to paragraphs 9 to 14 for headlight unit removal and refitting.

Front direction indicator side repeater light

20 The procedure is described as part of the bulb renewal procedure in Section 5.

Front foglight - pre-April 1997 models

Note: *Some models are fitted with front foglights which have no securing screws visible from the front of the lens. At the time of writing, no information was available for this type of foglight.*

Removal

21 To improve access, jack up the front of the vehicle and support on axle stands (see *"Jacking and Vehicle Support"*).
22 Trace the wiring back from the rear of the foglight, and disconnect the wiring connector.
23 Slacken and remove the foglight securing nut, and withdraw the light unit from the bumper. Recover any washers and spacers, noting their locations to ensure correct refitting.

Refitting

24 Refitting is a reversal of removal, ensuring that any washers and spacers on the securing stud are positioned as noted before removal.

Front foglight - April 1997 models onward

Removal

25 Remove the front bumper as described in Chapter 11.
26 Undo the three foglight unit retaining bolts and withdraw the unit from inside the bumper.

Refitting

27 Refitting is a reversal of removal.

Rear light cluster

28 The procedure is described as part of the bulb renewal procedure in Section 5.

Rear foglight - Estate models

29 The procedure is described as part of the bulb renewal procedure in Section 5.

High-level stoplight

Removal

30 Using a small screwdriver, depress the retaining tags on the side of the light unit cover and remove the cover.
31 Undo the two screws and withdraw the light unit.
32 Disconnect the wiring connections and remove the unit.

Refitting

33 Refitting is a reversal of the removal procedure.

Number plate light - Hatchback and Sedan models

Removal

34 Using a flat-bladed screwdriver, carefully prise the light unit from the rear bumper, and disconnect the wiring plug.

Refitting

35 Refitting is a reversal of removal.

Number plate light - Estate models

Removal

36 Remove the tailgate trim panel as described in Chapter 11.
37 Reach in through the aperture on the inside of the tailgate, depress the tags on the side of the light unit and withdraw the unit from the tailgate **(see illustrations)**.
38 Disconnect the wiring plug and remove the unit.

Refitting

39 Refitting is a reversal of removal.

8 Headlight beam alignment - general information

1 Accurate adjustment of the headlight beam is only possible using optical beam-setting equipment, and this work should therefore be carried out by a Peugeot dealer or suitably-equipped workshop.
2 For reference, the headlights can be adjusted using a suitable-sized Allen key to

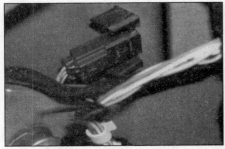

7.37a On Estate models, depress the tags on the side of the number plate light unit from inside the tailgate . . .

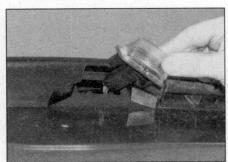

7.37b . . . then withdraw the light unit from the outside

rotate the adjuster assemblies fitted to the rear of each light unit. The outer adjuster alters the vertical height of the beam, whilst the inner adjuster alters the horizontal position of the beam. Prior to adjustment, ensure that the vehicle is unladen, and the adjuster units (see below) are both set to position "0".

3 Each headlight unit is equipped with a four or five-position vertical beam adjuster unit - this can be used to adjust the headlight beam, to compensate for the relevant load which the vehicle is carrying. The adjuster units may be incorporated into the vertical beam adjuster, or on certain models, an adjuster switch is provided on the facia. On models with adjusters mounted on the headlights, access to them can be gained with the bonnet open. The adjusters should be positioned as follows according to the load being carried in the vehicle:

Position 0	*Front seats occupied (1 or 2 people)*
Position -	*Front or rear seats occupied (3 people) (later models only)*
Position 1	*Front and rear seats occupied (5 people)*
Position 2	*Front and rear seats occupied and luggage compartment fully loaded*
Position 3	*Driver's seat occupied and luggage compartment fully loaded*

4 Ensure that both adjusters are set to the same position, and be sure to reset if the vehicle load is altered.

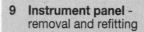

9 Instrument panel - removal and refitting

Removal

1 Disconnect the battery negative terminal (refer to *"Disconnecting the battery"* in the Reference Section of this manual).
2 Working in the engine compartment, pull the speedometer cable (where fitted) sharply to release the cable ball from the locating grommet in the bulkhead.
3 Unlock the steering column adjuster lever.
4 Working under the steering column, through the holes in the lower column shroud, unscrew the two upper securing nuts (and recover the washers), and lower the steering column **(see illustration)**. On later models without access holes, undo the three securing screws, and remove the lower column shroud
5 Unscrew the two upper and two lower instrument panel shroud securing screws, and withdraw the shroud **(see illustrations)**.
6 Unscrew the single upper and the two lower instrument panel securing screws, and pull the instrument panel forwards from the facia **(see illustrations)**.
7 Disconnect the wiring plugs, and the speedometer cable (where fitted) from the rear of the instrument panel (note the locations of the wiring connectors to ensure correct refitting), and remove the panel.

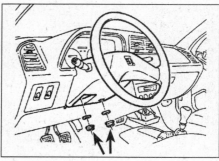

9.4 Working under the steering column, unscrew the two steering column upper securing nuts

Refitting

8 Refitting is a reversal of removal, bearing in mind the following points:
a) *Reconnect the speedometer cable to the rear of the panel before pushing the panel into position, and ensure that the seal is in position on the end of the cable.*
b) *Ensure that all wiring plugs are correctly reconnected to the rear of the instrument panel.*
c) *Engage the steering column with the upper locating studs whilst pulling on the adjuster lever.*
d) *Coat the speedometer cable ball with soapy water (eg washing-up liquid) to aid refitting, and ensure that it is correctly located in the bulkhead grommet.*

9.5a Unscrew the upper . . .

9.5b . . . and lower securing screws . . .

9.5c . . . and withdraw the instrument panel shroud

9.6a Unscrew the upper . . .

9.6b . . . and lower securing screws . . .

9.6c . . . and pull the instrument panel forwards

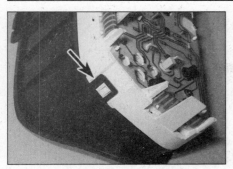

10.2a Instrument panel surround/lens securing clip (arrowed)

10 Instrument panel components - removal and refitting

General

1 Remove the instrument panel as described in Section 9, then proceed as described under the relevant sub-heading.

Gauges

2 Release the securing clips, and unscrew the three securing screws, then remove the panel surround/lens assembly from the instrument panel **(see illustrations)**.
3 Unscrew the screws or nuts, then withdraw the gauge from the front of the panel.
4 Refitting is a reversal of removal.

Illumination and warning light bulbs

5 Twist the relevant bulbholder anti-clockwise to release it from the rear of the panel. The bulbs are integral with the bulbholders.

11 Clock - removal and refitting

Removal

1 Disconnect the battery negative terminal (refer to *"Disconnecting the battery"* in the Reference Section of this manual).

2 Carefully prise the trim panel from the switches and clock.
3 Remove the two screws, and pull the clock forwards from the facia. Disconnect the wiring plug and remove the clock **(see illustrations)**.

Refitting

4 Refitting is a reversal of removal.

12 Cigarette lighter - removal and refitting

Removal

1 Disconnect the battery negative terminal (refer to *"Disconnecting the battery"* in the Reference Section of this manual).
2 Open the ashtray, then remove the four securing screws, and withdraw the ashtray assembly from the facia. Disconnect the wiring connectors from the cigarette lighter and withdraw the assembly.
3 Pull out the lighter element, release the tangs and push out the metal insert, then remove the plastic outer section of the lighter.

Refitting

4 Refitting is a reversal of removal.

13 "Lights-on" warning buzzer - general information

The purpose of this system is to inform the driver that the lights have been left on once the ignition has been switched off; the buzzer will sound when a door is opened. The system consists of a buzzer unit which is linked to the driver's door courtesy light switch.

The buzzer unit is located above the fuses in the facia fusebox, and access can be obtained once the fusebox cover has been removed. The unit is a push-fit in the panel, and can be identified by the slots in its cover.

Refer to Section 4 for information on courtesy light switch removal.

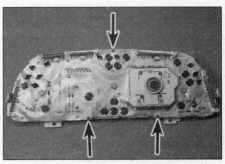

10.2b Instrument panel surround/lens securing screws (arrowed)

14 Horn - removal and refitting

Removal

1 Disconnect the battery negative terminal (refer to *"Disconnecting the battery"* in the Reference Section of this manual).
2 For improved access, apply the handbrake, then jack up the front of the vehicle and support it securely on axle stands (see *"Jacking and Vehicle Support"*).
3 Remove the securing screws, and where applicable drill out the rivets, securing the lower mud shield to the front bumper and the wheelarch liner. Withdraw the mud shield.
4 Reach up under the wheelarch, and disconnect the wiring plug from the horn.
5 Unscrew the securing nut, and withdraw the horn from its bracket **(see illustration)**.

Refitting

6 Refitting is a reversal of removal.

15 Speedometer drive cable - removal and refitting

Removal

Note: *On later models an electronic transducer provides road speed signals to the speedometer and engine management system and a speedometer drive cable is not fitted.*

11.3a Remove the securing screws . . .

11.3b . . . then withdraw the clock and disconnect the wiring plug

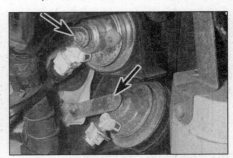

14.5 Horn securing nuts (arrowed) - viewed with front bumper removed for clarity

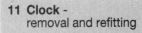

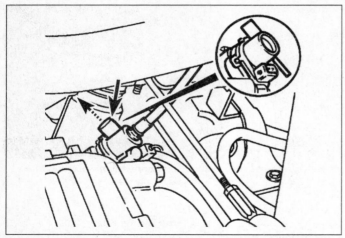

15.1 Pull the speedometer cable securing pin (arrowed) from the gearbox/transmission housing

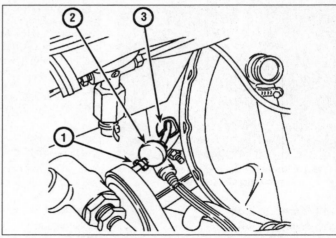

15.2 Pull sharply on the speedometer cable (1) to detach the ball (2) from the bulkhead grommet (3) - left-hand-drive model shown

1 Working in the engine compartment, pull the cable securing pin from the gearbox/ transmission housing, then release the end of the cable from the gearbox/transmission **(see illustration)**.
2 Pull the speedometer cable sharply to release the cable ball from the locating grommet in the bulkhead **(see illustration)**.
3 Pull the cable through the bulkhead grommet into the engine compartment, and withdraw it from the vehicle.

Refitting

4 Refitting is a reversal of removal, but coat the cable ball with soapy water (eg washing-

17.3 Unscrew the scuttle panel side securing nuts

up liquid) to aid refitting, and ensure that it is correctly located in the bulkhead grommet.

16 Wiper arm - removal and refitting

Removal

1 Operate the wiper motor, then switch it off so that the wiper arm returns to the at-rest position.
2 Stick a piece of masking tape along the edge of the wiper blade, to use as an alignment aid on refitting.
3 Lift up the wiper arm spindle nut cover, then slacken and remove the spindle nut. Lift the blade off the glass, and pull the wiper arm off its spindle. If necessary, the arm can be levered off the spindle using a suitable flat-bladed screwdriver.

Refitting

4 Ensure that the wiper arm and spindle splines are clean and dry, then refit the arm to the spindle, aligning the wiper blade with the tape fitted on removal.
5 Refit the spindle nut, tightening it securely, and clip the nut cover back into position.

17 Windscreen wiper components - removal and refitting

Wiper motor and linkage

Removal

1 Disconnect the battery negative terminal (refer to *"Disconnecting the battery"* in the Reference Section of this manual).
2 Remove the wiper arms (see Section 16).
3 Open the front doors, and pull the weatherstrips from the edges of the scuttle cover panels to expose the scuttle panel side securing nuts. Unscrew the nuts **(see illustration)**.
4 Remove the three securing screws, then pull the scuttle cover panels from the scuttle **(see illustrations)**.
5 Unscrew the three securing bolts, and remove the scuttle cover panel bracket from the wiper motor side of the scuttle **(see illustration)**.
6 Separate the two halves of the wiper motor wiring connector **(see illustration)**.
7 Unscrew the five securing bolts, and manipulate the motor/linkage assembly from the scuttle **(see illustrations)**.

17.4a Unscrew the outer (one screw on each side) . . .

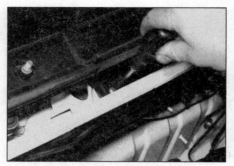

17.4b . . . and centre securing screws . . .

17.4c . . . then pull the cover panels from the scuttle

17.5 Unscrew the securing bolts (arrowed) and remove the bracket

17.6 Separate the two halves of the wiring connector

17.7a Unscrew the three upper bolts (arrowed) . . .

Refitting

8 Refitting is a reversal of removal.

Rain sensor

General

9 Certain later models are equipped with automatic windscreen wipers actuated by a rain sensor mounted on the windscreen. When the wiper switch is set to position 1, the wipers operate automatically and adapt to an appropriate speed depending on the amount of rain detected by the sensor.

Removal

10 Remove the interior mirror and mirror base by pulling downward **(see illustration)**.
11 Disconnect the rain sensor wiring plug from the top of the unit **(see illustration)**.

12 Pull out the green locking bar on each side of the sensor body and withdraw the unit from the mounting on the windscreen **(see illustrations)**.
Caution: Do not touch the rain sensor lens or the detection window on the windscreen once the sensor is removed.

Refitting

13 Locate the sensor on the windscreen mounting, maintain pressure to compress the seal and push in the green locking bars.
14 Reconnect the sensor wiring plug, then refit the interior mirror and base.
15 To check the operation of the sensor, spray water on the outside of the windscreen over the sensor detection window, with the windscreen wipers set to intermittent wipe.

18 Rear window wiper motor - removal and refitting

Hatchback models

Removal

1 Disconnect the battery negative terminal (refer to *"Disconnecting the battery"* in the Reference Section of this manual).
2 Remove the wiper arm (see Section 16).
3 Recover the trim plate, then unscrew the remaining trim plate **(see illustration)**.
4 Open the tailgate, then remove the securing screws and withdraw the tailgate trim panel.
5 Disconnect the fluid hose from the tailgate

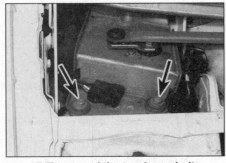

17.7b . . . and the two lower bolts (arrowed) . . .

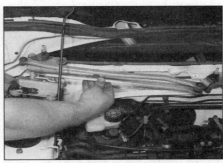

17.7c . . . and withdraw the motor/linkage assembly

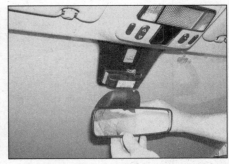

17.10 Remove the interior mirror and mirror base

17.11 Disconnect the rain sensor wiring plug

17.12a Pull out the green locking bars . . .

17.12b . . . and remove the rain sensor

18.3 Remove the trim plates from the motor spindle - Hatchback models

18.5 Disconnect the fluid hose from the washer nozzle - Hatchback models

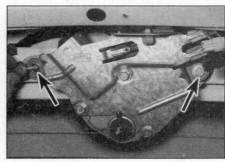

18.7 Unscrew the two motor bracket bolts (arrowed) - Hatchback models

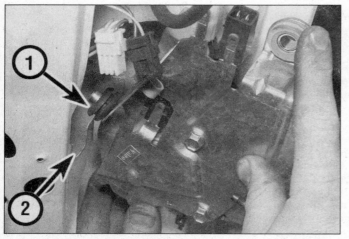

18.8 Release the lug (1) on the motor bracket from the slot (2) in the tailgate - Hatchback models

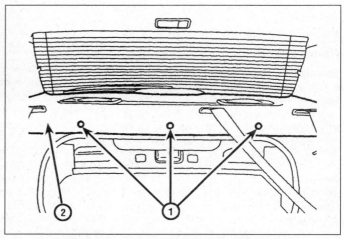

18.13 Remove the clips (1) securing the front of the parcel shelf (2) - Sedan models

washer nozzle, and release it from any relevant clips so that it can be moved clear of the wiper motor **(see illustration)**.

6 Disconnect the motor wiring connectors.

7 Unscrew the two bolts securing the motor bracket to the tailgate **(see illustration)**.

8 Slide the assembly to the right-hand side of the tailgate to release the lug at the rear of the bracket from the slot in the tailgate **(see illustration)**.

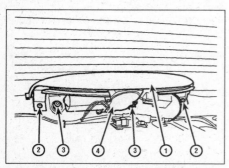

18.14 Rear window wiper motor mounting details - Sedan models

1 Motor cover
2 Motor cover fasteners
3 Motor securing bolts
4 Motor

9 Manipulate the motor assembly out through the aperture in the tailgate.

Refitting

10 Refitting is a reversal of removal.

Sedan models

Removal

11 Proceed as described in paragraphs 1 to 3.

12 Working inside the vehicle, tilt the rear seat backs forwards.

13 Remove the clips securing the front of the rear parcel shelf to the body, and lift the parcel shelf clear of the body for access to the wiper motor (there is no need to remove the parcel shelf) **(see illustration)**.

14 Remove the two fasteners and withdraw the wiper motor cover **(see illustration)**.

15 Disconnect the motor wiring plug.

16 Unscrew the two securing nuts, and withdraw the rear wiper motor assembly.

Refitting

17 Refitting is a reversal of removal.

Estate models

Removal

18 Disconnect the battery negative terminal (refer to *"Disconnecting the battery"* in the

Reference Section of this manual).

19 Remove the wiper arm (see Section 16).

20 Where applicable, recover the trim plate, then unscrew the remaining trim plate.

21 Open the tailgate, then remove the securing screws and withdraw the tailgate trim panel.

22 Disconnect the fluid hose from the tailgate washer nozzle, and release it from any relevant clips so that it can be moved clear of the wiper motor.

23 Disconnect the motor wiring connector **(see illustration)**.

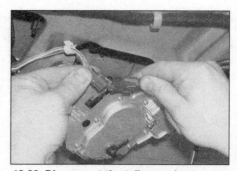

18.23 Disconnect the tailgate wiper motor wiring connector - Estate models

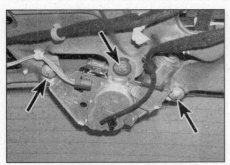

18.24 Undo the three wiper motor retaining bolts (arrowed) - Estate models

24 Unscrew the three bolts securing the motor bracket to the tailgate **(see illustration)**.
25 Manipulate the motor assembly out through the aperture in the tailgate.

Refitting

26 Refitting is a reversal of removal but apply a soapy water solution to the motor shaft sleeve to assist entry into the tailgate seal.

---

19 Windscreen/rear window/ headlight washer system - removal and refitting

---

Windscreen/rear window washer fluid reservoir

Removal

Note: *To minimise fluid spillage, it is recommended that the washer reservoir is emptied before removal.*
1 Disconnect the battery negative terminal (refer to *"Disconnecting the battery"* in the Reference Section of this manual).
2 Working in the engine compartment, unscrew the filler neck from the reservoir **(see illustration)**.
3 Jack up the front of the vehicle, and support it securely on axle stands (see *"Jacking and Vehicle Support"*).
4 Remove the right-hand roadwheel.
5 Remove the securing screws and clips, and withdraw the splash shield and the wheelarch

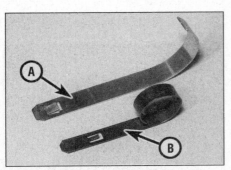

20.3a Peugeot special tools used to remove radio/cassette player

A Tool for Clarion unit
B Tool for Blaupunkt unit

---

liner to expose the fluid reservoir.
6 Disconnect the wiring plug from the washer pump located in the reservoir.
7 Disconnect the supply pipe(s) from the washer pump. Be prepared for fluid spillage if there is still fluid in the reservoir.
8 Slacken and remove the two reservoir retaining bolts, then lower the reservoir out from underneath the wheelarch.

Refitting

9 Refitting is a reversal of removal.

Washer pump

Removal

Note: *Prior to removing the pump, empty the contents of the reservoir, or be prepared for fluid spillage.*
10 Disconnect the battery negative terminal (refer to *"Disconnecting the battery"* in the Reference Section of this manual).
11 Jack up the front of the vehicle and support it securely on axle stands (see *"Jacking and Vehicle Support"*).
12 Remove the right-hand roadwheel.
13 Remove the securing screws and clips, and withdraw the splash shield and the wheelarch liner to expose the fluid reservoir.
14 Disconnect the wiring connector from the pump, then carefully ease the pump out of its sealing grommet.

Refitting

15 Refitting is a reversal of removal.

Windscreen washer jet

16 Open the bonnet, then unclip the washer jet from the bonnet, and disconnect it from its supply pipe.
17 On refitting, ensure that the jet is clipped securely in position. If necessary, the jet nozzles can be adjusted using a pin; aim the spray to a point slightly above the centre of the wiper swept area.

Tailgate washer jet

18 The tailgate washer jet is integral with the wiper arm.

Headlight washer fluid reservoir

Note: *On later models the headlight washers are supplied by the windscreen/tailgate washer fluid reservoir.*

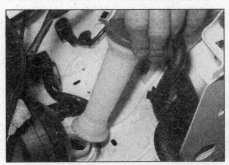

19.2 Unscrewing the filler neck from the washer fluid reservoir

19 The reservoir is located at the left-hand front corner of the engine compartment.
20 Proceed as described previously for the windscreen/tailgate washer fluid reservoir.

Headlight washer jet

21 Prise the jet from its location, and disconnect the fluid hose.

---

20 Radio/cassette player - removal and refitting

Removal

Note: *Once the battery has been disconnected, the radio/cassette unit cannot be re-activated until the appropriate security code has been entered. Do not remove the unit unless the appropriate code is known.*
1 Disconnect the battery negative terminal (refer to *"Disconnecting the battery"* in the Reference Section of this manual).
2 Measure the notches in the front lower edge of the radio/cassette player front panel. This will enable the correct tools to be constructed to release the unit from the facia. The slots may be either 10.0 mm or 14.0 mm wide.
Note: *Removal tools may well be supplied with the vehicle documents in the glovebox, or could be borrowed from a Peugeot dealer.*
3 Make up two tools (if necessary) as shown using thin strips of metal of the appropriate width **(see illustrations)**.
4 Insert the tools into the slots between the radio/cassette unit and the facia panel.

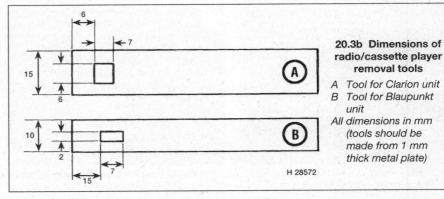

20.3b Dimensions of radio/cassette player removal tools

A Tool for Clarion unit
B Tool for Blaupunkt unit

All dimensions in mm (tools should be made from 1 mm thick metal plate)

H 28572

20.5 Insert the tools, then pull out to release the radio/cassette player

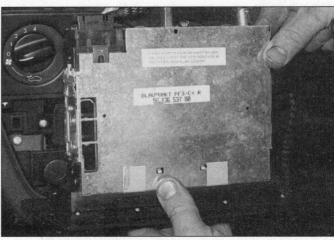

20.6 Pull the unit out and disconnect the wiring connectors and aerial lead

5 Push the tools fully inwards, then pull out to release the radio/cassette unit **(see illustration)**.

6 Disconnect the wiring and the aerial lead from the rear of the unit, then remove the unit from the vehicle **(see illustration)**.

Refitting

7 Reconnect the wiring plugs and the aerial lead to the rear of the unit, then push the unit back into its location in the facia until the retaining lugs lock.

8 Reconnect the battery negative terminal, then enter the appropriate code to activate the unit.

---

21 Loudspeakers -
removal and refitting

Front door-mounted speakers

Removal

1 Disconnect the battery negative terminal (refer to *"Disconnecting the battery"* in the Reference Section of this manual).

2 Prise the loudspeaker cover plate from the door, or remove the securing screws and withdraw the cover plate, as applicable.

---

3 Unscrew the screws, then withdraw the loudspeaker from the door panel and disconnect the wiring plug **(see illustrations)**.

Refitting

4 Refitting is a reversal of removal.

Rear parcel shelf-mounted speakers - Hatchback models

Removal

5 Disconnect the battery negative terminal (refer to *"Disconnecting the battery"* in the Reference Section of this manual).

6 Working in the luggage compartment, turn the locking ring, and disconnect the loudspeaker wiring from the connector on the left-hand side of the body **(see illustration)**.

7 Release the securing clips and remove the rear parcel shelf.

8 Working under the parcel shelf, remove the three loudspeaker securing screws, then withdraw the loudspeaker from the top of the parcel shelf, and disconnect the wiring plug **(see illustrations)**.

Refitting

9 Refitting is a reversal of removal.

21.3a Unscrew the securing screws ...

21.3b ... and withdraw the front loudspeaker

21.6 Disconnect the loudspeaker wiring connector - Hatchback models

21.8a Remove the three loudspeaker securing screws ...

21.8b ... and withdraw the loudspeaker - Hatchback models

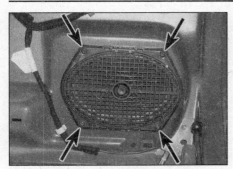

21.16 Undo the four screws (arrowed) to remove the tailgate loudspeaker - Estate models

Rear parcel shelf-mounted loudspeakers - Sedan models

Removal

10 Working inside the vehicle, tilt the rear seat back forwards.

11 Working in the luggage compartment, disconnect the loudspeaker wiring plugs.

12 Prise out the clips securing the rear parcel shelf, then release the edges of the parcel shelf from the side trim panels. Lift the parcel shelf, and pull it forwards from its location.

13 Unscrew the three securing screws, and withdraw the loudspeaker from its location.

Refitting

14 Refitting is a reversal of removal.

Rear tailgate-mounted loudspeakers - Estate models

Removal

15 Open the tailgate, undo the securing screws and remove the tailgate trim panel.

16 Undo the retaining screws and withdraw the loudspeaker from the tailgate **(see illustration)**.

17 Disconnect the wiring plugs and remove the loudspeaker.

Refitting

18 Refitting is a reversal of removal.

---

22 Radio aerial - removal and refitting

Aerial

Removal

1 Prise the cover panel from the roof console, to expose the two console securing screws.

2 Remove the two securing screws, then lower the console from the roof, and disconnect the wiring plugs.

3 Slacken and remove the nut from the base of the aerial, and disengage the aerial lead collar from its stud. The aerial can then be lifted away from the outside of the vehicle, noting the rubber seal which is fitted to its base.

Refitting

4 Check that the rubber seal is in good condition, and renew if necessary.

5 Refitting is a reversal of removal, ensuring that the locating pin is correctly located in its hole.

Aerial lead upper section

Removal

6 Remove the aerial as described previously in this Section.

7 Working inside the vehicle, locate the radio aerial wiring connector. The connector is located at the lower right-hand side of the facia on right-hand-drive models, or at the lower left-hand side of the facia on left-hand-drive models. Separate the two halves of the connector **(see illustration)**.

8 Tie a length of string to the aerial end of the lead, then withdraw the lead through the overhead console aperture, and untie the string from its end.

9 Leave the string in position - it can then be used to draw the lead back into position on refitting.

Refitting

10 Tie the length of string to the end of the aerial lead, and use the string to draw the lead back into position.

11 Further refitting is a reversal of removal, but refit the aerial with reference to paragraphs 4 and 5.

Aerial lead lower section

12 To remove the lower section of the aerial lead, it is necessary to remove the facia assembly as described in Chapter 11. The lead can then be freed from its retaining clips, and removed from the vehicle.

---

23 Anti-theft alarm system and engine immobiliser - general information

Note: *This information is applicable only to the anti-theft alarm system fitted by Peugeot as standard equipment.*

General

Some models in the range are fitted with an anti-theft alarm system as standard equipment.

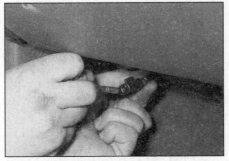

22.7 Separate the two halves of the radio aerial wiring connector

The alarm is automatically armed and disarmed using the remote central locking transmitter (where applicable). When the system is activated, the alarm indicator light, located on the facia, will flash continuously. In addition to the alarm function, the system also incorporates an engine immobiliser.

Additionally, certain models are fitted with a coded engine immobiliser device, operated by a key pad in the centre console, or an electronic immobiliser activated by a transponder in the ignition key.

Anti-theft alarm system

Note that if the doors are operated using the key, the alarm will not be armed or disarmed (as applicable). If for some reason the remote central locking transmitter fails whilst the alarm is armed, the alarm can be disarmed using the key. To do this, open the door with the key, then enter the vehicle, noting that the alarm will sound as the door is opened, and switch on the ignition switch whilst depressing the small alarm button, mounted on the right of the steering column. Note that the ignition switch must be turned on and the button depressed within 10 seconds of opening the door.

The alarm system has switches on the bonnet, tailgate and each of the doors. It also has ultrasonic sensing, which detects movement inside the vehicle, via sensors mounted on either side of the vehicle interior. If required, the ultrasonic sensing facility can be switched off, whilst retaining the switched side of the system. To switch off the ultrasonic sensing, with the ignition switched off, depress the alarm switch (mounted on the right of the steering column) until the alarm indicator light on the facia is continuously lit. Now, when the doors are locked using the remote central locking transmitter, and the alarm is armed, only the switched side of the alarm system is operational (and the alarm indicator light will revert to its flashing mode). This facility is useful, as it allows you to leave the windows/sunroof open, and still arm the alarm. If the windows/sunroof are left open with the ultrasonic sensing not switched off, the alarm may be falsely triggered by a gust of wind.

To deactivate the complete alarm system, a master switch is provided in the engine compartment, behind the right-hand headlight. The switch is operated by a dedicated key, and is protected by a plastic cover.

Should the alarm system become faulty, the vehicle should be taken to a Peugeot dealer for examination.

Coded engine immobiliser - pre-April 1997 models

Caution: Do not forget the immobiliser code - if the correct code cannot be entered, the engine management electronic control unit must be renewed.

This device cuts out the engine management system, and prevents the engine from being started unless a confidential code is keyed into the pad located in the centre console.

The code can be chosen by the owner, and full details are given in the vehicle handbook.

When the ignition is turned on, if the green light on the key pad is illuminated, the system is not working, and the engine can be started normally. If the red light is illuminated, the system is working (the engine cannot be started, and the alarm will sound if starting is attempted).

To de-activate the system, enter the correct code, which should be confirmed by four flashes from the green light, and four beeps. The red light should go out, and the engine can then be started.

If the wrong code is entered, the red light will stay on, and the engine cannot be started.

Electronic immobiliser - April 1997 models onward

On later models, the coded engine immobiliser is replaced by an electronic immobiliser. The electronic immobiliser consists of a transponder fitted to the ignition key, an analogue module fitted around the ignition switch and a control module located in the facia.

When the ignition key is inserted in the switch and turned to the ignition on position, the control module sends a pre-programmed recognition code signal to the analogue module on the ignition switch. If the recognition code signal matches that of the transponder on the ignition key, an unlocking request signal is sent to the engine management ECU allowing the engine to be started. If the ignition key signal is not recognised, the engine management system remains immobilised.

When the ignition is switched off, a locking signal is sent to the ECU and the engine is immobilised until the unlocking request signal is again received.

The recognition code is programmed into the system during manufacture and is contained on a confidential card supplied with the vehicle. The card should be kept in a safe place - never in the vehicle. The confidential card will be required if any work is to be carried out on the system by a Peugeot dealer, or if replacement keys are required.

Disconnecting the vehicle battery

Refer to "Disconnecting the battery" in the Reference Section of this manual).

24 "Dim-dip" lighting system (UK models only) - general information

To comply with UK regulations, a "dim-dip" lighting system is fitted to all UK models. The system operates through a dim-dip relay, and a resistor unit.

The dim-dip relay is supplied with current from the sidelight circuit, and is energised by a feed from the ignition switch. When energised, the unit allows battery voltage to pass through the resistor unit to the headlight dipped-beam circuits; this illuminates the headlights with approximately one-sixth of their normal power, so that the vehicle cannot be driven using sidelights alone.

25 Air bag system - general information, precautions and system de-activation

General information

A driver's air bag is fitted as standard equipment on certain models, and is an option on all other models. The air bag is fitted in the steering wheel centre pad. Additionally, on later models, a passenger's air bag located in the facia, and side air bags located in the front seats are also optionally available.

The system is armed only when the ignition is switched on, however, a reserve power source maintains a power supply to the system in the event of a break in the main electrical supply. The steering wheel and facia air bags are activated by a "g" sensor (deceleration sensor), and controlled by an electronic control unit which is integral with the steering wheel. The side air bags are activated by severe side impact and operate independently of the main system and of each other. A separate electrical supply and control unit is provided for each side air bag.

The air bags are inflated by a gas generator, which forces the bag out from its location in the steering wheel, facia or seat back frame.

Precautions

⚠️ **Warning: The following precautions must be observed when working on vehicles equipped with an air bag system, to prevent the possibility of personal injury.**

General precautions

The following precautions **must** be observed when carrying out work on a vehicle equipped with an air bag:

a) *Do not disconnect the battery with the engine running.*

b) *Before carrying out any work in the vicinity of the air bag, removal of any of the air bag components, or any welding work on the vehicle, de-activate the system as described in the following sub-Section.*

c) *Do not attempt to test any of the air bag system circuits using test meters or any other test equipment.*

d) *If the air bag warning light comes on, or any fault in the system is suspected, consult a Peugeot dealer without delay.* **Do not** *attempt to carry out fault diagnosis, or any dismantling of the components.*

Precautions to be taken when handling an air bag

a) *Transport the air bag by itself, bag upward.*

b) *Do not put your arms around the air bag.*

c) *Carry the air bag close to the body, bag outward.*

d) *Do not drop the air bag or expose it to impacts.*

e) *Do not attempt to dismantle the air bag unit.*

f) *Do not connect any form of electrical equipment to any part of the air bag circuit.*

Precautions to be taken when storing an air bag unit

a) *Store the unit in a cupboard with the air bag upward.*

b) *Do not expose the air bag to temperatures above 80°C.*

c) *Do not expose the air bag to flames.*

d) *Do not attempt to dispose of the air bag - consult a Peugeot dealer.*

e) *Never refit an air bag which is known to be faulty or damaged.*

De-activation of air bag system

The system must be de-activated before carrying out any work on the air bag components or surrounding area:

a) *Switch off the ignition.*

b) *Remove the ignition key.*

c) *Switch off all electrical equipment.*

d) *Disconnect the battery negative terminal (refer to "Disconnecting the battery" in the Reference Section of this manual).*

e) *Insulate the battery negative terminal and the end of the battery negative lead to prevent any possibility of contact.*

f) *Wait for at least ten minutes before carrying out any further work.*

Activation of air bag system

To activate the system on completion of any work, proceed as follows:

a) *Ensure that there are no occupants in the vehicle, and that there are no loose objects around the vicinity of the steering wheel. Close the vehicle doors and windows.*

b) *Insert the ignition key, and switch on the ignition.*

c) *Reconnect the battery negative terminal.*

d) *Switch off the ignition.*

e) *Switch on the ignition once more, and check that the air bag warning light in the steering wheel illuminates for approximately 3 seconds and then extinguishes.*

f) *Switch off the ignition.*

g) *If the air bag warning light does not operate as described in paragraph e), consult a Peugeot dealer before driving the vehicle.*

26.7 Turn the steering wheel for access to the two air bag unit securing screws (arrowed)

26 Air bag system components - removal and refitting

⚠️ *Warning: Refer to the precautions given in Section 25 before attempting to carry out work on any of the air bag components.*

Note: *The following information is applicable to vehicles fitted with a driver's air bag in the steering wheel. At the time of writing, no information was available concerning the passenger's air bag in the facia, or the side air* bags located in the front seats. On vehicles equipped with a passenger's air bag or side air bags, consult a Peugeot dealer before carrying out any work in the vicinity of the air bag components.

General

1 The air bag sensors are integral with the electronic control unit, which is itself integral with the steering wheel. The air bag warning light is integral with the air bag unit.

2 Any suspected faults with the air bag system should be referred to a Peugeot dealer - under no circumstances attempt to carry out any work other than removal and refitting of the air bag unit and/or the rotary connector, as described in the following paragraphs.

Air bag electronic control unit

3 The unit is integral with the steering wheel, and cannot be removed independently. Refer to Chapter 10 for details of steering wheel removal.

Air bag unit

Removal

4 The air bag unit is an integral part of the steering wheel centre boss.

5 De-activate the air bag system as described in Section 25.

6 Move the steering wheel as necessary for access to the two air bag unit securing screws. The screws are located at the rear of the steering wheel boss.

7 Remove the two air bag unit securing screws **(see illustration)**.

8 Gently pull the air bag unit from the centre of the steering wheel.

9 Carefully unclip the wiring connector from the air bag unit (use the fingers only, and pull the connector upward from the air bag unit).

10 If the air bag unit is to be stored for any length of time, refer to the storage precautions given in Section 25.

Refitting

11 Refitting is a reversal of removal, bearing in mind the following points:
 a) *Do not strike the air bag unit, or expose it to impacts during refitting.*
 b) *Tighten the air bag unit securing screws to the specified torque.*
 c) *On completion of refitting, activate the air bag system as described in Section 25.*

Air bag rotary connector

Removal

12 Remove the air bag unit, as described previously in this Section.

13 Remove the steering wheel as described in Chapter 10.

14 Remove the three securing screws, and withdraw the lower steering column shroud. Where applicable, manipulate the steering column adjuster lever as necessary to enable removal of the shroud.

15 If necessary, lower the column, then unclip the upper column shroud.

16 Carefully unclip the red rotary connector wiring plug from its bracket using a thin screwdriver blade inserted between the bracket and the connector **(see illustration)**.

17 Release the securing clip, and separate the two halves of the plug.

18 Remove the two screws securing the left-hand steering column stalk switch, then slide the switch from its bracket so that the end of the switch clears the indicator cancelling finger.

19 Unscrew the three securing screws, and withdraw the rotary connector from the steering column, feeding the wiring harness through the stalk switch bracket. Note the routing of the wiring harness.

Caution: Do not pull out the supply plug ("1" in illustration 26.16) when removing the rotary connector.

Refitting

20 Refitting is a reversal of removal, bearing in mind the following points:
 a) *Before refitting the steering column shrouds, ensure that the rotary connector wiring harness is correctly routed as noted before removal. Ensure that the wiring plug securing clip (securing the two halves of the plug together) is securely engaged.*
 b) *Refit the steering wheel as described in Chapter 10, and refit the air bag unit as described previously in this Section.*

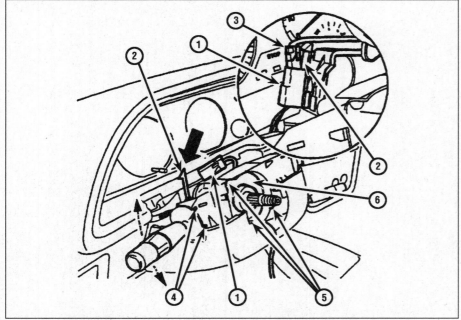

26.16 Air bag rotary connector mounting details

1 Red rotary connector wiring (supply) plug
2 Plug securing clip
3 Rotary connector plug
4 Stalk switch securing screws
5 Rotary connector securing screws
6 Rotary connector

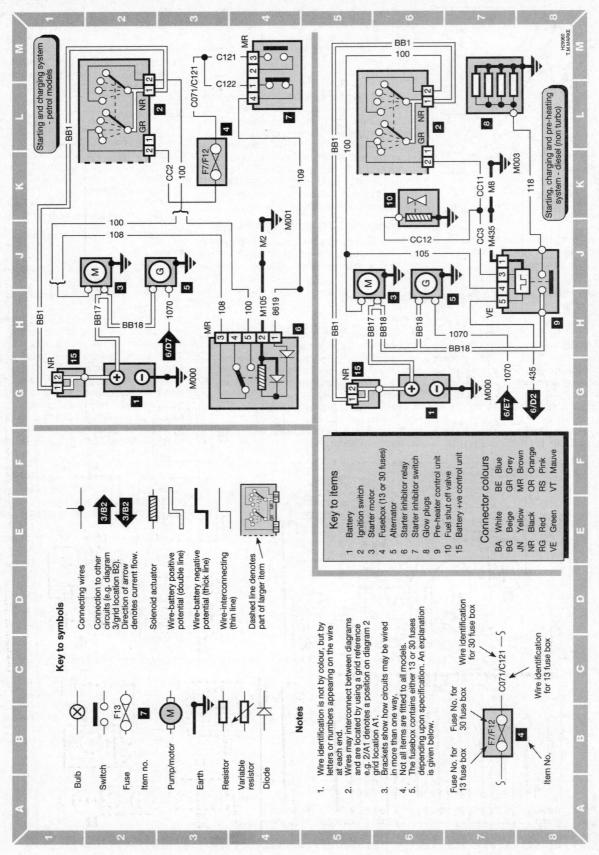

Diagram 1: Notes, key to symbols, typical starting, charging and pre-heating systems – up to April 1997

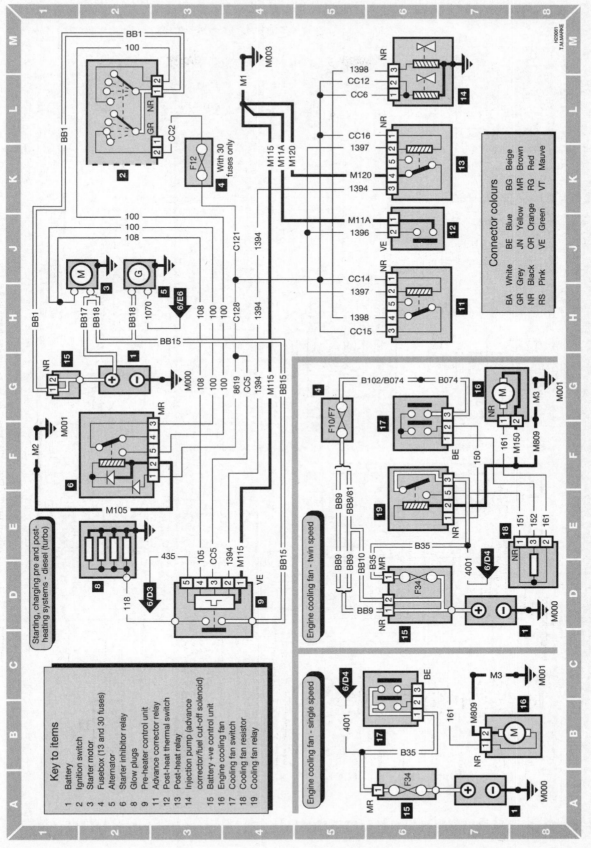

Key to items
1 Battery
2 Ignition switch
3 Starter motor
4 Fusebox (13 and 30 fuses)
5 Alternator
6 Starter inhibitor relay
7 Glow plugs
8 Pre-heater control unit
9 Advance corrector relay
10 Post-heat thermal switch
11 Post-heat relay
12 Injection pump (advance corrector/fuel cut-off solenoid)
13 Battery +ve control unit
14 Engine cooling fan
15 Cooling fan switch
16 Cooling fan resistor
17 Cooling fan relay

Connector colours

BA	White	BG	Beige
GR	Grey	MR	Brown
NR	Black	RG	Red
RS	Pink	VT	Mauve
BE	Blue		
JN	Yellow		
OR	Orange		
VE	Green		

Starting, charging pre and post-heating systems - diesel (turbo)

Engine cooling fan - twin speed

Engine cooling fan - single speed

Diagram 2: Typical starting, charging, cooling fan, pre- and post-heating systems – up to April 1997

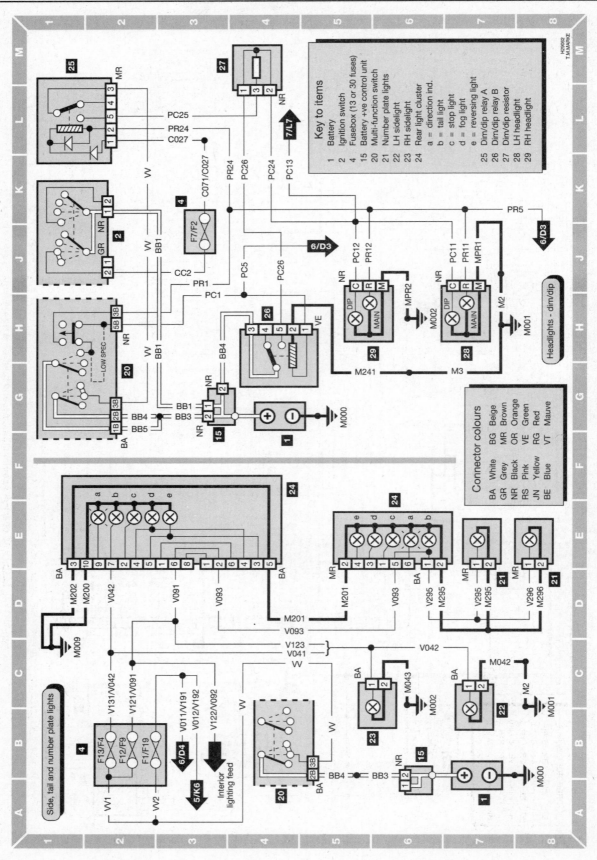

Diagram 3: Typical exterior lighting – up to April 1997

Key to items

1 Battery
2 Ignition switch
4 Fusebox (13 or 30 fuses)
15 Battery +ve control unit
20 Multi-function switch
21 Number plate lights
22 LH sidelight
23 RH sidelight
24 Rear light cluster
  a = direction ind.
  b = tail light
  c = stop light
  d = fog light
  e = reversing light
25 Dim/dip relay A
26 Dim/dip relay B
27 Dim/dip resistor
28 LH headlight
29 RH headlight

Connector colours

BA	White	BG	Beige
GR	Grey	MR	Brown
NR	Black	OR	Orange
RS	Pink	VE	Green
JN	Yellow	RG	Red
BE	Blue	VT	Mauve

Headlights - dim/dip

Side, tail and number plate lights

Interior lighting feed

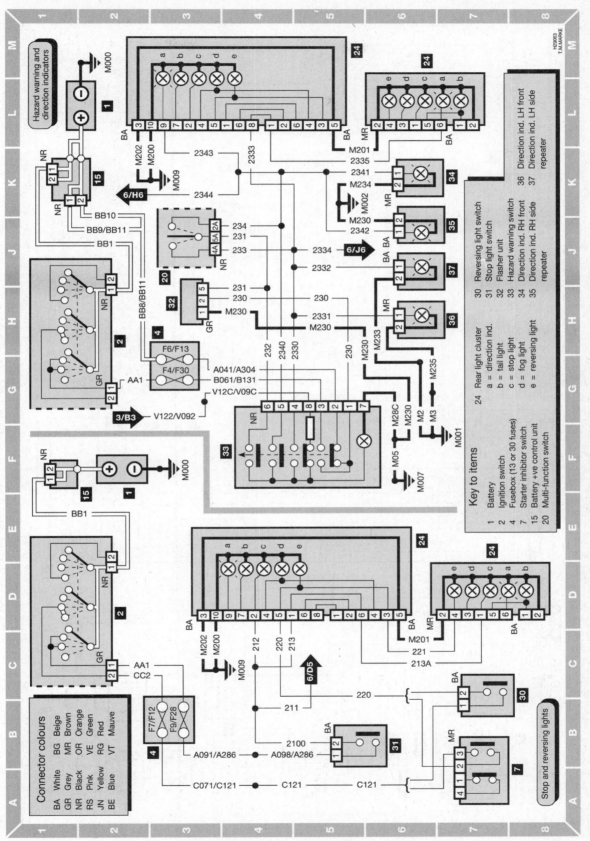

Diagram 4: Typical exterior lighting (continued) – up to April 1997

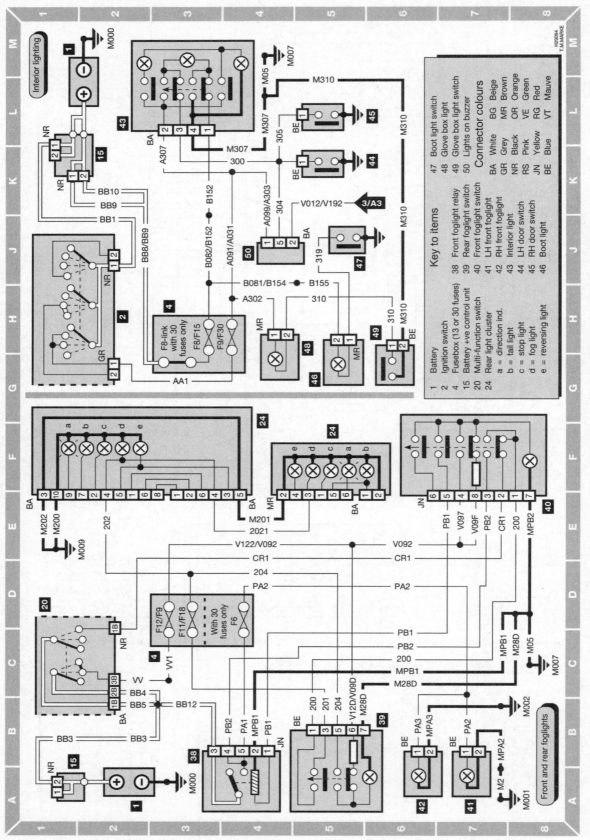

Diagram 5: Typical exterior lighting (continued) and interior lighting – up to April 1997

Key to items

1 Battery
2 Ignition switch
4 Fusebox (13 or 30 fuses)
15 Battery +ve control unit
20 Multi-function switch
24 Rear light cluster
   a = direction ind.
   b = tail light
   c = stop light
   d = fog light
   e = reversing light

38 Front foglight relay
39 Rear foglight switch
40 Front foglight switch
41 LH front foglight
42 RH front foglight
43 Interior light
44 LH door switch
45 RH door switch
46 Boot light
47 Boot light switch
48 Glove box light
49 Glove box light switch
50 Lights on buzzer

Connector colours

BA White
GR Grey
NR Black
RS Pink
JN Yellow
BE Blue
BG Beige
MR Brown
OR Orange
VE Green
RG Red
VT Mauve

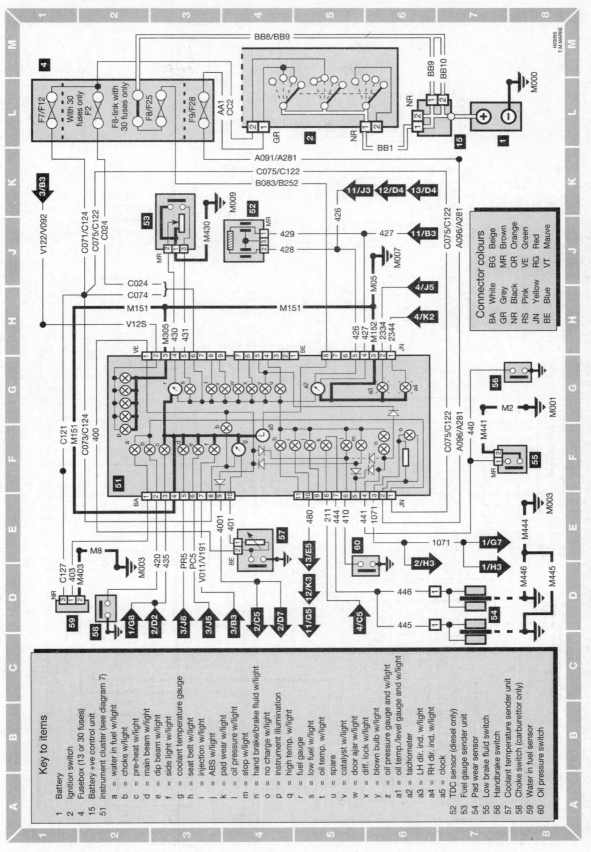

Diagram 6: Typical instrument cluster (low specification models) – up to April 1997

Connector colours

BA = White   GR = Grey
GR = Grey   MR = Grey
NR = Black   OR = Orange
RS = Pink   VE = Green
JN = Yellow   RG = Red
BE = Blue   VT = Mauve

BG = Beige
MR = Brown

Key to items

1 = Battery
2 = Ignition switch
4 = Fusebox (13 or 30 fuses)
15 = Battery +ve control unit
51 = Instrument cluster (see diagram 7)

a = water in fuel w/light
b = choke w/light
c = pre-heat w/light
d = main beam w/light
e = dip beam w/light
f = side light w/light
g = coolant temperature gauge
h = seat belt w/light
i = injection w/light
j = ABS w/light
k = pad wear w/light
l = oil pressure w/light
m = stop w/light
n = hand brake/brake fluid w/light
o = no charge w/light
p = instrument illumination
q = high temp. w/light
r = fuel gauge
s = low fuel w/light
t = oil temp. w/light
u = spare
v = catalyst w/light
w = door ajar w/light
x = diff. lock w/light
y = blown bulb w/light
z = oil pressure gauge and w/light
a1 = oil temp./level gauge and w/light
a2 = tachometer
a3 = LH dir. ind. w/light
a4 = RH dir. ind. w/light
a5 = clock

52 = TDC sensor (diesel only)
53 = Fuel gauge sender unit
54 = Pad wear sensor
55 = Low brake fluid switch
56 = Handbrake switch
57 = Coolant temperature sender unit
58 = Choke switch (carburettor only)
59 = Water in fuel sensor
60 = Oil pressure switch

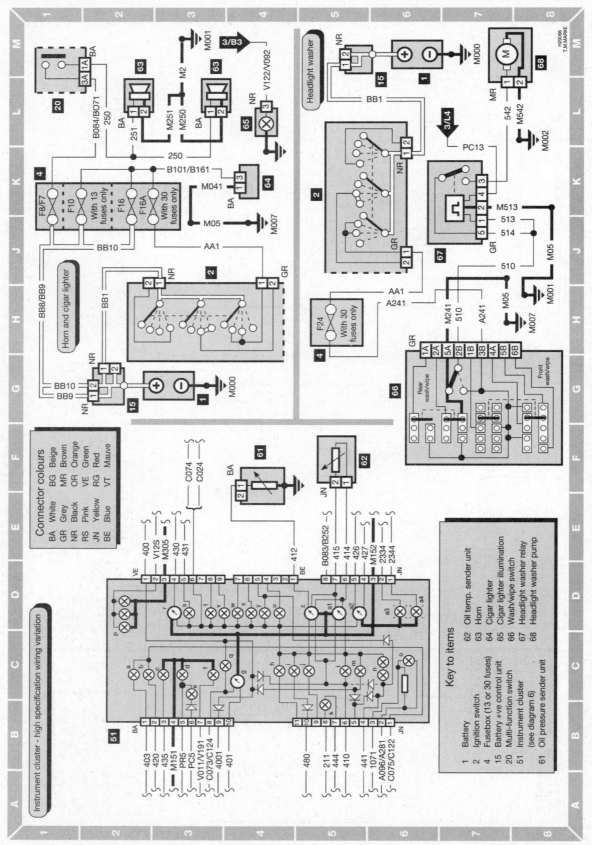

Diagram 7: Typical instrument cluster (high specification wiring variation), horn, cigar lighter and headlight washers – up to April 1997

Connector colours

BA	White	BG	Beige
GR	Grey	MR	Brown
NR	Black	OR	Orange
RS	Pink	VE	Green
JN	Yellow	RG	Red
BE	Blue	VT	Mauve

Key to items

1	Battery
2	Ignition switch
4	Fusebox (13 or 30 fuses)
15	Battery +ve control unit
20	Multi-function switch
51	Instrument cluster (see diagram 6)
61	Oil pressure sender unit
62	Oil temp. sender unit
63	Horn
64	Cigar lighter
65	Cigar lighter illumination
66	Wash/wipe switch
67	Headlight washer relay
68	Headlight washer pump

Instrument cluster – high specification wiring variation

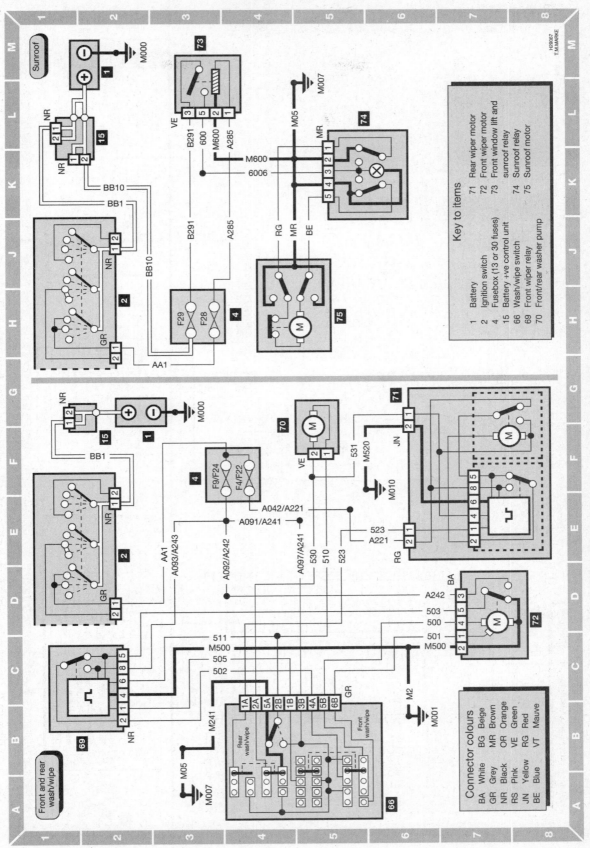

Diagram 8: Typical wash/wipe and sunroof - up to April 1997

Sunroof

Front and rear wash/wipe

Key to items

1 Battery
2 Ignition switch
4 Fusebox (13 or 30 fuses)
15 Battery +ve control unit
66 Wash/wipe switch
69 Front wiper relay
70 Front/rear washer pump
71 Rear wiper motor
72 Front wiper motor
73 Front window lift and sunroof relay
74 Sunroof relay
75 Sunroof motor

Connector colours

BA White
GR Grey
NR Black
RS Pink
JN Yellow
BE Blue
BG Beige
MR Brown
OR Orange
VE Green
RG Red
VT Mauve

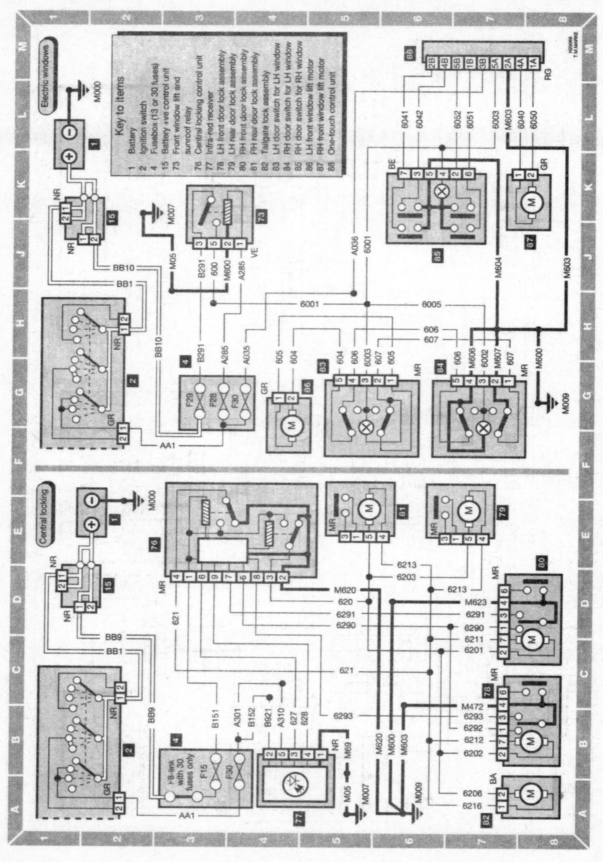

Electric windows

Central locking

Key to items
1 Battery
2 Ignition switch
4 Fusebox (13 or 30 fuses)
15 Battery +ve control unit
73 Front window lift end
76 Sunroof relay
77 Central locking control unit
77 Infra-red receiver
78 LH front door lock assembly
79 LH rear door lock assembly
80 RH front door lock assembly
81 RH rear door lock assembly
82 Tailgate lock assembly
83 LH door switch for LH window
84 RH door switch for LH window
85 RH door switch for RH window
86 LH front window lift motor
87 RH front window lift motor
88 One-touch control unit

Diagram 9: Typical central locking and electric window - up to April 1997

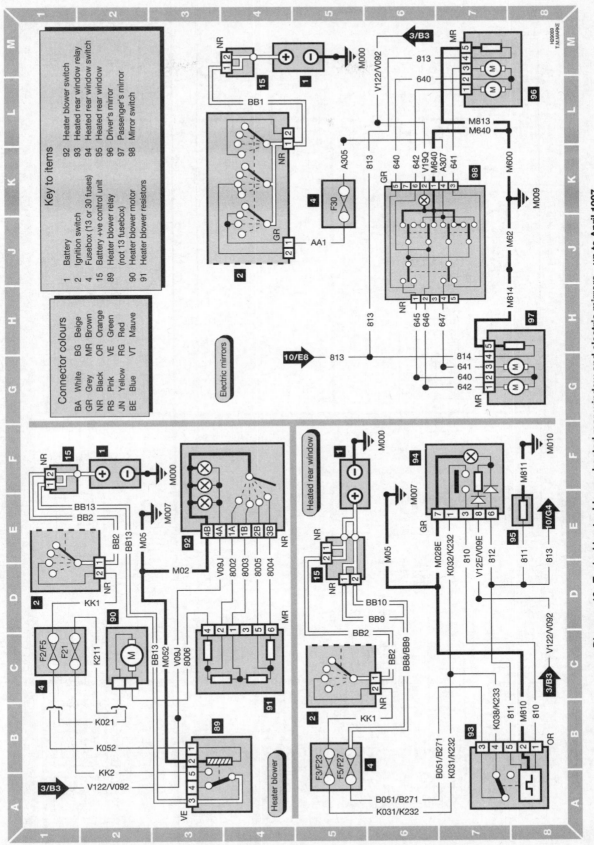

Key to items

1	Battery
2	Ignition switch
4	Fusebox (13 or 30 fuses)
15	Battery +ve control unit
89	Heater blower relay (not 13 fusebox)
90	Heater blower motor
91	Heater blower resistors
92	Heater blower switch
93	Heated rear window relay
94	Heated rear window switch
95	Heated rear window
96	Driver's mirror
97	Passenger's mirror
98	Mirror switch

Connector colours

BA	White	BG	Beige
GR	Grey	MR	Brown
NR	Black	OR	Orange
RS	Pink	VE	Green
JN	Yellow	RG	Red
BE	Blue	VT	Mauve

Electric mirrors

Heated rear window

Heater blower

Diagram 10: Typical heater blower, heated rear window and electric mirrors - up to April 1997

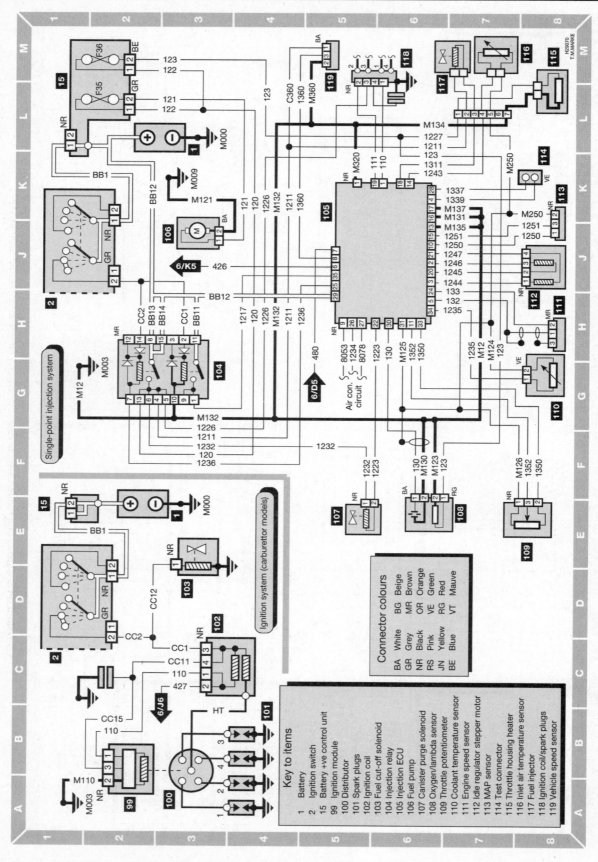

Diagram 11: Typical ignition system (carburettor models) and single-point fuel injection system - up to April 1997

Connector colours

BA	White	BG	Beige
GR	Grey	MR	Brown
NR	Black	OR	Orange
RS	Pink	VE	Green
JN	Yellow	RG	Red
BE	Blue	VT	Mauve

Key to items

1 Battery
2 Ignition switch
15 Battery +ve control unit
99 Ignition module
100 Distributor
101 Spark plugs
102 Ignition coil
103 Fuel cut-off solenoid
104 Injection relay
105 Injection ECU
106 Fuel pump
107 Canister purge solenoid
108 Oxygen/lambda sensor
109 Throttle potentiometer
110 Coolant temperature sensor
111 Engine speed sensor
112 Idle regulator stepper motor
113 MAP sensor
114 Test connector
115 Throttle housing heater
116 Inlet air temperature sensor
117 Fuel injector
118 Ignition coil/spark plugs
119 Vehicle speed sensor

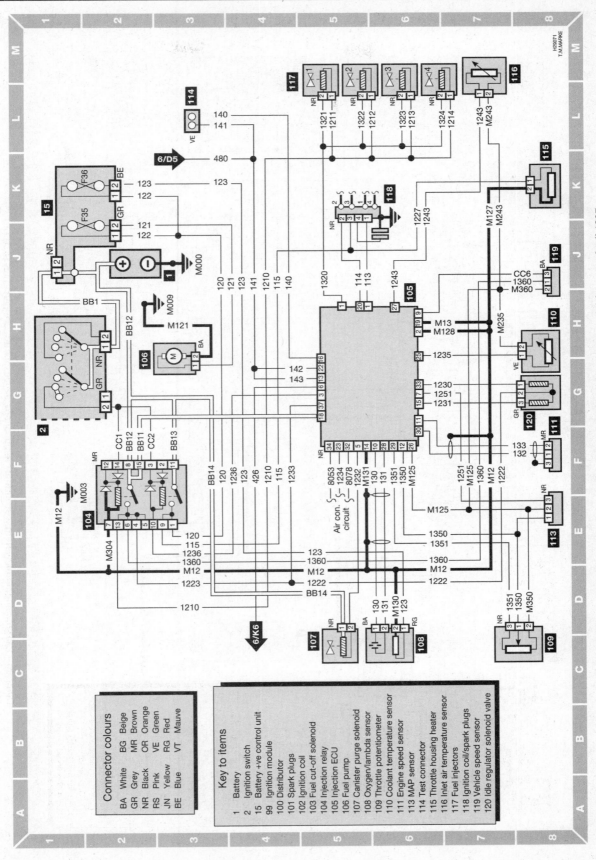

Diagram 12: Typical multi- point fuel injection system (1.6 litre models) - up to April 1997

Connector colours

BA	White	BG	Beige
GR	Grey	MR	Brown
NR	Black	OR	Orange
RS	Pink	VE	Green
JN	Yellow	RG	Red
BE	Blue	VT	Mauve

Key to items

1 Battery
2 Ignition switch
15 Battery +ve control unit
99 Ignition module
100 Distributor
101 Spark plugs
102 Ignition coil
103 Fuel cut-off solenoid
104 Injection relay
105 Injection ECU
106 Fuel pump
107 Canister purge solenoid
108 Oxygen/lambda sensor
109 Throttle potentiometer
110 Coolant temperature sensor
111 Engine speed sensor
113 MAP sensor
114 Test connector
115 Throttle housing heater
116 Inlet air temperature sensor
117 Fuel injectors
118 Ignition coil/spark plugs
119 Vehicle speed sensor
120 Idle regulator solenoid valve

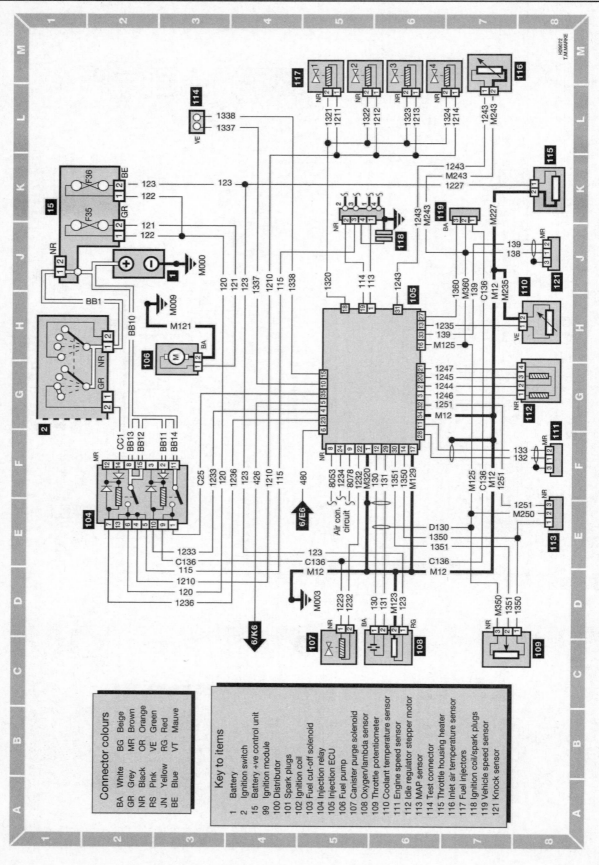

Diagram 13: Typical multi- point fuel injection system (1.8/2.0 litre models) - up to April 1997

Connector colours

BA	White	BG	Beige
GR	Grey	MR	Brown
NR	Black	OR	Orange
RS	Pink	VE	Green
JN	Yellow	RG	Red
BE	Blue	VT	Mauve

Key to items

1 Battery
2 Ignition switch
15 Battery +ve control unit
99 Ignition module
100 Distributor
101 Spark plugs
102 Ignition coil
103 Fuel cut-off solenoid
104 Injection relay
105 Injection ECU
106 Fuel pump
107 Canister purge solenoid
108 Oxygen/lambda sensor
109 Throttle potentiometer
110 Coolant temperature sensor
111 Engine speed sensor
112 Idle regulator stepper motor
113 MAP sensor
114 Test connector
115 Throttle housing heater
116 Inlet air temperature sensor
117 Fuel injectors
118 Ignition coil/spark plugs
119 Vehicle speed sensor
121 Knock sensor

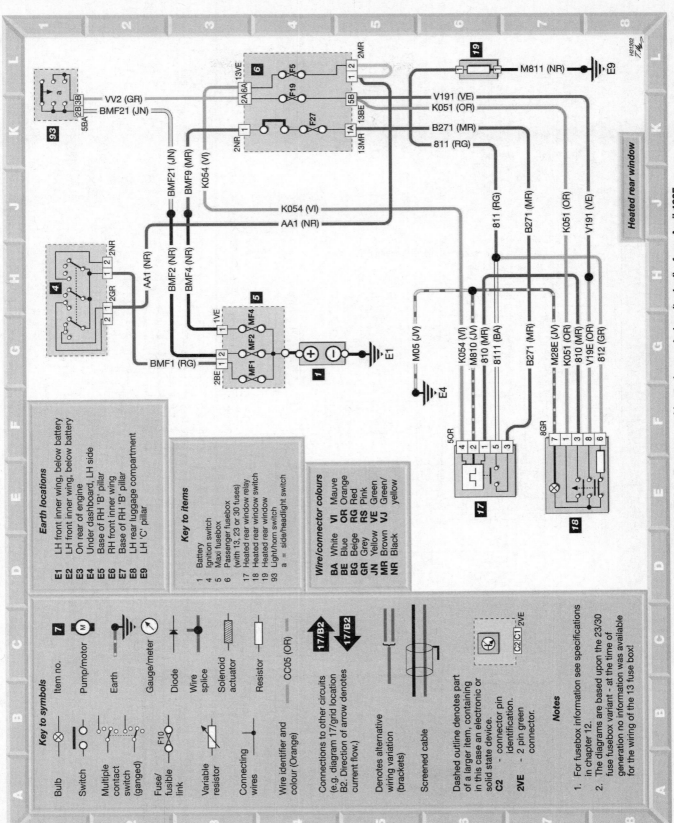

Diagram 14 : Information for wiring diagrams and heated rear window (typical) - from April 1997

Heated rear window

Key to symbols

Item no.	7
Pump/motor	M
Earth	
Gauge/meter	
Diode	
Wire splice	
Solenoid actuator	
Resistor	
Bulb	
Switch	
Multiple contact switch (ganged)	
Fuse/fusible link	F10
Variable resistor	
Connecting wires	
Wire identifier and colour (Orange)	CC05 (OR)
Connections to other circuits (e.g. diagram 17/grid location B2. Direction of arrow denotes current flow.)	17/B2
Denotes alternative wiring variation (brackets)	
Screened cable	
Dashed outline denotes part of a larger item, containing in this case an electronic or solid state device.	
C2 - connector pin identification.	C2 C1 2VE
2VE - 2 pin green connector.	

Earth locations

E1 LH front inner wing, below battery
E2 LH front inner wing, below battery
E3 On rear of engine
E4 Under dashboard, LH side
E5 Base of RH 'B' pillar
E6 RH front inner wing
E7 Base of RH 'B' pillar
E8 LH rear luggage compartment
E9 LH 'C' pillar

Key to items

1   Battery
4   Ignition switch
5   Maxi fusebox
6   Passenger fusebox (with 13, 23 or 30 fuses)
17 Heated rear window relay
18 Heated rear window switch
19 Heated rear window
93 Light/horn switch
a = side/headlight switch

Wire/connector colours

BA White   VI Mauve
BE Blue   OR Orange
BG Beige   RG Red
GR Grey   RS Pink
JN Yellow   VE Green
MR Brown   VJ Green/
NR Black   yellow

Notes

1. For fusebox information see specifications in chapter 12.
2. The diagrams are based upon the 23/30 fuse fusebox variant - at the time of generation no information was available for the wiring of the 13 fuse box

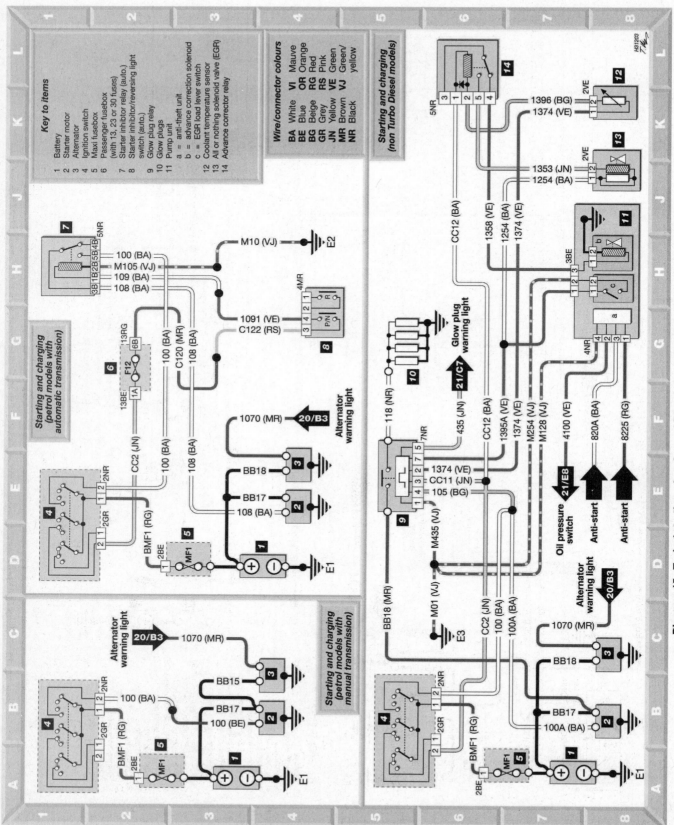

Diagram 15 : Typical starting, charging and Diesel pre and post heating - from April 1997

Key to items

1 Battery
2 Starter motor
3 Alternator
4 Ignition switch
5 Maxi fusebox
6 Passenger fusebox (with 13, 23 or 30 fuses)
7 Starter inhibitor relay (auto.)
8 Starter inhibitor/reversing light switch (auto.)
9 Glow plug relay
10 Glow plugs
11 Pump unit

a = anti-theft unit
b = advance correction solenoid
c = EGR load lever switch
12 Coolant temperature sensor
13 All or nothing solenoid valve (EGR)
14 Advance corrector relay

Wire/connector colours

BA White   VI Mauve
BE Blue   OR Orange
BG Beige   RG Red
GR Grey   RS Pink
JN Yellow   VE Green
MR Brown   VJ Green/yellow
NR Black

Starting and charging (non Turbo Diesel models)

Starting and charging (petrol models with automatic transmission)

Starting and charging (petrol models with manual transmission)

Alternator warning light

Glow plug warning light

Oil pressure switch

Anti-start

Anti-start

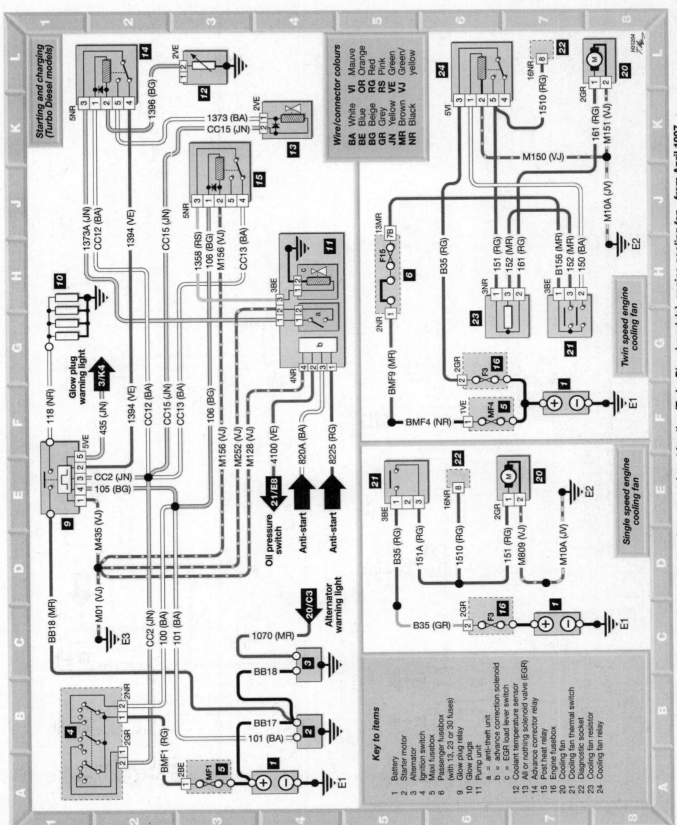

Diagram 16 : Typical starting, charging, pre and post heating (Turbo Diesel models), engine cooling fan - from April 1997

Starting and charging (Turbo Diesel models)

Twin speed engine cooling fan

Single speed engine cooling fan

Glow plug warning light

3/K4

Oil pressure switch
21/E8

Anti-start

Anti-start

Alternator warning light
20/C3

Wire/connector colours

BA	White	VI	Mauve
BE	Blue	OR	Orange
BG	Beige	RG	Red
GR	Grey	RS	Pink
JN	Yellow	VE	Green
MR	Brown	VJ	Green/yellow
NR	Black		

Key to items

1   Battery
2   Starter motor
3   Alternator
4   Ignition switch
5   Maxi fusebox
6   Passenger fusebox (with 13, 23 or 30 fuses)
9   Glow plug relay
10 Glow plugs
11 Pump unit
    a = anti-theft unit
    b = advance correction solenoid
    c = EGR load lever switch
12 Coolant temperature sensor
13 All or nothing solenoid valve (EGR)
14 Advance corrector relay
15 Post heat relay
16 Engine fusebox
20 Cooling fan
21 Cooling fan thermal switch
22 Diagnostic socket
23 Cooling fan resistor
24 Cooling fan relay

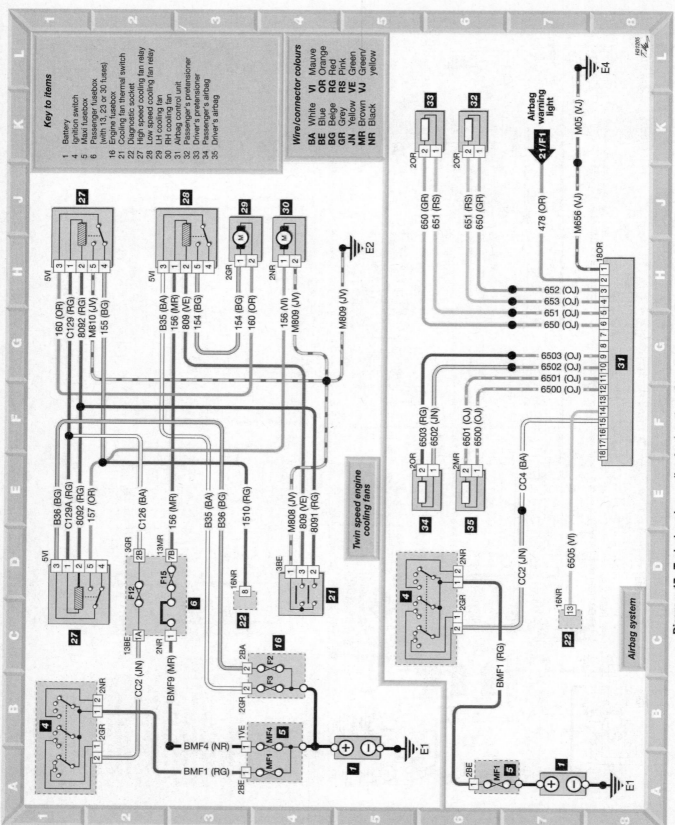

Key to items

1 Battery
4 Ignition switch
5 Maxi fusebox
6 Passenger fusebox (with 13, 23 or 30 fuses)
16 Engine fusebox
21 Cooling fan thermal switch
22 Diagnostic socket
27 High speed cooling fan relay
28 Low speed cooling fan relay
29 LH cooling fan
30 RH cooling fan
31 Airbag control unit
32 Passenger's pretensioner
33 Driver's pretensioner
34 Passenger's airbag
35 Driver's airbag

Wire/connector colours

BA	White	VI	Mauve
BE	Blue	OR	Orange
BG	Beige	RG	Red
GR	Grey	RS	Pink
JN	Yellow	VE	Green
MR	Brown	VJ	Green/yellow
NR	Black		

Twin speed engine cooling fans

Airbag warning light

Airbag system

Diagram 17 : Typical engine cooling fan (continued) and airbag system - from April 1997

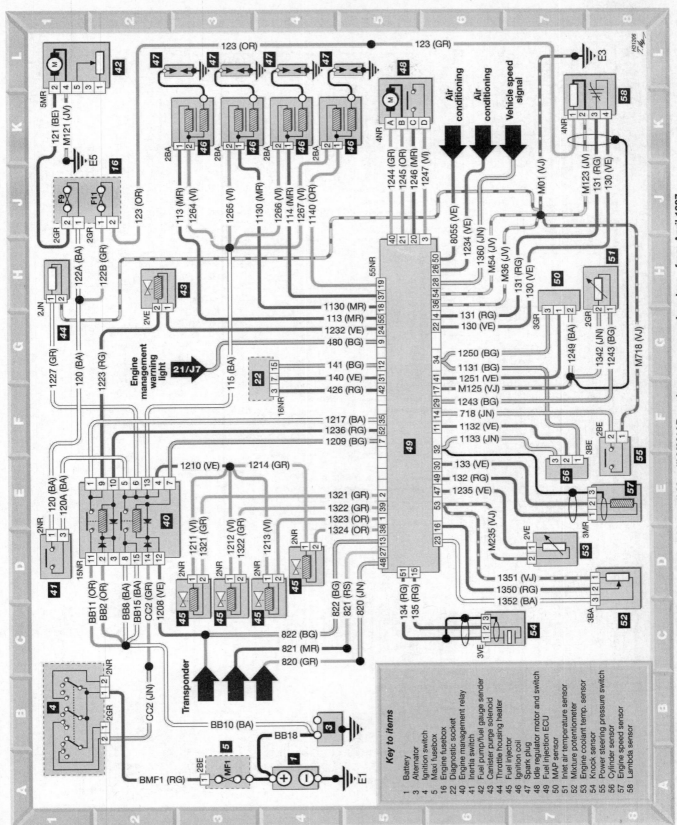

Diagram 18 : Typical Magneti Marelli MM1AP engine management system - from April 1997

Key to items

1. Battery
2. Alternator
4. Ignition switch
5. Maxi fusebox
16. Engine fusebox
22. Diagnostic socket
40. Engine management relay
41. Inertia switch
42. Fuel pump/fuel gauge sender
43. Canister purge solenoid
44. Throttle housing heater
45. Fuel injector
46. Ignition coil
47. Spark plug
48. Idle regulator motor and switch
49. Fuel injection ECU
50. MAP sensor
51. Inlet air temperature sensor
52. Mixture potentiometer
53. Engine coolant temp. sensor
54. Knock sensor
55. Power steering pressure switch
56. Cylinder sensor
57. Engine speed sensor
58. Lambda sensor

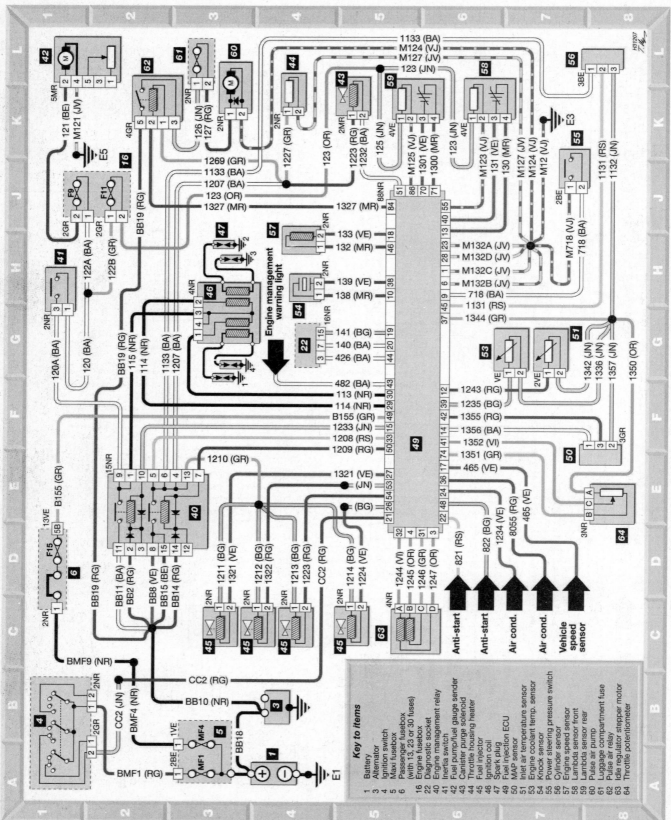

Diagram 19 : Typical Bosch MP7.3 engine management system - from April 1997

Key to items

1 Battery
3 Alternator
4 Ignition switch
5 Maxi fusebox
6 Passenger fusebox
   (with 13, 23 or 30 fuses)
16 Engine fusebox
22 Diagnostic socket
40 Engine management relay
41 Inertia switch
42 Fuel pump/fuel gauge sender
43 Canister purge solenoid
44 Throttle housing heater
45 Fuel injector
46 Ignition coil
47 Spark plug
49 Fuel injection ECU
50 MAP sensor
51 Inlet air temperature sensor
53 Engine coolant temp. sensor
54 Knock sensor
55 Power steering pressure switch
56 Cylinder sensor
57 Engine speed sensor
58 Lambda sensor front
59 Lambda sensor rear
60 Pulse air pump
61 Pulse air relay
62 Luggage compartment fuse
63 Idle regulator stepper motor
64 Throttle potentiometer

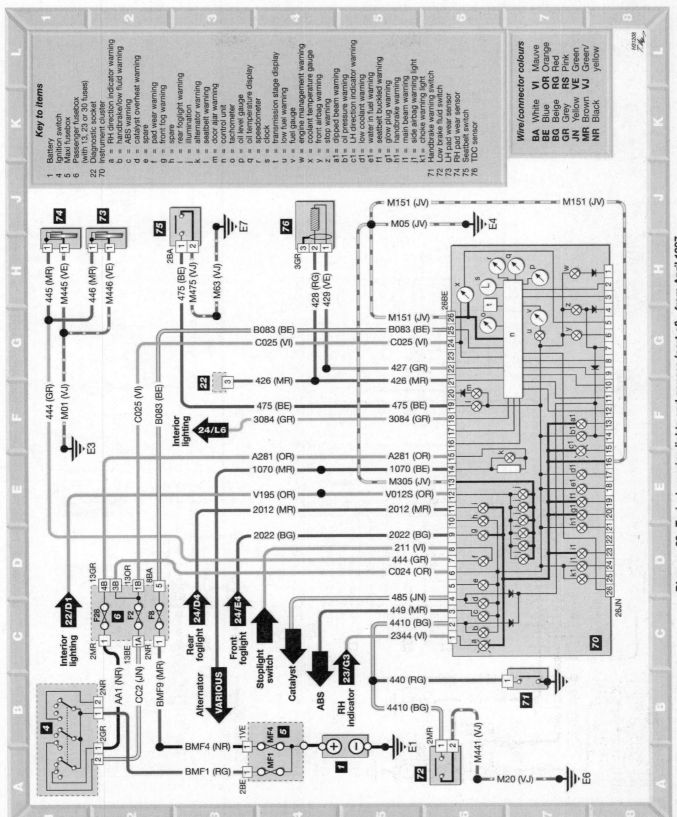

Diagram 20 : Typical warning lights and gauges (part of) - from April 1997

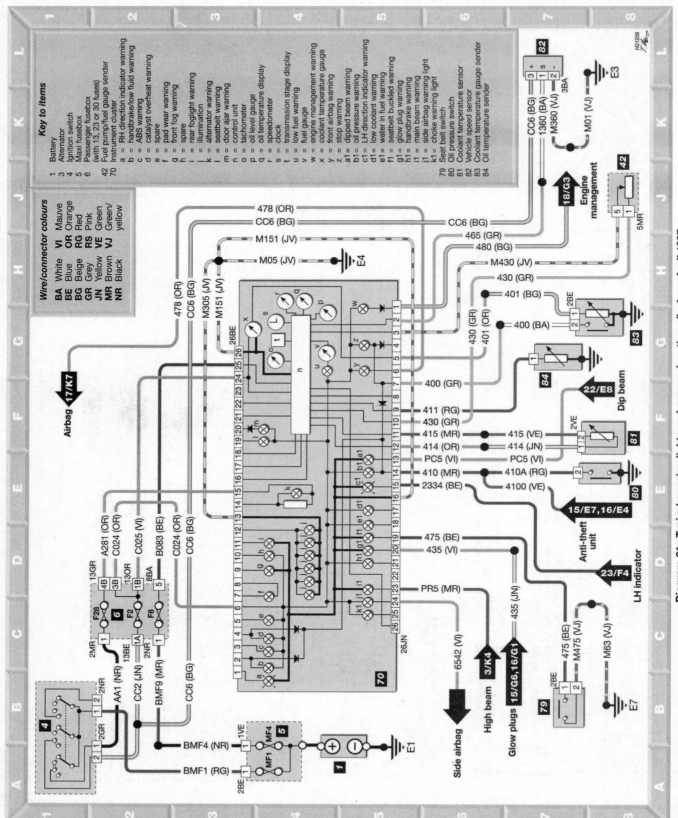

Key to items

1 Battery
3 Alternator
4 Ignition switch
5 Maxi fusebox
6 Passenger fusebox
   (with 13, 23 or 30 fuses)
42 Fuel pump/fuel gauge sender
70 Instrument cluster
   a = RH direction indicator warning
   b = handbrake/low fluid warning
   c = ABS warning
   d = catalyst overheat warning
   e = spare
   f = pad wear warning
   g = front fog warning
   h = spare
   j = rear foglight warning
   j = illumination
   k = alternator warning
   l = seatbelt warning
   m = door ajar warning
   n = control unit
   o = tachometer
   p = oil level gauge
   q = oil temperature display
   r = speedometer
   s = clock
   t = transmission stage display
   u = low fuel warning
   v = fuel gauge
   w = engine management warning
   x = coolant temperature gauge
   y = stop warning
   z = dipped beam warning
   a1 = oil pressure warning
   b1 = low coolant warning
   c1 = LH direction indicator warning
   d1 = water in fuel warning
   e1 = seatbelt buckled warning
   f1 = glow plug warning
   g1 = handbrake warning
   h1 = main beam warning
   i1 = side airbag warning light
   k1 = choke warning light
79 Seat belt switch
80 Oil pressure switch
81 Coolant temperature sensor
82 Vehicle speed sensor
83 Coolant temperature gauge sender
84 Oil temperature sender

Wire/connector colours

BA = White   VI = Mauve
BE = Blue   OR = Orange
BG = Beige   RG = Red
GR = Grey   RS = Pink
JN = Yellow   VE = Green
MR = Brown   VJ = Green/
NR = Black   yellow

Diagram 21 : Typical warning lights and gauges (continued) – from April 1997

H31209

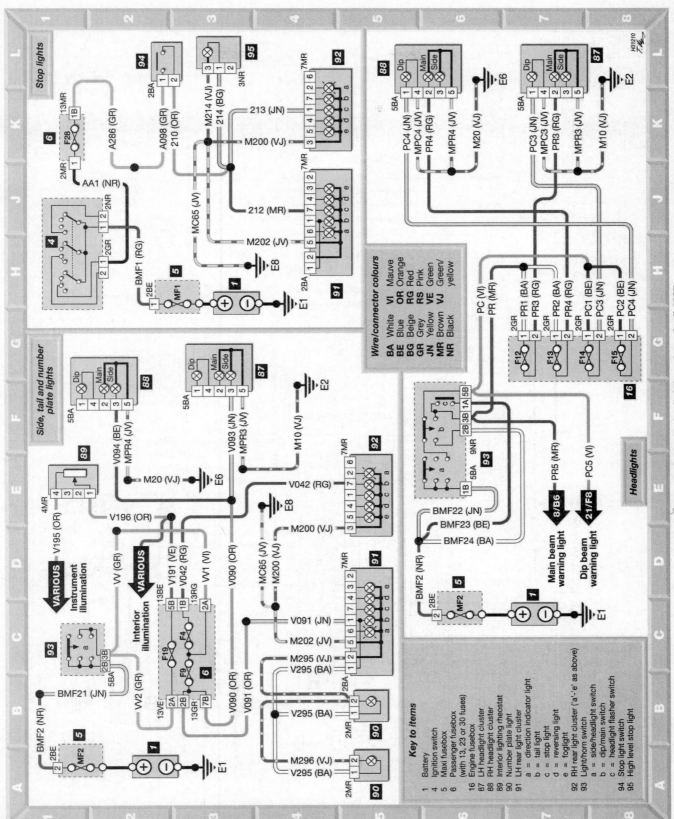

Diagram 22 : Typical exterior lighting - from April 1997

Wire/connector colours

BA	White	**VI**	Mauve
BE	Blue	**OR**	Orange
BG	Beige	**RG**	Red
GR	Grey	**RS**	Pink
JN	Yellow	**VE**	Green
MR	Brown	**VJ**	Green/
NR	Black		yellow

Stop lights

Side, tail and number plate lights

Instrument illumination

Interior illumination

Headlights

Main beam warning light

Dip beam warning light

Key to items

1 Battery
2 Ignition switch
4 Maxi fusebox
5 Passenger fusebox
   (with 13, 23 or 30 fuses)
6 Engine fusebox
16 LH headlight cluster
87 RH headlight cluster
88 Interior lighting rheostat
89 Number plate light
90 LH rear light cluster
91 LH rear light cluster
   a = direction indicator light
   b = tail light
   c = stop light
   d = reversing light
   e = foglight
92 RH rear light cluster ('a'-'e' as above)
93 Light/horn switch
   a = side/headlight switch
   b = dip/main switch
   c = headlight flasher switch
94 Stop light switch
95 High level stop light

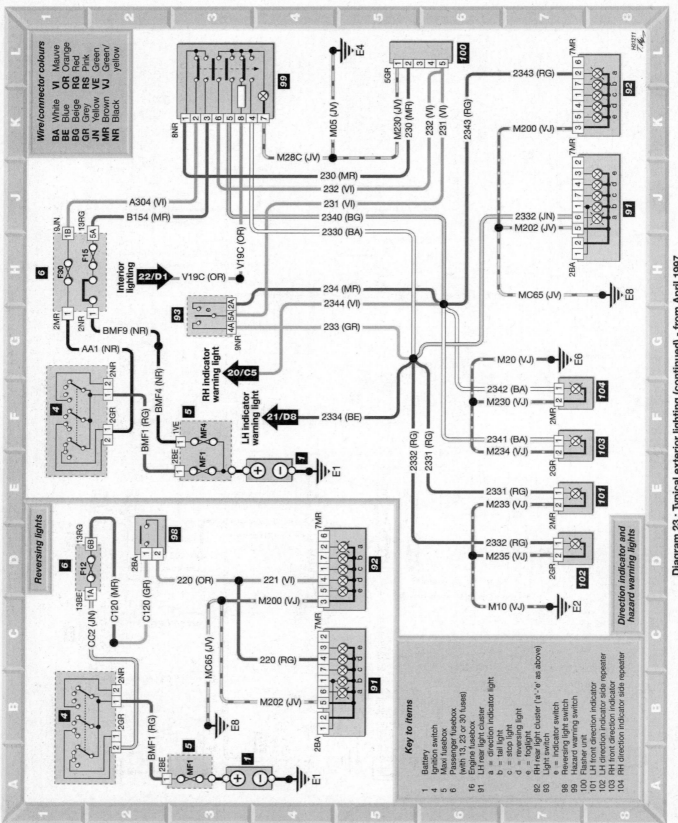

Diagram 23 : Typical exterior lighting (continued) - from April 1997

Wire/connector colours

BA	White	VI	Mauve
BE	Blue	OR	Orange
BG	Beige	RG	Red
GR	Grey	RS	Pink
JN	Yellow	VE	Green
MR	Brown	VJ	Green/yellow
NR	Black		

Key to items

1 Battery
4 Ignition switch
5 Maxi fusebox
6 Passenger fusebox (with 13, 23 or 30 fuses)
16 Engine fusebox
91 LH rear light cluster
    a = direction indicator light
    b = tail light
    c = stop light
    d = reversing light
    e = foglight
92 RH rear light cluster ('a'-'e' as above)
93 Light switch
    e = indicator switch
98 Reversing light switch
99 Hazard warning switch
100 Flasher unit
101 LH front direction indicator
102 LH direction indicator side repeater
103 RH front direction indicator
104 RH direction indicator side repeater

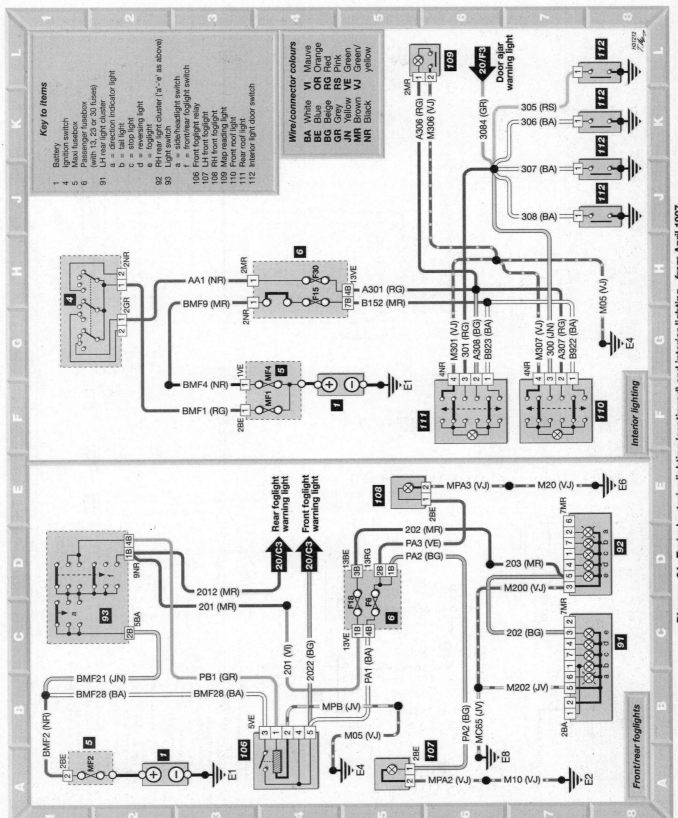

Key to items

1   Battery
4   Ignition switch
5   Maxi fusebox
6   Passenger fusebox
    (with 13, 23 or 30 fuses)
91 LH rear light cluster
    a = direction indicator light
    b = tail light
    c = stop light
    d = reversing light
    e = foglight
92 RH rear light cluster ('a' - 'e' as above)
93 Light switch
    a = side/headlight switch
    f = front/rear foglight switch
106 Front foglight relay
107 LH front foglight
108 RH front foglight
109 Map reading light
110 Front roof light
111 Rear roof light
112 Interior light door switch

Wire/connector colours

BA White   VI Mauve
BE Blue   OR Orange
BG Beige   RG Red
GR Grey   RS Pink
JN Yellow   VE Green
MR Brown   VJ Green/
NR Black   yellow

Interior lighting

Front/rear foglights

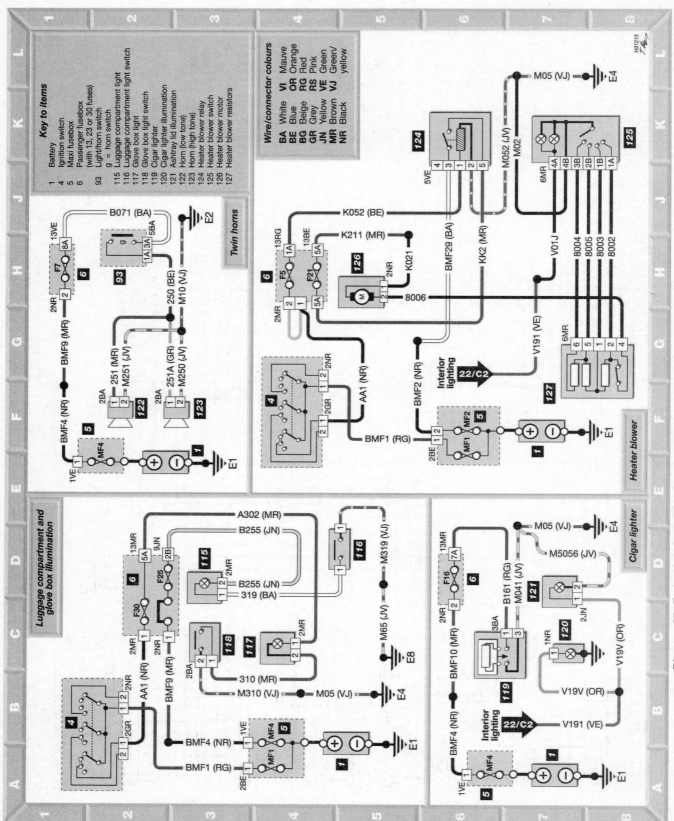

Diagram 25 : Typical interior lighting (continued), horn, cigar lighter and heater blower - from April 1997

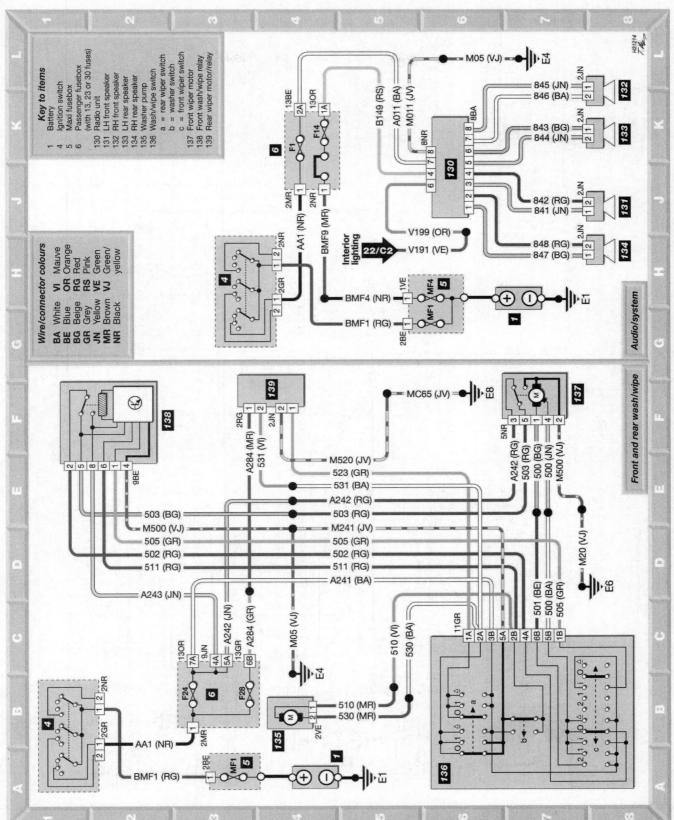

Key to items

1   Battery
4   Ignition switch
5   Maxi fusebox
6   Passenger fusebox
    (with 13, 23 or 30 fuses)
130 Radio unit
131 LH front speaker
132 RH front speaker
133 LH rear speaker
134 RH rear speaker
135 Washer pump
136 Wash/wipe switch
     a = rear wiper switch
     b = washer switch
     c = front wiper switch
137 Front wiper motor
138 Front wash/wipe relay
139 Rear wiper motor/relay

Wire/connector colours

BA	White	VI	Mauve
BE	Blue	OR	Orange
BG	Beige	RG	Red
GR	Grey	RS	Pink
JN	Yellow	VE	Green
MR	Brown	VJ	Green/yellow
NR	Black		

Audio/system

Front and rear wash/wipe

Diagram 26 : Typical front and rear wash/wipe and audio system – from April 1997

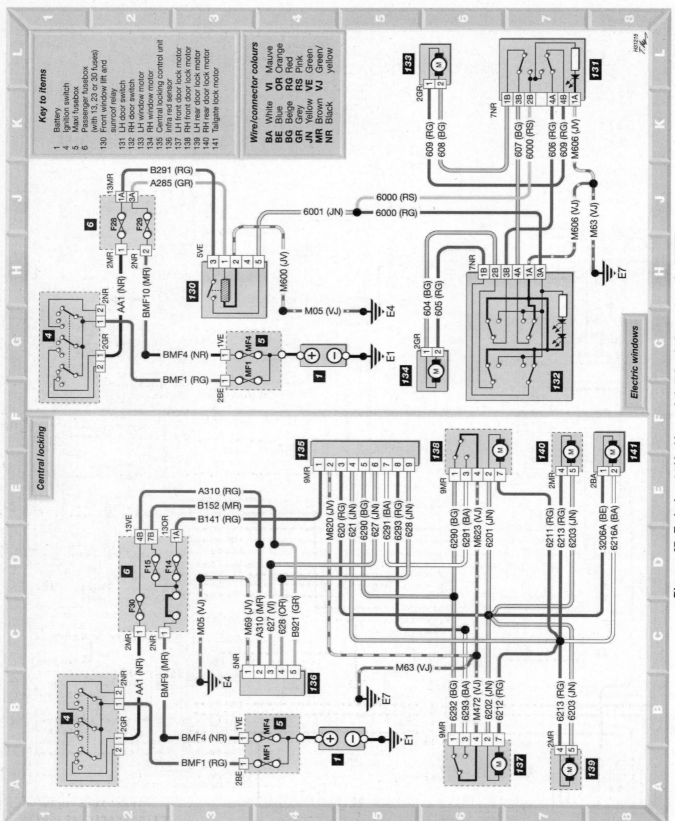

Diagram 27 : Typical central locking and electric windows – from April 1997

Wire colours

Ba	White	Nr	Black
Be	Blue	Or	Orange
Bg	Beige	Rg	Red
Gr	Grey	Rs	Pink
Jn	Yellow	Ve	Green
Vi	Violet	VJ	Green/
Mr	Brown		Yellow

Key to items

1 Battery
2 Ignition switch
3 Maxi fusebox
4 Engine fusebox
5 Passenger fusebox
6 Starter motor
7 Alternator
8 Additional heater
9 Additional heater relay
10 Engine management control unit
11 Coolant temperature sensor
12 Fuel injector
13 Engine speed sensor

14 Air conditioning pressostat
15 Air conditioning compressor relay
16 Air conditioning compressor
17 Vehicle speed sensor
18 Cylinder reference sensor
19 High pressure sensor
20 Instrument cluster
   a = alternator warning light
   b = control unit
   c = coolant temperature gauge
   d = engine management warning light
   e = preheater warning light
21 Accelerator pedal position sensor

22 Air flow sensor
23 Fuel temperature sensor
24 Inertia switch
25 Common connection point
26 Diagnostic socket
27 Preheater control unit
28 Glow plugs
29 Fuel pump/fuel gauge sender unit
30 High pressure regulator
31 Engine management double relay
32 EGR solenoid
33 3rd piston deactivator

H33043

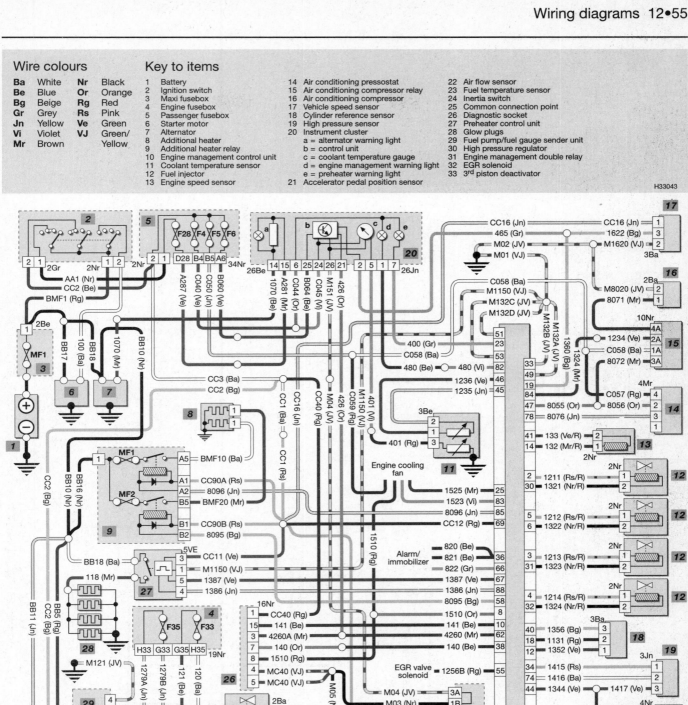

Typical Diesel engine management system (2.0 HDi)

Dimensions and Weights

Note: *All figures are approximate, and may vary according to model. Refer to manufacturer's data for exact figures.*

Dimensions

Overall length:
   Hatchback models . . . . 3995 mm
   Sedan/Saloon models . . . . 4240 mm
   Estate models . . . . 4338 mm
Overall width . . . . 1692 mm
Overall height (unladen):
   Hatchback models . . . . 1380 mm
   Sedan/Saloon models . . . . 1386 mm
   Estate models (including roof bars) . . . . 1415 mm
Wheelbase . . . . 2580 mm

Weights

Kerb weight . . . . 1020 to 1170 kg*
Maximum gross vehicle weight** . . . . 1480 to 1665 kg*
Maximum roof rack load . . . . 75 kg (100 kg for Estate with roof bars)
Maximum towing weight (braked trailer)** . . . . 900 to 1200 kg*
Maximum trailer nose weight . . . . 50 kg*
*Depending on model and specification.
**Refer to Peugeot dealer for exact recommendations.

Length (distance)

Inches (in)	x 25.4	= Millimetres (mm)	x 0.0394	= Inches (in)
Feet (ft)	x 0.305	= Metres (m)	x 3.281	= Feet (ft)
Miles	x 1.609	= Kilometres (km)	x 0.621	= Miles

Volume (capacity)

Cubic inches (cu in; in³)	x 16.387	= Cubic centimetres (cc; cm³)	x 0.061	= Cubic inches (cu in; in³)
Imperial pints (Imp pt)	x 0.568	= Litres (l)	x 1.76	= Imperial pints (Imp pt)
Imperial quarts (Imp qt)	x 1.137	= Litres (l)	x 0.88	= Imperial quarts (Imp qt)
Imperial quarts (Imp qt)	x 1.201	= US quarts (US qt)	x 0.833	= Imperial quarts (Imp qt)
US quarts (US qt)	x 0.946	= Litres (l)	x 1.057	= US quarts (US qt)
Imperial gallons (Imp gal)	x 4.546	= Litres (l)	x 0.22	= Imperial gallons (Imp gal)
Imperial gallons (Imp gal)	x 1.201	= US gallons (US gal)	x 0.833	= Imperial gallons (Imp gal)
US gallons (US gal)	x 3.785	= Litres (l)	x 0.264	= US gallons (US gal)

Mass (weight)

Ounces (oz)	x 28.35	= Grams (g)	x 0.035	= Ounces (oz)
Pounds (lb)	x 0.454	= Kilograms (kg)	x 2.205	= Pounds (lb)

Force

Ounces-force (ozf; oz)	x 0.278	= Newtons (N)	x 3.6	= Ounces-force (ozf; oz)
Pounds-force (lbf; lb)	x 4.448	= Newtons (N)	x 0.225	= Pounds-force (lbf; lb)
Newtons (N)	x 0.1	= Kilograms-force (kgf; kg)	x 9.81	= Newtons (N)

Pressure

Pounds-force per square inch (psi; lbf/in²; lb/in²)	x 0.070	= Kilograms-force per square centimetre (kgf/cm²; kg/cm²)	x 14.223	= Pounds-force per square inch (psi; lbf/in²; lb/in²)
Pounds-force per square inch (psi; lbf/in²; lb/in²)	x 0.068	= Atmospheres (atm)	x 14.696	= Pounds-force per square inch (psi; lbf/in²; lb/in²)
Pounds-force per square inch (psi; lbf/in²; lb/in²)	x 0.069	= Bars	x 14.5	= Pounds-force per square inch (psi; lbf/in²; lb/in²)
Pounds-force per square inch (psi; lbf/in²; lb/in²)	x 6.895	= Kilopascals (kPa)	x 0.145	= Pounds-force per square inch (psi; lbf/in²; lb/in²)
Kilopascals (kPa)	x 0.01	= Kilograms-force per square centimetre (kgf/cm²; kg/cm²)	x 98.1	= Kilopascals (kPa)
Millibar (mbar)	x 100	= Pascals (Pa)	x 0.01	= Millibar (mbar)
Millibar (mbar)	x 0.0145	= Pounds-force per square inch (psi; lbf/in²; lb/in²)	x 68.947	= Millibar (mbar)
Millibar (mbar)	x 0.75	= Millimetres of mercury (mmHg)	x 1.333	= Millibar (mbar)
Millibar (mbar)	x 0.401	= Inches of water (inH$_2$O)	x 2.491	= Millibar (mbar)
Millimetres of mercury (mmHg)	x 0.535	= Inches of water (inH$_2$O)	x 1.868	= Millimetres of mercury (mmHg)
Inches of water (inH$_2$O)	x 0.036	= Pounds-force per square inch (psi; lbf/in²; lb/in²)	x 27.68	= Inches of water (inH$_2$O)

Torque (moment of force)

Pounds-force inches (lbf in; lb in)	x 1.152	= Kilograms-force centimetre (kgf cm; kg cm)	x 0.868	= Pounds-force inches (lbf in; lb in)
Pounds-force inches (lbf in; lb in)	x 0.113	= Newton metres (Nm)	x 8.85	= Pounds-force inches (lbf in; lb in)
Pounds-force inches (lbf in; lb in)	x 0.083	= Pounds-force feet (lbf ft; lb ft)	x 12	= Pounds-force inches (lbf in; lb in)
Pounds-force feet (lbf ft; lb ft)	x 0.138	= Kilograms-force metres (kgf m; kg m)	x 7.233	= Pounds-force feet (lbf ft; lb ft)
Pounds-force feet (lbf ft; lb ft)	x 1.356	= Newton metres (Nm)	x 0.738	= Pounds-force feet (lbf ft; lb ft)
Newton metres (Nm)	x 0.102	= Kilograms-force metres (kgf m; kg m)	x 9.804	= Newton metres (Nm)

Power

Horsepower (hp)	x 745.7	= Watts (W)	x 0.0013	= Horsepower (hp)

Velocity (speed)

Miles per hour (miles/hr; mph)	x 1.609	= Kilometres per hour (km/hr; kph)	x 0.621	= Miles per hour (miles/hr; mph)

Fuel consumption*

Miles per gallon, Imperial (mpg)	x 0.354	= Kilometres per litre (km/l)	x 2.825	= Miles per gallon, Imperial (mpg)
Miles per gallon, US (mpg)	x 0.425	= Kilometres per litre (km/l)	x 2.352	= Miles per gallon, US (mpg)

Temperature

Degrees Fahrenheit = (°C x 1.8) + 32   Degrees Celsius (Degrees Centigrade; °C) = (°F - 32) x 0.56

It is common practice to convert from miles per gallon (mpg) to litres/100 kilometres (l/100km), where mpg x l/100 km = 282

Spare parts are available from many sources, including maker's appointed garages, accessory shops, and motor factors. To be sure of obtaining the correct parts, it may sometimes be necessary to quote the vehicle identification number. If possible, it can also be useful to take the old parts along for positive identification. Items such as starter motors and alternators may be available under a service exchange scheme - any parts returned should be clean.

Our advice regarding spare part sources is as follows.

Officially-appointed garages

This is the best source of parts which are peculiar to your car, and are not otherwise generally available (eg badges, interior trim, certain body panels, etc). It is also the only place at which you should buy parts if the vehicle is still under warranty.

Accessory shops

These are good places to buy materials and components needed for the maintenance of your car (oil, air and fuel filters, spark plugs, light bulbs, drivebelts, oils and greases, brake pads, touch-up paint, etc). Parts like this sold by a reputable shop are of the same standard as those used by the car manufacturer.

Motor factors

Good factors will stock all the more important components which wear out comparatively quickly and can sometimes supply individual components needed for the overhaul of a larger assembly. They may also handle work such as cylinder block reboring, crankshaft regrinding and balancing, etc.

Tyre and exhaust specialists

These outlets may be independent or members of a local or national chain. They frequently offer competitive prices when compared with a main dealer or local garage, but it will pay to obtain several quotes before making a decision. Also ask what 'extras' may be added to the quote - for instance, fitting a new valve and balancing the wheel are both often charged on top of the price of a new tyre.

Other sources

Beware of parts or materials obtained from market stalls, car boot sales or similar outlets. Such items are not invariably sub-standard, but there is little chance of compensation if they do prove unsatisfactory. In the case of safety-critical components such as brake pads there is the risk not only of financial loss but also of an accident causing injury or death.

Vehicle identification

Modifications are a continuing and unpublicised process in vehicle manufacture, quite apart from major model changes. Spare parts manuals and lists are compiled upon a numerical basis, the individual vehicle identification numbers being essential for correct identification of the part concerned. When ordering spare parts, always give as much information as possible. Quote the car model, year of manufacture, body and engine numbers as appropriate.

The *Vehicle Identification Number* (VIN) plate is inside the luggage compartment, riveted onto the rear of the body (just beneath the lock). Where there are two plates, the right-hand plate carries the VIN and vehicle weight information, as well as paint and trim colour codes. The left-hand plate is the homologation plate. This plate gives details of the vehicle which are required by law for export to certain countries (**see illustration**).

The vehicle identification (chassis) number is stamped into the body, along the top edge of the right-hand wing, and can be viewed with the bonnet open (**see illustration**). On some models, the chassis number may also be etched into the windscreen and window glass.

The *engine number* is situated on the front face of the cylinder block, and can be found in the following locations:
 a) 1.1, 1.4 and 1.8 litre petrol models -

stamped on a plate which is riveted to left-hand end of the block.
 b) 1.6 litre petrol models - stamped directly onto the left-hand end of the cylinder block.
 c) 2.0 litre petrol models - stamped directly onto the front face of the cylinder block, on the machined surface located just to the left of the oil filter.
 d) 1.8 and 1.9 litre Diesel engines - stamped on a plate which is riveted to the centre of the block.

Note: *The first part of the engine number gives the engine code - eg "KDX".*

The *paint code* is stamped onto the left-hand suspension turret (**see illustration**).

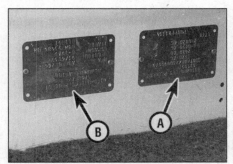

The VIN plate (A) is found in the luggage compartment. Plate (B) is the homologation plate (seen from inside the car)

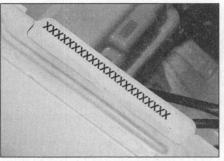

The chassis number is stamped onto the right-hand wing

The paint code is found on the left-hand front suspension turret

Whenever servicing, repair or overhaul work is carried out on the car or its components, observe the following procedures and instructions. This will assist in carrying out the operation efficiently and to a professional standard of workmanship.

Joint mating faces and gaskets

When separating components at their mating faces, never insert screwdrivers or similar implements into the joint between the faces in order to prise them apart. This can cause severe damage which results in oil leaks, coolant leaks, etc upon reassembly. Separation is usually achieved by tapping along the joint with a soft-faced hammer in order to break the seal. However, note that this method may not be suitable where dowels are used for component location.

Where a gasket is used between the mating faces of two components, a new one must be fitted on reassembly; fit it dry unless otherwise stated in the repair procedure. Make sure that the mating faces are clean and dry, with all traces of old gasket removed. When cleaning a joint face, use a tool which is unlikely to score or damage the face, and remove any burrs or nicks with an oilstone or fine file.

Make sure that tapped holes are cleaned with a pipe cleaner, and keep them free of jointing compound, if this is being used, unless specifically instructed otherwise.

Ensure that all orifices, channels or pipes are clear, and blow through them, preferably using compressed air.

Oil seals

Oil seals can be removed by levering them out with a wide flat-bladed screwdriver or similar implement. Alternatively, a number of self-tapping screws may be screwed into the seal, and these used as a purchase for pliers or some similar device in order to pull the seal free.

Whenever an oil seal is removed from its working location, either individually or as part of an assembly, it should be renewed.

The very fine sealing lip of the seal is easily damaged, and will not seal if the surface it contacts is not completely clean and free from scratches, nicks or grooves. If the original sealing surface of the component cannot be restored, and the manufacturer has not made provision for slight relocation of the seal relative to the sealing surface, the component should be renewed.

Protect the lips of the seal from any surface which may damage them in the course of fitting. Use tape or a conical sleeve where possible. Lubricate the seal lips with oil before fitting and, on dual-lipped seals, fill the space between the lips with grease.

Unless otherwise stated, oil seals must be fitted with their sealing lips toward the lubricant to be sealed.

Use a tubular drift or block of wood of the appropriate size to install the seal and, if the seal housing is shouldered, drive the seal down to the shoulder. If the seal housing is unshouldered, the seal should be fitted with its face flush with the housing top face (unless otherwise instructed).

Screw threads and fastenings

Seized nuts, bolts and screws are quite a common occurrence where corrosion has set in, and the use of penetrating oil or releasing fluid will often overcome this problem if the offending item is soaked for a while before attempting to release it. The use of an impact driver may also provide a means of releasing such stubborn fastening devices, when used in conjunction with the appropriate screwdriver bit or socket. If none of these methods works, it may be necessary to resort to the careful application of heat, or the use of a hacksaw or nut splitter device.

Studs are usually removed by locking two nuts together on the threaded part, and then using a spanner on the lower nut to unscrew the stud. Studs or bolts which have broken off below the surface of the component in which they are mounted can sometimes be removed using a stud extractor. Always ensure that a blind tapped hole is completely free from oil, grease, water or other fluid before installing the bolt or stud. Failure to do this could cause the housing to crack due to the hydraulic action of the bolt or stud as it is screwed in.

When tightening a castellated nut to accept a split pin, tighten the nut to the specified torque, where applicable, and then tighten further to the next split pin hole. Never slacken the nut to align the split pin hole, unless stated in the repair procedure.

When checking or retightening a nut or bolt to a specified torque setting, slacken the nut or bolt by a quarter of a turn, and then retighten to the specified setting. However, this should not be attempted where angular tightening has been used.

For some screw fastenings, notably cylinder head bolts or nuts, torque wrench settings are no longer specified for the latter stages of tightening, "angle-tightening" being called up instead. Typically, a fairly low torque wrench setting will be applied to the bolts/nuts in the correct sequence, followed by one or more stages of tightening through specified angles.

Locknuts, locktabs and washers

Any fastening which will rotate against a component or housing during tightening should always have a washer between it and the relevant component or housing.

Spring or split washers should always be renewed when they are used to lock a critical component such as a big-end bearing retaining bolt or nut. Locktabs which are folded over to retain a nut or bolt should always be renewed.

Self-locking nuts can be re-used in non-critical areas, providing resistance can be felt when the locking portion passes over the bolt or stud thread. However, it should be noted that self-locking stiffnuts tend to lose their effectiveness after long periods of use, and should then be renewed as a matter of course.

Split pins must always be replaced with new ones of the correct size for the hole.

When thread-locking compound is found on the threads of a fastener which is to be re-used, it should be cleaned off with a wire brush and solvent, and fresh compound applied on reassembly.

Special tools

Some repair procedures in this manual entail the use of special tools such as a press, two or three-legged pullers, spring compressors, etc. Wherever possible, suitable readily-available alternatives to the manufacturer's special tools are described, and are shown in use. In some instances, where no alternative is possible, it has been necessary to resort to the use of a manufacturer's tool, and this has been done for reasons of safety as well as the efficient completion of the repair operation. Unless you are highly-skilled and have a thorough understanding of the procedures described, never attempt to bypass the use of any special tool when the procedure described specifies its use. Not only is there a very great risk of personal injury, but expensive damage could be caused to the components involved.

Environmental considerations

When disposing of used engine oil, brake fluid, antifreeze, etc, give due consideration to any detrimental environmental effects. Do not, for instance, pour any of the above liquids down drains into the general sewage system, or onto the ground to soak away. Many local council refuse tips provide a facility for waste oil disposal, as do some garages. If none of these facilities are available, consult your local Environmental Health Department, or the National Rivers Authority, for further advice.

With the universal tightening-up of legislation regarding the emission of environmentally-harmful substances from motor vehicles, most vehicles have tamperproof devices fitted to the main adjustment points of the fuel system. These devices are primarily designed to prevent unqualified persons from adjusting the fuel/air mixture, with the chance of a consequent increase in toxic emissions. If such devices are found during servicing or overhaul, they should, wherever possible, be renewed or refitted in accordance with the manufacturer's requirements or current legislation.

Note: It is antisocial and illegal to dump oil down the drain. To find the location of your local oil recycling bank, call this number free.

The jack supplied with the vehicle should only be used for changing the roadwheels – see "Wheel changing" at the front of this manual. When carrying out any other kind of work, raise the vehicle using a hydraulic (or "trolley") jack, and always supplement the jack with axle stands at the vehicle jacking points.

When using a hydraulic jack or axle stands, always position the jack head or axle stand head under one of the relevant jacking points **(see illustrations)**.

To raise the front of the vehicle, position the jack with an interposed block of wood underneath the centre of the front subframe **(see illustration)**. **Do not** jack the vehicle under the sump, or any of the steering or suspension components.

To raise the rear of the vehicle, position the jack head underneath the centre of the rear axle tubular crossmember **(see illustration)**. **Do not** attempt to raise the vehicle with the jack positioned underneath the spare wheel,

as the vehicle floor will almost certainly be damaged.

The jack supplied with the vehicle locates in the jacking points in the ridge on the underside of the sill. Ensure that the jack head is correctly engaged before attempting to raise the vehicle.

Never work under, around, or near a raised vehicle, unless it is adequately supported in at least two places.

FRONT

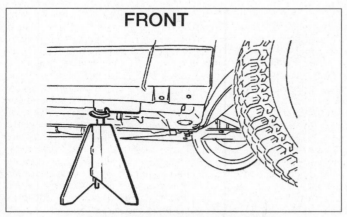

Location points for axle stand - FRONT

REAR

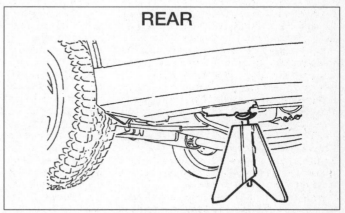

Location points for axle stand - REAR

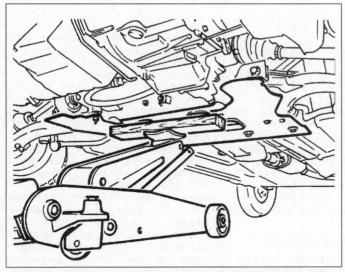

When raising the front of the vehicle, locate the jack underneath the centre of the front subframe. Note the use of the block of wood placed on the jack head

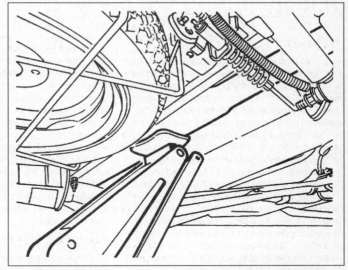

When raising the rear of the vehicle, position the jack head underneath the rear axle tubular crossmember

Disconnecting the battery

Several systems fitted to the vehicle require battery power to be available at all times, either to ensure their continued operation (such as the clock) or to maintain control unit memories which would be wiped if the battery were to be disconnected. Therefore, whenever the battery is to be disconnected, first note the following, to ensure that there are no unforeseen consequences of this action:

a) First, on any vehicle with central locking, it is a wise precaution to remove the key from the ignition, and to keep it with you, so that it does not get locked in if the central locking should engage accidentally when the battery is reconnected.

b) If the vehicle is equipped with a Peugeot factory option anti-theft alarm system, the system should be deactivated before disconnecting the battery. To deactivate the system on pre-1997 models, a master switch is provided in the engine compartment, behind the right-hand headlight. The switch is operated by a dedicated key, and is protected by a plastic cover. Lift up the cover and turn off the switch using the dedicated key. When reconnecting the battery, as soon as the battery is connected, the alarm is automatically activated. Use the remote transmitter to turn off the alarm, then activate the alarm siren using the dedicated key. To deactivate the system on later models, switch on the ignition switch and then within ten seconds, depress the alarm switch on the side of the steering column shroud and hold for approximately two seconds. The alarm indicator light should then flash rapidly for three seconds indicating the alarm is deactivated. To reactivate the system once the battery is reconnected, lock then unlock the vehicle using the remote transmitter; the alarm will be functional again the next time the vehicle is locked with the remote transmitter.

c) If a security-coded audio unit is fitted, and the unit and/or the battery is disconnected, the unit will not function again on reconnection until the correct security code is entered. Details of this procedure, which varies according to the unit fitted, are given in the vehicle owner's handbook. Ensure you have the correct code before you disconnect the battery. If you do not have the code or details of the correct procedure, but can supply proof of ownership and a legitimate reason for wanting this information, a Peugeot dealer may be able to help.

d) On petrol injection engines, the electronic control unit is of the "self-learning" type, meaning that as it operates, it also monitors and stores the settings which give optimum engine performance under all operating conditions. When the battery is disconnected, these settings are lost and the ECU reverts to the base settings programmed into its memory at the factory. On restarting, this may lead to the engine running/idling roughly for a short while, until the ECU has re-learned the optimum settings. This process is best accomplished by taking the vehicle on a road test (for approximately 15 minutes), covering all engine speeds and loads, concentrating mainly in the 2,500 to 3,500 rpm region.

Devices known as 'memory-savers' (or "code-savers") can be used to avoid some of the above problems. Precise details vary according to the device used. Typically, it is plugged into the cigarette lighter, and is connected by its own wires to a spare battery; the vehicle's own battery is then disconnected from the electrical system, leaving the "memory-saver" to pass sufficient current to maintain audio unit security codes and any other memory values, and also to run permanently-live circuits such as the clock.

⚠️ *Warning: Some of these devices allow a considerable amount of current to pass, which can mean that many of the vehicle's systems are still operational when the main battery is disconnected. If a "memory saver" is used, ensure that the circuit concerned is actually "dead" before carrying out any work on it!*

Introduction

A selection of good tools is a fundamental requirement for anyone contemplating the maintenance and repair of a motor vehicle. For the owner who does not possess any, their purchase will prove a considerable expense, offsetting some of the savings made by doing-it-yourself. However, provided that the tools purchased meet the relevant national safety standards and are of good quality, they will last for many years and prove an extremely worthwhile investment.

To help the average owner to decide which tools are needed to carry out the various tasks detailed in this manual, we have compiled three lists of tools under the following headings: *Maintenance and minor repair*, *Repair and overhaul*, and *Special*. Newcomers to practical mechanics should start off with the *Maintenance and minor repair* tool kit, and confine themselves to the simpler jobs around the vehicle. Then, as confidence and experience grow, more difficult tasks can be undertaken, with extra tools being purchased as, and when, they are needed. In this way, a *Maintenance and minor repair* tool kit can be built up into a *Repair and overhaul* tool kit over a considerable period of time, without any major cash outlays. The experienced do-it-yourselfer will have a tool kit good enough for most repair and overhaul procedures, and will add tools from the *Special* category when it is felt that the expense is justified by the amount of use to which these tools will be put.

Maintenance and minor repair tool kit

The tools given in this list should be considered as a minimum requirement if routine maintenance, servicing and minor repair operations are to be undertaken. We recommend the purchase of combination spanners (ring one end, open-ended the other); although more expensive than open-ended ones, they do give the advantages of both types of spanner.

☐ *Combination spanners:*
   Metric - 8 to 19 mm inclusive
☐ *Adjustable spanner - 35 mm jaw (approx.)*
☐ *Spark plug spanner (with rubber insert) - petrol models*
☐ *Spark plug gap adjustment tool - petrol models*
☐ *Set of feeler gauges*
☐ *Brake bleed nipple spanner*
☐ *Screwdrivers:*
   Flat blade - 100 mm long x 6 mm dia
   Cross blade - 100 mm long x 6 mm dia
   Torx - various sizes (not all vehicles)
☐ *Combination pliers*
☐ *Hacksaw (junior)*
☐ *Tyre pump*
☐ *Tyre pressure gauge*
☐ *Oil can*
☐ *Oil filter removal tool*
☐ *Fine emery cloth*
☐ *Wire brush (small)*
☐ *Funnel (medium size)*
☐ *Sump drain plug key (not all vehicles)*

Repair and overhaul tool kit

These tools are virtually essential for anyone undertaking any major repairs to a motor vehicle, and are additional to those given in the *Maintenance and minor repair* list. Included in this list is a comprehensive set of sockets. Although these are expensive, they will be found invaluable as they are so versatile - particularly if various drives are included in the set. We recommend the half-inch square-drive type, as this can be used with most proprietary torque wrenches.

The tools in this list will sometimes need to be supplemented by tools from the *Special* list:

☐ *Sockets (or box spanners) to cover range in previous list (including Torx sockets)*
☐ *Reversible ratchet drive (for use with sockets)*
☐ *Extension piece, 250 mm (for use with sockets)*
☐ *Universal joint (for use with sockets)*
☐ *Flexible handle or sliding T "breaker bar" (for use with sockets)*
☐ *Torque wrench (for use with sockets)*
☐ *Self-locking grips*
☐ *Ball pein hammer*
☐ *Soft-faced mallet (plastic or rubber)*
☐ *Screwdrivers:*
   Flat blade - long & sturdy, short (chubby), and narrow (electrician's) types
   Cross blade - long & sturdy, and short (chubby) types
☐ *Pliers:*
   Long-nosed
   Side cutters (electrician's)
   Circlip (internal and external)
☐ *Cold chisel - 25 mm*
☐ *Scriber*
☐ *Scraper*
☐ *Centre-punch*
☐ *Pin punch*
☐ *Hacksaw*
☐ *Brake hose clamp*
☐ *Brake/clutch bleeding kit*
☐ *Selection of twist drills*
☐ *Steel rule/straight-edge*
☐ *Allen keys (inc. splined/Torx type)*
☐ *Selection of files*
☐ *Wire brush*
☐ *Axle stands*
☐ *Jack (strong trolley or hydraulic type)*
☐ *Light with extension lead*
☐ *Universal electrical multi-meter*

Sockets and reversible ratchet drive

Torx key, socket and bit

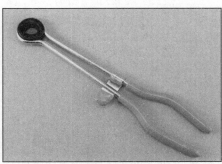

Brake bleeding kit

Hose clamp

Angular-tightening gauge

Special tools

The tools in this list are those which are not used regularly, are expensive to buy, or which need to be used in accordance with their manufacturers' instructions. Unless relatively difficult mechanical jobs are undertaken frequently, it will not be economic to buy many of these tools. Where this is the case, you could consider clubbing together with friends (or joining a motorists' club) to make a joint purchase, or borrowing the tools against a deposit from a local garage or tool hire specialist. It is worth noting that many of the larger DIY superstores now carry a large range of special tools for hire at modest rates.

The following list contains only those tools and instruments freely available to the public, and not those special tools produced by the vehicle manufacturer specifically for its dealer network. You will find occasional references to these manufacturers' special tools in the text of this manual. Generally, an alternative method of doing the job without the vehicle manufacturers' special tool is given. However, sometimes there is no alternative to using them. Where this is the case and the relevant tool cannot be bought or borrowed, you will have to entrust the work to a dealer.

- [ ] *Angular-tightening gauge*
- [ ] *Valve spring compressor*
- [ ] *Valve grinding tool*
- [ ] *Piston ring compressor*
- [ ] *Piston ring removal/installation tool*
- [ ] *Cylinder bore hone*
- [ ] *Balljoint separator*
- [ ] *Coil spring compressors (where applicable)*
- [ ] *Two/three-legged hub and bearing puller*
- [ ] *Impact screwdriver*
- [ ] *Micrometer and/or vernier calipers*
- [ ] *Dial gauge*
- [ ] *Stroboscopic timing light*
- [ ] *Dwell angle meter/tachometer*
- [ ] *Fault code reader*
- [ ] *Cylinder compression gauge*
- [ ] *Hand-operated vacuum pump and gauge*
- [ ] *Clutch plate alignment set*
- [ ] *Brake shoe steady spring cup removal tool*
- [ ] *Bush and bearing removal/installation set*
- [ ] *Stud extractors*
- [ ] *Tap and die set*
- [ ] *Lifting tackle*
- [ ] *Trolley jack*

Buying tools

Reputable motor accessory shops and superstores often offer excellent quality tools at discount prices, so it pays to shop around.

Remember, you don't have to buy the most expensive items on the shelf, but it is always advisable to steer clear of the very cheap tools. Beware of 'bargains' offered on market stalls or at car boot sales. There are plenty of good tools around at reasonable prices, but always aim to purchase items which meet the relevant national safety standards. If in doubt, ask the proprietor or manager of the shop for advice before making a purchase.

Care and maintenance of tools

Having purchased a reasonable tool kit, it is necessary to keep the tools in a clean and serviceable condition. After use, always wipe off any dirt, grease and metal particles using a clean, dry cloth, before putting the tools away. Never leave them lying around after they have been used. A simple tool rack on the garage or workshop wall for items such as screwdrivers and pliers is a good idea. Store all normal spanners and sockets in a metal box. Any measuring instruments, gauges, meters, etc, must be carefully stored where they cannot be damaged or become rusty.

Take a little care when tools are used. Hammer heads inevitably become marked, and screwdrivers lose the keen edge on their blades from time to time. A little timely attention with emery cloth or a file will soon restore items like this to a good finish.

Working facilities

Not to be forgotten when discussing tools is the workshop itself. If anything more than routine maintenance is to be carried out, a suitable working area becomes essential.

It is appreciated that many an owner-mechanic is forced by circumstances to remove an engine or similar item without the benefit of a garage or workshop. Having done this, any repairs should always be done under the cover of a roof.

Wherever possible, any dismantling should be done on a clean, flat workbench or table at a suitable working height.

Any workbench needs a vice; one with a jaw opening of 100 mm is suitable for most jobs. As mentioned previously, some clean dry storage space is also required for tools, as well as for any lubricants, cleaning fluids, touch-up paints etc, which become necessary.

Another item which may be required, and which has a much more general usage, is an electric drill with a chuck capacity of at least 8 mm. This, together with a good range of twist drills, is virtually essential for fitting accessories.

Last, but not least, always keep a supply of old newspapers and clean, lint-free rags available, and try to keep any working area as clean as possible.

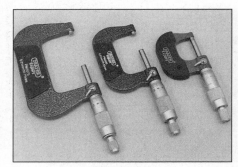

Micrometers

Dial test indicator ("dial gauge")

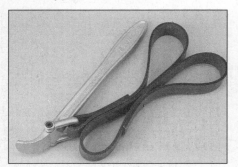

Strap wrench

Compression tester

Fault code reader

This is a guide to getting your vehicle through the MOT test. Obviously it will not be possible to examine the vehicle to the same standard as the professional MOT tester. However, working through the following checks will enable you to identify any problem areas before submitting the vehicle for the test.

Where a testable component is in borderline condition, the tester has discretion in deciding whether to pass or fail it. The basis of such discretion is whether the tester would be happy for a close relative or friend to use the vehicle with the component in that condition. If the vehicle presented is clean and evidently well cared for, the tester may be more inclined to pass a borderline component than if the vehicle is scruffy and apparently neglected.

It has only been possible to summarise the test requirements here, based on the regulations in force at the time of printing. Test standards are becoming increasingly stringent, although there are some exemptions for older vehicles.

An assistant will be needed to help carry out some of these checks.

The checks have been sub-divided into four categories, as follows:

1 Checks carried out **FROM THE DRIVER'S SEAT**

2 Checks carried out **WITH THE VEHICLE ON THE GROUND**

3 Checks carried out **WITH THE VEHICLE RAISED AND THE WHEELS FREE TO TURN**

4 Checks carried out on **YOUR VEHICLE'S EXHAUST EMISSION SYSTEM**

---

1 Checks carried out **FROM THE DRIVER'S SEAT**

Handbrake

☐ Test the operation of the handbrake. Excessive travel (too many clicks) indicates incorrect brake or cable adjustment.

☐ Check that the handbrake cannot be released by tapping the lever sideways. Check the security of the lever mountings.

Footbrake

☐ Depress the brake pedal and check that it does not creep down to the floor, indicating a master cylinder fault. Release the pedal, wait a few seconds, then depress it again. If the pedal travels nearly to the floor before firm resistance is felt, brake adjustment or repair is necessary. If the pedal feels spongy, there is air in the hydraulic system which must be removed by bleeding.

☐ Check that the brake pedal is secure and in good condition. Check also for signs of fluid leaks on the pedal, floor or carpets, which would indicate failed seals in the brake master cylinder.

☐ Check the servo unit (when applicable) by operating the brake pedal several times, then keeping the pedal depressed and starting the engine. As the engine starts, the pedal will move down slightly. If not, the vacuum hose or the servo itself may be faulty.

Steering wheel and column

☐ Examine the steering wheel for fractures or looseness of the hub, spokes or rim.

☐ Move the steering wheel from side to side and then up and down. Check that the steering wheel is not loose on the column, indicating wear or a loose retaining nut. Continue moving the steering wheel as before, but also turn it slightly from left to right.

☐ Check that the steering wheel is not loose on the column, and that there is no abnormal

movement of the steering wheel, indicating wear in the column support bearings or couplings.

Windscreen, mirrors and sunvisor

☐ The windscreen must be free of cracks or other significant damage within the driver's field of view. (Small stone chips are acceptable.) Rear view mirrors must be secure, intact, and capable of being adjusted.

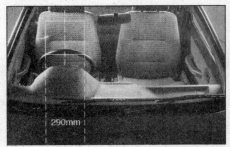

☐ The driver's sunvisor must be capable of being stored in the "up" position.

Seat belts and seats

Note: *The following checks are applicable to all seat belts, front and rear.*

☐ Examine the webbing of all the belts (including rear belts if fitted) for cuts, serious fraying or deterioration. Fasten and unfasten each belt to check the buckles. If applicable, check the retracting mechanism. Check the security of all seat belt mountings accessible from inside the vehicle.

☐ Seat belts with pre-tensioners, once activated, have a "flag" or similar showing on the seat belt stalk. This, in itself, is not a reason for test failure.

☐ The front seats themselves must be securely attached and the backrests must lock in the upright position.

Doors

☐ Both front doors must be able to be opened and closed from outside and inside, and must latch securely when closed.

2 Checks carried out WITH THE VEHICLE ON THE GROUND

Vehicle identification

☐ Number plates must be in good condition, secure and legible, with letters and numbers correctly spaced – spacing at (A) should be at least twice that at (B).

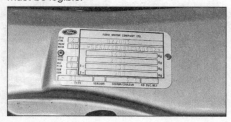

☐ The VIN plate and/or homologation plate must be legible.

Electrical equipment

☐ Switch on the ignition and check the operation of the horn.

☐ Check the windscreen washers and wipers, examining the wiper blades; renew damaged or perished blades. Also check the operation of the stop-lights.

☐ Check the operation of the sidelights and number plate lights. The lenses and reflectors must be secure, clean and undamaged.

☐ Check the operation and alignment of the headlights. The headlight reflectors must not be tarnished and the lenses must be undamaged.

☐ Switch on the ignition and check the operation of the direction indicators (including the instrument panel tell-tale) and the hazard warning lights. Operation of the sidelights and stop-lights must not affect the indicators - if it does, the cause is usually a bad earth at the rear light cluster.

☐ Check the operation of the rear foglight(s), including the warning light on the instrument panel or in the switch.

☐ The ABS warning light must illuminate in accordance with the manufacturers' design. For most vehicles, the ABS warning light should illuminate when the ignition is switched on, and (if the system is operating properly) extinguish after a few seconds. Refer to the owner's handbook.

Footbrake

☐ Examine the master cylinder, brake pipes and servo unit for leaks, loose mountings, corrosion or other damage.

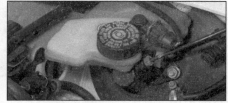

☐ The fluid reservoir must be secure and the fluid level must be between the upper (**A**) and lower (**B**) markings.

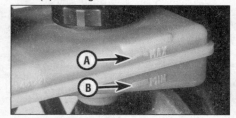

☐ Inspect both front brake flexible hoses for cracks or deterioration of the rubber. Turn the steering from lock to lock, and ensure that the hoses do not contact the wheel, tyre, or any part of the steering or suspension mechanism. With the brake pedal firmly depressed, check the hoses for bulges or leaks under pressure.

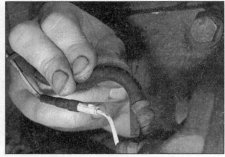

Steering and suspension

☐ Have your assistant turn the steering wheel from side to side slightly, up to the point where the steering gear just begins to transmit this movement to the roadwheels. Check for excessive free play between the steering wheel and the steering gear, indicating wear or insecurity of the steering column joints, the column-to-steering gear coupling, or the steering gear itself.

☐ Have your assistant turn the steering wheel more vigorously in each direction, so that the roadwheels just begin to turn. As this is done, examine all the steering joints, linkages, fittings and attachments. Renew any component that shows signs of wear or damage. On vehicles with power steering, check the security and condition of the steering pump, drivebelt and hoses.

☐ Check that the vehicle is standing level, and at approximately the correct ride height.

Shock absorbers

☐ Depress each corner of the vehicle in turn, then release it. The vehicle should rise and then settle in its normal position. If the vehicle continues to rise and fall, the shock absorber is defective. A shock absorber which has seized will also cause the vehicle to fail.

Exhaust system

☐ Start the engine. With your assistant holding a rag over the tailpipe, check the entire system for leaks. Repair or renew leaking sections.

3 Checks carried out WITH THE VEHICLE RAISED AND THE WHEELS FREE TO TURN

Jack up the front and rear of the vehicle, and securely support it on axle stands. Position the stands clear of the suspension assemblies. Ensure that the wheels are clear of the ground and that the steering can be turned from lock to lock.

Steering mechanism

☐ Have your assistant turn the steering from lock to lock. Check that the steering turns smoothly, and that no part of the steering mechanism, including a wheel or tyre, fouls any brake hose or pipe or any part of the body structure.
☐ Examine the steering rack rubber gaiters for damage or insecurity of the retaining clips. If power steering is fitted, check for signs of damage or leakage of the fluid hoses, pipes or connections. Also check for excessive stiffness or binding of the steering, a missing split pin or locking device, or severe corrosion of the body structure within 30 cm of any steering component attachment point.

Front and rear suspension and wheel bearings

☐ Starting at the front right-hand side, grasp the roadwheel at the 3 o'clock and 9 o'clock positions and rock gently but firmly. Check for free play or insecurity at the wheel bearings, suspension balljoints, or suspension mountings, pivots and attachments.
☐ Now grasp the wheel at the 12 o'clock and 6 o'clock positions and repeat the previous inspection. Spin the wheel, and check for roughness or tightness of the front wheel bearing.

☐ If excess free play is suspected at a component pivot point, this can be confirmed by using a large screwdriver or similar tool and levering between the mounting and the component attachment. This will confirm whether the wear is in the pivot bush, its retaining bolt, or in the mounting itself (the bolt holes can often become elongated).

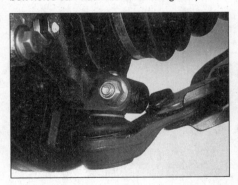

☐ Carry out all the above checks at the other front wheel, and then at both rear wheels.

Springs and shock absorbers

☐ Examine the suspension struts (when applicable) for serious fluid leakage, corrosion, or damage to the casing. Also check the security of the mounting points.
☐ If coil springs are fitted, check that the spring ends locate in their seats, and that the spring is not corroded, cracked or broken.
☐ If leaf springs are fitted, check that all leaves are intact, that the axle is securely attached to each spring, and that there is no deterioration of the spring eye mountings, bushes, and shackles.

☐ The same general checks apply to vehicles fitted with other suspension types, such as torsion bars, hydraulic displacer units, etc. Ensure that all mountings and attachments are secure, that there are no signs of excessive wear, corrosion or damage, and (on hydraulic types) that there are no fluid leaks or damaged pipes.
☐ Inspect the shock absorbers for signs of serious fluid leakage. Check for wear of the mounting bushes or attachments, or damage to the body of the unit.

Driveshafts (fwd vehicles only)

☐ Rotate each front wheel in turn and inspect the constant velocity joint gaiters for splits or damage. Also check that each driveshaft is straight and undamaged.

Braking system

☐ If possible without dismantling, check brake pad wear and disc condition. Ensure that the friction lining material has not worn excessively, (A) and that the discs are not fractured, pitted, scored or badly worn (B).

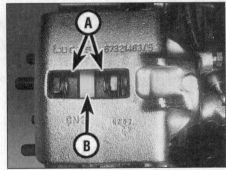

☐ Examine all the rigid brake pipes underneath the vehicle, and the flexible hose(s) at the rear. Look for corrosion, chafing or insecurity of the pipes, and for signs of bulging under pressure, chafing, splits or deterioration of the flexible hoses.
☐ Look for signs of fluid leaks at the brake calipers or on the brake backplates. Repair or renew leaking components.
☐ Slowly spin each wheel, while your assistant depresses and releases the footbrake. Ensure that each brake is operating and does not bind when the pedal is released.

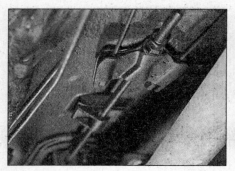

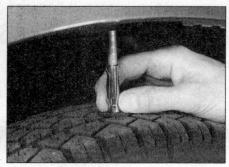

☐ Examine the handbrake mechanism, checking for frayed or broken cables, excessive corrosion, or wear or insecurity of the linkage. Check that the mechanism works on each relevant wheel, and releases fully, without binding.

☐ It is not possible to test brake efficiency without special equipment, but a road test can be carried out later to check that the vehicle pulls up in a straight line.

Fuel and exhaust systems

☐ Inspect the fuel tank (including the filler cap), fuel pipes, hoses and unions. All components must be secure and free from leaks.

☐ Examine the exhaust system over its entire length, checking for any damaged, broken or missing mountings, security of the retaining clamps and rust or corrosion.

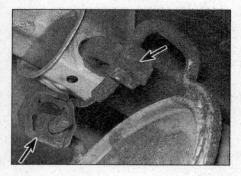

Wheels and tyres

☐ Examine the sidewalls and tread area of each tyre in turn. Check for cuts, tears, lumps, bulges, separation of the tread, and exposure of the ply or cord due to wear or damage. Check that the tyre bead is correctly seated on the wheel rim, that the valve is sound and properly seated, and that the wheel is not distorted or damaged.

☐ Check that the tyres are of the correct size for the vehicle, that they are of the same size and type on each axle, and that the pressures are correct.

☐ Check the tyre tread depth. The legal minimum at the time of writing is 1.6 mm over at least three-quarters of the tread width. Abnormal tread wear may indicate incorrect front wheel alignment.

Body corrosion

☐ Check the condition of the entire vehicle structure for signs of corrosion in load-bearing areas. (These include chassis box sections, side sills, cross-members, pillars, and all suspension, steering, braking system and seat belt mountings and anchorages.) Any corrosion which has seriously reduced the thickness of a load-bearing area is likely to cause the vehicle to fail. In this case professional repairs are likely to be needed.

☐ Damage or corrosion which causes sharp or otherwise dangerous edges to be exposed will also cause the vehicle to fail.

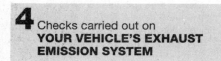

4 Checks carried out on **YOUR VEHICLE'S EXHAUST EMISSION SYSTEM**

Petrol models

☐ Have the engine at normal operating temperature, and make sure that it is in good tune (ignition system in good order, air filter element clean, etc).

☐ Before any measurements are carried out, raise the engine speed to around 2500 rpm, and hold it at this speed for 20 seconds. Allow the engine speed to return to idle, and watch for smoke emissions from the exhaust tailpipe. If the idle speed is obviously much too high, or if dense blue or clearly-visible black smoke comes from the tailpipe for more than 5 seconds, the vehicle will fail. As a rule of thumb, blue smoke signifies oil being burnt (engine wear) while black smoke signifies unburnt fuel (dirty air cleaner element, or other carburettor or fuel system fault).

☐ An exhaust gas analyser capable of measuring carbon monoxide (CO) and hydrocarbons (HC) is now needed. If such an instrument cannot be hired or borrowed, a local garage may agree to perform the check for a small fee.

CO emissions (mixture)

☐ At the time of writing, for vehicles first used between 1st August 1975 and 31st July 1986 (P to C registration), the CO level must not exceed 4.5% by volume. For vehicles first used between 1st August 1986 and 31st July 1992 (D to J registration), the CO level must not exceed 3.5% by volume. Vehicles first used after 1st August 1992 (K registration) must conform to the manufacturer's specification. The MOT tester has access to a DOT database or emissions handbook, which lists the CO and HC limits for each make and model of vehicle. The CO level is measured with the engine at idle speed, and at "fast idle". The following limits are given as a general guide:

  At idle speed -
    CO level no more than 0.5%
  At "fast idle" (2500 to 3000 rpm) -
    CO level no more than 0.3%
    (Minimum oil temperature 60°C)

☐ If the CO level cannot be reduced far enough to pass the test (and the fuel and ignition systems are otherwise in good condition) then the carburettor is badly worn, or there is some problem in the fuel injection system or catalytic converter (as applicable).

HC emissions

☐ With the CO within limits, HC emissions for vehicles first used between 1st August 1975 and 31st July 1992 (P to J registration) must not exceed 1200 ppm. Vehicles first used after 1st August 1992 (K registration) must conform to the manufacturer's specification. The MOT tester has access to a DOT database or emissions handbook, which lists the CO and HC limits for each make and model of vehicle. The HC level is measured with the engine at "fast idle". The following is given as a general guide:

  At "fast idle" (2500 to 3000 rpm) -
    HC level no more than 200 ppm
    (Minimum oil temperature 60°C)

☐ Excessive HC emissions are caused by incomplete combustion, the causes of which can include oil being burnt, mechanical wear and ignition/fuel system malfunction.

Diesel models

☐ The only emission test applicable to Diesel engines is the measuring of exhaust smoke density. The test involves accelerating the engine several times to its maximum unloaded speed.

Note: *It is of the utmost importance that the engine timing belt is in good condition before the test is carried out.*

☐ The limits for Diesel engine exhaust smoke, introduced in September 1995 are:
Vehicles first used before 1st August 1979:
  Exempt from metered smoke testing, but must not emit "dense blue or clearly visible black smoke for a period of more than 5 seconds at idle" or "dense blue or clearly visible black smoke during acceleration which would obscure the view of other road users".
Non-turbocharged vehicles first used after 1st August 1979: 2.5m^{-1}
Turbocharged vehicles first used after 1st August 1979: 3.0m^{-1}

☐ Excessive smoke can be caused by a dirty air cleaner element. Otherwise, professional advice may be needed to find the cause.

Engine   1

- [ ] Engine fails to rotate when attempting to start
- [ ] Engine rotates, but will not start
- [ ] Engine difficult to start when cold
- [ ] Engine difficult to start when hot
- [ ] Starter motor noisy or excessively-rough in engagement
- [ ] Engine starts, but stops immediately
- [ ] Engine idles erratically
- [ ] Engine misfires at idle speed
- [ ] Engine misfires throughout the driving speed range
- [ ] Engine hesitates on acceleration
- [ ] Engine stalls
- [ ] Engine lacks power
- [ ] Engine backfires
- [ ] Oil pressure warning light on with engine running
- [ ] Engine runs-on after switching off
- [ ] Engine noises

Cooling system   2

- [ ] Overheating
- [ ] Overcooling
- [ ] External coolant leakage
- [ ] Internal coolant leakage
- [ ] Corrosion

Fuel and exhaust systems   3

- [ ] Excessive fuel consumption
- [ ] Fuel leakage and/or fuel odour
- [ ] Excessive noise or fumes from exhaust system

Clutch   4

- [ ] Pedal travels to floor - no pressure or very little resistance
- [ ] Clutch fails to disengage (unable to select gears)
- [ ] Clutch slips (engine speed rises, with no increase in vehicle speed)
- [ ] Judder as clutch is engaged
- [ ] Noise when depressing or releasing clutch pedal

Manual transmission   5

- [ ] Noisy in neutral with engine running
- [ ] Noisy in one particular gear
- [ ] Difficulty engaging gears
- [ ] Jumps out of gear
- [ ] Vibration
- [ ] Lubricant leaks

Automatic transmission   6

- [ ] Fluid leakage
- [ ] Transmission fluid brown, or has burned smell
- [ ] General gear selection problems
- [ ] Transmission will not downshift (kickdown) on full throttle
- [ ] Engine won't start in any gear, or starts in gears other than "P" or "N"
- [ ] Transmission slips, shifts roughly, is noisy, or has no drive in forward or reverse gears

Driveshafts   7

- [ ] Clicking or knocking noise on turns (at slow speed on full-lock)
- [ ] Vibration when accelerating or decelerating

Braking system   8

- [ ] Vehicle pulls to one side under braking
- [ ] Noise (grinding or high-pitched squeal) when brakes applied
- [ ] Excessive brake pedal travel
- [ ] Brake pedal feels spongy when depressed
- [ ] Excessive brake pedal effort required to stop vehicle
- [ ] Judder felt through brake pedal or steering wheel when braking
- [ ] Brakes binding
- [ ] Rear wheels locking under normal braking

Suspension and steering systems   9

- [ ] Vehicle pulls to one side
- [ ] Wheel wobble and vibration
- [ ] Excessive pitching and/or rolling around corners, or during braking
- [ ] Wandering or general instability
- [ ] Excessively-stiff steering
- [ ] Excessive play in steering
- [ ] Lack of power assistance
- [ ] Tyre wear excessive

Electrical system   10

- [ ] Battery will not hold a charge for more than a few days
- [ ] Ignition/no-charge warning light stays on with engine running
- [ ] Ignition/no-charge warning light fails to come on
- [ ] Lights inoperative
- [ ] Instrument readings inaccurate or erratic
- [ ] Horn inoperative, or unsatisfactory in operation
- [ ] Windscreen/tailgate wipers failed, or unsatisfactory in operation
- [ ] Windscreen/tailgate washers failed, or unsatisfactory in operation
- [ ] Electric windows inoperative, or unsatisfactory in operation
- [ ] Central locking system inoperative, or unsatisfactory in operation

Introduction

The vehicle owner who does his or her own maintenance according to the recommended service schedules should not have to use this section of the manual very often. Modern component reliability is such that, provided those items subject to wear or deterioration are inspected or renewed at the specified intervals, sudden failure is comparatively rare. Faults do not usually just happen as a result of sudden failure, but develop over a period of time. Major mechanical failures in particular are usually preceded by characteristic symptoms over hundreds or even thousands of miles. Those components which do occasionally fail without warning are often small and easily carried in the vehicle.

With any fault-finding, the first step is to decide where to begin investigations. This may be obvious, but some detective work may be necessary. The owner who makes half a dozen haphazard adjustments or replacements may be successful in curing a fault (or its symptoms), but will be none the wiser if the fault recurs, and ultimately may have spent more time and money than was necessary. A calm and logical approach will

be found to be more satisfactory in the long run. Always take into account any warning signs that may have been noticed in the period preceding the fault - power loss, high or low gauge readings, unusual smells, etc - and remember - failure of components such as fuses or spark plugs may only be pointers to some underlying fault.

The pages which follow provide an easy-reference guide to the more common problems which may occur during the operation of the vehicle. These problems and their possible causes are grouped under headings denoting various components or systems, such as Engine, Cooling system, etc. The Chapter and/or Section which deals with the problem is also shown in brackets. Whatever the fault, certain basic principles apply. These are as follows:

☐ *Verify the fault*. This is simply a matter of being sure that you know what the symptoms are before starting work. This is particularly important if you are investigating a fault for someone else, who may not have described it very accurately.

☐ *Don't overlook the obvious*. For example, if

the vehicle won't start, is there fuel in the tank? (Don't take anyone else's word on this particular point, and don't trust the fuel gauge either!) If an electrical fault is indicated, look for loose or broken wires before digging out the test gear.

☐ *Cure the disease, not the symptom*. Substituting a flat battery with a fully-charged one will get you off the hard shoulder, but if the underlying cause is not attended to, the new battery will go the same way. Similarly, changing oil-fouled spark plugs for a new set will get you moving again, but remember that the reason for the fouling (if it wasn't simply an incorrect grade of plug) will have to be established and corrected.

☐ *Don't take anything for granted*. Particularly, don't forget that a "new" component may itself be defective (especially if it's been rattling around in the boot for months), and don't leave components out of a fault diagnosis sequence just because they are new or recently-fitted. When you do finally diagnose a difficult fault, you'll probably realise that all the evidence was there from the start.

1 Engine

Engine fails to rotate when attempting to start

- ☐ Battery terminal connections loose or corroded ("*Weekly Checks*").
- ☐ Battery discharged or faulty (Chapter 5A).
- ☐ Broken, loose or disconnected wiring in the starting circuit (Chapter 5A).
- ☐ Defective starter solenoid or switch (Chapter 5A).
- ☐ Defective starter motor (Chapter 5A).
- ☐ Starter pinion or flywheel ring gear teeth loose or broken (Chapters 2A, 2B, 2C and 5A).
- ☐ Engine earth strap broken or disconnected (Chapter 5A).

Engine rotates, but will not start

- ☐ Fuel tank empty.
- ☐ Battery discharged (engine rotates slowly) (Chapter 5A).
- ☐ Battery terminal connections loose or corroded ("*Weekly Checks*").
- ☐ Ignition components damp or damaged - petrol models (Chapters 1A and 5B).
- ☐ Broken, loose or disconnected wiring in the ignition circuit - petrol models (Chapters 1A and 5B).
- ☐ Worn, faulty or incorrectly-gapped spark plugs - petrol models (Chapter 1A).
- ☐ Preheating system faulty - Diesel models (Chapter 5C).
- ☐ Choke mechanism incorrectly adjusted, worn or sticking - carburettor petrol models (Chapter 4A).
- ☐ Faulty fuel cut-off solenoid - carburettor petrol models (Chapter 4A).
- ☐ Fuel injection system fault - fuel-injected petrol models (Chapter 4B or 4C).
- ☐ Stop solenoid faulty - Diesel models (Chapter 4D).
- ☐ Air in fuel system - Diesel models (Chapter 4D).
- ☐ Major mechanical failure (eg camshaft drive) (Chapter 2A, 2B or 2C).

Engine difficult to start when cold

- ☐ Battery discharged (Chapter 5A).
- ☐ Battery terminal connections loose or corroded ("*Weekly Checks*").
- ☐ Worn, faulty or incorrectly-gapped spark plugs - petrol models (Chapter 1A).
- ☐ Preheating system faulty - Diesel models (Chapter 5C).
- ☐ Choke mechanism incorrectly adjusted, worn or sticking - carburettor petrol models (Chapter 4A).
- ☐ Fuel injection system fault - fuel-injected petrol models (Chapter 4B or 4C).
- ☐ Other ignition system fault - petrol models (Chapters 1A and 5B).
- ☐ Fast idle valve incorrectly adjusted - Diesel models (Chapter 4D).
- ☐ Low cylinder compressions (Chapter 2A, 2B or 2C).

Engine difficult to start when hot

- ☐ Air filter element dirty or clogged (Chapter 1A or 1B).
- ☐ Choke mechanism incorrectly adjusted, worn or sticking - carburettor petrol models (Chapter 4A).
- ☐ Fuel injection system fault - fuel-injected petrol models (Chapter 4B or 4C).
- ☐ Low cylinder compressions (Chapter 2A, 2B or 2C).

Starter motor noisy or excessively-rough in engagement

- ☐ Starter pinion or flywheel ring gear teeth loose or broken (Chapters 2A, 2B, 2C and 5A).
- ☐ Starter motor mounting bolts loose or missing (Chapter 5A).
- ☐ Starter motor internal components worn or damaged (Chapter 5A).

Engine starts, but stops immediately

- ☐ Loose or faulty electrical connections in the ignition circuit - petrol models (Chapters 1A and 5B).
- ☐ Vacuum leak at the carburettor/throttle body or inlet manifold - petrol models (Chapter 4A, 4B or 4C).
- ☐ Blocked carburettor jet(s) or internal passages - carburettor petrol models (Chapter 4A).
- ☐ Blocked injector/fuel injection system fault - fuel-injected petrol models (Chapter 4B or 4C).

Engine idles erratically

- ☐ Air filter element clogged (Chapter 1A or 1B).
- ☐ Vacuum leak at the carburettor/throttle body, inlet manifold or associated hoses - petrol models (Chapter 4A, 4B or 4C).
- ☐ Worn, faulty or incorrectly-gapped spark plugs - petrol models (Chapter 1A).
- ☐ Uneven or low cylinder compressions (Chapter 2A, 2B or 2C).
- ☐ Camshaft lobes worn (Chapter 2A, 2B or 2C).
- ☐ Timing belt incorrectly tensioned (Chapter 2A, 2B or 2C).
- ☐ Blocked carburettor jet(s) or internal passages - carburettor petrol models (Chapter 4A).
- ☐ Blocked injector/fuel injection system fault - fuel-injected petrol models (Chapter 4B or 4C).
- ☐ Faulty injector(s) - Diesel models (Chapter 4D).

Engine misfires at idle speed

- ☐ Worn, faulty or incorrectly-gapped spark plugs - petrol models (Chapter 1A).
- ☐ Faulty spark plug HT leads - petrol models (Chapter 1A).
- ☐ Vacuum leak at the carburettor/throttle body, inlet manifold or associated hoses - petrol models (Chapter 4A, 4B or 4C).
- ☐ Blocked carburettor jet(s) or internal passages - carburettor petrol models (Chapter 4A).
- ☐ Blocked injector/fuel injection system fault - fuel-injected petrol models (Chapter 4B or 4C).
- ☐ Faulty injector(s) - Diesel models (Chapter 4D).
- ☐ Distributor cap cracked or tracking internally - petrol models (where applicable) (Chapter 1A).
- ☐ Uneven or low cylinder compressions (Chapter 2A, 2B or 2C).
- ☐ Disconnected, leaking, or perished crankcase ventilation hoses (Chapter 4E).

Engine (continued)

Engine misfires throughout the driving speed range

- ☐ Fuel filter choked (Chapter 1A or 1B).
- ☐ Fuel pump faulty, or delivery pressure low (Chapter 4A, 4B or 4C).
- ☐ Fuel tank vent blocked, or fuel pipes restricted (Chapter 4A, 4B or 4C).
- ☐ Vacuum leak at the carburettor/throttle body, inlet manifold or associated hoses - petrol models (Chapter 4A, 4B or 4C).
- ☐ Worn, faulty or incorrectly-gapped spark plugs - petrol models (Chapter 1A).
- ☐ Faulty spark plug HT leads - petrol models (Chapter 1A).
- ☐ Faulty injector(s) - Diesel models (Chapter 4D).
- ☐ Distributor cap cracked or tracking internally - petrol models (where applicable) (Chapter 1A).
- ☐ Faulty ignition coil - petrol models (Chapter 5B).
- ☐ Uneven or low cylinder compressions (Chapter 2A, 2B or 2C).
- ☐ Blocked carburettor jet(s) or internal passages - carburettor petrol models (Chapter 4A).
- ☐ Blocked injector/fuel injection system fault - fuel-injected petrol models (Chapter 4B or 4C).

Engine hesitates on acceleration

- ☐ Worn, faulty or incorrectly-gapped spark plugs - petrol models (Chapter 1A).
- ☐ Vacuum leak at the carburettor/throttle body, inlet manifold or associated hoses (Chapter 4A, 4B or 4C).
- ☐ Blocked carburettor jet(s) or internal passages - carburettor petrol models (Chapter 4A).
- ☐ Blocked injector/fuel injection system fault - fuel-injected petrol models (Chapter 4B or 4C).
- ☐ Faulty injector(s) - Diesel models (Chapter 4D).

Engine stalls

- ☐ Vacuum leak at the carburettor/throttle body, inlet manifold or associated hoses - petrol models (Chapter 4A, 4B or 4C).
- ☐ Fuel filter choked (Chapter 1A or 1B).
- ☐ Fuel pump faulty, or delivery pressure low - petrol models (Chapter 4A, 4B or 4C).
- ☐ Fuel tank vent blocked, or fuel pipes restricted (Chapter 4A, 4B, 4C or 4D).
- ☐ Blocked carburettor jet(s) or internal passages - carburettor petrol models (Chapter 4A).
- ☐ Blocked injector/fuel injection system fault - fuel-injected petrol models (Chapter 4B or 4C).
- ☐ Faulty injector(s) - Diesel models (Chapter 4D).

Engine lacks power

- ☐ Timing belt incorrectly fitted or tensioned (Chapter 2A, 2B or 2C).
- ☐ Fuel filter choked (Chapter 1A or 1B).
- ☐ Fuel pump faulty, or delivery pressure low (Chapter 4A, 4B, or 4C).
- ☐ Uneven or low cylinder compressions (Chapter 2A, 2B or 2C).
- ☐ Worn, faulty or incorrectly-gapped spark plugs - petrol models (Chapter 1A).
- ☐ Vacuum leak at the carburettor/throttle body, inlet manifold or associated hoses - petrol models (Chapter 4A, 4B or 4C).
- ☐ Blocked carburettor jet(s) or internal passages - carburettor petrol models (Chapter 4A).
- ☐ Blocked injector/fuel injection system fault - fuel-injected petrol models (Chapter 4B or 4C).
- ☐ Faulty injector(s) - Diesel models (Chapter 4D).
- ☐ Injection pump timing incorrect - Diesel models (Chapter 4D).
- ☐ Brakes binding (Chapters 1 and 9).
- ☐ Clutch slipping (Chapter 6).

Engine backfires

- ☐ Timing belt incorrectly fitted or tensioned (Chapter 2A).
- ☐ Vacuum leak at the carburettor/throttle body, inlet manifold or associated hoses - petrol models (Chapter 4A, 4B or 4C).
- ☐ Blocked carburettor jet(s) or internal passages - carburettor petrol models (Chapter 4A).
- ☐ Blocked injector/fuel injection system fault - fuel-injected petrol models (Chapter 4B or 4C).

Oil pressure warning light on with engine running

- ☐ Low oil level, or incorrect oil grade ("Weekly Checks").
- ☐ Faulty oil pressure warning light switch (Chapter 5A).
- ☐ Worn engine bearings and/or oil pump (Chapter 2D).
- ☐ High engine operating temperature (Chapter 3).
- ☐ Oil pressure relief valve defective (Chapter 2A, 2B or 2C).
- ☐ Oil pick-up strainer clogged (Chapter 2A, 2B or 2C).

Engine runs-on after switching off

- ☐ Excessive carbon build-up in engine (Chapter 2D).
- ☐ High engine operating temperature (Chapter 3).
- ☐ Faulty fuel cut-off solenoid - carburettor petrol models (Chapter 4A).
- ☐ Fuel injection system fault - fuel-injected petrol models (Chapter 4B or 4C).
- ☐ Faulty stop solenoid - Diesel models (Chapter 4D).

Engine noises

Pre-ignition (pinking) or knocking during acceleration or under load

- ☐ Ignition timing incorrect/ignition system fault - petrol models (Chapters 1A and 5B).
- ☐ Incorrect grade of spark plug - petrol models (Chapter 1A).
- ☐ Incorrect grade of fuel (Chapter 1A or 1B).
- ☐ Vacuum leak at the carburettor/throttle body, inlet manifold or associated hoses - petrol models (Chapter 4A, 4B or 4C).
- ☐ Excessive carbon build-up in engine (Chapter 2D).
- ☐ Blocked carburettor jet(s) or internal passages - carburettor petrol models (Chapter 4A).
- ☐ Blocked injector/fuel injection system fault - fuel-injected petrol models (Chapter 4B or 4C).

Whistling or wheezing noises

- ☐ Leaking inlet manifold or carburettor/throttle body gasket - petrol models (Chapter 4A, 4B or 4C).
- ☐ Leaking exhaust manifold gasket or pipe-to-manifold joint (Chapter 4A, 4B, 4C or 4D).
- ☐ Leaking vacuum hose (Chapters 4A, 4B, 4C, 4D, 5B and 9).
- ☐ Blowing cylinder head gasket (Chapter 2A, 2B and 2C).

Tapping or rattling noises

- ☐ Worn valve gear or camshaft (Chapter 2A, 2B or 2C).
- ☐ Ancillary component fault (coolant pump, alternator, etc) (Chapters 3, 5A, etc).

Knocking or thumping noises

- ☐ Worn big-end bearings (regular heavy knocking, perhaps less under load) (Chapter 2D).
- ☐ Worn main bearings (rumbling and knocking, perhaps worsening under load) (Chapter 2D).
- ☐ Piston slap (most noticeable when cold) (Chapter 2D).
- ☐ Ancillary component fault (coolant pump, alternator, etc) (Chapters 3, 5A, etc).

2 Cooling system

Overheating

☐ Insufficient coolant in system ("*Weekly Checks*").
☐ Thermostat faulty (Chapter 3).
☐ Radiator core blocked, or grille restricted (Chapter 3).
☐ Electric cooling fan or thermoswitch faulty (Chapter 3).
☐ Pressure cap faulty (Chapter 3).
☐ Ignition timing incorrect/ignition system fault - petrol models (Chapters 1A and 5B).
☐ Inaccurate temperature gauge sender unit (Chapter 3).
☐ Airlock in cooling system (Chapter 1A or 1B).

Overcooling

☐ Thermostat faulty (Chapter 3).
☐ Inaccurate temperature gauge sender unit (Chapter 3).

External coolant leakage

☐ Deteriorated or damaged hoses or hose clips (Chapter 1A or 1B).
☐ Radiator core or heater matrix leaking (Chapter 3).
☐ Pressure cap faulty (Chapter 3).
☐ Water pump seal leaking (Chapter 3).
☐ Boiling due to overheating (Chapter 3).
☐ Core plug leaking (Chapter 2C).

Internal coolant leakage

☐ Leaking cylinder head gasket (Chapter 2A, 2B or 2C).
☐ Cracked cylinder head or cylinder bore (Chapter 2A, 2B or 2C).

Corrosion

☐ Infrequent draining and flushing (Chapter 1A or 1B).
☐ Incorrect coolant mixture or inappropriate coolant type (Chapter 1A or 1B and "*Weekly Checks*").

3 Fuel and exhaust systems

Excessive fuel consumption

☐ Air filter element dirty or clogged (Chapter 1A or 1B).
☐ Choke cable incorrectly adjusted, or choke sticking - carburettor petrol models (Chapter 4A).
☐ Fuel injection system fault - fuel injected petrol models (Chapter 4B or 4C).
☐ Faulty injector(s) - Diesel models (Chapter 4D).
☐ Ignition timing incorrect/ignition system fault - petrol models (Chapters 1 and 5B).
☐ Tyres under-inflated ("*Weekly Checks*").
☐ Brakes binding (Chapters 1 and 9).

Fuel leakage and/or fuel odour

☐ Damaged or corroded fuel tank, pipes or connections (Chapter 4A, 4B, 4C or 4D).
☐ Carburettor float chamber flooding (float height incorrect) - carburettor petrol models (Chapter 4A).

Excessive noise or fumes from exhaust system

☐ Leaking exhaust system or manifold joints (Chapters 1 and 4A, 4B, 4C or 4D).
☐ Leaking, corroded or damaged silencers or pipe (Chapters 1 and 4A, 4B, 4C or 4D).
☐ Broken mountings causing body or suspension contact (Chapter 1A or 1B).

4 Clutch

Pedal travels to floor - no pressure or very little resistance

☐ Broken clutch cable (Chapter 6).
☐ Incorrect clutch cable adjustment (Chapter 6).
☐ Broken clutch release bearing or fork (Chapter 6).
☐ Broken diaphragm spring in clutch pressure plate (Chapter 6).

Clutch fails to disengage (unable to select gears)

☐ Incorrect clutch cable adjustment (Chapter 6).
☐ Clutch disc sticking on gearbox input shaft splines (Chapter 6).
☐ Clutch disc sticking to flywheel or pressure plate (Chapter 6).
☐ Faulty pressure plate assembly (Chapter 6).
☐ Clutch release mechanism worn or incorrectly assembled (Chapter 6).

Clutch slips (engine speed rises, with no increase in vehicle speed)

☐ Incorrect clutch cable adjustment (Chapter 6).
☐ Clutch disc linings excessively worn (Chapter 6).
☐ Clutch disc linings contaminated with oil or grease (Chapter 6).
☐ Faulty pressure plate or weak diaphragm spring (Chapter 6).

Judder as clutch is engaged

☐ Clutch disc linings contaminated with oil or grease (Chapter 6).
☐ Clutch disc linings excessively worn (Chapter 6).
☐ Clutch cable sticking or frayed (Chapter 6).
☐ Faulty or distorted pressure plate or diaphragm spring (Chapter 6).
☐ Worn or loose engine or gearbox mountings (Chapter 2A, 2B or 2C).
☐ Clutch disc hub or gearbox input shaft splines worn (Chapter 6).

Noise when depressing or releasing clutch pedal

☐ Worn clutch release bearing (Chapter 6).
☐ Worn or dry clutch pedal bushes (Chapter 6).
☐ Faulty pressure plate assembly (Chapter 6).
☐ Pressure plate diaphragm spring broken (Chapter 6).
☐ Broken clutch disc cushioning springs (Chapter 6).

5 Manual transmission

Noisy in neutral with engine running

- ☐ Input shaft bearings worn (noise apparent with clutch pedal released, but not when depressed) (Chapter 7A).*
- ☐ Clutch release bearing worn (noise apparent with clutch pedal depressed, possibly less when released) (Chapter 6).

Noisy in one particular gear

- ☐ Worn, damaged or chipped gear teeth (Chapter 7A).*

Difficulty engaging gears

- ☐ Clutch fault (Chapter 6).
- ☐ Worn or damaged gear linkage (Chapter 7A).
- ☐ Incorrectly-adjusted gear linkage (Chapter 7A).
- ☐ Worn synchroniser units (Chapter 7A).*

Jumps out of gear

- ☐ Worn or damaged gear linkage (Chapter 7A).
- ☐ Incorrectly-adjusted gear linkage (Chapter 7A).
- ☐ Worn synchroniser units (Chapter 7A).*
- ☐ Worn selector forks (Chapter 7A).*

Vibration

- ☐ Lack of oil (Chapter 1A or 1B).
- ☐ Worn bearings (Chapter 7A).*

Lubricant leaks

- ☐ Leaking differential output oil seal (Chapter 7A).
- ☐ Leaking housing joint (Chapter 7A).*
- ☐ Leaking input shaft oil seal (Chapter 7A).*

Although the corrective action necessary to remedy the symptoms described is beyond the scope of the home mechanic, the above information should be helpful in isolating the cause of the condition, so that the owner can communicate clearly with a professional mechanic.

6 Automatic transmission

Note: *Due to the complexity of the automatic transmission, it is difficult for the home mechanic to properly diagnose and service this unit. For problems other than the following, the vehicle should be taken to a dealer service department or automatic transmission specialist. Don't be in a hurry to remove the transmission if a fault is suspected, as most testing is carried out with the unit still fitted.*

Fluid leakage

- ☐ Automatic transmission fluid is usually dark in colour. Fluid leaks should not be confused with engine oil, which can easily be blown onto the transmission by airflow.
- ☐ To determine the source of a leak, first remove all built-up dirt and grime from the transmission housing and surrounding areas using a degreasing agent, or by steam-cleaning. Drive the vehicle at low speed, so airflow will not blow the leak far from its source. Raise and support the vehicle, and determine where the leak is coming from. The following are common areas of leakage:
  a) Fluid pan or "sump" (Chapter 1 and 7B).
  b) Dipstick tube (Chapter 1 and 7B).
  c) Transmission-to-fluid cooler pipes/unions (Chapter 7B).

Transmission fluid brown, or has burned smell

- ☐ Transmission fluid level low, or fluid in need of renewal (Chapter 1A or 1B).

General gear selection problems

- ☐ Chapter 7B deals with checking and adjusting the selector cable

on automatic transmissions. The following are common problems which may be caused by a poorly-adjusted cable:
  a) Engine starting in gears other than Park or Neutral.
  b) Indicator panel showing a gear other than that being used.
  c) Vehicle moves when in Park or Neutral.
  d) Poor gear shift quality or erratic gear changes.
- ☐ Refer to Chapter 7B for the selector cable adjustment procedure.

Transmission will not downshift (kickdown) at full throttle

- ☐ Low transmission fluid level (Chapter 1A or 1B).
- ☐ Incorrect selector cable adjustment (Chapter 7B).

Engine won't start in any gear, or starts in gears other than Park or Neutral

- ☐ Incorrect starter/inhibitor switch adjustment (Chapter 7B).
- ☐ Incorrect selector cable adjustment (Chapter 7B).

Transmission slips, shifts roughly, is noisy, or has no drive in forward or reverse gears

- ☐ There are many probable causes for the above problems, but the home mechanic should be concerned with only one possibility - fluid level. Before taking the vehicle to a dealer or transmission specialist, check the fluid level and condition of the fluid as described in Chapter 1A or 1B. Correct the fluid level as necessary, or change the fluid and filter. If the problem persists, professional help will be necessary.

7 Driveshafts

Clicking or knocking noise on turns (at slow speed on full-lock)

- ☐ Lack of constant velocity joint lubricant, possibly due to damaged gaiter (Chapter 8).
- ☐ Worn outer constant velocity joint (Chapter 8).

Vibration when accelerating or decelerating

- ☐ Worn inner constant velocity joint (Chapter 8).
- ☐ Bent or distorted driveshaft (Chapter 8).

8 Braking system

Note: *Before assuming that a brake problem exists, make sure that the tyres are in good condition and correctly inflated, that the front wheel alignment is correct, and that the vehicle is not loaded with weight in an unequal manner. Apart from checking the condition of all pipe and hose connections, any faults occurring on the anti-lock braking system should be referred to a Peugeot dealer for diagnosis.*

Vehicle pulls to one side under braking

☐ Worn, defective, damaged or contaminated brake pads/shoes on one side (Chapters 1 and 9).
☐ Seized or partially-seized front brake caliper/wheel cylinder piston (Chapters 1 and 9).
☐ A mixture of brake pad/shoe lining materials fitted between sides (Chapters 1 and 9).
☐ Brake caliper or backplate mounting bolts loose (Chapter 9).
☐ Worn or damaged steering or suspension components (Chapters 1 and 10).

Noise (grinding or high-pitched squeal) when brakes applied

☐ Brake pad or shoe friction lining material worn down to metal backing (Chapters 1 and 9).
☐ Excessive corrosion of brake disc or drum. May be apparent after the vehicle has been standing for some time (Chapters 1 and 9).
☐ Foreign object (stone chipping, etc) trapped between brake disc and shield (Chapters 1 and 9).

Excessive brake pedal travel

☐ Inoperative rear brake self-adjust mechanism - drum brakes (Chapters 1 and 9).
☐ Faulty master cylinder (Chapter 9).
☐ Air in hydraulic system (Chapters 1 and 9).
☐ Faulty vacuum servo unit (Chapter 9).

Brake pedal feels spongy when depressed

☐ Air in hydraulic system (Chapters 1 and 9).
☐ Deteriorated flexible rubber brake hoses (Chapters 1 and 9).
☐ Master cylinder mounting nuts loose (Chapter 9).
☐ Faulty master cylinder (Chapter 9).

Excessive brake pedal effort required to stop vehicle

☐ Faulty vacuum servo unit (Chapter 9).
☐ Disconnected, damaged or insecure brake servo vacuum hose (Chapter 9).
☐ Primary or secondary hydraulic circuit failure (Chapter 9).
☐ Seized brake caliper or wheel cylinder piston(s) (Chapter 9).
☐ Brake pads or brake shoes incorrectly fitted (Chapters 1 and 9).
☐ Incorrect grade of brake pads or brake shoes fitted (Chapters 1 and 9).
☐ Brake pads or brake shoe linings contaminated (Chapters 1 and 9).

Judder felt through brake pedal or steering wheel when braking

☐ Excessive run-out or distortion of discs/drums (Chapters 1 and 9).
☐ Brake pad or brake shoe linings worn (Chapters 1 and 9).
☐ Brake caliper or brake backplate mounting bolts loose (Chapter 9).
☐ Wear in suspension or steering components or mountings (Chapters 1 and 10).

Brakes binding

☐ Seized brake caliper or wheel cylinder piston(s) (Chapter 9).
☐ Incorrectly-adjusted handbrake mechanism (Chapter 9).
☐ Faulty master cylinder (Chapter 9).

Rear wheels locking under normal braking

☐ Rear brake shoe linings contaminated (Chapters 1 and 9).
☐ Faulty brake pressure regulator (Chapter 9).

9 Suspension and steering

Note: *Before diagnosing suspension or steering faults, be sure that the trouble is not due to incorrect tyre pressures, mixtures of tyre types, or binding brakes.*

Vehicle pulls to one side

☐ Defective tyre (*"Weekly Checks"*).
☐ Excessive wear in suspension or steering components (Chapters 1 and 10).
☐ Incorrect front wheel alignment (Chapter 10).
☐ Damage to steering or suspension components (Chapter 1).

Wheel wobble and vibration

☐ Front roadwheels out of balance (vibration felt mainly through the steering wheel) (Chapters 1 and 10).
☐ Rear roadwheels out of balance (vibration felt throughout the vehicle) (Chapters 1 and 10).
☐ Roadwheels damaged or distorted (Chapters 1 and 10).
☐ Faulty or damaged tyre (*"Weekly Checks"*).
☐ Worn steering or suspension joints, bushes or components (Chapters 1 and 10).
☐ Wheel bolts loose (Chapters 1 and 10).

Excessive pitching and/or rolling around corners, or during braking

☐ Defective shock absorbers (Chapters 1 and 10).
☐ Broken or weak spring and/or suspension part (Chapters 1 and 10).
☐ Worn or damaged anti-roll bar or mountings (Chapter 10).

Wandering or general instability

☐ Incorrect front wheel alignment (Chapter 10).
☐ Worn steering or suspension joints, bushes or components (Chapters 1 and 10).
☐ Roadwheels out of balance (Chapters 1 and 10).
☐ Faulty or damaged tyre (*"Weekly Checks"*).
☐ Wheel bolts loose (Chapters 1 and 10).
☐ Defective shock absorbers (Chapters 1 and 10).

Excessively-stiff steering

☐ Lack of steering gear lubricant (Chapter 10).
☐ Seized track rod end balljoint or suspension balljoint (Chapters 1 and 10).
☐ Broken or incorrectly-adjusted auxiliary drivebelt - power steering (Chapter 1).
☐ Incorrect front wheel alignment (Chapter 10).
☐ Steering rack or column bent or damaged (Chapter 10).

Excessive play in steering

☐ Worn steering column intermediate shaft universal joint (Chapter 10).
☐ Worn steering track rod end balljoints (Chapters 1 and 10).
☐ Worn rack-and-pinion steering gear (Chapter 10).
☐ Worn steering or suspension joints, bushes or components (Chapters 1 and 10).

Suspension and steering (continued)

Lack of power assistance

- ☐ Broken or incorrectly-adjusted auxiliary drivebelt (Chapter 1).
- ☐ Incorrect power steering fluid level ("*Weekly Checks*").
- ☐ Restriction in power steering fluid hoses (Chapter 1A or 1B).
- ☐ Faulty power steering pump (Chapter 10).
- ☐ Faulty rack-and-pinion steering gear (Chapter 10).

Tyre wear excessive

Tyre treads exhibit feathered edges

- ☐ Incorrect toe setting (Chapter 10).

Tyres worn in centre of tread

- ☐ Tyres over-inflated ("*Weekly Checks*").

Tyres worn on inside and outside edges

- ☐ Tyres under-inflated ("*Weekly Checks*").

Tyres worn on inside or outside edges

- ☐ Incorrect camber/castor angles (wear on one edge only) (Chapter 10).
- ☐ Worn steering or suspension joints, bushes or components (Chapters 1 and 10).
- ☐ Excessively-hard cornering.
- ☐ Accident damage.

Tyres worn unevenly

- ☐ Tyres/wheels out of balance ("*Weekly Checks*").
- ☐ Excessive wheel or tyre run-out (Chapter 1).
- ☐ Worn shock absorbers (Chapters 1 and 10).
- ☐ Faulty tyre ("*Weekly Checks*").

10 Electrical system

Note: *For problems associated with the starting system, refer to the faults listed under "Engine" earlier in this Section.*

Battery won't hold a charge for more than a few days

- ☐ Battery defective internally (Chapter 5A).
- ☐ Battery terminal connections loose or corroded ("*Weekly Checks*").
- ☐ Auxiliary drivebelt worn or incorrectly adjusted (Chapter 1A or 1B).
- ☐ Alternator not charging at correct output (Chapter 5A).
- ☐ Alternator or voltage regulator faulty (Chapter 5A).
- ☐ Short-circuit causing continual battery drain (Chapters 5A and 12).

Ignition/no-charge warning light stays on with engine running

- ☐ Auxiliary drivebelt broken, worn, or incorrectly adjusted (Chapter 1A or 1B).
- ☐ Alternator brushes worn, sticking, or dirty (Chapter 5A).
- ☐ Alternator brush springs weak or broken (Chapter 5A).
- ☐ Internal fault in alternator or voltage regulator (Chapter 5A).
- ☐ Broken, disconnected, or loose wiring in charging circuit (Chapter 5A).

Ignition/no-charge warning light fails to come on

- ☐ Warning light bulb blown (Chapter 12).
- ☐ Broken, disconnected, or loose wiring in warning light circuit (Chapter 12).
- ☐ Alternator faulty (Chapter 5A).

Lights inoperative

- ☐ Bulb blown (Chapter 12).
- ☐ Corrosion of bulb or bulbholder contacts (Chapter 12).
- ☐ Blown fuse (Chapter 12).
- ☐ Faulty relay (Chapter 12).
- ☐ Broken, loose, or disconnected wiring (Chapter 12).
- ☐ Faulty switch (Chapter 12).

Instrument readings inaccurate or erratic

Instrument readings increase with engine speed

- ☐ Faulty voltage regulator (Chapter 12).

Fuel or temperature gauges give no reading

- ☐ Faulty gauge sender unit (Chapters 3 and 4A, 4B, 4C or 4D).
- ☐ Wiring open-circuit (Chapter 12).
- ☐ Faulty gauge (Chapter 12).

Fuel or temperature gauges give continuous maximum reading

- ☐ Faulty gauge sender unit (Chapters 3 and 4A, 4B, 4C and 4D).
- ☐ Wiring short-circuit (Chapter 12).
- ☐ Faulty gauge (Chapter 12).

Horn inoperative, or unsatisfactory in operation

Horn operates all the time

- ☐ Horn push either earthed or stuck down (Chapter 12).
- ☐ Horn cable-to-horn push earthed (Chapter 12).

Horn fails to operate

- ☐ Blown fuse (Chapter 12).
- ☐ Cable or cable connections loose, broken or disconnected (Chapter 12).
- ☐ Faulty horn (Chapter 12).

Horn emits intermittent or unsatisfactory sound

- ☐ Cable connections loose (Chapter 12).
- ☐ Horn mountings loose (Chapter 12).
- ☐ Faulty horn (Chapter 12).

Windscreen/tailgate wipers failed, or unsatisfactory in operation

Wipers fail to operate, or operate very slowly

- ☐ Wiper blades stuck to screen, or linkage seized or binding (Chapters 1 and 12).
- ☐ Blown fuse (Chapter 12).
- ☐ Cable or cable connections loose, broken or disconnected (Chapter 12).
- ☐ Faulty relay (Chapter 12).
- ☐ Faulty wiper motor (Chapter 12).

Wiper blades sweep over too large or too small an area of the glass

- ☐ Wiper arms incorrectly positioned on spindles (Chapter 1A or 1B).
- ☐ Excessive wear of wiper linkage (Chapter 12).
- ☐ Wiper motor or linkage mountings loose or insecure (Chapter 12).

Wiper blades fail to clean the glass effectively

- ☐ Wiper blade rubbers worn or perished ("*Weekly Checks*").
- ☐ Wiper arm tension springs broken, or arm pivots seized (Chapter 12).
- ☐ Insufficient windscreen washer additive to adequately remove road film ("*Weekly Checks*").

Electrical system (continued)

Windscreen/tailgate washers failed, or unsatisfactory in operation

One or more washer jets inoperative

- [ ] Blocked washer jet (Chapter 12).
- [ ] Disconnected, kinked or restricted fluid hose (Chapter 12).
- [ ] Insufficient fluid in washer reservoir ("*Weekly Checks*").

Washer pump fails to operate

- [ ] Broken or disconnected wiring or connections (Chapter 12).
- [ ] Blown fuse (Chapter 12).
- [ ] Faulty washer switch (Chapter 12).
- [ ] Faulty washer pump (Chapter 12).

Washer pump runs for some time before fluid is emitted from jets

- [ ] Faulty one-way valve in fluid supply hose (Chapter 12).

Electric windows inoperative, or unsatisfactory in operation

Window glass will only move in one direction

- [ ] Faulty switch (Chapter 12).

Window glass slow to move

- [ ] Regulator seized or damaged, or in need of lubricant (Chapter 11).
- [ ] Door internal components or trim fouling regulator (Chapter 11).
- [ ] Faulty motor (Chapter 11).

Window glass fails to move

- [ ] Blown fuse (Chapter 12).
- [ ] Faulty relay (Chapter 12).
- [ ] Broken or disconnected wiring or connections (Chapter 12).
- [ ] Faulty motor (Chapter 11).

Central locking system inoperative, or unsatisfactory in operation

Complete system failure

- [ ] Blown fuse (Chapter 12).
- [ ] Faulty relay (Chapter 12).
- [ ] Broken or disconnected wiring or connections (Chapter 12).
- [ ] Faulty control unit (Chapter 11).

Latch locks but will not unlock, or unlocks but will not lock

- [ ] Faulty master switch (Chapter 12).
- [ ] Broken or disconnected latch operating rods or levers (Chapter 11).
- [ ] Faulty relay (Chapter 12).
- [ ] Faulty control unit (Chapter 11).

One solenoid/motor fails to operate

- [ ] Broken or disconnected wiring or connections (Chapter 12).
- [ ] Faulty solenoid/motor (Chapter 11).
- [ ] Broken, binding or disconnected latch operating rods or levers (Chapter 11).
- [ ] Fault in door latch (Chapter 11).

A

ABS (Anti-lock brake system) A system, usually electronically controlled, that senses incipient wheel lockup during braking and relieves hydraulic pressure at wheels that are about to skid.

Air bag An inflatable bag hidden in the steering wheel (driver's side) or the dash or glovebox (passenger side). In a head-on collision, the bags inflate, preventing the driver and front passenger from being thrown forward into the steering wheel or windscreen.

Air cleaner A metal or plastic housing, containing a filter element, which removes dust and dirt from the air being drawn into the engine.

Air filter element The actual filter in an air cleaner system, usually manufactured from pleated paper and requiring renewal at regular intervals.

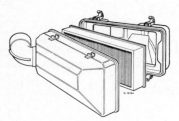

Air filter

Allen key A hexagonal wrench which fits into a recessed hexagonal hole.

Alligator clip A long-nosed spring-loaded metal clip with meshing teeth. Used to make temporary electrical connections.

Alternator A component in the electrical system which converts mechanical energy from a drivebelt into electrical energy to charge the battery and to operate the starting system, ignition system and electrical accessories.

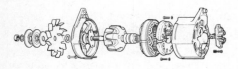

Alternator (exploded view)

Ampere (amp) A unit of measurement for the flow of electric current. One amp is the amount of current produced by one volt acting through a resistance of one ohm.

Anaerobic sealer A substance used to prevent bolts and screws from loosening. Anaerobic means that it does not require oxygen for activation. The Loctite brand is widely used.

Antifreeze A substance (usually ethylene glycol) mixed with water, and added to a vehicle's cooling system, to prevent freezing of the coolant in winter. Antifreeze also contains chemicals to inhibit corrosion and the formation of rust and other deposits that

would tend to clog the radiator and coolant passages and reduce cooling efficiency.

Anti-seize compound A coating that reduces the risk of seizing on fasteners that are subjected to high temperatures, such as exhaust manifold bolts and nuts.

Anti-seize compound

Asbestos A natural fibrous mineral with great heat resistance, commonly used in the composition of brake friction materials. Asbestos is a health hazard and the dust created by brake systems should never be inhaled or ingested.

Axle A shaft on which a wheel revolves, or which revolves with a wheel. Also, a solid beam that connects the two wheels at one end of the vehicle. An axle which also transmits power to the wheels is known as a live axle.

Axle assembly

Axleshaft A single rotating shaft, on either side of the differential, which delivers power from the final drive assembly to the drive wheels. Also called a driveshaft or a halfshaft.

B

Ball bearing An anti-friction bearing consisting of a hardened inner and outer race with hardened steel balls between two races.

Bearing

Bearing The curved surface on a shaft or in a bore, or the part assembled into either, that permits relative motion between them with minimum wear and friction.

Big-end bearing The bearing in the end of the connecting rod that's attached to the crankshaft.

Bleed nipple A valve on a brake wheel cylinder, caliper or other hydraulic component that is opened to purge the hydraulic system of air. Also called a bleed screw.

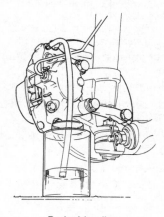

Brake bleeding

Brake bleeding Procedure for removing air from lines of a hydraulic brake system.

Brake disc The component of a disc brake that rotates with the wheels.

Brake drum The component of a drum brake that rotates with the wheels.

Brake linings The friction material which contacts the brake disc or drum to retard the vehicle's speed. The linings are bonded or riveted to the brake pads or shoes.

Brake pads The replaceable friction pads that pinch the brake disc when the brakes are applied. Brake pads consist of a friction material bonded or riveted to a rigid backing plate.

Brake shoe The crescent-shaped carrier to which the brake linings are mounted and which forces the lining against the rotating drum during braking.

Braking systems For more information on braking systems, consult the *Haynes Automotive Brake Manual*.

Breaker bar A long socket wrench handle providing greater leverage.

Bulkhead The insulated partition between the engine and the passenger compartment.

C

Caliper The non-rotating part of a disc-brake assembly that straddles the disc and carries the brake pads. The caliper also contains the hydraulic components that cause the pads to pinch the disc when the brakes are applied. A caliper is also a measuring tool that can be set to measure inside or outside dimensions of an object.

Camshaft A rotating shaft on which a series of cam lobes operate the valve mechanisms. The camshaft may be driven by gears, by sprockets and chain or by sprockets and a belt.

Canister A container in an evaporative emission control system; contains activated charcoal granules to trap vapours from the fuel system.

Canister

Carburettor A device which mixes fuel with air in the proper proportions to provide a desired power output from a spark ignition internal combustion engine.

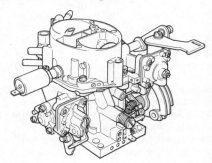

Carburettor

Castellated Resembling the parapets along the top of a castle wall. For example, a castellated balljoint stud nut.

Castellated nut

Castor In wheel alignment, the backward or forward tilt of the steering axis. Castor is positive when the steering axis is inclined rearward at the top.

Catalytic converter A silencer-like device in the exhaust system which converts certain pollutants in the exhaust gases into less harmful substances.

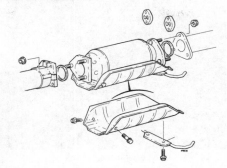

Catalytic converter

Circlip A ring-shaped clip used to prevent endwise movement of cylindrical parts and shafts. An internal circlip is installed in a groove in a housing; an external circlip fits into a groove on the outside of a cylindrical piece such as a shaft.

Clearance The amount of space between two parts. For example, between a piston and a cylinder, between a bearing and a journal, etc.

Coil spring A spiral of elastic steel found in various sizes throughout a vehicle, for example as a springing medium in the suspension and in the valve train.

Compression Reduction in volume, and increase in pressure and temperature, of a gas, caused by squeezing it into a smaller space.

Compression ratio The relationship between cylinder volume when the piston is at top dead centre and cylinder volume when the piston is at bottom dead centre.

Constant velocity (CV) joint A type of universal joint that cancels out vibrations caused by driving power being transmitted through an angle.

Core plug A disc or cup-shaped metal device inserted in a hole in a casting through which core was removed when the casting was formed. Also known as a freeze plug or expansion plug.

Crankcase The lower part of the engine block in which the crankshaft rotates.

Crankshaft The main rotating member, or shaft, running the length of the crankcase, with offset "throws" to which the connecting rods are attached.

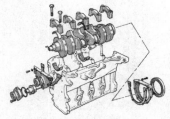

Crankshaft assembly

Crocodile clip See Alligator clip

D

Diagnostic code Code numbers obtained by accessing the diagnostic mode of an engine management computer. This code can be used to determine the area in the system where a malfunction may be located.

Disc brake A brake design incorporating a rotating disc onto which brake pads are squeezed. The resulting friction converts the energy of a moving vehicle into heat.

Double-overhead cam (DOHC) An engine that uses two overhead camshafts, usually one for the intake valves and one for the exhaust valves.

Drivebelt(s) The belt(s) used to drive accessories such as the alternator, water pump, power steering pump, air conditioning compressor, etc. off the crankshaft pulley.

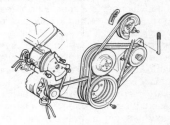

Accessory drivebelts

Driveshaft Any shaft used to transmit motion. Commonly used when referring to the axleshafts on a front wheel drive vehicle.

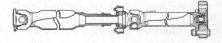

Driveshaft

Drum brake A type of brake using a drum-shaped metal cylinder attached to the inner surface of the wheel. When the brake pedal is pressed, curved brake shoes with friction linings press against the inside of the drum to slow or stop the vehicle.

Drum brake assembly

E

EGR valve A valve used to introduce exhaust gases into the intake air stream.

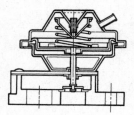

EGR valve

Electronic control unit (ECU) A computer which controls (for instance) ignition and fuel injection systems, or an anti-lock braking system. For more information refer to the *Haynes Automotive Electrical and Electronic Systems Manual.*

Electronic Fuel Injection (EFI) A computer controlled fuel system that distributes fuel through an injector located in each intake port of the engine.

Emergency brake A braking system, independent of the main hydraulic system, that can be used to slow or stop the vehicle if the primary brakes fail, or to hold the vehicle stationary even though the brake pedal isn't depressed. It usually consists of a hand lever that actuates either front or rear brakes mechanically through a series of cables and linkages. Also known as a handbrake or parking brake.

Endfloat The amount of lengthwise movement between two parts. As applied to a crankshaft, the distance that the crankshaft can move forward and back in the cylinder block.

Engine management system (EMS) A computer controlled system which manages the fuel injection and the ignition systems in an integrated fashion.

Exhaust manifold A part with several passages through which exhaust gases leave the engine combustion chambers and enter the exhaust pipe.

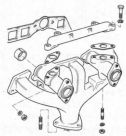

Exhaust manifold

F

Fan clutch A viscous (fluid) drive coupling device which permits variable engine fan speeds in relation to engine speeds.

Feeler blade A thin strip or blade of hardened steel, ground to an exact thickness, used to check or measure clearances between parts.

Feeler blade

Firing order The order in which the engine cylinders fire, or deliver their power strokes, beginning with the number one cylinder.

Flywheel A heavy spinning wheel in which energy is absorbed and stored by means of momentum. On cars, the flywheel is attached to the crankshaft to smooth out firing impulses.

Free play The amount of travel before any action takes place. The "looseness" in a linkage, or an assembly of parts, between the initial application of force and actual movement. For example, the distance the brake pedal moves before the pistons in the master cylinder are actuated.

Fuse An electrical device which protects a circuit against accidental overload. The typical fuse contains a soft piece of metal which is calibrated to melt at a predetermined current flow (expressed as amps) and break the circuit.

Fusible link A circuit protection device consisting of a conductor surrounded by heat-resistant insulation. The conductor is smaller than the wire it protects, so it acts as the weakest link in the circuit. Unlike a blown fuse, a failed fusible link must frequently be cut from the wire for replacement.

G

Gap The distance the spark must travel in jumping from the centre electrode to the side

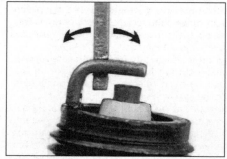

Adjusting spark plug gap

electrode in a spark plug. Also refers to the spacing between the points in a contact breaker assembly in a conventional points-type ignition, or to the distance between the reluctor or rotor and the pickup coil in an electronic ignition.

Gasket Any thin, soft material - usually cork, cardboard, asbestos or soft metal - installed between two metal surfaces to ensure a good seal. For instance, the cylinder head gasket seals the joint between the block and the cylinder head.

Gasket

Gauge An instrument panel display used to monitor engine conditions. A gauge with a movable pointer on a dial or a fixed scale is an analogue gauge. A gauge with a numerical readout is called a digital gauge.

H

Halfshaft A rotating shaft that transmits power from the final drive unit to a drive wheel, usually when referring to a live rear axle.

Harmonic balancer A device designed to reduce torsion or twisting vibration in the crankshaft. May be incorporated in the crankshaft pulley. Also known as a vibration damper.

Hone An abrasive tool for correcting small irregularities or differences in diameter in an engine cylinder, brake cylinder, etc.

Hydraulic tappet A tappet that utilises hydraulic pressure from the engine's lubrication system to maintain zero clearance (constant contact with both camshaft and valve stem). Automatically adjusts to variation in valve stem length. Hydraulic tappets also reduce valve noise.

I

Ignition timing The moment at which the spark plug fires, usually expressed in the number of crankshaft degrees before the piston reaches the top of its stroke.

Inlet manifold A tube or housing with passages through which flows the air-fuel mixture (carburettor vehicles and vehicles with throttle body injection) or air only (port fuel-injected vehicles) to the port openings in the cylinder head.

J

Jump start Starting the engine of a vehicle with a discharged or weak battery by attaching jump leads from the weak battery to a charged or helper battery.

L

Load Sensing Proportioning Valve (LSPV) A brake hydraulic system control valve that works like a proportioning valve, but also takes into consideration the amount of weight carried by the rear axle.

Locknut A nut used to lock an adjustment nut, or other threaded component, in place. For example, a locknut is employed to keep the adjusting nut on the rocker arm in position.

Lockwasher A form of washer designed to prevent an attaching nut from working loose.

M

MacPherson strut A type of front suspension system devised by Earle MacPherson at Ford of England. In its original form, a simple lateral link with the anti-roll bar creates the lower control arm. A long strut - an integral coil spring and shock absorber - is mounted between the body and the steering knuckle. Many modern so-called MacPherson strut systems use a conventional lower A-arm and don't rely on the anti-roll bar for location.

Multimeter An electrical test instrument with the capability to measure voltage, current and resistance.

N

NOx Oxides of Nitrogen. A common toxic pollutant emitted by petrol and diesel engines at higher temperatures.

O

Ohm The unit of electrical resistance. One volt applied to a resistance of one ohm will produce a current of one amp.

Ohmmeter An instrument for measuring electrical resistance.

O-ring A type of sealing ring made of a special rubber-like material; in use, the O-ring is compressed into a groove to provide the sealing action.

O-ring

Overhead cam (ohc) engine An engine with the camshaft(s) located on top of the cylinder head(s).

Overhead valve (ohv) engine An engine with the valves located in the cylinder head, but with the camshaft located in the engine block.

Oxygen sensor A device installed in the engine exhaust manifold, which senses the oxygen content in the exhaust and converts this information into an electric current. Also called a Lambda sensor.

P

Phillips screw A type of screw head having a cross instead of a slot for a corresponding type of screwdriver.

Plastigage A thin strip of plastic thread, available in different sizes, used for measuring clearances. For example, a strip of Plastigage is laid across a bearing journal. The parts are assembled and dismantled; the width of the crushed strip indicates the clearance between journal and bearing.

Plastigage

Propeller shaft The long hollow tube with universal joints at both ends that carries power from the transmission to the differential on front-engined rear wheel drive vehicles.

Proportioning valve A hydraulic control valve which limits the amount of pressure to the rear brakes during panic stops to prevent wheel lock-up.

R

Rack-and-pinion steering A steering system with a pinion gear on the end of the steering shaft that mates with a rack (think of a geared wheel opened up and laid flat). When the steering wheel is turned, the pinion turns, moving the rack to the left or right. This movement is transmitted through the track rods to the steering arms at the wheels.

Radiator A liquid-to-air heat transfer device designed to reduce the temperature of the coolant in an internal combustion engine cooling system.

Refrigerant Any substance used as a heat transfer agent in an air-conditioning system. R-12 has been the principle refrigerant for many years; recently, however, manufacturers have begun using R-134a, a non-CFC substance that is considered less harmful to the ozone in the upper atmosphere.

Rocker arm A lever arm that rocks on a shaft or pivots on a stud. In an overhead valve engine, the rocker arm converts the upward movement of the pushrod into a downward movement to open a valve.

Rotor In a distributor, the rotating device inside the cap that connects the centre electrode and the outer terminals as it turns, distributing the high voltage from the coil secondary winding to the proper spark plug. Also, that part of an alternator which rotates inside the stator. Also, the rotating assembly of a turbocharger, including the compressor wheel, shaft and turbine wheel.

Runout The amount of wobble (in-and-out movement) of a gear or wheel as it's rotated. The amount a shaft rotates "out-of-true." The out-of-round condition of a rotating part.

S

Sealant A liquid or paste used to prevent leakage at a joint. Sometimes used in conjunction with a gasket.

Sealed beam lamp An older headlight design which integrates the reflector, lens and filaments into a hermetically-sealed one-piece unit. When a filament burns out or the lens cracks, the entire unit is simply replaced.

Serpentine drivebelt A single, long, wide accessory drivebelt that's used on some newer vehicles to drive all the accessories, instead of a series of smaller, shorter belts. Serpentine drivebelts are usually tensioned by an automatic tensioner.

Serpentine drivebelt

Shim Thin spacer, commonly used to adjust the clearance or relative positions between two parts. For example, shims inserted into or under bucket tappets control valve clearances. Clearance is adjusted by changing the thickness of the shim.

Slide hammer A special puller that screws into or hooks onto a component such as a shaft or bearing; a heavy sliding handle on the shaft bottoms against the end of the shaft to knock the component free.

Sprocket A tooth or projection on the periphery of a wheel, shaped to engage with a chain or drivebelt. Commonly used to refer to the sprocket wheel itself.

Starter inhibitor switch On vehicles with an automatic transmission, a switch that prevents starting if the vehicle is not in Neutral or Park.

Strut See MacPherson strut.

T

Tappet A cylindrical component which transmits motion from the cam to the valve stem, either directly or via a pushrod and rocker arm. Also called a cam follower.

Thermostat A heat-controlled valve that regulates the flow of coolant between the cylinder block and the radiator, so maintaining optimum engine operating temperature. A thermostat is also used in some air cleaners in which the temperature is regulated.

Thrust bearing The bearing in the clutch assembly that is moved in to the release levers by clutch pedal action to disengage the clutch. Also referred to as a release bearing.

Timing belt A toothed belt which drives the camshaft. Serious engine damage may result if it breaks in service.

Timing chain A chain which drives the camshaft.

Toe-in The amount the front wheels are closer together at the front than at the rear. On rear wheel drive vehicles, a slight amount of toe-in is usually specified to keep the front wheels running parallel on the road by offsetting other forces that tend to spread the wheels apart.

Toe-out The amount the front wheels are closer together at the rear than at the front. On front wheel drive vehicles, a slight amount of toe-out is usually specified.

Tools For full information on choosing and using tools, refer to the *Haynes Automotive Tools Manual*.

Tracer A stripe of a second colour applied to a wire insulator to distinguish that wire from another one with the same colour insulator.

Tune-up A process of accurate and careful adjustments and parts replacement to obtain the best possible engine performance.

Turbocharger A centrifugal device, driven by exhaust gases, that pressurises the intake air. Normally used to increase the power output from a given engine displacement, but can also be used primarily to reduce exhaust emissions (as on VW's "Umwelt" Diesel engine).

U

Universal joint or U-joint A double-pivoted connection for transmitting power from a driving to a driven shaft through an angle. A U-joint consists of two Y-shaped yokes and a cross-shaped member called the spider.

V

Valve A device through which the flow of liquid, gas, vacuum, or loose material in bulk may be started, stopped, or regulated by a movable part that opens, shuts, or partially obstructs one or more ports or passageways. A valve is also the movable part of such a device.

Valve clearance The clearance between the valve tip (the end of the valve stem) and the rocker arm or tappet. The valve clearance is measured when the valve is closed.

Vernier caliper A precision measuring instrument that measures inside and outside dimensions. Not quite as accurate as a micrometer, but more convenient.

Viscosity The thickness of a liquid or its resistance to flow.

Volt A unit for expressing electrical "pressure" in a circuit. One volt that will produce a current of one ampere through a resistance of one ohm.

W

Welding Various processes used to join metal items by heating the areas to be joined to a molten state and fusing them together. For more information refer to the *Haynes Automotive Welding Manual*.

Wiring diagram A drawing portraying the components and wires in a vehicle's electrical system, using standardised symbols. For more information refer to the *Haynes Automotive Electrical and Electronic Systems Manual*.

Note: *References throughout this index are in the form - "Chapter number" • "Page number"*

Haynes Manuals – The Complete UK Car List

Title	Book No.
ALFA ROMEO Alfasud/Sprint (74 - 88) up to F *	0292
Alfa Romeo Alfetta (73 - 87) up to E *	0531
AUDI 80, 90 & Coupe Petrol (79 - Nov 88) up to F	0605
Audi 80, 90 & Coupe Petrol (Oct 86 - 90) D to H	1491
Audi 100 & 200 Petrol (Oct 82 - 90) up to H	0907
Audi 100 & A6 Petrol & Diesel (May 91 - May 97) H to P	3504
Audi A3 Petrol & Diesel (96 - May 03) P to 03	4253
Audi A4 Petrol & Diesel (95 - Feb 00) M to V	3575
Audi A4 Petrol & Diesel (Mar 00 - Aug 04) W to 04	4609
AUSTIN A35 & A40 (56 - 67) up to F *	0118
Austin/MG/Rover Maestro 1.3 & 1.6 Petrol (83 - 95) up to M	0922
Austin/MG Metro (80 - May 90) up to G	0718
Austin/Rover Montego 1.3 & 1.6 Petrol (84 - 94) A to L	1066
Austin/MG/Rover Montego 2.0 Petrol (84 - 95) A to M	1067
Mini (59 - 69) up to H *	0527
Mini (69 - 01) up to X	0646
Austin/Rover 2.0 litre Diesel Engine (86 - 93) C to L	1857
Austin Healey 100/6 & 3000 (56 - 68) up to G *	0049
BEDFORD CF Petrol (69 - 87) up to E	0163
Bedford/Vauxhall Rascal & Suzuki Supercarry (86 - Oct 94) C to M	3015
BMW 316, 320 & 320i (4-cyl) (75 - Feb 83) up to Y *	0276
BMW 320, 320i, 323i & 325i (6-cyl) (Oct 77 - Sept 87) up to E	0815
BMW 3- & 5-Series Petrol (81 - 91) up to J	1948
BMW 3-Series Petrol (Apr 91 - 99) H to V	3210
BMW 3-Series Petrol (Sept 98 - 03) S to 53	4067
BMW 520i & 525e (Oct 81 - June 88) up to E	1560
BMW 525, 528 & 528i (73 - Sept 81) up to X *	0632
BMW 5-Series 6-cyl Petrol (April 96 - Aug 03) N to 03	4151
BMW 1500, 1502, 1600, 1602, 2000 & 2002 (59 - 77) up to S *	0240
CHRYSLER PT Cruiser Petrol (00 - 03) W to 53	4058
CITROËN 2CV, Ami & Dyane (67 - 90) up to H	0196
Citroën AX Petrol & Diesel (87 - 97) D to P	3014
Citroën Berlingo & Peugeot Partner Petrol & Diesel (96 - 05) P to 55	4281
Citroën BX Petrol (83 - 94) A to L	0908
Citroën C15 Van Petrol & Diesel (89 - Oct 98) F to S	3509
Citroën C3 Petrol & Diesel (02 - 05) 51 to 05	4197
Citroën CX Petrol (75 - 88) up to F	0528
Citroën Saxo Petrol & Diesel (96 - 04) N to 54	3506
Citroën Visa Petrol (79 - 88) up to F	0620
Citroën Xantia Petrol & Diesel (93 - 01) K to Y	3082
Citroën XM Petrol & Diesel (89 - 00) G to X	3451
Citroën Xsara Petrol & Diesel (97 - Sept 00) R to W	3751
Citroën Xsara Picasso Petrol & Diesel (00 - 02) W to 52	3944
Citroën ZX Diesel (91 - 98) J to S	1922
Citroën ZX Petrol (91 - 98) H to S	1881
Citroën 1.7 & 1.9 litre Diesel Engine (84 - 96) A to N	1379
FIAT 126 (73 - 87) up to E *	0305
Fiat 500 (57 - 73) up to M *	0090
Fiat Bravo & Brava Petrol (95 - 00) N to W	3572
Fiat Cinquecento (93 - 98) K to R	3501
Fiat Panda (81 - 95) up to M	0793
Fiat Punto Petrol & Diesel (94 - Oct 99) L to V	3251
Fiat Punto Petrol (Oct 99 - July 03) V to 03	4066
Fiat Regata Petrol (84 - 88) A to F	1167
Fiat Tipo Petrol (88 - 91) E to J	1625
Fiat Uno Petrol (83 - 95) up to M	0923
Fiat X1/9 (74 - 89) up to G *	0273
FORD Anglia (59 - 68) up to G *	0001
Ford Capri II (& III) 1.6 & 2.0 (74 - 87) up to E *	0283
Ford Capri II (& III) 2.8 & 3.0 V6 (74 - 87) up to E	1309
Ford Cortina Mk III 1300 & 1600 (70 - 76) up to P *	0070
Ford Escort Mk I 1100 & 1300 (68 - 74) up to N *	0171
Ford Escort Mk I Mexico, RS 1600 & RS 2000 (70 - 74) up to N *	0139
Ford Escort Mk II Mexico, RS 1800 & RS 2000 (75 - 80) up to W *	0735
Ford Escort (75 - Aug 80) up to V *	0280
Ford Escort Petrol (Sept 80 - Sept 90) up to H	0686
Ford Escort & Orion Petrol (Sept 90 - 00) H to X	1737
Ford Escort & Orion Diesel (Sept 90 - 00) H to X	4081
Ford Fiesta (76 - Aug 83) up to Y	0334
Ford Fiesta Petrol (Aug 83 - Feb 89) A to F	1030
Ford Fiesta Petrol (Feb 89 - Oct 95) F to N	1595
Ford Fiesta Petrol & Diesel (Oct 95 - Mar 02) N to 02	3397
Ford Fiesta Petrol & Diesel (Apr 02 - 05) 02 to 54	4170
Ford Focus Petrol & Diesel (98 - 01) S to Y	3759
Ford Focus Petrol & Diesel (Oct 01 - 04) 51 to 54	4167
Ford Galaxy Petrol & Diesel (95 - Aug 00) M to W	3984
Ford Granada Petrol (Sept 77 - Feb 85) up to B *	0481
Ford Granada & Scorpio Petrol (Mar 85 - 94) B to M	1245
Ford Ka (96 - 02) P to 52	3570
Ford Mondeo Petrol (93 - Sept 00) K to X	1923
Ford Mondeo Petrol & Diesel (Oct 00 - Jul 03) X to 03	3990
Ford Mondeo Petrol & Diesel (July 03 - 07) 03 to 56	4619
Ford Mondeo Diesel (93 - 96) L to N	3465
Ford Orion Petrol (83 - Sept 90) up to H	1009
Ford Sierra 4-cyl Petrol (82 - 93) up to K	0903
Ford Sierra V6 Petrol (82 - 91) up to J	0904
Ford Transit Petrol (Mk 2) (78 - Jan 86) up to C	0719
Ford Transit Petrol (Mk 3) (Feb 86 - 89) C to G	1468
Ford Transit Diesel (Feb 86 - 99) C to T	3019
Ford 1.6 & 1.8 litre Diesel Engine (84 - 96) A to N	1172
Ford 2.1, 2.3 & 2.5 litre Diesel Engine (77 - 90) up to H	1606
FREIGHT ROVER Sherpa Petrol (74 - 87) up to E	0463
HILLMAN Avenger (70 - 82) up to Y	0037
Hillman Imp (63 - 76) up to R *	0022
HONDA Civic (Feb 84 - Oct 87) A to E	1226
Honda Civic (Nov 91 - 96) J to N	3199
Honda Civic Petrol (Mar 95 - 00) M to X	4050
HYUNDAI Pony (85 - 94) C to M	3398
JAGUAR E Type (61 - 72) up to L *	0140
Jaguar MkI & II, 240 & 340 (55 - 69) up to H *	0098
Jaguar XJ6, XJ & Sovereign; Daimler Sovereign (68 - Oct 86) up to D	0242
Jaguar XJ6 & Sovereign (Oct 86 - Sept 94) D to M	3261
Jaguar XJ12, XJS & Sovereign; Daimler Double Six (72 - 88) up to F	0478
Jeep Cherokee Petrol (93 - 96) K to N	1943
LADA 1200, 1300, 1500 & 1600 (74 - 91) up to J	0413
Lada Samara (87 - 91) D to J	1610
LAND ROVER 90, 110 & Defender Diesel (83 - 07) up to 56	3017
Land Rover Discovery Petrol & Diesel (89 - 98) G to S	3016
Land Rover Discovery Diesel (Nov 98 - Jul 04) S to 04	4606
Land Rover Freelander Petrol & Diesel (97 - Sept 03) R to 53	3929
Land Rover Freelander Petrol & Diesel (Oct 03 - 06) 53 to 56	4623
Land Rover Series IIA & III Diesel (58 - 85) up to C	0529
Land Rover Series II, IIA & III 4-cyl Petrol (58 - 85) up to C	0314
MAZDA 323 (Mar 81 - Oct 89) up to G	1608
Mazda 323 (Oct 89 - 98) G to R	3455
Mazda 626 (May 83 - Sept 87) up to E	0929
Mazda B1600, B1800 & B2000 Pick-up Petrol (72 - 88) up to F	0267
Mazda RX-7 (79 - 85) up to C *	0460
MERCEDES-BENZ 190, 190E & 190D Petrol & Diesel (83 - 93) A to L	3450
Mercedes-Benz 200D, 240D, 240TD, 300D & 300TD 123 Series Diesel (Oct 76 - 85) up to C	1114
Mercedes-Benz 250 & 280 (68 - 72) up to L *	0346
Mercedes-Benz 250 & 280 123 Series Petrol (Oct 76 - 84) up to B *	0677
Mercedes-Benz 124 Series Petrol & Diesel (85 - Aug 93) C to K	3253
Mercedes-Benz C-Class Petrol & Diesel (93 - Aug 00) L to W	3511
MG A (55 - 62) *	0475
MGB (62 - 80) up to W	0111
MG Midget & Austin-Healey Sprite (58 - 80) up to W *	0265
MINI Petrol (July 01 - 05) Y to 05	4273
MITSUBISHI Shogun & L200 Pick-Ups Petrol (83 - 94) up to M	1944
MORRIS Ital 1.3 (80 - 84) up to B	0705
Morris Minor 1000 (56 - 71) up to K	0024
NISSAN Almera Petrol (95 - Feb 00) N to V	4053
Nissan Bluebird (May 84 - Mar 86) A to C	1223
Nissan Bluebird Petrol (Mar 86 - 90) C to H	1473
Nissan Cherry (Sept 82 - 86) up to D	1031
Nissan Micra (83 - Jan 93) up to K	0931
Nissan Micra (93 - 02) K to 52	3254
Nissan Primera Petrol (90 - Aug 99) H to T	1851
Nissan Stanza (82 - 86) up to D	0824
Nissan Sunny Petrol (May 82 - Oct 86) up to D	0895
Nissan Sunny Petrol (Oct 86 - Mar 91) D to H	1378
Nissan Sunny Petrol (Apr 91 - 95) H to N	3219
OPEL Ascona & Manta (B Series) (Sept 75 - 88) up to F *	0316
Opel Ascona Petrol (81 - 88)	3215
Opel Astra Petrol (Oct 91 - Feb 98)	3156
Opel Corsa Petrol (83 - Mar 93)	3160
Opel Corsa Petrol (Mar 93 - 97)	3159
Opel Kadett Petrol (Nov 79 - Oct 84) up to B	0634
Opel Kadett Petrol (Oct 84 - Oct 91)	3196
Opel Omega & Senator Petrol (Nov 86 - 94)	3157
Opel Rekord Petrol (Feb 78 - Oct 86) up to D	0543
Opel Vectra Petrol (Oct 88 - Oct 95)	3158
PEUGEOT 106 Petrol & Diesel (91 - 04) J to 53	1882
Peugeot 205 Petrol (83 - 97) A to P	0932
Peugeot 206 Petrol & Diesel (98 - 01) S to X	3757
Peugeot 206 Petrol & Diesel (02 - 06) 51 to 06	4613
Peugeot 306 Petrol & Diesel (93 - 02) K to 02	3073
Peugeot 307 Petrol & Diesel (01 - 04) Y to 54	4147
Peugeot 309 Petrol (86 - 93) C to K	1266
Peugeot 405 Petrol (88 - 97) E to P	1559
Peugeot 405 Diesel (88 - 97) E to P	3198
Peugeot 406 Petrol & Diesel (96 - Mar 99) N to T	3394
Peugeot 406 Petrol & Diesel (Mar 99 - 02) T to 52	3982
Peugeot 505 Petrol (79 - 89) up to G	0762
Peugeot 1.7/1.8 & 1.9 litre Diesel Engine (82 - 96) up to N	0950
Peugeot 2.0, 2.1, 2.3 & 2.5 litre Diesel Engines (74 - 90) up to H	1607

* Classic reprint

Title	Book No.
PORSCHE 911 (65 - 85) up to C	0264
Porsche 924 & 924 Turbo (76 - 85) up to C	0397
PROTON (89 - 97) F to P	3255
RANGE ROVER V8 Petrol (70 - Oct 92) up to K	0606
RELIANT Robin & Kitten (73 - 83) up to A *	0436
RENAULT 4 (61 - 86) up to D *	0072
Renault 5 Petrol (Feb 85 - 96) B to N	1219
Renault 9 & 11 Petrol (82 - 89) up to F	0822
Renault 18 Petrol (79 - 86) up to D	0598
Renault 19 Petrol (89 - 96) F to N	1646
Renault 19 Diesel (89 - 96) F to N	1946
Renault 21 Petrol (86 - 94) C to M	1397
Renault 25 Petrol & Diesel (84 - 92) B to K	1228
Renault Clio Petrol (91 - May 98) H to R	1853
Renault Clio Diesel (91 - June 96) H to N	3031
Renault Clio Petrol & Diesel (May 98 - May 01) R to Y	3906
Renault Clio Petrol & Diesel (June 01 - 04) Y to 54	4168
Renault Espace Petrol & Diesel (85 - 96) C to N	3197
Renault Laguna Petrol & Diesel (94 - 00) L to W	3252
Renault Laguna Petrol & Diesel (Feb 01 - Feb 05) X to 54	4283
Renault Mégane & Scénic Petrol & Diesel (96 - 99) N to T	3395
Renault Mégane & Scénic Petrol & Diesel (Apr 99 - 02) T to 52	3916
Renault Megane Petrol & Diesel (Oct 02 - 05) 52 to 55	4284
Renault Scenic Petrol & Diesel (Sept 03 - 06) 53 to 06	4297
ROVER 213 & 216 (84 - 89) A to G	1116
Rover 214 & 414 Petrol (89 - 96) G to N	1689
Rover 216 & 416 Petrol (89 - 96) G to N	1830
Rover 211, 214, 216, 218 & 220 Petrol & Diesel (Dec 95 - 99) N to V	3399
Rover 25 & MG ZR Petrol & Diesel (Oct 99 - 04) V to 54	4145
Rover 414, 416 & 420 Petrol & Diesel (May 95 - 98) M to R	3453
Rover 45/MG ZS Petrol & Diesel (99 - 05) V to 55	4384
Rover 618, 620 & 623 Petrol (93 - 97) K to P	3257
Rover 75/MG ZT Petrol & Diesel (99 - 06) S to 06	4292
Rover 820, 825 & 827 Petrol (86 - 95) D to N	1380
Rover 3500 (76 - 87) up to E *	0365
Rover Metro, 111 & 114 Petrol (May 90 - 98) G to S	1711
SAAB 95 & 96 (66 - 76) up to R *	0198
Saab 90, 99 & 900 (79 - Oct 93) up to L	0765
Saab 900 (Oct 93 - 98) L to S	3512
Saab 9000 (4-cyl) (85 - 98) C to S	1686
Saab 9-3 Petrol & Diesel (98 - Aug 02) R to 02	4614
Saab 9-5 4-cyl Petrol (97 - 04) R to 54	4156
SEAT Ibiza & Cordoba Petrol & Diesel (Oct 93 - Oct 99) L to V	3571
Seat Ibiza & Malaga Petrol (85 - 92) B to K	1609
SKODA Estelle (77 - 89) up to G	0604
Skoda Fabia Petrol & Diesel (00 - 06) W to 06	4376
Skoda Favorit (89 - 96) F to N	1801
Skoda Felicia Petrol & Diesel (95 - 01) M to X	3505
Skoda Octavia Petrol & Diesel (98 - Apr 04) R to 04	4285
SUBARU 1600 & 1800 (Nov 79 - 90) up to H *	0995
SUNBEAM Alpine, Rapier & H120 (67 - 74) up to N *	0051
SUZUKI Supercarry & Bedford/Vauxhall Rascal (86 - Oct 94) C to M	3015
Suzuki SJ Series, Samurai & Vitara (4-cyl) Petrol (82 - 97) up to P	1942
TALBOT Alpine, Solara, Minx & Rapier (75 - 86) up to D	0337

Title	Book No.
Talbot Horizon Petrol (78 - 86) up to D	0473
Talbot Samba (82 - 86) up to D	0823
TOYOTA Avensis Petrol (98 - Jan 03) R to 52	4264
Toyota Carina E Petrol (May 92 - 97) J to P	3256
Toyota Corolla (80 - 85) up to C	0683
Toyota Corolla (Sept 83 - Sept 87) A to E	1024
Toyota Corolla (Sept 87 - Aug 92) E to K	1683
Toyota Corolla Petrol (Aug 92 - 97) K to P	3259
Toyota Corolla Petrol (July 97 - Feb 02) P to 51	4286
Toyota Hi-Ace & Hi-Lux Petrol (69 - Oct 83) up to A	0304
Toyota Yaris Petrol (99 - 05) T to 05	4265
TRIUMPH GT6 & Vitesse (62 - 74) up to N *	0112
Triumph Herald (59 - 71) up to K *	0010
Triumph Spitfire (62 - 81) up to X	0113
Triumph Stag (70 - 78) up to T *	0441
Triumph TR2, TR3, TR3A, TR4 & TR4A (52 - 67) up to F *	0028
Triumph TR5 & 6 (67 - 75) up to P *	0031
Triumph TR7 (75 - 82) up to Y *	0322
VAUXHALL Astra Petrol (80 - Oct 84) up to B	0635
Vauxhall Astra & Belmont Petrol (Oct 84 - Oct 91) B to J	1136
Vauxhall Astra Petrol (Oct 91 - Feb 98) J to R	1832
Vauxhall/Opel Astra & Zafira Petrol (Feb 98 - Apr 04) R to 04	3758
Vauxhall/Opel Astra & Zafira Diesel (Feb 98 - Apr 04) R to 04	3797
Vauxhall/Opel Calibra (90 - 98) G to S	3502
Vauxhall Carlton Petrol (Oct 78 - Oct 86) up to D	0480
Vauxhall Carlton & Senator Petrol (Nov 86 - 94) D to L	1469
Vauxhall Cavalier Petrol (81 - Oct 88) up to F	0812
Vauxhall Cavalier Petrol (Oct 88 - 95) F to N	1570
Vauxhall Chevette (75 - 84) up to B	0285
Vauxhall/Opel Corsa Diesel (Mar 93 - Oct 00) K to X	4087
Vauxhall Corsa Petrol (Mar 93 - 97) K to R	1985
Vauxhall/Opel Corsa Petrol (Apr 97 - Oct 00) P to X	3921
Vauxhall/Opel Corsa Petrol & Diesel (Oct 00 - Sept 03) X to 53	4079
Vauxhall/Opel Corsa Petrol & Diesel (Oct 03 - Aug 06) 53 to 06	4617
Vauxhall/Opel Frontera Petrol & Diesel (91 - Sept 98) J to S	3454
Vauxhall Nova Petrol (83 - 93) up to K	0909
Vauxhall/Opel Omega Petrol (94 - 99) L to T	3510
Vauxhall/Opel Vectra Petrol & Diesel (95 - Feb 99) N to S	3396
Vauxhall/Opel Vectra Petrol & Diesel (Mar 99 - May 02) T to 02	3930
Vauxhall/Opel Vectra Petrol & Diesel (June 02 - 06) 02 to 56	4618
Vauxhall/Opel 1.5, 1.6 & 1.7 litre Diesel Engine (82 - 96) up to N	1222
VW 411 & 412 (68 - 75) up to P *	0091
VW Beetle 1200 (54 - 77) up to S	0036
VW Beetle 1300 & 1500 (65 - 75) up to P	0039
VW 1302 & 1302S (70 - 72) up to L *	0110
VW Beetle 1303, 1303S & GT (72 - 75) up to P	0159
VW Beetle Petrol & Diesel (Apr 99 - 01) T to 51	3798
VW Golf & Jetta Mk 1 Petrol 1.1 & 1.3 (74 - 84) up to A	0716
VW Golf, Jetta & Scirocco Mk 1 Petrol 1.5, 1.6 & 1.8 (74 - 84) up to A	0726
VW Golf & Jetta Mk 1 Diesel (78 - 84) up to A	0451
VW Golf & Jetta Mk 2 Petrol (Mar 84 - Feb 92) A to J	1081
VW Golf & Vento Petrol & Diesel (Feb 92 - Mar 98) J to R	3097

Title	
VW Golf & Bora Petrol & Diesel (April 98 - 00) R to X	
VW Golf & Bora 4-cyl Petrol & Diesel (01 - 03) X to 53	4169
VW Golf & Bora Petrol & Diesel (04 - 07) 53 to 07	4610
VW LT Petrol Vans & Light Trucks (76 - 87) up to E	0637
VW Passat & Santana Petrol (Sept 81 - May 88) up to E	0814
VW Passat 4-cyl Petrol & Diesel (May 88 - 96) E to P	3498
VW Passat 4-cyl Petrol & Diesel (Dec 96 - Nov 00) P to X	3917
VW Passat Petrol & Diesel (Dec 00 - May 05) X to 05	4279
VW Polo & Derby (76 - Jan 82) up to X	0335
VW Polo (82 - Oct 90) up to H	0813
VW Polo Petrol (Nov 90 - Aug 94) H to L	3245
VW Polo Hatchback Petrol & Diesel (94 - 99) M to S	3500
VW Polo Hatchback Petrol (00 - Jan 02) V to 51	4150
VW Polo Petrol & Diesel (02 - May 05) 51 to 05	4608
VW Scirocco (82 - 90) up to H *	1224
VW Transporter 1600 (68 - 79) up to V	0082
VW Transporter 1700, 1800 & 2000 (72 - 79) up to V *	0226
VW Transporter (air-cooled) Petrol (79 - 82) up to Y *	0638
VW Transporter (water-cooled) Petrol (82 - 90) up to H	3452
VW Type 3 (63 - 73) up to M *	0084
VOLVO 120 & 130 Series (& P1800) (61 - 73) up to M *	0203
Volvo 142, 144 & 145 (66 - 74) up to N *	0129
Volvo 240 Series Petrol (74 - 93) up to K	0270
Volvo 262, 264 & 260/265 (75 - 85) up to C *	0400
Volvo 340, 343, 345 & 360 (76 - 91) up to J	0715
Volvo 440, 460 & 480 Petrol (87 - 97) D to P	1691
Volvo 740 & 760 Petrol (82 - 91) up to J	1258
Volvo 850 Petrol (92 - 96) J to P	3260
Volvo 940 Petrol (90 - 96) H to N	3249
Volvo S40 & V40 Petrol (96 - Mar 04) N to 04	3569
Volvo S70, V70 & C70 Petrol (96 - 99) P to V	3573
Volvo V70 / S80 Petrol & Diesel (98 - 05) S to 55	4263

AUTOMOTIVE TECHBOOKS

Title	
Automotive Electrical and Electronic Systems Manual	3049
Automotive Gearbox Overhaul Manual	3473
Automotive Service Summaries Manual	3475
Automotive Timing Belts Manual – Austin/Rover	3549
Automotive Timing Belts Manual – Ford	3474
Automotive Timing Belts Manual – Peugeot/Citroën	3568
Automotive Timing Belts Manual – Vauxhall/Opel	3577

DIY MANUAL SERIES

Title	
The Haynes Air Conditioning Manual	4192
The Haynes Manual on Bodywork	4198
The Haynes Manual on Brakes	4178
The Haynes Manual on Carburettors	4177
The Haynes Car Electrical Systems Manual	4251
The Haynes Manual on Diesel Engines	4174
The Haynes Manual on Engine Management	4199
The Haynes Manual on Fault Codes	4175
The Haynes Manual on Practical Electrical Systems	4267
The Haynes Manual on Small Engines	4250
The Haynes Manual on Welding	4176

* Classic reprint

CL22.4/07

Preserving Our Motoring Heritage

< *The Model J Duesenberg Derham Tourster. Only eight of these magnificent cars were ever built – this is the only example to be found outside the United States of America*

Almost every car you've ever loved, loathed or desired is gathered under one roof at the Haynes Motor Museum. Over 300 immaculately presented cars and motorbikes represent every aspect of our motoring heritage, from elegant reminders of bygone days, such as the superb Model J Duesenberg to curiosities like the bug-eyed BMW Isetta. There are also many old friends and flames. Perhaps you remember the 1959 Ford Popular that you did your courting in? The magnificent 'Red Collection' is a spectacle of classic sports cars including AC, Alfa Romeo, Austin Healey, Ferrari, Lamborghini, Maserati, MG, Riley, Porsche and Triumph.

A Perfect Day Out

Each and every vehicle at the Haynes Motor Museum has played its part in the history and culture of Motoring. Today, they make a wonderful spectacle and a great day out for all the family. Bring the kids, bring Mum and Dad, but above all bring your camera to capture those golden memories for ever. You will also find an impressive array of motoring memorabilia, a comfortable 70 seat video cinema and one of the most extensive transport book shops in Britain. The Pit Stop Cafe serves everything from a cup of tea to wholesome, home-made meals or, if you prefer, you can enjoy the large picnic area nestled in the beautiful rural surroundings of Somerset.

John Haynes O.B.E., Founder and Chairman of the museum at the wheel of a Haynes Light 12. >

< *Graham Hill's Lola Cosworth Formula 1 car next to a 1934 Riley Sports.*

The Museum is situated on the A359 Yeovil to Frome road at Sparkford, just off the A303 in Somerset. It is about 40 miles south of Bristol, and 25 minutes drive from the M5 intersection at Taunton.
Open 9.30am - 5.30pm (10.00am - 4.00pm Winter) 7 days a week, *except Christmas Day, Boxing Day and New Years Day*
Special rates available for schools, coach parties and outings Charitable Trust No. 292048

Title	Book No.
PORSCHE 911 (65 - 85) up to C	0264
Porsche 924 & 924 Turbo (76 - 85) up to C	0397
PROTON (89 - 97) F to P	3255
RANGE ROVER V8 Petrol (70 - Oct 92) up to K	0606
RELIANT Robin & Kitten (73 - 83) up to A *	0436
RENAULT 4 (61 - 86) up to D *	0072
Renault 5 Petrol (Feb 85 - 96) B to N	1219
Renault 9 & 11 Petrol (82 - 89) up to F	0822
Renault 18 Petrol (79 - 86) up to D	0598
Renault 19 Petrol (89 - 96) F to N	1646
Renault 19 Diesel (89 - 96) F to N	1946
Renault 21 Petrol (86 - 94) C to M	1397
Renault 25 Petrol & Diesel (84 - 92) B to K	1228
Renault Clio Petrol (91 - May 98) H to R	1853
Renault Clio Diesel (91 - June 96) H to N	3031
Renault Clio Petrol & Diesel (May 98 - May 01) R to Y	3906
Renault Clio Petrol & Diesel (June 01 - 04) Y to 54	4168
Renault Espace Petrol & Diesel (85 - 96) C to N	3197
Renault Laguna Petrol & Diesel (94 - 00) L to W	3252
Renault Laguna Petrol & Diesel (Feb 01 - Feb 05) X to 54	4283
Renault Mégane & Scénic Petrol & Diesel (96 - 99) N to T	3395
Renault Mégane & Scénic Petrol & Diesel (Apr 99 - 02) T to 52	3916
Renault Megane Petrol & Diesel (Oct 02 - 05) 52 to 55	4284
Renault Scenic Petrol & Diesel (Sept 03 - 06) 53 to 06	4297
ROVER 213 & 216 (84 - 89) A to G	1116
Rover 214 & 414 Petrol (89 - 96) G to N	1689
Rover 216 & 416 Petrol (89 - 96) G to N	1830
Rover 211, 214, 216, 218 & 220 Petrol & Diesel (Dec 95 - 99) N to V	3399
Rover 25 & MG ZR Petrol & Diesel (Oct 99 - 04) V to 54	4145
Rover 414, 416 & 420 Petrol & Diesel (May 95 - 98) M to R	3453
Rover 45/MG ZS Petrol & Diesel (99 - 05) V to 55	4384
Rover 618, 620 & 623 Petrol (93 - 97) K to P	3257
Rover 75/MG ZT Petrol & Diesel (99 - 06) S to 06	4292
Rover 820, 825 & 827 Petrol (86 - 95) D to N	1380
Rover 3500 (76 - 87) up to E *	0365
Rover Metro, 111 & 114 Petrol (May 90 - 98) G to S	1711
SAAB 95 & 96 (66 - 76) up to R *	0198
Saab 90, 99 & 900 (79 - Oct 93) up to L	0765
Saab 900 (Oct 93 - 98) L to R	3512
Saab 9000 (4-cyl) (85 - 98) C to S	1686
Saab 9-3 Petrol & Diesel (98 - Aug 02) R to 02	4614
Saab 9-5 4-cyl Petrol (97 - 04) R to 54	4156
SEAT Ibiza & Cordoba Petrol & Diesel (Oct 93 - Oct 99) L to V	3571
Seat Ibiza & Malaga Petrol (85 - 92) B to K	1609
SKODA Estelle (77 - 89) up to G	0604
Skoda Fabia Petrol & Diesel (00 - 06) W to 06	4376
Skoda Favorit (89 - 96) F to N	1801
Skoda Felicia Petrol & Diesel (95 - 01) M to X	3505
Skoda Octavia Petrol & Diesel (98 - Apr 04) R to 04	4285
SUBARU 1600 & 1800 (Nov 79 - 90) up to H *	0995
SUNBEAM Alpine, Rapier & H120 (67 - 74) up to N *	0051
SUZUKI Supercarry & Bedford/Vauxhall Rascal (86 - Oct 94) C to M	3015
Suzuki SJ Series, Samurai & Vitara (4-cyl) Petrol (82 - 97) up to P	1942
TALBOT Alpine, Solara, Minx & Rapier (75 - 86) up to D	0337

Title	Book No.
Talbot Horizon Petrol (78 - 86) up to D	0473
Talbot Samba (82 - 86) up to D	0823
TOYOTA Avensis Petrol (98 - Jan 03) R to 52	4264
Toyota Carina E Petrol (May 92 - 97) J to P	3256
Toyota Corolla (80 - 85) up to C	0683
Toyota Corolla (Sept 83 - Sept 87) A to E	1024
Toyota Corolla (Sept 87 - Aug 92) E to K	1683
Toyota Corolla Petrol (Aug 92 - 97) K to P	3259
Toyota Corolla Petrol (July 97 - Feb 02) P to 51	4286
Toyota Hi-Ace & Hi-Lux Petrol (69 - Oct 83) up to A	0304
Toyota Yaris Petrol (99 - 05) T to 05	4265
TRIUMPH GT6 & Vitesse (62 - 74) up to N *	0112
Triumph Herald (59 - 71) up to K *	0010
Triumph Spitfire (62 - 81) up to X	0113
Triumph Stag (70 - 78) up to T *	0441
Triumph TR2, TR3, TR3A, TR4 & TR4A (52 - 67) up to F *	0028
Triumph TR5 & 6 (67 - 75) up to P *	0031
Triumph TR7 (75 - 82) up to Y *	0322
VAUXHALL Astra Petrol (80 - Oct 84) up to B	0635
Vauxhall Astra & Belmont Petrol (Oct 84 - Oct 91) B to J	1136
Vauxhall Astra Petrol (Oct 91 - Feb 98) J to R	1832
Vauxhall/Opel Astra & Zafira Petrol (Feb 98 - Apr 04) R to 04	3758
Vauxhall/Opel Astra & Zafira Diesel (Feb 98 - Apr 04) R to 04	3797
Vauxhall/Opel Calibra (90 - 98) G to S	3502
Vauxhall Carlton Petrol (Oct 78 - Oct 86) up to D	0480
Vauxhall Carlton & Senator Petrol (Nov 86 - 94) D to L	1469
Vauxhall Cavalier Petrol (81 - Oct 88) up to F	0812
Vauxhall Cavalier Petrol (Oct 88 - 95) F to N	1570
Vauxhall Chevette (75 - 84) up to B	0285
Vauxhall/Opel Corsa Diesel (Mar 93 - Oct 00) K to X	4087
Vauxhall Corsa Petrol (Mar 93 - 97) K to R	1985
Vauxhall/Opel Corsa Petrol (Apr 97 - Oct 00) P to X	3921
Vauxhall/Opel Corsa Petrol & Diesel (Oct 00 - Sept 03) X to 53	4079
Vauxhall/Opel Corsa Petrol & Diesel (Oct 03 - Aug 06) 53 to 06	4617
Vauxhall/Opel Frontera Petrol & Diesel (91 - Sept 98) J to S	3454
Vauxhall Nova Petrol (83 - 93) up to K	0909
Vauxhall/Opel Omega Petrol (94 - 99) L to T	3510
Vauxhall/Opel Vectra Petrol & Diesel (95 - Feb 99) N to S	3396
Vauxhall/Opel Vectra Petrol & Diesel (Mar 99 - May 02) T to 02	3930
Vauxhall/Opel Vectra Petrol & Diesel (June 02 - 06) 02 to 56	4618
Vauxhall/Opel 1.5, 1.6 & 1.7 litre Diesel Engine (82 - 96) up to N	1222
VW 411 & 412 (68 - 75) up to P *	0091
VW Beetle 1200 (54 - 77) up to S	0036
VW Beetle 1300 & 1500 (65 - 75) up to P	0039
VW 1302 & 1302S (70 - 72) up to L *	0110
VW Beetle 1303, 1303S & GT (72 - 75) up to P	0159
VW Beetle Petrol & Diesel (Apr 99 - 01) T to 51	3798
VW Golf & Jetta Mk 1 Petrol 1.1 & 1.3 (74 - 84) up to A	0716
VW Golf, Jetta & Scirocco Mk 1 Petrol 1.5, 1.6 & 1.8 (74 - 84) up to A	0726
VW Golf & Jetta Mk 1 Diesel (78 - 84) up to A	0451
VW Golf & Jetta Mk 2 Petrol (Mar 84 - Feb 92) A to J	1081
VW Golf & Vento Petrol & Diesel (Feb 92 - Mar 98) J to R	3097

Title	Book No.
VW Golf & Bora Petrol & Diesel (April 98 - 00) R to X	3727
VW Golf & Bora 4-cyl Petrol & Diesel (01 - 03) X to 53	4169
VW Golf & Bora Petrol & Diesel (04 - 07) 53 to 07	4610
VW LT Petrol Vans & Light Trucks (76 - 87) up to E	0637
VW Passat & Santana Petrol (Sept 81 - May 88) up to E	0814
VW Passat 4-cyl Petrol & Diesel (May 88 - 96) E to P	3498
VW Passat 4-cyl Petrol & Diesel (Dec 96 - Nov 00) P to X	3917
VW Passat Petrol & Diesel (Dec 00 - May 05) X to 05	4279
VW Polo & Derby (76 - Jan 82) up to X	0335
VW Polo (82 - Oct 90) up to H	0813
VW Polo Petrol (Nov 90 - Aug 94) H to L	3245
VW Polo Hatchback Petrol & Diesel (94 - 99) M to S	3500
VW Polo Hatchback Petrol (00 - Jan 02) V to 51	4150
VW Polo Petrol & Diesel (02 - May 05) 51 to 05	4608
VW Scirocco (82 - 90) up to H *	1224
VW Transporter 1600 (68 - 79) up to V	0082
VW Transporter 1700, 1800 & 2000 (72 - 79) up to V *	0226
VW Transporter (air-cooled) Petrol (79 - 82) up to Y *	0638
VW Transporter (water-cooled) Petrol (82 - 90) up to H	3452
VW Type 3 (63 - 73) up to M *	0084
VOLVO 120 & 130 Series (& P1800) (61 - 73) up to M *	0203
Volvo 142, 144 & 145 (66 - 74) up to N *	0129
Volvo 240 Series Petrol (74 - 93) up to K	0270
Volvo 262, 264 & 260/265 (75 - 85) up to C *	0400
Volvo 340, 343, 345 & 360 (76 - 91) up to J	0715
Volvo 440, 460 & 480 Petrol (87 - 97) D to P	1691
Volvo 740 & 760 Petrol (82 - 91) up to J	1258
Volvo 850 Petrol (92 - 96) J to P	3260
Volvo 940 Petrol (90 - 96) H to N	3249
Volvo S40 & V40 Petrol (96 - Mar 04) N to 04	3569
Volvo S70, V70 & C70 Petrol (96 - 99) P to V	3573
Volvo V70 / S80 Petrol & Diesel (98 - 05) S to 55	4263

AUTOMOTIVE TECHBOOKS

Title	Book No.
Automotive Electrical and Electronic Systems Manual	3049
Automotive Gearbox Overhaul Manual	3473
Automotive Service Summaries Manual	3475
Automotive Timing Belts Manual – Austin/Rover	3549
Automotive Timing Belts Manual – Ford	3474
Automotive Timing Belts Manual – Peugeot/Citroën	3568
Automotive Timing Belts Manual – Vauxhall/Opel	3577

DIY MANUAL SERIES

Title	Book No.
The Haynes Air Conditioning Manual	4192
The Haynes Manual on Bodywork	4198
The Haynes Manual on Brakes	4178
The Haynes Manual on Carburettors	4177
The Haynes Car Electrical Systems Manual	4251
The Haynes Manual on Diesel Engines	4174
The Haynes Manual on Engine Management	4199
The Haynes Manual on Fault Codes	4175
The Haynes Manual on Practical Electrical Systems	4267
The Haynes Manual on Small Engines	4250
The Haynes Manual on Welding	4176

* Classic reprint

CL22.4/07

Preserving Our Motoring Heritage

< The Model J Duesenberg Derham Tourster. Only eight of these magnificent cars were ever built – this is the only example to be found outside the United States of America

Almost every car you've ever loved, loathed or desired is gathered under one roof at the Haynes Motor Museum. Over 300 immaculately presented cars and motorbikes represent every aspect of our motoring heritage, from elegant reminders of bygone days, such as the superb Model J Duesenberg to curiosities like the bug-eyed BMW Isetta. There are also many old friends and flames. Perhaps you remember the 1959 Ford Popular that you did your courting in? The magnificent 'Red Collection' is a spectacle of classic sports cars including AC, Alfa Romeo, Austin Healey, Ferrari, Lamborghini, Maserati, MG, Riley, Porsche and Triumph.

A Perfect Day Out

Each and every vehicle at the Haynes Motor Museum has played its part in the history and culture of Motoring. Today, they make a wonderful spectacle and a great day out for all the family. Bring the kids, bring Mum and Dad, but above all bring your camera to capture those golden memories for ever. You will also find an impressive array of motoring memorabilia, a comfortable 70 seat video cinema and one of the most extensive transport book shops in Britain. The Pit Stop Cafe serves everything from a cup of tea to wholesome, home-made meals or, if you prefer, you can enjoy the large picnic area nestled in the beautiful rural surroundings of Somerset.

John Haynes O.B.E., Founder and Chairman of the museum at the wheel of a Haynes Light 12.

< Graham Hill's Lola Cosworth Formula 1 car next to a 1934 Riley Sports.

The Museum is situated on the A359 Yeovil to Frome road at Sparkford, just off the A303 in Somerset. It is about 40 miles south of Bristol, and 25 minutes drive from the M5 intersection at Taunton.
Open 9.30am - 5.30pm (10.00am - 4.00pm Winter) 7 days a week, *except Christmas Day, Boxing Day and New Years Day*
Special rates available for schools, coach parties and outings Charitable Trust No. 292048